Current Biography Yearbook

1987

EDITOR
Charles Moritz

ASSOCIATE EDITORS
Henry Sloan
Kieran Dugan
Judith Graham
Michael Collins

THE H. W. WILSON COMPANY
NEW YORK

FORTY-EIGHTH ANNUAL CUMULATION—1987

PRINTED IN THE UNITED STATES OF AMERICA

International Standard Serial No. (0084-9499)

Library of Congress Catalog Card No. (40-27432)

PREFACE

The aim of *Current Biography Yearbook 1987,* like that of the preceding volumes in this series of annual dictionaries of contemporary biography, now in its fifth decade of publication, is to provide the reference librarian, the student, or any researcher with brief, objective, accurate, and well-documented biographical articles about living leaders in all fields of human accomplishment the world over. Whenever feasible, obituary notices appear for persons whose biographies have been published in *Current Biography,* and every attempt is made to pick up obituaries that have inadvertently been omitted in previous years.

Current Biography Yearbook 1987 carries on the policy of including new and updated biographical sketches that supersede or update earlier, outdated articles. Sketches have been made as accurate and objective as possible through careful researching by *Current Biography* writers in newspapers, magazines, authoritative reference books, and news releases of both government and private agencies. Immediately after they are published in the eleven monthly issues, articles are submitted to biographees to give them an opportunity to suggest corrections in time for publication of the *Current Biography Yearbook.* To take account of major changes in the careers of biographees, sketches have also been revised before they are included in the yearbook. With the exception of occasional interviews, the questionnaire filled out by the biographee remains the primary source of direct information.

Some persons who are not professional authors but who have written books are included under *Nonfiction* in addition to their vocational fields. The annual bestowal of Nobel Prizes has added articles to the volume. The pages immediately following contain *Explanations; Key to Reference Abbreviations; Key to Pronunciation;* and *Key to Abbreviations.* The indexes at the end of the volume are *Biographical References; Periodicals and Newspapers Consulted; Classification by Profession;* and *Cumulated Index—1981–1987. Current Biography Cumulated Index 1940–1985* cumulates and supersedes all previous indexes, and the reader will need to consult only that index in order to locate a name within that period of time.

For their assistance in preparing *Current Biography Yearbook 1987,* I should like to thank the associate editors.

Charles Moritz

Explanations

Authorities for biographees' full names, with some exceptions, are the bibliographical publications of The Wilson Company. When a biographee prefers a certain name form, that is indicated in the heading of the article: for example, Niemöller, (Friedrich Gustav Emil) Martin means that he is usually referred to as Martin Niemöller. When a professional name is used in the heading, as, for example, Anne Bancroft, the real name (in this case Annemarie Italiano) appears in the article itself.

The heading of each article includes the pronunciation of the name if it is unusual, date of birth (if obtainable), and occupation. The article is supplemented by a list of references to sources of biographical information, in two alphabets: (1) newspapers and periodicals and (2) books. (See the section *Biographical References*, found in the rear of this volume.)

Key to Reference Abbreviations

References to some newspapers and periodicals are listed in abbreviated form; for example, "Sat Eve Post 217:14 S 30 '44 por" means *Saturday Evening Post,* volume 217, page 14, September 30, 1944, with portrait. (For full names, see the section *Periodicals and Newspapers Consulted,* found in the rear of this volume.)

January—Ja	July—Jl	Journal—J
February—F	August—Ag	Magazine—Mag
March—Mr	September—S	Monthly—Mo
April—Ap	October—O	Portrait—por
May—My	November—N	Weekly—W
June—Je	December—D	Review—R

Key to Pronunciation

ā	āle	ō	ōld		*menu* (mə-nü); German ü, as in *grün*
â	câre	ô	ôrb		
a	add	o	odd		
ä	ärm	oi	oil	ə	the schwa, an unstressed vowel representing the sound that is spelled
		o͞o	o͞oze		
ē	ēve	o͝o	fo͝ot		
e	end	ou	out		
					a as in sofa
g	go	*th*	*th*en		e as in fitted
		th	thin		i as in edible
ī	īce				o as in melon
i	ill	ū	cūbe		u as in circus
		û	ûrn; French eu, as in *jeu* zhû), German ö, oe, as in *schön (shûn), Goethe* (gû´te)		
к	German *ch* as *ich* (iк)			zh	azure
N	Not pronounced, but indicates the nasal tone of the preceding vowel, as in the French *bon* (bôN)	u	tub	´	= main accent
		ü	Pronounced approximately as ē, with rounded lips: French u, as in	˝	= secondary accent

Key to Abbreviations

AAAA	Amateur Athletic Association of America
AAU	Amateur Athletic Union
AAUP	American Association of University Professors
A.B.	Arts, Bachelor of
ABA	American Bar Association
ABC	American Broadcasting Company
ACA	Americans for Constitutional Action
ACLU	American Civil Liberties Union
ADA	Americans for Democratic Action
ADP	Automatic data processing
AEC	Atomic Energy Commission
AFL	American Football League
AFL-CIO	American Federation of Labor and Congress of Industrial Organizations
AID	Agency for International Development
AIDS	Acquired immune deficiency syndrome
ALA	American Library Association
A.M.	Arts, Master of
AMA	American Medical Association
AP	Associated Press
ASCAP	American Society of Composers, Authors and Publishers
ASNE	American Society of Newspaper Editors
B.A.	Bachelor of Arts
BBC	British Broadcasting Corporation
B.D.	Bachelor of Divinity
B.F.A.	Bachelor of Fine Arts
B.L.S.	Bachelor of Library Science
B.S.	Bachelor of Science
CAA	Civil Aeronautics Administration
CAB	Civil Aeronautics Board
C.B.	Companion of the Bath
CBC	Canadian Broadcasting Corporation
C.B.E.	Commander of (the Order of) the British Empire
CBS	Columbia Broadcasting System
C.E.	Civil Engineer
CEA	Council of Economic Advisers
CENTO	Central Treaty Organization
CIA	Central Intelligence Agency
C.M.G.	Companion of (the Order of) St. Michael and St. George
CNN	Cable News Network
CORE	Congress of Racial Equality
DAR	Daughters of the American Revolution
D.C.L.	Doctor of Civil Law
D.D.	Doctor of Divinity
D.Eng.	Doctor of Engineering
D.F.C.	Distinguished Flying Cross
D.J.	Doctor of Jurisprudence
D.Litt.	Doctor of Literature
D.Mus.	Doctor of Music

D.Pol.Sc.	Doctor of Political Science
D.S.C.	Distinguished Service Cross
D.Sc.	Doctor of Science
D.S.M.	Distinguished Service Medal
D.S.O.	Distinguished Service Order
ECOSOC	Economic and Social Council (of the United Nations)
EDP	Electronic data processing
EEC	European Economic Community
EEOC	Equal Employment Opportunity Commission
EPA	Environmental Protection Agency
ERA	Equal Rights Amendment
E.R.A.	Earned run average
FAA	Federal Aviation Administration
FAO	Food and Agriculture Organization (of the United Nations)
FBI	Federal Bureau of Investigation
FCC	Federal Communications Commission
FDA	Food and Drug Administration
FHA	Federal Housing Administration
FPC	Federal Power Commission
FTC	Federal Trade Commission
GAO	General Accounting Office
GATT	General Agreement on Tariffs and Trade
G.B.E.	Knight or Dame, Grand Cross Order of the British Empire
G.C.B.	Knight or Dame, Grand Cross of the Bath
GOP	Grand Old Party (Republican)
GSA	General Services Administration
HHS	Department of Health and Human Services
H.M.	His Majesty; Her Majesty
HUD	Department of Housing and Urban Development
ICBM	Intercontinental ballistic missile
ICC	Interstate Commerce Commission
IGY	International Geophysical Year
IMF	International Monetary Fund
INS	International News Service
IRA	Irish Republican Army
IRS	Internal Revenue Service
J.D.	Doctor of Jurisprudence
K.B.E.	Knight of (the Order of) the British Empire
K.C.	King's Counsel
K.C.B.	Knight Commander of the Bath
KGB	Committee of State Security (Soviet secret police)
L.H.D.	Doctor of Humane Letters
Litt.D.	Doctor of Letters
LL.B.	Bachelor of Laws

LL.D.	Doctor of Laws	PLO	Palestine Liberation Organization
		PTA	Parent-Teacher Association
M.A.	Master of Arts		
M.B.A.	Master of Business Administration	Q.C.	Queen's Counsel
M.B.E.	Member of (the Order of) the British Empire		
MBS	Mutual Broadcasting System	RAF	Royal Air Force
M.C.E.	Master of Civil Engineering	RBI	Run batted in
M.D.	Doctor of Medicine	RCA	Radio Corporation of America
M.E.	Master of Engineering	RKO	Radio-Keith-Orpheum
METO	Middle East Treaty Organization	ROTC	Reserve Officers' Training Corps
M.F.A.	Master of Fine Arts		
MGM	Metro-Goldwyn-Mayer	SAC	Strategic Air Command
M.Lit.	Master of Literature	SALT	Strategic Arms Limitation Talks
M.L.S.	Master of Library Science	SCAP	Supreme Command for the Allied Powers
M.P.	Member of Parliament		
M.Sc.	Master of Science	SDI	Strategic Defense Initiative ("Star Wars")
Msgr.	Monsignor, Monseigneur		
MTV	Music Television	SEATO	Southeast Asia Treaty Organization
NAACP	National Association for the Advancement of Colored People	SEC	Securities and Exchange Commission
NAB	National Association of Broadcasters	SHAEF	Supreme Headquarters, Allied Expeditionary Force
NAM	National Association of Manufacturers	SHAPE	Supreme Headquarters, Allied Powers Europe
NASA	National Aeronautics and Space Administration	S.J.	Society of Jesus (Jesuit)
NATO	North Atlantic Treaty Organization	S.J.D.	Doctor of Juridical Science
NBA	National Basketball Association	SLA	Special Libraries Association
NBC	National Broadcasting Company	S.T.B.	Bachelor of Sacred Theology
NCAA	National Collegiate Athletic Association	S.T.D.	Doctor of Sacred Theology
NEA	National Education Association	TVA	Tennessee Valley Authority
NFL	National Football League		
NHL	National Hockey League	UAR	United Arab Republic
NIH	National Institutes of Health	UK	United Kingdom
NIMH	National Institute of Mental Health	UN	United Nations
NLRB	National Labor Relations Board	UNESCO	United Nations Educational, Scientific, and Cultural Organization
NMU	National Maritime Union		
NOAA	National Oceanographic and Atmospheric Administration	UNICEF	United Nations Children's Fund
		UPI	United Press and International News Service
NOW	National Organization for Women		
NSA	National Security Agency	U.S.	United States
NSC	National Security Council	USFL	United States Football League
		USIA	United States Information Agency
OAS	Organization of American States	USO	United Service Organizations
O.B.E.	Officer of (the Order of) the British Empire	USSR	Union of Soviet Socialist Republics
OECD	Organization for Economic Cooperation and Development	VA	Veterans Administration
		VFW	Veterans of Foreign Wars
OMB	Office of Management and Budget	VISTA	Volunteers in Service to America
OPEC	Organization of Petroleum Exporting Countries		
OSHA	Occupational Safety and Health Administration	WHO	World Health Organization
PBS	Public Broadcasting Service	YMCA	Young Men's Christian Association
PEN	Poets, Playwrights, Editors, Essayists and Novelists (International Association)	YMHA	Young Men's Hebrew Association
		YWCA	Young Women's Christian Association
Ph.B.	Bachelor of Philosophy		
Ph.D.	Doctor of Philosophy	YWHA	Young Women's Hebrew Association
PLC	Public limited company		

Current Biography Yearbook

1987

Allen, Debbie

Jan. 16, 1950- Dancer; singer; actress; choreographer. Address: b. c/o William Morris Agency, 1350 Ave. of the Americas, New York City, N.Y. 10019

According to Debbie Allen, "Luck is when opportunity meets preparation." Few performers have been as prepared to take advantage of show-business opportunities as the versatile Miss Allen, a triple-threat dancer, singer, and actress who has also compiled an impressive list of credits as a choreographer, director, and producer. Ever since she was plucked in storybook fashion from the chorus line and given a starring role in the 1973 Broadway musical *Raisin*, she has remained in the public eye, winning over audiences with her Texas-sized talents and her coruscating presence on stage. She triumphed as Anita in the 1980 Broadway revival of *West Side Story*, parlayed two lines in the movie *Fame* into a central role in its television incarnation, and gave a virtuoso performance in the 1986 Broadway revival of *Sweet Charity* as the quintessential romantic loser who keeps landing on her feet. To Mel Swope, the producer of the television series *Fame*, Debbie Allen "is a genius. This lady is stretched to the absolute limit and it doesn't show."

A native of Houston, Texas, Deborah Allen was born on January 16, 1950, the third of the four children of Andrew Allen, a dentist, and Vivian (Ayers) Allen, an artist and writer who received a Pulitzer Prize nomination for poetry in 1953. They separated when Debbie was only seven. Debbie's sister, Phylicia Rashad, plays Bill Cosby's wife on the television series *The Cosby Show*, and her brother Andrew ("Tex") Allen is a jazz composer and musician. Although segregation was still the rule in the Houston of the 1950s and early 1960s, and most movie theatres and the local amusement park were off limits to blacks, Debbie Allen rhapsodizes about her childhood there, recalling: "Growing up in a place where you could see the sun, the sky, and have a lot of trees and grass, you felt like you really had a place in this universe."

Debbie Allen began taking dance lessons when she was three, but it was seeing a performance of Alvin Ailey's ballet *Revelations*, with its pulsating score based on traditional black folk music that crystalized her desire for a career in musicals. When she was eight, her mother, whom Miss Allen calls "my guide and mentor," tried to enroll her in the Houston Foundation for Ballet, but without any success because, Debbie believes, of still-existing segregation policies. Undaunted, Vivian Ayers arranged for Debbie to study privately with a former

teacher from the Ballet Russe. She also took her three older children to live for a year in Mexico City, where Debbie trained at the Ballet Nacional de México, attended performances of the Ballet Folklórico de México, and became fluent in Spanish. After what Debbie Allen laments was "a lot of good time lost," she was admitted to the Houston Foundation for Ballet at the age of fourteen and given a full scholarship, becoming the only black in the company.

Debbie Allen's pursuit of a dance career hit another snag when, during her senior year in high school, she was refused admission to the North Carolina School of the Arts—despite being asked to demonstrate technique to the other auditioners—because, according to the dance director, she was "built wrong." The rejection—which she blames on a racial quota system—was a stinging blow, and she stopped dancing for a year. Instead, she enrolled in Howard University, in Washington, D.C., studying Greek classics, speech, and theatre arts. In 1971 she graduated *cum laude* with a bachelor of fine arts degree. While she was at Howard, the choreographer Mike Malone, whom Miss Allen credits with getting her to resume dancing, recruited her for his dance troupe and gave her a part in his production of *The Music Man* at the Burn Brae Dinner Theater. She also danced with student groups at Howard University, studied at the National Ballet School, and headed the dance department at what is now the Duke Ellington School of the Performing Arts, where she taught and befriended "the most wonderful, talented little chickens." She later drew upon the Ellington School of the Performing Arts experience for her role as a dance teacher in the television series *Fame*.

For a time Miss Allen considered staying in teaching, but in 1971 she headed for New York, where the choreographer Louis Johnson cast her as a dancer in *Purlie*, a musical adaptation of Ossie Davis' hit comedy, *Purlie Victorious*. She appeared in two dance numbers, one at the start of the show and the other before the final curtain. She had so much time between her appearances that she recalls leaving the theatre during the play's Philadelphia run, getting grazed by a taxi, being taken by ambulance to the hospital for treatment, and returning in time for the finale. Determined to find a broader showcase for her talents, she left *Purlie* after six weeks and joined George Faison's modern dance troupe, the Universal Dance Experience, as a principal dancer. During the year that she spent with the company she also worked as Faison's assistant and played a firefly unable to keep her fire lit in *Ti-Jean and His Brothers*, which Faison choreographed for the New York Shakespeare Festival in 1972.

By 1973 Debbie Allen was back on Broadway—this time in *Raisin*, a musical version of Lorraine Hansberry's poignant drama *A Raisin in the Sun*. Originally cast in the chorus, Miss Allen "added a kick and turn" to her dance assignment whenever possible and was given the featured role of Beneatha Younger, a young woman determined to escape ghetto life by becoming a doctor, during the show's out-of-town tryouts when Shezwae Powell, the original Beneatha, was dropped from the cast. When the show opened on October 18, 1973, the reviewer Martin Gottfried, writing in *Women's Wear Daily* (October 19, 1973), took note of Debbie Allen's "special talent for dance and delightful quality altogether." Similarly, Douglas Watt of the New York *Daily News* (October 19, 1973) called her "a dandy dancer," and Richard Watts of the *New York Post* (October 19, 1973) commented on her "attractively humorous and zestful performance." In an interview with Joyce Wadler for the *New York Post* (July 10, 1975), Miss Allen traced her Broadway success back to her birthplace: "Maybe we have a different attitude coming from Texas; I mean, we don't do any of that lost souls trying to find ourselves routine. Child, that wouldn't go down in Texas. We hustle, hustle all the time."

After leaving the cast of *Raisin* in 1975, Debbie Allen began landing television jobs—first in commercials (she and her sister worked together in an advertisement for Pampers disposable diapers) and then with Mimi Kennedy and Ellen Foley in *3 Girls 3*, a widely praised comedy-variety series about a trio of singer-dancer-actresses seeking their niche in show business. The *New York Times* television reviewer John J. O'Connor expressed the critical consensus when he called the show's opening episode "easily the freshest, liveliest, and most exciting premiere of a series that television has concocted in years." The show languished in the ratings, however, and ran only from June 15 to June 29, 1977.

With her usual resilience, Debbie Allen soon found other gainful employment by appearing as Ben Vereen's dancing partner in the 1977 television special *Stompin' at the Savoy* and as Jimmie Walker's girlfriend in a made-for-television movie, *The Greatest Thing that Almost Happened*, shown on October 26, 1977. She then went on the road as the long-suffering Miss Adelaide in a national company's revival of *Guys and Dolls*, starring Leslie Uggams and Richard Roundtree. On her return to New York, she rehearsed eight to twelve hours a day for three weeks to play the title role in *Anna Lucasta* for two weekends at Woody King's New Testament Theater.

Even more disappointing for Debbie Allen than the demise of *3 Girls 3* was the failure of *Alice*, director Vinnette Carroll's disco version of *Alice in Wonderland*. Tapped for the title role by coproducer Mike Nichols, she hoped that the show would propel her into the charmed circle of performers who are able to select what they want to do from a wide variety of projects. But *Alice* never jelled into a cohesive whole, resulting in poor reviews, apathetic audiences, and a Philadelphia closing on June 11, 1978, that left Miss Allen "devastated." "Nothing is ever simple," she told writer Evelyn Renold in 1986. "Just when you've figured out how to build this house, here comes a tornado and tears everything apart."

But the unstoppable Debbie Allen, recouping her self-confidence, was seen in the theatre, on television, and in the movies in 1979. In February of that year she played Nan Branch Haley, Alex Haley's wife, in the much-acclaimed miniseries *Roots: The Next Generation*. The next month she replaced Charlene Woodard in *Ain't Misbehavin'*, a celebration of the songs and personality of the legendary jazzman and tunesmith Fats Waller, which had been playing to packed houses since its Broadway opening on May 9, 1978. Her numbers included the crackling dance "How Ya Baby" and the long-time favorite "Keepin' Out of Mischief Now." November marked her film debut in *The Fish that Saved Pittsburgh*, a little-noticed comedy, starring Julius Irving and Stockard Channing, about a basketball team that seeks advice from an astrologer. In addition to playing a cheerleader, she worked behind the scenes on the film's choreography.

In 1980 the unqualified triumph that Debbie Allen had been waiting for came when she dazzled critics and audiences with her portrayal of Anita in a Broadway revival of *West Side Story*, a retelling of Shakespeare's *Romeo and Juliet* with the rival houses of the Capulets and the Montagues replaced by rival street gangs on New York City's West Side. Choreographed and directed by Jerome Robbins, with a book by Arthur Laurents, music by Leonard Bernstein, and lyrics by Stephen Sondheim, the revival, according to Walter Kerr in the

New York Times (February 15, 1980), made the musical seem "by some odd metamorphosis . . . to have grown younger, more innocent, more endearing with the years." Debbie Allen brought high-voltage sass to the role of the spirited girlfriend of a Puerto Rican gang leader, the part that in the original 1957 production helped to launch the career of Chita Rivera. Many of the movers and shapers behind the scenes of the original production of *West Side Story* were again on board for the revival, including Robbins, Bernstein, and the scenic designer Oliver Smith. Chita Rivera helped Miss Allen to master Robbins' sizzling dances, including the show-stopping "America," Anita's ambivalent tribute to the U.S.A.

When the revival of *West Side Story* opened in New York on February 14, 1980, many reviewers reserved their special praise for Debbie Allen. In a March 3, 1980 article for *New York*, the hypercritical John Simon called her "a dream Anita, delightful in every respect and incomparable when dancing or joking." Clive Barnes of the *New York Post* (February 15, 1980) called her "an exultant yet compassionate spitfire as Anita," and his fellow critic Walter Kerr (the *New York Times*, February 15, 1980), found her Anita to be "wonderfully tart-tongued as she mocks the easy slogans of the bloodthirsty Sharks. She's better still when . . . she whips across the stage floor dizzyingly in her lilac dress trimmed with red, squandering high-kicks and heel-thrusts as though there were no tomorrow night." Her performance earned Debbie Allen an Antoinette Perry Award nomination and a Drama Desk Award.

In 1981 Debbie Allen temporarily hung up her dancing shoes to take a role in *Ragtime*, the film adaptation of E. L. Doctorow's kaleidoscopic vision of early twentieth-century America. Prevailing over stiff competition, she won the role of Sarah, a washerwoman whose lover, Coalhouse Walker, fights for justice after his new Model-T is wrecked by racists when he visits her and their newborn baby in an affluent New York suburb. In a large cast that also included James Cagney, Mary Steenburgen, and James Olsen, Miss Allen held her own, sketching a believable portrait of a distraught woman trying to cope with disastrous circumstances beyond her control. Her later film assignments were few and far between, she believes, partly because of the notorious lack of roles for blacks in Hollywood movies.

As it happened, Debbie Allen's film breakthrough came in a bit part as a dance instructor, Lydia Grant, in the 1980 hit *Fame*, which dealt with the aspirations of a group of students at New York City's High School for the Performing Arts. Her cameo appearance limited her to two lines, one of which was the word "Wicked!"—said while watching a male student audition—but, as Jamie Gold noted in retrospect in the *Washington Post* (February 21, 1982), "If your instrument's refined and you know where you're coming from, you can say 'Wicked!' so well that who knows? Maybe you get asked to be in the TV spinoff."

In NBC's adaptation of *Fame*, Lydia Grant emerged as a tough, exuberant, supportive dance teacher—a role seemingly tailor-made for Debbie Allen. Yet she took the part solely on the unusual condition that she be allowed to choreograph the dances for the show. After triumphing in a trial assignment, she emerged as perhaps the prime mover of *Fame*. Although each episode blended comedy, drama, and performance—including singing, acting, and instrumentals—it was dance that underscored the action and carried it forward. Exulting in the challenge of "creating something new each week," Debbie Allen arrived at the MGM studios each day at 6 in the morning and eventually created dozens of dances, primarily jazz, that had the ebullient, interracial cast of *Fame* dancing in class, down the halls, on cafeteria tables, and on the school's seemingly cavernous stage. On location in New York City, she created a "body language" number that involved imitating its inhabitants and a fantasy routine in Times Square that used balloons like banners for her high-stepping troupe.

Although critically acclaimed, *Fame* languished near the bottom of the ratings, hampered by its mid-season replacement status, stiff competition from the popular CBS series *Magnum, P.I.*, and a national viewing public possibly nonplussed by the most ethnically diverse cast on television. Nevertheless, the show won five Emmy awards (including Miss Allen's for best choreography), prompting NBC to continue *Fame* in its 1982–83 schedule. At the end of the year, Debbie Allen won her second Emmy for best choreography, but the ratings had not improved, and NBC dropped the show in the spring of 1983. *Fame*, however, abruptly came back to life in August when its producer, MGM/UA Television, joined with Metromedia, Inc., to distribute twenty-four episodes of the series to independent and network-affiliated local stations. Comfortably ensconced in non-prime-time slots, *Fame* began to thrive. By October 1983 it was seen on 116 independent stations, including twenty-nine of the top thirty syndication markets, and had been sold to syndicators in Great Britain, Continental Europe, and Australia, where for a time it was the number-one show. When *Fame* entered its fourth season in September 1984, Miss Allen had been named one of the show's producers, and in 1985–86 she directed several of its episodes.

Adding more responsibility to an already crowded schedule, Debbie Allen played a tough prison guard on a made-for-television movie, *Women of San Quentin*, which aired on NBC on October 23, 1983. In the fall of 1985 she cowrote, choreographed, and performed in *Dancin' in the Wings*, a one-hour television special that also featured Sammy Davis Jr. and Shirley Hemphill. The next year she was cast in Richard Pryor's semi-autobiographical movie *Jo Jo Dancer, Your Life Is Calling*, as a hard-bitten, promiscuous woman who marries Pryor's Jo Jo with calamitous results.

In *Sweet Charity*, the vehicle that brought Debbie Allen back to Broadway on April 27, 1986, she stepped exuberantly into the role created by Gwen Verdon in 1966. Indeed, she learned director-choreographer Bob Fosse's supercharged dance numbers—including *I'm a Brass Band*, *There's Gotta Be Something Better than This*, and *If My Friends Could See Me Now*—from Gwen Verdon. Cy Coleman's pulsating score and Dorothy Fields' inventive lyrics also provided a splendid showcase for Miss Allen's singing abilities, particularly in the bewildered *Where Am I Going?* and *I'm the Bravest Individual*, a duet with costar Michael Rupert.

Based on Federico Fellini's film *Nights of Cabiria* (1957), *Sweet Charity* is the story of Charity Hope Valentine, a kind-hearted, naïve dance-hall hostess whose romantic encounters inevitably end in disappointment. Whereas Gwen Verdon had stressed the character's Chaplinesque pathos, Debbie Allen took a 1980's approach, emphasizing Charity's spunk and resiliency. Her interpretation disturbed critics such as *Time* magazine's William A. Henry 3d, who felt that Charity was not believable without a "doormat vulnerability." Most critics, however, were rapturous in their praise of Debbie Allen. Douglas Watt of the New York *Daily News* proclaimed, "Debbie Allen is a joy forever, whether dancing on air, singing brightly, or acting with a saucy appeal, this small wonder dazzles from start to finish." Brendan Gill wrote in the *New Yorker* (May 12, 1986) that "there are many unexpected consolations in this world; I appear to have missed Halley's comet, but at least I haven't missed Debbie Allen." The show won an Antoinette Perry award for Best Revival, and Miss Allen was nominated for Best Actress in a Musical.

Debbie Allen is a five-foot-two-inch, 108-pound "stick of dynamite," according to one interviewer. She wears her black hair short, often with curls over her forehead. She has a raucous laugh, and, according to writer Ann Foley, she "radiates warmth and exuberance." In December 1975 she married Winfred Wilford, a CBS Records executive. They were divorced in 1983, and in 1984 Miss Allen married Norm Nixon, a basketball player with the San Diego Clippers whom she met on the set of *The Fish that Saved Pittsburgh*. They and their daughter Vivian Nicole, who was born in May 1984, live in Santa Monica, California. Her honors include a Golden Globe award for best actress in a TV series (*Fame*) and a cultural citation from Harvard, which she calls her "lah-de-dah award."

Debbie Allen left *Sweet Charity* in the fall of 1986 to return to *Fame* for its final season, as both an actress and a director (of eleven episodes). She also directed episodes of *Family Ties* and *The Bronx Zoo* on the CBS network. She plans to continue directing, and she hopes to do more films and an original Broadway show with a part created especially for her. Two people she would love to portray are the legendary entertainer Josephine Baker (who visited her backstage during the run of *Raisin*) and Florence Mills, the popular star of *Shuffle Along* and *Bye-Bye Blackbird* in the 1920s. In collaboration with her husband, Miss Allen con-

ceived "The Debbie Allen Show," a proposed CBS series in which she would star, in her words, "as a very different character than the one [she has] been playing—more kooky, more fun."

References: Ebony p74+ Mr '83 pors; Encore 7:26+ O 2 '78 pors; N Y Daily News p36 F 16 '79 por; N Y Daily News Mag p8+ Ap 13 '86 pors; N Y Times C p4 F 22 '80 por; Newsday II p3 My 25 '86 pors; People p110 Mr 10 '80 pors, p71+ Ap 19 '82 pors; Washington Post B p1+ Je 15 '77 pors; Washington Post Television Mag p3 F 21 '82 por

Amis, Kingsley

Apr. 16, 1922– British writer. Address: b. c/o Jonathan Clowes, 22 Prince Albert Rd., London NW1 7ST, England

NOTE: This biography supersedes the article that appeared in *Current Biography* in 1958.

The British writer Kingsley Amis is perhaps best known for his satiric novels, but the body of his work encompasses poetry, short stories, essays, thrillers, television plays—such a diversity of form and content, in fact, that the critic Philip Gardner has referred to him as "a man of letters rather than simply a writer." Amis' first novel, *Lucky Jim*, which was published in 1954 and remains his most popular book to this day, earned him a reputation as a satirist in the tradition of Angus Wilson and Evelyn Waugh, but he has also been compared to Henry Fielding, Samuel Butler, and H. G. Wells. "What I think I am doing is writing novels within the main English-language tradition, that is, trying to tell interesting, believable stories about understandable characters in a reasonably straightforward style: no tricks, no experimental foolery," Amis has said, as quoted in *Contemporary Novelists* (1976). His "prime object," he went on, is "to portray human nature as it has always been." For his most recent effort, *The Old Devils*, Amis was awarded the Booker Prize, Britain's highest honor for fiction, in 1986.

Kingsley William Amis was born on April 16, 1922, in Clapham, in southwest London, England, the only child of William Robert Amis, a senior clerk in the export department of Colman's Mustard, and Rosa Annie (Lucas) Amis. From his conservative, lower-middle-class, Baptist parents, Amis learned "all the standard Protestant virtues," which he enumerated, in an interview with Dale Salwak for *Contemporary Literature* (Winter 1975), as "conscientiousness, thrift, hard work, patience particularly." Both his upbringing and his environment were "insular almost to a fault" and "fiercely non-crazy," Amis wrote years later in his essay "A Memoir of My Father." By his own account an "undersized," "timid," and "very lonely" boy, he did not come into his own until he began attending school, first at St. Hilda's, then at Norbury College, where at the age of eleven he saw his first story, "The Sacred Rhino of Uganda," published in the school magazine.

Recognizing his son's ability, William Amis agreed to pay the fees for Kingsley's first year of instruction at the City of London School, a topnotch private prep school, confident that the boy would win a scholarship for the succeeding terms, which he did. Amis has recalled his tenure, from 1934 to 1941, at the school warmly, writing on one occasion, as quoted in the *Dictionary of Literary Biography* (1983): "I have never in my life known a community where factions of any kind were less in evidence, where differences of class, upbringing, income group and religion counted for so little." Amis did well enough in his special subjects—classics and English—to earn a scholarship to St. John's College, Oxford.

Amis arrived at Oxford in April 1941, but he was able to complete only a year of his studies in English before he was drafted into the British Army and commissioned as an officer in the Royal Corps of Signals. During his three and a half years in the military, part of it spent in Belgium, France, and Germany, Amis rose to the rank of lieutenant. His war experiences served as the basis for several short stories, three of which were collected and published under the title *My Enemy's Enemy* (Gollancz, 1962; Harcourt, 1963).

At the war's end, Amis returned to St. John's College, and two years later, in 1947, he earned his B.A. degree, with first class honours, in English. The same year saw the publication of his first book of verse, *Bright November*, by Fortune Press. Continuing his studies at the graduate level, Amis remained at Oxford for a time, although he failed to win an advanced degree after his thesis, "English

Poetry, 1850–1900, and the Victorian Reading Public," was rejected.

In 1949 Amis accepted a job as a lecturer in English at the University College of Swansea, in South Wales, a post he held until 1961. During his first six years there, he devoted most of his spare time to writing witty, colloquial poems, many of which were published in popular poetry anthologies or in his own collections *A Frame of Mind* (School of Art, Reading University, 1953) and *A Case of Samples: Poems, 1946–56* (Gollancz, 1956; Harcourt, 1957). It was during that period, too, that he completed his first published novel, *Lucky Jim* (Gollancz, 1954; Doubleday, 1954). In writing *Lucky Jim*, the story of Jim Dixon, an irresolute young college instructor who clings precariously to a thankless job in a provincial university and bumbles his way along in academic life, Amis undoubtedly drew on his own experiences at Swansea and on his encounters with colleagues at other universities, although the book cannot be said to be autobiographical in any strict sense.

For a first novel, *Lucky Jim* attracted unusually wide critical attention, much of it favorable. Many reviewers were impressed by its deft characterizations, detached, sardonic style, and satiric bite, which some ranked with the best of P. G. Wodehouse and Evelyn Waugh. Perhaps more important, as the novelist and critic Anthony Burgess observed a decade later in his *The Novel Now* (1967), Amis had not only created in Jim Dixon "the most popular antihero of our time," he had also "caught the public mood of post-war restiveness in a book which, though socially significant, was, and still is, extremely funny." Never out of print, *Lucky Jim* has been translated into scores of languages, among them Catalan and Serbo-Croat, and has sold over one million paperback copies in the United States alone. A film version, starring Ian Carmichael, Hugh Griffith, and Terry-Thomas, was released by British Lion in 1957.

At least partly because of what was perceived as Jim Dixon's philistinism, Amis was inevitably linked with the so-called "Angry Young Men," a group of up-and-coming British writers, among them John Osborne, Alan Sillitoe, and John Braine, who were known for their caustic and unpitying criticism of contemporary British society. In an article for the London *Sunday Times* (December 25, 1955), the aged and venerable novelist Somerset Maugham attacked those young rebels for creating heroes lacking in manners and morals. "They are mean, malicious and envious . . . ," he wrote. "They are scum." Amis himself has always denied that he was part of that emergent group of novelists and playwrights. As he explained to Malcolm Oram in an interview for *Publishers Weekly* (October 28, 1974), those who read *Lucky Jim* as a polemic on contemporary culture had misunderstood it: "The idea that Jim was an 'outsider' just won't do. He was an *insider*." Ironically, in the light of Maugham's stinging rebuke, Amis was the recipient of the Somerset Maugham Award for *Lucky Jim* in 1955.

Critics generally agree that the three comic novels—*That Uncertain Feeling* (Gollancz, 1955; Harcourt, 1957), *I Like It Here* (Gollancz, 1958; Harcourt, 1958), and *Take a Girl Like You* (Gollancz, 1960; Harcourt, 1961)—that followed *Lucky Jim* were variations on the same theme of commonsensical adjustment to a wider society. Brigid Brophy, in her *Don't Never Forget: Collected Views and Reviews* (1966), went so far as to accuse Amis of "rewriting much the same novel under different titles and with different names for the characters." On the other hand, James Gindin, in his critical study *Postwar British Fiction* (1962), contended that Amis' successive protagonists, although outwardly similar (each, for example, is a gifted mimic), were progressively "more competent" and "more in control of the world." As for Amis himself, Gindin went on, he appeared to prefer "a comic acceptance of the contemporary world as it is" to social rebellion.

Amis spent the 1958–59 academic year in the United States as a visiting fellow in creative writing at Princeton University. While there, he gave a series of lectures on science fiction—a genre that had fascinated him since his boyhood—which were eventually published as *New Maps of Hell: A Survey of Science Fiction* (Harcourt, 1960; Gollancz, 1961). Over the next five years, he pursued that longstanding interest as the coeditor, with Robert Conquest, of the science fiction anthology series *Spectrum*. Amis' year at Princeton inspired the seriocomic novel *One Fat Englishman* (Gollancz, 1963; Harcourt, 1964), which recounts the adventures of Roger Micheldene, a gluttonous, vehemently anti-American British publisher on a business trip to the fictional Budweiser College, in Pennsylvania, where he is ultimately destroyed by his own excesses. Although he can "sympathize" with Micheldene, Amis has often described the character as the least admirable of all his heroes. As he told Malcolm Oram, "One theme of the book is to attack anti-Americanism by putting it into the mouth of an unpleasant, violently prejudiced person."

In 1961 Amis left University College of Swansea to accept a post as fellow and director of studies in English at Peterhouse College, Cambridge. As he explained later in his essay "No More Parades," he had high and, as it turned out, naive expectations of academic life at one of England's premier universities, but where he had anticipated lively and learned discussions with his colleagues, he found instead boring faculty gossip. Unable to accept what he saw as a general lowering of scholarly standards, he resigned his post two years later. Except for the two semesters he spent as a visiting professor of English at Vanderbilt University in 1967–68, Amis has since devoted himself exclusively to writing.

According to the general critical consensus, Amis produced little of significance during his first few years as a full-time professional writer. His next substantial effort, *The Anti-Death League* (Cape, 1966; Harcourt, 1966), caught both reviewers and readers off guard. A departure in style and tone from his earlier works, *The Anti-Death League* is part spy thriller, part sentimental love story, and part philosophical "novel of ideas." Although there is some comic relief, mainly in the form of a few zany characters, the pervading mood is somber and chillingly fatalistic. Some critics, inevitably comparing the new novel to *Lucky Jim*, rejected its "grander ambitions" and suggested that it represented Amis' "valediction to the world of Lucky Jim." But Anthony Burgess, writing in *Life* magazine (August 28, 1970), advised those admirers of *Lucky Jim* who were "puzzled" as to how Amis, "after that uproarious first novel, arrived at this position," to "read *Lucky Jim* again."

Burgess was among those readers who found a related philosophical preoccupation in *The Anti-Death League* and *The Green Man* (Cape, 1969; Harcourt, 1969). As he observed in his article for *Life*, "Both posit the existence of a malign ultimate reality, against which there is little defense." An extravagant blend of a pyschological study of human relations and a hair-raising ghost story, *The Green Man* describes the gradual mental and physical decline of Maurice Allington, the proprietor of a haunted pub who begins to see apparitions—first, the resident ghost, a depraved seventeenth-century parson, and, finally, God himself in the guise of, in Amis' words, "a young, well-dressed, sort of after-shave lotion kind of man." Many reviewers admitted to being somewhat nonplussed by *The Green Man*, their assessments ranging from Alan Ross's "ingenious, convincingly documented" ghost story to Jonathan Yardley's "mildly diverting entertainment pasted over with embarrassingly obvious thematic trumpeting."

By the late 1960s Amis was openly at odds with the liberal-left cultural/political establishment that he had formerly embraced. In the 1967 essay "Why Lucky Jim Turned Right," which is among the short pieces included in the collections *Lucky Jim's Politics* (Conservative Political Centre, 1968) and *What Became of Jane Austen?* (Cape, 1970; Harcourt, 1971), he chronicled his disillusionment with leftist orthodoxy and its followers, who "[buy] unexamined the abortion-divorce-homosexuality-censorship-racialism-marijuana package." He especially deplored the failure of governmental policies to better the human condition. "Many of the evils of life—failure, loneliness, fear, boredom, inability to communicate—are ineradicable by political means . . . ," he wrote. "All you can reasonably hope for is keeping things going . . . an injustice righted here, an opportunity extended there. This is not a very romantic sounding programme. In fact, it is not a programme at all. I like that." At least partly because it is "the party of non-politics," Amis has since conferred "grudging toleration" upon the Conservative party.

Amis satirized the "trendy Lefty" in *I Want It Now* (Cape, 1968; Harcourt, 1969), a slight novel, according to the critical consensus, whose hero is a hedonistic, opportunistic television talk-show host. *I Want It Now* was set partly in Greece, which Amis had recently visited while doing background research for a sequel to the late Ian Fleming's James Bond thrillers. The author of *The James Bond Dossier* (Cape, 1965; Harcourt, 1965), a serious examination of the Bond series, which he greatly admired, Amis was recruited for the unusual assignment by Gildrose Productions, which owns the copyright on Fleming's books. He has since confessed that his decision to accept the offer was motivated, at least in part, by the "major fringe benefit" of knowing "how cross the intellectual Left will get." Published under the pseudonym Robert Markham, *Colonel Sun* (Cape, 1968; Harper, 1968) suffered in comparison to the earlier Bond books, mainly because in "humanizing" the consummate spy-hero, Amis had robbed him of the very qualities that had endeared him to hundreds of thousands of readers the world over.

As Amis' political pessimism began to infiltrate his novels, the split between those who applauded his efforts to explore new forms and themes and those who, as Christopher Porterfield put it, had "never forgiven him for not devoting his career to rewriting *Lucky Jim*," widened. That split was never more evident than in the critical reaction accorded *Girl, 20* (Cape, 1971; Harcourt, 1972), a savage dissection of human failings, as embodied in an aging, lecherous "cultural frontiersman." Philip Gardner, in his critical study *Kingsley Amis* (1981), numbered the novel "among Amis' finest achievements," and Julian Symons, writing in the *Washington Post* (September 10, 1973), rated it as one of the few books in which Amis' talent had "yet been seen at anything like full stretch." But James P. Degnam saw *Girl, 20*, which he described in the *Hudson Review* (Summer 1972) as "a bad novel by any standard and Amis' worst book by far," as further evidence of "the steady decline" in the quality of the writer's work. "Without the Lucky Jim type," he went on, Amis' satire "loses the moral seriousness and moral core that made his early comic satires so original and important."

A firm believer in Kipling's dictum that a professional writer "should range as widely as possible," Amis next tried his hand at a detective story, with the publication of *The Riverside Villas Murder* (Cape, 1973; Harcourt, 1973), a painstakingly detailed period mystery set in the 1930s and featuring an appealing adolescent hero. As a reviewer for the London *Times Literary Supplement* (April 6, 1973) wryly noted, the book "offers no comfort to those who look for consistency in Kingsley Amis' work." Critics could not even agree if it was a "straight" detective story or a parody of the genre.

Similar dissension among the ranks of the reviewers continued throughout the 1970s and into the 1980s. During those years Amis wrote six more novels that were variously hated, loved, praised, pilloried, and invariably compared by at least one critic to *Lucky Jim*. Both *Jake's Thing* (Hutchinson, 1978; Viking, 1979), in which a sixtyish Oxford don resorts to sex therapy in an attempt to revive his flagging interest in the opposite sex, and *Stanley*

and the Women (Hutchinson, 1984; Summit, 1985), about a burned-out, middle-level executive who comes to view women as the bane of an otherwise rational world, were lambasted by some critics, especially in the United States, as misogynistic. *The Alteration* (Cape, 1976; Viking, 1977) and *Russian Hide-and-Seek* (Hutchinson, 1980), Amis' experiments with the "alternate world" subgenre of science fiction in which the author revises history to create a different society, were interpreted by Blake Morrison, among other reviewers, as confirmation of Amis' developing interest in "serious politico-historical fiction." For *The Alteration*, his reconstruction of the world based on the premise that the Protestant Reformation never took place, Amis won the John W. Campbell Award for science fiction.

Over the years, Amis has often been taken to task for the lack of affection he shows for his main characters, but in his two novels about the problems and frustrations of old age, *Ending Up* (Cape, 1974; Harcourt, 1974) and *The Old Devils* (Century Hutchinson, 1986; Summit, 1987), some critics detected traces of "a new depth of human feeling," as John Vaizey put it. That is particularly true in *The Old Devils*, an endearing comedy of manners about the intertwined lives of four Welsh couples, longtime friends, who face the onset of the "golden years" with something less than enthusiasm. As Michiko Kakutani observed in her review for the *New York Times* (February 25, 1987), while Amis had not lost his comic edge, he seemed to have discovered "a compassion for his characters, and as a result *The Old Devils* possesses a depth and emotional chiaroscuro new" to his work. "Instead of making fun of his characters' dilemmas," she continued, "Mr. Amis has chosen this time to write each of them—men and women—from the inside, and this decision . . . burnishes the entire novel with the luster of redemption."

Throughout his career Amis has continued to write poetry, which he has called "a higher art." His most recent collection of verse, *Collected Poems: 1944-1979*, was published in Britain by the Hutchinson Publishing Group in 1979 and in the United States the following year by the Viking Press. A frequent contributor to several periodicals, he was for a time the author of a column, "Kingsley on Drink," for *Penthouse* magazine and the London *Daily Express*. Amis has also written several plays for radio and television, a number of short stories, and the pictorial biography *Rudyard Kipling and His World* (Cape, 1975; Scribners, 1976), among other works, and he is the coeditor, with James Cochrane, of *The Great British Songbook* (Michael Joseph, 1986).

Kingsley Amis, who stands five feet eleven inches tall, has graying light brown hair and blue eyes. For relaxation, he favors reading (he is especially fond of thrillers and science fiction) and listening to music, from baroque to jazz. He has two sons—Philip Nicol William, a design consultant, and Martin Lewis, a novelist—and a daughter, Sally, a carpenter, from his marriage to Hilary Ann Bard-well, which ended in divorce. A second marriage, to the writer Elizabeth Jane Howard, also ended in divorce, in 1983. Amis lives in a self-contained ground-floor flat in a house in north London that he shares with his first wife and her third husband, Lord Kilmarnock. The novelist was named a Commander of the Order of the British Empire in 1981.

References: Contemporary Literature 16:1+ Winter '75; London Sunday Times p29 S 28 '86; Pub W 206:6+ O 28 '74 por; Time 69:106 My 27 '57 por, 126:74+ S 20 '85 por; Vanity Fair 50:156 Mr '87 por; Contemporary Authors new rev vol 8 (1983); Contemporary Novelists (1976); Dictionary of Literary Biography vol 15 (1983); Gardner, Philip. Kingsley Amis (1981); International Who's Who, 1987–88; Who's Who, 1987–88

Andrew, Duke of York

Feb. 19, 1960– Address: Buckingham Palace, London SW 1, England

A lengthy commitment to a career in the Royal Navy and marriage to a suitable young woman were seen by many Britons as signs of the new maturity of Andrew, their "roughneck prince." Currently fourth in the line of succession to the throne, the Duke of York, who was known as Prince Andrew until his marriage in 1986 to Sarah Ferguson, signed on for a long-term hitch in the Royal Navy in 1979, but his public image, tarnished over the years by his penchant for pranks and for beautiful but often inappropriate women, was less than shining until the Falkland Islands war in 1982. His pro-

fessionalism and courage as a helicopter pilot during that conflict against Argentina won him the respect and admiration of his fellow sailors and of the British people. Now, with a popular wife at his side and the prospects of a successful naval career before him, he is assuming his share of royal responsibilities and settling in to what his father calls "the family business."

The third child and second son of Queen Elizabeth II and Prince Philip, the Duke of Edinburgh, Prince Andrew was born at Buckingham Palace, the Queen's official London residence, on February 19, 1960. He was the first child born to a reigning monarch since the birth of Princess Beatrice to Queen Victoria in 1857. At the time of his birth, Andrew—whose full forename is Andrew Albert Christian Edward (Andrew after Prince Philip's father, Prince Andrew of Greece, and Albert after the Queen's father, King George VI)—was second in the line of succession to the throne, preceded by his older brother, Prince Charles, heir apparent to the throne of Great Britain, who was born in 1948. He also has an older sister, Princess Anne, born in 1950, and a younger brother, Prince Edward, born in 1964.

Feeling that there had been an overexposure of Prince Charles and Princess Anne, who had been hounded by reporters and photographers virtually from their births, the royal family set out to provide as normal a childhood as possible for Prince Andrew. Although official photographs—the first was taken by Cecil Beaton when the prince was a month old—were occasionally released to the press, Andrew was deliberately kept out of the public eye. So successful were the Queen and Prince Philip's efforts that frustrated journalists eventually began to speculate that there was something wrong with the child. Those rumors were put to rest when, apparently on the spur of the moment, Andrew was included in the official photographs of Queen Elizabeth the Queen Mother on her sixtieth birthday. According to Nicholas Courtney, in his book Prince Andrew (1983), those pictures showed a "jolly" baby, "always full of smiles," who "rarely cried."

A robust and boisterous little boy, Andrew thrived in the more relaxed atmosphere of a royal nursery presided over by Mabel Anderson, the daughter of a Liverpool policeman. Less formal and starchy than the formidable Scottish nannies who had looked after Charles and Anne, "Mamba," as Andrew called her, proved to be the ideal nanny for the mischievous prince, whose impish pranks included using the Queen's hat as a football, turning around the signs meant to direct guests at a royal garden party, and even putting itching powder in his mother's bed. Unlike his older brother and sister, Andrew spent several hours a day with his parents, who arranged their crowded schedules to allow time for their son every morning and again in the evening. The Queen herself taught him the alphabet and numbers; Prince Philip played games with him and taught him to swim.

When he was five years old, Andrew began his formal schooling in the royal classroom in Buckingham Palace, then under the direction of Katherine Peebles, familiarly known as "Mispy." Five children from aristocratic families, among them the prince's cousin, David Viscount Linley, joined Andrew in his lessons. To give her son some experience with youngsters from more modest backgrounds, the Queen encouraged him to enroll in a Wolf Cub Scout pack, which met weekly in the palace grounds. In 1968 Andrew was sent to Heatherdown Preparatory School, an exclusive boarding school near Ascot where the daily routine consisted of academic instruction in the mornings and sports in the afternoons.

After five years at Heatherdown, Andrew enrolled at Gordonstoun, the spartan and mentally and physically competitive public school in Scotland that was the alma mater of both his father and his older brother. As he had done at Heatherdown, the prince took courses in a variety of subjects, ranging from history and foreign languages to carpentry and mechanics. Brief, incognito trips to France and Germany during that time helped him to polish his language skills. A born athlete, Andrew also took part in a number of sports, including soccer, tennis, sailing, hockey, and cricket. He played cricket well enough to be a member of Gordonstoun's first eleven for three years, and during his last year at the school he captained the side.

Following a visit to Canada to watch his sister, Anne, perform in the equestrian events of the 1976 Summer Olympic Games, Andrew decided to take advantage of Gordonstoun's student exchange program with Lakefield College School, near Peterborough, Ontario. The prince seems to have enjoyed his two terms at Lakefield enormously, at least partly because of the opportunities for skiing and playing ice hockey. He concluded his stay in Canada with a 300-mile trip by canoe down the Coppermine River to the Arctic. That journey through the wilderness of the Northwest Territories inspired several of Andrew's landscape paintings, one of which was eventually shown publicly in an art exhibition called "Royal Performance at Windsor Castle." According to the art critic for the London Sunday Telegraph, the painting displayed "an adventurous sense of abstraction and composition beyond the usual amateurism of royal performance."

In February 1978, shortly after his return to Gordonstoun, Andrew reached his majority, which entitled him to a government annuity of £20,000 annually, although all but £600—his yearly allowance while he completed his education—was invested. It was at about this time that the prince, who had earned his wings as a glider pilot two years earlier, joined his older brother, Charles, in parachute training. His first jump tested both his skill as a parachutist and his coolness under pressure, for as his chute opened the lines became snarled. It took the prince two hundred feet of drop to disentangle them. "Of course I was nervous," he said afterwards, as quoted by Nicholas Courtney.

"If you are not nervous, you will do something stupid. I am thoroughly enjoying all this and I'm dead keen to get up again." He went up again the very next day, this time carrying the regulation fifty-five-pound army pack, and soon earned his parachuting insignia and certificate.

Historically, the male members of the royal family have signed on for tours of duty of varying length with the Royal Navy. In keeping with that tradition, Prince Andrew took the preliminary aptitude tests for naval flight training in December 1968. Accepted as a trainee helicopter pilot, he used his Easter school holidays in 1979 to learn the rudiments of flying, then buckled down to study for his "A," or advanced level, exams in English, history, and economics and political science. Taking the tests under a pseudonym to avoid possible charges of favoritism, he passed with results good enough for university admission, but he chose instead a twelve-year commission in the Royal Navy.

On September 12, 1979 Prince Andrew began his military training at the Britannia Royal Naval College in Dartmouth, where his father, older brother, and many forebears had preceded him. Inevitably compared to Charles, who had been enormously popular among his fellows at the college, Andrew was thought by some to be rather arrogant and overbearing. "He never lets you forget who he is," the wife of one of the instructors told a newspaper reporter, as quoted in Courtney's Prince Andrew. No concessions to his rank were made, however, and throughout the arduous, six-month basic training course, Andrew was treated like any other midshipman. The only outward sign of his status was the constant presence of the plain-clothes police officer who served as his bodyguard.

After passing his professional and academic exams at Dartmouth, in February 1980 the prince joined the crew of the aircraft carrier HMS Hermes, the Royal Naval College's training ship, for a stint of sea duty. On his return, he took a four-week commando course with the Royal Marines, then completed his studies at Dartmouth. Before going on for helicopter training, Andrew signed up for a series of aviation survival courses and put in a number of hours piloting fixed-wing aircraft. He began his helicopter training in earnest in October 1980 at the Royal Naval Air Station at Culdrose in Cornwall. Six months later, at the annual "passing-out parade," or graduation ceremony, at Culdrose, Prince Philip personally awarded Andrew his wings and the traditional silver salver for finishing first in his class. Andrew then returned to Culdrose for advance flight training on the Royal Navy's Sea King helicopters.

Since he was, at the time of his twenty-first birthday, in the midst of his naval training, Prince Andrew marked the occasion quietly at a private family dinner. The official celebration came on June 19, 1981, during Royal Ascot Week, at a grand ball honoring Andrew and his father, who had turned sixty on June 10, at Windsor Castle. The summer of 1981 was a time of celebrations for the royal family. A daughter, Zara, was born to Princess Anne and her husband, Captain Mark Phillips, in May. When the baby was christened on July 27, Prince Andrew acted as godfather. Two days later, he and Prince Edward served as Prince Charles's "supporters," a position comparable to that of "best man," at the wedding of the Prince of Wales and Lady Diana Spencer. At twenty-one, Prince Andrew was eligible to act as a Counsellor of State, and royal obligations became a part of his life. His first official engagement in his own right was a speech at a dinner following the centenary rugby match between Oxford and Cambridge universities on December 8, 1981. Because of his duties as a serving officer in the Royal Navy, however, Andrew was given a lighter schedule than other members of his family.

Shortly after he was commissioned to the rank of sublieutenant, on September 1, 1981, Prince Andrew was posted to the 820 Squadron on the aircraft carrier HMS *Invincible*. Just a few months later, on April 5, 1982, Andrew sailed with his ship to the South Atlantic. HMS *Invincible* was one of the forty vessels that made up the initial task force dispatched to recapture the Falkland Islands, a British dependent territory about 480 miles northeast of Cape Horn, from Argentina, which had invaded the islands in pursuance of its claim to sovereignty. Although there were some calls in Parliament to excuse the prince from combat missions, Andrew insisted that he be treated no differently than his brother officers. "It simply never occurred to me that, because I'm a member of the royal family, I wouldn't take part if it came to fighting or seeing it through," he told a reporter for the London *Daily Telegraph*, as quoted by Nicholas Courtney. On action stations throughout the conflict, Andrew piloted Sea King helicopters on antisubmarine and transport operations. His most harrowing moments came when he flew his aircraft on decoy missions designed to draw Argentina's low-flying, radar-directed Exocet missiles away from the British fleet. One of his biggest worries was the possibility of being hit by British Sea Wolf defensive missiles. "Sea Wolfs locked onto our helicopter three times while we were hovering," he explained to the correspondents traveling with the task force. "It really makes the hair stand up on the back of your neck." In September, three months after Argentina surrendered, Prince Andrew and the crew of HMS *Invincible* finally returned home to a tumultuous heroes' welcome led by the Queen.

Shortly before his ship had sailed for the Falklands, Prince Andrew had met and, according to most reports, begun a love affair with Kathleen ("Koo") Stark, an American-born actress. On his return, the two, along with Miss Stark's mother, traveled under assumed names to the Caribbean to spend a few days at Princess Margaret's vacation home on Mustique Island. Andrew was recognized almost immediately by one sharp-eyed reporter, and it was not long before the British press discovered that Miss Stark had starred in the 1978 soft-porn feature *Emily*. Within hours, stills from the

film appeared on the front pages of the London tabloids, and television crews were on their way to the island. His quiet holiday at an end, Andrew quickly returned home. A "handsome and boisterous charmer," as Ralph Martin described the prince in his book *Charles and Diana* (1985), Andrew clearly enjoyed the company of beautiful young women. Over the years, he had been linked romantically with about a dozen women, mostly models and actresses. His amorous escapades had earned him the nickname "Randy Andy," but as Sue Arnold observed in an article for *Vanity Fair* (June 1986), "Behind the Superprince lover-boy image stands a pretty ordinary, straightforward chap all but coerced into his Lothario role by media . . . hellbent on creating a newsworthy character."

Late in 1982 Andrew undertook his second official engagement—the switching on of the Christmas illuminations on Regent Street, a popular annual event attended by huge crowds. His expanded official schedule over the next few years included a visit to St. Helena Island in 1984 to mark its 150th anniversary as a Crown Colony, a return to the Falklands in 1985 to open the new Mount Pleasant airport, and several goodwill missions to Canada and the United States. The goodwill aspect of his trip to California in April 1984 to promote British exports and raise money for the British Olympic team was almost lost in the controversy that erupted after the prince, while touring a model housing project in Los Angeles, playfully sprayed a group of reporters with white paint. Despite a formal apology, he was denounced in local newspapers as a "spoiled rich kid." One television announcer, as quoted in *U.S. News & World Report* (July 28, 1986), went so far as to call Andrew's four-day stay "the most unpleasant royal visit since they burned the White House in the War of 1812."

The California incident aside, Prince Andrew handled his royal duties with exceptional grace and aplomb, but it was in his naval career that he really found fulfillment. "I feel about six inches taller when I come to sea," he explained in a television interview, as quoted in the New York *Daily News* (November 11, 1984), "because you can leave all those other cares at home and get on with the job I enjoy doing, which is flying." In September 1983 Andrew transferred to the 702 squadron on HMS *Osprey* for advanced flight training on Lynx helicopters. Promoted to the rank of lieutenant upon completing the course, he was assigned in May 1984 to HMS *Brazen*'s Lynx helicopter squadron, where he served until March 1986. He has since taken classes at the Royal Naval College, Greenwich, and the Royal Naval Air Station, Yeovilton, to qualify as a helicopter warfare instructor. Andrew's enthusiasm for the Royal Navy was made even more evident in October 1986, when he transferred from the service's medium-term special list to the general list, thus becoming eligible for more promotions.

On leave during Royal Ascot week in June 1985, Andrew chose as his companion for the festivities the cheerful, twenty-six-year-old daughter of Prince Charles's polo manager, Ronald Ferguson. While they had not traveled in the same circles, Miss Ferguson, an editor in a London publishing house, had known the prince from her childhood, and the pair soon became inseparable. Wary of the press, the two managed to avoid the spotlight for several months. It was only after "Fergie," as she is known to friends, was spotted holding hands with the prince at Sandringham, where she had joined the royal family for the New Year's holiday, that journalists and photographers descended on the young woman. Although the press reported that Miss Ferguson had previously been involved in two serious relationships, the public nonetheless seemed to accept her as the first suitable potential partner for Prince Andrew, whose possible ascension to the throne was now quite remote, given the birth of two sons to the Prince and Princess of Wales. Miss Ferguson may have been technically a commoner, but as a writer for the London *Times* put it, "Some commoners are less common than others."

The official announcement, on March 19, 1986, of the engagement of Prince Andrew and Sarah Ferguson was greeted enthusiastically by the British people. Mindful of the public's interest in the prince and his down-to-earth bride-to-be, the palace agreed to allow television cameras to follow the couple for over three months. The resulting documentary, broadcast in Britain and Canada in the early summer of 1986, served as a prelude to the pair's wedding, with full royal pomp, in Westminster Abbey on July 23, 1986. Two hours before his marriage, Prince Andrew was created Duke of York, Earl of Inverness and Baron Killyleagh. (Duke of York is the title traditionally conferred on a British monarch's second son.) Following a honeymoon cruise of the Azores in the royal yacht, *Britannia*, the Duke and Duchess resumed their official duties and their careers. Andrew officially took his seat in the House of Lords on February 11, 1987.

A handsome, athletically built six-footer with brown hair and intense blue eyes, Andrew is thought by many to resemble his father in looks and temperament. He has a keen sense of humor and is said to do a superb imitation of the stereotypical upperclass "twit." Fond of most outdoor sports, he especially enjoys skiing, sailing, and shooting. In recent years he has devoted much of his spare time to photography. Exhibitions of Andrew's work have been held at the Hamilton Gallery, in 1983, and at the Royal Albert Hall, in 1986. *Photographs*, a selection charting his progress from a "through-the-window" beginner to what one reviewer called "a very respectable high-amateur status," was published by Hamish Hamilton in 1986. Andrew is patron of the British Schools Exploring Society, the Jubilee Sailing Trust, the Aycliffe School, and the SS *Great Britain* appeal, and in June 1986 he was named a governor of Gordonstoun School.

References: *Ladies Home J* 93:102+ Mr '76 por; *McCall's* p20+ F '83 por; *N Y Daily News* "You" p8 N 11 '84 por; *People* 17:42+ Ap 26 '82 pors; *Vanity Fair* 49:55+ Je '86; Courtney, Nicholas. *Prince Andrew* (1983); Edgar, Donald. *Prince Andrew* (1980); Fisher, Graham, and Fisher, Heather. *Prince Andrew* (1981); Morton, Andrew, and Seamark, Mick. *Andrew, the Playboy Prince* (1983)

Arias Sánchez, Oscar
(ä´ryäs)

Sept. 13, 1941– President of Costa Rica. Address: *Casa Presidencial, San José, Costa Rica*

Oscar Arias Sánchez, president of Costa Rica since May 1986, has assumed the role of peacemaker in strife-torn Central America in his determination to prevent his country—known as the "Switzerland" or "Denmark" of the Americas—from being used as a battleground in the conflict between neighboring Nicaragua's Marxist Sandinista government and United States-supported Contra rebels seeking to overthrow it. Educated in the United States and Great Britain, Arias served with distinction as Costa Rica's minister of planning from 1972 to 1977 and as general secretary of the moderately socialist National Liberation party from 1979 to 1984. As president he has tried to maintain Costa Rica's neutrality, political stability, high cultural level, and relative prosperity, despite serious economic problems. With reference to his country's relationship with the United States, which has contributed more economic assistance per capita to Costa Rica than to any other country except Israel, Arias has said: "I value nothing more than friendship—friendship between people, friendship between nations. Friendship implies loyalty, but loyalty is not synonymous with servitude or unconditionality." The Costa Rican president's efforts to end the strife in Central America earned him the Nobel Peace Prize in October 1987.

The scion of one of Costa Rica's most prosperous coffee-producing families, Oscar Arias Sánchez was born in Heredia, near San José, the Costa Rican capital, on September 13, 1941, to Juan Rafael Arias Trejos and his wife, the former Lilian Sánchez. His brother, Rodrigo Arias Sánchez, serves as presidential chief of staff in his administration. His paternal grandfather, Juan Rafael Arias Bonilla, was a prominent legislator and government minister, and his grandfather on his mother's side, Julio Sánchez Lepiz, the founder of the family's coffee-growing enterprise, also served in the national legislative assembly.

After receiving his early education in Costa Rica, at the Escuela República Argentina in Heredia and at the Colegio Saint Francis in Moravia, where he was a member of the soccer team, Arias went to the United States, originally to study medicine at Boston University. While there, he took a great interest in the televised Kennedy-Nixon debates that preceded the 1960 presidential elections, and he decided to make John F. Kennedy, whom he met on Cape Cod, his role model. Returning to his native country, Arias studied with the faculty of law and economic science at the University of Costa Rica in San José, and during his student years there became actively involved in the Partido de Liberación Nacional (PLN). His essay "La Crisis de Berlin," a description of events surrounding the Soviet blockade of the western sector of the German metropolis in 1948 and 1949 as a confrontation between freedom and totalitarianism was written in 1961 for a competition sponsored by the San José newspaper *La Nación*. Published by Luis Alberto Monge and Father Benjamin Núñez in their journal *Combate*, it favorably impressed PLN leaders.

In 1964 Arias met José Figueres Ferrer, the elder statesman of the PLN, and worked with him in organizing study groups dealing with national affairs. During the 1965–66 election campaign, Arias helped the PLN candidate, Daniel Oduber, in his abortive effort to win the national presidency. After completing his studies at the University of Costa Rica with a *Licenciatura en ambas*, Arias went to England to study under a British government grant at the University of Essex and the London School of Economics and Political Science. He returned to Costa Rica in 1969 to write a dissertation about the socioeconomic origins of the Costa Rican political leadership that earned him a doctorate from the University of Essex. It was published in 1974 under the title *¿Quién gobierna en Costa Rica?* From 1969 to 1972, Arias held a professorship in the school of political science at the University of Costa Rica. His book *Grupos de Presión en Costa Rica* (dealing with pressure groups in Costa Rica) was published in 1970 and earned him the Premio Nacional de Ensayo in the following year.

When José Figueres was returned to the presidency of Costa Rica in May 1970 after a twelve-year absence, he invited Arias to join his economic council. In August 1972 Figueres appointed Arias to his cabinet as minister of national planning and political economy, and when Daniel Oduber succeeded Figueres as president in May 1974, he retained Arias in the cabinet post until July 1977. Considered one of the most successful planning ministers in Costa Rica's history, Arias put into effect an elaborate program designed to stimulate national economic growth, technological development, and full employment. Among the cornerstones of his tenure were the construction of the Plaza de la Cultura, a cultural park in the center of San José, and the promotion, in November 1976, of a symposium at which prominent persons in various fields discussed the future socioeconomic and political development of Costa Rica. Its conclusions were published in 1977 in the book *La Costa Rica del año 2000*.

In February 1978 Arias was elected to represent Heredia in the national legislative assembly, where he was a leading critic of the administration of Rodrigo Carazo Odio, the standardbearer of the conservative Partido Unidad Social Cristiana, who was widely regarded as one of the least effective presidents in recent Costa Rican history. In the legislative assembly, Arias introduced various projects to reform the national constitution and to streamline the electoral process. He relinquished his parliamentary seat in May 1981 to take an active part in the campaign of Luis Alberto Monge, who was elected president as the PLN candidate in February 1982. Meanwhile, rising in the ranks of the PLN, in which he represented the more conservative wing, Arias was chosen in August 1975 as the party's international secretary, and in July 1979 he was elected to the top PLN post, that of general secretary, to which he was reelected in June 1983.

In addition, Arias was from 1970 to 1972 a vice-president of the board of directors of the Banco Central de Costa Rica, and he continued to serve as a member of the bank's board until 1977. From 1972 to 1974 he was a member of the *ad hoc* commission of the National University of Heredia; from 1974 to 1977 he was a director of the technological institute of Costa Rica and a member of the national council of university rectors; in 1976 he served on the board of directors of the International University Exchange Fund, with headquarters in Geneva; and in 1977 he was a member of the North-South Roundtable, convening in Rome. Over the years, Arias also took part in a variety of international conferences and seminars dealing with Third World affairs and other matters, and as a leading democratic socialist he represented Costa Rica at various congresses of the Socialist International.

Arias' views on the major issues facing Costa Rica in recent years were outlined by J. S. Fuerst, who interviewed him for *Commonweal* magazine (May 9, 1986). According to Fuerst, "Arias . . . stands for greater equalization of income by increasing real wages, by raising taxes on the middle and upper classes, by enhancing education, health, and housing services, and by intensifying the program of cooperatives—both consumer and producer." But although Arias considers cooperatives an effective alternative course to both private ownership and government enterprise, Costa Rican efforts during the presidency of Monge to transfer unwieldy state-owned enterprises to cooperative sponsorship were hindered by the United States Agency for International Development (AID), which insisted on subsidizing only transfers to private enterprise. "We have got to convince the U.S. that a more extensive use of cooperatives is most important for Costa Rica," Arias told Fuerst. "It is the way to bring grass-roots democracy to people. . . . And it is more efficient than state-owned enterprises."

While rejecting Communist demands for widespread land distribution, Arias believes that farmers and workers could best be helped by such means as wage increases and keeping up the level of farm prices, by the creation of jobs through new developments in agriculture and industry, and by grass-roots participation in decision-making on the local level. He is also a staunch supporter of educational reforms and of cultural exchange programs. "What Costa Rica needs as much as anything is improvement of its education," he told J. S. Fuerst. "We cannot use the U.S. as a guide. . . . We have to have technical vocational schools. We have to combine them with the cooperative movement for a kind of work-study program. Perhaps most of all we need a substantial improvement in the quality of teachers. We must raise salaries, offer more scholarships for foreign study. . . ." Although critical of the Sandinista regime of Nicaragua because of its authoritarianism and its restrictions on civil liberties at home, as well as indications that it was fomenting unrest in Costa Rica through the domestic Communist organization, Arias resisted right-wing pressure to adopt a militant anti-Sandinista stand, and he consistently supported efforts to resolve Central American hostilities through negotiations.

Arias relinquished the post of secretary general of the PLN in January 1984 to seek nomination as the party's candidate for the presidency in the national elections scheduled for February 1986. Although the incumbent, Luis Alberto Monge, was one of the most popular presidents in Costa Rica's history, largely as a result of his policy of neutrality combined with his sharply critical attitude toward Nicaragua's Sandinistas, he was prevented by the constitution from running for a second consecutive term. After some interparty factional strife, in which he provoked resentment as an upstart by the party's traditional bosses, Arias was nominated as the presidential candidate at a PLN conference on January 27, 1985. According to James LeMoyne, writing in the *New York Times* (February 4, 1986), Arias "rolled up his usually carefully pressed sleeves and bruised his way through the opposition of the party's aging bosses to win the presidential

nomination. The fight left damaging divisions in the . . . party until the prospect of a likely defeat late in the campaign rallied party leaders behind Mr. Arias."

On the eve of the elections, Costa Rica was plagued by a national debt of some $4.5 billion that it had accumulated while supporting a welfare state during a period of depressed commodity prices and slow economic growth. Economic collapse was averted only by an infusion of large-scale foreign loans and United States aid. In December 1985 some $80 million in American and international credits were suspended until Costa Rica fulfilled demands by the World Bank to reduce the number of government employees and to cut certain import taxes, as well as the budget of the National Production Council, which subsidizes basic food commodities. Furthermore, despite an official policy of neutrality, United States-backed Contra forces were operating against Nicaragua's Sandinista regime from Costa Rican soil during Monge's presidency, while American Green Beret troops were training Costa Rica's civil guards. The presence of some 250,000 Central American refugees in Costa Rica, most of them from Nicaragua, was creating further social, health, and employment problems.

Arias' chief opponent for the elections was Rafael Angel Calderon Fournier, a former foreign minister and an unsuccessful candidate in the 1982 presidential election, representing the right-of-center Partido Unidad Social Cristiana (PUSC). At first the two leading candidates appeared to be about equal in strength, and their platforms were similar, both emphasizing economic recovery and the preservation of Costa Rica's traditional neutrality and friendship toward the United States while expressing hostility toward Nicaragua. Adopting the campaign slogan "roofs, jobs, and peace," Arias promised the voters improvements in housing, employment, and social services, and pledged to meet the country's staggering foreign debt without dismantling the welfare state that had given Costa Rica its high standard of living.

In the final weeks of the campaign, Arias gained substantially in the opinion polls after taking a more assertive stance as the "peace" candidate. When Calderon suggested at one point that he favored sending border guards to fight in Honduras in the event that Nicaragua invaded that country, Arias called him a "hawk" who would drag Costa Rica into a war. In response, Calderon asserted that Arias represented a corrupt and complacent ruling party that should be replaced by a new leadership for the benefit of the nation. Shortly before the election, Arias emphasized that Costa Rica was "a welfare state and not a garrison state."

In the elections of February 2, 1986, in which 1,185,222 Costa Ricans—about 80 percent of the eligible voters—went to the polls, Arias emerged as the victor, with 620,315 votes, or 52.3 percent of the total, while Calderon received 542,434 votes, or 45.8 percent. Of the fifty-seven seats in the unicameral legislative assembly, twenty-nine went to the

PLN and twenty-five were claimed by the PUSC, while the remaining three seats went to leftist splinter groups whose share of the popular vote was less than 2 percent. In his victory speech, Arias expressed satisfaction that the people had "chosen bread" over rifles, and he warned the approximately 3,000 Nicaraguan Contras on Costa Rican soil that he would not allow them to abuse the nation's hospitality or to put its sovereignty at risk.

Sworn in on May 8, 1986 for a four-year term as Costa Rica's forty-seventh and youngest president, Arias declared in his inaugural address: "We will keep Costa Rica out of the armed conflicts of Central America and we will endeavor through diplomatic and political means to prevent Central American brothers from killing each other." Referring to Costa Rica as an oasis of peace and freedom, Arias extolled the virtues of democracy and emphasized the need for Latin American economic recovery and the preservation of Costa Rica's neutrality to the assembled dignitaries, who included United States Vice-President George Bush and ten Latin American heads of state. He pledged to support the so-called Contadora peace treaty, sponsored by Colombia, Panama, Mexico, and Venezuela, which would require democratic elections, demilitarization, and internal reconciliation for all of Central America.

On May 24 and 25, 1986, Arias met with the presidents of Guatemala, El Salvador, Honduras, and Nicaragua in a Central American summit conference at Esquipulas, Guatemala to discuss the proposed Contadora peace accord for the region. In their final declaration, the five leaders recognized the need for the Contadora pact to be signed eventually but admitted that fundamental differences on key points remained to be resolved, notably in regard to arms control and limitations on international military maneuvers in the region, and Nicaragua's refusal to sign the pact as long as the United States continued to fund the Contra rebels. At Arias' request, a phrase that described the five signatories as "freely elected by the will of their respective peoples," which he felt did not apply to Nicaraguan President Daniel Ortega Saavedra, was omitted from the final draft. The declaration called for continued dialogue to enhance democracy and pluralism in Central America, to promote regional cooperation for social and economic development, and to establish means for the resolution of differences without outside interference. The leaders also agreed to initiate a Central American parliament.

On the economic front, Arias instituted measures to stimulate the infusion of money from abroad, including a "tax holiday" for foreign investors and the establishment of a free-trade zone near San José, but the national economy continued to be vulnerable. Although Arias resumed making interest payments on the country's foreign debt, which had been suspended by Monge, the expenditures of some $250 million a year—about 30 percent of export earnings—exceeded what Costa Rica could expect in new grants and loans from abroad. In September and October 1986 labor unions representing all sectors of the work force, from banana plantation and dock workers to civil servants and schoolteachers, staged massive demonstrations to protest salary increases that fell far short of the double-digit inflation rate. In response, the government called for a "great national pact" to deal with wage problems, but with little immediate effect. Similarly, the government's removal, in July 1986, of subsidies for basic grain products and the imposition of farm price ceilings led to demonstrations by farmers, compelling Arias to reinstate the subsidies in October.

Despite his strong criticism of Nicaragua's Sandinista government, Arias has vigorously opposed United States funding of the Contra rebels, contending that the money could be put to better use in promoting the survival of liberal democracy in Central America by peaceful means. "The more you give to the Contras, the more [Nicaraguan President] Ortega gets from the Soviets," he has said, as quoted by Stephen Kinzer in the *New York Times* (September 16, 1986). His program of "stability with growth and social justice" would, in his view, be impossible to achieve if there was no peace.

As a means of safeguarding his country's neutrality, Arias has moved decisively against Contra activities in Costa Rica. During the summer and early fall of 1986 the Arias government arrested several Contra activists and dismissed government officials who permitted a secret Contra hospital to operate on Costa Rican soil. "We're going to throw them out no matter who they are if we catch them helping the Contras," Arias has asserted. In September 1986 Costa Rican civil guards occupied a secret 6,520-foot airstrip near the Nicaraguan border that was being used for Contra supply flights. It had been built under the supervision of associates of former White House aide Lieutenant Colonel Oliver North, who was later dismissed in connection with the Iran-Contra scandals. When in November 1986 Contra leaders met in San José to discuss future plans, Arias denied visas to two of their top men, Adolfo Calero and Enrique Bermúdez, whom he considered military rather than political figures.

At a meeting on February 15, 1987 with the presidents of Honduras, Guatemala, and El Salvador, Arias put forth his proposals for a new regional peace plan for Central America, based on the Contadora proposals but broader in scope. The ten-point plan, described by Arias as a "risk for peace," called for immediate cease-fires in all guerrilla wars in the region—in Guatemala and El Salvador as well as in Nicaragua. All outside military aid to rebel groups would be suspended; there would be a general amnesty; and negotiations between conflicting parties would be initiated. This would be followed by free elections in the region, guarantees for improved human and civil rights, and a general reduction in military forces. In Arias' view, the plan would put the Sandinistas to a test. "If we arrive at an agreement and Nicaragua does not fulfill the obligations . . . ," he told John Moody in an interview for *Time* (June 29, 1987), "then it will put an end to this ambiguity which has permitted the Sandinistas to receive the support of both democratic and totalitarian governments." Democratic Senator Christopher Dodd of Connecticut, who was present at the initial meeting, termed Arias' proposals "an important first step for the Central Americans to get out of the bleachers and into the playing field in order to begin solving their own problems," and Flora Lewis noted in her *New York Times* column (May 27, 1987) that "the beauty of the Arias plan is that it will clarify the issues so badly muddled by shifting United States policy statements and covert actions."

At first, the Arias plan received wide support, in Latin America, the United States, and Western Europe, and even the PUSC opposition in Costa Rica endorsed it. Nicaraguan President Ortega, after an initial negative reaction, also indicated that he was receptive to it. On March 12, 1987, the United States senate, in a nonbinding resolution sponsored by Democratic Senator Terry Sanford of North Carolina, endorsed the Arias plan by a vote of ninety-seven to one, although Republican spokesmen warned that their support of a negotiated settlement should not be interpreted as abandonment of Reagan administration policies.

Eventually, however, the Arias plan became subject to increasing criticism. On June 17, 1987, Arias was invited to the White House in Washington, D.C. to consult with President Ronald Reagan and other officials in a sixty-five minute meeting that was later described by Costa Rican sources as "sharp, tense, and blunt." Reagan reportedly found a number of "loopholes" in the plan and maintained that it made undue concessions to the Sandinistas. The plan also caused concern in El Salvador, whose president, José Napoleon Duarte, feared that the agreement would force his government to make concessions to imprisoned leftist rebels. Meanwhile, Sandinista spokesmen accused the United States of trying to isolate Nicaragua and to sabotage the possibility of a negotiated settlement. Discussions of the Arias plan at a summit meeting originally scheduled for June 25, 1987 were postponed.

Finally, on August 7, 1987, after some prodding by the Costa Rican president, the five Central American heads of state, meeting in Guatemala City, signed a regional peace plan essentially based on the Arias proposals and scheduled to go into effect on November 7, 1987. At the same time they shunted aside a plan presented three days earlier by President Reagan and Jim Wright, the speaker of the House of Representatives, that placed greater demands on the Sandinistas, imposed a shorter deadline than was provided for under the Arias plan, and left the door open for renewed United States aid to the Contras. Although the Arias plan left some questions unresolved, it was widely hailed as a breakthrough toward peace, and even President Reagan welcomed what he called "this commitment to peace and democracy by the five Central American presidents."

On September 20, 1987, Arias embarked on an eight-day visit to the United States to promote his peace plan, consult with President Reagan and other United States officials, and address Congress and the UN General Assembly. He made no reference to a recent proposal by Reagan to ask Congress for $270 million in new aid to the Contras but urged his American hosts to "give peace a chance."

Arias received appropriate recognition for his peace efforts when on October 13, 1987, the Norwegian Nobel committee named him the winner of the Nobel Peace Prize, citing his "outstanding contribution to the possible return of stability and peace to a region long torn by strife and civil war." Although the award was widely hailed, it was seen as a setback for the Reagan administration, whose continued efforts to aid the Contras now appeared to be doomed.

Oscar Arias Sánchez was married in 1973 to Margarita Penón Góngora, a biochemist who graduated from Vassar College in the United States. Their children are Silvia Eugenia and Oscar Felipe. Described in the *Nation* as "a man of intelligence and enormous pride," Arias has, according to James LeMoyne in the *New York Times*, "some of the reserve and intellectual independence" that is reflected in his British academic training. His published works include *Democracia, Independencia y Sociedad Latinoamericana* (1977), *Los Caminos para el Desarrollo de Costa Rica* (1977), and *Nuevos Rumbos para el Desarrollo Costarricense* (1980), as well as diverse articles in periodicals and scholarly journals. "It takes Oscar a long time to make up his mind sometimes," one friend has said of him. "But when he does he's very single-minded."

References: *Christian Sci Mon* p14 My 8 '86; *Commonweal* 113:272+ My 9 '86; *N Y Times* A p3 F 4 '86, A p12 S 23 '87 por; *Nation* 243:698+ D 20 '86; *Newsweek* 105:44+ O 26 '87 por; *Time* 130:44+ O 26 '87 por; *Who's Who in the World,* 1987–88

Ashcroft, Peggy

Dec. 22, 1907– British actress. Address: b. c/o The Royal Shakespeare Company, Barbican Theatre, Barbican Centre, Silk St., London EC2Y 8BQ, England; h. "Manor Lodge," Frognal Lane, London N.W. 3, England

NOTE: This biography supersedes the article that appeared in *Current Biography* in 1963.

Indisputably the supreme English-speaking actress of our time, in the view of the majority of theatre critics and historians and most of her colleagues, Dame Peggy Ashcroft has been a dominant force in British theatre for more than fifty years. Acclaimed for her brilliant technique, her emotional

Peggy Ashcroft

Speech Training and Dramatic Art (now the Central School of Speech and Drama) in London.

Miss Ashcroft's early love of language developed into a passion for the theatre at the Woodford School in Croydon, where she studied elocution with Gwen Lally, a former classical actress, and appeared regularly in the school's annual Shakespearean productions—usually in the male lead. By her mid-teens she had decided to pursue a career on the stage. "I think it was that I discovered it was very exciting to become someone else," she explained to Michael Billington in an interview for the London *Sunday Telegraph Magazine* (November 28, 1982). Despite her own interest in the theatre, Violet Ashcroft disapproved of her daughter's intention, but she reluctantly agreed to allow the girl to attend the Central School. Enrolling at the school in 1923, Miss Ashcroft trained mostly under Elsie Fogerty herself and eventually earned a diploma in dramatic art. For their performances in a scene from *The Merchant of Venice,* she and a classmate, Laurence Olivier, were awarded the school's gold medal.

While she was a student at the Central School, Peggy Ashcroft made her professional stage debut, on May 22, 1926, when she stepped in at the last minute for the ailing Muriel Hewitt in the Birmingham Repertory Company's staging of J. M. Barrie's *Dear Brutus.* She had already essayed the part of Margaret in a school production of the play, but the experience of performing the role with a troupe of seasoned professionals left her with a profound sense of how much she had yet to learn. On her own, following the death of her mother later in the year, Miss Ashcroft took whatever parts she could find. "My rule—straight out of drama school—was to accept whatever was offered," she told Melvin Bragg, who interviewed her for a London *Observer* (August 24, 1986) profile. "I did it even if I hated it. Then people made offers, and *then* you could begin to choose."

After playing a succession of ingenues in London's fringe theatres, Miss Ashcroft made her West End debut in November 1927, as Betty in Nigel Playfair's production of Congreve's Restoration comedy *The Way of the World.* A series of roles in relatively insignificant plays followed, among them Anastasia Vulliamy in *The Fascinating Foundling,* Mary Bruin in *The Land of Heart's Desire,* Edith Strange in *Earthbound,* and perhaps most notably, Lucy Deren in Molly Kerr's modern tragedy *Requital,* before she landed the part that first brought her wide recognition: Naomi in Ashley Duke's adaptation of Lion Feuchtwanger's bestselling novel *Jew Süss,* which opened at the Duke of York's Theatre in September 1929. As Süss's innocent and adoring daughter, Miss Ashcroft more than held her own opposite the great actor-manager Matheson Lang, in the title role. Largely because of her "singular capacity to suggest a pure and noble being bruised and broken by an immense sorrow," the veteran drama critic Harold Hobson has included the sentimental melodrama among his "half-dozen most memorable visits" to the theatre.

honesty, and her incomparable understanding of and respect for the music of language, she has been for thousands of theatregoers the definitive incarnation of Shakespeare's "golden girls," as she has called them, but because of her extraordinary versatility and her uncommon willingness to take risks, she has been an equally effective interpreter of Ibsen, Chekhov, Beckett, Albee, and Pinter.

More concerned about the development of her craft than the progress of her career, Miss Ashcroft has worked mainly in "art" theatres, and she was involved in the pioneering theatrical movements that led to the establishment of the English Stage Company, the National Theatre, and the Royal Shakespeare Company (RSC). A longtime RSC associate artist, she has been since 1968 the only actor on the "direction" committee that is ultimately responsible for the company's artistic policy. For her services to the theatre, Miss Ashcroft was designated a Dame of the Order of the British Empire in 1956, and in 1962 she became the first British actress to have a theatre—the Ashcroft Theatre in Croydon—named after her in her lifetime.

Peggy Ashcroft, whose full name is Edith Margaret Emily Ashcroft, was born in Croydon, just south of London, England, on December 22, 1907, the daughter of William Worsley Ashcroft, an estate agent who was killed in World War I, and his wife, the former Violet (or Violetta) Maud Bernheim. As a young child learning to read, she was fascinated by the sound and rhythm of verse and frequently memorized poems for her own amusement. She was encouraged in that precocious pursuit by her poetry-loving grandfather and her mother, an enthusiastic amateur actress who had studied with the renowned speech specialist Elsie Fogerty, the founder of the Central School of

On the strength of her performance in the long-running *Jew Süss*, Miss Ashcroft was recruited in May 1930 to play Desdemona in a lavish West End production of *Othello*, starring Paul Robeson as the Moor. Among the many admirers of her radiant Desdemona was the actor John Gielgud. "It was as if all the lights in the theatre had suddenly gone up," he wrote, of her first entrance, in his book *Early Stages* (1939). Remembering Miss Ashcroft's luminous quality, Gielgud later hired the actress, who had been playing a variety of roles in a series of mostly short-lived West End productions, to star in his staging of *Romeo and Juliet* for the Oxford University Dramatic Society, which opened to universal acclaim—particularly for Miss Ashcroft's rapturous Juliet—in February 1932.

A few months later Peggy Ashcroft began her first season as the leading lady at the Old Vic in London. In the course of the nine-month 1932–33 Old Vic season, she played six major Shakespearean roles—Juliet, Imogen, Rosalind, Portia, Perdita, and Miranda—as well as Cleopatra in Shaw's *Caesar and Cleopatra*, Kate Hardcastle in *She Stoops to Conquer*, Lady Teazle in Sheridan's *The School for Scandal*, and the title role in John Drinkwater's historical epic *Mary Stuart*. It was, in Miss Ashcroft's words, a "killing venture" made even more difficult by her decision to take a few weeks off in mid-season to learn the arduous leading part (said to be among the longest in modern drama) in Theodore Komisarjevsky's stage adaptation of Arthur Schnitzler's sexually frank *Fräulein Elsa*.

Having earned a reputation as a competent and versatile performer, Miss Ashcroft made the leap to recognition as a major actress in October 1935, when John Gielgud resurrected his production of *Romeo and Juliet* for a stand at the New Theatre in London. Playing opposite Gielgud and Laurence Olivier, who alternated in the roles of Romeo and Mercutio, she brought Juliet to life with an interpretation that was at once "extraordinarily endearing" and "frightfully direct," as Gielgud put it. The critics, including the influential James Agate and W. A. Darlington, were unanimous in their praise of "the sweetest Juliet of our time." "She does more than make Shakespeare's expression of Juliet's thoughts seem natural," Peter Fleming observed in his review, as quoted by Richard Findlater in the book *These Our Actors* (1983). "She makes it seem inevitable."

It was while she was performing with Gielgud and Edith Evans, among others, in Komisarjevsky's production of Chekhov's *The Seagull* at the New Theatre in May 1936 that Miss Ashcroft, by her own account, first realized the rewards of ensemble playing and "the true value" in practice of a permanent acting company. Consequently, upon her return to London in 1937 following her Broadway debut, as Lise in Maxwell Anderson's fantasy *High Tor*, she jumped at the chance to join Gielgud's company for a season at the Queen's Theatre. Her assignments for the engagement were the roles of Lady Teazle, Portia, the confused little Queen in

Richard II, and Irina in Michel Saint-Denis' staging of Chekhov's *The Three Sisters*. Miss Ashcroft has since described her months at the Queen's Theatre, working with such actors as Gielgud, Anthony Quayle, Michael Redgrave, Gwen Ffrangcon-Davies, Alec Guinness, Glen Byam Shaw, and George Devine under the direction of Komisarjevsky, Tyrone Guthrie, and perhaps most important, Saint-Denis, as "by far the most formative part of my acting experience." Indeed she was so taken by Saint-Denis' emphasis on preparation and attention to detail that when the Queen's troupe disbanded, she and a few of the other actors reunited under the director, formed an acting ensemble, and took out a lease on the Phoenix Theatre. The group's first efforts—Bulgakov's *The White Guard*, in October 1938, and *Twelfth Night*, with Miss Ashcroft as Viola, two months later—were well received by the critics, but failed to attract an audience. Within months, the venture collapsed.

For the next half-dozen years or so, Miss Ashcroft was, for casting directors and audiences alike, the ideal ingenue. Numbered among her credits during that period were Dinah Sylvester in Clemence Dane's *Cousin Muriel*, Mrs. de Winter in the stage adaptation of Daphne du Maurier's best-selling novel *Rebecca*, Cecily Cardew in Oscar Wilde's *The Importance of Being Earnest*, Ophelia in *Hamlet*, and Titania in *A Midsummer Night's Dream*. Miss Ashcroft finally escaped from romantic typecasting when she tackled the role of the alcoholic Evelyn Hart in *Edward, My Son*, an episodic melodrama by Robert Morley and Noel Langley. In the view of most critics, it was her unflinching portrayal of that disillusioned "wreck," to use her description, that made this otherwise ordinary play an extraordinary success, both in London, in 1947, and in New York, in 1948. For her interpretation, Miss Ashcroft received the Ellen Terry Award for the best performance by an actress in London in 1947.

Miss Ashcroft followed up with a sharply etched character study of Catherine Sloper, the gauche, inarticulate spinster who takes revenge on her faithless suitor in *The Heiress*, adapted by Ruth and Augustus Goetz from Henry James's *Washington Square*. As Harold Hobson observed in his *Theatre in Britain* (1984), the play was "of great importance" in the history of postwar British theatre because it proved beyond a doubt that "Britain now had an actress worthy of comparison with the great feminine figures of the Continental stage." In *The Heiress*, he went on, "Peggy Ascroft showed herself to be complete mistress of that moment of supreme emotion. . . . For [her] performance, superlatives seem pale and feeble things. In her hands the tragedy of this unloved girl became one of the theatre's most moving experiences."

Irresistibly drawn to what she has called the "mystery" of the great classical parts, Miss Ashcroft spent most of the 1950s working in classical repertory at the Shakespeare Memorial Theatre in Stratford-upon-Avon and the Old Vic in London. She made her debut at the Memorial Theatre, then under the artistic direction of Anthony Quayle, in 1950, turning in a Cordelia that was, for most reviewers, "goodness incarnate" in *King Lear* and a Beatrice that was more feminine and vulnerable than most in *Much Ado About Nothing.* Later in the decade, her impatient and adventurous Portia, opposite Michael Redgrave's Shylock in Gielgud's Victorian staging of *The Merchant of Venice,* reminded older critics of the legendary Ellen Terry, and her "miraculously youthful" (she was, at the time, forty-nine years old) characterizations of Rosalind, in *As You Like It,* and Imogen in *Cymbeline,* astounded viewers. By most accounts, she was less successful as Cleopatra in Glen Byam Shaw's opulent production of *Antony and Cleopatra.* Her unorthodox approach to the queen, whom she portrayed as a cunning, ruthless Greek (which, historically, she was, as Miss Ashcroft has pointed out in several interviews), disappointed some reviewers, who concluded that she was temperamentally unsuited to the role. At the Old Vic, her parts included Viola in *Twelfth Night,* Mistress Page in *The Merry Wives of Windsor,* and most notably, the title role in Saint-Denis' staging of *Electra,* which many of her colleagues still refer to as "her Hamlet."

Although she devoted most of her time in the 1950s to the classical repertoire, Miss Ashcroft did not neglect newer works, choosing to play Hester Collyer in Terence Rattigan's emotional drama *The Deep Blue Sea,* the mysterious Miss Madrigal in Gielgud's extravagantly praised production of Enid Bagnold's offbeat comedy *The Chalk Garden,* for she which was voted best actress of 1956 by the London *Evening Standard,* and the dual role of Shen Te, the heart-of-gold prostitute, and her bestial cousin, Shui Ta, in the British premiere of Bertolt Brecht's *The Good Woman of Setzuan,* one of the first productions of the English Stage Company.

Peggy Ashcroft scored perhaps her greatest triumph of the decade in November 1954, when she played the title role in Ibsen's *Hedda Gabler* at the Westminster Theatre in London and, later, at the New Theatre in Oslo, Norway. Stripping away the glamour and the aura of romantic tragedy often associated with the character, Miss Ashcroft brought out Hedda's mordant wit and calculated cruelty. The drama critic of the Oslo *Aftenposten* wrote of her performance: "It is curious to have to register the fact that an English actress has shown the Norwegian public how Hedda should be played. . . . There is the most intimate connection between the Hedda Gabler of Peggy Ashcroft and the intentions of Ibsen himself." King Haakon of Norway was so moved by Miss Ashcroft's interpretation that he personally awarded her the King's Gold Medal.

Further evidence of Miss Ashcroft's affinity for what she has called Ibsen's "extraordinary tragic world" came in 1959, with her electrifying performance as Rebecca West, the ambivalent "antiheroine," to use the actress' word, in the English Stage Company's production of Ibsen's *Rosmersholm.* Since then, she has given an affect-

ing human dimension to such varied Ibsen characters as Mrs. Alving in *Ghosts,* for the Royal Shakespeare Company in 1966, Ella Rentheim in *John Gabriel Borkman,* for the National Theatre in 1975, and the Rat Wife in *Little Eyolf,* for the BBC in 1982. Fascinated by the way in which Chekhov's characters reveal themselves—"layer by layer, like Peer Gynt's onion," as she once put it—she was equally effective in that dramatist's studies of frustrated middle-class lives. Her Madame Ranevskaya in the RSC's 1961 production of *The Cherry Orchard,* was notable for its "harrowing truthfulness." Three years later, her Madame Arkadina in Tony Richardson's staging of *The Seagull* for the English Stage Company was similarly acclaimed for its subtlety and humanity.

By her own description "an actress in search of a company," Peggy Ashcroft had for years spoken out in favor of the creation of a more or less permanent acting ensemble comprised of "a group of people with the same outlook and style." Such a company offered, in her opinion, "the only hope of reaching perfection in our theatre." It is not surprising, then, that she was among the first actors to join Peter Hall's fledgling Royal Shakespeare Company in 1960, nor that she was the first of those actors to sign a long-term contract with the troupe. In her first season with the company, Miss Ashcroft displayed "iron strength of presence and queenly control of phrasing," to quote Richard Findlater, as Paulina in *The Winter's Tale* and, in a novel reinterpretation, tenderness and humor as an obviously smitten and "cautiously blossoming" Katharina, opposite Peter O'Toole's Petruchio, in John Barton's vigorous staging of *The Taming of the Shrew.*

Other classical parts Miss Ashcroft has portrayed—invariably to stunning effect—for the RSC over the years include the title role in Webster's intricate tale of vengeance, *The Duchess of Malfi;* Emilia in Franco Zeffirelli's operatic staging of *Othello,* starring John Gielgud; Queen Katherine in the rarely performed *Henry VIII;* and most recently, a serenely melancholy Countess of Rousillon in Trevor Nunn's bewitching Edwardian production of *All's Well That Ends Well,* which was one of the most popular attractions of the company's inaugural season at its new Barbican Theatre in London in 1981–82.

Miss Ashcroft also appeared in several productions of the company's perennial favorite *The Hollow Crown,* John Barton's anthology about the kings and queens of England. But she is perhaps best remembered for her tour de force performance in the marathon part of Margaret of Anjou in the RSC's 1963 landmark production *The Wars of the Roses,* Barton's condensation of the *Henry VI* trilogy and *Richard III* into three plays. In a display of blazing virtuosity that left both audiences and critics awestruck, she aged thirty-five years over the course of ten hours' playing time, from an alluring but willful young princess to a bloodthirsty warrior-queen to a bedraggled crone. Universally hailed as "the work of a great actress in the prime of her powers," to quote Peter Roberts' review for

Plays & Players (October 1963), Miss Ashcroft's astonishing performance earned her the London *Evening Standard's* best-actress award.

Although Peggy Ashcroft clearly relishes the challenge of playing Shakespeare, one of the chief attractions of the RSC, in her opinion, is its policy of staging, in addition to the Shakespeare canon that is the core of its repertoire, a wide variety of contemporary works. "One simply cannot do Shakespeare year in and year out . . . ," she explained to David Addenbrooke in a conversation for his book *The Royal Shakespeare Company* (1974). "Our company can play Shakespeare as full-bloodedly and wholeheartedly as they do only because they are not committed to playing Shakespeare for the whole of their lives, or for three years on end."

Welcoming the "fresh problems and new difficulties" that were, in her words, "all quite different from those of Viola or Lady Teazle," Miss Ashcroft embarked on a series of contemporary plays in 1966. Over the next ten years, her credits for the RSC included the possessive matriarch in *Days in the Trees*, Marguerite Duras' examination of futility and loneliness; Volumnia in Günter Grass's complex and sardonic *The Plebeians Rehearse the Uprising*, about an abortive workers' revolt in East Germany; and the eccentric Lidya in Aleksei Arbuzov's geriatric comedy *Old World*, for which she received the Society of West End Theatre's award for best actress of 1976. She also took leading roles in the company's productions of Edward Albee's chilling examinations of American family life, *All Over* and *A Delicate Balance*, and of Harold Pinter's double bill about stifled lives, *A Slight Ache* and *Landscape*.

Since joining the RSC in 1960, Miss Ashcroft has appeared almost exclusively with the company. On the few occasions when she has accepted an outside assignment, it has most often been with the English Stage Company, on whose artistic council she sits, or the National Theatre, now under the direction of her longtime colleague Peter Hall. Her credits for the two subsidized repertory companies include the schizophrenic murderess Claire Lanner in Marguerite Duras' psychological thriller *The Lovers of Viorne*, for the English Stage Company in 1971, and the battered but chirpily optimistic Winnie in Samuel Beckett's *Happy Days* and the formidable grande dame Fanny Farrelly in a revival of Lillian Hellman's *Watch on the Rhine*, for the National Theatre in, respectively, 1975 and 1980. Her sole venture into the commercial West End in the past twenty-five years came in 1972, when she joined Ralph Richardson in *Lloyd George Knew My Father*, William Douglas Home's lighthearted comedy about the eccentricities of the British upper class.

Because of the fragmentary and "somewhat mechanical" techniques of filmmaking, Peggy Ashcroft has generally felt less at home on the motion picture soundstage than in a theatre. Over the course of her long career, she has made fewer than a dozen films, beginning with *The Wandering Jew*

in 1933 and including *Quiet Wedding* (1940), *The Nun's Story* (1958), *Sunday Bloody Sunday* (1971), and *Joseph Andrews* (1977). Until recently, her most memorable film role may well have been the crofter's wife in Alfred Hitchcock's classic thriller *The Thirty-Nine Steps* (1935), but in the early 1980s, David Lean, the veteran film director, persuaded the reluctant actress to take on the part of Mrs. Moore in *A Passage to India* (1984), his visually lush adaptation of E. M. Forster's elusive novel. Her delicately calibrated characterization of that venerable matron "impatient both with the world and with her persisting ignorance of it," to quote Stanley Kauffmann, was widely praised and earned her best-actress awards from the New York Film Critics Circle and the British Academy of Film and Television Arts and best-supporting-actress honors from the Academy of Motion Picture Arts and Sciences and the Hollywood Foreign Press Association.

Besides recreating for the small screen her stage roles in *The Cherry Orchard*, *The Wars of the Roses*, and *Days in the Trees*, Miss Ashcroft has appeared in several important television productions, including the first live transmission of a Shakespearean production—*Twelfth Night*, from the stage of the Phoenix Theatre in 1939. More recently, she has played a stubborn and arrogant Viennese dowager in Stephen Poliakoff's *Caught on a Train* (BBC, 1980); an elderly wife in *Cream in My Coffee* (London Weekend Television, 1980), Dennis Potter's poignant evocation of a thwarted life; Queen Mary in *Edward and Mrs. Simpson* (ITV, 1980); and Barbie Batchelor, the eccentric missionary in *Jewel in the Crown* (Granada, 1982; PBS, 1984), the award-winning miniseries based on Paul Scott's panoramic portrait of the British in India, *The Raj Quartet*. Peggy Ashcroft was so intrigued by the character of Barbie, whom she has described as the "outsider" who reflects "the 'other' attitude to India," that she determinedly sought out the part. In the view of many critics, among them Ann Walmsley of *Maclean's* (October 8, 1984), it was Dame Peggy's interpretation that gave the fourteen-part series "continuity and conscience." For each of the aforementioned performances, Miss Ashcroft was named best television actress of the year by the British Academy of Film and Television Arts.

Dedicated to the continued development of the theatre and of the arts in general, Peggy Ashcroft has served on the executive committee of Actors' Equity, and she was for three years, from 1962 until 1965, a member of the Arts Council. Her intense feeling for poetry led her in 1943 to take the initiative in founding the Apollo Society, which has helped to revive interest in poetry through staged readings, recordings, and radio broadcasts. An active adherent of the Labour party, she has been associated with Arts for Labour, an organization charged with advising Labour party leaders on formulating "a socialist policy" for the arts. Deeply committed to human rights and nuclear disarmament, among other liberal causes, Miss Ashcroft has given countless readings and one-woman shows to raise money for such organizations as Amnesty International, Campaign for Nuclear Disarmament, and the International Committee for Artists' Freedom.

A striking woman who appears to be some years younger than her chronological age, Peggy Ashcroft has short, softly curled gray hair, lively blue eyes, a radiant smile, and a friendly, unpretentious manner. "She has no airs and graces," John Gielgud has said of his longtime friend and colleague, as quoted in the London *Sunday Telegraph Magazine* (November 28, 1982). "She rarely talks of her work even to me, except when we're in the theatre. She's not at all gossipy, not interested in her hair or clothes, or the impression she's making. She's so *unactressy*." Because she dislikes "talking about [herself]," Miss Ashcroft rarely grants interviews, and relatively little is known about her private life. She is fond of literature, art (she has a collection of works by the British painter and etcher Walter Sickert), and music (especially Mozart), and she enjoys walking. An admitted cricket ad-

dict, she has helped organize theatrical teams, and she herself played on the Royal Shakespeare Company's eleven in a charity match in 1963. Dame Peggy's three marriages—to Rupert Hart-Davis, in 1929, Theodore Komisarjevsky, in 1934, and Jeremy Nicholas Hutchinson, in 1940—ended in divorce. From her last marriage, she has two children, Nicholas, a theatrical director, and Eliza, and several grandchildren. The actress lives alone in a book-filled nineteenth-century house in the Hampstead section of London.

References: Guardian Wkly p20 N 22 '81 por; London Observer p45 Mr 10 '85 por, p19 Ag 24 '86; Plays & Players 11:8+ Je '64 pors; Washington Post B p1+ S 4 '73 por, C p1+ Mr 19 '85 pors; Addenbrooke, David. The Royal Shakespeare Company (1974); Burton, Hal, ed. Great Acting (1967); Findlater, Richard. The Player Queens (1976), These Our Actors (1983); Keown, Eric. Peggy Ashcroft (1955); Speaight, Robert. Shakespeare on the Stage (1973); Who's Who, 1987–88; Who's Who in the Theatre (1981)

Astor, Brooke

1902(?)– Philanthropist; author. Address: b. The Vincent Astor Foundation, 405 Park Ave., New York City, N.Y. 10022

The civic-minded and arts-oriented octogenarian socialite Brooke Astor devotes most of her abundant energy to the Vincent Astor Foundation, the philanthropy established by her late husband in

1948 for the "amelioration of human misery." A ubiquitous participant in New York City life, Mrs. Astor has displayed a combination of imagination and discernment in allocating over $135 million in grants in support of what she calls the city's "crown jewels"—the New York Public Library, the Metropolitan Museum of Art, the Bronx Zoo, Rockefeller University, and the Pierpont Morgan Library—as well as projects for the disadvantaged. The historian Arthur Schlesinger Jr. has described her as "a great lady" with "the look and spirit of a gamine." "She is wealthy and could so easily waste her days in aimless social diversion," Schlesinger wrote in *Architectural Digest* (May 1986). "But she is a truly civilized woman. She not only reads books but writes them. . . . She enjoys the graces of living, but her consuming purpose is to improve the quality of life for others."

In addition to the presidency of the Vincent Astor Foundation, Mrs. Astor's charity trusteeships include membership on the corporate board of the Astor Home for emotionally disturbed children in Rhinebeck, New York. Before she became a philanthropist, she was a magazine journalist, and she continues to pursue a writing career. She is a consulting editor of *House and Garden*, a contributor to other magazines, and the author of two autobiographies and two novels partly inspired by her life experiences. The more successful of the novels is the latest, *The Last Blossom on the Plum Tree* (Random House, 1986), a comedy of manners evoking life in international high society in the heady days preceding the Wall Street Crash of 1929. She sees her writing as "inclined to be something to cheer people up."

Brooke Astor, who is coy about her age, was born Roberta Brooke Russell in Portsmouth, New

Hampshire, shortly after the turn of the century. Various sources yield differing birth dates up to 1905, but internal evidence points to the year 1902. Her father was John Henry Russell, a Marine Corps major general who served as commandant at a succession of Marine posts around the world. Her mother was Mabel (Howard) Russell, a socialite of intellectual bent. "My father formed my character", she has said, "My mother formed my mind." Like Emily, the protagonist of *The Last Blossom on the Plum Tree*, she was taught by her parents to develop "good manners and good humor" and to consider self-pity "the most ignoble of emotions."

The description of Mrs. Astor's first sixteen years of life chronicled in her memoir *Patchwork Child* (Harper & Row, 1962), reads like a grand tour of the world. The family moved from Annapolis, where the father taught at the Naval Academy, to Marine posts in Honolulu (where Brooke had a Japanese nurse who introduced her to the folklore of the East), Panama, Newport, Shanghai, and Peking. In Shanghai, the poverty of the sampan people deeply touched Brooke, young as she was. In Peking, where she lived between the ages of seven and eleven, she became interested in Oriental art and philosophy.

Deprived of abiding peer friendships by her nomadic life, Brooke developed a lively inner life. At six she began to write, and at seven to keep a diary. During her years in China she filled copybooks with stories, plays, and poems. While precociously learning how to behave in high international social circles, she would retreat to playing with her dolls. Except for one year in a British school in Peking, her education was in the hands of governesses.

When the family returned to the father's house in Washington, D.C., Brooke's mother, worried about her daughter's introversion, got rid of her dolls and enrolled her in Miss Madeira's School, an elite secondary institution. While there, Brooke founded the Facio Club, a literary society that gave readings and published a monthly student magazine, for which she wrote and drew illustrations.

Brooke wanted to study Latin and Greek, but her mother dissuaded her. "She thought I was going to become a 'bluestocking' . . . a bore and not attractive, someone who wouldn't learn to flirt at all," she recounted to an interviewer for *New York Newsday* (September 4, 1986). "I didn't finish high school. . . . I was a dropout, taken away by my mother." Following a sojourn with her parents in Santo Domingo, she "went to another school— which shall be nameless—that was in Washington, too, and that was devoted more to giving you French and drawing lessons and that sort of thing." For self-improvement, she devoted herself to reading.

Invited by a Facio Club acquaintance to attend a Princeton prom, Brooke met wealthy J. Dryden Kuser, the manager of the *Daily Princetonian* and the president of the New Jersey Audubon Society. At sixteen, she married Kuser, who in time became a New Jersey state senator. As she reveals in

Footprints (Doubleday, 1980), the sequel to *Patchwork Child*, the marriage was a most unhappy one, marked by drunkenness and, at times, violence on Kuser's part, and it ended in divorce in 1930. By that marriage, she had her only child, a son, Anthony, who is now a consultant on international affairs after having served as United States ambassador to Kenya.

On the positive side, Brooke's marriage to Kuser brought her in touch with many influential politicians and journalists, and it drove her into outside activity. She reviewed books for *Vogue* and wrote articles for *Pictorial Review*, sat on the boards of the Virginia Day Nursery and the Maternity Center Association—the first of the many charity boards on which she would sit in her lifetime—and did such volunteer social work as accompanying a nurse on her rounds of poor families with young children, in New York City. Settling in New York City after her marriage to Kuser ended, she studied creative writing in Columbia University's extension program and hosted a writing workshop in her home at 1 Gracie Square. One of the participants in the workshop was the journalist Arthur Krock, who became a lifelong friend and introduced her to his colleagues in journalism, Herbert Bayard Swope and Ralph Pulitzer.

Meanwhile, Brooke was corresponding with Charles ("Buddie") Marshall, a stockbroker whom she had met when riding to hounds with her first husband. Following Marshall's divorce from his first wife, he and Brooke married, in 1932. The actress Lillian Gish, a close friend of Brooke's, has described her twenty-year marriage to Buddie Marshall as "one of the greatest love stories" she had "ever been near." The couple bought a house in Westbury, Long Island and a penthouse at 10 Gracie Square, and they spent their summers in a castle in Portofino, Italy. Marshall indulged Brooke's love of travel, taking her to Hungary, Egypt, Turkey, Lebanon, and Israel, among other countries. Sharing her concern for the underprivileged, he taught her to implement that concern in a disciplined, organized way. He assisted her as well in her cultural pursuits, including the organizing of chamber music concerts. Through a friend, Harry Bull, the editor of *Town and Country*, she became a contributor to that magazine. During World War II she was hostess for the U.S.O., served as a Red Cross Grey Lady, and assisted in an army library. After the war she became the feature editor of *House and Garden* magazine, her first paying job. She was also on the board of *Newsweek*, of which Marshall was a founder. At home, she played the piano and sang for Marshall in the evenings, and they played croquet together.

In 1953, a year after the death of Buddie Marshall, Brooke married Vincent Astor, the heir to the fortune of John Jacob Astor, the fur trader and financier who was the richest man in America at the time of his death in 1848. (It was Vincent Astor's third marriage. His first wife, Helen, was the sister of Buddy Marshall's first wife, Alice.) Civic-spirited like his wife, Vincent Astor funded a playground in Harlem, converted part of Ferncliff, his 500-acre estate in Rhinebeck, New York, into a model state experimental farm, and turned a smaller property he owned in Rhinebeck into the Astor Home for invalid children. Deeded to the Roman Catholic Archdiocese of New York in 1952, the home began concentrating on the care of emotionally disturbed children, the function that it still fulfills under the direction of an order of Catholic nuns.

Brooke Astor assisted her husband in his philanthropic work and served on the boards of Recording for the Blind and the Women's Auxiliary of New York Hospital. Regarding the Vincent Astor Foundation, which he had set up in 1948 as the principal beneficiary of his will, Vincent told Brooke that she was "going to have a hell of a lot of fun" with it after his death. That death, in 1959, was, as she said, "like a volcano" in Brooke Astor's life, an eruption that left her with the means to accomplish virtually anything she wanted. Astor willed her $2 million outright, the income on $60 million (the principal to be disposed of in her will), and control of another $60 million in the form of the assets of the Vincent Astor Foundation.

Soon after Vincent Astor's death, Brooke Astor was named a trustee of the New York Public Library, a special family interest ever since John Jacob Astor helped get the library started a century before. Between 1959 and 1983 Astor contributions to the library totaled about $20 million. In 1983 Mrs. Astor resigned from numerous other charity boards to concentrate on pulling the library out of a budget crisis. Her energetic fund-raising and her own gift of $10 million helped the library to emerge from the crisis not only with its cut services restored but with a renovated Forty-second Street building.

Because the Astor fortune was built primarily on profits from New York City real estate, Mrs. Astor decided early on that the Vincent Astor Foundation funds would be spent exclusively in the five boroughs of the city. It would be difficult to cite any cultural institution in the city not affected by that decision, but some stand out. In 1965 New York University rewarded Mrs. Astor for her contributions by electing her, along with Mrs. Albert D. Lasker, one of the first two women trustees in the university's 134-year history. Thanks to Astor Foundation funds, the Metropolitan Museum of Art was able, in 1981, to open the Chinese Garden Court and the Ming Room, the first permanent exhibits created jointly by the United States and China after their rapprochement. In the late 1970s, in recognition of the several millions of dollars in Astor Foundation contributions to the Bronx Zoo, a baby elephant at the zoo was named "Astor." More recently, Mrs. Astor helped to rehabilitate the Cooper-Hewitt Museum and the South Street Seaport.

Mrs. Astor's attention to cultural projects has been accompanied by a concern for the disadvantaged, such as those living in the Bedford Stuyvesant section of Brooklyn, where Astor seed money began the fight against blight. In 1961 the United Neighborhood Houses of New York announced that the Vincent Astor Foundation had given it $1 million for a three-year project involving nine settlement houses in Manhattan and Brooklyn dedicated to steering vulnerable pre-teenagers away from gangs and juvenile delinquency. In 1964 Mrs. Astor donated part of the Astor estate in Rhinebeck to the Roman Catholic Archdiocese of New York for charitable uses. In 1966, acting on her awareness of the detrimental effect of environmental ugliness on the quality of life of the poor, she was instrumental in the creation of imaginative parks, which she called "outdoor living rooms," in the George Washington Carver housing development in Harlem and the Jacob Riis Plaza housing project on the Lower East Side. Two years later she dedicated the new $1,250,000 clubhouse, financed by her, for the Boys Brotherhood Republic in the Lillian Wald housing project on the Lower East Side. It was at that time that Urban America Inc. elected her to its board of trustees.

Over twenty-seven years, Brooke Astor has overseen the awarding of an average of 100 grants a year to civic projects, groups, or institutions (never individuals) in New York City. With inflation, the total annual value of the grants has risen to $9 million. Among the recipients have been the Coalition for the Homeless, the St. Francis Friends of the Poor, which runs a residence for the homeless, and the Animal Medical Center, which treats pets of the elderly poor. To see where the need is greatest, she personally visits schools, hospitals, hostels for the homeless, landmarks in need of repair, slum sites, and other places, institutions, and organizations, usually in the company of Linda Gillies, the director of the Vincent Astor Foundation, or of Annette Reed, a younger philanthropist who is her protégé. Her intention is to dissolve the resources of the Vincent Astor Foundation during her lifetime because she "wants to have the fun of doing it" and also because she is "very careful." "I never give to anything I don't see," she told the interviewer for New York Newsday.

"She is no Mrs. Gotrocks playing Lady Bountiful," William M. Dietel, the president of the Rockefeller Brothers Fund, has said of Mrs. Astor. "She has courage as well as imagination. She does her homework. If [she] says a particular institution or program is worthwhile, she gives it a special imprimatur and attracts interest and additional support from other philanthropists concerned with New York." The host of institutions and agencies that have recognized Mrs. Astor's cultural and humanitarian achievements with awards and other honors range from the federal Department of Housing and Urban Development to architectural and library associations, universities, and religious organizations.

As a writer, Mrs. Astor displays considerable wit and has a crisp, clear style. The memoir is her forte. Her first effort to channel her memoiristic talent into sustained fiction was The Bluebird Is at Home (Harper, 1965), the story of a young woman, the daughter of a career foreign service officer, who marries into wealth. That effort, inspired in part by the author's turbulent first marriage, sold well but received tepid notices. Her second, *The Last Blossom on the Plum Tree* (1986), dedicated to the memory of Charles Marshall, her second husband, was much more successful, partly because of the guidance given her by her new editor, Jason Epstein of Random House. *The Last Blossom on the Plum Tree*, set in New York and its nobbier suburbs and on the Italian Riviera, vividly evokes the now vanished carefree life of the very rich just before the Depression. The title alludes both to the ending of a social and economic era and to the last chance at romance for its heroines, two wealthy American dowagers. Reviewers cited the book's "good humor," its "touching" depiction of the "sorrows and occasional serendipitous joys of aging," its "refreshingly old-fashioned" style, and the "modern sensibility" the author "brings to a theme more often explored in European literature than American—the fascination of the much older woman for the younger man."

Brooke Astor is a slim woman, five feet seven and a half inches tall, with blond hair and bright blue eyes. According to Arthur Schlesinger Jr., she is "approachable . . . , impulsive, and responsive," she "bubbles over with humor and enthusiasm," and she is "devoid of snobbery or disdain." Others who know her say that she is "genetically cheerful" and that her mind "cuts through hypocrisy like a knife through butter."

When not traveling abroad, Mrs. Astor divides her time between her Park Avenue apartment, Holly Hill, her sixty-eight-acre country estate in Westchester County, New York, and her summer home in Maine. An amateur horticulturalist who employs a staff of gardeners, she fills her residences with flowers and chintzes with flower motifs. She also collects nineteenth-century paintings of dogs, and she has several pet dogs. Among her favorite recreations are the opera, social dancing, and entertaining at small dinner parties, and spending time with her twin grandsons, Philip and Alexander. Although her grandmother-in-law was the founder of New York society's "400," she abhors that set's traditional rarefied teas and galas and sees the democratization of high society as making for "much more interesting company." In politics, she is a lifelong Republican.

"Power, for me, is the ability to do good things for others," Mrs. Astor told Lois Metzger in an interview for an article in *Harper's Bazaar* (September 1985). "I have the means to do it, thanks to Vincent's money, and the act of giving makes me powerful inside. I would tell anyone, if you have enough money for three meals a day and you're not too busy, you ought to do something for others. Visit the elderly who are lonely. Teach some child to read. . . . If you can't give money, give of yourself, and if you have both, give both. Giving will make you strong and happy—it's done so for me." A practicing Episcopalian, the sprightly octogenarian believes "that adversity and tragedy are sent to test one's faith and courage." Her rare moments of de-

pression have come when she has wondered if she "will have time" to do "all the things [she wants] to do."

References: *Architectural Digest* 42:34+ F '85, 43:158+ My '86 pors; *Harper's Bazaar* 118:270+ S '85 por; *N Y Herald Tribune* p1+ My 30 '65 por; *N Y Newsday* p81 S 4 '86 por; *N Y Times* p60 Je 16 '68 por; *N Y Times Mag* p51+ My 20 '84 pors; *Vogue* 172:196+ Je '82 pors; Astor, Brooke. *Footprints* (1980), *Patchwork Child* (1962); *Who's Who in the East, 1983–84; Who's Who of American Women, 1983–84*

Babbitt, Bruce E(dward)

June 27, 1938– Former Governor of Arizona; lawyer. Address: b. c/o Congressional Exploratory Election Committee, 2095 E. Camelback Rd., Phoenix, Ariz. 85016

Arizona politicians joke that theirs is the one state in the union where mothers are unable to tell their sons that they might grow up to be president. Yet despite memories of Barry Goldwater's disastrous campaign in 1964, Arizona has once again produced a dark horse candidate for the presidency, this time the former governor Bruce Babbitt, who is a Democrat. The wealthy scion of an old Flagstaff family, Babbitt began his political career in 1974 as a reform-minded attorney general who unexpectedly succeeded to the governorship in March 1978 after the death of Wesley H. Bolin. Winning two terms in his own right, Babbitt enacted innovative programs of water management and child welfare that won the grudging admiration even of his conservative critics. A former civil rights lawyer who combines his party's traditional concern with social justice with an emphasis on government austerity, Babbitt has led the effort among younger Democrats to forge a new liberalism for the post-Reagan era. Although he may lack charisma, Babbitt's youthful vigor and impressive grasp of public policy have gained him national attention as prospective presidential material. Having chosen not to run for a third term as governor, in early January 1987 Bruce Babbitt became the first candidate officially to form a campaign committee, and on March 11, in Manchester, New Hampshire, he formally announced his candidacy for the presidency.

Once described by a *New York Times* (March 8, 1978) reporter as "a patrician figure who blends new and old Arizona," Bruce Edward Babbitt was born in Los Angeles on June 27, 1938, the second of the six children of Paul J. and Frances Babbitt. He grew up in Flagstaff, Arizona, where his pioneering family had originally made its fortune by establishing and running Indian trading posts. That fortune is today estimated to be worth around $20 million.

For a politician, Bruce E. Babbitt once said, he is "hopelessly overeducated." He earned a B.S. degree, *magna cum laude,* in 1960 from Notre Dame in South Bend, Indiana, where he served as student body president and majored in geology. Then, as part of the prestigious Marshall Scholars program, he studied geophysics at the University of Newcastle in England, from which he obtained his M.S. degree in 1962. Babbitt had originally intended to pursue a career exploiting Arizona's mineral wealth, but he changed his plans after a trip through the mines of Bolivia. He told a reporter, "I saw so much misery, such human deprivation while in Bolivia, that I thought how can I live in an ivory tower filled with such people problems?" Consequently, he enrolled in Harvard Law School, taking time off to join the historic civil rights march on Selma, Alabama, in 1964.

After obtaining his law degree from Harvard in 1965, Babbitt became a civil rights lawyer in Washington, D.C. He served as an assistant to the director of VISTA from 1965 to 1967, but the waste and inefficiency he saw there soon soured him on the Johnson administration's "Great Society" programs, and he returned to Arizona to join a corporate law firm in Phoenix.

Back home in Arizona, Babbitt found his liberal sensitivities outraged by a different kind of social injustice. In the state's vigorous but unregulated boom that took place after World War II, there had developed a deeply entrenched system of corruption in Arizona's closely knit business community. Crooked land deals, security and insurance fraud, bribery, antitrust violations, and other forms of white-collar crime were all commonplace. Backed by factions among both the old families and the new migrants, Babbitt decided to battle the corruption, and ran sucessfully for attorney general in 1974 on a so-called "clean up the mess" platform.

As attorney general, Babbitt aggressively prosecuted price-fixing and other antitrust violations and helped to create a system of state grand juries that convicted more than fifty people involved in land fraud schemes. He also won three convictions (later overturned by the Supreme Court) in the mob-style murder in 1976 of Don Bolles, a Phoenix reporter who was investigating land fraud. At one time, Babbitt himself was reportedly the target of a mob murder contract.

As he was nearing the end of his term as attorney general, an unusual series of events made Bruce E. Babbitt governor of Arizona. In October 1977, the Democratic Governor Raul H. Castro resigned to become President Jimmy Carter's ambassador to Argentina. Since Arizona has no lieutenant governor, Castro was succeeded by the secretary of state, Wesley A. Bolin, who died after only five months in office. On March 4, 1978, at 7:30 in the morning, Babbitt was awakened and informed that, as the person next in line of succession, he was now governor of Arizona. Although an "accidental" governor, he showed that he intended to be more than a figurehead by vetoing three bills in his first four months of office. When he ran for election in November 1978, he won 52 percent of the vote against a former state senator, Evan Mecham, a Republican.

In his first full term of office, Babbitt made headlines by ordering the Arizona National Guard to seize a Tucson plant owned by the American Atomics Corporation, which had failed to remove radioactive tritium, a substance used in making illuminated signs and watch faces, that had been leaking into the surrounding neighborhood. Citing the threat to the community, Babbitt declared a state of emergency in September 1979 and employed the members of the National Guard to seal and remove the tritium.

In a virtuoso display of political leadership, Babbitt engineered the passage of a major groundwater management program in 1980. Water has always been a major political issue in arid Arizona, which has to depend on irrigation for its survival. In the absence of a statewide program of water conservation, farmers had been pumping ground water at such a rate that the state might well have been pumped dry within the decade.

Concerned by that alarming prospect, Secretary of the Interior Cecil D. Andrus, with Babbitt's behind-the-scenes support, threatened to cut off federal funds for the Central Arizona Project, a long-awaited irrigation system, unless the state adopted new ground-water regulations. Citing pressure from the federal government, Babbitt got the Arizona state legislature to set up a special commission, with himself as its chairman, to draft the law. Dazzling the legislature with his command of detail, the governor got the complex legislation, which ensures that the ground-water supply will be stabilized by the year 2225, drafted and approved within eight months.

Riding high on that success, Babbitt easily won reelection to the governorship in 1982, defeating a

strong Republican candidate, Leo Corbet, with an impressive 62 percent of the vote. But in his second term, he ran afoul of organized labor by sending the National Guard to a Phelps-Dodge plant during a bitter strike by the United Steelworkers in 1983. Dubbing him "Governor Scabbitt," the union leaders maintained that his action was solely aimed at breaking the strike, and to this day, Bruce E. Babbitt remains unpopular with organized labor.

In January 1985 Babbitt shocked Arizonans by dedicating his entire state of the state address to one issue, the need to devote more resources to the protection and education of children. He proposed a new fund of over $32 million to provide better prenatal and postnatal health care, improved after-school programs, and a more rigorous inspection of day-care facilities. The governor also advocated tougher penalties for child abuse and sexual molestation, and announced the establishment of a cabinet-level Office of the Child. At the time, skeptical critics scoffed at Babbitt's unusual move, but he managed to persuade a conservative legislature to provide the funds, and since then Arizona's innovative child welfare programs have received high marks.

Babbitt's impressive performance as a moderate Democratic governor of an ultraconservative state rapidly gained him an influential role in the national Democratic party. In the wake of Walter F. Mondale's 1984 defeat, Babbitt and other young Democrats formed the Democratic Leadership Council, a group devoted to rethinking the party's political philosophy and strategy. In 1985 Babbitt became cochairman of the Democratic Leadership Council as well as head of the National Governors' Association, another influential national group.

Within those organizations, Babbitt has been harshly critical of the performance of the national Democratic party. The Democrats, he contends, have abdicated their innovative role in American politics by promoting an outdated concept of liberalism. To revive its sagging national appeal, Babbitt believes, the Democratic party has to combine its traditional concern for social justice with a stronger commitment to a leaner, more efficient government, and an effective national defense.

Although he sympathizes with Reagan's drive to streamline the federal government, Babbitt strongly objects to the way the president has gone about it. Viewing Reagan as being antigovernment, he says of himself, "I support government at all levels." Babbitt believes that what is needed is a new allocation of state and federal responsibilities, with each level doing what it does best. The federal government should administer the entitlement programs, in sharp contrast to the policy of Reagan, who wants to shift them to the states, and the states should manage education, highways, and crime control.

The most controversial aspect of Babbitt's political thinking is undoubtedly his emphasis on means testing for entitlement programs such as Social Security and Medicare, for he believes that government benefits have to be more closely tied to economic need, He was quoted as saying in 1985: "Is it unreasonable to suggest that W. R. Grace, the Mellons, the Hunts, and other members of the Forbes 400 do not need exactly the same Medicare entitlement as a widow living in a cold water flat?" To that end, Babbitt proposes such measures as a tax on Social Security benefits and higher Medicare deductibles for high-income families, as well as the elimination of mortgage-interest deductions for second homes. Democrats have traditionally opposed means tests on the grounds that they would erode middle-class support for welfare programs, but Babbitt believes that the government can no longer afford to buy their backing with such benefits. With the funds saved by means testing, Babbitt would extend entitlement programs for the truly needy, including expanded Medicare coverage for catastrophic and long-term illness, and extended Medicaid for all women and children under the poverty line. He would also like to provide day-care entitlements for working parents and to increase funding for prenatal nutrition programs.

While advocating a strong federal commitment to social welfare, Babbitt wants government to stay clear of centralized economic planning. He opposes a national industrial policy, protectionist trade legislation, and corporate bailouts. Instead he advises using a progressive corporate income tax to encourage small businesses and reducing price supports for agribusinesses.

On foreign policy issues, Babbitt belongs to the "hawk" faction of the Democratic party. He supported the Grenada invasion and approves of Reagan's policy on El Salvador, but opposes aid to the Contras, whom he sees as an ineffectual group whose efforts only strengthen the Sandinista regime in Nicaragua. His chief foreign policy concern is Mexico. With an eye on Hispanic voters, he has charged Reagan with "cavalier neglect" of the nation's neighbor to the South. Babbitt, who speaks fluent Spanish and has many Latin American political contacts, wants the United States to take a more active role in helping Mexico to cope with its formidable economic problems.

Beginning in 1985 Babbitt's name began to be mentioned as a presidential contender, especially after he bypassed a run for Barry Goldwater's Senate seat in 1986. Although not a favorite of the labor and education lobbies, he does well with other Democratic constituencies such as environmentalists, women, Hispanics, and blacks. More important, he enjoys strong support in the Sun Belt, an area that the Democrats will have to win in a presidential election.

In 1986 Bruce E. Babbitt actively tested the presidential waters. In August he made a much-publicized bicycle tour of Iowa, where the first presidential trial will be held in February 1988, and followed that up with a mountain-climbing tour of New Hampshire, where the second primary is scheduled to take place a few weeks later. He also organized a hiking and boating trip through the Grand Canyon for his supporters, leading one

observer to ask jokingly if he was running for the presidency or for the Olympic Games. Encouraged by his cordial reception, Babbitt formally established a campaign committee in January 1987 and formally announced his candidacy for the presidency on March 11 in Manchester, New Hampshire.

Pledging not to accept any contributions from political action committees, Babbitt launched his campaign with the assertion that the next president must "dare to be different" and "risk offending some potential supporters." Among proposals that he advanced in the course of his campaign have been a scheme for "gainsharing," under which part of an employee's pay would be in the form of stock in the employer's company. He called for "very tough" environmental protection laws, a comprehensive nuclear test ban treaty with a "mutual moratorium" on space-based weapons, a "simple international agreement for balanced trade" between the United States and its major trading partners, and a "progressive consumption tax" similar to the value-added tax used in some Western European countries. On the issue of abortion, Babbitt indicated that he favored freedom of choice, even though he is a Roman Catholic. To enhance his relatively weak standing in the opinion polls, Babbitt mounted the first television advertising campaign of the 1988 presidential race and sought professional advice on improving his image. In October 1987 he appeared in a comedy skit on the NBC-TV program *Saturday Night Live*.

Babbitt has chosen to develop his presidential potential less by cultivating strategic political contacts than by developing new ideas. What he may lack in charisma—some observers insist that he comes across as too professorial—he tries to make up for with intelligent, audacious, and original thinking. A consummate policy maker, he has a superb grasp of the detail and complexity involved in contemporary government. Often compared with Jimmy Carter, Babbitt regrets that both Carter and Reagan have given a mastery of details a bad name, the former by his devotion to them, the latter by his aversion. Babbitt has predicted that from now on, presidential campaigns will not be "a contest of platitudes."

Some critics doubt that Babbitt's experience in running a small-scale state government has really prepared him for national office, while others familiar with his governorship maintain that he has trouble delegating authority and consulting with others on his political moves. As a cool, somewhat remote figure, he may well have difficulty connecting with the average voter. Nevertheless, Bruce E. Babbitt promises to bring to the 1988 presidential campaign a much-needed emphasis on important issues.

A tall, lean Donald Sutherland look-alike, Bruce E. Babbitt favors conservative gray suits. He is married to a Phoenix lawyer, Hattie Coons, whom he met while he was a government lawyer and she was a college student in Texas. They have two sons, Christopher and Timothy, and live in a comfortable, ranch-style house in Phoenix, along with a pet snake named Logo. A committed outdoorsman, Babbitt enjoys backpacking, hiking, and horseback riding.

References: Atlan 259:37+ Ap '87; Chicago Tribune V 1+ Jl 3 '87 pors; New Repub 192:9+ My 27 '85; N Y Times A p17 Mr 8 '78 por; Washington Post A p1+ Je 23 '86 por; Almanac of American Politics, 1983; Who's Who in America, 1986-87; Who's Who in American Politics, 1987-88

Baker, Howard (Henry, Jr.)

Nov. 15, 1925– United States government official. Address: b. The White House, 1600 Pennsylvania Ave., Washington, D.C. 20500

NOTE: This biography updates the article that appeared in *Current Biography* in 1974.

When a president asks a favor, Howard Baker finds it difficult to say no. Thus, when Ronald Reagan in February 1987 asked the former senator from Tennessee, a moderate pragmatist with a casual style, to replace the more abrasive Donald Regan as White House chief of staff and help the administration to cope with the Iran-Contra scandal, Baker did not hesitate to comply. The scenario was ironic, for one of the assets the president saw in Baker was his reputation for statesmanlike bipartisanship and compromise—the very reputation that had made Baker persona non grata to Reagan's New Right supporters in 1980, when the Tennessean sought to be Reagan's running mate after abor-

tively seeking the Republican presidential nomination himself.

Baker went to Washington in 1967 as the first Republican ever popularly elected to the United States Senate from Tennessee. During three terms of office, he earned a reputation as "the quintessential mediator, negotiator, and moderator," in the words of James Baker 3d, President Reagan's first chief of staff, now secretary of the treasury. After achieving national prominence as the ranking Republican on the Senate Watergate investigatory committee, in 1973, Howard Baker was the Senate minority leader (1977–81) and majority leader (1981–85). Just as he had helped President Jimmy Carter, a Democrat, get the Panama Canal treaties through the Senate (a sore point with hard-line conservatives), he played a critical role in the passage of President Reagan's tax and budget program. At the end of his third term, in 1985, Baker, still eyeing higher office, returned to private legal practice to begin preparing for the 1988 presidential campaign. Although he has at least temporarily shelved his presidential aspirations, Washington insiders do not rule out a dark-horse candidacy for the charming Tennessean, a man of easy articulateness. In the meantime, he is relishing his work as Reagan's top aide. As his wife, Joy, has observed, "It's like being president without having to make the run."

Howard Henry Baker Jr. is relatively liberal for his background. The scion of an old, prosperous, and politically powerful Appalachian family, he was born on November 15, 1925, in the Cumberland mountain town of Huntsville, Tennessee, a Republican enclave that had resisted secession at the time of the Civil War, "The place is built around the Bakers," a neighbor once told a Baker profiler. "It's like a feudal setting, and Howard was raised very much like the lord of the manor." His grandfather was a judge, his grandmother was the first woman sheriff in the state, and his father was United States representative from Tennessee's second congressional district from 1951 until his death in 1964. "My father had a profound impact on me in a way I don't think I could ever explain," Baker recalled in a 1979 interview with Steven Rattner of the New York Times. Howard Baker Sr. was succeeded in his unfinished last term in Congress by his second wife, Irene Bailey Baker, Howard Jr.'s stepmother. (His natural mother was Dora Baker, née Ladd.)

At the public elementary school in Huntsville, Baker was a champion debater. After graduating from the McCallie School, a Chattanooga military academy, in 1943, he entered the Navy's wartime V-12 officer training program and studied electrical engineering at the University of the South and Tulane University. With the rank of lieutenant j.g., he did a brief tour of duty on a PT boat in the South Pacific before World War II ended. After the war, switching from engineering to law, he finished his work for a bachelor's degree at the University of Tennessee. Showing the flair for coalition politics that would later make him a molder of consensus

in the Senate, Baker won election as student body president at the university on the pledge to conciliate differences between the fraternities and the rest of the campus population.

After taking his law degree in 1949, Baker joined the Knoxville law firm founded by his grandfather and soon earned the nickname "Old Two-to-Ten," an allusion to the light sentences that his shrewd cross-examinations as a criminal defense lawyer often won for his clients. As the corporate lawyer for a group of coal companies, he obtained a $1 million settlement from the United Mine Workers. While practising law, he invested profitably in banking and real estate, amassing a fortune beyond his inherited wealth. In 1951 he married Joy Dirksen, the daughter of the late Senator Everett McKinley Dirksen of Illinois.

Baker entered electoral politics in 1964, running to fill the unexpired term of Senator Estes Kefauver, who had died the previous summer. Although he disassociated himself from the presidential bid that year of conservative Senator Barry M. Goldwater (who proposed the privatization of the Tennessee Valley Authority), he ran a highly conservative campaign of his own, promising to fight to limit foreign aid and federal interference in local education and civil rights matters and warning against a drift "toward state socialism." "I was a young man in his first race, which was a tumultuous campaign," he later said, explaining his extremist, untypical 1964 platform. He lost the 1964 race to the more liberal Ross Bass while attracting more votes than any previous Tennessee Republican in a statewide election.

Running for a full term in the Kefauver-vacated seat in 1966, Baker took a more moderate stance and even supported fair-housing laws and other liberal legislation. His opponent was Governor Frank G. Clement, who had defeated Bass in the Democratic primary. Endorsed by Democratic newspapers the governor had alienated, Baker cut into the traditionally Democratic vote, especially among blacks and young people, to win by nearly 100,000 votes (56 percent of the total) and become the first Republican senator ever to be popularly elected from Tennessee. Some of the credit for his victory was claimed by Richard M. Nixon, the future president, who stumped the state in his behalf. Baker was reelected to the Senate with 62 percent of the vote in 1972 and 56 percent in 1978.

Baker's description of himself in the Senate as "moderate to moderate conservative" was supported by the ratings given his voting record by the liberal Americans for Democratic Action and the conservative Americans for Constitutional Action. In 1972 his ADA rating was zero and his ACA rating was 70. During the remainder of the 1970s he had an average rating of 15 percent from the ADA and 67 percent from the ACA. He was in general a champion of federal fiscal conservatism, except where defense spending was concerned.

Situating himself at the center of the Republican spectrum, Baker was liberal on environmental issues and moderate to liberal on civil rights. As a member of the Committee on the Environment and Public Works, he helped to draft important environmental protection legislation, including several anti-strip-mining measures (a sensitive issue in Tennessee), the Clean Air Act of 1970 and later modifications of that act, and a modified version of the 1980 "Superfund" bill to clean up contamination from toxic waste. On civil rights, he considered school busing "a grievous piece of mischief" but was one of only three Southern senators to vote for the 1968 open-housing act. He also supported voter-rights legislation. Given the sentiment in his constituency, he considered it "impossible . . . politically" to support gun-control legislation, but he backed strong law enforcement measures, including a controversial "no-knock" provision. Wary of détente with the Soviet Union at the time, he voted against SALT II. On American military involvement in Southeast Asia, he was a hawk.

In other areas, Baker opposed the common situs picketing favored by the labor lobby and supported the supersonic transport, the antiballistic missile, natural-gas deregulation, maintenance of the oil depletion allowance, financial aid to higher education, the protection of endangered species, and voluntary prayer in public schools. One of his proudest achievements was legislation authorizing federal revenue sharing with the states. His habit of walking a fine line on controversial issues was demonstrated in his voting for the Equal Rights Amendment but against extending the deadline for its ratification and in his opposing an antiabortion amendment to the Constitution while favoring the right of states to impose strict limits on public funding of abortions for the poor.

Baker shot to national prominence in 1973 as the ranking Republican on the Senate select committee set up to investigate the Nixon administration's Watergate scandal. As an old friend of Richard Nixon, Baker knew that he was vulnerable to being viewed as "Nixon's man" on the committee. For that reason he was painstakingly objective, constantly raising the question, "What did the president know and when did he know it?" With his telegenic looks, calm manner, casual but articulate speech, wry humor, and skill in cross-examination, he impressed viewers of the hearing (which were televised nationally in their entirety) more favorably than any other member of the panel, with the possible exception of Senator Sam Ervin Jr., the elderly and homespun chairman. "Named to the committee by the then minority leader Hugh Scott as punishment for having challenged Mr. Scott for the leadership post, Senator Baker, to all appearances, escaped with his reputation greatly enhanced, despite extraordinarily difficult circumstances," Steven Rattner wrote in his New York Times profile. "The Baker tendency toward weighty, serious statements served him well, leaving most Americans with the impression that he had nothing at heart but the interests of the country."

Although most journalists reported positively on Baker's lawyer-like performance in the hearings, some thought that he pulled his punches as the hearings progressed. The truth was, as he later revealed, that in the beginning he was pro-Nixon, believing the president was innocent, and changed his mind as evidence mounted. The litmus test was the reaction of right-wing Republicans, who blamed him for contributing to the pressure that forced President Nixon to resign. The New Right's animosity toward him would become full-blown when, later, he supported ratification of the Panama Canal treaties, under the terms of which the Canal will eventually be ceded to Panama.

The favorable public exposure that Baker gained on the Watergate committee served as the launching pad for his bids for higher office, but the enmity of the national New Right movement contributed to the failure of those bids to some degree in 1976 and in large measure in 1980. Delivering the keynote address at the Republican convention in 1976, Baker hoped to get the vice-presidential spot on Gerald R. Ford's ticket, but he was passed over in favor of Robert Dole. In the New Hampshire presidential primary four years later, he finished third, behind Ronald Reagan and George Bush, and early national polls put him second only to Reagan. As the Reagan campaign gained momentum, Baker switched his efforts toward the vice-presidential slot, but the Republican right wing's vengeance on "Panama Howie" effectively removed him from consideration. Personally popular with most of his colleagues of both parties, he was more successful in the cloakroom politics of the Senate, winning election as minority leader in 1977 and majority leader in 1981, following the Reagan-led Republican electoral landslide.

While expressing doubts about some of Reagan's policies, Baker as majority leader cast himself in the role of the president's "spear carrier" in the Senate. Playing a crucial part in moving the administration's tax and budget agenda through the upper chamber, he passed the greatest test to which his talents as a negotiator had ever been put by bridging the differences between liberals and conservatives within his own party. His favorite tactic was to closet the combatants together for hours, sometimes into the night, let them argue to the point of exhaustion, and then come in with an appealing compromise. President Reagan on one occasion told the press, "I'm frank to say that I don't think we could have had the successes that we've had up there [on Capitol Hill] without his leadership."

As Senate Republicans grew increasingly fractious toward the end of President Reagan's first term, Baker's conciliatory leadership style proved less effective. With rival senators warring over the simplest resolutions, his consensus-building tactics became more and more time-consuming and increasingly futile. Although "a proven winner at leading people who want to be led," as one Capitol Hill observer reported, Baker's "gentle touch and personal popularity" did little to prevent the Senate's "continuing slide into individualism and disarray." Tiring of his role in the Senate, Baker returned to private life in 1984, to spend more time with his wife, who had fallen ill with cancer, to prepare for his 1988 presidential campaign, and to return to the practice of law. As a member of the prestigious firm of Vinson and Elkins, he went from his relatively modest Senate salary to a law practice income estimated at $1.5 million a year.

In polls taken early in 1987, Baker ranked third, behind George Bush and Robert Dole, as a contender for the 1988 Republican presidential nomination. Realizing that the money and effort it would cost to become a front-runner would be enormous, he remained willing to try, but he also became more amenable to other opportunities for a return to public life. When President Reagan offered to name him to succeed the ailing William Casey as director of the Central Intelligence Agency, he turned down the offer but let it be known that he could be drafted for a seat on the Supreme Court or the position of secretary of state, should George Shultz resign. Then the Iran-Contra scandal broke, and the administration came under press and Congressional fire for covert and illegal sale of tax-payer-bought arms to Iran and diversion of the funds into secret private accounts, some allegedly for the benefit of the Contras, the Nicaraguan rebels, in violation of a Congressional amendment. Beleaguered, Reagan decided he would have to replace his hard-driving chief of staff, Donald Regan, whose managerial style had alienated not only Congress but many of the president's closest supporters, including the First Lady. After first approaching former Secretary of Transportation Drew Lewis and Senator Paul Laxalt, both of whom had other plans, Reagan turned to Baker at Laxalt's suggestion, and Baker agreed to become White House chief of staff.

Baker's presence in the White House immediately lifted morale there, as well as the administratin's credibility on both Capitol Hill and in the nation. Baker helped the president to draft a penitent nationally televised speech on the Iran-Contra affair, established a committee to prepare the White House's case at the Senate hearings on the matter, and set about making Reagan more accessible to Congress and the press. On the personnel front, he jettisoned the troubled candidacy of Robert Gates for CIA director in favor of that of William Webster (previously director of the FBI) and reorganized the White House staff. Aware that administrative detail was not his forte, he delegated that side of his job to his deputy, Kenneth Duberstein, in order to concentrate on working on policy and political strategy with the president or in his behalf.

By the beginning of September 1987 Baker's honeymoon with administration insiders and his former colleagues on Capitol Hill seemed to be over and he was being blamed for a range of administration problems, "from inconsistent policy statements to legislative defeats to staff amateurism," as David Eisenhower pointed out in the *New York Times Magazine* (September 6, 1987). According to Eisenhower, Baker was report-

ed "to have minimal influence on President Reagan and to be unable to halt his drift toward a confrontation with the Congress." Baker remained buoyant, however. "There was no talk from him of 'controlling the damage' from the Iran-Contra hearings. . . . If he seemed weary, it was because he and his crew were busy preparing for . . . the fall session of Congress and the pending showdowns on a trillion-dollar budget, Persian Gulf strategy, trade protectionism, Contra aid, and, above all, the confirmation of Robert H. Bork . . . [President Reagan's unsuccessful nominee for] justice of the United States Supreme Court." When the stock market crashed in October—at least in part because of the international climate of financial pessimism caused by the runaway American federal deficit—President Reagan for the first time seemed to soften his hard line against a tax increase. The presidential advisers said to be most responsible for that change were Jim Baker, the secretary of the treasury, and Howard Baker.

Arriving at the White House at 8:00 A.M., Baker discusses the day's agenda with Reagan and spends much of the rest of the day "padding back and forth," as he puts it, between the Oval Office and his own office down the hall until he leaves for home, around 6:30 P.M. He is often in communication with Capitol Hill, where his popularity and connections, while superficially diminished, remain strong assets to the president, as does his legislative savvy. The last-mentioned trait was recently demonstrated in his foisting the initiative for breaking the 1987 budget stalemate on the reluctant Democrats. In foreign policy, he has encouraged Reagan to respond positively to Soviet leader Mikhail Gorbachev's arms control proposals while counseling a tough posture in the Persian Gulf.

Howard Baker is five feet seven inches tall and heavier than he was when he charmed the national Watergate audience. There is a twinkle in his brown eyes, except when he is tired, and he has a ready, somewhat lopsided grin. He and his wife, Joy, have two grown children, Darek and Cynthia, and two grandchildren. The Bakers maintain two homes, an apartment in Washington and a large estate in Huntsville, where every election day they drive to the polls in the late Senator Dirksen's old DeSoto.

As Steven Rattner pointed out in his *New York Times* profile, Baker is respected "even in cynical Washington . . . as a decent and kind man, unfailingly polite, who prides himself on rarely losing his temper." According to Rattner, "He mixes well, remembers faces and names, yet at the same time he is an intensely private man who displays little of his inner self even to close aides. . . . What he does enjoy are small groups where his relaxed manner works nicely." Baker plays tennis and golf, but he most enjoys being at home, reading, watching television, or working in his darkroom. A talented photographer, he has staged several successful one-man shows. Speaking of his equanimity, Baker's stepmother once said, "He's like the Tennessee River. He flows right down the middle."

References: N Y Times A p28 Mr 17 '87 por; N Y Times Mag p31+ N 4 '79 pors; U S News 102:16+ Mr 17 '87 por; Almanac of American Politics, 1984; Politics in America (1984); Who's Who in America, 1986–87

Barry, Marion S.

Mar. 6, 1936– Mayor of Washington, D.C. Address: b. 1350 E Street, N.W., Washington, D.C. 20004; h. 3607 Suitland Rd., S.E., Washington, D.C.

The first black militant to be elected mayor of a major American city, Marion S. Barry began his third term as chief executive of Washington, D.C. in January 1987, with a four-day inaugural celebration paid for from private funds. As mayor of Washington, Barry is responsible for the well-being of its 650,000 residents, 70 percent of whom are black. He also oversees a bureaucracy of 33,000 people and a budget of $2 billion. There are, however, significant limits to the mayor's authority over the affairs of what he calls "the last colony." Although Congress, which began a century of complete control over Washington's government in 1874, has granted the District of Columbia limited home rule, city officials must still submit their budget as well as proposed legislation for its approval.

Marion S. Barry was born on March 6, 1936, into a family of sharecroppers in the rural community of Itta Bena, Mississippi. His father, Marion S. Barry, died when he was four, and his mother, Mattie B. Barry, then moved to Memphis, Tennessee, where she married David Cummings. Barry's mother worked as a domestic, while his stepfather

took a job as a butcher, to support him and his seven younger sisters. Barry himself contributed to the family income by taking odd jobs as a cotton picker, waiter, paperboy, and carhop.

Although the boys in Barry's impoverished neighborhood had low expectations, he was an achiever, who made good grades and earned the badge of an Eagle scout. Until he reached his junior year in high school, Barry was unaware that such a thing as higher education existed, but, after graduating, he entered the all-black LeMoyne College in Memphis. He obtained a bachelor of science degree in chemistry in 1958, and during the next two years earned a master's degree at Fisk, the predominantly black university in Nashville. Barry spent the academic year of 1960–61 at the University of Kansas, where he was a teaching assistant; he then transferred to the University of Tennessee, with the intention of working towards a doctorate.

Marion Barry's involvement in the civil rights movement grew gradually. He joined LeMoyne's college chapter of the NAACP as a sophomore and became its president as a senior, a post in which he served as the group's spokesman during a controversial effort to force one of the school's white trustees to retract patronizing remarks he had made about blacks while serving as Memphis' defense attorney in a bus-desegregation trial. Barry's first real contact with the broader civil rights movement took place in 1959 at Fisk, where he helped to organize a college chapter of the NAACP and became involved in a workshop in nonviolence.

Early in 1960 Barry organized the first lunch counter sit-ins in Nashville, and, in April of that year, he and other student leaders met with Martin Luther King Jr. at Shaw College in Raleigh, North Carolina. The outcome of that gathering was the establishment of the Student Nonviolent Coordinating Committee (SNCC). Dedicated to direct action through demonstrations, sit-ins, and boycotts, the organization established Atlanta, Georgia, as its base and made Marion Barry its first national chairman.

Barry taught for a while at Knoxville College, a black institution in the city of that name, but he stopped his teaching and his doctoral studies in 1964 in order to work full time for SNCC. His first assignment was New York City until June 1965, when he moved to Washington, D.C. Barry soon had the town in an uproar, and its newspapers, alluding to the African-style shirt he adopted, began referring to him as a "dashiki-clad militant."

On January 24, 1966 Barry led a one-day bus boycott against D.C. Transit, which had proposed raising its fares. The action was so effective that the company's request was later turned down. One month after that, he announced the formation of the "Free D.C. Movement," a response to efforts by the Metropolitan Board of Trade to undermine pending legislation to replace complete Congressional control of the capital with a form of limited home rule. The movement's attacks on "moneylord" merchants and its threats of boycotts against those businesses that would not display signs in favor of home rule led many prominent businesses to dissociate themselves from the board's stand and to provide Free D.C. monetary as well as moral support. But Barry's action also prompted accusations of extortion and blackmail, and even some strong supporters of home rule suggested that the newcomer's agitation hurt more than it helped the bill, a version of which was passed in 1973.

In January 1967 Barry resigned as head of SNCC's Washington office. "The civil rights direction of protest is dead," he declared. "Now we must concentrate on control—economic and political power." Over the next few months he designed a program to aid Washington's poor blacks, and in July 1967 he won approval from Secretary of Labor Willard Wirtz, for a $300,000 grant to support a one-month pilot project. Youth Pride, as the nonprofit operation became known, put 1,100 unemployed black youths in bright green work suits and sent them out to clean 1,400 streets and 1,200 alleys, and to kill 25,000 rats.

Youth Pride's early success won it a Labor Department grant of $2 million to carry it through the winter, and in August 1968 the organization received another $3.8 million. As executive director of operations for Youth Pride, Barry quickly expanded the operation to include a profit-oriented arm, Pride Economic Enterprises, of which he became president. With support from private companies, foundations, and the Small Business Administration, Youth Pride took over six gas stations, a landscaping and gardening company, a painting and maintenance company, and a fifty-five-unit apartment complex.

Critics attacked Youth Pride, Inc., from its very beginning. Joel Broyhill, a Republican representative from Virginia, described it as a multimillion-dollar enterprise promoted by liberals "convinced that permissiveness and coddling of criminals and back alley creeps is the surefire shortcut to peace and safety on our streets," and the United States Attorney's office was soon looking into rumored graft and corruption. Youth Pride's officials denied any conscious wrongdoing, and Barry charged that "it's that old stereotype of black folks with their hands always in the till. Nothing but witch-hunting." He also pointed to the difficulties inherent in teaching job skills to as many as 1,400 previously unemployed young men. Known in the argot of the Washington ghetto as "dudes," many brought with them problems of inadequate education, drug addiction, and criminal behavior.

During his first years in the city, Barry's relationship with Washington's police force was stormy. In 1969 he was even charged with assaulting two police officers during a dispute over a parking ticket, but the department also used Barry's portrait on posters that encouraged members of minority groups to join the force. And it was police matters that provided Barry with his first electoral success. In February 1970 he was elected to the citizens' board governing the Pilot Police District Project, an experiment in creating rapport between precinct officers and the black community to which they were assigned.

In 1971 Barry left his post as chairman of the citizens' board in order to seek election to the school board. Running for an at-large seat against Anita F. Allen, the incumbent board president, Barry portrayed his opponent as committed and competent but unable to provide leadership. By contrast, Barry, as a private citizen, had played an important role during the autumn of 1970 in mediating a dispute between the board and the city's teachers. Mrs. Allen, who enjoyed informal Republican support, charged, in turn, that Barry was seeking to control the Democratic party. With campaign assistance from the Democratic organization of Walter E. Fauntroy, the District's congressional delegate, and from the teachers' union, Barry was able to take 58 percent of the vote in the November election.

Barry won election to the school board two more times and served as its president between 1972 and 1974. He won his third victory in January 1974, and less than six months later, on June 5, announced that he would run for the post of city council president in the fall municipal election, the first to be held under the home rule recently granted to the District. His opponent in that race was to be Sterling Tucker, who had been vice-chairman of that body for the previous five years and was executive director of the city's Urban League. Barry changed his mind, however, when Walter E. Washington, who had been appointed the city's mayor by Presidents Lyndon B. Johnson and Richard M. Nixon, declined to endorse either candidate. Withdrawing from the race for the council presidency, he sought, instead, an at-large seat on that body.

Easily elected to the city council in 1974, Barry became a full-time politician and resigned from Youth Pride, Inc. Two years later he won re-election to the council with an overwhelming 78 percent of the vote. While on the council, he made himself expert on the economic problems of the city and reached out not only to blacks but also to other minority groups. He worked, for example, with the Gay Activists' Alliance to develop one of the strongest municipal ordinances in the nation for protecting the civil rights of homosexuals. His service on the council almost cost him his life when Hanafi Muslims shot him in the chest during their seizure of the District Building on March 9, 1977. The bullet just missed his heart, but Barry was back at work by the end of the month.

On January 21, 1978 Marion Barry announced his intention to run for mayor of Washington, D.C. His principal opponents in the Democratic primary campaign were the incumbent, Walter E. Washington, who had become the city's first elected mayor in 1974, and Sterling Tucker, the president of the city council. No real ideological differences separated the three, and, in the opinion of many, the less well-positioned Barry was the underdog. Nevertheless, Barry received a last-minute endorsement from the influential *Washington Post* and union backing from Washington's police, firefighters, and teachers. On September 12 he managed to squeeze out a victory with 35 percent of the vote in the primary. Although votes from blacks made up 62 percent of Barry's total, he received less than 30 percent of all the votes cast by members of his race. According to observers, the key to the outcome of the contest was Barry's impressive showing among Washington's white minority, which comprised approximately 35 percent of the electorate.

Victory in the Democratic primary made Barry's election as mayor a foregone conclusion, and on November 7 he took two out of every three votes cast in his race against the Republican candidate, Arthur A. Fletcher, who had served as assistant secretary of labor in the Nixon and Ford administrations. Barry's inauguration took place on January 2, 1979, following a parade down the 14th Street corridor, where blacks had rioted in 1968. The new mayor took the oath of office from Thurgood Marshall, the black associate justice of the United States Supreme Court, and then delivered an inaugural address in which he pledged "to bring all of the people of this city into a full governing partnership with my administration."

Problems, most of which he inherited or were beyond his control, bedeviled Barry's first years in office. A major snowstorm and a protracted teachers strike, the latter of which he took credit for ending, were early difficulties. Much more serious was Washington's financial crisis, including a deficit that had mushroomed to $409 million. To deal with it, Barry had to cut jobs and services, call for more federal aid, and submit Washington to its first audit so that the city could enter the bond market to raise revenues.

Although critics charged that Barry had abandoned his poor, black supporters, and although his popularity dipped considerably during his first year in office, he managed to convince most Washingtonians of the necessity of his drastic actions. Barry also strengthened his electoral base by moving his residence to a $125,000 brick house in the Hillcrest neighborhood of Ward 7, an enclave of working-class and middle-class blacks located in the city's far eastern corner, for that district, where he had been weak in 1978, became one of his strongholds in the 1982 election. Barry entered the race with a $1.3 million war chest, and he was able to take 60 percent of the votes in the September 14 primary, in which his chief opponent was Patricia Roberts Harris, a black woman who had served President Jimmy Carter as secretary of housing and urban development and secretary of health and human services. The mayor then went on to defeat the Republican candidate, E. Brooke Lee Jr., by a five-to-one margin in the general election.

During his second term Barry saw continued progress in certain areas: Washington regained its fiscal health, the downtown area underwent a renewal, and both unemployment and crime declined. Unfortunately, the four years were also marred by serious troubles. The public housing stock deteriorated, while the administration left $8

million in federal money unspent. Conditions in the city's teeming prisons worsened, while the mayor postponed making the inevitably unpopular decision on the location of a new jail. On June 14, 1986 arson caused a fire at the Lorton Correctional Facility, and on July 10 further arson and disturbances there led to injuries for thirty-two inmates and guards.

Scandals also took their toll on Barry's second term. Ten top city officials, including the mayor's chief aide, Ivanhoe Donaldson, were convicted of crimes of malfeasance, and Mary Treadwell, who had been a coleader of Youth Pride, Inc., and who, from 1972 to 1976, had been Barry's second wife, was convicted for defrauding the United States government. On several occasions, Barry found himself in compromising circumstances. A female city worker, with whom he had a social relationship, was convicted of selling cocaine, and a discounted mortgage offered by the bank for which his present wife worked and an expensive gift of clothing presented to her by a lawyer engaged in city business also raised some eyebrows.

Despite all his problems, Barry encountered little resistance on his way to a third term. Instead, as his troubles mounted, black Washingtonians rallied to the defense of their beleaguered mayor. On September 9, 1986 he won the Democratic primary with approximately 71 percent of the vote. During the ensuing general campaign, Carol Schwartz, the white city councilwoman who ran as the Republican candidate, attacked Barry's administration charging that "we are capable of better, and deserve better." Mrs. Schwartz, whose three children attended public schools, especially rankled Barry by making an issue of the mayor's decision to enroll his child in a private school. Nevertheless, on November 4 Barry garnered 61 percent of the vote in turning back her challenge and those of four other candidates. In 1986, however, the mayor's votes came mostly from blacks; in contrast to previous elections, he had only sparse support from the city's white neighborhoods.

Perhaps because of escalating rumors of municipal corruption involving bribery, fraud, racketeering, and obstruction of justice, a public opinion poll taken by the *Washington Post* in early September 1987 indicated that Barry's approval rating among Washingtonians had slipped from 50 percent to 44 percent within one year. His third term was also clouded by his failure to take appropriate action for snow removal after a blizzard in January and by his impolitic remarks about the city's poor taking undue advantage of free ambulance service and his advice to a welfare mother who had complained about inadequate housing for herself and her fourteen children to "stop having all those babies."

Marion Barry stands six feet one inch tall and weighs over 200 pounds. His once athletic physique has suffered from a weight problem in recent years. Barry's initial, "S.," originally had no special significance, but in 1957 he adopted the middle name "Shepilov," after a purged member of the leadership of the Soviet Communist party. The mayor dresses fashionably, favoring three-piece suits in dark blue and gray "power tones." He enjoys playing poker and an occasional game of tennis.

In 1978 Marion Barry, who was briefly married while a student, took Effi Slaughter, the former wife of a jazz musician, as his third wife. Mrs. Barry, who is now the vice-president of JAM Corporation, a public relations and advertising firm, is an intensely private person who avoids the almost endless round of public appearances that leads her husband to call himself the "Mobile Mayor." The couple has one son, Marion Christopher, who was born on June 17, 1980.

References: Ebony 23:82+ D 1 '67 pors, 36:74+ My '81 pors; New Repub 179:10+ D 2 '78; People 11:69+ F 5 '79 pors; Washington Post C p1 D 10 '78 pors; Washington Post mag p16+ D 16 '79 pors, p20+ Ap 6 87 pors; Who's Who in America, 1986–87; Who's Who in the East, 1986–87

Becker, Boris

Nov. 22, 1967– German tennis player. Address: b. c/o Association of Tennis Professionals, 611 Ryan Plaza Dr., Arlington, Tex. 76011; c/o Deutscher Sportbund, Otto Fleck Schneise, 12-D 6000 Frankfurt-am-Main, 71 West Germany

In his first two years on the professional tennis circuit, Boris Becker climbed from the ranks of the unknowns to number two, behind Ivan Lendl, in the Association of Tennis Professionals' computer ratings. A power player known for his scorching serve, Becker came from nowhere to win the men's singles title at Wimbledon in 1985 with an astonishing display of gutsy, acrobatic shots and composure under pressure. Idolized as a national hero in his homeland of West Germany, he surmounted the stress of celebrity, a punishing tournament schedule, and the "sophomore blues" to repeat as Wimbledon champion in 1986. 1987, however, was a frustrating year for Becker, for he won only two major tournaments. Perhaps his most disappointing defeat came at Wimbledon, where he was ousted in the second round by an unseeded player. As a result of his string of losses, Becker dropped to number four in the world rankings.

The son of Karl-Heinz and Elvira Becker, Boris Becker was born in Leimen, a few miles southwest of Heidelberg, West Germany, on November 22, 1967. His father, an architect and an avid amateur tennis player, designed the local tennis center where young Boris began his training when he was just three years old. Recognizing the boy's natural aptitude for the game, the instructors at the Leimen tennis club selected him for intensive, one-on-one training sessions. By the time he was nine, Becker was a regular entrant in the nationwide junior tournaments organized by the West German Tennis Federation. Even at that young age he was an unusually aggressive and competitive player. His temperament on the court, which his manager, Ion Tiriac, has since described as "complete bananas," once earned him a temporary suspension from the tennis federation's youth program.

Throughout his childhood, Becker was as likely to be found on the soccer field as on the tennis court, but when he was about twelve, he decided to concentrate on tennis. Working daily with Günther Bosch, he progressed so rapidly that the tennis federation, in its assessment of the boy's ability in 1981, could find few faults. The official report listed as his strong points his command of the fundamentals of the game, the strength of his serves and ground strokes, and, perhaps most important, his fearless determination. The following year Becker fulfilled the federation's expectations when he won his country's junior championship, a title he held until he turned professional in 1984. In his first major international competition, in 1983, he battled his way to the runner-up spot in the United States Junior Championship.

In April 1984 Bosch asked his friend Ion Tiriac, a one-time Romanian Davis Cup player and the former coach of Ilie Nastase, Guillermo Vilas, and Björn Borg, to take a look at his young protégé. "His footwork had to improve, and he had some growing to do," Tiriac has recalled, as quoted in the *New York Times* (July 9, 1985). "But he didn't have any holes. The only question was whether he could make the sacrifices and take the aggravation of the [professional tennis] tour." After conferring with Karl-Heinz and Elvira Becker, Tiriac, a glowering and rather sinister-looking man who claims kinship with the historical Count Dracula, signed on as Boris Becker's manager for an undisclosed percentage of the player's future earnings.

With Tiriac responsible for his tournament schedule and business affairs and Bosch in charge of his training regimen, Boris Becker joined the professional senior circuit immediately after he graduated from his local *Realschule* (academic high school with modern curriculum) in 1984. Tiriac, who is widely respected in tennis circles for training his players for the long haul, drew up a demanding, all-surface tournament schedule for Becker. "The first year, I was brutal with him," Tiriac admitted to Michael Stone in an interview for *New York* magazine (September 2, 1985). "I made him play everything; find out how good he is. . . . I couldn't care less if he loses in the first round. I want to build something to last."

Tiriac left plenty of room in the schedule for practice and physical conditioning, including a two-week break every three months so that Becker could concentrate on his footwork and on building up strength in his legs. Under the watchful eyes of his two mentors, Becker worked hard on improving his inconsistent ground strokes and occasionally erratic backhands and on perfecting his already intimidating serve. Because their young charge was, in Tiriac's words, "very stubborn," it took the pair three months to teach him to change the mechanics of his serve so he could get to the net more quickly. Clocked at over 150 m.p.h., Becker's cannonball serve is easily the most devastating weapon in his considerable arsenal. Becker launches his explosive serve from midair. Throwing the ball high and slightly forward, he leaps up and smashes down on the ball when it is perhaps ten feet in the air. "This special serve is unique in tennis," Bosch explained to Dudley Doust, as quoted in the London *Sunday Times* (July 6, 1986). "It comes from high and you have less time to see it."

During his first year on the professional circuit, Becker's awesome serve helped lift him from 566th to sixty-fifth place in the Association of Tennis Professionals' computer rankings. Teamed with the veteran Wojtek Fibak, he had a number of wins in doubles competition, and although he failed to win a singles title, he played well enough to reach the quarterfinals of the Australian Open and to qualify for Wimbledon, where he was forced to withdraw from his third-round match, against Bill Scanlon, after tearing a tendon in his left ankle.

Returning to the tour following surgery on his injured ankle, Becker got off to an impressive start with a decisive victory over Sweden's Stefan Edberg to take the World Young Masters crown, in January 1985. Over the next few months, he entered a score of Grand Prix tournaments, but it was not until June 1985 that he finally won his first Grand Prix title by trouncing Johan Kriek, 6-2, 6-3, in the final of the Stella Artois Grass Court Championships at the Queen's Club, near London, En-

gland. On the strength of his win there, British bookmakers made the unseeded Becker their fourth choice to win the men's singles title at Wimbledon the following week.

Obviously at home on the fast grass courts of the All England Lawn Tennis and Croquet Club in Wimbledon, Becker soon endeared himself to the crowd with his gutsy perseverance and his acrobatic, throw-caution-to-the-winds play. He made short work of his first two opponents, Hank Pfister and Matt Anger, but courted disaster in the third round, when Joakim Nystrom twice served for the match against him. Retaining his composure in the face of defeat, Becker broke Nystrom's serve and eventually closed out the grueling five-set contest by pressuring his opponent into making three successive errors. Down two sets to one to Tim Mayotte, a serve-and-volley grass-court specialist, in the round of sixteen, Becker twisted his ankle midway through the fourth set. Rather than forfeit the match, he took a short time out to have his injured ankle taped, then, limping noticeably, returned to the court. Coolly adapting his game to his decreased mobility, he "went for the big shots," as he put it, and defeated Mayotte, 6-3, 4-6, 6-7, 7-6, 6-2. After prevailing over Henri Leconte in the quarterfinals, he came up against the formidable Anders Jarryd, who jumped to an early lead in their semifinal skirmish. Becker fought back gamely and pulled even with the Swede before rain forced a suspension of the match. When play resumed the following day, Becker went on the attack, breaking his foe's serve six times in the last two sets to take the match, 3-6, 7-6, 6-3, 6-3.

Becker's come-from-behind defeat of Jarryd earned him the right to meet Kevin Curren, who had advanced to the final by successively routing top seeds Jimmy Connors and John McEnroe in straight sets, for the men's singles crown. In what turned out to be a classic serve-and-volley confrontation, with aces and service breaks almost equally divided between the two, Becker outlasted Curren, 6-3, 6-7, 7-6, 6-4, to become the men's singles champion. Almost two years younger than the previous youngest champion—Wilfred Baddeley, the victor in 1891—Becker was also the first unseeded player and, of even more importance to his jubilant countrymen, the first West German to take the singles title. (Wilhelm Bungert, the only other West German to reach the final, lost to John Newcombe in 1967.) "I think this will change tennis in Germany," an ecstatic Becker told reporters in a post-match press conference. "They never had an idol and now maybe they have one."

When he returned to Germany a few days later, Becker was caught up in a seemingly endless round of victory celebrations. But even as the new Wimbledon champion basked in the adulation of his compatriots, skeptics were pointing out that he had won the title without beating any of the top four seeds—Connors, McEnroe, Ivan Lendl, and Mats Wilander. Writing in the London *Sunday Times* (July 14, 1985), veteran tennis correspondent Nick Pitt warned his readers not to expect "a Becker era" in the sport. The experienced players "will take Becker's power and use it against him," Pitt explained. "There are the clay-court experts, the thinkers like Wilander, who can nullify his serve, make him rally, and run him into the ground." In Pitt's view, however, the "worst enemy" would be mental: "Becker has the kind of certainty that never bends or cracks. It shatters. One day he will be invaded by self-doubt, and winning tournaments will be a desperate struggle."

In the months following his Wimbledon championship, Becker confounded prognosticators with his erratic play. Although he racked up some impressive wins on grass, clay, and hard courts over such world-class players as Mats Wilander and Anders Jarryd, he failed to earn a single tournament title between August 1985, when he tamed Wilander, 6-4, 6-2, in the final of the Association of Tennis Professionals Championships, and March 1986. During that long dry spell, however, he managed to make it to an advanced round of several Grand Prix events before succumbing to an older, more experienced player. In the 1985 United States Open, for example, Becker sailed through to the round of sixteen, where his game collapsed (he made sixty-four unforced errors) under the relentless baseline pressure of Joakim Nystrom. In the finals of the Benson and Hedges contest in Wombley, England, in November 1905 and the Nabisco Grand Prix Masters tournament in New York City in January 1986, it was Ivan Lendl who stopped the young German cold.

Becker got his own back in the final of the Volvo-Chicago tennis tournament in March 1986, when he ended Lendl's winning streak at twenty-nine matches. By attacking Lendl's second serve and repeatedly rushing the net, Becker so unsettled the Czech that he twice lost his service in the second set. Lendl never regained his self-confidence and fell to Becker, 7-6, 6-3. To make the victory even sweeter, Becker had advanced to the final by rallying to beat the veteran Jimmy Connors, 7-6, 4-6, 6-4, in the semifinals. But despite his increasing ability to handle the pressure of the big matches against the best players in the world, Becker continued to show a disturbing tendency to lose in early rounds to such unheralded players as Michiel Schapers, who upset him in the second round of the Australian Open in November 1985, and Mikael Pernfors, who embarrassed him, 2-6, 6-4, 6-2, 6-0, in the quarterfinals of the French Open in June 1986. Seemingly unruffled by his early-round losses, Becker told reporters, as quoted in the Washington Post (March 31, 1986), "Sometimes I lose early, then next week I beat everybody. Consistency comes with age."

To the delight of his delirious countrymen, Becker displayed the most consistency of his career to that date in the 1985 Davis Cup competition, which was held at various locations in West Germany in the latter half of the year. In the quarterfinals against a second-string American squad in August, Becker humiliated Eliot Teltscher and Aaron Krickstein, both in straight sets, to lead the

West Germans to their first team victory over the United States in Davis Cup play. Two months later, he won two singles matches and a doubles contest as West Germany swept Czechoslovakia in the semifinals to advance to the title round against the powerful defending champion, Sweden.

Playing on a lightning-fast artificial surface in Munich, Becker twice evened the best-of-five series by defeating two of the world's best serve-and-volley players, Stefan Edberg and Mats Wilander, in his two singles matches, but he and his partner, Andreas Maurer, proved to be no match for Wilander and Nystrom, who dominated the doubles event, 6-4, 6-2, 6-1. Of the seven games taken by the West German pair, five were won almost exclusively on the strength of Becker's booming serve. But as Roger Williams noted in the Washington Post (December 22, 1985), each of Becker's aces and blazing forehand winners was "matched—or more—by mis-hit returns, double faults and flubbed volleys." "Maurer and Becker played as if they barely knew each other," Williams continued. "Wilander and Nystrom moved like a dance team." Sweden went on to win the last singles match, against the hapless Michael Westphal, and retain the Davis Cup.

Some observers contended that Becker's inconsistency on the tennis courts was due, at least in part, to his extraordinary popularity in his native land. A poll published in the early autumn of 1985 put the tennis player's name recognition among the German people at 98.1 percent, second only to that of Volkswagen. With hundreds of fans milling around his hotels and as many as fifty reporters and photographers covering even his practice sessions, Becker has occasionally found it hard to concentrate on his game. "The Germans wanted me to live for them," he said, as quoted in Time magazine (June 30, 1986). "They worshipped me too much. When I entered my own hometown, people stood there and gazed up at me as if they were expecting blessings from the Pope. When I looked at the eyes of my fans at the Davis Cup matches last December, I thought I was looking at monsters. Their eyes were fixed and had no life in them. When I saw this kind of blind, emotional devotion, I could understand what happened to us a long time ago in Nuremberg. . . . It's very, very difficult to be German sometimes," he went on. "Because of their guilt, the Germans feel they have to do something special. I have to behave better than my opponents. Unfortunately, heroes have very short lives."

Because he had won only two of the nineteen tournaments he had entered in the previous twelve months and had failed to reach the final of a single Grand Slam event, Becker was under unusual pressure to repeat as the men's singles title-holder at Wimbledon in the summer of 1986. Seeded fourth, the lowest for any defending champion since Jan Kodes was seeded sixth in 1974, Becker started uncertainly, opening his first-round meeting against Argentina's Eduardo Bengoechea with a double fault, but he soon settled down to take that contest and the four succeeding matches, dropping only one set along the way. In his semifinal duel, Becker unnerved the flashy Henri Leconte with his unbreakable serve to take the match, 6-2, 6-4, 6-7, 6-3.

Becker's opponent in the final was the top-seeded Ivan Lendl, who had been beaten only twice in fifty-four Grand Prix matches in 1986. Playing confidently and cagily, Becker confounded Lendl with sizzling aces and a variety of dazzling returns that kept the Czech scrambling. When Lendl, down two sets to none, threatened to take the third set, Becker saved three successive set points—one of them with a crosscourt backhand from his knees—and went on to take the set and the match, 6-4, 6-3, 7-5. His second Wimbledon title was "much more satisfying than the first one," Becker told reporters later. "I thought about how difficult it would be to win a Grand Slam or Wimbledon again. But when I got here, it was like home. . . . And although you cannot say I am the best tennis player in the world, you have to say that, maybe, I am the best on grass."

Becker's jubilation was perhaps tempered somewhat by his subsequent losses to Lendl in the final of the Volvo International in August and to Miloslav Mecir in the semifinals of the United States Open in September. Toward the end of the year, however, he was well on his way toward proving that he was indeed the best player on all surfaces. In the space of a few weeks, he won three straight tournaments—the Australian Open, the Seiko Super, and the French Open—on three continents. His winning streak, which reached twenty-one successive matches, was snapped in the final of the Nabisco Grand Prix Masters by Lendl, who capitalized on soft, sliced shots to an increasingly exasperated Becker's tentative backhand to triumph, 6-4, 6-4, 6-4. Undaunted, forty hours later Becker was on a court in Stuttgart, West Germany, where he fought off a determined challenge by Jonas B. Svensson of Sweden to collect his third consecutive Waterford Crystal Young Masters trophy.

The second seed in the 1987 Australian Open, Becker was upset in the fourth round by the unheralded Wally Masur in a five-set match marred by the German's unsportsmanlike conduct. (He was subsequently fined $2000 for, among other things, breaking three rackets and verbally abusing the umpire.) Shortly thereafter, Gunther Bosch resigned as Becker's coach. A stickler for discipline, Bosch reportedly objected to his charge's increasingly lackadaisical attitude toward training and to the distracting presence on the tour of the player's constant companion, Bénédicte Courtain. Becker was widely criticized in the West German press for letting Bosch leave, but Ion Tiriac supported his client's decision. "He just doesn't want to be a machine," Tiriac explained, as quoted in *Time* (June 29, 1987). "He wants to take charge of himself and make his own mistakes."

Troubled by recurrent illness, Becker played erratically during the first half of 1987, but he still managed to win the Pilot Pen Classic, snapping

Stefan Edberg's fifteen-match winning streak, and to advance to the semifinals of the Paris Open, where he was trounced by Mats Wilander, 6-4, 6-1, 6-2. By late June, however, he seemed to have recovered his old form, as he came from behind to best Jimmy Connors in the final of the Stella Artois grass-court championship at the Queen's Club in England. The top seed at Wimbledon a few days later, he dispatched his first-round opponent, Karel Novacek, in straight sets only to fall to Peter Doohan, a relatively unknown Australian grass-court specialist, in the second round, 7-6, 4-6, 6-2, 6-4. It was the earliest departure for a defending champion since 1967. Becker bounced back to take both his singles matches, including an epic six-and-one-half-hour duel with John McEnroe, in Davis Cup play against the United States squad in July, but he fared poorly in subsequent major tourneys, losing to Brad Gilbert in the round of sixteen in the United States Open and to Pat Cash, the 1987 Wimbledon champion, in the semifinals of the Australian Indoor Championship.

A tall and husky young man with broad shoulders, "tree-trunk legs," and the strength of a defensive lineman, Boris Becker stands six feet three inches tall and weighs 190 pounds. He has light-blue eyes, a thatch of strawberry-blond hair, and a boyish, freckled face. His unassuming, good-natured manner and easy smile give him "a kind of Howdy Doody innocence," according to *New York Times* reporter Peter Alfano, that belies his intensity on the court. Becker, who once described his schedule as "practicing, eating, sleeping, and practicing," rarely takes time off, but when he does he enjoys reading, going to the movies and listening to rock music. "I like talking, eating, fooling around, having a nice time, even giving autographs," he told Frederick C. Klein, who interviewed him for the *Wall Street Journal* (December 5, 1986). "I only don't like it when they [his fans] . . . gang up on me."

A "hot property" in his homeland, Becker has signed some of the richest promotional deals in history, including a six-year contract, for a reported $24 million, with Puma, the West German sporting-goods firm. He also has lucrative arrangements with Phillips, the Dutch electronics conglomerate, a German watch manufacturer, and Deutsche Bank. Becker's annual earnings from prize money and endorsements have been estimated to be as high as $4.5 million. For tax purposes, Becker, like many of his fellow tennis pros, maintains an official residence in Monte Carlo, although he is there only during his infrequent and brief respites from the tour.

References: *German Tribune* p15 Jl 21 '85 por, p14 F 22 '87 por; *Guardian* p28 Jl 14 '85 por; *Inside Sports* 8:56+ Jl '86 pors; *N Y Post* p33 Jl 8 '85 por; *N Y Times* A p1+ Jl 8 '85 por, V p1+ Je 22 '86 por; *Scala* no 10:14+ '85 pors; *Time* 126:64 Jl 22 '86 pors, 127:60 Je 30 '86 por, 129:58+ Je 29 '87 pors; *International Who's Who*, 1987–88

Bernstein, Robert L(ouis)

*Jan. 5, 1923– Publisher; human rights activist.
Address: b. Random House, Inc., 201 E. 50th St.,
New York City, N.Y. 10022*

Robert L. Bernstein, who has been the president of Random House since 1966 and its board chairman since 1975, was once described in *Publishers Weekly* as a man "with a passion for freedom to publish." Since joining the firm in 1958 in response to an invitation from its founder, the late Bennett Cerf, Bernstein has helped to build Random House, now an independent subsidiary of Newhouse Publications, into what one publishing executive, quoted in the *New York Times* (May 5, 1985), has called "without any question, still the dominant and most influential force in American publishing." Complementing Bernstein's role as a publisher has been his energetic commitment to human rights throughout the world.

A second-generation American of German and Lithuanian family background, Robert Louis Bernstein was born in New York City on January 5, 1923, to Alfred Bernstein, who was in the textile business, and Sylvia (Bloch) Bernstein. He has a younger sister, Barbara (Mrs. Herman Rosenberg). While growing up in Manhattan's West Seventies, Bernstein attended the Lincoln School, a progressive private institution affiliated with Columbia University. It was as a student at Lincoln that Bernstein first became aware of the underprivileged through field trips to such areas as the coal mining regions of West Virginia as well as visits to some of the poorer sections of New York City. He remembers spending much of his time in the Depression-era shantytown in Riverside Park on Manhattan's Upper West Side, where squatters were living in shacks made of cardboard and corrugated tin.

After graduating from the Lincoln School in 1940, Bernstein entered Harvard University, where he completed his undergraduate studies as a history major *cum laude* in about two and a half years. He obtained his B.A. degree in 1944, a year after he had joined the United States Army Air Corps for service in World War II. Although he had at first intended to become a teacher, he decided by the time he was discharged from military service in 1946 that teaching would not pay him enough. Having become interested in communications during his years at Harvard, Bernstein decided to try to make his way in that field. After writing some fifty letters to radio and television stations and walking the streets of New York, visiting various offices, he took a job as a receptionist with radio station WNEW.

Soon afterwards, through a friend, Bernstein obtained his first job in publishing, as an office boy with the firm of Simon & Schuster, and he decided that he had found the field in which he felt most at home. "Ideas, that's all the business is," he recalled in an interview for a profile by Hope MacLeod in the *New York Post* (October 25, 1976). "You're really learning every minute. It's exciting." One of his main functions, he believes, was "as a catalyst," talking with people, stimulating their thinking, and getting them excited about ideas. Rising through the ranks at Simon & Schuster, Bernstein became its general sales manager in 1950 and remained in that post for seven years.

In late 1957 Bernstein was dismissed from his post as general sales manager as a result of a major cutback and staff shakeup at Simon & Schuster, and the experience so embittered him that he was at that time determined never to work for anyone again. But before he left Simon & Schuster he had met Bennett Cerf, the bon vivant, raconteur, and president of Random House. Much impressed by Bernstein, Cerf persuaded him to become the firm's sales manager in January 1958.

Random House had its origin in the Modern Library, a unit of the publishing firm of Boni & Liveright that specialized in low-cost hardbound reprints of classic and semiclassic literary works. In 1925 Bennett Cerf and Donald S. Klopfer bought the Modern Library, then consisting of 112 titles, from Horace Liveright for $215,000 in borrowed money, and within two years recouped their investment. In 1927 they decided to publish luxury editions of books that they chose "at random," and they called the firm Random House.

In 1933 Random House acquired the publishing rights for the plays of Eugene O'Neill and the poems of Robinson Jeffers. A landmark for the firm was the historic decision by United States District Judge John M. Woolsey, in December of that year, giving Random House the legal right to publish James Joyce's novel *Ulysses*, which had been seized by United States Customs as obscene. The court ruling, engineered behind the scenes by Cerf and Klopfer, placed Random House in the vanguard of the struggle against censorship. The company soon acquired publication rights for the works of such other distinguished writers as William Faulkner, Marcel Proust, Sinclair Lewis, Robert Penn Warren, Havelock Ellis, Budd Schulberg, and Quentin Reynolds, and for a number of Broadway plays. In 1947 it established a college department with the publication of the first edition of the *American College Dictionary*, and during the 1950s it introduced the Landmark series of books on American historical themes by such best-selling authors as John Gunther, Thomas B. Costain, C. S. Forester, and Pearl Buck; the World Landmark series, dealing with events of world history; the All-about Books series, concerning science and nature; and Beginner Books, featuring children's literature, such as Laurent de Brunhoff's Babar elephant stories and Dr. Seuss's whimsical books.

When Robert L. Bernstein joined Random House as its sales manager in early 1958, its annual sales volume was about 7.5 million. Continuing to prosper, its Modern Library division had sold by that time over forty million copies of some 300 titles. An additional eighty titles made up the Modern Library Giants, which were bulkier in format and more expensive. In 1959 Random House went partly public by selling 30 percent of its stock to outsiders. That decision was followed by a series of acquisitions, of which the most important was that of Alfred A. Knopf, Inc., widely regarded as the most distinguished literary publishing firm in the United States. Under terms of an agreement announced in April 1960 the Knopf firm, while retaining a high degree of autonomy, merged with Random House, which acquired all of its stock. In addition, Random House acquired Knopf's college division as well as Vintage Books, its quality paperback line. In the same year Random House bought the major textbook publishing firm of L. W. Singer, and in 1961—the year in which Bernstein became vice-president in charge of sales—the company acquired Pantheon Books, which published nonfiction, including scholarly works by European authors. In 1962 Bernstein was promoted to the office of first vice-president.

As a result of executive changes voted at a Random House board of directors meeting in November 1965, Cerf was designated chairman of the board, Klopfer became vice-chairman, and Bernstein was chosen to succeed Cerf as president on January 1, 1966. "It's time the younger generation got into the picture," Cerf remarked, as quoted by Maurice Dolbier in the New York *Herald Tribune* (December 12, 1965). "There never was a time in the publishing business when there was a more obvious need for young men with exciting new ideas and perspectives. Bob Bernstein has proved that he fulfills these requirements. . . . It'll relieve wear and tear on me." At the time, the annual sales volume of Random House had more than quadrupled over the preceding eight years, to thirty-four million, of which over 60 percent represented sales in the burgeoning educational market, while the Modern Library and Vintage Books accounted for about 15 percent. Random House was represented by over 150 salesmen in four separate sales forces.

In addition to occupying the presidency of Random House, Bernstein became its chief executive officer in 1967. He was also elected chairman of the board in 1975, succeeding the retiring Donald S. Klopfer, who had assumed the post in 1970, a year before Bennett Cerf's death.

Meanwhile, in the mid-1960s, some major conglomerates became interested in acquiring book publishing firms with the aim of bringing together electronic "hardware" and publishing "software" for joint educational ventures, and Random House, which was prospering, was coveted by several prospective buyers. In a merger announced in January 1966 the publishing firm became a wholly owned subsidiary of the Radio Corporation of America. Random House was "an excellent acquisition," according to Howard Hawkins, an RCA executive who was quoted in the *New York Times* (August 1, 1975). "We maintain an arms-length relationship with them. We believe in complete editorial independence, though we work with them closely on financial systems and performance." But Bernstein felt thwarted by the complex management decisions imposed on Random House by RCA, which frustrated the publisher's efforts to acquire other companies. "Under RCA," Bernstein said, as quoted in the *New York Times* (May 5, 1985), "we were a $40 million business in an $8 billion company, so we were not important to them. . . . Everything was done by committees."

Under RCA, Random House grew from a $40 million company to one that had annual revenues of $180 million, but by the late 1970s its profits had leveled off, and RCA was looking around for a buyer for the publishing firm. Finally, in early 1980, Random House was purchased from RCA for $70 million by Newhouse Publications, a $2.7 billion communications concern whose holdings included a chain of newspapers as well as the Condé Nast magazines, the syndicated *Parade* magazine, and several radio stations and cable television systems. Founded in 1922 by the late Samuel I. Newhouse, it was carried on by his sons, Samuel I. Jr. and Donald, who incorporated Random House as an independent subsidiary in their publishing empire. Under Newhouse, Bernstein was given greater flexibility than he had had with RCA, especially in his efforts to expand Random House through acquisitions and internal growth, and he was able to maintain a high degree of editorial independence under guidance.

In the years that followed acquisition by Newhouse, Bernstein instituted a number of important changes at Random House. He added to the staff such highly recommended and knowledgeable experts as Howard Kaminsky, a former chief executive of Warner Books, and Peter Osnos, a former editor at the *Washington Post*. He founded Villard Books, a hard-cover publisher of commercial fiction and nonfiction, and he purchased Times Books from the New York Times Company. To rescue the money-losing Ballantine Books paperback line, acquired in 1973, Bernstein merged it with Fawcett Books, which he bought from CBS, thus creating one of the major mass-market publishers. In addition, he considerably expanded the company's college division, acquiring major lines of college textbooks; assumed distribution for some ten smaller publishers, such as Warner Books, Reader's Digest Press, Sierra Club, and Grove Press; introduced juvenile and adult books on audio and video cassettes, including a six-tape cooking course by Julia Child; and acquired companies producing educational games and audio-visual aids for schools. In May 1987 a history-making agreement was reached under which Random House would acquire a consortium of three of Great Britain's leading publishing houses—Jonathan Cape, Chatto & Windus, and the Bodley Head—the first purchase of major European trade book publishers by an American firm.

Bernstein's achievements and policies have greatly contributed to the growing prosperity of Random House. Its revenues during the first half of the 1980s increased annually by some 15 percent as compared with 7 percent under RCA, and during 1984 its revenues totaled $370 million and pretax profits averaged about 10 percent. "I think it represents one of the great buys of our time," Samuel I. Newhouse Jr. has said of the Random House purchase, as quoted in the New York Times (May 5, 1985).

On the other hand, some critics have suggested that Random House under Bernstein had become "complacent and smug," that it was losing its "competitive edge" in relation to such other publishing giants as Simon & Schuster, and that some of its editors were "pseudo-intellectual snobs" who tended to shun overtly commercial books. Although, as of the mid-1980s, Random House had published twenty-seven Nobel Prize-winning authors and thirty-eight Pulitzer Prize winners, some observers noted a lack of flexibility in its publishing policies. For example, Random House consistently refused to consider publishing Judith Krantz's novel Scruples, a major best seller with titillating entertainment value but questionable literary quality.

Although Bernstein's "laid-back" style of management and his unwillingness to "knock heads" seem to have given the impression to some rival publishers that he is essentially a figurehead manager, his associates and employees insist that he is very much in control. They point out that he is in constant contact with the various department heads, presides over weekly executive board meetings, approves all advances to authors in excess of $100,000, and personally negotiates with such heavyweight Random House writers as Norman Mailer, Gore Vidal, James A. Michener, and Robert Ludlum. "Negotiating with Bob, I always have a sense of fair play while aware he will vigorously pursue his company's interests," Owen Laster, who heads the literary department of the William Morris Agency, has said, as quoted in the New York Times (May 5, 1985). Although Bernstein is said to have a limited attention span for some details, he is, according to Laurence J. Kirshbaum, the president of Warner Books, an "outstanding" editor who "hires the best talent in the industry and lets the horses run."

Apart from publishing, Bernstein's major concern has been his passionate involvement in the cause of human rights, especially during the past two decades. "Vietnam is what made me realize I couldn't sit around and just talk . . . ," he told Hope MacLeod in the New York Post interview. "My sons were getting nearer and nearer draft age. I finally realized that if I was going to try to keep my sons out of the war I would have to keep other sons out of the war." Eventually he took part in marches, demonstrations, and political activities. His human rights efforts are directed equally against abuses in the Soviet sphere and in Western nations. Although he has generally kept his publishing and human rights concerns separate, they have on occasion overlapped. Under the Alfred A. Knopf imprint he has published works of such activists as the Soviet dissidents Andrei D. Sakharov, Yelena Bonner, and Arkady N. Shevchenko and the Argentine-born journalist Jacobo Timerman. Bernstein was behind the Knopf suit resulting in a court ruling that rejected government efforts to censor the book The CIA and the Cult of Intelligence (1974) by Victor L. Marchetti and John D. Marks for security reasons. In 1976 he received the New York Civil Liberties Union's Florina Lasker award and announced that he would divide the accompanying $1,000 among the defense funds of four persecuted dissidents abroad: the poet Kim Chi Ha in South Korea, Mihajlo Mihajlov in Yugoslavia, Nelson Mandela in South Africa, and Vladimir Bukovsky in the Soviet Union.

While serving as chairman of the Association of American Publishers in the early 1970s, Bernstein became chairman of its International Freedom to Publish Committee, which was organized to investigate human rights abuses against writers in various countries. In 1975 he founded the Fund for Free Expression, composed of publishers, editors, and writers, through which he helped to establish the Helsinki Watch Committee, which monitors compliance with the human rights provisions of the Helsinki Final Act of 1975; the Americas Watch Committee, which monitors and promotes observance of human rights in the Western Hemisphere; and the related Asia Watch Committee.

Bernstein's abiding interest in human rights has taken him on a number of trips abroad, including several visits to China and the Soviet Union. In 1975 he was in Oslo, Norway to hear Yelena Bonner deliver the Nobel Peace Prize acceptance speech for her husband, Andrei D. Sakharov, whom Soviet authorities refused to allow to attend. In 1977 Bernstein decided not to attend the Moscow Book Fair in protest against harassment of Soviet writers. When in 1979, and again in 1985, Bernstein was scheduled to go to the Moscow fair, Soviet authorities denied him permission, but in 1987 he was granted a visa, as were several of his colleagues in the publishing field. Meanwhile, American publishers became more receptive to publishing books by Soviet authors as a result of the new policy of *glasnost,* or openness, fostered in the USSR under Mikhail S. Gorbachev. In Bernstein's view, although the Soviet system was still resistant to change, Gorbachev's actions deserved "credibility in the West."

Bernstein drew criticism from members of the Reagan administration in 1981, when he testified before a congressional committee that in his view the president's nominee for assistant secretary of state for human rights, Ernest W. Lefever, was not sufficiently committed to human rights to qualify for the post. Lefever failed to obtain the position. In the spring of 1985 Bernstein visited a combat zone of Nicaragua near the Honduras border with two companions to investigate charges by Americas Watch that Contra forces fighting the Sandinista government were committing terrorist acts against unarmed civilians. Responding to charges by Assistant Secretary of State Elliott Abrams that Americas Watch had become "wholly politicized," Bernstein insists that the three "Watch" committees are nonpolitical and that their main emphasis is to "influence American foreign policy toward protecting human rights wherever they are violated." Bernstein has used the Op-Ed columns of the *New York Times* to appeal to Soviet leader Mikhail Gorbachev to free all of his country's political prisoners and to call on President Ronald Reagan to oppose tyranny in such countries as Chile, South Africa, South Korea, Romania, El Salvador, Pakistan, and Turkey.

In a shakeup at Random House in October 1987, Howard Kaminsky, who had been considered a likely successor to Bernstein, resigned as the company's publisher of adult books, reportedly under pressure, and was succeeded by Joni Evans, formerly the head of trade-book publishing at Simon & Schuster. Bernstein attributed the resignation to "management differences" between himself and Kaminsky and indicated that "four or five" people were being groomed to succeed him as head of Random House.

In addition to being chairman of the Fund for Free Expression and the Helsinki Watch Committee, a member of the Americas Watch Committee and the Asia Watch Committee, and a past chairman of the Association of American Publishers, Bernstein serves on the boards of the Aaron Diamond Foundation, the Dr. Seuss Foundation, and the Chamber Music Society of Lincoln Center. His clubs are the Century Association and the University Club in New York City.

On November 23, 1950, Robert L. Bernstein married Helen Walter, who was then a researcher for the now defunct *Reporter* magazine. They have three grown sons, Peter Walter, Tom Alfred, and William Samuel. Bernstein is six feet three inches tall, weighs about 180 pounds, and has graying auburn hair that was formerly flaming red. Although he has been described as having a "gentle, softspoken manner," he is, by his own account, "also aggressive." His favorite recreations include tennis, swimming, and skiing. Of his political view-

point, Bernstein has said, as quoted by Edwin McDowell in the *New York Times* (August 6, 1986): "Most people would probably call me a liberal, but I think of myself as an old conservative who believes in old values. The trouble is, many conservatives applaud my human rights views when applied to the Soviet Union or Cuba, yet abhor them when applied to Central America."

References: N Y Post p25 O 25 '76 por; N Y Times III p1+ My 5 '85 por, C p21 Ag 6 '86 por; Washington Post C p4 Je 6 '69 por; International Who's Who, 1986-87; Who's Who in America, 1986-87

Biden, Joseph (Robinette), Jr.
(bī'den)

Nov. 20, 1942– United States Senator from Delaware. Address: b. 489 Russell Bldg., Washington, D.C. 20510

Few American politicans can match Senator Joseph Biden's combination of youth, experience, and influence. Although only in his mid-forties, the Delaware Democrat is in his third term in the upper chamber. The recapture of control of the Senate by the Democrats in the 1986 elections enabled him to assume the chairmanship of the powerful Judiciary Committee, after Edward M. Kennedy, who had been in line for the post, chose instead to take over the leadership of the Labor and Human Resources Committee. Biden is enormously popular in his home state, and had the makings of an "image-perfect" candidate beyond its boundaries. Despite Delaware's small size, Biden occupied a strong position among the handful of leaders in contention for the Democratic presidential nomination in 1988. He announced his candidacy for the presidency on June 9, 1987, but withdrew three and a half months later, following revelations that in his Senate speeches and, earlier, in his law school work, he had appropriated material from others without giving credit to his sources.

Of largely Irish descent, Joseph Robinette Biden Jr. was born on November 20, 1942, in Scranton, Pennsylvania, to Joseph (Robinette) Biden and his wife, Jean (Finnegan) Biden. The family later moved to Wilmington, Delaware, where the father managed a Chevrolet dealership. Biden attended St. Helena's Roman Catholic parochial school and Archmere Academy. As a youngster, he stuttered, but he worked at oratory to overcome the problem, and by the time of his high school graduation, he had become a skilled enough speaker to be selected to give the commencement address.

Biden played football at the University of Delaware until his junior year, when his father, who was dissatisfied with his son's B-minus average, told him to drop off the team, but Biden continued to apply himself to his studies with a casualness only made possible by his raw ability. "Joe was the kind of guy," his roommate remembers, "who could read someone else's notes and do better on the exam than the guy who made the notes."

After graduating from the University of Delaware in 1965 with an B.A. degree, Biden enrolled in law school at Syracuse University, an institution that he chose partly because his future wife, Neilia Hunter of Skaneateles, New York, whom he had met in the Bahamas during a spring break, was a student there. Biden found law school to be "the biggest bore in the world" and recalls that he "almost flunked out," but thanks to "doing all-nighters all the time," he managed to earn his J.D. degree in 1968.

After his admission to the Delaware bar in 1968, Biden practiced criminal law in Wilmington, first as a public defender and then as a partner in his own firm, Biden and Walsh. He also became involved in politics and, in 1970, won election as a Democrat to the New Castle County Council. His easy victory surprised many, because that district normally went Republican and also because Biden, who had taken part in antisegregation sit-ins at Wilmington's Towne Theatre during his high school years, had run on a liberal platform that included support for public housing in the suburbs.

Even as a college student, Biden had aspired to become a United States senator, and the new councilman immediately began to make plans for seeking that office in 1972. Despite his inexperience and youth, he encountered little resistance within his own party, since no other Democrat was eager to challenge the popular Republican incumbent, J. Caleb Boggs, whose two terms as senator had followed three terms as Delaware's at-large member of the House of Representatives and two as its governor. Although Biden himself liked Boggs, who years before had offered to nominate him for an

appointment to the United States Naval Academy, he also perceived his weaknesses, for Boggs had not established clear positions on issues, and rumors persisted that he did not intend to sit for a full term. Indeed, Boggs had agreed to run only at the insistence of President Richard Nixon.

The Biden campaign was a low-budget, family-centered operation. The candidate's sister, Valerie, acted as the campaign manager, her husband was budget director, and Biden's mother organized the thirty to forty coffee hours that her son attended each week to improve his name recognition. Biden's younger brother, James, raised money, and teenage volunteers distributed the campaign literature by hand in order to save the cost of postage. Biden however, did receive some financial assistance from the AFL-CIO and from the national party, and Patrick Caddell, who was handling polling in behalf of Democratic presidential candidate George McGovern, performed similar services for Biden.

Biden's campaign theme was summed up in brief radio spots that stressed public distrust of officeholders and candidates. "Politicians have done such a job on the people that the people don't believe them anymore," he asserted in one message, "and I'd like a shot at changing that." He argued that for trust to be restored, politicians had to become more accountable. "My philosophy of government is to narrow responsibility so I know whom to crucify." On the issues, Biden called for an end to the war in Vietnam, more equitable taxation, legislation in behalf of consumers and the environment, and greater expenditures for mass transit and health care.

Biden trailed Boggs 47 percent to 19 in polls taken early in August, but the two men were neck and neck by late October. Finally, on election day, the challenger squeezed by his opponent, taking 116,006 ballots to Boggs's 112,844. The narrow victory made Biden the second-youngest person ever voted into the upper house; indeed, he did not reach the minimum age prescribed by the Constitution for service in the Senate until several weeks after the election.

Shortly before Christmas, a personal tragedy annihilated Biden's feelings of elation and almost ended his public career. On December 18, in Hockessin, Delaware, the car in which his wife and children were bringing home a Christmas tree for the holiday celebration, crashed into a tractor-trailer. Mrs. Biden and their infant daughter, Amy, were killed instantly, and their two sons were injured. In the following weeks Biden considered surrendering his newly won seat, but Senator Mike Mansfield of Montana, the Democratic leader, persuaded him to accept his duties. Biden finally took his oath of office in the hospital room in which his sons were recovering.

The tragic accident so profoundly affected Biden that he decided to keep his boys at home in Wilmington, and his sister and brother-in-law moved into his house in order to help with their care. He himself embarked on a grueling schedule involving daily commuting between Wilmington and Washington, D.C., a practice that he has continued even though each 100-mile leg of the trip requires a two-hour ride on the Metroliner.

Unsure when he took office that he would be able to be both a senator and family man, Biden believed that he might quit after six months. Contrasting the claims on his attention of the people of his state with those of his children, he remarked, "They can always get another senator," but the children "can't get another father." Biden not only managed to finish his first term but also won two more. In 1978 he defeated James H. Baxter, a poultry farmer, by a margin of 93,930 to 66,479. In 1984 he avoided a serious challenge when Pierre S. ("Pete") Du Pont 4th, who was completing the maximum service of two terms allowed to Delaware's governor, chose not to run against him. That year Biden scored an almost 50,000-vote victory over John M. Burris, a businessman and former Republican leader of the Delaware house of representatives.

The first issue that Biden tackled as a senator was the reform of campaign finances. During his campaign, people with money had implied that they would support him in return for a promise of his aid on matters of concern to them. He recalled how tempting their offers were and admitted that, in view of his meager finances, he might have accepted had it not been for his "Scotch Presbyterian wife who had a backbone like a ramrod." Likewise, he wondered how many people who had committed themselves to political careers compromised their ideals instead of taking the heroic steps that would qualify them for "the second edition of *Profiles in Courage*." Not surprisingly, Biden supported passage in 1974 of legislation to provide full federal subsidies for federal general election campaigns and to place a ceiling on campaign contributions and spending.

In 1975 Biden shocked some observers when, despite his identification with the cause of civil rights, he broke from the liberals' ranks on the issue of school busing. In September of that year, the senator won Senate endorsement of an amendment that forbade the Department of Health, Education, and Welfare to require busing for desegregation except in compliance with a specific court order. Arguing that busing was a "bankrupt concept" that violated "the cardinal rule of common sense," Biden contended that other previously intimidated lawmakers would soon agree with his position. "I've made it reasonable," he commented, "for longstanding liberals to begin to raise the questions I've been the first to raise in the liberal community here on the floor."

On most matters of public policy, Biden has taken moderately liberal positions. According to the *National Journal*, in 1985 he voted more liberally than 76 percent of the Senate on economic issues, 80 percent of the Senate on social questions, and 74 percent of the Senate on foreign policy. He voted against Senate sponsorship of a constitutional amendment mandating a balanced budget and characterized proposals to eliminate federal subsidies for the Amtrak rail system as a waste of $3 billion investment rather than as a way to cut the budget deficit. Resisting the desire of the Reagan administration to reduce various benefits under the Social Security system, Biden declared that "the best measure of the humaneness of a society is the way in which a society treats its elderly." Moreover, in 1983 he worked vigorously on a measure that reconstituted the United States Commission on Civil Rights to allow the Congress to appoint half its members.

In contrast with his generally liberal inclinations, Biden has continued to vote for antibusing measures, including a 1982 bill to prevent the Justice Department from taking any legal action that could lead to court-ordered busing. Although he has opposed federal funding for abortions, he supports the right of women to have them and in 1983 voted against Senate endorsement of a constitutional amendment that would have allowed individual states to ban the procedures. "It's the only consistent position intellectually," he says, "which is that if you say government should be out, then government should be out."

In regard to foreign policy, Biden has opposed military aid to El Salvador and to the Contras of Nicaragua. He has been a strong supporter of Israel and has resisted efforts by the administrations of Presidents Jimmy Carter and Ronald Reagan to sell respectively F-15s and AWACs to Saudi Arabia. Although wary of the Soviets, Biden supported the SALT II treaty and, despite the Senate's failure to ratify it, has tried to convince the Reagan administration to abide by the principles of the pact. He also voted against the MX missile system and for the nuclear freeze.

Biden had been serving on the powerful Judiciary and Foreign Relations Committees and became the ranking Democrat on the Judiciary Committee in 1981. So effectively has he worked with Strom Thurmond, until 1986 the Republican chairman of the Judiciary Committee, that the South Carolinian conservative called him "My Henry Clay." Biden's work on the Judiciary Committee gave him his most important legislative triumph when, in 1984, he served as the Democratic floor manager for the passage of the Comprehensive Crime Control Act. Civil libertarians believe the package, which had been in the works for eleven years, could have been much worse, from their perspective, if it had not been for Biden's efforts. Although he persuaded Democrats to allow judges to hold more prisoners without bail, for example, he also persuaded Republicans to drop Draconian provisions, such as a federal death penalty.

Overall, Biden has emerged as one of the most acidulous critics of the appointments and policies of the Reagan administration. In 1981, at the confirmation hearings held on William P. Clark's appointment as deputy secretary of state, his sharp questioning revealed that the new president's nominee could not identify key leaders in southern Africa. In 1985 Biden vehemently expressed his reasons for opposing the nomination of Edwin Meese 3d to be attorney general. Speaking as the ranking Democrat on the Judiciary Committee, Biden found the candidate to be "likable" and "ethical," but concluded that allegations involving Meese's financial affairs and his promotion to colonel in the Army Reserve suggested behavior "beneath the office" to which he aspired.

The senator is a frequent foe of the legal and judicial appointments that the president sends to the Judiciary Committee. In the summer of 1985 Biden led the effort to block a promotion for William Bradford Reynolds, who had very narrowly interpreted his responsibilities as civil rights chief at the Justice Department, and in 1986 he was floor manager of the Democrats' almost successful effort to keep Daniel Manion, another controversial Reagan nominee, from being named a federal appellate judge. In July 1986 Biden opposed the nomination of Associate Justice William H. Rehnquist to be chief justice of the United States Supreme Court. His questioning of Rehnquist was especially severe and focused on his unsuccessful effort to have the nominee, who was a law clerk with the Supreme Court in 1954, declare what position he would have taken then on the Brown v. the Board of Education case, in which the Court struck down the legal rationale for segregation.

But Biden's most publicized clash with the Reagan administration took place in July 1986 after the president refused to support extensive economic sanctions against South Africa. During testimony by Secretary of State George P. Shultz before the Foreign Relations Committee, Biden remarked that Archbishop Desmond Tutu's characterization of Reagan's statement as "nauseating" showed "restraint." When Shultz retorted that Tutu's comment was "nuts" and charged that the senator was calling for violence, Biden denied the accusation and chided the administration for lacking "moral backbone." At one point the exchange between the pair became so heated that Shultz blurted out at the senator, "Just because I'm secretary of state, you can't kick me around. I'm a taxpayer."

Critics of Biden contend that, apart from the 1984 anticrime package, his legislative record indicates only modest achievement. They allege that the senator has more style than substance and that he has not demonstrated the ability or the inclination to complete what he undertakes. His detractors charge that after becoming an expert on arms control matters in the late 1970s, Biden lost interest in the subject, and they note that the senator seemed so uninterested when he held an important post on the Budget Committee that he eventually removed himself from that body. They point out that despite his rhetoric Biden had supported the large majority of Reagan's judicial appointments and that his poor timing of a critical vote was the factor that brought Manion Senate approval. Finally, his critics argue that Biden's recent vociferous attacks are merely ploys to gain him the attention necessary to promote his ambition for higher office.

As far back as 1983 Patrick Caddell, the Democratic pollster, tried to persuade Biden that a younger candidate could constitute a strong challenge in the next presidential race, but when he came up for reelection in 1984, the senator decided that the honor of competing against a popular incumbent president was not worth relinquishing his secure seat in the upper chamber. Nevertheless, Biden seemed primed to make a serious bid for the Oval Office in 1988, especially since Senator Edward M. Kennedy of Massachusetts had taken himself out of the running. Dismissing the charges of his critics, he has noted that the issues from which he moved away were those on which no progress could be made during the Reagan presidency. Biden also argued that his colleagues recognized his substance as well as his style, and he saw his stance as that of a generalist. "I don't think presidents get elected on specifics," he has said. "I think presidents get elected on broader notions of what their vision for America is."

Biden hoped to be able to capitalize on a change in the national mood, believing that "1988 will be a time of idealism when people will say, 'Let's try to make the world better again. Let's get up and work.'" But he also thinks that his party must revitalize and reshape itself if Democrats are to take control once again. During the past several years, he has charged Democrats with making their organization a "fossilized shadow of its former self" by being self-satisfied and refusing to think critically about adapting traditional programs to new times. Biden has also complained that the Democrats' perceived softness with regard to defense has driven the electorate toward the Republicans, despite the fact that most voters believe the G.O.P.'s position to be excessively tough. At the same time, he characterized Senator Gary Hart and other advocates of reorientation as "Atari Democrats," who lacked "real heart" and compassion.

The withdrawal, in May 1987, of Gary Hart from the presidential race, in which he had been considered the front-runner, enhanced Biden's standing among presidential aspirants. On June 9, 1987, at Wilmington, Delaware, he formally announced his candidacy for the Democratic nomination. Appealing especially to the "baby boom" generation that grew up after World War II, he lashed out, in language reminiscent of that of John F. Kennedy, against "cynicism and indifference" and asserted, "For too long as a nation we have sacrificed moral values to the mere accumulation of material things." Outlining the issues that he considered of prime importance, he called for a "middle-of-the-road" trade policy that would be neither protectionist nor completely free, opposition to the Reagan administration's "Star Wars" missile defense system, an emphasis on the "integrity" of government, and a social agenda that would stress the welfare of children, alleviation of poverty, and the battle against illegal drugs.

As chairman of the Senate Judiciary Committee, Biden presided over the confirmation hearings on President Reagan's nomination to the Supreme

Court of Judge Robert H. Bork, who was eventually rejected by the Senate. Although he was opposed to Bork's confirmation from the outset, Biden won praise for the fairness with which he conducted the proceedings.

Biden came increasingly under fire following revelations that in a speech in August 1987 he had virtually lifted a significant passage from a campaign advertisement by British Labour party leader Neil Kinnock and that on other occasions he had used passages from Robert F. Kennedy and Hubert H. Humphrey without giving credit to his sources. It was also revealed that as a first-year law student he had once been disciplined for plagiarism and that in an appearance in New Hampshire in April 1987 he had greatly overstated his academic achievements. On September 23, 1987, Biden announced his withdrawal from the presidential race, declaring that his candidacy had been overwhelmed by the "exaggerated shadow" of the mistakes that he made in his "zeal to rekindle" the "compassion and commitment" of younger Americans.

Senator Biden is handsome despite his receding hairline, and he has the tall and trim build of an athlete. Moreover, people find it hard to dislike his irrepressible, boyish personality and his capacity for laughing at his own foibles. Despite a penchant for long-windedness, Biden is one of his party's best orators. His impassioned conviction as a speaker rivals that of Governor Mario Cuomo of New York, and some believe that the senator from Delaware has communications skills on a par with those of Ronald Reagan.

On June 17, 1977, Senator Joseph Biden Jr. married Jill Tracy Jacobs, the divorced daughter of a Philadelphia banker, whom he had met in 1975 when she was completing her training as a teacher at the University of Delaware. The couple has a daughter, Ashley Blazer, who was born in 1981. Biden occasionally took his wife or one of his teen-aged sons, Joseph 3d ("Beau") and Robert Hunter ("Hunt"), along on his speaking tours to let them judge whether or not they were willing to undergo the pressures of a campaign, and he often relies on his wife's judgment. "I trust her instincts more than anyone else's," he has said. "She is the one who has the veto power. A lot of men have been able to divorce their professional lives from their family lives. I can't."

References: Atlan 259:37+ Ap '87 por; Chicago Tribune V p1+ Ag 14 '87 por; Esquire 97:64+ Je '82 pors; People p38+ Ag 25 '86 pors; Washington Post A p1+ Jl 28 '86 por; Almanac of American Politics, 1986; Congressional Directory, 1985–86; Who's Who in America, 1986–87

Biller, Moe

Nov. 5, 1915– Labor union official. Address: b. APWU National Headquarters, 817 14th St., N.W., Washington, D.C. 20005

Crusty, outspoken Moe Biller, the president of the 320,000-member AFL-CIO-affiliated American Postal Workers Union (APWU), is a man whom people either love or hate. A "unionist of the old school," as a writer for the New York Times put it, Biller came to national prominence as well as notoriety in 1970 as a leader of the first strike in the long history of the United States Postal Service (USPS). Despite what has become a growing chorus of dissent from APWU members who object to his sometimes abrasive, heavy-handed executive style, he has used his popularity among the rank and file of his powerful New York home local to twice win re-election as the union's chief officer.

Moe Biller was born Morris Biller on November 5, 1915, in the New York borough of Manhattan. He attended Seward Park High School on the Lower East Side, where he won such distinctions as the geometry award and membership in the Arista Honor Society. Following his high school graduation, Biller studied for a time at Brooklyn College (1936–38) and at the City College of New York (1946). On May 8, 1937 he went to work at the Knickerbocker postal station in lower Manhattan, first as a substitute employee, running errands on

a bicycle, and then as a distribution clerk. Apart from two years out (1943–45) for wartime service in the United States Army, Biller has been with the post office ever since.

Moe Biller first became involved in the activities of Local 10 of the old Manhattan-Bronx Postal Union, the forerunner of the New York metropolitan area APWU formed in 1980, immediately after joining the post office. He served in a variety of executive positions, including chairman of the membership committee, sergeant-at-arms, and as a member of the seniority committee. Biller got his first taste of contract bargaining in 1938, when he negotiated sick leave and vacation benefits for substitute employees, and he began his long climb through the union's executive hierarchy in 1952, when he won election as first vice-president of Local 10. Two years later he became executive vice-president, and in 1959 he was elected president of the Manhattan-Bronx Postal Union, consisting of 25,000 members. It was in that post that he first moved into the front lines of the union's battles with the United States Postal Service.

Biller's critics have vilified him for his role in the now infamous 1970 postal strike, but the irony is that despite his rhetoric, he was not really responsible for what happened. It was the militant National Association of Letter Carriers (NALC) who walked off the job on March 17, 1970, to back their contract demands. A sympathetic Biller announced that although he anticipated that members of his union would not cross NALC picket lines, no decision on APWU participation in the strike was possible until its membership had been polled. By the time that an affirmative vote was taken on March 21, the strike was already crumbling. President Richard M. Nixon had sent in troops to move the mails, and USPS lawyers had obtained a court injunction against further picketing by the union.

Given the obvious futility of continuing the strike, Biller advised his union membership to return to work. They did so, others followed, and the strike died. Nevertheless, that the workers' bitterness and frustrations lingered was made abundantly clear on April 2, when negotiators for the USPS and the seven unions involved announced a tentative settlement. Biller responded by posting bulletins at sixty-five New York post offices accusing the union negotiators of having betrayed their memberships.

The situation took on a new dimension on April 17, when President Nixon announced a broad "compromise" plan to reform the United States postal system by turning it into a public corporation. The Nixon proposal included higher wages, granted the postal unions the right (unique among federal employees) to bargain collectively, and devised a strategy to trim the postal deficit. Congressional critics created an amended version of the Nixon bill named the Udall-Derwinski substitute postal reform bill after its cosponsors Representatives Morris Udall of Arizona and Edward Derwinski of Illinois. Because it was much less generous to the postal unions, when AFL-CIO President George Meany expressed support for the substitute bill, Biller angrily accused him of "selling out postal workers."

The five largest postal unions reacted to the August 13 signing into law of President Nixon's Postal Reorganization Act of 1970 by forming a merger committee. As a result, on July 1, 1971, the unions joined to form the American Postal Workers Union (APWU), of which Moe Biller became the northeast regional coordinator. None of those developments mollified union hardliners, however, and tempers were still so frayed a year after the aborted 1970 strike that when 3,300 New York postal workers assembled on July 26, 1971 to discuss their new contract, the meeting ended in what reporter Damon Stetson of the *New York Times* described in its edition of the following day as "a shouting, brawling melee." Moe Biller and Vincent Sombrotto were pursued by an angry, taunting mob as they fled the hall by ducking out a back door. Although such an ignominious retreat did not please the feisty Biller, he had more pressing concerns on his mind in those days.

It was apparent to Biller that in addition to increasing revenues by raising postal rates, management now intended to trim the post office's deficit by reducing services and by relying on early retirements and increased automation to cut the work force. The issue of labor cuts inevitably became a major source of friction between the USPS and its unions because, while the average postal worker's salary increased by 28 percent in the three years between 1975 and 1978, the total unionized work force declined by 5 percent. As post-office labor relations deteriorated, Biller and other union heads were faced with members who were increasingly eager to defy the law against striking. Postal workers disrupted the nation's mail with impunity when they shut down the New Jersey bulk and foreign mail center for four days in 1974; but when another strike occurred in July 1977, 157 workers were fired in New Jersey and California.

The speedy resolution of grievances filed on their behalf became a major issue in the contract negotiations of 1978. The union hired the noted labor attorney Theodore W. Kheel to work out an acceptable way of expediting the grievances, but when another APWU attorney agreed in a federal court hearing that Kheel's proposals were not workable, it became apparent that there were serious disagreements between the union's national executive and its more militant regional leaders like Biller, who supported Kheel's ideas. The 1978 contract negotiations stalled in the face of President Jimmy Carter's "voluntary" 5.5 percent cap on federal pay raises, and as the July 20 deadline drew nearer, a national postal strike loomed as a distinct possibility. On June 21 Moe Biller met with other APWU regional leaders. Afterwards, he announced plans for what he termed "massive demonstrations" and "job actions" to step up pressure for a new contract with a 12 percent wage increase and an improved cost-of-living-allowance (COLA) provision. Especially important to New York area workers was a demand for pay differentials to compensate them for their higher costs of living. "Carter can't jawbone us into taking peanuts," Biller warned.

When the APWU president, Emmet Andrews, echoed Biller's threat and noted the union's "no contract, no work" policy, postal officials hastily completed contingency plans to have troops move the mail. It appeared that both management and labor were ready for a decisive showdown, but on July 21 the unexpected happened when negotiators in Washington, D.C. announced a tentative contract offering a 19.5 percent pay increase over three years in return for union concessions in other key areas. Joining the APWU's national bargaining committee in rejecting the proposal out of hand, Biller set July 31 as the date for a strike vote by his crucially important New York local. Postal lawyers blocked the balloting by obtaining a temporary injunction in a New Jersey court, postal workers in Jersey City and Kearney staged another impromptu strike, and Postmaster General William F. Bolger responded by promptly firing thirty-seven workers and suspending 116 others.

Thwarted in their strike plans, Biller and other militant leaders vented their anger at an August convention of the APWU in Denver. Emmet Andrews, the union president, was roundly booed for an hour by the 3,000 delegates when he tried to defend the proposed contract, and it was rejected by a margin of five to one when put to a vote. With prospects for a new postal agreement viewed as slim, an arbitrator was called in, as was required by federal law. Although Biller was obliged to accept the contract imposed on September 15, which included a 21.3 percent pay raise over three years, he was still not content, partly because his quarrel with management was personal. The mutual hostility between Biller and Postmaster General William F. Bolger dated back to the 1970 postal strike, when Bolger had been a regional postmaster in New York.

In the wake of the imposition of the new contract, Biller repeatedly criticized Bolger for his "dictatorial tactics" in refusing to make concessions on the rehiring of fired strikers or on dealing with the occupational health and safety deficiencies at the Jersey City bulk mail facility, where a worker had been crushed to death in a conveyor belt accident on December 15, 1979. Bolger, for his part, blamed Biller and the unions for the lethargic mail service characteristic of the New York City area. On January 2, 1980, while meeting with the city's political leaders, Bolger vowed to correct the situation and pledged himself to achieve a 90 percent overnight delivery rate on local mail within six months. Paradoxically, while moving to increase the use of automation and extending post-office hours, Bolger remained intent on slashing costs by reducing the frequency of door-to-door delivery and by increasing postal rates.

An incensed Moe Biller announced on April 24, 1980 that he would seek to unseat Emmet Andrews as president of the APWU. In a press release he cited the union's need for "creative leadership" at a time when, as he put it, "we are facing major survival tests in the postal service including: a cutback to five-day mail delivery, the future of electronic

telecommunications in the postal service, the strong anti-public employee attitude sweeping America, and the continued demands for health and physical safety within postal facilities."

Biller had little trouble ousting Andrews in a nationwide mail vote held in October. He took office on November 8, 1980, three days after his sixty-fifth birthday, and immediately served notice that stormy times lay ahead if changes were not made at the post office. "I'm not taking office with a chip on my shoulder, but I don't like the anti-union tactics of the present postal administration and I don't—and my members don't—want a repeat of the 1978 disaster," he said.

Unfortunately for the plans of Moe Biller, the United States took a turn to the political right just a few weeks later and elected Ronald Reagan to the White House. High on the new president's agenda of fiscal reforms was a plan to slash $632 million from the $1.5 billion federal postal subsidy for the 1982 fiscal year, a move that Biller predicted would cost 40,000 postal workers their jobs. He vowed to make job security a major issue in the contract negotiations that were due to begin in Washington on April 20, 1981, but that starting date was delayed almost two months when William F. Bolger unsuccessfully petitioned the National Labor Relations Board in an effort to force the unions involved to negotiate jointly for a new contract. The plan also encountered surprisingly stiff political opposition on Capitol Hill. Senator Barry Goldwater, chairman of the influential Senate Commerce Committee's communications subcommittee, voiced his opposition, and Bolger ran into another unexpected roadblock when prolabor Democrats in the House introduced a bill to delay plans to introduce machine-readable, nine-digit postal codes.

Contract negotiations that finally began on June 16, only a little over a month before the existing collective agreement was due to expire, on July 20, bogged down over the United States Postal Service's insistence on a wage freeze and reduced fringe benefits. With his usual colorful phraseology, Biller termed management's offer "a regressive bunch of garbage." Given the intransigence of both sides, the dispute appeared to be headed once again for binding arbitration until negotiators unexpectedly reached an eleventh-hour accord. The $4.8 billion contract—the largest in the history of the federal public service—included an 11 percent pay raise over three years, bringing the average postal worker's annual salary to more than $22,000.

Despite some initial grumbling, the new contract was accepted by the APWU membership, leaving Biller free to turn his attention to other matters. He championed the cause of air traffic controllers who had been fired as a result of their 1981 strike, waged a campaign against the private courier companies competing for business with the post office, and supervised the collection of a $350,000 union "war chest" to aid the election campaigns of prolabor politicians. Harold Washington was one of the first candidates to benefit when he defeated incumbent Jane Byrne in the 1983 Chicago mayoralty race.

In November 1983 Moe Biller was reelected to a second term as president of the APWU. Speaking with reporters at the AFL-CIO's annual convention in February 1984, he expressed optimism about the upcoming talks for a new collective agreement, due to begin in Washington on April 24, but as it turned out, his hopes were dashed by a Postal Service board of governors decision to press the issue of "wage comparability" in the negotiations. Quite simply, what that amounted to was a rollback in the wages paid postal workers to bring them in line with private sector wages. Citing post office profits in both 1982 and 1983, Biller adopted the bargaining slogan "No Givebacks" and vowed to fight for a 20 percent pay hike, increased job security, and improved fringe benefits.

In what was by now a wearyingly familiar pattern, negotiations dragged on for eighty-four days with little progress being made. The only concession that post-office negotiators seemed willing to make was to abandon the "comparability" demand in return for union agreement to a "two-tier" pay system, whereby new employees would be paid 20 percent less than employees with at least one year of experience. Rejecting the proposal, Moe Biller and Vincent Sombrotto stormed out of the negotiations just hours before the July 22 midnight deadline.

Delegates attending an August 1984 convention of the APWU in Las Vegas authorized the national executive to take whatever action was necessary, including a national strike, in order to get a new contract. Although it proved to be unnecessary and a new contract was eventually concluded, the usually combative Biller favored having an arbitrator impose another collective agreement. Observers noted his apparent reluctance to risk a major confrontation with the White House after the 1981 mass firing of striking air traffic controllers. And it might also have been noted that Biller was facing a potentially serious challenge to his union leadership.

In winning reelection as APWU president the previous fall, Biller had defeated David Daniel, the candidate of the union's self-proclaimed "democratic" reform element—the Trine Council. When the United States Labor Department ordered another vote after it had investigated complaints of alleged election campaign irregularities, Biller charged he was being harassed for political reasons. After winning the revote, he hit back hard against his perceived enemies, asking some embarrassing questions about the circumstances behind the awarding of a $300,000 postal contract to the San Francisco law firm of a top post office official and about a $62,000 retirement bonus being paid to Postmaster Bolger. When both Moe Biller and William F. Bolger appeared on the same edition of NBC-TV's *Meet the Press* program one Sunday in September, the two men exchanged angry words before engaging in a brief scuffle.

No sooner had the furor over that incident died down than Moe Biller was again in hot water with the government. In February 1985 he, Vincent Sombrotto, and Kenneth Blaylock, the president of the American Federation of Government Employees, were cited by the Office of the Special Counsel, the enforcement arm of the Merit Systems Protection Board, for alleged violations of the Hatch Act (the law prohibiting federal employees from engaging in partisan politics) arising out of their unions' support for the 1984 Democratic presidential candidate, Walter F. Mondale. Despite cries of outrage from leaders of the American labor movement, Biller, Sombrotto, and Blaylock were officially "suspended" in October 1985 from their government jobs for sixty days. The suspensions were the first in the forty-six-year history of the Hatch Act.

Grateful, perhaps, for words of support from Jackie Presser, the president of the International Brotherhood of Teamsters, Moe Biller attended the Teamsters' annual convention in Las Vegas, Nevada in July 1986. In a brief, ill-advised speech before the 2,000 delegates, he called on the labor movement to fight the "anti-labor forces" that had "come down on the back of Jackie Presser," who was facing indictment by a federal grand jury in Cleveland on racketeering and embezzlement charges. Other labor leaders, as well as members of Biller's own union, expressed their strong disapproval of the speech. Ken Leiner, a national officer of the APWU, said, for example, that he and many other members did not feel "that the indictment of Jackie Presser is an issue that needs the solidarity of the labor movement." Those sentiments were echoed at a northeast regional APWU meeting on July 12, 1986 in Allentown, Pennsylvania, where delegates voted to censure Biller for his speech. Biller reacted angrily, telling a *New York Times* correspondent, Kenneth Noble, that criticism of him came from APWU rivals who were seeking to discredit him. "I'm not a gutless wimp like some of those characters," he blustered.

In spite of that incident and speculation by observers such as Jonathan Tasini of *Business Week* magazine about "the quiet revolution" going on within the APWU, Biller was reelected in November 1986 to a third term as president. He again defeated the union reform candidate, David Daniel, outpolling him 49,179 votes to 40,124. Secure again for another three-year term, Biller turned his energies to the coming negotiations for a new collective agreement in 1987. On July 21, 1987, the Postmaster General, Preston R. Tisch, Moe Biller, and Vincent Sombrotto announced that a contract settlement had been reached between the United States Postal Service and its two leading unions. Under its terms, postal workers would be given average wage increases of $1,700 to $1,866 over a forty-month period.

Moe Biller is the father of two sons, Michael and Steven, by his first marriage, to Anne Feifer, on August 24, 1940. She died in December 1978. On January 4, 1987 he married Colee Farris. In addition to working with the APWU, Biller serves as a member of the board of directors of United Way International, the advisory board of Cornell University's Trade Union Women Studies Program, and the United States Labor Department's Advisory Council on Occupational Health and Safety. Among the many awards he has received during his long career are the 1977 Distinguished Service Award of the New York City Labor Council and the 1982 Spirit of Life Award from the City of Hope Medical Center.

References: N Y Times p51+ N 2 '80, A p15+ Ag 23 '84; Who's Who in America, 1986-87

Bloom, Harold

July 11, 1930– Literary critic; university professor. Address: b. 2976 Ezra Stiles College, Yale University, New Haven, Conn. 06520; h. 179 Linden St., New Haven, Conn. 06511

Only the superlative degree seems adequate to observers of academe in placing Harold Bloom among his colleagues: "the most notorious literary critic in America," "the most original," "the most controversial," "the best-known," "the best talker." He is also the most individual and the most independent: "a one-man band," "a one-man department of the humanities." Criticism to Bloom is itself a literary genre, as The Anxiety of Influence (1971), A Map of Misreading (1975), Kabbalah and Criticism (1975), Agon (1982), and his many other books may demonstrate. His theory of literary influence not as a benign inspiration but as a "fierce process" of usurpation and revisionism, which he

tends to present in terms of somewhat obfuscating paradigms, has outraged many fellow critics. Although Bloom has said, probably not with displeasure, "I am the pariah of my profession," even among his more exasperated opponents there are few who do not acknowledge his brilliance and the force of his deep, personal caring about poetry and criticism. Since 1955 he has been teaching at Yale University, where he currently has the title of Sterling Professor of the Humanities.

Harold Bloom was born in New York City, New York, on July 11, 1930, the youngest by many years of the five children of William and Paula (Lev) Bloom. He had an Orthodox upbringing, though in recent years he has spoken of himself as a Jewish Gnostic. His parents had moved to New York City's East Bronx from Eastern Europe, and Yiddish was the language of Bloom's boyhood home. But at the age of five he began to acquire a knowledge of English that soon flourished on his love of reading. "I became cathected upon poems very early, when I was about ten years old," Bloom wrote in an essay in Agon, "and I have spent forty years trying to understand that initial cathexis."

His preference for poetry and his desire to become a teacher of literature may account for why Bloom referred to his high school, the academically well-regarded Bronx High School of Science, as "that ghastly place," when he talked with David Remnick of the Washington Post (August 20, 1985). Finishing first in a statewide New York regents examination, he was awarded a full scholarship to Cornell University. The most important for him of his teachers there probably was M. H. Abrams, the influential author of books on Romanticism and literary criticism. Bloom dedicated one of his early books to Abrams, but before long he departed from many of his former teacher's views, such as his "sweetness and light" approach in reading poetry.

In his interview with Remnick, Bloom spoke of his "astonishing memory" for the poetry he has read: "When I was a student I would get a bit drunk and recite Hart Crane's 'The Bridge' frontwards, then backwards, quite like a tape recorder running wild." Another recollection of himself as a student appears in an Agon essay: "When I was a young man, deeply in love with the whole range of Romantic poetry, British and American. . . . " But Yale University, which Bloom entered after taking his B.A. degree at Cornell in 1951, was then the citadel of the New Critics. Many members of Yale's English faculty, which included Cleanth Brooks, Robert Penn Warren, and W. K. Wimsatt, followed T. S. Eliot's conservative, Catholic or Anglo-Catholic favoritism toward seventeenth-century metaphysical and religious poets to the neglect of the Romantics, whose dependence upon individual vision, or inner light, allied them with dissenting Protestants, as Bloom later pointed out.

Displaying the rebellious spirit that has characterized all of his literary studies, Bloom chose to write his doctoral dissertation on the Romantic poet Percy Bysshe Shelley, whom he saw as an impassioned intellectual skeptic. In 1955 he was awarded his Ph.D. degree and appointed an instructor of English at Yale. Four years later he published *Shelley's Mythmaking* (Yale Univ. Press, 1959), which he had developed from his dissertation. In examining the mythmaking aspect of many of Shelley's principal poems—his effort to replace received myths with his own experience of reality—Bloom turned to the distinction that Martin Buber made between "I-It" and "I-Thou" attitudes. Mythmaking in "Hymn to Intellectual Beauty," for example, is an encounter not between a subject and an object, but between subject and subject: a relationship, or communion, of existences, one Thou affording a glimpse, however brief and perishable, of the Eternal Thou.

With his defense of Shelley against a host of detractors, Bloom began his attack on anti-Romanticism. In *The Visionary Company* (Cornell Univ. Press, 1961; revised edition, 1971) he sought to establish Romanticism as the central tradition of English poetry and as a continuing force in literature. He defined the tradition through interpretative readings, or prose paraphrases, of the important poems of the six major Romantic poets of the late eighteenth and early nineteenth centuries—William Blake, William Wordsworth, Samuel Taylor Coleridge, Lord Byron, Shelley, and John Keats. There is also a chapter on some of the lesser poets of the period.

While maintaining that the Romantics were not poets of nature, Bloom showed in *The Visionary Company* that one of their common themes was the relationship, or dialectic, between nature and the imagination in the process of creating poetry. As if in defiance of the New Criticism treatment of a poem as a self-contained, nonreferential "well-wrought urn," he sought out other shared themes, patterns of crisis and quest, analogues, borrowings, recurring images. In his epilogue to *The Visionary Company*, moreover, he countered the structuralist assertion that "myths have no authors and come into existence only when incarnated in a tradition" by arguing that "the myths of Romanticism have authors and then are embodied by tradition," and tracing the transmission of John Milton's "Il Penseroso" to the American Romanticist Wallace Stevens's Crispin through kindred figures in the poems of intervening English Romantic poets. Bloom edited an anthology, *English Romantic Poetry* (Doubleday, 1961), to accompany his book.

Two books other than the one on Shelley that Bloom devoted to a single English poet are *Blake's Apocalypse: A Study in Poetic Argument* (Doubleday, 1963) and *Yeats* (Oxford Univ. Press, 1970). The latter is an exhaustive, systematic study of Yeats's work, especially as it relates to the Romantic tradition extending from Milton to Robert Browning. Various aspects of that tradition were also Bloom's concern in *The Ringers in the Tower* (Univ. of Chicago Press, 1971), a collection of twenty-one essays that had first appeared, mainly during the 1960s, in periodicals and in introductions to anthologies and other books.

Milton had clearly emerged in *The Visionary Company* as the precursor of the Romantic poets: "It is one of the great characteristics of the Romantic period that each major poet in turn sought to rival and surpass Milton, while also renewing his vision." That rivalry became more intense in *The Ringers in the Tower*: "Somewhere in the heart of each new poet there is hidden the dark wish that the libraries be burned in some new Alexandrian conflagration, that the imagination might be liberated from the greatness and oppressive power of its own dead champions. Something of this must be involved in the Romantics' loving struggle with their ghostly father, Milton." As Bloom noted in his preface, the unifying theme of *The Ringers in the Tower* "is poetic influence (perhaps rather poetic misprision) conceived as an anxiety principle or variety of melancholy, particularly in regard to the relation between poets in the Romantic tradition."

"Having hit a kind of universal nerve with a little book, *The Anxiety of Influence*, published [by the Oxford Univ. Press] in January 1973," Bloom said in a lecture at the University of California in 1981, "I have had a number of years in which to reflect upon the joys and sorrows of giving offense." In his interview for the *Washington Post* he explained that he began to develop his theories about literary influence in 1965, "in the midst of a personal crisis," during which he started to read Sigmund Freud and Ralph Waldo Emerson almost continuously. When his book on influence was eventually published, he told David Remnick, "the nastiness with which it was received was unprecedented."

Basic to the theory set forth in *The Anxiety of Influence* is Bloom's contention that a poem's substance is intrapoetic relations, that a poem is both a response to and a defense against another poem, an antecedent. The relationship is ambivalent, but necessarily adversarial because the "ephebe" or "belated" poet must clear a space in which to fulfill himself. Bloom offers as an analogue the Satan of Milton's *Paradise Lost*, who struggles against God, and as a Freudian paradigm, the parricidal Oedipus. Satan goes so far as to consider himself "self-begot, self-rais'd." Just as every man, according to Freud, has the unconscious wish to be his own father, the poet would like to be his own literary precursor, the possessor, as Satan boasts of being, of his "own quick'ning power."

As Bloom conceives poetic influence, the poet copes with his precursor by an act of misreading, or misprision, that is, in fact, a misrepresentation, a falsification, a "wilful revisionism." To the six "revisionary ratios," by which such a poet creatively corrects a prior text, Bloom applies the terms clinamen (swerving), tessera (completing), kenosis (emptying), daemonization (displacing), askesis (diminishing), and apophrades (the return of the dead). They are kinds of strategies that have "the same function in intrapoetic relations that defense mechanisms have in our psychic life."

The map in *A Map of Misreading* (Oxford Univ. Press, 1975), which intends to show how to read a poem in accordance with the theory proposed in

The Anxiety of Influence, has not only six revisionary ratios and six psychic defenses, but also six sets of images, six rhetorical tropes, and three stages of creation. Bloom demonstrates how the interplay of his map's images and tropes produces meaning by testing his map on Browning's baffling "Childe Roland to the Dark Tower Came," of which he had given a detailed and illuminating reading in *The Ringers in the Tower*. With his map as a guide he also examines the way Milton influenced the English Romantics, some of whom in turn influenced each other, and how Emerson influenced Walt Whitman, Stevens, John Ashbery, and other American poets.

Following Bloom in his endeavor to gain "power over the text" is not easy, but as he has said, repeatedly, with Emerson, "Nothing is got for nothing." In *A Map of Misreading* and elsewhere Bloom makes clear that he is not involved in a search for sources, similarities in style, and verbal echoes: "I continue *not* to mean the passing-on of images and ideas from earlier to later poets. Influence, as I conceive it, means that there are *no* texts, but only relationships *between* texts." It is a relationship, moreover, in which "poets need not *look* like their fathers."

Remarkably erudite, Bloom has ready access to a vast store of religious, philosophical, historical, and literary information, much of it esoteric, that supplies him with paradigms and underpinnings in the explication of his theory of poetic influence. In the work on the Kabbalah of the sixteenth-century Jewish mystic Isaac Luria, along with that of the modern Jewish scholar Gershom Scholem, he discovered "a dialectic of creation astonishingly close to revisionist poetics," as he maintained in *Kabbalah and Criticism* (Seabury, 1975). He later stated, moreover, in *Agon* that the "sole concern" of *Kabbalah and Criticism* was "to use Kabbalah, or Jewish Gnosticism, and Scholem's analyses as paradigms for a theory of reading poetry." But Leon Wieseltier objected in the *New York Review of Books* (February 19, 1976): if Bloom had demanded from the Kabbalah "no more than models, paradigms, and maps, *Kabbalah and Criticism* would have been a *tour* de force which, like all his other books, would stand or fall on the validity of his theory of influence. Unfortunately, however, . . . he advances the further and unfelicitous claim that Kabbalah itself is a theory of influence because it is likewise 'a theory of writing.'"

Bloom's employment of arcane Lurianic Kabbalah terminology, which he had also found useful in earlier books, aroused some protest from reviewers of both *Kabbalah and Criticism* and *Poetry and Repression; Revisionism from Blake to Stevens* (Yale Univ. Press, 1976). Arguing in the latter that the "true subject" of a poem is its "repression of the precursor poem," Bloom furthers the study of intrapoetic relations begun in *The Anxiety of Influence*. One reviewer recommended the last chapter, on Wallace, as "a stunner, a celebration of the Sublime." Most of the essays in *Figures of Capable Imagination* (Seabury, 1976) illustrate Bloom's theory of influence by detailing

Emerson's role as the poetic father of modern American Romantic poets, notably Stevens, A. R. Ammons, and Ashbery. Again Emerson, along with Whitman, emerges as the progenitor as Bloom traces the "revisionary swerves" between poet and precursor in his interpretative reading of Stevens's poetry in *Wallace Stevens: the Poems of Our Climate* (Cornell Univ. Press, 1976).

Emerson, Whitman, Stevens, and other poets are once more among the protagonists of Bloom's familiar world of "literary arenas" and of "contests with anteriority" in the essays that make up *Agon: Toward a Theory of Revisionism* (Oxford Univ. Press, 1982). As readers of his earlier books know, Bloom has long been interested in the theology of Valentinus, the second-century founder of a Gnostic sect, as well as in Kabbalist commentary. And while Freud's mythmaking and methods of interpretation greatly appealed to him, he specified in *Agon*, "My mode of interpreting literary texts can be described more accurately as a Valentinian and Lurianic approach than as being Freudian, Nietzschean or Viconian." (A reincarnated Valentinus is one of the characters in Bloom's only novel, *The Flight to Lucifer; A Gnostic Fantasy* [Farrar, 1979].)

Bloom's undiminished regard for Freud is nevertheless confirmed in some of the essays in *Agon* and in one of the lectures he gave as the first Wellek Library Lecturer, at the University of California at Irvine in the spring of 1981. The lectures were published in *The Breaking of the Vessels* (Univ. of Chicago Press, 1982), which owes its title to the second, or catastrophic, stage of the Kabbalistic myth of the world's creation, degeneration, and restoration. A recent essay by Bloom in the *New York Times Book Review* (March 23, 1986) is titled "Freud, the Greatest Modern Writer."

In 1974, the year after—and apparently as a result of—the publication of *The Anxiety of Influence*, Bloom left Yale's Department of English, where he had obtained his full professorship in 1965, to become DeVane Professor of the Humanities. Since 1983 he has had the title of Sterling Professor of the Humanities. The theory of how to read a poem that Bloom developed, beginning with *The Anxiety of Influence*, was antithetical to the School of Deconstruction, which in his opinion exerts a despiritualizing effect on criticism and which has several distinguished subscribers who teach or have taught at Yale. He joined some of them, including Paul de Man and Jacques Derrida, in writing *Deconstruction and Criticism* (Seabury, 1979), which attempts to clarify the Deconstructionist philosophic approach to literature and its way of analyzing meaning. Eager to deny allegations that he himself is a practitioner of Deconstruction, which has German and French origins, Bloom said in the *Washington Post* interview, "I am purely an American and Emersonian phenomenon." His books are unstinting in their praise of the great English critics Dr. Samuel Johnson, William Hazlitt, and Oscar Wilde.

In charge of one of the most ambitious publishing ventures of its kind, Bloom is currently editing and writing the introductions for Chelsea House's projected multihundred-volume series of critical anthologies, scores of which are already in print. The undertaking, as suggested in *Newsweek* (August 19, 1986), is one for which he seems to be well-suited because he is an insomniac and "a nonstop reader" who claims that he has "been doing nothing but read for 50 years now." But a possible diversion is baseball. Among the tributes paid to Bloom are honorary degrees from Boston College and Yeshiva University, the Melville Cane Award of the Poetry Society of America for *Yeats* in 1971, the Zabel prize of the American Institute of Arts and Letters in 1982, and a "genius" grant from the Catherine and John D. MacArthur Foundation in 1985. He taught or lectured at Hebrew University in Jerusalem in 1959, Breadloaf Summer School in Vermont in 1965-66, Society for the Humanities at Cornell University in 1968-69, and the New School for Social Research in New York City in 1982.

Harold Bloom married Jeanne Gould on May 8, 1958; they have two sons, Daniel Jacob and David Moses. In his article, "The Tyranny of the Yale Critics," in the *New York Times Magazine* (Febru-

ary 9, 1986) Colin Campbell described Bloom as "large, shaggy-haired and courteous" and reported that "as a teacher, he's known as a sage, genius, and comic rolled into one—Zarathustra cum Zero Mostel." Remnick, who in the *Washington Post* also noted the Zero Mostel resemblance, similarly gave a profile of Bloom as a teacher that is free of the antagonistic tone of his books: "Nowhere is Bloom's personality more evident and powerful than in the classroom. He is an affectionate and generous teacher, an easy grader, in fact. . . . Some students say they adore Bloom, some admit they cannot make head or tail of his lectures." One former student remembers his having "a kind of personal power as a figure that's hard to escape."

References: *N Y Times Bk R* p20+ F 9 '86 por; *Newsweek* 108:56+ Ag 18 '86 por; *Washington Post* C p1+ Ag 20 '85 pors; *Contemporary Authors* 1st rev vols 13–16 (1975); *Contemporary Literary Criticism* vol 24 (1983); *Contemporary Literary Critics* (1982); *Directory of American Scholars* (1982); *Who's Who in America, 1985–86*; *World Authors 1970–1975* (1980)

Bogosian, Eric

Apr. 24, 1953– Playwright; actor; performance artist. Address: b. c/o George Lane, William Morris Agency, 1350 Ave. of the Americas, New York City, N.Y. 10019

In 1986, after surviving a precarious decade during which he perfected his special brand of black humor before tiny theatre audiences in downtown New York but "scraped the bottom" both financially and emotionally, Eric Bogosian finally cast his spell on the uptown establishment with his one-man show *Drinking in America*. It won both the Drama Desk Award and Obie Award for that year. With that show and his most recent hit, *Talk Radio*, Bogosian has established himself as a protean one-man "museum of humanity," to quote a phrase he once applied to the prime source of his material, New York City. Bogosian has a mime's command of body movement, a mastery of regional and ethnic speech, and a voice endowed with an enormous tonal range. His gallery of characters includes visionary winos, workaholic immigrants, credit-card-carrying yuppies, predatory Hollywood agents, bigoted vigilantes, and in *Talk Radio*, a late-night radio talk show host who plays both psychoanalyst and drill sergeant to a neurotic audience.

In performance, Bogosian uses striking juxtapositions to emphasize the gaps and similarities between his characters. "The wino lying in the street becomes in an instant the Hollywood agent being awakened by a New York call," Allan Wallach observed in *Newsday* (January 20, 1986). Bogosian's interlocked characters collectively embody the

dark side of the American dream and the betrayal of the ideals that Bogosian feels were expressed but insufficiently assimilated during the turbulent 1960s. "There's no question we're in a decadent phase in our country," he told Samuel G. Freedman of the *New York Times* (January 19, 1986). "I don't provide any answers to that, but I do know something's missing and we're rushing to replace it with booze or drugs or power or money."

Eric Bogosian was born in Boston, Massachusetts on April 24, 1953, to Henry and Edwina Bogosian. He grew up in nearby Woburn, where his father worked as an accountant and his mother as a hairdresser. The Bogosian household, according to David Handelman (*Rolling Stone*, June 19, 1986), was a "demonstrative" one where "dinner was always a battle for attention." Apart from that, Bogosian recalls that his childhood was lonely. "I was definitely nerd city," he told Evelyn Renold of the New York *Daily News Magazine* (March 9, 1986). He eventually gained acceptance from his peers by becoming a "junior hippie" and student actor. Although Bogosian made his acting debut as the elder Capulet in a Woburn High School production of *Romeo and Juliet,* he made the special intensity of his theatrical gifts more evident in a play, written by himself, in which one of his characters committed suicide by burning out his eyes with hot coals. Fred Zollo, a childhood friend who is now a New York producer and collaborator with Bogosian, told David Handelman: "We used to call him 'Egosian'. But at the same time, he was very down on himself. He wanted to be with the Out Crowd—the drug addicts, the motorcycle bunch. There's a strong romantic streak in him that finds something exciting in doing dangerous things."

After graduating from high school, Bogosian, Zollo, and another friend, Nick Paleologus, who is now a Massachusetts state senator, established the Woburn Drama Guild. In his interview with Evelyn Renold, Zollo recalled a play in which Bogosian, portraying a mental patient, strangled his doctor, who was played by Paleologus. "At the end," Zollo said, "Eric strangled Nick—so convincingly that Nick's mother leaped to her feet in the middle of this crowded auditorium and yelled 'Don't kill my son!' Nick stopped, everything stopped, except Eric, who continued to strangle him."

After spending two years at the University of Chicago, Bogosian transferred to Oberlin College in Ohio, from which he graduated in 1976 with a degree in theatre. He moved immediately to New York, dreaming of critical acclaim and grant money, but the 1970s recession vaporized his pot of gold, and as Bogosian remembered in the *Rolling Stone* interview, "There were no grants left, no critics, nothing." To cut down on expenses, he lived for a time on the premises of the Chelsea Westside Theater, where he obtained a job as a gofer. He then advanced "a step up from gofer" at the Kitchen, the premier avant-garde space of the time. Within a year he had become one of its directors and had established its contemporary dance program.

Meanwhile, Bogosian and his colleagues worked to develop "a new pictorialism, a new romanticism," as he told David Handelman, adding that "what it boiled down to was content, because there hadn't been any in a long time." He began frequenting "some pretty strange places to find color," among them a bar for transvestites and a Bowery coffee shop patronized by pimps and prostitutes. Bogosian stresses that much of his material does not come from research, however, but from America's "many classic stereotypes." "I started off doing accents," he told Stephen Holden in an interview for the *New York Times Magazine* (May 24, 1987). "I would talk off the top of my head, and the next thing I knew I would be making up what this guy would say . . . eventually I decided to make a piece that said in effect, 'Here's your classic this and your classic that.'"

Eric Bogosian gave his first solo performance, "Careful Moment," at St. Mark's Church in the Bowery in 1977. In it he impersonated a game show host, delivered a lecture, danced to the recorded accompaniment of the Jackson Five, and "beat a guy up on stage." During the next five years he attracted a small following with more than twenty plays and performance pieces such as "Men in Dark Times" and "Sheer Heaven." In "The Ricky Paul Show" he took on the persona of a misanthropic, audience-baiting comedian who sometimes goaded his listeners until they began throwing bottles at the stage. He then began "to understand the power of the spoken word, especially when uttered in the face of the fragility of people's beliefs," as he expressed it in his autobiographical introduction to the published version of *Drinking in America* (Vintage Books, 1987). Tiring, however, of the Ricky Paul persona, he wrote, directed, and performed in a sixteen-scene play called *The New World* in which he appeared with fourteen other actors. When the equipment for *The New World,* in which he invested his entire savings of about two thousand dollars, was stolen, he decided to "get practical" and concentrate on solo pieces because of their low overhead. "But I didn't want to become Ricky Paul," he explained in his introduction to *Drinking in America,* "I wanted the pieces to exist in the theatre and, when I went home, I wanted to go home as me."

At home Bogosian's lifestyle "based on the possibility of an imminent fatal truck accident," as he once put it, was characterized by dancing all night, hard work, attendance at "all the films, all the clubs," and "big doses of sex, drugs and rock-and-roll." Fred Zollo recalled for David Handelman that Bogosian "did this down-and-out lifestyle, working very hard at being insane to see what it would look like. He feared that he was close to being an alcoholic—or worse. But even at the height of his quasi-addiction or usage, I never thought he was in danger." The drug-related death in 1982 of the comedian John Belushi, one of Bogosian's idols, prompted a self-examination followed by reformation, and he now calls himself "super clean" and drinks nothing stronger than club soda. "I'm a pretty conservative guy morally," he told Samuel G. Freedman, "but we don't live in a moral world, so there's a tension."

In 1981 Bogosian began to work on a new one-man show, "Men Inside," in an attempt, he explained in *Drinking in America,* to "sort out all these people inside me." During a 1982 meeting on another subject, Joseph Papp, the director of New

York's Public Theater, asked Bogosian to perform a few pieces, for his benefit, from *Men Inside*. Seeing a rare opportunity to take "the bull by the horns," Bogosian "jumped up and did a bunch of characters" so impressively on the spot that Papp quickly scheduled a presentation of *Men Inside* at his Public Theater. The show's catalog of men, ranging from a barker at a freak show to a "success guru" telling his audience, "Life is a struggle, man is an island . . . love is loving yourself first," established Bogosian as an artist on the rise. In her review for the *Village Voice* Sally Banes wrote that his "personae are so various, each with its distinctive accent, pacing and vocabulary, that one marvels first at the speed and pliancy of the voice itself, and at the facial expressions and bodily gestures that plastically express the states of that voice. Then one marvels again at the crash-speed hairpin turns voice and body take as they careen along the grotesque landscape of masculine identity. He's like a man possessed, a medium, a schizophrenic."

Another solo show, *FunHouse*, which followed a year later, was a bravura series of monologues depicting further carefully observed characters recruited from life's shadows. Among them were a mafioso suffering from heartburn, a TV evangelist who promises to "end starvation in the world" if viewers will pitch in only $18 a month, and a salesman for torture devices who says, "Some people like to work with telephone books and broken fingers, but hey, we're not in the dark ages, we have electricity." When Bogosian reached that point at one performance, an audience member stormed out shouting, "That's not funny." "I never said it was funny," Bogosian replied. A few weeks later, he explained to Samuel G. Freedman (*New York Times*, September 30, 1983), "The hard part is to make my point without being genuinely sick. I want to shock people. My work is all about reminding people of the time these things did shock us. How many times can we say, 'Oh, that's too bad'? But I want to remain sensitive, to rethink these things. I hate it when I hear people say, 'I just can't deal with it anymore.'"

The success of *FunHouse* helped to win Bogosian a contract with the William Morris Agency and brought him to the attention of the established theatre world uptown. It also gained him further employment. He appeared in a commercial for a granola bar, made guest appearances on television, and obtained a role in the film *Special Effects* (New Line Cinema, 1986). Bogosian thus joined what Cathleen McGuigan once described in *Newsweek* (March 24, 1986) as "the small but growing band of avant-garde performers—part satirist, part actor—who are being swept out of downtown Manhattan lofts and into the mainstream of TV, film and theatre." As Bogosian told Samuel G. Freedman, all this had an effect on him that "was a stronger rush than any cocaine." He added, "I was suddenly sling-shotted into what I thought it was 'all about.' I was sitting around thinking how great I was. . . . Whatever deal I had, I wanted a better deal. I was getting very off-center personally

and I wanted to get back to center." Bogosian's trip back to "center" churned up a variety of demented characters in his imagination around whom he constructed *Drinking in America*, a ninety-minute tour de force that confirmed his reputation with some critics as the Lenny Bruce of the 1980s. *Drinking in America* was first seen by the public at the Institute of Contemporary Art in Boston, Massachusetts. It was subsequently performed at PS 122 in New York City and was taken on tour in Great Britain.

Drinking in America opened at New York's American Place Theatre on January 20, 1986 and, as Bogosian has explained, explored a society growing increasingly addicted—to intoxicants, to power, to sex—and becoming ever more corrupted in the process. In each high-energy performance Bogosian transformed himself into a portrait gallery of decadence and his expanding audience kept the 285-seat theatre packed during what became a sixteen-week run. The subtext and counterweight of his portraits, Bogosian told one inquiring reporter, was "the whole 60's dialogue—what is war about? what are race relations about? how can we live better in this new world?" and the fact that such dialogue now "seems to be all forgotten." For Bogosian it suggested that "[we] didn't think as deeply about these things as we all thought we did."

Bogosian evoked the Sixties at the New York opening of *Drinking in America* by reading from a journal supposedly unearthed from old college memorabilia, that is filled with such platitudes of the flower child era as "there's no point to a liberal arts degree now" and "I want to change the world, and I know I can do it." His rapid-fire montage of metamorphoses replaced the flower child with such characters as a Hollywood agent breakfasting on cocaine and bourbon while closing a variety of sleazy deals, a young punk who describes stealing a van with friends and setting it on fire in a spectacle that was "like spiritual or something" and a wino who bitterly congratulates an affluent passerby and declares, "If I wasn't here, buddy, you wouldn't be there, 'cause you can't have a top unless you have got a bottom. . . . We're two sides of the same coin. You got a coin for me, buddy?"

The cumulative effect of *Drinking in America*, as Frank Rich observed in a *New York Times* review (January 21, 1986), was "a hangover of outrage that a theatergoer can't easily shake." Writing for the *Nation* (February 22, 1986), Paul Berman called Bogosian "a man of a thousand skills, a master of several accents (if not quite as many as he attempts) and [of] all kinds of postures and speech patterns." Michael Feingold told his readers in the *Village Voice* (January 28, 1986): "Those of you who thought you resided in the United States of America are in for a shock. You're actually living—I think almost everyone in the modern world is—in the tiny principality of Bogosian. Though it only occupies the space of one average-size male human body, Bogosian is devastatingly inclusive." *Drinking in America* won the 1986 Drama Desk

Award for Outstanding Solo Performance and the 1986 Obie Award for Best New American Play. A condensed version was broadcast on Home Box Office/Cinema cable television as "Eric Bogosian Takes a Look at Drinking in America."

While performing *Drinking in America*, Bogosian had been putting the finishing touches on another piece, *Talk Radio*, which he developed in collaboration with the Portland, Oregon artist Tad Savinar over a four-year period, with Bogosian in charge of the writing and Savinar responsible for the sets. In developing the show, Bogosian studied what he has called the "attack guys"—half-serious radio shock artists such as New York's Howard Stern and the late Denver talk show host Alan Berg, who became magnets for loonies and served as a conduit for listener hostility. *Talk Radio*, which opened at the New York Public Theater on May 28, 1987, featured Bogosian playing not many characters but only one—the acid-tongued, homophobic, bigoted, and immensely popular late-night radio talk show host Barry Champlain. The new show made it clear to Mel Gussow of the *New York Times* (May 29, 1987) that Bogosian had taken "a long leap from performance artist to playwright."

Talk Radio deals with the repellent but entertaining Champlain's last night on the air before his show goes national and involves many characters, both onstage and offstage, who revolve around him. "Barry is the most insecure guy in the world," Bogosian informed Stephen Holden. "He's someone who never stops talking. He probably eats in the same diner every day, where everyone he knows treats him with total adulation. He drinks about fifty cups of coffee and smokes several packs of cigarettes." In the studio, Barry's mood shifts rapidly as he alternately soothes and bullies telephone callers or coaxes some secret from them before suddenly cutting them off with the brutality of "an executioner." "You listen to this show," he tells one caller, "because you feel superior to the other losers who listen." He tells another that his audience consists of "the cowardly and the narrow-minded, the bitter, bigoted people who hide behind anonymous phone calls, full of hatred and poisonous bile . . . the grotesquely ignorant people like you, Betty, who make me puke." Eventually nearing his own breaking point, Barry barks into the mike, "I despise each and every one of you. The only thing you believe in is me."

As in *Drinking in America*, Bogosian used *Talk Radio* to comment on the contemporary debasement of traditional values. In an essay he wrote for the arts and leisure section of the *New York Times* (July 26, 1987), he underscored the complicity between radio host and audience, noting that Barry's job is "very clear: to get people to tune in and keep them listening. . . . The audience is so large that all sincerely held beliefs become part of an enormous play script. . . . On talk radio, the callers are very serious. And they are discussing important topics. What could be more important than nuclear disarmament or loneliness or racism? What does it

mean when a society fashions this very important dialogue into show biz? What happens when an actor leads the discussion?"

On another occasion Bogosian noted some affinity between himself and the radio talk show hosts. "We are lonely by nature," he told David Firestone in *Newsday* (May 23, 1987), "and I think underneath it all, [the radio hosts] are kind of like a bad boy who wants attention but kind of does it in the wrong way, by scribbling on the wall or pulling on little girls' ponytails. It's better to get any attention at all than to be ignored."

"I have a horrible self-perception," Bogosian told Evelyn Renold during his interview with her. When he is in a film or appears on a television show, he immediately sees "this Armenian guy with a big nose and fuzzy hair." More detached observers have described him as "a small, shapely, incandescently energetic young man with blue eyes, [and] a thatch of curly hair" and as "bluntly handsome." In October 1980 Eric Bogosian married the Australian graphic designer Jo Anne Bonney, and they have a son, Harris Wolf, born in March 1987. They have exchanged Bogosian's ground-floor flat in New York's Little Italy, now used by him as an office, for a better apartment and have also bought a New Jersey country house on a ten-acre estate. Bogosian's plans for the future include "anything that involves putting pieces together," including directing and producing. He is currently working on a screenplay for Twentieth Century-Fox and is writing a script for New York's off-Broadway showcase Playwrights Horizons. His new solo piece, "Sex, Drugs and Rock 'n' Roll," is scheduled to be televised on Home Box Office in the near future. Bogosian earned praise from an unexpected quarter in May 1987 when radio talk show host Gary Dee, a model for Barry Champlain, attended a performance of *Talk Radio* and, during the audience discussion afterwards, declared it both "accurate" and "brilliant" and finally came up to shake Bogosian's hand. "A chill went down my spine," Bogosian told David Firestone. "But I would venture to say that Dee was left with a few questions to think about when the evening was over."

References: *Chicago Tribune* 13 p10+ Je 28 '87 por; *N Y Daily News Mag* p14+ Mr 9 '86 por; *N Y Times* II p1 Ap 13 '86 pors; *N Y Times Mag* p34 My 24 '87 pors; Bogosian, Eric. *Drinking in America* (1986); *Who's Who in American Art* (1986)

Boland, Edward P(atrick)

Oct. 1, 1911– United States Representative from Massachusetts. Address: b. 2426 Rayburn Office Bldg., Washington, D.C. 20515

Ever since he first arrived in Washington, D.C., in January 1953, Congressman Edward P. Boland, a

Edward P. Boland

moderate Democrat from western Massachusetts, has shunned publicity. He is widely respected by his colleagues for his intuitive grasp of the issues and for his mastery of the legislative process, but his influence at the national level has been somewhat diminished—at least in the eyes of the public—by what Sidney Blumenthal of the *Washington Post* has called his "almost clinically inexpressive" demeanor. Recent events, however, have pushed the reticent Boland into the national spotlight. As a former chairman of the House Select Committee on Intelligence and the author of the so-called Boland amendments, a series of laws restricting covert American aid to the Nicaraguan rebels, or Contras, he has played a major role in the Congressional investigation of the Iran-Contra scandal, which involved the covert sale of weapons to Iran and the secret diversion of some of the profits from that sale to the Contras.

Edward Patrick Boland was born on October 1, 1911, in Springfield, Massachusetts, the son of an Irish immigrant railroad worker and his wife. Reared in the Irish working-class neighborhood known as "Hungry Hill," he attended Classical High School and the Bay Path Institute, a privately controlled coeducational business school in his hometown, then continued his education at Boston College Law School. At some point in the early 1930s, he took a job as a playground director for the city of Springfield and, in that capacity, organized a sandlot baseball league for the local schoolboys. With the help of those teenage athletes, who campaigned tirelessly in his behalf, Boland was elected to the Massachusetts House of Representatives in 1934.

After serving six years in the state legislature, Boland won election to a six-year term as Hamp-

den (Massachusetts) County register of deeds. His tenure was temporarily interrupted in 1942, when he enlisted in the United States Army. He spent the duration of the war in military service, stationed mainly in the Pacific. Discharged with the rank of captain in 1946, Boland was reelected to a second term as register of deeds, but after three years he left that office to become the military aide to Massachusetts Governor Paul A. Dever.

When Foster Furcolo, the incumbent Democratic representative from Massachusetts' Second Congressional District, declined to run for a third term in 1952, Boland declared his candidacy for the vacant seat in the United States House of Representatives. Because the second district was located entirely within the boundaries of Hampden County, Boland entered the race with a built-in political base, but he nonetheless had to struggle against the strong Republican tide that swept Dwight D. Eisenhower to victory in the presidential contest. Although both Eisenhower and Henry Cabot Lodge, the Republican senatorial candidate, carried the district by huge margins, Boland hung on to win election to the House by some 6,500 votes. He has since been returned to office seventeen times, often against only token Republican opposition. Indeed, he is so popular with his constituents that on seven occasions the Republican party has not even fielded a candidate against him.

With well over a decade's experience in the rough-and-tumble world of Massachusetts politics, Boland brought to Capitol Hill a solid grounding in political gamesmanship. "They play a hard, cruel game [in the Massachusetts House of Representatives]," Thomas P. ("Tip") O'Neill, who had served in the state legislature with Boland, explained to Sidney Blumenthal in an interview for the *Washington Post* (June 15, 1987). "If you come to Washington, you have a five- or six-year advantage on your freshman congressmen." O'Neill was also elected to Congress in 1952, and he and Boland became workweek roommates and close political associates. As traditional Democrats, the two men had a common philosophy, but their temperaments and personal styles could not have been more different. According to Blumenthal, they were the capital's "odd couple"—"O'Neill, tall and stout, was the sloppy one; Boland, short and thin, was the neat one."

The gregarious and ambitious O'Neill rose rapidly through the ranks of the Democratic party hierarchy in the House of Representatives to become majority leader, in 1973, and Speaker of the House, in 1977. Boland's friendships with Tip O'Neill and with President John F. Kennedy, whom Boland served as a campaign coordinator in the 1960 general election, undoubtedly contributed to the legislator's success in obtaining federal grants and pilot projects for the Second Congressional District. Largely as a result of his efforts, in the past thirty years Springfield has metamorphosed from an ailing factory town into an industrial and commercial center with a thriving, diversified economy.

Boland's voting record over the course of his congressional career is a testament to his moderate convictions and his loyalty to the Democratic party line. In the view of some longtime Washington observers, he bridged the gap between the old-line Democratic pols and the party's younger, more ideological liberals. During the administrations of Presidents Eisenhower, Kennedy, and Lyndon B. Johnson, the congressman was a staunch supporter of job-creating public works projects, urban redevelopment programs, and increased federal aid to education. He also voted for the landmark civil rights bills and the "Great Society" social welfare programs passed into law in the 1960s. A fervent anti-Communist, he was an early advocate of increased United States involvement in the Vietnam war, but as the years passed he gradually turned against continued American participation in the conflict and, in 1973, joined his colleagues in voting to override Richard Nixon's veto of the War Powers Act that limits a president's authority to commit troops abroad.

According to a biographical profile of the congressman in *Politics in America* (1986), during his long career in the House, Boland has twice had an opportunity to advance to a formal leadership position. On both occasions he hesitated, apparently waiting for the go-ahead from O'Neill. In 1970, for instance, after Majority Leader Carl Albert became Speaker of the House, Boland and O'Neill were among several representatives mentioned as likely candidates to succeed Albert in the Democratic leadership post. In the end, neither man ran, but O'Neill, who had backed the favorite, Hale Boggs, was rewarded with an appointment as majority whip. Similarly, in 1978, when George H. Mahon stepped down as chairman of the House Appropriations Committee, Boland, then second in seniority, was considered by many to be the ideal alternative to the ranking Democrat, Jamie L. Whitten, whose attacks on environmental and consumer agencies had offended some liberals. Once again, however, Boland hesitated, and Speaker O'Neill, not knowing how much his friend wanted the job, approved Whitten's succession to the chairmanship.

The relationship between O'Neill and Boland has been strained at times, but when it came to choosing a chairman of the newly created Select Committee on Intelligence—one of the most sensitive leadership posts in the House—the Speaker immediately turned to his longtime friend and colleague. "I knew of nobody more trustworthy than Eddie," O'Neill explained to Sidney Blumenthal. "[He is a man] of the greatest sincerity, dedicated to the country and dedicated to keeping his mouth shut." Established in the wake of public disclosures of widespread abuses of power by the Central Intelligence Agency, the committee was charged with monitoring the operations of the CIA and other federal intelligence-gathering agencies. Convinced that earlier arrangements, which had divided jurisdiction over intelligence activities among several committees, had led to many leaks of classified information to the press, Boland had been one of the chief sponsors of the bill consolidating oversight responsibility into a single select panel, and he was determined to prevent further breaches of security.

On assuming the chairmanship of the House Select Committee on Intelligence in July 1977, Boland reminded his fellow panel members that their primary purpose was "to protect the rights of Americans." At least partly for that reason, he was, he said, "less interested in . . . dragging out past abuses" than in overseeing the CIA's current operations. "Eddie Boland tends to be of the old school," one liberal Democrat told Steven V. Roberts of the *New York Times* (May 1, 1983). "He sees his role as being supportive of the administration. He's less skeptical than some others, and that's why he was chosen to be chairman." For his part, Boland denied that he was "of the old school," but as he explained to Steven V. Roberts, "I think there's more of a willingness and a desire to cooperate on my part and get along with different administrations. I think there's responsibility on the part of the chairman to cooperate with any administration that's in."

Throughout his tenure as chairman, Boland tried to bring a "consensus approach" to the committee, and for a time, the panel generally backed the sitting administration's foreign operations, such as the effort, begun by President Jimmy Carter and expanded by President Ronald Reagan, to aid the *mujahidin*, or "holy warriors," who were fighting the Soviet military occupation of Afghanistan. By 1981, however, that bipartisan approach was being severely tested by mounting evidence that the CIA was covertly assisting the Nicaraguan rebels in their struggle to overthrow the leftist Sandinista government.

In response to questions from the committee, the Reagan administration insisted that the CIA was only trying to interdict weapons shipments. Boland was prepared to give the government the benefit of the doubt, but he nonetheless persuaded the committee to propose a measure that insured the continuation of aid to the Contras only as long as the appropriated funds were not used "for the purpose of overthrowing the government of Nicaragua or provoking a military exchange between Nicaragua and Honduras." This "first Boland amendment," which was attached to the Defense Appropriations Act of 1983, was unanimously passed by the House and signed into law by President Reagan in December 1982.

A few months later, Boland, troubled by reports that the Reagan administration was violating the law by providing covert aid to the Nicaraguan rebels, dispatched committee member Wyche Fowler Jr. to Central America to investigate. When Fowler returned with what Boland described as "very strong" evidence that the United States was deeply involved in covert activities aimed at overthrowing the Sandinista government, the House intelligence committee recommended barring further aid to the Contras, after a secret date. In presenting the bill to the full House in July 1983, Boland said, "This secret war is bad U.S. policy—because it does not work, because it is in fact counterproductive to U.S. interests, because it is illegal." Boland's reasoned argument convinced his fellow legislators to pass what has since become known as the "Boland cap," which set a $24 million ceiling on funding for the Contras in fiscal 1984. The measure also urged the president to seek a negotiated settlement of the conflict through the Organization of American States and established a new $80 million program to help Central American governments stop the flow of arms to leftist guerrillas in the region.

Over the next several months, press reports detailing the CIA's continuing involvement in covert activities, including the mining of Nicaraguan harbors and the production of a guerrilla training manual that advocated, among other things, the "selective use of violence to neutralize" Sandinista officials, further eroded congressional support for aid to the Contras. Appalled by the revelations, Boland introduced the toughest of the amendments that bear his name—the "Boland cutoff," a flat ban on aid to the Nicaraguan rebels in the 1985 fiscal year. "The secret war hasn't brought Central America closer to peace or Nicaragua closer to democracy," he argued during the debate on the House floor. "What it does is provide the Sandinistas with the perfect excuse to foist unfair elections, a huge army, censorship and the draft on the Nicaraguan people."

Boland left the House Select Committee on Intelligence at the end of the congressional session in 1984, but he has continued to speak out against "this war in Nicaragua." In June 1985 he proposed extending the prohibition against military aid to the Contras indefinitely, but his appeal was turned down by the House, many of whose members had been angered by Nicaraguan President Daniel Ortega's recent trip to Moscow for meetings with top Soviet officials. More recently, he declined to join the majority in approving a $100 million aid package, including some $70 million in military aid, arguing that the funds would "not buy a Contra victory," only "continued fighting to no apparent conclusion."

Although the Boland amendments expired in 1986, they were crucial elements of Congress' investigation of the Iran-Contra affair, as members of the House and Senate's select committees attempted to discover whether Reagan administration officials had broken the law by assisting the private network that sent money and weapons to the Contras. Named to the House Select Committee to Investigate Covert Arms Transactions with Iran in December 1986, Boland occasionally found himself defending the amendments in the face of increasing criticism from some witnesses and from conservative political columnists, among them George F. Will, who contended that the measures were "unconstitutional in intent." To George F. Will and other critics, he responded simply, "It is the law."

In the ten weeks of joint public hearings, which began on May 5, 1987, the congressman focused on the clash between "policy and constitutional principle," as he put it, devoting most of his allotted questioning time to the Reagan administration's efforts to evade the various Boland amendments in effect from fiscal 1983 through fiscal 1986. Unlike some of his colleagues on the panel, he refrained from making speeches justifying the law or denouncing the administration for failing to abide by it. On the House floor, however, he demanded quick action on a bill that tightened the requirements for notifying Congress of covert operations in order to settle what he has called a "serious and fundamental" disagreement over existing laws.

On other recent issues of national importance, Boland has generally continued to vote with his party. He has, for example, opposed funding for the deployment of the MX missile, the production of binary chemical weapons, and the development of the multi-billion-dollar Strategic Defense Initiative, popularly known as "Star Wars," which envisions a "shield" in space that would protect the United States from missile attack. He has also voted to impose sanctions on South Africa as a form of protest against apartheid and to prohibit American aid for military or paramilitary operations in Angola. Domestically, Boland has been among the most outspoken supporters of social welfare legislation, including a catastrophic health insurance plan and programs to provide job training for veterans and the chronically unemployed, and housing, food, and social services for the homeless. As chairman of the Appropriations Committee's subcommittee on housing and urban development and independent agencies, he has, among other things, pushed through bills to fund public housing—the only housing program for "the desperately poor," in his view—and cleared the way for the approval of the construction of a space shuttle to replace *Challenger*, which exploded shortly after lift-off in January 1986.

A quiet man whose black hair and swift gait belie his years, Edward P. Boland keeps in trim by working out daily in the House gymnasium. Little is known about his private life. Self-effacing and exceedingly private, he rarely holds press conferences or gives interviews. "He honors the New England code: only talk when it improves the silence," Christopher Matthews, a former press secretary to Tip O'Neill, told Sidney Blumenthal. The longtime bachelor surprised his constituents when, on August 9, 1973, he wed Mary K. Egan, a lawyer and then president of the Springfield (Massachusetts) city council. Locals joked that Boland had married Miss Egan to prevent her from running against him for his House seat. The congressman maintains an apartment in Washington, but he returns to his home in Springfield every weekend to spend time with his wife and their four children: Martha Mary, Edward Patrick, Kathleen Mary, and Michael James.

References: Washington Post A p13 Ag 10 '83 por, C p1+ Je 15 '87 por; Almanac of American Politics, 1986; Politics in America (1986); Who's Who in America, 1986-87; Who's Who in American Politics, 1987-88; Who's Who in the East, 1986-87

Bonner, Yelena

Feb. 15, 1923- Soviet human rights activist.
Address: Chkalova St., Moscow, USSR

Yelena Bonner, the sexagenarian wife of the Nobel Peace Prize winner and leading Soviet human rights activist Andrei D. Sakharov, has been described by her friend Robert L. Bernstein, the chairman of Random House, as "one of the great women of the world." Although she is soft-spoken and deferential in public to her spouse, a writer for Newsweek has pointed out that this occasionally headstrong and abrasive lady "can stare down any Soviet bureaucrat (and) outsmart any KGB thug." Vilified by the Soviet media as a Western agent, the feisty Bonner and her husband have emerged from their bleak years of exile undaunted, victors in what an observer has termed "one of the most extraordinary struggles in history between a state and an individual—or, in this case, two individuals."

Yelena Bonner was born on February 15, 1923, in Moscow, USSR, the older of the two children of Ruth Grigorievna Bonner and Gevork Alikhanov, both ardent members of the Communist Party of the Soviet Union (CPSU). Bonner was only fourteen and had just finished the seventh grade when, in 1937, her mother and father were arrested in the

great purge instigated by the Soviet dictator Joseph Stalin. "Never did I believe—either as a child or as an adult—that my parents could have been enemies of the state. Their ideals and their internationalism had been lofty models for me," she recalled in her moving memoirs Alone Together (Knopf, 1986).

Because of their father's execution and their mother's imprisonment (until 1954), Yelena Bonner and her ten-year-old brother, Igor, went to Leningrad to live with a grandmother and an aunt and uncle, but when the aunt and uncle were also purged, Yelena, Igor, and a cousin were raised by their grandmother. Yelena Bonner finished school while working as a cleaning lady and, later, as a file clerk at a factory. In 1940 she enrolled in night courses at a teachers institute and became involved with Communist party youth groups. With the outbreak of war with Germany she volunteered for the army, and while serving at the front on October 21, 1941 sustained a concussion and other wounds that left her nearly blind in her right eye and suffering from failing vision in the left. After her recovery she was assigned to a hospital train and by the end of World War II had been promoted to the rank of lieutenant.

For the next two years Yelena Bonner was in and out of hospitals, as she struggled to retain her failing eyesight. When her condition stabilized in 1947, she enrolled at the First Leningrad Medical Institute, where she fell in love with a classmate, Ivan Vasilyevich Semyonov. They married and eventually had two children, a daughter, Tatyana, who was born in 1950, and a son, Alexei, born in 1956. In 1953 Yelena Bonner graduated as a physician and then practiced as a district doctor, a maternity home pediatrician, and, in Iraq, as a foreign aid health worker. Concurrently, she wrote for professional journals and edited several publications, including the collected poems of Vsevolod Bagritsky, her childhood sweetheart who died fighting the Nazis.

Despite her ongoing involvement as an organizer of the young Communist group, Komsomol, Yelena Bonner was never a member of the CPSU in those years, for it was only after the party denounced Stalinism that, in 1965, she joined. In the same year Yelena Bonner and her husband separated: he stayed on at the medical school in Leningrad as a teacher, while she pursued her own career and continued her political activities. But like her parents before her, Yelena Bonner was a freethinker who chafed under the party's rigid dogmatism, and when the Red Army invaded Czechoslovakia in 1968, she was left feeling confused and disillusioned. In the words of Newsweek (December 16, 1985), she began "working constantly in the front lines of dissent, helping to publish underground newsletters." Her alienation from the party became final in 1970, when at the trial of a fellow dissident, she met Andrei D. Sakharov, a prominent leader of the nascent Soviet human rights movement. Kindred spirits, they married in 1971, and in keeping with her convictions, she resigned from the CPSU the following year.

By now, Yelena Bonner and the members of her family were being closely watched by the KGB, and she herself was being harassed by the secret police for her ties to two dissidents who had been put on trial for publishing a clandestine journal. When she was summoned to the police station five times in a span of sixteen days in late November 1973, an irate Sakharov, who felt that the tactic was a means of pressuring him, wrote to Yuri Andropov, then the head of the KGB, complaining that further questioning of his wife was immoral, illegal, and pointless. Furthermore, he informed Western reporters that he would take full responsibility for Yelena Bonner's refusal to reappear before the police. Although the KGB backed off for the time being, the Sakharovs were well aware that the sometimes subtle, sometimes overt, cat-and-mouse game with the KGB would intensify.

Despite her repeated visits to Soviet hospitals, Yelena Bonner's eyesight was again failing so noticeably in early 1975 that her desperate husband applied in March 1975 for a visa to allow her to travel to an eye clinic in Italy. The visa was finally issued after four months of delays, and then only after Sakharov appealed to the outside world for support. Yelena Bonner left Moscow on August 16 for what was to be a four-month visit—the first of three she made between 1975 and 1980—that also proved fruitful in an unexpected way. It was announced in 1975, while she was in the last stages of her treatment in Italy, that Andrei D. Sakharov had been chosen to be the recipient of the Nobel Peace Prize, the first Russian ever to be accorded that honor. When her husband was denied permission to travel to Oslo, Norway, for the ceremony on December 10, she went in his place and read a statement on his behalf.

On December 20 Yelena Bonner returned home, taking care to leave the $143,000 Nobel Prize money in a Western bank, where it would be safely out of the reach of KGB agents. Emboldened by their celebrity, the Sakharovs broke into the international news again on April 15, 1976 after they scuffled with police who tried to prevent them from attending the trial in Omsk of a Tatar nationalist who had been charged with anti-Soviet subversion. Yelena Bonner admitted striking a policeman during the melee but complained that on the following day, when she and Sakharov returned to the scene of the trial, she had been grabbed by the neck by a security policeman who threw her down the courthouse steps.

Despite close KGB surveillance, the Sakharovs and seven other prominent Moscow dissidents formed a "watchdog" group in May 1976 to monitor Soviet compliance with the 1975 Helsinki accords on human rights. The move encouraged dissidents in other cities, who soon established watchdog committees in Kiev and Vilna. Chagrined by their gestures of defiance, the KGB increased its harassment of the Sakharovs, but though such tactics failed to intimidate Yelena Bonner, glaucoma succeeded in doing so. By April 1977 her vision had deteriorated to the point where she was forced to seek another visa to go to Italy for treatment. Following the usual delays and Sakaharov's renewed public protests, the precious sixty-day visa was at last issued in mid-August, and Yelena Bonner departed for the West at the end of the month. She was back home November 23 and soon after that, applied for yet another visa to return for a checkup. The authorities were not disposed to process the application quickly, so that they could display their displeasure with the Sakharovs, who had been fined for a courthouse scuffle in May with police trying to bar them from attending the trial of fellow dissident Dr. Yuri Orlov. As a result, the visa was not issued until 1979.

Increasingly impatient and frustrated by its repeated inability to control the pair and to limit Andrei D. Sakharov's criticism of the Soviet invasion of Afghanistan, the KGB moved unexpectedly on January 22, 1980. Sakharov was arrested and sent into internal exile at the city of Gorky, an industrial center (closed to Westerners) of 1.3 million people about 250 miles east of Moscow. Since she was allowed to go with her husband and free to travel back and forth between Moscow and Gorky, Yelena Bonner became Sakharov's principal contact with the outside world. On April 16, 1980 she met with Western reporters in the Soviet capital to relay Sakharov's message that even in internal exile he would continue speaking out on important matters.

True to his word, and in spite of intimidation from what Yelena Bonner derisively referred to as "Gorky's gangsters," the KGB, Sakharov joined his wife in July 1980 in an appeal to the authorities on behalf of the fiancée of Bonner's son, Alexei, who had been trying for two years to get an emigration visa to join him in the United States. When another year passed without the issuing of any visa, the Sakharovs began a hunger strike on November 22, 1981, despite the fact that both of them were in frail health. Uneasy with the international attention the strike attracted and fearful that Sakharov or his wife might die as a result of the fast, the KGB ended it on December 4 by taking the couple to a hospital, where they were force-fed. Two weeks later Yelena Bonner was back in Moscow looking gaunt, but smiling because the visa had been issued.

The life of the Sakharovs in Gorky soon took on a mind-numbing monotony, with Sakharov confined to the city and subjected to the intrusive and constant harassment of the KGB. Particularly irksome were the repeated KGB attacks of vandalism on their car and the secret filming of their daily routine. For her part, Yelena Bonner made regular visits to Gorky, where she endured persistent police searches in which hers and Sakharov's personal papers, and portions of a memoir he was writing, were routinely seized from her bags.

The KGB was unrelenting, too, in tightening the screws on Yelena Bonner and her fellow dissidents in Moscow. As she later noted, so many members of the Helsinki watchdog group were imprisoned that it got to the point where she had to spend the annual political prisoners' day all by herself. On

September 8, 1982 a harried Yelena Bonner announced that the watchdog group was disbanding, for with sixteen members of the Moscow group in jail or in exile, along with all the members of four provincial satellite groups, it was no longer practical to continue.

Under that kind of protracted stress Yelena Bonner's health began to fail. She was laid-up with angina pectoris in November, and by the end of the year was feeling so ill that she turned to Soviet doctors for treatment, despite her mistrust of them. On May 9, 1983 she announced that she and Sakharov had decided to immigrate to the West if it would end their "nightmarish existence." Any hopes they entertained that they might be allowed to leave were quickly dashed, however, when the government press agency *Tass* within hours carried an item stating that Sakharov would not be permitted to leave since he allegedly knew Soviet military secrets.

Bowed but not broken, the Sakharovs went on with their lives. In September 1983, at Sakharov's urging, Yelena Bonner defiantly filed papers at a Moscow courthouse charging that she had been defamed by a KGB-inspired writer named Nikolai Yakovlev. Not surprisingly, the action died quietly when a judge declined to hear it on the orders of his superiors. In the face of such official intransigence, and chilled by the prospect of spending the rest of his life in internal exile, Sakharov grew increasingly concerned about his wife's deteriorating health. He fought back the only way he could: on May 2, 1984 he began another hunger strike aimed at forcing the authorities to grant Yelena Bonner an exit visa to go to the West for treatment of her heart and eyes. She joined him in the protest ten days later.

The KGB fought back with a press campaign to vilify Yelena Bonner, who was attacked as an evil influence on her husband and as a Western agent. Then she was formally charged with eight counts of anti-Soviet activities, and on August 10, after a two-day secret trial, she was sentenced to five years in internal exile at Gorky, where, ironically, her mother had been exiled in the 1940s. Those authorities who were responsible may have assumed that isolating the Sakharovs would end their effectiveness, but they soon discovered just how wrong they were in their assumption. Yelena Bonner first appealed the verdict against her, and when that proved fruitless, she applied unsuccessfully in March 1985 for a pardon as well as a visa to go to the West for medical treatment, and to visit her mother and children in Boston, Massachusetts. There followed an intense six-month battle with the Soviet bureaucracy. Sakharov and Bonner repeatedly began hunger strikes (which the KGB invariably ended by hospitalizing and force-feeding them) in a desperate bid to gain issuance of a visa.

As had occurred previously, in October 1985 the ninety-day exit visa was unexpectedly issued. Yelena Bonner has said that the next few months went by in a blur. After bidding a tearful farewell to Sakharov, she flew to Italy on December 2 for an eye checkup and an audience with Pope John Paul II. "It is not necessary to ask me anything. I want to return home," she told reporters at Milan airport. "I have given a signed piece of paper that I will not talk to the press or give a press conference." All that she remembers of her airplane flight to the United States is that she arrived in Boston on December 7 and was met there by her family and a crush of media people.

Three days after her arrival, Yelena Bonner went into a hospital for a minor operation to remove a tumor from her lip. She then kept a low profile until after she successfully underwent sextuple bypass surgery on January 13, 1986. Released from the hospital a week after the operation, she was readmitted with minor complications on January 23. She recovered, however, and by mid-February was well enough to travel, do some sightseeing, and make a few public appearances. In the last week of March she had a small operation to correct a circulatory problem in her leg. In Washington a few days later, in her anger over continued secret KGB filming of her husband, she broke her pledged silence to call for his release. "For him to undergo further life in Gorky is a threat to his life," she said. She was quietly received at the White House on March 31 by John M. Poindexter, the national security adviser, when President Ronald Reagan declined to see her for diplomatic reasons. Yelena Bonner did not conceal her disappointment at the stiffly formal meeting with Poindexter, who she correctly sensed was not very well informed about the plight of the Sakharovs.

Far more satisfying to Yelena Bonner was a reunion on May 14—the first in ten years—in New York with the Soviet emigrés Ludmilla Alexeyeva and Anatoly Shcharansky, two old friends who cofounded the Helsinki watchdog group in Moscow. A week later, she attended an Andrei Sakharov Day party on Capitol Hill, which was held in honor of Sakharov's sixty-fifth birthday, and received a letter from President Reagan in which he pledged his continued efforts to "do everything possible" to free Sakharov. Buoyed by that news, Yelena Bonner reluctantly left for the Soviet Union on May 24, carrying with her a gift for her husband: a radio-controlled toy car. In an open letter of thanks to the American people, Yelena Bonner termed the improvement in her health "a miracle" and asked that friends and supporters in the West disbelieve all reports about her and her husband unless they were confirmed by them in regular telephone calls to Yelena Bonner's family in Boston.

After visiting with the British Prime Minister Margaret Thatcher and with the French President François Mitterrand, Bonner consulted with her eye doctor in Italy before returning home on June 2, accompanied by American friends and politicians. Asked by reporters at the Moscow airport how it felt to be back in the Soviet Union, she admitted, "It's complicated. I was staying with my family there, but my husband was here. If I didn't have a husband here I wouldn't have come back." On the following day she and Sakharov were reunited in Gorky. That nothing much had changed there became clear a few days later when the West German newspaper *Bild* obtained a copy of a KGB audio tape purportedly of the Sakharovs quarreling in their apartment. But it also became apparent that the couple had again outwitted their tormentors, for it was announced in the United States that Sakharov's memoirs had been smuggled out to the West for publication in 1987, and that Yelena Bonner had left behind after her American visit a 70,000 word memoir. Entitled *Alone Together*, it had been written in whirlwind fashion while she was recuperating from heart surgery. The book, which was excerpted in *Time* magazine (October 13, 1986), was published simultaneously in ten Western countries. The novelist John Updike was not the only critic who noted that *Alone Together* suffered from its "hurried, fragmentary" nature, when he evaluated the book for the *New Yorker* (January 19, 1987), but reviewers were unanimous in praising the moral courage of the Sakharovs.

Having feared the worst, the Sakharovs were stunned when just before Christmas of 1986, workers installed a telephone at their Gorky apartment. On the next afternoon Sakharov received a personal telephone call from Mikhail Gorbachev informing him that both he and Yelena Bonner would be permitted to return to Moscow to live and work. Western observers viewed the move as a sign of Gorbachev's serious intent to pursue a policy of *glasnost*, or openness, in Soviet society. Lending credence to that view was the conspicuous absence of the KGB when the Sakharovs arrived back in Moscow on December 30. Sakharov had no sooner stepped off the train when he was mobbed by Western reporters and asked to reiterate the opinions that had brought about his exile.

In an interview a few days later with *Newsweek* correspondent Joyce Barnathan (January 5, 1987), Yelena Bonner and Andrei D. Sakharov admitted that the long years in exile had taken a toll on their health, and although the couple acknowledged the crucial role that world public opinion had played in bringing about their release, Yelena Bonner pleaded that they be left in peace for a while. "If our lives are worth anything to anybody, then we shouldn't have such tension that we have owing to the press," she said. Even so, within days the Sakharov's tiny Chkalova Street apartment had again become what a writer for *Time* (February 23, 1987) referred to as "the nerve center of the [Soviet] human rights movement." When in early February 1987 the government announced the mass release from exile and labor camps of forty-two Soviet dissidents, a delighted Yelena Bonner expressed the hope that "this is only the beginning and that soon all prisoners of conscience will be freed." Her optimism was reinforced in the middle of March by the release of eight more Soviet dissidents, and by the visit to Moscow in early April of Prime Minister Margaret Thatcher, who engaged with Gorbachev in forceful debate on human rights, among other issues.

Yelena Bonner is a bespectacled, intense-looking woman of about five feet four inches in height, who usually weighs about 150 pounds. She has renounced chain-smoking at her doctor's behest. In her leisure time she likes to read, in the original English, the novels of Agatha Christie, Rex Stout, and John Le Carré.

References: New Yorker 62:88+ Ja 19 '87; Newsweek 109:39+ D 16 '85; Washington Post p1 D 8 '87; Bonner, Elena. Alone Together (1986)

Brenner, David

Feb. 4, 1945(?)– Comedian. Address: b. Sound Advice, 110 W. 57th St., New York City, N.Y. 10019

After changing his career to stand-up comedy in 1969 and doing yeoman duty in small comedy clubs for several years, the hard-working David Brenner, a former producer of television documentaries, found niches for himself in Las Vegas and Atlantic City casinos and on television talk shows. In 1986-87 he hosted his own syndicated TV show, *Nightlife*, a thrice-weekly late-night half hour of music, talk, and comedy taped before a live audience in New York City and broadcast over more than 100 stations nationwide. Brenner, a lean and gangling man with an ear-to-ear smile, is a pleasant raconteur, eschewing offensive material and sticking to humorous personal anecdotes or self-deprecating jokes about his prominent nose ("I have always admired people who use only one Kleenex"), his deprived childhood (such as the family debate over whether to buy him a new pair of shoes or get his teeth fixed), the colorful chums of his youth in Philadelphia's meaner streets (one of whom grew up to be a vegetarian "because he won't eat anything that can have children"), and the ludicrous aspects of common experience ("Have you seen the Evangelist who cures people on television? And he wears a toupee? I don't get it! He can fix a guy's legs and he can't put some hairs on his own head?"). After five years at the Sands Hotel in Atlantic City, where he was official spokesman as well as a stellar performer, Brenner moved to the Golden Nugget, another Atlantic City casino, early in 1987.

David Brenner, a self-described "poor boy from South Philadelphia" who celebrates his birthday on February 4, is reticent about the year of his birth. Published sources give the year 1945, but internal evidence in those sources points in the direction of a date somewhere in the late or perhaps even middle 1930s. Brenner is the youngest of the three children of Louis Yehuda Brenner and Estelle Anne (Rosenfeld) Brenner, whom he describes respectively as his "best pal" and "best sweetheart" in his memoir *Soft Pretzels with Mustard* (Arbor House, 1983), named after a Philadelphia gastronomical eccentricity.

Brenner's father was a vaudeville comedian and song-and-dance man who quit the stage when he was young and, in Brenner's words, spent the rest of his working life "spinning dreams about show business" while earning a bare, on-and-off subsistence for his family as a bookie, gambler, and insurance salesman. "Dad kept trying to talk me out of a show-business career," Brenner has recalled "but then he'd say, 'There's no thrill like hearing a thousand people laughing at you.'" The comedian told Thomas C. Hunter, the compiler of the autobiographical omnibus *Beginnings* (1978), that his father had the family "laughing all the time" and that the laughter was therapeutic, "because if you make fun of what hurts, it takes away some of the sting." He had "to run a gauntlet of snarling kids" after school every day, but when he "made it home there was always a laugh." Brenner took after his father, to the point where his mother was, as she once told an interviewer, "afraid to get out of bed on April Fool's Day."

The Brenners lived in an uncle's row house in South Philadelphia until David was seven, when they moved in with David's maternal grandmother in the city's more middle-class West End. As Brenner relates in *Soft Pretzels with Mustard*, the grandmother, a domineering woman who was "money-crazy to the point of insanity," made life unbearable for his "wonderfully gentle mother." The acrimony climaxed in a scene between the two women during which Brenner became so agitated that his tear ducts hemorrhaged and he "was crying blood." As the family prepared to flee the grandmother's house, when David was nine, the father, to "get even," drove nails through the woman's prized collection of brass pots and pans. "I asked my mother," Brenner writes in his memoir, "why such things were happening to us. After all, we were good people. She answered softly, 'Sometimes being good isn't enough in this world. Sometimes you need money.' Not taking my eyes off my father, I said, 'Someday, Mom, I'm going to have a lot of money. This is never going to happen to us again.' It never has. It never will. . . . That's the best way of getting even."

Larry Kart of the *Chicago Tribune* (December 11, 1983) regards the experience recounted by Brenner as a "first-generation 'primal scene' par excellence," one that "explains why Brenner's image and his style of comedy are at odds with the images and styles of most second- and third-generation comics," for whom "'the good life' was somebody else's battle" and who "proceed to toy with the spoils, building their humor around the host of anxieties about status and properly stylish behavior that seem to be their birthright." For Brenner, on the contrary, Kart points out, "'making it' is a gut necessity" having nothing to do with "whether one has done it in the right, 'stylish' way." "Shifting between wry, sweet reminiscences of childhood and routines about the minor foul-ups of everyday life, he never questions the goodness of 'the good life.'"

From the grandmother's home the Brenners moved into a small, derelict row house in a tough, changing neighborhood. There David spent the rest of his childhood, hustling to earn money at menial after-school jobs and however else he could. The determination to become "rich enough to see that [he and his family] got the best" was reinforced when, during his sixteenth year, his hospitalized father "couldn't even afford the damn ward" and was bedded in a hospital hallway. "I never had a career idea in my head—not once," he told Thomas C. Hunter. "I never had a direction except to get away from being poor."

In school Brenner was a bright but, in his words, "bored" and "disruptive" student. "I was always popular, always," he told Joyce Wadler in an interview for the *Washington Post* (June 11, 1978). "From fourth grade to high school I was class president and most popular class clown. I always did well with the girls. My ego was enormous." At his high school graduation he was "literally drunk" and "just wanted to get the hell out of there and get to the parties."

Following compulsory service in the army, Brenner went on scholarship to Temple University, in Philadelphia, where he majored in mass communications because he had always been interested in writing and wanted "to do something creative." After taking his degree with honors, he worked in Philadelphia as, successively, a documentary writer at radio station WRCV and head of the documentary department at television station KYW-TV, a Westinghouse Broadcasting affiliate. Later he was a producer at WBBM-TV in Chicago and at WNEW-TV and the Public Broadcasting Laboratory in New York City. In all, he made 115 documentaries, some of which won awards. The first was about, in his words, the subject he "knew best, white neighborhoods becoming black." The last was about welfare programs for the poor, a subject on which "we have all the answers—we simply don't want to implement them."

"In every job I ever had," Brenner recounts in *Soft Pretzels with Mustard,* "I would look at my boss or the owner and ask myself if I wanted to end up like him. I never have worked for anyone whom I wanted to look like, dress like, or be like in any manner or form." He decided to venture a change in career not because he "had a burning desire to be an entertainer" but because he had to get away from what he was doing. When trying to decide on a new field, he took a vacation in the West Indies, where he listened to the news on the radio during three straight days of rain. "It was so depressing all the reports about everything that was wrong in the world," he recalled for Thomas C. Hunter. "I thought to myself, If you don't laugh, you'll never get through the day with that news. . . . So . . . let me be a comedian for a year. I've got $9,000 in the bank. I'll go back to the way I used to live."

Brenner bombed in his first (unpaid) public performance, parodying folk singers in a folk haunt in Greenwich Village, New York City's bohemian quarter. His first professional engagement was at Pips Coffee House in Sheepshead Bay, Brooklyn, where he appeared several times a weekend for $30 over a period of months. During the trial year (later extended to a year and a half) he had set for himself, he performed almost nightly in other venues in New York City, including Catch a Rising Star and the Improvisation, showcases for new talent where he received no payment, as well as small Greenwich Village clubs, and, in his words, "other places all over town—little clubs, nothing bars, joints." Carrying a tape recorder with him at all times, he constantly expanded and honed his material. Unafraid of failure, because he knew he could always go back to producing, he came across to audiences from the beginning as pleasant and relaxed, and his gawky appearance and beak-like nose helped create a mood for laughter. "At first I thought it was going to be an extra arm," he would say about his nose. "I kept waiting for the hands to appear."

Brenner's savings were exhausted when, in the nick of time, he got his big break, a guest performance on *The Tonight Show Starring Johnny Carson,* NBC's popular late-night talk and variety program, on January 8, 1971. Within twenty-four hours of his appearance with Carson, he was offered $10,000 worth of jobs, including a spot on the CBS Sunday night *Ed Sullivan Show,* then the most coveted variety showcase on television, and a booking in the main room of the Sahara Hotel in Las Vegas. At the Sahara he opened for Sonny and Cher, and he subsequently toured with those two comedy-oriented singers until they broke up in 1974.

"About 1975 I hit a low spot," Brenner recalls in *Beginnings.* "I was a very good opening-act comedian for a lot of big names, and I was doing okay on the talk shows. The *Tonight Show* was always behind me. So were Mike Douglas and Merv Grif-

fin—and David Frost when he had his show. But the rest of the industry was cold on me." Tripling his television appearances, Brenner was a guest on the four major talk shows 104 times in the forty-three months beginning January 1976, more than any other performer. Fifty-four of the TV appearances were as a guest or substitute host on the Carson Show. (He never repeated a line in his first twenty-three *Tonight* appearances, and he once taped seventeen hours of television in one week without telling the same joke twice.) In addition to appearing on the talk shows, he was often one of the celebrity participants in the game show *Hollywood Squares.* The television exposure whetted the demand for him as a live headliner, especially in Las Vegas, where he was voted Entertainer of the Year. In addition, he won the American Guild of Variety Actors Comedy Award in 1976. By 1978 he was working as a headliner forty-eight weeks a year—half the time in Las Vegas and earning about $50,000 a week. Starring as a hairdresser opposite Leslie Ann Warren, Brenner made seven episodes of a television situation comedy called *Snip* in 1976. Rejected as too offbeat for network broadcast in the United States, the seven episodes ended up on Australian television.

In February 1981 Brenner and the comedienne Joan Rivers, another frequent Carson guest and substitute host, began performing in clubs together. By 1982 they were working together about 70 percent of the time and selling out most of the rooms they worked. They determined who opened with the flip of a coin each night, the loser opening the show and the two working in tandem for the last third, an ad-lib session with the audience. "Joan and I are as opposite as two performers can be," Brenner told Larry Kart of the *Chicago Tribune.* "She's rapid-fire, while I'm a builder with a slow-paced delivery. She's bombastic and caustic, while I'm very gentle and don't attack anyone. . . . And Joan's humor can be dirty in a clean way, while I work squeaky clean." On his own, Brenner drew capacity audiences in a tour of thirty college campuses in 1985.

Joan Rivers and Brenner entered new, competitive stages of their careers in the fall of 1986. Miss Rivers, who had been Johnny Carson's permanent guest host since 1983, went on her own with the nightly hour-long *The Late Show Starring Joan Rivers* on the fledgling Fox Broadcasting Company network. Brenner was tapped to host the thrice-weekly half-hour show *Nightlife,* produced by Motown Productions on a budget of $39 million for 195 shows and distributed by King World Productions to 108 stations across the country, of which more than a third were ABC network affiliates. The King Brothers, Roger and Michael, noting the success of the hip variety show *Late Night with David Letterman* (which follows Carson nightly on NBC), sized up the late-night audience as a predominantly young one. Seeing Brenner as demographically suitable, they plied him with such inducements as a percentage of the profits and a studio in Manhattan, which he prefers over Los

Angeles. "They've told me they're in this for the long haul," Brenner informed Fred Bernstein of *People* (September 22, 1986), "and they want me to think about what we'll be doing in 1990."

Taped "live" before an audience in Manhattan earlier in the evening and scheduled for broadcast at different times in different markets, *Nightlife* was pitted against Carson and/or Rivers in some markets. Downplaying the competitive aspect, Brenner explained to Michael E. Hill of the *Washington Post* (August 31, 1986): "King World did extensive research into what the public needs in programming. They found the public wants alternative programming at a half-hour length late at night. . . . Billy Preston [the show's musical director] will attract some new faces to television. . . . You know they [producer Bob Tischler and director Dave Wilson, both *Saturday Night Live* veterans] will do different things. . . . Say we find a guy in Washington who's responsible for lighting the Capitol dome and keeping it lit all night. That's a *Nightlife* person. . . . We're a different animal from the other shows. They're like two land masses squared off across from each other. We're going through the channel between."

"One night I may do a monologue and have only one guest because we can get away with that in a half-hour format," Brenner told Kevin Goldman of *Newsday* (September 8, 1986). "Other nights we'll have multiple guests or take the show on location to places that are open all night." Bob Tischler informed Goldman that the show would make frequent use of pretaped pieces, including one on growing up in Philadelphia, and that "there will be a lot of audience participation." Brenner, as quoted by Fred Bernstein of *People*, promised to defer to guests. "If there's an actor who doesn't feel comfortable doing talk shows," he said, "I'll tell him, 'When it's done you can see it, and if you don't like it, we won't use it.'" It was a promise he kept only too well, in the view of some critics. Monica Collins of *USA Today* (October 21, 1986), characterizing *Nightlife* as "stodgy and mainstream," observed that Brenner, "from the old school of Vegas and backslapping, panders to his guests instead of challenging them and drawing them out." In *Time* (November 3, 1986), Richard Zoglin wrote: "Brenner's new show—a cramped half hour of music, talk, and comedy—has managed to strip the celebrity interview of its last vestiges of real-life conversation." Zoglin went on to note that Brenner "has made stabs at Lettermanesque irreverence" and on-location larking (such as taking members of the studio audience to a haberdashery to help him choose a new wardrobe) "but comes across like Robert Goulet trying to do a rap song." A survey of thirteen markets taken in mid-October 1986 indicated that *Nightlife* was reaching an average of 2.1 million households per show, giving Brenner 8 percent of the TV audience in his time slot, compared to 22 percent for Carson and 10 percent for Miss Rivers. During the 1986–87 television season the Brenner and Rivers shows each attracted about two million viewers, one-third the Carson audience, and neither show endured into 1987–88.

When Brenner performed at the Westbury Music Fair on Long Island in October 1986, Bill Kaufman of *Newsday* reported that he paced the stage "like a lone eagle searching for a place to roost." "As stand-up comics go, Brenner is a raconteur rather than a master of slickly timed and paced one-liners," Kaufman wrote. "His obviously unframed act, which gives the distinct impression that much of it is last-minute patchwork, builds slowly, allowing him to acquaint the audience with his collection of early pals and colorful characters. The comedian is not especially witty, but, much like the late storyteller Myron Cohen, he establishes his kinship with the audience by tapping memories that many can associate with their own lives."

Brenner's humor, free of shock, insult, profanity, smut, and heavy social message, is addressed to a mass mainstream audience. "I have the premise that an entertainer's job is to entertain," he has said. "If one person walks out of the audience upset, then I haven't really done my job." "I'm a monologist," he told Larry Kart of the *Chicago Tribune*, "an observationist. I talk about simple everyday things, like getting your orange juice out of the refrigerator. And I always work clean. As Johnny Carson says, why develop material you can't use on television?"

Much of Brenner's humor comes from questioning common expressions that are taken for granted. To the panhandler asking for "spare change" he imagines himself saying, "Oh, am I glad I ran into you. I was about to throw all these quarters into the street." Regarding a radio meteorologist's announcement that the air in New York City is "unacceptable," he says, "What do we do, suck in air from Colorado?" His father gave him his comment on the phrase "Have a nice day": "Why are you giving me only one nice day? Why not a nice life? Or at least a weekend." Brenner writes almost all of his own material, often building on his ad-libs during performances, all of which he records and studiously replays. He keeps an idea file as well as a file listing every routine, where he performed it (so as not to repeat it there), what the audience response was, and where to retrieve the tape.

In addition to *Soft Pretzels with Mustard*, Brenner has written *Revenge Is the Best Exercise* (Arbor House, 1983), a conventional joke book, and *Nobody Ever Sees You Eat Tuna Fish* (Arbor House, 1986), a sequel to his first memoir in which he again mingles humor with poignancy. The title of his comedy album *Excuse Me, Are You Reading that Paper?* (MCA, 1983) comes from the following staple in his act: "I sat down on a newspaper in the subway and a guy asked if I was reading it. I said yes, stood up, turned the page, and sat down again."

David Brenner is six feet two inches tall and weighs under 160 pounds. Although he flaunts jewelry less ostentatiously than he once did, he still tends to be daringly experimental in dress. Brenner maintains many of his prefame friendships, and he is close to his nonagenarian father. (His mother died in March 1986.) He has been married and divorced twice, and he is the father of a boy born out of wedlock in 1982, Cole Jay, of whom he is seeking custody.

A self-described "addicted New Yorker," Brenner lives with his girlfriend Victoria Campbell, a make-up artist for *Nightlife*, in a four-story townhouse that he owns on a landmark block on Manhattan's Upper East Side. When Joyce Wadler interviewed him at home for the *Washington Post* he told her, "I sometimes say to people, 'Four hundred years of Brenner poverty stops here.' . . . Everything in this house a joke bought. The same

jokes that used to get me thrown out of school made me rich. Weird, huh? Weird!"

References: Biog N p262 Mr/Ap '75 por; Chicago Tribune VI p2+ Mr 25 '79 por, VI p14+ Je 13 '82 por, XIII p10+ D 11 '83 por; N Y Daily News Leisure p5+ Je 11 '78 por; People 26:12+ S 22 '86 pors; Brenner, David. Soft Pretzels with Mustard (1983), Nobody Ever Sees You Eat Tuna Fish (1986); Contemporary Theatre, Film, and Television vol 2 (1986); Hunter, Thomas C. Beginnings (1978); Smith, Ronald Lande. The Stars of Stand-up Comedy (1986); Who's Who in America, 1986–87

Brinkley, David (McClure)

July 10, 1920– Television journalist. Address: b. ABC News, 1717 DeSales St., N.W., Washington, D.C. 20036

NOTE: This biography supersedes the article that appeared in Current Biography in 1960.

David Brinkley, the host of the American Broadcasting Company's Sunday morning television news/commentary/interview show *This Week with David Brinkley*, has in his words, "done the news longer than anyone on earth." After serving an apprenticeship with United Press, Brinkley joined the National Broadcasting Company as a radio writer in Washington, D.C., in 1943. At NBC, as he has said, television journalism and he "quite literally . . . grew up together." Brinkley was the Washington correspondent on the network's

Camel News Caravan from 1951 to 1956, when he teamed up with Chet Huntley to cover political conventions and elections for NBC and do its nightly *Huntley-Brinkley Report*, probably the first TV newscast to provide context and treat viewers as adults. During their fourteen-year partnership, Huntley and Brinkley became one of the best-known name combinations in the United States, and Brinkley's distinctive delivery, a wry cadenced drawl that shapes itself around the simple declarative sentences that mark his news writing, soon set a trend among imitative young broadcasters. As his colleague Roger Mudd has observed, Brinkley "brought a level of political sophistication and literary craftsmanship and a lively sense of humor that television had never known before and that hasn't been equaled since," Brinkley moved from NBC to ABC in 1981.

David McClure Brinkley was born in Wilmington, New Hanover County, North Carolina, on July 10, 1920, the youngest of the five children of William Graham Brinkley and Mary MacDonald (West) Brinkley. In response to a query from *Current Biography*, Brinkley described his family as "an old Southern family with generations of physicians and Presbyterian preachers, none famous." His father, a railroad employee, died when Brinkley was eight. Considerably younger than his two brothers and two sisters, and a loner, Brinkley turned to books for companionship. "If there is anything worth knowing about me . . . ," he told Philip J. Hilts for a profile in the *Washington Post's Potomac* magazine (January 27, 1974), "it is that at the age of ten or twelve I became a semipermanent fixture at the Wilmington, North Carolina public library. I would go every day after school and stay till it closed. . . . That's really where I learned what little I know. I once took out Oswald Spengler's *Decline of the West*. The librarian said I was the only one in Wilmington who would ever read it, so she gave it to me. I still have it." Among the trove of other books he cherished were those of E. B. White, whose journalistic style he strove to emulate.

At New Hanover High School, Brinkley's extracurricular activities were band, school newspaper,

English club, and rifle team. Academically, he did not apply himself—except in English, because, as he told the editors of Current Biography, he "liked to write and was pretty good at it." Encouraged to go into journalism by one of his teachers, Mrs. L. Burrows Smith, he interned at the local morning newspaper while he was in high school. Three decades later, when he won the 1964 Golden Key Award (a double award given annually by six educational organizations to a citizen who has contributed significantly to the national welfare, and to one of his or her teachers), Brinkley chose Mrs. Smith to receive the companion Golden Key as the teacher who had the greatest formative influence on him. According to an article in the Kentucky School Journal (March 1964) on the occasion of the award, Brinkley dropped out of school in his senior year to become a full-time reporter for the Wilmington paper. In the article, Mrs. Smith was paraphrased as saying that "the high school failed him, rather than the other way round." "David was quite an individualist," Mrs. Smith explained as quoted in the article. "We had no counselors then as we do today, and teachers were too busy to find time to learn what a student's problems were and help him solve them."

In 1939–40 Brinkley was enrolled as a special student in English at the University of North Carolina at Chapel Hill. Although sources disagree on the exact chronology of his activities between 1940 and 1943, when he joined NBC, the activities themselves are not in doubt: he served in the United States Army as a supply sergeant at Fort Jackson, South Carolina; was a peripatetic Southern stringer for the fledgling United Press news service (which later became United Press International); and while working for UP he was a part-time special student of English at Emory and Vanderbilt universities. "Because I could write better than anybody they had in the office, they [his superiors at the UP bureau in Atlanta] put me to writing the radio wire, which was sold to radio [stations] . . . ," he recounted to Claudia Dreifus in an interview for Newsday (March 8, 1981). "My writing attracted a little attention among broadcasters around the country, and CBS offered me a job in Washington. So I quit UP and went to Washington to take the CBS job. On arrival—I don't know what happened, there was some kind of mix-up—they'd never heard of me. I couldn't even find anybody who had offered me the job. So . . . I walked across the street to NBC and got hired in five minutes."

NBC hired Brinkley chiefly because of his flair for writing for the ear, for spoken delivery. Accordingly, his first NBC assignment was writing news scripts for staff radio announcers; in addition, he did reportorial legwork at the White House and on Capitol Hill. After several years of such yeomanry, he was given the chance to do some broadcasting himself, not so much on radio—then still the electronic mass medium, reserved for the "golden voices"—as on television, at that time still a novelty watched by the few small localized audiences able to afford the gadget. "I had a chance to learn while nobody was watching," he later observed.

Television began to assume national dimensions during the 1948–49 season, when coaxial cables linking the East and Midwest made simultaneous broadcasting to different regions of the country possible for the first time, but the medium still had a limited audience and was less attractive to ambitious broadcasters, than radio. John Cameron Swayze, an NBC radio newscaster who was offered the choice of resigning or moving to television, chose the latter, and in February 1949 he became the anchorman of NBC's nightly fifteen-minute Camel News Caravan. That broadcast, originating from Radio City in Manhattan, consisted for the most part of Swayze's reading the news, or reciting it from memory. There was at first little if any on-the-spot coverage and much reliance on film footage imitative of movie newsreels, featuring such staged and frivolous events as fashion shows, ship launchings, beauty contests and politicians taking advantage of photo opportunities.

The Camel News Caravan was enhanced by a brief report from Washington by David Brinkley, a regular spot in the show from 1951 to 1956. During those years NBC established film crews in major American cities and several foreign capitals, but, except for protracted wars and natural catastrophes, remote coverage continued to be of predictable events, such as Air Force maneuvers, high society affairs, award banquets, campaign speeches, and official ceremonies. "Television news was still nothing to be taken seriously . . . ," Brinkley told James F. Fixx in an interview for McCall's (October 1966). "It was essentially a newsreel. . . . That's what we put on the air in the early days, because we thought of ourselves as a newsreel that was faster. . . . We were very proud of the fact that we got a piece of film on the air within an hour or two instead of a week. Most of the time, of course, it was dull film, and it was made no less dull by being fast."

Brinkley was among the NBC television news reporters who discussed topical issues in the network series Comment in the summer of 1954. Singling Brinkley out in a review of Comment in the New York Herald Tribune (June 27, 1954), John Crosby wrote: "For this sort of work I would unhesitatingly pick Brinkley, who has a pungent and economical style of prose, an engaging face, and a dry, sardonic tone of voice which carries great authority." As television boomed, so did Brinkley's career. A turning point came in 1956, when he and Chet Huntley were brought together. NBC, then being bested in the news ratings by CBS, put great stock in its coverage of the Republican and Democratic national conventions that year. With a number of suggested names before them, including those of Chet Huntley and David Brinkley, the network executives "didn't have any one person they were willing to trust alone" to compete against CBS's Walter Cronkite in covering the conventions, as Brinkley recounted to James F. Fixx of McCall's. "Covering a convention is a very hard job. You have to keep about eight tennis balls in the air at one time. You have to listen while you're talking, you have to know everybody, and you have to know everything about the political situation. NBC wasn't willing to believe that either of us could do it. So in effect they were hedging their bet by putting us both on, figuring if one of us blew it, the other could help him out. They wouldn't want to admit that now, but it's true. And as it turned out, it worked." While Walter Cronkite drew the best notices for coverage of the conventions in 1956, as he had in 1952, Huntley and Brinkley showed the form that would soon move them ahead of Cronkite, and NBC News ahead of CBS News. Assessing the NBC coverage of the Democratic National Convention in Chicago, Jack Gould wrote in the *New York Times* (August 17, 1956): "Mr. Brinkley quite possibly could be the forerunner of a new school of television commentator. He is not an earnest Voice of Authority. He contributes his observations with assurance but not insistence. [His] extraordinary accomplishment has been not to talk too much. He has a knack for the succinct phrase that sums up the situation."

Realizing the appeal of its new team, NBC assigned Huntley and Brinkley to replace John Cameron Swayze. On October 29, 1956 *The Camel News Caravan* became *NBC News*, later renamed the *Huntley-Brinkley Report*, anchored by Huntley in New York and Brinkley in Washington. At first fifteen minutes long, the show was later extended to half an hour. By the end of 1956 it had full sponsorship, and within two years it was television's top-ranked news program, a status it would continue to hold through most of its fourteen-year run. Reuven Frank, the show's producer, conceived its trademark closing lines: "Good Night, Chet." "Good Night, David . . . and Good Night for NBC News"—a touch of warmth calculated to offset the generally serious demeanor of the two broadcasters. While serious in their treatment of the news, neither man was pompous, and Brinkley was the less solemn of the two, spicing his reports and commentaries with wry wit and delivering them with an air and a look sometimes suggesting skepticism, or even boredom, especially where politicians and bureaucrats were concerned. "The only way to do news on television is not to be terrified of it . . . ," he explained to James F. Fixx in the *McCall's* interview. "Most of the news just isn't that important. In fact, very little of it is. And I think the proper attitude is not be awed by it."

In 1958 Brinkley received the DuPont Award for his "inquiring mind sensitive to both the elusive fact and the background that illuminates its meaning." The *Huntley-Brinkley Report* won Emmys in 1959 and 1960, and in the latter year Huntley and Brinkley's coverage of the political conventions for NBC captured 51 percent of the viewing audience. CBS was second with 36 percent and ABC was third with 13 percent. On both election night in 1960 and inauguration day in 1961 NBC was watched by 52 percent of the viewers.

At the New York end of the *Huntley-Brinkley Report*, Chet Huntley was involved with a multitude of correspondents, camera crews, and other personnel in reporting world news, but in Washington, Brinkley was relatively free of dependence on others. He personally knew the Washington scene as well as anyone, had many friends inside government, and was the chief writer as well as the narrator of his scripts. His style of delivery spawned what Claudia Dreifus in *Newsday* described as "a whole slew of David Brinkley clones . . . newscasters with a quiet, acid tone in their voices."

Among Brinkley's projects outside of *The Huntley-Brinkley Report* was *David Brinkley's Journal*, a weekly NBC public affairs program that aired from October 1961 to August 1963. On that live show, with filmed segments, he covered a wide range of topics, both heavy and light. The program won a George Foster Peabody Award in its first season and an Emmy in its last. Brinkley was "very proud to have been a part" of network television's sustained live coverage of the aftermath of President John F. Kennedy's assassination in November 1963, which he considered "one of television's best hours."

The *Huntley-Brinkley Report* ended with Huntley's retirement in July 1970. (He died four years later.) While experimenting with rotating anchors—Brinkley, John Chancellor and Frank McGee—over the following thirteen months, NBC lost first place in the news ratings to CBS. In August 1971 Chancellor became sole anchor, and for five years thereafter Brinkley appeared on *NBC Nightly News* (as the program was retitled) only as a commentator. During those years he became a popular speaker on college campuses, where, as he told an interviewer for *TV Guide* (April 15, 1972), he was heartened to find in students "an evolved consciousness . . . quite often creative" on political and social issues. "I think if about five previous generations, including mine, had done the same things," he said, "this country would be in much better shape now than it is."

In June 1976 Brinkley returned to coanchoring *NBC Nightly News*, with John Chancellor, and he remained coanchor until October 1979. At that time NBC was behind ABC as well as CBS in news ratings. In the fall of 1980 NBC launched the weekly program *NBC Magazine with David Brinkley*. Pitted against overwhelming CBS escapist competition (first the hit prime-time soap opera *Dallas* and then the fantasy-adventure series *The Incredible Hulk*), the new Brinkley program failed to survive.

On September 4, 1981 Brinkley announced that he was leaving NBC, not because of a conflict with William Small the new president of NBC News, but simply in order to continue "to do what [he has] always done—cover politics." (Roger Mudd, Tom Brokaw, and John Chancellor had assumed the key on-air positions at NBC News, and they were the ones slated to cover the 1982 and 1984 election campaigns.) Later he confessed to Tom Shales of the *Washington Post* (November 12, 1982): "I shed a few tears. I'm not a crybaby, but I did cry a little. It's like leaving a family."

Two weeks after Brinkley made his announcement, ABC News executives confirmed that he had signed a four-year contract with them for assignments including a weekly news and discussion show, political commentary for *World News Tonight*, and coverage of the 1982 and 1984 elections. The hour-long weekly show, *This Week with David Brinkley*, went on the air on Sunday morning November 15, 1981. Seeking to vary the "funereal" Sunday morning news interview ritual, the program was multifaceted, beginning with a short newscast by Brinkley, followed by a background report on the program's central topic, a panel interview with invited guests, and a roundtable discussion by Brinkley, correspondent Sam Donaldson, and news analyst George F. Will. When the program created news with a timely scoop interview, live by satellite, with Libyan leader Muammar al-Qaddafi in December 1981, Thomas Griffith wrote in *Time*: "After a wobbly start, the Brinkley show looks like a true innovation in television journalism." Within less than a year, *This Week with David Brinkley* overtook the hoary Sunday morning interview stalwarts *Meet the Press* (NBC) and *Face the Nation* (CBS) in the ratings.

Although he strives for impartiality in his political journalism, Brinkley has been called everything from a left-wing radical to a right-wing reactionary. He has taken sides on issues—he was critical of the Vietnam war in its later years, for example, during the 1970s he became increasingly critical of the overbearing role of a big government unresponsive to people's needs—but he is a partisan of no political group other than that which views Washington as "ten square miles surrounded on all sides by reality." To those who read editorializing into his facial expressions (including an arched eyebrow) and his delivery in newscasts, he has responded: "The smirks and sneers are entirely in the eye of the beholder."

On June 10, 1972 David Brinkley married Susan Melanie Benfer, a former real estate operator with a young daughter, Alexis. He was previously married to and divorced from Ann Fischer, by whom he has three grown sons, Alan, Joel, and John. Joel followed his father into journalism and in 1980 won a Pulitzer Prize for a series of reports on Cambodian refugees. Brinkley is an amateur carpenter, and in the *Current Biography* questionnaire he listed as his favorite recreations "reading, writing, travel, architecture, wildflowers, and outdoors."

"There seem to be two David Brinkleys," Barbara Matusow wrote in her book *The Evening Stars* (1983), "one faithful and mischievous, the other remote, sour, even forbidding." Brinkley is six feet two inches tall and weighs 183 pounds. His eyes are blue and his brown hair is graying. He is a Presbyterian, a member of the Cosmos Club and the National Press Club, both in Washington, D.C., and a trustee of Colonial Williamsburg. Brinkley has been working on a book on Washington during World War II that he expects will be ready for publication by Alfred A. Knopf, Inc., in 1988.

References: *Broadcasting Now* 103:95+ N 15 '82 por; *McCall's* 94:56+ O '66 por; *New Yorker* 44:34+ Ag 3 '68 por; *Newsday Mag* p19+ Mr 8 '81 por; *Contemporary Authors* vols 97–100 (1981); *Encyclopedia of Twentieth-Century Journalists* (1986); *Who's Who in America*, 1986–87

Broderick, Matthew

Mar. 21, 1962– Actor. Address: b. c/o Arnold Stiefel Co., 9200 Sunset Blvd., Suite 415, Los Angeles, Calif. 90069

Having won important roles in two motion pictures and a hit Broadway play within two years of his graduation from high school, in 1980, Matthew Broderick has often and, given his boyish appearance, perhaps inevitably, been linked to the group of up-and-coming young actors collectively known as "the brat pack." But unlike the majority of his peers, Broderick brings more than good looks and the transient bloom of youth to his roles. A dedicated professional who has, in his words, "never wanted to be limited to those things that make a lot of money," he has deliberately selected from the scores of parts offered to him only those that challenge and develop him as an actor. In his brief career, he has tackled an unusually wide variety of roles, ranging from a homosexual street kid to Neil Simon's loquacious alter ego, Eugene Jerome, in *Brighton Beach Memoirs*, for which he earned a Tony award, and *Biloxi Blues*.

Matthew Broderick was born on March 21, 1962, in New York City, the youngest of the three children of James Broderick, a character actor perhaps best known for his role as the father in the television series *Family*, and Patricia (Biow) Broderick, a playwright and director. He has two older sisters—Janet, a potter, and Martha, a psychotherapist. As a child, Matthew often accompanied his father to rehearsals and performances. "I used to love just being backstage," he told Jesse Kornbluth in an interview for a *New York* (March 25, 1985) magazine profile. "I'd hang around, sitting in the audience during rehearsals. I was like a groupie." But despite his infatuation with the theatre, young Broderick balked when, at the age of seven, he was offered a part opposite his father in a summer stock production. "I became so hysterical that I had to be taken home," he recalled to Jerry Parker of *Newsday* (June 12, 1983). "I was terrified of acting. I think it might have to do with the fact that I wasn't such a good reader. Maybe I was afraid I wouldn't be able to read the script."

Except for an appearance as Santa Claus in an elementary school Christmas pageant, Matthew Broderick shunned the stage until his sophomore year at the Walden School, the Manhattan prep school he had chosen to attend primarily because of its excellent theatre program. During his first year there, he had restricted his extracurricular activities to soccer and softball, but after a knee injury forced him to forgo most sports, he auditioned for and won the part of Snout in the school's production of *A Midsummer Night's Dream*. Over the next two years, he appeared in featured roles in nine more Walden theatrical productions. As he became more involved in theatre and more confident of his growing ability as an actor, he gradually lost interest in his studies. Admittedly "very manipulative," he repeatedly "weaseled" his way out of assignments and course requirements. By the time he was a senior, he had resolved to try his luck as an actor rather than continue his education on the college level. "It wouldn't have worked for me," he told Gene Siskel, the film critic of the *Chicago Tribune* (June 26, 1986). "I would have ended up doing the minimum amount of studying to just pass, and I would have resented even giving up that much time. I love acting."

Shortly after his graduation from high school in 1980, Broderick made his first professional stage appearance, as his father's costar in a limited-run production of Horton Foote's *On Valentine's Day* at the Herbert Berghof studio. Over the next year, Broderick doggedly made the theatrical rounds, "auditioning like a madman," as he put it, without success. Heartened by the example of his father, who had suffered a similar string of rejections in his youth, he refused to become discouraged. To better his chances, he took classes with Uta Hagen, the actress and acting coach. Broderick's persistence finally paid off when he landed a costarring role, opposite the Academy Award-winning actress Sally Field, in the motion picture *No Small Affair*, about a romance between a fifteen-year-old boy and an older woman. After two weeks on the set, however, Martin Ritt, the film's director, became ill. The project was temporarily shelved, and Matthew Broderick was once again unemployed.

In the fall of 1981 Broderick tried out for the role of David, a homosexual street urchin in *Widows and Children First!*, the final play in *Torch Song Trilogy*, Harvey Fierstein's seriocomic drama, comprised of three interconnected one-act plays, about the growth to maturity of a "drag queen." Over the strong objections of his agent, who feared that the young actor might become typecast, he signed on for an eight-week engagement in the piece at the Richard Allen Center, a tiny Off-Off-Broadway theatre near Lincoln Center. At first, audiences shunned *Torch Song*, but about a month into the run, both the *New York Times* and the *Village Voice* published glowing reviews. Suddenly a hot ticket, *Torch Song Trilogy* moved to Off Broadway in January 1982, beginning its regular commercial run at the Actors Playhouse in Greenwich Village, where it drew rave notices. Widely admired for the "naturalness" and "spontaneity" he brought to the role of the troubled teenager, Matthew Broderick came in for a respectable share of the praise. Jack Kroll, writing in *Newsweek* (March 15, 1982), went so far as to rate Broderick's portrayal "one of the most original, witty, and touching performances [he'd] ever seen from a young actor." *Torch Song* eventually transferred to Broadway and won a Tony as the best play of the 1982–83 season, but by that time, Broderick had left the cast.

Not long after he completed his run in *Torch Song Trilogy*, Broderick auditioned for the central role of Eugene Jerome in Neil Simon's Broadway-bound *Brighton Beach Memoirs*. Originally rejected as being too old to play the precocious fifteen-year-old Eugene, he was later called back to read a second time for *Brighton Beach* and for Simon's proposed new movie, *Max Dugan Returns*, as well. Following his own tryouts, Broderick was asked to read a scene with Zeljko Ivanek, who was being considered for the part of Eugene's older brother. "I thought it was an audition for Zeljko, and that I didn't have the part, so I was real loose," Broderick recalled to Leslie Bennetts in an interview for the *New York Times* (April 5, 1983). "Then when I was leaving, the casting director said, 'Well it's been a good day for you, hasn't it? I think you got them both.'" The man who personally selected Broderick for the two roles was none other than Neil Simon himself. In explaining his decision to Leslie Bennetts, Simon said, "You just see somebody and say, 'That's the kid.' It's like when you fall in love and say, 'That's her.' That's how I felt about Matthew. He has the attitude that I was looking for for both parts, sort of New York and streetwise, but sweet. And his gift of timing is incredible. He acts way beyond his years, especially in comedy."

In mid-1982 Broderick flew to California to begin work on *Max Dugan Returns*, Simon's comedy about a young widow (Marsha Mason) struggling to come to terms with her adolescent son (Broderick) and her long-lost father (Jason Robards). He returned to New York almost every weekend to visit his father, who was then gravely ill with cancer. Always close, the two had forged an even stronger bond since Matthew had become a professional actor and often spent hours discussing roles, career options, and the politics of the theatre. It was at his father's suggestion that Matthew refused to do a screen test for the leading role in the high-tech thriller *WarGames*—a part he eventually landed anyway on the strength of his performance in the early rushes of *Max Dugan Returns*.

Broderick continued his practice of spending his weekends in New York throughout the filming of *WarGames*. "Some people say acting is a kind of therapy," he said, as quoted by David Richards of the *Washington Post* (May 25, 1983). "It didn't seem to help me. Doing *WarGames* was like time out. On the set, I'd forget the tragedy that was happening at home. But whenever I'd come home from shooting, it was just as horrible as it had been the weekend before. It was just like these . . . two different times." James Broderick died on November 1, 1982, the first day of rehearsals, in Los Angeles, for *Brighton Beach Memoirs*. "My father wanted me to phone him after the first reading of the play and tell him how it had gone," Broderick told Richards. "I did, and he asked a lot of questions. He died that very night."

After undergoing a successful tryout in Los Angeles, *Brighton Beach Memoirs* opened at the Alvin Theatre on Broadway on March 27, 1983. Set in a middle-class Jewish household in Brooklyn in the depths of the Great Depression, Neil Simon's autobiographical memory play revolves around Simon's alter ego, the wisecracking Eugene Jerome, who not only takes part in the action but also observes it and comments on it with an alternately bewildered and discerning eye. Broderick's portrayal of a young man coming of age in a troubled time won over even those few critics who were disappointed in the play itself. As Eugene, he "possesses both the polished performing skills and the magnetism that are essential to keep *Brighton Beach Memoirs* rolling," Frank Rich noted in his review for the *New York Times* (March 28, 1983), although he tempered his praise with the quibble that the actor "sometimes has the too-calculated delivery of a stand-up comic." For the *New Yorker*'s Brendan Gill, however, it was Broderick's ingenuous delivery of the "surefire one-liners" that gave the play a "pleasing humaneness" and kept it from degenerating "into slapstick." Gene Siskel agreed. "Jerry Lewis at his prime couldn't give the comic performance that Broderick delivers," Siskel wrote in the *Chicago Tribune* (June 26, 1983). "Maybe a teenage Walter Matthau could have done it, but few others. He is that good, pushing his voice and body into a constant but controlled tremble, playing a youngster in perpetual fear of being blamed for breathing and other major offenses. When you are in New York, it's the one performance to see." Broderick's interpretation brought him a 1983 Tony award for best actor in a featured role, an honor he accepted in his father's memory.

Max Dugan Returns dropped out of sight shortly after its release in April 1983, but *WarGames* proved to be one of the biggest box-office hits of that summer. Cast as David Lightman, a seventeen-year-old whiz who inadvertently taps into the Pentagon's computerized early warning system and nearly triggers World War III, Broderick turned in another winning portrayal. In the view of some critics, his ability to project innocence and what Gary Arnold called "innate youthful decency" compensated for the film's implausible plot twists.

Broderick's salary soon reflected his notices. For *Max Dugan Returns*, he was reportedly paid $30,-000, for *WarGames*, $50,000, and for *Brighton Beach Memoirs*, $1,000 a week. After winning the Tony, he negotiated a new contract to continue in the play for six months at a significantly higher salary, but he soon took a leave of absence to play an impish thief in the medieval fantasy *Ladyhawke* (1985), for which he received an estimated $750,-000. Reviewing the film for the *New Yorker* (May 13, 1985), Pauline Kael wrote, "Put on the screen for comic relief, Broderick has more of a fairy-tale quality than anyone else, and he gives this limp movie with its disco-medieval score its only traces of inspiration." But the simplest and perhaps most telling tribute came from his director, Richard Donner, who said, as quoted by Jesse Kornbluth, "He found a character better than had been written."

After fulfilling his contractual obligations to *Brighton Beach Memoirs*, Broderick took on the comparatively small but meaty role of Brother Vaughan, the wastrel son of a genteel Texas family in the independent feature *1918* (1985). Written by Horton Foote, a longtime friend of the Broderick family, *1918* concerns the survival of a family in a small Gulf Coast community that is reeling from the effects of World War I and the influenza pandemic. The seventh play, chronologically, in Foote's cycle "The Orphan's Home," nine plays based on stories his father had told him about his own life, *1918* was the first part of the series to be translated to the screen by Foote, with his family's and friends' assistance. The second was *On Valentine's Day* (1986), which was set one year earlier than *1918*, and which once again featured Broderick as the reprobate Brother Vaughan. Both films, along with Foote's *Courtship*, were broadcast in April 1987 on PBS's *American Playhouse* under the umbrella title *Story of a Marriage*.

Broderick's television credits also include Harold (Hally) in *Master Harold . . . and the Boys*, Athol Fugard's shattering drama about apartheid's corrosive effects on the human spirit. Caught between a drunken, racist father and an inattentive mother, Hally takes out his rage and bitterness on "the boys," the two black waiters in his father's tearoom who have been his surrogate family since his childhood. When *Master Harold* was televised by the Public Broadcasting Service in November 1985, Broderick, who was coached in his South African accent by Fugard himself, was unanimously acclaimed for his "fascinatingly complex" interpretation of the lonely, self-hating Hally.

On March 28, 1985, Broderick returned to Broadway, as Eugene Jerome in *Biloxi Blues*, the second installment in Neil Simon's autobiographical trilogy. *Biloxi Blues* finds Eugene—six years older than he was in *Brighton Beach Memoirs*—in basic training at an army camp in Biloxi, Mississippi. His intentions, he tells the audience in one of his many asides, are to become a writer, survive the war, and lose his virginity, though not necessarily in that order. As Frank Rich and Robert Brustein observed, Broderick had become to Neil Simon what Jean-Pierre Léaud was to the late French filmmaker François Truffaut—the ideal surrogate. "Unfortunately," Brustein went on to explain in his review for the *New Republic* (May 20, 1985), Broderick was "also beginning to personify Simon's shrewd capacity to manipulate audiences. [His] broad takes, his shuffling walk, his urban accent, even the way he often appears to be breaking up on stage, sometimes seem more calculated than real." To Rich, however, he was no longer the "practical stand-up comic masquerading in little boy's clothing" that he had been in *Brighton Beach*, but, as he wrote in the *New York Times* (March 29, 1985), "an assured actor at one with a full-bodied role. His comic timing, now as much physical as verbal, has attained a textbook perfection."

Broderick left *Biloxi Blues* in August 1985 to take the title role in *Ferris Bueller's Day Off* (1986), John Hughes's lightweight but nonetheless enormously successful teen comedy. Cast as a "likable goof-off" who plays truant from high school on a beautiful spring day, Broderick did the best he could with a flimsy role, but for most reviewers *Ferris Bueller's Day Off* remained little more than a "minor summer diversion," to quote the *Christian Science Monitor*'s David Sterritt. Broderick's most recent film venture was *Project X* (1987), a suspense drama about a young airman assigned to a top-secret military training program using chimpanzees to test pilot endurance.

After completing *Project X*, Broderick took a brief vacation (his first in five years), and then rejoined Horton Foote and his more or less permanent acting ensemble in an Off-Broadway production of the fourth play in Foote's "The Orphan's Home" cycle, *The Widow Claire*, which opened at the Circle in the Square Theatre on December 17, 1986. Taking place during a single summer night in 1911, *The Widow Claire* is a wistful comedy about a shy young man's tentative courtship of a widow some six years his senior. Most critics found Broderick's restrained interpretation of the inarticulate Horace Robedaux to be as effective as his flamboyant portrayal of the voluble Eugene Jerome. He and his costar, Hallie Foote, were especially adept at conveying the almost imperceptible progress of the pair's romance, displaying what John Beaufort of the *Christian Science Monitor* (December 31, 1986) called "an extraordinary sensitivity to the implications beneath the externals."

A slightly built man, Matthew Broderick stands five feet eight inches tall and has large, "basset-hound" brown eyes, dark-brown hair, and a sly grin. Because of his film work, he maintains an apartment in Los Angeles, but he considers the Greenwich Village apartment in which he grew up and which he currently shares with his mother, to be his home. In his leisure time, he enjoys playing softball, riding his fifteen-speed bicycle, stargazing with one of his three telescopes from the roof of his apartment building, and visiting with neighborhood friends. "My best friends are still my best friends," he told Deborah Mason in an interview for *Vogue* (August 1983). "The only difference is that now they expect me to pay for everything." While vacationing in Northern Ireland with his girlfriend, the actress Jennifer Grey, in August 1987, Broderick suffered a broken leg and other injuries when the car he was driving collided with another automobile, killing its two occupants. Charged with one count of manslaughter and reckless driving, the actor, whose case was scheduled to be heard on February 15, 1988, faced a sentence of up to ten years in prison, if convicted.

References: *Chicago Tribune* XII p11+ Je 26 '83 pors; *N Y Times* C p9 Ap 5 '83 por; *New York* 18:48+ Mr 25 '85 pors; *Newsday* II p3+ Je 12 '83 pors; *People* 19:11+ My 6 '83 pors; *Seventeen* 42:247+ Ag '83 por; *Time* 121:70 Je 6 '83 pors; *Washington Post* B p1+ My 26 '83 pors; Brower, Millicent. *Young Performers on the Stage, in Film, and on TV* (1985)

Buffett, Warren E(dward)

Aug. 30, 1930 Corporate executive; investor.
Address: b. Berkshire Hathaway Inc., 1440 Kiewit Plaza, Omaha, Neb. 68131

The low-key demibillionaire portfolio investment virtuoso Warren E. Buffett, who is known on Wall Street as "the oracle of Omaha" with "the Midas Touch," has made most of his fortune and the high returns for his shareholders by ignoring the Street's conventional wisdom and strategies and departing from its style. Buffett is the chairman of Berkshire Hathaway Inc., a long-term investment company with more than $2 billion in corporate holdings, notably in insurance, retail, and communications. Since he took over the company nearly a quarter of a century ago—when it was a small New England textile firm—Berkshire Hathaway's per-share book value has grown from $19.46 to more than $2,000. A shrewd discerner of long-term business and industrial worth, Buffett built up his conglomerate by buying into undervalued companies that had a solid management in place, letting that management stay, and watching the companies reach their potential. His profile was relatively low until he participated in Capital Cities Communications' takeover of the American Broadcasting Companies in 1985 and 1986, a transaction from which he emerged with an 18 percent share of the stock in the combined companies. He again made head-

Warren E. Buffett

lines in the fall of 1987, when he came to the rescue of Salomon Inc., the Wall Street investment giant, which was threatened by corporate raiders.

Warren Edward Buffett was born in Omaha, Nebraska on August 30, 1930, into a family prominent in the city's political and business life. His mother was Leila (Stahl) Buffett and his father was Howard Homan Buffett, a stockbroker and four-term Republican United States representative. As a congressman, Howard Buffett was such an upright fiscal conservative that he turned back to the United States Treasury his share of a raise that Congress voted itself. In Omaha, the Buffetts owned a grocery store founded by a grandfather.

Buffett grew up in Omaha and, when his father was a congressman, in Washington, D.C., where he was an eager-beaver paperboy for the *Washington Post,* covering several delivery routes simultaneously. He also retrieved lost golf balls at a suburban golf course, and sold them. With one of his two sisters, he started playing the stock market on a very modest scale when he was eleven. A year later he tried his hand at turning out a horse-racing handicap sheet, and as a high school student in Washington he was a partner with another student in a small pinball machine business that grossed fifty dollars a week. Before graduating from high school, he bought forty acres of farm land in Nebraska.

Majoring in business, Buffett began his undergraduate studies at the University of Pennsylvania, which he attended from 1947 to 1949, and took his B.S. degree at the University of Nebraska in 1950. At the University of Nebraska he began reading the books of Benjamin Graham, a pioneer in the "value" (as opposed to "growth") approach to portfolio management. Graham, a professor at the

graduate school of business at Columbia University in New York City and the author of *The Intelligent Investor* and, with David Dodd, *Security Analysis,* taught his readers and students to "seek stocks that the market has undervalued and then patiently wait for them to rise." Buffett did his graduate work under Graham at Columbia, taking his M.B.A. degree in 1951. Among the lessons taught him by Graham was the following, paraphrased by him: "You're not right or wrong because 1,000 people agree with you or disagree with you. You're right because your facts and your reasoning are right."

Buffett worked as an investment salesman with Buffett, Falk and Company, his father's brokerage firm in Omaha, from 1951 to 1954, and he was a security analyst under Benjamin Graham at the Graham-Newman Corporation in New York City from 1954 to 1956. In the latter year, when he was twenty-five, he returned to Omaha and pooled $5,000 of his own money and $100,000 from relatives and friends to form the Buffett Partnership, an investment fund that he managed for thirteen years. The other shareholders were limited partners, making no investment decisions.

Donald Keough, now the president of Coca-Cola, was a young executive in Omaha in the 1950s. "I had five small kids and left for work each day," Keough recalled for a profile of Buffett by Bernice Kanner in *New York* (April 22, 1985). "Buffett had three and stayed home. He had a marvelous hobby, model trains, and my kids used to troop over there and play with them. One day, Warren popped over and asked if I'd thought about how I was going to educate these kids. . . . I told him I planned to work hard and see what happened. Warren said that if I gave him $5,000 to invest, he'd probably be able to do better [for me]. My wife and I talked it over, but we figured we didn't know what this guy even did for a living—how could we give him $5,000? We've been kicking ourselves ever since. I mean, if we had given him the dough, we could have *owned* a college by now."

Among Buffett's coups in the Buffett Partnership was his investment in the American Express Company in 1963, when AmEx shares were selling cheap because the credit card company, then the victim of a major swindle, was considered near bankruptcy by many on Wall Street. In the places that he ate and shopped in Omaha, Buffett noticed that customers were continuing to use their American Express cards just as they had before the scandal broke. Ignoring the gossip from Wall Street and following his own common sense, he bought 5 percent of AmEx stock, which soon revived and over the following five years rose from 35 to 189 points on the stock market.

"While the [investment] gunslingers of the Sixties were promoting each other over drinks at Oscar's [on Wall Street] then going back to their offices so they could watch the tape, Buffett was compiling the best records in the industry from Omaha, Nebraska," the pseudonymous Adam Smith wrote in his book *Supermoney,* "No quote machines, no ticker, no Oscar's, no chewed fingernails, no tranquilizers, no Gelusil, no backgammon after the close, no really big spectacular winners . . . [just] quiet, simple stocks, easy to understand, with a lot of time left over for the kids, for handball, for listening to the tall corn grow."

When, with uncanny prescience, Buffett dissolved the Buffett Partnership in 1969, just in time to escape a general dive in stock prices in the early 1970s, the value of the original investment had multiplied thirty-fold. Looking back over the history of the partnership, John Train wrote in his book *The Money Masters*: "He [Buffett] never had a down year, even in the severe bear markets of 1957, 1962, 1966, and 1969. That achievement stands alone in modern portfolio management."

One of the companies in which the Buffett Partnership invested was Berkshire Hathaway, a struggling New Bedford, Massachusetts textile manufacturer. Taking a special interest in that company, Buffett personally bought control of it, installed a new management (an unusual action for him), and acquired a second mill, in Manchester, New Hampshire. After the dissolution of the partnership, he slowly, over the years, built Berkshire Hathaway into a rich conglomerate with diversified holdings, including insurance companies, banks, steel service industries, and department and other retail stores as well as an apparel company. The textile operations became an ever less profitable facet of the enterprise, but Buffett kept the mills going as long as possible, despite stockholder opposition, because they were major employers in New Bedford and Manchester and many of the employees were too old for retraining. He did not close them down until 1985.

In the early 1970s Buffett began investing in news media and what he saw as an extension of that media, advertising agencies. Two of Berkshire Hathaway's early media acquisitions were the Omaha Sun (now defunct) and the Interpublic Group of Companies, the owner of the McCann-Erickson advertising agency. "Long ago," Carl Spielvogel, the chairman and chief executive officer of Backer & Spielvogel, the advertising agency, told Vartanig G. Vartan of the *New York Times* (March 20, 1985), "Warren [Buffett] identified communications companies as the bridge between the manufacturer and the consumer. These companies—newspapers and the rest of the media—have taken the place of what was once personal selling." Vartan quoted David S. Gottesman, a managing partner of the First Manhattan Company and a friend of Buffett's for two decades: "Warren understood the concept of the media business way back then, and he was virtually alone. He saw what many of us failed to see, namely the advantage of a good franchise and the potential for growth. Furthermore, he has great discipline as to what represents value."

Beginning in 1973 Berkshire Hathaway Inc. began buying into the Washington Post Company, ultimately acquiring 13 percent of that company's stock, which increased in value from approximately $11.6 million to more than $250 million today. In the low-profile manner that has always been his wont, Buffett has been, in the words of a former Post executive, the "financial guru" of Katharine Graham, the chairman of the Post company, and a mentor to Donald Graham, Mrs. Graham's son, who succeeded his mother as publisher of the *Washington Post* newspaper. Buffett also bought 8 percent of the shares of Affiliated Publications, which owns the *Boston Globe*, for $3.5 million (now valued at $55.7 million), and 4 percent of Time Inc., the publisher of *Time* magazine and other national magazines and owner of several cable television enterprises, for $20.4 million (now valued at more than $52 million).

Outside of media, Buffett invested $60 million in the General Foods Corporation in 1983, when that corporation's stocks were depressed. "You've got strong brand names, you're selling three times earnings when other food companies are selling at six to seven times earnings, and you're loaded with cash," Buffett explained when Philip Smith, the president of General Foods, asked him why he was interested in the company. "If you don't know what to do with it, someone else will."

The personal touch that Buffett brings to investing was exemplified in his purchase of 90 percent of the stock in Omaha's Nebraska Furniture Mart in 1983. Buffett had been shopping on and off at the mart for years and admired the gritty industriousness of its nonogenarian owner, Rose Blumkin. "I would rate him the best," Mrs. Blumkin told Bernice Kanner for the *New York* profile of Buffett. "He hadn't been here in maybe seven, eight years when he walks in and says, 'Today is my birthday and I want to buy your store. How much do you want for it?' I told him $60 million [soon reduced to $55 million]. He goes, gets a check, and is back right away. He never brought no lawyers and never took inventory till a year later. His word is as good as gold." Mrs. Blumkin remained chairman of the company and in charge of its daily sales operation. Another such instance was Buffett's purchase of See's Candy Shops, a small San Francisco chain whose fudge he had been buying for years.

In the mid-1980s, as the Dow Jones average rose into the stratosphere and stayed there (before finally crashing in October 1987), Buffett stuck with his largest holdings but refrained from purchasing any new stock. Instead, he turned to bonds. In his 1985 annual report to Berkshire Hathaway shareholders he stunned his audience by revealing that he had spent $139 million on long-term bonds issued by the Washington Public Power Supply System (WPPSS), a nuclear power plant construction corporation in Washington state so notoriously trouble-ridden it had acquired the popular nickname "Whoops." In 1986 he bought an additional $700 million of medium-term tax-exempt bonds, which he considered the "least objectionable alternative" to stocks.

Buffett also turned to merger arbitrage, not in the conspiratorial and hostile manner of an Ivan Boesky but openly and in a friendly way. In 1985 he became involved in Capital Cities Communications' takeover of the American Broadcasting Companies, the media giant that includes the ABC television network. According to the agreement reached in March 1985 and effective in January 1986, Capital Cities bought ABC for $3.5 billion. By providing $517 million in financing to Capital Cities, Berkshire Hathaway became the owner of 18 percent of Capital Cities/ABC Inc., a percentage that gives Buffett voting control of the enterprise, if he chooses to exercise it (which would be a departure from his normal laissez-faire policy).

Buffett's investment in Capital Cities, the largest he has ever made, does not strictly conform to Benjamin Graham's value approach to portfolios, as Bernice Kanner pointed out in her New York article. "Cap Cities is not exactly a twenty-cent dollar—the kind of bargain investment Buffett traditionally favors," Miss Kanner wrote. "But then, twenty-cent dollars are getting harder to find. And in other ways this deal meets Buffett's usual criteria. ABC has a franchise—there are only three networks—and Buffett has been a longtime friend of Thomas Murphy, Cap Cities' cost-conscious chairman."

Threatened by the corporate raiders who had been taking over one giant American corporation after another, John Gutfreund, the chairman of Salomon Inc., the parent company of Salomon Brothers, Wall Street's largest investment banking house, responded favorably in September 1987 to Buffett's offer to buy a 12 percent stake in Salomon for $700 million. Ronald O. Perelman, the chairman of Revlon Inc., then outbid Buffett, offering to pay the same amount for a 10.9 share, but according to Bill Powell and Carolyn Friday of Newsweek (October 12, 1987), Gutfreund regarded Buffett as "the white knight."

The executives who work with Buffett appreciate his laissez-faire style. "I've invited him to sit on the board," Jack Byrne, the chief executive officer of Geico Corporation, the major property and casualty insurer, in which Buffett owns a third interest, told Bernice Kanner. "He won't. He won't even visit the company more than every fourteen or fifteen months, though once he's here with my managers, it's like plugging him in." Byrne described Buffett as the "perfect takeover insurance," explaining: "No one would ever make a run at us, because he has said—and backed it up through the years—that I am the only one to sell his stock. That kind of faith is unequaled in the business world." In her New York article Miss Kanner quoted John J. Burns Jr., an asset management executive who has worked with Buffett, as saying, "He's a straight shooter with great integrity and a blunt mind that cuts through the baloney." In the same source William Phillips, the chairman of Ogilvy & Mather International, the advertising agency, in which Buffett had a 9 percent investment until recently, was quoted: "Warren's kept his perspective clear by living in Omaha, away from it all, and looking at what's important rather than what's urgent or fashionable."

Buffett's annual reports to the Berkshire Hathaway shareholders are refreshingly honest, chatty, funny, and self-deprecating reckonings that have a cult following in the financial world. The reports are sprinkled with quotations or paraphrases from a range of sources including Goethe ("When ideas fail, words come in handy"), Pogo ("The future isn't what it used to be"), and Pascal ("All men's misfortunes spring from the single cause that they are unable to stay quietly in one room"). In the report issued in April 1985 Buffett cited Billy Rose on a disadvantage of overdiversification: "If you have a harem of forty women, you never get to know any of them very well."

Warren E. Buffett and Susan Thompson, a former cabaret singer, were married on April 19, 1952. They have three grown children: Susan, Howard, and Peter. According to John Train in his book on Buffett, The Midas Touch (1987), the investor and his wife are amicably separated, and Buffett lives with Astrid Menks, his housekeeper/companion, in the three-story house he bought in Omaha in 1958, a mile and a half from his tiny, spartan office. In the office he is assisted by five employees, who keep records and file reports without the aid of calculators and computers. The calculator is Buffett himself, who has an amazing ability to do complicated mathematical figuring in his head. For a man of his net worth (which, according to estimates, is approaching a billion dollars), he is unusually frugal, as averse to unnecessary interior decoration as he is to what he calls the "hokum" of most stockholder relations.

Buffett is described by friends, associates, and interviewers as a genial man with a folksy manner who does not smoke and who prefers cherry-flavored Coca-Cola or Pepsi-Cola to alcoholic drinks. He is a voracious reader of newspapers, business publications, corporate reports, and nonfiction books on a variety of subjects. For recreation he plays golf and bridge, and he used to play racquetball before he suffered a back injury a few years ago. Within his close circle of friends are Katharine Graham, the chair of the Washington Post Company, Laurence Tisch, the entertainment conglomerate tycoon, and the octogenarian Joseph Rosenfield, the retired department store entrepreneur.

Politically, Buffett is a middle-of-the-road Democrat who contributes to various population-control and nuclear nonproliferation causes as well as the Pugwash Movement, which promotes better relations between the United States and the Soviet Union. Berkshire Hathaway charity money goes to a variety of beneficiaries chosen by the stockholders, including St. Cecilia's elementary school in Omaha's inner city and the Rhino Rescue Trust. According to Jaclyn Fierman in Fortune (October 12, 1987), Buffett plans to leave most of his money to charities, partly because he believes, in her paraphrase, that "wealthy parents can help children live up to their potential" if they "don't leave it all to the kids."

References: Fortune 111:3+ Ap 29 '85 por, 115:7 Ap 27 '87 por; N Y Times D p1+ Mr 20 '85 por; New York 18:52+ Ap 22 '85 por; Newsweek 105:56 Ap 1 '85 por, 110:66 O 12 '87 por; Train, John. The Midas Touch (1987); Who's Who in America, 1986-87

Calero (Portocarrero), Adolfo
(kä-lä´ rō)

1932(?)- Nicaraguan rebel leader. Address: c/o Fuerzas Democráticas Nicaragüenses, Tegucigalpa, Honduras

Described in Newsweek (March 2, 1987) as "the most powerful Contra warlord," Adolfo Calero remains a leading figure in the struggle by United States-supported rebels to overthrow Nicaragua's Marxist Sandinista regime, though his influence has been on the decline because of his hardline conservatism, allegations of corruption, and a shifting balance of power within the administration of President Ronald Reagan. Stung by the Iran-Contra affair and hampered by a liberal-dominated Congress in his effort to provide military aid for the Contras, President Reagan has tried to find a politically more palatable solution to the Nicaraguan imbroglio. Responding to none too subtle pressure from the United States State Department, Calero resigned in February 1987 as a member of the three-man directorate of the Union Nicaragüense de Oposición (UNO), the fractious umbrella organization of anti-Sandinista groups. Nevertheless, he remains a powerful figure within the Nicaraguan exile community because of his leadership of the Honduras-based Fuerzas Democráticas Nicaragüenses (FDN), the largest and most important of the Contra guerrilla armies.

Despite his high media profile, Adolfo Calero Portocarrero remains a shadowy figure. He was born in Nicaragua about 1932 to well-to-do parents who sent him to the United States to be educated. He graduated from the University of Notre Dame in 1953 with a degree in business administration and then went on to do graduate work in industrial management at Syracuse University in the state of New York. Returning to his native country, Calero earned a law degree from the Universidad Centroamericana in Managua.

Calero's involvement in politics dates from the 1950s, when he became active as an organizer for the Partido Conservador Nicaragüense (Nicaraguan Conservative party). During that period he entered the hotel business in Managua, eventually becoming the owner of several hotels. He also served for a time as director of the local chamber of commerce and as a member of the national development organizations known as INDE and FUNDE, and he helped to found the Human Development Institute in his country. In the late 1950s Calero became manager of the Nicaraguan subsidiary of the Coca-Cola Company, and under his supervision its bottling plant, which handled other soft drinks in addition to Coca-Cola, prospered.

The Pulitzer Prize-winning New York Times foreign affairs reporter Shirley Christian, who came to know Calero while she was based in Managua in the late 1970s, described him in her book Nicaragua: Revolution in the Family (Random House, 1985) as "a favorite dispenser of news, opinion, and gossip to diplomats and journalists." Politically well-connected, Calero was a close personal friend of Pedro Joaquín Chamorro, editor of the daily La Prensa, who was one of the most influential conservative critics of the regime of dictator Anastasio Somoza Debayle. Furthermore, Calero was on speaking terms with Somoza himself, despite the fact that in 1959 he had helped Chamorro to organize antigovernment strikes by Nicaraguan businessmen.

As opposition to Somoza escalated dramatically in the 1970s, demands for political reforms by Chamorro and Calero helped to bring about a split in conservative ranks. In 1970 Calero had been offered a seat as an alternate in the congress, Nicaragua's national legislature, as part of an agreement between Somoza and the Conservative party leader Fernando Aguero, but he rejected it and helped to organize the Partido Conservador Auténtica (Genuine Conservative party). In 1978 Calero became his party's representative in the new Frente Amplio de Oposición (Broad Opposition Front), an umbrella group that called for Somoza's resignation and the establishment of a government of national unity.

Meanwhile, plans for reconciliation talks among the quarreling right-wing factions had been interrupted when Chamorro was assassinated on January 16, 1978. Suspecting that Somoza's gunmen had been responsible for the murder, Calero responded quickly by helping to organize an anti-government protest strike that dragged on for three weeks, closing an estimated 80 percent of stores and factories in the country's major cities. Although Somoza survived the crisis, it soon became clear that his days in power were numbered. Faced with near anarchy in the streets, a growing military presence of the leftist Frente Sandinista de Liberación Nacional (FSLN), or Sandinist National Liberation Front, and the erosion of his popularity among his trusted national guard and conservative supporters, Somoza, in desperation, began to arrest even his most moderate opponents.

In the days from September 2 to 5, 1978, Somoza imprisoned about 600 persons, including Calero and some sixty other key opposition business and political leaders. It was only after Somoza met with President Jimmy Carter's special envoy William Jorden on September 28 in Managua that he reluctantly agreed to free Calero and six other leading conservative critics. Calero's importance as a leading opposition spokesman was reinforced in March 1979, when he was named the leader of the Partido Conservador Demócrata (Democratic Conservative party), a reform-minded coalition composed of three right-of-center political groups.

In failing health and faced with the determined political opposition of left and right alike, Somoza finally fled to Miami on July 17, 1979, abandoning power to the leftist guerrillas of the FSLN. No sooner had the initial euphoria died down than many conservative and wealthy Nicaraguans who had gone along with the revolution became uneasy with the new regime's policies and its cordial relations with Cuba and the Soviet Union. Those who could do so, quietly began leaving the country. Optimistically believing that the situation would eventually improve, Calero chose not to join the exodus although, as Shirley Christian has pointed out, he made "no secret" of his distaste for the Sandinista government.

Calero continued to operate his soft drink bottling plant during that period, despite sugar rationing and bottle shortages. In fact, he actually expanded operations at a time when most other private companies were either stagnant or cutting back, leading some Sandinistas to hail him for showing faith in the country and the revolution. But, as politically active and outspoken as ever, Calero had become a thorn in the side of the FSLN leadership. In August 1981 he embarrassed the regime by writing a letter in behalf of his political party to foreign ministers of member nations of the Organization of American States (OAS), asking that the ministers convene a meeting of the international organization to deal with the Sandinista government's noncompliance with a 1979 pledge to allow political pluralism in Nicaragua. Calero reiterated his criticism of the regime's authoritarianism in September 1982, when he and José Castillo, another prominent conservative leader, addressed a long letter to the FSLN's nine-member directorate rejecting an invitation to meet and discuss their political differences. They maintained that there was

nothing to talk about until the regime honored its pledge to the OAS.

Two months later Calero incurred the wrath of President Daniel Ortega and other Sandinista leaders when he boldly proposed that the regime open formal negotiations with the armed Contra groups operating in exile. Ortega rejected the idea out of hand, aware of internal dissension within those exile groups, most of them backed by the United States Central Intelligence Agency. The extent of that disarray was made clear a few weeks later, when spokesmen for the Miami committee of the key Contra group Fuerzas Democráticas Nicaragüenses announced that José Francisco Cardenal and Mariano Mendoza had been replaced as leaders of the FDN by an eight-member directorate. Seven of the new directors were identified; the eighth remained anonymous, leading to speculation that it was Adolfo Calero.

Meanwhile, Calero and his wife were out of the country spending Christmas with relatives in Miami and New Year's Day in Costa Rica, visiting the owner of the bottling plant of which Calero was manager. Aware of persistent rumors that he was now persona non grata in Nicaragua and that he would be arrested on his return there, Calero appealed to the FSLN leadership for a safe-conduct guarantee. State security agents indirectly, but forcefully, answered his request when on January 27, 1983 they occupied Calero's home in Managua. A few weeks later they seized the Coca-Cola bottling plant.

Unable to return to Nicaragua, Calero toured FDN guerrilla camps in Honduras before going on to Washington, D.C., where he called a news conference to announce that he had joined the FDN leadership. The news was welcomed by many members of the Contra movement, since Calero was not the stereotypical bearded guerrilla and, as James Conaway observed in the Washington Post (February 4, 1984), his presence afforded "Third World politics . . . a corporate sheen." Contra leaders met in Tegucigalpa, Honduras, on October 7, 1983 to form a Nicaraguan government in exile, with Calero as president.

Encouraged, Calero set about broadening and strengthening his power base. He met in mid-October with Alfonso Robelo, one of the leaders of the Alianza Revolucionaria Democrática (ARDE), the Costa Rica-based guerrilla group headed by Edén Pastora, the former Sandinista leader known as Commander Zero. Relations between Pastora and Robelo had become strained, and Calero was hopeful of winning Robelo over to the FDN. Although that initiative met with only limited success, Calero did manage to smooth over relations with leaders of three smaller Contra groups, and on December 1, 1983 they met in Panama with Richard B. Stone, President Reagan's special envoy to Central America, and jointly asked him to arrange peace talks with the Sandinistas. "What we have is a conflict among Nicaraguans that has to be resolved by Nicaraguans," Calero explained. "We asked Mr. Stone to use his good offices to establish contacts, and he agreed to do so."

Meanwhile, the Contras, backed by $24 million in aid that had been approved by the United States Congress in September 1983, received yet another welcome boost in mid-January 1984. A presidential commission headed by former Secretary of State Henry A. Kissinger issued a report that indirectly endorsed continued American aid to the Contras as a means of pressuring the Sandinista government to negotiate with anti-Communist exiles. Calero now boasted that the NDF had 17,000 men under arms—largely peasants and workers and also including Miskito Indians from Nicaragua's northern coastal region. He denied that former members of Somoza's hated national guard constituted more than a minuscule portion of its ranks. True to his pledge of stepped-up military operations against the Sandinistas, the NDF, supported by the CIA, began in early 1984 to mine Nicaraguan seaports in what Calero said was an effort to halt the flow of Soviet arms and supplies to the Sandinistas.

Liberals in the United States Congress were not impressed by Calero's rhetoric, nor were they in favor of increased involvement in Central America, since memories of the Vietnam conflict were still all too vivid. As a result, Contra aid was officially cut off in June 1984, although funds amounting to $14 million were approved for the fiscal year beginning on October 1 on the stipulation that the money could not be spent unless Congress renewed approval after March 1, 1985. Frustrated, Calero termed that latest setback "a Communist victory," and he directed a vigorous lobbying campaign at liberals unfriendly to the Contra cause. He warned that if the rebels did not get renewed American military aid they might easily be routed by the Sandinistas, who had been well armed by the Soviet Union.

Unsuccessful in his efforts to obtain further United States government aid, Calero moved in a new direction, pursuing private funding. On January 31, 1985 FDN officials in Miami announced plans to issue interest-bearing bonds. The proposal ran into unexpected opposition from two liberal members of Congress, who introduced a bill to prohibit American citizens from donating money or supplies to the Contras if Congress voted against aid to them. Close on the heels of that development, in June 1985, despite President Reagan's spirited lobbying, Congress approved only a limited amount for "non-lethal" aid to the Contras. Denied adequate funding, the guerrilla movement floundered badly. The Union Nicaragüense de Oposición (UNO), a loosely structured umbrella organization of Contra groups formed in 1985, seemed to be on the verge of disintegrating in a welter of political and personality conflicts. Compounding Calero's problems was the fact that congressional investigators in the United States were now looking into allegations that he and other top NDF leaders were involved in illegal arms deals, drug trafficking, and international terrorism. Calero reacted angrily to the charges. "We welcome any investigation; let there be a thousand investigations," he said. "We have absolutely noth-

ing to hide." It was soon becoming evident that Calero's popularity within the Nicaraguan exile community had faded badly. Reagan administration officials, recognizing that fact, began quietly to search for a new, moderate Contra spokesman who would be more acceptable to both Congress and the American public.

It was against that grim backdrop that Calero, Arturo Cruz, and Alfonso Robelo, the three top UNO leaders, met in Miami in mid-May 1986 in a last-ditch attempt to resolve the critical differences between them. Robelo and Cruz, former Sandinistas who were generally considered to be politically moderate, were dissatisfied by what they regarded as Calero's unilateral control of the powerful FDN, which was seen by some critics as still dominated by former members of Somoza's national guard. Heightening the drama in Miami was the fact that in Washington, Congress was about to consider a $100-million Contra aid package proposed by President Reagan. "It is like three men sitting down to play poker," one United States official said of the Contra leaders' talks. "Calero has a stack of chips in front of him that reaches up to his shoulders. Cruz and Robelo have one chip each, and that makes for a difficult game."

Negotiations dragged on for twenty days, until Calero, Cruz, and Robelo surprised observers on May 20, 1986 by announcing that they had resolved their major differences. Under the terms of the agreement that was hammered out, Calero conceded to Cruz and Robelo greater power to name UNO officials, and all future decisions by the three-member directorate would be on a majority basis. The UNO had, for the time being, survived, and United States officials were relieved. Some of the satisfaction of the moment was, however, blunted when at the news conference announcing the agreement, Calero was served with a subpoena naming him in a $24 million federal court lawsuit filed in Miami by two American broadcast journalists based in Costa Rica. Tony Avigron of National Public Radio and his wife, Martha Honey, of ABC, accused Calero and other Contra leaders of smuggling cocaine to finance their military operations and of plotting terrorist acts in Central America.

As it turned out, the uneasy peace within the UNO hierarchy lasted only a few months. When Calero, Cruz and Robelo met again in Miami during the first week in October 1986, James LeMoyne reported in the New York Times (October 5, 1986) that "a furious struggle for political control" of the UNO appeared to be underway. The disagreement was over Calero's reluctance—or inability—to share power in the FDN with Cruz and Robelo. Calero's followers, mainly FDN field commanders, ill at ease about the idea of taking orders from former Sandinistas, formed an independent military command council as well as a new political wing they called the Nicaraguan Democratic Effort.

By January 1987 tensions among the Contra leaders had led to an impasse, with Cruz threatening to resign from the UNO directorate. Political observers pointed out that the loss of Cruz could permanently cripple White House efforts to secure congressional approval of additional Contra funding. To avert that possibility, Assistant Secretary of State Elliott Abrams met with Calero and reportedly suggested that his departure from the UNO would "be in the best interests of the movement at this time." In compliance with the suggestion, on February 16, 1987 Calero announced his resignation from the UNO, but not from the FDN, where the real power resided. Calero had made the decision, he explained, so as "not to be an obstacle." According to Newsweek (March 2, 1987), Washington's shift in support from Calero to Cruz "seemed to signal that the Contras' singleminded pursuit of military victory would be replaced by something like a two-track policy, with attention also given to the search for a political solution." The Reagan administration's move was sharply criticized by such right-wing stalwarts as Republican Senator Jesse Helms, who called Calero "the only person within the UNO who truly represents the freedom fighters."

Concurrent with the UNO's internal troubles and, in effect, spotlighting them was the deepening crisis in Washington, D.C., over the so-called Iran-Contra affair, involving secret and officially unauthorized sales, engineered by White House officials, of armaments to Iran and the diversion of some of the profits from that transaction to the Nicaraguan Contras. On May 20, 1987, Adolfo Calero appeared before a congressional panel investigating the affair. He testified that between July 1984 and March 1985, while Congress had officially cut off support for the Contras, "Country Two"—believed to be Saudi Arabia—had provided a total of $33.6 million in aid to the Nicaraguan rebels. Retired United States Air Force Major General Richard V. Secord, who had earlier appeared before the committee, had testified that the Contras received about $3.5 million from sales of arms to Iran, but Calero disputed this. He asserted that he had no idea where any of the money he had received had come from, and if there had been any Iranian money received by the Contras, it was at most $200,000. The rest, he alleged, had gone to Secord.

Calero also revealed to the panel that in mid-1985 he had provided former National Security Council aide Lieutenant Colonel Oliver L. North, who was his chief link with the White House, with some $90,000 in blank traveler's checks. The money was ostensibly intended to finance a secret operation to free kidnapped Americans in Lebanon. Congressional investigators discovered that about $25,000 worth of checks had gone toward that abortive scheme, while at least $2,440 had been cashed by North personally.

Despite protest demonstrations that marked his public appearances in the United States, Calero's testimony before the Iran-Contra hearings seemed, in fact, to boost his sagging fortunes, and, like North, he became something of an instant celebrity. On July 29, 1987, when he appeared in Chicago as guest of honor on an evening boat cruise on Lake Michigan organized by the United Republican Fund, 248 persons paid $35 each to "rub shoulders" with him. A week later he was one of the top Contra leaders invited to the White House to discuss with President Reagan ways of convincing Congress to renew aid to the Contras, scheduled to run out in September. In the words of Time (August 17, 1987), the Contra leaders were "blindsided" by news that the president, with the cooperation of House Speaker Jim Wright, had put forward a peace proposal at the same time that the leaders of the five Central American nations were considering a broad regional plan advanced by President Oscar Arias Sánchez of Costa Rica. Reagan's proposal called for an immediate cease-fire, dialogue between the Sandinistas and the Contras, and a reduction of the United States presence in the region. Skeptics dismissed the American plan as merely another attempt to influence Congress to renew Contra aid, while the Central American leaders simply chose to ignore it. Calero, for his part, served notice that the effectiveness of any peace plan would ultimately be determined by himself and other Contra leaders. "Any decision on a cease-fire would have to be either accepted or rejected by us," Calero said.

Adolfo Calero and his wife, María Lacayo de Calero, have a daughter and other relatives in Miami. His brother Mario served as procurement official for the Contras in New Orleans, according to a Playboy (October 1987) interview with Richard V. Secord, who expressed a somewhat negative view of the Contra leadership. Calero has been described as tall, articulate, and avuncular, with thinning silvery hair. According to James Conway, writing in the Washington Post, he was "wearing a three-piece pin-striper, a red, white, and blue tie, and a Notre Dame class ring" when he visited Washington, D.C., in February 1984. Before his departure from Nicaragua, Calero was, according to Shirley Christian, a genial bon vivant who "was highly visible . . . , went to lots of parties and all the embassy receptions, invited people to his beach house regularly, had an opinion on everything, was always available to journalists, and traveled abroad frequently. . . . He . . . knew such important things as whose ancestors were liberals and whose were conservatives, and who didn't keep up his dues at the country club. . . . "

References: U S Department of State Report CIS S381–28.10 p927+ Ap '85; Washington Post C p1+ F 4 '84 por; Christian, Shirley. Nicaragua: Revolution in the Family (1985)

Carter, Benny

Aug. 8, 1907– Musician; composer; arranger; bandleader; educator. Address: h. 8321 Skyline Dr., Los Angeles, Calif. 90046

As a bandleader, arranger, multi-instrumentalist, and composer, Benny Carter has been a shaper of jazz music for over half a century. He helped to launch the idiom's "golden age" in the 1930s, when he created one of history's most perfect and influential alto saxophone styles. His playing, razor-sharp, unpredictable, and tuneful at the most demanding tempos, provided altoists and other musicians with a vocabulary free of the sentimental devices that had begun to encumber some older approaches to improvisation. It also paved the way for Carter's groundbreaking arrangements, such as his 1930 version of "Keep a Song In Your Soul," and his original songs, such as "Lonesome Nights," written in 1933. These works, distinguished by lush reed section passages suspended over pulsing, four-beats-to-the-bar rhythms, became blueprints of the "swing" style that dominated jazz throughout the 1930s. They have become classics along with other Carter compositions, such as "When Lights Are Low" (1936) and "Melancholy Lullaby" (1939), which has been called "the loveliest of all the big band themes."

Throughout the 1930s and 1940s Carter organized big bands that had some of the function of musical academies for such now legendary members as Ben Webster and Sid Catlett. But Carter "never had any luck" with them financially, as one musician has recalled, and in 1946 he dissolved the last of them and began to concentrate almost exclusively on writing music for Hollywood films. He added composition for television to his activities in the late 1950s and also began to arrange and conduct for such singers as Ray Charles and Peggy Lee. In more recent years Carter has entered academia as a lecturer, at Princeton and other universities, and has reintegrated himself fully into the jazz world, producing a string of recording gems that include Further Definitions (1961) and Benny Carter: A Man and His Music (1986). Peter Watrous observed in the Village Voice (March 10, 1987) that throughout his career Carter has written "about paradise," offering "a haven for those who need it."

Bennett Lester Carter was born in New York City's San Juan Hill area, near the present location of Lincoln Center, on August 8, 1907, to Sadie (Bennett) Carter, who worked as a domestic, and Norrell Carter, who was employed variously as a janitor, night watchman, longshoreman, and postal clerk. Benny attended an integrated San Juan Hill elementary school that, he has said, "at least in the fighting, was free of prejudice. Blacks fought blacks, whites fought whites, and each group fought the other."

Carter's musical education began with piano lessons from his mother and one of his two older sisters when he was about ten years old. He afterwards studied with a private teacher for a year but then put music aside until he was fourteen, when his formal education ended with his expulsion from the eighth grade. Carter told Morroe Berger, Edward Berger, and James Patrick, the authors of the 1982 biography Benny Carter: A Life in American Music, that the expulsion marked the first time he had had trouble in school. "I had a fight with a kid," he told his biographers. "A teacher intervened to help him. He kicked me from behind as I was going down a staircase, calling me a dirty nigger. I turned and punched him. I was expelled on the spot, I guess, but I didn't mind much because by then I was engrossed in music." Carter's return to music was inspired by his wish to emulate a local trumpeter, Bubber Miley, and an older cousin, the Pittsburgh-based Theodore "Cuban" Bennett, who was "a fantastic trumpet player" and was stylistically ahead of his time, Carter told Stanley Dance, who quoted him in his The World of Swing (1963). Carter bought his first trumpet on a one-dollar weekly installment plan over a period of thirty-three weeks. On the weekend after finally bringing it home, however, he was disheartened by the difficulties of playing it. "When Monday came and I still couldn't play it," he told Josh Mills, as quoted in the New York Sunday News (July 11, 1976), "I took it back to the shop and traded it in for a [C melody] saxophone, because someone told me it was easier to learn. None of them, of course, are easy." Carter began to study intermittently with several saxophone teachers. He also practiced much of the time by himself, adopting as his early model the C melody saxophonist Frankie Trumbauer.

When his family moved from San Juan Hill to Harlem in 1923, in the midst of the cultural boom known as the "Harlem Renaissance," Carter was plunged into a "bubbling musical world," according to his biographers. His playing developed, and he began to be hired on a short-term basis by musicians such as the pianist Willie "the Lion" Smith, who in 1924 persuaded Carter to give up the C melody saxophone for the alto.

Carter flowered quickly as an altoist and began to be increasingly sought after by well-known bands. In 1925 he traveled to the all-black Wilberforce University in Ohio at the invitation of Horace Henderson, the brother of the New York bandleader Fletcher Henderson and the leader of his own Wilberforce-based band, the "Collegians." Carter's biographers stress that he went to Wilberforce as a "professional musician" though it has become a tradition for writers to assert that he went there intending to study theology. He left the Wilberforce campus for good in 1926, when the Collegians went on their annual summer tour.

In the next few years Carter played with a variety of bands, including Fletcher Henderson's, Charlie Johnson's, and, briefly, Duke Ellington's. His alto playing astonished his fellow musicians, and one called him "the greatest since high-button shoes." By this time Carter had begun seriously to arrange music. "I started off writing saxophone choruses, along the chord structures I knew the rhythm section would be playing," Carter told Stanley Dance. "From there on, I would take each part from an orchestration, put them on the floor and study them, part by part. . . . It was many years before I learned to make a score. I used to do each part for the orchestra. That was the hard way. So this was the meagre beginning, as I've heard somebody say!"

Two of Carter's earliest arrangements, of "Charleston Is the Best Dance After All" and "Easy Money," were recorded in 1928, by Charlie Johnson and Fletcher Henderson respectively. They "sound like a Carter solo harmonized in three or four parts," according to Morroe Berger and the co-authors of the Carter biography. Berger felt that the early arrangements for Henderson overemphasized the saxophone, failed to balance the orchestra's sections against each other, and were "lackluster."

This began to change when, in January 1930, Carter won one of the coveted places in the Fletcher Henderson orchestra. It was "the acid test," Carter has said, because the band was playing "the hardest music and the best music around." Carter passed his test, and during his subsequent fifteen-month tenure with Henderson he became widely known, alongside Duke Ellington's brilliant altoist Johnny Hodges, as one of the two great models of alto saxophone style of the era. For some he was *the* stylist.

As an arranger, meanwhile, Carter found a way to build on the work of his predecessor in the Henderson band, Don Redman. Gunther Schuller observed in his book *Early Jazz: Its Roots and Musical Development* (1968) that with his 1930 arrangement of "Keep a Song in Your Soul" Carter, emphasizing syncopation based on a four-beat bar rather than the traditional two-beat bar, forged the

"final key to the 'Henderson style'" and to the style of the incipient swing era. "Carter," Schuller wrote, "obviously has found the long-sought-after solution for making a section swing. . . . Once [a soloist] could detach himself from explicitly stating the four beats and thus get 'inside' the beats a vast field of rhythmic emancipation lay ahead." Carter's contribution to Henderson's band—the combination of his arranging triumphs and the spectacular lyricism of his own soloing—kept the unit in the front rank of early 1930s jazz, despite competition from the likes of Duke Ellington.

Carter left Fletcher Henderson's band in March 1931 and worked for five months in a band led by the drummer Chick Webb. He next directed McKinney's Cotton Pickers for eight months, taking time out to record his now classic "Blues in My Heart" as "King Carter" in 1931. In the following year he formed the first incarnation of "Benny Carter and his Orchestra" and recorded with the 1932 edition of the all-star Chocolate Dandies. In the next two years he assembled under his baton an extraordinarily gifted group of young musicians, including drummer Sid Catlett, saxophonists Ben Webster and Chu Berry, and pianist Teddy Wilson. "We broke our necks to get into Benny's band," trumpeter Doc Cheatham has said. Bassist Hayes Alvis later recalled working with Benny as "the happiest period" of his life and added, "If you are able to hold a chair with Benny, you are made. Every bandleader will hire you after you made the grade with Benny Carter."

Trombonist Dicky Wells traced the quality of Carter's bands to the leader's writing and his personal charisma. "His bands used to sound so good because of the book," Wells once said. "All he would ask you to do was play the notes. . . . If you accidentally played a wrong note he'd stop the band and ask you what note you played. 'The one on the paper,' you'd answer. 'You'd better look again,' he'd say. He was very well liked because he knew how to rub his men down, get what he wanted out of them, and leave them smiling."

In this period, Carter sang occasionally and recorded, using the clarinet, which he had first played in Charlie Johnson's band, and also the trumpet, which he had begun to study in earnest after being assured by Doc Cheatham that it would not upset his saxophone technique. One of his earliest recorded trumpet solos, on the Chocolate Dandies' recording of his composition "Once Upon a Time," is, according to his biographers, "one of the greatest . . . in jazz history." His clarinet seems to have been equally successful. Whitney Balliett asserted in the *New Yorker* (September 22, 1962) that "one of the persistent sorrows of jazz" is Carter's abandonment of that instrument after the 1930s. "Carter's clarinet on the celebrated Chocolate Dandies sides," Balliett continued, "has a timeless air. . . . These recordings suggest that Carter might easily have been *the* jazz clarinetist. . . . Like his saxophone, it offered the ideal sound for the instrument."

As an arranger Carter continued to make the ideal choices for the swing style. On his 1933 recording of his composition "Lonesome Nights," for instance, his famed "block chord" technique, in which for each of four saxophones he wrote parts that formed four-part chords, created a mesmerizing melodic depth without skipping a beat or diminishing the overall "swing." With that recording and another 1933 effort, "Symphony in Riffs," Carter became "the arranger everybody followed," according to Schuller. Despite these achievements and wide acclaim, Carter was forced at the end of 1934 to dissolve his band in the face of the economic crunch of the Great Depression. He then survived as a free-lance arranger and recording sideman.

In 1935 Carter was hired by the British Broadcasting Corporation as a staff arranger. His departure for England came at about the time of the unofficial launching of the "swing era" by Benny Goodman and his orchestra in a triumphant performance at Los Angeles' Palomar Ballroom. Some of Carter's arrangements, sold to Goodman and other bandleaders or traded between them, were important generating sparks in the swing boom. "Lonesome Nights," for instance, reappeared in Goodman's repertoire as "Take My Word." Playing it with the definitive instrumentation that had built Carter's big-band sound, Goodman defined his own sound to a significant degree. "In the background of every swing band," one big-band leader later testified, "there was a Benny Carter arrangement lurking some place."

Carter remained in Europe until 1938 and recorded twenty-six songs, many of them his own compositions, with the best British players. On those records, in addition to doing all the arrangements, Carter played trumpet, clarinet, alto and tenor saxophone, and piano. To such activities were added tours of mainland Europe, where everywhere he "met with resounding acclaim and did much to advance the cause of jazz," according to Edward Berger in the New Grove Dictionary of American Music (1980). A 1937 recording date in Paris with tenor saxophone giant Coleman Hawkins produced classic renderings of Carter's "Crazy Rhythm" (1937) and Fats Waller's "Honeysuckle Rose." Carter's alto solo on "Crazy Rhythm," according to Edward Berger, "presaged future developments on this instrument" with its "long lines, legato phrasing and understated attack."

Carter returned to America in 1938 and quickly put a big band together that appeared for the next three years at the Savoy ballroom in Harlem. He appeared elsewhere with smaller bands, one of which included the trumpeter Dizzy Gillespie—a leader of the controversial "bebop" revolution taking place in jazz at the time. Carter recounts complaints from one club owner about what "that trumpet player [was] playing," but he "ignored that, and Dizzy played" and became known to a widening audience. Conversely, Carter's saxophone style began to include bop nuances, though he used them in his own way, to coin musical "ideas . . .

as fresh as those of the modernists," in the phrase of Gary Giddins (Village Voice, July 5, 1976). In 1942 Carter organized a new big band and took it on tour to the West Coast. He brought along future greats of modern jazz, such as drummer Max Roach and trumpeter Miles Davis. He received a hero's welcome in the Los Angeles jazz community, where his band opened at Billy Berg's Swing Club. The band was booked into a steady stream of engagements through 1944, and one critic declared it the "most promising . . . since Count Basie came out of Kansas City."

Carter's musical conquest of Los Angeles reached the Hollywood studios when he was invited to work on the sound track for Stormy Weather (1943). Twentieth Century-Fox music department head, Al Newman, marveled at the fact that though Carter "hardly had any experience in string writing, and none in movie work . . . , he came up with some of the best string writing [Newman had] heard in years." At about this time Carter also cowrote a popular song, "Cow Cow Boogie," sung by Ella Mae Morse, which became such a hit that it helped to make Capitol Records solvent. During the rest of 1943 Carter contributed to the scores for such films as the Laurel and Hardy comedy Jitterbugs and Busby Berkeley's The Gang's All Here. In 1944 Carter appeared, along with his band, in MGM's Thousands Cheer, for which he also helped to arrange the score. Meanwhile, his big band continued to tour and to garner critical raves despite the fact that it was "in very bad shape financially," as Carter has recalled. He finally disbanded it in 1946, thinking that he "could put [the band] down and start again later, but [he] never did."

Settling in California, Carter concentrated on arranging and writing for the movie studios for the next decade, though he periodically led small groups in clubs and played on numerous sound tracks. By 1957 he had composed and arranged music for fifteen films, including the Marx Brothers' Love Happy (1950), and he had a small role in one of them, The Snows of Kilimanjaro (1952).

Carter used his success as one of the first black musicians to break into the lucrative film scoring market and, eventually, to be credited for his work, to open the door for other blacks, among them his former sideman J. J. Johnson. He also succeeded in using his influence to push successfully for the merging of the segregated Musicians' Union's white and black locals.

Carter participated in the jazz world mainly by leading small groups from time to time, touring with "Jazz at the Philharmonic"—an all-star package put together by impressario Norman Granz—and arranging for such singers as Sarah Vaughan, Louis Armstrong, Ella Fitzgerald, Carmen McRae, Peggy Lee, and Ray Charles. In 1963 one of the songs that Carter arranged for Charles, "Busted," became a tremendous hit and a Grammy-award winner.

Carter began writing for television in 1958. During the next thirteen years he wrote music for about ninety-five episodes of twenty series, including *M Squad*, *Bob Hope Presents the Chrysler Theater*, *Ironside*, *The Name of the Game*, *It Takes a Thief*, and *The Hanged Man*. Carter's wide-ranging activity in film and television writing moved Stanley Crouch to assert in the *Village Voice* (May 11, 1982) that "the substance and humor of his sensual serenades have indelibly textured American music."

Carter began gradually to increase his recording output in the late 1950s and early 1960s. During 1957 and 1958 he recorded the selections that appeared on *Benny Carter, Jazz Giant* (Contemporary Records, 1958). At this time he had begun to be seen largely as an historical presence in jazz because of his concentration on film and television work, but the critic Nat Hentoff, in his liner notes for the album, emphasized that "hearing Benny in this free context may . . . remind many of how influential a figure he is. . . . Benny's kind of statement doesn't disintegrate with changes in trends and styles."

Carter produced what many consider to be his finest album, *Further Definitions* (MCA), in 1962. Conceived in part as a reprise of their 1937 encounter in Paris, the album featured a new pairing of Carter and Coleman Hawkins. In his *New Yorker* article Whitney Balliett described Carter's solos on the record as "perhaps the freest, most jubilant he has recorded." Balliett cited in particular Carter's composition "Blue Star," which concluded with a long, written passage that was a "distillation of all his solos" and "close to a classic performance."

Carter's return to jazz was greatly accelerated in 1969, when he was first contacted by his future biographer, Morroe Berger, a Princeton sociologist who felt that Carter was "the one great contributor to jazz who has not received the kind of acclaim accorded to Duke Ellington and Louis Armstrong." Berger arranged for Carter to lecture at Baldwin-Wallace College in Berea, Ohio, in 1970. This led to his being invited to lecture regularly at other institutions, especially Princeton University, where he was a visiting professor in the fall of 1973 and the recipient in 1974 of an honorary Doctor of Humanities degree. In 1975 the United States State Department, at Berger's recommendation, sent Carter on a successful concert and lecture tour of the Middle East. On his return he recorded three new albums, *The King* (Pablo, 1976), on which he was reunited with Dizzy Gillespie for a series of brilliant duets, and, with Count Basie and his orchestra, *Basie Jam #2* (Pablo, 1977) and *Basie Jam #3* (Pablo, 1979). The *Village Voice*'s Gary Giddins spoke for many critics when he wrote that Carter "is back with a vengeance, playing not only as well as ever but better than usual."

Carter was booked for an extended engagement at a New York City establishment for the first time in thirty-four years when he appeared at Michael's Pub in 1976. Afterwards he returned regularly to New York clubs and East Coast jazz festivals, astonishing critics with the seemingly ceaseless evolution of his talents and moving John S. Wilson to declare him a perennial "giant among giants" in an article in the *New York Times* (April 17, 1981). The all-star American Jazz Orchestra—organized by Gary Giddins with the aim of keeping jazz classics current through live performance—saluted Carter's music, with Carter himself conducting and playing, at the Great Hall of New York City's Cooper Union in February 1987. The critics hailed Carter's razor-sharp conducting and his soaring trumpet and alto saxophone playing. The concert's climax was provided by Carter's "Central City Sketches," a five-part suite he had written for the occasion that was variegated in tempo and "sumptuous," according to one reviewer. "Few concerts of great expectations are packed with the fulfillment that Benny Carter provided . . . ," Stuart Troup observed in *Newsday* (February 28, 1987). Carter's recent recordings, such as *Benny Carter: A Gentleman and His Music* (1986), have also dazzled the critics. Kevin Whitehead, in his May 1986 review of the album in *Downbeat*, could only conclude that the creativity of Benny Carter "—like the progress of the stars—[defies] easy explanation."

In *Jazz Masters of the Thirties* Rex Stewart described Benny Carter as a man "of imposing stature" with a "deceptively mild" countenance and a "gentility [that] almost seems out of a forgotten age." He added that Carter's "ready wit, smile, his soft, quick speech also give slight indication of the iron will encased in his brilliant mind." Carter was first married in 1925, to Rosa Lee Jackson, who died of pneumonia three years later. He and Margaret Johnson, whom he married in California in 1956, were divorced in 1978. He resides with his present wife, Hilma Ollila Arons Carter, in a large home on a Hollywood hill.

Carter received an award from the Académie du Disque in France in 1976 for his album *The King*. Among his numerous other awards he especially prizes a cup he won for leading the Wilberforce Collegians to victory in a battle of the bands with McKinney's Cotton Pickers in 1928. Carter, who says he reveres the past but does not "want to live in it," has filled his schedule well in advance with bookings for jazz festivals and concert dates in Europe, Japan and the United States. His leisure-time pursuits include a continuing self-education in music and in other areas.

References: N Y Sunday News III p13 Jl 11 '76 por; N Y Times C p17 Je 5 '86 por; New Yorker 38:49 S 22 '62, 52:65 Jl 5 '76; Newsday II p37 Ap 29 '82 por; Village Voice p65 My 11 '82; Berger, Morroe, and others. Benny Carter: A Life in American Music (1982); Dance, Stanley. The World of Swing (1963); Stewart, Rex. Jazz Masters of the Thirties (1982)

Cerezo (Arévalo), (Marco) Vinicio
(se-rā´-sō)

Dec. 26, 1942– President of Guatemala. Address:
b. Oficina del Presidente, Guatemala City,
Guatemala

"We have gone almost six months in Guatemala without a serious rumor of a coup d'etat," President Vinicio Cerezo joked in July 1986. "It's almost getting boring." His humor, however, seemed bittersweet. Cerezo, who was inaugurated in January 1986, is the first elected civilian to lead Guatemala since the military seized power there in 1970 and only the second in some thirty years. His accession to office has stirred hopes that democracy will take root in that Central American nation and that political violence, which has left thousands murdered or missing, will fade away. But observers are aware that the army and the wealthy still hold much of the real power in oligarchic Guatemala, and that the self-described "moderate leftist" president can push reform only so far without risking the overthrow of his government.

Moreover, Guatemala's new president inherited a backlog of grave economic problems. About half the country's income from exports goes to pay off the country's $2.5 billion foreign debt. Some 50 percent of the nation's population is jobless or underemployed, and inflation has been a major problem.

Relatively little is known about the youth and early career of Marco Vinicio Cerezo Arévalo. The son of Marco Vinicio Cerezo Sierra and Esperanza Arévalo de Cerezo, he was born on December 26, 1942, into a family distinguished both for its public service and for its resistance to Guatemalan dictators. His father was a member of the nation's Supreme Court; his uncle, Celso Cerezo, was, in the 1940s, the youngest member of Guatemala's first freely elected Congress; his grandfather reportedly was poisoned in retaliation for opposing the dictator Jorge Ubico; and his great-grandfather was wounded in an attempt to overthrow an earlier dictator, Manuel Estrada Cabrera, in 1921.

Cerezo was twelve years old when the United States Central Intelligence Agency sponsored its 1954 overthrow of the elected socialist government of Jacobo Guzmán Arbenz. After the coup, Cerezo's father was dismissed from the Supreme Court and spent several months in jail. It was at that time that Cerezo committed himself to a political career. "We lost a sense of liberty and of law," Cerezo recalls. "I decided then to try to get it back." He pursued his law studies at the University of San Carlos in Guatemala City, and while there joined the Christian Democratic party, in part, he says, because that organization was not bound by a rigid political doctrine. By the mid-1960s Cerezo and his youthful allies had taken over the Christian Democrats, and he became the chief organizer for the party as well as general secretary of its student organization. Later he represented it at various European and Latin American meetings. After qualifying as a lawyer in 1968, Cerezo went on to earn a master's degree in public administration two years later. He also studied political science at Loyola University in New Orleans, and he undertook additional studies in Venezuela, Chile, West Germany, and Italy.

In 1974 Cerezo won election to the Guatemalan Congress, but in a disputed and possibly fraudulent election four years later, he lost a race for the mayoralty of Guatemala City. Life soon became dangerous for the young reformer. While General Fernando Romeo Lucas García held control of the government between 1978 and 1982, Cerezo survived three assassination attempts. The first took place in January 1980, when snipers engaged Cerezo and his bodyguards in a ten-minute gun battle outside the offices of the Christian Democrats. After that incident, he sent his wife and four children to live in Washington, D.C. During the next five years he kept alive by staying on the move, changing residences approximately twenty-five times.

Cerezo's precarious existence typified Guatemalan political life in recent decades. After the last civilian president left office in 1970, the army tightened its already iron grip on the nation's politics. Violence increased dramatically while the military carried out operations against leftist insurgents in the following years. The army and other elements of the nation's security forces engaged in assassination, torture, and kidnapping, and they often looked the other way when independent rightwing "death squads" took action against almost anyone suspected of opposing the interests of the wealthy private businessmen and landowners who sponsored them. At the same time, the guerrillas were meting out their own version of justice as well. The Rand Corporation estimates that as many as 30,000 Guatemalans died in politically related violence between 1966 and 1982, and some human rights groups allege that 50,000 died in the first half of the 1980s. According to Americas Watch, 38,000 Guatemalans have vanished since 1954, and their number accounts for 42 percent of all Latin American *desaparecidos* (those who have disappeared) in that period.

Guerrilla forces, organized in four major groups, have an estimated 2,000 to 3,000 armed combatants operating primarily in the rural areas where 61 percent of Guatemalans—half of them Indians—dwell. Their retaliatory attacks, according to a Western intelligence official, have been aimed at the army, security forces, and civil patrols. In November 1980 the four rebel groups combined under an umbrella organization called Guatemalan National Revolutinary Unity, and they are beginning to increase their ability to launch terrorist attacks.

Guatemala's violence alienated the nation's allies, and in 1977 President Jimmy Carter suspended credits for American military aid to Guatemala. That disorder, combined with widespread corruption, also threatened to lead to the economic collapse of the country, which had been the most prosperous in Central America as recently as 1969. The guerrilla war forced an increase of 600 percent in government expenditures between 1973 and 1981, and because Guatemala had almost no taxation, its leaders financed the spending by means of high-interest, short-term loans. Guatemala could still hope to rescue its economy by restructuring its loans to allow for a longer repayment period, but in 1984 the International Monetary Fund had suspended its agreement with the nation because of its failure to meet certain economic goals.

By 1982 some younger officers in the Guatemalan army had come to recognize the perilous course their nation was following. When General Lucas attempted to impose his defense minister as the country's new president, they stepped in to nullify the rigged election. They named as the new president Efraín Ríos Montt, a retired general who had been cheated out of that office in the 1974 election. When the evangelistically religious and eccentric Ríos Montt began a crackdown on corruption and promised agrarian reform, however, the Guatemalan defense minister, General Oscar Mejía Víctores, overthrew him on March 23, 1983. Nevertheless, Mejía continued his predecessor's pledge to hold free elections. According to most observers, Mejía and his supporters hoped that a restoration of at least the trappings of democracy would win the outside support needed to keep Guatemala afloat.

Plans for the restoration of civilian rule in Guatemala led to the election of a constituent assembly in 1984 and to a call for a presidential election in 1985. The preliminary round of the latter contest took place on November 3, 1985, with Cerezo and Jorge Carpio Nicolle as the leading contenders. Cerezo's Christian Democrats had the backing of the liberal wing of both the Catholic Church and the army, as well as financial support from the Coordinating Committee of Agricultural, Commercial, Industrial and Financial Associations (CACIF), the organization representing Guatemala's oligarchy. Carpio, a wealthy businessman and newspaper publisher, seen as the "Reaganomics" candidate of the new right, led the National Union of the Center, which he had founded two years earlier. The right-wing National Liberation Movement and a conservative coalition of the Revolutionary party and the Democratic Party of National Cooperation also put forward strong candidates, while representatives of several weaker factions completed the field. Political terror during the Lucas government had previously taken the lives of the country's two leading civilian politicians—the former Foreign Minister Alberto Fuentes Mohr, who was machine-gunned to death in 1979 as he drove by a military base in Guatemala City shortly after registering his new Social Democratic party, and Manuel Colóm Argueta, a former mayor of the capital, who was killed two months later, after having registered his own new center-left party.

With 39 percent of the vote in the eight-candidate race, Cerezo established a commanding lead over his chief rival, who managed to win only 20 percent of the ballots cast in the November election. Carpio, however, rejected Cerezo's contention that another election would "only be a formality," and refused the Christian Democrat's suggestion that he withdraw from a second election, which the failure of any single candidate to win a majority had made legally necessary. In the ensuing campaign, Carpio accused Cerezo of being a leftist, but the latter's prediction of easy victory proved true. On December 8, Cerezo took 68.4 percent of the valid votes to defeat Carpio by a landslide margin of 1,133,517 to 524,306, polling more votes than any other candidate in the history of Guatemala.

On January 14, 1986, Vinicio Cerezo took the oath of office as Guatemala's president before a jubilant crowd in the National Theatre. To mark the occasion, his wife, who had constantly worn some black during the campaign as a symbol of mourning for Guatemala's dead, dressed in a bright white suit. Although the tone of his inaugural address was somber, his words also conveyed a message of hope. "No leader of this nation has ever taken over a country in worse condition," he said. "We are in a terrible crisis." He warned his countrymen that a period of "great austerity and great sacrifice" would follow. Referring to the transition to civilian rule, he said, "We are a people that has been thrown out of its house. Today we are coming back to it."

Thus far, Cerezo has followed a cautious course, having recognized from the beginning that there are real limits on what he can hope to accomplish. Before taking office, he predicted, "In the first six months I'll have 30 percent of the power. In the first two years I'll have 50 percent, and I'll never have more than 70 percent of the power during my five-year term." Guatemala's army and wealthy elite will allow him to go only so far. Cerezo admits that, as president, he can imprison army officers and seize the lands of the rich only at his own risk, but, he contends, "there are other fundamental things" on which he can work—"the respect for the law, not killing people, only arresting someone for cause and not outside the law, promoting a fiscal reform to allow public investment in health and education." One important step he has taken is the legalization of labor unions, allowing workers to organize and conferring on them the right to strike. Unions had been fiercely repressed under successive military regimes, and many of the "missing" have been union organizers.

The Reagan administration has thus far exhibited a coolness towards Cerezo, primarily because he refuses to collaborate with any campaign against the Nicaraguan Sandinistas. "Guatemala will not be an instrument of the U.S. in Central America," he has declared, and he has refused to endorse "violent solutions" to problems involving Nicaragua. In an official rebuff, President Ronald Reagan failed to attend Cerezo's inauguration (he was meeting with the conservative Ecuadorian president on that day instead) and sent Vice-President George Bush to Guatemala City in his place. Furthermore, the $77 million in economic aid and $10.3 million in military aid proposed for Guatemala by the Reagan administration is the smallest amount planned for any Central American republic, although Guatemala is the largest and most populous country in the region.

Cerezo describes his foreign policy as an "active neutrality" designed to bring Guatemala out of its isolation. He has tried to keep alive the Contadora plan for peace in Central America, on which Colombia, Mexico, Panama, and Venezuela have been conferring since 1983. To that end, Cerezo acted as the host of a regional summit meeting attended by the presidents of Costa Rica, El Salvador, Honduras, and Nicaragua in the Guatemalan town of Esquipulas in May 1986. His efforts did not achieve the goal of having the Contadora treaty signed by June 6, but the participants agreed to continue their dialogue. They also endorsed Cerezo's proposal for the creation of a Central American parliament whose seat would rotate among Costa Rica, El Salvador, Guatemala, Honduras, Nicaragua, and Panama.

The president has made only limited progress against the political violence that claimed as many as 700 Guatemalan lives during his first six months in office. Observers also believe that right-wing groups are becoming more active in order to undermine the new democratic government. In the countryside the army's campaign against supposed subversives has continued, and guerrilla activity has intensified. Rebel leaders, some of whom Cerezo knew in his student days, have indicated their willingness to engage in negotiations in Guatemala City under the auspices of the Spanish or Mexican embassies, but Cerezo has said that talks and amnesty must wait "until we have reestablished the rule of law" and until the rebels have put down their weapons and have become part of the political process.

Although the army's former chief of staff, General Rodolfo Lobos Zamoro, described by GAM as one of the "intellectual authors" of Guatemala's political violence, was in line for the post of minister of defense, Cerezo prevented his installation and named, instead, one of his own allies, General Jaime Hernández, former chief of the country's honor guard. But Cerezo's ability to control the army is limited by a series of decrees promulgated by his predecessor four days before the inauguration, legalizing military control of the countryside, limiting the jurisdiction of civilian cabinet members over security concerns, and prohibiting prosecution of military officers for any political crimes committed during the previous four years.

Perhaps one of the greatest challenges facing the new president is the one posed by the relatives of those who have disappeared. In 1983 distraught family members formed the Mutual Support Group for the return of missing relatives (GAM), the only surviving human rights group in Guatemala. In April 1985 two of its organizers were killed. Héctor Gómez, a baker active in the GAM, was abducted as he left a meeting, and his body was found the next day with its tongue cut out. Five days later, another GAM leader, Rosario Godoy de Cuevas, who had spoken at the Gómez funeral, was snatched from a shopping center with her brother and her two-year-old son. Her raped and mutilated body was found in her car; the baby's fingernails had been torn out.

Unhappy with Cerezo's acceptance of the Mejía decrees, the organization, which has as its spokeswoman Nineth de García, has been pressing for the investigation and prosecution of those responsible for the kidnappings. Cerezo maintains that prosecution is a function of the courts and not of the president, although under the constitution, written during Mejía's regime, civilian courts have no power to try military personnel. At the time of his election, Cerezo promised GAM that he would establish a government commission to investigate the cases of the disappeared, but he reversed that commitment in the summer of 1986, and a commission has not yet been formed.

On February 4, 1986, Cerezo had a special police battalion seize the offices of the Department of Technical Investigations (DIT), whose members are believed responsible for many of the political killings and kidnappings in Guatemala. Of the 600 members in the security force, 115 were immediately dismissed, while the remainder were offered the opportunity to be retrained for new jobs in the National Police. Cerezo, however, has been unable to take action against the military's feared intelligence branch, G-2, which keeps files on alleged subversives and whose 2,000 agents have been implicated in widespread assassinations. In addition, there are several private death squads, such as the *Mano Blanco* (White Hand) and the Secret Anti-Communist Army, which are financed by right-wing Guatemalan businessmen. Nineth de García has called the dissolution of the DIT "a diversionary tactic that changes nothing."

Cerezo's plans for Guatemala's economic recovery focus on export-led growth. He has devalued the Guatemalan quetzal and streamlined the regulations controlling exports. To raise money for the government, he has imposed new taxes, including a 30 percent impost on coffee exports. The freeze that hurt Brazil's coffee crop has raised prices for the crop and has mitigated the impact of the tax. But Cerezo has warned the nation's businessmen that their acceptance of levies to meet urgent needs is the only way to avoid a confrontation with the masses unable to obtain work or food. On the other hand, Cerezo's removal of controls on the prices of many basic goods combined with the devaluation of the currency to raise the cost of living index by 37 percent in the first quarter of 1986.

In perhaps his boldest move to date, Cerezo has begun to address Guatemala's pressing land question. Fewer than 1 percent of its people own over one-third of its land, and many Guatemalans starve while vast tracts of land go uncultivated. When 20,000 landless peasants marched in protest before the National Palace in May 1986, Cerezo came out to join them and declared that "your presence here with me is a message to all those who have benefited from the riches of our country. . . . All we ask is that they remember that we exist, that we have needs and that we want to grow food so we can have more to share with everyone." Four months later the president, who had pledged to CACIF not to pursue land reform, called for a program of "rural development" that would not touch private property but would instead distribute government-owned, unused land to migrant farm workers.

During 1987 Guatemala continued to be faced by economic problems, crime, political violence, labor unrest, and the ever-present threat of the powerful army. On the other hand, the Cerezo government could claim credit for a successful economic stabilization program. The inflation rate, which stood at 40 percent in 1983, was reduced to about 13 percent by the spring of 1987, while the gross national product was on the upswing. In October the Cerezo government instituted negotiations with leftist rebels to end a twenty-five-year conflict and introduced substantial increases in business taxes.

On his first state visit to Washington, D.C., in May 1987, Cerezo asked President Ronald Reagan to consult with Central American leaders in the formulation of United States policy toward Nicaragua. "The administration has to take the views of Central American countries seriously," he asserted, "because we are going to suffer the consequences of American policy."

On August 7, 1987, at a summit meeting in Guatemala City, Cerezo and the four other Central American presidents signed a regional peace pact encompassing the main points of a plan put forward in February by President Oscar Arias Sánchez of Costa Rica. It called for cease-fires in all conflicts in the region, expansion of civil liberties and other democratic reforms, an end to outside aid to insurgents, and a promise to hold free elections. It differed from a proposed plan announced a few days earlier by President Ronald Reagan, which placed greater demands on Nicaragua's Sandinista government and left the door open for United States aid to the Contra rebels. "It's a long road to build peace," Cerezo said of the Arias plan, which subsequently earned its author the Nobel Peace Prize. "Today in Guatemala we can affirm that Utopia is starting to become a reality." Addressing the UN General Assembly on September 22, 1987, Cerezo called on the United States and other nations to respect the wishes of Central American leaders and support the peace plan.

Many experts agree that if his government is to be viable, Cerezo will have to strike a balance between the strong competing interest groups in his country. As William Walker, a State Department deputy assistant secretary for inter-American affairs has expressed it, "The new president will have some very, very tough decisions to make and some very delicate relationships to work on. But if anyone stands a chance of pulling it off, it is someone like him."

Since 1965 Vinicio Cerezo has been married to the former Raquel Blandón. They met as students at a demonstration in front of the National Palace, when he rescued her from the police as they attempted to seize her for burning a copy of a controversial election law. Supporters describe the president's wife, who is a law professor and an active Christian Democrat, as a brilliant thinker, and critics call her a leftist. She declares herself "the people's advocate," and some compare her to Argentina's Eva Perón. Cerezo and his wife are the parents of four children; their oldest son, Marco Vinicio, attends the Sorbonne in Paris, while his two brothers, Carlos Rafael and Alexi Mauricio, and his sister, Quetzali Raquel, are students in Washington, D.C.

President Cerezo has curly dark hair, a moustache, and a flashing smile. Informal by choice, he frequently wears denim jackets and prefers to be called "Vinicio." Trim and athletic, Cerezo has served as a diving instructor, and he is a founding member of a football team at the University of San Carlos. He holds a black belt in karate, which he says he practices for "personal discipline" rather than for self-defense. For the latter he depends on bodyguards and on the pistol he constantly carries in his shoulder holster. "The only way they are going to get me out of the palace," he has said, "is to carry me out dead."

References: Insight p26+ Ja 20 '86 pors; N Y Rev of Bks 33:39+ Ag 14 '86; N Y Times A p3 D 10 '85 por; N Y Times Mag p32+ N 9 '86 pors; Time 126:60 N 18 '86 por; International Who's Who, 1987–88

Chamberlain, Richard

Mar. 31, 1935– Actor. Address: b. c/o Creative Artists Agency, 1888 Century Park East, Suite 1400, Los Angeles Calif. 90069

NOTE: This biography supersedes the article that appeared in Current Biography in 1963.

Over the course of a career that has spanned three decades, Richard Chamberlain has metamorphosed from a teenage heartthrob, as the young hero of the television series Dr. Kildare, into the undisputed "king of prestige television," as the star of many award-winning made-for-television movies and miniseries. Two of those miniseries were among the most popular in the history of television, Shōgun and The Thorn Birds. Believing that "one must never allow oneself to become comfortable," as he once expressed it, Chamberlain left the relative security of Hollywood in the mid-1960s to perfect his craft in Britain, where he became, in 1969, the first American actor since John Barrymore to play Hamlet on the British stage. On his return to the United States, he distinguished himself in theatrical productions of such classics as Richard II and Cyrano de Bergerac, among other plays, before taking on an ambitious variety of roles, ranging from Lord Byron to King Edward VIII to the American explorer John Charles Frémont, in film and television. "The fun of acting is playing different parts, being different people," Chamberlain has explained, as quoted in the Los Angeles Times (March 16, 1980). "If you're just going to play one part all your life, you might as well sell insurance."

George Richard Chamberlain was born in Los Angeles, California, on March 31, 1935, the second of the two sons of Elsa and Charles Chamberlain,

who owned a small plant that manufactured supermarket fixtures. Reared in what he would later describe as "a highly predictable middle-class atmosphere" in nearby Beverly Hills, Chamberlain attended the local public schools, but because of a dyslexic condition, he dreaded his classes. As he told Charles Higham in an interview for the Saturday Evening Post (April 1974), it was not until his late teens that he "learned the pleasure of study."

After he graduated from Beverly Hills High School, Chamberlain enrolled at Pomona College, a small liberal arts college in Claremont, California, where he majored in art. In his spare time, he was a sprinter on the college track team and a bit player in campus productions of such plays as King Lear, Arms and the Man, and The Lady's Not For Burning, even though he was, by his own account, a "simply terrible actor." He recalled his college days in an interview for TV Guide (March 16, 1963): "I was a hermit. I sat in my little room and I painted pictures. I was in some sort of a cocoon. . . . Then I discovered acting. The stage seemed like a place where you could escape from the cocoon. It seemed like a place where you could be free. Free to express your emotions . . . free to move . . . free to shout. It seemed like a way to have fun without getting involved in real life."

Shortly after receiving his B.A. degree in art from Pomona College in 1956, Chamberlain was drafted into the United States Army. He spent most of the next two years in Korea, serving as a company clerk. Discharged from the military with the rank of sergeant in 1958, he returned to the Los Angeles area and began taking acting, singing, and dancing lessons in the hope of taking up a theatrical career. To pay for his classes, he worked at a series of odd jobs, including chauffeur, supermarket clerk, and construction worker. While he continued his training, he doggedly made the rounds of theatrical and motion picture agents and producers, but as he told one reporter, he would invariably "freeze up" during interviews and auditions. Late in 1959 he finally landed his first paying job as an actor—a bit part in an episode of the hit television series Gunsmoke. He then secured small parts in segments of the TV series Bourbon Street Beat, Mr. Lucky, Thriller, The Deputy, and Alfred Hitchcock Presents, among others. He also appeared in the motion pictures The Secret of the Purple Reef (1960) and A Thunder of Drums (1961).

A Thunder of Drums, a western, was produced by MGM, which had signed Chamberlain to a seven-year contract after selecting him to play the lead in the pilot film for a proposed television series called "The Paradise Kid." Although that project was shelved, Chamberlain remained under contract, and when the studio decided to create a TV series based on the popular "Dr. Kildare" movies of the 1940s, he was among the dozens of young actors tested for the pivotal role of the idealistic intern James Kildare. Although Chamberlain's first reading was, by all accounts, rather colorless and one-dimensional, Norman Felton, the show's executive producer, perceived in the actor "a great warmth and personal charm." Perhaps more important, the veteran actor Raymond Massey, who had worked with Chamberlain before and who was slated to play Kildare's mentor, Dr. Gillespie, found him "compatible." After a second reading, the producers decided to cast the unknown actor in the title role. "It was one of the great breaks of all time," Chamberlain said later.

From its debut, on September 28, 1961, to its demise five years later, Dr. Kildare ranked among NBC's top-rated shows. As more than one critic has pointed out, the series focused on the emotive aspects of the practice of medicine and tended to gloss over the starkness of its clinical side. A gentle, selfless, and warmhearted man who was dedicated to the well-being of his patients, Kildare was, in the words of the television critic and historian Robert S. Alley, a representative of professional care "not . . . as it is, but as it should be." As for Chamberlain's performance, a reviewer for TV Guide (March 16, 1963) complained that he projected "neither mysterious nor heroic qualities, but rather the somewhat blank innocence of inexperience." Chamberlain himself often described his character as "a prig" and "an irreclaimable bore," and he tried time and again to persuade the show's writers to make Kildare "more subject to faults and weaknesses—like the rest of us," as he recalled in an interview for a Saturday Evening Post (September 30, 1963) profile.

While Dr. Kildare was riding high in the Nielsen ratings, Richard Chamberlain was among television's most popular performers. He reportedly received more than 12,000 fan letters a week and invariably ranked at or near the top of the list in viewers' popularity polls. Voted the favorite male performer of 1963 in an audience survey conducted by TV Guide, he also won three Photoplay Gold Medals and awards from the Hollywood Foreign Press Association and the Hollywood Women's Press Association. Eventually, Chamberlain came to feel hedged in by all that idolatry and, perhaps more to the point, by his identification in the minds of his viewers with the character of James Kildare. "Being a national institution, I had to live like him and seem like him all the time . . . ," he explained to Catherine Stott, as quoted in the Guardian (March 7, 1969). "It was agony talking to the press because I could never speak my mind—I always had to say that everything was lovely and beautiful and true. . . . Even my reactions to life became stereotyped because of Kildare's."

In an effort to extend his range, Chamberlain continued his professional training throughout Dr. Kildare's five seasons, often going straight from the set to a class or rehearsal hall. Taking advantage of the annual breaks in the television series' shooting schedule, he starred in two motion pictures for MGM—the courtroom drama Twilight of Honor (1963), in which he played an earnest, small-town defense attorney whose first major case is a grisly sex murder, and Joy in the Morning (1965), about the marital problems of a struggling law student.

He also made guest appearances on several TV variety shows, including Hollywood Melody and The Bob Hope Show, and in 1963 he recorded the album Richard Chamberlain Sings, which became a modest hit.

When Dr. Kildare, a victim of dwindling ratings, was canceled following the 1965–66 television season, Chamberlain decided to focus his attention on the theatre. In December 1966 he made his New York stage debut, as Jeff Claypool in Breakfast at Tiffany's, a musical comedy loosely based on Truman Capote's novella of the same name. The troubled production, in which he costarred with another television veteran, Mary Tyler Moore, closed during previews because of continuing problems with the book. Undaunted, Chamberlain spent much of the next year acting in stock company productions of such perennial favorites as Philip Barry's The Philadelphia Story and Noel Coward's Private Lives, and in a touring production of the hit musical West Side Story. He also snared a feature role in Petulia, Richard Lester's critically acclaimed but financially unsuccessful film about the barrenness of contemporary American life. When the film was released in 1968, Chamberlain earned the best notices of his career to that date for his portrayal of the kooky heroine's neurotic and sexually impotent husband.

Invited to London in 1967 for a guest spot on Eamonn Andrews' popular television talk show, Chamberlain decided to remain in England for "any kind of training [he] could find." Almost immediately, he was chosen to play Ralph Touchett, the consumptive American hero in the BBC's six-part adaptation of Henry James's The Portrait of a Lady. That assignment was, in Chamberlain's view, "the turning point" of his career, for his performance prompted Peter Dews, then the artistic director of the Birmingham Repertory Theatre, one of Britain's most prestigious regional repertory companies, to offer him the title role in the company's upcoming production of Hamlet.

Embarking on what he has described as "a night-and-day crash course on how to play Shakespeare," Chamberlain worked privately with Peter Dews for weeks to develop his vocal strength and master the technique of verse-speaking. On opening night, he was, by his own admission, "catatonic with fear," but he nonetheless delivered a graceful and assured interpretation of the prince. "Anyone who comes to this production prepared to scoff at the sight of a popular American television actor, Richard Chamberlain, playing Hamlet will be in for a deep disappointment," Michael Billington wrote in his review of the first-night performance for the London Times (March 13, 1969). Although he lodged some complaints, chiefly about Chamberlain's limited vocal range, Billington found much to admire in his "zestful attack" and in his unconventional interpretation of Hamlet as "an open-hearted natural extrovert who for the first time of his life is confronted by an insuperably difficult moral problem." Chamberlain reprised the role in an all-star television production for the

Hallmark Hall of Fame that was first broadcast by NBC on November 1, 1970. The soundtrack of that telecast, issued by RCA was subsequently nominated for a Grammy award as the "best spoken word" recording of the year.

Remaining in England for about three years, Chamberlain took professional classes and appeared in a number of film and television productions. His screen credits for that period include a young French radical in *The Madwoman of Chaillot* (1969), Bryan Forbes's star-studded version of Jean Giraudoux's fragile, stylized fantasy; Octavius in a critically acclaimed production of *Julius Caesar* (1971), with Charlton Heston, John Gielgud, and Jason Robards in the leading roles; Lord Byron in Robert Bolt's ill-conceived historical drama *Lady Caroline Lamb* (1972); and Peter Ilich Tchaikovsky in *The Music Lovers* (1970), Ken Russell's frenetic motion picture about the anguished life and loves of the Russian composer.

On his return to the United States in 1971, Chamberlain signed on to play the title role in *Richard II* for the Seattle Repertory Theatre. His warm, sympathetic interpretation of the poet-king earned him virtually unanimous critical applause. Hailing Chamberlain as "a potential new Barrymore," T. E. Kalem cheered in his review for *Time* (April 26, 1971), "For the first time in years, a man capable of becoming a great and serious classical actor has appeared on the U.S. stage. . . . It is proof of Chamberlain's high emotive gift that members of an audience, so rapt that they never coughed, had cause, more than once, to wipe their eyes." There were minor flaws in Chamberlain's performance, Kalem conceded, "but these faults can be amended. The important point is that he is, in the language of sport, a natural. With further discipline, and firm resolve, he can become one of the lords of the stage."

A year later Chamberlain offered a different interpretation of Richard II in a new production of the play, staged by Jonathan Miller, for the Center Theatre Group at the Ahmanson Theatre in Los Angeles. As Dan Sullivan observed in his review for the *Los Angeles Times* (March 26, 1972), the actor's revised characterization was "harsher and more aggressive—more brass, fewer strings." Although he was reportedly convincing in his portrayal, Chamberlain found Miller's conception of Richard as "a kind of petulant child" to be "disconcerting." "I felt that sort of unsympathetic treatment wasn't really fair to the character or the play in the long run," he explained to Charles Higham in the interview for the *Saturday Evening Post*. "I think it's far more deeply and convincingly tragic to have a man who's seeking growth than a man who's defeated from the outset."

Following an acclaimed engagement in *Richard II* at the Eisenhower Theater of the John F. Kennedy Center for the Performing Arts in Washington, D.C., in May 1972, Chamberlain had the distinction of being the first American ever to star in a production at the venerable Chichester Festival in Britain when he took the part of Thomas Mendip, an itinerant soldier in fifteenth-century England in Christopher Fry's romantic comedy in verse *The Lady's Not for Burning*. Later in the year, he began a long run as the Narrator (El Gallo) in the musical *The Fantasticks* at the Arlington Park Theater, near Chicago.

In November 1973 Chamberlain tackled the complex, larger-than-life role of the swaggering eponymous hero in Edmond Rostand's classic romance *Cyrano de Bergerac*. That he was more than equal to the task was evident in the glowing notices accorded the Center Theatre Group's staging. The *Los Angeles Times*'s Dan Sullivan went so far as to call it "probably the most satisfying show" that the company had ever produced at the Ahmanson Theatre. Sullivan was especially pleased by Chamberlain's decision to play Cyrano not as "a clown or somebody's country cousin" but as "a true aristocrat" who is "an outsider only by virtue of that extraordinary nose." "That's good psychology," Sullivan concluded, "and good acting strategy, too."

Chamberlain continued his successful association with the Center Theatre Group in December 1975, playing the part of T. Lawrence Shannon, the tortured, defrocked clergyman turned tour guide in the company's staging of Tennessee Williams' *The Night of the Iguana*, a bleak exposure of loneliness. When the production transferred from the Ahmanson Theatre in Los Angeles to the Circle in the Square on Broadway in 1976, Chamberlain surprised New York critics with his finely etched performance of a man "frayed physically and emotionally." "He has masked his extraordinary good looks with a seediness that goes to the character's burnt-out soul . . . ," Martin Gottfried wrote in the *New York Post* (December 17, 1976). "His recollection of a past gentility, real or imagined, is as heartbreaking as Blanche's" in *A Streetcar Named Desire*. The actor was equally memorable—and, with his whiskeyed voice and fevered gaze, "almost unrecognizable," in Mel Gussow's opinion—as Wild Bill Hickok in a workshop production of *Fathers and Sons*, Thomas Babe's drama about the persecution and assassination of the legendary frontier marshal, at New York's Public Theater two years later. He repeated his performance in a sold-out engagement at the Soleri Theater in Beverly Hills in 1980.

Throughout the 1970s Chamberlain interspersed his stage assignments with motion picture and television appearances. Among other film roles, he played the dashing Aramis in Richard Lester's lighthearted remake of *The Three Musketeers* (1973) and in its sequel, *The Four Musketeers* (1975); the lovelorn Prince Edward in *The Slipper and the Rose* (1977), a lavish British musical based on the Cinderella story; a villainous electrical contractor in Irwin Allen's multimillion-dollar disaster spectacle *The Towering Inferno* (1974); and a scientist in the sci-fi thriller *The Swarm* (1978), which had to do with South American killer bees attacking the United States. He earned the best notices for his understated portrayal of a liberal corporate attorney inexplicably called upon to defend a group of aborigines accused of murdering a member of their tribe in *The Last Wave* (1978), Peter Weir's award-winning apocalyptic parable. Chamberlain's most recent film ventures are *King Solomon's Mines* (1985), a campy remake of H. Rider Haggard's novel that was panned as a *"Raiders of the Lost Ark* ripoff," and its equally unconvincing sequel, *Allan Quartermain and the Lost City of Gold* (1987).

Besides re-creating for the small screen his stage role in *The Lady's Not for Burning*, Chamberlain has starred in the television adaptations of Alexandre Dumas' *The Count of Monte Cristo*, for which he received an Emmy nomination as the outstanding lead actor in a dramatic special for the 1974-75 season, and *The Man in the Iron Mask*, which was first broadcast by NBC in 1977. He also starred as King Edward VIII in *Portrait: The Woman I Love* (ABC, 1972), the novelist F. Scott Fitzgerald in *F. Scott Fitzgerald and the Last of the Belles* (ABC, 1973), and the Writer in *The Good Doctor*, (PBS, 1978), Neil Simon's comedy anthology adapted from the early short stories of Anton Chekhov. In 1978 Chamberlain launched his miniseries career when he appeared as the trapper Alexander McKeag in *Centennial*, NBC's ambitious twenty-six-and-one-half-hour adaptation of James Michener's bloated and best-selling epic about the settlement of the American West.

Chamberlain finally reclaimed his place as one of television's most bankable stars in *Shōgun*, the multimillion-dollar, twelve-hour serialization of James Clavell's swashbuckling evocation of medieval Japan. Cast in the part of John Blackthorne, the shipwrecked English adventurer who, under the tutelage of the supreme warlord Toranaga, gradually develops into a true samurai, the actor earned his second Emmy award nomination and a Golden Globe for his powerful interpretation of a man caught between two worlds. When it was first telecast by NBC in September 1980, *Shōgun* attracted an estimated audience of 130,000,000 viewers, making it the second-most-watched miniseries, after *Roots*, in television history. A two-and-one-half-hour theatrical version of *Shōgun* was later released internationally.

Deluged with film and television offers following the phenomenal success of *Shōgun*, Chamberlain determinedly sought only one role—Father Ralph de Bricassart, the ambitious, guilt-ridden Catholic priest in Colleen McCullough's blockbuster *The Thorn Birds*, the panoramic family saga set in the desolate Australian outback that was a runaway best seller in 1977. In an interview for *TV Guide* (March 26, 1983), he explained that he was especially attracted by the challenge of portraying "a man whose heart is torn in half in a lifelong struggle" between his devotion to God and the Church and his passion for Meggie Cleary, the novel's spirited heroine. On a more personal level, he added, he had found "amazing parallels" between Father Ralph's failure to live up to the image of the perfect priest and his own search for perfec-

tion as an actor. Chamberlain's intuitive feel for his character's anguish paid off in a touching performance that won over even those critics who had previously found fault with his work. For his efforts, the actor reaped another Golden Globe, for best television actor in a miniseries, and his third Emmy award nomination.

Chamberlain's most recent TV credits include the roles of Dr. Frederick Cook, the physician and Arctic explorer in *Cook and Peary: The Race to the Pole* (CBS, 1983); Raoul Wallenberg, the Swedish diplomat credited with saving the lives of some 100,000 Jews in Hungary during World War II, in *Wallenberg: A Hero's Story* (NBC, 1985); John Charles Frémont, the American frontiersman who became the Republican party's first candidate for president, in the six-part miniseries *Dream West* (CBS, 1986), based on the novel by David Nevin; and Giovanni Jacopo Casanova, the eighteenth-century writer and amorist in *Casanova* (ABC, 1987). In the early 1980s Chamberlain set up his own production company, Cham Enterprises ("Cham" is the name with which he has signed his paintings since his college days), to develop and produce television movies with contemporary settings.

While Chamberlain feels an obligation to television because it has nourished his career, he nonetheless acknowledged, in an interview for the *Los Angeles Times* (July 26, 1984), "I need to do theatre. If I don't, I feel something is missing." After an absence of seven years, he returned to the stage in March 1987 to star, with Blythe Danner, Judith Ivey, and Geraldine Page, in a limited run of Noel Coward's *Blithe Spirit*. It was the first major Broadway revival of the astringent farce since its premiere in 1941. Cast as Charles Condomine, the debonair mystery writer who inadvertently conjures up the ghost of his first wife while researching a book on spiritualism, Chamberlain struggled in rehearsals to find " a new way" to play Coward so that he and his fellow actors would not look like "museum pieces cavorting around the stage." His solution, sanctioned by the director, Brian Murray, was to pay more attention to the subtext and to the playwright's ambivalence about relationships. Chamberlain's unorthodox approach to his character failed to impress New York critics, most of whom agreed with the *Times*'s Frank Rich that the role was "not a natural fit."

Richard Chamberlain stands six feet one inch tall and weighs a lean 170 pounds. Still boyishly handsome, he has the finely chiseled features of "a natural aristocrat," as one reporter put it, slightly slanting pale-blue eyes, and light-brown hair. He keeps fit by running daily with his two dogs and by swimming, surfing, and playing tennis. He also enjoys horseback riding and white water rafting. Numbered among his less strenuous pursuits are reading, painting, and making stained-glass windows. A soft-spoken, introspective man who prefers to keep his private life "very private," he shuns the Hollywood party circuit, preferring to spend his rare leisure hours socializing with friends or going to the movies. Admittedly ambitious and devoted to his craft, Chamberlain found it difficult to balance his professional and personal lives until undergoing several years of what he has called "psychological work," including sessions with a Gestalt therapist and with the holistic physician William Brugh Joy. The actor divides his time between a Japanese-style home in Beverly Hills, a Manhattan apartment, and a vacation hideaway on the island of Oahu, Hawaii.

References: Christian Sci Mon p6 Ja 8 '75 pors; Guardian p11 Mr 7 '69 por; Horizon 26:46+ N/D '83 pors; Look 26:137+ N 20 '62 pors; N Y Daily News mag p14+ Mr 1 '87 pors; N Y Times II p5+ Mr 29 '81 por; Newsday II p4+ F 4 '73 pors; People 14:96+ S 22 '80 pors; Sat Eve Post 263:14+ Mr 30 '63 pors; TV Guide 31:12+ Mr 26 '83 por; Who's Who in America, 1986-87; Who's Who in the Theatre (1981)

Cisneros, Henry G(abriel)

June 11, 1947- Mayor of San Antonio. Address: b. P.O. Box 9066, San Antonio, Tex. 78285; h. 2002 W. Houston St., San Antonio, Tex. 78207

As a twenty-five-year-old White House fellow in 1972, native San Antonian Henry Cisneros was dubbed a "national resource" by Elliot L. Richardson, then the United States secretary of health, education, and welfare. The dynamic young Harvard-trained urbanologist, elected the first Hispanic mayor of a large American city only nine years later, has maintained an unwavering dedication to carrying out the task for which he so rigor-

ously pursued his impressive academic credentials: ensuring San Antonio's growth and prosperity before considering any bid for higher elective office. Reelected three times since 1981 by its voters, Cisneros has succeeded in largely defusing the tensions of the city's historic ethnic polarization between Anglos and Chicanos, building a broad-based coalition for change through the sheer force of his personal magnetism, intellectual ability, political acumen, tireless boosterism, and "strategic vision" for the future of the tenth-largest municipality in the United States.

In the face of some criticism from Hispanic activists who consider him too much of a centrist, Cisneros, a self-avowed moderate, has successfully deployed a two-pronged urban policy agenda based on employment-directed economic development and inclusion of all socioeconomic groups in the political process. He was named a member of the Reagan administration's National Bipartisan Commission on Central America in 1983 and elected president of the National League of Cities two years later. In 1984 he was interviewed by Democratic presidential candidate Walter F. Mondale as a possible choice for the vice-presidential nomination, an event that only served to fuel speculation that he would one day fulfill what the Texas pollster George Shipley considers Cisneros' political destiny as "a truly nationally qualified natural."

Descended on his father's side from early Spanish settlers in the American Southwest, Henry Gabriel Cisneros was born on June 11, 1947, in San Antonio's Prospect Hill section, a middle-class Hispanic enclave bordering the city's crowded West Side barrio. His father, George Cisneros, was a civilian administrator for the United States Army who later became a colonel in the army reserve. His mother, Elvira (Munguia) Cisneros, was the daughter of Romulo Munguia, a Mexican printer, journalist, and intellectual who had been a follower of the revolutionary Venustiano Carranza during the oppressive regime of Mexican dictator Porfirio Diaz. In 1926 Munguia had fled his native country, settling in San Antonio with his wife and children, and eventually he started his own print shop and became an avid promoter of Mexican-American commerce, education, and culture.

The first of the five children of George and Elvira Cisneros, Henry Cisneros grew up in the midst of a supportive extended family, in a neighborhood that he later described as "a sort of Norman Rockwell" creation. His industrious father took frequent adult education courses and made a number of improvements on the family home, inspiring his eldest son by his example. Elvira Cisneros imposed on her children a summertime regimen of chores, reading, spirited family debates, and creative projects, in the firm belief that her three sons and two daughters would fulfill a special destiny that she prophetically envisioned for them. Eventually, each of Henry's brothers and sisters pursued careers as absorbing as his own, ranging from biology to music, architecture, and journalism.

Henry Cisneros attended the Roman Catholic parochial school of San Antonio's Church of the Little Flower, where he skipped the third grade, and went on to graduate at sixteen from Catholic Central High School. Too young and too spindly to be accepted by the United States Air Force Academy, Cisneros abandoned his dream of becoming a pilot and enrolled at Texas A & M University in the fall of 1964. The rigorous traditions of A & M only served to sharpen his resolve to "perform in a competitive way," as he told Kemper Diehl and Jan Jarboe, the authors of his biography, *Cisneros: Portrait of a New American* (1985). "A & M in that era was one of the last pure meritocracies left," he recalled. "If you could perform in the classroom, if your military performance was up to speed, if you had leadership capabilities, then there was no limit."

Far from being a revolutionary during the chaotic era of the late 1960s, Cisneros pursued a carefully calculated middle course, distinguishing himself as commander of the combined Aggie Band and taking part in a staggering array of extracurricular activities. Because he was having difficulties with calculus, he switched his major from aeronautical engineering to city management in his sophomore year. In 1967 Cisneros was selected to attend a student conference at West Point, an occasion that he has described as a turning point in his career plans. By the time he graduated from A & M with a B.A. degree in 1968, Cisneros had already decided, according to his brother George, that he would some day become mayor of San Antonio.

In the summer of 1968 Cisneros returned to San Antonio, where Roy Montez, the director of the local department of President Lyndon B. Johnson's Model Cities program for urban revitalization, hired him as an analyst. That same year he also worked for a time as an assistant to the city manager of Bryan, Texas. In January 1969 Cisneros won a promotion to assistant director of the Model Cities department in his home city, a position that gave him his first taste of the factionalism that divided San Antonio's conservative Anglo establishment from its disenfranchised West Side Hispanic majority.

During Cisneros's tenure in the Model Cities department, the Good Government League (GGL), a probusiness interest group that had virtually controlled San Antonio politics since the mid-1950s, began to lose Hispanic support. The issues that occupied the attention of the Model Cities program during the late 1960s—lack of city funding for street improvements, drainage projects, public libraries, and alleviation of substandard conditions in public housing projects—foreshadowed the 1970s-era concerns of Communities Organized for Public Service (COPS), an advocacy group inspired by the community organizer Saul Alinsky, and they later provided grist for Cisneros' city council campaign speeches.

The experience that Cisneros gained from his first urban management job brought him to the conclusion that politicians were more likely than bureaucrats to be successful catalysts for the amelioration of West Side poverty and unemployment. Resolving to add a doctorate in administration and finance to the M.A. degree in urban planning that he had earned at Texas A & M in 1970, he applied to George Washington University for the doctoral program in urban administration. In January 1970 Cisneros set out for Washington, D.C., where he soon landed a full-time job as an administrative assistant to the executive vice-president of the National League of Cities. The following year he applied for the White House fellows program, a Johnson administration project that gave promising young political hopefuls an opportunity to serve as assistants to members of the cabinet or the White House staff. Although his youth and the high academic level of the competition presented formidable obstacles, Cisneros was selected for the 1971 program and assigned to serve under Elliot L. Richardson, the secretary of health, education, and welfare, who became his intellectual and political mentor.

Richardson, who praised Cisneros highly for his political potential, his grasp of the issues, and his "genuineness," convinced his twenty-three-year-old protégé that returning to San Antonio on completion of the program in order to develop a sound political base was a vital first step in climbing the political ladder. From 1972 to 1974 Cisneros lived in Boston, where, with a Ford Foundation grant, he earned a master's degree in public administration from the John F. Kennedy School of Government at Harvard University in 1973, worked as a teaching assistant at the Massachusetts Institute of Technology, and completed doctoral classes at M.I.T. In August 1974 Cisneros turned down an offer of a full-time teaching job at M.I.T. and returned home to accept an assistant professorship at the University of Texas at San Antonio, where he taught courses in labor economics and urban studies. In 1975 he received his doctorate in public administration from George Washington University.

Bristling with credentials, Cisneros appeared on the local political scene ready to do battle with the forces of establishment complacency. With the Good Government League machine in tatters and Hispanic factions angling for political power, desperate GGL leaders sought an attractive Mexican-American candidate for the city council to garner Hispanic votes. Cisneros' uncle Ruben Munguia, who had since taken over Munguia Printers from his father, lobbied to get his nephew placed on the GGL ticket. In 1975, eight months after his return to San Antonio, Cisneros was elected to the city council in a zealously independent campaign that served to distance him from the nearly defunct GGL.

At twenty-seven the youngest city councilman in San Antonio history, Cisneros was subsequently reelected in 1977 and 1979, serving a total of six years. He strategically aligned himself with Communities Organized for Public Service (COPS), the grass-roots Hispanic advocacy group founded in 1973, on such mutually beneficial issues as capital improvements for the West Side, allocation of federal community development funds, and decreasing utility costs. During a bid by environmentalists to limit commercial development above the underground Edwards Aquifer, San Antonio's only source of water, Cisneros, although opposed to the construction, drew fire from COPS leaders when he abstained in a vote to institute an eighteen-month moratorium on it because he doubted the legality of such a move. He campaigned alongside COPS once again in a successful bid to change the at-large system of electing city council members to a single-member districting system in 1976, a move that gave ethnic minorities a six-to-five council majority in the 1977 election.

Already so popular with local voters that he won reelection in 1977 with 92 percent of the vote, Cisneros nevertheless suffered two demoralizing defeats—the council's repudiation, by a six-to-five vote, of his effort to become mayor pro tem and the overwhelming rejection by voters of a 1978 bond issue that he supported. He again clashed with COPS leaders in March 1979, when he refused to support their resolution calling for the city to stop doing business with a leading contractor until he agreed to repair homes that were said to be faultily constructed. Although he sympathized with the homeowners, he did not believe that the city should impose sanctions against a major developer. Cisneros spent much of his final city council term mending fences, both with COPS and with the business community's Economic Development Foundation (EDF), which had earlier been alleged by COPS leaders to have promoted San Antonio to prospective relocating industries as a "cheap labor town." Cisneros led COPS and EDF in a successful effort to attract the high-tech Minneapolis firm Control Data to San Antonio, and a truce between battling factions was tentatively extended.

By 1980 Cisneros felt that it was imperative that he make his move on city hall. Mayor Lila Cockrell, the first woman to be elected mayor of a city with a population over 750,000, had presided over the San Antonio city council since 1975. While the popular mayor deliberated over whether to seek a fourth term, Cisneros amassed names of potential supporters and met with volunteers to discuss economic development, the overriding theme of his campaign. Citing personal reasons, Mrs. Cockrell withdrew from the race in December 1980, leaving Cisneros to run against the wealthy businessman and three-term councilman John Steen, and a field of six other hopefuls. On April 4, 1981, Cisneros became the first Mexican-American to be elected mayor of San Antonio since 1842, receiving 62 percent of the vote. The mandate that his impressive victory gave him among Anglos as well as Hispanics led him to declare, on the day after the election, "We have managed to transcend the ethnic factor, and there's a great sense of anticipation that we're going to be able to work together, and that the coalition we built can be put to work for San Antonio."

Cisneros' record in the ensuing years indicated that he had successfully managed to deflect ethnic animosities, for the most part, while pursuing his aggressive agenda of gaining new manufacturing jobs for San Antonio. His "strategic vision" involved economic development and incentives to woo new and relocating light industries to the city and enhancement of San Antonio's stature as a center for technological education. The newly elected mayor achieved a striking victory early in his first term by persuading the conservative coordinating board of the Texas College and University System to approve an engineering program at the University of Texas at San Antonio that was designed to provide an educational base for high-tech development.

Cisneros also wrote a detailed plan, entitled "San Antonio's Place in the Technology Economy," for building a major technology sector for the city, and he lectured widely on diversification in such key areas as manufacturing, tourism, the military, and medical research and services. He spurred the establishment of a high-technology high school and a health careers high school in Bexar County, of which San Antonio is the county seat, and he was instrumental, with the help of EDF and COPS, in attracting such high-tech companies as Advanced Micro Devices, Mark Industries, Tandy Corporation, and Sprague Electric Company to San Antonio during his first mayoral term. At the same time that John Naisbitt, the author of *Megatrends*, was researching his best selling book on the replacement of the industrial economy by an information-based technological economy, Cisneros was reaching similar conclusions. In a public television series, Naisbitt called Cisneros "the best informed public official" on the trend that appeared to be revolutionizing the American economy. Rather than concentrating all his efforts on high technology, however, Cisneros realistically chose to focus as well on such projects as a biosciences research park and a communications "teleport" heralded as the wave of the future.

Although his prodevelopment policies have endeared him to businessmen, Cisneros has not forgotten his ethnic roots. "We must capitalize on the Sun Belt growth," Cisneros insists, "and we must do it in such a way that everybody shares." His theory that "trickle-down economics" can be an effective remedy for minority joblessness has alienated him from Hispanic activists who favor more direct remedies for the plight of the disadvantaged, and other San Antonians have complained that the mayor's pursuit of development and his continual traveling have caused him to devote less energy and money to basic local services. Nevertheless, Cisneros has cautioned that "just creating a prosperous economy is not sufficient," and he insists that he favors government intervention where it is necessary to ensure equity for the poor.

Cisneros launched his 1983 reelection campaign by unveiling his "Target '90" program, a comprehensive plan for San Antonio involving some 500 citizens of the area assigned to work toward specific goals on the various issues facing the city. That July, having won reelection in April with more than 93 percent of the vote, he was named by President Ronald Reagan to the twelve-member National Bipartisan Commission on Central America, headed by former Secretary of State Henry A. Kissinger, and he was surprisingly outspoken as a voice of opposition to the administration's Central American policies. The appointment boosted his "national profile as an Hispanic voice," according to Marshal Ingwerson, writing in the *Christian Science Monitor* (May 24, 1984). Reports that Cisneros was Democratic presidential candidate Walter F. Mondale's second choice as a running mate in 1984 further magnified his visibility.

Nevertheless, Cisneros has continued to demur when questioned about his national ambitions. Reelected as mayor in April 1985 with a 73 percent mandate against five opponents, he has enhanced his national stature by making periodic headlines. In interviews with reporters in March 1986, for example, Cisneros criticized proposed budget cuts by the Reagan administration in federal aid to cities and denounced the Senate's immigration reform bill, which he felt could increase discrimination against native-born Hispanic Americans. In November 1986, at the conclusion of his one-year term as president of the National League of Cities, Cisneros told the 10,000 participants at the organization's annual conference in San Antonio, that "inclusive" politics, taking into consideration the interests of all elements of society, was the key to the future of American cities. Among his recent projects have been a bill to increase mass transit taxes for the financing of a major league sports stadium; the establishment of Sea World, a giant aquatic park, in San Antonio; and an abortive effort to obtain the designation of the city as the site of the 1991 United States Olympic festival.

Elected in April 1987 to a fourth term as mayor, with 67 percent of the vote, Cisneros indicated that he hoped to remain chief executive of San Antonio through 1990, the year his Target '90 plan was scheduled to bear fruit. He has ruled out seeking the governorship of Texas or any other statewide office in 1990, explaining that he wanted to devote more time to civic projects and to caring for his ailing youngest child.

Tall, lean, and telegenic, Henry Cisneros dresses impeccably and is said to be high-strung, driven, and sometimes petulant. He maintains a demanding schedule that includes time for jogging, reading, and family activities. On June 1, 1969, he married Mary Alice Perez, his high school sweetheart. He and his wife live with their two daughters, Theresa Angelica and Mercedes Christina, and their son, John Paul Anthony, born in 1987 with defects of the heart and digestive system, in what was formerly his grandfather Munguia's modest West Side home. One of the most poorly paid mayors in the United States, he is limited by the city charter, according to his biographers, to $3,000 a year plus the annual city council compensation of $1,040. (One source states, however, that his remuneration is about $20,000 a year.) Although the post was intended to be primarily ceremonial, Cisneros works at it full time.

Cisneros derives most of his income from his position as a visiting professor at Trinity University in his home city, while on leave from the University of Texas at San Antonio. He makes frequent speaking appearances in San Antonio and elsewhere, and he writes a syndicated newspaper column on urban affairs. His published works include the book *The Entrepreneurial City* (Ballinger, 1986). Among other civic activities, Cisneros has served as a trustee of the San Antonio City Public Service Board and the Fire and Police Pension Fund, as a member of the Twentieth Century Fund educational task force, and as a board member of the San Antonio Symphony Society. He received honorary degrees from Texas Tech University in 1982 and Amherst College in 1987. Although he lobbies continually to improve the lot of Hispanics, Cisneros, in the words of Marshall Ingwerson of the *Christian Science Monitor*, views himself as "mayor first" and "a member of his ethnic community second."

References: Advertising Age 52:44+ Je 22 '81 por; Am City & County 100:24+ Ja '85 pors; Christian Sci Mon p1+ My 24 '84 por; Esquire 102:480+ D '84 por; N Y Times A p12 Ap 6 '81 por; Read Digest 125:193+ D '84 por; Texas Monthly 15:87+ S '87 pors; Diehl, Kemper, and Jarboe, Jan. Cisneros: Portrait of a New American (1985); Who's Who in America, 1986–87; Who's Who in American Politics, 1985–86

Clapton, Eric

Mar. 30, 1945– British rock and blues guitarist; singer; songwriter. Address: b. c/o Warner Bros. Records, Inc., 75 Rockefeller Plaza, New York City, N.Y. 10019

"The objective, really, is to make everyone feel like they've just been struck by a bolt of lightning," the British guitarist and singer Eric Clapton once said of his playing style. As the mainstay of the international supergroups Cream, Blind Faith, and Derek and the Dominos, then as a solo performer fronting his own bands, Clapton has achieved his objective on numberless occasions and become the archetype of the rock 'n' roll guitar hero, playing with a brilliance that inspired his early followers to write "Clapton is God" on walls around London in the mid-1960s. With sales for his records regularly reaching into the millions, Clapton has become one of the most influential guitarists in the history of rock 'n' roll.

Only an occasional singer for much of his career, Clapton blossomed in that role on the album considered to be his masterwork and one of the masterpieces of rock, *Layla and Other Assorted*

Eric Clapton

Love Songs (RSO, 1970). The pressures of apotheosis, however, continually raised fears in Clapton that his "music was suffering because of how potent [his] image [was]," and helped to drive him into heroin addiction immediately after he completed *Layla*. He dropped from public view for two and a half years between 1970 and 1973 and then resumed his career with a series of uncharacteristically mellow and, some felt, mediocre albums during the rest of the decade. In the 1980s Clapton's former fire was rekindled with the release of such albums as *Behind the Sun* (RSO, 1985) and *August* (RSO, 1987). His fellow guitarist Carlos Santana has said that "the center of Eric Clapton's music, to me, is obviously the blues. But he has another plus—he's very lyrical. All of a sudden, his guitar is a voice in itself—or a trumpet or an orchestra. . . . You know, he doesn't play fast, but like my conga player, Armando Peraza, says, 'He gets inside the note.'"

Eric Patrick Clapton was born to Patricia Clapton on March 30, 1945, in Ripley, a small town about thirty miles south of London, in Surrey, England. "I was born illegitimately, I think," Clapton told the journalist Phillip Norman in an interview for *Show* (March 1970). "I looked at my birth certificate . . . and where it said 'Father' there was just a dash." Clapton's mother left him to be brought up by his grandparents, the plasterer John Clapp and his wife, Rose. In school, Eric displayed a precocious gift for painting and drawing and was an avid student until his mother returned to his grandparents' household in 1957. "From that moment on," Clapton has recalled, "I was moody and nasty and wouldn't try. We had to go through this whole thing of pretending she was my sister." Clapton failed the grammar school entrance exams that would

have put him on a college-bound course and enrolled in Surbiton Secondary Modern School.

The vista of a way out of the "village that was never going to change" opened before him when he saw the American rocker Jerry Lee Lewis perform on British television. "It was like seeing someone from outer space," Clapton told Robert Palmer in an interview for *Rolling Stone* (June 20, 1985). "There on TV was something out of the future. And I wanted to go there!" Settling on the guitar as his means of transport, he tried to carve one out of wood and then persuaded his grandparents to buy him a plastic one. In 1959 they bought him a Hafner acoustic guitar for his fourteenth birthday, but finding it virtually impossible to play, he put it aside and decided to concentrate on his other talents. Although he enrolled at Kingston College of Art in 1961, he also began spending a great deal of time in London coffee houses, listening to such performers as England's seminal bluesmen, Alexis Korner, Cyril Davis, and 'Long John' Baldry.

Enraptured by the blues, Clapton became increasingly inattentive to the demands of his studies at the art school and was expelled in 1962. He then worked as a manual laborer, spending his evenings practicing on an electric guitar that he had persuaded his grandparents to buy for him or frequenting the local blues clubs. He joined a blues band called the Roosters in March 1963. By the time it broke up that August he had, apart from music, "no other interests at all." "I Love the Woman," a Freddy King single played for him by a fellow Rooster, marked the first time, he told Robert Palmer, that he heard "that electric-lead-guitar style, with the bent notes—T-Bone Walker, B. B. King and Freddie King, that style of playing." "Hearing that Freddie King single," he added, "started me on my path."

That path led Eric Clapton to his first major band—the Yardbirds, which he joined in the latter part of October 1963. His budding virtuosity helped to make it one of the most influential and popular groups of the early 1960s. Although the guitarist had yet to evolve the fat tone and violin-like *sostenuto* that characterized his later work, his playing with the Yardbirds in 1963 and early 1964 displayed a blues feel and confidence hitherto unknown in rock circles. Clapton acquired the nickname "Slowhand" because his powerful playing regularly broke his guitar strings, which he then changed onstage to the accompainment of a slow handclap from listeners who were the harbingers of his later cult following. The Yardbirds' first album, *Five Live Yardbirds* (Charly, 1964), and what was to be their studio and American debut album, *For Your Love* (Epic 1965), included the songs that broke them into the pop charts—such as "For Your Love"—alongside blues classics that the purist Clapton preferred. Especially important for what it portended of the Clapton-to-come was "Got to Hurry," an instrumental shuffle in the Freddie King mold that displayed many of the hallmarks of the mature Clapton style: the rapid-fire runs; the sustained, violin-like tone; the extreme string-bending; and, of course, the famous vibrato technique that he had learned from his study of B. B. King's now classic recordings from the late 1950s and early 1960s.

Encouraged by the success of other local bands such as the Rolling Stones, the Yardbirds began to "see a future in being internationally famous," as Clapton has put it, and began to concentrate on recording commercial songs that he viewed as a betrayal of his blues principles. The friction that developed between himself and the group resulted in his departure in March 1965. To collect his thoughts, Clapton left London for Oxford, where he stayed with Ben Palmer, a Roosters alumnus, and spent a month doing little but practicing the guitar. When he returned to London, he received a call from an old admirer, John Mayall, who was known for his uncompromising and fervent dedication to pure blues, and Clapton joined Mayall's band, the Bluesbreakers, in March 1965. Helped along by an immediate marriage of sensibilities between Mayall and Clapton, the guitarist developed so quickly that after a few months he was established as the musical focus of the Bluesbreakers, playing his Les Paul guitar with a technique unheard of since the groundbreaking electric guitar recordings made by Paul himself in the early 1950s. In the Eric Clapton issue of Guitar Player (July 1985) Mayall recalled that although Clapton obviously had come under "quite a few influences" it was "just the way Eric played and put things together" that made him unprecedented. "He was a very moody player," Mayall added, "—by that I mean he could conjure up these incredible moods and intensity. . . . [He could] send shivers down your spine. . . . Of course everyone in England took severe notice of that." With Clapton on board, the popularity of the Bluesbreakers skyrocketed, and fans accustomed to pop stars with limited musical abilities began the wave of "Clapton is God" graffiti that ushered in the era of the guitar hero. The clubs where the Bluesbreakers played, according to former Mayall drummer Hughie Flint, "were full of young dudes at the front, sort of all playing [air guitar] . . . looking at their lord and master."

Clapton's fanatic following pushed the Mayall band's 1966 album, Bluesbreakers (on the London label), to the number six position on the English pop charts—an unprecedented feat for a blues record. With Mayall content to take a back seat to his illustrious sideman, the album became both a triumph of ensemble playing and a Clapton showcase, each song peaking in virtuosic, even visionary Clapton breaks and solos that established him once and for all as the most authentic and brilliant of the British bluesmen.

Having scaled one musical peak, Clapton began to feel "there was more to do" and "different places to go." He therefore left the Bluesbreakers in the middle of 1966 to form Cream with the drummer Ginger Baker, the Gene Krupa of rock, and Jack Bruce, a brilliant bassist who had played with Mayall in the fall of 1965. During his stint with Mayall, Jack Bruce had opened new horizons for Clapton with his irreverent, improvisatory approach to the blues classics, but Clapton originally envisioned Cream as an orthodox blues band. It soon became apparent that Bruce and Baker entertained other ambitions, as indicated by the name of the band, with its sly reference to each man's preeminence on his instrument. "I hadn't taken into consideration the power of the personalities at all," Clapton told Dan Neer of the Music Paper (January 1987). "I'm not necessarily that kind of person, but if I'm put with those elements, it brings that out of me." Equipped with a consummate group ego, Cream set out, in Clapton's words, "to start a revolution in musical thought . . . to change the world, to upset people, and to shock them."

The three men largely succeeded in their aims, setting lasting trends with virtually every musical decision they made. Bruce and Baker had worked together previously, with intermittent personal acrimony but consistent musical splendor, as a jazz rhythm section. As a result, while retaining the blues as the source of much of its material, inspiration, and tonal focus, Cream became the first rock band to explode the three-minute pop song formula with extended improvisational solos, especially in the epic live performances that began with its debut in 1966 at the Windsor Jazz and Blues Festival. The response proved, as Clapton has recalled, that rock audiences "actually wanted to go off somewhere. And we had the power to take them." The eclecticism of Cream opened the way for many other developments in pop music, including the syntheses of "progressive rock" and the cacaphonous distillations of "Heavy Metal."

On the group's first album, Fresh Cream (RSO, 1967), Clapton used the technical innovations, pentatonic tonality, and emotional fire of the American blues masters in his own imaginative tours de force. He thus established a new standard for the rock guitar solo, making it a virtually independent compositional form. His guitar work competed and combined with Bruce's bass lines and Baker's pyrotechnics to push Cream into unexplored musical territory and make Fresh Cream "a departure so radical as to suggest a visitation from the enigmatic monolith in 2001," Tom Wheeler wrote in Guitar Player's special issue on Clapton.

Disraeli Gears, Cream's second album, which was released at the end of 1967 on the RSO label, included the group's first top forty hit, "Sunshine of Your Love," on which Clapton shared vocal duties with Jack Bruce. It was followed in 1968 by Wheels of Fire (RSO), an enormously successful two-record set featuring both live recordings and new studio cuts. Clapton produced a classic with his wah-wah pedal work on "White Room" and paid tribute to blues great Robert Johnson with a masterful rendering of Johnson's "Crossroads." On the strength of those albums and its live performances, Cream achieved a level of international popularity exceeded only by the Beatles and the Rolling Stones, and Clapton himself became an international demigod. His trademark Les Paul guitar blasting from stacks of Marshall amplifiers "became the setup," according to Guitar Player's Dan Forte. Clapton himself has recalled that the attire he wore at one concert sometimes presaged that worn by the audience at the next. "For some incredibly uncanny reason," he said during the American tour, "a musician is more important than a politician these days. . . . so much responsibility is attached, it's too much, a drag."

The adulation swept him along for a time, however, and in the 1985 Rolling Stone interview he admitted to Robert Palmer: "During Cream I was riding high on the 'Clapton is God' myth . . . I was pretty sure we were the best thing happening that was popular. Then we got our first kind of bad review. . . . The ring of truth just knocked me backward. . . . There toward the end . . . [we no longer really had] a band with Cream; we were three virtuosos, all of us soloing all the time." After reading the review, he told Palmer, "I fainted. After I woke up, I immediately decided that that was the end of the band." Cream made its farewell tour of the United States in October and November of 1968 and gave its final performance at the Albert Hall in London, also in November. A farewell album, Goodbye, was released by RSO in March 1969 and included the lyrical hit single, "Badge," a collaboration between Clapton and George Harrison of the Beatles.

In February 1969 Clapton formed a new and short-lived supergroup, Blind Faith, with Ginger Baker, bassist Rick Grech, and the multitalented musician Steve Winwood, who previously was the front man for Traffic and the Spencer Davis Group. A measure of the high expectations the band aroused was the crowd, estimated as at least 36,000, in attendance at its free debut concert in London's Hyde Park in June 1969. Partly because the band had been "a rush job," in Clapton's recollection, both that concert and the band's debut album, Blind Faith (RSO), was dominated by Winwood, who handled all the vocals, played keyboards, wrote half the quartet's repertoire, and even traded guitar licks with Clapton on "Had to Cry Today." Clapton's guitar work on the album continued to display its lightning filigree and sinewy strength, but was noticeably restrained. "I was in awe of Steve," he explained to Dan Neer, "and respectful of his space and this made me rein in a lot more than I'd ever done before." While the album climbed to number one on both the British and American charts, Blind Faith embarked on a sold-out twenty-four-city American tour, the pressures of which destroyed it as a group. "We were blown up and hyped so much," Clapton told Neer, "we were just terrified all the time. . . . We went on stage shaking and white, and had a dreadful time." By mutual consent, Blind Faith disbanded in January 1970.

In an attempt to seek the sort of less-pressured musical environment denied him with Blind Faith, Clapton joined the tour's opening act, the relatively unknown husband-and-wife team of Delaney and Bonnie Bramlett and their group, Delaney and Bonnie and Friends.

The result of that collaboration was a disappointing live album for Polydor, Delaney & Bonnie & Friends, with Eric Clapton (1970). It was followed in the same year by Clapton's first solo album, Eric Clapton, on which the guitarist, backed by the Friends, managed some scorching guitar work amid a welter of mostly indifferent material. He also definitely emerged as a singer, overcoming insecurity about his limited vocal range, and produced a pop hit with his version of J. J. Cale's "After Midnight." Just as some critics were beginning to lament his decline, Clapton set the stage for some of his greatest music by hiring three members of Delaney's band after they were fired in a pay dispute with their employer.

The three musicians—bassist Carl Radle, drummer Jim Gordon, and keyboardist Bobby Whitlock—spent a year with Clapton at his estate in England, writing songs, playing "night and day and [taking] all kinds of dope," as Clapton has recalled. As Derek and the Dominos, they began recording what is still considered Clapton's greatest work, Layla and Other Assorted Love Songs, at Criteria Studios in Miami, Florida. There, the slide guitar maestro Duane Allman of the Allman Brothers Band arrived to watch the proceedings and was invited by Clapton to play. Already at the peak of his vocal and instrumental powers on songs such as "Bell Bottom Blues," recorded before Allman's arrival, Clapton reached new heights in the virtuosic guitar dialogue that ensued on "Why Does Love Got To Be So Sad," "Key to the Highway," and the rest of the tracks on the completed double album. The album's climax, "Layla," was reportedly inspired by a troubled love affair that Clapton had at the time with George Harrison's wife, Patti, and was dedicated "to the wife of my best friend." It is "perhaps the most powerful and beautiful song of the '70s," Dave Marsh observed in The Rolling Stone Illustrated History of Rock & Roll, 1950-1980. "Clapton," Marsh noted, "composed his own perfect blues without resorting to the traditional blues form. He matched Robert Johnson blow for blow, sorrow for sorrow."

Not long after the Criteria sessions, during which, he has said, any "drug you wanted" could be obtained "at the newsstand," Clapton developed a serious heroin addiction. Derek and the Dominos fell apart in the course of an American tour and an attempt to make a second album. "That's when I went on my journey into the smack," Clapton told Palmer. "I basically stayed in the house with my girlfriend for about two and a half years. . . . All that time, though, I was running a cassette machine and playing. . . . as if there was something struggling to survive." Clapton was brought out of seclusion by the guitarist and songwriter Pete Townshend, of the Who. He organized an all-star concert with personnel including Steve Winwood and then pleaded with Clapton until he agreed to leave his house and appear in the concert at the Rainbow Theatre in London. Clapton performed indifferently at the concert and was unable to shake the heroin habit until 1974, when, through Townshend, he underwent a controversial, but highly effective electro-acupuncture treatment for drug and alcohol addiction developed by Dr. Meg Patterson. In the following year he appeared as the Preacher in Ken Russell's film version of Townshend's rock opera, *Tommy*.

After his rehabilitation, Clapton spent the 1970s recording a series of albums, released on the RSO label, in which he tried to construct an identity distinct from that of the idolized guitar hero by "minimizing" his solos. *461 Ocean Boulevard* highlighted Clapton's slide guitar skills, emphasized his singing, and did much to introduce Jamaican reggae music to a wide audience through his hit single cover of Bob Marley's "I Shot the Sheriff." The albums that followed, *There's One in Every Crowd* (1975), *E.C. Was Here* (1975), *No Reason to Cry* (1976), *Slowhand* (1977), and *Backless* (1978), disappointed fans accustomed to his persona of guitar hero, for his old intensity seemed to diminish sometimes to the vanishing point in a stream of laid-back melodies. Yet they also spotlighted Clapton's developing singing ability. He was now a regular on the pop charts with songs such as "Lay Down Sally" from *Slowhand* and "Promises" from *Backless*.

The return of Eric Clapton as master bluesman and guitar hero was heard again on the live album *Just One Night* (RSO, 1980), in which he delivered some of his most moving onstage playing. The resurgence of one aspect of his character that, as he has said, "is made up of an obsession to push something to the limit," also manifested itself in a drinking habit which, before he finally broke it, helped to force his hospitalization in 1981. The new fire afterwards worked its way into the music Clapton made on the albums *Another Ticket* (RSO, 1981), *Money and Cigarettes* (Warner Brothers, 1983), *Behind the Sun* (Warner Brothers, 1985), and *August* (Warner Brothers, 1986). In addition to its lustrous guitar licks, those albums featured trim arrangements and impressive songwriting from Clapton, and produced such hits as *August*'s "It's in the Way That You Use It" and "Tearing Us Apart."

Members of the press have attributed Clapton's new verve to a variety of reasons, including his deepening commitment to Christianity, to which he had converted before his period of heroin addiction; his marriage in 1979 to the former Mrs. George Harrison, whose affections he had regained some time before; and the father-son relationship that developed between him and the blues-immortal Muddy Waters in the late 1970s. Clapton himself has credited his resurgence to the same soft melodies that once aroused doubts among his followers. "If you're a blues player," he told Robert Palmer, " . . . it seems you can't face it all the time. Sometimes you need to hear some harmonic softeners, some quiet, some subtle, to kind of quench the fire and calm yourself. . . . When I got back to being *me*, it was almost a shock to realize how tough my stuff was in comparison."

Eric Clapton is five feet ten inches tall and slim in build. Known for his chameleon-like tendency to take on, for a time, the musical tastes and even some of the personal idiosyncrasies of those around him, he has changed his appearance over the years from the crew-cut, button-down days of the Yardbirds through the shoulder-length perms, paisley shirts, and bell-bottom jeans of the Cream era to the casual country look of the early 1980s. Today, he cuts an elegant figure with his short hair, closely trimmed beard, and designer suits. His main hobby is fishing, a sport in which he indulges whenever the opportunity presents itself. Clapton still makes his home in England and seems unwilling to maintain the multiple residences that many rock stars seem to think essential to their lifestyles. He is still married to Patti Boyd-Harrison.

References: *Guitar Player* 19:10+ Jl '85 pors; *Melody Maker* p34+ Je 21 '69 pors; *Music Paper* p28+ Ja '87 pors; *Rolling Stone* p33+ Je 20 '85 pors; *Show* 1:48+ Mr '70 pors; Miller, Jim, ed. *The Rolling Stone Illustrated History of Rock & Roll, 1950–1980*; Tobler, John. *Guitar Heros* (1978)

Clark, Dick

Nov. 30, 1929– Television personality; producer. Address: b. Dick Clark Productions, 3003 W. Olive Ave., Burbank, Calif. 91505.

NOTE: This biography supersedes the article that appeared in *Current Biography* in 1959.

The winner of four Emmy awards, Dick Clark, "America's oldest living teenager," has either introduced or given national exposure to many of the country's most popular rock and roll records and performers over a thirty-year career. Clark, who is best known as the host of *American Bandstand*, the longest-running musical or variety series on television, and as the master of ceremonies of the TV quiz show *$100,000 Pyramid*, is also a television and movie producer, actor, author, and entrepreneur who heads eight entertainment-industry corporations under their umbrella company, Dick Clark Productions. Income from those enterprises as well as from the restaurants, radio stations, and the show-business newsletter he owns, gives him an estimated net worth of $180 million—an impressive sum for a man who says of himself, "I can't sing, or dance. I just talk."

Since American Bandstand began production in 1952, 600,000 teenagers have danced to pop records before the show's cameras. Among the stars who have made their national television debut on *American Bandstand*—usually lip-syncing to their recordings—have been Buddy Holly and the Crickets, Chuck Berry, Simon and Garfunkel, Johnny Cash, Ike and Tina Turner, Dionne Warwick, Smokey Robinson and the Miracles, Aretha Franklin, Stevie Wonder, the Beach Boys, Neil Diamond, the Doors, the Jackson Five, Barry Manilow, the Talking Heads, Prince, Madonna, Cyndi Lauper, and Julio Iglesias.

Richard Wagstaff Clark was born in Bronxville, New York, on November 30, 1929, to Richard and Julia Clark. He grew up in nearby Mount Vernon, New York, where he attended A.B. Davis High School. Clark had an older brother, Bradley, who was killed when his plane was shot down in World War II. Since he had idolized his athletic brother, he tried to emulate him by going out for football, swimming and track, but he failed to make any of the varsity teams. As he recalled in his autobiography, *Rock, Roll & Remember* (Thomas Y. Crowell Company, 1976), he assuaged his loneliness by listening to the radio. Among his favorite programs were Martin Block's "Make Believe Ballroom," Art Ford's all-night show, "The Milkman's Matinee," and WMCA's "Battle of the Baritones," from which he later borrowed the idea for "Battle of the Songs" and "Battle of the Bands" on *Bandstand*. He became a fan of Steve Allen, Garry Moore, and Arthur Godfrey. From Godfrey he learned that "a radio announcer does not talk to 'those of you out there in radio land'; a radio announcer talks to *me* as an individual." When his parents took him to New York City to see a live radio broadcast of the Jimmy Durante-Garry Moore show, he told his mother afterwards, "That's what I want to do."

His parents encouraged him to join the high school dramatic club, which turned out to be a decisive step, for performing bolstered his self-confidence. A "determined extrovert," he was elected president of his class, and was voted by his schoolmates "Man Most Likely to Sell the Brooklyn Bridge." Shortly before he graduated, he moved with his family to Utica, New York, where his father took a job at WRUN, a radio station owned by a relative, Bradley Barnard. He worked at the station during that summer, running the office mimeograph machine and helping in the mailroom. His first experience on the air was as a pinch-hitter for a vacationing FM announcer, doing hourly weather forecasts. Later, WRUN assigned him to doing station breaks and the news on its larger AM outlet.

In 1946 Clark went off to Syracuse University, where he majored in advertising and minored in radio. While in college, he won a prize for writing a slogan for Gem razor blades ("A man's best friend is a Gem") and filled a disc-jockey slot on the student-run radio station, WAER-FM. During his senior year he worked on weekends at the downtown commercial Syracuse radio station WOLF as a news announcer and disc jockey for "the WOLF Buckaroos," spinning Gene Autry and Eddie Arnold records.

After graduating from Syracuse in 1951, Clark moved back to his parents' house in Utica. His father, who was by then station manager at WRUN, gave him a job as a summer replacement announcer, but he did not want to work for his father, and to declare his independence, even changed his name for a short time to "Dick Clay." Leaving the family's radio station, he landed a job at Utica's only television station, WKTV, which was small enough to enable him to learn every aspect of television production. In addition to announcing the news, he wrote commercials, moved scenery, and hosted a country music show called "Cactus Dick and the Santa Fe Riders."

In 1952 he moved to Philadelphia and changing his name from "Dick Clay" back to Dick Clark, took a job with radio station WFIL because of its proximity to New York and also because it had a television affiliate that offered room for advancement. In August 1952 the station gave him his own weekday show, *Dick Clark's Caravan of Music*, and a few months later, in October, its television affiliate launched a successful afternoon show called *Bandstand*, hosted by Bob Horn and Lee Stewart, that was basically a radio music-and-interview program adapted to the television format. Meanwhile, Clark was informed by the management that the name of his radio program was now *Bandstand* too, though he had to play "easy listening" records instead of the records for teenagers featured on its television counterpart. In the fall of 1955 Clark acted as a substitute host on the televised *Bandstand* while Bob Horn took a vacation, and when, in the summer of 1956, Horn was arrested for drunken driving, jailed, and fired, Clark was given Horn's job.

By May 1957 *Bandstand* was ranked as the most popular daytime show in Philadelphia. Among the local performers who got their start on the show were Bobby Rydell, Frankie Avalon, Chubby Checker, James Darren, and Fabian. In August 1957 ABC network officials gave the show a test run coast-to-coast, and in October the show was assigned a regular slot on national TV. The name of the show was changed to *American Bandstand* to emphasize its new nationwide audience, but otherwise its format remained unchanged. *American Bandstand's* first sponsor was General Mills, and its other sponsors included Clearasil, Bosco, Popsicles, Almond Joy, and Dr. Pepper.

Many of the performers who appeared on *Bandstand,* either in person or through the proxy of their records, became stars, and it was one of the first television showcases for black entertainers. A list of performers who got their first important exposure on the show would include James Brown, Bill Haley, Jerry Lee Lewis, Connie Francis, Johnny Mathis, Sam Cooke, Neil Sedaka, the Supremes, and the Everly Brothers.

The show's format was simple. As Dick Clark later explained: "I played records, the kids danced, and America watched." Eight million Americans watched, to be more specific, every afternoon from 3:00 to 4:30, and the show brought in, at one point, almost a million fan letters in one week, thanks to such popular features as Clark's letting the teenagers on the set rate the records he played, and having top performers lip sync their records. Clark became known for his terse commentary: "I'd give it an 85. I like the beat, and it's easy to dance to." Even the teenagers who regularly appeared on the show became stars of a sort, receiving thousands of fan letters weekly, and turning up in fan comic books. They also helped to popularize a long list of teen dances, including the Twist, the Pony, the Bristol Stomp, the Watusi, the Harlem Shuffle, the Stroll, and the Calypso.

In 1958 ABC aired a prime-time Saturday night version called *The Dick Clark Saturday Night Show,* during which a rapt teenaged audience did not dance, but watched from their seats while rock performers lip synched their latest hits and Dick Clark proclaimed the top ten records of the week. Beechnut Spearmint Gum was the full-time sponsor of *The Dick Clark Saturday Night Show* for all of its two-and-one-half-year run.

In June 1958 ABC sent Dick Clark and the Saturday-night show to Miami, Atlanta, Los Angeles, Atlantic City, and Binghamton, New York. The October 1958 performance in Atlanta was one of the first racially integrated rock concerts, which went peacefully despite threats from the local Ku Klux Klan and the presence of the National Guard. In 1959 Clark began to host another show, *Dick Clark's World of Talent,* on ABC-TV, on which aspiring performers were rated by a panel composed of Jack E. Leonard and two celebrity guests.

At about that time, Clark began investing in the record industry. "The basic reason," he explained in his autobiography, "is that I couldn't make enough money doing *Bandstand.*" Consequently, he became a partner in companies handling talent management, music publishing, record pressing, record label-making, record distribution, domestic and foreign song rights, motion pictures, show promotion, and merchandising of products for teenagers. In one lucrative week, he made a total of $200,000. Later Clark bought 25 percent of Jamie

Records and established SRO Artists to manage one of its stars, Duane Eddy. He formed two music publishing firms, Sea Lark and January Music, acquired a third-interest in Chips Distributing Company, and helped to found Swan Records. In 1959 he continued to buy and establish music publishing companies, bought a second record-pressing plant, and a new record firm. At the age of thirty he was a millionaire.

Dick Clark's clean-cut, all-American image was temporarily besmirched, when the "payola" scandals broke in 1959. A Congressional subcommittee investigating "payola"—the practice of taking money for playing a new record—subpoenaed him in February 1960. Denying that he had ever accepted payola, he demonstrated that he selected records with the help of computers, on the basis of their popularity, not payments, although he did admit that he had a financial interest in 27 percent of the records aired on *American Bandstand* over a period of twenty-eight months. By the time he was called to testify before the full committee in May, ABC executives made Clark divest himself of all his record-company interests "as a matter of company policy" and sign notarized statements confirming that he had never taken or demanded money in exchange for airplay. Although some of the media hinted that Clark's baby face might be a mask for corruption—the *Washington Post* even coined the word "Clarkola"—and although Clark acknowledged that he had accepted a fur stole and some jewelry from two record companies as gifts to his wife, he was never found guilty of any crime. He later contended that ABC's requirement that he divest himself of his business interests cost him more than $8 million.

In late 1959 and early 1960 Clark produced his first touring rock music show, *Dick Clark's Caravan of Stars,* which criss-crossed the country by bus with such stars as the Drifters, the Supremes, Chubby Checker, Paul Anka, and the Shirelles. A precursor of today's live rock concerts so popular with teenagers, *Caravan* grossed $5 million a year.

But the world was changing, and by 1963 the music scene that *American Bandstand* had so successfully exploited was fading. The Beatles, who made their first New York appearance in February 1964, ushered in a new age in rock music, and California bands such as the Beach Boys were redefining the meaning of "cool." Sensing the shift with his usual acumen, Clark and the rest of the *American Bandstand* crew moved to Los Angeles in March 1964, where he founded Dick Clark Productions. Since, by his own admission, he "lost touch" with rock music during the psychedelic sixties, he began concentrating on other activities, including the creation of two music TV shows, *Where the Action Is* and *Happening.* In 1964 he was master of ceremonies for *Missing Links,* a daytime game show on ABC, in which celebrities guessed the missing words to a story that was read aloud. That year he also hosted *The Object Is,* another daytime game show on ABC, in which guests had to guess the names of famous personalities from "object" clues.

Clark has appeared as an actor in several youth-oriented and mostly routine and forgettable films. The first was the 1960 release, *Because They're Young*, where he played the part of high-minded Neil, a new high school teacher. In his second film, *The Young Doctors* (1961), he played a young intern in a big-city hospital, alongside fellow cast members Ben Gazzara, Fredric March, and Eddie Albert. Ronald Reagan was the narrator. In 1968 alone, Clark appeared in four films: *Psych-Out*, *The Savage Seven*, *Killers Three* and *Wild in the Streets*. All but *Wild in the Streets* he produced himself. Clark was also a guest star on the September 4, 1967, episode of CBS-TV's *Coronet Blue* series, entitled "The Flip Side of Tommy Devon."

Throughout the 1970s Clark produced many television shows while he continued to preside over *American Bandstand*. From 1973 to 1975 he produced a Friday night music show for ABC-TV called *In Concert*. Another music show, *Dick Clark Presents the Rock and Roll Years*, ran on ABC-TV from November 1973 to January 1974. *Dick Clark's Live Wednesday*, a one-hour live variety series for which he was host and executive producer, appeared on NBC-TV for four months in late 1978. He was also executive producer for *Easy Does It*, a summer variety series telecast by CBS in 1976. His television unit produced *The Captain and Tenille* show which ran on ABC in prime time opposite the formidable competition of *Rhoda* and *Little House on the Prairie* during the 1977-78 season. One of his most popular assignments was as host of *The $10,000 Pyramid*, later played in denominations of $20,000, $25,000, $50,000 and $100,000, which alternated on CBS and ABC in 1973 and 1974.

Dick Clark has also produced and hosted a long list of television specials, including *Dick Clark's Good Ol' Days*; *Supercars and Classic Cars*; *Hollywood's Private Home Movies*; *Animals Are the Funniest People*; *The Most Beautiful Girl in the World*; *The First Time Ever* (featuring Roberta Flack); *The Janis Joplin Story*; *Sting Man*; *Copacabana*; and *Elvis*. The yearly *Dick Clark's New Year's Rockin' Eve*, which he has hosted and produced since 1972, has become an annual tradition, like the dropping of the ball in Times Square.

During the 1980s Clark has emerged as a preeminent show business entrepreneur, involved with television production, film production, radio production and syndication, live concerts, and publishing. His umbrella corporation, Dick Clark Productions, has a staff that fluctuates from about thirty-five to 200 people, depending on the demands of current projects. Described by Clark as an "entertainment boutique," the company is housed in a three-story mock-Tudor office building near the NBC studios in Burbank, California. In 1984 Dick Clark Productions was responsible for more than 170 hours of television programming, and now averages about 150 hours a year.

Radio, which gave Clark his start, is still yielding him a considerable amount of revenue, thanks to his *Dick Clark National Music Survey*, which is broadcast on nearly 600 stations to an estimated audience of 8.5 million, and his *Dick Clark's Rock, Roll and Remember* radio show, which has an estimated 29.5 million listeners. The latter program is syndicated by United Stations, cofounded by Clark, which is now the second-largest radio network in the United States. Clark also continues to package live stage productions, including the *Good Ol' Rock and Roll* touring revue.

In 1986 Clark marked his thirtieth year of hosting *American Bandstand* and became the only television personality simultaneously to host programs on all three networks: *American Bandstand* on ABC, *Pyramid* on CBS, and *TV Bloopers and Practical Jokes* on NBC. In 1986 Clark had fifty new projects in various stages of progress, including network daytime programs, syndicated television programs, network prime-time specials, network prime-time series, late-night network programs, and made-for-television movies. He recently entered the home video market, when the first volume of *Dick Clark's Best of Bandstand* home video tapes was released in 1985. Prolific though he and his company are, Clark has earned an unenviable reputation as a producer of what a critic for *Newsweek* (August 18, 1986) rhymed as "lots of schlock and rock" and what *TV Guide* (December 30, 1978) labeled as musical "junk food." But Clark does not regret being what Brandon Tartikoff, president of entertainment at NBC, characterized as "the McDonald's of television." His uncanny, long-run ability to keep on top of trends has made him a very rich man, with a net worth estimated by *Newsweek* magazine in 1986 of over $100 million. Profits from Dick Clark Productions amounted in 1985 alone to $12 million on revenues of $55 million.

His income is expected to increase substantially in the future, since his company, Dick Clark Productions "went public" in November of 1986 and is now on the New York Stock Exchange. According to the prospectus, Clark will not only be compensated as president and chief operating officer with a salary of $750,000 for the first two years and $800,000 for the next three, but will also control 80 percent of the voting stock. He is to be paid additionally when he performs, again when he produces, and again when his name is licensed to outside enterprises.

Despite the invidious epithets of some of his critics, Clark has managed to garner four Emmy awards, one for the 1978-79 season as "Outstanding Host in a Game or Audience Participation Show" for his work on *The $20,000 Pyramid*; for the 1982-83 season for coproducing *The Woman Who Willed a Miracle* and for *American Bandstand* as "Outstanding Daytime Series"; and yet another Emmy, again for *Pyramid*, during the 1985-86 season. As for bestowing honors on others, he has hosted the Golden Globe Awards, the American Music Awards, the Academy of Country Music Awards, and the ACE Awards for cable programming.

In addition to his autobiography, *Rock, Roll & Remember*, which he wrote with Richard Robinson, Clark has written and collaborated on other books. They include *Looking Great, Staying Young* (Bobbs-Merrill, 1980), cowritten with Bill Libby; *Dick Clark's Program for Success in Your Business and Personal Life* (Cornerstone Library, 1980); *Dick Clark's The First 25 Years of Rock & Roll* (Delacorte Press, 1981), cowritten with Michael Usland; and *The History of American Bandstand* (Ballantine, 1985). His most recent book is *Dick Clark's Easygoing Guide to Good Grooming* (Dodd, Mead, 1986).

Dick Clark has been married three times. In 1952 he married his high school sweetheart, Bobbie Mallery. They had one child, Richard Jr., and were divorced in 1961. Clark remarried in 1962, to Loretta Martin, the secretary to one of the performers on the traveling *Caravan of Stars*. They had two children, Duane and Cindy, and were divorced in 1971. He remarried again in 1977, this time to Kari Wigton, who is also his business partner.

Although his face now bears a few wrinkles, and his hair is streaked with grey, Clark still looks two decades younger than his chronological age. His secret, he maintains, is to "have an open mind and a closed refrigerator," but he concedes that youthful looks run in his family.

A lifelong workaholic, Dick Clark makes some 200 phone calls a day, and flies across the continent every ten days. His wealth has brought him a multimillion dollar mansion and an eighty-acre ranch in Malibu, California (which Clark and his wife share with Clark's father and four dogs) and a condominium in New York's Trump Tower. Among his other worldly goods are several fine cars, including a Rolls-Royce, a Mercedes, and a Jaguar. Although Clark freely admits he appreciates money ("I'm in a commercial business," he has said, "What's wrong with giving people what they want?"), he also entertains higher ambitions. One of his *pro bono* projects was the hosting of the *Live Aid* rock concert special on ABC-TV in July 1985. That internationally broadcast concert, featuring a huge contingent of superstars and name bands, was held to raise money for African famine relief. Someday he would like to produce a dramatic series on prime-time television. "There's so much I want to do," he assured a reporter from *People* magazine (February 14, 1977). "Most of all I want to be remembered as a hell of a lot more than some guy who did Clearasil commercials on the damn tube."

Reliability is the major trait on which Dick Clark has built his success. "If you need a show for next May, call Dick," says Rick Ludwin, vice-president for specials and variety programs at NBC. "If you have to plug an hour, he'll do it on time and within budget. I don't know anyone else who can do that."

References: *Newsweek* 108:26+ Ag 18 '86 pors; *Wall Street J* p1+ Mr 25 '85 por; *American Film Institute Catalog of Motion Pictures: Feature Films 1961–1970* (1976); Clark, Dick, and Robinson, Richard. *Rock, Roll & Remember* (1976); Eberly, Philip K. *Music in the Air* (1982); McNeil, Alex. *Total Television* (1984); *Who's Who in America, 1984–85*

Coetzee, J(ohn) M.
(kō-ĕt′zē)

Feb. 9, 1940– South African novelist; critic; translator. Address: h. P.O. Box 92, Rondebosch, Cape Province 7700, South Africa

The South African novelist J.M. Coetzee articulates "with laconic brilliance . . . one of the basic problems of our time—how to understand the mentality behind brutality and injustice," according to his fellow novelist Anthony Burgess. In the politically charged fiction that he has published since 1974, Coetzee combines allegory with such devices as stream-of-consciousness narration and the skewing of narrative viewpoint to that of deranged, confused, or otherwise unreliable protagonists. In so doing, he breaks with the more naturalistic and directly political writing tradition established by such leaders of the previous generation of South African writers as Alan Paton, Nadine Gordimer, and Athol Fugard. Through the grim atmosphere conveyed in his books—broken at times by Beckett-like black humor—there are protagonists ranging from genocidal colonizers to conscience-stricken beneficiaries of repressive post-colonial systems and to the disenfranchised themselves.

Leaving unnamed the totalitarian states that are the settings of most of his fiction, Coetzee at once describes, and distances himself from, the tumult of South Africa and achieves, in the opinion of critics, a universality rarely found in the writing of his peers. His intensity and perspective, combined with pristine linguistic virtuosity, have won him an international following as well as Great Britain's distinguished Booker McConnell prize, awarded to him for his fourth book, *The Life and Times of Michael K.*

John M. Coetzee—who is reticent about revealing what his middle initial stands for—was born in Cape Town, South Africa, on February 9, 1940. His father was a lawyer, his mother a schoolteacher, and he has a brother who is a journalist. A remote ancestor, Jacobus Coetzee, arrived in southern Africa in the eighteenth century and wrote down part of the history of the Hottentot tribe, not as the Hottentots saw it but, as Coetzee ironically describes it, "from above." Coetzee's grandparents on both sides were Afrikaner farmers but his father was anglicized. Coetzee grew up speaking English at home and Afrikaans to other relatives and acquaintances. He has recalled that his "intense relationships" of his early years were with the works of such writers as James Joyce, Samuel Beckett, Ezra Pound, and Rainer Maria Rilke. During his boyhood, he lived with his parents in about a dozen towns in the Cape Province's 100,000-square-mile tableland, the Karoo, while attending English-language schools.

After graduating from a Roman Catholic boys' school, Coetzee disregarded guidance tests that marked him as a prospective "quantity surveyor" and entered the University of Cape Town, where he made his first attempts at writing poetry and graduated in 1961 with degrees in literature and mathematics. He has recalled that he read T. S. Eliot and Ezra Pound and "tried doggedly to understand what people saw in Shakespeare." In mathematics he found some relief, but he eventually had similar difficulties with probability theory as he had with Shakespeare, being unable to apply it to reality as he knew it.

In 1962 Coetzee left by ship for England to work for the International Business Machines corporation as a computer programmer. In the evenings he read the works of Ford Madox Ford and Samuel Beckett and tramped around "the cold streets of London seeking the meaning of life." He abandoned poetry in mid-1963 and mathematics a year and a half later. During 1964–65 Coetzee worked as a systems programmer for International Computers in Bracknell, England. In September 1965 he sailed for the United States, where he enrolled in a graduate English program at the University of Texas at Austin. There he taught freshman English, developed an interest in linguistics, discovered the notebooks in which Samuel Beckett had written his novel *Watt*, and began to speculate about what was required to produce a great book. In the university libraries he also discovered reports by the early white settlers of their "civilizing mission" in South Africa, including accounts of exploration, the teaching of Christianity, the compilation of "makeshift grammars" of South African tribal languages by missionaries, and records of punitive expeditions against the tribes.

In that new intellectual landscape, Coetzee found himself troubled by moral questions raised by the Vietnam War, the assassination of South African Prime Minister H. F. Verwoerd, the "architect of Grand Apartheid," and the rampage of Charles Whitman, a University of Texas student, who shot and killed a number of people from a bell tower on the campus. Such violence, retribution, and madness, all of which were later prominent in his books, inspired in Coetzee thoughts of his own relationship to them.

In 1968, the year before he obtained his Ph. D. degree with what he described in an autobiographical sketch in *World Authors 1975–1980* as an "over-hasty dissertation on Beckett's prose style," Coetzee went east to become an assistant professor of English at the State University of New York at Buffalo. While there, he resolved on New Year's day 1970, to begin writing a novel. But throughout his stay in the United States he missed his home country, and in 1971 he returned to South Africa with the beginnings of two novellas. The stories were published together by South Africa's Raven Press in 1974 and by Penguin Books in 1985 under the title *Dusklands*. Meanwhile, he joined the faculty of the University of Cape Town as a lecturer in 1972, becoming an associate professor in 1980 and a professor of general literature in 1984.

The first of the two novellas in *Dusklands*, entitled "The Vietnam Project," is in the form of a report submitted to an official named Coetzee by one Eugene Dawn, a think-tank employee responsible for inventing new ways of destroying enemy morale through psychological warfare, who becomes gradually deranged as a result of his duties. The companion story, "The Narrative of Jacobus Coetzee," presents as its main character a fictional counterpart of Coetzee's ancestor in an apparent attempt to account for the South African present. It chronicles Jacobus Coetzee's destruction of an entire Hottentot tribe that had in his estimation, "humiliated" him. According to Barend J. Toerien's interpretation in *World Literature Today* (Summer 1978), *Dusklands* was "a device which allowed [Coetzee] to show the jelling of rigid attitudes and the props needed to establish and maintain the master/slave relationship, which is still the crutch of the South African establishment." It also seemed to reflect the "definite sense of closing horizons" that Coetzee felt upon his return to South Africa, especially in such ironic examples of tunnel (or gunbarrel) vision as Jacobus Coetzee's definition of savages as "those who do not have guns" and his description of all he has killed, including the Hottentots, as part of his "dispersed pyramid to life." Although it attracted little attention from reviewers outside of South Africa until after Coetzee's later books became known, *Dusklands* was found by some to be comparable in its impact to Joseph Conrad's novella *Heart of Darkness*.

Having presented his view of the rise of modern South Africa as embodied in his forefather,

Coetzee began to explore what seemed to be the scenario for its disintegration. *In the Heart of the Country* (Secker & Warburg, 1977), published in the United States as *From the Heart of the Country* (Harper & Row, 1977), completed at about the time of the Soweto uprisings of 1976 and 1977, dealt with the attempts of a madwoman, Magda, to come to terms with the apparent breakdown of a world once ordered with allegorical neatness into relationships of white and black, master and servant, father and child. The reader is introduced to that disintegrated world through 265 intense, stream-of-consciousness diary entries, comprising a kind of distress signal, which seem to be all that remain for Magda once the structure imposed on reality by the social and moral hierarchy is destroyed. She murders (or dreams of murdering) her father—with whom she seems to have an incestuous relationship—because he has (or she thinks he has) an affair with a black woman working on their farm. She is subsequently raped (or thinks she is) by the woman's husband and abandoned by everyone to live in her isolated farmhouse, trying to understand why she chooses not to leave it and whether or not there is significance in her choice and in her self. She concludes that she and the others she discusses "are outside the law" and therefore live "only by the law [they] recognize" in themselves, their "inner voice."

Although some reviewers thought that Magda rambled excessively, most praised *In the Heart of the Country*'s emotional power and stylistic grace. Sheila A. Roberts, a South African critic whose words were reprinted in *World Literature Written in English* (Spring 1980), took Magda to be a type of the "ineffectual dreaming liberal" and regarded the book as an exploration of why, despite liberal rhetoric, white South Africans "are still maintaining or silently condoning" their system. Barend J. Toerien in *World Literature Today* (Summer 1978) praised the book for its "brooding intensity" and "crazy humor" and interpreted Magda's continual revisions of her story and her desperate attempts to follow her "inner voice" as a less political and more universal search for self and meaning, perhaps even for God. It is a search consistent with Coetzee's own professed relationship to storytelling: "Writing is not carried out in a vacuum. The book is what you are about to become, or have become, or used to be." *In the Heart of the Country* won South Africa's highest honor for writing, the CNA Literary Award, in 1977. A film version entitled *Dust*, written and directed by Marion Hansel and starring Jane Birkin and Trevor Howard, was released in 1986.

In a review in the *New Republic* (March 11, 1985), Coetzee praised the Afrikaner poet Breyten Breytenbach for those parts of his *True Confessions of an Albino Terrorist* in which he "tries to feel his way into the experience of the condemned man, into the experience of death itself, . . . into the moral world of the men who order deaths, build prisons, carry out tortures, and then into the very interior of the mad thinking of 'security'

itself." With the two books that won Coetzee his international audience, *Waiting for the Barbarians* (Penguin Bks., 1980) and *The Life and Times of Michael K* (Secker & Warburg, 1983, Viking 1984), he makes similar attempts in stories in which spiritual and social turmoil of the kind found in Magda's narrative seemed to have found a physical location.

In *Waiting for the Barbarians* the unnamed "magistrate" of a frontier town in an unnamed "empire" confronts the incarnation of "the mad thinking of security" when a contingent from the "Third Bureau division of the civil guard" arrives, led by a torturer, Colonel Joll. Rumors of a massing of "barbarian" tribes against the empire have prompted the dispatch of Joll to "apply pressure." Joll's truth-getting methods, detached as they are bloody, prompt the magistrate to rethink his ideas about barbarism, about the empire and about Joll: "Is it only in the provinces that headsmen and torturers are still thought of as unclean? . . . [Does Joll] have a private ritual of purification . . . to enable him to return and break bread with other men?" Joll remains inscrutable, as does the passive (or indifferent) barbarian woman with whom the magistrate eventually has an affair. Throughout, the magistrate himself is in a state of confusion and questions his own motives without ever quite understanding them. After returning the woman to her tribe, he is driven from office as an enemy of the empire and delivered for a time into the attentive hands of the colonel. When Joll's forces are defeated by the tribes they rouse, the magistrate is reinstated and left to await the barbarian armies. His constituents adopt a surprising attitude, attributed on another occasion to Afrikaners whom Coetzee interviewed for an article that appeared in the *New York Times Magazine* (March 9, 1986): "They do not talk like people perched on the lip of a volcano. All of them believe the world around them is changing . . . but nowhere do they seem to envisage an eruption of change that might sweep them and their children away."

Some critics accused Coetzee of an unforgivable complacency, maintaining that his allegories, with their nondogmatic, even sympathetic portraits of characters implicated in oppression, merely described evil without truly attempting to disturb it. But many viewed *Waiting for the Barbarians* more broadly, agreeing with assessments such as that of Martin Seymour-Smith in *British Book News* (April 1981), who felt that it had applications far beyond South Africa and noted that Coetzee had "learned much from the masters of the novel of more or less oblique protest—Vargas Llosa, Asturias, García Márquez." In Seymour-Smith's view, the book "ought to be read by all those interested in decency and its perpetuation amongst men." *Waiting for the Barbarians* earned Coetzee the 1980 CNA Literary Award as well as the James Tait Black Memorial Prize and the Geoffrey Faber Award.

The July 1985 issue of *World Press Review* published a brief profile of Coetzee in which he indicated a distrust of all ideologies, whether critical, revolutionary or totalitarian. "I thrive on informed criticism," he asserted. "But people on the Left accuse me of remaining too aloof from South African realities, and those on the Right say I am too connected with them." In his *New Republic* essay on Breytenbach, Coetzee called an antigovernment mission that landed the poet in jail a "quixotic foray . . . valuable though that is for its pages of analysis of the appeal of direct political action to the intellectual." The value of apolitical but intense attachment to basic values—filial love, love of the earth, individual freedom—is explored in detail in Coetzee's fourth novel, *The Life and Times of Michael K.*

Michael K., condemned to a life as a victim by birth defects—a harelip and, in the view of those around him, simplemindedness—and by his low social status in a repressive society, is not a quixotic intellectual but, in the view of some critics, the embodiment of the idea that freedom is the ultimate good. He begins an odyssey through a country embroiled in civil war when his mother, sensing that she is dying, asks him to return her to the farm where she was born. After her death, K forges on with her ashes but is menaced by bandits, government soldiers, and rebels. He is flung into—and ingeniously escapes from—brutal refugee camps, internment camps, labor camps, prison and, toward the end of the book, a detention center where a staff doctor tries to offer him charity and understanding—both of which K interprets as new forms of confinement. An interlude during which K finds a kind of peace in planting pumpkin seeds and sleeping in a womblike burrow, almost a seed himself, ends when an army deserter arrives and tries to make him a servant.

Although *The Life and Times of Michael K* is filled with South African place names, the country is never actually named, nor is K's race specified. Coetzee further places his story outside a strictly South African context with references to Nazi Germany, including brutal camp guards who claim only to be doing their jobs. K himself, inarticulate and passive to the point of being boring, as some critics have observed, moves through Coetzee's landscape exposing the brutality of some characters and the sensitivity of others. His color and his nature seemed similarly to change in the eyes of reviewers. Some took "CM," as he is categorized by one official in the novel, to mean "Caucasian Male," others took it to mean "Colored Male." Cynthia Ozick, in a laudatory review in the *New York Times Book Review* (December 11, 1983), described the K who plants pumpkin seeds as "Robinson Crusoe . . . the lord of his life." The critic Bruce Allen found in him "the embodiment of the survival instinct," while Vivian Gornick, writing in the *Village Voice* (March 20, 1984), concluded that "we know very little of who or what Michael is. Coetzee tries to make him a holy idiot, but what emerges is a human being who . . . has been kept in a childlike state all his life: exactly what a man like Coetzee might observe of a man like Michael, the two of them passing each other daily on the streets of Capetown."

Coetzee's compatriot Nadine Gordimer concluded that in Michael K, Coetzee had gone beyond the allegorical characters of his earlier books by creating an "unclassifiable" figure with certain idiosyncracies, while at the same time fashioning a story that traced the harried lives of many blacks in South Africa. She considered Coetzee's portrayal of oppressors, who are just as helplessly confined by policies they no longer believe in as the people victimized by those policies, to be a brave statement for a South African to make. She noted, however, that the universal helplessness portrayed in the book, and especially Michael's passivity, "denies the energy of the will to resist evil." In her view, Coetzee, "while fiercely moved far beyond commonplace understanding of their plight, does not believe in the possibility of blacks establishing a new regime that will do much better." Nevertheless, she found that Coetzee achieved a "prehensile comprehension" of what he investigated and that *The Life and Times of Michael K*, with its "passionate vitality," was very likely a great novel. Responding to critics' comparisons of Michael K with Franz Kafka's Josef K, the protagonist of *The Trial*, Coetzee merely commented, according to Claire Tomalin, writing in the London *Sunday Times* (October 30, 1983), that Kafka had no "right of proprietorship" over the name.

Coetzee's writing style, in that as in his other books, was widely admired. In her *New York Times* review, Cynthia Ozick noted that the "grain of his sentences is flat and austere, but also so purifying to the senses that one comes away feeling that one's eye has been sharpened, one's hearing vivified, not only for the bright proliferations of nature, but for human unexpectedness." *The Life and Times of Michael K* earned for Coetzee Great Britain's most prestigious award, the Booker McConnell prize, as well as a CNA Literary Award, in 1983.

In his novel *Foe* (Secker & Warburg; Viking, 1986), Coetzee retold Daniel Defoe's classic *Robinson Crusoe* as a parable of colonization and took the theme of inarticulateness with which he dealt in *Michael K* to its logical extreme. The narrator, an Englishwoman named Susan Barton, tells the story of being shipwrecked on an island inhabited by a white man named Cruso and a black native called Friday, whose tongue had been cut out. The three are eventually rescued, but Cruso dies at sea, and Susan Barton arrives in England accompanied only by Friday. Wishing to tell her story but uncomfortable with writing, she relates her narrative to "Mr. Foe," a writer whom she does not trust to recount it fairly. According to Hermione Lee, writing in the London *Observer* (September 7, 1986), "A meditation develops on the parallels between writing and colonization. . . . At the center is the impenetrable silence of the black slave, 'subjected' by having his story told for him." She considered the book a "theoretical exercise" in some respects but found the image of Friday's silence spreading "to the ends of the earth" to be "unforgettable." Coetzee collaborated with André Brink in editing *A Land Apart: A South African Reader* (Faber, 1986), an anthology of fiction "compiled amid the tumult of the uprisings of 1985."

J. M. Coetzee is "a slightly built man with a prematurely graying beard, soft eyes, an even softer voice and an extraordinarily reticent manner," according to Allister Sparks, writing in the *Washington Post* (October 29, 1983). He is said to be "in a quandary" about his status as a public figure who is expected to make pronouncements on social issues but prefers to let his books speak for him. Currently Coetzee is still professor of general literature at the University of Cape Town, and he lives within walking distance of the campus, on the slopes of Table Mountain, on a road that does not appear on any map. He has reared his two children, Nicholas, and Gisela, the offspring of a marriage that ended in divorce. At the university, Coetzee is highly regarded as a literary critic, linguist, translator, and teacher, as well as novelist. A regular contributor to literature and language journals, he has published translations of poetry and prose from the Dutch, which he speaks fluently in addition to German, French, and Afrikaans. A batsman and bowler for the faculty cricket team at the university, Coetzee is also an aficionado of rugby, and he once wrote an essay on its sociology. In 1985 Coetzee received the Prix Fémina Etranger, and in the same year the University of Strathclyde in Scotland conferred an honorary doctorate on him. In 1987 Coetzee received the prestigious Jerusalem Prize for the Freedom of the Individual in Society. In his April 9 acceptance speech in Jerusalem, Coetzee called for the dismantlement of apartheid in South Africa. Apartheid, he said, created not only "deformed and stunted relations between human beings" but also a "deformed and stunted inner life." The result was to make South African literature " a literature in bondage . . . ,a less than fully human literature . . . , exactly the kind of literature you would expect people to write from a prison."

References: London Observer p7 O 30 '83 por; N Y Times Bk R p9 Ap 15 '84; Washington Post C p1+ O 29 '83; Contemporary Literary Criticism vol 23 (1983), vol 33 (1985); International Who's Who, 1986–87; Who's Who, 1986–87; World Authors, 1975–1980 (1985)

Conner, Dennis

1943– Yacht racer. Address: b. c/o St. Martin's Press Inc., 175 5th Ave., New York City, N.Y. 10010

The America's Cup, the most coveted of regatta prizes, is "the holy grail" to Dennis Conner, a yachtsman of middle-class origins who pursues the blueblood sport with a full-time dedication and aggressiveness that offends some of its more gentrified participants. Conner, who has been winning world match races since 1973, successfully defended the America's Cup as skipper of *Freedom* in 1980. Three years later he became the first American in 132 years to lose the Cup, to Australia, and he reclaimed the trophy as the skipper of *Stars & Stripes '87* in February 1987. Not the least of Conner's talents is his ability to organize around him a winning team—or syndicate, as it is known in the sport—of financial backers, yacht designers, high-tech scientists, crewmen, and others, and to infuse that team with his own enthusiasm. For him, leaving a single "stone unturned" is giving oneself "an excuse to lose." "I don't like to sail," he told Tom Callahan of *Time* (February 9, 1987). "I like to compete. I guess I don't *dislike* it, but my sailing is just the bottom line, like adding up the score in bridge. My real interest is in the tremendous game of life. . . . Funding, staffing, operating, planning, logistics, everything—isn't that the game of life?" Because of the "amateur" nature of the sport, Conner classifies yacht racing as his "hobby," despite the time and energy he devotes to it; his livelihood is

a wholesale and retail carpeting and drapery business in San Diego.

The son of a Convair jet engineer who also did some commercial fishing, Dennis Conner was born in San Diego, California, in 1943. Raised just half a block from the San Diego Yacht Club, he "hung around the place the way some kids hang around the local pool parlor," as he recounts in his autobiographical book about sailing, *No Excuse to Lose* (W. W. Norton, 1978), written with John Rousmaniere. Chubby and physically awkward as a boy, he had "a bit of an inferiority complex," which was exacerbated by the fact that he, in the midst of wealthy yachtsmen, "could never own [his] own boat as a kid." "But since sailing was one of the few things that I could do really well, and since it was important for me to excel at something, I kept at it, racing in many different types of boats as a crew." In high school he lettered in track and basketball but "wasn't really the star of the show." After graduating from high school, "like any kid not knowing what to do with himself," he studied business at San Diego State College, apparently without taking a degree. He worked summers in sail lofts but spent most of his free time in boats. Crewing for a number of owners in a variety of sailboats, he became "well rounded in a way that young boat owners are not." One of those for whom he crewed was the late Alan Raffee, who owned a carpeting business. Conner went to work for Raffee and eventually became his business partner, before starting his own business.

In 1970, when he was twenty-seven, Conner became a boat owner, with a $1,700 share in a thirty-three-foot-long PC class vessel, in which he won that year's PC class national championship. In 1971 he bought his own second-hand Star class boat, and in it he won the Star world championship in 1971 and 1972. At the same time, he was beginning to compete in match races. The major North American match race series, after the America's Cup, then held out of Newport, Rhode Island, is the Congressional Cup, centered in Long Beach, California. Conner first tried out for the Congressional Cup in 1971, when he was beaten in the West Coast eliminations. In his second try, in 1972, he was runner-up, and in 1973 he finally won, after a four-way tie. In 1975 he won again, easily, with eight victories against a single loss, and in 1976 he lost to Dick Deaver.

In the trials for the 1974 America's Cup defense, Conner began as number-two man under Ted Turner aboard *Mariner*, moved up to skipper of *Valiant*, and replaced Turner as skipper of *Mariner*. He was, finally, starting helmsman and tactician on *Courageous* when that boat won the final trials and went on to beat Australia's *Southern Cross*, 4-0. His sailing style in the 1974 regatta prompted the Australian syndicate head Alan Bond to characterize him as a "cowboy" who used "rodeo tactics." Jerry Kirshenbaum, writing in *Sports Illustrated* (March 24, 1975), remarked the "sheer aggressiveness" of Conner's "cunning starts, adroit tacks, and well-executed spinnaker runs."

Even before he went east for the 1974 America's Cup, Conner was, as the professional lingo goes, "organizing for" the boat that he would sail in the 1975 Southern Ocean Racing Conference, the most important distance-racing series in North America. Sailing the thirty-four-foot *Stinger*, designed for him by Doug Peterson, he won the 1975 SORC by 29.25 points. In the small-boat Olympics in Kings-

ton, Canada, in 1976, Conner and his number-one crewman, Conn Findlay, sailing Conner's Tempest yacht, finished in third place. Later in the same year Conner again won the Star world championship.

In preparation for his second America's Cup, this time as skipper, Conner in 1980 used two twelve-meter boats to try out hulls and sails, and he and his crew practiced for 3,000 hours in Newport and San Diego. In the event itself, sailing *Freedom*, he beat Australia 4-1. Two years later, preparing again to defend the Cup and looking for the ideal vessel, he had three boats built, tested them against each other, and decided on *Liberty*. Ted Turner and others accused him of "overkill" and pointed out that his obsessiveness had forced his rivals for the first time to resort routinely to organizational and fund-raising syndicates, which pushed costs beyond the range of any single individual. Conner responded, "What they're saying is, 'If I were willing to give as much as Dennis does, I could be as good as he is.' That's just an excuse to lose."

One group in agreement with Conner's all-out effort to mobilize space-age technology behind yachting competition was the Australian syndicate headed by Alan Bond, who had been trying to win the America's Cup for a decade and had invested $16 million in that attempt. It had been a Bond-sponsored boat that Conner had beaten in 1980. The Bond syndicate's 1983 boat, *Australia II*, with its winged keel, caused a sensation when it was officially measured in June 1983. As Conner recounts in his second book, *Comeback: My Race for the America's Cup* (St. Martin's Press, 1987), written with Bruce Stannard, *Australia II* "was pulverizing the competition in the foreign trials." He protested the keel, pointing out that America's Cup rules specify that twelve-meter boats entered in the race "shall draw no more than nine feet," but nothing came of his protest.

In the first race of the 1983 America's Cup, *Australia II* and *Liberty* were nip and tuck over most of the 24.3-mile course, which *Liberty* finished a minute and ten seconds faster than *Australia II*. Conner also won the second and third races, but *Australia II* rallied, taking the last four races and becoming the first foreign competitor to capture the America's Cup.

Setting his sights on recapturing the America's Cup, Conner spent virtually his every waking moment in the years leading up to the 1987 regatta in the most intense Cup campaign in history. To begin with, he founded the Sail America Foundation for International Understanding under the auspices of the San Diego Yacht Club and traveled the United States amassing corporate and individual funding totaling $16 million. In 1985 he and his crew moved to Honolulu in order to train in wind and water conditions very similar year round to those in the Indian Ocean off of Freemantle, Perth, Australia, where the Cup would be contested. Most important, he organized yachting's largest-ever and most high-tech design team, headed by the veteran sailor and sailmaker John Marshall and including three top yacht designers and nearly thirty scientists and engineers from the Grumman Corporation, the Scientific Applications International Corporation, and elsewhere.

The major constraint in developing a faster boat was the twelve-meter rule—which specifies certain mathematical relationships between hull dimensions and sail area—formulated by the International Yacht Racing Union in London. In deciding on the optimum design, the Sail America team members took into consideration the facts that the elimination rounds of the 1987 America's Cup would be held in the relatively mild winds of Australia's spring, in October, November, and December 1986, and that the final event would take place in the strong winds of the Australian summer, in January 1987. In performing tank tests with one-third-scale models, they pioneered the use of a computer code that made possible the accurate prediction of the wave drag of various hulls. The product of their efforts was an ingenious keel that would meet the twelve-meter rule limiting keel depth but minimize drag by causing the water to behave as if the keel were deeper. The trick was accomplished with delicately adjusted winglets.

The first full-scale boats created by the Sail America team, Stars & Stripes '85 and Stars & Stripes '86, were tested off the coast of Hawaii for ten months and in the Indian Ocean for seven months. Both boats were of unprecedented size in their class and had unprecedented power and speed as well as stability in heavy winds. Stars & Stripes '85 was the faster of the two under most conditions, and its crew had utmost confidence that it could beat any known competitor in the four-of-seven series in January 1987. The catch was that it had a slim chance—given the weather and water conditions expected in the Indian Ocean in the last months of 1986—of surviving the round-robin eliminations in which thirteen challengers would generally be two or three feet shorter. For that reason, the Sail America team revised the design and built a third boat, small enough to compete successfully in the round robins but still longer than the boats the team had observed competing in the twelve-meter world championships at Perth in late 1985 and early 1986. None of those boats was as large as the size the team had decided was optimal for summer conditions.

When Conner first saw the completed Stars & Stripes '87, he was, as he recounts in Comeback, "a bit taken aback by the pug nose, the gondola look," but he knew that "fast boats have their own way of looking good." With the fast boat went fast sails, designed by Conner's close friend Thomas Whidden in a Freemantle warehouse set up by Sail America. In the first America's Cup 1987 elimination round, at Freemantle in October 1986, Stars & Stripes '87 sailed to eleven victories against only one defeat. Competitors in and spectators of those races were surprised at Conner's departure from his wonted style. "My racing style is to be aggressive as I have been in the past," he later explained to Sarah Ballard when she interviewed him for Sports

Illustrated (February 16, 1987), "but this time I didn't have a boat that could do that. So I had to play with the personality of the boat I had. My boat can't tack, it can't turn, it can't stop, it can't go, and it can't go downwind. It can do one thing—it goes fast in a straight line. I had to adapt my style to the boat."

In the second elimination round, Conner, confronted by light winds disadvantageous to Stars & Stripes' design (and holding back from full speed in order to surprise the Australians later), lost four races. Coming out of the third and last round, he was in third place, with twenty-seven wins and seven losses. As preplanned, in the break between the round robins and the semifinals the span of Stars & Stripes '87's winglets was increased by 3.5 feet, making the boat potentially forty seconds faster over a 24.1 mile course in high winds and two minutes faster in low winds, primarily by increasing the upwind speed. Downwind, it would lose some speed, but Conner and his engineers had the great daring to take the risk. To make the boat slip even more quickly through the water, the hull was coated with a grooved, experimental plastic film to reduce drag, and the rudder was altered for greater maneuverability.

In the semifinals of America's Cup 1987, Conner skippered Stars & Stripes '87 to victories over USA, 4-0, and New Zealand 7 (popularly called Kiwi Magic), 4-1. Observing the races against New Zealand 7, the Australian skipper Iain Murray noted that Conner was "always in the right spot." Against Kookaburra III, skippered by Murray, in the final round Conner was at the peak of his powers. Despite the rudder modifications, Stars & Stripes '87 was still less maneuverable than Kookaburra III. In the starting maneuvers of each race, Murray tried to engage Conner in tacking duels, hoping to force him either to foul out or to cross the starting line early. Conner outwitted Murray by veering off into the spectator fleet and using it as a shield until just before the gun, when, with almost unbelievable timing, he would dart over the line.

The first race against Kookaburra III took place in light air and wildly shifting breezes. Using a light-air mainsail borrowed from USA, Conner again succeeded in being in the right place at the right time, riding all the favorable breezes and winning by a margin of one minute, forty-one seconds. When the second race took place, the wind known as the "Freemantle Doctor" (because of the cooling effect it has on the otherwise hot summer temperature of Freemantle) was at full strength, gusting sometimes to thirty knots and providing Stars & Stripes with its natural habitat. Stars & Stripes '87 won that race by one minute, ten seconds and the third race, in twelve to eighteen knots of breeze, by one minute, forty-six seconds. "The fourth and last race, on February 4," Conner recounts in Comeback, "was virtually over at the start, when Murray tried to push me over the line early but I was able to carefully luff and stall, gaining a six-second lead by the gun." The America's Cup was rewon when Stars & Stripes '87 finished that race one minute, fifty-nine seconds ahead of *Kookaburra III*. Just as when he had faced the press after his 1983 loss, there were tears in Conner's eyes as he accepted the trophy for the San Diego Yacht Club. When he returned home, 40,000 people lined the victory parade route in San Diego, and there were similar subsequent public acclamations in Washington, D.C., and New York City. On February 19, 1987, he was awarded the United States Yacht Racing Union's Yachtsman of the Year award at the New York Yacht Club.

Unlike many other competitive yachtsmen, Conner has not made any money from endorsement of products in connection with yachting. After the death of Alan Raffee in an airplane crash in the late 1970s, Conner left the Raffee family carpeting business and bought Vera's Draperies, a company that he still runs as a wholesale business. In addition, in partnership with Frank Trovato, Conner in 1985 founded Dennis Conner Interiors, which sells carpets and other floor coverings in addition to the Vera company's draperies. Conner is president of the enterprise, which employs thirty-seven drapers and other workers, and Trovato is vice-president and general manager. Trovato made most of the daily decisions when Conner was preoccupied with the America's Cup 1987. When possible Conner flew back to San Diego once a month to work on business strategy, and he telephoned Trovato once a week.

Dennis Conner is six feet one inch tall and heavy-set, with thick brown hair and heavy hands whose appearance belies the delicacy with which he uses them at the helm. Conner and his wife, Judy, have two daughters, Julie and Shanna. Mrs. Conner told Tom Callahan of *Time* that Conner "never relaxes," that "hell to Dennis would be a day on the beach at Acapulco." "He's a hard-driving guy," Adam Ostenfield, the starboard tailer on *Stars & Stripes '87*, said, as quoted by Sarah Ballard in *Sports Illustrated*. "And that's what he's made us into." According to Miss Ballard, Conner is "not an eloquent speaker." "Except when he is describing a twelve-meter match race, he has trouble squeezing his tumbling thoughts into tidy verbal packages," she wrote. "His delivery contains the hint of a stammer that worsens when his emotions are near the surface." Malin Burnham, the head of the Sail America syndicate, told Miss Burnham: "He can get so emotional, he spaces out. He loses touch with the world."

References: N Y Times C p1+ S 12 '83 pors, C p13 Ja 12 '87 pors; Sports Illus 66:66+ F 9 '87 pors, 66:10+ F 16 '87; Time 129:42+ F 9 '87 pors; Conner, Dennis, and Rousmaniere, John. No Excuse to Lose (1978); Conner, Dennis, and Stannard, Bruce. Comeback (1987)

Cruise, Tom

July 3, 1962– Actor. Address: b. c/o Andrea Jaffe, Suite 401, 9229 Sunset Blvd., Los Angeles, Calif. 90069

By combining clean-cut sex appeal with on-screen intensity and an aura of vulnerability, Tom Cruise, one of the reigning new film stars of the 1980s, has attracted a considerable amount of critical attention and established his box-office preeminence among the "brat pack" of young actors with whom he came to prominence. According to one Hollywood producer, "Guys want to be like him, and girls want to be with him." As a result, Cruise has exerted what has been called a "tidal pull" on his generation, packing his compeers into movie theatres to watch such films as *Risky Business* (1983), *Top Gun*, the biggest-grossing movie of 1986, and *The Color of Money* (1986), the critically acclaimed film that brought Cruise to the attention of older moviegoers.

Using his box-office clout as leverage, Cruise has achieved a salary estimated at $2 million per movie, accompanied by the perquisites of choosing his own projects and suggesting script changes. Nonetheless, he remains an extremely thoughtful performer, "avaricious," according to one observer, in his desire to grasp the essence of a character and dedicated to his conviction that his craft is the "most important thing" in his life. He prepares

himself physically as well as mentally for each role, losing or gaining weight, or even removing a cap from a damaged tooth. Writing in *Cosmopolitan* (January 1984), Lawrence Eisenberg praised Cruise's "chameleonlike way of becoming . . . disparate characters" and detected a "quality of self-mockery just below the surface" of his performances. "Despite the element of anger and raunchiness present in all of [his] characters," Eisenberg continued, Cruise "projects a potent wholesomeness, . . . an optimistic air of knowing how to survive."

Thomas Cruise Mapother 4th was born on July 3, 1962, in Syracuse, New York, the third of the four children and the only son of Thomas Cruise Mapother 3d, an electrical engineer, and Mary Lee Mapother, a teacher of dyslexic and hyperkinetic children and an amateur actress. She herself suffered from dyslexia, as did her children. Cruise has recalled that, when learning to read in kindergarten, he was unable to tell "whether letters like C or D curved to the right or the left" and though he performed skits and imitated television characters at home, he found himself ill at ease in school. His difficulties were exacerbated by the fact that the Mapothers moved frequently, following job opportunities in Missouri, New Jersey, New York, and Canada, and as a result, he attended eight grade schools and three high schools. "When you're a new kid, all you want to do is blend in with everybody and make friends," Cruise told David Hutchings in an interview for an article that appeared in People (September 5, 1983). Dyslexia and placement in remedial reading courses "separated you and singled you out." To prove himself among his peers and to make new friends, Cruise flung himself into sports, taking part in football, hockey, wrestling, lacrosse, tennis, baseball, and skiing.

After the divorce of his parents when he was eleven, Tom Cruise's mother took her children to her hometown, Louisville, Kentucky, where for five years she struggled to support them by taking on a variety of jobs, including selling appliances and serving as a hostess at electronics conventions. According to Christopher Connelly of Rolling Stone (June 19, 1986), the Mapothers wrote poems and read them to each other as gifts one Christmas when they were unable to afford any other kind of present.

"After a divorce, you feel so vulnerable," Cruise told Connelly during the Rolling Stone interview. Although he felt more acutely than ever a need to be accepted by his new acquaintances in Louisville, he never confided in them because he was convinced that they would fail to understand his special kind of childhood, so different from their own. One day, while walking to school, he told his sisters: "Let's just get through this. If we can just get through this somehow." At the age of fourteen, in his quest for what he has called a more "structured environment," Cruise enrolled at a Franciscan seminary in Cincinnati, with thoughts of becoming a priest, but he left after one year when he realized that he "loved women too much to give that up."

Cruise's mother remarried when he was sixteen, and the new family settled in Glen Ridge, New Jersey. There, Cruise was temporarily sidelined from sports when he injured himself while running up and down stairs in an effort to lose weight for a wrestling match. Looking for something to do, he followed up on a glee club instructor's suggestion that he audition for the high school musical, Guys and Dolls, and was cast in a leading role as Nathan Detroit. On opening night he discovered that he felt "at home on stage . . . relaxed," and realized that he finally "had a way to express [him]self." At home that night, he asked his mother and stepfather to give him ten years to "make it" in show business.

After appearing in a local dinner theatre production of Godspell, Cruise moved in with a friend in New York, where he worked as a busboy and took other odd jobs between auditions. He has been described by one of the Hollywood insiders he encountered at the time as "very New Jersey, less polished than he is now. . . . He was like a greaser—he had big muscles, he had his hair greased back. He had an angry edge to him." Although Cruise "may have been raw," Christopher Connelly noted in his Rolling Stone article, "he was handsome, and those who saw him then recall an urgency in his performing that was hard to dismiss." Within a few months of his move to New York, Cruise won a minor film role, as a teenager who advises a lovesick friend (Martin Hewitt) to set his girlfriend's (Brooke Shields) house on fire, in Franco Zeffirelli's ill-advised production of Endless Love (1981). That led to a role in Harold Becker's Taps (1981), a story of cadets who, under the spell of an irascible but charismatic commander, stage a bloody defense of their code of Honor, Duty and Loyalty, battling police and National Guardsmen after their school is put up for sale to developers and the commander is dismissed.

As the sidekick of a murderously fanatic cadet, David Shawn, Cruise performed so well during the course of filming that the two roles were combined and he became the new Shawn. Cruise "was so strong that the other guy didn't have a chance," co-star Sean Penn recalled for the Rolling Stone interview. Becker himself has said that Cruise's "strut down the field" showed "the crispness that a kid at a military academy might work three or four years for."

According to Sean Penn, Cruise accepted the casting shift with great reluctance, not wanting to hurt the career chances of the other actor. "To the end he was like that," Penn said. "He really was a total innocent." In playing what a reporter for Newsweek (June 9, 1986) called a "scarily dangerous" character in Taps, Cruise has said that he drew on aggression and anxiety built up in childhood. "The character is just fear," he explained to Cameron Crowe, who questioned him for Interview (May 1986). "That's what he does when he's afraid—he fights." To insure that Shawn would come to life on the screen, Cruise established what has become for him a commitment to physical as well as psychological realism, gaining fifteen pounds to give Shawn "visual impact" and successfully lobbying the director to add a scene showing the gung ho cadet lifting weights.

Taps was for the most part coolly received when it was released, but critics were impressed by Cruise's performance and filmmakers began to offer him what he has described as "a lot of insane characters." To avoid being typecast, he accepted the leading role in *Tijuana* or *Losin' It* (1983), a postpubescent sexploitation comedy about California teenagers who travel to Mexico for some fun and games. Although the film was withdrawn from theatres because of a listless response at the box office, it has been shown on cable television, to the acute embarrassment of Cruise and his costar, Shelley Long. If nothing else, *Losin' It* was a cautionary experience that taught Cruise to be more careful about choosing scripts and jobs. He told Edwin Miller, in an interview for an article that appeared in *Seventeen* (October 12, 1986): "You may feel you can make a script into something good, but you've got to examine all the elements of a project. Who's directing? Who's producing?"

In signing the contract for his next film, *The Outsiders* (1983), Cruise settled for relatively low pay and a minor role in order to work with the Academy Award-winning director Francis Ford Coppola. On location in Oklahoma, Cruise met Emilio Estevez, Matt Dillon, and Rob Lowe, who (along with *Taps* alumni Sean Penn and Timothy Hutton and several others) were often referred to in the press as a "brat pack" of "hot" young actors. Scripted by Kathleen Knutsen Rowell from a young adult novel by S.E. Hinton, *The Outsiders* portrays gang warfare between upper- and lower-class Tulsa teenagers, the preppy Socs, or "Socials," versus the Greasers. To prepare for his role as a Greaser, Cruise had a cap removed from a front tooth and avoided showering for most of the nine weeks of shooting. Although popular at the box office, *The Outsiders* disappointed many critics who accused Coppola of drowning S. E. Hinton's authenticity and humor in an egotistical display of epic style. Cruise, however, was grateful for the film. He told Cameron Crowe that in creating his Greaser character he learned that he had a flair for comedy.

In the midst of his location work on *The Outsiders*, Cruise flew to Los Angeles, still wearing his Greaser costume, to meet with the writer-director Paul Brickman. For four months, in preparing for what eventually became the film *Risky Business* (1983), Brickman had been trying to cast the part of the central character, Joel Goodsen, a young man who experiments with the free enterprise system by turning his suburban home into a brothel while his parents are away on vacation. When he arrived in Brickman's office, as Cruise recounted to Cameron Crowe, he was "pumped up and talking in an Oklahoma accent. . . . Paul just sat there," looking at him. After making a rocky start on a "cold read," both men ended up reading through half the script. "It was fun, we were all laughing," Cruise recalled. Although Cruise did not "test well" with Rebecca De Mornay, already cast as the call girl with whom Joel falls in love, he impressed Brickman with his detailed conception of

Joel Goodsen's character and mannerisms—among them a "kind of a duckwalk" and a fear of "*everything.*" Brickman concluded that Cruise had the "right combination of heat and innocence" and the "sheer physical intensity" he was looking for.

Once cast, Cruise shed almost fourteen pounds in five weeks by jogging and dieting. He then quit his exercise regime to "put on a little layer of baby fat." Joel Goodsen is "very vulnerable," Cruise told David Hutchings. "I didn't want any physical defenses up for him. No muscle armor at all." During filming, Cruise and Brickman developed one line of the script—"Joel dances in underwear through the house"—into a scene that became a popular icon, spoofed by Ron Reagan Jr. on *Saturday Night Live*, copied for a Campbell's soup commercial, and imitated by teenagers throughout the country. Wearing nothing but dark glasses, white socks, briefs, and a button-down shirt, Joel "rocked" his parents house as the family stereo blasted Bob Seger's "Old Time Rock & Roll." "With kids, to be a rock star is the ultimate," Cruise told Hutchings. "When their parents leave, they turn the music up."

Risky Business took in $65 million at the box office and won critical approval as well, though a few detractors accused it of pandering to the same exploitative American materialism that it claimed to satirize. Among its defenders was Tom Shales, who wrote in the *Washington Post* (August 30, 1983) that, between them, Cruise and Brickman had managed to "utterly revitalize the screen image of the young man who undergoes moviedreamy sexual initiation," and called a scene on a Chicago commuter train "one of the most blissfully erotic sequences in recent American filmdom." Another critic, Roger Ebert, as quoted in the *People* article, concluded that Cruise "occupies [*Risky Business*] the way Dustin Hoffman occupied *The Graduate.*"

In his next film, Michael Chapman's *All the Right Moves* (1983), Cruise played Stef Djordjevic, an athletically gifted youth who hopes to use his prowess to win a football scholarship and gain an education that will enable him to escape his economically crippled hometown. Cruise, who has described himself as "detail oriented," arrived early at the film's Johnstown, Pennsylvania, location, dyed his hair, attended the local high school under an assumed name, and worked out with its football squad. Although *All the Right Moves* was thought to be too predictable and formulaic by the critics, Cruise's portrayal of Djordjevic impressed reviewers. Rex Reed of the *New York Post* (October 21, 1983) credited Cruise with "a rare mixture of masculinity and sensitivity," concluding that of "all the current teen idols," Cruise was "the most sophisticated, the most appealing, the most capable of tackling a wider dramatic range . . . an actor, not a talking poster."

After making *All the Right Moves*, Cruise told Cameron Crowe, he felt he had "done the two extremes of high school life" and wanted a change. He disappeared from public view for over two years while mulling over various projects and working on *Legend*, which was released in Britain by Universal (1985) and in the United States by Twentieth Century-Fox (1986). A $30 million fantasy film directed by Ridley Scott, *Legend* kept Cruise in London for a year with production problems, including a fire that destroyed most of the set. Cruise, who has said he "grew up on fantasy films," starred as the magical character Jack O' the Green in a production featuring unicorns, elves, and other mythological beings. After its opening three weeks, during which it became America's top-grossing film on the strength of Cruise's popularity, *Legend* floundered and failed at the box office. It was dismissed by critics for what Richard Corliss described in *Time* (May 12, 1986) as "landscapes too remote," "quests too familiar," and "special effects too rudimentary," and despite his professed affection for the film, Cruise admitted that as Jack O' the Green he had become "another color in a Ridley Scott painting."

Before shooting was completed on *Legend*, Cruise was sent a script for what eventually became *Top Gun* (1986), a flight school saga in the tradition of macho-star vehicles of the 1940s and 1950s. In researching the film at San Diego's Miramar Naval Air Station, *Top Gun*'s producers, Don Simpson and Jerry Bruckheimer, decided that the young pilots they saw were "rock and rollers in the sky," or "Tom Cruises." They asked Cruise to star as Lieutenant Pete ("Maverick") Mitchell, a brilliant, egotistical pilot who struggles to adapt to the Navy's code of behavior, but he was dissatisfied with the script, and it was agreed that he would rework it with Bruckheimer and Simpson without any obligation to sign for the movie. He finally signed after being taken up for a flight with the Navy's elite Blue Angels demonstration team, for flying in the F-14, he soon discovered, "is one of those experiences that is bigger than life itself." Back on the ground he prepared intensively, rising each morning at four in order to run and on Wednesdays joining the fighter pilots for a hard-drinking "Animal Night" at the officers club, where he took note of the flyers' gestures and body language.

Top Gun earned a remarkable $8.1 million in its opening weekend at American theatres, and most critics acknowledged the visceral excitement of its flight combat and midair collision sequences, which gained a reputation as the most spectacular ever filmed. Some reviewers, however, were disturbed by what they perceived as the film's rampant jingoism in portraying, according to Robert Lindsey of the *New York Times* (May 7, 1986), a "bellicose" and "Rambo-esque triumph over the forces of Communism." Jacob V. Lamar Jr., reviewing *Top Gun* in *Time* (November 24, 1986), called the film "a 110-minute commercial for the Navy," and Joseph Gelmis wrote in *Newsday* (May 16, 1986) that the filmmakers had overestimated "our sympathy for the arrogant Maverick. When a nice guy dies because of his compulsive grandstanding, we resent it." The strength of Cruise's performance, however, seemed to have been his ability

to project what David Ansen described in *Newsweek* (June 9, 1986) as an uncanny ability to convey an endearing boyishness in spite of the cocksure arrogance of Maverick Mitchell. *Top Gun* went on to gross more than $150 million. Ansen concluded, "It seems the 80s generation has found its all-American type."

Following *Top Gun*, Cruise fulfilled a daydream he had when first breaking into the film business, that of working under the director Martin Scorsese. The film that emerged, *The Color of Money*, was released in the autumn of 1986 and featured Paul Newman in a return to the role of "Fast Eddie" Felsen, which he had created in the 1961 classic *The Hustler*. Cruise played Vincent Luria, an arrogant but naive and straightforward pool prodigy whom Newman's Fast Eddie, himself a former prodigy, works to transform into a hustler. Discussing his creative approach to Vincent Luria with the *Washington Post*'s Paul Attanasio (October 17, 1986), Cruise said, "A lot of times, looking at a character, first you decide what they're afraid of." Luria, he felt, was "afraid of being alone, because, in some sense he's always alone. Vincent has a lot of fears—that's why he moves so fast. When you see him walking, it's a skip and a jump." At one point, during the filming of a lesson in pool hustling given Luria by Newman's Fast Eddie, Cruise improvised one of Luria's impulses by abruptly walking over to embrace the older actor. Newman, according to Scorsese, "didn't know what was going on and the expression on his face was perfect." Cruise also taught himself to play pool for the movie and did all but one of Luria's spectacular shots and "thunderbolt" breaks.

His performance in *The Color of Money* brought Cruise almost universal critical acclaim for the first time in his career. Several critics noted, and Scorsese confirmed, that the mentor/protégé relationship between Newman and Cruise did not end on the screen. "I think there's an element of that," Scorsese has said, "of the older guy passing on the torch to the younger actor." In August 1987 Cruise was scheduled to begin work on the film "Rainman."

On May 9, 1987, Tom Cruise married the actress Mimi Rogers in a Unitarian ceremony. Cruise is five feet nine inches tall, muscular, well-groomed, and "conscientiously polite." According to several sources, his courteous, almost deferential demeanor extends not only to distinguished coworkers such as Scorsese (who "had to keep hitting him to get him to stop" saying "sir") but also to strangers. The actress Lea Thompson characterized Cruise as self-confident and "very giving," recalling that he urged the director to expand her character in *All the Right Moves*. Crediting Cruise's childhood and upbringing with his "extreme responsibility and loyalty," producer Don Simpson called Cruise "the youngest patriarch I've ever encountered," explaining, "His road was never paved; it was always full of potholes, and he jumped over them all."

References: *Interview* p42+ My '86 pors; *N Y Daily News* p5 O 16 '83 pors; *Newsday* II p4+ O 12 '86 pors; *Newsweek* 107:72+ Je 9 '86 pors; *People* 20:107+ S 5 '83 pors, 25:105+ Je 2 '86 pors; *Rolling Stone* p37+ Je 19 '86 pors; *Seventeen* p63+ F '84 pors; *Washington Post* B p1+ Ag 30 '83 pors, B p1+ O 17 '86 por; *International Motion Picture Almanac*, 1986

Crystal, Billy

Mar. 14, 1948– Comedian; actor. Address: b. c/o Jack Rollins, Rollins, Joffe, Morra & Brezner Inc., 801 Westmount Dr., Los Angeles, Calif. 90069

If, as the veteran all-round entertainer Steve Allen believes, the humorous character sketch is comedy's "major leagues," then Billy Crystal should surely be destined for comedy's big-league Hall of Fame. Crystal, a gifted mimic who feels "at home in other bodies," is an actor as well as a comedian and is theatrical even in his standup humor. He does not tell jokes or do pat impressions but evokes full-blown alter egos, including composite Jewish relatives, old jazz musicians, and other characters drawn from his experience, such fictional creations as the transvestite "Penny Lane," and uncannily palpable caricatures of a host of show-business figures, including Sammy Davis Jr. (singing, in one bit, "We Are the World" with Yiddish asides). Whoopi Goldberg, another comic who does personalities rather than one-liners, has said of Crystal: "There's no character he can't do. He does me better than *I* do me."

Crystal, who began his career with a small-time improvisational trio in 1969 and went solo four and a half years later, now draws top dollar at the best resorts and clubs in the United States. He cultivated a national following playing the homosexual Jodie Dallas in the outrageous ABC television situation comedy *Soap* in 1977–81, hosted *The Billy Crystal Comedy Hour* on NBC in 1982, and achieved superstardom as the most outstanding member of the cast of the NBC comedy show *Saturday Night Live* during the 1984–85 television season. The running hit of SNL that season was Billy Crystal's perennial routine "Fernando's Hideaway," a mock morning talk show fatuously hosted by a fading Latin-American matinee idol and Lothario (Crystal) who is given to saying, "Remember, it's better to look good than to feel good, and darling, you look *mahvelous*." Crystal has also done dramatic as well as comedic acting in made-for-television movies. On the big screen, he starred in the coolly received comedy *Rabbit Test* (1978) as well as the comedy/action drama *Running Scared* (1986), which had mixed reviews but better box office.

Billy Crystal was born in the borough of Manhattan, New York City, on March 14, 1948, the youngest of the three children, all sons, of Jack and Helen Crystal. As he says in his slim autobiography, *Absolutely Mahvelous* (Putnam's, 1986), written with Dick Schaap, he was "bred for show business." His paternal grandfather was a Yiddish actor, and his mother loved the theatre and performed in shows at temple. One of his uncles, Milt Gabler, founded Commodore Records in the late 1930s and later headed Decca Records. (Dedicated to the recording of pure jazz, Commodore bucked the trend to swing music and was instrumental in the Dixieland revival.) His father (who died in 1963) managed Gabler's Commodore Music Shop, on Fifty-second Street in Manhattan, and was a producer of jazz concerts at the Central Plaza, a Jewish catering hall and ballroom on the Lower East Side. Joel Crystal, Billy's older brother, teaches art at Long Beach (Long Island) High School. Richard, the middle brother, is a television producer. "Fernando's Hideaway" was his idea, when he was working on *The Billy Crystal Comedy Hour*.

Billy grew up in the Bronx (for two years) and in Long Beach, Long Island, where his mother still lives, when she is not wintering in Miami. Jazz musicians "were part of the family," he recalls. "The musicians called me 'Face,'" he writes in *Absolutely Mahvelous*. "I met Billie Holiday when I was five. Miss Billie called me *Mister* Billy. The first blind man I ever saw was W. C. Handy. My father used to bring home jazz musicians at Passover. We had swinging seders." Pee Wee Russell taught him to play the clarinet, and Willie (the Lion) Smith, Eddie Condon, Henry (Red) Allen, and Zutty Singleton played at his bar mitzvah. He "loved their [the musicians'] jive talk" and "started imitating them." Donning the adults' hats and overcoats, he also did impressions of visiting relatives. "We had this mixture of Jewish ethnic people with great love and a sense of humor [and] black jazz musicians . . . all at the bar mitzvah together."

Jack Crystal guided his sons' television viewing toward "tasty things" like Laurel and Hardy movies, Billy remembers, and away from the kind of comedy represented by the Three Stooges, and he brought home from his store the recordings of such comedians as Bill Cosby, Mike Nichols and Elaine May, Woody Allen, and Jonathan Winters. Listening to Cosby tell funny family stories, Billy realized that he had his own such stories, that he could "talk about Uncle Max" and other relatives. Encouraged by their mother, he and his brothers would perform together in the living room for their extended family, lip-synching Spike Jones's records and imitating the televised or recorded routines of Mel Brooks and Carl Reiner, Ernie Kovacs and his "Nairobi Trio," and Sid Caesar, among other celebrated comedians.

Unlike many who became professional comedians, Billy Crystal was diligent in school, never a cutup. Without resorting to clowning, he was voted the wittiest student in his class at Long Beach High School. In 1964 he emceed the school's annual variety show and contributed to it his own rendering of Bill Cosby's "Noah" routine. At that time he was more interested in baseball than in show business, and he might have become a Triple-A player were it not for his diminutive size. (He is five feet six inches tall and weighs about 130 pounds.) After playing shortstop for and captaining the high school team, he went to Marshall University, in Huntington, West Virginia, on a baseball scholarship. No sooner had he arrived at the university than it eliminated its baseball program for lack of funds. Finding the university to be "too far Off Broadway" for his sensibility, he stayed only one year, during which he hosted a call-in show on the campus radio station. "I used to call in to myself," he recounts in Absolutely Mahvelous. "I'd put my questions on tape and then I'd do the answers live."

In the fall of 1966 Crystal transferred to Nassau Community College, in Garden City, Long Island, where his girlfriend and future wife, Janice Goldfinger, was beginning her freshman year. He majored in theatre at the two-year college, and he spent three summers acting in productions of the school's Alumni Theatre Group. He also directed one of the group's productions, The Apple Tree. Victor Abravaya, the administrative assistant to the chairman of the theatre and dance department at Nassau Community College, told Wayne Robbins of Newsday (February 8, 1976) that Crystal had "the most drive" of any student in his class and that "when Billy has his mind set on something, there's no stopping him." After graduating from Nassau Community College, Crystal studied television and motion picture directing under Martin Scorsese at New York University. While at NYU, he worked as the house manager for the Off-Broadway hit musical You're a Good Man, Charlie Brown.

In 1969 Crystal and two fellow alumni of Nassau Community College, Dave Hawthorne and Al Finelli, formed an improvisational comedy troupe called successively We The People, Comedy Jam, and Three's Company. The trio played Greenwich Village clubs, small Eastern colleges, and trade shows for four and a half years, making barely enough money to cover expenses. Crystal, married and with a baby daughter (his first of two) to support, did part-time teaching at Long Beach Junior High School for two of those years.

Three's Company was managed by Buddy Morra and Larry Brezner, then the junior partners in Rollins, Joffe, Morra & Brezner, a talent management firm with a very impressive track record. (It still represents Crystal as well as such other comedians as Woody Allen, Robin Williams, and David Letterman.) Morra and Brezner were urging Crystal to "try stand-up" on his own, but the prospect filled him with "self-doubt and anxiety." "I spent some time in therapy when I wanted to break up the group but didn't know how," he told Wayne Robbins of Newsday. "The last year of Three's Company I could hardly function. [Finally] the therapist told me. 'Go do it.' So I did." The turning point was his initial, tentative solo professional booking, a $25 gig at an NYU fraternity party. For that occasion, Crystal, who says he "needs deadlines," put together on short notice an act built around impressions of the braggadocian prizefighter Muhammad Ali and the grandiloquent sportscaster Howard Cosell. "I was supposed to do twenty minutes, and I did more than an hour," he recounts in his autobiography. "I exploded. I went nuts and the kids went crazy. . . . Buddy and Larry said, 'Let's go to work.'"

At the start of his solo career, Crystal worked nights for a pittance if not gratis at Catch a Rising Star, a Manhattan comedy showcase, and spent his days taking care of his daughter Jennifer, while his wife went out to work as a secretary. For a time, he also toured the Playboy clubs. Among those who caught his act were the producers of Saturday Night Live, an irreverent weekly television comedy show broadcast from New York City over the NBC network beginning in October 1975. Their plan was to use Crystal in six of the broadcasts in 1975-76, but that plan was abandoned when Crystal walked off the set just before the first broadcast, when he was told he would have to cut the seven-minute monologue he had prepared down to two minutes. He did so reluctantly and sadly, on the advice of Buddy Morra, as he recounts in Absolutely Mahvelous, and "crawled back to Long Island shaken."

NBC's Saturday Night Live had to shorten its title briefly because of conflict with the title of ABC's Saturday Night Live with Howard Cosell, which had begun airing in September 1975. The NBC show regained its full original title when Cosell's program folded in midseason. (Crystal was a guest performer on the last Cosell broadcast, in January 1976.) Saturday Night Live went on to become NBC's sole smash hit of the 1975-76 season. Crystal finally appeared on it in April 1976, doing "Face," his monologue of a composite of old black musicians. As he recalls, he "got good reviews, great reaction" but "wasn't on the show again for the next eight years."

With his wife and first-born daughter, Crystal moved to Los Angeles, where the television producer Norman Lear and several ABC executives caught his act one night at the Comedy Store, an "improv" club similar to New York's Catch a Rising Star. Lear gave him a guest role in his situation comedy *All in the Family* and then cast him as Jodie Dallas, the first openly homosexual character in the history of television, in the prime-time half-hour weekly situation comedy *Soap*, a spoof of soap operas that ran on the ABC network from 1977 to 1981. With its risqué humor and innovative flouting of taboos (from impotence and extramarital sex to the humorous humanizing of organized criminals), *Soap* offended church and family-oriented groups but nevertheless attracted a large and loyal audience. As originally written, the Jodie character was an egregiously effeminate stereotype that drew objections from homosexual organizations. With the cooperation of the writers, Crystal toned the character down, to the point where the National Gay Task Force eventually applauded Jodie as "the one sane, sensitive person on the whole show." Although he felt he was "doing good work," doing one character season after season bored Crystal, and he "never felt good about the success [he] was getting" in *Soap*. "It wasn't what I wanted," he said in retrospect. "It wasn't me. You wait a long time for the right thing."

Among those who enjoyed watching Crystal on *Soap* was the comedian Joan Rivers, who cast him as Lionel, the world's first pregnant man, in the far-fetched comedy *Rabbit Test* (Avco Embassy, 1978), a motion picture that she cowrote and directed. That picture was a critical dud, dismissed by most critics as sophomoric and "tasteless." In the made-for-television film *Human Feelings* (NBC, 1978), a comic updating of the Sodom and Gomorrah story, God, played by Nancy Walker, threatens to destroy Las Vegas if six righteous people cannot be found there within one week. In that film, Crystal was cast as the angel who, disguised as the mortal Myles Gordin, is dispatched to scour the city for the redeeming six. With thirty minutes of new material added, *Human Feelings* was repeated as a two-hour pilot on NBC in 1980. Crystal also had several roles in TV dramatic films: that of David, one of the endangered supersonic transport passengers in *SST—Death Flight* (ABC, 1977); of Danny Doyle, one of the six estranged husbands who spend the summer together at a Malibu Beach house in *Breaking Up Is Hard to Do* (ABC, 1979); and of Lieutenant Jake Beser in *Enola Gay* (NBC, 1980), the story of Colonel Paul Tibbets and the crew of the plane that dropped the atomic bomb on Hiroshima. In interludes away from the big and small screens, Crystal returned to the live comedy circuit, and he played the Master of Ceremonies in a summer stock production of the musical *Cabaret* in Ohio in 1981.

Just before the premiere of the *The Billy Crystal Show* on NBC, Crystal previewed the program for Kay Gardella of the *New York Daily News* (January 26, 1982) in these words: "The show looks like an illustrated monologue. As I talk, scenes will develop in a warm and informal way. Since my two idols are Red Skelton and the late Ernie Kovacs, I try to combine elements of both of them. Like Skelton, I do my own characters. For instance, there's eighty-three-year-old Julius. . . . Then there's Tony Monetti, the old fighter; Willie, an autograph hound who hangs around Sardi's; Tony Terrio, a street punk, and Dr. Stan Green, a radio type who takes phone calls like Allen Burke or Joe Pine [two pioneers of television talk show irascibility]."

Among the guests on the premiere of *The Billy Crystal Comedy Hour*, in prime time on Saturday, January 30, 1982, was Robin Williams, who joined Crystal in several comedy skits, including "The Punk Honeymooners," with Crystal spoofing Ralph Kramden and Williams, Ed Norton. Reviewing that first program, Marvin Kitman wrote in *Newsday* (February 2, 1982): "He [Crystal] seems to be able to do everything. But he doesn't have the big ego to go with all the talent. He seems to be, underneath the nice guy image, a nice guy. . . . The tale of the old jazz musician . . . was endearing and tender. . . . His stories sparkle with *joie de vivre*." Starting out against such competition as a two-hour version of the hit series *Love Boat*, the Golden Globe awards, and a TV showing of the popular theatrical movie *Silver Streak*, Crystal's program had low ratings and was terminated with its fifth airing, on February 27, 1982.

When Crystal guest-hosted *Saturday Night Live* in March 1984, he and the producers began talking about his becoming a regular cast member. At first he was dubious about the wisdom of uprooting his family from California in order to fill a slot in a show that had been in decline since the 1970s, when its brash, untamed young cast came seemingly out of nowhere to create a national sensation by saying things never heard on television before. As the early comic formulas wore thin, the show's novelty wore off and its ratings dropped. The producers assured Crystal that the cast would be reshuffled with a watchful eye to well-crafted professionalism, and when he learned that he would be part of an input of new but experienced comic talent including his friends Martin Short, Christopher Guest, and Harry Shearer, he knew that "the caliber of the work would be high." (Guest and Shearer are, like Crystal, performers who write practically all of their own material.) He agreed to join the cast for the 1984–85 season.

When *Saturday Night Live* rebounded in the ratings in 1984–85, observers on all sides gave most of the credit to Crystal and his gallery of impersonations, including a Borscht Belt comic, a seventy-five-year-old baseball player, a phlegm-voiced Jewish weatherman ("The forecast for Thursday: Don't be such a big shot. Take a jacket"), an elderly hippie with a Yiddish accent who recounts his seeing Sly and the Family Stone, "the whole *mishpochah*," at the Woodstock rock 'n' roll festival, and impressions of the appearance (with the aid of makeup man Peter Montagna) as well as the voice and mannerisms of such show-business figures as Joe Garagiola, Yul Brynner, and Joe Franklin. "You look mahvelous," the catch phrase of his Fernando character, echoed across the United States and became the best-known comedy line of the year.

"What sets the Crystal brand of humor apart from much that has come before," Daniel B. Wood of the *Christian Science Monitor* (April 10, 1985) observed, "is . . . that [it] is built from real characters, usually people Crystal knew. . . . Not that Crystal doesn't appear in the occasionally crude or irreverent skit, but by SNL standards he often has that lighter, more poignantly comic flair that arises out of true human impulse." In an interview with Wood, Dick Ebersol, *Saturday Night Live*'s executive producer, described Crystal as "a very humane comedian" as well as "the most professional, hardest-working, most dedicated person" he had ever worked with. "When you talk about someone who's a star like he is, writes three-fourths of his own material, and works eighteen hours a day, it's simply mind-boggling," Ebersol said. "SNL is one of the last shows if not the only show in show business where someone that's as multi-talented as he is can show off his talents."

Crystal parlayed his Fernando bit into the hit song "Mahvelous," an A&M LP with the same title, and a four-minute music video. In the video, Crystal, as Fernando, crooned "Mahvelous" and backed himself up with impersonations of Sammy Davis Jr., Tina Turner, Grace Jones, and Prince. The Fernando character is loosely based on the late actor Fernando Lamas, who used to make Crystal giggle when he would appear as a guest on *The Tonight Show Starring Johnny Carson* and do "that macho thing where he would sit and fix a crease in his pants before saying hello to Johnny." Esther Williams, Lamas' widow, was, along with her husband before his death in 1982, originally amused by the continuing impersonation, but she told an interviewer for *People* (September 30, 1985) that she had come to feel it a cruel mockery that "this dignified man should be remembered as a silly woman chaser." Crystal insisted that while Lamas inspired the Fernando character, he was not its essence, which was the satirization of "every talk show in the morning ever invented." "The late Mr. Lamas was an intelligent man," he told an interviewer for *Playboy* (September 1985). "My guy is an idiot."

During 1984 and 1985 Crystal performed regularly at the Sands Hotel in Atlantic City, and shortly after the 1984–85 television season ended he played the Bottom Line club in Greenwich Village. "Billy Crystal has always been a funny actor rather than a comedian . . . ," Wayne Roberts wrote in his review of the Bottom Line engagement in *Newsday*. "He is strongest in intelligently paced conceptual pieces and in the development of well-rounded characters. . . . Crystal is also one of the most visually oriented funny men. . . . His greatest stage assets are his face and his hands. His face

is so elastic that it can span not just moods but generations. . . . The hands are as sure and as swift as those of a Gold Glove shortstop, always one move ahead of the ball—or, in Crystal's case, adding narrative weight as well as punctuation to his stories."

The television special *A Comedy Salute to Baseball,* broadcast on NBC in July 1985, was co-written and hosted by Crystal, whose guests included comedian Bob Newhart and a bevy of baseball players and managers. The movie director Peter Hyams, witnessing Crystal's agility playing infield in a show-business baseball game and already having sensed that his standup work was "acting and not mimicry," offered him a starring role in the action comedy/drama *Running Scared*. In August 1985 Crystal announced that he would not be returning to *Saturday Night Live* for the 1985–86 season, explaining, "They didn't know what was going to happen with [the television show]. The movie came up and I really wanted to do it."

Running Scared (MGM, 1986), written by Gary DeVore and Jimmy Huston, is the story of two renegade Chicago undercover policemen (Crystal and Gregory Hines) who bungle a drug bust and take an enforced vacation in Florida, where they make a down payment on a bar and decide on early retirement. Before retiring, they must return to Chicago for a final tour of duty, during which they joke their way through a hair-raising gamut of life-threatening encounters with the underworld. The critical consensus was that Crystal comes across in the movie as "free-spirited" and "surprisingly sure" in his acting but "stifled" by an unimaginative "copycat" script riddled with genre clichés as well as hip banter that doesn't "quite match . . . the violent action." Among the more generous of the reviewers was Mike McGrady of *Newsday* (June 21, 1986), who thought that Crystal and Hines "generate a splendid flow, and despite the breakneck speed of events, it's that personal electricity that gives the movie its heat."

With fellow comedians Robin Williams and Whoopi Goldberg, Crystal cohosted the Home Box Office television special *Comic Relief,* a benefit concert for the homeless, in March 1986. Five months later he starred on the HBO special *On Location: Billy Crystal—Don't Get Me Started,* an hour-long show that included the tape of a performance he had given at Hofstra University in May 1986. Stephen Holden, of the *New York Times* saw the special as bringing Crystal into "the serious comedy territory occupied by Lily Tomlin, Woody Allen and only a handful of others." Marvin Kitman of *Newsday* thought that Crystal's satirical portraits were getting "stronger each time" and that Peter Montagna, his makeup man, "deserves an Emmy" for helping him to "look like 'Spitting Image' puppets." During the summer of 1986 Crystal took his act on tour across the United States, and in September 1986 he spent several nights sitting in for Johnny Carson as host of the NBC television network's *The Tonight Show*. He hosted the live

Grammy awards show on the CBS television network in February 1987.

Billy Crystal has been described as "elfin" in stage presence, "vulnerable" but "resilient" in ego, and "straight as a baseball bat" in lifestyle. Crystal and his wife, the former Janice Goldfinger, who were married in 1970, currently live with their two daughters, Jennifer and Lindsay, in Pacific Palisades, California, but they hope to move back to New York again. Among Crystal's close Hollywood friends are Rob Reiner, Robin Williams, and Jamie Lee Curtis. Softball, tennis, cooking Japanese food, and collecting New York Yankees memorabilia are among his recreations. "I'm comfortable being old . . . being black . . . being Jewish," Crystal writes in *Absolutely Mahvelous.* "And I look good very good in dresses. I like twisting my face and my voice and my mind into different characters. . . . But I do have a specialty. When I'm in trouble, under pressure, I fall back on being old and Jewish. I rattle phlegm. . . . I feel good."

References: Contemporary Newsmakers Issue 3 p27+ por; N Y Daily News TV Week p2+ Ag 26 '84 por, P p4 Mr 3 '85 por, mag p7+ Je 15 '86 por; Newsday II p3+ F 8 '76 pors, II p3 O 21 '84 por; People 9:87+ Ap 10 '78 pors, 23:41+ S 30 '85 pors; USA Weekend p4+ Ag 1-3 '86 pors; Washington Post B p1+ Je 24 '85 pors; Crystal, Billy. Absolutely Mahvelous (1986)

Curran, Charles E(dward)

Mar. 30, 1934– Roman Catholic theologian.
Address: Cornell University, Ithaca, N.Y. 14853;
c/o Catholic University of America, 620
Michigan Ave. N.E., Washington, D.C. 20017

In keeping with Pope John Paul II's conservative thrust, the Vatican in August 1986 revoked the license of the Rev. Charles E. Curran to teach moral theology in the School of Religious Studies at the Catholic University of America, the only pontifical university in the United States. Father Curran, the first American ever to be so disciplined by Rome, is perhaps the best-known Roman Catholic moral theologian in the United States, a popular professor at the papally chartered university since 1965 and the author of sixteen books, most of which are compilations of his lectures and contributions to professional journals. Unlike Hans Küng, the Swiss theologian condemned by the Holy See in 1979, Curran is not a revolutionary offering a radical reevaluation of the church itself but a mainstream reformer who believes that theology "should always be in dialogue with the world" and "in tension with the church." The points of contention in his case were nuanced, relatively minor qualifications of what were traditionally absolute "noninfallible hierarchial teachings" in the areas of sexual and medical ethics, including artificial birth control and sterilization (which in his view "are not intrinsically evil but good or evil insofar as they are governed by the principles of responsible parenthood and stewardship"). The crux of the matter seems to have been his insistence on the right to dissent openly on debatable issues, an insistence that in Rome's view was a source of "scandal." While fighting for reinstatement at Catholic University, Curran is teaching at Cornell University.

Charles Edward Curran was born in Rochester, New York, on March 30, 1934. With his mother, a devout Catholic of German descent, he attended daily Mass as a child. From his father, an insurance adjuster and Democratic politician of Irish ancestry, he "inherited . . . cynicism," as he told Jim Castelli of *People* (April 7, 1986). "If you're cynical enough, you don't fall for everything that comes down the pike." As a result, he would never fall "for all that folderol" he would encounter in Rome.

When Curran was twelve he began thinking of the priesthood as a way "of being involved in some sort of spiritual service to people," and at thirteen he entered St. Andrew's Minor Seminary in Rochester. After completing his secondary education at St. Andrew's, he earned his B.A. degree at St. Bernard's Seminary. His aspiration was simply to become a Rochester diocesan priest, a pastor or curate, but his supervisors singled him out for higher theological studies at pontifical universities. Sent to Rome, he took two doctorates there in 1961. One was from the Lateran University, where his thesis was "Invincible Ignorance of the Natural

Law According to St. Alphonsus." The other was from the Gregorian University, where his dissertation was "The Prevention of Conception After Rape: An Historical Theological Study."

From 1961 to 1965 Curran taught moral theology at St. Bernard's Seminary in Rochester. "I learned theology the old way and I taught it for a couple of years," he recounted to Lois Romano of the Washington Post (September 4, 1986). "Then I did a lot of counseling with Catholic couples who were my own age at the time and experiencing these problems (with church positions on sexual issues). It was in talking to them that all of a sudden I really began to question the whole thing. . . . These are problems that everyone has to deal with. Everybody's family has had to deal with the issue of divorce. . . . A good number of families are increasingly having to deal with the question of a homosexual child." Regarding such problems, his response was "in no way in favor of any kind of promiscuity" but rather "to look at church teachings in light of these changes." His evolving point of view was evident in his contribution to Ecumenical Dialogue at Harvard (Harvard University Press, 1964), edited by S. H. Miller and G. E. Wright.

Curran's liberated approach to moral theology made him too innovative for the training of undergraduate seminarians, in the view of his superiors at St. Bernard's. With the approval of his bishop, in 1965 he moved to the theology faculty of the Catholic University of America in Washington, D.C., where he continued to unsettle the establishment. Following the publication of his book Christian Morality Today (Fides, 1966), the conservative, bishop-dominated board of trustees of Catholic University voted not to renew his contract, in 1967. In protest of the vote, faculty and students boycotted classes, forcing the board to reconsider. Curran was not only reinstated but promoted from assistant to associate professor.

Most close observers trace Curran's problems with the Vatican back to 1968, when Pope Paul VI issued his encyclical Humanae Vitae ("Human Life"), condemning all methods of contraception except the natural "rhythm" method. Spearheading American Catholic resistance to the encyclical, Curran rallied some 600 theologians and academics behind the signing of a public statement asserting that "spouses may responsibly decide according to their conscience that artificial contraception in some circumstances is permissible and indeed necessary to preserve and foster the values and sacredness of marriage." As the Rev. Richard McBrien, the chairman of the theology department at Notre Dame University, has remarked, "They have been watching him ever since," making him the scapegoat for the fact that "85 percent of Catholic couples practicing birth control do not abide by the papal teachings."

Curran edited the books Absolutes in Moral Theology (Corpus Books, 1968), Contraception: Authority and Dissent (Herder, 1968), and with R. E. Hunt, Dissent in and for the Church (Sheed, 1969).

He was a contributor to Law for Liberty (Helicon, 1967), edited by James E. Biechler; The Situation Ethics Debate (Westminster Press, 1968), edited by Harvey Cox; The New Day (John Knox, 1968), edited by William Jerry Boney and Lawrence E. Molumby; and Norm and Context in Christian Ethics (Scribner, 1968), edited by Gene H. Outka and Paul Ramsey.

In 1969 and 1970 Curran served as president of the Catholic Theological Society of America. In his outgoing address before 300 members of the society in Detroit in June 1970, he attacked a revision of the Roman Catholic code of canon law proposed by the Vatican, labeling it a threat to "any future progress in the area of ecumenism" and an "insult to the Oriental churches." He considered the proposed revision an example of "Latin or Western cultural imperialism based on the antiquated notion of centralization that fails to take into consideration the principles of subsidiarity and shared responsibility." It should, he said, be subjected to the same collegial drafting process as the documents produced at Vatican Council II, where the bishops of the world debated each decree together, point by point, until they reached consensus. "Especially in those matters that touch on an understanding of the basic structure of the church, the function of law in the church, and a constitutional law for the church," he asserted, "American theology and the American church have a responsibility of great magnitude."

Catholics of right and left, conservatives and liberals, traditionalists and progressives, generally come together, albeit narrowly, on the subject of abortion. When the United States Supreme Court repudiated most state antiabortion laws in 1973, sixty leading American Catholic theologians and scholars, rallied by Father Curran, issued a statement reaffirming the Catholic doctrine that "individual human life is present before the time of the viability of the fetus." Like Curran, many of the signers were among those who had jeopardized their careers five years before by challenging the papal encyclical banning artificial birth control. Curran pointed out to Marjorie Hyer of the Washington Post (February 18, 1973) that while all of the signers "felt an obligation to speak out on this particular issue in disagreement with the apparent moral reasoning of the court," the statement represented a limited area of consensus. Some of the signers agreed with the church's official unconditional opposition to abortion, under penalty of excommunication from the sacraments. Curran believes that "truly individual human life" begins not at conception (the traditionalist view) but fourteen to twenty-one days later. Before that time, "conflict situations" may justify abortion, but "only for the sake of the life of the mother or for a value commensurate with life itself." Curran pointed out to Miss Hyer that "throughout history the church has held that other values, such as fidelity to the faith and chastity, are commensurate with life itself"—until, on the abortion issue, no values are pondered other than the fetus' right to existence.

Citing the hierarchy's relative lack of concern about the sacredness of life in Vietnam, Curran told Miss Hyer: "Catholic theology seems to pay more attention to life inside the womb than outside it."

In a speech before the 1974 convention of the Canon Law Society of America, Curran addressed himself to the problems posed by the church's stand on the indissolubility of marriage. While recognizing the importance of upholding that conjugal ideal, he urged that those unable to live up to it be allowed to remarry with the church's blessing. Reporting on the speech in his column in the conservative Catholic weekly *Twin Circle* (November 8, 1974), Dale Francis characterized Curran as an "apostle of confusion." Similar denunciations of Curran regularly appeared in such arch-traditionalist Catholic periodicals as *The Wanderer*, which editorially urged its readers to voice their disapproval to the Holy See. Throughout the 1970s the Congregation for the Defense of the Faith was flooded with mail against Curran, much of it organized by such groups as Catholics United for the Faith. The tenor of the more reasoned complaints was that the liberalization of theological speculation initiated by Vatican Council II (1962–65) was exceeding the intentions of the council fathers when they opened the church to a renewing "air of change" and that Father Curran was among the most arrant of the dissident American theologians "undermining the deposit of faith" through their abuse of the council mandate.

Among the books published by Curran in the early 1970s were *Catholic Moral Theology in Dialogue* (University of Notre Dame Press, 1972), *Politics, Medicine, and Christian Ethics: A Dialogue with Paul Ramsey* (Fortress Press, 1973), and *Ongoing Revision: Studies in Moral Theology* (Fides Publishers, 1975). *New Perspectives in Moral Theology* (Fides, 1974) was a compilation of seven previously published essays by Curran on subjects ranging from analyses of current debates about natural law to the ethics of abortion, divorce, and sterilization. In the essays he tried to make a distinction between "absolute norms" and the "radical demands of the gospel." Reviewing the book in the *Christian Century* (November 20, 1974), Daniel Cobb remarked Curran's "clarity of style and of substance," his "thorough research and criticism," and his "concern for the human and humane as the stance of Christian ethics," and he judged him to be "the ablest of current American Catholic moral theologians."

In his book *Issues in Sexual and Medical Ethics* (University of Notre Dame Press, 1978), Curran went against the Vatican grain by offering such opinions as "Christians, sometimes without any personal fault, are not always able to live up to the goal of indissolubility in Christian marriage." A reviewer of *Transition and Tradition in Moral Theology* (University of Notre Dame Press, 1979) for *Christian Century* (April 30, 1980) found Curran's arguments to be "persuasive" and "insightful," especially on the ethics of homosexu-

ality. Curran's most succinct statement on that subject is perhaps the following: "I believe human sexuality has a meaning in terms of the person and the personal relationship to another person. I talk about the irreversible homosexual, and I don't think you can say that this person is called to celibacy. Homosexual relationships striving for permanency can be acceptable and legitimate for homosexuals." Like masturbation, however, homosexuality falls "short of the full meaning of human sexuality" in Curran's opinion.

That "human beings do have the power and responsibility to interfere with the sexual faculty and act" was among Curran's dissenting opinions in *Moral Theology: A Continuing Journey* (University of Notre Dame Press, 1982), part of which was devoted to ethical questions relating to aging, in vitro fertilization, embryo transfer, and the contraceptive revolution. He presented his arguments justifying abortion under some circumstances up to three weeks after impregnation and the carefully monitored use of artificial insemination as well as arguments against surrogate motherhood and the politics of the "New Christian Right" in America. "Curran's surveys of options in contemporary ethics are penetrating and concise," Mark Ellingsen wrote in his review in the *Christian Century* (March 9, 1983). "The most intriguing and suggestive feature of the book is the convergence one can discern between Roman Catholic and contemporary Protestant moral theology, a convergence Curran himself recognizes." Writing in *America* (September 18, 1982), the Jesuit theologian Richard A. McCormick called Curran "a conservative theologian in the best sense of that word: respectful of tradition, but not enslaved by it."

Also in 1982, the University of Notre Dame Press published *American Catholic Social Ethics: Twentieth Century Approaches*, in which Curran discussed the thought of William Engelen (and his relationship to the German Catholic Central Verein), Paul Hanley Furfey (and the Catholic Worker movement), and James W. Douglass (and the Catholic peace movement), among others. Walter W. Benjamin in his review of that book in the *Christian Century* (September 28, 1983) observed that Curran's position on the use of coercion and the just-war theory "echoes Niebuhrian realism and shows the influence of Paul Ramsey." Although Curran made "no attempt . . . to give an artificial unity" to the nine previously published essays brought together in *Critical Concerns in Moral Theology* (University of Notre Dame Press, 1984), the essays did share a common premise: that Christian morality is basically humanistic morality. In some of the essays he offered critiques of the moral theology of Bernard Haring and Edna McDonogh, among others, and examined traditional church teachings on war and peace in the light of "The Challenge of Peace," a recent pastoral letter of the American bishops. Reviewing the collection in the *Journal of the American Academy of Religion* (September 1985), Lisa Sowle Cahill wrote: "Curran is always a skillful analyst of trends and disputes in Catholic ethics. . . . These essays, ironic and patient in tone . . . show the ways in which the thought of 'revisionist' Catholic theologians is continuous with their heritage." In 1985 the University of Notre Dame Press published Curran's books *Directions in Catholic Social Ethics* and *Directions in Fundamental Moral Theology*.

In an essay evaluating the life of the Catholic Church in the twenty years since Vatican II in *America* (September 28, 1986), Curran reflected on developments in moral theology that stress "the person as agent and subject and not just the morality of particular acts," that are "much more closely linked with Scripture and with the whole of theology," and that are allied with a diversity of philosophical approaches outmoding "the monolithic manualistic philosophy of the past." Citing such controversial revisionist developments as feminist theology and the liberation theology followed by priests and other Catholics radicalized on the side of the poor and oppressed in the Third World, he suggested that "the church must be willing to live with a greater pluralism and diversity [in noninfallible matters] than heretofore."

The mail against Curran flooding into the Holy See over the years reached receptive ears in the Curia, the Vatican bureaucracy, but official action against him did not begin until the ascendancy of Pope John Paul II, the former Karol Cardinal Wojtyla of Poland, who was elected pontiff in September 1978. Coming from a totalitarian country where Catholics guard their faith as a precious, besieged treasure, John Paul brought with him to Rome no patience for those in the "free" world who were in his view toying with the integrity of that faith from within. Chagrined at the spiritual disarray of Catholicism in the West and perceiving that permissiveness was creating a crisis of authority in the church, John Paul set about restoring a conservative "balance" in doctrine and discipline. He reaffirmed traditional teachings on birth control, abortion, divorce, and other sexual matters, approved a partial revival of the old Tridentine Latin Mass, tightened the leash on religious orders and national hierarchies, and instituted intensive monitoring and disciplining of revisionist theologians. A year of "penitential silence" was imposed on the Brazilian Franciscan liberation theologian Leonardo Boff, and in Europe the French theologian Jacques Pohier and the Flemish Dominican Edward Schillebeeckx were reprimanded. The most severe punishment was the expulsion of the radical Swiss theologian Hans Küng from the Catholic faculty of the University of Tübingen in West Germany.

In the United States in the early and mid-1980s the effects of Pope John Paul II's "restoration" policy included the dismissal of proabortion nuns, and the excommunication of the director of the Rhode Island branch of Planned Parenthood, and Seattle Archbishop Raymond Hunthausen's loss of most of his episcopal powers because he emphasized social and political issues to the soft-pedaling of the Vatican line on sexual issues. The investigation of

Father Curran, seething unofficially since 1968, became official in 1979 and dragged on for six years. In corresponding with Curran in the early 1980s, the Congregation for the Defense of the Faith, the Curia office charged with guarding orthodoxy and punishing heterodoxy, specified four areas (contraception and sterilization; abortion and euthanasia; masturbation, premarital sexual acts, and homosexual acts; and the indissolubility of marriage) in which he was accused of deviating from official church teaching. Refusing to recant, he insisted on his right to dissent on matters of faith and morals on which Rome has not spoken *ex cathedra*. (Since Vatican Council I, in 1869–70, there has been only one *ex cathedra* pronouncement, Pope Pius XII's 1950 decree on the Assumption of the Virgin Mary.) In September 1985 Joseph Cardinal Ratzinger, the prefect of the Congregation for the Defense of the Faith, wrote to Curran definitively, informing him that he had been found guilty of "violating the conditions necessary for a professor to be called a Catholic theologian" and explaining why. Father Richard A. McCormick, the Jesuit theologian, who was privy to the correspondence, remarked of Ratzinger's letter that if the contention undergirding it "were to be applied to theologians throughout the world . . . the vast majority would not qualify as Catholic theologians."

When Curran made public the definitive letter from Cardinal Ratzinger in March 1986, a legion of theologians, including nine past presidents of the Catholic Theological Society of America, spoke out in his behalf, while traditionalists sided with the Vatican. On August 18, 1986, the Vatican formally announced that Curran could no longer teach theology at the Catholic University of America, where graduate degrees in theology, philosophy, and canon law are granted under a papal charter. Among the theologians who publicly deplored the action were Richard McBrien ("If the church already knows all the answers, what's the point of getting a doctoral degree?") and Avery Dulles ("It seems the Vatican is trying to teach noninfallible doctrine as if it were infallible"). Earlier, Bishop Matthew H. Clark of Rochester (Curran's bishop) had said: "If Father Curran's status as a Roman Catholic theologian is brought into question, I fear a serious setback to Catholic education in this country."

Contending that he was protected by his contract as a tenured professor, Curran set in motion a formal faculty investigation of his case. While the investigation was in progress, he remained on a sabbatical leave with the intention of returning to his usual teaching schedule in January 1987, but on November 20, 1986, he told the press that school officials had "unilaterally removed" his name from the newly published class schedule for the next semester. Seeing that action as "a *de facto* suspension . . . totally outside the legal process," he sought out the services of the same lawyer who defended him back in 1967. Asked about a possible violation of academic freedom at the university, Robert Kirkwood, the executive director of the Middle States Association of Colleges and Schools, told a reporter: "If the ultimate conclusion is that the university is no longer in control of its affairs, then the question of accreditation would come up." Pending the outcome of court and faculty proceedings in Washington, Curran accepted a visiting professorship in Catholic studies at Cornell University in 1987-88.

Father Charles E. Curran, known as "Charlie" to his students and peers, is six feet tall and spare of build, with an easygoing manner and a quick sense of humor, as ready with a laugh as with a Latin quote from St. Thomas Aquinas. Shunning clerical garb, he dresses lay style, in jacket and tie. Those who have studied under him say that as a teacher he is stimulating and witty and presents church teachings "clearly, fairly, and objectively," sometimes questioning but never misrepresenting. According to a representative of the theology department at the Catholic University of America,

he was still living in his two-room suite above the department, in Caldwell Hall, in December 1986. Self-described as "not a brooder," he has learned to live with his ecclesiastical problem as easily, he has said, as he gets over a bad review of a book. He remains convinced that the hierarchical teaching office of the church will ultimately have to allow dissent on important noninfallible issues. "According to Catholic theological tradition," he has explained, "the word and work of Jesus must always be made present and meaningful in the contemporary historical and cultural circumstances."

References: N Y Times A p16 Mr 24 '86; Newsweek 108:64 S 1 '86 por; People 25:133+ Ap 7 '86 pors; Time 127:73 Mr 24 '86 por, 128:65 S 1 '86 por; Washington Post B p1+ S 4 '86 por; Contemporary Authors vols 23-24 (1970)

Danilova, Alexandra

(da-nyĕl´ō-və)

1903(?)- Ballet teacher; choreographer. Address: b. c/o Lewis Ufland Public Relations, 136 E. 57th St., New York City, N.Y. 10022

At the zenith of her career, as the Ballet Russe de Monte Carlo's prima ballerina in the 1940s, Alexandra Danilova was acclaimed by the veteran dance critic Walter Terry as "the greatest of those ten or twelve women, currently performing in America, who have a claim to the title 'ballerina.'" Admired more for her impeccable style, elegant

line, and radiant personality than for her technical virtuosity, Danilova brought to each of her many and varied roles an innate musicality and a sensitivity to dramatic nuance that made the most elemental movement an expression of consummate artistry. Of the more than 100 roles she essayed in her forty-odd years as a performer, she is perhaps best remembered for her exuberant, irresistible soubrettes—Swanilda in Coppélia, the Street Dancer in Le Beau Danube, and the Glove Seller in Gaité Parisienne—and for her touchingly vulnerable Swan Queen.

Over the course of her long and illustrious career, Danilova has been associated with some of the most influential companies in the history and development of ballet, including Sergei Diaghilev's adventurous Ballets Russes, the Ballet Russe de Monte Carlo, which through its cross-country tours—many of them headlined by Danilova—contributed immeasurably to the growth and popularity of ballet in the United States, and most recently, George Balanchine's iconoclastic New York City Ballet, for which she has mounted two productions. Since retiring from the stage in 1957, Danilova has transmitted her wisdom and experience to hundreds of young dancers as an instructor at the School of American Ballet and as a coach and choreographer.

The younger of the two daughters of Dionis and Claudia (Gotovtzeva) Danilov, Alexandra Danilova was born in Peterhof, near what is now Leningrad, Russia in 1903. (Some sources give her year of birth as 1904.) Danilova has "no idea" what her father did for a living, but as she recounted in her autobiography, Choura: The Memoirs of Alexandra Danilova (Knopf, 1986), at the time of her birth Peterhof consisted only of the tsar's palaces and accommodations for his retinue, so she suspects that her parents "must have been connected in some way with the court." After her mother and father died when she was about two years old, Alexandra and her older sister, Elena, lived successively with their grandmother and their godmother before they were separately adopted, Alexandra by Lidia Mstislavna Gototsova, a wealthy woman whom she came to regard as her aunt. It was with "Aunt" Lidia and her second husband, General Mikhail Ivanovitch Batianov, one of the highest ranking officers in the Russian army, that Alexandra spent most of her childhood.

Danilova first became interested in dance when, at the age of seven, she won praise from her teacher for her extraordinarily graceful performance as a butterfly in the annual Christmas pageant at her grammar school. "I started to spend hours at the mirror, performing every sort of movement," she told an interviewer for a *Ballet News* (May 1982) profile. Recognizing the girl's natural talent, Aunt Lidia encouraged her to try out for the Imperial Ballet School in St. Petersburg. One of only seventeen youngsters chosen from among the 250-odd aspirants, Danilova began her training at the celebrated school on Theatre Street in the autumn of 1911. An energetic and impish child, she was, by her own account, "so busy making mischief" during her first year as a student there that she had to repeat most of the curriculum, which included courses in history, literature, and other academic subjects as well as daily classes in basic ballet technique, but she eventually settled down enough to win a scholarship funded by the tsar.

Under the watchful eyes of such now legendary instructors as Olga Preobrajenska and Agrippina Vaganova, Danilova progressed rapidly, invariably finishing each year first in her class. She also gained valuable onstage experience as a performer, in children's roles in productions of various ballets and operas at the Maryinsky Theatre. Her training was temporarily interrupted in 1917 by the Russian Revolution, but after about a year she and her fellow students returned to their school, since renamed the State Ballet School, with renewed dedication. Two years later, in 1920, Danilova was accepted into the corps de ballet of the newly retitled Soviet State (now Kirov) Ballet, the resident company at the old Maryinsky Theatre. "The theatre was a refuge for us, almost a paradise," she wrote in *Choura*. "Outside lay only the chaotic aftermath of the war and the Revolution. But regardless of how the government had changed, what went on inside the theatre was more or less the same. The repertoire was carefully maintained."

Among Danilova's assignments during her first two years with the company were corps and soloist roles in the Petipa classics *Paquita, Swan Lake, The Sleeping Beauty, La Bayadère, Raymonda,* and *The Nutcracker* and in new works by Mikhail Fokine, Pavel Petrov, Fyodor Lopokov, who was then the troupe's artistic director, and other young choreographers. On the strength of her impressive performance as the slave girl Ta-Hor in Fokine's dramatic *Une Nuit d'Egypte*, she was awarded the title role in Lopokov's version of *Firebird*. Her success in that part led to "one new role after another" and won her a promotion, in 1922, to the rank of so-

loist. Throughout most of that period, Danilova was also appearing regularly in the Evenings of Young Ballet series organized by former schoolmate George Balanchine as a showcase for his unconventional choreography. Threatened with expulsion from the State Ballet, whose tradition-bound directors objected to Balanchine's choreographic experiments, Danilova left the Young Ballet in 1923, but not before she had appeared in leading roles in the world premieres of four of Balanchine's earliest efforts—*Waltz, Adagio, Marche Funèbre,* and the romantic pas de deux *Poème.*

Increasingly frustrated by the lack of artistic and political freedom in the Soviet Union, Danilova jumped at the chance to join Balanchine and two other friends from school—Nicholas Efimoff and Tamara Geva—on a tour of European vacation spots in the summer of 1924. Billed as the Soviet State Dancers, they performed a varied repertoire of classical pas de deux and new pieces by Balanchine at dance halls, summer theatres, and private parties on the Continent before landing a month's engagement at the Empire Theatre in London. There they were seen by Sergei Diaghilev, the founder and artistic director of the Ballets Russes, who was so taken by their speed, agility, and daring that he hired all four for the Ballets Russes's upcoming 1924–25 season.

Because the roster of the Ballets Russes included at that time such experienced and popular ballerinas as Tamara Karsavina, Vera Nemchinova, Lydia Lopokova, and Felia Doubrovska, Danilova was given only secondary parts at first, but as the months passed, she gradually assumed leading roles in most of the ballets in the company's large and eclectic repertoire, among them such Fokine staples as *Firebird, Les Sylphides, Schéhérazade, Le Carnaval, Petrouchka,* and *Le Spectre de la Rose* as well as new pieces by Bronislava Nijinska, then the company's resident choreographer, and Leonid Massine, in whose *La Boutique Fantasque* she discovered one of her most felicitous roles, as the saucy Can-Can Dancer. She also appeared in Massine's *Soleil de Nuit, Les Matelots, Zéphyr et Flore,* and *Les Femmes de Bonne Humeur,* a comical period piece that she found especially appealing, and in his *Le Pas d'Acier* and *Ode,* both of which he created for her.

By her own account, Danilova scored her first great personal success in Balanchine's *The Triumph of Neptune,* a parodistic pantomime that was given its world premiere by the Ballets Russes in London in December 1926. Her interpretations of the twin roles of the Fairy Queen and Neptune's Daughter earned her a promotion to principal dancer. Among the other roles that Balanchine tailored to her talents during her tenure with the Ballets Russes were the Shepherdess and the Butterfly in *L'Enfant et les Sortilèges;* the Servant in *Barabau,* a burlesque based on an Italian nursery song; the Black Dancer in the divertissement *Jack-in-the-Box;* the Serving Maid-Goddess in *The Gods Go a-Begging;* the Lady in the offbeat and angular *Le Bal;* and Terpsichore in *Apollon*

Musagète, the revolutionary piece that, in the view of most dance historians, marked the birth of neoclassicism on the ballet stage. Although Balanchine had created Terpsichore's light and airy variation especially for Danilova, Diaghilev, in deference to Lord Rothermere, who had donated a large sum of money to the company's 1928 London season, awarded the role in the world premiere of the work to Alice Nikitina, Rothermere's mistress. After that, the two ballerinas alternated in the part.

With Diaghilev's death in August 1929 and the subsequent dissolution of his Ballets Russes, Danilova wrote in *Choura*, "the ground collapsed" beneath her feet. "It seemed I didn't belong anywhere," she went on. "I suddenly felt very small and insignificant." She especially worried that Balanchine, with whom she had been living since 1926, might "go off and work for big companies," leaving her stranded. Except for short seasons with the Monte Carlo Opera Ballet in 1929 and 1930, Danilova was unable to find steady employment until she was invited to London in 1931 to dance in *Waltzes From Vienna*, an operetta about the rivalry between Johann Strauss and his son that was to run in the West End for more than a year. From London, she wrote a letter to Balanchine suggesting that they "go their own ways." "Life was separating us . . . ," she explained in her autobiography. "George and I had a perfect understanding. We both had a deep respect for art—that was our strongest bond, and it remained."

Determined to "make a new life" for herself, Danilova signed on, in 1933, with the Ballets Russes de Monte Carlo, founded by René Blum, formerly the director of the Monte Carlo Opera Ballet, and the Russian-born impresario Colonel W. de Basil. The star attractions of the company were the teenage prodigies Irina Baronova, Tatiana Riabouchinska, and Tamara Toumanova—the so-called "baby ballerinas"—and most of the new ballets went to them. Danilova was relegated to reprising her roles from the Diaghilev repertoire, among them the gold-digging Doll in *Petrouchka*, the flirtatious Mariuccia in *Les Femmes de Bonne Humeur*, and perhaps most important, the title role in Fokine's *Firebird*, which she danced with such supreme authority that it soon became hers exclusively. In her highly individual interpretation, the Firebird was strong and, in her words, "rather ferocious"—more "like an eagle" than a delicate, exotic creature.

During the mid-1930s, on tours of Europe and the United States with de Basil's Ballets Russes, Danilova won critical and popular acclaim for her performances in an unusually wide variety of works, ranging from a one-act *Swan Lake* to David Lichine's romantic *Francesca da Rimini* to Nijinska's masterpiece *Les Noces*, but her most famous part was undoubtedly the jealous Street Dancer in Massine's character comedy *Le Beau Danube*. Often partnered by the choreographer himself, she combined depth of characterization, musical grace, and what Edwin Denby called "temperamental vivacity" to make the role, originally created for Lydia Lopokova, forever her own. Recalling her sparkling portrayal years later, Massine said simply that she was "like champagne."

In 1938 Danilova left de Basil's increasingly contentious company to become a charter member of the Ballet Russe de Monte Carlo, a spinoff of the de Basil troupe that was organized by the disaffected Massine and Sergei I. Denham, a Russian-American financier. The centerpiece of the company's debut season was a lavish new production of *Coppélia*, staged especially for Danilova by Nicholas Sergeyev, a former *régisseur* of the Imperial Ballet. Instilling her technically impeccable performance in the central role of Swanilda with mischievous humor and feminine charm, the ballerina made her interpretation of the irrepressible village lass "one of the unforgettable experiences in dance," according to Walter Terry. Partnered most often by Frederic Franklin or Igor Youskevitch, she danced Swanilda scores of times for the Ballet Russe and other companies over the next dozen years or so, invariably to ecstatic notices. Commenting on one of her last appearances in the part, as a guest artist with the Sadler's Wells Ballet in London in 1949, a reviewer for the Manchester *Guardian* (March 16, 1949) noted with pleasure that time had "entirely failed" to dim the lustre of her classical technique and the "superb and elegant outrageousness"—the "inimitable mixture of good manners and naughtiness"—that gave her dancing, particularly in soubrette roles, its special quality.

Among the other classical roles in Danilova's personal repertoire with the Ballet Russe de Monte Carlo were Giselle and Myrtha in *Giselle* and Odette in the second act of *Swan Lake*. Temperamentally unsuited to the part of the infatuated peasant girl Giselle, she nonetheless turned in a convincing portrayal notable for its attention to dramatic nuance, expecially in the challenging mad scene. She has credited some of her success as Giselle to Bronislava Nijinska, who coached her in the part. "Nijinska taught me how to act with my body . . . ," she explained in *Choura*. "A great actress expresses what she is feeling with her body and her voice, not by making monkey faces, and Nijinska helped me to find that expression in dance." Nevertheless, by her own account, Danilova found Myrtha, the steely Queen of the Wilis in *Giselle*, more to her liking. The critics apparently agreed, for more than twenty-five years after she last danced the part, Walter Terry still considered her to be "the perfect Myrtha."

Danilova's extraordinary ability to "act with her body" was perhaps never more evident than in her eloquent interpretation of the doomed Swan Queen. As Walter Terry observed in his New York *Herald Tribune* (February 19, 1947) review of a performance of *Swan Lake* at the old Metropolitan Opera House, she etched an indelible portrait of the bewitched Odette by emphasizing the three aspects of her character in telling movements—fluttering, feathery beats for the enchanted bird, an upward tilt of the head and regal gestures for the queen, and soft, pliant arabesques and yielding body for the woman. "The frame for this portrait was the manner" of Danilova's presentation, Terry concluded, "a manner which can only be described by the term 'ballerina' and the authority, the assurance, the graciousness and the meticulousness of action which the word implies."

The reigning star of the Ballet Russe de Monte Carlo throughout the 1940s, Danilova racked up one triumph after another. In addition to those mentioned above, her most congenial roles, among the dozens she essayed, were the Sugar Plum Fairy in The Nutcracker pas de deux; the Daughter in Frederick Ashton's amusing The Devil's Holiday; Zobeide, the imperious concubine in Fokine's sensual Schéhérazade; the title role in a full-length production of Raymonda that she and George Balanchine reconstructed for the company; and perhaps most unforgettably, the coquettish Glove Seller in Massine's delightful confection Gaité Parisienne. Walter Terry rated her performance in the last-named part "one of the great characterizations in contemporary ballet."

During the mid-1940s, while Balanchine was working with the company as a guest choreographer, he created leading roles for Danilova in the second of his three versions of Mozartiana and in three new ballets—the jazzy, syncopated Danses Concertantes, Pas de Deux, a lyrical duet in the grand manner, and the Gothic fantasy Night Shadow. As the Sleepwalker in Night Shadow, she was called upon—in the duet with the obsessed Poet that is the heart of the ballet—to execute a dizzying series of skimming bourrées, seemingly directed only by the touch of the Poet's hand.

Beginning in the early years of World War II, the Ballet Russe de Monte Carlo spent most of its time on tour in the United States, where it "planted the seeds of ballet," as Danilova put it, in cities and towns throughout the country. By the end of the decade, however, the company was foundering, weakened by the departures of many of its principal dancers, including Alicia Markova, Anton Dolin, and Maria Tallchief. Discouraged by the growing influence of Sergei Denham's protégée, Nina Novak, Danilova herself left the Ballet Russe in December 1951. She returned briefly, as a guest artist, in 1957, making her New York farewell performance in two of the ballets most associated with her—Le Beau Danube and Gaité Parisienne.

After leaving the Ballet Russe, Danilova made guest appearances with a number of ballet companies in the United States and abroad, among them London's Festival Ballet and the Slavenska-Franklin Ballet. In 1954 she formed her own troupe, Great Moments of Ballet, which over the next two years toured North and South America and the Far East. Comprised at the beginning of Danilova, Moscelyne Larkin, Roman Jasinski, and Michael Maule, the group presented a carefully chosen program of excerpts from the classics and new pieces, some of them choreographed by members of the tiny company. Danilova last appeared onstage in 1958, as the vivacious flower girl Lisa in the Broadway musical comedy Oh, Captain!, which enjoyed a respectable run of nearly 200 performances despite generally unenthusiastic reviews.

Danilova's career took a new turn late in 1958, when she agreed to stage the dances in the Metropolitan Opera's new production of La Gioconda. Her fresh and inventive version of the shopworn "Dance of the Hours" stopped the show and prompted the Met's management to engage her as its resident choreographer for the next several seasons. Her credits for the opera company include the ballet interludes in The Gypsy Baron, La Périchole, and Adriana Lecouvreur and the polonaise in Boris Godounov. Danilova's innate musicality, always one of her most notable traits as a dancer, stood her in good stead as a choreographer, and on the strength of her string of successes at the Metropolitan Opera, she was asked to mount a full-length production of The Nutcracker for the Washington Ballet in 1961. She has subsequently staged, among other works, Les Sylphides, for the Pennsylvania Ballet and, under the title Chopiniana, for the New York City Ballet; Raymonda, for the Minnesota Dance Theatre; Paquita, for the Cincinnati Ballet and the Dance Theatre of Harlem; and Coppélia, which she has mounted for more than a dozen companies worldwide, including the New York City Ballet, for which she devised, in collaboration with Balanchine, a sharper, accelerated version designed to appeal to contemporary audiences. Her hand was especially evident in the exquisitely detailed mimed scenes of the first two "story" acts and in the refreshingly human characterizations of the central characters, particularly Dr. Coppelius.

At Balanchine's request, Danilova, who had been teaching off and on since the early 1950s, joined the faculty of the School of American Ballet, the official school of the New York City Ballet, in 1964. The following year she inaugurated the annual workshop program in which graduating students perform before an audience of dance professionals as part of their final examination. "The idea is to get them out of class and into the theatre . . . ," she has explained, as quoted in the Ballet News profile. "Not every talent is good in class." For those workshops, she has staged excerpts from Coppélia, Raymonda, Paquita, and Aurora's Wedding and even choreographed some short pieces, including Les Saisons and Scènes de Ballet, an elaborate series of dances for a large company that Balanchine labeled "too professional."

One of the most respected and admired instructors at the School of American Ballet, Danilova teaches her students not only how to execute classical movements, but also how to interpret them by stressing musicality, attention to detail, and port de bras. In her painstakingly structured and varied classes, she gives her students variations and combinations of steps that she learned from Vaganova, Nijinska, Fokine, Nicolai Legat, and Lubov Egorova, often demonstrating a particular exercise herself with characteristic sparkle and grace, but she also tries to prepare her pupils for the modern styles of choreographers like Balanchine, Jerome Robbins, and Peter Martins, whose works comprise the bulk of City Ballet's repertoire. Danilova's uncommon gifts as a teacher and coach were captured in Anne Belle's documentary *Reflections of a Dancer: Alexandra Danilova, Prima Ballerina Assoluta* (1986), which was recently selected by *American Film* magazine as one of the ten best dance films available on videotape, and in the motion picture *The Turning Point* (1977), Herbert Ross's loving re-creation of the world of professional dancers, in which she portrayed with humor and style a Russian-born ballerina who teaches her most famous role to a young dancer.

Alexandra Danilova is a trim, petite woman with a heart-shaped face, large, heavily lidded, dark blue eyes, perfectly coiffed blond hair, and, as Jennifer Dunning noted when she observed one of her classes several years ago, "still-slender, beautifully shaped legs." An optimist by nature, she is unfailingly cheerful, projecting what the dance critic and historian John Gruen has called "an intoxicating *joie de vivre.*" In her leisure hours, she enjoys visiting museums and art galleries, attending plays, concerts, and dance performances, and reading, especially history. A naturalized American citizen since 1952, Danilova lives alone in an apartment in midtown Manhattan, not far from the School of American Ballet. Her first marriage, to the Italian industrialist Giuseppe Massera, ended with her husband's death; her second, to Casimir Kokitch, a soloist with the Ballet Russe de Monte Carlo, terminated in divorce. "I sacrificed marriage, children, and country to be a ballerina, and there was never any misunderstanding on my part—I knew the price," she wrote in *Choura.* "I gave 100 percent of myself to my art, and my art has repaid me." Danilova is the recipient of several major dance awards, including the first Capezio Award ever bestowed upon a ballerina, in 1958, and the 1984 Dance Magazine Award.

References: Ballet N 3:11+ My '82 pors; Ballet R 4:32+ no 4 '73, 4:50+ no 5 '73; Dance 35:39+ Mr '61 pors, 58:20 Mr '84 pors; Chujoy, A., and Manchester, P. W., eds. Dance Encyclopedia (1967); Concise Oxford Dictionary of Ballet (1982); Gruen, John. The Private World of Ballet (1975); Tracy, Robert. Balanchine's Ballerinas: Conversations With the Muses (1983); Twysden, A. E. Alexandra Danilova (1945); Who's Who in America, 1985–86

Depardieu, Gérard

(de-pär-dyû´)

Dec. 27, 1948– Actor. Address: b. c/o Art Média, 10 Avenue George V, 75008 Paris, France

Breaking the stereotype of the suave French matinee idol, the ubiquitous Gérard Depardieu, "Europe's hunk," brings to the screen a rough-hewn and intense physicality as well as an unpredictability deriving from "a wonderful inner madness," as Bertrand Blier, who directed him in *Going Places* (1973) and the Academy Award-winning *Get Out Your Handkerchiefs* (1977), has pointed out. A hulking and beefy six-footer with an ex-boxer's battered Neanderthaloid face, Depardieu seems a natural as the pathetically vulnerable lug in *The Last Woman* (1976) and the petty hoodlum in *Loulou* (1980), but such roles represent only a fraction of his adventurous filmography, which ranges from tender melodrama to black comedy and erotic satire. The fifty-three characters he has portrayed before the cameras since 1968 are a varied lot, including the repertory actor involved in hoodwinking the Germans in occupied Paris in *The Last Métro* (1980), the textile executive driven to despair by the pressures of his job in *Mon oncle d'Amérique* (1980), the eponymous French revolutionary in *Danton* (1982), a man gulled into believing a runaway teenager is his son in *Les Compères* (1983), the enigmatic title character in *The Return of Martin Guerre* (1981), and the transvestite in *Ménage* (1986). When asked by interviewers if he

can explain why he, the most unlikely of sex symbols, has become the French cinema's most popular leading man, especially with female moviegoers, Depardieu has suggested that perhaps it is because audiences enjoy (as he does), or are provoked by, the risks he takes in playing "characters who are not always to [his] advantage" and in pushing his characterizations "to their limits."

DEPARDIEU

Gérard Depardieu was born on December 27, 1948, in Chateauroux, in the region of central France traditionally known as the Berri. "The Berri is a country . . . where sorcery still exists," he told Norma McLain Stoop of *After Dark* (March 1977). "I have two grandmothers who make magic. Me, too." Gérard and his five siblings grew up in a crowded two-room household amidst the constant quarreling of their mother, Eliette (Marillier) Depardieu, and father, René Depardieu, an illiterate itinerant sheet-metal worker who devoted more time to fishing and drinking than earning money. Drifting into the streets, Gérard was a petty thief by the age of eight. A chronic truant, he was barely literate when, at twelve, he dropped out of school. In retrospect, he sees his early delinquency in a positive light, as a good preparation for acting. "Having to confront policemen and judges is an excellent way to train your imagination," he has explained. "In a few seconds you have to improvise a role with talent and emotion."

Leaving home at thirteen, Depardieu worked variously as a dishwasher, an attendant at a home for the retarded, a traveling salesman, and a beach attendant on the Riviera. In addition, he was an amateur boxer and sometimes worked as a sparring partner. When he was in his mid-teens he followed an older actor friend to Paris and took acting classes under Charles Dullin and Jean-Laurent Cochet. At first he had trouble deciphering scripts, but his reading ability quickly progressed. "I got into acting to try not to be taken for what I looked like—a hoodlum," he told Joan Dupont when she interviewed him for a profile in the *New York Times Magazine* (June 14, 1987).

In his late teens Depardieu made his motion picture debut in the short film *Le Beatnik et le minet,* directed by Roger Leenhardt, and his television debut in the series *Rendez-vous à Badenberg.* Beginning in 1968 he was in several French-language productions of British and American plays directed by Jean-Laurent Cochet at the Théâtre National Populaire. One of the plays was Edward Bond's *Saved.* Marguerite Duras, who was looking for a "scary" type to play the malevolent traveling salesman in *Nathalie Granger* (1972), a film that she had written and was directing, saw Depardieu in *Saved* and cast him in her film, which starred Jeanne Moreau. "I had never seen anything like him," Miss Duras told Joan Dupont. "Natural genius, incredible intelligence, and completely unspoiled. He didn't dare talk in those days. I'm not sure he knew how to read and write. During the filming, Jeanne Moreau said, 'I wonder where Marguerite found a Shakespearean actor?' She felt that dimension right away."

Depardieu's vehicle to stardom was *Going Places* (1973), Bertrand Blier's adaptation of his novel *Les Valseuses,* a gross picaresque tale of two alienated, nihilistic young brutes (Depardieu and Patrick Dewaere) who steal and womanize their way across France. When that film reached the United States, Vincent Canby of the *New York Times* (May 14, 1978) judged its characters to be de-

rivative of "old movies, early Belmondo, James Dean, and any number of early Godard characters." Among Depardieu's other roles in the early 1970s were a boxer in *Vincent, François, Paul, and the Others* (1974) and the young factory owner who steals to meet his payroll in *The Wonderful Crook (Pas si méchant que ça,* 1974). Reviewing the latter in *New York* (February 7, 1977), John Simon described Depardieu as "superbly moving as a befuddled, decent man."

In Bernardo Bertolucci's *1900* (1975), a five-hour epic about the rise of fascism in Italy, Depardieu was cast as Olmo, a peasant on an estate who is born on the same day as the heir to the estate, Alberto (Robert De Niro). The two characters are inseparable as children but grow up to oppose each other politically, after Olmo becomes a Communist and Alberto, as the lord of the estate, aligns himself with the Mussolini regime. Critics faulted the film for being "immensely long," "heavy-going," "exasperatingly uneven," and propagandistic but found in it "powerful moments" and the overall "grandeur of a classic visionary folly." Stanley Kauffmann of the *New Republic* (November 26, 1977) credited Depardieu with having "at least some animal vigor," and Norma McLain Stoop of *After Dark* described his characterization of Olmo as "deeply felt," making "every motive, every action (however surprising) completely understandable."

Depardieu played a burglar who becomes involved with the madame of a brothel specializing in sadomasochism in Barbet Schroeder's *Maîtresse* (1975) and a boxer killed by his double in André Techine's *Barocco* (1976), an underworld caper film. In Marco Ferreri's *The Last Woman (La Dernière Femme,* 1975), Depardieu was cast as a beer-bellied factory engineer whose wife has left him and who treats a succession of mistresses as if they were no more valuable than the high-tech gadgets that fill his apartment. When Valerie, the woman of the title, breaks through his cocoon of chauvinistic assumptions he is devastated and, in a paradoxical act of machismo, emasculates himself with one of his gadgets, an electric knife. "If the script calls for a revolting slob, the performance is impeccable," John Simon snidely observed in *New York* (June 21, 1976). Seeing "brilliance" in Depardieu's performance, Vincent Canby of the *New York Times* (June 7, 1976) judged him to be "quite suddenly . . . France's most talented young actor." In another Ferreri movie, *Bye Bye Monkey (Rêve de singe,* 1977), filmed on location on Manhattan's Lower East Side, Depardieu portrayed a young man who is victimized by members of a feminist consciousness-raising theatre group. "Depardieu is effective as the youth unable to cope with any true emotion," the reviewer for *Variety* (May 24, 1978) noted.

In Bertrand Blier's *Get Out Your Handkerchiefs (Préparez vos mouchoirs,* 1977) the Depardieu character offers his sexually unsatisfied and depressed wife to a stranger (Patrick Dewaere), but she remains unaroused until she finally forms a liaison with a thirteen-year-old boy. Blier also directed Depardieu in *Buffet froid* (1978), an absurdist farce consisting of random "side-dish" sketches that keep the viewer waiting for the entrée. "Mr. Depardieu, the most engagingly ambivalent presence in the modern cinema," Vincent Canby wrote in the *New York Times* (September 4, 1987), "gives *Buffet froid* an import not really justified by Mr. Blier's material."

So rapidly did Depardieu move from one role into another that six films starring him were showing simultaneously in Paris in 1978. In the opinion of David Denby of *New York* (October 2, 1980), his "loosest, most detailed physically" performance was in the title role of Maurice Pialat's *Loulou* (1979), a ne'er-do-well thief for whom his lover, Nelly (Isabelle Huppert), leaves her middle-class husband. In Alain Resnais' *Mon oncle d'Amérique* (1979), a cinematic investigation of behaviorist ideas, Depardieu played a young man who rises from peasant origins to become a business executive but who has a nervous breakdown when his firm is swallowed up in a merger, and he is demoted. For Vincent Canby of the *New York Times* (December 17, 1980), Depardieu stood out in *Mon oncle d'Amerique* as "especially comic and appealing."

"Last year the French cinema, and in particular that part of it generally associated with the New Wave, made a comeback, both critically and, more important, commercially," Richard Roud wrote in the *Guardian* (March 2, 1981). "In Britain we have already seen three of the four films that made 1980 a great year for the French cinema: Alain Resnais' *My American Uncle*, Jean-Luc Godard's *Slow Motion*, and Maurice Pialat's *Loulou*. . . . But there is still one more film to come, and that is François Truffaut's *The Last Métro* . . . the greatest box-office success of them all." Depardieu won a César, the French equivalent of the Oscar, for his role in *The Last Métro* (*Le Dernier Métro*), that of Bernard Granger, an actor in Nazi-occupied Paris who plays opposite Marion Steiner (Catherine Deneuve) as her Jewish husband directs a production from his hiding place in the cellar of the theatre. As Archer Winsten observed in his review of *The Last Métro* in the *New York Post* (February 11, 1981), "Depardieu's burly physique gives realism" to the scene in the film in which Granger attacks the villainous theatre critic Daxiat, an anti-Semite and collaborationist.

In his second Truffaut film, *The Woman Next Door* (*La Femme d'à coté*, 1981), Depardieu was cast as a married man who renews his rocky liaison with a former lover (Fanny Ardant). "Depardieu can be dangerously volatile and clumsily endearing," David Ansen observed in *Newsweek* (October 19, 1981), "but the mixture doesn't add up to a full person. Truffaut's innate charm tames him, as it tames her [Miss Ardant]." Truffaut himself once said that there is "a go-between, pimpish side" to Depardieu, an ability to "bring . . . people together." Depardieu agreed, saying that his aim is to "get people talking, [to] act as a kind of switchboard for their energies, [to] be infectious."

Daniel Vigne's *The Return of Martin Guerre* (*Le Retour de Martin Guerre*, 1981), set in a sixteenth-century French farming village, is based on a true story, legendary in France, that begins with the young farmer Martin Guerre disappearing from the village. Eight years later a man who says he is Guerre shows up in the village and is put on trial as an impostor falsely claiming Guerre's land, wife, and child. As David Ansen of *Newsweek* (June 27, 1983) pointed out, Depardieu plays the Guerre who returns "robustly, wittily, and tenderly," with "a combination of earthy appetite, guileless charm, romantic ardor, and litigious cunning [that] is uniquely his own." In the *New York Times* (August 21, 1983), Janet Maslin remarked that Depardieu's performance is "so clever that it can support either interpretation [that he is the true Martin Guerre or the impostor] until the film is virtually over."

In Andrzej Wajda's *Danton* (1982) Depardieu was cast in the role of the French revolutionary, an advocate of toleration, whose attempt to humanize his fanatical and icy rival Robespierre led to his death at the guillotine. As Rita Kempley observed in the *Washington Post* (October 21, 1983), in that role Depardieu "is enormous and sensual . . . expansive, often full of good wine, a grand orator, the heart and soul of the revolution, the embodiment of unchecked freedom." For his performances in *The Return of Martin Guerre* and *Danton*, Depardieu was voted the best actor of 1983 by the National Society of Film Critics.

As Leo Seligson remarked in *Newsday* (March 28, 1984), Depardieu brought "his usual manic intensity" to his comic role in *Les Compères* (1983), in which his personality dominated that of the slender and more withdrawn Pierre Richard. In the film the two men seek the runaway teen-aged son of a former mistress of both, each believing himself to be the boy's father. The slapstick that ensues reminded some reviewers of Laurel and Hardy. Two other 1983 releases in which Depardieu starred are less highly esteemed: *The Moon in the Gutter* (*La Lune dans le caniveau*), which Depardieu called "The Moon in the Sewer," and *Fort Saganne*, a lavish costume adventure picture set in North Africa.

Depardieu directed himself in the title role of a film version of Molière's *Le Tartuffe* (1984), which he had previously done on the stage. Made up as a wigged, rouged, and mascaraed effete, he rendered the best Tartuffe that Stanley Kauffmann, for one, had ever seen. "To see this performance . . . ," Kauffmann wrote in the *New Republic* (March 18, 1985), "is to see a born actor coming into his birthright." In Maurice Pialat's *Police* (1984) Depardieu starred as a tough, sexist, and lonely police detective who falls in love with the girlfriend of a criminal he brings to justice. Seeing him in *Police*, Janet Maslin of the *New York Times* (September 20, 1986) was struck "once again" by his ability to combine "brutishness, intelligence, and profound emotion with a subtlety that has no equal." Depardieu himself has said that he felt he made *Police* "in a state of grace." For his role as the detective, he was voted best actor at the 1985 Venice Film Festival.

In 1986 Depardieu toured France, Belgium, and Italy in the stage musical *Lily Passion*. Three of his films released that year were seen by a total of sixteen million people. One was Bertrand Blier's comedy *Ménage* (*Tenue de soirée*), in which Depardieu played a bisexual thief who seduces both partners in an unhappy marriage. "I think my part in *Ménage*," Depardieu told Marcia Froekle Coburn in an interview for the *Chicago Tribune* (November 3, 1986), "is . . . all about innocence. The burglar, Bob, is a childlike person—open, available, full of wonder. [The film] isn't about homosexuality or misogyny. It only seems that way. It is, above everything else, about the problems of the couple." Stanley Kauffmann of the *New Republic* (November 3, 1986) wrote of Depardieu in *Ménage* that "force spills from him so easily that it almost hides his talent."

Another 1986 release was Claude Berri's *Jean de Florette*, set in Provence during the 1920s. In that film Depardieu is the title character, a hunchback who inherits a farm and tries to make a success of it despite the human and natural obstacles arrayed against him. "The acting is magnificent: Depardieu . . . achieves a kind of epic martyrdom," Jack Kroll wrote in his review in *Newsweek* (July 13, 1987). The third 1986 release was *Les Fugitifs*, in which Depardieu and Pierre Richard played the title characters. Again under the direction of Maurice Pialat, Depardieu made *Sous le soleil de Satan* (1987), based on Georges Bernanos' novel of the same name (translated into English as *Under the Sun of Satan*), the story of a country priest's encounter with evil. That film won the Golden Palm award at the Cannes Film Festival.

Gérard Depardieu is six feet two inches tall and has dark-blond hair and a ruddy complexion. A hearty eater, he is, at approximately 260 pounds, more than a little overweight. On April 11, 1970, Depardieu married Elisabeth Guignot, whom he met in acting school and who played his wife in *Jean de Florette*. In addition to acting, Elisabeth Guignot is a singer and composer of pop music. (Depardieu himself has recorded an album of her songs.) The Depardieus, who have two children, Guillaume and Julie, own a home in Bougival, near Paris, and a farm on the coast of Normandy, where Depardieu butchers his own livestock. The ambiguity of Depardieu's tough-gentle presence on the screen is reflected in a statement the actor made in an interview with Dan Yakir for the *New York Times* (February 1, 1981): "Acting is a woman's language, the desire to be liked, to seduce. So, if I'm an actor at all, I'm a female actor—maybe the most feminine of all."

References: *After Dark* 9:31+ Mr '77 pors; *Chicago Tribune* V p3 N 3 '86 por; *N Y Times* II p1+ F 1 '81 por; *N Y Times Mag* p39+ Je 14 '87 pors; *People* 15:62+ pors; *International Who's Who*, 1986–87

Ditka, Mike

Oct. 18, 1939– Professional football coach. Address: b. Chicago Bears, 55 E. Jackson St., Chicago, Ill. 60604

"Attack—always." That is the football philosophy of Coach Mike Ditka, an old-fashioned, no-frills exponent of the brawling, do-or-die school. As a player, Ditka was an All-American end at the University of Pittsburgh before turning professional. As a pro, he played end with the great Chicago Bears team of the early 1960s, with the Philadelphia Eagles in 1967 and 1968, and then for four years with the Dallas Cowboys team that won Super Bowl victories in 1970 and 1971. Following a coaching apprenticeship under Tom Landry in Dallas, he returned in 1982 to his first love, the Bears, who had over the years deteriorated into a 6-10 team. Learning to control his notorious irascibility, he imbued the Chicago players with some of his intensity and coached the resuscitated team to a five-year record of 50-23, to the National Football Conference playoffs in 1984, 1985, and 1986, and to triumph in the Super Bowl in January 1986.

The oldest of four children, Ditka was born Michael Keller Ditka on October 18, 1939, in Carnegie, Pennsylvania. He grew up in the nearby Beaver Valley town of Aliquippa, where his father, Mike Sr., now retired, worked in the Jones and Laughlin steel mill as a welder for the Aliquippa and Southern Railroad. Mike Sr., the son of Ukrainian immigrants, had changed the family name from Dyzcko to Ditka to approximate in spelling the way the name was pronounced in Aliquippa. Some relatives opted for Disco or Discoe. Mike Jr.'s mother is Charlotte (Keller) Ditka, whose ancestry is Irish, German, and, to a lesser degree, English.

His younger siblings are Ashton, David, and Mary Ann.

The Ditkas lived in a small one-family condominium in a row of such houses in a government-subsidized housing project in Aliquippa. Mike Jr. rose early, to serve as altar boy at the first mass at St. Titus Church, and throughout his elementary school years he was usually in bed by 9:30, in keeping with his father's strict regimen, which was enforced with an old leather Marine belt. The major lesson absorbed by Ditka in Aliquippa was the work ethic—that "you only get what you work for."

"We played sports day and night," Ditka recounts in his autobiography, *Ditka* (Bonus Books, 1986), written with Don Pierson, who covers the Bears for the *Chicago Tribune*. "I was a better baseball player than football player because I was small. We played everything. In the spring, it was baseball until the sun went down. Football was the same way. Our fingers would crack and break open from playing basketball on the cold and wet court with a wet basketball. It didn't matter. That's all we had, so we played." As the captain of his Little League baseball team, he "hated to lose," as he still does. "I was just too intent on winning. Our whole society is built that way. I really believe this: if you accept defeat, you're going to be defeated a hell of a lot more than you're going to win. You can be gracious in defeat . . . on the outside, but you better be doing flip-flops inside." Having a temper, Ditka was not a gracious loser in his Little League days, and many of the spankings he received from his father were for ungentlemanly conduct on the field.

Ditka began playing organized football in the fifth grade at St. Titus parochial school. At Aliquippa High School—where he was voted most popular in his class—he was at first too scrawny (five feet seven, 130 pounds) as well as too slow for football. Encouraged by Coach Paul Ashman to bide his time, he practiced body-building, lifting weights and doing pushups so strenuously that, according to his father, "you could hear the house rock." As a 135-pound sophomore, he made the junior varsity. Sprouting several inches and adding thirty pounds going into his junior year, he started at linebacker and also played offensive end on the Aliquippa team that won the Western Pennsylvania interscholastic championship. As a 180–185-pound senior, he started at middle linebacker and switched to fullback.

Ditka's perseverance was fueled by his awareness, inculcated by his father, that "football was [his] ticket out" of the mines and mills of Beaver Valley. "I saw the way my dad and my grandfather came home from work all the time," he recounts in his autobiography. "The clothes, the dirt, the filth. My dad had burn marks on his arms. All his clothes had holes in them from the sparks. That wasn't what I wanted." The only escape that he saw was through a college scholarship, which would have to be athletic because his otherwise good academic average was lowered by poor grades in mathematics.

Playing semipro baseball as a catcher (and sometime shortstop and outfielder) from the age of fifteen, Ditka attracted the attention of Cincinnati and Milwaukee scouts, but choosing a professional baseball career would have meant going directly from high school into the minor leagues, not into college. Like many another ethnic Catholic high school football star, he dreamed of going to the University of Notre Dame. Notre Dame approached him, but nothing came of the overture, and he narrowed his options to Pennsylvania State University and the University of Pittsburgh. He chose Pitt because he thought he might become a dentist and an athlete he knew at Pitt told him that if he did his undergraduate work at that university it would be easier for him to enter dental school there.

At the University of Pittsburgh Ditka made good grades in all of his predental courses except physics and chemistry. As in high school, he played baseball and basketball as well as football, but he concentrated on football not only because it was his ticket to a scholarship but also because it best suited his competitive, chip-on-shoulder spirit, his attraction to "the challenge of . . . going head-to-head, man-to-man." He became outstanding in the sport, he explains in *Ditka*, "not because [he] was faster or could catch the ball better" but because he taught himself "to do a lot of things that other guys didn't."

On defense with the Pitt Panthers, Ditka was an end and middle linebacker, positioned in a three-point stance against offensive tackles. He liked defense better than offense because in tackling he found "the combat" that he liked. As an offensive end, he caught forty-five passes, and as a punter he averaged forty yards per boot.

Even in practice at Pitt, Ditka was a manic, all-out player, going so far on one occasion as to knock himself unconscious by charging blindly into a solid steel blocking sled. In response to his pleading, his position coach, Ernie Hefferle, later let him practice against teammates instead of blocking sleds. "When he walked on the field, Lord have mercy, everybody was his enemy," Hefferle told Don Pierson for an article in the *Chicago Tribune* (November 17, 1985). Finally Hefferle would not allow Ditka to scrimmage in practice, lest he end up on the injured list before the following Saturday's game. In both practice sessions and games, Ditka was outspoken and sometimes violent in criticizing teammates for lack of effort, especially in his senior year, when he was team captain and when Pitt errors deprived the team of nineteen points that would have meant an undefeated season. According to reports, during one halftime he slammed an errant teammate up against a locker and on another occasion he punched out two guards in the huddle. Ditka views such reports as exaggerated. In his autobiography he remembers scolding the guards, not punching them, for example. "The stories about me at Pitt get better every year. I keep reading about all the bars I was in. I was hardly in any bars until my senior year. We cut a wide swath then, though." Generally, he says, he was regarded as a "nice guy" in college.

Following his junior year at Pitt, Ditka, a consensus All-American, opened himself to the 1961 professional draft. Picked by both the Chicago Bears of the old, established National Football League and the Houston Oilers of the fledgling American Football League, he felt he had no choice but to go with "the best league." Inexperienced at negotiating, and without an agent, he signed a one-year deal with the Bears for $12,000 (plus a $6,000 bonus), one half of what one of the team's third-string quarterbacks was making. The following day the Oilers, not knowing he had signed with the Bears, offered him a two-year contract worth $50,000. Although he felt cheated by the contract with the Bears, he was content, because he understood and respected the old-fashioned thriftiness of "Papa Bear" George Halas, the Chicago president, a crusty but sentimental pro-football pioneer who was as ornery at running a team as Ditka was at playing for one, and he "always got along" with George Allen, then Halas' assistant in charge of the draft. Besides, Ditka considered himself "kind of like a Bear." "The Bears were hitters and I liked to hit and that was it," he explains in Ditka. His second contract with the Bears was for a straight $18,-000. By holding out, he ultimately exacted a $25,000 contract, still measly by pro standards for a player of his calibre.

In 1961, his initial season with the Bears, Ditka beat out Fran Tarkenton for Rookie of the Year. Playing offensive tight end, he contributed mightily to the winning of the Bears' last NFL title under George Halas in 1963. As a receiver, he made several extraordinary runs that season, bouncing off of tacklers as if they were trampolines. The run that made the highlight films was, in his view, the least talented of the lot, a fifty-yard lucky "fluke" against Pittsburgh that set the Bears up for the game-tying field goal. After dislocating his left shoulder, he played the 1964 season in a harness and, virtually one-handed, caught seventy-five passes, then an NFL record for tight ends and still an all-time Bears mark.

The Bears were 5-9 in 1964. In scrimmage before the 1965 season Ditka's right foot was smashed. Because the foot was not set properly or was dislocated again in the cast, it became permanently deformed, and the complications affect him to this day. Despite the injury, he played every game in 1965, a 9-5 season for the Bears, and caught thirty-six passes, not very far below his average. One of the catches was the greatest of his career: in a game against the 49ers, he dove, slapped the ball to his chest with one hand, and slid into the end zone for a touchdown. Slowed by his injured foot, he caught only thirty-two passes in 1966, when the team went 5-7-2. During a game in Los Angeles in 1966, a fan trespassed onto the field, pursued by security guards. Excusing himself from the huddle, Ditka decked the intruder.

Nineteen-sixty-six was Ditka's option year with the Bears. Meanwhile what he called a "personality conflict" had been developing between him and Halas, who resented Ditka calling him, however facetiously, a "cheap Bohemian" who threw "nickels around like they were manhole covers." After the 1965 season, the Houston Oilers of the AFL offered Ditka a $300,000 contract that included a $50,000 signing bonus and other inducements. He signed, and then played out his option season with the Bears. The signing became moot when the leagues merged and the NFL picked up all the contracts that NFL players had signed with AFL teams.

Following the 1966 season, Halas traded Ditka to the Philadelphia Eagles for quarterback Jack Concannon. Although he agreed to the trade, Ditka "cried like hell" to be "leaving friends" and "going from the penthouse to the outhouse," as he confesses in his autobiography. "But it was important that it happened. I really believe there is a plan for everybody's life. . . . I think I was put in Philadelphia . . . to learn a little humility."

Playing with the Philadelphia Eagles in 1967 and 1968—both lopsided losing seasons—Ditka, favoring his still painful right foot, pulled muscles and tore ligaments and tendons. He did not play often, partly because of his physical problems and partly perhaps as punishment for his public criticism of the team's lack of "a winning attitude . . . from top to bottom." The more he sat on the bench, the more he sought escape in alcohol, and the more he drank the worse his physical condition became. By the end of the 1968 season he was, in his words, "a mess." Although there was a year remaining on his contract, he left Philadelphia with the intention of retiring. Four days later Tom Landry, the coach of the Dallas Cowboys, called him to say that he was willing to gamble on Ditka's having "a few years" left as a player, and Ditka changed his mind about retirement. Before the beginning of the 1969 season, he went to Dallas in a trade for Dave McDaniel. "I couldn't understand why [Dallas] traded for me," he writes in his autobiography. "Looking back, I was traded for a reason. The Good Lord put me there. . . . Life has cycles and that was the start of a new cycle . . . an upbeat cycle." During that cycle he would refind himself religiously as well as athletically, in significant measure through the inspiration of Tom Landry, a "born again" Christian.

The Cowboys already had an excellent tight end in Pettis Norman, and Ditka went to Dallas chiefly to complement Norman. Outside of short yardage and goal line plays, he saw little action in 1969, when Dallas lost to Cleveland in the playoffs. After that season he made up his mind that he was going to get back in shape, and he did so under the conditioning program of Alvin Roy, the Dallas strength coach. Partly as a runner, he played on the Cowboys' victorious Super Bowl teams of 1970 and 1971. He made a touchdown in their first Super Bowl victory, and he regards 1971 as "the best year he ever played." Then, in 1972, he developed excruciating back pains (a distant complication of his foot problem), so that he "couldn't run at all" and "what had been [his] trademark, [his] strength and quickness, was gone." Realizing that "it was all over," he wrapped up a playing career in which his totals in 158 games included 427 receptions for 5,812 yards (an average of 13.6) and forty-three touchdowns. Becoming an assistant coach with the Cowboys in 1973, he took a salary drop from $44,-000 to $22,000, but it was in his opinion "the best opportunity he ever had." Landry taught Ditka how to utilize the analysis of game films in coaching, and Landry credits Ditka with reminding him that "sometimes you have to fit the system to the players," rather than vice-versa. "Coaching is not getting the best of the best," Ditka later told Don Pierson. "It's getting people who don't have the true talent to come up to a level that's going to help your football team."

As an assistant coach in Dallas, Ditka was an offensive coordinator, first working with receivers and then with special teams and helping Landry to develop Dallas' "shotgun" formation. In 1981 he handled the passing game. Over the years, meanwhile, he was in occasional contact with George Halas, and the relationship between the two men mellowed. After the 1981 season, responding to an overture from Ditka, Halas called him to Chicago and signed him to a $100,000 contract, by far the smallest in the NFL for a head coach, which didn't bother Ditka. "Nobody else in the National Football League would have hired me . . . ," he points out in Ditka. "There's an NFL image you have to be and maintain and I probably wasn't it."

The team that Ditka took over in Chicago had had only two winning seasons in thirteen. A major problem was discord in the ranks, manifested not only in player-management contract disputes but also in the contempt that defensive players showed for the offense. In trying to rally the team, Ditka first emulated Tom Landry's stoic sideline manner. When that did not work, his frustration erupted into one prolonged temper tantrum, marked by screaming and the hurling of headsets, clipboards, and other handy objects and culminating in his breaking his right hand by punching a steel trunk in the locker room following two consecutive overtime defeats in 1983 (the year George Halas died). Realizing that he was trying too hard to vindicate Halas' hiring of him, he decided that he had to let "some fun" back into his game. With his right hand in a cast the following Sunday, he signaled the beginning of a moderation of his attitude by wryly asking his players to go out against the Denver Broncos and "win this one for Lefty." They did, 31–14.

Once Ditka had separated the wheat from the chaff in his organization, had drafted or traded for offensive players who wouldn't be bullied by the defense, and had begun to curb his own temper, his ability to communicate with his men, to motivate them, and to create an atmosphere in which disparate personalities could harmonize became apparent. In such an atmosphere, strong individualists like Jim McMahon, the punkish prima donna quarterback, and Buddy Ryan, the strong-willed

defensive coordinator, could not only coexist but flourish. Ditka's disagreements with McMahon and Ryan never became lasting problems because he was not, and never has been, a holder of grudges. "I can accept deviation from people around me," he explained to Ira Berkow of the New York Times (January 20, 1986), "because I see a lot of myself in people like McMahon and Ryan. They're both winners. And I'm open to suggestion."

Chicago sports columnists were merciless to Ditka during the strike-shortened 1982 season, when the Bears went 3-6. Moving from an early deficit in 1983, the Bears won their last six games and finished 8-8. Quarterback trouble in 1984 forced Ditka to rely heavily on the single wing, in which the multiple-threat fullback Walter Payton—"the very best football player" Ditka had "ever seen . . . the complete player"—carried the load. With a 10-6 record that season, followed by a preliminary playoff victory, the Bears made the National Football Conference title game, which they lost to the 49ers, the ultimate Super Bowl victors.

Coming out of the 1984 season, Chicago's defense was acknowledged to be the best in the NFL. The addition of the 308-pound rookie defensive tackle William ("Refrigerator") Perry in 1985 might have been a redundancy had not Ditka had the strategic imagination, and the concern for Perry, to bolster the Bears' goal-line offense by turning Perry into a rushing back who captured the national imagination. Along with Payton and other Bears, Perry became a conspicuous figure in television and other endorsements, in which the team led the league. Into the league's seventh-ranked offense that year Ditka inserted an astute mixture of multiple formations, sophisticated passing plays, and fierce run-blocking. The Bears went 15-1 (tying the NFL record for regular-season victories set by San Francisco the previous year), rolled over the Giants and Rams in the playoffs with scores totaling 45-0, and defeated the New England Patriots in the Super Bowl 46-10. Among the laurels heaped on Ditka were his elections as the AP and Sporting News NFL Coach of the Year, as the UPI's National Football Conference Coach of the Year, and, coincidentally, as a member of the National Football Foundation's College Football Hall of Fame.

In 1986 the Bears finished 14-2 and captured their third straight division title before being eliminated in the playoffs. Following the 1986 season, there were reports that Ditka was planning to leave Chicago after 1987, for which he has a contract for an estimated $325,000. According to the reports, he was unhappy over the firing of general manager Jerry Vainisi, a close friend of his, by Michael McCaskey, George Halas' grandson, the club president. On August 29, 1987, Ditka ended the speculation by announcing that he had signed a new, three-year contract with the Bears. The details were not revealed, but his average annual salary under the contract was widely assumed to be between $400,000 and $500,000.

To Ditka, the philosophy behind his and the Bears style of football is, "Ask no quarter, give no quarter." Like Tom Landry, he believes in a multiple, ball-centered offense that keeps the opposing defense off balance with changing formations, movements, and snap counts. Within that scheme, he prefers a two-back to a one-back attack. Encouraging self-analysis as well as physical exertion by his players, he meets regularly with his veterans to listen to their gripes and suggestions. His greatest strength is not as a technician but as a motivator who knows when to pat a man on the back and when to issue a diatribe and how to transmit his rage to his players. "He's good at finding the red button in each of us," Mike Singletary, the Bears' All-Pro linebacker, has said. In Ditka's view, an emotional pep talk to players is useless unless it is "something they can understand and relate to." Before a game, he usually in one way or another exhorts the players to "win it for each other." A typical exhortation ends with a prayer to the "Heavenly Father . . . in the name of Jesus Christ" for "the courage and commitment to use [our God-given] talents to the best of our ability so that we may give the glory back to you." After a game, he leads the team in a prayer that is more often than not a thanksgiving for relative freedom from injury.

Mike Ditka is a brawny man with darting gimlet eyes and a small, bristly mustache. His most persistent nicknames are "Hammer" (from his college basketball days) and "Iron Mike." In Dallas, teammates dubbed him "Chip" and "Monk," allusions to his chubby cheeks, and Chicago players often call him "Redhead," a reference to the orange tint that is now sometimes detectable in his thick head of graying, naturally auburn hair, which he brushes straight back. To help induce composure, he has been wearing a tie at games since 1984. When pacing the sideline he still growls and seethes, but with relative poise, seldom exploding as he used to. Interviewers have described him off the field as "pleasant," "thoughtful," and able to laugh at what he singles out as his "one physical problem—a big mouth." Actually, he has major physical problems deriving from the right-foot injury he sustained when playing for the Bears. Related to that injury is deteriorating arthritis in his right hip, and physicians recently found that three joints in the foot itself are out of place. He has been advised to bring a liability suit against the Bears, but he so disdains the greed that is rampant in our litigation-prone society that he cannot countenance such a step.

Ditka and Diana Tratham were married in 1977, after his divorce from his first wife, whom he met in high school and married in college. From his first marriage he has four grown children. He acknowledges that his own failings contributed to the breakup of that marriage. One of the weaknesses he has worked hard at subduing is that for alcohol, especially since his arrest on a drunk driving charge in 1985. Nicotine is a lesser problem: although he smokes cigars, he does not inhale.

The tempestuous Bears coach and his wife share their modest house in Grayslake, Illinois with a sheep dog and two schnauzers. Ditka's favorite recreations are golf and gin rummy. He enjoys watching television shows like *Hill Street Blues*, reading political adventure novels such as those of Frederick Forsyth, and collecting old cars (although he is not mechanically inclined). His favorite cuisine is seafood. Among his heroes, besides Tom Landry and George Halas, are Stan Musial, Vince Lombardi, and President Ronald Reagan. In Chicago, he co-owns Ditka's, a restaurant on Ontario Street; has his own radio show; and appears regularly on the television program *Bears Extra*. He has also made two music videos (in which he sings and dances) spoofing his "Iron Mike" reputation and "Grabowski," his ideal "lunch-pail" player. In his practice of his Roman Catholic faith he is a daily communicant, and his favorite charity is Misericordia Hospital in Chicago. He is much in demand as a motivational speaker, at $10,000 a speech.

References: Chicago Tribune IV p1+ N 17 '85 pors, III p1 Ag 30 '87 por; Inside Sports 8:26+ Jl '86 por; Newsday p16 O 20 '85 pors, p5 Ja 26 '86 pors; Newsweek 106:74+ D 2 '85 por; People 27:66+ Ja 5 '87 pors; Sports Illus 63:78+ D 16 '85 por; Ditka, Mike, with Pierson, Don. Ditka (1986)

Dole, Robert J(oseph)

July 22, 1923– United States Senator from Kansas. Address: b. 141 Hart Senate Office Bldg., Washington, D.C. 20510

NOTE: This biography updates the article that appeared in *Current Biography* in 1972.

In his quarter-century on Capitol Hill, the witty and supercharged Republican Robert Dole has grown from a congressman ranked "to the right of Genghis Khan" to the statesman-like leader of his party in the Senate and a top contender for the Republican presidential nomination. Elected to the Senate in 1968 after four terms of relative obscurity in the House of Representatives, the then acerbic lawyer from Russell, Kansas immediately acquired a high profile as a fiercely partisan senatorial defender of President Richard Nixon. Barely surviving the Watergate scandal that brought down the Nixon presidency, Dole won a tough reelection fight in 1974 and became President Gerald R. Ford's running mate in the unsuccessful Republican presidential campaign of 1976. The public image of "mean-spirited" party "hatchet man" with which he emerged from the 1976 campaign gave way in the early 1980s to that of a pragmatic Senate Finance Committee chairman and Senate majority leader respected even by liberals for his rationality and sense of responsibility on tax and budget issues. Dole's legislative record as a whole bears testimony to his personal conception of "fairness." While voting consistently with Reagan Republicans on such issues as defense, the Strategic Defense Initiative, funding the Nicaraguan Contras, gun control, school prayer, and abortion, he has broken with many of them to defend the food-stamp program, support civil rights legislation, and fund programs for the handicapped.

In his presidential bid, Dole has an asset in his wife, Elizabeth Hanford Dole, the Reagan administration's secretary of transportation, who announced in September 1987 that she was leaving her cabinet post to stump for him. As an advocate of "conservatism with compassion," Dole wants to change the perception of the GOP as the party of the affluent and uncaring. The intensity he brings to that task is typical of his driving personality, a goad traceable in part to his determination to overcome World War II injuries that left him with a useless right arm. When Thomas B. Edsall of the *Washington Post* (March 9, 1987) asked him what set him apart from the other presidential candidates, Dole said: "I'm a producer. . . . I've been tested in my lifetime, both personally and legislatively. I'm a survivor. I keep coming back."

Robert Joseph Dole was born into a hard-working blue-collar family in the town of Russell, the seat of rural Russell County, Kansas, on July 22, 1923. His father, Doran Ray Dole, ran an egg and cream distribution station and, later, a grain elevator. His mother, Bina (Talbot) Dole, sold Singer sewing machines, traveling the county with them in her old Chevrolet. During the Depression Mrs. Dole rented out the Dole home to oil-field workers, moving herself and the rest of the family into the basement. An ambitious woman, fearsome in confrontations with others, she lived by the pragmatic slogan, "Can't never did anything." Like their parents, Robert and his brother and two sisters rose at dawn to do their assigned chores. After school Robert delivered newspapers, and evenings he worked

as a soda jerk in the town drugstore, where the sense of humor he inherited from his father brightened his repartee with customers. Tall and husky, Dole was a natural athlete and a sports and fitness enthusiast, working out constantly with homemade weights and competing fiercely in basketball, football, and track.

At first aspiring to be a physician, Dole was a premedical student at the University of Kansas from 1941 until 1943, when he was called up for service in World War II. As a second lieutenant, he was leading an assault on a last-ditch German machine gun nest in the Po Valley of Italy on April 14, 1945, when he was struck by an exploding shell that destroyed his right shoulder, fractured vertebrae in his neck and spine, and riddled his body with metal slivers. An experimental dose of streptomycin, then a new wonder drug, saved him from near fatal infections, but not from almost total paralysis. The prognosis that he might never walk again did not take into account his will to recover. Over the course of three years in army hospitals—and three major operations—he began standing and, cautiously, moving about. His right arm and hand were beyond recuperation, but his left hand, while lacking abductor and adductor control, had some residual feeling, and he gradually mastered the use of that "good" hand. He returned to civilian life a different, driven man, in a hurry to overcompensate for the time and physical integrity he had lost. That obsession has never left him. Just the daily ordeal of buttoning a shirt reminds him, as he has said, "that you've got to keep pushing, because you're not quite a whole person."

Never a dedicated scholar before his injury, Dole returned to college after the war determined to excel academically in law. "The only thing I've got left is my head," he told his brother, Kenneth, "so I'd better use it." With the help of his first wife, Phyllis—a physiotherapist whom he married in 1948 and who did all of his writing for him until he learned to write lefthanded—he studied at the University of Arizona and at Washburn University of Topeka (Kansas). At the latter he earned his B.A. and L.L.B (*magna cum laude*) degrees.

On the Republican ticket, Dole won election to the Kansas state legislature in 1951. After one two-year term as a legislator, he served four terms as the prosecuting attorney of Russell County, the last ending in 1961. In 1960, after a close primary race, he easily won the general election to represent Kansas' Sixth Congressional District (later renumbered the First) in the United States Congress, and he was reelected three times. He spent his four terms in the House of Representatives futilely opposing most of what he regarded as the spendthrift liberal legislation of the Kennedy and Johnson administrations. While he favored government aid to agriculture, to the hungry, and to the handicapped, he opposed such other federal programs as Medicare, aid to Appalachia, the 1964 antipoverty program, and federal aid to mass transit. His only major breaks from conservative ranks were his votes for the Civil Rights Act (1964) and the Voting Rights Act (1965).

When United States Senator Frank Carlson of Kansas announced his retirement in 1968, Dole handily won the Republican nomination to succeed Carlson and the general election that followed. He gained prominence in the Senate sooner than most freshmen through his aggressive and often abrasive defense of the policies of President Richard Nixon. His sharp tongue-lashings aroused resentment in moderates and liberals who questioned the president's Vietnam war strategy or opposed his controversial appointments to the Supreme Court. Even some Republicans considered him a brash upstart, but others liked the fire he introduced into the Senate's clubroom atmosphere. Among the latter was Senator Barry Goldwater, who observed, "He's the first man we've had around here in a long time who will grab the other side by the hair and drag them down the hill."

Dole's reward for his service to Nixon was his appointment to the chairmanship of the Republican National Committee in 1971, a position from which he conducted a vigorous partisan campaign against the Democrats. Fortunately for him, Dole did not work well with Nixon's White House staff, and he was eased out of the committee chairmanship in January 1973, just in time to escape involvement in the Watergate scandal, which forced Nixon to resign. Still, Dole's identification with Nixon very nearly cost him reelection in 1974, when his Democratic opponent, Dr. William Roy, exploited the Watergate scandal in his campaigning. While portraying himself as an innocent victim of guilt by association, Dole did some mudslinging of his own, referring to Roy, an obstetrician who had performed "therapeutic" terminations of pregnancies, as an "abortionist" who favored abortion on demand. Dole won the election by less than a 2 percent margin.

Less rigidly conservative than he had been in the House, Senator Dole was appreciated on both sides of the aisle as a pragmatic legislator who worked well with his colleagues and on occasion joined them in supporting liberal causes. A case in point was his work with former Democratic presidential candidate George McGovern—whom he had blasted when he was party chairman—in overhauling and expanding the food-stamp program in the mid-1970s. Because that program was popular with his farm constituency, Dole had political motives in supporting it, but in working with McGovern on the select committee on nutrition he developed a genuine, strong commitment to feeding the needy and to persuading his fellow Republican conservatives that true conservatism is not "anti-people."

Perhaps no one was more surprised than Robert Dole himself when in August 1976 President Gerald R. Ford—who was filling out the remainder of Nixon's second term as president—chose him as his vice-presidential running mate in the election that year. Ford's choice reflected a number of considerations. While Dole brought no geographic balance to the ticket, his long record of support for agriculture gave him appeal in the farm states. In addition, his voting record was conservative enough to make him acceptable to the Reagan wing of the party, which had put up a hard fight for the presidential nomination; Ronald Reagan's endorsement of Dole over the other candidates on the short list of vice-presidential possibilities apparently weighed heavily with Ford. Most important, President Ford wanted to exploit his position as the incumbent by taking the dignified high road in his campaign, and to do so he needed an aggressive fighter on the low road. As Ford wrote in his memoirs, "I sent Dole to the briar patch, and I stayed in the Rose Garden."

It was in the campaign of 1976 that Dole acquired his "hatchet man" reputation. Logging 65,000 miles in forty-four states, he went after the Democrats with scathing wit, referring to Jimmy Carter, the Democratic presidential candidate, as "Southern-fried McGovern" and joking that Walter F. Mondale, Carter's running mate, had such close ties to labor that George Meany, the dour and baggy-faced union leader, lent him his makeup man for the televised vice-presidential debate. In that debate the "nastiness" of which he had been accused in the campaign reached a new low in his lament for "all the killed and wounded in all Democrat wars in this century."

After the Ford-Dole ticket went down to defeat by only 2 percent of the vote, many observers ascribed much of the blame to Dole's campaign style. Dole considered that judgment unfair, pointing out that polling data showed that "in areas where we were supposed to be helpful, we were helpful." He did acknowledge, however, that his calling the world wars and Korea and Vietnam "Democrat wars" was regrettable. "I went for the jugular—my own," he remarked of the fatal debate with Mondale.

Dole emerged from the 1976 defeat determined to change his public image. Hiring a public relations firm, studying videotapes of his campaign performances, and submitting to behavior modification under specialists at a New York City firm called Speech Dynamics, he worked on projecting a warmer, less acerbic persona. "We changed [his sense of humor]," Dorothy Sarnoff, the head of Speech Dynamics, told Thomas B. Edsall of the Washington Post. "We took the snideness away from him. We changed the way he dressed to a more classy look."

The debut of the "new" Bob Dole, in the 1980 presidential primaries, fizzled, chiefly because of poor campaign organization, and after a very poor showing in the New Hampshire primary Dole pulled out of the race. Ronald Reagan's landslide election to the presidency later that year gave Dole a more promising opportunity to work on a statesmanlike image. For the first time in twenty-six years the Republicans were in control of the Senate, and as chairman of the Senate Finance Committee Dole had more control than any other senator over a flood of revenue legislation introduced during Reagan's first term. Of his string of brilliant legislative victories in the Ninety-seventh Congress the two most impressive were the Economic Recovery Tax Act of 1981, the tax-slashing keystone of the Reagan domestic program, which Dole supported despite misgivings, and an antidote to that measure, the Tax Equity and Fiscal Responsibility Act of 1982. Never a convert to supply side economics, he emerged as a leading critic of Reagan's fiscal policies and blocked Reagan's effort to end the food-stamp program. Seeing that the sweeping tax cuts enacted in 1981 were leading to projections of an alarming growth in the budget deficit, Dole in 1982 looked for some way to recoup revenues that would be palatable to the president, who was opposed to any tax increases. What he hit on was an ingenious "tax reform" package that repealed some of the 1981 tax breaks and increased corporate taxes. The resulting revenue from taxes on interest, dividends, tips, telephone use, tobacco, and the like restored 45 percent of the previous year's cuts and added nearly $100 billion in revenue, all under the guise of "closing loopholes" and ensuring tax "equity." By all accounts, Dole's shepherding of the 1982 measure past all of the powerful special interest groups that opposed it was nothing less than masterful.

Two other major pieces of legislation that Dole played a key role in pushing to enactment in the Ninety-seventh Congress were the extension of the Voting Rights Act in 1982 and the bipartisan act providing for the bailout of the Social Security program in 1983. A consistent supporter of civil rights, Dole served as floor manager for the measure that made Dr. Martin Luther King Jr.'s birthday a national holiday.

Dole became Senate majority leader in November 1984, succeeding the retiring Howard Baker. As majority leader he shifted his stance, becoming a Reagan loyalist. As such, he faced a difficult task negotiating the administration's conservative second-term legislative agenda through an increasingly fractious Senate. Often bypassing discussion and consensus-building in favor of swift action, he cleverly employed procedural rules to keep a tight rein on floor debates. Some Democrats complained that they were not being given a fair chance to voice their objections or to modify bills. When Robert Byrd, the minority leader, accused him of abusing his powers, Dole replied, "I didn't become majority leader to lose."

His position as majority leader gave Dole the influence and visibility that he needed to launch another, more viable bid for the presidential nomination. When the Republicans lost control of the Senate after the 1986 elections and Dole was *ipso facto* demoted to minority leader, it was widely assumed that his ascendancy was at an end. The vagaries of politics, however, brought him a new opportunity in the form of the Iran-Contra scandal of 1986–87, which brought the Reagan administration under press and Congressional fire for covert and illegal sale of tax payer-bought arms to Iran and diversion of the profits into secret private bank accounts, some for the benefit of the Contras, the

Nicaraguan rebels, in violation of a Congressional amendment. Jumping into the political vacuum created by the chaos in the White House, Dole acted as an informal spokesman for the Republican party during the critical early months of the Iran-Contra crisis. Applying a lesson learned from Watergate, he successfully pressed President Reagan to cooperate with a special Congressional investigation, to appoint a special prosecutor, and to initiate a thorough review of National Security Council operations. Dole's deft assistance in the handling of the crisis impressed Republican leaders, including the party strategist John Deardourff, who admired the way Dole "stepped right up to bat, admitted there was a serious problem, and proposed ways to solve it."

"Irangate" helped Dole most by slowing the political momentum of his chief rival for the 1988 presidential nomination, Vice-President George Bush. Early polls of Republican voters had made Bush the front runner by a comfortable two-to-one majority, but as the Iran-Contra affair dragged on and speculation about Bush's possible involvement mounted, Dole gained steadily on him. In August 1987 national polls showed Dole trailing by only some 15 percent, and in Iowa, where the first primary would be held, he led Bush, 28 percent to 25. During that August, Dole traveled to twenty-eight states, setting up campaign organizations and raising funds. In September he went to Nicaragua to confront Daniel Ortega, the Marxist Nicaraguan president, in debate. On his return to Washington he led the unsuccessful Republican effort to secure the confirmation of Judge Robert H. Bork, President Reagan's nominee to the Supreme Court. When the stock market crashed in October 1987, in part as a result of the runaway federal deficit, Dole cautiously joined those favoring limited tax increases, along with budget cuts, to reassure the market. Like President Reagan, Dole had previously hewed to a hard line against any rise in taxes. Dole formally declared his candidacy for the presidential nomination on November 9, 1987.

Political analysts saw Dole's candidacy as needing the enunciation of a broad political "vision" transcending such Dole preoccupations as the deficit, which were not good vote-getters. Some thought that he had such a theme in his political philosophy of "conservatism with compassion." Polls suggested that his brand of Republicanism, which combines traditional conservative values with a populist emphasis of "fairness," was more attractive to border-line Democrats and independent voters than the more coldly economic program of Representative Jack Kemp or the ambiguous ideological stance of George Bush. Dole believes strongly that the Republican party has to shed its image as the "cadre of the elite, the wealthy, [and] the insensitive . . . " by pursuing tax reform and fiscal restraint with due regard for the needs of poor and low-income Americans.

While he has mellowed over the years, Dole remains a complex man, charming but still sometimes aloof and abrasive, with partisan instincts and a combative sense of humor. "I have to watch my tongue," he admitted during an interview with Gail Sheehy for *Vanity Fair* (April 1987). A key influence in his growth both as a person and as a politician has been his second wife, Elizabeth Hanford Dole, whom he married in 1975, three years after divorcing his first wife, Phyllis. A political power in her own right, Mrs. Dole has been credited with planing some of her husband's rough edges. Together, she and he are one of the most attractive couples in Washington society.

The Doles work twelve-hour days, six days a week, relaxing occasionally by reading, going to the theatre, and watching the evening news on television. Bob Dole's chief indulgence is regular sunbathing, on a Senate veranda and the terrace of his Watergate apartment. On Sundays, he and his wife attend the Foundry Methodist Church in Washington. For short getaway trips, they go to a condominium they own in Florida. They have a pet miniature schnauzer named Leader. From his first marriage, Dole has a grown daughter, Robin.

Robert F. Dole is six feet one and a half inches tall, weighs 175 pounds, and has graying hair and dark, intense eyes that often have a mischievous glint. He conveys such an impression of vigor that those associating with him tend to forget his handicap. To keep well-wishers from grabbing his fragile right hand, he habitually carries in that hand a pen or rolled-up piece of paper. With money from his lecture fees, Dole in 1983 established the Dole Foundation, which finances rehabilitation programs for the mentally and physically handicapped. Gail Sheehy asked the politician and diplomat Robert Ellsworth, Dole's closest friend and confidant aside from his wife, how he would assess the shaping of Dole's character. "Dole has not been given anything by the gods, ever," Ellsworth replied, "yet he's emerged from it all as truly whole, internally powerful." According to Miss Sheehy, even those closest to Dole often forget that his right arm is virtually useless. He compensates for his disability so well that his wife sometimes asks him to hang a picture or perform some other task requiring two good arms. Senator Alan Simpson remarked of Dole to Miss Sheehy: "What can you do to a guy who's lain in a hospital bed for three years? You can't spook him. He's invulnerable."

References: Chicago Tribune mag p8+ O 5 '86 pors; N Y Times A p1+ Ag 20 '76 por; N Y Times Mag p65+ D 12 '82 pors; Newsday mag p10+ Ja 1 '84 pors; Vanity Fair 50:112+ Ap '87 por; Washington Post A p1+ Mr 9 '87 pors; Who's Who in America, 1986-87

Donaldson, Sam

Mar. 11, 1934– Broadcast journalist. Address: b. ABC News, 1717 DeSales St., N.W., Washington, D.C. 20036

When President Jimmy Carter left the White House in January 1981, he joked that he wished he could leave his successor, Ronald Reagan, two things: Menachem Begin, the combative Israeli prime minister, and Sam Donaldson, ABC's aggressive and pugnacious chief White House correspondent. A veteran journalist with more than thirty years' experience in radio and television news broadcasting, Donaldson covered Capitol Hill, the Vietnam war, and four presidential campaigns before moving to the White House beat in 1977. His tenacity and his abrasive, no-nonsense manner, which prompted the *Washington Journalism Review* to dub him "the junk yard dog" of the White House press corps, have angered some viewers, but he is widely admired by his colleagues for having revitalized presidential news coverage. In 1987 Donaldson's fellow journalists voted him the best all-around television news correspondent in the nation's capital for the third consecutive time.

The youngest of the two sons of Samuel Andrew and Chloe (Hampson) Donaldson, Samuel Andrew Donaldson was born on March 11, 1934, in El Paso, Texas. Three days later, his mother took him home to the family's cotton farm in nearby Chamberino,

New Mexico. His father having died of a heart attack several months before his birth, young Sam was reared by his mother and his brother, Thomas, fifteen years his elder. Chloe Donaldson, a former schoolteacher, guided her younger son's intellectual development, encouraging him to read and to

speak in public, beginning with recitations of the Scriptures at the local Baptist church. Skeptical of the quality of education available at the rural community's school, each weekday Mrs. Donaldson drove Sam to school in El Paso, some twenty-five miles away.

Bright and inquisitive, Donaldson was fascinated by the radio from an early age. "We would sit in the kitchen by the coal stove on cold winter nights and listen to the war news," he recalled in his memoir *Hold On, Mr. President!* (Random House, 1987). "I would sometimes pretend to be delivering it." Recognizing her son's developing interest in broadcasting, Chloe Donaldson gave the boy a shortwave radio receiver for his eleventh birthday. The following year he took the examination for a ham radio operator's license. "I failed it, and that almost broke my heart . . . ," Donaldson wrote. "Looking back, I realize I didn't study hard enough for the exam because I wasn't that interested in circuits and Ohm's law. I was interested in talking on the radio."

After Sam graduated from the Dudley Grade School in El Paso in 1948, his mother enrolled him at the New Mexico Military Institute in Roswell, New Mexico, in the hope of instilling discipline in the boy. Donaldson's initial antipathy for the military lifestyle eventually gave way, and he became a model cadet, rising to the rank of sergeant by the end of his second year. While he was a student there, he developed a passion for flying, which became for him "both an adventure and an escape." Paying for his lessons with money his mother sent him, ostensibly to buy blankets for his bunk, he "went up every chance [he] got." (Donaldson finally earned his private pilot's license in 1955.)

On his graduation from the New Mexico Military Institute in 1951, Donaldson continued his education as a telecommunications major at Texas Western College, now the University of Texas at El Paso. An indifferent student, he was, by his own admission, more interested in "having fun" than in studying. About the only thing he took seriously at that time in his life was radio broadcasting. To gain practical on-the-air experience, Donaldson signed on as a part-time disc jockey at KELP, a tiny, 250-watt AM station in El Paso. Shortly after that, he moved on to a larger local station, KEPO, where he worked long shifts as a news reader, occasional interviewer, and host of his own one-hour deejay program, *Sam's Show*. In his senior year Donaldson landed a job as an announcer at KROD-TV, the CBS affiliate in El Paso. "I didn't like it as well [as radio]," he wrote in *Hold On, Mr. President!* "I didn't get to do as much, and I sensed the lack of that magic link with the audience radio provides. Ask anyone who has worked in both, and they'll tell you the real freedom and romance in broadcasting is to be found in radio."

After receiving his B.A. degree from Texas Western College in 1955, Donaldson entered the University of California at Los Angeles for a year of postgraduate study. During his stay there, he devoted most of his spare time—and virtually all of his spare cash—to publishing and promoting *Television Film,* a magazine that he cofounded with his friend Al Preiss. Realizing that he could not raise enough money to meet his share of the ongoing publication expenses, he eventually sold out to Preiss, who continues to publish the periodical under the name of *Television International Magazine*. In the summer of 1956 Donaldson returned to El Paso, where he helped establish a local chapter of the Young Republicans. As a leader of the group, he organized a motorcade and campaign rally for the visiting Republican vice-presidential candidate, Richard M. Nixon.

Late in 1956 Donaldson reported to Fort Bliss in El Paso for active duty in the United States Army. Commissioned as an ROTC second lieutenant in the air defense artillery, he voluntarily extended his tour of duty from six months to two and a half years. During that time he served as a training officer in the deployment and operation of anti-aircraft missiles, then as an assistant in the base information office. At one point, he requested a temporary posting to Camp Desert Rock, Nevada, so that he could observe an atomic bomb test. "It was a thrilling and terrifying experience . . . ," Donaldson recalled years later in his memoir. "Those people who argue that nuclear war is acceptable have never seen the force of those weapons firsthand. The atomic bomb is not just another weapon."

Following his discharge from the army in April 1959, Donaldson moved to Dallas, where he worked for a time as a mutual-funds salesman—a job he admittedly "hated"—before he returned to broadcasting, as a general announcer at KRLD-TV, the CBS affiliate in Dallas. Thinking that he had, as he put it, "learned as much as [he] was going to learn" at KRLD, he resigned in September 1960 and set off for New York. Rejected by every television and radio station in the city because he lacked the experience in print journalism then considered essential, he eked out a living working as an extra in television dramas and commercials while he continued his search for employment. Finally, in the summer of 1961, he was hired by WTOP-TV, the CBS affiliate in Washington, D.C., to fill in for the station's announcers during their vacations. He performed his duties, which ranged from reading commercials to commenting on events of local interest, so well that at the summer's end he was offered a permanent post in the news department.

At first a general assignment reporter, Donaldson covered a wide variety of stories, from routine local features to the Cuban missile crisis. Beginning in 1962, he also wrote and delivered a nightly commentary spot called "The Sound Look." By his own admission his commentaries were "bland" and "not very tough," but they nonetheless occasionally nettled some government officials. For example, after he indirectly criticized the FCC's failure to approve the establishment of additional broadcasting outlets in Austin, Texas, whose sole television station was owned by the wife of President Lyndon B. Johnson, the irate president reportedly tried to have the reporter fired. While Donaldson's bosses defended him on that occasion, they demoted him not long afterwards because of his lobbying efforts in behalf of the American Federation of Television and Radio Artists (AFTRA), which was then trying to unionize WTOP's news division. An active member of AFTRA, Donaldson eventually served two terms as president of the union's Washington-Baltimore local.

Donaldson's demotion was short-lived, and within months he was once again drawing such important assignments as the civil rights movement and Senator Barry M. Goldwater's 1964 presidential bid. He also anchored the station's weekend newscasts and, beginning in September 1967, its weekday evening news program, which was at the time the most widely watched local news broadcast in the capital. Just a few weeks later, however, he left WTOP to join ABC News's Washington bureau. Many of his new colleagues at ABC were admittedly discouraged by the network's poor ratings and shoestring budget, but Donaldson saw the situation as a golden opportunity to advance quickly. Devoting himself to his job, he worked long hours and willingly took on all the "late and dirty" assignments that no one else wanted. As John Lynch, then ABC's Washington bureau chief, told John Weisman in an interview for a TV Guide (July 29, 1978) profile of Donaldson, he "became the catalyst for ABC's bureau. He was always hanging around the desk, looking for stories, grabbing the phones, waiting for something to happen."

The strategy paid off handsomely for Donaldson in assignments that would not normally have been entrusted to a network newcomer. The skill and political expertise he displayed in covering both the Democratic and Republican national conventions in 1968 earned him the prestigious Capitol Hill beat—the best assignment in Washington, according to Donaldson. After two years of reporting on the House and Senate, he volunteered for a three-month tour as a war correspondent in Vietnam. Back in the United States in time for the 1972 election campaign, he once again covered the national nominating conventions of the two major political parties, and then followed George S. McGovern, the Democratic standard-bearer, as he stumped the country.

It was not until 1973, however, that Sam Donaldson became a familiar figure to the national television audience as a regular member of the ABC news team assigned to the Senate Watergate hearings, which the three networks carried live in rotation. "Watergate proved to be the most difficult story I've covered when it came to keeping my own emotions and feelings from coloring my reporting," Donaldson admitted in Hold On, Mr. President!. "As the facts of Watergate accumulated, I became convinced that Richard Nixon was participating in a criminal conspiracy to obstruct justice and ought to be punished for it through the constitutional and legal process. I tried to keep this personal view out of my reporting, but in retrospect, I didn't always succeed."

After President Nixon's resignation in August 1974, Donaldson went through what he has called "the greatest period of decompression" he has experienced in his long career. Despite a variety of challenging assignments, including a documentary on the hidden costs of government regulations for ABC News Close-up, he did not come out of the doldrums until January 1976, when he was assigned to cover Jimmy Carter, a dark horse candidate for the Democratic presidential nomination. Donaldson spent the next eleven months traveling with Carter, thus becoming the obvious choice for the high-profile post of network White House correspondent after Carter's inauguration as president in January 1977.

As Donaldson outlined it in Hold On, Mr. President!, the task of the White House press corps is "to challenge the president . . . to explain policy, justify decisions, defend mistakes, reveal intentions for the future, and comment on a host of matters about which his views are of general concern." To that end, Donaldson asks specific, pointed (some would say confrontational) questions and maintains an attitude of "continuing, unrelenting skepticism," as he once put it. "It's my job to ruffle feathers," Donaldson explained, as quoted in TV Guide (December 25, 1982). "Docile reporters may produce 'better stories' from the White House point of view, but not from the public's." His adversarial approach has on more than one occasion led to important newsbreaks. In March 1979, for example, as President Carter was about to leave the Middle East for home following several days of what appeared to be inconclusive talks with Egyptian President Anwar el-Sadat and Israeli Prime Minister Menachem Begin regarding a peace treaty between Egypt and Israel, Donaldson, refusing to accept the official White House line, shouted above the Cairo airport din, "Mr. President, is it peace?" When Carter hesitated, the reporter persisted. "But it sounds like peace—if the Israeli cabinet agrees?" he asked. "Right," Carter replied.

Donaldson's aggressive, irreverent style has been at the root of his frequent differences of opinion with the White House press secretaries for both Jimmy Carter and Ronald Reagan, but even the presidential spokesmen have publicly admitted their respect for the reporter's intelligence, accuracy, and professionalism. "Sam is one of the best," Marlin Fitzwater, President Reagan's press secretary, told Louise Sweeney of the Christian Science Monitor (April 13, 1987). "He's a serious student of the issues, always inquisitive about the facts, and aggressive in their pursuit. But I think the most praiseworthy of Sam's traits is the fact that he's always relevant." Moreover, Fitzwater added, Donaldson "often has a degree of confidence that allows him to report a story just based on his own knowledge. And there aren't many reporters who have that confidence, and who are right."

Of the many major stories that Donaldson has covered in his ten years as ABC's White House correspondent, perhaps the most important in terms of their effects on the presidents involved were the

Iranian hostage crisis, which dominated the last fourteen months of Carter's presidency, and the assassination attempt against Ronald Reagan in March 1981. During the hostage crisis, which began when militant supporters of the Ayatollah Khomeini seized the American Embassy in Tehran in November 1979 and ended with the hostages' release in January 1981, Donaldson regularly put in sixteen-hour days, as he prepared and delivered live reports on the situation for the network's regularly scheduled news broadcasts and for its *The Iran Crisis: America Held Hostage*, a special late-night recap that eventually developed into the highly praised live interview program *ABC News Nightline*. It was, as Donaldson has since acknowledged, "the hardest, most sustained effort" he has ever made as a journalist.

The attempt on Ronald Reagan's life provided another kind of journalistic challenge, for as Donaldson has observed, "when someone shoots at the president, you can't wait until you have the details confirmed." One of a handful of veteran correspondents on hand to hear the president deliver a routine speech at a Washington hotel, Donaldson was just a few feet away when John W. Hinckley Jr. fired several shots, striking Reagan in the chest. At the time, however, he saw "no evidence" that the president had been hit, and in his first ad-libbed telephone report from the scene, which was broadcast by ABC Radio just four minutes after the attack, he said that although he could not be certain, he did not believe that Reagan had been shot. It was not until he returned to the studio and began discussing the incident live with Frank Reynolds that he learned that the president had indeed been wounded. "I was flabbergasted, embarrassed, and angry . . . ," Donaldson recalled in his memoir. "To discover I had been wrong all along and had misled our audience, well, I was horrified."

At least partly because of the tightening of security after the assassination attempt, the access of the press corps to President Reagan has since been severely curtailed. "We are permitted to be close enough to see—they want the pictures shown—but not close enough to ask questions in any civilized way," Donaldson has complained. After Reagan's staff moved to limit the longstanding custom of allowing impromptu questions during photo opportunities, the reporter accused the administration of trying to "manage the news" coming out of the White House. To Donaldson, the new restrictions on the press suggested that the president's staff did not want the public "to see Ronald Reagan in action unless he's on the same carefully prepared sound stage that he had worked on for so long in Hollywood."

In addition to serving as ABC's White House correspondent, Donaldson anchors the network's Sunday evening newscasts and appears as one of the three regular panelists on its Sunday morning public affairs program, *This Week With David Brinkley*. At first troubled by his participation in the Brinkley show's round-table discussion segment, where the panelists debate political view-

points with rotating guest commentators, he eventually decided that he was not compromising his integrity or his credibility with the viewers by performing the dual role of reporter and commentator. Donaldson has made no secret of his desire to be relieved of the White House beat after Reagan's second term. "I really believe that turnover is good for everyone," he explained, as quoted in the *Washington Journalism Review* (February 1986). "I need a new challenge, and I think it would be good for ABC News and the viewers to have [a reporter] come to the White House and not be so blasé and not say, 'I know how this is going to go.'"

A lean six-footer, Sam Donaldson has blue eyes, dark-brown hair threaded with gray, and what has been described as a "foxy" smile. His most distinctive features, however, are his thick, dark eyebrows, which "seem to be raised in a permanent query," as Louise Sweeney observed. A workaholic, he has little time for hobbies, although he enjoys playing bridge and tending the roses that he grows at his home in McLean, Virginia. He shares that home with his third wife, Jan Smith, a reporter for the Independent News Network whom he wed on April 16, 1983. His two earlier marriages—to Patricia Oates, in 1954, and Billy Kay Butler, in 1963—ended in divorce. Donaldson has a son, Samuel, by his first wife, and three children, Jennifer, Thomas, and Robert, by his second.

References: *Newsweek* 109:58+ Mr 2 '87 pors; *People* 17:55+ Je 14 '82 pors; *Playboy* 30:57+ Mr '83 pors; *Time* 121:78+ Ap 11 '83 por; *TV Guide* 26:8+ Jl 29 '78 por; *Washington Post* C p1+ Jl 24 '84 pors; *Contemporary Authors* vol 11 (1984); *Who's Who in America*, 1986–87; *Who's Who in TV & Cable* (1983)

Doubleday, Nelson

July 20, 1933- Baseball executive; former publisher. Address: b. New York Mets, Shea Stadium, Roosevelt Ave. and 126th St., Flushing, N.Y. 11368

Nelson Doubleday, the scion of one of the major American publishing dynasties, has parlayed an unlikely partnership between the family book company and a major-league baseball franchise into a winning investment. Doubleday is the grandson of F. N. Doubleday, the founder of Doubleday & Company Inc., and the great-great-grandnephew of Abner Doubleday, the apocryphal "inventor" of baseball. Working his way up the executive ladder in the publishing company, he became its president in 1978. Two years later the company bought the then lowly New York Mets, the National League baseball team, and Doubleday became chairman of the Met board as well. Over the next six years, the Mets developed into a championship team, while Doubleday & Company showed signs

Nelson Doubleday

Head, Long Island, and the Eaglebrook School and Deerfield Academy in Deerfield, Massachusetts. Friends have explained the mixture of "patrician" and "good old boy, Northern style" in his personality to the profound effect his father's death had on him in 1949. "Overnight he went from being a fun-loving if somewhat spoiled kid who loved to play ball and practical jokes—he delighted in ordering gags such as exploding cigarettes from magazines—to being the man of the family as well," Nancy Perry reported in Fortune (January 5, 1987). "He has been struggling to reconcile the two personas ever since."

At Princeton University, Doubleday started out as an English major but switched to economics. A member of the Colonial Club at Princeton, he excelled in club sports, especially baseball, football, and hockey. After graduating, he worked briefly at entry level at Doubleday & Company, at the time the largest hard-cover book publisher in the country; served in the United States Air Force for three years (1956–59); and then resumed his grooming for leadership at the publishing house. Following stints as an assistant in the promotion and subsidiary-rights departments, he managed the trade publications division, chaired the new broadcast subsidiary, and, in 1967, became executive vice-president in charge of sales.

Privately owned and intimately run, with its own printing plant in Garden City, New York, Doubleday & Company had acquired the reputation of being the most inscrutable house in the publishing world. The once close relationship between Nelson Doubleday and his sister became strained when Neltje pressed for going public with the company stock. In coalition with his mother and with John Sargent, Neltje's ex-husband and the company's president and chief executive officer since 1961, Nelson opposed her effort. In July 1973, when he turned forty, he assumed full control of the stock left him by his father, and at a stockholders meeting two months later Neltje's bid for a public stock offering was voted down. With the addition of the shares left him by his mother when she died early in 1978, Nelson had the controlling interest in the company.

In May 1978 Nelson Doubleday was elected to succeed John Sargent as the president and chief executive officer of Doubleday & Company. Still a giant among hard-cover publishers, with a list of some 700 books a year, the company at that point had been steadily registering annual sales and profits gains. For the fiscal year ending April 30, 1978 it reported sales of $350.9 million and net earnings of $16.6 million, up 7 and 10 percent respectively from the previous year. The chief source of income was not its renowned line of trade books but its empire of book clubs, led by the venerable and gargantuan Literary Guild. The next most lucrative enterprise was Laidlaw Brothers, its textbook subsidiary. Approximately 15 percent of the company's income came from the paperback imprints of the Dell Publishing Company, a recently acquired subsidiary. Among the other operations

of foundering. In 1986 Nelson Doubleday carried off a double coup, personally buying the baseball team from Doubleday & Company for a record $100 million in partnership with Fred Wilpon and, in a separate transaction, selling the publishing company to Bertelsmann A.G., the West German communications conglomerate, for a reported $475 million.

Nelson Doubleday is the son of the late Nelson Doubleday Sr., who built the company founded by F. N. (Frank Nelson) Doubleday into a mass-market giant among trade publishers, and the late Ellen McCarter (Violett) Doubleday. His ancestor Abner Doubleday actually existed and may have contributed to the popularization of baseball, but he certainly did not invent the game. Nelson was born on July 20, 1933, in Oyster Bay, Long Island. During Nelson's infancy the aging Rudyard Kipling, one of the Doubleday company's many illustrious authors, dedicated his poem "If" to him. Growing up in Oyster Bay, Nelson and his sister, Neltje (who now has the last name Kings, from her second marriage), lived, in Neltje's words, the "very isolated life" of "two rich kids sitting in a big house with lots of nannies and maids." According to Neltje, Nelson, a "very silent" child, was much more interested in baseball than in books. "He went to day camp and hated it," she remembered, as quoted by Christine Dugas in Business Week (August 4, 1986). "He wasn't much of a participator. But he liked to listen to Dodgers [baseball] games on the radio." Like his father, Nelson was "not a reader," Neltje said. "I think in many ways he mimicked our father, who always said, 'I don't read books, I sell them.'"

Doubleday received his elite primary and secondary education at the Green Vale School in Glen

were bookstores, a packaging firm, an export agency, and several FM radio stations.

Meanwhile, Nelson Doubleday had been dabbling financially in his other, perhaps truer, love—sports. Specifically, he had become a minor shareholder in the California Golden Seals and New York Islanders hockey teams, and in the same year that he took the helm at Doubleday & Company he bought a major interest in the Islanders. Under him, Doubleday & Company in 1980 became the majority owner of the New York Mets baseball team, putting up 80 percent of the then record $21.1 million paid for the franchise by a triumvirate of investors. (The others were the City Investing Corporation and Fred Wilpon of Sterling Equities Inc., who became president of the team. Later Doubleday & Company bought City Investing's shares, bringing its ownership percentage to 95.) The price tag surprised close observers of the baseball scene, because the Mets, in a downward spiral ever since winning the World Series in 1969, were ensconced in last place in the National League East at the time. With an infusion of $8 million from Doubleday & Company and $2 million from the other investors, the Mets were rebuilt, chiefly through a nurturing of young talent in the team's farm system and astute trades that bypassed the exorbitantly priced and treacherous free-agent route.

Looking to payments for broadcast rights to games, especially on cable TV, as a means of putting the Mets back into the black financially, Nelson Doubleday did not take kindly to the suggestion of Bowie Kuhn, the baseball commissioner, that the owners of teams in lucrative markets, such as New York, Montreal, and Philadelphia, share their home-game television revenues with the more numerous teams from Cincinnati, Milwaukee, and other poorer venues. Led vigorously by Doubleday, a campaign by the minority of rich-city owners resulted in Kuhn's replacement by Peter V. Ueberroth in 1984.

The return on Doubleday & Company's investment in the Mets began to become tangible in 1984, when the team became a profit-making pennant contender. With records of 90-72 and 98-64 respectively, the Mets finished second in their division in both 1984 and 1985. In 1986, when the team recaptured the world championship, attendance at Shea Stadium, its home field, rose to 3 million (four times the 1980 figure) and receipts exceeded $6 million.

While the Mets were resurging, the parent company was slumping. The early years of Nelson Doubleday's presidency of Doubleday & Company coincided with increasingly hard times in the publishing industry generally, and Doubleday was among the firms most severely affected. In the early 1970s the company had registered net profits in the magnitude of $8 and $9 million on sales approximating $250 million. By the beginning of the 1980s the sales had doubled, partly reflecting monetary inflation, but the profit figure did not rise accordingly. In the fiscal year ending April 30, 1982 the company's cash assets were down $10 million from the previous year, and its profit on sales of $505 million would have been less than $3 million but for creative accountancy. ($10 million-plus from the sale of a radio station was listed as income rather than capital gain.) In 1983-84 sales were $493 million and earnings were $8.4 million. The following year the profit on sales of more than $400 million was only $300,000.

Some observers of Doubleday & Company's decline blamed Nelson Doubleday for paying too much attention to the New York Mets. The truth of the matter, however, was that laissez-faire was his wonted, all-round style. Just as he left the running of the baseball team to general manager J. Frank Cashen, and field manager Davey Johnson, he tended to delegate power at the parent company—until 1985, when, alarmed, he took drastic action to stop the company's downward plunge. With the help of John R. McLaughlin, the head of Doubleday's Dell subsidiary and a paragon of efficient management, he tightened operations at Dell, eliminating jobs and some imprints; reorganized and streamlined the other mass-market divisions and the textbook subsidiary; and sold the radio subsidiaries for approximately $100 million and the international marketing division for an undisclosed amount. The company's annual list was reduced to 400 books, and staff was cut accordingly.

In September 1985 Nelson Doubleday stepped aside, becoming chairman of the board of Doubleday & Company while handing over the duties of chief executive to John R. McLaughlin. A year later Doubleday & Company (with sales of $472 million and earnings of $7 million, $5 million of which was from the Mets) was still not a very hot property, but Bertelsmann A.G., eager to expand its beachhead in the United States, agreed to buy the company for almost $500 million in cash and assets. The Mets were not part of that transaction, because Nelson Doubleday and Fred Wilpon personally arranged to buy the baseball franchise from the publishing company before it was sold to Bertelsmann. As equal partners, Doubleday and Wilpon paid $85 million outright and agreed to assume about $15 million in team liabilities, including player contracts. The total of $100 million was the highest amount ever paid for a sports franchise.

Nelson Doubleday has a round, tanned face, and his wavy, once dark hair is almost completely gray. Over six feet tall, weighing over 200 pounds, and dressing in loud striped shirts, the ebullient Doubleday cuts a robust and colorful figure at Shea Stadium, where he likes to mingle with fans in the hot dog line and never visits the dugout. In her profile of Doubleday in Fortune, Nancy J. Perry described him as "a fine Scotch blend: two parts Locust Valley, Long Island WASP—pampered . . . and exceedingly preppie—and one part earthy Scot, with deep voice, hearty chuckle, bawdy humor." In interviewing him, Miss Perry found him to be "a man's man" who "likes people, parties, practical jokes" but who can become "brusque, dismissive" if you "tread too close, push too far, ask for instance if you might chat with his wife or daughters."

Following his divorce from his first wife, the former Florence McKim, Doubleday married Sandra P. Barnett, a real estate broker, in 1973. The fact that none of his four daughters or their husbands is employed by Doubleday & Company made Doubleday's decision to sell the company much easier than it would otherwise have been. The baseball executive and his wife live alternately in Hobe Sound, Florida, and in a large house on Duck Pond Road in Locust Valley. Hunting ducks is one of his favorite recreations, and wild-duck motifs decorate his office walls and his neckties. He also takes an annual pheasant-hunting vacation in England, excels at backgammon, and plays ten-handicap golf.

References: American Heritage 35:9 Je/Jl '84; Bsns W p74+ Ag 4 '86 por; Fortune 115:32+ Ja 5 '87 por; N Y Times III p1+ Jl 15 '79, p25 Jl 28 '84 por, A p1+ Ag 15 '86 por, C p4 S 29 '86 por, C p17 O 2 '86, p1+ O 18 '86 por; New York 13:13+ F 11 '80, 16:50+ F 7 '83 pors; Pub W 223:58+ Ja 28 '83 por; Lang, Jack, and Simon, Peter. The New York Mets (1986); Who's Who in America, 1984–85

Douglas, Michael

Sept. 25, 1944– Actor; motion picture producer. Address: b. c/o Ron Meyer, Creative Artists Agency, 1888 Century Park East, Suite 1400, Los Angeles, Calif. 90067

An actor with twenty years of experience in playing what he has described as "generally humane, morally responsible guys" in theatrical productions, films, and television series, Michael Douglas branched out into independent feature production in 1975 with the Academy Award-winning One Flew Over the Cuckoo's Nest. Since then, as a producer and actor-producer, he has shown an uncanny knack for choosing projects that reflect changing trends and public concerns. Over the past twelve years, he has been involved in such controversial and politically influential motion pictures as The China Syndrome and such crowd-pleasing escapist fare as Romancing the Stone and The Jewel of the Nile. In recognition of his "extraordinary career," Douglas was named producer of the year in 1984 by the National Association of Theatre Owners.

Michael Kirk Douglas was born on September 25, 1944, in New Brunswick, New Jersey, the older of the two sons of the actor Kirk Douglas and his actress wife, Diana (Dill) Douglas. His brother, Joel, who followed him into the motion picture business, has served as the line producer on most of his films. Shortly after Michael's birth, the Douglases moved to Hollywood, California, where the father and mother hoped to establish themselves as screen actors. As their film careers took opposite turns, Kirk and Diana Douglas drifted apart, and about 1950 they divorced. Both were eventually remarried, Diana to William Darrid, a theatrical producer and writer, and Kirk to the former Anne Buydens. Michael Douglas has two half brothers—Eric, an actor, and Peter, a writer—from his father's second marriage.

In his mother's custody following the divorce, Michael Douglas spent his boyhood in New York City, Los Angeles, California, and after her remarriage, in what he has described as "a very warm and loving home" in Westport, Connecticut. The mother's frequent moves meant that young Michael, by his own admission an indifferent student, attended a number of schools, ranging from a private elementary day school in Manhattan to a tough public junior high school in West Los Angeles to the Black-Foxe Military Institute, also in Los Angeles. He completed his secondary education at the Choate School, an elite college preparatory school for boys in Wallingford, Connecticut. Throughout that period, the boy regularly spent the summers with his father, either at his home in Hollywood or on location. In an interview for Playboy magazine (February 1986), Douglas admitted that "it was hard" being the son of an internationally famous movie star: "I saw my father as a gladiator, nailed to a cross, as an artist who cut his ear off—and he would be shown doing these superhuman things. I'd think, 'How can I possibly be a man? How can I be the man this man was?'"

Although he had been accepted by Yale, Douglas opted for the University of California at Santa

Barbara. More interested in "beaches and bikinis," as he put it, than in his studies, he flunked out in his freshman year. For the next eighteen months he worked at a succession of odd jobs, including gas station attendant and second assistant director on his father's film *Cast a Giant Shadow* (1966), then sought and won readmission to the University of California. Because he thought he'd "make better grades doing something [he] knew," Douglas decided to major in drama. He appeared in several campus theatrical productions over the next few years, among them *As You Like It* and *Candida*, for which he was named the school's best actor in 1967, and even tried his hand at directing. His staging of the one-act play *Muzeeka*, John Guare's biting social satire, earned him the university's best director honors in 1968. During his summer vacations from college, Douglas took part in the annual National Playwrights Conference program at the Eugene O'Neill Theatre Center in Waterford, Connecticut, a showcase for the work of promising young writers. His list of credits over several seasons at the center includes roles in more than a dozen plays, most notably, *Summertree*, Ron Cowen's examination, through a series of flashbacks, of the life of a young man killed in the Vietnam war.

After receiving his B.A. degree from the University of California in 1968, Douglas moved to New York City to continue his dramatic training, first with Sanford Meisner at the Neighborhood Playhouse, where he appeared in workshop productions of Pirandello's *Six Characters in Search of an Author*, and Thornton Wilder's *Happy Journey to Trenton and Camden*, among other plays, and then with Wynn Handman at the American Place Theatre. A few months after he arrived in New York, Douglas got his first big break when he was cast in the *CBS Playhouse* production of Ellen M. Violett's moralistic drama *The Experiment*, which was televised nationwide on February 25, 1969. In the pivotal role of the free-spirited scientist who compromises his liberal views to accept a lucrative job with a buttoned-down high-tech corporation, he turned in a "remarkably lucid and attractively relaxed" performance, according to Jack Gould in his review of the program for the *New York Times* (February 26, 1969). Douglas "could easily go as far as his father," Gould concluded. "He has a promising knack for intuitive versatility."

Douglas' convincing portrayal won him an audition for the lead in *Hail, Hero!*, the initial project of CBS's newly organized theatrical film production company, Cinema Center Films. Nevertheless, the young actor's screen test went unnoticed until his agent telephoned the director, David Miller, to point out that he had auditioned the son of Kirk Douglas, whom Miller had directed in *Lonely Are the Brave*. Miller promptly assigned the role to Douglas. In an interview with Al Cohn for *Newsday*'s Sunday magazine (December 23, 1979), the actor conceded that having a famous father helps "get you your first part because the publicists will capitalize on who you are." Later, however, "it starts becoming a negative. The only other advantage of the 'in' is that you know about the industry from the inside. So if you do have some success, you are much more able to deal with it."

Based on John Weston's controversial novel of the same title, *Hail, Hero!* (1969) starred Michael Douglas as Carl Dixon, a well-meaning, almost saintly young pacifist determined not only to justify his beliefs to his conservative parents but also to test them under fire in the jungles of Indochina. While the majority of critics maintained that Douglas more than held his own opposite such veteran actors as Arthur Kennedy and Teresa Wright, few felt that his performance, "admirable" though it was, redeemed the otherwise "confused" and "simplistic" film. Similar reservations greeted the release, in 1970, of his second feature, *Adam at 6 A.M.*, about a young man's search for his roots. For most reviewers, Douglas' "finely individualized" portrayal, to use Judith Crist's description, of the protagonist was the movie's strongest—some would say only—asset.

Douglas fared no better in *Summertree* (1971), a somewhat heavy handed film version of Ron Cowen's play that was produced by Kirk Douglas' Bryna Company, and *Napoleon and Samantha* (1972), a sentimental children's melodrama from the Walt Disney studio. In between film assignments, he took what stage work he could find in summer stock and Off-Broadway productions, among them *City Scenes*, Frank Gagliano's surrealistic vignettes of contemporary life in New York City, John Patrick's short-lived romance *Love is a Time of Day*, and George Tabori's *Pinkville*, in which he played a young innocent brutalized by his military training. He also appeared in the made-for-television thriller *When Michael Calls*, which was first broadcast by ABC-TV on February 5, 1972, and in episodes of such popular series as *Medical Center* and *The FBI*.

Impressed by Douglas' performance in a segment of *The FBI*, Quinn Martin, the series' producer, signed the actor for the part of Karl Malden's sidekick in the new police series *The Streets of San Francisco*, which had its premiere in September 1972. To prepare for their roles as, respectively, Detective Lieutenant Mike Stone, a streetwise veteran of the police force, and Assistant Inspector Steve Keller, a college-educated criminologist, Malden and Douglas often accompanied local police officers on patrol. Their homework, coupled with their on-screen rapport, paid off in sharply etched characterizations that earned the pair Emmy award nominations in three successive seasons. The series itself started slowly, but after programmers switched its time slot from Saturday to Thursday nights, the show took off to become one of the top-rated entries on ABC's prime-time program roster in the mid-1970s.

During the annual breaks in the shooting schedule for *The Streets of San Francisco*, Douglas devoted most of his time to his film production company, Big Stick Productions, Ltd., which produced several short subjects in the early 1970s. Long interested in producing a film version of Ken

Kesey's grimly humorous novel *One Flew Over the Cuckoo's Nest*, to which Kirk Douglas owned the movie rights, he purchased the property from his father and began scouting around for financial backing. After a number of major motion picture studios turned him down, Douglas formed a partnership with Saul Zaentz, a record industry executive, and the two set about recruiting a cast and crew. Douglas still had a year to go on his contract for *The Streets of San Francisco*, but its producers agreed to write his character out of the story so that he could concentrate on filming *Cuckoo's Nest*.

With Milos Forman behind the camera and a cast headed by Jack Nicholson, in the role of Randle Patrick Murphy, who is committed to a mental institution after feigning insanity to avoid a jail sentence, and Louise Fletcher, as the sadistic Nurse Ratched, filming of *One Flew Over the Cuckoo's Nest* finally got under way in January 1975. To insure its authenticity, Douglas arranged for most of the movie, which describes the systematic destruction of the rebellious Murphy, to be shot on location at the Oregon State Mental Hospital in Salem. A critical and commercial success, *One Flew Over the Cuckoo's Nest* won five Academy Awards, including those for best picture, director, actor, and actress, and went on to gross more than $180 million at the box office.

Because of his extraordinary coup in sweeping the four top Oscar categories for 1975, Douglas suddenly found himself in demand as an independent producer. One of the many scripts submitted to him for consideration over the next few months was Mike Gray's chilling account of the attempted coverup of an accident at a nuclear power plant. Attracted by the combination of social relevance and hair-triggered suspense, Douglas immediately bought the property, but until he teamed up with the actress Jane Fonda, he was unable to raise enough cash to begin production. Deemed "uncommercial" by most potential investors, the project especially appealed to Miss Fonda, who had recently formed her own motion picture production company, IPC Films, for the purpose of making "message" movies in an entertaining way.

A Michael Douglas-IPC Films coproduction, *The China Syndrome* (1979) starred Jack Lemmon as Jack Godell, the whistle-blowing chief engineer at the fictitious Ventana nuclear power plant, Jane Fonda as Kimberley Wells, an ambitious television feature reporter who hopes that her coverage of the plant accident will break her into hard news, and Michael Douglas as her hot-tempered, maverick cameraman. Under the direction of James Bridges, Douglas earned his best notices to date, turning in a performance of such power and intensity that Vincent Canby, writing in the *New York Times* (November 2, 1979), contended that he "could well be on his way to becoming one of our best young leading actors."

The reviews for the film itself were generally favorable, although some viewers criticized its "exaggerated" and "ponderously alarmist" portrayal of the risks of nuclear power. Then, just two weeks after the movie opened, life imitated art when a partial meltdown occurred at the Three Mile Island nuclear plant near Harrisburg, Pennsylvania. "I saw how the whole thing paralleled our film," Douglas told Arthur Knight in an interview for *Penthouse* magazine (December 1979). "It took on proportions for me that were religious. It was an ordained sort of event." To avoid the appearance of capitalizing on the accident, Douglas pointedly refused to include references to it in the film's promotional advertisements, but as he explained to Knight, "If the picture had not been there, the nuclear industry might have been able to bury the accident. . . . Our film prodded and forced the news teams to answer the call." Nominated for three major Academy Awards, *The China Syndrome* was named one of the best English-language films of the year by the National Board of Review.

His success as a producer notwithstanding, Douglas is, by his own admission, "an actor first and a producer second," and in the late 1970s he decided to concentrate for a time on acting. His screen acting credits for that period include, in addition to *The China Syndrome*, *Coma* (1978), Michael Crichton's thriller about foul play in a Boston hospital; *It's My Turn* (1981), a feminist comedy vehicle for Jill Clayburgh; *The Star Chamber* (1983), a gripping tale of modern-day vigilante justice; and *Fatal Attraction* (1987), a psychological thriller about the disastrous results of a philandering husband's weekend fling with an emotionally unstable woman, played by Glenn Close. He was perhaps most effective as Michael Andropolis, the compulsive quitter who sacrifices everything to take one last shot at the Olympics as a marathoner in the otherwise undistinguished *Running* (1979), and as Zach, the dictatorial director in Sir Richard Attenborough's pallid screen version of the hit Broadway musical *A Chorus Line* (1985). Douglas recently completed work on Oliver Stone's "Wall Street," tentatively scheduled for release in December 1987, in which he portrays an unscrupulous corporate raider.

Douglas' careers as actor and producer came together again in 1984 with the release of the tongue-in-cheek romantic fantasy *Romancing the Stone*. Douglas had begun developing the project, based on a script by Diane Thomas, several years earlier, but it was, in his words, "a hard sell" until Steven Spielberg's 1981 pulp adventure *Raiders of the Lost Ark* grossed more than $230 million in ticket sales. Lighter and, in the view of most critics, funnier than the frenetically paced *Raiders of the Lost Ark*, to which it has frequently been compared, *Romancing the Stone* owes its special charm to an inspired gender twist: its central character is not a dashing adventurer in the Indiana Jones vein, but Joan Wilder, a dowdy writer of gothic romances transformed overnight into a feisty heroine when she travels to the jungles of Colombia to find buried treasure and thereby rescue her kidnapped sister. With Kathleen Turner as Joan Wilder and Douglas himself as Jack Colton, the reluctant soldier of fortune who is her ally and foil, *Romancing the Stone* was a resounding hit, taking in more than $100 million at the box office. Its inevitable sequel, *The Jewel of the Nile* (1985), which takes the Turner and Douglas characters to new adventures in the deserts of North Africa, "[failed] to maintain the same giddy level of humor and suspense," as the New York *Daily News's* Kathleen Carroll, among others, observed, largely because of its weaker script and "run-of-the-mill" plot. Commercially successful despite the generally unenthusiastic reviews, *The Jewel of the Nile* grossed nearly $60 million in its first three months.

Since he became involved in motion picture production in the early 1970s, Douglas has selected only those scripts that have interested him personally. "It is a love affair," he explained to an interviewer for *American Film* (July/August 1979). "You read projects and you flirt with them and . . . all of a sudden you fall in love. You've got to have that because like any relationship it's going to be really hard to keep your interests and energy going two and a half years later unless you're in love." It took Douglas nearly that long to persuade Columbia Pictures executives to approve the production of *Starman*, an unlikely but ultimately irresistible tale about a romance between a young widow and a disembodied extraterrestrial who has temporarily assumed human form. Coproduced by Douglas and Larry J. Franco, *Starman* was the sleeper of the 1984 Christmas holiday season. Indeed it proved to be so popular with audiences that it spawned, in 1986, a television series of the same name, which Douglas coproduced. In October 1986 Douglas formed a partnership, Mercury-Douglas, with Michael Phillips, the producer of such hit films as *The Sting* and *Close Encounters of the Third Kind*. The pair intends to produce sixteen movies over the next four years.

A lanky six-footer, Michael Douglas has caramel-colored hair, deep-set, blue-green eyes, and a hint of his father's famous cleft chin, but as Louise Bernikow observed in an article for *Gentlemen's Quarterly* (December 1985), his face, like the roles he has played, "is not butch, not tough" like Kirk Douglas'. "It doesn't express the kind of masculinity associated with movies of an earlier time," she explained. "This face is fine and lean and unavoidably sensitive." Described by those who know him as "genuine" and "generous," Douglas devotes much of his free time to campaigning for handgun control and a nuclear freeze, among other liberal causes. He is a founder of the Committee of Concern, a group of entertainers that, in his words, tries "to inform people about Central American issues without turning them off." The soft-spoken, easygoing actor dislikes the glitzy Hollywood lifestyle, preferring to spend his rare leisure hours in the company of his friends and family. He and his wife, the former Diandra Luker, whom he married on March 20, 1977, recently moved with their son, Cameron Morrell, to an apartment overlooking Central Park on Manhattan's Upper West Side. They also maintain residences in Los Angeles and

in Santa Barbara, California. Douglas is a trustee of the University of California at Santa Barbara and the Eugene O'Neill Memorial Theatre Foundation.

References: *American Film* 4:29+ Jl/Ag '79 pors; *Gentlemen's Quarterly* 55:206+ D '85 pors; *Moviegoer* 5:14+ Ja '86 pors; *N Y Sunday News* mag p16+ D 9 '79 pors, mag p4+ D '85 por; *N Y Times* II p19+ S 7 '69 por; *Newsday* mag p14+ D 23 '79 por; *People* 11:96+ Ap 16 '79 pors; *Playboy* 33:51+ F '86 pors; *Rolling Stone* p28+ Ja 16 '86 por; *TV Guide* 22:25+ F 16 '74 por; *US* 3:32+ D 30 '85 pors; *Who's Who in America*, 1986–87

Durang, Christopher

Jan. 2, 1949– Playwright; actor. Address: b. c/o Helen Merrill Agency, 337 W. 22d St., New York City, N.Y. 10011

The absurdist farces of the young American playwright Christopher Durang would be unbearably sad if they were not played for their humor. His protagonists, when not being destroyed by the routine malevolence of fate, are being assaulted in a no less malevolent manner by parents or other ill-willed or incompetent authority figures into whose hands they fall. Durang is always asking why, if God exists, the world is so nasty, and why people inflict such horrors on those closest to them. His *Sister Mary Ignatius Explains It All for You* achieved notoriety because of its assault on the Roman Catholic parochial schools of his youth, and all his plays appear to be attempts, through the guise of laughter, to exorcise the demons of his past. Durang seems unlikely ever to be a popular playwright like Neil Simon—only two of his works have made it to Broadway, and then for only short runs—but they have a following among both the critics and the public.

Christopher Ferdinand Durang was born on January 2, 1949, in the upper-middle-class enclave of Montclair, New Jersey, the only child of Francis Ferdinand Durang, an architect, and Patricia Elizabeth Durang. Named after Christopher Robin of the A. A. Milne children's classics and of mainly Irish ancestry, despite his French surname, he was reared in Berkeley Heights, New Jersey, and spent twelve years in Roman Catholic schools.

An exposure to the performing arts came to Christopher Durang early. Two of his aunts, both professional musicians, took him along when they sang in hospitals, and he began singing at an aunt's piano recitals at the age of six. Inspired by the Broadway shows to which his parents took him regularly, he acted out plays of his own devising in the attic of the family home, where he created characters drawn from movies and television. His first play, a two-page adaptation of *I Love Lucy*, was produced when he was only in the second grade. By the time he reached the fourth grade, he was writing twelve-page dramas, and in the eighth grade he turned out his first full-length musical, the satirically titled *Banned in Boston*.

During interviews that he granted to various reporters during the early 1980s, Durang described himself as having been "a very religious, very well-behaved child." The gallows humor that darkens his plays he attributed largely to the traumas he suffered during his childhood, when he "saw people being horrible to one another, over and over." He told Steven Watson of *Newsday* (June 2, 1985): "My father always had a drinking problem, and my mother had an Rh negative [in her blood] that resulted in several stillborn children."

Although he was a militant radical at the Benedictine prep school that he attended, taking part, for example, in marches protesting the Vietnam war, Durang had contemplated entering a monastery before he was admitted to Harvard College in 1967 on the strength of his playwriting talent. He soon found himself confused and despondent in Cambridge. His parents, who had earlier separated, divorced while he was away at school, and he found the Catholics at Harvard, as he informed Chet Flippo of *New York* magazine (March 15, 1982), to be "very traditional and very kind of clubby . . . stultifying" so that he "stopped believing for all the various reasons one does stop believing." Moreover, he stopped writing plays.

"My sophomore and junior year, I was close to paralysis," Durang recalled in an interview with David Richards of the *Washington Post* (October 30, 1983). "I stayed in my room a lot or went to the movies. I stopped going to classes. Every day, I just sort of couldn't get up. I had this job, very proletarian, to help pay for my board. I cleaned bathrooms—two hours a day, five days a week. It was very contemplative." He almost flunked out of

school before snapping out of it in his senior year, when he resumed writing plays and was accepted by Yale University's drama school. Intimations of the fully formed Durang were already apparent in *The Nature and Purpose of the Universe*, which was presented at Smith College in 1971. In that play, as staged in New York in 1979, a heavenly messenger in the form of a Fuller Brush salesman promises to rescue a sorely tried housewife from her miseries. By the time deliverance appears, ostensibly in the form of death, the heroine is ready to welcome it with open arms, but to her chagrin, a "merciful" God "spares" her. "My mother brought some of her friends to see it," Durang recalled to Chet Flippo. "After they saw it, their faces were so funny to see. They really looked as if they had just been slapped and as if someone had come up and defecated right in front of them. . . . " Also produced at that time, in Cambridge, Massachusetts, was *'Dentity Crisis*, which savaged the pretensions of psychiatry, although he later described his therapy in college as having been "very helpful."

At Yale, Durang had seven of his plays staged, including three he wrote in collaboration with Albert Innaurato, later well known as the author of *Gemini* and other plays. *The Idiots Karamazov*, their parody of Dostoevski's classic novel, packed with literary allusions and rife with intellectual gamesmanship, was professionally produced by the Yale Repertory Theater in 1974 with Meryl Streep, a fellow Yale student, as the narrator and Durang as Alyosha, the saintly brother. Mel Gussow, who reviewed it for the *New York Times* (November 11, 1974), declared himself "impressed with their [the authors'] wit as well as their scholarship."

After receiving a master's degree from Yale in 1974, Durang stayed on in New Haven as a drama teacher at Southern Connecticut College and as a teacher of playwriting at Yale until 1976, when he took the plunge and moved to New York. His first substantial notices there were for a double bill presented in May 1976 of *Titanic* (earlier staged at Yale) and *Das Lusitania Songspiel*, which he had concocted with a fellow Yale student, Sigourney Weaver, who appeared in both plays. The former, a send-up of disaster movies, struck Edith Oliver of the *New Yorker* (May 24, 1976) as a "merry and (innocently) obscene farce. . . . Few sexual perversions were neglected in a plot of blind complexity." The latter is a mock Bertolt Brecht-Kurt Weill revue in which Christopher Durang appeared with Sigourney Weaver. A revised version of *Das Lusitania Songspiel* was produced in New York in 1980, again starring the same team but this time expanded to forty-five minutes. At the end, the stars threw fruit and vegetables at the audience. Clive Barnes of the *New York Post* (January 11, 1980) pronounced it "very good indeed. And deliciously outrageous. . . . For my money these two are as funny as Nichols and May."

Durang's next play, *The Vietnamization of New Jersey*, was presented by the Yale Repertory Theater in 1977. A parody of David Rabe's *Sticks and*

Bones in particular and of soul-searching anti-Vietnam-war dramas in general, it incorporated suicide, adultery, and homosexuality, as an eccentric family "welcomes" the return of their veteran son and his Vietnamese wife. "Bad taste and lots of it," declared a reviewer for *After Dark* (April 1977). "Durang's other comic excesses . . . are also outrageous. But, God help me, they *are* funny."

Meanwhile, Durang had been putting the compulsive moviegoing of his student days to good use in writing a play called *A History of the American Film*. As described by Brendan Gill of the *New Yorker* (April 10, 1978), Durang recapitulates America's cinematic history by having "five typical moviegoers, who are also, from time to time, movie actors, work their way in and out of parody versions of one or another of a number of classic American films." Following its workshop presentation, Durang was approached by the Mark Taper Forum in Los Angeles, the Hartford Stage Company, and the Arena Stage in Washington, D.C., and he accepted all three offers. Reviewing the Washington production, Edwin Wilson of the *Wall Street Journal* (May 26, 1977) found that "the history of the movies provides a profile of our nation through the 20th century . . . , moving from wide-eyed innocence . . . to the neurotic self-absorption of the post-war period." *A History of the American Film* opened on Broadway in the early spring of 1978, but it was buried under an avalanche of negative reviews. According to Jack Kroll of *Newsweek* (April 10, 1978), "Along the way from the regional theatre to New York . . . , Broadway greed has destroyed the delicate balance of a delicately balanced idea. The play became smartass instead of smart." John Simon of *New York* (April 17, 1978) agreed: "Bloated to ANTA Theatre size, drawn out and overproduced in sundry ways, it sadly betrays itself as the campy, campus cabaret it is: bright and funny in places, but largely self-indulgent, repetitious, and sophomoric."

Although *A History of the American Film* brought Durang a Tony nomination, he was, according to friends, devastated by its failure. To compound his troubles, his mother had suffered recurrence of the breast cancer that was first discovered in 1972 and was to cause her death in 1979. Pressed to give up his career and take care of her, Durang soon was commuting to her bedside "three and four times a week and recuperating the other three days," as he told David Richards. "My mother was a practicing Catholic, but her faith was not sufficient solace for her. Basically she didn't want to die." (Durang's father has since been incapacitated by a stroke that left him only intermittently lucid.)

His harrowing experiences led Durang to write *Sister Mary Ignatius Explains It All for You*, which made its Off-Broadway debut in December 1979. Bound to offend traditionalist Catholics, Durang has a teaching nun, equipped with handmade charts, lecturing the audience in the idiom of the pre-Vatican Council II catechism for children, but adding her own idiosyncratic observations. Sister Mary is not only simplistic, arbitrary, and authoritarian but also insane, as the audience gradually comes to realize. The questions, presumably from her "audience," that she reads from index cards are fielded and returned in feisty fashion: to someone with a brain tumor who is dying and wants advice, Sister Mary replies: "Now I thought I had explained what happens after death to you already. There is heaven, hell, and purgatory. What is the problem?" Later she says: "Are all our prayers answered? Yes, they are. What people who ask the question often don't realize is that sometimes the answer to our prayer is 'no.'"

On the scene appear four of her former students: two men—one an alcoholic, the other a homosexual—and two women—one of whom has had two abortions, the first after having been raped, the second after having been seduced by her psychiatrist, and the other an unwed mother. The first woman, after telling of her mother's agonizingly slow death from cancer, rejects the sister's citation of the Book of Job as an adequate explanation and brandishes a gun, threatening to kill her. Sister Mary diverts her attention, whips out her own gun, and shoots the woman dead. She also shoots the homosexual to save his soul, since he had earlier that day confessed his sin, but seemed certain to backslide.

Sister Mary made little impression in its obscure showcase production, although it won an Off-Broadway (Obie) award, but when it was again shown on a double bill in October 1981, it began a run that lasted for two and a half years. The opener, *The Actor's Nightmare*, is a black comedy in which a man unexpectedly finds himself onstage, seeking to master his lines in a kaleidoscopic sequence of plays by Shakespeare, Coward, and Beckett, until, cast as Thomas More in *A Man for All Seasons*, he is unable to stave off his all-too-real execution.

In his drama column for the *New Republic* (December 9, 1981), Robert Brustein told his readers: "I recommend the evening to you warmly. It represents another strong advance in the progress of a singularly outrageous satirist, whose pen is dipped in venom and bile, and also in the blood of his own personal wounds." In reviewing the double bill for the *New York Times* (October 22, 1981), Frank Rich observed: "In this one-act comedy [Durang] goes after the Catholic Church with a vengeance that might well have shocked the likes of Paul Krassner or Lenny Bruce, and yet he never lets his bitter emotions run away with his keen theatrical sense." But Richard Gilman of *The Nation* (December 11, 1981) spoke for many when he complained that "so excessive is Durang's spleen, and so lacking is he in taste . . . that the laughs come reluctantly, with embarassment and even guilt." Gilman lamented a pervading viciousness "that grinds up wit, social observation, and moral criticism."

Among those who were not amused was Archbishop John May of St. Louis, who deplored a local production of *Sister Mary* as a "vicious diatribe against all things Catholic [that] . . . caricatures and ridicules every Catholic doctrine and every Catholic value," and called on all Catholics to boycott it. Others took note of the public funds—$12,-000—allotted by the Missouri Arts Council to the theatre company that mounted the play. Although the play's run survived political pressure to close it in St. Louis, Boston, Nassau County, New York, and other places, Durang says that he knows of one production in Florida and another in Oklahoma that were canceled because of complaints.

Now a self-styled agnostic, Durang does not consider *Sister Mary* to be anti-Catholic. He told Joseph C. Koenenn of *Newsday* (July 17, 1985): "Obviously the play is critical of Catholicism or a dogmatic Catholicism that existed before the Second Vatican Council and seems to be coming to the fore again. To criticize that dogmatism is not to criticize the whole church." And in justifying his position to David Richards, he said: "People can agree or disagree with me, but I was raised Catholic and I feel that I have the right to write from my own past."

Durang's next play, *Beyond Therapy*, which opened Off Broadway at the Phoenix Theater in January 1981, may have been inspired by his return to psychotherapy around the time of his mother's death. A farce, it brought together a woman and a bisexual man through an ad in a personals column and pitted the former's male therapist against the latter's female therapist. In his review for the New York *Daily News* (January 6, 1981), Douglas Watt expressed the critical consensus when he noted that "it soon becomes clear that Durang's smartass dialogue is an end in itself and has nowhere to go." When it was transplanted to Broadway in a revised version in the spring of 1982, Allan Wallach of *Newsday* (May 27, 1982) found that the revamped edition had not corrected "Durang's tendency to let his plot meander, nor did it do much to change his blithe disregard for characterization." Although Edith Oliver, one of the few dissenters, called it a "delightful little farce" in the *New Yorker* (June 7, 1982), the play had only an abbreviated run on Broadway, at the Brooks Atkinson Theater. It resurfaced as a movie in 1987, with a script by Durang and with direction by Robert Altman, to a mostly chilly reception from the film critics.

First produced at the American Repertory Theater in Cambridge, Durang's *Baby with the Bathwater* opened Off Broadway in December 1983. It deals with Mom and Dad and Dad's mistress raising Daisy as a girl, although Daisy ascertains in late adolescence that he is actually a boy, undergoes psychotherapy for decades, and finally fathers a child. Frank Rich wrote in the *New York Times* (November 9, 1983) that the playwright "conquers bitterness and finds a way to turn rage into comedy that is redemptive as well as funny. . . . Daisy is the first Durang hero who works through his rage to become an adult."

The Marriage of Bette and Boo, an expanded version of a short work that Durang wrote during his student days at Yale, opened at Joseph Papp's Public Theater in New York in May 1985. The avowedly autobiographical play, made up of thirty-three brief scenes, included Durang himself in the cast, in the role of Matt, son of Bette, who has given birth to four successive stillborn babies, each dumped on the hospital floor by the obstetrician. There are onstage deaths from stroke and cancer. Near the end, Matt concludes: "I don't believe that God punishes people for specific things. He punishes people in general for no reason." Durang received an Obie for his performance in the play.

Although Frank Rich of the *New York Times* (May 17, 1985) found that *The Marriage of Bette and Boo* said "little the author hasn't said with greater wit and emotional ferocity before," Allan Wallach of *Newsday* (May 17, 1985) discovered that "this time the laughter curdles in the throat. The pain in this new comedy is so enormous that it's several sizes too large for the cartoonlike characters." In the *New Republic* (July 1, 1985), Robert Brustein wrote that *The Marriage of Bette and Boo*, "for all its anger and reproaches, is suffused with an aura of understated forgiveness, and it is this element that seems to me new in Durang's work."

Scheduled to open Off Broadway at Playwrights Horizons in November 1987, Durang's newest project, "Laughing Wild," is a two-character play that he has described as "an intense comedy." Although he was still working on the script in the early autumn of 1987, he divulged that its first two sections consist of monologues delivered by its female character and male character, while the third brings the two players together. In his first appearance onstage since *Bette and Boo*, Durang himself was slated to undertake the role of the male character.

Christopher Durang is about five foot six or seven inches in height and has dark hair and blue eyes. Interviewers have often described his boyishly handsome appearance as that of a cherub, acolyte, or choirboy, though in recent years he has gained some weight and his hair has begun to gray. His favorite author is the late *New Yorker* humorist James Thurber. Chet Flippo, who interviewed Durang in 1982 in the Manhattan Upper East Side apartment where he lived alone, described the playwright's flat as dark and gloomy, particularly the "TV room," which was painted "some kind of incredible, depressing, dark-brown color that seems actually to *defeat* light." Soon after, Durang was reported as having moved to a more suitable apartment in Greenwich Village.

References: *Chicago Tribune* VI p11 Je 20 '82 por; *N Y Times* II p4 My 23 '82 por; *New York* 15:40+ pors; *Newsday* II p13 Je 2 '85 por; *Washington Post* F p1+ O 30 '83 por; *Contemporary Authors* vol 105 (1982); *Contemporary Dramatists* (1982); *Contemporary Theatre, Film, and Television* vol 3 (1986)

Dutoit, Charles
(dyü-twa´)

Oct. 7, 1936- Swiss conductor. Address: b. c/o Orchestre Symphonique de Montréal, 200 Ouest, Boulevard de Maisonneuve, Montreal, Quebec H2X 1Y9, Canada

Few orchestral conductors have enjoyed as rapid a rise in critical esteem as Charles Dutoit, the music director of the Montreal Symphony Orchestra. In less than a decade, Dutoit has established himself as the world's leading interpreter of French impressionist music, and as one of the most celebrated music directors of his generation, a winner of international recording awards and a cultural hero in Canada, France, and his native Switzerland.

Charles Dutoit was born on October 7, 1936, in Lausanne, Switzerland, to Edmond Dutoit and the former Berthe Laederman, neither of whom was very musically inclined. Dutoit's main interests as a boy were mathematics and science, and it was not until he was eleven that he suddenly became fascinated with the rhythms of marching bands. At first he wanted to play the trombone, but after his practicing disturbed the other members of the family, his father insisted that he find a quieter instrument, and the boy settled on the violin. When he started lessons at the age of thirteen, he was at first repelled by the sounds he made on the instrument. But Dutoit persisted, playing and practising unevenly, and finding encouragement from a group of fellow young musicians and the recordings and radio concerts that they listened to together. He credits Fritz Kreisler's recording of the Beethoven Violin Concerto with having had a profound impact on his playing and understanding of the instrument. After he joined a neighborhood

orchestra, he advanced quickly through the ranks of the violins. His first opportunity to conduct came through an accident. When his conductor had to leave a rehearsal early, Dutoit, then fourteen, took over and did so well that he also conducted the actual performance.

His main interest, however, remained science and mathematics. It was only after he discovered the work of Stravinsky that music overrode his other interests. "I heard [the] *Rite Of Spring* and *Les Noces* and became fascinated by the complicated design of scores," he told Glenn Plaskin during an interview for the *New York Times* (May 9, 1982). "It was at this point that I began to take music more seriously." He entered the Lausanne Conservatory where, in addition to studying violin, he majored in theory and studied with Hans Haug, among others.

It was while he was working as an usher at performances of L'Orchestre de la Suisse Romande, at the age of seventeen, that Dutoit succumbed to the spell of the legendary Swiss conductor Ernest Ansermet. "I was mesmerized by his approach to music," he told Glenn Plaskin. "He achieved an incredible orchestral sheen and had an organic sense of rhythm that he translated into a total body expression, like dance." Although Dutoit never took formal instruction from his idol, he attended his concerts, lectures, and rehearsals over the next two years. Ansermet's specialization in modern composers had an immediate effect on Dutoit. "As I had played in a chamber orchestra for several years, my special interest was naturally Haydn and Mozart," he recalled for Andrew Keener in the British publication *Gramophone* (June 1982), "and suddenly to swing in the direction of this twentieth-century French and Russian music—Ravel, Debussy, Stravinsky—was a revelation!"

After graduating from the Lausanne Conservatory when he was seventeen, Dutoit entered the Academy of Music in Geneva. There he studied conducting with the conductor-composer Samuel Baud-Bovy and abandoned the violin in favor of the viola. "With the viola," he explained to Herbert Kupferberg in *Ovation* magazine (January 1984), "there is an opportunity to learn more. You sit in the center of an orchestra or a quartet; you listen with both ears." He studied the viola with Ron Golan and continued playing in various orchestras. There was a Dutoit string quartet for a brief time in the mid-1950s until its founder joined a chamber orchestra. Dutoit also began learning foreign languages, partly as an extension of his own mixed French-Swiss, German, English, and Brazilian heritage, and eventually acquired fluency in Swedish, Spanish, German, English, Portuguese, and Korean.

At the Lucerne (Switzerland) Festival of 1956, while still much under the spell of the wizardry of Ernest Ansermet, Dutoit first saw the renowned Austrian conductor who became the next great influence on his career, Herbert von Karajan. "The magnetic presence of this man was overpowering," he has recalled of his first experience of watching von Karajan at work. "Coming from Ansermet, I entered Von Karajan's world of mystical concentration and obscure forces."

In addition to pursuing his studies in Geneva, Dutoit attended the Accademia Musicale Chigiana in Siena, Italy, and the Conservatorio Benedetto Marcello in Venice. He acquired some practical experience in conducting during 1957 and 1958 by leading an amateur orchestra in Renan, Switzerland, but remained an active performer. In 1958, the year in which he joined the Lucerne Chamber Orchestra as a violist, Dutoit won first prize in conducting at the Geneva Academy's competition. He made his first visit to the United States during the summer of the following year to attend the Berkshire Music Festival at Tanglewood, where he studied with Charles Munch.

In the fall of 1959 Dutoit returned to Switzerland, where he was appointed choral conductor at the University of Lausanne. His four-year tenure there, and his appointment in 1963 as conductor of the Lausanne Bach Choir, proved important steps in his orchestral career. "That's how I studied the choral repertoire," Dutoit recalled in an interview with Andrew Keener in *Gramophone* (June 1982), "and I still think it's the best way: you conduct the repertoire in rehearsal, and then you observe and learn from the principal conductor's interpretation of it."

In 1963 Dutoit made his official orchestral conducting debut with the Bern Symphony Orchestra in a performance of Stravinsky's *Le Sacre du printemps*. Among the members of the audience was Herbert von Karajan, at that time director of the Vienna State Opera, who was so impressed by the performance that he invited Dutoit to conduct later that year at the Vienna Festival, in a production of Falla's *Three-Cornered Hat* with choreography by George Balanchine and sets by Pablo Picasso. In 1964 Dutoit returned to Bern as assistant conductor under Paul Kletzki, and in that year was also appointed artistic director of the Radio-Zurich Orchestra. Two years later he succeeded Kletzki as music director of the Bern Symphony Orchestra and was appointed associate director of the Zurich Tonhalle Orchestra under Rudolf Kempe.

His three prestigious appointments made Charles Dutoit one of the most visible young conductors in Switzerland and served as a springboard for his international career. During 1967 he began making the rounds of Europe as a guest conductor, and soon added engagements in South America, Mexico, and Japan. In the late 1960s he also began his recording career with a series of chamber orchestra performances for the Paris-based Erato label, among them a prize-winning interpretation of Stravinsky's *L'histoire du soldat*. It was not until August 31, 1972, that Dutoit made his American debut, in a concert with the pianist Martha Argerich at the Hollywood Bowl in Los Angeles, in a program featuring the Schumann Piano Concerto, Bartók's *Concerto For Orchestra*, and Berlioz' *Roman Carnival Overture*. Adding to his many other commitments, he became music director of Mexico's National Orchestra, and music director of the Göteborg (Sweden) Orchestra.

Charles Dutoit regards the journeyman phase of his career as a necessary part of his education as a conductor. "When you are a guest conductor," he explained to Allan Kozinn in *Keynote* magazine (April 1984), "you are always making a fresh start, and you realize that you can never achieve all you want in the time you have. It is frustrating. But it's also interesting, because one learns a lot from different orchestras. You learn about different ways of playing, and different sounds, and you have to learn these things if you want to gain enough experience to create your own world." By his own estimation, he had worked with over 150 orchestras by the late 1970s.

That ability to get quick results from unfamiliar orchestras served Dutoit well when he arrived in Montreal. His first contact with the Montreal Symphony Orchestra (or *L'Orchestre symphonique de Montréal,* as its management prefers it be known) was as a guest conductor in February 1977, and his debut was so successful that he was immediately invited to become its music director. The Montreal Symphony was then in the midst of a crisis in management and finance that had culminated in 1976 with the resignation of its music director, the Spanish conductor Rafael Frühbeck de Burgos. The orchestra was also regarded as an ensemble that had been established by the city's English-speaking population, and had suffered during the growth of Quebec's French separatist movement in the late 1960s and early 1970s.

The opportunity to direct the Montreal Symphony came along at an especially fortunate time for Dutoit, for despite the enjoyment he derived from his work as a guest conductor, he looked forward to taking over an orchestra of his own. "It is important for a young conductor to have his own orchestra, where he can work from scratch and create the sound he wants," he told Allan Kozinn in *Keynote.* Dutoit also felt he had reached a time for a change. "I was forty," he recalled for Stephen Godfrey in the *Toronto Globe and Mail* (June 28, 1984), "which is the turning point for so much. You have the advantage of the experience and the years ahead in which to use it. It's not too soon and not too late."

Dutoit began reshaping the orchestra during his first season, in the fall of 1977. By replacing members of the string section and all of the principal winds through retirements, he managed to renovate those key sections of the orchestra within two years. He engendered some criticism for an informal policy favoring the hiring of French musicians. "I hire a French musician if he is good," Dutoit explained when questioned about that policy in the *New York Times* (May 9, 1982), "but even if he is two or three percent less good than an outsider, I hire him anyway, because I can compensate the loss with the stability of knowing that a local player has roots in Montreal and will stay with the orchestra." Indeed, much of Dutoit's success in managing the orchestra has been the stability he has achieved within its ranks and the fact that a key criterion for his selection of the fifty players he had added as of 1985 was their willingness to remain with the Montreal Symphony rather than using it as a stepping stone to another orchestra. Dutoit's approach seems to work. In October of 1983, for example, Timothy Hutchins, the Montreal Symphony's principal flautist, turned down a tempting offer from the New York Philharmonic to replace its principal flautist, Julius Baker, who had retired. For his part, Dutoit has indicated a willingness to stay with the Montreal Symphony indefinitely, and his contract was recently extended until 1991.

Equally eager to update the orchestra's image, in 1980 Dutoit inaugurated the first full summer season in its history, both as a way of bringing the ensemble to the public in a less formal setting and of maintaining the momentum built up during the spring. He also planned and executed an elaborate and aggressive public relations compaign, involving the orchestra's first outdoor concerts, television commercials, and personal appearances to win public and corporate support, with the result that subscriptions and overall attendance increased substantially.

The provincial governments, which had previously balked at increasing their support, agreed during the mid-1980s to provide funding for one of Dutoit's key priorities, a new $30-million concert hall. The conductor's own celebrity within the province of Quebec increased during the early 1980s to a level of popular recognition paralleled only by Zubin Mehta in New York, and his face decorated billboards throughout Montreal as part of advertisements celebrating civic pride. Another expression of appreciation came in 1985, when Dutoit was awarded an honorary doctorate of arts and music by Laval University for his contribution to Quebec's artistic life.

Dutoit's most notable success with the Montreal Symphony, however, stems from recordings. In 1980 he arranged for a three-record contract with London/Decca, selecting French impressionist music, partly because of the lack of competition in that area from more celebrated ensembles, and partly because of the label's past triumphs with Ansermet's recordings. Already known as a severe taskmaster in rehearsal, Dutoit prepared the Montreal Symphony for its first recordings by programming Ravel's complete orchestral works during the year leading up to the recording sessions. Their 1982 debut album, the complete ballet of Ravel's *Daphnis et Chloé*, sold over 30,000 copies and won five major international record awards, including two from the Grand Prix du Disque. Its sales and those of the recordings that followed exceeded Decca's expectations and resulted in an extension of the contract to four recordings a year after 1983. Among the albums that followed, Falla's *Three-Cornered Hat* was singled out for the 1984 High Fidelity International Record Critics' Award, while the Berlioz *Symphonie fantastique* received the Grad Prix du Disque. The orchestra's recording in 1982 of Ravel's *Bolero* also achieved distinction as the first album by a Canadian orchestra ever to

sell 100,000 copies and earn a Platinum Record Award.

Hailed by *Gramophone* as "the finest French orchestra today," the Montreal Symphony was suddenly in worldwide demand. The revitalized orchestra embarked on its first American tour in November 1981, and it has since begun a series of international tours scheduled for seven out of every eight years, instead of the previous one year out of eight. Dutoit made his debut with the New York Philharmonic in February 1982, in a program of Stravinsky, Franck, and Haydn. He has since then not only conducted the rest of America's "big five" orchestras, Chicago, Boston, Philadelphia, and Cleveland, but has also recorded with the ensemble made famous by his mentor Ernest Ansermet, L'Orchestre de la Suisse Romande, in his native land.

Dutoit took on his first long-term post in the United States in 1983, when he became principal guest conductor of the Minnesota Orchestra. His *Petrouchka* during his debut concert on October 5, 1983, featuring Beethoven, Ravel, and Stravinsky, was described by Michael Anthony in *Ovation* magazine (January 1984) as "impressive . . . taken as though in one big, rhythmically vivid sweep, a grand and dramatic account with particular emphasis on the music's sardonic nature." Since 1984 his other guest appearances in the United States have included performances with the Pittsburgh Symphony, the Los Angeles Chamber Orchestra, and the St. Louis Symphony. Dutoit's operatic work has been limited because of his other obligations. "I'd like to do more opera," he said in the *Ovation* interview, "but I just won't go in for one evening and take over a show. I like to work with a production from the very start." He did, however, make his Covent Garden debut in June 1983, conducting all seven performances of a new production of Gounod's *Faust*. Dutoit also brought the Montreal Symphony to Carnegie Hall on May 21, 1983, for a program that included a concert performance of Act Two of Saint-Saëns' *Samson et Dalila* with Jessye Norman and James McCracken.

Despite the luster of his reputation in the French repertory, Dutoit points out in his interviews that his interests and his orchestra's repertoire extend into many other areas. In addition to promoting a contemporary music series devoted to Canadian and non-Canadian composers alike, the Montreal Symphony has performed and recorded romantic and postromantic works by such figures as Weber, Mahler, and Holst. His professional background in chamber orchestras still manifests itself in his high praise for such early music specialists as Christopher Hogwood and Nikolaus Harnoncourt, from whom, he says, "there is a lot to learn." Dutoit's own "wish list" would include recordings of the complete piano concertos and operas of Mozart, whom he describes as "the top of creation."

In 1983 Charles Dutoit married his third wife, the former Marie-Josée Drouin, the executive director of the Hudson Institute of Canada, and one of the country's leading economists. His two earlier marriages ended in divorce. "My wife gives me the intellectual balance that an artist needs," he told the *Ovation* interviewer. "I have an analytical brain, and it's good to have someone with me who's not in the music business. It gives me a different approach to the whole world." The couple has two children, a boy and a girl.

References: *Gramophone* 60:17 Jl '82; 61:1167 Ap '84; *Guardian* p11 Ap 13 '84; *Keynote* 8:12 Ap '84; N Y Times II p19+ My 9 '82; *Ovation* 4:14+ Ja '84; *Toronto Globe and Mail* p14+ Jl 28 '84; *International Who's Who* 1985–86; *Who's Who* 1985–86

Eisner, Michael D(ammann)

Mar. 7, 1942– Corporation executive. Address: b. Walt Disney Co., 500 S. Buena St., Burbank, Calif. 91521

Among executives who have gone to the rescue of foundering corporations, few have had quicker or more spectacular success than Michael D. Eisner, chairman and chief executive officer of the Walt Disney Company since September 1984. Acknowledged to be one of the most creative and energetic leaders in the motion picture industry, Eisner moved Disney out of the state of "suspended animation" that followed the death, in 1966, of its famous founder, Walt Disney, and brought it back into the front rank of motion picture companies. His appointment followed a fierce battle with corporate raiders that almost tore the company apart. But Eisner's leadership has brought it stability and unparalleled prosperity. The company's earnings

more than tripled in less than three years, its activities have greatly expanded, and it has become a stock market favorite. Eisner's triumphant record as "the prince who awakened Sleeping Beauty" has positioned him to amass a personal fortune of well over $100 million.

Michael Dammann Eisner was born into an affluent Jewish family in Mt. Kisco, New York, on March 7, 1942. His father, Lester Eisner, was a Harvard-educated lawyer and investor, and his mother, the former Margaret Dammann, was the daughter of a cofounder of the American Safety Razor Company. While growing up in his family's luxurious New York City apartment, he was always required to wear a jacket and tie to dinner. His father made him read for two hours each day before permitting him to watch television. Despite his prosperous circumstances, Eisner also learned frugality. "I was brought up to believe that money is not frivolous," he has recalled.

After attending the Lawrenceville school in New Jersey Eisner, disregarding his family's wishes that he go to Princeton, chose instead to attend Denison, a small university in Granville, Ohio. There he majored in English literature and theatre, impressed, he recalled, by "a Maxwell Anderson essay about how what remains behind in societies is not the wars or the politics but the art." During his junior year he wrote his first play, to impress a female fellow student, and that summer he obtained his first studio job, as a page with NBC.

Following his graduation in 1964 with a B.A. degree, Eisner went to Paris, intending to write a novel, but stayed only ten days. Returning to New York, he took a job as a Federal Communications Commission logging clerk at NBC. After six weeks, he moved to the programming department of CBS studios, where he was in charge of ensuring that commercials were inserted in the proper places in children's television programs.

Hoping to obtain a more challenging job, Eisner sent out 200 résumés but got only one response, from Barry Diller, then a young programmer at ABC, who was to play a key role in his career. Diller persuaded the network to hire Eisner as assistant to the national programming director in New York. In the following year he obtained a break when he was named in-house producer of a television special called *Feelin' Groovy at Marine World*, a program for which no one else wanted responsibility. It was Eisner's idea to invite Bing Crosby to take part in the program, and before long, ABC executives were entrusting him with increasing responsibilities.

In 1968 Eisner became director of specials and talent, and in the following years he was put in charge of the network's Saturday morning children's programs, an assignment in which he had his first big success. Described as "childlike" in his interests and enthusiasm, he thoroughly enjoyed children's programming. Among his projects were an animated show featuring a singing group called the Jackson Five and another that featured the Osmond Brothers.

Over the next few years, Eisner assumed a key role in what has been described as the most dramatic change in network television history—ABC's rise from a perennial third to first place in the ratings. His own advancement reflected that rise. From 1968 to 1971 he was director of program development for the East Coast. In the latter year he was named vice-president for daytime programming, a post he held until 1975, when he became vice-president for program planning and development. In 1976 he was promoted to senior vice-president for prime-time production and development.

Although ABC's chief programmer, Fred Silverman, had received most of the credit for the network's historic ratings turnaround, according to ABC's president, Fred Pierce, it was Eisner who was the driving force behind it. As daytime chief programmer he had been responsible for such hits as the soap opera series *All My Children* and *One Life to Live*. Later, in prime time, he moved to even greater success, programming such series as *Happy Days*, *Welcome Back Kotter*, *Barney Miller*, and *Starsky and Hutch*. Like Silverman, Eisner had an uncanny, almost instinctive feeling for what programs appealed to mass audiences. He was able to grasp the elements of good storytelling, and he could simplify the material for television viewers.

By the mid-1970s, Eisner had received many job offers, including one from Barry Diller, who had left ABC in 1974 to become board chairman of Paramount Pictures Corporation. In late 1976, with ABC firmly in first place, Eisner accepted Diller's offer of the presidency of Paramount, with the additional title of chief operating officer. Eisner was not typical of major film studio presidents, most of whom were recruited from the ranks of lawyers, agents, and business executives. But he more than made up for his lack of experience in motion pictures with his boundless energy, exuberance, and wealth of imagination. "Michael is unequivocally the most creative executive I've ever met," Don Simpson, a former executive at the studio, told Tony Schwartz, as quoted in *New York* magazine (July 30, 1984). "He is disorganized, sloppy, absent-minded, he has an optional memory, and the only way he considers a deal fair is if he wins. But . . . his instincts are solid gold."

In the same article, Simpson recalled one of the first meetings over which Eisner presided: "We went into a boardroom at nine in the morning. . . . At the time we had absolutely nothing good in development. . . . Eisner said, 'We're going to come up with twenty projects today even if we have to stay here till midnight. Leave if you want to, but then don't bother coming back.' Several people looked at him like he was crazy. But by 5:30, we had fifteen projects."

Such experiences reflected not only Eisner's creativity and decisiveness, but his years in television, with its ravenous appetite for material and its need to develop it quickly and economically. He steered clear of big-budget movies, and under his supervision the cost of making a Paramount film

averaged $8.5 million as compared with $12 million for the industry as a whole. "You've got to get hysterical and pretend you're playing with your own money," Eisner told an interviewer for *Newsweek* (April 9, 1984).

While other heads of studios concentrated on making deals, marketing, or signing up stars, Eisner and Diller, as former programmers, shared the conviction that what matters most in a movie is the story, and they spent much of their time reading, arguing about, and choosing scripts. Diller's decision to shift Paramount's emphasis from distributing films produced at other studios—which had once made up four-fifths of its releases—to turning out its own pictures gave him and Eisner much more choice and control over Paramount's output. While other studios were mostly financing and distributing films, Paramount was making some fifteen a year, more than most other studios, because its costs per film were less.

Even before the full effect of that change was being felt, Eisner had played a key role during his first two years at Paramount in revitalizing the company and moving it from last to first place among the six major studios. Paramount broke records for domestic film rentals with an eighteen-month string of twenty profitable movies. They included such box-office hits as *Saturday Night Fever*, *Grease*, and *Heaven Can Wait*. In October 1978 five Paramount films were among the top ten, and the studio's share of the market had doubled to 20 percent. Earnings for fiscal 1978 increased 66 percent over the previous year.

During the period from 1978 to 1984 Paramount turned out an unrivaled succession of hits and critical successes, among them *Raiders of the Lost Ark* (1981), which Eisner succeeded in obtaining for Paramount despite Diller's lack of enthusiasm and which eventually grossed about a quarter of a billion dollars. Others included *Ordinary People*, *Terms of Endearment*, *An Officer and a Gentleman*, *The Elephant Man*, *Reds*, *Flashdance*, *Trading Places*, *Beverly Hills Cop*, and three *Star Trek* movies.

Eisner ranged far and wide for movie ideas. He was inspired to make *Footloose* (1984), one of Paramount's most commercially successful movies, about a town that bans dancing, after he read Nathaniel Hawthorne's nineteenth-century classic novel *The Scarlet Letter* and another Hawthorne story, "The Maypole of Merrymount." During a dinner conversation, Eisner heard about a script by three unknown writers for a parody of the *Airport* movies that had been rejected by every other studio. He arranged for its purchase and agreed to permit the three writers to direct the movie. The result was the hilarious comedy *Airplane!* (1980), which cost the studio $6 million and earned $83 million. A few of Eisner's favorites at Paramount were failures. One was *White Dog*, a film based on a novel by Romain Gary about a dog trained to attack black people that was never released to theatres. Another was *Breaking Glass*, a British punk rock version of *A Star Is Born* that had only a brief run.

Although Eisner was more respected than liked in the industry, and many found him and Diller difficult to do business with, his success as president of Paramount was unquestioned. He was credited with having played a crucial role in bringing to Paramount six consecutive fiscal year records for domestic and foreign film rentals. In national television, the company also enjoyed growing success during his tenure, with an increase from two shows in 1976 to nine during the 1981–82 season. Eisner helped to produce two Emmy award-winning television series, *Cheers* and *Family Ties,* and a nationally syndicated news program about show business, *Entertainment Tonight.* He also helped to bring the company into cable television. Success brought Eisner huge monetary rewards, in salary and bonuses, as well as an avalanche of favorable publicity. An article in *Newsweek* (April 9, 1984), reviewing his achievements and those of Diller, cited Paramount as the "best all-around movie studio."

In September 1984 Eisner surprised many by quitting Paramount to become chairman and chief executive of Walt Disney Productions—renamed the Walt Disney Company in 1986. He had left Paramount because of friction with Martin Davis, the new chairman of its parent company, Gulf & Western Industries, and because he felt that he had outgrown a job in which he was merely number two man. Diller, who could not get along with Davis either, had left previously to become chairman of Twentieth Century-Fox, but Eisner was not offered his job as chairman of Paramount.

Because of his reputation at Paramount, Eisner virtually had his pick of jobs. He was considered "the hottest property in town," according to John Taylor, author of *Storming the Magic Kingdom* (1987), a book about the battle over control of Disney. Eisner was anxious to head Walt Disney Productions because he felt that his abilities fit perfectly with the company's tradition. He revered Walt Disney and loved children's programming, which had brought him success early in his career, and he very much wanted to produce family entertainment. Furthermore, the company's poor performance provided a challenge. "In addition to more important quality reasons, I wanted to go to a company where you couldn't fall off the floor," he said. In the fall of 1982 Disney's chief executive, Ronald Miller, had approached Eisner about heading its failing film division, but Eisner declined when Miller refused to offer him greater responsibilities.

But by the spring of 1984 Eisner was in the market for a new position. He approached Roy Disney, a nephew of Walt Disney, who had recently resigned as a director because he was unhappy about the company's decline. Before his death in 1966, Walt Disney had built an American institution dedicated to family entertainment, but it had failed to keep pace with the times. Children and adolescents of the 1970s and 1980s thrilled to *Star Wars* and *Raiders of the Lost Ark,* rather than to Disney's saccharine offerings. The bulk of the company's revenues was now coming from its huge theme parks, Disneyland in California and Walt Disney World and the Experimental Prototype Community of Tomorrow (Epcot) in Florida, and even from them the returns were disappointing. In 1983 the film and television division, on which Disney's business had been built, accounted for only 13 percent of revenues, and in the same year CBS-TV canceled the weekly *Wonderful World of Disney,* leaving the company without a network program for the first time in almost thirty years. Disney's overall earnings declined for three successive years. Myron Magnet summed up its plight succinctly in *Fortune* (January 5, 1987): "Kids stayed away, profits dwindled, the stock slid."

In late February 1984 Disney's shares were selling for forty nine dollars, although financial analysts figured that the selling price of its assets actually would make their value over twice as much. The discrepancy made Disney a prime target for corporate raiders who typically gained control of a company whose shares were undervalued and sold off its assets, making enormous profits and dismembering the company in the process. When two major raiders, Saul P. Steinberg and Irwin L. Jacobs, moved in on Disney, the company fought back by buying off Steinberg with $32 million in so-called "greenmail."

But Disney's dismal earnings and its six-month battle with the corporate raiders left its management irrevocably weakened. Major stockholders and directors demanded new leadership. The idea of appointing Eisner met with strong opposition, largely because of his insufficient business experience. But he won out when his supporters convinced his opponents that his creativity was the single most important factor needed to "reanimate" Disney.

On September 23, 1984, Eisner was formally named chairman and chief executive officer. His contract made him the highest-paid executive in the motion picture industry, with a salary of $750,-000 a year in addition to bonuses and stock options. Although some observers thought that it would take Eisner and his number two man, Frank Wells, years to turn Disney around, according to *Business Week* (April 18, 1986), "under his wizardry, the sleepy company awakened within months." From the beginning, Eisner understood that his most important and difficult job would be to build a successful motion picture and television company.

On his first day Eisner approved the script for *Down and Out in Beverly Hills,* the first R-rated film ever made at Disney studios and the first hit movie to be made there under his aegis. Shortly afterward, he also approved production of *Golden Girls,* the highly rated, Emmy award-winning NBC-TV situation comedy. It went on the air in the fall of 1985, as did two Saturday morning cartoon features, *The Adventures of the Gummi Bears* and *The Wuzzles.* In February 1986 he brought Disney back into network evening television with the *Disney Sunday Movie* on ABC.

Eisner also put Disney into large-scale syndication, selling to television stations some of the hundreds of old programs, cartoons, and feature films that lay unused in the company's vaults. Other stored library material was presented on the Disney Channel, the company's pay cable outlet. He also created an international television division to sell Disney productions to foreign broadcasters. In 1986 he visited China where he sold a two-year series of old cartoons to be shown on Chinese television, with Mickey Mouse and Donald Duck speaking dubbed-in Mandarin. In addition, he released the animated Walt Disney classic *Pinocchio* on videocassettes.

By the end of his first year at Disney, net earnings had increased by more than 75 percent, and income from television, films, and video had multiplied. As Aljean Harmetz observed in a feature article in the *New York Times Magazine* (December 29, 1985): "Eisner has already managed to convince Hollywood that he is turning Disney into something it never was before, a major movie studio."

Down and Out in Beverly Hills was followed by the release of *Ruthless People*, a second R-rated comedy hit starring Bette Midler, which some critics found "screamingly funny," while others pronounced it "rude," "vulgar," and "offensive." Tastes at Disney had clearly changed. A third R-rated film, *The Color of Money*, brought Paul Newman his first Academy Award. These and seven other Disney films released in 1986 suddenly vaulted the studio, a perennial also-ran, into a highly respectable third place at the box office, exceeded only by Paramount and Warner Brothers.

Film successes helped to raise the Disney Company's net income by about 43 percent in 1986. But Eisner also had some failures, including two prime-time television programs, *The Ellen Burstyn Show* and *Sidekicks*, which had to be canceled. Critics have pointed out that despite Eisner's overall success in films and television, almost three-fourths of the company's income continued to come from theme parks and hotels.

To increase attendance at the theme parks, Eisner has added some new attractions, including a $17 million, three-dimensional musical video, *Captain EO*, starring Michael Jackson and produced by George Lucas, who also designed a $32 million spaceship ride at Disneyland. In addition, Eisner approved a fifty-acre water park, a $300 million movie studio with facilities for tours, and a 900-room resort hotel, all at Walt Disney World, that were expected to open in 1988. The success of the four-year-old Tokyo Disneyland, which the company had designed, prompted Eisner in 1987 to sign an agreement for a 17 percent stake in a $2.5 billion Euro Disneyland on the outskirts of Paris, scheduled to open in 1992. In March 1987 Eisner announced the acquisition of the Disney Company's first television station, KHJ-TV in Los Angeles. Among the Disney Company's major projects for 1987 was the rerelease, in some forty countries around the world, of the classic feature-length cartoon *Snow White and the Seven Dwarfs*, which had rescued the company from financial ruin in 1937.

The Disney Company's spectacular earnings growth continued into 1987. Its stock, after adjustment for a four-for-one split in 1986, had more than quintupled in value by the fall of 1987, and that increase greatly enhanced Eisner's personal fortune. Like Mickey Mouse and the other characters who decorate the $300 million worth of Disney products, including watches and T-shirts, that he markets worldwide, Eisner himself has become a highly visible symbol of the company. As host of the *Disney Sunday Movie* he appears briefly on each week's program, sometimes joking with actors costumed as Mickey, Goofy, and other cartoon characters. Although he concedes that he "can't act," he appears relaxed, good-humored, and personable.

Six-foot-three inches tall and slender, with thinning dark curly hair, Eisner is decidedly informal in his manner. His expensive suits are often rumpled and his ties askew. He best expressed his childlike enthusiasm when he was chosen as Disney's chairman and said that he felt like he had been set free in a toy store: "I don't know which toy to take home because they're all fabulous and they all work and I'm so excited I can't sleep at night." Fiercely devoted to his family, Eisner has been married to the former Jane Breckenridge for some twenty years. He recalls that the happiest moment of his life was when his first child was born, and he regularly spends Saturday mornings watching his sons, Breck, Eric, and Anders, play basketball, football, and soccer. He has often put helping them with their schoolwork or taking them to Indian Guide meetings ahead of business matters. Eisner also finds time to serve on the boards of Denison University, the California Institute of the Arts, the American Hospital of Paris Foundation, the National Committee on United States-China Relations, the Missing Half (a nonpartisan organization devoted to bringing nonvoters to the polls), the Public Awareness and Education Council of the Committee for Food and Shelter, Inc., and Landmark West School.

References: Bsns W p62+ Mr 9 '87 por; N Y Newsday mag p1+ Ap 19 '87 por; N Y Times Mag p13+ D 29 '85 por; New York p25+ Jl 30 '84 pors; Vanity Fair 46:76+ Jl '83 por; Who's Who in America, 1986–87

Eldridge, Roy

Jan. 30, 1911– Musician; conductor; singer.
Address: c/o Pablo Records, 451 N. Canon Dr.,
Beverly Hills, Calif. 90210

The virtuoso trumpet player and bandleader Roy Eldridge is an undisputed giant in the history of jazz, a distinctive innovator widely regarded as the link between Louis Armstrong and John Birks ("Dizzy") Gillespie, who once acknowledged him to

Roy Eldridge

be "the Messiah of our generation." "I was never trying to be a bridge between Louis Armstrong and something," Eldridge once protested to the music critic John S. Wilson. "I was just trying to outplay anybody, and to outplay them my way." That way, "emotionally" based on the example of Armstrong's trumpet, but technically more influenced by Coleman Hawkins and other tenor saxophonists, was "to play all the high notes"—and "Dizzy just took over from there."

Known as "Little Jazz" because of his short stature, Eldridge used his nickname as the title of his theme song as a bandleader beginning in the late 1930s, after he had served apprenticeships with Teddy Hill and others and had come to prominence as a soloist with Fletcher Henderson. Crossing the color line to join Gene Krupa's big band in 1941 and to play later with Artie Shaw, he was the leading trumpeter of the swing era. He is perhaps best remembered from that era for his soaring trumpet on a recording of "Rockin' Chair" and for his warm duet with Anita O'Day on "Let Me Off Uptown," one of the many disks on which he can be heard singing, in a gritty voice that echoes the crackle of his trumpet. Although overshadowed by the ascendancy of Gillespie and bebop music in the postwar years, Eldridge remained vigorous in clubs, festivals, concerts, and, to a lesser degree, recording sessions until October 1980, when he suffered a heart attack.

David Roy Eldridge was born to Alexander and Blanche (Oakes) Eldridge on January 30, 1911, in Pittsburgh, Pennsylvania, a city that he remembers as having "plenty of prejudice—like the last six rows in the theatre being for blacks only." His mother played piano and his brother Joseph, a saxophonist, also became a professional musician and

bandleader. Eldridge began playing drums when he was six, and soon afterward he turned to the trumpet. He also learned to play the flugelhorn and piano. Although a local teacher named P. M. Williams coached him on the trumpet, he was for the most part self-taught musically, and he did not learn to read music until well into adulthood. The instrument that had the most influence on his trumpet style was the more facile tenor saxophone, as played by his brother and Coleman Hawkins and, later, by Benny Carter, Chu Berry, Lester Young, Ben Webster, Ike Quebec, and other saxophonists he worked with and admired. "Knocked out" by the way the saxophones "would run changes, would run through all the passing chords and things," he learned, as he once put it, to "play nice saxophone on the trumpet."

Eldridge began performing publicly as a child in Pittsburgh, and early in his teens he was leading a band called, incongruously, Roy Elliott and his Panama Band from New York. Dropping out of high school, he went on the road with the Sheesley Shows carnival band in 1927, and soon afterward he toured the black theatrical circuit with a revue called *Rock Dinah*. He was also a member of the Chocolate Dandies and the Hot Chocolates. Before the end of 1928 he had his first big break, a spot with the Dixie Stompers (then led by Horace Henderson, Fletcher Henderson's brother) on the strength of his ability to play a trumpet version of Coleman Hawkins' solo on "Stampede." When Hawkins heard Eldridge's first recordings a decade later, the older musician, who was then being lionized in Europe, became determined to work with him, not realizing that what attracted him to Eldridge's trumpet was the transposition of some of his own phrasing.

The trumpet players who earliest influenced Eldridge were the fast and flexible Rex Stewart, a member of his brother's band, and, above all, the white player Red Nichols, a member of the so-called New York school of jazz. "That's what I was exposed to, you see," he explained to Harriet Choice, the jazz critic for the *Chicago Tribune* (July 15, 1979). "I didn't hear Louis [Armstrong] until later on. . . . In fact, the first time [trumpeter] Hot Lips Page heard me, I was playing with my little band in Oklahoma. He couldn't believe it. He said, 'Where'd this little cat come from playing like an ofay?' I mean, I couldn't growl on the trumpet. I hadn't heard enough of Louis [Armstrong] to latch on to what was really going on."

In the late 1920s and early 1930s Eldridge played with the bands of Lawrence ("Speed") Webb, Elmer Snowden, and Cecil Scott and with McKinney's Cotton Pickers, then under the direction of Don Redman. He did not begin to acquire what he calls the "emotional base" of his trumpet style until 1931 or 1932, when he first saw Louis Armstrong play, as he recounted to Harriet Choice: "I had all the technical stuff together, but as [the drummer] Chick Webb said about me, 'He's fast, but he ain't sayin' nothing.' But then I really got a chance to hear Louis, and he taught me how to tell a story whether I was playing fast or slow. You've got to introduce the story, tell it, and then bring it to a climax. . . . That's what I learned from Louis." In addition to Armstrong's staccato, the maturing Eldridge was influenced by the more fluid phrasing of trumpeter Henry ["Red"] Allen.

His ability to meet the technical challenge of the saxophone increasingly gave Eldridge an edge over other trumpeters, and by the mid-1930s he was a featured soloist with the Harlem bands of Charlie Johnson and Teddy Hill. Throughout the 1930s he intermittently led his own bands, of varying sizes, at such venues as Minton's Playhouse, the Famous Door, and the Savoy Ballroom in Harlem and the Three Deuces club in Chicago. He also occasionally co-led his brother's combo, and he played with the Original Cotton Pickers.

Eldridge gained his national reputation as a soloist with the Fletcher Henderson band in 1936 and 1937. At that time the mainstream craze for swing music was beginning, largely impelled by the financially desperate Henderson's sale of some of his best arrangements to the white orchestra leader Benny Goodman. When the white jazz drummer Gene Krupa formed his big band in 1941, he daringly breached the racial barrier to hire Eldridge, who had been leading his own band at Kelly's Stables in New York City and the Arcadia Ballroom in Chicago. After the Krupa organization disbanded, in 1943, Eldridge played with Artie Shaw's white swing band, in 1944 and 1945.

As a black traveling the white dance-hall circuit with white bands, Eldridge often found himself barred from the hotels in which the musicians stayed, and on at least one occasion he had difficulty gaining entrance even to the dance hall where the Shaw band was booked. Although Shaw was aggressively supportive, the insults to Eldridge's pride made his swing-band experience "not worth the glory, not worth the money, not worth anything," as he told an interviewer for Down Beat at the time. He was much more comfortable with small groups in Harlem or in the row of jazz clubs then flourishing on Fifty-Second Street in midtown Manhattan.

The best known of Eldridge's swing-band solos is preserved on the Krupa recording of "Rockin' Chair." In his interview with Harriet Choice of the Chicago Tribune, Eldridge remembered with special fondness his recorded duets with the singers Anita O'Day, Mildred Bailey, and Billie Holiday and with the tenor saxophonists Coleman Hawkins, Ben Webster, and Chu Berry. "I always had a good feeling with tenors," he said. "After all, my playing was more like a sax than a trumpet anyway. Most of the recordings I did with Coleman were live concerts, and when we stretched out it was something else." Recording sessions in general were "a lot of fun," except for the ones when, even with Teddy Wilson conducting, Benny Goodman "wasn't so nice," arrogating to himself Eldridge's parts.

Surveying Eldridge's recordings retrospectively, back to the 1930s, James Lincoln Collier in his book

The Making of Jazz: A Comprehensive History (1979) observed that "no matter what his surroundings, his playing is instantly recognizable," with "the saxophone conception . . . everywhere evident." "He uses a great many downward-plunging figures made of eighth notes weighted on the first of each pair, in the Hawkins manner, and he roughens his tone in places, as Hawkins, Berry, and Webster consistently did, to create intensity and climaxes," Collier wrote. "His sound otherwise, however, is strictly brass. He attacks cleanly and forcefully, often biting off notes sharply at the end. At other times he employs a relatively fast terminal vibrato, which becomes broader and slower on medium-tempo numbers, so broad at times that it gives the effect of hesitation. His greatest fault, which dogged him through much of his career, was a tendency toward scatter-shot playing, with ideas tumbling one on the heels of the next in a disorderly fashion." As Eldridge matured, Collier noted, he developed more control, as evidenced by a 1938 recording with Chu Berry of "46 West 52nd Street," the title of which is an allusion to the retail shop of Commodore Records. "Roy's playing here is filled with saxophone figures, long skeins of eighth notes, often chromatic runs, which fall more naturally under a saxophonist's fingers than a trumpet player's. By 1940, in the classic version of 'I Can't Believe That You're in Love with Me,' with Hawkins, Benny Carter, and [Sid] Catlett, he has a sure and ordered conception. Here is Eldridge at his best—the rasps, the sudden leaps into high places, the headlong plunges—and the organization is sound. Note especially how he begins preparing his second chorus in the twenty-fifth bar, so that the first chorus is felt as a stepping-stone to the second one."

In the late 1930s and early 1940s, when the trumpet dominated American jazz, no player of the instrument took more creative, electrifying risks than Eldridge, and none other than Armstrong was as imitated by younger players. "He strongly influenced all the men who came after him," James Lincoln Collier wrote in his history of jazz, "most particularly Dizzy Gillespie, who at one stage of his career aped Eldridge's manner so successfully that at times it was difficult for listeners to tell them apart." In To Be or Not . . . to Bop (Da Capo Press, 1979), the memoirs of Gillespie, written with Al Fraser, the alto saxophonist and band leader Howard Johnson was quoted as remembering that he did not write out Eldridge's solos for Gillespie when Gillespie was in his band: "If Dizzy played Roy's solos, he played 'em on his own. Dizzy admired Roy greatly . . . although his style is different. . . . Roy played fast, and Dizzy played fast, but it was a different kind of fast. Now how do I explain this? Roy would play fast in spots, in spurts, and go to a more or less Louis Armstrong style of punch in phrasing. Dizzy played fast almost all the time. He'd double up—what they called 'double up,'—any place in the arrangement. Roy's style was more understandable to the people at the time because Dizzy was way ahead of his time, even then. But it was still patterned after Roy's style."

"Roy was from the old school," Gillespie says in his book regarding the transition from swing to bebop. "He didn't know the continuity of the music, how it happened, why a guy comes up like me, like himself. He probably figured he just got it out of the air, but he didn't. He was inspired by Louis Armstrong, Rex Stewart, Red Allen, and all these guys. He didn't know the chronology of the music, how these guys come, so he didn't treat me too well. Sometimes, I'd meet him out in front of the Three Deuces and say, 'Hey, Roy.' He'd make like he didn't hear me [while] all the trumpet players were trying to play like me, instead of trying to play like him. Roy Eldridge is the most competitive musician I've ever seen. Every time he picks up his horn and another trumpet player's there, he wants to blow him out. . . . Roy used to always get the best of us by playing real high; he'd challenge me. But now trumpet players who play high have to do something else within that. You just can't get up and scream any more, though it has an effect on a big audience like Jazz at the Philharmonic [impresario Norman Granz's traveling concert troupe] where people are out to make a whole lotta noise."

Among Eldridge's contributions to Gillespie's book (which is more of an oral-history pastiche than an autobiography) were his recollections of contacts with Gillespie at the Savoy Ballroom and Minton's Playhouse in Harlem. "I was with my own band at the Savoy," he recalled. "And Dizzy, Charlie Shavers [and others] used to come around. They could play all [my] things . . . better than I could, you know. But Dizzy had his thing going. I talked to him once down at Minton's and he was asking me how I did certain things and I told him. And the one thing I appreciate about Diz, even though he used to play something like me, is that he . . . started a whole new kind of thing. . . . He deserves a lot of credit because the cat really stuck to his guns. I remember when they didn't like him and said, 'Awww, he's playing off key. . . . ' But he stuck to what he was doing and he came out all right."

Gillespie's coming "out all right" meant the victory of the bebop, or bop, revolution in the middle and late 1940s under the leadership of Gillespie, Charlie Christian, and Charlie Parker. The bop revolutionaries introduced startlingly new harmonies and shifted the accent in phrasing. Their slow tempos were delusive, allowing the soloist to insert batches of sixteenth and even thirty-second notes. Thus, as John Lincoln Collier has pointed out, within the superficial slow-tempo context they were really playing very fast. "Gillespie, it should be remembered, took as his model Roy Eldridge, who had himself begun trying to be the fastest gun in the West. . . . In the end the bop musicians simply became habituated to machine-gun tempos."

Partly because of the speed of the tempos, the bop players began to reverse swing music's tendency to divide a beat into two unequal parts, one of which virtually disappeared. As Collier explains, at fast tempos it is almost impossible to make markedly unequal divisions of a beat,

"because the short note of the pair becomes in effect a sixteenth, and at a tempo above about 250, sixteenth notes are impossible on a wind instrument except in double-tonguing, when the result is equal sixteenths, which was not the goal of the bop musicians. In pursuing long strings of more or less equal notes, many bop musicians could not separate the line from the beat, but the best players succeeded, by playing behind or well away from the beat, making leaps that, in Collier's words, "for a moment appear to escape the gravity pull of the ground beat" and set free a "whole patch" of phrases, "like a sudden shower of hailstones on the roof."

The rhythmic change introduced by the boppers that bothered older jazz musicians the most was the shift in the emphasis in phrasing. Before bop, even the most experimental of jazz improvisers playing in 4/4 time began and ended their phrases on the first and third beats, because that was what seemed natural to Western ears. To those ears, the bop musicians seemed to be "offbeat" in accenting the second beat or even the last half of the fourth beat, the weakest point in a measure.

With the hegemony of bop (and the coincidental ascendancy of the saxophone), Eldridge found himself, as James Lincoln Collier puts it, "at the height of his powers, in his mid-thirties, passé." On the waning momentum of the swing movement, he remained in demand, leading his own band and touring Europe with Gene Krupa and Jazz at the Philharmonic and with the Benny Goodman sextet, but, according to Collier, he was discouraged and suffered a "near-nervous breakdown" while abroad. The respect for his music that he encountered during an extended stay in Paris (1950–51) evidently restored his confidence.

Back in the United States, Eldridge resumed a busy schedule, with his own combos and with other groups and individuals, including Coleman Hawkins, with whom he played on and off for seventeen years. Reviewing his American Recording Society album *Swing Goes Dixie* in the *New Yorker* (June 1, 1957), Whitney Balliett described Eldridge as "fiery and indefatigable," with a "wild and dancing and nervous" style. "He seems to bite at, instead of merely blow, his notes, which rise in sudden breathtaking swoops to the upper registers of his instrument or plummet to the low registers, where he often achieves a bleary, guttural sound," Balliett wrote. "[Although] his unruly imagination now and then outruns his sizable technique . . . his solos are marvels of spontaneous construction, which march with a steady, unbreakable logic from oblique, studied beginnings to soaring hats-off climaxes." Covering a concert by Eldridge at the Museum of Modern Art four years later, Balliett reported that the trumpeter by then possessed several closely related styles, all occasionally heard in the course of a single solo: his early staccato approach, his insouciant and "enveloping" tone of the 1940s, and his 1950s "effort to fold into his playing some of Sonny Rollins' hard-bop techniques."

In 1962 Eldridge opened the Newport Jazz Festival, and in the mid-1960s he toured with Count Basie's big band and gave many concerts with Ella Fitzgerald, including one at the Royal Box in London. By the late 1960s he was content to lead his quintet in gigs at such Manhattan clubs as the Half Note, the Village Vanguard, and the Down Beat, close to his home in Hollis, Queens, and to his wife since 1936, the former Viola Lee Fong (by whom he has a daughter, Carole Elizabeth). "I've had all the glamour I want—and all the traveling," he told John S. Wilson of the *New York Times* (January 31, 1969) one night at the Half Note. "I'm always so glad to get back to New York. I walk my dogs, cook what I want to eat, and play enough club dates and bar mitzvahs as a sideman to keep going." Wilson reported that Eldridge was "still a trim, dapper man" with "a touch of gray showing in his close-cropped mustache and at the edges of his neatly slicked-down black hair" and that "the fire that roared through his playing in the early days continues to flare up, but it is balanced by the provocatively edgy warmth that appears when the fires are banked."

In 1969 Eldridge began an eleven-year engagement as the leader of the house band at Jimmy Ryan's, a club on West Fifty-Fourth Street in Manhattan known for specializing in Dixieland music. Eldridge adapted to the new situation by learning the Dixieland routines without submitting to them, as the assiduous John S. Wilson informed the readers of the *New York Times* in 1971: "The band may be pumping its way through 'Royal Garden Blues' when, with a sudden ripping burst of sound, Mr. Eldridge razzle-dazzles his way into an electrifying solo, filled with the crackling phrases and bright, sharp clusters of notes that have always been his hallmark. It shakes up the tune, it shakes up the band, and it lifts [the] audience out of its seats with an outburst of cheers. And when Mr. Eldridge is not putting his personal stamp on the old Dixieland tunes, he is apt to be answering requests for specialties of his own, such as 'After You've Gone,' an astounding bit of virtuosity that he began developing when he had his own band at the Three Deuces in Chicago more than thirty years ago and later featured during his stay with Gene Krupa. He still plays it with the driving, fiery brilliance that made it a jazz classic."

During his long engagement at Jimmy Ryan's, Eldridge occasionally gave performances in other venues, including the London House in Chicago in 1971, Avery Fisher Hall at Lincoln Center in New York City, where he and Ella Fitzgerald reunited for a concert in 1976, and the Blackstone Hotel in Chicago, where he took part in a Louis Armstrong memorial concert sponsored by the Jazz Institute of Chicago in 1979. A "Salute to Roy Eldridge" presented at New York University's Loeb Auditorium in 1979 included a number of jazz luminaries in addition to Eldridge himself, as did the "Portrait of Roy Eldridge" presented at Town Hall in Manhattan as part of the Kool Jazz Festival in 1981. Still recuperating from his 1980 heart attack, Eldridge

confined his contribution to the Town Hall event to singing.

In 1981 Inner City Records issued in the United States the album *I Remember Harlem*, an Eldridge session with Don Byas, the tenor saxophonist, that had been recorded on the Vogue label in Paris thirty years before. In that session Eldridge sang vocals in French and English besides playing the trumpet. In addition to the title cut, the album included "O Shut Up," a modernist mockery of the Dixieland heritage; "The Heat Is On," Eldridge's variation of "I Never Knew"; several homages to Louis Armstrong; and three Eldridge piano solos in boogie, rubato improvisation, and stride styles. In hearing "O Shut Up," Gary Giddens of the *Village Voice* (May 27, 1981), could not think of "a better example of what makes Eldridge the most electrifying of jazz trumpeters." Recalling how the trumpeter as a young man had challenged Armstrong with his flamboyant performances of "King of the Zulus" and "Saint Louis Blues," Giddens pointed out that "it was a genuine if respectful competitiveness that kept his motor wound, as it does today, and in one area at least—excitement—he may have surpassed Armstrong." Whereas the older trumpeter's notes were "shaped and radiant," Eldridge "never had a pure or golden sound tone," but rather a "vocal rasp" that seemed to "start in the viscera and work its way through his small body, carving a path in his throat and bursting forth with breathtaking gravity." Also, Eldridge's high notes were "not brilliant like Armstrong's" but "shaded by a rapid shake" and seemingly "a spontaneous, uncontainable explosion of feeling."

In 1982 three collections of Eldridge recordings were released: the Columbia two-disk album *Roy Eldridge: The Early Years*; the single MCA "Jazz Heritage" LP *All the Cats Join In*, largely devoted to Eldridge's sessions as a soloist with big swing bands; and the four-record album *Louis Armstrong—Roy Eldridge/Jazz Masterpieces*, produced by the Institute of Jazz Studies and distributed by the Franklin Mint Record Society.

In the photograph illustrating Gary Giddens' article in the *Village Voice*, Roy Eldridge is shown holding a miniature pet dog and wearing horn-rimmed glasses, a Greek sea captain's cap, and a colorful cravat. According to the *New York Times*'s John S. Wilson, writing in October 1982, Eldridge seemed "fit, vigorous, and energetic," but had "not resumed playing his horn since [his] illness." In her 1979 *Chicago Tribune* article, Harriet Choice noted that "a party atmosphere prevails" wherever Eldridge is. According to her, "He is delightfully frisky on the bandstand, kidding with his colleagues and laughing the hardest when the joke's on him. Offstage his sense of humor is everywhere, in his choice of words, in the sly 'heh-hehs' that accompany his anecdotes, and in his amazing ability to emphasize the good moments through bad times." If recent sources are correct, Eldridge moved during the 1970s from Hollis, Queens, to Convent Avenue in Manhattan. Painting and photography are among his hobbies, and the honors he has accrued include a citation from the Muscular Dystrophy Association, the Westinghouse Trophy, the Esquire Silver Award, first place in two *Down Beat* polls (1944 and 1946) and three *Metronome* polls (1944–46), and enrollment in the *Down Beat* Hall of Fame. Eldridge is a Presbyterian.

References: *Chicago Tribune* VI p4 Jl 15 '79 por; *N Y Post* p50 Jl 30 '66 por; *N Y Times* p30 Ja 31 '69 por, C p5 Je 30 '81 por, II p25 O 17 '82 por; *Village Voice* p76+ My 27 '81 por; *Washington Post* G p1 S 21 '69 pors; Collier, James Lincoln. *The Making of Jazz* (1979); Kinkle, Roger D. *Complete Encyclopedia of Popular Music and Jazz 1900–1950* vol 2 (1974); Mapp, Edward. *Directory of Blacks in the Performing Arts* (1978); Southern, Eileen. *Biographical Dictionary of Afro-American and African Musicians* (1982); *Who's Who in America, 1984–85*

Elkin, Stanley (Lawrence)

May 11, 1930– Writer; university professor.
Address: b. Dept. of English, Washington University, St. Louis, Mo. 63130

Riding what one critic called the "razor's edge between realism and fantasy," Stanley Elkin received serious attention within the writing profession for about two decades without attracting wide audiences. Elkin creates "high art" from the symbols of popular culture and the grotesque details of everyday life, writing paradoxically, as Caryn James observed in the *Village Voice* (October 26, 1982) about "the regular guy with an all-American dream of making it big" in "sentences . . . convoluted enough to give a Jamesian pause." A humorist with lyrical instincts, Elkin once inspired the critic and novelist William H. Gass to write, "Nothing but genre blindness could prevent us from seeing that there is no warmer, wealthier poetry being written in our time."

Some critics, such as the novelist John Irving, have been ambivalent about Elkin's digressive disregard for plot, crediting him with "some of the best prose-writing in English today" while accusing him of self-indulgent density. In his book *Reading Stanley Elkin* (1985), Peter J. Bailey traces this uncertainty to an early shift in Elkin's work from the "plot-centered" Jewish-American social realism, as represented by Philip Roth and Saul Bellow, toward the antirealism of Thomas Pynchon, Robert Coover, and Donald Barthelme. According to Bailey, Elkin's "work has come increasingly to dramatize the evolution of his own attitude toward language. . . . The real tension underlying all his work . . . is that of the imagination refusing to allow invention to flag—that of the creative mind's insistence that new pleasures and insights can still be wrung from the old materials and the old words."

Stanley Lawrence Elkin was born on May 11, 1930, in Brooklyn, New York, the older of the two children and only son of Philip Elkin and Zelda [Feldman] Elkin. Like some of Elkin's characters, his father was a salesman, a "dynamic and humorous man" who "told a lot of good stories." Living on Chicago's South Side after the age of three, Elkin first showed an aptitude for writing "about the time [he] was toilet trained," when he scribbled on letterheads from his father's business, "charged by the fact that every page looked like the page that preceded it." While attending grammar school, he began writing stories, or "the same story a lot of times," as he joked in an interview for *Current Biography*. Discovering Whit Burnett's anthology *This Is My Best* (1942), Elkin became aware that there was a "world of real writers" to which he could aspire.

Upon graduation from Chicago's South Shore High School, Elkin entered the University of Illinois at Urbana, majoring at first in journalism, with the assumption that newspapers and magazines were "where stories were written." On the advice of a freshman composition teacher, Elkin soon switched to the English department. Outside the classroom, Elkin wrote for *Illini Writers*, the undergraduate literary magazine, and performed in radio dramas on the college station WILL.

After receiving his B.A. degree in 1952, Elkin enrolled in the University of Illinois graduate school, which granted him an M.A. degree in English in 1953. His instructors included John T. Flanagan, an authority on American literature and folklore, and the poet Randall Jarrell, who was a visiting professor there for one semester. Elkin's doctoral work was interrupted by service in the United States Army from 1955 to 1957. Stationed at Fort Lee, Virginia, he wrote a training manual on forklift trucks and, "as a way of forgetting that [he] was in the army," acted in plays at the Virginia Museum Theatre.

Returning to Illinois after his discharge, Elkin continued his doctoral work and read manuscripts for *Accent* magazine, which published several of his stories. His early work, mainly with Jewish themes, included the stories "A Sound of Distant Thunder" (1957) and "The Party" (1958), in which, as Doris G. Bargen noted in *Dictonary of Literary Biography* (1984), "the traditional reverence for the past strikes the protagonists as anachronistic while full immersion into mainstream American culture appears to them as a betrayal. Rejecting past and present, they opt for the timeless, for beauty, symbolized by chinaware in one case and by fairy tales in the other." Elkin obtained his Ph.D. degree from the University of Illinois in 1961, on acceptance of his dissertation, "Religious Themes and Symbolism in the Novels of William Faulkner."

Meanwhile, in 1960, Elkin became an instructor in the English department at Washington University in St. Louis. Except for brief leaves of absence, he has remained there ever since, becoming a professor in 1969. He took his first leave of absence in 1962, to work on a novel. As he told Doris G. Bargen for the *Dictionary of Literary Biography* profile, he spent the next year in Rome and London on what he called "a Mother's grant," since his travels were generously funded by Zelda Elkin.

Elkin's first novel, *Boswell: A Modern Comedy* (Random House, 1964), which he wrote during his sojourn in Europe, models its protagonist on the eighteenth-century biographer of Samuel Johnson. In this parodic novel, the contemporary Boswell surrounds himself with celebrities to assuage his anxieties about death, represented here by a professional wrestler nicknamed the Grim Reaper. Rather than focusing his attention on one Johnsonian figure like his eighteenth-century counterpart, Elkin's Boswell attempts to achieve immortality through "The Club," a scheme to bring together such diverse notables as a Nobel laureate, the world's wealthiest man, an "international revolutionist," and an Italian *principessa*. Reviewing *Boswell* in *Book Week* (June 21, 1964), Robert Maurer suggested that readers would find it difficult to empathize with Boswell's "bizarre" means of adjusting to "mediocrity and . . . approaching death" but conceded that "Elkin writes marvelously well. Humor explodes in bursts. Scenes crackle with gusto and imaginative fertility, and his people pop off the page with overabundant flesh."

Criers and Kibitzers, Kibitzers and Criers (Random House, 1966) is a collection of nine stories that Elkin had published in magazines since the late 1950s. Described as his most realistic work, the stories, according to the publisher's note, have as their common theme "the tragic inadequacy of a simplistic response to life." In the words of H. L. Rosofsky, who reviewed the collection for the *Library Journal* (January 15, 1966), they "run the gamut from the 'Oy veh' school of the modern Jewish writer to the free-wheeling fantastic style of the more 'far out' authors on today's literary scene. The characters come alive, each in his own element."

The book opens with a title story in which the owner of a small supermarket discovers that his recently deceased son had stolen money from the cash register. In "I Look Out for Ed Wolfe," an orphan sells all his possessions to find out how much he is worth after being fired from a debt collection agency for being too tough with the delinquents. And in "The Guest" a drifter demonstrates his disdain for his patronizing hosts. Other stories include "In the Alley" and "Among the Witnesses," originally published in the *Chicago Review* and *Accent*, respectively, which together had earned for Elkin the Longview Foundation award in 1962. David Galloway, writing in the *Southern Review* (Summer 1968), rated *Criers and Kibitzers, Kibitzers and Criers* as "one of the most important collections of short stories published in recent years" and cited its "blend of farce and pathos. . . . sheer mastery of style and martinet-like understanding of the human condition."

Elkin's second novel, *A Bad Man* (Random House, 1967), is set in a prison, where the favor-peddling department store executive Leo Feldman confronts the authoritarian order of Warden Fisher. The "Fisher of bad men" enforces a conformist notion of "goodness" with arbitrary but interlocking regulations. In the words of Raymond M. Olderman in *Beyond the Wasteland* (1972), this novel presents the reader "with a choice between Fisher's sterility and Feldman's madness," of which the antisocial but life-affirming "Feldmanian self-aggrandizement" is clearly preferable. In commenting on *A Bad Man* in the *New York Times Book Review* (October 15, 1967), Josh Greenfield noted that "Elkin is at once a bright satirist, a bleak absurdist, and a deadly moralist, with a brisk and busy imagination."

The hero and title character of Elkin's third novel, *The Dick Gibson Show* (Random House, 1971), shares the desire of other Elkin protagonists to manifest their identity by exalting the self. But unlike the elitist Boswell and the nonconformist Leo Feldman, Gibson seeks his apotheosis paradoxically, attempting, in the words of Peter J. Bailey, to "transcend" the "normal and everyday . . . by becoming their very symbol, turning himself into the quotidian's champion, the mythic embodiment of the anti-mythic view." Intending to give voice to the ordinary family, to unify Americans through his radio programs, Gibson is stymied by the fragmentation and narcissism of his audience. Ironically, Gibson's call-in talk show contributes to that alienation by encouraging people to become their own stars, filling the airwaves with their private obsessions. Although Elkin won widespread acclaim for his satiric portrayal of the world of radio, some critics were dissatisfied with the book's episodic form. As Geoffrey Wolf observed in *Newsweek* (April 10, 1971), Elkin's style recalls "the principles of radio—accident, surprise, random occurrence" but "seems to accept radio's risk, . . . that the audience's attention will wander."

In the novella *The Making of Ashenden* (Covent Garden Press, 1972), the perfect aristocrat Brewster Ashenden falls in love with the equally aristocratic and overachieving Jane Loes Lipton, but cannot marry her unless he becomes "pure again," by regaining his virginity. The necessary purification occurs when Ashenden is forcefully seduced by a 700-pound female Kamchatkan brown bear in heat. Unfazed by this sequence, Doris G. Bargen, writing in the *Dictionary of Literary Biography* (1978), found the author's stylistic control "amazingly tasteful and moving." And Bruce Allen observed in the *Hudson Review* (Spring 1974), "The man-bear sex scene is vigorous, raunchy, painful, smelly—and downright *touching.*"

The Making of Ashenden was reprinted in *Searches and Seizures* (Random House, 1973), a collection published in Great Britain as *Eligible Men: Three Short Novels* (Gollancz, 1974) and republished as *Alex and the Gypsy: Three Short Novels* (Penguin, 1977). Also included in those editions were "The Bailbondsman" and "The Condominium," the former ranked by William Plummer among "the great works in the language—right up there perhaps, with [Faulkner's] 'The Bear' and [Melville's] 'Bartleby.'" Its protagonist, Alexander Main, a Cincinnati bailbondsman, is fascinated by crime, museum skeletons of extinct carnivores, and the phoenix-like liver fluke, last remnants of the ferocious passion that animated his Phoenician forebears. Threatened by the creeping humanitarianism of the 1960s ("the heart is winning the battle of history") and disillusioned by a growing awareness that crime itself is "a cooperation," Main forces his secretary, a former bail-jumper, to become a fugitive again so that there will be "someone to hunt."

In "The Condominium," Marshall Preminger, a lecturer, who at thirty-seven is still a virgin, inherits a condominium upon the death of his father. Moving into the building to avoid losing his father's investment, Preminger experiences an emotional crisis, his identity shaken by a gradual adoption of his father's role and by revelations of his father's "swinging" lifestyle. Described by Doris G. Bargen as the most realistic of the three novellas, "The Condominium" reminded Raymond M. Olderman, in his essay "The Politics of Vitality" in *Fiction International* (1974), of Saul Bellow's "angst, . . . that lost diamond, scuffed by a bad old world."

Reviewing the novellas in the *Washington Post Book World* (October 28, 1973), L. J. Davis cited "The Condominium" as revealing "what Elkin is capable of when he is able to liberate himself from the chains of his own artistry and contemplate his plot as closely as he contemplates his faultless metaphors." But, despite "Elkin's acuity, formidable skill and astonishing inventiveness," the novellas founder, in Davis' view, on the manipulation of artificial characters, "superbly sculptured statuary adorned with rich garlands of prose . . . trundled from place to place like demonstration models."

The homogenization of contemporary American life is the subject of Elkin's fourth novel, *The Franchiser* (Farrar, Straus, 1976). An orphan, like several other Elkin protagonists, Ben Flesh grows up among the eighteen physically afflicted Finsberg children—several sets of twins and triplets—of a theatrical costume business executive. Backed by prime-rate loans from the Finsberg estate, Flesh buys Mister Softees, Midas Mufflers, and other franchises "to costume" America in "all its ubiquitous, familiar neon signatures and logos." Although standardization continues until Flesh himself is unable to tell Michigan from Alabama, Flesh's empire building is cut short by the energy crisis, described by Doris G. Bargen as a "painful analogue to the multiple sclerosis" that affects both Ben Flesh and the novelist.

Citing the "wheeling, dealing, spieling, yet feeling" narrative voice as *The Franchiser*'s main attraction, Thomas Le Clair of the *New Republic* (June 12, 1976) rhapsodized, "Sentence for sentence, nobody in America writes better than Stanley Elkin." John Leonard praised it in the *Saturday Review* (May 29, 1976) as the best of Elkin's novels and termed it "a frenzied parable" of cultural assimilation and expansion, of "manifest destiny on credit." Some reviewers, including Robert Towers, writing in the *New York Times Book Review* (June 13, 1976), expressed irritation with the "verbally incontinent" Ben Flesh, but few went so far as Geoffrey Stokes in the *Village Voice* (August 20, 1979), who dismissed the novel as "a lumpily indigestible porridge of small boffos and Big Thoughts."

Many of Elkin's detractors were disarmed by *The Living End* (Dutton, 1979), a "triptych" composed of three novellas, each building upon the previous one to tell a story about the afterlife. The first section, "The Conventional Wisdom," centers on Ellerbee, a virtuous liquor-store owner sent to Hell for such minor sins as keeping his store open on Sundays and for viewing Heaven as a theme park. In the second novella, "The Bottom Line," God lectures Hell's "iambic angels in free fall" on the difficulty of His job, goes to a school concert to scout musicians for Heaven, and twice inflicts punishment on the wrong people.

"The State of the Art," the final novella, interweaves the efforts of the damned to endure their suffering with depictions of life among the sanctified, including a very Jewish Joseph, who refuses to believe that his son is the Messiah. At the time of the Apocalypse, God reveals the identity of John F. Kennedy's assassin, informs His listeners on how to shop for used cars and how to do the latest disco steps, and expresses His frustration that He "never found [His] audience." As Geoffrey Stokes observed in the *Village Voice*, "Elkin is ultimately addressing the obligations of all creators. And suddenly—when the eternally disfigured Christ learns that his suffering occurred solely because God thought it would make a better story—the laughter stops, and the very funny, very serious Elkin goes deeper than he's ever gone before."

Terence des Pres, writing in the *Washington Post Book World* (July 1, 1979), praised Elkin's "blend of irreverence and care, of hard-core realism and fabulous invention" and his ability to exploit the vigor of clichés. Contrasting Elkin's vision with those of Thomas Pynchon and William Gaddis, des Pres wrote: "Elkin does not identify with the laughter of the gods, he does not dissociate himself from the human spectacle by taking out a franchise on the cosmic joke. Hard and unyielding as his comic vision becomes, Elkin's laughter is remission and reprieve, a gesture of willingness to join the human mess, to side with the damned, to laugh in momentary grace at whatever makes life Hell."

Elkin won the National Book Critics Circle Award for George Mills (Dutton, 1982), a novel that spans 1,000 years and over forty generations of blue-collar workers, each of whom is named George Mills. As described by Bart Testa in the Toronto Globe and Mail (May 14, 1983), George Mills is "the perennial bystander whose role in the dramas of kings, sultans, seers, shakers and movers is to hold the horses, haul the ashes and carry the valises to the limousine." Thomas Le Clair observed in the New Republic (December 27, 1982) that "Elkin has powered his routines beyond comedy and beyond pathos to the emotional clarity that comes when the writer no longer worries about amusing and prompting his audience." But Frances Taliaferro, in Harper's magazine (November 1982), noted the familiar problem of digression, citing chapters that "stand well enough on their own to qualify as short stories, but as structural elements of the novel . . . seem as arbitrary and anomalous as flying buttresses tacked onto a split-level house."

"Disease, not health, is at the core of things," a doctor is quoted as saying in Elkin's novel The Magic Kingdom (Dutton, 1985). Centered on a Disney World tour for terminally ill children, the book includes such characters as a woman with "tainted genes" who masturbates continuously in lieu of conventional sex, to avoid producing freaks of nature, and a doctor who goes to Florida in search of Holocaust survivors to confirm his theory of the "latency of all pathologies." Reviewing The Magic Kingdom in the Chicago Tribune (April 21, 1985), Lynne Sharon Schwartz observed, "It is a novel at once outraged and outrageous but in its vigor and its outcome, redemptive, a verbal feast held at the gallows. . . . In a hyperbolic finale, . . . the passion to live and be fruitful is unexpectedly and movingly triumphant."

Elkin's next novel, The Rabbi of Lud (Scribner's, 1987), was described in Publishers Weekly (September 11, 1987) as a "self-mocking send-up of Judaism and New Jersey suburbia" that "evokes Philip Roth." His book-length screenplay, The Six-Year-Old Man, of which an early version was printed in Esquire (December 1968), was slated to be published by Bamberger Books, also in 1987. Several of Elkin's works have been considered for the screen over the years. His novella "The Bailbondsman" was the basis for the film Alex and the Gypsy (1976), starring Jack Lemmon. Elkin has written several screenplays, as yet unproduced, and he contributed dialogue to the script of the science fiction film Demon Seed (1977). His radio play "The Coffee Room" has been presented on National Public Radio. He and Shannon Ravenel collaborated on compiling and editing The Best American Short Stories (Houghton Mifflin, 1980), for which he wrote the introduction.

As Merle Kling Professor of Modern Letters at Washington University since 1983, Elkin teaches a graduate course in writing each fall. He has been a visiting professor at several other institutions, including Yale University, Smith College, and the University of California at Santa Barbara. A Guggenheim fellow in 1966-67, Elkin also received the Paris Review humor prize in 1964, a Rockefeller Foundation grant in 1968-69, a grant from the National Endowment for the Arts and Humanities in 1972, the American Academy of Arts and Letters Award in 1974, and the Richard and Hinda Rosenthal Award in 1980. A collection entitled Stanley Elkin's Greatest Hits (Dutton, 1980) received the Sewanee Review prize in 1981. Washington University conferred an honorary L.H.D. degree on him in 1986. Elkin is sometimes confused with the historian Stanley M. Elkins and the late suspense novelist Stanley Ellin.

Stanley Elkin lives in University City, Missouri, which he described in Esquire (November 1980) as one of "over ninety incorporated municipalities surrounding St. Louis, . . . filling it in like some jigsaw of the irrefutable, Mondrian's zones and squares like a budgeted geometry." Married on February 1, 1953, to Joan Marion Jacobson, a painter, Elkin has three children, Philip Aaron, Bernard Edward, and Molly Ann. His friends include Washington University colleagues William Gass and Howard Nemerov. A heart attack survivor at thirty-eight, Elkin was also diagnosed as having multiple sclerosis shortly after his forty-second birthday. He walks with a cane and since 1979, when it became difficult for him to hold a pen, has worked with a word processor, a gift from Washington University. Elkin usually writes from breakfast "until it's not happening anymore," and he averages about five and a half hours at a stretch. In a profile in Publishers Weekly (March 29, 1985), Miriam Berkley compared Elkin to "a village elder" who appears older than his chronological age, with the "crinkly fringe of nearly white hair around his chin, cheeks and balding pate, . . . the wire rim glasses that frame his watchful eyes, the red suspenders he sports, and his air—perhaps illusory—of calm."

References: Book World p1+ O 10 '82 por; Esquire 94:108+ N '80 por; Pub W 227: 74+ Mr 29 '85 por; Bailey, Peter J. Reading Stanley Elkin (1985); Contemporary Authors new rev vol 8 (1983); Contemporary Novelists (1986); Dictionary of Literary Biography vol 2 (1978), vol 28 (1984); Who's Who in America, 1986-87; World Authors 1970-75 (1980)

Fichandler, Zelda

*Sept. 18, 1924– Theatre producer; director.
Address: b. Arena Stage, 6th and Maine Ave.,
S.W., Washington, D.C. 20024; h. 3120 Newark
St., N.W., Washington, D.C. 20008*

Of America's 250 regional theatres, one of the first
in time and foremost in quality is Arena Stage of
Washington, D.C. As an official of the National Endowment for the Arts recently acknowledged,
"Under the visionary leadership of Zelda Fichandler, [Arena Stage] has been a flagship for the
resident theatre field since its inception." Mrs. Fichandler is called the "guiding spirit" and "driving
force" of the theatre that she cofounded in 1950
and has since served as producing director. A challenging and adventurous enterprise, modest but
ambitious, Arena Stage soon began to pioneer in
producing new plays as well as classics and reviv-
als of modern works, in gaining a loyal audience,
developing new playwrights and training actors,
and in creating an ensemble with its own style and
collective consciousness, building a home designed for its special purposes, and assuring financial support for its survival and artistic growth. For
more than a decade its national and international
acclaim has made "regional theatre" a misnomer.

"Our aim is no less than this," Mrs. Fichandler
has said of Arena Stage, "to bring life to life. . . .
We live to illuminate life and make it more
enjoyable." The director Alan Schneider, who had
a long and close relationship with Arena Stage,
once named Zelda Fichandler, Margo Jones, and
Tyrone Guthrie as the "three seminal figures in the
greater American theatre." But he pointed out that
unlike Guthrie, who "imported the castle fully built
and dumped it down in Minneapolis," Zelda Fic-

handler "built the castle from the ground up, brick
by brick, and made it truly American in a sociological sense."

Zelda Diamond Fichandler was born in Boston,
Massachusetts, on September 18, 1924, to Harry
and Ida (Epstein) Diamond. The Harry Diamond
Laboratories of the United States Army were
named in honor of her father, a scientist and engineer whose accomplishments included the development of blind-instrument landings for aircraft.
An atmosphere of disaffection in her home in
Washington, D.C., where she grew up, helps to account for Zelda Diamond's early strong attraction
to the theatre, which, she has said, gave her "a
point of entry into the world." When interviewed
by David Richards of the *Washington Post* (November 17, 1985), she recalled, "In this middle-
class Jewish family, I was the maverick. I wasn't
docile. I never fit in. My father was a self-made
man. He thought people were self-starters, self-
makers, self-motivators. I was very socially mind-
ed. I believed in support programs for the needy,
that sort of thing, and that was a cause of friction."
She defended her views with biting, sarcastic re-
torts that masked her timidity and shyness.

By the age of nine Zelda had made up her mind
that she would become an actress, as she declared
in a prize-winning essay that she sent to the Washington *Star*, which was sponsoring a contest for
young readers on the subject of their intended careers. While attending a local drama school she
played Helga in "Helga and the White Peacock,"
and with that role, presumably, she took up what
she had called "a lifetime project," an effort to
overcome an inordinate fear of facing audiences,
of speaking in public. She sensed that the theatre
would provide her with a way of gradually gaining
self-confidence and diminishing her fear.

When she was sixteen years old, Zelda Diamond
graduated from Woodrow Wilson High School in
Washington and entered Cornell University to major in Russian language and literature. She left in
1945 with a Phi Beta Kappa key and a B.A. degree.
Back in Washington at the end of World War II, she
worked as a research analyst in the Russian division of military intelligence. On February 17, 1946,
she married Thomas C. Fichandler, an economist
who served in the Social Security Administration
and later headed the Washington office of the
Twentieth Century Fund.

If she had not found her lifework in the theatre,
Zelda Fichandler has said, she would have become
a psychiatrist. She was briefly a premedical student but then enrolled in courses in theatre arts at
George Washington University. At that time, in the
late 1940s, Washington had no professional theatre,
the National Theatre having closed down because
of a dispute over racial segregation. A drama professor of Zelda Fichandler at the university, Edward Mangum, who had organized one of the city's
dozens of amateur groups, used to talk with his student about the need of a professional theatre.
"Something went 'bong' in my head," Mrs. Fichandler recalled in her *Washington Post* inter-

view. "Everything seemed to come together—my political conscience, my interest in literature, my dramatic sense, my curiosity about people."

One of Zelda Fichandler's early dreams for a theatre, a showboat on the Potomac River, went unrealized. But the plans she discussed with her husband and Mangum resulted in the founding of Arena Stage in 1950, the year in which she also earned her M.A. degree in theatre arts at George Washington University. It was Washington's first integrated professional theatre. Risking their shoe-string of $15,000, the Fichandlers and Mangum decided that Arena's first home would be the old Hippodrome, a movie house in a run-down neighborhood of Washington. On August 16, 1950, on the squared stage that they had built in the center of 247 tiered seats, they presented their first play, Oliver Goldsmith's She Stoops to Conquer, whose cast included Lester Rawlins and George Grizzard. Before the season was over, they had ventured seventeen different plays. One of them, Mr. Arcularis, by Conrad Aiken and Diana Hamilton, initiated Arena Stage's policy of introducing new scripts. Among the several plays that Zelda Fichandler herself directed in 1950–51 were Synge's The Playboy of the Western World, Shakespeare's Twelfth Night, and Oscar Wilde's The Importance of Being Earnest.

After the first year Mangum moved from Washington, but Zelda Fichandler, with her husband, who served Arena Stage for a time as business manager and then as executive director, continued, with the title of producing director, to develop both a resident company and an audience. During its five years at the former Hippodrome, Arena Stage offered Washingtonians fifty-five productions. So many of them played to a full, or nearly full, house that in 1955, at the end of the Zelda Fichandler-directed American premier run of The Mousetrap, Arena Stage remained dark for a year, until a larger theatre could be found.

Moving their company to a part of the unoccupied Heurich Brewery in Washington's Foggy Bottom, the Fichandlers were ready in November 1956 to open the Old Vat; as the theatre came to be called, with the American premiere of the full-length version of Arthur Miller's A View from the Bridge. Arena Stage presented forty-eight plays during its five seasons at the Old Vat. With some of them, including John Osborne and Anthony Creighton's Epitaph for George Dillon, Zelda Fichandler began the practice at Arena Stage of giving a second chance to promising plays that had met with financial disaster on the New York stage. Despite the greater seating capacity of the Old Vat, Arena Stage could not meet its expenses from ticket sales. By choosing a not-for-profit status, as it did in 1959, it was able to look to foundations and other sources for funds.

On October 31, 1961, after having raised some $800,000 through private and public contributions, Arena Stage moved into its new, handsome permanent playhouse on a site along the Washington Channel in the city's developing Southwest section. Architect Harry Weese's innovative and functional theatre derives from Zelda Fichandler's insistence upon an open stage, in keeping with her definition of a theatre as "a design of space that relates audience to players." Writing in the Washington Post and Times Herald (October 29, 1961), Frederick Gutheim credited Mrs. Fichandler with having "shown real architectural courage in planning this first deliberately designed non-proscenium theatre." Arena Stage is recognized as having the first theatre in the United States built to answer the needs indicated by the collective experience of a resident company.

Adjoining the Arena Theater is the $1,500,000 Weese-designed Kreeger Theater, which opened in late November 1970. Notably different from the Arena, whose stage is surrounded by four tiers of about 800 seats, the Kreeger has a 500-seat fan-shaped auditorium and an end-thrust stage with a back wall, curtains, and other equipment of a conventional performing area. Mrs. Fichandler had taken off several months in 1966–67 from her work as producing director to concentrate on operational plans for the Kreeger. "My heart will always belong to the stage next door, that ring," she admitted, however, to Richard C. Coe of the Washington Post (January 17, 1971). She described the Kreeger as "more intimate than the Arena, warmer, less formidable, less disturbing and insistent." There are two other performing spaces in the Arena Stage complex—a 180-seat cabaret called the Old Vat Room and the 130-seat Scene Shop, which is used partly for exploratory work. Arena Stage also maintains centers in the Washington area for its community outreach program, the Living Stage Theatre Company, which has been praised especially for its work with disabled children.

To inaugurate the rectangular stage that Zelda Fichandler calls "the ring," Arena Stage had presented the American commercial premiere of Brecht's The Caucasian Chalk Circle, which Alan Schneider directed. Beginning with Tennessee Williams' The Glass Menagerie in April 1951, Schneider directed over forty plays for Arena Stage, including Samuel Beckett's Krapp's Last Tape. Another now well-known director, the Rumanian Liviu Ciulei, staged his first play in English at Arena Stage in 1974. Later, as the artistic director of the Tyrone Guthrie Theater, he looked back at working with Zelda Fichandler as an unusual experience: "Quality is considered a normal thing at the Arena."

Several prominent American actors have also enjoyed a mutually beneficial association with Arena Stage. The "dean" of the company, Robert Prosky, played some 130 roles in twenty-three seasons at Arena Stage before moving on to larger audiences in 1984 in the movie The Natural and David Mamet's Broadway drama Glengarry Glen Ross. Recalling his early days in Washington, he told Richards of the Washington Post (May 20, 1984), "Zelda saw something in me, God knows what, and kept nurturing it." Viveca Lindfors and Jane Alexander appeared together in Brecht's

Mother Courage in December 1970 at Arena Stage, and Miss Lindfors returned in 1972 to give her one-woman show, *I Am a Woman.* Under Zelda Fichandler's direction Miss Alexander portrayed Irina in Chekhov's *The Three Sisters* in February 1966. On December 12, 1967, a lustrous date in Arena Stage's history, she played opposite James Earl Jones in the first performance of *The Great White Hope,* Howard Sackler's drama about a black boxing champion victimized by racists. The play—with director Edwin Sherin and much the same cast—moved to New York the following year for a long Broadway run and won Tony awards for itself, Miss Alexander, and Jones.

The discovery of new plays and the development of untried playwrights together make up one of the major goals that Zelda Fichandler set for Arena Stage. *The Great White Hope* was the first of the plays that she fostered to be welcomed on Broadway. Others that followed the path from their American premiere at the Arena to the New York stage include Arthur L. Kopit's *Indians* (1969), Michael Weller's *Moonchildren* (1971), the musical *Raisin* (1973), based on Lorraine Hansberry's *A Raisin in the Sun,* Christopher Durang's *A History of the American Film* (1977), and Patrick Meyer's *K2* (1982). The Broadway presentation of *K2* brought a Tony to Arena Stage's Ming Cho Lee for his stage design.

Arena Stage meanwhile had begun to become known internationally when, in 1973, the United States Department of State chose it to be the first theatre company to tour the Soviet Union with American drama. For audiences in Moscow and Leningrad, Zelda Fichandler staged Jerome Lawrence and Robert E. Lee's *Inherit the Wind,* and Alan Schneider staged Thornton Wilder's *Our Town.* Both Mrs. Fichandler and Schneider had the advantage on the tour of a knowledge of Russian. Visiting Moscow shortly before the tour Mrs. Fichandler was much impressed by the work of the Russian director Yuri Lyubimov, who recently, in early 1987, made his American debut at the Kreeger Theater with his adaptation of Dostoevski's *Crime and Punishment.*

On another trip abroad, in February 1981, Mrs. Fichandler directed the Arena Stage company in a presentation of Arthur Miller's *After the Fall* at the Hong Kong Arts Festival. That production was for a proscenium stage. Later in the month she restaged the play for the Arena's four-sided stage. When, in the spring of 1987, Arena Stage traveled to Israel to perform Miller's *The Crucible,* which Zelda Fichandler directed, the Jerusalem Sherover Theater provided a four-sided stage for the occasion.

Among Mrs. Fichandler's foremost objectives for Arena Stage has been the development of an acting company whose performers work in ensemble through training that is directly related to the actual production of professional theatre. Through her association over the years with the Theatre Communications Group and many theatre panels, symposia, and conferences she has been able to put forth her conviction that "the acting company is the organic method of producing theatre as an artform," along with her other views on the theatre, such as how drama is related to the rest of the world. In 1972, upon completing a series of lectures as visiting professor at the University of Texas, she became university professor and professor of theatre arts at Boston University. Since September 1984, while continuing her work at Arena Stage, she has been chairperson of acting and directing at New York University's Tisch School of the Arts.

Finding a way to support Arena Stage's kind of ensemble was part of the business responsibilities of Thomas C. Fichandler, but as in every other aspect of Arena Stage, Zelda Fichandler took part vigorously in the fund-raising struggle. Because of its exploratory nature, she argued that Arena Stage must be free to fail at times and in order to maintain its standard of quality must invest on occasion in productions beyond its immediate means. Box-office receipts and subscription sales assured an average house capacity of 90 percent or more. But ticket revenues and related earnings paid only about 70 percent of the expenses of the theatre, which then had to look to funds from foundations, corporations, individual sponsors and the government to make up the difference. In May 1984 Arena Stage launched a drive to raise $6,000,000 for an endowment, which would yield enough interest to guarantee its continued artistic development. By the summer of 1986 Arena Stage had not only surpassed its endowment goal but also, as a result of a series of annual fund drives that it conducted simultaneously with its endowment campaign, had raised a total of another $6,000,000. It uses that fund to pay the operating costs that exceed its ticket sales.

Some of the gifts and grants to Arena Stage have been tributes to Zelda Fichandler. Her dozens of honors include doctorates from Hood College, Georgetown University, George Washington University, and Smith College and the Brandeis University Creative Arts Award. In 1971 she won the Margo Jones Award for "significant contribution to the dramatic arts through the production of new plays," and in 1976 she and Arena Stage received the first Tony Award to be given for achievement outside the New York City theatre. Among her more recent honors are three conferred in 1985: the Acting Company's John Houseman Award for "commitment and dedication to the development of young American actors," the Double Image Theatre Award "in recognition of her peerless achievement in the art of the theatre," and the Common Wealth Award for "distinguished service in the dramatic arts."

Zelda and Thomas C. Fichandler are the parents of two sons, Hal, a lawyer, and Mark, who is associated with the New York producer Alexander H. Cohen. Their marriage ended in 1975, but Thomas C. Fichandler continued to work at Arena Stage until his retirement in 1986. Slim, dark-haired and dark-eyed, personable, and highly articulate, Mrs. Fichandler can count public relations among the many services she has performed for Arena Stage. "A mercurial woman," as David Richards described her, "Fichandler can be moody, insightful, stubborn, flirtatious, withdrawn, and frankly intimidating. But Arena's capacity for renewal is clearly a function of her complicated temperament, relentless in its questioning curiosity." Also writing in the *Washington Post*, Meryle Secrest mentioned another aspect of her personality: "She's kind and humorous."

When asked by the *Chicago Tribune* (June 30, 1987) to discuss the value of maintaining live art in a technological age, Mrs. Fichandler replied: "The theater is a place of language and a place of experi- ence and a place of imagination. Theater usually takes its technology from its current day. . . . Today there is a broader spectrum of technology available to us, but theater is essentially still a storytelling medium, and people still go to it because they experience their lives as story, as a tale. And they go to see . . . other people's stories, which they can compare and relate to their own."

References: Christian Sci Mon p36 N 25 '85 por; N Y Times p6 Ag 13 '85 por; Washington Post F p3 Ja 21 '73 por, E p1+ O 20 '74 por, mag p10 Ap 17 '83 por, G p1+ N 17 '85 por; Notable Names in the American Theatre (1976); Who's Who in the Theatre (1981)

Finnbogadóttir, Vigdis

Apr. 15, 1930– President of Iceland. Address: Office of the President, Reykjavik, Iceland.

Vigdis Finnbogadóttir, the president of Iceland, has the distinction of being the first woman ever elected head of state in a democratic nation. With little political experience but many cultural achievements to her credit, she defeated three male candidates to win the largely ceremonial post in 1980, and easily won reelection in 1984. As a teacher and lecturer, President Vigdis, as she is called by her people, has devoted her career to preserving and interpreting the culture of her tiny island republic, which is known for its rich literary tradition dating back to early medieval times. Theatre being her special passion, she served from 1972 to 1980 as director of Iceland's national the- atre, the Reykjavik Theatre Company, where she played a special role in encouraging Icelandic playwrights.

Supporters who valued her cultural knowledge and also wanted to see a woman elected to high office, urged her in 1980 to run for president, a non-political post that symbolizes national unity. She won the election with almost 34 percent of the vote, succeeding Kristjan Eldjarn to become Iceland's fourth president since its independence from Denmark in 1944. In her two terms of office, President Vigdis has proved to be a charming and effective ambassador for her country, traveling widely and, most recently, acting as host for the Reagan-Gorbachev summit in October 1986. In the words of the Manchester *Guardian*, she is, in short, "one of the most disarming and intelligent of world leaders," and her career has not been harmed by her classic Nordic good looks.

Vigdis Finnbogadóttir was born on April 15, 1930, in Reykjavik, the capital of Iceland. Her father, Finnbogi Rutur Thorvaldsson, was a civil engineer and professor at the University of Iceland. Her mother, Sigridur Eiriksdóttir, was chairman of the Icelandic Nurses Association for thirty-six years. In Iceland, surnames are created by adding "sson" or "dóttir" to the father's first name; thus Vigdis is called "Finnbogadóttir" after her father. But because of the complexity of that naming system, Icelanders are known by their first names, so that Vigdis finds it strange to be referred to as "President Finnbogadóttir" in the Western press. In Iceland, it is also customary for women to keep their maiden names after marriage.

On finishing high school, Vigdis could not decide whether to stay at home and study to become a doctor, or go to the continent of Europe for her further education. Both her parents had studied abroad, and she had grown up hearing about Europe, especially during the war years. "I remember as a child I hoped they wouldn't destroy it all before I could come and see it, and I think that was what finally influenced me to go abroad," she explained during an interview for the *Christian Science Monitor* (September 16, 1982).

Consequently, after completing junior college at Menntaskolinn í Reykjavik in 1949, Vigdis went to the University of Grenoble, where she studied French, and then to the Sorbonne in Paris, where she took courses in literature and dramaturgy. Her increasing interest in theatre led her eventually to Copenhagen, Denmark, to study theatre history. Finally, she returned to the University of Iceland to round out her education with courses in English literature and education.

After acquiring her own extensive education, Vigdis became a teacher herself, first serving as a French instructor at her alma mater, and then building up the French department at a new experimental school, the Menntaskolinn vid Hamrahlid. She also taught French on the public television station of Reykjavik. During a sabbatical year, she returned to France to study its cultural influence on Iceland in the nineteenth century. During her summer holidays from teaching, Vigdis served as a tourist guide for the Icelandic Tourist Bureau, taking foreign journalists and writers around the island and helping them collect research material on Iceland. Eventually she developed and ran a program of training guides for the bureau.

Meanwhile, Vigdis' interest in the theatre continued unabated. "I was very enthusiastic about avant-garde theatre," she explained during an interview for the *Washington Post* (September 7, 1982). She joined Grima, the first experimental theatre group ever to be established in Iceland, but she never wanted to be on the stage herself. "Which is a very funny thing, since I am standing on a stage now," she said in the same interview, referring to her public role as Iceland's president.

In 1972 Vigdis was appointed director of the Reykjavik Theatre Company, and under her guidance the national theatre flourished. She made a special effort to encourage Iceland's own playwrights, discovering that "it was a lot of fun finding writers." She also saw to it that contemporary plays were translated and performed, and she served as the host of a popular television series on drama for Icelandic state television. She gained further visibility by her lectures on Icelandic culture, which she gave at home and abroad, and by presiding over the Alliance Française. In 1976 she became a member of the Advisory Committee on Cultural Affairs in the Nordic countries and became its chairman in 1978.

During those same years of involvement in the performing arts, Vigdis remained largely aloof from politics, although in 1961 she took part in a demonstration against the United States naval base at Keflavik and in 1974 helped to organize a petition campaign for its removal. Otherwise, she remained detached from her nation's often turbulent political scene. The Manchester *Guardian* once pigeonholed her as being "non-political but left-inclined." Her lack of political identification combined with her cultural expertise made Vigdis a natural candidate for the presidency of Iceland, a largely ceremonial position that is meant to foster national unity, above and beyond party politics,

and her efforts to preserve and to interpret Icelandic culture, as well as her gender, gained her many supporters. When first approached about running, Vigdis was reluctant, but friends finally persuaded her that it was time for a woman to run. "I wanted to prove that women could do it," she explained to a reporter for the *New York Times* in an interview (September 8, 1982).

Facing three formidable male candidates, Vigdis campaigned vigorously for four months, visiting farms and factories, "jumping into airplanes and like an ogress covering the country in three steps," she recalls. For her, the best part of the campaign was the opportunity to meet and to know her own people. The fact that Vigdis had been divorced and later adopted a child as a single mother proved to be no handicap in the campaign. In fact, she feels that her "eccentricity" in raising a child on her own may have helped her with the voters, who also seemed to approve of her emphasis on Iceland's cultural strengths. Looking back on the campaign, she said during the *New York Times* interview, "I think I was elected because I tried to talk about our identity, our history, our country, our ecology— how we have survived."

With 90 percent of the electorate voting, Vigdis won the presidency of Iceland on June 30, 1980, with 33.8 percent of the vote, and was inaugurated as the fourth president of Iceland on August 1, succeeding Kristjan Eldjarn. Her election as the first female head of state chosen by the democratic process made news across the world, and congratulations poured in. Although Vigdis feels that the people of Iceland voted for her as a person and not as a woman, she admits that "the nation showed considerable courage being the first to realize that it was not the main point whether I, as a candidate, was a man or a woman." The fact that she received less than 50 percent of the vote shows that many Icelandic women did not vote for her, which Vigdis thinks may partly reflect their own low self-esteem. She said in her *Christian Science Monitor* interview: "Many ladies do not have confidence in themselves because in the male society they are used to having men run the whole thing. They don't have confidence in themselves, so why should they have confidence in another woman?"

The duties that Vigdis assumed as the new president of Iceland are largely ceremonial, for in the Icelandic political system, the chief power rests with the prime minister. As Vigdis explained in the *New York Times*, "The role of the president is to be a symbol for the nation of unity and identity." But the president does have some important political duties, such as signing all bills passed by the Althing, the Icelandic parliament. Should she veto one, a right that is rarely exercised, it immediately goes before the people in a national referendum. In times of crisis, it is also her duty to oversee the formation of a new government.

But by far the greatest part of Vigdis' time is spent in other ways. She travels frequently in Iceland, giving speeches, meeting with its citizens, and attending theatre and museum openings. Several days a week she opens her office to people who are seeking advice and help. "Anybody in Iceland can make an appointment to see the president," she notes proudly. Although she is not always able to help, she thinks simply listening is important. "Psychologically, it is good for someone to talk to the president, and know afterward that the president knows about their problem," she has said.

Perhaps Vigdis' most important role has been as a cultural ambassador abroad. In September 1982 she made a much-publicized trip to the United States to promote an exhibition on "Scandinavia Today," which highlighted the culture of Denmark, Iceland, Sweden, Norway, and Finland. Honored by being asked to give the keynote address at the Kennedy Center opening of the exhibition in Washington, D.C., she devoted her speech to the theme of cooperation among the Nordic countries, to which she refers as the "golden ring." During her visit to the capital, she met with President Ronald Reagan before going on to tour other American cities, including Minneapolis, New York, and Seattle, where the "Scandinavia Today" exhibit was scheduled to appear. Vigdis has made several goodwill trips to England as well. She attended the wedding of Prince Charles in July 1981 and met with Prime Minister Margaret Thatcher in February 1982. Since England and Iceland had waged a "cod war" over fishing rights only a few years earlier, those official visits helped to restore good feeling between the two nations. Always enthusiastic about British theatre, Vigidis made a special point to visit the National Theatre and to meet the playwright Tom Stoppard, whose works she had translated and staged at the Reykjavik Theatre Company.

In 1984, when her first term of office was up, Vigdis won reelection with no opposition, an effortless victory that a reporter for the New York Post (September 3, 1986) credited to the "easy-going style which has endeared her to her countrymen." Her successful missions as a cultural ambassador no doubt also contributed to her popularity. As a Time (October 31, 1983) writer observed, her trips have "enabled her to put Iceland on the international scene." With her charm and her fluent command of several languages, the writer added, she has been "the best ambassador Iceland has ever had."

The one and only controversy of Vigdis' presidency occurred in 1985. The Icelandic women's liberation movement, which has gained a lot of strength since the 1970s, decided to stage a strike to protest unequal wages and other forms of discrimination against women. A similar protest held on October 24, 1975, in which tens of thousands of women walked off the job and refused to do their housework, had effectively demonstrated that without its women, Iceland could not function. The purpose of the 1985 demonstration was to repeat that lesson on the tenth anniversary of the memorable 1975 strike.

President Vigdis announced her intention to observe the women's strike by staying out of the of-

fice, a decision that at first caused little criticism. But on the day of the strike, the Althing passed a bill forbidding the stewardesses of Icelandair to join the protest, on the grounds that disrupting the nation's air traffic would be a major economic disaster. At first Vigdis refused to sign the bill, but under pressure from Prime Minister Steingrimur Hermannsson, she finally agreed to endorse it and then left the office. The stewardesses ignored the parliamentary bill anyway and joined the strike. Their action served to confirm the reputation of Icelandic women for being strong and independent. Yet President Vigdis believes that they still have many prejudices to fight, as do all women. "My message to the girls of the world is this: get educated," she has said. "Never accept a shorter education than your brothers."

On April 25, 1987 Steingrimur Hermannsson and his center-right coalition lost the general election, giving the Women's Alliance, the powerful feminist party, the balance of power in forming a new government. When he was forced to resign a few days later, Vigdis invited him to take charge of a caretaker Cabinet until a new coalition could take over. The outgoing prime minister accepted her invitation. Doubling its seats in the Alfing, the Women's Alliance garnered 10 percent of the vote, but its leaders made clear their refusal to enter the government unless their pay, which in Iceland is 40 percent less than that of men, be made equal.

Fiercely proud of her island nation, Vigdis tries to dispel the stereotypes of Iceland as "a very cold place, full of ice, with very few people living there." Although small, the country is cosmopolitan. Despite an inflation rate that is the highest in Europe, Iceland enjoys full employment, a high standard of living, and a thriving cultural life. One aspect of Icelandic culture that Vigdis particularly prizes is its literary tradition dating back to the Old Norse of the Vikings. Iceland has always been a nation of writers, she believes, because its barren land gave creative persons so little else with which to work. Since people lacked many materials for arts and crafts, they had to resort to words to express themselves.

Its strong cultural identity has helped Iceland to survive as an independent nation, despite its small size and its precarious position midway between the United States and the Soviet Union. At an equal distance from Moscow and New York, Reykjavik has been a favored spot for summit conferences. Its most recent one took place in October 1986, when President Vigdis played host to Ronald Reagan and Mikhail Gorbachev. Since they are poised between the world's two superpowers, Icelanders have a strong desire to be peacemakers. President Vigdis has pointed out, in Time, "We are people of peace and we have never been at war with anybody."

Because Iceland is such a small, democratic, and informal nation, occupying its presidency has not radically changed Vigdis' lifestyle. She still drives her own car and can still stroll in the downtown area without attracting too much attention. During her coffee breaks, she likes to visit the Reykjavik Theatre Company and sit in on rehearsals. Divorced at the age of thirty-two after nine years of marriage, Vigdis later adopted a daughter, Astridur. When Astridur was nine, she told the *Christian Science Monitor* interviewer: "I have protected her as much as possible from the limelight. So she doesn't quite realize my position." When her famous mother has to be away on state business, Astridur has been known to complain, "I don't like to be the daughter of a president." President Vigdis' chief leisure interest is, not surprisingly, the theatre.

References: *Christian Sci Mon* p15 S 16 '82 por; *N Y Times* C p16 S 8 '82 por; *Washington Post* B p1 S 7 '82 por; *Cur World Leaders* 24:870+ N '81 pors; *International Who's Who*, 1986–87

FitzGerald, Frances

Oct. 21, 1940– Journalist; author. Address: b. c/o Simon & Schuster Inc., 1230 Ave. of the Americas, New York City, N.Y. 10020

With the exception of *The Pentagon Papers*, the leaked Defense Department dossier on Indochina, no book did as much to turn American public opinion against American military intervention in Vietnam as Frances FitzGerald's Pulitzer Prize-winning *Fire in the Lake* (1972), an incisive interpretation of the Vietnam war and its baffling incongruences. "She [Miss FitzGerald] was the first Westerner to grasp the complexities of the Eastern culture," as Robert Manning, the editor of the *Atlantic*, has said, "and to explain them in a lucid style to Americans." Miss FitzGerald, whom a colleague has described as "a cultural anthropologist working as a reporter," turned her attention to America's changing view of itself and its role in the world as presented in classroom history texts over the past two centuries in the provocative work *America Revised* (1979). Her third book, written with her wonted wit and attention to telling detail, was *Cities on a Hill* (1986), in which she sought to identify and understand broad cultural changes in the United States since 1960 through the prism of four discrete, more or less intentional and separatist communities. William Shawn, the former editor of the *New Yorker*, is among the many who consider Miss FitzGerald to be "one of the best nonfiction writers of her generation."

Frances FitzGerald, who is known to her family and friends as Frankie, was born on October 21, 1940, in a hospital on New York City's East Side just four blocks from the apartment in which she now lives. Her father, the late Desmond FitzGerald, a descendant of Protestant Anglo-Irish aristocrats, adventurers, and explorers, was a Wall Street lawyer and, later, a deputy director of the Central Intelligence Agency. Desmond, who trained Chinese troops in the China-Burma-India theatre of military operations during World War II, had, like his seagoing grandfather before him (a collector of Oriental art), a fascination for Asian culture, some of which Frankie absorbed.

Frankie FitzGerald's mother is Marietta FitzGerald Tree (née Mary Endicott Peabody), one of the blue-blooded Peabodys, an old Boston family, rich in a tradition of public service and *noblesse oblige*, boasting among its members down the years an Episcopal bishop, founders of the Groton School and Radcliffe College, a governor of Massachusetts, and numerous other luminaries, especially in preaching and teaching. The maternal grandmother, Mary (Parkman) Peabody, a descendant of the historian Francis Parkman, made national headlines in 1964, when, at the age of seventy-two, she was jailed in Florida for taking part in a civil rights demonstration. From her grandmother, Frankie learned, in her words, that "the more a person receives from the world, the more he owes it," and that "to waste time is immoral."

Marietta Tree, who is now a city planner, was a prominent figure, often described as "the goddess of liberal causes," in the Democratic party in the 1950s and 1960s. A close friend and confidante of the late Adlai Stevenson, she served with him at the United Nations (where she was the first American woman to bear the title of ambassador) and was with him when he collapsed and died on a London street in 1965. Soon after her divorce from Desmond FitzGerald in 1947, Marietta married the British multimillionaire and former member of parliament Ronald Tree, with whom she had a second daughter, Penelope, who became a fashion model and, in the late 1960s, a jet-set celebrity. Frankie also has step-siblings (Desmond and Joan FitzGerald) from her father's second marriage.

Frankie FitzGerald grew to maturity with what she has described as a "terror of mediocrity, of not being the best at whatever [she] did," the feeling that "one had to be absolutely Beethoven." The palatial Tree townhouse in Manhattan and country estate in England served as salons where Marietta Tree played hostess to statesmen and politicians (including Winston Churchill, Anthony Eden, and Herbert Lehman), leaders in journalism and communications (including Joseph Alsop and William Paley), and other major players in the world of power—people who encouraged Frankie's ambitions and would provide her with important connections in the years to come. With her mother, Frankie was active in Adlai Stevenson's campaign for the presidency in 1952, and Stevenson took her to visit Albert Schweitzer in Africa five years later, when she was sixteen.

Outside of reading, Frankie FitzGerald's favorite activity in childhood was horseback riding. After graduating from the exclusive Dalton School in Manhattan, she chose to go to the Foxcroft School in Middleburg, Virginia, at least partly because it was the only prep school acceptable to her elders that would allow her to keep a horse. It was under a demanding English teacher at Foxcroft that she began to take writing seriously. A diligent, hardworking student, she was at the head of her class at Foxcroft. Before graduating, she made her social debut. Then, as a major in Middle Eastern history at Radcliffe College, she studied under Sir Hamilton Gibb, wrote her thesis on King Faisal I's abortive reign in Syria in 1920, and took her B.A. degree *magna cum laude* in 1962.

"I think I always wanted to be a writer," Miss FitzGerald told Barbara Rowes of *People* (December 3, 1979), "but I thought I would become a novelist." Rejecting the idea of going from Radcliffe into the study of law at Harvard University, she decided, after talking with George Plimpton and Bob Silvers (who were back from working on the *Paris Review*), to go to France to write a novel. In Paris, she found employment with the Congress for Cultural Freedom, an organization headed by the Russian émigré composer Nicolas Nabokov (a friend of her mother's) that published magazines and conducted seminars for non-Communist European intellectuals. (It was not until 1967 that the organization was exposed as a CIA front.) "It was in France," Frankie told Jane Howard in an interview for *Life* (October 27, 1972), "that I suddenly discovered poetry for the first time, and I sort of learned about Catholicism there too; I realized that religion hadn't only to do with one's social conscience: it was mystery and magic too." As for her novel, she felt "totally frustrated" trying to write it and decided that fiction was not for her.

After returning to New York City in 1964, Frankie FitzGerald met Clay Felker, then the editor of the New York *Herald Tribune*'s Sunday magazine. On assignment from Felker, she wrote profiles for the magazine—on subjects ranging from a Puerto Rican gang leader to her maternal grandmother and the architect Philip Johnson—until the *Herald Tribune* folded in 1966. Soon she was contributing regularly to *Vogue* and the *Village Voice*, and later she became a contributor to the *New York Review of Books* and the *New York Times Magazine*, among other publications.

Desmond FitzGerald advised his daughter to find a subject on which she could write with "passion" and "dedication," and she found that subject in the Vietnam war. When she arrived in Saigon (now Ho Chi Minh City) in February 1966, she recalled in an interview with Paul Friedman for *Esquire* (July 1980), she was "very naive" and had no strong opinions about the civil war in which the United States was waging massive intervention on the side of the non-Communist government in the south, where National Liberation Front rebels were fighting to unify the country under the rule of the Hanoi government of Ho Chi Minh in the north. "I honestly didn't know what it [the war] was all about. I thought I would stay in Vietnam a month or two, write a couple of pieces to pay for the trip, and then come home. But once I got there, I couldn't leave." She stayed for almost a year.

"Nobody was interested in the politics of the war at the time," Miss FitzGerald told Robert Friedman. "Everyone [of the correspondents] was chasing the American units around—that's what people thought you should do when you're covering a war. But I never fancied myself a war correspondent in that sense. I never put on a uniform and went out with the troops." Moving out of the hotel in Saigon where most of the press corps lived, she rented an apartment and began researching documents, interviewing officials in charge of "development" programs, and getting to know the people. Her French served her well in the cities; in the hamlets, where she experienced firsthand America's loss of the minds and hearts of the peasants, she was assisted by an interpreter, a young Vietnamese woman from a strict Confucian family who was just back from university studies in the United States. Thus, as a correspondent who knew her in Vietnam told Friedman, "she was able to understand better than any of us why the American government was doomed to fail."

Gradually it began to become clear to Miss FitzGerald that the basic conflict in Vietnam was really a clash of two cultures—that of an indigenous society struggling for self-determination on the one hand and, on the other, the alien culture of a bullying Western power unable to view the country other than as a mere pawn in an anti-Communist global strategy. She found her most important clue to understanding the conflict in a book given to her by Daniel Ellsberg (later famous for leaking the Pentagon Papers to the press), at that time a liaison officer at the United States Embassy in Saigon. The book was *Sociologie d'une guerre* (1952), by the French anthropologist Paul Mus. In his book, Mus explained how Ho Chi Minh's Communist revolution was consonant with the Confucian character of Vietnamese society and why the efforts to stop it were futile. (The French had tried and failed before the Americans took their turn.)

Miss FitzGerald began writing quick articles on the war when she was in Vietnam, and after she returned to the United States, in 1967, she wrote a more conscientious article for the *Atlantic Monthly* on "the maze of Vietnam politics" that brought her an Overseas Press Club Award and served as the sketch for her book on the war. She was unaware that Paul Mus was alive and teaching at Yale University until Mus, after reading the *Atlantic* article, contacted her. Until Mus's death in 1969, she traveled frequently to New Haven to discuss Vietnamese history and culture with him.

After several years of research, a large amount of which was done in the Widener Library at Harvard University, and a second visit to Vietnam, in 1971, Miss FitzGerald completed *Fire in the Lake: The Vietnamese and the Americans in Vietnam* (Little, Brown, 1972), which she dedicated to Paul Mus and to her father. The book opened with a detailed description of Vietnam's traditional agrarian society, based on Confucian ideas of "correctness" and of absolutes operative in ordered, communal hierarchies and centered in nature and the family (including ancestor worship). Set against this was the American pattern, that of the "progressing," urbanized, industrial West. American war relocation programs and sponsorship of the Saigon government, which was out of touch with the rural, nationalistic population, exacerbated the irreconcilable differences between the two ways of thinking and living and made the parallels between Marxism and Confucianism more significant. "Physical death is everywhere," Miss FitzGerald wrote, "but it is the social death caused by destruction of the family that is of overriding importance. . . . The land and the family were the two sources of national as well as personal identity. The Americans have destroyed these sources for many Vietnamese, not merely by killing people but by forcibly separating them, by removing the people from the land and depositing them in the vast swamp-cities."

The title "*Fire in the Lake*," an expression taken from the *I Ching*, the ancient Chinese "Book of Changes," is symbolic of revolution in traditional Vietnamese usage. "Behind the dam of American troops and American money," Miss FitzGerald concluded in the book, "the pressure is building towards one of those sudden historical shifts when 'individualism' and its attendant corruption gives way to the discipline of the revolutionary community. . . . The narrow flame of revolution [will] cleanse the lake of Vietnamese society from the corruption and disorder of the American war. . . . It is the only way the Vietnamese of the south can restore their country and their history to themselves." Beneath Miss FitzGerald's ostensibly calm and reasoned indictment of American intervention in Vietnam, her moral outrage ran "like a furious undercurrent," as Robert Friedman observed in *Esquire*. Friedman pointed out that the central theme of *Fire in the Lake*—a theme that would recur in her subsequent work—was the failure of American intelligence in both the espionage and common meanings of the word.

Within days of its publication, *Fire in the Lake* went into a second printing. Attempting to explain the book's immediate great popularity, Michael Mok in *Publishers Weekly* (October 16, 1972) proffered the suggestion that it somehow managed "to get under the skin of this ugly war which has left so many Americans feeling bewildered and morally bankrupt." Others cited Miss FitzGerald's originality, compassion, and ability to deliver the results of hard research with a style that often bordered on poetry in its use of Taoist symbolism. "If Americans read only one book to understand what we have done to the Vietnamese and to ourselves," Arthur M. Schlesinger Jr. said, "let it be this one." Some purists quibbled over points of Miss FitzGerald's scholarship, but the overwhelming majority of reviewers credited her with achieving what she had set out to write—not an academic tome but a book that would be readable as well as profound. In addition to the Pulitzer Prize for general nonfiction, which was shared with Robert Coles (the author of *Children of Crisis*), *Fire in the Lake* won a Front Page award, a National Institute for Arts and Letters award, a National Book Award, a Sidney Hillman award, and the Bancroft Prize.

After completing *Fire in the Lake*, Miss FitzGerald devoted an increased amount of her time and energy to antiwar activism, organizing in New York City for Senator George S. McGovern, the Democratic presidential peace candidate in 1972, and speaking tirelessly around the country in behalf of the Indochina Peace Committee. On assignment for the *New Yorker*, she reported from Cuba (in 1973) and North Vietnam (in 1974, the year before the war ended). In 1974, with the help of her father's former boss at the CIA, Richard Helms, then the ambassador to Tehran, she interviewed the top government officials in Iran and wrote for *Harper's* a prescient article describing the Shah's narrow base of support and predicting his fall. That article brought Miss FitzGerald her second Overseas Press Club award.

As "a way of going at the American idea of self," Miss FitzGerald in *America Revised* (Little, Brown, 1979) surveyed United States history as it has been presented, and distorted, in textbooks for schoolchildren from Noah Webster's day to the present. While the textbooks of the nineteenth century were rabidly opinionated and biased (in one, typically, Spanish colonists were described as "naturally weak and effeminate"), they were often energetically and excitingly written, and they reflected and helped to shape a national consensus. A high percentage of American children during the early decades of the twentieth century learned American history from a single book, David Saville Muzzey's idiosyncratic *American History*, which was written by Muzzey with an attractive "tone of self-assurance, his assumption of his own legitimacy in the American tradition."

Now, Miss FitzGerald pointed out, publishers race every several years to come out with new textbooks in accordance with changing social and political needs and prejudices. Usually written, at least in effect, by committees with an eye to pleasing or at least not offending a wide spectrum of special interest groups, from minorities to the Moral Majority and the military-industrial complex, they tend to be reductionistic and dull. Although they are more concerned with such problems as discrimination, poverty, and unemployment than the texts of yore, they approach the problems from a peculiar "natural disaster" premise, presenting them for solution by everyone without ascribing blame to anyone. Afraid to describe the dynamics of conflict, they resort to "bland fictions" about an unreal society "without malice or stupidity, where Dick (black or white) comes home with a smiling Jane to a nice house in the suburbs"—lies which are "propagated for the purpose of creating good citizens [but which] may actually achieve the opposite." In addition, these "towers of Babel" dispense a progressive ethics that is detached from heritage. "The textbooks' naiveté about child psychology is matched only by their lack of respect for history . . . ," Miss FitzGerald observed. "Since the progressive era, those responsible for the majority of American-history texts have been paying mere lip service to the truism that one must know history in order to understand the present and the future."

The "pious and upbeat" histories of Muzzey and his predecessors were flawed by male WASP chauvinism, but, according to Miss FitzGerald, they did not assume "that students have the psychology of laboratory pigeons," and they constituted a "familiar tapestry" that offered a semblance of common history, common culture, and common values. That tapestry "has been ripped apart and converted into a glum, pluralistic patchwork" suggesting to children "that the center cannot, and should not, hold." To present problems to the young not only dishonestly—that has always been true to some degree—but also with no appeal to imagination and emotion and without the resource of accumulated wisdom is, in her opinion, to invite or reinforce cynicism, apathy, and despair.

In a summary and assessment of *America Revised* in *American Heritage* (December 1979), Bernard Weisberger described Miss FitzGerald's habitual strength as "cultural anatomy—the careful dissection of the webs of habit and belief that hold a people together" and that book in particular as "an X-ray of American culture that is not to be missed by anyone seriously interested in our national future or our past." Other reviewers remarked Miss FitzGerald's wit, inspired research, and "characteristic incisive gaze and trenchant turn of phrase."

When teaching a class in journalism at the University of California, Berkeley, in 1978, Miss FitzGerald became interested in the homosexual community in the San Francisco neighborhood called "the Castro," after Castro Street. A year later, while lecturing at Lynchburg College in Virginia, she visited the Liberty Baptist church in Lynchburg, the home parish of Jerry Falwell, the fundamentalist founder of the Moral Majority and one of the most articulate spokesmen of the religious right. After writing magazine articles on the Castro and on Falwell's church, she looked for other recently developed communities exemplifying "cultural differences in the white middle class" and serving to illuminate "some of the changes that had taken place" in the larger society in the 1960s and 1970s. She found such enclaves in Sun City, an all-adult retirement community in Florida, and the Rajneeshpuram, a controversial "New Age" commune in Oregon. (The commune, led by an eccentric renegade guru from India and populated by many American ex-professionals, commandeered the town of Antelope in the early 1980s and was trying to take over the government of Wasco County when federal and state prosecutors put it out of business.)

Miss FitzGerald reported on the four communities in *Cities on a Hill: A Journey Through Contemporary American Cultures* (Simon & Schuster, 1986), the title of which is an allusion to John Winthrop's admonition to his Puritan company crossing the Atlantic to found the Massachusetts Bay Colony: "We must consider that we shall be a City Upon a Hill; the eyes of all people are upon us." Examining each of the groups in turn and finally in historical context, she saw them as coming "out of the same impulse in American life, the impulse to cut all ties," to reinvent ourselves. All believed that they could start over, embark on a new life without reference to the old, and in so doing lay the groundwork for transforming the wider society. Some critics thought that her effort at historical connections was strained, especially the connection to such spiritual frontier groups as the utopian communities of the 1830s, but even those critics admired her "stylish brashness." "While FitzGerald bends the evidence to fit her thesis," the reviewer for *Publishers Weekly* (August 15, 1986) wrote, "her report brilliantly succeeds in getting inside the minds of these communities."

Frances FitzGerald is five feet nine inches tall and has blond hair, green eyes, a soft voice, and aristocratic bearing. Although self-assured, she is modest in manner, sometimes to the point of seeming shy or diffident. Her mastery of foreign languages extends to considerable German and a little Greek. Although not a natural athlete, she has over the years regularly worked out in gyms and enjoyed swimming and scuba diving, among other physical activities. Her taste in music ranges from Broadway musicals to Shubert *Lieder*, and her favorite reading includes history and Victorian novels. She often spends holidays and vacations in a family cottage in Maine.

The walls of Miss FitzGerald's Manhattan apartment are lined with books, seashells, and Koranic verses in Persian and Arabic calligraphy, there are Oriental rugs on the floor, and some choice Oriental art objects are positioned here and there. Frugal and self-reliant, she lives very simply by the standards of her class, preferring to clean her apartment herself, to take public transportation, and to forego expensive couture and coiffure.

She has had numerous discreet romantic liaisons over the years, but has never married. Friends have described her as "a driven woman," who "can party" but "always goes home to her typewriter." "I work very hard," her colleague in journalism Gloria Emerson told Judith Viorst in an interview for *Redbook* (March 1975), "but it's nothing compared to how Frankie works." According to Miss Emerson, "Sloth is worse than syphilis [to her]. There is nothing voluptuous, nothing indulgent about her. She's never let the curse or a headache keep her from doing her duty." Miss FitzGerald herself told an interviewer for *Vogue* (February 1979): "Your life is only improved by being able to think about

subjects, or to do something, yourself." Pamela Peabody, the wife of Frankie's uncle Mike, produced a documentary on Miss FitzGerald, her mother, and her grandmother, *The Female Line*, which was televised by the Public Broadcasting Service in 1980.

References: Guardian p13 N 8 '72 por; N Y Post p28 Jl 21 '72 por; Newsweek 80:62 Ag 7 '72 por; People 14:62+ S 15 '80 pors; Time 100:58+ Ag 28 '72 por; Vogue 161:108+ Ja '73 pors; Washington Post B p1+ Ag 29 '72 por; Contemporary Authors 1st rev vol 41 (1979); Who's Who in America, 1986–87

Fox, Michael J.

June 9, 1961– Actor. Address: b. c/o NBC-TV, 3000 W. Alameda Ave., Burbank, Calif. 91523

Endowed with the same energy and drive that his characters display on the screen, Michael J. Fox has achieved the distinction of starring simultaneously in the top-grossing film of 1985, *Back to the Future*, and in the second-most-popular situation comedy of the mid-1980s, *Family Ties*, for which he received Emmy awards in 1986 and 1987. Demonstrating "an incredible comic sensibility," "agile timing," and "infallible charm," in the words of various admiring critics, he continues to attract large audiences, even in mediocre films. Once aiming no higher than supporting roles, the quondam short and chubby youth has been transformed into a teeny-bopper's sex symbol.

Noting Fox's "large, expressive face and . . . wise guy's élan," Paul Attanasio of the *Washington Post* (July 3, 1985) praised his ability to "modulate" his "big TV-style delivery" in film roles "while making use of the shortcuts that TV teaches, that way of conveying a character in a few broad strokes." According to Lloyd Sachs of the *Chicago Sun-Times*, (February 8, 1987), Michael J. Fox, Tom Cruise, and Matthew Broderick are prototypes of the "more clean-cut, value-oriented young leading man" that has reemerged in the 1980s in the wake of the ascendancy of the "brat pack." The director Paul Schrader believes that Fox is shooting for "a career in the direction of . . . Jimmy Stewart, primarily light comedy but turning to heavier fare if the situation is just right." The initial "J" in Fox's show business name is a gesture he made in honor of Michael J. Pollard, a character actor whom he much admires.

Michael Andrew Fox was born on June 9, 1961, in Edmonton, Alberta, Canada, the fourth of five children of Bill Fox, a retired veteran of the Canadian army who later served fifteen years with the Edmonton police, and Phyllis Fox, a payroll clerk whom her famous son describes as a "5-foot-2, round and sexy Irish lady." "My parents are their best friends in the world," Fox told Mark Morrison of *Rolling Stone* (March 12, 1987), in describing their relationship ("always together—an unmovable force") as a crucial aspect of his happy childhood. His humor is homegrown too, as he observed in the *Rolling Stone* interview. "The oldest form of theater is the [family] dinner table. It's got five or six people, new show every night, . . . same players. Good ensemble; the people have worked together a lot."

Because he often had to relocate with his family before he reached the fifth grade, when the Foxes moved to Burnaby, a suburb of Vancouver, Fox had to learn to adapt to new environments quickly. His flair for changing "negative attention . . . into positive attention" appeared each time that "the New Short Kid" metamorphosed into "Funny Mike or Smart Mike." Fox aspired to become a hockey player, a graphic artist, or a writer in his quest for a career "that didn't have any rules," as he once put it. Although Fox was a good student through junior high school and was elected class president in the ninth grade, his mother often expressed concern because her son was "so small and crazy." But his grandmother always prophesied, "Don't worry, he'll get through it, and then he'll be famous someday."

At the age of fourteen Michael J. Fox played guitar in a rock band called the Helix, which specialized in the performance of songs by Bachman Turner Overdrive and other well-known Canadian bands. The Helix had such a strong Canadian identity that a maple leaf was painted on Fox's guitar. With typical self-deprecating humor, Fox admitted to Lloyd Sachs that he "was in a band mainly to get girls."

Michael J. Fox's theatrical career grew out of a course in drama that he took in high school, when his teacher, Ross Jones, who had received a casting notice for the Canadian Broadcasting Corporation's sitcom Leo and Me, suggested that he audition for it. Although his role was originally intended for a ten-, eleven-, or twelve-year-old, the members of the casting staff were charmed by the cleverness and drive of the diminutive Michael J. Fox, who was sixteen at the time. "When he came in, I swear the air changed," CBC casting director Heather Jones recalled for Stephen Godfrey of the Toronto Globe and Mail (June 20, 1987). "He could make saying his name funny. He wasn't intimidated by the studio, and he was as natural on camera as off." Since he was committed to playing the lead in the school production of Rumpelstiltskin on the same day that call-backs were held for the CBC, Fox considered giving up his first professional opportunity, but "the CBC changed their schedule to suit him," as Ross Jones told Stephen Godfrey.

First telecast in October 1978 in British Columbia, Leo and Me starred Brent Carver as an Italian playboy responsible for rearing his orphaned nephew, Jamie, who was played by "Mike Fox." During the series of twelve shows, Fox's rapid physical development necessitated changes in the presentation of Jamie. As described by Stephen Godfrey, the early episodes of Leo and Me presented Fox as "barely five feet tall" and as "encased in baby fat," sporting a "pageboy haircut and a high, unbroken voice." Jamie experienced the onset of puberty in front of the camera, growing from a "cute and endearing" child to a teenager who competes with his uncle in a disco contest.

After admiring a production at the Vancouver Arts Club theatre, Fox persuaded its director to cast him in a serious play. And so it happened that at the age of seventeen, he made his professional stage debut in The Shadow Box, Michael Cristofer's grim drama about a hospice for the terminally ill. As the fourteen-year-old Steve, Fox continued his pattern of playing characters younger than his own chronological age. The artistic director Bill Millerd remembers him as "a natural" who was "focused" and "always knew what he wanted to do." For Fox, the experience proved to be magical. "I felt like I had found God," he recalled during his Chicago Tribune interview.

With acting jobs taking up much of his time, Fox began to skip school so often that he even failed his beloved drama class, and one of his exasperated teachers warned him that he was "not going to be cute forever." But Maureen Stapleton and Art Carney, who played his parents in the Paramount Television movie Letters From Frank (1979), encouraged Fox to seek new outlets for his theatrical ambitions. At seventeen, in 1979, Fox dropped out of high school during the twelfth grade, and moved to Los Angeles. His early assignments there included the Disney film Midnight Madness (1980), a forgettable college comedy about a scavenger hunt; guest appearances on television programs, such as Lou Grant and Trapper John, M.D., and a supporting role in Class of 84 (1981), a Canadian Blackboard Jungle remake about drug and vice rackets that the Motion Picture Guide described as a "sadistic, humiliating production" and that Fox concedes may be "possibly one of the worst films of all times . . . violent and depressing."

Cast as a young racial bigot in Alex Haley's Palmerstown, U.S.A., a dramatic series that had a run of seven episodes on CBS-TV in 1980, Fox began to live beyond his means, squandering his entire income of perhaps $60,000. "I was an idiot, trying to paint this picture in my head of [a] young successful guy," Fox disclosed during his Rolling Stone interview. His lack of self-discipline also led to a weight problem. By working steadily and eating steadily he found himself carrying 140 pounds on what was then a mere 5-foot frame, so that he began to look like "a pasta salesman," as he once put it.

Dieting assistance came unexpectedly when Palmerstown, U.S.A. was canceled. As much as $35,000 in debt, Fox had to live on macaroni and cheese and was forced to sell off a sectional couch piece by piece to raise money for his everyday expenses. "My phone suddenly stopped ringing," he told a reporter for People (August 12, 1985). "I'm sure it happens to every actor, but I'd never planned for it." According to Fox, his phone had been disconnected and he was using a pay phone outside a Pioneer Chicken store when he learned that NBC's Family Ties was casting the role of Alex P. Keaton in 1982. "I was on the phone with my agent, saying it had to be so many thousand per week, wishing I just had $1.99 to go in and buy chicken and biscuits," he has recalled.

His first audition failed to impress Family Ties producer Gary David Goldberg, who perceived him as "too self-assured, too arrogant . . . [not] enough of a kid," but the casting director, Judith Weiner, urged that Fox be given another chance. Once he had chosen Fox, Goldberg then had to sell the casting decision to the network. The NBC executive Brandon Tartikoff reportedly said "The kid's good, but can you see his face on a lunch box?" But Fox turned out to be the key ingredient in a hit series. Originally centered on Michael Gross and Meredith Baxter-Birney as 1960s activists turned upper-middle-class parents, Family Ties began to emphasize Alex P. Keaton because of audience reactions, particularly after the third episode in which Alex ran the household while the parents were away. "Without Fox, we wouldn't be on the air," Goldberg admitted to TV Guide's Al Martinez (April 14, 1984).

Scheduled in a time slot that followed the top-rated Cosby Show on Thursday nights, Family Ties rose to second place in the all-powerful Nielsen ratings. Citing Alex and his father as characters "so real that they transcend the medium and turn the sitcom dross into the gold of real drama," Benjamin J. Stein of the Wall Street Journal (December 12, 1983) welcomed the show as a throwback to the "golden age" of television comedies like Ozzie and Harriet, The Mary Tyler Moore Show, and All in the Family in which the personalities of "rich, highly textured characters" are "the engines that [drive] the plot."

During his first two season breaks from Family Ties, Fox appeared in the television movies Poison Ivy and High School USA. Set in a Maine summer camp, Poison Ivy (NBC, 1985) starred Fox as Dennis Baxter, a girl-crazy counselor who falls in love with the camp's assistant nurse, Rhonda (Nancy McKeon). The simplicity, innocuousness, and prankishness of Poison Ivy also characterized High School USA, an NBC potential pilot about a midwestern high school. When he was offered a role in John Hughes's Pretty and Pink, Fox had to decline in order to film the two-hour 1985 season opening segment of Family Ties.

When Steven Spielberg first considered Michael J. Fox for Bob Zemeckis' Back to the Future (1985) and Fox was unable to fit the film into his schedule, Spielberg cast Eric Stoltz of Mask instead, but discovered after five weeks of shooting that Stoltz was "too intense for the comedy." Goldberg agreed to let Fox moonlight on Back to the Future during the Family Ties season, launching seven exhausting weeks in which Fox played Alex on Family Ties from breakfast until dinner, then transformed himself into Marty McFly of Back to the Future until 2:30 A.M. "I found myself dealing with three personalities, and mine got the worst of it," Fox has recalled of that ordeal, because to salvage as much footage as possible from the previous weeks of shooting, Fox had to perform scenes from the exact places where Stoltz had stood. When the film was completed, Fox worried about its reception. "There's never been a Spielberg flop, and God, Lord, don't let it be my movie," he confided to Robert Basler of the Washington Post (July 21, 1985). But far from being a flop, Back to the Future beat Rambo as the top-grossing film of 1985, taking in $200 million at the box office.

Filmed before Back to the Future but released shortly afterwards to capitalize on the blockbuster's success, Teen Wolf (1985) earned $40 million, proving to producers that Fox's drawing power helped even movies of minor significance. In it, Fox starred as Scott Howard, a high school student who inherits werewolf genes from his father and who becomes a sports hero when his lupine characteristics improve his basketball playing. When

he reviewed Teen Wolf in Newsweek (August 23, 1985), Bill Kaufman rated Michael J. Fox "perfect as the teen wolf," and applauded his "youthful vigor." For a brief period in 1986, Fox considered appearing in a biographical film about James Cagney, after Cagney's manager informed him that the veteran actor wanted Fox to play him. But the Cagney scripts that Fox had read so far were not only poorly plotted but also portrayed the man as "Saint Jimmy," as he put it. "Maybe it's best just to leave our relationship the way it is—me admiring him and not trying to play him," he has said.

Extending his range, Fox appeared as Joe Rasnick in Paul Schrader's Light of Day (1987), a musical drama about tensions within a working-class family and its son and daughter's rock band. Torn between his feuding mother (Gena Rowlands) and his sister (Joan Jett), Rasnick plays the secondary but crucial role of maintaining the band and acting as a mediator. According to Schrader, Fox's part was essentially difficult because it required an actor "who could be in the center" and "in just about every scene" without receiving much attention, yet "still be sympathetic, not look like a wimp." Although Light of Day at first rode high on the crest of Fox's popularity, it eventually failed, both at the box office and in the opinion of critics. David Ansen of Newsweek (February 9, 1987) found "the smooth-mannered Fox and the rough-hewn Jett" to be "unlikely siblings," with "accents . . . from opposite sides of the town, if not the country." But Brian D. Johnson of the Canadian weekly Maclean's (February 9, 1987) liked Fox's "grit," "strength and conviction" justaposed with "moments . . . when the good natured magnanimity of his Family Ties character shines through." Janet Maslin predicted in the New York Times (February 6, 1987) "that he will be well suited to dramatic roles when the right one comes along."

Returning to light comedy in The Secret of My Success, a 1987 release directed by Herbert Ross, Fox played Brantley Foster, a Kansan just out of college who rises quickly from the mailroom to the boardroom by taking advantage of interoffice memos that suggest hidden opportunities amidst the disarray of bureaucracy. Bedroom farce is added to the corporate climbing when Foster is seduced by the wife of his boss (who happens to be his uncle) and when he falls in love with his uncle's mistress. Ross cites Fox's personality as a key factor in the success of the film, which jumped to number one at the box office when it was released. "It's impossible to perceive him in a negative light," Ross explained to Paula Span of the Washington Post (April 9, 1987). "Any other actor might be seen as a hustler; Michael can overcome that and imbue the character with all kinds of good qualities."

In Fox's next film, Bright Lights, Big City, an adaptation of Jay McInerney's best-selling first novel, Fox plays the protagonist, an alienated magazine fact checker at a magazine that resembles the New Yorker, who spends his nights club-hopping in a cocaine-induced fog. Shooting began in April 1987, under the direction of Joyce Chopra. A self-described "director groupie" who teaches himself film technique by watching videotapes of classic movies, Fox plans to direct a film for Steven Spielberg in the near future. The Spielberg offer came in response to a short film, *The Iceman Hummeth*, a satire of hockey violence directed by Fox for David Letterman's celebrity film festival in December 1986. Noting the sequence of *The Iceman Hummeth*, in which his character "beat[s] up some pretty big guys," Fox observed that enjoyment of the directorial power to "create [one's] own little fantasy and control everything involved in it" may reflect "one's insecurities."

In addition to his film work and *Family Ties*, Fox can be seen in a popular Pepsi commercial for which he reportedly received "seven figures." His price per film now exceeds $1.5 million, and his *Family Ties* salary has increased to $35,000 per episode. Despite his success, Fox believes that his family will keep him from developing a star-sized ego. "If I went home and started any of that, there would be a lawn mower in front of me before you could blink," he has said. Fox often telephones his parents and leaves California regularly to visit the Canadian home that he helped them to buy.

Sandy-haired Michael J. Fox stands five-foot-four inches tall and weights about 120 pounds. Because he is a heavy smoker, he asks not to be photographed smoking to avoid becoming a negative role model for his younger fans. Although the media have reported romantic links between Fox and several women, including the actress Nancy McKeon, whom he dated for over two years, Fox refuses to discuss details of his private life. "Once you let the public into your relationships . . . people get hurt. Genuine feelings are involved, real emotional investments," Fox once explained to an interviewer. He expects to marry "right before [becoming] fat and bald" and, always the gentleman, qualifies his desire for three or four kids: "I know it's easy for the guy to say and if I could have a couple of them for her, I would."

References: *Chicago Sun-Times* p5+ F 8 '87 pors; *Chicago Tribune* XIII p4+ Je 8 '86 pors; *GQ* 56.227+ D '86 pors; *Maclean's* 100:40+ F 9 '87 pors; *N Y Daily News City Lights* p23 Jl 20 '86; *Newsweek* 59:76+ My 11 '87; *People* 24:82+ Ag 12 '85 por, 24:86+ D 23 '85 por, 24:87+ Ap 20 '87 pors; *Rolling Stone* p31+ Mr 12 '87 pors; *Seventeen* 45:90+ Jl '86; *Teen* 29:57+ Ag '85; *Toronto Globe and Mail* C p1 Je 20 '87 pors; *TV Guide* 35:12+ Mr 7 '87 pors; *USA Weekend* p4+ F 20 '87; *Washington Post* C p1+ Ap 9 '87 por; *Contemporary Newsmakers* (1986) por

Frankel, Max

Apr. 3, 1930– Journalist. Address: b. *New York Times*, 229 W. 43d St., New York City, N. Y. 10036

Since November 1986 the Pulitzer Prize-winning journalist Max Frankel has been executive editor of the influential *New York Times*, generally acknowledged to be the quality newspaper in New York City and the newspaper of record in the United States. A career-long *Times* man, Frankel began with the paper as a campus stringer at Columbia University in the early 1950s and went on to become full-time reporter, foreign correspondent, chief Washington correspondent, Washington bureau chief, Sunday editor, and editorial page editor. His current appointment was reported to be popular with most of the *Times's* 750 reporters and editors, some of whom were said to be relieved when the brilliant but more authoritarian A. M. ("Abe") Rosenthal, Frankel's predecessor in the post, made no attempt to remain beyond his statutory retirement. As the New York correspondent for the British publication the *Economist* observed at the time, in appointing Frankel, Arthur Ochs ("Punch") Sulzberger, the *Times's* publisher, was "opting for continuity and integrity and perhaps a little less abrasiveness." Frankel himself announced, "From this moment on . . . I have no editorial opinions," but some observers, noting what they perceived to be a recent incipient

"neoconservative" tendency in the coverage of news and cultural events in the *Times*, hoped that Frankel would nudge the paper back to the center. In July 1987 Harrison Salisbury, the retired *Times* editor, credited Frankel with introducing "a more benign and gracious manner of running the paper."

Max Frankel was born to Jacob A. and Mary (Katz) Frankel in Gera, Germany, on April 3, 1930. In 1938 the Frankels, forced to leave Nazi Germany, crossed over into the Soviet Union. According to a profile of Frankel in *Time* (October 20, 1986), Jacob Frankel was arrested by the Soviets on suspicion of being a German spy and was given the choice of Soviet citizenship or a sentence to hard labor in Siberia. Because the intention of the family was to reach the United States, he refused the offer of citizenship and was sent to Siberia. He would not be reunited with his wife and son until World War II was over.

Obtaining exit visas from the Soviet Union, Mary Frankel and her son arrived in the United States in 1940. Like many other German-Jewish refugees, they settled in the Washington Heights section of New York City. As a ten-year-old in elementary school, Frankel was humiliated at being sent to the first grade to learn the rudiments of reading and spelling in English. "I was like Gulliver in those little chairs," he recalled to Barbara Matusow of the *Washington Journalism Review* (January/February 1987). "I couldn't stand it." Conscious of "what other refugee kids sounded like," and not wanting "to sound like them," he said, he was determined to lose his German accent and "be more American than anyone else."

When Jacob Frankel rejoined his family in New York City after World War II, he opened a dry-goods store in Harlem. Although the chronology seems inconsistent with Max Frankel's age at the time and his academic progress, by Barbara Matusow's account he attended junior high school in Harlem. "Max again experienced humiliation at school," she wrote. "A gang of schoolboys repeatedly stole his pens and money, but he says he was too ashamed to tell his mother. When he complained to the principal, the boys beat him up after school. Finally, he refused to go back to school, so his mother let him fake an address in order to go to a junior high in another neighborhood."

Frankel received his secondary education at the High School of Music and Art in Manhattan, where music teachers impressed with his singing voice encouraged him to seek a career in opera. He rejected the suggestion, he has explained, because "the enterprise appeared too risky" and he did not "want to wind up singing at weddings." Introduced to journalism in a course at the high school, he decided to pursue a career in that field. In 1948 he became a naturalized citizen of the United States.

As a student of journalism at Columbia University, Frankel was editor in chief of the *Columbia Daily Spectator* and campus correspondent for the *New York Times*. He spent virtually all of his free hours at the *Times*, becoming acquainted with its star reporters, whose articles he scrupulously analyzed for rhetorical technique. "If you're not a natural," he explained to Barbara Matusow, "you learn to take things apart and see how others do it." After graduating from Columbia with a B.A. degree and Phi Beta Kappa key in 1952, Frankel went on to take an M.A. degree in American government at the university in 1953.

Frankel was hired as a full-time reporter for the *Times* in 1952. After serving in the United States Army from 1953 to 1955, he returned to the newspaper as a rewrite man and reporter. On the night rewrite desk in 1956, he scored a minor coup with his quick but impressive job on the sinking of the ocean liner *Andrea Doria*. Later in 1956 he was sent to Europe to cover the Hungarian and Polish rebellions. Among his dispatches as a member of the *Times*'s Moscow bureau from 1957 to 1960 was a series of colorful articles on Siberia that were described in the Soviet government newspaper *Izvestia* as coming "quite close to objectivity." After returning to the Western Hemisphere, he covered the United Nations and the Caribbean area, including Cuba, for a year.

In 1961 Frankel was assigned to the *Times*'s Washington bureau as diplomatic correspondent, a position in which he won the Overseas Press Club Award for foreign reporting (1965). In 1963, when he threatened to leave the *Times* to become a columnist for the New York *Herald Tribune*, he was induced to stay by a large raise and the title of chief correspondent. According to Gay Talese in his book *The Kingdom and the Power* (1969), Frankel almost quit the *Times* again in 1964, when Tom Wicker rather than he was named to succeed James Reston as the Washington bureau chief. Frankel told Barbara Matusow, however, that he had been considering an attractive offer from the *Reporter* magazine before the Wicker appointment and that the appeal of the offer was reinforced by his discontent over certain conditions at the *Times*. "I felt boxed in in terms of straight coverage," he said. "I had no scope for my analytic skills. And the copy desk was murderous. Every morning there would be a battle over some [wrong] thing they had written in or taken out." Frankel issued a much more serious resignation threat in 1968, when James Greenfield, an outsider, was being considered to succeed Tom Wicker as bureau chief when Wicker moved to New York as an associate editor. In the end, Frankel was chosen to succeed Wicker.

As chief of the Washington bureau, Frankel paid more attention to bureau management than his immediate predecessors, in addition to writing his analyses of Washington and foreign affairs. In the latter category he won the George Polk Memorial Award for "best daily newspaper or wire service interpretation" in 1970, and the following year he received the Raymond Clapper Memorial Award for "exceptionally meritorious" Washington correspondence. In 1972 he accompanied President Richard Nixon on his historic trip to China, filing twenty-four stories that brought him the 1973 Pulitzer Prize for international reporting.

In an article published in *Commentary* (March 1971), Daniel Patrick Moynihan (now a United States senator), a former adviser to President Nixon and a friend of Frankel's, charged that an "Ivy League" press was setting standards for presidential performance too high for any president to live up to and that therefore threatened effective government. In a fifteen-page, single-spaced letter to Moynihan, Frankel replied that the problem was created not by the unrealistic expectations of journalists but by "the habit of regular deception in our politics and administration . . . the damnable tendency toward manipulation that forces us so often into the posture of apparent adversaries."

In Washington, Frankel was close to many high government officials, especially Henry A. Kissinger, who was then secretary of state, but he resisted Kissinger's efforts to persuade him to suppress coverage of such events as the resumed American bombing of North Vietnam. When, in 1972, some of his superiors and their lawyers at the Times balked at publication of the Pentagon Papers, the purloined Defense Department documents revealing the secret history of United States involvement in the Vietnam war, Frankel wrote a cogent memorandum that helped to change their minds. In the Times's subsequent successful defense of its publication of the papers before the United States Supreme Court, Frankel's memo was an important affidavit.

In contrast to its expeditious publication of the Pentagon Papers, the Times lagged conspicuously behind the Washington Post in its coverage of the Nixon administration's Watergate scandal in 1972. At that time Frankel was preoccupied with preparing for his transit back to New York as editor of the Times's Sunday edition, the bulkiest (weighing almost five pounds and numbering about 450 pages) journalistic product on earth, demanding a full day's attention from the dedicated reader. When Frankel took it over early in 1973, the Sunday edition had a circulation of 1.4 million and accounted for approximately half of the 78 million lines of advertising sold annually by the Times, at a rate 60 percent higher than the weekday and Saturday editions. As the Sunday editor, he had control of all sections—including the Book Review, the Magazine, and the Arts and Leisure and Travel and Resorts sections—except the front news section, which was then, along with the weekday and Saturday editions, the responsibility of the news department.

Frankel restyled and enlivened the Sunday edition, and he did the same to the editorial and Op-Ed pages after he became editorial page editor in 1977, following the unification of the news and Sunday departments. With Frankel's lighter, more pragmatic touch, the opinion pages became less doctrinaire than they had been under his predecessor, John B. Oakes, a passionate and predictable liberal on a gamut of issues. When Frankel made sweeping staff changes, those affected nicknamed him and his deputy, Jack Rosenthal, "Max the Axe" and "Jack the Knife," even though many close observers traced the action upstairs, to Punch Sulzberger. In the house organ Times Talk (February 1987), Jack Rosenthal recounted how, as the nightly editorial deadline approached, Frankel "would become ever calmer" while editing a piece, but if there was time enough "he'd press the author to read it over and over, looking for ways to tighten

or improve." His "ingenious" mind could not "let go of a problem," but instead "kept turning, almost always producing a solution." If an editorial board member gave him an argument, however, he was likely to relent and say, "I'm not convinced, but go ahead and try it."

Under the autocratic seventeen-year executive editorship of Abe Rosenthal (no relation to Jack) the once staid and money-losing New York Times acquired a more contemporary format and style and a wider variety of sections, covering virtually all aspects of local, national, and international life, from science and technology to culture and fashion. Readership and advertising increased, and the newspaper went from red to upward black financially. In other words, as the correspondent for the Economist (October 18, 1986) observed, the paper was "rarely affected" by the "discontent and politicking" behind the scenes. "Mr. Rosenthal's accomplishment is due in large part to assembling a first-rate staff," the correspondent wrote. "Managing his talented stable of editors and reporters, many of them prima donnas, has not been easy. There have been defections, accompanied by accusations that he had favorites or discriminated against individuals. Staff morale has frequently been low." Later, Jonathan Alter of Newsweek (March 9, 1987) recalled how Rosenthal "ruled with such complete authority that grown men and women, reporters whose job it was to cover wars and stand up to foreign tyrants, quaked in his presence."

When, in anticipation of Rosenthal's statutory retirement at age sixty-five, Frankel was in October 1986 named to succeed him the following month, no close Times observer expected any drastic change in the paper. The common prediction was that under Frankel there would be greater equilibrium, in the relation of hard news to features (sometimes given a slight edge under Rosenthal, according to some critics), in political viewpoint (away from Rosenthal's sometimes "passionate" effort to avoid set leftist positions), and, above all, in staff management. "I would expect the paper to be a little more steady on the line," Harrison Salisbury said, as quoted in Time (October 20, 1986). "It would not dart and jab as much as Abe's paper has." In personnel relations, according to the Time report, Frankel, "a patient, low-key man," was "expected to calm the newsroom waters." The report quoted a colleague regarding Frankel: "Consensus is his middle name."

Others regard Frankel as "judicious" and "the smartest guy at the paper" as well as "generally softer than Abe" and "less harsh on people who make errors." "He has a subtle mind that sees all the shadings," Roger Wilkins, who had written editorials under Frankel, told Barbara Matusow. "If you lost an argument with him, you knew the reasons. Everything was well thought-out." The star political columnist Tom Wicker said: "I look for the paper to become more centrist under him. He is much less likely to bring his own enthusiasms and prejudices to the paper and much less likely to tolerate it in someone else." When Edwin Diamond of *New York* magazine (October 27, 1986) asked one *Times* employee how the paper would differ under Frankel, he received the reply: "Abe was the iron fist in the iron glove. Max is the iron fist in the velvet glove."

Even before his nomination as executive editor became effective, Frankel began introducing himself to everyone in every department under his jurisdiction, asking questions about their jobs, their opinions, their problems, and themselves. "My key to management," he has explained, "is precision of self-expression and a good sense about what motivates other people. . . . I try to understand what people are proud of, what they're afraid of, what makes them tick." "He's good at getting people to loosen up," one *Times* investigative reporter said in his interview with Barbara Matusow. "These gestures are having a tremendous effect. . . . People . . . feel like part of the process."

In his first general memo as executive editor, Frankel said that it was "a joy and a privilege to lead this magnificent news staff in the production of the greatest newspaper on earth," and he advised his staffers to "have fun" in their work. In staff gatherings, however, he rarely failed to stress greater efficiency as well as budgetary concerns. Believing in a two-stage managerial strategy—acquaintance with all operations, followed by retreat, to "let people do their own thing"—he reorganized the chain of command to involve people down to desk editors in decision-making.

In July 1987 it became obvious that under Frankel the *Times* would be much more accountable for its errors. In a story filed from Washington on July 10, a *Times* reporter mistakenly paraphrased Lieutenant Colonel Oliver L. North as telling a Congressional committee that President Ronald Reagan was *deliberately* kept in the dark about a Central Intelligence Agency plan to set up a secret and probably illegal fund for clandestine activities. The *Times* correction, on July 13, appeared not at the bottom of page one—previously the newspaper's most prominent spot for corrections—but at the top of the page, under a two-column headline.

Max Frankel and Tobia Brown were married on June 19, 1956. (Mrs. Frankel died on March 16, 1987.) Frankel has three children: David, Margot, and Jonathan. He lives in the Riverdale section of New York City and vacations on Fire Island. The pipe-smoking Frankel's recreations include singing, painting, punching away at his home computer, and playing tennis. "I would not call him a natural [at tennis]," his friend Daniel Schorr, the National Public Radio commentator, told Barbara Matusow of the *Washington Journalism Review,* "but he has mastered it. . . . He takes lessons. [Frankel] has never lost the sense of insecurity of coming into an alien society. He's an adapter. He learned the *Times,* its sensitivities and quirks. . . . If anything can be mastered by learning, he'll do it." Frankel has described himself as a "naturally organized" man, given to "files and lists" and unafraid of "numbers, statistics, and budgets." "I have

always been good and quick at numbers," he told Barbara Matusow.

In public Frankel usually maintains a formal demeanor, and he is a no-nonsense worker, sometimes abrupt with those under him. In private, with friends, he is, according to those who know him, fun-loving and affectionate. In his article in *Times Talk,* Jack Rosenthal noted that Frankel "hates to waste time" and to indulge in what he regards as time-wasting activities, including shopping. "When he finds shoes he likes, he buys three pair, to avoid having to do it again soon." Frankel is a member of the Council on Foreign Relations.

References: N Y Times A p1+ O 12 '86 por; New York 19:37+ O 27 '86 por; Time 107:87 Ap 19 '76 por, 128:77+ O 20 '86 por; Times Talk p1+ F '87 pors; Washington J R 9:24+ Ja/F '87 pors; Contemporary Authors vols 65–68 (1977); Catledge, Turner. My Life and The Times (1971); Talese, Gay. The Kingdom and the Power (1969); Who's Who in America, 1986–87

Friedkin, William

Aug. 29, 1939– Filmmaker. Address: c/o PMK Public Relations, 84 W. 3rd St., Los Angeles, Calif. 90048

William ("Billy") Friedkin, the director of films such as the Academy Award-winning *The French Connection* (1971), the box-office smash *The Exorcist* (1973), and his most recent hit, *To Live and Die in L.A.* (1985), is acknowledged to be one of the master technicians and most spellbinding storytellers among American filmmakers. He is also a controversial figure, who is accused of being a merciless manipulator of audiences by some, but praised by others for the visceral power of his vision of a moral zone where good and evil have become almost indistinguishable.

"There is a thin line between the policeman and the criminal," Friedkin has said. "My characters are usually in extremely pressured situations and have few alternatives. Usually their problems are self-created, or created by fate. The mystery of fate fascinates me a great deal. The way I've explored that is through the crime genre because it involves tense and pressured situations." In some less well-known films, such as *The Night They Raided Minsky's* (1968), Friedkin has exposed the lighter side of the crime genre with a sure comedic touch. Riskier explorations of his theme, in films such as *Sorcerer*, his personal favorite, and *Cruising*, which set off a bitter wave of protest in the New York gay community, brought about a decline in Friedkin's commercial and critical success in the late 1970s and early 1980s. *To Live and Die in L.A.* signaled for most observers Friedkin's return to his old form, in a milieu that he had helped to create. As *New York Times* critic Janet Maslin has noted, "Friedkin was making sleek, sensational, ice-cold thrillers long before rock videos and 'Miami Vice' were fashionable. And he couldn't be more in his element now than they are."

William Friedkin was born in Chicago, Illinois, on August 29, 1939, the only child of Louis and Rae (Green) Friedkin. His family was lower-middle class and Jewish, and his father, who died when Friedkin was in his teens, "never made more than $50 a week" at any of the various sales jobs he held, Friedkin told Michael E. Hill in an interview for the *Washington Post* (July 27, 1986). Rae Friedkin, an operating-room nurse, was "a gentling, square influence," but it was her brother-in-law, Harry Lang, who had the most lasting effect on the future director's world view. Lang was a much decorated police officer who, with his partner, brought in Frank Nitti, the gangster, with eight bullet wounds in his stomach, but Lang was later discovered to be on Nitti's payroll and was dismissed from the police department. "I still have my childhood feelings about him," Freidkin told Hill. "He was a fascinating and frightening figure."

While attending the Graham Stewart School on Chicago's North Side, Friedkin was caught stealing from Goldblatt's, a store near his home where he and his friends shoplifted regularly. He never tried to shoplift again, but, as he told Gene Siskel of the *Chicago Tribune* (March 25,1979), "virtually every young man of my generation escaped a life of crime by an act of God. A great many guys I went to grammar school with . . . have ended up doing time. They got fouled up."

As a somewhat disaffected student at Senn High School in "the pre-Sputnik period," Friedkin concentrated on developing his basketball skills, with the hope of eventually making it into the professional ranks. But he stopped growing when he was six feet tall, a height that he felt closed the door on

basketball greatness, and he trained his sights instead on a career as a muckraking journalist. He started by getting a job in the mailroom at Chicago's WGN-TV station, advanced to studio floor manager before the end of the year, and in 1956, at only seventeen, began directing television shows and documentaries.

After finishing high school by the skin of his teeth, Friedkin went on to direct over 2,000 live television shows (sometimes at a rate of five a day) and a dozen documentaries. In making the documentaries he worked closely with Bill Butler, a cameraman at WGN-TV who later became a successful Hollywood director of photography. Both men were fortunate enough to be making documentaries when the first lightweight Arriflex cameras and Nagra tape recorders were available in the United States. "The documentary influence that has pervaded all my films was really influenced by the equipment," Friedkin told Gene Siskel in an another interview for the *Chicago Tribune* (November 9, 1980). "I learned on equipment that almost begged for you to get up and move around." His first film, *The People vs. Crump*, a brief documentary made for Chicago's WBKB-TV, depicted the rehabilitation of a man on death row so persuasively that it helped to win the commutation of his sentence. The film received a Golden Gate Award at the San Francisco Film Festival in 1962. Although it was never telecast, it inspired the management of WBKB to set up a documentary unit with Friedkin in charge. Friedkin went on to direct three documentaries for the producer David L. Wolper: *The Thin Blue Line*, *The Bold Man*, and *Mayhem on a Sunday Afternoon*, all of which were aired on ABC-TV.

The other source of his training was his exposure to such film classics as *The Treasure of the Sierra Madre*, *All About Eve*, *Paths of Glory*, and, above all, *Citizen Kane*, for it was seeing *Citizen Kane* that crystallized Friedkin's ambition to become a Hollywood director. Still considering it "the best-made film" he has ever seen, he describes it and his other favorites as "subversive" films that "shatter our best-held illusions, films that get behind human nature" to reveal a kind of central hypocrisy, "the foremost element in human behavior that continues to impress itself" on Friedkin.

Aware that the golden age of live television and of ready opportunities to "do first-rate drama or documentary work" was coming to an end, Friedkin left television in 1966 and was soon hired by the Hollywood movie producer Steve Broidy to direct a film starring the pop music duo Sonny and Cher. Entitled *Good Times* (Columbia, 1967), the film, closely if zanily modeled on Sonny and Cher's actual situation as rising stars, lent itself to Friedkin's documentary approach, with its quick cuts, psychedelic lights, instant costume changes, and reverse negative exposures. Such technical trickery stretched the flimsy plot to its utmost and enveloped *Good Times*, which became a box-office "sleeper" hit, in an aura of pop art.

In his next film, *The Night They Raided Minsky's* (1968), Friedkin established several practices that he would follow for most of his career: he based the film on a real event, did his shooting on location, and, to make every detail authentic, conducted research that included the interrogation of some of the survivors of that historic occasion. The film provided a lighter aspect of Friedkin's obsession with crime, the police, and "all the moral values in the spectrum."

The event that inspired *The Night They Raided Minsky's* was a raid in 1925 on a burlesque house run by the four Minsky brothers in New York City. Morton Minsky, one of the Minsky *frères,* acted as a consultant to Friedkin. The completed film confirmed Friedkin's status as a directorial wunderkind. One critic wrote in *Newsweek* (December 30, 1968) that "Friedkin does some really marvelous things with the cast," which included Jason Robards, Britt Ekland, and Bert Lahr (in a cameo appearance). William Wolf of *Cue* magazine (December 28, 1968) marveled at the fact that "through inspired direction not often associated with a comedy of this genre, Friedkin mixes the proper proportions of horseplay, atmosphere, and character for maximum enjoyment. His blend of black-and-white and color sequences, bridging actual bygone scenes and his simulated ones, is masterful." Friedkin himself, who called the film his "apprenticeship," discovered that in working with veteran show business professionals he had to try to get his effects without pushing and that the actors always seemed to be testing him. " I blow a lot of takes," he has explained. "And it all works against me."

Friedkin next took on a greater challenge by turning his attention to *The Birthday Party,* an early absurdist work by his favorite playwright, Harold Pinter, obtaining the film rights as well as a screenplay from Pinter after months of negotiations. Like the play, the film charts the mental disintegration of Stanley, the lone guest at a seaside hotel who finds himself menaced by two newly arrived and sinister guests who accuse him of having betrayed "the Organization" and finally take him away. The film was released in late 1968 to mixed reviews. A number of critics complained that it had not attained "a life of its own," but Derek Malcolm, writing in the *Guardian* (February 12, 1970), praised it for "enclosing us in Pinter's most menacing waking nightmare more completely than a stage production ever could."

Turning to another film adaptation of a play, Friedkin next directed *The Boys in the Band* (1970), based on the play of the same name by Mart Crowley, who also produced the movie. Shot on location in New York with its original stage cast, the film centers on a group of gay men at a birthday party that begins with bitchy levity and ends with bleak self-confrontation. While some gay organizations later criticized the film's portrayal of its characters, Friedkin maintained that the move "is not about the gay world but about human problems." In *New York* magazine (October 25, 1971) Judith Crist discerned in *The Boys in the Band* the latest stage in Friedkin's "steadily developing artistry and . . . versatility."

William Friedkin moved from admired precocity to acknowledged mastery with his next film, *The French Connection* (1971). The movie was based on an actual narcotics case in which a huge international heroin deal was uncovered by two New York detectives, Eddie Fagan and Sonny Grosso, both of whom had small roles in the movie and acted as consultants. Friedkin shot most of *The French Connection* in blighted areas of New York City. Against that backdrop, the action unfolds at a breakneck pace. In the most acclaimed sequence, "Popeye" Doyle, played by Gene Hackman, commandeers an automobile and sets off through crowded streets to chase an elevated subway train that is being terrorized by a gunman. Friedkin has said that he created the scene not only to bring the movie to a climax but to convey the essence of the "obsessive, self-righteous, driving, driven" Popeye Doyle. The parallels and contrasts that Friedkin drew between the hard-bitten Doyle and the elegant Frenchman who masterminds the drug deal evoked high marks from critics for portraying the characters as virtually mirror images of each other. Writing in the *New York Times* (November 21, 1971), Stephen Farber further noted the "salient ironic fact that [the sociological situation of] the underpaid cop . . . defending law and order for the privileged and complacent" is brought out clearly by the contrast between "Popeye's pathetic existence and the high-style living enjoyed by the gangsters."

The sheer velocity of *The French Connection* left so many interpretations churning in its wake that Friedkin made a point of insisting for the benefit of would-be exegetes, "I'm not a thinker. I'm making commercial films." At the end of the year the film won five Academy Awards, for best director, best picture, best actor, best screenplay based on another medium, and best editing. It was also nominated for best sound and best cinematography.

Fresh from his *French Connection* triumph, Friedkin was asked by William Peter Blatty, the author of the 1971 best seller *The Exorcist,* to direct the film version. Blatty's novel was based on an exorcism in Georgetown, Maryland, in 1949—the last time that the rite was sanctioned by the Roman Catholic Church in the United States. It "took hold of me," Friedkin has said, "I became physically ill. I was amazed at the power this thing had." He abandoned plans for a vacation and for a lecture tour, researched his subject for a year, hired two Jesuit priests as his advisers, and began shooting *The Exorcist* on August 14, 1972. Its filming was plagued by many disruptions, including injuries, illnesses, one death among the actors, and the loss of an entire set in a fire. As a result, *The Exorcist* took sixteen months to complete, ran millions of dollars over budget, and left Friedkin wondering if it had been "jinxed."

Such fears were quickly dispelled when *The Exorcist* finally opened in December 1973 and earned $5 million in its first three weeks. In New York City the crowds broke all attendance records and waited for hours in subfreezing cold to see the film, while scalpers hawked tickets for more than three times their face value. By February 1974 *The Exorcist* was grossing about $2 million a week at thirty theatres across the United States, and it eventually earned over $84 million in the United States alone.

The film's many graphic sequences, including scenes in which the central character, a young girl possessed by the devil, undergoes grotesque metamorphoses, vomits green fluids, and masturbates with a bloody crucifix, forced audiences, as Foster Hirsch reported in the *New York Times* (May 5, 1974), to "respond exactly the way Friedkin wants [them] to, with a series of escalating shudders, moans, gasps, and shrieks. His pacing is expert: when Friedkin lets up for a minute or two, [audiences] relax with great explosive sighs." Newspaper reports about fainting spells, seizures of vomiting, and even flight from the theatre by less hardy members of the audience only lengthened the lines that formed outside movie theatres, and one Brazilian policeman was reportedly shot in the leg while trying to control an impatient crowd.

Critical and institutional response to what one journalist called "the Exorcist cult" ranged from approval to condemnation. Joseph Gelmis of *Newsday* adjudged *The Exorcist* to be "one of the most terrifying horror movies ever made" and in *Newsweek* its religion editor, Kenneth L. Woodward, wrote that "at a time of moral confusion among sophisticates . . . [The Exorcist] speaks to a basic moral need." Others dismissed the film as immoral, exploitative, crass, and, in the phrase of Vincent Canby of the *New York Times*, the "sensationalism of a basically foolish mind." Some clerical and government officials called for its "R" rating to be changed to an "X" rating, and in Washington, D.C., the "X" rating was imposed and enforced by the police. The public obsession with *The Exorcist* nonetheless continued, and the Catholic Information Center in Washington, D.C., reported being inundated by daily calls for information on exorcism, while at least one young girl who, convinced she was demoniacally possessed, called to demand the ritual. When asked about all the brouhaha, Friedkin replied, "I certainly don't understand what's happening between [the movie] and its audience. [But] it is important to me to have made a film that is controversial and provocative." He has explained: "I know how to do it. I just throw everything at the audience and give them a real thrill. That's what they want. They don't want to go into a theatre and treat it like a book."

Friedkin's series of back-to-back blockbusters was followed by his first commercial failures, *Sorcerer* (1977), *The Brinks Job* (1978), *Cruising* (1980), and *Deal of the Century* (1983). In *Sorcerer* Friedkin had set out to "consciously say something much more relevant than anything [he] had ever done before" by spending $21 million to film a long-contemplated remake of Henri-Georges Clouzot's *The Wages of Fear* (1953). Dedicated to Clouzot, *Sorcerer* retells the grim tale of four renegades attempting to drive two truckloads of nitroglycerin through a South American jungle. Friedkin's favorite among his films, *Sorcerer* brings to the fore his fascination with the unpredictability of fate and, given the unsavory backgrounds of each of his protagonists, with the peculiar no man's land located between good and evil. Most critics complained, as Vincent Canby did in the *New York Times* (June 25, 1977), that the opening background sketches "diminish the impact of the sometimes stunning melodrama that unfolds in the Latin American petroleum republic." Jack Kroll, however, writing in *Newsweek* (July 4, 1977), commended the film's "clenched power" and "cruel and compelling beauty."

Returning to the re-creation of actual events, Friedkin brought a light comedic touch to *The Brink's Job*, the story of a spectacular 1950 heist that netted its eleven perpetrators $2.7 million. The Brinks caper had fascinated Friedkin since his childhood. The film led Frank Rich to speculate in *Time* magazine (December 11, 1978) that there were really "two William Friedkins." The Friedkin "audiences love to hate," Rich wrote, the director of *The French Connection*, *The Exorcist* and *Sorcerer*, was "a steely, at times brilliant cinematic technician who will heartlessly pull out any stop in the effort to make moviegoers squirm." The other is "a sweet fellow who once directed *The Night They Raided Minsky's*."

The other Friedkin returned in *Cruising* (1980), the story of policeman Steve Burns, played by Al Pacino, who goes undercover in the world of New York's gay, heavy-leather, sadomasochistic bars in search of a murderer who seduces and kills gay men. Written as well as directed by Friedkin and based to some degree on a series of murders of gays that were unsolved at the time of the filming, *Cruising* follows the erosion of Burns's sexual identity and even of his identity as an enforcer of the law. It finally hints that he himself has committed some of the crimes he has been assigned to investigate.

Even before *Cruising* was completed, gay activists picketed on-location filming in New York's West Village and smashed windows of restaurants and bars that were to be used as sets. Friedkin's crew even received a bomb threat. After the film was released, in February 1980, the National Gay Task Force and other groups demonstrated outside New York theatres. Reviewers generally agreed with their charges that the film was exploitative and even potentially encouraged violence against gays. Although acknowledged to be technically flawless and frightening in its depiction of violence, *Cruising* was also thought to be conceptually muddled.

After the completion of *Cruising*, Friedkin turned briefly from the screen to the stage to direct the play *Duet for One* (1981), Tom Kempenski's dramatization of the concert cellist Jacqueline du Pré's struggle to come to terms, through psychoanalysis, with the multiple sclerosis that ended her career. Friedkin's direction was praised in *Variety* (December 23, 1981) for enlivening a potentially "static talkfest" but was elsewhere accused of overwhelming it. Friedkin next directed the film *Deal of the Century* (1983), a satire on international arms trading that was universally reviled for its poorly timed slapstick. The director made a critical and commercial comeback with his next film, *To Live and Die in L.A.* (1985), for which he cowrote the screenplay. The moral ambiguities of *The French Connection* inform the actions of the film's hero, Robert Chance, a Los Angeles Secret Service agent, played by Robert Petersen, who is trying to track down the killer of his former partner. Most reviewers found the film heartless but could not help admiring Friedkin's directorial sleight of hand.

In the mid-1980s Friedkin returned to television, directing a music video for Barbara Streisand, an episode of the *Twilight Zone*, and, in July 1986, a two-hour made-for-television film entitled *C.A.T. Squad* that was notable for its complete lack of foul language, car chases, or violence. Friedkin told one interviewer at the time that "films have gone too far with violence and graphic sex" and asserted that he "would never again portray violence in a graphic way in a film." The movie was still as "cynical as all get-out," Michael Hill noted in his *Washington Post* article, adding that once again it was "sometimes hard to tell good guys from the bad." In 1987 Friedkin was at work on a new film, *Rampage,* an investigation of psychiatry and the insanity plea in the criminal justice system.

William Friedkin has been described as pale, magisterial, immaculately groomed, and "prematurely world-weary." He has a nine-year-old son from his first marriage, to French actress Jeanne Moreau, and a three-year-old son from his second marriage, to actress Lesley-Anne Down, which ended in divorce in 1985. Friedkin's hobbies include going to the movies, listening to music, and reading history and philosophy. He enjoys his success and its trappings, saying, "I love money and all the chotchkas that go with it." About his Oscar for best director of 1971, he once said, "Winning the Academy Award isn't everything; its the only thing. It's as important to me as being president." In 1971 he was given the Directors Guild of America's top directorial award, and he won Golden Globe Awards as best director in 1972 and 1974.

References: Chicago Tribune VI p25+ Mr 25 '79 pors, VI p5+ N 9 '80, X p7 N 24 '85; *N Y Daily News* p80 Jl 17 '86; *Toronto Globe and Mail* C p1+ Ap 12 '86 pors; *Washington Post* L p9+ O 22 '72, *TV Week* p9 Jl 27 '86; *Biographical Dictionary of Film* (1981); *International Dictionary of Films and Filmmakers, vol 2* (1986); *Who's Who in America,* 1986–87

Friendly, Fred W.

Oct. 30, 1915– Broadcast journalist; educator. Address: b. Columbia University Graduate School of Journalism, New York City, N. Y. 10027

NOTE: This biography supersedes the article that appeared in *Current Biography* in 1957.

In a career spanning more than fifty years, Fred W. Friendly, now Edward R. Murrow professor emeritus at Columbia University's Graduate School of Journalism, has been associated with some of the most honored programs in the history of broadcast journalism. With such innovative public affairs series as *See It Now,* which he coproduced with Edward R. Murrow in the 1950s, and the long-running and hard-hitting *CBS Reports* documentaries, Friendly forever changed the concept and scope of television news. "This little black box didn't get invented at this time in our technological evolution just to show pictures of horse operas . . . ," he once remarked. "It is just asking to be used. We can take the people there and show them what is happening." An early and vocal critic of commerical television's capitulation to the marketplace, Friendly left network television in 1966 and joined the Ford Foundation, where as an adviser on communications he helped to lay the groundwork for the development of noncommercial public television.

Fred W. Friendly was born Ferdinand Friendly Wachenheimer on October 30, 1915, in New York City, the only child of Samuel Wachenheimer, a jewelry manufacturer, and Therese (Friendly) Wachenheimer. (He adopted his mother's maiden name as his surname—initially at the insistence of his employer—when he began his career in broadcasting in 1937.) In the mid-1920s Friendly moved with his parents to Providence, Rhode Island, where he attended the local public schools. Following his graduation from Hope Street High School, he continued his education at Nichols Junior College in Dudley, Massachusetts. A business administration major, Friendly edited the college yearbook and took part in campus dramatic productions in his spare time.

Interested in radio from his childhood, in 1937 Friendly landed a job as an announcer and newscaster for radio station WEAN in Providence. During his four-year tenure there, in addition to his other duties, he wrote and narrated a series of short dramatized biographies of such historical figures as Harvey Firestone, the American industrialist, and the inventors Thomas Edison and Guglielmo Marconi. A recording company eventually bought the series from Friendly and released it in 1942 under the title Footprints in the Sands of Time.

When World War II broke out, Friendly enlisted in the United States Army. He served until 1945 as an instructor in the Signal Corps in both the European and Pacific theatres of operations and as a correspondent for CBI Roundup, the Far East equivalent of the Army newspaper Stars and Stripes. For displaying unusual heroism in the line of duty, Master Sergeant Friendly was awarded the Legion of Merit, four battle stars, and, shortly after his discharge, the Soldier's Medal, for his efforts in rescuing the survivors of a dock explosion in Bombay, India, where he was then working as a correspondent for CBS. According to a profile by Allene Talmey in Vogue (February 1, 1954), Friendly's "mild Providence personality underwent a curious forced growth" during the war. By the time he returned to civilian life in 1945, she wrote, he was "a fairly flamboyant, unorthodox character."

Resuming his career in radio broadcasting, Friendly introduced his panel quiz show Who Said That? on the NBC radio network on July 4, 1948. The show, which he edited and produced with his wife, Dorothy (Greene) Friendly, a former researcher for Life magazine, featured a trio of prominent people, who were asked to identify the source of famous quotations. Despite a warm critical response and a select, loyal audience, the unsponsored program was canceled by the network a year later.

Meanwhile, in 1948, an agent named J. G. Gude introduced Friendly to the celebrated broadcast journalist Edward R. Murrow, thus beginning a partnership that was to assume almost legendary proportions within the industry. As Eric F. Goldman observed of that remarkable association in the New York World Journal Tribune's book review section of March 26, 1967, Friendly and Murrow, "in their very different ways, had the same fire in their bellies—a fire made up of all kinds of elements but including that age-old American emotion which insists that when something new comes

along, it should be used to help the ordinary American become less ordinary." Friendly proposed to Murrow that they collaborate on a record album that would be, in effect, an oral history of the period from 1932 to 1945, featuring the voices of Franklin D. Roosevelt, Winston Churchill, Adolf Hitler, Joseph Stalin, General Douglas MacArthur, Will Rogers, and the Duke of Windsor, among others. Taken with the idea, Murrow sold it to Columbia Records, and shortly thereafter, I Can Hear It Now, as the album was called, became one of the best-selling nonmusical albums of the year. The pair followed their success with two similar albums, covering the 1920s and the post-World War II period, and years later Friendly was to collaborate with Walter Cronkite on yet another volume, I Can Hear It Now—The Sixties. Hear It Now, a short-lived radio program based on the same idea, earned Friendly and Murrow a Peabody citation in 1951.

Recognizing the enormous potential of television, the Murrow-Friendly team launched See It Now, a half-hour weekly news review, on the CBS television network in November 1951. With Murrow acting as the on-screen narrator and Friendly as the behind-the-scenes producer, See It Now set out to cover significant news events in an in-depth way. The first program, marking the recent linking by microwave of the East and West coasts, featured simultaneous live shots of the Atlantic and Pacific Oceans on a split screen. On subsequent programs, Murrow and Friendly took viewers to Europe for a trip on the Orient Express, to the battlefields of Korea, to Ann Arbor, Michigan, for an interview with Dr. Jonas Salk on the day he announced the discovery of a polio vaccine, and to Africa, for a comprehensive analysis of that continent's diverse cultures. Edited down from 250,000 feet of film, See It Now's "Report from Africa," which was first broadcast in May 1956, was widely praised for its "stunning photography" and its "unblinking attention" to the painfully complex problems of emerging nations.

Notwithstanding See It Now's superb coverage of topics of international importance, it was Friendly's willingness to tackle controversial domestic political issues that earned the show its honored place in the history of broadcast journalism. In 1953, for example, at the height of the McCarthy era's red-baiting, See It Now took up the cause of Milo Radulovich, an officer in the United States Air Force Reserve who was suspended from duty and recommended for dismissal because some of his relatives were suspected of having Communist sympathies. As a result of the program's exposé of this case of "guilt by association," the Air Force reversed its decision and restored Radulovich to active duty. The following year See It Now took on Senator Joseph R. McCarthy himself with a devastating examination of the methods he had used in his rise to power. Some critics immediately hailed the "Report on Senator McCarthy" as "television's coming of age," and within a few days of the broadcast, on March 6, 1954, CBS received more than

100,000 responses from viewers, most of them favorable. Top CBS executives, however, were less enthusiastic about programs that regularly dealt with political controversy than they were about action-filled adventure series and big-money quiz shows, such as The $64,000 Question, which made its debut on the network in June 1955. Demoted to an irregular slot on the program roster, See It Now was eventually canceled, in July 1958.

As Thomas Whiteside noted in his profile of Fred W. Friendly for the New Yorker (February 17, 1962), See It Now was "the first television documentary series of any consequence that attempted to deal with current affairs." After its first season on the air, it was chosen to receive television's most prestigious honor, the George Foster Peabody Award, for its "strikingly effective format for presenting the news and personalities in the news with humor, sometimes with indignation, always with careful thought." Over the course of its seven-year run, the program won thirty-five major awards, including the TV Guide Medal, the Page One award of the New York Newspaper Guild, the National Headliners Club award, and the Overseas Press Club award.

After the cancellation of See It Now, Murrow and Friendly remained at CBS as the coproducers of a weekly public affairs program called Small World. Moderated by Murrow, the show featured conversations between people in different parts of the world who were linked by radio or phone hookups—an innovative idea at the time. Small World was axed after just one season, but by then the quiz shows on which the networks had banked so heavily were being rocked by scandal. Judging that the audience was ready for a return to quality programming, Frank Stanton, then the president of CBS, asked Friendly to produce a new documentary show, CBS Presents, later renamed CBS Reports. Murrow was pointedly ignored. Even more of an independent spirit than Friendly, the reporter had not endeared himself to the network's managers, with whom he had frequently clashed. Friendly freely admitted that he had "great apprehension" about proceeding without Murrow, but he was gratified that CBS had enough confidence in him to assign his new program a primetime Thursday-night slot.

Using television to its maximum potential was Friendly's goal, and within the next few years, as executive producer of CBS Reports, he set a standard for television documentaries that remains a measure of quality to this day. Within two short years, he could point with pride to an arm's-length list of award-winning documentaries that put even See It Now to shame. "Those old See It Nows—they're nostalgic and amateurish," he told a reporter for Newsweek (May 8, 1961). "We made some of them in four or five days. CBS Reports has ten full-time producers, and they do about two shows each year. When we did Harvest of Shame, [producer] David Lowe lived with the migrant workers for one full year." Harvest of Shame, a searing look at the grim lives of migrant farm work-

ers, won for Friendly his tenth Peabody Award. CBS Reports itself was to win over forty major awards, making it the most garlanded series on network television.

Because of Friendly's penchant for such potentially explosive subjects as racial discrimination, gun control, right-wing political groups, and the Vietnam war, CBS Reports often found itself the center of public controversy. Just as the American Farm Bureau Federation condemned Harvest of Shame as a "rigged documentary" and a "highly colored propaganda job," so other powerful special interest groups denounced other programs. Following the broadcast of The Business of Health: Medicine, Money and Politics, the board of trustees of the American Medical Association issued a statement charging that it was filled with "misrepresentations, bias and distortions" that made a "caricature of medicine and its aims." Another show, Who Speaks for Birmingham?, so angered several influential white citizens of that Alabama city that they filed a $1.5 million damage suit against CBS on the ground of character defamation. Among CBS Reports' less controversial but no less compelling broadcasts over the years were its interviews with such diverse personalities as President Dwight D. Eisenhower, Admiral Hyman Rickover, Carl Sandburg, Walter Lippmann, and its Town Meeting of the World series of satellite-linked discussions among past and present world leaders. Recalling those heady days in an interview for a New York Times Magazine (April 23, 1967) profile of Friendly, CBS producer Gene de Poris told Harvey Swados, "[Friendly] had an incredible knack of always throwing hot dice. He really knew the future book—he was the one guy who sensed when to do a show so that it was ready for a news break."

In March 1964 Friendly was appointed president of CBS News, succeeding Richard Salant. Because it meant giving up what he has called "the best job in the world," as producer of CBS Reports, Friendly accepted the promotion with mixed feelings. "I feel like I've been shot into orbit and have no retrorockets to come down with," he joked, as quoted in Time (March 13, 1964). "If this isn't fun, I'll be a flop." His first order of business, he announced, was to invite Edward R. Murrow to rejoin CBS News. Next, he dispatched three experienced correspondents and five camera crews to South Vietnam to cover the escalating conflict there and assigned Eric Sevareid, one of the network's most respected reporters, to cover the trial of Jack Ruby, who had shot and killed Lee Harvey Oswald, the accused assassin of President John F. Kennedy. His other immediate plans for the news division included comprehensive coverage of the upcoming Senate debate on pending civil rights legislation.

"I want this to be 'the reason-why network,'" Friendly proclaimed when he took the helm of CBS News, but years later he was to criticize not only the media in general but also his own role as a network news president in particular for what he termed the "dramatic shortage of news analysis" following the passage, in 1964, of the Gulf of Tonkin resolution, which gave the president the power to "take all necessary measures . . . to prevent aggression" in South Vietnam, and during the early years of direct American combat involvement in the Vietnam war. "It was not our war to win or lose, but it was our war to understand and explain," Friendly maintained in an article for the *Columbia Journalism Review* (Winter 1970-71). The "disturbing problem was our inability to understand the complexities of the Vietnam puzzle and to assemble a comprehensive profile early enough to make a difference."

It was Friendly's anger over interference in the operation of the news division by upper-level CBS executives that led to his dramatic resignation in February 1966. At issue was the live coverage of events of national importance—in this case, the Senate Foreign Affairs Committee's public hearings on the Vietnam war. CBS News, under Friendly's direction, had broadcast General James Gavin's testimony live from gavel to gavel, and Friendly wanted to continue the practice when George F. Kennan, the chief architect of President Harry S. Truman's foreign policy and a critic of increased American military involvement in the war in Southeast Asia, took the stand as the next witness. He was overruled by the newly appointed CBS group vice-president, John A. Schneider, who ordered the network to resume its less expensive regular daytime program schedule, which included reruns of the situation comedies *I Love Lucy* and *The Real McCoys*. Charging that Schneider's decision was a "business, not a news judgment," Friendly submitted a biting letter of resignation in which, among other things, he chastised Schneider for making a "mockery" of CBS's longtime crusade for "broadest access to Congressional debate."

The following year, in his book *Due to Circumstances Beyond Our Control* (Random House), Friendly placed the blame for what he regards as a bizarre, pusillanimous decision not so much on the network executives themselves, but on "the mercantile advertising system that controls television." Reviewing the book for the New York *World Journal Tribune Book Week* (March 26, 1967), Eric F. Goldman expressed the assessment of many other critics when he called it "forceful . . . enormously informed, tartly analytical, astute, passionate, and disturbing." With this "major book," Goldman concluded, Friendly "has stoked the fire of criticism of TV in a way which in the long run, I suspect, will serve the people of the United States as effectively as the memorable TV hours which he did so much to create."

The day after he resigned from CBS, Friendly received a telephone call from McGeorge Bundy, who was about to leave government service after many years to become president of the Ford Foundation. Bundy offered Friendly a position as adviser on communications to the foundation, which had distinguished itself with its continuing support of educational television. Friendly immediately accepted. Beginning in 1968 he served simultaneously as Edward R. Murrow Professor of Journalism and chairman of the broadcast program at Columbia University. In these positions, Friendly devoted himself over the next few years to promoting the concept of noncommercial television. He is acknowledged to have been the driving force behind the Ford Foundation's bold proposal for funding educational television. Submitted to the Federal Communications Commission in 1966, the plan, which Friendly described as "television's last chance," called for the creation of a nonprofit corporation to operate a ring of domestic satellites. The corporation would sell its transmission services to the commercial networks and, with the profits, subsidize educational television.

In 1967 the board of trustees of Columbia University approved a two-year experimental, coast-to-coast series of noncommercial public affairs television programs. Financed by a $10 million grant from the Ford Foundation, the series, which was to be called the *Public Broadcasting Laboratory*, was to be, in Friendly's words, "a practical demonstration" of public television's potential. To avoid being both donor and recipient of a Ford Foundation grant, Friendly hired Av Westin, a former *CBS Reports* producer, to execute the program. The experiment paid off, for by the end of the decade Congress had chartered the Corporation for Public Broadcasting.

Meanwhile, Friendly was thriving as a professor at Columbia. "I wish someone had told me about teaching before, it's such a fantastic experience," he told Harvey Swados. When one of his students asked him to describe the origins of the FCC's Fairness Doctrine, Friendly was—for once—stumped for a reply. His curiosity on the question led to what he called "a 20,000-mile excursion through the fifty-five-year thicket of regulatory history" and resulted in his book *The Good Guys, the Bad Guys and the First Amendment: Free Speech vs. Fairness in Broadcasting* (Random House, 1976). As the title indicates, while he recognized the complexity of the issue, Friendly came down on the side of free speech, although he recommended expanding the number of television channels to allow for a fuller airing of different points of view.

Friendly explored one controversial First Amendment ruling in depth in *Minnesota Rag: The Dramatic Story of the Landmark Supreme Court Case That Gave New Meaning to Freedom of the Press* (Random House, 1981). The case in question, *Near v. Minnesota*, pitted a right-wing bigot, Jay M. Near, and his weekly newspaper, the *Saturday Press*, against the state of Minnesota, which had shut down the publication under its Public Nuisance Act. In 1931 the Supreme Court ruled that the First Amendment forbids such "prior restraint" of the press. In the course of his research, Friendly discovered, to his surprise, that most of Near's charges of corruption in local government were true. As Aryeh Neier pointed out in his review of *Minnesota Rag* for the *Nation* (June 6, 1981), "It is this revelation that suggests the singular importance of *Near v. Minnesota* as a constitutional document. The decision stands for the proposition that, with rare exception, our press must be free from government censorship. And the freedom to publish even extends to unscrupulous bigots like Jay M. Near."

In December 1980 Friendly retired as the Ford Foundation's adviser on communications, although he has continued to work on the series of seminars on the mass media and public policy that he initiated in 1974. Cosponsored by the Ford Foundation and major news organizations, those seminars bring together journalists and representatives from other sectors of society for dialogues on such topics as investigative reporting, libel, medical ethics, and international terrorism. Many of the more than 100 conferences held to this date have been videotaped and televised nationwide on PBS and CBS. Friendly was also involved in the production of *The Constitution: That Delicate Balance*, a thirteen-week series that examined contemporary issues in the light of constitutional law. Originally broadcast in the fall of 1984, the series, in videotape form, has since become part of the curricula in the journalism and law schools of many colleges and universities.

A lean, rangy man with boundless energy, Fred W. Friendly is six feet two inches tall and has blue eyes and receding gray hair. He is known for his relentless drive and his passionate commitment to quality journalism. "He is not just a teacher, but an igniter," a former student once remarked. "He has sent many of us out as journalists with a desire to do our best and with the knowledge that it is not an easy job." From his first marriage, which ended in divorce, Friendly has three children, Andrew, Lisa, and David; from his second, to the former Ruth W. Mark, a widowed schoolteacher whom he married in June 1968, he has three stepsons, Jon, Michael and Richard. All are involved in the performing arts and/or journalism.

References: N Y Times Mag p31+ Ap '67 pors; New Yorker 37:41+ F 17 '62; Newsweek 63:56 Mr 16 '64 por, 67:97 Ap 18 '66 por, 69:92 Mr 27 '67 por; Time 83:62+ Mr 13 '64 por; Contemporary Authors new rev vol 14 (1985); International Who's Who, 1986–87; Who's Who in America, 1986–87

Gaddis, William

Dec. 29, 1922– Novelist. Address: b. c/o Candida Donadio & Associates, 231 W. 22d St., New York City, N.Y. 10001

The American novelist William Gaddis' efforts to use fiction to "escape whole the limitations of [his] own mind," as he once wrote, have resulted over the last thirty years in three novels of enormous scope that, though unknown to much of the reading public, are already numbered among the landmarks of contemporary letters. Long an underground classic, his first book, *The Recognitions* (Harcourt, 1955) is considered by some to be the best of the post-World War II American novels, and is credited with having introduced a new American genre—that of the blackly humorous, encyclopedic "Mega Novel" that, according to the critic Frederick Karl, captures in its openendedness something "very close to what America is." *The Recognitions* was followed twenty years later by *JR* (Knopf, 1975), a National Book Award-winning satire about American business enterprise that is told almost entirely through a cacaphonous babble of dialogue. In 1982 *JR* helped to win Gaddis a Catherine and John D. MacArthur Foundation Fellowship, better known as a "genius award," with a five-year $280,000 stipend that subsidized him while he completed his third novel, *Carpenter's Gothic* (Viking, 1985). A bleaker and much shorter work than his preceding novels, *Carpenter's Gothic* was described by Cynthia Ozick in the *New York Times Book Review* (July 7, 1985) as "Gaddis-in-little" but "Gaddis to the

brim . . . an extra turret added on to the ample, ingenious, audacious Gothic mansion Gaddis has been building in American letters."

William Thomas Gaddis, who was born in Manhattan on December 29, 1922, spent his early years in the village of Massapequa on Long Island, where his family owned property. In *Contemporary Authors* (1987), Steven Moore observed: "Gaddis grew up without a father. Haunting all three [of his] novels, in fact, is the spirit of a dead or absent father who leaves a ruinous state of affairs for his children, a situation that can be extrapolated to include Gaddis' vision of a world abandoned by God and plunged into disorder."

Working against, but also dramatizing that sense of disorder was "the entire Protestant ethic," which was instilled in him during his childhood, when he attended a boarding school in Berlin, Connecticut. That ethic, Gaddis told Lloyd Grove of the *Washington Post* (August 23, 1985), "has been very much in me from my boarding school days on. My mother's family was Quaker. I was brought up pretty much in New England. I was taught that 'This is what you do and you do it right. These are the rules.'"

After completing the seventh grade, Gaddis left boarding school to continue his education at Farmingdale High School on Long Island. In September 1941 he entered Harvard College, where he studied English literature. Late in his freshman year, he developed a kidney ailment brought on by the treatment of a "tropical fever of unknown origin" he had suffered from at Farmingdale High School. The illness forced him to leave for a year of recuperation, and, to his great disappointment, disqualified him from joining the armed forces after the United States entered World War II. When he returned to Harvard, he joined the staff of and edited its highly irreverent *Lampoon* magazine. He contributed poetry, essays, reviews, and short stories to the magazine until 1945, when he was asked to leave by the dean of Harvard College in connection with a fracas involving himself, another student, and the Cambridge police.

Returning home to New York, Gaddis quickly found work as a fact checker for the *New Yorker* magazine. The work there, he has said, was "terribly good training, a kind of post-graduate school for a writer." During the next two years, Gaddis became acquainted with members of the beat generation of writers, including Allen Ginsberg, Jack Kerouac, and William Burroughs. In 1947 he left New York for a year and traveled south to Mexico, where he began what he has described as "one aspect of" *The Recognitions*, and later moved on to the Panama Canal Zone, where he began another version of the book while working as a crane operator at the Miraflores docks. He traveled next to Costa Rica, then in the midst of a civil war. On arriving there, he was sent to a young captain named Madero and given a "banged-up" Springfield rifle that was stolen from him before the day was out. During another, longer assignment he helped to level an airstrip for planes bringing arms from Guatemala in order to supply ammunition to the elected Costa Rican government. He made his way back to New York on a Honduran banana boat in 1948. In their introduction to the festschrift *In Recognition of William Gaddis* (1984), John Kuehl and Steven Moore, its editors, recounted that, back from his adventures, Gaddis wore a white Panama suit and kept his right arm in a sling, though there was nothing wrong with it, for the

purpose of preparing himself to "write explosively when [the arm] was released from its bandage like a bird from a cage."

Gaddis spent the summer of 1948 on Long Island, and the New York City scenes and characters in *The Recognitions* are largely drawn from his experiences at this time. At that early stage in its development, Gaddis conceived of his evolving work as in part a parody of Goethe's *Faust*. At the end of the summer, after announcing to his boon companions that he would be the "first to publish," Gaddis left New York, where he had just had an unhappy love affair, for Europe. He wrote what is now the beginning of *The Recognitions* in Spain. After spending two years there, he traveled to Paris, where he set the manuscript of *The Recognitions* aside and wrote radio scripts for UNESCO. Somehow he also found the time to read prodigiously. After spending a year in Paris, he made a short visit to North Africa before returning to the United States. Most of those ports of call found their way into his gestating novel.

His intellectual ports of call included Sir James Frazer's *The Golden Bough*, a monumental study of myth and ritual, the reading of which led him to do research on the early Christian church and to study closely *The Recognitions*, a third-century religious romance attributed to Pope Clement I that recounts Clement's quest for salvation and his Faustian bargain with an Egyptian magus. From Frazer, Gaddis developed the idea of Christianity as a counterfeit religion, dishonest about its concealed pagan origins, using that concept to present what he perceived as the forged and bankrupt spirituality of the modern world. Gaddis transformed Clement's quest into the search for artistic and spiritual truth of his protagonist, Wyatt Gwyon, a talented but commercially unsuccessful painter who becomes a forger of Flemish masterworks in order to establish some contact with an age when art was sanctioned by God. Gaddis' labyrinthine plot follows Gwyon from the New England home of his clergyman father to art school in Munich, to Paris, and then to New York City shortly after World War II. There he begins to forge the Flemish old masters and strikes a bargain with a Mephistophelean art dealer. Forgery of every sort crops up in Gaddis' vast gallery of characters, which includes six other persons who serve as types, alter egos, or "forgeries" of Wyatt.

"There's that lovely phrase in *As You Like It*," Gaddis told Miriam Berkley during an interview for *Publishers Weekly* (July 12, 1985) in explaining his all-inclusive impulses in constructing *The Recognitions*, "'All's brave that youth mounts and folly guides.' Today, the idea of undertaking a thing like that appalls me. I thought, with the naive kind of confidence that youth has, that the world is made up of falsehood and fraud, and I'm going to expose it. And everyone will be amazed. Once one gets a theme in one's mind it becomes obsessive. If it happens to be forgery, then everywhere you look all you see is forgery, falsification—of religious values, of art—plagiarism, stealing. Gradually this panorama emerged. I thought, 'I've got to get it all in here.'"

After Gaddis returned to the United States in early 1951 a segment of his work-in-progress appeared in *New World Writing* (April 1952), prompting the literary agent Bernice Baumgarten to offer to represent him. After she arranged for Gaddis to be granted an advance and put under contract by Harcourt Brace and Company in 1952, he retired to a farmhouse in Montgomery, New York. There, by working daily and well into the nights, he completed *The Recognitions*. After he made cuts and revisions at the suggestions of his editors, the novel was finally published by Harcourt Brace in 1955, in an edition of 956 pages.

Despite a penny-pinching promotional campaign that later prompted Gaddis to remark that his publisher "didn't *publish* [*The Recognitions*]; he *privated* it," the novel was widely reviewed. Some critics regarded it as pretentious, overambitious, undisciplined, and tedious, but several reviewers admired its erudition, energy, and imagination. Stunned by the negative reviews, Gaddis dropped from public view for twenty years, a period during which, he has said, he became effectively "posthumous."

During those years the critical consensus on his novel changed dramatically. As early as 1957, only two years after its publication, Anthony West hailed *The Recognitions* as "the most interesting and remarkable novel written by a young American in the last twenty-five years." It was reissued in paperback in 1962 and translated into Italian in 1967. Although Gaddis continued to derive only about $100 a year from *The Recognitions* in royalties, it attracted a loyal cult following and increasing critical scrutiny. By 1971 the critic Tony Tanner could write in his book *City of Words: American Fiction 1950–1970* that William Gaddis had been "instrumental in inaugurating a new period in American fiction in which the theme of fictions/ recognitions has come to occupy the forefront of the American writer's consciousness. . . . *The Recognitions* probes into so many ideas and states of mind and stylistic possibilities which are peculiarly relevant to the decades which followed it, that it seems surprising more notice was not taken of it." Another critic, David Madden, in trying to explain the novel's long neglect, speculated in his *Rediscoveries* (1971) that "some readers got mired down" in the allusions, anecdotes, and wide-ranging subject areas that comprise the "surface stuff" of the novel.

During his twenty-year absence from the literary world, Gaddis supported himself as a freelance writer, turning out speeches for corporate executives and scripts for industrial and military films. Although the growing reputation of *The Recognitions* brought him a National Institute of Arts and Letters grant in 1963 and a National Endowment for the Arts grant in 1967, he continued to run into financial difficulties. At one point Gaddis, needing dental work, was forced to ghostwrite professional journal articles for a dentist in ex-

change for root canals. He made more conventional arrangements with the United States Army, for which he worked on propaganda films until 1964, when he quit in disapproval of its stepped-up involvement in Vietnam. He then began writing for Eastman Kodak.

Meanwhile, in his literary work, Gaddis was involved in a variety of projects, including a play about the Civil War and a novel about business enterprise, and in his investigations of what he called "expanding prospects of programmed society and automation in the arts . . . which may bring . . . an escape from the tomb of the 9–5." He described his projects in a note for *World Authors 1950–1970* (1975) as "beginnings that have redeemed . . . years unproductive of any accomplishment but getting a living . . . [a] tangle of apparently disparate projects which continue their struggles to devour, and develop, and illuminate one another." Those projects were finally subsumed in his second novel, *JR*, which was published by Alfred A. Knopf in both paperback and hard cover in 1975.

Dispensing with narrative conventions, Gaddis told the story of JR almost exclusively through dialogue, populating his pages with characters who are identified mainly by their verbal idiosyncrasies: their choice of slang, jargon, and epithet. He did so, he explained to Miriam Berkley, in order "to remove the author almost entirely, and force the story to tell itself—and, in effect, to ask the reader to become a participant, to create these figures in his own mind from the evidence on the page."

The grand design of *JR* consists of an enormous river of talk that sweeps along its gigantic cast through 726 pages of a convoluted plot. It charts the rise of eleven-year-old JR from an elementary school hustler who swindles his classmates out of a single share of stock they have pooled their resources to buy and parlays that single share into a paper empire, to a runny-nosed tycoon at the helm of the American business empire that he inadvertently brings crashing down around him. "The important thing about JR," Gaddis explained to Miriam Berkley, "is that he *not* be a genius. I wanted him to epitomize the amoral—which is to say simple, naked, cheerful greed." Eddying around the edges of JR's wheeling and dealing are what George Stade described in the *New York Times Book Review* (June 1, 1975) as "ruined careers and marriages . . . children neglected, lost or abandoned . . . obsession, madness, murder and suicide . . . casual slaughter and continuous betrayal . . . artists who can't work . . . teachers who won't teach, men of affairs who mismanage them . . . collisions, interruptions, malfunctions and breakdowns . . . an accelerating entropy that no one can escape, let alone control. . . . "

The reception accorded *JR* by most critics was considerably more enthusiastic than the one that was accorded *The Recognitions*, perhaps partly to make up for the erroneous judgements of twenty years earlier. A few reviewers, including Robert Towers, writing in the *New Republic* (September 2, 1985), objected to Gaddis' unrelenting exploitation of his "uncannily accurate ear for banality, greed, hypocrisy, and stupidity." "Twenty pages into [*JR*]," Towers complained, "I felt as if I had been trapped inside a telephone booth with a maniac . . . and there were still 700 pages to go." The majority of critics, however, gave *JR* a high rating. Alicia Metcalf Miller, reviewing it for the *Cleveland Plain Dealer* (October 1975), observed that "if Gaddis is a moralist, he is also a master of satire and humor. *JR* is a devastatingly funny book. Reading it, I laughed loudly and unashamedly in public places." The novelist William H. Gass has called *JR* "perhaps the supreme masterpiece of acoustical collage" and "a culmination of the oral tradition." *JR* was given the National Book Award as the best novel of 1975 by William H. Gass and Mary McCarthy, the members of the fiction award selection committee for that year.

After the cordial critical reception accorded *JR*, there was a growing acceptance of Gaddis in academia, and essays and dissertations devoted to his work began to appear more frequently. In 1976, the same year in which he received a Rockefeller Foundation Fellowship, he was hired to teach one semester each year as Distinguished Visiting Professor at Bard College. In 1981 he obtained a Guggenheim fellowship, and in 1982 he received his MacArthur Foundation Fellowship. In the latter year, Steven Moore's *A Reader's Guide to William Gaddis' "The Recognitions,"* the first full-length critical study of his work, appeared.

Meanwhile, Gaddis had begun work on a third novel, whose themes were presaged in one of his infrequent essays, "The Rush for Second Place," which he developed from lectures he gave at Bard College on the theme of failure in American literature. Published in *Harper's* in April 1981, the article is an invocation of thinkers and writers ranging from John Maynard Keynes to Aleksander Solzhenitsyn in an effort to take the measure of an America that Gaddis feels has been brought to the brink of disaster by its cheerful fulfillment of Keynes's prediction, made in 1930, "For at least another hundred years we must pretend to ourselves and to everyone that fair is foul and foul is fair; for foul is useful and fair is not. Avarice and usury . . . must be our gods for a little longer still."

Carpenter's Gothic, Gaddis' bleakest novel, was published by Viking in 1985. A much shorter work than its predecessors, its publication was accompanied by the simultaneous reissue of *The Recognitions* and *JR*. Seeking to increase his readership and to "keep the record straight," Gaddis indulged in promotional activity for the first time by granting interviews and posing for photographs. The plot of *Carpenter's Gothic* centers on the disastrous marriage between the domineering Paul Booth, self-described "media consultant," and his wife Liz, a mine company heiress whom he has married for her money. The power of "sheer deceit," as Gaddis had described it in "The Rush for Second Place," seems to be embodied by Paul's client Elton Ude, a fundamentalist evangelist opposed to evolution, science, Marxism , and abor-

tion, who launches an imperialist crusade in Africa through his anti-Marxist overseas food program. Ude sets off a chain of events that brings the world to the brink of nuclear war.

As in *JR*, the events in *Carpenter's Gothic* are imparted by the torrential flow of the dialogue. Lorna Sage, in evaluating it for the *London Observer* (February 16, 1986), noted that in the end what remains is the characters' "coinciding greeds and desires, those bullying, pleading, lying voices that lace their way over the globe, speaking *through* people . . . and destroying them." Although she expressed the hope that "perhaps this time [Gaddis will] win more readers, since the world is clearly getting more like he always thought it was" and although *Carpenter's Gothic* sold briskly in comparison to its predecessors, a number of critics found his vision, however accurate, to be too bleakly pessimistic and misanthropic. Some viewed *Carpenter's Gothic*—and Gaddis' entire oeuvre—less as an act of misanthropy than as a call to arms for men of good will. Steven Moore wrote in *Contemporary Authors*: "It is clearly ridiculous to accuse Gaddis—as some critics have—of contributing to the very moral chaos he deplores." Quoting from Maynard Mack's essay "The Muse of Satire," Moore asserted that like the work of the classical satirists, Gaddis' fiction invites his readers to join what the critic Louis I. Bredvold called "the invisible church of good men . . . few though they may be . . . for whom things matter."

In his mid-sixties William Gaddis is gray-haired, trim, and "country casual in dress," according to Miriam Berkley. She also found him to be "close to handsome . . . eyes blue (gaze disconcertingly direct), chin cleft, voice husky." Gaddis has two grown children from a former marriage and is said to leave interviewers' questions about his personal life unanswered. When Lloyd Grove asked him about his reticence, Gaddis summed up his objections by saying, "I don't want to be seen in *People* magazine, romping with my dog. . . . " In his interview with Miriam Berkley, Gaddis called the artist the "human dregs" of his work, echoing Wyatt Gwyon's assertion in *The Recognitions* that the artist is "the human shambles that follows [the work] around." Gaddis insisted that "the writer cannot run after a book saying 'this is what I really meant.' For me it is very much a proposition between the reader and the page. That's what books are about."

References: N Y Post p33 D 4 '75 por; Pub W 228:56+ Jl 12 '85 por; Washington Post Bk World p7 Je 2 '68 por, B p1+ A 23 '85 pors; Contemporary Authors new rev ser vol 21 (1987); Kuehl, John, and Moore, Steven. In Recognition of William Gaddis (1984)

Gale, Robert (Peter)

*Oct. 11, 1945– Physician. Address: b.
International Bone Marrow Registry, University
of California, Los Angeles, Calif. 90024*

Dr. Robert Gale, an associate professor of medicine and the head of the bone marrow transplant unit at the Medical Center of the University of California, Los Angeles, was getting ready to go to work on the morning of April 28, 1986, when he heard, on the morning radio news, the first reports of the devastating accident at the Soviet nuclear power plant in Chernobyl, in the Ukraine. Although those first reports were sketchy, it was clear that massive amounts of radiation had been released, destroying the bone marrow of many people, in a process similar to the ravages of the cases of leukemia that he so often treated. As chairman of the Milwaukee-based international bone marrow transplant registry and as one of America's leading bone marrow transplant specialists, Gale immediately decided to offer his help to try to save some of the victims of the disaster.

The next few weeks thrust Gale into the headlines, as he became a critical actor in the horrifying but fascinating Chernobyl drama that captured the attention of the world. Racing against time to save radiation victims, Gale and his Soviet colleagues watched many of their patients die when the radiation sickness was too far advanced to be helped by a transplant operation. They agreed to cooperate in future studies and in the monitoring of the long-run effects of Chernobyl. Gale's face became known to, and loved by, millions of Soviet citizens, and passers-by stopped him in the streets of Moscow to express their gratitude at his having come so far to help their country in that tragic time of need. A

poem was printed in *Pravda* that contained the lines: "God is in a man who walked into a radiated complex . . . Who didn't save himself, But saved Odessa and Kiev . . . God is . . . in Dr. Gale . . . who came to Russia."

Robert Peter Gale was born on October 11, 1945, in Brooklyn Heights, New York, the son of a stockbroker. He grew up in an affectionate, mutually supportive, and highly cultured family, and remembers being taken to a performance of Wagner's *Götterdämmerung* at the Metropolitan Opera when he was only twelve and loving every minute of that mammoth work. Although Gale always wanted to be a doctor, his interests ranged widely, and for a time he also studied industrial art. He attended Hobart College in Geneva, New York, from 1962 to 1966, graduating with an A.B. degree and with high honors in biology. After Hobart, he enrolled at the School of Medicine of the State University of New York at Buffalo, which granted him his M.D. degree in 1970. He then moved to Los Angeles, serving his internship and his residence at the UCLA department of medicine and continuing his graduate studies there as well, in microbiology and immunobiology. He obtained a Ph.D. degree from UCLA in 1978. From 1977 until 1983 Gale served as the director of UCLA's program in transplantation biology, teaching at the same time in the division of hematology and oncology, where he was promoted to his current post of associate professor in 1979.

Gale became interested in immunobiology and in seeking a cure for leukemia as a way of combining his pursuit of scientific research with the practice of traditional medicine. To expand the frontiers of medical knowledge and to administer aid to suffering human beings, he puts in an exhausting daily schedule in UCLA's leukemia ward. Gale estimates that about half of the leukemia patients he treats with bone marrow transplants will live more than five years after the operation and that because of recent advances in research, between 60 and 70 percent of children diagnosed as having leukemia will survive.

The bone marrow transplant operation is still a relatively new procedure. Because leukemia destroys bone marrow, the ultimate source of the body's blood and immune defense cells, in the transplant operation, healthy bone marrow is taken by syringe from the pelvic bones of a donor and injected into the veins of a patient. Ideally, the new bone marrow will produce healthy cells to replace those crowded out by the cancerous ones. Although the operation itself is relatively simple, somewhat like a blood transfusion, the match between donor and recipient must be much more exact than in the case of a donation of blood, so that the ideal bone marrow donor is an identical twin. The more common donor is another sibling, although there is only a 25 percent chance that the bone marrow of two siblings will match. If the transplanted marrow is not perfectly matched, there is a danger that it will not engraft and produce new cells. Another danger is that the graft will work "too well," that the newly produced white cells will perceive the host body as foreign and attack it, sometimes to the point of death.

Gale's work as head of the transplant team at the UCLA Medical Center was highly regarded across the United States by the mid-1980s, although the National Institutes of Health reprimanded him in 1985 for some transplants performed in 1978 and 1979 on the grounds that he had not obtained the necessary advance clearance required for cases and treatment considered as research rather than as standard operating procedure. Dr. James B. Wyngaarden, director of the National Institutes, decreed that UCLA would be required to file reports on Gale's work every six months, through March 1988, during which time Gale would continue to be eligible for research grants from the institutes and also be able to serve on institutes committees. Gale defended his actions by pointing out that the treatments he administered in 1978 and 1979—the bone marrow transplants—were not done as experiments but rather as procedures considered the most likely to help the individual patients in question. By 1985 the transplant operation had become a fairly routine procedure.

The new phase of Gale's life after the Chernobyl disaster was anything but routine, however. Making the immediate decision to offer his services to the Soviets did not guarantee that his offer would be accepted. Moreover, the Soviet Union was not a member of the international bone marrow transplant registry (although it has since indicated that it wishes to join the thirty-two-nation group), and as a consequence, Gale had no easy professional line of communication. The Soviet government had at first refused initial Western offers of humanitarian aid. Gale therefore decided to contact Dr. Armand Hammer, the chairman of Occidental Petroleum Corporation, who had developed a close relationship with Soviet leaders ever since his first visit to the Soviet Union in 1921 and whom Gale had met through Hammer's work as chairman of the president's cancer advisory panel. When Gale called Hammer on April 29 to inform him of his assessment of medical needs in the wake of the Chernobyl accident, Hammer immediately cabled a letter to General Secretary Mikhail Gorbachev, outlining the doctor's offer of help and offering to pay for all expenses involved.

The answer came at 7:30 in the morning on May 1, when Gale received a telephone call from the then-acting Soviet ambassador to the United States, Oleg Sokolov, indicating the Soviet eagerness for Gale to go to Moscow as soon as possible. Gale quickly packed his bag and left that afternoon. Having decided to bring with him a team of specialists who, working with their Soviet colleagues, could undertake the unprecedented task of performing a series of bone marrow transplants on short notice. Gale requested that the Soviets grant visas to two members of the UCLA team, Dr. Richard Champlin and Dr. Paul Terasaki, and to the Israeli biophysicist Dr. Yair Reisner. Gale talked to all three, to confirm their willingness to

go, and then left on the fifteen-hour flight to Moscow.

On his arrival, Gale was greeted by the chief of protocol of the ministry of health, Dr. Ivan Nikitin, and by Dr. Victor Voskresenskiy, the medical attaché for the Soviet embassy in the United States. He was taken to his lodgings at the Sovietskaya Hotel, an old but elegant hotel with red carpets and large rooms that are generally reserved for foreign diplomats. There, that same evening, Dr. Alexandr Baranov visited Gale to apprise him of the situation. The Moscow team had so far performed nine transplants on radiation victims. Six had been bone marrow transplants, and three had involved the use of fetal liver cells, a substitute procedure when a matched donor cannot be found. (The cells that will perform the bone marrow function in a human being are located in the developing liver in early fetal life.) Neither the hospital nor the doctors were prepared to perform so many operations; in the two years before the Chernobyl accident, they had cared for no more than two transplant patients at one time.

The next morning Gale was taken to Moscow's Municipal Hospital Six, a stark, brown-brick building in a state of disrepair. After meeting with the head of the Soviet team, Dr. Angelina Guskova, he came to appreciate her knowledge and expertise, particularly the method that she devised for estimating the amount of radiation absorbed by an individual. Those calculations, involving a formula based on the drop in the patient's white blood cell count and the extent of breakdown in the chromosome structure of the blood and bone marrow, were essential for making decisions concerning operability. Gale suggested that victims who had received a radiation dose of 500 or more rads should be operated on; those in the highest range, with dosages as high as 1,500 rads, were beyond all help and were given antibiotics and pain killers to tide them over until their death.

That first morning, Gale helped to perform one transplant operation and met all the patients on the special ward, including a doctor about Gale's own age who had heroically returned again and again to the burning Chernobyl plant to rescue its workers. He had extensive burns all over, both from radiation and from the fire, and Gale saw immediately that he had little time left to live. Gale wrote in his account for *Life* magazine (August 1986), accompanied by his own photographs: "Doctors spend huge amounts of time, professionally and socially, discussing what would happen if someone dropped a bomb or a nuclear submarine radiated its crew, and here I was, awestruck, face-to-face with people who'd been accidentally radiated."

The Soviets quickly agreed to Gale's request that Champlin, Terasaki, and Reisner be allowed to come, to contribute their special skills to the momentous task. Gale had already made several calls to UCLA, requesting medicines and supplies, for the Moscow hospital lacked needed antibiotics, as well as the equipment and chemicals needed for large-scale bone marrow transplants. Champlin brought some of the needed supplies with him, and Gale contacted other sources throughout the world to procure $800,000 worth of high-tech medical machinery. Despite the fact that Israel has no diplomatic ties with the Soviet Union, making Israelis ineligible for Soviet visas, Reisner was allowed into the country without incident, and Gale's team was complete.

Gale and his team worked from twelve to fifteen hours a day, and there were times when he got no more than three hours sleep at night. He was often up at five o'clock in the morning, placing or receiving international phone calls, and then would go jogging, together with Champlin, up and down the thoroughfare in front of their hotel. On one occasion they ran for six miles to Red Square. By nine o'clock, they were in the hospital, making the rounds with Guskova and Baranov, and they did not leave until late at night. The strain of the work, with its constant grim reminder of radiation and death, inevitably took its toll, and as Gale recounted in *Life,* one of his colleagues "began to come unglued." As a precautionary measure, two cases of Watney's Ale were ordered in with the next shipment of medical equipment.

Even with new equipment brought in from abroad, facilities at Hospital Six remained woefully inadequate. Lacking an automated blood-cell counter, the hospital staff had to count blood cells under a microscope, a thirty-minute procedure for what could be done with the right equipment in twenty seconds. There were constant mechanical breakdowns even during surgery. But the Soviet and American teams developed a fine working relationship, under trying circumstances that Gale has compared to "a battlefield situation." He went on to explain," We had to decide whom to save, who could not be saved. . . . We were running against the clock." Many transplant recipients died before the transplant had enough time to grow and produce healthy cells.

Gale felt those deaths very keenly, for he had come to know each of the patients individually. When he was introduced to them as an American doctor, they thanked him profusely for coming. Men and women who had been leading normal lives until April 25, 1986, were reactor workers, firemen, paramedics, security guards, and doctors. Many had showed great heroism in the trying hours of the accident, fighting the raging fire, rescuing others at a great risk to themselves. And Gale also came to know the family members, who played a more active role than is common in American hospitals, bringing cooked food to their relatives, trying to add a personal touch to those agonizing days. In June 1986, when Soviet television presented a memorial program for the twenty-six Chernobyl victims who had died by that date, Gale watched with much emotion. He told Michael Ryan of *Parade* magazine (September 7 1986): "I knew many of them personally, and, on television, I could see them not as patients but as individuals, with their wives and children, in their firefighters' or military uniforms. I felt it very personally."

During his first two busy weeks in Moscow, Gale was virtually inaccessible to reporters, since the professional agreement he had reached with his hosts included the understanding that he would not become a source of information for the Western press. In fact, American doctors knew little beyond what was happening in Moscow's Hospital Six and often questioned Western reporters to obtain news of the larger picture. Before he returned to Los Angeles in mid-May, Gale finally held a press conference that was covered in the Western media and in *Pravda,* the Communist party newspaper. He also had an opportunity to meet Mikhail Gorbachev, who, effusive in his thanks to Gale and the American team, told him how moved he was by the gestures of sympathy and solidarity made by American citizens, many of whom had written letters and sent money to aid the Chernobyl victims.

In late May and in July, Gale returned on two more trips to the Soviet Union, to perform more operations and to observe the progress of the transplant patients, some of whom died. He also worked out an agreement with Soviet doctors for continued international cooperation in monitoring the 100,000 people who had lived within 18.7 miles of Chernobyl, the radius that scientists consider to be the danger zone. "I concentrated on about thirty-five people," Gale told Don Kirk of *USA Weekend* (July 18, 1986), "but as a physician I feel equally about these other 100,000." On his second trip, Gale was finally able to fulfill what by then had become an "obsession" with him, to see for himself the Chernobyl reactor and its surrounding area, when, on June 3, he, Mikhail Shandala, the deputy minister of health, and Gale's two translators, Dr. Voskresenskiy and Dr. Fetisov, took an Aeroflot helicopter from Kiev. Gale sat next to the helicopter pilot, wearing a mask for protection from radiation particles.

The sight of the Chernobyl reactor and the abandoned nearby city of Pripyat stunned Gale. His own account in *Life* magazine conveys his feelings: "Things obviously had been left in haste—laundry by open windows, a soccer ball lying in a field. . . . This was it. This is what it would look like. . . . And I thought: This is a tremendous lesson. I felt a sense of awe and a pressing need to try to memorize this. . . . This was something terribly important, like Hiroshima, Nagasaki, Dachau— and somehow I felt I had to transmit this message." It impressed on him the harsh truth of what he said to Gorbachev when the two had met: that considering the limited nature of the accident and the extent of the medical resources required to deal with it, it would be impossible to respond in any meaningful way to a nuclear accident of greater magnitude, let alone the horror of a nuclear war.

That is the burden of the message that Gale took with him from his experiences and that he conveys in the interviews he has granted since his return from the Soviet Union. Although he insists that his trips were medical, not "political," (and Gale found that he had to resist the overtures of Soviet dissidents, to speak in their behalf), he hopes, "Perhaps

Chernobyl can bring our two leaders together. . . . Can you imagine what would happen if there were *intentional* use of nuclear weapons? This is too small a planet."

Robert Gale's passionate concern for human life strikes those who meet him for the first time. His obsessive love for his work consumes his time and energy. The day after he returned from his trips to Moscow, he was back in the leukemia wards of UCLA visiting his patients. He is married to Tamar, an Israeli archeologist whom he met in Jerusalem in 1974, and the couple have three children, Tal,

Shir, and Elan. The family converses in Hebrew at their home in Los Angeles' fashionable neighborhood of Bel Air. Gale is said to be working on a book about his experiences at Chernobyl that is scheduled for publication in the spring of 1988.

References: Maclean's 100:5+ Jl 6 '87 por; N Y Times Mag p22+ Jl 13 '86 pors; USA Weekend Mag p4+ Jl 18–20 '86 pors; Parade Mag p17 S 7 '86 por; American Men and Women of Science (1982); Who's Who in Frontiers of Science and Technology (1985)

Gehry, Frank O(wen)

Feb. 28, 1929– Architect. Address: b. Frank O. Gehry and Associates, Inc., 11 Brooks Ave., Venice, Calif. 90291

There are those who claim that Frank O. Gehry is really an artist who just happens to design buildings, but Gehry, rejecting what he considers to be that dismissive appraisal, often feels compelled to insist that he is first and foremost an architect. He is, moreover, an architect with a more than usual feeling for buildings as sculptural objects ("spatial containers" he terms them) and one who has often collaborated with visual artists, with whom he finds "a great common language."

A late modernist rather than one of the postmodern architects, Gehry nevertheless shares with the latter their rejection of brute architecture and preference for designs geared to a human scale. But he does not accept their deliberate eclecticism of

style, and his work is a defiantly original response to his commitment not "to make something cute and pretty" but to achieve "a certain toughness." A recent guide to the architecture of the Los Angeles area revealed that the largest number of buildings by a single architect are by Gehry.

Gehry's work of the late 1970s into the early 1980s—shopping malls, school and museum complexes, office buildings, and private residences—use low-budget, unpretentious materials and harmonize with their settings in the typical American urban sprawl. A certain notoriety has attached to his bold use of chain-link fencing, plywood, raw concrete, and sheets of corrugated metal in many of those designs. He confesses that he actually hates chain link as "cheapskate architecture," but uses it deliberately because it is omnipresent on the American scene. Another of his contributions has been what the architectural critic Paul Goldberger calls the unfinished building, in which the construction elements are left visible to the observer. Such works, seemingly still in progress, provide freshness and surprise. Recently, there have been signs that Gehry is moving toward a "straighter" architecture, returning to the more orthodox modernism of certain of his designs of the 1960s and early 1970s.

Frank Owen Gehry, who is so identified with southern California, is in fact Canadian by birth. He was born in Toronto on February 28, 1929, the son of Irving and Thelma (Caplan) Gehry. It may be possible to relate his oscillations between avantgarde design and buildings of more orthodox style and construction to a childhood of alternating family chaos and order. His father was a businessman who has been described by Gehry's sister, the urban designer Doreen Nelson, as having been both charismatic and unstable, a man who "subjected the family to frightening cycles of boom and bust," both economically and psychically. His influence proved a troubling one for his son. Their mother, on the other hand, was highly organized and helped to support the family, eventually by becoming an interior decorator. Meantime, she encouraged her son's development by taking him to museums and concerts. Building blocks and Erector sets were his favorite childhood toys, and one of his most vivid memories is that of his grandmother, in Toronto, building houses and cities with him.

The family settled in Los Angeles in 1947, and Gehry attended the University of Southern California, where he enrolled first as a fine arts major, from 1949 to 1951. He returned in 1954 to obtain his bachelor's degree in architecture, after a year spent working as a designer of commercial spaces for Victor Gruen Associates in Los Angeles. After a year of military service in the United States Army Special Services Division (1955–56), Gehry embarked on postgraduate work, not in architecture but in city planning, at the Harvard Graduate School of Design (1956–57). His developing career included affiliations with Robert and Company, architects, in Atlanta (1955–56); Hideo Sasaki Associates, Boston (1957); Pereira & Luckman, Los Angeles (1957–58); and, as a project director, for Victor Gruen again (1958–61) and for André Remondet in Paris (1961). It was in 1962, the year of his father's death, that he established his own firm, Frank O. Gehry and Associates, Inc., in Los Angeles. Their first project was the 1963 Kay Jewelers Office Building in that city, which like the Steeves House in Brentwood, California, designed in collaboration with Greg Walsh in 1959, manifests the influence of Frank Lloyd Wright and of Japanese architecture. The little O'Niel Hay Barn, built in Orange County, California in 1966, was his first work conceived of as sculptural form, in this case one built, within a few weeks, of telephone poles and corrugated metal. From then on, an inventory of Gehry buildings reveals a range of styles and types that justifies his reputation as an authentic original and documents his self-defined principle of an architecture "in the pursuit of firmness, commodity, and delight."

That commitment perhaps provides the key to one of Gehry's best-known buildings—the house in Santa Monica that he redesigned for his own use in 1978 and 1979. Taking what he calls a "dumb little house with charm," a two-story 1920s bungalow, he surrounded it on three sides with a shell of chain-link fencing, corrugated metal, and unpainted plywood. Walls and ceilings were stripped, and the laths were left exposed. Out of the original windows, now framed to become objects, one can see into and be seen from the new part of the house. There is further playful spatial ambiguity in that there are now two doors, for behind the new one stands the old original. You enter, but are still outside. For all its surreal effects the house is nevertheless eminently livable, retaining the comfortable spirit of the old suburban home within its new carapace. "A major work of architecture," according to no less an authority than Paul Goldberger, it has for the architect Philip Johnson "a disturbing kind of satisfaction that you don't get in anyone else's spaces." Neighbors, however, vociferously protested its bizarre presence in their midst.

Frank O. Gehry's concern for space specifically designed to enliven the life it will contain, also guided the creation of his mini-campus for Loyola Marymount University Law School (1981–84). Located in a nondescript downtown Los Angeles neighborhood, its original buildings reflected the area's banality and offered the students no place or incentive to linger between classes or to meet for informal discussions. Members of the faculty feared that the quality of learning might be impaired. Working with the university administration, Gehry came up with a plan designed to promote cross-campus flow. Two small classroom buildings, a moot court, and a chapel, cluster around a Zen-inspired courtyard, against the backdrop of a larger combined classroom, office, and student-center building. Although the student center presents to the neighborhood an appropriately quiet, gray stucco façade, on its inner, or campus, side it is faced in bright ocher stucco. In accord with Gehry principles, relatively inexpensive materials were used, for example Finnish plywood on the chapel's street façade. Its campus-facing side is glass, revealing exposed wooden structural elements. An adjacent "campanile" (actually bell-less) and the four stubby concrete columns, without bases and capitals, outside the moot court make dignified but unself-conscious allusions to classical architecture and academic tradition. As the architect Robert A. M. Stern has summed it up, in his book *Pride of Place*, the mini-campus becomes a scholarly retreat, one that fosters a sense of identity and worth, but one always consonant with the realities of its surroundings. One of Gehry's own strong beliefs, in fact, is that "architecture ought to deal with reality."

Another of the Gehry's precepts is evident here: his preference for assemblages of small individual structures as opposed to the monolithic glass-box type of modern architecture. Before Loyola Law School, there was his 1974 commission to do the corporate headquarters of Rouse Company. On a lakeside site in Columbia, Maryland, he built a village-like cluster of small structures, each devoted to a departmental division of the firm. It was, nevertheless, one of his more matter-of-fact constructions, and although his plan did include an abstract glass sculpture by Larry Bell, James W. Rouse and his associates rejected it as too avant-garde. Later there was Gehry's more daring Wosk Residence (1982–84). Charged with reconverting the top floor-and-a-half of a Beverly Hills apartment house into a studio-apartment for the owner's daughter, Gehry designed a grouping of several small structures (each being a separate room) of different shapes and colors. The result, an offbeat mini-village, actually brings the entire building into harmony with its neighboring small-scale, richly detailed private homes.

Among a number of attention-getting suburban residences the architect has designed to take advantage of their southern California beach sites is the Guest House and Gallery built for the art collector Norton Simon (1976). The tranquillity of the ocean-front view and the classical antiquities on display is underscored by the modest building materials that were predominantly used and by the human proportions of the design. A similar respect for space and light makes his shopping malls, like Santa Monica Place (1973–80) or the three-level Galleria in Oklahoma City (1983), unique. The former, one of his largest and most costly projects, has been described as a festive high-tech environment and praised for its avoidance of the usual drab, closed-in look of urban malls.

Two of Gehry's works besides his own home have involved the transformation of existing buildings into vibrantly exciting spaces. The California Aerospace Museum (1982–84), his renovation of an old Los Angeles armory, has been termed by Gehry "a fantasy . . . a baroque space shuttle." Its dominant features are the way separate building units, different in shape, size, and color, come together as a whole, and the dramatic façade over which a jet fighter is cantilevered in nose-dive position. In 1983 Gehry turned an old Los Angeles garage and warehouse into a theatre for a multimedia performance, *Available Light*, devised by the avant-garde dancer Lucinda Childs and the minimalist composer John Adams. The set design featured a two-level platform for simultaneous action and a scrim of his "favorite" chain link. Although he lost the design competition for the new Los Angeles Museum of Contemporary Art, Gehry's warehouse renovation was eventually turned into an annex, dubbed Temporary Contemporary, for the museum.

There is a distinctly altruistic side to Frank Gehry, particularly with respect to the well-being of children. He once worked with the artists Claes Oldenburg and Coosje van Bruggen on plans for a camp—never completed—for terminally ill children, with a kitchen, for example, shaped like a milk can. Over the years he has worked with the Los Angeles school system, the National Endowment for the Arts, and the Smithsonian Institution in developing programs to introduce young people to the concepts and problems of urban planning. Three of his own projects are museums that are specifically laid out to encourage hands-on experiences for children: Arts Park (1978) in the San Fernando Valley; the Cabrillo Marine Museum (1979) in San Pedro, California; and the Los Angeles Children's Museum (1980). For an invitational competition to design an art museum and an adjoining children's library—the Médiathèque-Centre d'Art Contemporain—in Nîmes, France, he submitted a plan that presented the structures as sculptural objects with appropriate allusions to one of the city's famous Roman landmarks, the Maison Carrée.

One of Gehry's less audacious recent buildings is the Frances Howard Goldwyn Regional Branch Library in Hollywood (1983–84), a grouping of glass boxes, indeed, but one that does not abandon the established Gehry principles of providing comfortable spaces in which people can move easily, and in which advantage is taken of natural light here emanating through a central fountain court. Other mainstream projects currently under way include a building for the Yale University medical school, mixed-purpose building complexes in Cleveland and Dallas, and an office building in Venice, California, that will incorporate as its entranceway feature a forty-five-foot-tall binocular-shaped structure designed by Oldenburg and van Bruggen.

All of Gehry's projects begin with a sort of free-association process in which he connects what he knows about his client with his own notions of the forms and structures required. "Starting with pure fantasy is a reputable way to arrive at doing the real thing," he reasons. His fantasizing entails drawings, which are for him a way of getting to an idea, "a frantic kind of searching." Far from typical architectural renderings, they are art works in their own right and have been exhibited as such at the Musée des Arts Décoratifs in Paris in 1973, at the Cooper-Hewitt Museum in New York in 1977, and in a one-man show at the Max Protetch Gallery in New York in 1982.

Between 1969 and 1973 Gehry, who has always enjoyed working directly with materials, devised a line of furniture made of layers of corrugated cardboard. Playful shapes, yet functional, strong enough to sit or lie on, Easy Edges, as he called them, were extremely inexpensive and proved enormously popular. In fact, Gehry could have become wealthy marketing them, but withdrew the line in favor of getting on with his work as an architect, although between 1979 and 1982 he elaborated another, less popular series of cardboard furniture called Experimental Edges. In 1983 he was commissioned by the Formica Corporation to create designs for their plastic laminate ColorCore. Dissatisfied with what he had at first worked out, he took a sample of the new material and broke it. The resulting chips suggested fish scales to him, and developing that suggestion, he went on to fashion laminate lamps in the forms of fish and, later, of snakes.

Gehry's sensitivity to the problems of museum planning, coupled with his interest in painting and sculpture, has engaged him in a number of much-praised exhibition designs for the Los Angeles County Museum of Art. Starting in 1965 with "Art Treasures from Japan," he planned installations for, among other shows, "The Treasures of Tutankhamen" (1978), "The Avant-Garde in Russia 1910–1930" (1980), "Seventeen Artists in the Sixties" (1981), and "German Expressionist Sculpture" (1983). When he took part in the 1980 Venice Biennale, his own design for a screened-in enclosure in which models of his recent works were exhibited constituted an integral part of the show. In 1986 a major retrospective of his work opened at the Walker Art Center in Minneapolis, and was scheduled to travel to Houston, Toronto, and Atlanta before closing in 1988 at the Los Angeles Museum of Contemporary Art. Models of his buildings, photographs, and architectural drawings, and examples of his cardboard furniture were exhibited, but the main features of the show were the five room-size structures that replicated and summarized themes and materials of his actual architecture, enabling museum visitors to experience his spaces. One of them, the centerpiece of the installation, was a gigantic fish-shaped enclosure, constructed of copper with lead scales, appropriately housing examples of his fish and snake lamps.

For his extremely varied body of work Gehry received the 1983 Arnold W. Brunner Prize awarded annually by the American Academy and Institute of Arts and Letters to "an architect who has made a significant contribution to architecture as an art." In June 1987 he and Patrick Naggar won the first annual House and Garden Design Awards for outstanding achievement in residential design in the United States. A corporate member of the American Institute of Architects, he was elected in 1974 to its College of Fellows for his design achievements, and in May 1987 he was made a member of the American Academy and Institute of Arts and Letters. In 1984 he held the Eliot Noyes Design Chair at Harvard University's Graduate School of Design. He has also taught or served as visiting critic at the University of Southern California, U.C.L.A., Southern California Institute of Architecture, Parsons School of Design, and Yale, where one of his students characterized him as "a man who wanted to free people up rather than sell his own doctrines." It is a fact that he has as yet established no school of followers.

In his studio, now located in a structure designed by the architect himself in the seedily chic artists' enclave of Venice, California, Gehry spends long hours at work. "I love my kids, my wife, but I'm so intensely involved . . . I never remember anything personal," he has confessed. Despite his reputation as a maverick, his first consideration is for working out his clients' problems, and he prides himself on projects that come in on time and on budget, and that are planned with due consideration for their architectural context. "Actually," he has joked, "I'm very conventional. I even go to Brooks Brothers." By a first marriage Gehry had two children. In 1975 he remarried, and he and his second wife, the former Berta Aguilera of Panama, have two sons. His owlish mien is reinforced by his glasses and his direct glance. This "rumpled, humorous and intense man," as he was described in the *New York Times Magazine* (May 16, 1982), is, interviewers agree, immensely likable and easy to talk to. As for his intensity, Frank O. Gehry finds that now that he is not so compelled to prove himself, he feels that he can "relax a little."

References: *Maclean's 100:U3+ S 28 '87; N Y Times Mag p48+ My 16 16 '82 por; Washington Post G p1+ My 2 '87 por; Contemporary Architects (1980); Gehry, Frank O. Buildings and Projects (1985) por; Who's Who in America, 1986–87*

Gephardt, Richard (Andrew)

Jan. 31, 1941– United States Representative from Missouri. Address: b. 1436 Longworth House Office Bldg., Washington, D.C. 20515

On February 23, 1987, Representative Richard A. Gephardt of Missouri became the first Democrat officially to declare his intention to run for president of the United States in 1988. Less than two months later, he became the first candidate from either political party to have raised enough money from at least twenty states to become eligible for matching federal funds for individual contributions up to $250. Whether or not he will succeed in his effort to be the first member since James A. Garfield in 1880 to make the leap from the House of Representatives to the White House remains to be seen. He is still a dark horse and a nationally unknown quantity, but he has campaigned extensively in Iowa, whose primary on February 8, 1988, will be the first major test of the race. Indeed, Gephardt had made frequent visits there even before he made his official announcement. Political commentators believe that Gephardt is the candidate who has gained the most from Gary Hart's withdrawal from the race and that he also stands to benefit from the decision of Senator Sam Nunn of Georgia not to run.

Richard Andrew Gephardt was born in St. Louis, Missouri, on January 31, 1941, the second son of

Louis Andrew and Loreen (Cassell) Gephardt, who were both the grandchildren of German immigrants. When Gephardt reported that his father was the driver of a milk truck and his mother a legal secretary, his critics accused him of trying to

curry public favor by making his background seem more humble that it actually was. The elder Gephardt, they have noted, left his milk truck after a decade on the job and became involved in real estate, where he prospered.

Gephardt, who was an Eagle Scout, completed his secondary education at Southwest High School in St. Louis and then enrolled at Northwestern University in Evanston, Illinois, where he majored in speech and drama. A big man on campus, he was vice-president of the freshman class, a member of the Honor Society, president of the Beta Theta Pi fraternity while a junior, and president of the student senate in his senior year. After graduating with a B.S. degree in 1962, Gephardt continued his education at the Law School of the University of Michigan, where he obtained a J.D. degree three years later.

After graduating from law school, Gephardt decided to try his hand at politics in the south St. Louis community where he had grown up. "Making money has never turned me on," he has said. "I'm not interested in fancy cars and what money can buy." He and his bride, the former Jane Ann Byrnes, began attending Democratic party meetings in their home ward. Although the Gephardts were the only people under fifty in attendance, they eventually won the respect and trust of the regulars.

When the death, in 1968, of the politician who had been the Democratic committeeman for St. Louis's fourteenth ward for forty years created an opportunity for Gephardt, he took over the post and remained in it for three years. In 1971 he won election to the St. Louis board of aldermen, and together with several other younger members, worked to reinvigorate the stagnating city by sponsoring zoning laws that helped to preserve ethnic neighborhoods and by building a base of support in the German-American working-class communities of the south side. At the same time, he managed not to alienate the older political regulars who dominated the board. While carving his niche in local politics, Gephardt also practiced law. He became a partner in Thompson & Mitchell, the city's second-largest law firm, where he had worked as a messenger boy in his youth. He also managed to find time to perform military service in the Missouri Air National Guard, as a captain and legal officer between 1965 and 1971.

Gephardt had set his sights on running for mayor of St. Louis in 1976, but, on the day that he had intended to tell his law partners of his plan, Leonor Sullivan, the long-time representative from Missouri's Third Congressional District, unexpectedly announced her intention to retire. The young alderman, who had aspired to the seat but would never have challenged the twelve-term Democratic incumbent for it, immediately changed his plans. The primary to determine the Democratic candidate for the Third Congressional District pitted Gephardt against Donald J. Gralicke, a state senator and head of an electrical workers' union local, and two other candidates. Gralicke had mustered

support among Democratic operatives in the suburban areas included in the district, but Gephardt was stronger in south St. Louis and ran a much better media campaign. In the end, Gephardt's 16,000-vote advantage within the city was his margin of victory over Gralicke, and he won the election with 56 percent of the 87,000 votes cast.

In the 1976 general election, Gephardt faced Joseph L. Badaracco, a veteran Republican politician with the advantage of wide name recognition, who had served eight years on the board of aldermen, had been its president for six of them, and had been an unsuccessful candidate for mayor of St. Louis in 1973. The Republican contender tried to portray his Democratic opponent as an elite downtown lawyer and member of the "establishment," but Gephardt was able to convince the electorate that he would pursue the moderate policies of Leonor Sullivan. On election day he took 64 percent of the almost 181,000 votes cast.

Richard Gephardt has not faced a serious challenge since that first election. In 1978 he took 82 percent of the vote against Lee Buchschacher in his first bid for reelection, and, in the face of the Reagan landslide two years later, he managed to tally 78 percent against Robert A. Cedarburg. When he ran against Richard Foristel in 1982, Gephardt once again took 78 percent of the vote. After being unopposed in 1984, Gephardt garnered 69 percent of the vote against Roy Amelung in 1986.

Observers thought that in 1982 Gephardt might challenge Missouri's incumbent Republican United States Senator, John C. Danforth, but early in 1981 he announced that he would not make the run. Although Danforth seemed unstoppable at the time, it turned out that he barely survived against Harriet Woods, a liberal state senator who took advantage of the state's unhappiness with the effect of "Reaganomics." Content with his secure base in the House, Gephardt likewise passed up the 1986 senatorial election, in which Christopher S. ("Kit") Bond, the popular former Republican governor, defeated Harriet Woods for the right to replace the Democrat Thomas Eagleton, who was retiring.

Representative Richard Gephardt rose quickly in the ranks of the House, and Richard Bolling, the chairman of its Rules Committee, immediately took his fellow Democrat and Missourian under his wing. With Bolling's support, Gephardt gained the almost unprecedented honor for a freshman legislator of a seat on the powerful Ways and Means Committee. Moreover, between 1979 and 1984, Gephardt had the unusual opportunity and responsibility of serving simultaneously on the Budget Committee as well as on Ways and Means.

After Ronald Reagan's election to the White House, Richard Gephardt emerged as one of the recognized leaders of the generation of younger Democrats in the House of Representatives. In 1981 the party's leaders tapped him to draft a Democratic response to the president's proposals regarding taxes and spending. In the same year they named him head of the task forces gathered to shepherd major bills on the floor of the House. After the 1984 and 1986 elections, Gephardt's fellow Democratic congressmen selected him to be chairman of their caucus, the fourth-highest post in the party's House leadership, ranking behind only the speaker, the majority leader, and the majority whip.

One key to Richard Gephardt's acknowledged leadership is his willingness to listen. Long before he was chosen caucus chairman, he was canvassing younger members for their views on the issues. "You have to talk to people, you have to include them, you have to make them part of things," Gephardt has explained, and Representative Barbara B. Kennelly of Connecticut has said: "His silence is one of his greatest strengths. He's a listener." A House aide has expressed the same thought, but less circumspectly: "Gephardt's a beautiful listener. He will suffer some of the greatest boobs in the House."

A second key to Gephardt's influence is his ability to prod his older colleagues without offending them. Dan Rostenkowski, the Democratic chairman of the House Ways and Means Committee, recalls that Gephardt, in his first years, was "an eager volunteer . . . kind of pesky." But Rostenkowski soon recognized that the junior congressman was also extremely able. Likewise, when Gephardt became a focal point for a number of younger Democrats dissatisfied with the party's House leadership, he was able to use his ties with both junior and senior members to work out a plan for more frequent meetings that would allow the voices of the juniors to be heard by the seniors.

Gephardt's ability to fashion compromises and to build coalitions grows from his self-described position as a "terminal centrist." A former aide has said that "Dick has an intuitive belief that the correct position on any issue is in the middle," and to a large extent, Gephardt's attitude also reflects the middle-of-the-road constituency that sends him so enthusiastically to Congress. The Third District divides into three sections; 35 percent is in the traditional and mostly Roman Catholic ethnic neighborhoods of south St. Louis; 40 percent in suburban St. Louis County, which favors Republican candidates, and 25 percent in politically marginal Jefferson County. Overall, the Third is modestly middle-class and predominantly white.

On February 28, 1985, in response to the overwhelming defeat suffered in the preceding November by the Democratic candidate for president, Walter Mondale, Gephardt announced the formation of the Democratic Leadership Council. With Gephardt as chairman and other younger Democrats from the South and West—including Senator Sam Nunn and Governors Charles S. Robb of Virginia and Bruce Babbitt of Arizona—making up the bulk of its membership, the council set for itself the goal of wooing the party back to a more popular centrist position. On the following weekend, Gephardt hosted a three-day session at the Greenbrier Resort in Sulphur Springs, West Virginia, where scores of House Democrats planned strategy and heard speakers, like Lee A. Iacocca, describe what the party had to do to enhance its credibility.

His critics have accused Gephardt of being ready to abandon Democratic principles and have chided him for considering changes in programs like Social Security. They admire his technical skills as a legislator but wonder about his compassion. An aide to former House Speaker Thomas P. ("Tip") O'Neill remarked of Gephardt and other "new breed" Democrats: "Tip looks at a bill, and his first question is, 'Is it fair?' I think this group asks, 'Will it sell?'" But Gephardt denies that he has abandoned the Democratic faith in active government. "The basic ideal is right," he concedes of the Democrats' outlook. "When people need help, we've got to try to help them." He notes that he and other young Democrats, who were responsible for administering locally the Great Society programs of the last generation, came to see other incentives as well as for federal aid. "It's just a question of pragmatism," he remarks, "what works, what doesn't work, especially in times of budget problems."

He resists political labels. "It may be terribly inaccurate to say that I'm a liberal or I'm a conservative or even that I'm a moderate", he has said. "I don't think those terms get us very far." Gephardt once endorsed constitutional amendments to ban abortion and school busing; he has opposed gun control legislation; he has supported the causes of school prayer and tuition credits for parents of children in private schools; and he has endorsed the invasion of Grenada and the air raid on Libya. On the other hand, he has also supported the idea of a nuclear freeze, has used his post as Democratic caucus chairman to lead opposition to the MX missile, and has worked to stop the extension of military aid to the Nicaraguan Contras.

As he has taken on a greater national role, Gephardt seems to have become somewhat more liberal on issues. His ranking from the liberal Americans for Democratic Action (ADA) rose from scores of 50 and 35 in 1977 and 1978 to marks of 85 and 75 in 1983 and 1984, and the AFL-CIO likewise raised his ratings for the same years from 70 and 75 to 94 and 92. Some of his former backers have been upset by the congressman's decision that a constitutional amendment to ban abortion, would not solve the underlying problem. He still, however, opposes federal funding for abortion and other observers have criticized as opportunistic his support for the mandatory controls on agricultural production that are the key to the Save the Family Act sponsored by Senator Thomas Harkin of Iowa.

Among the earliest politicians to latch on to such key issues as control of hospital costs and tax reduction, in 1979 Gephardt helped to defeat President Jimmy Carter's plan to impose mandatory limits on hospital costs, but he and Republican David Stockman later urged legislation that would control those costs by encouraging competition between insurance plans. In 1982 Gephardt joined with Senator Bill Bradley, the New Jersey Democrat, in proposing a "Fair Tax Act," the first step in the drive to tax reform. He then played an important role in drafting the legislation that became the Tax Reform Act of 1986.

His best-known initiative, however, has been the "Gephardt amendment," which would direct the government to identify those nations having large trade surpluses with the United States and to take action against any country that has achieved its advantage by unfair practices. In particular, unless an amicable solution could be reached through negotiation, the president would have to impose tariffs and take other punitive action that would reduce any offender's surplus by 10 percent per year. Its critics contend that the amendment would invoke retaliation and that the restrictive practices of foreign countries are responsible for only a small percentage of America's trade deficit. The House strongly supported the measure in 1986, and, by a vote of 218 to 214, added it to the Omnibus Trade Bill in 1987. The Senate, however, seemed hostile to the controversial proposal.

When Gephardt decided to declare his candidacy for the presidency, he chose to make the announcement in a half-hour speech that he delivered at St. Louis's Union Station, a former railroad depot, refurbished into a modern shopping area, where Harry S. Truman accepted his upset victory in the 1948 presidential election. Representative Thomas S. Foley of Washington, the House majority whip, and Representative Dan Rostenkowski also addressed the gathering, and almost a score of other members of Congress joined the thousands of Gephardt supporters at the festivities.

Many who were present at Gephardt's declaration of candidacy were nostalgically reminded of the rhetoric of John F. Kennedy. "I'm not doing this because I want an office but because I want to change this country," the Missourian said of his decision. "I want this country to be great again." Gephardt took Ronald Reagan to task for having given the people a "call to selfishness" and for not inspiring them to rise to a higher standard. "Now," the candidate remarked, "America must ask: 'What will it take for us to be good? How can we do better? How can we be the best?'"

The overall platform of Richard Gephardt calls for closer cooperation between business and labor, modeled on Japanese practices. It emphasizes education, both in the form of increased spending for schools and of retraining workers for new skills, and it urges controls on agricultural production to restore prosperity for the nation's farmers. Above all, it underscores the spirit of the Gephardt amendment and takes a hard line against what the congressman perceives to be the unfair trade practices of some countries.

The political demise of Gary Hart, the former senator from Colorado who had been the most prominent Democratic aspirant to the White House and Gephardt's most formidable foe in Iowa, changed the nature of the race for the presidency, to the benefit of Gephardt. A poll published for the *Des Moines Register* on May 3, 1987, the day on which reports of Hart's relationship with Donna Rice first surfaced, indicated that the Colorado Democrat enjoyed the backing of 65 percent of the party faithful in the state, Jesse Jackson 9 percent, and Gephardt 7 percent. A new poll taken for the newspaper shortly after Hart's withdrawal showed Gephardt with the support of 24 percent of Iowa's Democrats, Jackson with 13 percent, and Governor Michael S. Dukakis of Massachusetts with 11 percent.

Despite Gephardt's repeated assertions that he does not "know how it plays politically," commentators believe that his denunciations of the "predatory trade practices" of foreign nations like Japan and Korea allowed Gephardt to distinguish himself from other Democrat hopefuls after Hart stumbled. Hart himself had attacked the Gephardt amendment, and none of the six candidates, including Jackson, Babbitt, Dukakis, Senator Paul Simon of Illinois, Senator Albert Gore of Tennessee, and Senator Joseph Biden of Delaware, who engaged with Gephardt in a nationally televised debate from Houston on July 1, 1987, would endorse his amendment. Observers speculate, however, that the Missourian's advantage may prove short-lived unless he extends his campaign beyond a single issue.

In his speeches and debates in the summer and fall of 1987, Gephardt affirmed his position as a middle-of-the-roader. Described as a "neo-isolationist" by New York Republican Representative Jack F. Kemp, an old friend but political adversary, in a debate in New Hampshire in August, Gephardt referred to Ronald Reagan's "rogue foreign policy" and called the administration's support for the Nicaraguan Contra rebels "a seven-year exercise in macho and mayhem." On the other hand, speaking in Washington, D.C., a month later, Gephardt declared that the Democratic party must overcome its reputation for "soft-headedness and faintheartedness" on national security issues."

Richard Gephardt has been married to the former Jane Ann Byrnes of Nebraska since August 13, 1966. They met when she was a freshman and he a senior at Northwestern, but began their dating while he was at the law school of the University of Michigan and she was still in the Chicago area. Gephardt is a Baptist who attends church regularly, while his wife and their three children—Matthew Richard, Christine Leigh, and Katherine Hope—are Roman Catholics. Matthew has successfully recovered from what was diagnosed as terminal cancer in 1972, when he was less than two years of age. That brush with tragedy helped to shape the family's outlook on life. "You realize how fragile life is," Gephardt says. "You have this momentary opportunity. You've got to deal with the present in the best way you can."

A conservative dresser, Gephardt is well-groomed, with razor-cut red hair. He has a well-modulated voice and though he was once considered a boring speaker, his oratorical skills have improved considerably. According to the *Washington Post*, Gephardt is "the perfect television-age candidate." While Congress is in session, Gephardt and his family live in a comfortable but modest home in Virginia. They also own a house in St.

Louis, where the congressman's mother lives. For recreation, Gephardt enjoys jogging and a little tennis, and he has been, since childhood, a devoted fan of the St. Louis Cardinals baseball team.

References: Chicago Tribune V p1+ Jl 17 '87 por; Fortune 111:106+ My 13 '85; N Y Times A p1+ F 24 '87 por; People 27:40+ Ap 13 '87 por; Almanac of American Politics, 1986; Politics in America (1986); Who's Who in America, 1986–87; Who's Who in American Politics, 1985–86

Ginsberg, Allen

June 3, 1926– Poet. Address: P. O. Box 582, Peter Stuyvesant Station, New York City, N. Y. 10009

NOTE: This biography updates the article that appeared in Current Biography in 1970.

Allen Ginsberg, America's most famous living exponent of the tradition of Walt Whitman and William Carlos Williams, has been the country's laureate of alienation and protest since the 1950s, when he wrote his two best-known poems, "Howl" and "Kaddish." The latter is generally considered to be his finest work, but it has not had the public impact of "Howl," an apocalyptic and visceral outpouring of rage at what Ginsberg perceived to be the inferno of contemporary society. Uttered in a strophic style, or in what the poet calls his "Hebraic-Melvillian breath," "Howl" culminates in beatific transcendence.

With "Howl," Ginsberg emerged as the first and leading poetic voice of the Beat Generation, the bohemian literary movement of the 1950s, and he has

been a conspicuous figure in the counterculture, including the peace movement, ever since. Of the original circle of Beat writers, only he and Gary Snyder remain as energizing forces in the American culture of today. "If the poetics of Ginsberg has mellowed to a conventional meter in which daily life is too amply recorded," the literary scholar Paul Cristensen has written, "the thread of his moral conscience born in the fury of 'Howl' and 'Kaddish' shapes and enlivens his most recent work. . . . Ginsberg's unique achievement has been to voice the despair and anxiety of several generations of Americans as America formed itself into a superpower."

Allen Ginsberg was born on June 3, 1926, in Newark, New Jersey, the son of Louis and Naomi (Levy) Ginsberg. Louis Ginsberg, who died in 1976, was a high school English teacher and poet of conservative bent who regarded his son, with perplexity, as "such an experimenter." Allen inherited his "mad idealism" from his mother, a Russian-born dedicated Marxist who died in a mental institution in 1956. He described his parents as "old-fashioned delicatessen philosophers" in an interview with Ron Grossman for the Chicago Tribune (November 30, 1986). He recalled: "My father would go around the house either reciting Emily Dickinson and Longfellow under his breath or attacking T. S. Eliot for ruining poetry with his 'obscurantism.' My mother made up bedtime stories that went something like: 'The good king rode forth from his castle, saw the suffering of the workers, and healed them.' I grew up suspicious of both sides." The trauma of witnessing his mother's protracted mental and emotional deterioration as well as the confused passions she evoked in him would be exorcised in the intense elegy "Kaddish for Naomi Ginsberg (1894–1956)," better known simply as "Kaddish."

With his brother, Eugene, who became a lawyer, Ginsberg grew up in Paterson, New Jersey. With the halfhearted goal, inspired by his mother, of defending the underprivileged at the bar, Allen Ginsberg enrolled at Columbia University in New York City on a YMHA scholarship in 1943. Originally intending to major in prelaw, he changed his major to literature and became the star student of Mark Van Doren and Lionel Trilling, whose relative traditionalism, the legacy of George Edward Woodberry, dominated the study of literature at Columbia at that time.

More influential in Ginsberg's artistic as well as personal development was the off-campus circle of underground (and, in some cases, underworld) literati in which he became involved. At its center were Jack Kerouac, a former Columbia student four years older than he, and the considerably older William S. Burroughs, a sophisticated cosmopolitan "hipster" who introduced his younger friends to Manhattan's sybaritic subculture, to exotic drugs, and to the literature of rebellion, and who in 1959 would publish his notorious surreal satire of American life called Naked Lunch. The members of the circle, including Herbert Hunke, John Clellon Holmes, Lucien Carr, and Neal Cassady, were seminal personalities of the "Beat Generation," which would begin to surface as a movement in the mid-1950s with the publication of "Howl" and Kerouac's bohemian-hobo novel *On the Road*. In his essay on Ginsberg in the *Dictionary of Literary Biography* (1980) John Ower pointed out that the sophisticated, balanced mixture and "prophetic seriousness and comic detachment" of "Howl" was reached "only after the poet's radical Romantic stance had contributed to his personal problems."

Ginsberg's major personal problems rose out of immature homosexual passion and brushes-by-association with the law. In the aftermath of a murder committed by Lucien Carr in 1945, Ginsberg was suspended from Columbia for a year, during which he worked as a merchant seaman, a Times Square restaurant dishwasher, and a reporter for a New Jersey newspaper. Returning to Columbia, he maintained an A-minus average and took his B.A. degree in 1948. It was in 1948 that he had, during masturbation, his first mystical vision, a paranormal illumination in which he experienced a supernal voice reciting from William Blake's "Songs of Experience." Early the following year Herbert Hunke moved into Ginsberg's Manhattan apartment. When Hunke, a *poète maudit* who stole to support his drug habit and stored his loot in the apartment, was arrested and sentenced to five years in jail, Ginsberg, circumstantially implicated, pleaded psychological disability and was committed to the Columbia Psychiatric Institute for eight months. There he became acquainted with fellow inmate Carl Solomon, the "lunatic saint" to whom he would dedicate "Howl." Solomon deepened Ginsberg's understanding of poetry as an act of prophecy and political resistance and was instrumental in introducing him to the writings of André Breton and the other French Surrealists, who sought inspiration from the irrational unconscious through dreams, automatic writing, and other such means.

After his release from the Columbia Psychiatric Institute, Ginsberg went home to Paterson to live with his father. During that stay in Paterson he became a friend of the physician and writer William Carlos Williams, who in his poetry and fiction celebrated common life in the United States. Williams impressed on Ginsberg, who had written traditional verse in college, the importance of paying attention to the world immediately around him and recording his plain observations in the rhythms of the American idiom. Catalyzed by Williams' advice, Ginsberg shifted in his poetry into the more spontaneous mode of composition that Kerouac had adopted in his fiction writing and had been urging Ginsberg to try. Ginsberg called the mode "speedworthy," connoting both acceleration of composition and the use of the amphetamine Benzedrine (called "speed" in slang) for that purpose. The model for such composition was, ironically, Neal Cassady, who was not a writer but a high-energy bisexual athlete and a spellbinding, lyrical talker spinning out riffs of words and ideas, like a bop musician, while engaged in such activities as driving across country at speeds above 100 miles per hour. As Paul Christensen pointed out in his Ginsberg entry in the *Dictionary of Literary Biography* (1983): "Cassady is the source for a technique of expression that fundamentally subverted calculated choice and revision of words, a technique which the Beats saw as a means of opposing a calculating and regimented society."

Ginsberg remained in the New York City area until 1953, supporting himself mainly by working as a market researcher. Deciding to follow Neal Cassady (who had married) to San Francisco, he left New York in December 1953 and, after visiting Cuba and Yucatan, arrived in California in 1954. In San Francisco he stayed with the Cassadys briefly, until Cassady's wife, Carolyn, evicted him. As if following Cassady's lead, Ginsberg acquired a live-in girlfriend, a well-paying job in market research, and a middle-class apartment, and tried living a life of bourgeois domesticity. After a year he decided, with the blessing of his psychotherapist, to shuck the straight life and all of its trappings, to quit his job, "get a room with Peter [Orlovsky] and devote [himself] to writing and contemplation, to Blake and smoking pot, and doing whatever [he] wanted."

In San Francisco, Ginsberg became part of what was known at the time as the San Francisco Poetry Renaissance, a literary scene presided over by Kenneth Rexroth and Lawrence Ferlinghetti and including Gary Snyder, Michael McClure, Philip Whalen, Robert Duncan, and Philip Lamantia. In October 1955 Rexroth hosted a poetry reading at the Six Gallery in San Francisco in which Snyder, McClure, Whalen, and Lamantia participated, along with Ginsberg, in his poetry-reading debut. On that occasion Ginsberg read his newly composed poem "Howl," an event that signaled the birth of the Beat revolution.

The title of "Howl" was suggested by Jack Kerouac, to whom the poem's outpouring of pent-up rage resembled the rising and falling cry of wolves or dogs in pain or distress. Ginsberg himself explained that the structure of "Howl," comprising a long series of breath units, ·or exhalations, "developed out of an extreme rhapsodic wail [he] once heard in a madhouse." The poem is written in Whitmanesque measure, with haiku-like compression of language within the lines. The language itself is colloquial, often shockingly so, although the obscenity and scatology are consonant with the charged rhetoric, in which bitterness is relieved by whimsical humor. As William Carlos Williams suggested in his introduction to the first edition of the poem, "Howl" is a Dantesque journey through a contemporary American hell, with three stages, beginning with descent and culminating in return. The first section is a lamentation for "the best minds of my generation destroyed by madness" in a sick urban society. In the second, Ginsberg invokes the myth of the Phoenician god Moloch, to whom children were sacrificed, to personify the sickness, a demonic power "whose mind is pure machinery . . . whose fingers are ten armies . . . whose factories dream and croak in the fog . . . whose soul is electricity and banks . . . who frightened me out of my natural ecstacy." The third section is a homage to Carl Solomon, an apostle of artistic rebellion against the new Moloch. A concluding footnote counters the latter-day Moloch's puritanism with an ecstatic litany of all that is holy in the world, including the body. Thus, the cycle that began with death, or descent into hell, ends with rebirth through transcendent vision.

When Ginsberg read "Howl" at the Six Gallery, the audience felt itself transformed into "a secret new community within the drab masses of mid-century America," as Paul Christensen recounted in the *Dictionary of Literary Biography*. "The performance Ginsberg gave was uncanny, and the poem itself established his reputation as a major voice of the era." Following the reading, Kenneth Rexroth's wife, Martha, privately distributed a mimeographed, fifty-copy edition of *Howl for Carl Solomon*, containing several poems in addition to "Howl." In 1956 Lawrence Ferlinghetti, who had recently founded City Lights Books, published the larger but still slim selection *Howl and Other Poems* in his Pocket Poets series. United States Customs officers and the San Francisco police seized the edition, and Lawrence Ferlinghetti was charged with publishing an obscene book. The court case, which Ferlinghetti won in 1957, gave the book immense publicity, and by the time the trial was over, Ginsberg was widely in demand for poetry readings and Beat and other anarchist-style literary happenings.

From the late 1950s on, Ginsberg based himself in New York (where he acquired a farm upstate, in Cherry Valley, in addition to the slum apartment that he still maintains on Manhattan's Lower East Side) while traveling widely in Europe, Latin America, North Africa, and the Far East as well as the United States. Into the early 1960s he experimented heavily with drugs, especially with hallucinogens (including LSD, under the guidance of Timothy Leary), partly as an aid to poetic creativity. Parts 1 and 2 of "Kaddish to Naomi Ginsberg (1894–1956)"—the title poem in *Kaddish and Other Poems* (City Lights, 1961)—were written under the influence of a combination of amphetamines and morphine. Twice as long as "Howl" and a more mature achievement, that poem is a confessional work in which he came to terms with his mother's tragic life and death and his Oedipal tie to her. In his younger years he had responded negatively to her paranoid fantasies of persecution and the terrible states to which they reduced her. Now, purging his traumatic memories of the past by narrating them in harrowing detail, he was able to recognize her as a martyr in the cause of forbidden passions and dreams, to express his love for her, and, after much anguish, to celebrate her death as a liberating transcendence.

Much less successful were the drug-related poems written between 1953 and 1960 that were collected in *Reality Sandwiches* (City Lights, 1963), in which Ginsberg seemed hung-up on the obsessions of his earlier adolescent self. Early poems, written before Ginsberg shifted into his spontaneous mode, were collected under the title *Empty Mirror* (Corinth Books, 1961). Still troubled by his perception of the universe as an inhuman mystery, Ginsberg sought the counsel of Martin Buber in Israel and of holy men in India and emerged with a new attitude, renouncing his mystical aspirations in favor of "direct vision, sense perception, contact with the now of life." That turning point was the occasion as well as the subject of the title poem of *The Change* (Writer's Forum, 1963). In his tours of American universities in the mid-1960s, Ginsberg began to preach the superiority of yoga and meditation to drugs, but he did not rule out the usefulness of such psychedelics as marijuana, peyote, and, occasionally, LSD as aids to poetic creativity and he continued to campaign for the liberalization of drug laws. While he warned against the use of addictive hard drugs, such as heroin, he deplored the government's manipulation of the publicized danger of those drugs, among others, for its own ends.

As a guru to the new countercultural generation known as the hippies—and their more politically militant cousins, the prankish Yippies—Ginsberg invented the term "flower power" in 1965 and was the moving spirit behind the Gathering of the Tribes for a Human Be-In, the first of the hippies' evangelical picnics, held in Golden Gate Park in San Francisco in January 1967. Later in 1967 he was arrested in an anti-Vietnam war demonstration in New York City, and during the demonstrations at the 1968 Democratic National Convention in Chicago he was tear-gassed by police while trying to induce calm by chanting mantras. At the conspiracy trial of the Chicago demonstration leaders, known as the Chicago Seven, he testified for the defense.

The poems in *Planet News: 1961–1967* (City Lights, 1968) constitute a poetic record of Ginsberg's travels in Eastern Europe, the Indian subcontinent, and other parts of Asia as well as in the United States. Included in the collection was "Wichita Vortex Sutra," inspired by his tour of Midwestern universities. Reviewing the book along with *T.V. Baby Poems* (Grossman, 1968) and *Ankor Wat* (Fulcrum, 1968), in the *New York Times* (May 17, 1969), Thomas Lask observed that Ginsberg had become "firmer" in his craft but continued to use elision, juxtaposition, and frequent lists, "as if he wanted to be sure that no bit of experience would be left out."

The collection *The Fall of America: Poems of These States, 1965–1971* (City Lights, 1973) brought Ginsberg the National Book Award. The poems in that collection are for the most part melancholy as well as angry, expressing Ginsberg's "car bus airplane dream consciousness" of a severe national crisis, manifested in the futile brutality of the Vietnam war, reckless ecological pollution, and mass-media mind control in the service of the military, political, and economic powers-that-be. "The poet's rather grim vision is indicated on the personal level by his awareness of his aging, by the injuries that he sustained during a car crash in 1968, and by the . . . deaths of Cassady (in 1968) and Kerouac (in 1969) . . . ," John Ower observed. "The deaths of Kerouac and Cassady become symbols of the loss by America of the Edenic and epic potentials celebrated by Whitman."

In 1974 Ginsberg helped to found the Jack Kerouac School of Disembodied Poetics of the Naropa Institute in Boulder, Colorado, a Buddhist university where he continues to teach summer courses in poetry and Buddhist meditation. That same year he was inducted into the American Institute of Arts and Letters. After the Vietnam war ended, Ginsberg concentrated his political energy on efforts to expose alleged CIA subsidization of drug trafficking; in attempts to reform American drug laws, the enforcement of those laws, and the treatment of addicts; in the environmental and antinuclear, and sexual freedom causes; and in speaking out against governmental covert action, including the FBI's harassment of the countercultural press, among other accretions of the "surveillance state." Recently, he added his voice to those protesting the Reagan administration's interference in Nicaragua, and he wrote the poem "Plutonium Ode" for declamation at a demonstration in which he participated at the Rocky Flats, Colorado, plutonium works. Ginsberg's loss of "any hope for the salvation of America" led him more deeply into Buddhism, under the guidance of Chogyam Trungpa, the Tibetan guru who supervises the Naropa Institute. In addition to instructing Ginsberg in Kagu Buddhist meditation, Trungpa has served as his general adviser, in artistic as well as spiritual matters.

From the beginning, there was a relationship between Beat poetry and music, especially jazz. Many of Ginsberg's early poetry readings included jazz accompaniment, and later he set poems by William Blake to simple music and chanted them in his public performances, accompanying himself on a small, hand-operated harmonium. Still later, he began singing, or chanting, some of his own poems to his own accompaniment on the harmonium. In 1977 he performed spontaneously composed blues poems as a member of the Rolling Thunder Revue (named after one of the songs), a touring troupe organized by the folk/rock musician Bob Dylan. Those compositions were among the simple ballads and blues lyrics meant to be sung or chanted in Mind Breaths (City Lights, 1978). Many of the poems, mostly meditations for spiritual renewal, were accompanied by score sheets indicating spare melodic lines.

After publishing his books for years with small alternative-press houses, Ginsberg signed a $160,000 contract with Harper & Row for six books. The first, Collected Poems 1947-1980, was issued in 1984. Reviewing the more-than-800-page collection in the New York Times Book Review (December 30, 1984), Lewis Hyde noted the gradual modulations of Ginsberg's poetic voice over the years. The poems in the collections Howl and Kaddish, he pointed out, were those of "a young man hungry for love and hungry for God . . . a man whose hunger had been satiated, if only for a moment." In striving for poetic perfection, he learned how to transcribe the American idiom (from William Carlos Williams), how to speak the language of hallucination (from the Surrealists), and how to shock with juxtaposition (from the paintings of Cézanne). While mastering the craft of modern poetry, he kept his original vision, so that his poetry remained a theodicy, spoken, in Hyde's words, "in the prophetic voice of one who believes that angels help the poets to write and that evil powers feed on the nation's tender hearts." In time, however, when his epiphanies failed to free him from his discontent, he seemed increasingly to doubt his vocation as an explorer of altered states of consciousness, and that doubt, in Hyde's words, "set him adrift as he had been in the years before 'Howl.'" He did not find his way again for a decade (roughly the 1960s), during which he indulged his wanderlust and wrote poetry that was predominantly travelogue. Finally, he began to practise—and not just talk about—Buddhism, and to write about that practice. His preoccupations—supernatural entities, family, love and longing—remained the same, but his poetry became "a meditation on such preoccupations, not an attempt to make them real."

The collection White Shroud (Harper & Row, 1986) brings together poems written by Ginsberg between 1980 and 1985, including several composed during a visit to China and the title poem, a sequel to "Kaddish," more peaceful than the latter in its reconciliation with death. Much of his current poetry is a psychological return to the themes of his earlier work. "It must be a part of aging, this need to try and make sense out of things," he told Ron Grossman. "One day you wake up, as Blake put it, 'disguised as an old person.' Lately, my dreams—which are a prime source of inspiration—have been reviewing the major epiphanies of my life."

Ginsberg has made scores of recordings, including an album in the Spoken Arts Treasury of 100 American Poets (volume XVI, 1969), William Blake's Songs of Innocence and Experience Tuned by Allen Ginsberg (MGM, 1970), First Blues: Songs (Vanguard, 1978), and many poetry readings in limited editions. His voice may also be heard, in a speech and in discussions, on the twenty-three-record set Dialectics of Liberation (Liberation Records, 1968).

Ginsberg's books of prose include Indian Journals (1970), Allen Verbatim: Lectures on Poetry, Politics, Consciousness (McGraw-Hill, 1974) and Journals: Early Fifties-Early Sixties (Grove, 1977), both edited by Gordon Ball. Columbia University and the Humanities Research Center at the University of Texas, Austin, have collections of his papers. The filmmaker Jerry Aranson is working on a documentary of Ginsberg's life. Ginsberg was a visiting professor at Columbia University in 1986-87, and he began teaching at Brooklyn College in the fall of 1987.

Whether in his tenement apartment on the Lower East Side, on his farm in Cherry Valley, or in his house in Boulder, Allen Ginsberg begins each day with a Buddhist contemplative exercise and a cup of hot tea with lemon. Now bald of pate, graying of beard, and usually attired in suit and tie, Ginsberg presents a far more conservative appearance than the one he assumed as the wild shaman of the Beats and hippies. He lives simply, spending a large portion of his income on travel and putting some of it into the Committee on Poetry, a foundation he set up to funnel aid to writers and friends in distress. Imamu Amiri Baraka has been one of the recipients of that aid.

Francis X. Clines in the *New York Times Magazine* (November 11, 1984) described Ginsberg as "a gentle, thoughtful man who works hard at his obligations to writing, to his family, and to what remains of the rambunctious community of free souls who helped him to find flight." He cherishes his friends with a poignancy that increases with the years and with his preoccupation with death (which is more pacifying than morbid), and he continues, as he has for many years, to take photographs of them, so as to free-frame visually, as he does artistically in his poetry, "the dearness of the vanishing moment."

References: N Y Times Mag p68+ N 11 '84 pors; Contemporary Authors new rev vol 2 (1981); Dictionary of Literary Biography vol 5 (1980), vol 16 (1983); Kramer, Jane. Allen Ginsberg in America (1969); Merrill, Thomas F. Allen Ginsberg (1969); Mottram, Eric. Allen Ginsberg in the 60's (1972); Tytell, John. Naked Angels: The Lives and Literature of the Beat Generation (1976); Who's Who in America, 1986–87; World Authors 1950–1970 (1975)

Goldstein, Joseph L(eonard)

Apr. 18, 1940– Physician; scientist; educator.
Address: b. Dept. of Molecular Genetics,
University of Texas Health Science Center at
Dallas, 5323 Harry Hines Blvd., Dallas, Tex.
75235; h. 3720 Holland Ave., Apt. H, Dallas, Tex.
75219

When Dr. Joseph L. Goldstein was asked to explain, for the benefit of the lay person, the research that he and Michael Brown had performed that in 1985 won for them the Nobel Prize in Physiology or Medicine, he replied: "We discovered a molecule, called a receptor, on the surface of cells that controls the blood cholesterol level." The modesty and simplicity of his response belie the fifteen years of labor that Goldstein and Brown invested in their quest toward further understanding of the blood cholesterol level and its relation to heart disease. Coronary heart disease kills more people in the Western world than any other disease, while atherosclerosis, or hardening of the arteries, kills one million Americans each year. The work of Goldstein and Brown has been influential in shaping the growing consensus that excess cholesterol causes heart disease and in outlining possible pathways for prevention and treatment. In 1984, partly in response to their work, the National Institutes of Health recommended changes in the fat content of the nation's diet.

Goldstein is currently chairman of the department of molecular genetics and the Paul J. Thomas Professor of Medicine and Genetics at the University of Texas Health Science Center at Dallas, where Brown is director of the Center for Genetic Disease. The two men work so closely together that their colleagues jokingly refer to them as "Brownstein" and describe them as being as "inseparable as Gemini twins," and they have also developed a legendary partnership at bridge. They have received, together, many prestigious awards from the American Chemical Society, the National Academy of Sciences, the Roche Institute of Molecular Biology, the American Heart Association, and the American Society for Human Genetics.

Writing in *Science* (January 10, 1986), Arno G. Motulsky, who is director of the Center for Inherited Diseases at the University of Washington, chose not only to single out Goldstein and Brown's pathbreaking research, but also to note their continuing dedication to seeing patients, making ward rounds, and teaching house staff and students in internal medicine. "Brown and Goldstein show how a synthesis of medicine and the basic sciences still remains possible," Motulsky observed. "The granting of the Nobel Prize to these broadly based medical scientists provides a role model for younger biomedical researchers who sometimes feel that only extreme specialization can lead to important results."

Joseph Leonard Goldstein was born on April 18, 1940, in Sumter, South Carolina, the only son of Isadore E. and Fannie (Albert) Goldstein. The family owned and operated a clothing store in Kingstree, South Carolina, a small town and winter resort in the eastern part of the state. After attending the local primary and secondary schools, Goldstein enrolled at Washington and Lee University in Lexington, Virginia, where he obtained a B.S. degree in chemistry, summa cum laude, in 1962. He then attended Southwestern Medical School of the University of Texas Health Science Center in Dallas. He was considered so brilliant that during his student days Donald Seldin, chairman of the Health Science Center's department of internal medicine, offered him a future faculty position if he would specialize in genetics and return to Dallas to establish a division of medical genetics in the department of internal medicine.

After receiving his M.D. degree in 1966, Goldstein moved to Boston, where he became first an intern and then a resident in medicine at Massachusetts General Hospital. It was there that he met Michael Brown, who had obtained his M.D. degree from the University of Pennsylvania in 1966. The men served together in the same internship and residency program, and they became close friends who engaged in long bull sessions on trends in medical science.

Goldstein and Brown shared an interest in medical research, and after completing their medical training, in 1968, they joined the staff of the National Institutes of Health in Bethesda, Maryland, to gain research experience. Goldstein worked in the laboratory of biochemical genetics under the direction of Marshall W. Nirenberg, who won the 1968 Nobel Prize in Physiology or Medicine for deciphering the manner in which the genetic code determines protein structure. In Nirenberg's laboratory, Goldstein and his colleague C. Thomas Caskey isolated, purified, and worked out the mechanism of action of several proteins required for termination of protein synthesis. Goldstein not only learned some sophisticated new biochemical techniques but also experienced the excitement of research in general and the effectiveness of the molecular biology approach to human disease in particular.

Concurrently, Goldstein had a limited clinical responsiblilty, serving as physician to the patients of Donald S. Fredrickson, then clinical director of the National Heart Institute, who was studying people with abnormally high levels of cholesterol in their blood, or hypercholesterolemia. Goldstein's curiosity was aroused when he cared for patients with the striking clinical syndrome of homozygous familial hypercholesterolemia, cases that he discussed intensively with Michael Brown,

who was then working at the NIH laboratory of biochemistry.

Familial hypercholesterolemia, or FHC, had first been identified as a genetically acquired disease in 1939, by Carl Müller of Oslo, Norway, who noted that the genetic defect caused an error of metabolism that resulted in high blood cholesterol levels and heart attacks, sometimes in very young people. In the 1960s it was Donald Fredrickson, as well as Avedis K. Khachadurian of the American University of Beirut, who demonstrated that the disease occurs in two forms, the "heterozygous" form, in which a person inherits a single defective gene for the disease, and the "homozygous" form, in which two defective genes are inherited. The heterozygous form is relatively common for a genetic disease, and afflicts about one in 500 people. Persons with that condition develop blood cholesterol levels two to three times the normal level, and male FHC heterozygotes face a 75 percent chance of suffering a heart attack before the age of sixty, compared to a 15 percent chance in the general population. Female FHC heterozygotes face a 45 percent, as opposed to a 10 percent, heart attack risk in the general female population.

Chances of developing the homozygous form of the disease are just one in a million, but its results are tragic and deadly. Blood cholesterol levels reach up to 650-1,000 milligrams per 100 milliliters of blood serum, four to eight times the normal level, and symptoms of atherosclerosis begin in childhood. Almost all sufferers from the disease die from heart attacks before the age of thirty.

After leaving the National Institutes of Health in 1972, Goldstein accepted a two-year special NIH fellowship in medical genetics, to work with Arno G. Motulsky, an internationally known authority on the genetic aspects of heart disease, at the University of Washington School of Medicine, in Seattle. There he directed a landmark study aimed at determining the frequency of various hereditary hyperlipidemias (disease of high blood-fat levels) in an unselected population of heart attack survivors. These were taken from 885 patients, who survived three months or more, out of 1,166 heart attack victims admitted to thirteen Seattle hospitals in an eleven-month period in 1970-71. When Goldstein and his team studied 500 of those survivors and 2,520 members of their families, they found that 31 percent of the survivors had high blood-fat levels, either high cholesterol or high triglycerides, or a combination of both, and that genetic causes accounted for 20 percent. Eleven percent had an inherited combination of both high cholesterol (FHC) and high triglycerides, and Goldstein and his colleagues labeled that disease familial combined hyperlipidemia.

Goldstein knew that the complex, combined hyperlipidemia would be a difficult area in which to begin research investigation, whereas the existence of patients with homozygous hypercholesterolemia—that is, with no normal genes at the locus of the then unknown defect—might more readily yield clues concerning gene functioning and cholesterol level. Therefore, when he returned to the University of Texas Health Science Center in 1972, as head of the medical school's first division of medical genetics and assistant professor in the department of internal medicine (still headed by his former teacher, Donald Seldin), Goldstein set to work to try to understand the basic defect in the genetic disease known as familial hypercholesterolemia. Michael Brown had joined the staff of the Health Science Center in the previous year at Goldstein's urging, while Goldstein was completing his study in Seattle.

"Cholesterol," Goldstein and Brown were to write years later, for their Nobel Prize lecture, "has exerted an almost hypnotic fascination for scientists from the most diverse areas of science and medicine. . . . Physiologists and cell biologists have been fascinated with cholesterol because of its essential function in membranes and animal cells. . . . The observation that elevated levels of blood cholesterol accelerate the formation of atherosclerotic plaques . . . has been of great interest to physicians. Cholesterol is a Janus-faced molecule." In fact, more than 93 percent of the cholesterol found in the human body is inside cells, where it takes part in functions vital to cell growth and survival, including the formation of cell membranes. It also plays a role in essential, specialized functions, such as the production of sex hormones, corticosteroids, and bile acids. But it is the remaining 7 percent of the body's cholesterol, circulating in the bloodstream, that is potentially dangerous if, rather than undergoing absorption into the cells, it sticks to the walls of blood vessels and thus interferes with the flow of blood to the heart and the brain.

Since the human body produces it own cholesterol—in the liver—it does not depend on cholesterol in the diet, which is found only in animal foods. Individual cells are also capable of generating their own cholesterol, but will do that only if none at all is available through the bloodstream. Excess cholesterol, not used by the cells or deposited on the walls of blood arteries, is excreted by the liver. Because cholesterol is soluble in fat but not in water, it attaches itself to water-soluble proteins, or lipoproteins, manufactured in the liver, in order to travel in the blood. There are several types of lipoproteins, but the most common as carriers of cholesterol are the low-density lipoproteins, or LDLs, in which the fat greatly outweighs the protein. High levels of low-density lipoproteins in the blood are associated with the danger of heart disease.

Goldstein and Brown began their research by studying tissue cultures of the human skin cells known as fibroblasts, which they grew from six FHC homozygotes, sixteen FHC heterozygotes, and forty normal persons. Like all animal cells, cultured fibroblasts need cholesterol as a major component of the cell membrane. What Goldstein and Brown were thus able to observe was the process by which the cells obtained cholesterol, observing that process to be the extraction of cholesterol from the lipoproteins in the serum of the culture medium, particularly LDLs. Their outstanding, pathbreaking discovery came in 1973, when they demonstrated the existence on the cells of "receptor" molecules that function to bind LDLs and bring them inside the cell.

Although the concept of cell receptors was previously known, it had never been studied in relationship to blood-fat and cholesterol. Goldstein and Brown found that each cell normally has 250,000 receptors that work at binding low-density lipoproteins; they demonstrated the presence of LDL receptors not only on cultured fibroblasts but also on circulating human blood cells and cell membranes from many different animal tissues. But their examination of cells taken from people with familial hypercholesterolemia showed that FHC heterozygotes have only 40 to 50 percent of the LDL receptors that are normally found on the cells, and FHC homozygotes have very few, if any at all. The liver keeps manufacturing cholesterol, sent into the blood bound on LDLs, but the cholesterol is only removed from circulation at a slow pace. Where normally an LDL molecule spends a day and a half in the bloodstream, in FHC heterozygotes it stays in the blood plasma for three days, and in FHC homozygotes for five days, spilling over, in the interim, into the blood tissues.

According to Joanne Silberner, writing in *Science News* (October 19, 1985), "Finding the LDL receptor was the initial step in a cascade of research," and Arno G. Motulsky reported in *Science* (January 10, 1986): "In a series of brilliant studies since 1974, each step in the pathway of cholesterol through the cell was meticulously defined." Throughout the 1970s the pair accumulated so many prestigious awards for their research that they became facetiously known by their colleagues and students as "the Gold Dust Twins." One of the most promising ramifications of their findings concerned the use of drugs for treating high cholesterol levels. The standard drug treatment had been the use of cholestyramine, synthesized over twenty years previously but never fully understood. It was now disclosed that cholestyramine works by increasing the number of LDL receptors in the liver, and the liver is then able to convert the cholesterol into bile acids and excrete them into the intestines.

The problem with cholestyramine—its limited effect—was also cleared up: the increased number of LDL receptors sends a message that more cholesterol is needed, and the liver being the cholesterol-producing factory, responds by producing more cholesterol, and that, in turn, shuts off the production of LDL receptors. That elucidation of the process involved clarified what was needed next: a drug that would block cholesterol synthesis by the liver. In 1976 a Japanese scientist, Akiro Endo, isolated just such an anticholesterol enzyme, compactin, from a penicillin mold, and Alfred W. Alberts of the Merck, Sharp and Dohme research laboratories worked with a different mold to isolate a structural relation, mevinolin. When Goldstein and Brown experimented with the use of mevinolin, combined with cholestyramine, they discovered that it reduced the plasma LDL levels in dogs by 75 percent, though they cautioned in 1981 that the long-term possible toxicity of the drug combination was not yet known. By February 1987 an advisory panel to the Food and Drug Administration recommended marketing approval for mevinolin, now called lovastatin, and some physicians were hailing it as a milestone. When, on September 1, 1987, the Food and Drug Administration approved lovastatin for marketing, the news made the front page of the *New York Times*. Its endorsement was accompanied by the proviso that lovastatin be resorted to only when diet and exercise alone have proved ineffective, and a prediction from Goldstein that it would take at least five or ten years before its effect could be seen on the American coronary death rate.

The 1985 Nobel Prize in Physiology or Medicine represented the culmination of the honors that the scientific community had long conferred on Goldstein and Brown. The Nobel committee's citation stated that the two men had "revolutionized our knowledge about the regulation of cholesterol metabolism and the treatment of diseases caused by abnormally elevated cholesterol levels in the blood." The practical applications of their research into FHC in particular were soon, by the time of the Nobel award, in the successful treatment, via a liver transplant, of Stormie Jones, a FHC homozygous child who had had a heart attack at the age of six and had survived two triple bypass operations. Her new liver was able to produce LDL receptors, and her cholesterol level dropped from 1,100 milligrams to 300 milligrams. Later treatment with lovastatin brought her cholesterol level down to 180, a normal scale.

There is not universal agreement among all scientists that dietary cholesterol behaves the same way in the human body as cholesterol that is manufactured in the liver, and some of them still question the relationship between cholesterol and heart disease. But Goldstein and Brown, on the basis of their experiments with animals, concluded that high-fat diets reduce the LDL receptors in the liver, thus demonstrating the relationship between dietary cholesterol and cholesterol levels in the blood. More generally, the work of Goldstein and Brown has established a new paradigm for the functioning and dysfunctioning of receptor cells, giving birth to a new field of "receptorology" and research into other receptor-related diseases, such as some forms of diabetes, myasthenia gravis (a muscle-wasting disease), and pernicious anemia.

In 1980 Joseph L. Goldstein was elected to membership in the National Academy of Sciences. He is also a member of the American Academy of Arts and Sciences and a Fellow of the American College of Physicians, among many other appointments and honors. He is, or has been, a member of the editorial boards of *Annual Review of Genetics, Arteriosclerosis, Cell, Journal of Biological Chemistry, Journal of Clinical Investigation,* and

Science. Apart from bridge, listening to classical music is his favorite recreation. He is a bachelor.

References: *Chicago Tribune* p1+ O 15 '85 por; *N Y Times* A p1+ O 15 '85 por; *Science* vol 231 Ja 10 '86 por; *US News* 102:64+ My 25 '87 por *American Men and Women of Science* vol 111 (1986); *International Who's Who, 1986–87; Who's Who in America, 1986–87; Who's Who in Frontiers of Science and Technology* (1985)

Gore, Albert, Jr.

Mar. 31, 1948– United States Senator from Tennessee. Address: b. 393 Russell Senate Office Bldg., Washington, D.C. 20510

Senator Albert Gore Jr. of Tennessee, the youngest of the candidates for the 1988 Democratic presidential nomination, is also the most aggressive. The last of the Democratic hopefuls to enter the field thus far, Gore was a long shot, relatively little known nationally, when he declared his candidacy on June 29, 1987. Later in the year, in his campaign speeches and his debates with his Democratic rivals, he emerged as the toughest of the lot on defense and relations with the Soviet Union and thus raised his national profile and began to consolidate his strength in the South.

Gore boasts a number of qualities that make him potentially an attractive presidential candidate for the Democratic party. He is handsome, articulate, liberal on domestic issues, and expert on arms control. His other strengths include a record of service in Vietnam, a famous political name, an unimpeachable family life, and religious ties that are fervent but not fanatic. Even Republicans recognize his assets. His opponent from the 1984 Senate race predicted that Gore would be on the national ticket, and the conservative commentator John McLaughlin has called him "too good to be true." David Rogers wrote of him in the *Wall Street Journal* (October 23, 1987): "The consummate politician, Mr. Gore is fiercely competitive, but seemingly blind to the ambition that drives him. Born into a political family, he bears the stamp of his populist father and brings to his campaign an intellect honed by the education of the ruling elite."

Albert Gore Jr. was born in Washington, D.C., on March 31, 1948, to Albert Gore Sr. and Pauline (La Fon) Gore, while his father was serving his tenth year as a Democratic representative from Tennessee. A strong supporter of New Deal legislation and a liberal, Albert Gore Sr. served four more years in the House and then won three consecutive terms as a senator from Tennessee. As a result, Albert Gore Jr. grew up in the nation's capital. He attended the exclusive St. Alban's Episcopal School for Boys, where he was an honors student and captain of the football team.

Gore enrolled at Harvard College and earned a B.A. degree *cum laude* in government in 1969, after submitting a senior thesis that dealt with "The Impact of Television on the Conduct of the Presidency, 1947–1969." He kept himself aloof from the turbulence that beset Cambridge, Massachusetts, in the final years of the 1960s. Martin Peretz, who was one of Gore's professors at the time and is now editor in chief of the *New Republic* has recalled: "People had an intense politics then that looked serious, but which was not always as serious as it was intense. Al stood out to me because he didn't get swept up in the élan of the student movement. He had independence of mind."

When, after graduation from Harvard, Gore was drafted for service in the military, he and his family were placed in an awkward position. Like his father, Gore opposed the war in Vietnam, and for a time he contemplated not going. His parents offered to support whatever choice he made, but he eventually accepted induction into the United States Army. That decision helped his father, who ran in 1970 for a fourth term in the Senate, to counter charges made by his Republican opponent, William Brock, that Gore's opposition to the war made him too liberal for Tennessee. Nevertheless, Albert Gore Sr. lost by a margin of 46,000 votes.

In Vietnam, Gore served as an army reporter with the 20th Engineering Battalion, which was stationed outside Saigon. He sent copies of his stories home to his wife, who passed them on to the editors of the *Tennessean*, a newspaper in Nashville. They, in turn, published some of the pieces and, when Gore completed his tour of duty in 1971, he was offered a job as a reporter. Between 1971 and 1976 Gore pursued a number of activities. His primary commitment was to the *Tennessean*, where he covered stories of local interest and the police beat. Eventually assigned to write on city politics, he proved to be a determined investigative report-

er, and a series of articles that he wrote in 1974 led to the conviction of several local political figures for bribery and corruption. Outside the newspaper, Gore became a home builder and land developer with the Tanglewood Home Builders Company and a livestock and tobacco farmer.

While working the night shift at the *Tennessean* in 1971–1972, Gore, who is a devout Baptist, studied philosophy and phenomenology at Vanderbilt University's Graduate School of Religion, in Nashville. "I went to divinity school," he has explained, "to study the spiritual issues that were most important to me at the time." The senator's supporters point with pride to the fact that Gore did not use his interest in religion as a means to escape military service. "To Al Gore's eternal credit," says one, "he went to divinity school *after* Vietnam."

In 1974 Gore enrolled in the Law School of Vanderbilt University, where he remained for two years, while writing editorials for the *Tennessean*. During that time he overcame an earlier feeling, nurtured by the Vietnamese War, the presidency of Richard M. Nixon, and perhaps his father's defeat, that politics would be the last profession he entered. When at the end of February 1976, the Democratic Representative Joe L. Evins unexpectedly announced his decision not to seek reelection from Tennessee's Fourth District, Gore immediately decided to run for the House.

Eight other candidates vied with Gore in the Democratic primary for the right to run for Evins' seat. He had, however, a considerable asset in his name, which, he admitted, brought him to the attention of some people who might otherwise have ignored a former newspaper reporter without previous experience in politics. Proving to be an able campaigner in his own right, Gore called for higher taxes on the rich, more public jobs, and less spending on defense. He also attacked the "private power trusts" that wanted to dismantle the Tennessee Valley Authority.

Stanley Rogers, the majority leader of the Tennessee House of Representatives, who emerged as Gore's chief rival for the Democratic nomination, criticized Gore's wealth, which amounted to a little over one-quarter million dollars. In addition, he tried to portray Gore, whose father had become chairman of the Island Creek Coal Company of Lexington, Kentucky, as the candidate of the energy monopolies. Rogers, however, had his base of support in the southern part of the district, which was also home to several other candidates. With his opponents drawing from the same constituency, Gore took advantage of his solid standing in Smith County, where his hometown of Carthage is located, and in the rest of the district's northern section to squeeze out a 3,559 vote victory over Rogers.

His success in the Democratic primary assured Gore of victory in the 1976 general election, in which he faced only minor opposition from an independent candidate, William H. McGlamery. Once established in Congress, he found his seat secure. In 1978 he ran unopposed for a second term, and, two years later was elected to a third term by a margin of 137,612 votes to 35,954 over the Republican contender, James Beau Seigneur. Redistricting switched Gore to Tennessee's Sixth District, and in 1982 he ran unopposed in his fourth race for the House.

When Howard H. Baker Jr., the leader of the Republican majority in the Senate, announced in January 1983 that he would not seek reelection from Tennessee in 1984, Gore quickly emerged as the likely Democratic nominee for that seat. Gore began his campaign almost two years before the election and, given his record and name, was able to build considerable momentum while the Republicans squabbled among themselves. When the GOP finally settled on Victor Ashe, a wealthy Knoxville lawyer and former state senator in the August 1984 primary, Ed McAteer, a conservative activist, decided to run independently. With the opposition divided, Gore swept to an easy victory, taking 1,000,607 votes to 557,016 for Ashe and 87,234 for McAteer.

Both as a representative and as a senator, Albert Gore Jr. has been, in his words, a "raging moderate." "I believe that people have partially discredited liberalism because they have lost faith in its competence," he remarked after winning his first election to Congress. "They have discredited conservatism because of its apparent complacency in the face of problems of unprecedented magnitude. There is a feeling there has been too much philosophy and not enough common sense." During his eight years in the House, Gore received average scores of 64 and 80 respectively from the liberal Americans for Democratic Action (ADA) and the Committee on Political Education of the AFL-CIO (COPE). He has continued to be a moderate liberal during his years in the Senate.

Gore has focused much of his attention on health-related issues, and he is now vice-chairman of Congress' Biomedical Ethics Board. When he led the first Congressional hearing on the dangers of toxic waste he helped to bring attention to the damage done by it in an area near Memphis, Tennessee, and in the Love Canal neighborhood of Niagara Falls, New York. Gore also played an important role in the development and passage of the 1980 "Superfund" bill (Public Law 96-510) to clear up chemical spills and dangerous land dumps.

In his final year as a member of the House, Gore sponsored the Organ Procurement and Transplantation Act of 1984, which prohibited the sale or purchase of human organs for transplantation, and also authorized $2 million annually to support a national computerized system for matching patients with scarce organs. In order to achieve passage of the measure, however, Gore had to withdraw his proposal to provide $30 million over two years to help patients, otherwise unable to pay, to obtain a drug needed to prevent the rejection of transplanted organs.

In regard to other issues, although Gore has opposed voluntary prayer in schools, he has voted to allow students a moment of silence to use as they wish. He has voted against banning the interstate sale of handguns, and he has voted against federal funding for abortions, despite the hardship that stance inflicts on the poor, because he believes that keeping the government from "participating in the taking of what is arguably human life" is a more important principle. In recent months the senator has said that he would oppose legislation favored by the Vatican, which would bar all medical intervention in reproductive processes, but he has also speculated that the Congress will consider some controls over surrogate motherhood. "There is a need for legislation," he has said, "but I don't think that we should be forced to choose between a completely laissez-faire approach on the one hand or an outright and total ban on the other extreme."

Perhaps the chief criticism of Albert Gore Jr. comes from those who believe that he stakes out "safe issues" and pursues media coverage too aggressively. "If it's in the news," one Congressional aide has remarked, "then young Albert will be there, on television." Commentators more sympathetic to Gore make remarks like those attributed to Norman Ornstein of the American Enterprise Institute: "He's picked issues that have him staked as the good guy fighting evil. What's wrong with that?" Gore himself believes that he has an affinity for problems for which he can offer solutions. "I like to examine issues with finite answers," he says. "That's where I'm most comfortable."

Despite his reputation for seeking issues that are clear and amenable to legislative solution, Gore has made probably his most important contributions in the decidedly complex area of nuclear arms and disarmament. He admits that the issue consumed no more than fifteen minutes of his time during his first four years in Congress, but his concern with it grew along with that felt by his constituents. When Gore gained an assignment to the House Intelligence Committee after his reelection in 1980, he gave himself wholeheartedly to the problem, and during the next thirteen months committed himself for eight hours a week to the study of the relevant technical literature and to briefings by experts. By the end of that period, his mastery of the material impressed even professional scholars in the field.

Gore first put his thoughts on the nuclear issue into print in material published in the *Congressional Record* in February 1982. The piece attracted immediate attention in the U.S.S.R., and, within a month, Soviet arms control experts, including Oleg Bykov of the Institute of World Economics and International Relations and Georgi Arbatov of the Institute of U.S.A. and Canada Studies, were asking visiting Americans about the "Gore Plan." Shortly after that, Gore's arguments moved to center stage in the debate going on within the American establishment on the subject of disarmament.

The core of Gore's arms proposal, which he spelled out in a *New Republic* article (May 5, 1982), addresses the problems caused by "counterforce weapons." According to the logic of "Mutually Assured Destruction" (MAD), he argued, neither the Soviet Union nor the United States will dare launch a nuclear attack on the other, so long as it knows that the victim can launch an equally devastating attack in retaliation. Recent developments, however, have threatened to destabilize that stalemate. The U.S.S.R. has deployed intercontinental ballistic missiles (ICBMs) with multiple warheads known as MIRVs (multiple independently targeted, reentry vehicles). The United States is deploying similar missiles in the form of land-based MXs and submarine-based Trident II D-5s. Such missiles are potential "first-strike" weapons because, by launching a small number of its MIRVs, either nation might be able to knock out most of the other's nuclear force. Both sides, therefore, have the capacity, or are moving toward being able, not only to cause incredible damage with a preemptive first strike but also to accomplish that objective while keeping enough warheads in reserve to threaten another all-out attack—perhaps on civilian rather than military targets—if the opponent should dare to retaliate on any scale.

According to Gore, since "counterforce weapons have made nuclear war 'thinkable' again," the critical step in disarmament must involve the removal of those destabilizers from American and Soviet arsenals. He not only argues that compliance with his proposal can be verified technically but adds that by scrapping their MIRVs both the United States and the Soviet Union "would be in a much better position to continue the arms control process in an atmosphere less fraught with mutual apprehension."

Since 1982 Gore has sought to develop a bipartisan approach concerned with both sides of the policy dilemma—"national power and security on the one hand and long-term human survival on the other," though his stance has made him part of what he calls "the beleaguered center," which is under assault from the left and the right. He especially disappointed the supporters of a "nuclear freeze" when, in 1983, he voted in favor of releasing $625 million in research and development funds for the MX missile. He says that his vote came in return for a White House promise of greater flexibility at the strategic arms reductions talks at Geneva. In 1985, as a senator, Gore voted to limit the deployment of the MX to 40 or 50 missiles.

Critical of Ronald Reagan's approach to the disarmament issue, Gore dismisses the president's Strategic Defense Initiative (SDI), or Star Wars Program, as an example of destabilizing counterforce weaponry, and he chided Reagan for announcing, late in May 1986, that the United States would no longer be bound by the unratified SALT II agreement. At the other extreme, Gore sees dangers in the radical disarmament proposals that surfaced during Reagan's meeting with Soviet Prime Minister Mikhail S. Gorbachev in Reykjavik, Iceland, in October 1986. He contends, in particular, that either a freeze, which would allow the Soviets to maintain their edge in short-range intermediate nuclear force (INF) systems, or complete nuclear

disarmament, would leave Western Europe vulnerable to nuclear blackmail or to threats from the Warsaw Pact's vastly larger conventional forces.

For Albert Gore Jr. the key to nuclear peace lies in the traditional concept of deterrence combined with a modernization of American defenses. A central feature of his middle-of-the-road policy on arms control has been, therefore, support of the Midgetman, which is a light missile, armed with a single warhead, and carried on a mobile launcher hardened against nuclear blast. The Scowcroft Commission, established by President Ronald Reagan in 1983 and led by former National Security Advisor Brent Scowcroft, proposed the Midgetman as the answer to a number of defense and arms control problems. In agreement with the commission, Gore argues that the Soviets cannot cripple an American defense based on Midgetmen without launching so many of their own missiles that they can retain no counterforce option. Furthermore, because the Midgetman has but a single warhead, it cannot constitute an American counterforce weapon.

Albert Gore Jr. is a ruggedly handsome man with thick brown hair. He jogs every day. The senator has a well-deserved reputation for keeping in touch with his constituents, and since his first election to Congress in 1976, has returned to Tennessee nearly every weekend. Overall, he has conducted 1,600 open meetings in the state. Since May 19, 1970, he has been married to the former Mary Elizabeth Aitcheson. They are the parents of four children, Karenna, Kristin, Sarah, and Albert 3d. Mrs. Gore, familiarly known as "Tipper," is a member of the Parents Music Research Center, which advocates that record companies voluntarily rate and label records with lyrics that are sexually explicit. Gore publicly supported her cause at a Senate Commerce Committee hearing in September 1985, at which he took the rock band Twisted Sister to task for writing obscene songs. If nominated in 1988, Gore will be the youngest presidential candidate since William Jennings Bryan in 1900. If elected, he will be the youngest president in American history.

References: Newsweek 109:20 F 16 '87 por; N Y Times B p19 Je 2 '83 por; Washington M 18:43+ N '86 por; Almanac of American Politics, 1986; Congressional Directory, 1986; Politics in America, 1986; Who's Who in America, 1986–87

Gottlieb, Robert A(dams)

Apr. 29, 1931– Editor; former publishing executive. Address: b. c/o The New Yorker, 25 W. 43rd St., New York City, N.Y. 10036

The announcement in January 1987 that Robert A. Gottlieb, the president and editor in chief of Alfred A. Knopf, Inc., would replace William Shawn as

Robert A. Gottlieb

editor of the *New Yorker* hit the magazine's staff "like an atom bomb," according to one insider. A petition by 154 of the *New Yorker*'s staff members, including editors, writers, and cartoonists, urged Gottlieb to withdraw from his new post. When he refused to do so, several members of the magazine's staff left in protest. They and the other petitioners acknowledged, however, the brilliance that had earned for Gottlieb, at Knopf, and before that at Simon & Schuster, favorable comparison with Maxwell Perkins, the late legendary editor at Charles Scribner's Sons, and had made him the preferred editor of writers ranging from Anthony Burgess to B. F. Skinner, the behaviorist.

The petitioners, who objected vehemently to the timing and manner of Gottlieb's appointment, were especially incensed at reports that Samuel I. Newhouse Jr., the publishing baron whose family firm, Newhouse Publications, owns both the *New Yorker* and Random House, the parent company of Alfred A. Knopf Inc., had forced William Shawn into retirement, passing over Charles McGrath, the *New Yorker*'s fiction editor, whom Shawn had groomed as his successor, to clear the way for Gottlieb. Many of the petitioners felt that the magazine's traditions could best be maintained by an insider and that Gottlieb would furthermore be handicapped by the fact that he had never turned out a weekly magazine. Defending the appointment, Steven T. Florio, the publisher whom Newhouse had brought in when he bought the *New Yorker* in 1985, said, as quoted in the *Chicago Tribune* (January 25, 1987), "It was incumbent on us not to pick the best person at the *New Yorker*, but the best person in the world for that job and we felt it was Bob Gottlieb." Previous to Shawn, there had been only one editor of the *New Yorker*—its founder, Harold Ross.

Robert Adams Gottlieb was born in New York City, on April 29, 1931, and raised on Manhattan's Upper West Side. He is the only child of Charles Gottlieb, a lawyer, and Martha (Keen) Gottlieb, a teacher, both of whom were compulsive readers. Gottlieb has recalled that his father's "idea of a real treat, something truly devilish, was to go on a spree at Brentano's and buy half a dozen books." Sickly, lonely and unhappy as a child, Gottlieb took refuge in reading at an early age. As he told Tony Schwartz in an interview in the *New York Times Book Review* (February 24, 1980), "When I was a kid, I would read three to four books a day after school, and I could read for sixteen hours at a time. Mind you, that's all I did. I belonged to three lending libraries and the public library."

Although Gottlieb also enjoyed the vintage movies he saw at the Thalia theatre on Manhattan's Upper West Side, the snowball fights outside the Ethical Culture School that he attended, and the weeks he spent at summer camp, books remained his ruling passion. As a teenager he reportedly read *War and Peace* in one day, and while attending Columbia University, from which he graduated with a B.A. degree and a Phi Beta Kappa key in 1952, he read Marcel Proust's monumental *Remembrance of Things Past* in seven days.

After leaving Columbia University, Gottlieb, now married, traveled to England for postgraduate study at Cambridge University. "At the time I was eager for celebrity," Gottlieb told Tony Schwartz. He achieved a degree of celebrity as a director of Cambridge Theatre productions, but in spite of his "outer triumph," he was having an "inner breakdown." "I needed to prevail," he explained to Schwartz. "I've never been consciously ambitious for money or position, but obviously I am a competitive person. I was ambitious in my work in the sense that I couldn't allow myself to fail. The idea of not winning was so terrifying to me that I couldn't contemplate it. That's a good formula for winning, but not a good one for living." After leaving Cambridge and returning to New York with his wife and child in 1954, he worked as a Christmas card salesman at Macy's department store while searching haphazardly for other employment.

In 1955, having overcome the idea that his sensibility was "too fine" for office work, Gottlieb went to the offices of Simon & Schuster for an interview with Jack Goodman, the company's editor in chief. When Goodman asked him to write a letter explaining why he wanted to go into publishing, Gottlieb wrote: "It's never occurred to me to be anything else." He was hired at $75 a week as Goodman's editorial assistant, a position that he especially appreciated because "there was no need to compete" and he thus could "use [all of his] energy for work."

Within two years, Gottlieb made his mark as an editor. His first major project was a manuscript with the working title of "Catch 18," the first novel of an advertising and promotion copywriter named Joseph Heller, which he accepted on the strength of a few chapters. Because Leon Uris had a book in the works entitled *Mila 18* Gottlieb suggested the now famous title of the work, *Catch-22*, and he worked closely with Heller to hone the manuscript. "His editing suggestions were always delivered in a very tactful way," Heller recalled for Tony Schwartz. "The most valuable ones were structural. He'd say, for example, that he thought one part of *Catch-22* should be moved up in the book. What eventually resulted was that I cut seventy pages, which is what he intended. . . . The thing about Bob is that I would not doubt for one second something he told me."

Catch-22 went on to become a durable best seller, and its phenomenal success established Gottlieb as an editorial wunderkind. As he told Dennis Brown, in an interview in the *St. Louis Post-Dispatch* (December 2, 1979), "By the time I was twenty-six I started to have very serious responsibilities at Simon & Schuster, and that's given me ten years more experience of authority than most people my age in the business have had. Also, I grew up in a place that was wonderfully happy then. . . . So none of my energy has ever been deflected into politicking or anything other than our real work." After Jack Goodman's death in 1957, Gottlieb took over the editing of many writers from his stable of authors, among them Walter Kerr, the drama critic, S. J. Perelman, the humorist, and Meyer Levin, the novelist of the Chicago scene.

After becoming vice-president and editor in chief of Simon & Schuster, Gottlieb built a close and productive family at the firm. Now established as a top editor and publisher, he became restless for a professional change. It came in 1968 with his appointment as executive vice-president and editor in chief of Alfred A. Knopf, Inc., perhaps the most prestigious publishing house in the United States. The Gottlieb era at Knopf began when leading writers ended often long-term relationships with other firms and moved to Knopf so that they could have Gottlieb as editor. Some followed him from Simon & Schuster, among them Jessica Mitford, Doris Lessing, Evan Connell, Ray Bradbury, Chaim Potok, and Joseph Heller. Others who moved over to Knopf from other firms to have books edited by Gottlieb included Anthony Burgess, John Cheever, John Le Carré, Michael Crichton, B. F. Skinner, Antonia Fraser, Margaret Drabble and Barry Commoner. For them, as well as for less established authors, Gottlieb had a Midas touch in editing and in making contractual arrangements. In his move to Knopf, Gottlieb took with him some of Simon & Schuster's top executives, notably, the associate publisher, Anthony Schulte, and the vice-president in charge of advertising, Nina Bourne. They had helped Gottlieb to develop many best sellers during his thirteen years at Simon & Schuster. The team had been "wooed and hired" by Robert L. Bernstein, the president of Random House, of which Knopf is now a subsidiary. Gottlieb's appointment was, in part, according to Henry Raymont, writing in the *New York Times* (March 4, 1968), the result of the problem of succession at family-owned publishing houses, "when

control passes from strong-willed older men, with a deep feeling for tradition, to a new generation geared to technological development and new tastes."

Random House and some of its younger editors wanted to move faster than the aging Alfred A. Knopf had been inclined to go in discovering and developing new American writers, and the parent company wanted Gottlieb's editorial skills and eye for top talent. Although the Knopf firm's cultivated founder—once described by H. L. Mencken as "the perfect publisher"—had built a company that rivaled the great British and German publishing houses, he had given little thought to choosing a successor. The executives of Radio Corporation of America, the conglomerate parent of Knopf and Random House, stepped in and made the decision for him by putting Gottlieb into the office of the executive vice-president and chief editor in 1968. While continuing to serve as chief editor, Gottlieb became president of Knopf in 1973.

Eric Pace, writing in the *New York Times* (August 16, 1973), found that Gottlieb represented a radical departure from the usual publishing executive. "Why has Mr. Gottlieb done so well himself?" Pace asked. "Not through the legendary publishing industry lunches in posh restaurants; he prefers to slip home at lunchtime or to have a hot dog in Central Park. And it is not through an imposing appearance. His hair is on the long side—and on the wild side; he has an unfashionable summertime pallor, and he suffers from a weakness for rumpled polo shirts." The usual uniform of the chief editorial voice at the venerable house of Knopf—the first American firm to publish Thomas Mann as well as Franz Kafka, Willa Cather, Elizabeth Bowen, and Dame Ivy Compton-Burnett—consisted of baggy chino pants or worn jeans and sneakers. Gottlieb had a simple formula for selecting books for publication at Simon & Schuster and at Knopf. "I just read and react," he has explained. "If I like a book, I will publish it. If I don't like it, I won't publish it." His temperament led him to share what he knew and felt, instead of trying to "satisfy some abstract marketing concept."

According to Dennis Brown, in the *St. Louis Post-Dispatch* article, Gottlieb kept his functions as editor and publisher separate. "No editorial work is done in the office," Gottlieb said, as quoted by Brown. "During the day I'm the head of a company; I'm a publisher. At night and on weekends I'm an editor. All my reading and editing is done at home. . . . " In Gottlieb's view, "you can't make an editor. . . . Editing is the application of the sensibility and common sense you were born with." An effective editor, he believes, is a "chameleon," capable of applying that sensibility and common sense in specific ways to individual writers. While carrying on the tradition of Alfred Knopf and his wife, Blanche, Gottlieb developed his own list of distinguished writers. But the placid routine of his nineteen years at Knopf came to an end with the news, in January 1987, that he had been appointed editor of the *New Yorker*. Rumors that Gottlieb would replace William Shawn as editor had been circulating from the time, two years earlier, when the Newhouse media chain had bought the *New Yorker*. The magazine had been losing advertising revenue, and its new owners had qualms about some of its editorial and business practices. They objected, for example, to its long, if not interminable, articles and to its policy of holding some stories for years before publication.

Internally, at the *New Yorker's* offices on West Forty-third Street, near the venerable Algonquin Hotel, Shawn had been looked upon as something of a god. At seventy-nine, he was perhaps the last of America's gentleman-editors in the nineteenth-century British tradition. Newhouse acknowledged Shawn's fifty years of respected service at the *New Yorker*—thirty-five as editor—but thought him an anachronism. Shawn had done little to choose a successor in the two years following the Newhouse takeover. In talks with the owners before Gottlieb's formal appointment, Shawn did give marked attention to Charles McGrath, the *New Yorker's* deputy editor and fiction editor, and most of the staff approved the choice, because an insider was deemed crucial to continuing the policies, standards, and internal administration that had made the *New Yorker* a great magazine.

Then, on January 12, 1987, it was learned that Shawn was out, Gottlieb was in. It was all done with the dispatch and efficiency of a Wall Street firm's announcement of a new board chairman. On the day that Shawn was virtually drummed out of service, Samuel I. Newhouse Jr. had gone to the editor's office and handed him a one-page memo, instructing him to tell the staff that he had retired and that Gottlieb was to succeed him. In the view of the owner, the move from one Newhouse property to another constituted the "inside appointment" that many on the *New Yorker* staff wanted.

The next day, in a "hallway speech" at the magazine, Shawn told 100 employees that he was retiring "involuntarily" and that his successor was Robert Gottlieb. Later, six staff members drafted a letter asking Gottlieb to decline the appointment. There was nothing personal in the request, the letter's 154 signers said, noting that they had the highest regard for his book-editing ability. But the job, they felt, should go to a member of the *New Yorker* staff and one who was an experienced magazine professional. Declining to step aside, Gottlieb said in a counter-memo, that he looked forward to meeting the staff. In the words of one editor, most staff members knew that there was no chance that Gottlieb might change his mind, but they wanted to state their concerns "in the strongest possible manner." For his part, Gottlieb asserted: "If I did not already love the *New Yorker*, I would not want to be there, and I think that, by temperament I am a conserver, not a revolutionary." In an effort to play the role of a peacemaker, the *New Yorker's* publisher and president, Steven T. Florio, disclosed that Gottlieb was "excited to be here" and had "gone out of his way to be cordial and very gra-

cious to Shawn. Even the most suspicious . . . are willing to give Bob a shot."

But in many of the opinion journals there was scant sympathy for the imbroglio on West Forty-third Street. "The real issue at stake here is not Newhouse's rudeness or how the staff, those tender buttons, will deal with an outsider," maintained an article in the *New Republic* (February 18, 1987) by Alfred Gingold, who parodied the *New Yorker* in his book *Snooze: The Best of Our Magazine*. "The real issue is the post-Shawn issues of the *New Yorker*." Gingold hoped that there would be shorter articles, especially by the film critic Pauline Kael, and he added: "With any luck, there'll be fewer stories about young women going through resonant mementos in the attic and weeping tastefully. With a bit more luck, the journalistic pieces will get more rigorous or, failing that, shorter."

The editors of the London magazines, the *Spectator* and the *Economist*, felt that a change at the *New Yorker* was long overdue. Paul Johnson, in his *Spectator* article "A Stately Dame in Flux," rejected the notion that "only an editor who has been a longstanding member of the staff" was eligible for the "apostolic succession." He expressed doubt "whether the *New Yorker* was ever quite the bastion of literature its supporters now claim" and added: "What the *New Yorker* needs is not the management style of a ritzy publishing house, with one eye on Madison Avenue, but a strong injection of Grub Street," where London's newspapers are published. "It should forget the table at the Algonquin, which is now a literary museum-piece anyway, and forge links with whatever deplorable hostelries young writers patronize." And it should also find itself one "really funny" cartoonist. Believing that its staff was "spoiled rotten," the writer for the *Economist* criticized what he called "a surprisingly naive protest" against Gottlieb's appointment. In the past, the *New Yorker* had "style and wit," he wrote. Now it was "self-indulgent." Once its long articles were daring, "now they are, all too often, simply interminable," he complained.

In mid-July 1987 members of the *New Yorker* staff told an interviewer for *Current Biography* that Gottlieb appeared to be firmly in control. They cited his directness and informality, and, in particular, his casualness of dress in sharp contrast with the style of Shawn, who was virtually never without a coat or tie. In differences of opinion between the editorial and business departments, Gottlieb and his editorial staff generally prevailed. Differences had also occurred in the Shawn era, but Gottlieb was not quite as "demonstrative" as Shawn had been in opposing change or matters that business, promotion, or advertising people might want. Some observers have suggested that the bright, bold *New Yorker* cover of July 13, 1987, showing two young women eating in a pizza parlor, heralded a more obtrusive—and more competitive—"Gottlieb look" for the magazine.

In general, the members of the *New Yorker* staff like Gottlieb's accessibility. The editor interviewed by *Current Biography* said that he always had access to Shawn, although others may have had difficulty in getting to him. "Gottlieb's management style, if one may call it that, is a lot more direct and informal," he said. "This means, in part, that he is accessible to everybody. He drops in at offices and talks with us all the time." Gottlieb may stop by an early-arriving editor's office and ask how things are going. The editor welcomes the visits as a chance, for one thing, to get his questions answered immediately, while with Shawn "everything was by appointment, through his secretary."

In conversations with *New Yorker* staff members shortly before he assumed the editorship, Gottlieb said that he had no master plan or grand design for the magazine. His approach has been relatively delicate and subtle, mainly in seeking tighter and shorter articles and perhaps a bolder look. According to an article by Edwin Diamond, a writer on media affairs, in *New York* magazine (June 8, 1987), "changes of a sort have surely but slowly come to the *New Yorker*," among them a "stick-to-it" schedule for articles and stories, in contrast to Shawn's tendency to change content almost daily. According to Diamond, Gottlieb's weakness is the absence of an "overarching, clear and compelling vision for the *New Yorker*." As one *New Yorker* staff member confided to the *Current Biography* interviewer, Gottlieb "is egocentric; if you ever meet him, let him do all the talking. Then he'll be your friend." Lynn Nesbit, a literary agent, told an interviewer for the *New York Times*, "Bob doesn't surround himself with people who challenge his authority. But his style is supportive; he makes all people who work with him feel they are part of the adventure, even though he is in control."

The actor who could play Gottlieb without makeup is Woody Allen, to whom the editor bears an uncanny resemblance. Gottlieb is five feet nine inches tall, and recent news pictures of him suggest some paunchiness. His campus, knockabout style of dress makes him look much younger than his chronological age. One of the world's fastest readers, Gottlieb boasts of having read some 600 Gothic novels, and he once set himself the task of reading every fiction best seller written in recent years, to learn what makes them sell.

Although he has helped scores of writers to do the best work of which they are capable, Gottlieb personally avoids writing, calling it one of the three most difficult things he has ever had to do. The other two were practicing the piano and going through psychoanalysis. Even writing a simple letter can be tedious and troublesome for him. He devotes much of his energy to what he calls his "second career"—his efforts in behalf of the New York City Ballet. He serves on its board of directors and calls his affiliation with it "part management, part slave." His reluctance to talk to the press may stem from his belief, as he told a newspaper interviewer, that "there is nothing in me that has to be nurtured the way an artist's talent does. My job is to protect and nurture others."

From his first marriage, which ended in divorce in the early 1960s, Gottlieb has a son, Roger. He makes his home in a town house in Turtle Bay, on Manhattan's East Side, with his present wife, the actress Maria Tucci, whose father, Niccolo Tucci, had published a number of stories in the *New Yorker* during the 1950s. They have two children, Elizabeth and Nicholas. "There are four things in my life," Gottlieb once told an interviewer, as quoted by Edwin McDowell in the *New York Times* (January 13, 1987). "Work, the ballet, reading, and my family. I don't do anything else. I don't have lunches, dinners, go to plays or movies. I don't meditate, escalate, deviate or have affairs. So I have plenty of time."

References: *Chicago Tribune* V p1+ Ja 25 '87 por; *Economist* p27 Ja 21 '87 por; *Maclean's* 100:46 Ja 26 '87 por; N Y *Newsday* II p4 Ja 15 '87; N Y *Times* p26 Ja 6 '68 por, A p1+ Ja 13 '87 por, C p21 Ja 14 '87 por, C p33 Ja 26 '87; N Y *Times* Bk R p7+ F 24 '80 por, p1+ O 4 '87; *New Repub* 196:10+ F 9 '87; *Pub W* 231:20 Ja 23 '87 por; *Spec* 258:20 Ja 24 '87 por; *St. Louis Post-Dispatch* F p2+ D 2 '79 por; Fadiman, Clifton, ed. *Fifty Years* (1965); *Who's Who in America,* 1986–87

Guth, Alan H(arvey)
(go͞oth)

Feb. 27, 1947– Physicist. Address: b. Massachusetts Institute of Technology, Dept. of Physics, Cambridge, Mass. 02139

The Massachusetts Institute of Technology physicist Alan Guth helped to revolutionize cosmology, a field in which he had only a casual interest until 1978–79, when his postdoctoral pursuit of particle theory at Cornell University led him into an "inflationary" scenario for the evolution of the universe, which solved some of the problems that plagued the standard "Big Bang" theory. In Guth's model, announced in 1980, the universe inflated at a spectacular rate in the fraction of a second following the primordial fireball, and in so doing it cooled so drastically as to undergo a transition like that of water changing to ice. Out of what had been a very hot vacuum there crystallized the matter of the universe as it is known today. Because the equations of Guth's inflationary universe theory indicated that matter is likely to have come literally out of nothing, he described the universe as "the ultimate free lunch." His subsequent refinements and extensions of his equations suggest that it might be possible one day to create in a laboratory a spin-off universe that would leave behind an evaporating black hole as its only remaining trace in our cosmos. "For all we know," Guth told Malcolm W. Browne of the *New York Times* (April 14, 1987), "our own universe might have been started in someone's basement."

Alan Harvey Guth, born in New Brunswick, New Jersey, on February 27, 1947, is the second of three children of Elaine (Cheiten) Guth and Hyman Guth, a dry cleaner. His earliest exposure to science came from watching Don Herbert's television program *Mr. Wizard* and from reading *Scientific American* magazine. By the time he reached the fourth grade, he was already drafting plans for rocket ships and using Newton's laws to estimate how high they would fly. At the end of his junior year he left Highland Park (New Jersey) High School to enter the Massachusetts Institute of Technology, where his extracurricular activities included, as they had in high school, debating, track, and the mathematics club. After taking his B.S. and M.S. degrees, both in 1969, he remained at M.I.T. to pursue his doctorate on a Karl Taylor Compton Fellowship. He received the Ph.D. degree in 1972, on completion of the thesis, "A Model for Mesons Based on Numerical Solutions to the Bethe-Salpeter Equation."

Mesons are elementary particles theorized to be agents of one of the three fundamental forces of nature (not counting gravity)—the so-called "strong interaction" that holds the atomic nucleus together. (The others are the "weak" force, regulating radioactive decay, and electromagnetism.) Guth continued to concentrate on abstract problems of particle theory in postdoctoral teaching and research positions at Princeton University (1971–74), Columbia University (1974–77), and Cornell University (1977–79). At Columbia in 1975 he began to learn about the magnetic monopole, an exotic particle theorized to be, in his words, "ridiculously massive" and to have a single magnetic charge, corresponding to an isolated north or south pole. At Cornell that theory led him into the realm of the very early universe when the so-called grand unified theories, or GUTs, were beginning to be discussed widely by physicists.

One of Guth's colleagues at Cornell, Henry Tye, suggested that they study the cosmological consequences of grand unified theories, particularly as they related to the production of magnetic monopoles in the Big Bang, the primordial explosion out of which our universe is thought to have emerged. "I had heard of GUTs," Guth told Joan Rachel Goldberg, who interviewed him for *Science Digest* (July 1985), "but I certainly didn't understand them. So I had to ask him, 'What's a grand unified theory?'" The basic idea of a grand unified theory, he learned, "is that what were perceived to be three independent forces . . . are actually parts of a single unified force." The unifier is a mathematical framework, a ground field in which "a symmetry relates one force to another." Because the forces "are very different in strength and character," the theory is constructed so that the symmetry, while "spontaneously broken in the present universe," is in principle possible at an extremely high temperature such as that which existed at the birth of the universe. GUTs theorists speculate that near the infinitely hot, infinitely dense point, or "singularity," which their equations indicate existed at the very beginning of the universe, gravity was also included in the unification of forces.

The "grand unified era" is thought to have lasted only for nanoseconds, ending when the universe began to expand and cool. That created a "Higgs field," which, like a prism separating white light into primary colors, triggered the breaking of symmetry between the basic forces. The strong atomic-nucleus force, for instance, separated from the others when the universe was about 10^{-35} of a second, or, one hundred millionth of a billionth of a billionth of a billionth of a second old. The remaining electro-weak force separated into the "weak force" and electromagnetism when the universe was 10^{-12} of a second old and 10^{15} degrees in temperature.

GUTs predicted that as the universe cooled and the forces separated there were imperfections in the process. The symmetry between the forces broke differently in different places, twisting portions of space into magnetic monopoles. Because of the size of those exotic particles, none of the accelerators available to physicists was able to generate even a fraction of the energy necessary for their formation. Although Guth verified for Tye the connection between GUTs and magnetic monopoles, the idea of predicting magnetic monopole production in the Big Bang sounded "crazy" to him, but Tye insisted, because success would mean a clarification of the linkages between the Big Bang theory, in which the strong and electro-weak forces are always separate, and the GUTs theory.

Guth did not become persuaded of the value of relating the two sets of theories until the spring of 1979, when Steven Weinberg, the Nobel laureate in physics that year, gave a lecture at Cornell. Weinberg's lecture concerned the use of ideas put forward by GUTs to calculate the number of protons and neutrons produced in the Big Bang and to account for the present-day preponderance of matter over antimatter in the universe. The lecture convinced Guth that it made "sense to talk about the Big Bang and GUTs," and he went to work with Tye on the connection. Soon the two men reached the conclusion that if both the grand unified theories and the standard cosmological model were correct, then far too many magnetic monopoles would have been produced in the very early universe, causing that universe to collapse back on itself before the planets and animal and human life could evolve. "This conclusion was first published by John Preskill of Harvard," Guth has pointed out, "but the work led Henry [Tye] and me to consider mechanisms which might suppress the production of monopoles. It was this study which led to the development of the inflationary model of the universe."

Guth moved to the Stanford Linear Accelerator Center in the fall of 1979, but he and Tye continued to work on the problem of magnetic monopole overproduction by telephone. Their solution focused on the moment of the breaking of the symmetry between the strong, weak, and electromagnetic forces with the appearance of the Higgs field as the universe cooled. When the temperature of the universe is extremely high (10^{27} degrees), the Higgs field effectively does not exist and its value is said to be zero. As the temperature drops below 10^{27} degrees the universe is expected to undergo a "phase transition" such as that which occurs when water changes to ice. The Higgs field "freezes," acquiring a value larger than zero, and breaks the symmetry between the strong force and the electro-weak force. A sea of latent particles then pops into existence and, battening on the Higgs field, gains mass. Unfortunately, the troublesome magnetic monopoles also appear at that point. Guth and Tye cracked the problem when it occurred to them that the universe might fall so rapidly in temperature that it might "supercool." Water, for example, can be supercooled well below its freezing point without turning to ice. A supercooled universe would minimize magnetic monopole production because the value of its Higgs field would remain at zero and the symmetry between its strong and electro-weak forces would not be broken at temperatures that would normally manufacture the monopoles. The supercooled universe would enter what is known as a "false vacuum" state in which the energy needed to make magnetic monopoles and other particles would be entirely concentrated in the Higgs field. That vacuum, existing by a kind of sleight of hand, is "false," because it contains so much latent energy. The theory of quantum mechanics predicts that the vacuum will be full of "virtual particles"—particles that do not quite exist but are statistically possible and can be brought into being by random fluctuations of energy.

Guth proceeded to investigate the path the universe might be expected to take from the "false vacuum" to the "true vacuum" in which the Higgs field finally releases the energy trapped within it, much as supercooled water releases a burst of latent heat when it freezes. On Thursday, December 6, 1979, he has recounted, ideas that were already in his head without his knowing it "seemed to come together in one fell swoop." The ideas percolated as he discussed GUTs and particle physics with Sidney Coleman of Harvard University during that day, and at home that evening he filled page after page of a notebook with calculations. Very late at night came what has been called his "Eureka moment," when, as he recounted to Joan Rachel Goldberg, he "solved those equations" and came to the "spectacular realization" that in its first fraction of a second of existence "the universe grew exponentially, inflating like a balloon."

Guth had reasoned that, like the inevitable ice crystal forming in a glass of supercooled water, sooner or later a portion of the Higgs field would "tunnel" out of the false vacuum, acquiring a positive value and creating a bubble of true vacuum. The energy density of the Higgs field, behaving as matter does in the present universe, is normally expected to slow the bubble's expansion. That the bubble forms at all, Guth reasoned, indicates that negative pressure within the false vacuum overcomes the positive energy density and creates a bubble, much as the negative temperature of subzero weather might cause a pipe to burst. As Alan H. Guth and Paul J. Steinhardt pointed out in an article in Scientific American (May 1984), "The bizarre notion of negative pressure leads to the even more bizarre effect of a gravitational force that is effectively repulsive." The paradoxical repulsion causes the bubble of true vacuum to inflate "at a speed that would rapidly approach the speed of light." Chilled by the enormous expansion, the energy that had been trapped in the Higgs field would crystallize in the form of matter.

By the time the true vacuum is fully formed and inflation ends, the size of the universe has increased by a factor of 10^{50}—from a fraction of the size of a proton to the size of a grapefruit—though only 10^{-32} of a second has passed. The rate of expansion would then slow to the rate predicted in the standard Big Bang theory, the chilled universe having been "reheated" into a fireball of 10^{27} degrees by the released energy density of the Higgs field.

What most excited Guth was his inflationary theory's solution of the "flatness problem" in the standard Big Bang theory. He had first heard about "flatness" from the Princeton University astronomer Robert Dicke, when Dicke spoke at Cornell in 1978. The problem was the Big Bang's failure to explain the almost exact observed equality between the actual mass density of the galaxies and particles in the universe and the critical density needed to prevent the universe from being "open" and expanding forever. Had the universe been open at the beginning, it would have expanded too fast for matter to congregate into stars or galaxies. If, as is still possible, it is only slightly open, it will expand and cool until stars and galaxies fizzle out. On the other hand, were the mass density greater than the critical density—as it would be in the event of too many magnetic monopoles—the universe would be "closed," in the way that a sphere is closed by its surface, and would contract back upon itself in a "big crunch." The near-perfect match between mass density and critical density that has been observed suggests a "flat" universe that, being neither open nor closed, is miraculously stable. This means, Guth concluded, that "at one second after the Big Bang the equality [of mass density and critical density] held to an accuracy of at least 14 or 15 decimal places." He compared such a prediction to "balancing a pencil on its point so precisely that it's still there a billion years later."

The mechanism of the equality of densities that emerged in the equations Guth worked out on that December night in 1979 was the exponential inflation of the universe, forcing a density match in a way comparable to a vise holding the "pencil" firmly upright. Although "a little queasy [about] inventing something that dramatic," Guth bicycled from his home to the Stanford Linear Accelerator Center the following morning in record time, so eager was he to discuss his equations with his colleagues.

In his book Perfect Symmetry: The Search for the Beginning of Time (1985), Heinz R. Pagels observed that "Guth had the answer—the inflationary universe epoch—before he knew the questions it answered." Early in 1980 one of Guth's colleagues, Marvin Weinstein, told him about the "horizon problem" in the Big Bang theory. One of the central proofs for the Big Bang was the "afterglow" of the primal fireball, a uniform background of microwave radiation coming from all points of the sky. The problem was that within the limits of the Big Bang theory, the approximately fifteen billion years of the universe's existence would not be sufficient time for radiation, traveling at the speed of light, to have crossed from one side of the expanding universe to the other. The maximum distance the radiation could have traveled since the Big Bang, known as the horizon distance, was less than one-ninetieth the distance between the opposite sides of space. Guth immediately saw that inflation solved that problem by hypothesizing creation of the universe from a subatomic bubble that would have had time to reach uniform temperature before its period of exponential expansion.

There was one noticeable flaw in Guth's theory as originally published in 1980. His equations predicted that the formation of a bubble of true vacuum would not be an isolated phenomenon but would take place at random throughout the false vacuum. The equations indicated that the bubbles would cluster and their boundaries would be extremely energetic and detectable. Because there is no evidence for such behavior in the present universe, Guth's model clearly had to be adjusted. In 1981 the emendation was provided by the Russian physicist Andrei Linde and, independently, by two physicists working in the United States, Andreas Albrecht and Paul Steinhardt. Linde told John Gribbin that the flaw in Guth's theory had made him "physically ill" because he "could not believe that God could miss such a good possibility to simplify the work of creation of the universe."

Even as emended by Linde, Steinhardt, and Albrecht, the new inflationary model of the universe was not perfect, but cosmologists remained enthusiastic about it because of its basic attractive feature: the fine-tuning of the standard Big Bang model, which had previously been useful only in explaining the universe when it was a second or more old and already expanded. Whatever initial conditions prevailed before the "Planck barrier"—when the universe was 10^{-43} of a second old—inflation would convert them into initial conditions of the Big Bang.

Guth returned to M.I.T. as a visiting associate professor in the department of physics in 1980. He became associate professor in 1981 and a full professor in 1986. At M.I.T. he continued to speculate on the instant of creation that preceded the Planck barrier. Extrapolating from quantum rules that predict the creation of particles out of nothing (when the universe "isn't looking," as John Gribbin put it), he began to investigate the possibility that the universe itself might have been created out of nothing more than a quantum fluctuation in an initial state devoid of space, time, or matter. The conservation laws of physics, one of which states that energy can be neither created nor destroyed, have a loophole. As Guth has pointed out, the negative value of gravity in the false vacuum exactly cancels the positive value of the energy density. "The total energy," he and Steinhardt wrote in their Scientific American article, "is then zero and is consistent with the evolution of the universe from nothing." Guth has also noted that the inflationary scenario suggests that "everything that we see and everything . . . connected to everything that we see comprises one island universe, which is only one of many island universes."

In their 1987 paper "An Obstacle to Creating a Universe in the Laboratory" (Physical Letters, 183B, 149) Guth and E. H. Farhi explored the possibility of artificially producing Big Bang conditions. "The odd thing," Guth told Malcolm W. Browne in a New York Times interview (April 14, 1987), "is that you might even be able to start a universe using energy equivalent to just a few pounds of matter. Provided you could find some way to compress it to a density of about 10 to the 75th power grams per cubic centimeter, and provided you could trigger the thing, inflation would do the rest." In building his scenario, Guth conceives the present universe as an immense sphere whose size, like that of the surface of the Earth, makes it appear flat to the up-close observer. Compressing the few pounds of matter would produce an "aneurysm" on the surface of the sphere. The aneurysm would pinch itself off, leaving behind a black hole which would eventually evaporate because of the phenomenon known as "Hawking radiation." The offspring universe would then inflate and enter a Big Bang era, and the fate of such a universe would be unknowable to its creator. "Once their common space-time is pinched off," Guth explained to Browne, "the two universes can never again have any point of contact or any channel of mutual communication." "It would be literally true," Guth added with a laugh, "that you can't get there from here."

Alan H. Guth, who is five feet seven inches tall, brown-eyed, and brown-haired and weighs 155 pounds, describes himself as "a happy person at heart." According to a note preceding the *Science Digest* interview, "Guth's face is still boyish. He seems shy, his voice hesitant, [but the] voice gathers strength as he continues, with a ready laugh often punctuating the tale of his Eureka moment." Guth lives in Brookline, Massachusetts, with the former Susan Barbara Tisch (whom he married on March 28, 1971) and their two children, Lawrence David (born in 1977) and Jennifer Lynn (born in 1984).

Guth was the recipient of an Alfred P. Sloan Foundation Fellowship in 1981, and he was made a fellow of the American Physical Society Fellowship in 1986. In addition to his duties at M.I.T., he does part-time work at the Harvard-Smithsonian Center for Astrophysics.

References: Chicago Tribune mag p16+ Ja 6 '85 pors; Discover 4:93+ Je '83 pors; N Y Times C p1+ Ap 14 '87 por; Science 82 p14+ D '82 pors; Science Digest 93:42+ Jl '85 por; Gribbin, John. In Search of the Big Bang: Quantum Physics and Cosmology (1986); Pagels, Heinz R. Perfect Symmetry: The Search for the Beginning of Time (1986)

Haacke, Hans (Christoph)

(hä´kə hänz)

Aug. 12, 1936– Artist. Address: b. c/o John Weber Gallery, 142 Greene St., New York City, N.Y. 10012

Since the early 1960s the provocative German-born postformalist graphic artist and sculptor Hans Haacke has been painstakingly researching and meticulously crafting systems art—mixed media works that appropriate the forms and materials of various inorganic and organic systems, which when placed in a gallery context make the viewer aware of normally ignored internal relationships. After first concentrating on physical and biological systems, Haacke became politicized and turned his visual wicked wit, cunning hand, and Brechtian moral indignation to social systems, presenting statistics, texts, photographs, and other cultural data in illuminating Conceptual montages, documentary schema that the art historian Lucy Lippard compared to "Duchampian Dada, subverting with found material." "From the grab bag of public information," Miss Lippard wrote in the *Village Voice* (February 25, 1981), "he spotlights aspects of society we have taken for granted, thereby performing the classic artist's function of teaching people how to see."

At his most controversial, Haacke creates art that, in his words, "bites the hand that feeds it." He is an art demystifier, perhaps the most unequivocal and influential of the artists who refuse to self-censor in conformity with the notion of art promulgated by the corporations, chiefly multinational, which are the major funders of art institutions today. According to that notion, art is a pure, rarified activity, suggesting a noble liberal humanism without touching on such real-life problems as the sometimes dubious ways that the corporate funders make their money. Over the past dozen years Haacke has repeatedly used his work to expose the mechanisms by which the art establishment is permeated by social, economic, and political forces.

Because much of his work embarrasses museum curators, he was not given a one-man museum show in the United States until 1986, when the New Museum of Contemporary Art in New York City mounted a fifteen-year retrospective. Brian Wallis, the adjunct curator of the New Museum, writing in *Art in America* (June 1986), said of Haacke: "His art functions on several levels, 're-writing' the fixed images or practices of corporate semiotics, utilizing a montage of specific but loosely connected information to produce both an intensive and an extensive reading. Intensively, his work provokes the viewer to . . . burrow into obscured factual information which forms the network connecting and supporting his images. . . . Extensively, his art provokes an extrapolation from the individual work outward . . . beyond the art world to other economic, social, and political power formations." A resident of the United States since 1965, Haacke is a tenured professor at the Cooper Union for the Advancement of Science and Art in New York City.

The grandson of an amateur painter, Hans Christoph Haacke was born on August 12, 1936, in Cologne, Germany. His father, a Social Democrat and a follower of anthroposophy, a system of mystical beliefs derived from theosophy, lost his job with the city of Cologne because he refused to join the Nazi party. Haacke's friend Jack Burnham, the English artist and critic who introduced him to the systems concept, sees Haacke's low-keyed handling of potentially explosive subjects in his best work and the deliberately low profile that he assiduously keeps as the habits of a lifelong "alien," who learned reticence under Hitler, who found the postwar choice between Stalinism and capitalistic consumerism unacceptable, and who has lived in the United States for twenty-two years while retaining his West German citizenship. Haacke himself explained to Grace Glueck of the *New York Times* (January 25, 1987) that he doesn't sign his work and forbids publicity photographs of himself because he does not want to play up to "the cult of personality"—and besides, "it's easier to get around when your face isn't known."

Growing up in the Bonn suburb of Bad Godesberg, Haacke attended the Pädagogium Otto Kuhne and the Nicholas Cusanus Gymnasium there. After taking a master of fine arts degree at the Hochschule für Bildende Künste in Kassel, West Germany, in 1960, he studied on scholarships at the printmaker Stanley William Hayter's Atelier 17 in Paris (1960-61), at the Tyler School of Art at Temple University in Philadelphia (1961-62), and at the Pratt Graphics Center in New York City (1962-63). He taught at the Pädagogische Hochschule in Kettwig, West Germany, in 1963-64 and at the Modeschule in Düsseldorf in 1964-65. From 1960 to 1965 he exhibited kinetic works with Gruppe Zero (a name connoting an empty space before a new beginning), a loose affiliation of Düsseldorf-based artists whose shows were happenings involving the audience in experiments with light, vibration, and color. In 1965 Haacke married Linda Snyder, an American, and settled with her in the United States, where he lectured at the University of Washington in Seattle (1965) and the Philadelphia College of Art (1966-67) before joining the faculty of Cooper Union in 1967.

Haacke's earliest exhibited works were paintings and prints, including intaglios of pale yellow dots on white grounds. Among his first sculptures were blocks and cylinders laminated with mirror-like aluminum foil and configured as a feedback loop in which they reflected infinite regressions of each other. Much of his early work showed the influence of Yves Klein's examinations of water, air, and fire, the Greek kinetic sculptor Takis' use of such physical forces as magnetic fields and electrical energy, and Klaus Rinke's meteorological art. Between 1962 and 1964 Jack Burnham introduced him to systems theory, and later Haacke read and absorbed the biologist Ludwig von Bertalanffy's book General Systems Theory (1968), which emphasized how all plant and animal life functions interrelatedly in open systems that remain flexible through change, or what Jack Burnham described as "the inflow and outflow of materials and energy."

Beginning in 1962 Haacke made a series of "dripper boxes," which spectators were invited to turn upside down, as they would an egg timer, causing water to flow through holes in interior grids. Between 1963 and 1965 he built a series of "weather cubes," sealed clear acrylic boxes in which water condensed or evaporated in response to changes in temperature in the gallery. The reverse of his condensation pieces was Ice Stick (1966), in which a sealed-off refrigeration coil collected and froze atmospheric water vapor in response to the temperature and humidity of the gallery and the number of spectators breathing on it. Other projects involving liquids included boxed waves activated by the spectator. He also did air sculptures, including sails billowed by compressed air and balloons and other spheres kept aloft by currents of air.

In a 1965 catalog statement, Haacke described his sculpture as phenomenological, "something which lives in time and makes the spectator experience time." Later he defined a system as "a grouping of elements subject to a common plan" and interacting in "real time" so as "to arrive at a joint goal" independent of perceptual interpretation. Moving from inorganic to organic systems in the late 1960s, Haacke made such art objects as Grass Cube, Chickens Hatching, Ant Co-op, Grass Grows, and Live Airborne System. In the last-mentioned, he lured with bread crumbs and photographed in flying formation a flock of seagulls at Coney Island.

Meanwhile, Haacke was active in the Art Workers Coalition, a group that took political stands, such as opposition to the war in Vietnam, in addition to fighting for the professional rights of artists in New York City, including the right to studio space in old loft buildings. "I began to see things as belonging together, the world as not compartmentalized, but one organic whole," he recounted to Grace Glueck of the New York Times. "Like other artists of the 1960s, I got politicized by the war and the racial situation. But while many of them [because of the strictures of abstract art] couldn't extend their work into the social field, there were no barriers for me. I decided to incorporate my concerns in my work, and went from biological to political-social systems."

At the Howard Wise Gallery in 1969 Haacke had an exhibition that included fifty years of New York City mayoral election results and a United Press International wire-service machine jigging out a constant, endless stream of news on ticker tape, which was looped from ceiling to floor at the end of each day and then stored in glass archival urns. In an interview at the time he explained: "Both [physical and biological systems] can be tangible and visible—whereas social systems and political systems are essentially invisible. If you want to present, demonstrate, or document them in a non-interpretative manner—without giving opinions about them—you have to resort to some sort of vehicle. . . . There has to be a fact, before you can ramble in your mind."

The 1969 Howard Wise Gallery exhibition was the occasion of Haacke's first Gallery-Goers Residence Profile. Maps of the world and New York City were displayed, and visitiors were asked to indicate on the maps their place of birth, with red pins, and their place of residence, with blue pins. What he found was "a cluster of people living downtown . . . and then some on the upper East Side . . . almost nobody coming from the Harlem area" and "pretty thin" representations from Queens, the Bronx, and Brooklyn. Later he photographed the 752 buildings visitors from Manhattan had specified as their residences and, in a gallery in Cologne, Germany, mounted the photos on a wall design representing the Manhattan street plan. Without commentary, the display documented the social class pattern of gallery going. The social implications of his demographic and other surveys of gallery-goers confirmed Haacke's realizations that "it is precisely the exchange of necessarily biased information between the members of a social set that provides the energy on which social relations evolve" and that he himself was conditioned by the system he was surveying.

From 1969 to 1973 Haacke did a number of polls of gallery-goers in which responses to demographic and sociopolitical questions were correlated in bar graphs, charts, and other statistical schema. His *MOMA Poll*, created for the June-September 1970 "Information" show at the Museum of Modern Art, asked visitors, by placing their ballots in one of two transparent boxes, to respond to the question: "Would the fact that Governor [Nelson A.] Rockefeller has not denounced President Nixon's Indochina policy be a reason for you not to vote for him in November?" Several elements combined to make that question in that context particularly provocative. The Rockefellers had been instrumental in the founding of the museum, and the governor and other family members were currently influential trustees. The Kent State shooting of four antiwar student demonstrators had taken place the month before, and many New York artists, under the banner of "Art Strike," had demanded the temporary closing of all museums in protest. During twelve weeks of tabulation, 69 percent of those responding opposed the governor. "Haacke realized that by being very specific to the context in which it was posed, his question had more weight and energy than it would have had if it had been asked outside the four walls of the museum," Catherine Lacey pointed out retrospectively in a 1984 Tate Gallery (London) catalog. "The specific sociopolitical context caused an articulation of prejudices, which, to an extent, disrupted the homogenous image of the museum as an apolitical space, an inviolate temple of culture."

In France in 1970 Haacke participated in an exhibition of experimental works by young American artists sponsored by the Fondation Maeght. Angered that the guest artists were treated "like dogs," and perversely inspired by the aristocratic ambiance and manicured grounds of the foundation's estate, he created three obtrusive ecological works, including *Goat Feeding in the Wood, Thus Changing It*. For his contribution to an evening of performance art, Haacke created an audiotape on which a female voice reported the prices of prints for sale at the bookstore of the not-for-profit foundation. All of the prints, whose aggregate value was $190,000, were by artists handled by the commercial Galerie Maeght in Paris. The director of the foundation tried, unsuccessfully, to stop the performance.

In one of the art world's most publicized recent contretemps, the Guggenheim Museum in New York City, forewarned, canceled a Haacke exhibition scheduled at the museum in 1971. Thomas Messer, the museum's director, found three works "inappropriate": a multiple-question visitors' poll and, above all, two *Real-Time Social Systems*, exposés, based on publicly available records, that untangled the intricate web of corporate and other identities behind which major New York City

slumlords were hiding from public accountability. The most controversial of the works, *Shapolsky et al. Manhattan Real Estate Holdings*, consisted of two photo-enlarged maps, one of Harlem and the other of the Lower East Side, and 142 photographs of building facades or empty lots, each accompanied by a typewritten sheet giving such data as purchase price, current assessed value, nominal owner (invariably a faceless corporation, such as "194 Avenue B Realty Corp."), and the names of the principals of those corporations (invariably Harry J. Shapolsky or a member of his family). Messer explained that the real-estate documentaries constituted "libelous muckraking" that violated the museum's policy against "active engagement toward social and political ends." The museum, he said, was "not the proper place in which to expose slumlords." Edward Fry, the curator in charge of the exhibition, publicly defended Haacke and was fired. Writing in *Arts Magazine* (May 1971), Joseph James Akston observed that the cancelation dramatized the pressures put upon artists everywhere "in the name of Culture supposedly removed from all kinds of real-life problems," and made clear "that the establishment expects art to be separated from socio-political confrontations" and to cater only "to the tastes of both a self-defining mandarin class and an affluent and complacent bourgeoisie."

"I wanted to do something about power in New York, and that is real estate," Haacke said of his *Real-Time Social Systems*. "At that time I was also part of the Art Workers Coalition, and there was the Guggenheim with its white walls and immaculate environment, situated in the most expensive part of town. I felt somehow one had to remind this other world that the majority of people in New York don't live that way." The *Real-Time Social Systems* documentaries were finally exhibited as part of a "Making Megalopolis Matter" show at the New York Cultural Center.

Rhine-Water Purification Plant, which consisted of a series of transparent containers in which polluted water pumped from the Rhine River was purified, was exhibited at the Museum Haus Lange in Krefeld, West Germany, in 1972 along with a related piece, *Krefeld Sewage Triptych*, which traced the path of the Krefeld sewer system, through which forty-two million cubic meters of untreated sewage were dumped into the Rhine annually. The chagrined city officials acknowledged the problem and took steps to correct it.

Haacke began focusing on the intimate nexus between big business and "artistic success" in the mid-1970s, with two documentary works in which he traced the provenance of Seurat's *Les Poseuses* (small version, 1888) and Manet's *Bunch of Asparagus* (1880) through their rise to "museum status." The Manet work is owned by the Wallraf-Richarz Museum in Cologne. Invited to contribute a work to the international celebration of the 150th anniversary of the Wallraf-Richarz Museum in 1974, Haacke submitted a proposal that showed *Bunch of Asparagus* on an easel and, on a wall behind, ten elegantly mounted panels detailing the ownership of the painting over the years, the prices paid, and the social and economic status of the owners and the museum's current trustees, including Hermann J. Abs, one of the major donors to the purchase of the painting. The museum balked at the profile of Abs, which included the important banking positions he had held under the Third Reich. In rejecting his proposal, Horst Keller, the director of the museum, explained to Haacke that "a grateful museum . . . must protect initiatives of such an extraordinary character" as Mr. Abs's. He further said Abs's worldly offices had nothing to do with his "spiritual initiative" and that "a museum knows nothing about economic power; it does, indeed, however, know something about spiritual power." The project was instead exhibited at the Paul Maenz Gallery in Cologne, with a reproduction standing in for Manet's painting.

In *On Social Grease* (1975) Haacke illuminated the philosophy behind big business' sponsorship of the arts by quoting from trade journals, corporation conference reports, and the speeches of politicians. He photoengraved the quotations in magnesium on aluminum plaques, a format suggestive of corporate nameplates. The title derived from a statement by Robert Kingsley of the Exxon Corporation: "Exxon's support of the arts serves as a social lubricant. And if business is to continue in big cities, it needs a more lubricated environment." "Embalmed as art," Gary Indiana later observed in the *Village Voice* (May 21, 1985), "these tossed-off bits of speechwriter's verbiage emit more sincerity, and hence more menace, than they were intended to. In plaque form the message is: art is a religion of unknowing that can make Big Business look like God. Haacke's work is sacrilegious, destructive of an entire belief structure. By contrast, much contemporary art is merely blasphemous, aimed at shattering (or, more typically, tweaking) aesthetic norms. It ultimately reaffirms the status quo by joining it, despite its own intentions."

In such works as *The Good Will Umbrella* (1976), Haacke exposed the ulterior motive of multinational corporations in their cultural underwriting. *Mobilization* (1975) consisted of large silkscreen sheets mimicking the highbrow *New York Times* op-ed ads of Mobil, the oil corporation, in format and typeface. On the sheets Haacke quoted the investment banker C. Douglas Dillon, a champion of Mobil and the president of the Metropolitan Museum of Art, and Raymond d'Argenio, Mobil's manager of public relations. D'Argenio was quoted as pointing out that Mobil's sponsorship of high-caliber PBS television specials builds "enough acceptance to allow us to get tough on substantive issues" and that a Mobil-sponsored "city-wide jump rope contest . . . gets even more publicity than Senator Jackson's 'obscene profits.'" (He was referring to the late Senator Henry Jackson, the chairman of a Senate committee investigating the oil industry at that time.)

During the late 1970s Haacke created several works unrelated to art sponsorship that pointed up the contradictions between the highbrow public-relations images projected by multinational corporations and some of their less than noble real-life activities. *A Breed Apart* (1978) adopted the format used by British Leland Ltd. in advertising its Jaguar automobile to show that company's Land Rover being used by police in racist South Africa. *The Right to Life* (1979) replicated American Cyanamid's smiling and shampooed Breck Girl above copy detailing the company's policy of compulsory sterilization for female employees of child-bearing age who wished to remain in high-paying jobs that exposed them to toxic substances.

Again tying art patronage to corporate policy, Haacke in *We believe in the power of the creative imagination* (1980) juxtaposed that slogan of the F-N Browning Company's international art competition with photographs of the F-N automatic rifle being used against South African blacks. In *Voici Alcan* (1983) he superimposed statements about the repressive labor policies of Alcan Aluminum Ltd.'s South African affiliate on two photographs of opera productions sponsored by Alcan. Those photos flank a post-autopsy portrait of Stephen Biko, the South African black leader killed by police interrogators. All three panels are framed in aluminum and topped by the Alcan logo. "The panels' uniform, banal streamlining purveys a pathetic reality," Gary Indiana commented in his *Village Voice* article, "reality 'sponsored,' 'presented' by faceless entities for whom an opera extravaganza and a convenient political killing are all in the day's work."

In 1982 Haacke took aim at the Reagan administration in *Oil Painting, Homage to Marcel Broothaers.* (Broothaers was a Belgian Conceptual artist.) Unlike his previous work, which involved minimal transformation of existing materials, this consists in one part of a realistic, fiercely imperial-looking oil portrait of President Ronald Reagan laboriously copied from a photograph. As conceived for showing by Haacke, the portrait is mounted in a gold frame under a picture lamp and stanchioned with a red velvet rope. From the portrait, a red carpet runs across the room to a facing wall covered with a photomural that changes with time and locale. In Kassel, West Germany, the mural was of a demonstration in Bonn against deployment of Cruise and Pershing II missiles; in New York, of an antinuclear march in Manhattan. The viewer, standing on the red carpet between the two images, is asked, more effectively than in words, "Which side are you on?" Another Haacke work relating to the Reagan administration, *U.S. Isolation Box, Grenada 1983*, shows a torture device used by the American military in a prison camp.

In his unfinished *Taking Stock* (1983-84) Haacke tied the economics of art to political power in a courtly Victorian-style portrait of Margaret Thatcher, the British prime minister, containing visual allusions to Saatchi & Saatchi, the global British advertising firm (known facetiously in London as Snatchit & Snatchit) that ran Mrs. Thatcher's election campaigns as well as public relations campaigns for the government of South Africa, the Tate

Gallery, the National Gallery, and other British institutions of fine art. Charles Saatchi is a major collector and aggrandizer of contemporary art, best known for buying up the works of Julian Schnabel when their price was cheap. Nine of the eleven Schnabel paintings in a solo exhibition at the Tate in 1982 came from the Saatchi collection. After *Taking Stock* was included in Haacke's retrospective exhibition at the Tate Gallery in 1984, Charles Saatchi resigned from the Tate's Patrons of New Art Committee.

MetroMobilitan (1985) is a small-scale fiberglas approximation of the entrance to the Metropolitan Museum of Art, with three Met-style banners. The central banner announces "Treasures of Ancient Nigeria," an exhibition sponsored at the Met by Mobil in 1982. The side banners carry Mobil statements justifying its policy of selling oil to the South African army and police. Behind the banners, partly hidden from view, is a giant photomural of a funeral procession for blacks shot by the South African police. On the entablature above is a quotation from the Metropolitan's brochure promoting art sponsorship as a "cost-effective" marketing device, "particularly where international, governmental or consumer relations may be a fundamental concern."

MetroMobilitan was created for a Haacke exhibition held at the John Webber Gallery in SoHo, Manhattan's arts quarter, in May 1985. In his review of the show in the *Village Voice*, Gary Indiana wrote: "Many of Haacke's elegant-looking art objects transport widely available cultural data . . . to the rarefied precinct of art, recasting them in standard materials and familiar Conceptual themes. Because of their content, the shift in context plays havoc with the communal fiction that art knows nothing about the social, economic, and ideological forces that permeate it. [His work] relies on the aura of art for its power and, things being what they are, probably needs it for protection."

The one-man retrospective show of Haacke's work that opened at the New Museum of Contemporary Art in SoHo in December 1986 included *Buhrlesque* (1985), in which the artist wittily connects the Bally shoes and other elegant leather goods manufactured by Oerlikon-Buhrle, the Swiss company, with the same company's armaments business with the South African Defense Force. Some of the small works exhibited were parodies of corporate ads. "He has become as cagey as his enemies over the years," Elizabeth Hess observed in her review of the show in the *Village Voice* (January 6, 1986). "Yet unlike them, Haacke uses art to reveal rather than conceal ideology." After the show left the New Museum in February 1987, it began a tour of galleries and museums in several other North American cities. Haacke planned to make a site-specific work "attuned to the muck" of each stop in the itinerary.

Hans Haacke and his wife, Linda, have two sons, Carl and Paul. The camera-shy artist, who looks much younger than his years, was described by Paul Richard of the *Washington Post* (May 6,

1976) as "in conversation, a friendly man" who "does not preach or browbeat." Haacke told Richard that he had long ago cut himself off from partisanship with any political group. Although his sympathies are leftist, he has, he says, "little patience with the orthodoxies of the left." His honors and awards include a Guggenheim fellowship (1973-74), a grant from the National Endowment for the Arts (1978), and the Skowhegan Medal of the Skowhegan (Maine) School of Painting and Sculpture (1987). Without his tenured professorship at Cooper Union, he has said, he "couldn't afford to do what [he] is doing." There are several books of criticism and appreciation of Haacke's work, including *Hans Haacke: Framing and Being Framed*, edited by Jack Burnham and published by New York University Press in 1975, and Haacke himself has written numerous essays on art for professional journals and his exhibition catalogs.

References: Christian Sci Mon p10 N 24 '69; N Y Times II p27+ Ja 25 '87; Washington Post C p15 My 6 '76; Contemporary Artists (1977); Who's Who in American Art, 1986; World Artists 1950–1980 (1984)

Habré, Hissène
(ä-brā´ ē-sen´)

1942- President of Chad. Address: Présidence de la République, N'Djamena, Chad.

With a series of stunning battlefield victories over Libyan and Libyan-backed armies in early 1987, Hissène Habré, the president of Chad since 1982, brought a measure of peace and national unity to his divided country for the first time in two decades. The 1987 triumphs were the culmination of fifteen years of guerrilla battles and political intrigues for the Paris-educated Habré, who rose to power in the course of a civil war that has wracked his sprawling, landlocked, drought-stricken central African homeland since 1965. Chad's artificially created borders, drawn by late nineteenth-century French colonists, enclose the territories of eleven ethnic groups speaking different languages and drawing on separate cultural traditions—a circumstance that made civil war almost inevitable after the country obtained its independence from France in 1960.

Habré's powerful personality and undisguised ambition, which for many years made him the most feared and controversial figure in Chadian politics, are seen by some as perhaps the only forces strong enough to hold together the nation that the World Bank lists as the planet's poorest against the internal and external forces that threaten to tear it apart. "We have enormous problems," Habré once admitted in an interview for the *UNESCO Courier* (March–April 1987). Acknowledging the threat of famine and economic collapse brought on by drought in 1984 and 1985 and by the fragmenting of political and administrative structures during a generation of war, Habré stressed, however, that "God has given Chad all it needs in life," including sources of fresh water such as Lake Chad, fertile soil in areas such as the cotton-growing south, and untapped oil reserves. "The basic job has been done," he insisted. "The Chadians are one again and we are united against the foreign invader. . . . Let me tell you that we have great ambitions for our country."

Hissène Habré was born in 1942 in Faya Largeau, a northern garrison town on a major caravan route linking Chad and Libya. His father, a poor shepherd, belonged to the Annakaza subclan of the Daza clan of the Toubous, a tribe of about one hundred thousand nomads and seminomads with a history of caravan raiding, slave trading and interclan feuding, as well as of the more peaceful but less profitable pursuits of date-growing and herding. Habré attended a mission-run primary school in Faya Largeau and graduated in 1962. He was then appointed to a minor post with the French military administration, which retained responsibility for Chad's rebellious northern provinces of Bourkou, Ennedi, and Tibesti until 1965. The local French commandant, impressed with Habré's intelligence and apparent incorruptibility, recommended him to independent Chad's first president, François Tombalbaye. As part of a plan to develop loyal northern leaders, Habré was given a scholarship to study administration in France. He left for Paris in 1965, the year in which full civil war broke out between Chad's northern rebels and the Tombalbaye government, which, having centralized power in one party dominated by Tombalbaye's southern Sara tribe, was compiling what one scholar called an "appalling record of incompetence, mismanagement, corruption and sheer brutality."

In Paris, Habré earned successive degrees at the Institute of Overseas Higher Studies and the faculty of law and economic science, capping his education with a doctorate from the faculty of law. In that period, Habré was strongly influenced by the radical student movement then rocking France, and he once described himself as a Maoist. But a Chadian who studied with him recalled that "Habré was never an ideologue. Even then, he believed only in himself, and was dreaming of becoming a prefect."

Habré's ambitions soon began to bear fruit. He was appointed subprefect of a strategically important town, Moussoro, immediately after his return to Chad in 1970. By then, the civil war had moved into high gear, pitting the Toubou and other poor, Arabized, Islamic tribesmen from the north against Tombalbaye's wealthier, westernized, Christianized Sara tribesmen who, numbering about one and a quarter million, constituted Chad's largest single ethnic group. French troops, sent home in 1965 and called back in 1968, provided Tombalbaye's government with a protective shield, but the president's own erratic and heavy-handed policies and his resistance to any dilution of his authority or real power-sharing outside of the Sara tribe, had irrevocably unified the north against him. The *Front de la Libération Nationale du Tchad* (FROLINAT), a loose coalition of northern rebel groups formed in 1966, increased steadily in militancy and popularity and helped to drive Tombalbaye to introduce a number of policies of desperation that alienated even southerners and French officials. In October 1971, in a major bid to reverse his fortunes, Tombalbaye dispatched Habré on a secret mission to Algiers to win over two top FROLINAT leaders, Abba Siddick and Goukouni Oueddei. Instead, after a few negotiating sessions, Habré defected to FROLINAT. Journalists and scholars have cited fear of facing Tombalbaye after having failed to gain Oueddei's and Siddick's defections and a Machiavellian interpretation of Chad's political scene as possible reasons for Habré's decision.

Habré instantly sought a key leadership position in FROLINAT, but according to a reporter for *Le Monde* (September 12, 1975), he was greeted with "immediate and obvious dislike" by Abba Siddick, who saw that "this newcomer was too gifted not to be a potential rival." Friction between the two men led to Habré's departure to join Oueddei in northern Chad's rugged Tibesti mountains, where Oueddei was based with his faction of FROLINAT, the *Forces Armées du Nord* (FAN). Early in 1972 Habré was made FAN's military commander, with the task of stepping up the rebellion against the government, while Oueddei continued as the faction's political head.

Tombalbaye meanwhile was struggling to retain power over his own increasingly restive supporters. He defused one plot against himself by arresting all his generals, including his army chief of staff, Félix Malloum, but Tombalbaye was killed in an April 13, 1975, coup that brought Malloum to power. Malloum's ties to the fallen regime, mysterious killings of jailed FROLINAT members, and what FROLINAT leaders regarded as a continued lack of effort to improve the lot of northerners, made Malloum's overtures of reconciliation unacceptable to Habré and other rebel leaders. French air and ground raids, however, bought time for Malloum by putting the rebels, who were poorly armed and weakened by faction fights, on the defensive, creating a stalemate between FROLINAT and Malloum that lasted until 1979. Bottled up with a thousand men in the Tibesti mountains, Habré was effectively barred from any southward thrust toward the civil war's strategic prize, N'Djamena, control of which brought control of Chad.

Habré finally broke the stalemate in April 1974 by attacking Bardai, a district capital, and taking three Europeans as hostages. By forcing the French government to negotiate directly with him, Habré made a bold move that eroded the Chadian government's already shaky legitimacy and catapulted FAN to preeminence among FROLINAT's feuding factions. Habré was suddenly a global media figure with enhanced stature in rebel politics. The kidnappings, however, soured his relationship with Goukouni Oueddei, whose more cautious, idealistic leadership was threatened by Habré's flamboyant tactics. Oueddei particularly criticized Habré's refusal to settle for anything other than arms in exchange for the last remaining hostage, Françoise Claustre, an anthropologist, and the wife of a high French official. Habré rejected Oueddei's arguments out of hand, held Mme. Claustre hostage for three years, and ordered the execution of a French officer sent to negotiate her release.

Fearing French wrath and hoping to win favor with Libya, whose armed support he felt would be essential to FROLINAT's success against the Malloum regime, Oueddei tried to persuade Habré to accept a Libyan offer to mediate the Claustre affair with France. The split between Oueddei and Habré was completed when the former also argued for acquiescence, at least temporarily, to Libya's 1973 seizure of the mineral-rich Aozou strip along the Chad-Libya border, which Libya claimed on the basis of an unratified 1935 treaty between France and Italy. Habré's declaration that FROLINAT should fight on two fronts rather than submit to Libyan landgrabbing at once forced a showdown between himself and Oueddei at a FAN meeting on October 18, 1976.

As the son and heir of the traditional Toubou religious leader, the Derde, Goukouni Oueddei commanded greater popular support, and he succeeded in dismissing Hissène Habré from FAN's leadership. In January 1977, with Libyan help, Oueddei negotiated the release of Mme. Claustre. In defeat, Habré took refuge, with about 200 diehard supporters, along Chad's border with Sudan, whose government opposed Libyan expansionism and therefore provided Habré with weapons and a safe base area.

The following year, with extensive Libyan military support, Oueddei launched a campaign against Malloum in which he regularly defeated the president's forces and advanced to within a few hundred kilometers of N'Djamena. Malloum shored up his regime by calling in French Foreign Legionnaires and combat aircraft, which arrived in Chad in March 1978. In August he moved to split his northern opposition by inviting the outcast Habré to become prime minister of a new "government of national union."

Habré accepted, but the arrangement proved short-lived. Habré was intent upon presenting himself as the champion of northern interests, and he refused to permit FAN's integration into the national army, the Forces Armées Tchadiennes (FAT), until all his political demands were met. In an increasingly strained atmosphere, fighting soon broke out, and by February 1979 Habré's more mobile and aggressive troops had succeeded in chasing FAT out of N'Djamena in battles that set off a wave of ethnic revenge killings and refugee movements throughout the southern half of Chad.

While the French stood by, unwilling to back decisively any faction, a score of rival northern armies, including at least two backed by Libya and one backed by Nigeria, converged on N'Djamena, supposedly to fight alongside Habré's forces, but actually to jockey for postwar political position. Meanwhile, the south was in a state of virtual secession, protected by several thousand FAT soldiers. For several months the entire country lingered in a state of intermittent anarchy. Finally, a series of mediation attempts by the Organization of African Unity (OAU) and such nations as France, Nigeria, Sudan, and Libya resulted, in November 1979, in the formation of a shaky coalition, the "Gouvernement d'Union National de Transition" (GUNT). Goukouni Oueddei was its president, Hissène Habré its defense minister, and the exiled General Malloum's chief southern rival, Lieutenant Colonel Abdelkader Kamougue, was GUNT's vice-president. Although GUNT was broadly representative, mistrust and enmity were too great to permit the agreed-upon peaceful transition to free elections. By early 1980 the coalition was disintegrating, with Habré charging that Oueddei was a puppet of the Libyans and Oueddei countering that Habré was a French stooge with dictatorial ambitions.

In March 1980, despite the arrival of a 500-man Congolese peacekeeping contingent, large-scale fighting once again broke out in N'Djamena. This time the fighting lasted for nine months, sending as many as 250 casualties a day into French military hospitals. More than 120,000 citizens, half N'Djamena's population, fled across the Chari River into the neighboring nation of Cameroon. Habré nonetheless refused to sign a cease-fire agreement until all the Libyan troops backing Oueddei had left Chad. Oueddei rejected that demand, and he was supported by most of the other factional chieftains, who resented and feared what was viewed as Habré's unbounded ambition for personal power. In April 1980 they voted to expel Habré from GUNT.

Unwilling to become entangled in the looming civil war among northern factions, both the French and the Congolese withdrew their forces by the end of May 1980. This left the way clear for Libyan forces to outgun Habré's FAN troops. By December 1980 they had established Oueddei and his allies solidly in control of N'Djamena. But Oueddei's obvious dependence on Libya, formalized in an agreement on January 6, 1981, to merge the two countries, provoked an outcry from France and from most African states. Both feared that the Libyan leader Colonel Muammar el-Qaddafi's goal was the establishment of a trans-Saharan empire merging black Africa into the Arab world. France and a large number of African states therefore mounted a successful diplomatic campaign to force a Libyan withdrawal. At the end of April 1981 an agreement was signed providing for the exchange of Oueddei's Libyan backers for an Organization of African Unity peace-keeping force, which was supposed to maintain the peace until free elections could be held, no later than August 1982.

Meanwhile, Habré and his men had regrouped in eastern Biltine province, along the Sudanese border. With arms supplied by Egypt, Sudan, and—according to rumor—the United States, Habré launched his first attacks on government outposts in January 1981. By mid-September he controlled all of eastern Biltine and Ouadai provinces. At the same time, he earned diplomatic respectability by expressing interest in a proposed OAU-sponsored national reconciliation conference, which Oueddei, fearing Habré's growing anti-Libyan, nationalist appeal, steadfastly refused to undertake. By the spring of 1982 Hissène Habré was once more on the road to N'Djamena. On June 7 his troops reentered the city, forcing Oueddei and his allies to flee across the Chari River to Cameroon, and Habré was installed as president.

With Libyan help, Oueddei meanwhile moved to Bardai, near the Aozou strip, and rebuilt his GUNT forces. In October 1982 he set up a "national peace government," which included representatives of several other northern factions. In the spring of 1983 Libyan-GUNT armies launched a major offensive, culminating in the recapture of Faya Largeau in early August. Habré responded to the renewed military threat by urgently requesting French troops. Although France was reluctant to commit troops, Libya's refusal to discuss withdrawal unless the French first ditched Habré, finally compelled the French government to send a force of paratroopers and fighter aircraft to maintain a balance of power by demarcating a line through the middle of Chad, at the sixteenth parallel, south of which Libyan forces would not be permitted to move uncontested.

The security provided by the French presence enabled Habré to begin turning his attention to southern Chad, a region whose allegiance to his regime was limited, at best. Using a combination of concessions and repression, he started the long process of pacifying a region whose deep historical resentments caused by northern slave-raiding had

been exacerbated by recently committed atrocities of both northern soldiers and civilians. Just as that process was getting under way, on September 17, 1984, France and Libya announced a joint agreement to withdraw. France's withdrawal contributed to a resurgence of southern rebel activity, which Habré was not able to end before the middle of 1986.

Ignoring their agreement with the French, the Libyans kept their 10,000-man force in northern Chad, but to avoid a confrontation, they heeded French warnings and remained above the sixteenth parallel. In northern towns that they had captured, such as Wadi Doum and Habré's birthplace, Faya Largeau, they tried to strengthen their hold by instituting people's committees like those existing in Libya. That move angered leaders of a number of GUNT factions and led to mounting criticism of Oueddei for not speaking out against Libyan interference. When Oueddei, in August 1985, finally started criticizing the Libyans and expressed a desire for face-to-face negotiations with Hissène Habré, the Libyans placed him under house arrest in Tripoli and replaced him, as head of GUNT, with a more pliable candidate, Achiekh Ibn Omar. In October 1985, in a shootout with his Libyan captors, Oueddei reportedly was wounded and two of his bodyguards were killed. When news of this incident reached Oueddei's supporters in the Tibesti mountains, they attacked Libyan bases, and most of them agreed to a merger with Habré's army in January 1987.

Habré now at times launched his forces beyond the sixteenth parallel with the goal of retaking Faya Largeau. On New Year's day 1987, Habré's men retook the oasis town of Fada, which had been the southernmost stronghold of the Libyans. The supplies left behind by retreating Libyan troops, according to one Western diplomat, inadvertently made Libya "Chad's biggest arms supplier." Next, after much painstaking intelligence gathering and planning, the Chadians carried out what Bernard E. Trainor described in the New York Times (April 4, 1987), as a "spectacular defeat of 5,000 Libyans" at Wadi Doum. The victory had been set up, Trainor noted, by routs, in early March, of two heavily armored Libyan columns on their way to retake Fada. "The Chadians," Trainor wrote, had known that "their light [Toyota] trucks were no match for the Libyans' Soviet-made T-55 tanks and armored personnel carriers. Their solution to this mismatch had been to hide in the desert, then suddenly speed across the sand and "attack the Libyans before they could react."

Now, with the fall of Wadi Doum after ninety minutes of fighting, Libya lost 1,269 soldiers, hundreds of millions of dollars in military equipment, and an airfield that had been the anchor of its Chadian supply line. Faya Largeau fell two days later without a battle, placing the entire central plain of northern Chad under Habré's control. In August 1987, in the midst of a domestic consolidation of power based on courting former enemies and appointing them to key cabinet posts according to what one observer called "ethnic arithmetic," Habré sent his troops north to retake the Aozou strip. "They blew in real fast, hell-bent for leather" in their Toyota trucks, according to one diplomat, and captured the strip's administrative center, Aozou, in the first week of August. The French, who had advised Habré against any military venture into the Aozou, refused to extend air cover into the strip and twenty days later Habré's troops were forced to abandon the recaptured town because of heavy Libyan bombing and tank attacks. Habré, once again going against French advice to seek arbitration over the Aozou strip in the international courts, now sent his troops 100 kilometers into Libya, where they knocked out the strategic Matan as-Sarra air base. Tripoli responded by staging a bombing raid against N'Djamena, but this time the French blocked the attack by using their antiaircraft equipment to shoot down a Libyan bomber. With the Chadian-Libyan conflict threatening to take on broader international proportions, a cease-fire was called on September 11 and both countries agreed to submit documentation of their claims to the Aozou by October 30. Libya, with a weaker case, was not expected actually to do so, and the fragile cease-fire developed as one of

"resting, rearming and waiting," according to James Brooke of the New York Times (October 9, 1987).

Hissène Habré is tall, slender, and prematurely graying and has piercing eyes and a quiet, compelling manner. Discussing his leadership of a 1983 battle against Oueddei's forces, one Western official said, "There is no way that the government troops could have stopped the rebels without Habré. Just to have Habré at the front lines must have given his troops an incredible psychological lift. . . . He exudes authority and confidence."

Since becoming Chad's chief executive in 1982, Habré has for the most part forsaken guerrilla uniforms for traditional African attire. Little is known about his personal life, other than that he married while working for the French military administration in Faya Largeau and fathered at least one child, a daughter.

References: Africa Report p41+ Mr–Ap '87 pors; Christian Sci Mon p6 Ag 3 '83 por; N Y Times IV p3 Ap 5 '87 por; New African p157+ N '77 pors, p9+ Mr '87; West Africa p862+ My 4 '87 pors; Africa South of the Sahara, 1986; Britannica Book of the Year, 1979, 1983; Who's Who in the World, 1987–88

Haig, Alexander Meigs, Jr.

Dec. 2, 1924– Business executive; retired United States Army officer; former government official. Address: b. Worldwide Associates, Inc., 1155 15th St., N.W., Suite 800, Washington, D.C. 20006

NOTE: This biography supersedes the article that appeared in Current Biography in 1973.

Alexander Meigs Haig Jr.—soldier, statesman, and corporate executive—has perhaps been closer to the reins of presidential authority in the United States than any other person not elected to public office. In March 1987 he formally announced his intention to seek the Republican presidential nomination for the 1988 elections, convinced that he could offer the necessary "leadership for America." A thirty-seven-year veteran of the United States Army, Haig compiled an impressive record that included service as a combat officer in Korea and Vietnam, as a staff officer at the Pentagon and at West Point, as army vice-chief of staff, and as commander of the North Atlantic Treaty Organization.

As a member of the White House staff of President Richard Nixon, first as military adviser to presidential aide Henry A. Kissinger, then as deputy assistant for national security affairs, Haig played an important role in the reorganization of the National Security Council and in the administration's efforts in the fall of 1972 to negotiate a settlement of the Vietnam conflict and the return of

American war prisoners. During the troubled days of the Watergate crisis, Haig, as White House chief of staff, was credited with keeping the executive branch of government functioning almost singlehandedly. As secretary of state during the first eighteen months of Ronald Reagan's presidency, Haig insisted on articulating a clearly defined foreign policy, understood by allies and adversaries alike.

Although Haig has been characterized by some as a "hawk" and a "hard-line right-winger," informed observers have insisted that he is not a rigid ideologue but a moderate, and that he tempers his conservatism with pragmatism. "Our foreign policy must reflect the values of the nation," Haig concluded in his book Caveat (1984). "Military power and economic strength are important, but they are not everything. Americans will support a policy that demands a world of peaceful change, the defense of human values, the liberation of human genius, the advancement of social justice."

Of Scottish and Irish ancestry, Alexander Meigs Haig Jr. was born on December 2, 1924, in Bala-Cynwyd, Pennsylvania, a Philadelphia suburb, to Alexander Meigs and Regina Anne (Murphy) Haig. He has an older sister, Mrs. Regina Meredith, who is an attorney, and a younger brother, the Rev. Frank R. Haig, a Jesuit priest and educator. His father, a lawyer who served as assistant city solicitor in Philadelphia, died when Haig was ten years old. Although his mother had to struggle at times to make ends meet, Alexander Haig had a fairly normal boyhood. To help out with the family finances, he took a newspaper route and later worked for the post office and the Atlantic Refining Company and as a department store floorwalker.

Haig received his early education at Roman Catholic parochial schools. After graduating in 1942 from Lower Merion High School in Ardmore, Pennsylvania he spent a year at Notre Dame University, where he majored in arts and letters and supplemented his savings by working in the university dining hall. Having chosen to realize a boyhood ambition to make his career in the military, he managed, through the help of an uncle who had congressional contacts, to obtain an appointment to the United States Military Academy at West Point in 1943. Although he at first encountered some difficulty in adjusting to military discipline, he soon conformed to it, and on June 3, 1947, he graduated in 214th place in a class of 310, with a B.S. degree and a second lieutenant's commission in the armored branch. The yearbook of his graduating class took note of his "strong convictions and even stronger ambitions."

After taking additional training at Ground General School at Fort Riley, Kansas, and at the Armored School at Fort Knox, Kentucky, Haig served as a rifle platoon leader in the first cavalry division of the Far East command. During 1949 he was an administrative assistant to General Douglas MacArthur's deputy chief of staff in occupied Japan, and in 1950-51 he was aide-de-camp to General Edward Almond, the commander of the Tenth Corps in Korea. In the early phases of the Korean conflict he saw combat in five campaigns, took part in the Inchon landings, and earned three medals.

After recovering from a bout of hepatitis, Haig served in 1951-52 as a tank commander at Fort Knox and completed the advanced course at the Armored School. From 1953 to 1955 he was a tactical officer at West Point, and he also took graduate courses in business administration at Columbia University. After serving as an exchange company officer at the United States Naval Academy at Annapolis in 1955-56, Haig was transferred to Europe, assigned to the 899th tank battalion and then to United States Army headquarters.

Returning to the United States in 1959, Haig graduated from the Naval War College at Newport, Rhode Island in 1960 and obtained an M.A. degree in international relations from Georgetown University in Washington, D.C., in 1961. He then worked on European and Middle Eastern affairs with the international plans and policy division at the Pentagon, and from 1962 to 1964 he was a staff officer in the office of the deputy chief of staff for military operations in the department of the army. In 1964 he was assigned as military assistant to Secretary of the Army Cyrus R. Vance, and when the latter was appointed deputy secretary of defense under Secretary Robert S. McNamara later that year, Haig remained with him, serving until 1965 as a deputy special assistant in the defense department. His duties during his years in the Pentagon included policy planning on questions involving Berlin and NATO, and on Latin American affairs.

After spending a year at the Army War College in Carlisle, Pennsylvania, Haig was assigned in 1966 to Vietnam and earned the Distinguished Service Cross in recognition of his "extraordinary heroism" while commanding a battalion of the first infantry division in the battle of Ap Gu, one of the important early engagements of the Vietnam conflict. On his return to the United States in June 1967, Haig was appointed a regimental commander with the corps of cadets at the United States Military Academy, and a year later, having in the meantime attained the rank of colonel, he became deputy commander at West Point.

In late 1968 Dr. Henry A. Kissinger, who was then engaged in reorganizing the foreign affairs staff for President-elect Richard Nixon, was urged by Joseph A. Califano, a key aide to President Lyndon B. Johnson, to appoint Haig as his military adviser on the National Security Council. He assumed his duties as military assistant to the assistant to the president for national security affairs in January 1969. "Haig soon became indispensable," Kissinger recalled in his book Years of Upheaval (1982). "He disciplined my anarchic tendencies and established coherence and procedure in a National Security Council staff of talented prima donnas. . . . He acted as my partner, strong in crises, decisive in judgment, skillful in bureaucratic infighting, indefatigable in his labors."

As Kissinger's chief military aide, Haig assumed responsibility for keeping the National Security Council functioning efficiently and acted as liaison between the Pentagon and the State Department. Working as many as fifteen hours a day, seven days a week, he screened all intelligence information coming to the president's desk, presented daily summaries on security conditions abroad for the president, and took charge of the National Security Council during Kissinger's absence. Although he had little formal authority, his pivotal position made him one of the key men in Washington, and in October 1969 he was promoted to brigadier general.

Because of Haig's expert knowledge of the Indochina conflict, President Nixon sent him in early 1970 on the first of several trips to Vietnam to obtain firsthand assessments of developments there. In June 1970 Haig was formally appointed deputy assistant to the president for national security affairs. While continuing to act as Kissinger's assistant, he now had more direct access to the president and was authorized to conduct presidential briefings while Kissinger was abroad. In January 1972 Haig went to the People's Republic of China as head of the advance party to prepare for President Nixon's historic mission in the following month. He was promoted to major general in March 1972.

Although Nixon was reluctant to relinquish a valuable man, he deferred to Haig's wish to return to active military duty by naming him in September 1972 to succeed General Bruce Palmer Jr. as army vice-chief of staff under the new chief of staff, General Creighton W. Abrams. At the same time, Nixon promoted Haig from two-star to four-star rank, passing over 240 high-ranking officers with greater seniority. The promotion was recommended by top defense department officials, who wanted to encourage "upward mobility" for some of the younger officers in the armed forces. Although Haig had been characterized by some critics as a "yes-man," he was, according to Robert S. McNamara, "one of those rare military officers who could be counted on to disagree when he felt policies were wrong."

Haig's takeover of the Pentagon post was, however, postponed until early January 1973, since at the time of his appointment he had been in the midst of negotiations for a settlement to end the Vietnam conflict. As Nixon's main emissary to South Vietnamese President Nguyen Van Thieu, he made more than a dozen trips to Saigon in the final months of 1972, and he also took part in secret talks in Paris and Pnompenh. It was Haig who persuaded Thieu to agree to the January 1973 cease-fire accord.

Haig's return to the Pentagon as army vice-chief of staff in January 1973 was destined to be short-lived. Deeply embroiled in the Watergate crisis, Nixon asked Haig to return to the White House in May of that year to help reorganize the staff following the resignations of the chief presidential aides H. R. Haldeman and John D. Ehrlichman. Although Haig's appointment to succeed Haldeman as White House chief of staff was at first temporary, Nixon asked him to retire from the military and devote himself exclusively to his White House duties. On August 1, 1973, after putting in twenty-six years of military service, Haig retired, with some reluctance, to try to help restore confidence in the crisis-ridden Nixon administration.

As White House chief of staff, Haig turned out to be more relaxed and less authoritarian than Haldeman. While Nixon's most trusted henchmen fell by the wayside, he helped to bolster staff morale and saw to it that the essential tasks of government were carried out. Leon Jaworski, who succeeded Watergate special prosecutor Archibald Cox and who worked closely with Haig throughout the Watergate investigation, formed a favorable opinion of him as "the man on the tightrope" who in effect "ran the country" as the president became immobilized by Watergate developments.

Haig was said to have played a key role in persuading Nixon to resign on August 9, 1974, in view of the impending release of White House tape recordings that implicated him in the conspiracy to cover up the Watergate break-in of June 1972. As one of the few close Nixon aides that remained untarred by Watergate, Haig prepared the groundwork for the transfer of power to the new president, Gerald R. Ford, after Nixon's resignation. After retaining Haig as his White House chief of staff for six weeks, Ford acceded to his wish to resume his military career. On September 16, 1974, he designated Haig to succeed General Andrew J. Goodpaster Jr. as commander in chief of United States forces in Europe, effective November 1, and as supreme allied commander in Europe, in command of NATO forces, effective December 15, and Haig returned to active duty in the United States Army on October 15, 1974. Although critics complained that Haig lacked command experience for the NATO post and entertained misgivings because of his close involvement with the Nixon White House, he soon won wide respect. As Leslie H. Gelb noted in the New York Times Magazine (May 3, 1981), Haig, as NATO commander, was "almost universally considered to be doing an excellent job."

During his four and a half years as commander of NATO, Haig devoted much of his effort to modernization of Western military forces to counter the massive Soviet buildup in Eastern Europe and exercised his diplomatic skills to reconcile the often diverse interests among the thirteen member nations. According to Time (December 29, 1980), "By skillful military management Haig forged the various NATO members into a more cohesive fighting unit. He conducted more realistic maneuvers. . . . Units were ordered to engage in simulated combat with no advance warning—a genuine test of readiness." Often at odds with President Jimmy Carter, particularly over what he considered an excessively accommodating policy toward the Soviet Union on the part of the administration, Haig finally left the NATO post because of "strong differences of opinion" with Carter's government. On July 1, 1979, he retired from military service with the reputation of having been the most effective NATO commander since Dwight D. Eisenhower.

Returning to Philadelphia, Haig accepted appointments as an adjunct professor of political science at the University of Pennsylvania and as a research director with the Foreign Policy Research

Institute. His series of public speaking engagements presenting his views on defense and foreign policy prompted his supporters to consider him as a possible presidential candidate for 1980 and to weigh the possibility of forming "draft Haig" committees, but before such a movement could gain momentum, Haig was approached by Harry J. Gray, a long-time friend, who was chairman of United Technologies Corporation of Hartford, Connecticut, a major defense contractor. Gray offered Haig the presidency of the firm, which he assumed in December 1979 with characteristic brio.

In June 1980, less than four months after undergoing double bypass heart surgery, Haig was a delegate for Connecticut at the Republican convention in Detroit, where he came to the attention of Ronald Reagan as a possible future member of his cabinet. Following his landslide victory, President-elect Reagan named Haig on December 16, 1980, as his secretary of state. During five days of confirmation hearings before the Senate Foreign Relations Committee, Haig summarized his views on global problems and justified his role as White House aide in helping Nixon to defend himself against Watergate charges, by asserting that the president was "entitled to the presumption of innocence." Haig admitted that he helped to implement the Nixon-Kissinger decision to conduct wiretaps on several government officials in 1969–70 to stop security leaks, and he defended his involvement in the secret bombings of North Vietnamese troop concentrations in Cambodia in March 1969 and the 1972 Christmas bombings of military targets in North Vietnam. He insisted that throughout his career he had never taken part in any action that he "considered to be illegal or immoral."

Endorsed by a fifteen-to-two vote of the Foreign Relations Committee and confirmed on January 21, 1981, by a ninety-three-to-six vote of the full Senate, Haig was sworn in as the fifty-ninth United States secretary of state. His appointment was looked upon with favor both at home and abroad. The Senate committee chairman, Charles Percy of Illinois, observed that Haig had "demonstrated an art of diplomacy probably unique to a military commander," and Richard Nixon, who admiringly called Haig "the meanest, toughest, most ambitious s.o.b." he had ever known, predicted that he would "make a hell of a secretary of state."

As the self-described "vicar" of foreign policy within the Reagan administration, Haig became a strong advocate of clearly defined and unambiguous strategies. He urged consolidation of authority within the state department for the conduct of international relations, but he expressed a "lack of enthusiasm" when after two months Vice-President George Bush, and not he, was placed in charge of the administration's "crisis management team."

When on March 30, 1981, President Reagan was seriously wounded in an assassination attempt, Haig, fearing that misleading actions and statements by the confused White House staff might ac-

cidentally touch off an international armed conflict, explained in response to reporters' questions about who was running the government: "As of now, I am in control here, in the White House, pending return of the vice-president, and in close touch with him." The comment was seen in segments of the media as an improper attempt by Haig to assume authority during the absence of Vice-President Bush, who was flying back from Texas to the nation's capital. Under the Constitution, the secretary of state is preceded in the order of succession for the presidency by the speaker of the House of Representatives and the president pro tem of the Senate. But, as was explained later, since the president had not surrendered his authority and the vice-president was only temporarily absent, the secretary of state, as the administration's most senior officer, was authorized to take charge of the "emergency watch" at the White House.

During his tenure as secretary of state, Haig focused attention on international terrorism, which he called the greatest threat to human rights. He engaged in talks with NATO officials and with Soviet Foreign Minister Andrei A. Gromyko, and he worked toward normalization of relations with the People's Republic of China, which in his view was "of overriding importance to international stability and world peace." In the Middle East he generally took a pro-Israeli stand despite some opposition from other administration officials. After the Argentine invasion of the British-controlled Falkland Islands in March 1982, Haig engaged in shuttle diplomacy between Buenos Aires and London in an effort to help settle the dispute.

Toward the Soviet Union, Haig adopted a new and tougher posture, particularly aimed against Soviet support of insurgency and so-called wars of liberation in developing countries. On the other hand, he was prepared to leave the door open for negotiations with the USSR. "Our unreconciled differences on human rights must . . . not be permitted to bring a global catastrophe," he said in a speech in August 1981. "We must compete with the Soviet Union to protect freedom, but we must also search for cooperation to protect mankind." Although he recognized the need "to deal with the socioeconomic conditions that create the breeding ground for external intervention and subversion" in the Third World, Haig opposed demands for large-scale infusion of resources from rich nations to the poor as "unrealistic." Instead he urged developing countries to rely for economic growth on private initiative, free markets, and foreign capital. Along those lines, he helped to develop the administration's Caribbean Basin Initiative, hailed in Time magazine (July 5, 1982) as "a positive Haig accomplishment."

Haig's insistence on "one voice" for United States foreign policy often set him at odds with other members of the Reagan administration, notably, Secretary of Defense Caspar W. Weinberger and William P. Clark, national security adviser. When those differences surfaced, especially in the formulation of United States Middle Eastern policy, Haig resigned on June 25, 1982, and was succeeded as secretary of state by George P. Shultz.

Shortly after leaving the State Department, Haig established Worldwide Associates, a consulting firm in Washington, D.C., of which he became president and board chairman. The firm provides services related to foreign and domestic affairs, security, trade, and international business transactions. He also renewed his association with United Technologies Corporation, as chairman of its European and Pacific advisory council, in addition to serving on the boards of directors of several other major manufacturing and financial firms. Haig's book *Caveat: Realism, Reagan and Foreign Policy,* in which he detailed his experiences as secretary of state, was published by Macmillan in 1984.

In April 1986 Haig formed the Committee for America, a political action group that supported candidates for Congress and important state offices. By late 1986, after the Reagan administration had suffered a series of foreign policy setbacks, Haig's name again began to circulate as a possible presidential candidate. On March 24, 1987, he formally announced his candidacy for the 1988 Republican presidential nomination. Quoting the stand-up comedian Mort Sahl, one of his early supporters, he declared that he was throwing his "helmet into the ring." As his campaign slowly got under way in the weeks that followed, Haig charged, among other things, that the government under Reagan suffered from "fiscal flabbiness" and intimated that the Iran-Contra affair proved that the president needed a strong "vicar" to deal with foreign policy.

Haig is a senior fellow of the Hudson Institute and the Institute for Policy Research in the Public Interest. He has been a visiting lecturer at Princeton, Yale, the University of Michigan, the United States Military Academy, and LeMoyne College. He serves on the President's Commission for Strategic Forces and on the boards of directors of the Atlantic Council, the Foreign Policy Association, and the George C. Marshall Foundation. His many military honors include the Silver Star with oak leaf cluster, the Distinguished Flying Cross with two oak leaf clusters, the Air Medal with twenty-seven oak leaf clusters, and the Defense Distinguished Service Medal. He also holds decorations from the governments of South Vietnam, West Germany, Italy, France, the Netherlands, Luxembourg, and Saudi Arabia.

Alexander Meigs Haig Jr. was married in Tokyo on May 24, 1950, to Patricia Antoinette Fox, the daughter of General Alonzo P. Fox, then a member of General Douglas MacArthur's senior staff. Their children are Alexander P. Haig, a lawyer, Major Brian F. Haig, a West Point graduate, and Barbara E. Haig, a staff officer with the National Endowment for Democracy. The Haigs have four grandsons. The soft-spoken general is tall and blue-eyed, with gray hair and a military bearing. A fastidious dresser, he conforms more to the stereotype of a pinstriped diplomat than to that of a military man.

He often surprises audiences with his whimsical humor and easy manner. On occasion he lapses into what journalists have termed "Haigspeak"—a jargon that combines military terminology, verbification of nouns, and multisyllabic words. When time permits, "Al" Haig enjoys playing tennis, and occasionally golf. Asked what he considered the greatest single challenge or achievement of his career, Haig responded: "The privilege and honor of leading American troops under fire to defend what this country stands for."

References: Atlan 247:11+ Mr '81 por; Chicago Tribune V:1+ S 11 '87 pors; N Y Times A p1+ Mr 24 '87 por; N Y Times Mag p23+ My 31 '81 pors; Newsday Mag p19+ Ap 25 '82 pors; Time 116:8+ D 29 '80 pors, 117:12+ Mr 16 '81 pors; Brownstein, Ronald, and Easton, Nina. Reagan's Ruling Class (1982); Morris, Roger. Haig: The General's Progress (1982); Political Profiles: The Nixon/Ford Years (1979); Who's Who in America, 1986–87

Hodel, Donald P(aul)

(hō del´)

May 23, 1935– United States Secretary of the Interior. Address: b. Office of the Secretary, United States Department of the Interior, 18th and C Sts., N.W., Washington, D.C. 20240

Since his confirmation as United States secretary of the interior in February 1985, Donald P. Hodel has been in the middle of an ongoing struggle between environmental preservationists and pro-development business interests. "The questions I get are unresolvable and somebody has to take the heat for them," Hodel told Cass Peterson in an interview for the *Washington Post* (August 23, 1985). So far, however, with the exception of a widely publicized feud with Lee Iacocca, the chairman of a federal advisory commission on the restoration of the Statue of Liberty and Ellis Island, over the future development of Ellis Island and intermittent controversy about offshore oil leasing, Hodel has received less criticism for his decisions than his former boss and predecessor as secretary of the interior, James G. Watt. The latter's policies favoring increased exploitation of resources embroiled the department in a series of bitter confrontations with environmentalists. After two years as Watt's deputy, Hodel was himself elevated to a cabinet post when President Ronald Reagan named him secretary of energy late in 1982. Before joining the Reagan administration, the Harvard-educated Oregonian, an attorney by training, served as administrator of the Bonneville Power Administration and as an energy consultant.

Donald Paul Hodel was born in Portland, Oregon, on May 23, 1935, the son of Philip E. and Theresia Rose (Brodt) Hodel. Interested in politics from an early age, he majored in government at Harvard University. While he was a student there, he joined the Harvard Young Republican Club, serving as its treasurer in 1955–56 and as its president the following academic year. On receiving his B.A. degree in 1957, Hodel returned to Oregon for graduate study at the University of Oregon Law School, where, during his final year, he edited the University of Oregon *Law Review*.

Hodel earned his J.D. degree in 1960, then joined the Portland law firm of Davies, Biggs, Strayer, Stoel & Boley. In 1963 he left that firm to become a corporate attorney for Georgia-Pacific, the lumber and paper products company. While he was practicing law in Portland, Hodel became actively involved in local Republican party politics. Beginning as a precinct organizer for the Clackamas County Central Committee in 1964, he was chosen committee chairman a little more than a year later. In 1966 and 1967 he was chairman of the Oregon Republican State Central Committee, and in 1968 he served on the state's Reagan for President Committee and attended the Republican National Convention as an alternate delegate.

Hodel's practical experience in energy-related matters began the following year, 1969, when he was named deputy administrator of the Bonneville Power Administration (BPA), a federal agency that markets the electrical power produced by the government's dams in the Pacific Northwest. As he acknowledged to an interviewer at the time of his appointment to the post, "The key that opened the door to this job for me was my chairmanship of the [Oregon] Republican party." After serving for three years as second-in-command, Hodel was promoted to administrator in 1972.

During his five years as the Bonneville Power Administration's top officer, Hodel played a key role in the region's long-term energy planning. His tenure, which continued until 1977, was stormy. Some of the agency's transmission towers were blown up by an extortionist, and Hodel received several death threats. According to Chip Brown, writing in the *Washington Post* (December 3, 1984), the administrator occasionally went so far as to leave a pebble on the hood of his car to make sure that no one had tampered with the engine in his absence.

Painting a grim picture of the economic hardships the Northwest would endure without enough energy supplies, Hodel endorsed a wide-ranging program to build a regional network of nuclear and coal-fired power plants. Central to the plan was the construction of five nuclear power stations by the Washington Public Power Supply System (WPPSS). The massive construction project, plagued by huge cost overruns and a whopping overestimation of the region's future energy needs, soon became known as "Whoops." Because costs escalated sharply and demand fell, four of the nuclear plants were eventually canceled, and WPPSS was forced to default on $2.25 billion in bonds. Critics of the billion-dollar boondoggle maintained that more money had been wasted on unnecessary power plants in the Northwest than in any other region of the country.

In retrospect, Hodel has some reservations about the wisdom of authorizing the WPPSS project, but the massive energy development program symbolized his passionate commitment to expanding the area's electrical power capacity, particularly by building nuclear power stations. In words that his political opponents have since used against him, Hodel cast the program in the terms of an ideological crusade. "Let the no-growth proponent explain to parents and their children why the schools must be closed soon because there isn't enough power to heat and light them," he said, as quoted in *Reagan's Ruling Class* (1982). "Let him tell housewives how to operate their homes during rotating blackouts. This is the sort of direct accountability that the no-growthers should have to assume."

In a speech he delivered at the Portland City Club in July 1975, Hodel lashed out at environmentalists who "clamor for a return to more primitive life, to choking off our individual and collective aspirations for ourselves and our children." During the early 1970s, he went on, the environmental movement had "fallen into the hands of a small, arrogant faction which is dedicated to bringing our society to a halt. I call this faction the Prophets of Shortage. They are the anti-producers, the anti-achievers. The doctrine they preach is that of scarcity and self-denial. By halting the needed expansion of our power system, they can bring this region to its knees."

In his last year as head of the Bonneville Power Administration, Hodel moderated his harsh words to an extent. While he continued to call for the development of increased electrical capacity, he began to temper his remarks with a recognition of the public's increasing interest in energy conservation.

In 1980 he even chaired a state commission looking into the feasibility of alternative sources of energy. In its final report, the commission concluded that renewable energy sources could easily meet Oregon's increasing power demands until the twenty-first century.

The election of Jimmy Carter to the presidency of the United States in 1976 spelled the end of Hodel's tenure as BPA chief. Shortly after Carter took office in January 1977, leaders of environmental groups throughout the Northwest, joined by Oregon Representative Jim Weaver, urged the president to dismiss Hodel, charging, among other things, that he had "blatantly ignored environmental laws." Less than a year later, Hodel resigned to become president of the National Electric Reliability Council, an industry group set up after the New York City blackout in 1965. According to Robert D. Hershey Jr., writing in the *New York Times* (November 6, 1982), Hodel earned "high marks" from industry insiders for his efficient management of the council, which he headed from 1978 to 1980. He has been credited with transforming the group, based in Princeton, New Jersey, from little more than a data bank into a consumer advocate overseeing the adequacy and dependability of the country's power supply.

In addition to directing the activities of the National Electric Reliability Council, from 1978 until 1981 Hodel was president of Hodel Associates and Company, an energy consulting firm that he founded with his wife, Barbara. Among their clients were Pacific Power and Light, Puget Sound Power and Light, Portland General Electric, and the Montana Power Company. The consultancy played an important part in bringing many formerly isolated electric utility companies throughout Texas into the national power grid.

Called back into public service by President Ronald Reagan, Hodel was appointed undersecretary of the interior, the number two man to James G. Watt, in February 1981. As Watt's top deputy, Hodel contributed to the formulation of such controversial policy initiatives as oil exploration in wilderness areas and auctions of million-acre sections of the ocean floor. It was during this period that the Department of the Interior drew intense fire from ardent conservationists for its "anti-environmental policies" and for allegedly turning what was intended to be a management agency into a sales office for public resources. As Philip Shabecoff observed in his profile for the *New York Times* (January 11, 1985), department officials relied on Hodel to tone down some of Secretary Watt's more inflammatory pronouncements. Charged with running the day-to-day operations of the department, the undersecretary earned a reputation for, in Shabecoff's words, "political shrewdness, pragmatism, an efficient management style and plain hard work."

Those qualities undoubtedly played a part in Reagan's decision, in November 1982, to name Hodel secretary of energy, over the vigorous objections of various environmental groups. In an effort at conciliation, shortly after taking office Hodel invited representatives of conservation and consumer groups to meet with him to express their views. Opposition from environmentalists was only one of the problems Hodel faced as secretary of energy. President Reagan had long been committed to disbanding the Department of Energy and turning its responsibilities over to other government agencies, but the selection of Hodel as secretary had put the beleaguered department under the leadership of an energy specialist for the first time in its history. (Of his predecessors in the post, only James R. Schlesinger had had some experience in the field, as chairman of the Atomic Energy Commission. Charles W. Duncan Jr. was a business executive and James B. Edwards, a dentist.) Consequently, Hodel's first priority was to boost department morale, which had slumped because of Reagan's proposal to abolish the agency and to make cutbacks in many department activities, particularly in the areas of renewable energy, emergency planning, and data collection.

As secretary of energy, Hodel "saw the eclipse" of his department's "planning for a sustainable national energy future while more and more of its budget was consumed by the production of nuclear weapons and the promotion of nuclear power," Ruth Norris wrote in *Audubon* magazine (September 1985). At the same time, he forged ahead with the job of filling the Strategic Petroleum Reserve, lobbied for the passage of a bill providing for the establishment of the country's first permanent disposal site for high-level nuclear waste, and shaped legislation to ease the regulation of natural gas. Hodel also insisted on setting aside funds for energy conservation and for the development of solar power even though other Reagan administration officials had given those items low budget priority—a decision that won him grudging praise from some environmentalists. He earned praise from his colleagues at the Department of Energy, too, for restoring staff morale and for his vaunted ability to grasp complex issues quickly. "Six months after he got to the Energy Department he knew more about the jobs of all the assistant secretaries here than the assistant secretaries themselves," Robert C. Odle Jr., one of the department's assistant secretaries, told Philip Shabecoff in an interview for his *Times* profile of Hodel.

On January 10, 1985, President Reagan nominated Donald Hodel to succeed William P. Clark as secretary of the interior, a job he is said to have wanted "very badly." His return to the department was enthusiastically applauded by pro-development groups and by energy industry leaders, such as Carl E. Bagge, the president of the National Coal Association, but it not surprisingly raised concern among environmentalists. "He has not shown any particular interest in conservation issues," Paul C. Pritchard, the president of the National Parks and Conservation Association, a private group, explained, as quoted in the *New York Times* (January 11, 1985), and Louise C. Dunlap, the president of the Environmental Policy Institute, feared that Hodel's reassignment might "signal a return of James Watt's anti-environmental policies."

More than two years into Hodel's tenure as chief steward of the nation's natural resources, environmentalists generally remain skeptical about his policies, but his low-key management style and accessibility appear to have secured him a measure of wary respect. "Conservationists tend to view Mr. Hodel as a James Watt in, say, striped bass clothing," Philip Shabecoff observed in the *New York Times* (March 3, 1986). "While they prefer his operating style and tend to view it as more effective than Mr. Watt's, they are not satisfied with his commitment to the preservation of public lands and resources and worry that he is eager to turn over those lands and resources to private interests."

Hodel himself has frequently said that his goals as secretary of the interior are the same as Watt's were because President Reagan gave them the same five "charges" when each took over the leadership of the department. As Shabecoff outlined them in his March 3, 1986 piece, those charges were: to preserve the nation's parks and other lands and resources; to enhance its energy and military resources; to increase its water resources; to improve federal relations with state and local governments; and to develop the country's Indian resources. Hodel has made it clear over the years that he is a Reagan loyalist and a staunch advocate of the president's policies even when he disagrees with them. "I am a supporter, as I always knew I would be, of whatever it is the president finally decided upon," he told a questioner at a 1985 round table discussion, as quoted in the *Audubon* article.

Even so, the direction in which Hodel has taken the Interior Department has not raised nearly the degree of animosity and commotion among environmentalists as the course that Watt charted during President Reagan's first term. Facing a vote of condemnation from the Senate, the outspoken Watt was forced to resign late in 1983. His successor, William P. Clark, while continuing the pro-development policies instituted by Watt, brought a nonconfrontational style to the department that Hodel has by and large maintained since he took over in 1985.

On issues not involving energy resources, Hodel has often gratified environmentalists. Among the decisions they especially favored were his appointment of the conservation-minded William Penn Mott Jr. to head the National Park Service, his purchase of a ranch to raise masked bobwhite quail, an endangered species, and his refusal to allow contaminated water from farms in the San Joaquin Valley to drain into the Kesterson National Wildlife Range. Nonetheless, as during Watt's tenure, the Department of the Interior's budget is widely perceived to be heavily weighted toward resource development and away from preservation. In 1986, for example, Hodel opposed major new acquisitions for the National Park System, but where Watt had called for a moratorium on land acquisition, Hodel justified deferring new purchases on fiscal

grounds, contending that they were, at least for the time being, too costly. Largely because of his disarming manner and low-key approach, he has been more successful than his predecessors in pursuing programs to open the outer continental shelf to oil and gas exploration, an initiative that had roused Congressional ire during Watt's tenure. Hodel did, however, draw heavy fire from California's Congressional delegation in September 1985, after he backed away from a tentative agreement limiting oil and gas drilling off the California coast.

The California offshore drilling controversy was Hodel's only highly publicized confrontation as secretary of the interior until his clash with Lee Iacocca, the enormously popular chairman of the Chrysler Corporation. In February 1986, Hodel fired Iacocca from his unpaid post as head of the government's advisory commission on the restoration of the Statue of Liberty and Ellis Island after he had refused to step aside voluntarily. Hodel said he dismissed the auto executive "to avoid any question of conflict of interest," as he put it, between Iacocca's simultaneous service as chairman of a private foundation raising money to restore the national landmarks and as director of the government commission recommending how the money should be spent. Speaking in his own defense, Iacocca maintained that he had been discharged because he had publicly denounced the proposed construction of a conference center and hotel complex on Ellis Island—a plan reportedly endorsed by the National Park Service—as a "luxury" project that would be paid for through "tax credits for the rich."

Hodel made the headlines again in February 1987, when he warned of new gasoline shortages "in the next two to five years" that could be as disruptive as those caused by the Arab oil embargo in the early 1970s. As a preventive measure, he recommended developing the potential oil resources in government-owned coastal areas and in the Arctic National Wildlife Refuge in Alaska. Two months later, on April 27, 1987, he announced a five-year plan for opening those areas to oil and gas exploration. "The outer continental shelf and the Arctic National Wildlife Refuge coastal plain are the foundation of America's energy future," Hodel explained to reporters. "Together, they mean the difference between a secure, environmentally sound oil and gas program for the country in the twenty-first century and the energy crisis we suffered in the 1970s, at the hands of OPEC."

Because Hodel had deferred leasing on vast tracts of the continental shelf, including Gray's Reef National Marine Sanctuary in the South Atlantic and the Channel Islands National Marine Sanctuary off Southern California, a spokesman for the American Petroleum Institute called the department's program "a disappointment," although he urged Congress to adopt it. Among the plan's more outspoken opponents was Sarah Chasis, a lawyer and an expert on offshore development issues for the Natural Resources Defense Council, who spoke for many environmentalists when she told Philip Shabecoff of the *New York Times*

(April 28, 1987), "The Hodel program fails to provide a reasonable balance between energy development and environmental protection, as required by law."

A tall man with a lean, athletic build, Donald P. Hodel has deep-set eyes and coal-black brows. Colleagues and reporters have described him as personable, articulate, and witty. In his spare time, he likes to ski and play basketball. He and his wife, the former Barbara Beecher Stockman, whom he married on December 10, 1956, have one son, David Beecher. Their older son, Philip Stockman, died in the mid-1970s. Hodel is the recipient of a number of awards and honors, including the first Interior Department Outstanding Service Award for energy conservation activities, in 1974, a De-

partment of Commerce Save Energy Citation, in 1975, and the Institute of Human Relations Award, which the American Jewish Committee bestowed upon him in 1985 for "his demonstrated concern for the environment and his continued efforts for the preservation of our country's natural resources."

References: Audubon 87:28+ S '85 por; N Y Times p9 N 6 '82 por, B p6 Ja 11 '85; US News 94:20+ Mr 28 '83 por, 98:59+ Ap 15 '85 por; Washington Post A p1+ D 3 '84 por; Brownstein, Ronald, and Easton, Nina. Reagan's Ruling Class (1982); Congressional Directory, 1985–86; Who's Who in America, 1986–87; Who's Who in American Politics, 1987–88

Hogan, Paul

1941 (?)- Australian comedian; actor. Address: b. c/o Terry Jackman & Associates, Level 15, 55 Lavender Place, Milson's Point, Sydney, N.S.W. 2060, Australia

In 1986 the popular Australian television comedian Paul Hogan shot to unexpected international stardom with the phenomenal commercial success of his first motion picture, "Crocodile" Dundee, a simple, wholesome comedy about a tough but amiable Aussie outbacker adrift in Manhattan's asphalt jungle. Released in Australia in the spring of 1986, the film broke box-office records there, and the following fall and winter it became the most profitable foreign film ever released in the United

States and was on its way to an expected worldwide gross of $200 million, including television and video profits. Critics attribute the success of "Crocodile" Dundee largely to the natural, easy charm of its star, a former construction worker whose Paul Hogan Show had the highest ratings on Australian television for nine years. American audiences caught their first glimpse of Hogan when he brought a refreshing friendliness to the television ads of the Australian Tourist Commission, beginning in 1984. He has also done export commercials for Foster's lager, first on British television and recently on American.

The second of three children of a career army sergeant turned postman, Paul Hogan was born in, or about, 1941 in Lightning Ridge, an opal-mining town in New South Wales, Australia, and he grew up in a working-class suburb of Sydney, the capital of New South Wales. As a boy he "never got into any real trouble," he has recalled, but "every time [he] threw something, a ball or a stick, it went through a window or cracked open some other kid's head." In high school he was considered, in his words, "a stirrer, someone who stirs things up."

Hogan dropped out of high school at fifteen and married at eighteen. To support his growing family, he worked at a succession of jobs, including chauffeur, prizefighter, salesman, and construction worker. He was earning seventy-five dollars a week building maintenance scaffolds on the Harbour Bridge in Sydney when, in 1972, fellow workers dared him to audition for New Faces, a mock television talent show of the Gong Show variety familiar to British and American audiences. Appearing on New Faces as a blindfolded, tap-dancing knife thrower, he made a hit with the humorous ad libs that he directed against the judges and was invited back twice to "just talk, be funny," as he recounted in an interview with Fred Robbins for the New York Daily News (December 11, 1986).

From New Faces Hogan went into a small weekly spot as a humorous blue-collar editorialist on the television news magazine A Current Affair (not to be confused with the American TV program of the same name), while still working at what he called his "proper job" as a bridge rigger. "Once a week I'd call in at the television channel and give my opinion on what was wrong with the country and how to fix it," he told Fred Robbins. "By the time the year ended I started making my own television show." John Cornell, who produced A Current Affair and became Hogan's partner and manager, traced Hogan's appeal to his broad but low-keyed and offhand sense of humor, his "almost magical . . . originality," and his "almost eerie sense of how the average citizen feels." Hogan himself felt that the key to his appeal was his unpretentiousness. "We're a very egalitarian society," he later explained. "If I meet the prime minister I call him mate. There are no 'Sirs,' no 'Misters.' If you want to play snobs or do airs and graces, you join a very exclusive club in Melbourne." As quoted by Charles Leerhsen and Carl Robinson in Newsweek (December 8, 1986), he said, "What set me apart was that at a time when half the people on Australian TV were speaking this ridiculous Oxford English accent that they don't even speak in England, and the other half were copying a kind of California-American accent, I was talking like the guys down at the pub. Like an Australian. Simple—but, believe it or not, everyone thought it was bloody amazing."

The Paul Hogan Show, produced by John Cornell, directed by Peter Faiman, and written by Ken Shadie (with input by Hogan) was a sketch-comedy a sort of cross between America's Saturday Night Live and Carol Burnett Show and Britain's Benny Hill Show. Dressed in a variety of costumes, from mismatched rugby uniforms to hobo clothes and beach-bum attire, Hogan played a range of Australian types. "They're all the same character, really," he once pointed out. "Me." Broadcast sporadically in sixty installments over a period of nine years, the show consistently drew the highest ratings in Australia, and it has subsequently been syndicated in some thirty countries worldwide.

At the beginning of his television career Hogan did commercials for Winfield cigarettes that made Winfield the number-one brand in Australia. (Although he continued to smoke Winfields himself, he stopped doing the cigarette ads at the request of public health officials.) Later in the 1970s he began promoting Foster's lager, an Australian beer, on British television. The three ads he has done gratis for the Australia Tourist Commission, seen in eight major United States markets since 1984, have been credited with almost doubling American tourism in Australia. In the travel commercials a friendly, casually dressed Hogan is photographed in happy beach and cookout scenes, inviting viewers to come have a look at "the land of wonder—Down Under." In one ad he instructs an American visitor in the proper intonation of the phrase "G'day", the all-purpose Australian greeting, and in another he promises to "slip another shrimp on the barbie [barbecue]" for his American guests.

To help launch the tourism campaign, Hogan made his first visit to New York City in 1984. The idea for "Crocodile" Dundee came to him shortly after that experience with Manhattan's hustle and bustle. "A week after I got back home," he recounted to Fred Robbins in the New York Daily News interview, "I was up fishing with some mates in the Northern Territory. And the thought struck me. These guys, they don't like to go to Darwin—a big, racy city as far as they're concerned—and Darwin has a population of about 50,000. If you took a few of those guys and carted them to New York, they would really think they're on another planet. [In the Northern Territory] you don't have the little things—elevators and escalators and flush toilets. And you don't have hookers in the streets, or transvestites. You don't have a drug scene at all."

"Crocodile" Dundee was made on a budget of $5.6 million (high by the standards of Australia but low by those of Hollywood), more than half of which came from the pockets of Hogan and John Cornell, the film's producer. Hogan, Cornell, and Ken Shadie wrote the screenplay, and Peter Faiman directed the film, which was shot in Australia and New York City. The motion picture bridges three cinema traditions, those of The Cowboy and the Lady, the fish out of water, and the conquering innocent. Michael J. Dundee is a personification of the legendary outback adventurer, a rugged, self-sufficient he-man who is as enshrined in Australian popular mythology as Paul Bunyan and Davy Crockett are in American folklore. Dundee is a crocodile poacher and wilderness guide who shows a visiting American reporter, Sue Charlton (Linda Kozlowski), around the outback and then travels with her to New York City. There, the canny and insouciant outsider has a series of encounters in which he turns the tables on urban snobs and urban thugs alike, with a minimum of violence and no explicit sex. It is an escapist movie, described by Hogan as "a wholesome sort of fairy tale, a romantic culture clash with an Australian hero and an American heroine." As he has pointed out, it's "not full of boob jokes or lavatory wall humor," and the leading character is "not a Rambo" but a guy who "looks at the world through rose-colored glasses and gives everyone the benefit of the doubt."

Released in Australia in the spring of 1986, "Crocodile" Dundee grossed two dollars for every person in the country within six months, becoming the biggest money-maker in Australian movie history. "Why the film works for Australian audiences has a lot to do with the mood of the country these days," the Australian writer C. C. O'Hanlon observed in the New York Times (September 21, 1986). "Times are lean in Australia—unemployment and inflation are rising fast, currency has taken a dive, minerals and agricultural products are being undercut, and . . . the country hasn't won a Wimbledon or a cricket Test in years. So along comes Michael J. (Crocodile) Dundee, a nostalgically dinkum Aussie character with all the traits of a true 'battler'—tough, reliable, outgoing, a friend to his mates, a sucker for a grouse-looking sheila, and shrewd to boot—that Australians like to think of as typical but no longer is. Dundee belongs to another decade, the 1950s maybe, a time Australians like to think was one of their best."

Wondering if the film's success in Australia could be duplicated in the United States, O'Hanlon asked Hogan if he thought that Americans "can . . . be seduced" by "a fairy tale in which Australia's loss of innocence is turned into a metaphorical romance between a contemporary New Woman and the last of a mythical outback breed." Hogan replied that there are aspects of the Australian character that might be instructive and appealing to an American audience. "We can show them a good time," he said. "We're less competitive. We're more weekend oriented, which is sort of sensible if you're only gonna live seventy years or so."

Paramount Pictures paid $8 million for the distribution rights (theatrical, television, cable, and video) to "Crocodile" Dundee in the United States. (Twentieth Century-Fox bought the international rights.) Paramount spent an additional $5 million in editing the picture for the American market and promoting it. After recovering from a cerebral hemorrhage he suffered while weight lifting, Hogan joined in the promotion, making a whirlwind thirty-day tour of major American cities. On its release in the United States late in September 1986, "Crocodile" Dundee was greeted with so-so reviews, most of which panned the film as "corny" and "hokey" while recognizing Hogan's Dundee as "a fun guy" and Hogan himself as "an easy, extremely likable screen personality—a mixture of warmth, sex appeal, disarming innocence, and dry humor." The film earned $19.5 million in its first ten days of American exhibition and more than $900,000 on a single weekday. Within weeks it grossed $117 million, a new United States record for both an autumn release and a foreign film, and within months the figure rose to $175 million, second only to that for Top Gun. Internationally, it had the largest gross of any film in 1986.

"Crocodile" Dundee drew large American audiences not only in the big cities but in smaller cities and suburban areas as well. "The most surprising thing is that the appeal of the movie defies demographics and geographics," Frank Mancuso, the chairman of Paramount, told Aljean Harmetz of the New York Times (January 12, 1987). "We're getting the infrequent moviegoers, people who go to the movies once or twice a year." Gene Siskel, the movie reviewer for the Chicago Tribune, who had panned the film at the time of its release while predicting its box-office success, said in explaining that success: "The lesson here is that there is a massive audience that wants clean, wholesome entertainment. It may be a slightly older audience and they may not go to the movies often, but they will go when they hear from their friends that it is safe to go back to the movies again."

With the success of "Crocodile" Dundee came a small flood of scripts for Hogan to consider, but he was preoccupied with the sequel to "Crocodile" Dundee, "'Crocodile' Dundee II," which went into production in the autumn of 1987. That same fall American television viewers saw for the first time a miniseries made for Australian TV several years before. In that four-part production, ANZACS: The War Down Under, Hogan, Andrew Clarke, and Mark Hembrow played Aussie volunteer soldiers in Europe in World War I. As for the work of others, Hogan prefers such entertainments as the film Back to the Future, and he disdains both what he calls "multiple-car-crash music-video movies for thirteen-year-olds" on the one hand and, on the other, state-subsidized Australian "intellectual" movies ("boring little films about nothing") that don't attempt to reach a mass audience. His prestige in Australia is such that some leaders of both political parties have shown an interest in running him for the Australian parliament. He has not reciprocated the interest, although in his view "politicians are media performers" and "a good game show host could be prime minister." His attitude toward the future is open and relaxed. Feeling "totally spoiled" because "everything works out" for him, he wants nothing more than "to make a lot of people laugh" and "make the laugh go around the world."

Hogan, whose nickname is Hoges, is, by his own description, "not a pretty boy . . . just a comedian who's not ugly," but with his tanned, weather-beaten face, blond hair, and muscles rippling beneath casual clothes, he has an undeniable sex appeal. Paul and Noelene Hogan were married in 1958, divorced in 1981, and remarried less than a year later. They have five children, four boys and a girl, ranging in age from twelve to twenty-six, and they are grandparents. The Hogans live in a suburb north of Sydney, in a large house with landscaped grounds, a swimming pool, a tennis court, and a garden, which Paul tends. The comedian drives a burgundy 1985 Porsche 944, which he is never photographed in, under orders from John Cornell, who worries about his undermining his proletarian image. Generally, Hogan's private personality is true to his public persona. Reading is not one of his favorite pastimes, for example, and although he can be icy in manner, his sense of humor comes through. "He doesn't have that big-star attitude," Linda Kozlowski, his costar in "Crocodile" Dundee, has testified. "When it comes to humor, I think he's a lot like the character in the film. He's understated, wry, and subtle." Hogan is reported to have an I.Q. of 140.

References: Chicago Tribune X p4 S 21 '86 por; Economist 300:33 O 11 '86 por; N Y Newsday III p1+ S 26 '86 pors; N Y Times C p13 O 14 '86 por, C p17 Ja 12 '87 por; People 26:55+ O 20 '86 pors; Toronto Globe and Mail A p15 Ap 3 '87 por; Washington Post C p8 N 20 '86 por

Hoiby, Lee

Feb. 17, 1926- Composer; concert pianist.
Address: h. Box 71, Long Eddy, N.Y. 12760

The contemporary American composer Lee Hoiby
has enjoyed remarkable success in writing in a
conservative, tonal idiom that rejects the dissonant
revolution in twentieth-century music. Although
Hoiby has written many critically praised works
for solo piano, chamber ensemble, and orchestra,
he is perhaps better known for his operas, including Summer and Smoke, based on the Tennessee
Williams play, and a musical version of Shakespeare's The Tempest. With his deeply melodic
sensibility, penchant for full, ripe orchestration,
and affinity for themes of love and redemption,
Hoiby is heir to the romantic tradition that has regained currency on the American music scene after spending years in the shadow of atonal
formalism. Both admirers and detractors of Hoiby's
style acknowledge his exceptional gift for graceful
vocal writing and his fine craftsmanship. In the
manner of romantic composers of the past, Hoiby
is also a virtuoso pianist who has had a second career on the concert stage in recent years.

Lee Hoiby was born on February 17, 1926, in
Madison, Wisconsin, the son of Henry and Violet
(Smith) Hoiby, both of whom were amateur musicians. He began his piano studies at the age of five
and made his debut as a composer at the age of six
with a piano work he called The Storm. Revealing
a precocious flair for the theatrical, the boy insisted
on turning off the lights in the living room before
performing the piece for an audience of family and
friends. As a child, he enjoyed improvising on the
piano and wrote down his first composition when
he was fifteen. He continued to compose in suc-

ceeding years while grooming himself for a career
as a concert pianist. Even before he graduated
from West High School in Madison, in 1944, Hoiby
was receiving intensive keyboard instruction from
Gunnar Johansen, the artist-in-residence at the
University of Wisconsin and specialist in Busoni,
whom Hoiby calls "the first great musical
influence" of his life.

At Johansen's urging, Hoiby attended Egon Petri's master classes in Ithaca, New York, in the
summer of 1944, and, after obtaining a bachelor of
music degree from the University of Wisconsin in
1947, went on to study with Petri at Mills College
in Oakland, California, where he received his master's degree in 1952. At the same time, Hoiby continued to pursue his interest in musical
composition, which was coming to supersede the
piano as the prime outlet for his creativity. After
studying composition with Darius Milhaud at Mills
College, he canceled his concert debut at New
York's Town Hall to serve an apprenticeship under
Gian-Carlo Menotti at the Curtis Institute of Music
in Philadelphia. "It was Menotti who encouraged
me to write for the orchestra (which, at first, did not
interest me at all) and to try my hand at opera
(which interested me even less)," Hoiby recalled
for David Ewen in American Composers: A Biographical Dictionary (1982). "When I resisted, he
pressured me into trying, and to my great surprise,
I discovered my love for the orchestra and my own
gift for opera. Without his insistence, I doubt if I
would ever have tried."

Unlike many fledgling composers, Hoiby enjoyed signal success in getting his works performed. Thomas Schippers and the NBC
Symphony introduced Hoiby's Nocturne for orchestra in New York City in October 1950, and
Erich Leinsdorf and the Rochester Symphony performed his ballet Hearts, Meadows, and Flags in
November 1952. His easily accessible style undoubtedly helped to find an audience for those and
his other early works, for in rejecting the atonality
that held sway over many American composers in
the early 1950s, Hoiby favored a deeply melodic
idiom with lush orchestrations in the manner of
late-nineteenth century romanticism. "I'm a mainstream composer and my style has never really
changed," Hoiby acknowledged during an interview with Gary Schmidgall in Opera News (June
1986), citing Menotti, Barber, Mahler, Debussy,
and Richard Strauss as among his major musical
influences.

While gratifying to audiences, Hoiby's unabashed conservatism drew fire from the more
dogmatic prophets of dissonance among his professional colleagues. "I was told, 'You must invent
new sounds,'" the composer recalled for Schmidgall. "It was as if I had been told, 'You can have a
garden—but grow only cactuses.'" When Hoiby received a Fulbright scholarship for study in Rome
in 1953, the director of the Accademia di Santa Cecilia actually refused to admit him because his
work was too tonal, and Hoiby was obliged to
spend the year working on his own. Looking back

on his sense of artistic isolation and alienation during that period, Hoiby told Schmidgall: "I didn't think there was anyone like me then, but in more recent years it has become clear that others too were in hibernation while this antihuman musical infection ran its course."

Some music critics, however, found the composer's imaginative use of traditional tonal techniques a welcome change from the dry academicism prevailing in much formalist composition. "It was a relief to hear a young composer apparently less interested in manner than in communication of feeling," noted one *New York Times* critic in reviewing a program of Hoiby's chamber music and songs that was presented at Columbia University's Composers Forum in May 1956. And critics found Hoiby's lyricism especially well suited to the vocal writing in which he began to specialize. In the spring of 1958 Hoiby introduced his first one-act opera, *The Scarf*, at Gian-Carlo Menotti's Festival of Two Worlds in Spoleto, Italy, and then brought the work to the New York City Opera in the following year. The opera had a suspenseful libretto about rural sorcery, sex, and murder by the American poet Harry Duncan based on Chekhov's short story *The Witch* and featured the long, arching melodies and old-fashioned lyric arias that were to become Hoiby hallmarks. Reviewing it for the *New York Times* (April 6, 1959), Howard Taubman admired its "ingratiating" writing for the voice and the "dramatic cogency" of Hoiby's handling of the orchestra.

The supernatural also figured prominently in Hoiby's next opera, *Beatrice*, a three-act work commissioned by the WAVE television and radio station in Louisville, Kentucky, and given its premiere in that city in October 1959. Marcia Naudi's libretto drew on Maurice Maeterlinck's play *The Miracle*, which deals with a medieval nun's fall from grace and her mystical redemption. Although a *New York Times* (June 19, 1960) reviewer of *Beatrice* judged its artlessly simple story as being inadequate to carry the weight of a full-length opera, he extolled Hoiby as a "great and specifically operatic talent. He has the innate sense of what will and will not go, vocally speaking, which many composers appear to lack."

Lee Hoiby's third opera, *Natalia Petrovna*, had its premiere at the New York City Opera—which has always been hospitable to new American works—in October 1964. Its libretto, by William Ball, was based on Turgenev's *A Month in the Country*, a subtle psychological study of unfulfilled love and desire. Although critics found *Natalia Petrovna* to be musically compelling in its conservative idiom structured around soaring phrases and lyrical ensemble scenes, they observed that Turgenev's underplotted and introspective play presented special problems in forging the musical and dramatic synthesis required of viable opera. To illuminate the Russian writer's nuances of character and psychological intricacies, for example, Hoiby and Ball were obliged to write long passages of bald, speech-like exposition. But reviewers admired Hoiby's gift for ensemble comic writing, as in the second-act scene where a doctor proposes marriage to the flighty young Lisavette and is met with a volley of coloratura giggles. The often exigent Paul Hume of the *Washington Post* (March 28, 1965) lauded *Natalia Petrovna*'s closing octet, based on an ostinato theme, as a passage of "overwhelming beauty" that amounts to a "supreme moment in opera." Later revised and retitled *A Month in the Country*, the opera was presented in Boston in its new format in January 1981.

Although he devoted most of his attention to opera in the late 1950s and early 1960s, Hoiby also composed many nonoperatic vocal works during that period, including the oratorio *A Hymn of the Nativity* (1960) and the symphonic song *Tides of Sleep* (1961), in addition to some chamber music and a ballet, *After Eden* (1966). He worked extensively in the theatre as well, writing songs for Off-Broadway productions of Dylan Thomas' *Under Milkwood* and Molière's *Tartuffe* in New York and *The Tempest* in Stratford, Connecticut, among other plays. In 1964, after seeing and admiring *Natalia Petrovna*, Tennessee Williams asked the composer to write the music to five songs for his new drama, *Slapstick Tragedy*. That collaboration proved so successful that Williams invited Hoiby to choose one of his plays to make into an opera, the first time he had ever sanctioned a musical adaptation of any of his major works. After exhaustively studying the Williams canon, Hoiby selected the three-act drama *Summer and Smoke* (1948), which, in his opinion, offered the best combination of romantic, comic, and serious material for opera. The play is a tragedy of repressed and frustrated love between Alma Winemiller, a sexually starved small-town singing teacher, and her neighbor, a dissolute young doctor named John Buchanan.

Enlisting the services of the well-known playwright Lanford Wilson as his librettist, Hoiby obtained a commission for *Summer and Smoke* from Thomas and David Daniels of St. Paul, Minnesota, and spent three years on its composition. *Summer and Smoke* was given its premiere at the St. Paul Opera on June 19, 1971 with highly acclaimed performances by Mary Beth Peil and John Reardon, who went on to star in the New York City Opera's production the following year.

Except for some reservations, critical reaction to *Summer and Smoke* was generally enthusiastic. Virtually all reviewers had something positive to say about Hoiby's voluptuously romantic score, but several questioned the wisdom of his choice of another introspective, fragile, and delicately nuanced play for objective operatic treatment. The *New Yorker*'s Winthrop Sargeant (April 8, 1972), for example, while pronouncing Hoiby "the most gifted of American composers," called the original source "too subtle for musical treatment," and noted that the score failed to evoke Alma's anguish as she fights her passion for Buchanan. *Musical America*'s Judith Gerstel (September 1971), on the other hand, regarded *Summer and Smoke* as "a triumph," whose "understated and quite beautiful score" is effectively "mood-evoking, expressive of inner human conflict" and "unresolved longing." The *New York Post* critic Harriett Johnson (March 20, 1972) concurred. Hoiby "has written a beautiful work," she informed her readers, "exquisitely set for the voice and with an instrumental fabric which is vividly evocative of the drama. As a wedding of words, mood and music, *Summer and Smoke* is our most successful American opera to date." In 1980 the Chicago Opera Theater revived *Summer and Smoke*, and the Chicago public television station WTTW filmed that production for national broadcast.

After putting the finishing touches on *Summer and Smoke*, Hoiby told Gary Schmidgall, he went through a period of creative limbo in the early 1970s when he feared that he was losing his touch as a composer. Listening to the music of such popular songwriters as Cat Stevens and Joni Mitchell helped to summon back his reluctant muse: "Their arching melodic line, combined with wonderfully simple harmonic means was just what I needed." He also got his creative juices flowing again by inaugurating his long-deferred career as a concert pianist. Beginning to perform in solo recitals and with orchestras around the country, Hoiby made his New York recital debut at Alice Tully Hall on January 17, 1978, at the age of fifty-one, in a program of Bach, Beethoven, Liszt, Chopin, and his own *Five Preludes*. He was accorded an enthusiastic audience response after an introspective performance that in the opinion of the *New York Times* critic Donal Henahan was noteworthy for its technical fluidity and musical sensitivity.

More recently, Hoiby has appeared as a collaborative pianist, touring with Mary Beth Peil in the fall of 1980 and performing his *Sonata for Violin and Piano* with Daniel Heifetz at the Library of Congress in October 1984. Faubion Bowers in *Musical America* (February, 1985) described the sonata as a virtuosic showpiece that is also musically compelling and predicted that it "should soon become a staple in every violinist's larder." In April 1984 Hoiby presented a highly successful program of his own piano and vocal works with the singers Kristine and Katherine Ciesinski at the 92d Street Y in New York. The concert introduced his *Bermudas*, a duet set to a poem by Andrew Marvell, a work that a *New York Times* (March 1, 1984) critic, Tim Page, described as "richly melodic, expertly crafted," and deserving of "a place in the permanent repertory."

Dividing his time between performing and composing, Hoiby completed many other vocal, piano, chamber music, and orchestral works from the mid-1970s to the mid-1980s. The piano music he wrote during that period includes a *Piano Sextet* (1974), a second piano concerto that the composer introduced as soloist in a televised performance with Chicago's American Chamber Symphony in June 1980, and the solo works *Narrative* (1984) and *Ten Variations on a Schubert Laendler* (1982). Hoiby also wrote two major choral works, the opera-oratorio *Galileo Galilei* (1975) and *The Lord is King* (1985), a monumental choral setting for a thousand voices, brass, organ, and percussion based on the Ninety-third Psalm that was commissioned to commemorate the 200th anniversary of the New York Episcopal Diocese. Among Hoiby's other vocal compositions are the one-act opera buffa *Something New for the Zoo* (1980) and a song cycle (1985) for the soprano Leontyne Price, a long-time admirer of the composer who has featured his work in her recitals for many years. In January 1985 Jean Stapleton and the Baltimore Opera Company gave the premiere performance of Hoiby's musical monodrama *The Italian Lesson*, based on the Ruth Draper monologue with the same title. David Patrick Stearns reported in *Opera News* (April 13, 1985) that Hoiby's "warm and affectionate" musical language "skillfully supports the stage action, tellingly inflecting the vocal lines but never fading into innocuousness."

In 1982 Lee Hoiby embarked on his most ambitious opera project to date when he accepted a commission from the Des Moines Metro Opera to write an operatic version of Shakespeare's *The Tempest*. The composer had been attracted to the operatic potentialities of the play ever since he wrote the incidental music for a staging of *The Tempest* in 1960, but found himself intimidated from attempting the project by the more than thirty failures to convert it to the lyric stage that are recorded in opera history. Composers have been thwarted by the dual challenge of matching music to the play's extraordinary poetry and the difficulty they have encountered in imposing thematic unity on the complex stage action. Nevertheless, seduced by "language as lyrical as anything Shakespeare wrote," language that "cries out for music," as the composer remarked to Gary Schmidgall, Hoiby enlisted Mark Shulgasser as his librettist and began the project that was to require four years of intensive work. In the course of his composing, Hoiby found himself attracted to Shakespeare's valedictory drama about shipwrecked mariners on a magic isle for philosophical as well as musical reasons. He discovered an "extremely optimistic" moral message in the play, concluding that "the right action is forgiveness, not revenge, and its reward is the ever possible rebirth of innocence." The composer explained to Schmidgall: "I have never before found a project so affecting to me in an existential way. Shakespeare forced me to get at my own core in a deeply personal and spiritual way. It was a four-year love affair, and I'm almost sorry to see it ending."

The Tempest was given its premiere by the Des Moines Metro Opera at the Blank Performing Arts Center in Indianola, Iowa, on June 21, 1986. In his *New York Times* review (July 12, 1986), John Rockwell discovered "arresting instrumental and vocal passages throughout" the opera, which, he noted, is written in a late-Romantic idiom reminiscent of Strauss's *Ariadne auf Naxos*. Rockwell added that Hoiby has "written some lush, beautiful and stratospherically difficult music" for the coloratura soprano in the role of Ariel, one of the opera's leading characters.

Lee Hoiby is a slightly built man with dark eyes and gray-streaked light-brown hair that recedes from a prominent forehead. He is reportedly warm, amiable, and nonegotistical, and Gary Schmidgall profiled him as "an artist at ease with himself, thoughtful, gentle-spirited, lacking the usual tics of the self-absorbed." Hoiby composes in solitude ("I can't write a note if anyone is listening") and sings every operatic role *plena voce* as he goes along, a practice that leaves him virtually speechless at the end of a good day. He confesses that he rarely attends opera, repelled by a "kind of falseness" that he finds in much of the nineteenth-century repertory, and that the premiere of one of his own works leaves him "a complete wreck, huddled in a high balcony seat or tempted to take a long, quiet walk during the performance." A lifelong bachelor, Hoiby is also a "confirmed country person" who loves to live near water. Several years ago he moved from New York City to a rambling house on the banks of the Delaware River in Long Eddy, New York.

References: N Y Times II p17+ Je 13 '71 por, II p23 O 19 '80; Opera N 50:10+ Je '86 pors; Ewen, David. American Composers: A Biographical Dictionary (1982)

Holladay, Wilhelmina (Cole)

Oct. 10, 1922– Philanthropist; museum founder and president; interior designer. Address: b. National Museum of Women in the Arts, 801 13th St., N.W., Washington, D.C. 20005; h. 3215 R St., N.W., Washington, D.C. 20007

The National Museum of Women in the Arts, which officially opened its doors to the public in Washington, D.C., on April 7, 1987, is largely the creation of its president, Wilhelmina Holladay, a Washington socialite who is director of interior design for her husband's Holladay Corporation. Some two decades earlier, while touring the art galleries and museums of Europe with her husband, Mrs. Holladay discovered to her dismay that, with a few exceptions, women artists were virtually unrecognized by the art establishment and the general public, even though the history of art is studded with the names of a number of distinguished female representatives, dating back to the Renaissance. In the years that followed, Mrs. Holladay collected a substantial number of works by female artists, which form the basis of the permanent holdings of the National Museum of Women in the Arts. Responding to feminists who insist that women's art should not be segregated, Mrs. Holladay has said that the National Museum of Women in the Arts constitutes "a forum for greater awareness of women in the arts and their contribution to the aesthetic aspect of life." She maintains that the "intent is not to separate art into male and female, but to uncover and celebrate the hidden contribution of women in the history of art."

Of patrician background, Wilhelmina Holladay was born in Elmira, New York, on October 10, 1922, to Chauncey E. and Claire Elizabeth (Strong) Cole. She spent her early years in Elmira, on the estate of her maternal grandmother, Gertrude (Mrs. Charles Henry) Strong, who was a major influence on her life. Mrs. Holladay remembers her grandmother as having been "fantastically aware of aesthetic values," she told Julia Cameron, as quoted in the *Chicago Tribune* (February 16, 1986). "She really raised me. As a little girl, I would say, 'Look, Grandma, isn't that flower beautiful?' and she would reply, 'Yes, dear, but why? Is it the color you find beautiful? The shape? The smell?' . . . She really created in me a heightened awareness of beauty. I learned to sort out my responses." Wilhelmina Cole grew up, as Sarah Booth Conroy noted in an article in the *Washington Post* (February 15, 1987), "determined to use the minutiae of everyday life as art: the dining table as a still-life painting, the interior decoration as a stage set."

Wilhelmina Cole studied art at Elmira College, earning a B.A. degree in 1944, and took additional courses in art history at Cornell University. Later, she did postgraduate work in the history of art at the University of Paris in 1953 and 1954, and at the University of Virginia in 1961 and 1962. Considering herself more a connoisseur than a creative artist, she believes that connoisseurship is "part of an instinctive sensitivity" to art. "I'm a Libra, and my horoscope is always mentioning color and art," she told Sarah Booth Conroy. "But it's amazing how much you learn. You develop an eye for proportion."

During World War II, Wilhelmina Cole worked in Washington, D.C., for a general who headed the Air Force division that was responsible for reallocating contracts for military equipment, and she remembers the nation's capital in wartime as a stimulating, lively place. In 1944-45 she was executive secretary to Howard Ludington, in Rochester, New York. Then, from 1945 to 1948, she was employed by the Chinese Nationalist government, assigned part of that time to work as social secretary to Madame Chiang Kai-shek at her estate north of New York City. Her duties included compiling biographical information about expected guests. She remembers the Chinese first lady as having been "very bright, very elegant, very demanding."

In Washington, D.C., Wilhelmina Cole met Wallace Fitzhugh Holladay, a young architect and engineer who was at that time an officer in the United States Navy, and who shared her aesthetic sensibility. They were married on September 27, 1946. After the birth of their first child, Mrs. Holladay took on a new career as a volunteer executive. "When I grew up, mothers didn't work, not unless they had a great talent they wanted to exercise," she told Sarah Booth Conroy. "It's different now, but I'm still old-fashioned. I was president of my child's school, helped in charitable events, worked hard on boards. . . . I have always wanted to be a productive individual. I would be bored to tears to sit on a cushion and be supported. I was taught to use time." From 1957 to 1959 Mrs. Holladay worked part time in the information room of the National Gallery of Art.

At her husband's request, in 1970 Wilhelmina Holladay became director of interior design for the development section of his Holladay Corporation, a mini-conglomerate that owns, among other properties, 50 percent of Washington's Grand Hotel, as well as a high-quality printing company. "I said I'd do it—if I were given unlimited funds and dictatorial powers," she told Sarah Booth Conroy. "Those are the essentials for success. And we are extremely successful." In addition, she became a member of several boards of the corporation's subsidiaries.

In the mid-1960s Wilhelmina Holladay and her husband were traveling in Europe, visiting museums and touring art galleries in search of paintings for their elegant home near Dumbarton Oaks in the Georgetown section of Washington. While in Vienna, they were much impressed by an inconspicuously hung Flemish still-life painting, dated 1594, of a pair of goblets, a scattering of gold coins, and a spray of tulips, by Clara Peeters, an artist of whom they had never heard. A week later, at the Prado in Madrid, they found additional paintings, by the same artist. Back home, Mrs. Holladay turned to H. W. Janson's *History of Art* (1962), then the standard text in its field, and found no mention of Clara Peeters or for that matter, of any other woman artist. Observing her indignation over the lack of attention given to women artists, her hus-

band suggested, "I think you've found a focus for your collecting."

In that way, the Holladays began what is believed to be the first major collection of works by women artists. "Painting by painting, artist by artist, we set out to track down great women artists who had been forgotten or ignored," she told Julia Cameron. "We found that some eras had been good to women artists and that others had been far more repressive. During the Renaissance, women artists flourished. . . . Then, in later ages, they were not even allowed to study. . . . A woman artist, Angelica Kauffmann, could found England's Royal Academy but, because she was a woman, her art could not be hung in it."

Mrs. Holladay considers herself an "appreciator" of art, rather than a collector in the conventional sense, and she has said that she acquired works of art simply on the basis of their appeal to her. Over the years, she and her husband assembled a collection of about 300 works representing some 150 women artists from nineteen countries, spanning a period of three and a half centuries. Among the artists represented in the collection are Lavinia Fontana, a court artist to Pope Clement VIII in the early seventeenth century who supported her husband and eleven children by painting portraits and Vatican altarpieces; Rachel Ruys, a contemporary of Rembrandt noted for her flower studies; Maria Sibylla Merian, a Swiss naturalist painter; Elisabeth Vigée-Le Brun, who was Marie Antoinette's favorite portrait painter; Rosa Bonheur, a nineteenth-century French painter of animal life; Lilla Cabot Perry, an American who worked with Claude Monet in France; and Mary Cassatt, a leading American representative of French impressionism.

Also included in the collection were works of such twentieth-century artists as the German "proletarian" sculptor and graphic artist Käthe Kollwitz; the American painter of Southwestern motifs Georgia O'Keeffe; the English sculptor Dame Barbara Hepworth; the American abstract expressionist Helen Frankenthaler; the American representational artist Alice Neel; the American primitive painter Anna Mary Robertson ("Grandma") Moses; and such representatives of the Washington artists' community as Joan Danziger, Sheila Isham, and Alma Thomas.

The Holladays compiled an exhaustive archive of catalogues, books, photographs, and biographical information on women artists. But although they added a large room to house their growing collection, eventually the Holladay house was not large enough to accommodate it. "We felt as though we were the collection's custodians," Mrs. Holladay told Sarah Booth Conroy. "It began to have a vitality of its own. We would have been sad to give it away. . . . " At the suggestion of the late Nancy Hanks, who was then chairman of the National Endowment for the Arts, the Holladays decided to donate their collection as the foundation of a new museum for women's art. "We didn't want our name on it," Mrs. Holladay said, "not only because we could raise more money for it that way, but also because I hope it will be everybody's museum and all will take joy in it. I have heard from women all over the world. They want to be taken seriously, for people to know their achievements."

The National Museum of Women in the Arts, with Wilhelmina Holladay as its founder, board chairman, and president, was incorporated in December 1981. To house its collection, which for the time being remained in the Holladays' Georgetown home, the museum in 1982 purchased for $5 million a stately six-story Renaissance Revival building, two blocks from the White House. Designed by Waddy Wood, the building was constructed in 1907 as a Masonic temple. Interior renovation of the 70,-000 square foot building was begun in the summer of 1985 at a cost of $8 million. The renovated building includes six large-scale and eight small-scale galleries, a great hall, a 4,000-volume library and research center, a 200-seat auditorium, conference rooms, a membership lounge, and a café.

Wilhelmina Holladay herself conducted the campaign to raise funds for the purchase, renovation, and endowment of the museum's building. "With the zeal of a missionary [she] . . . single-handedly engineered nearly every cog in the mammoth assembling of the . . . museum . . . ," Iris Krasnow wrote in the Chicago Tribune (April 19, 1987). "She has been at it for four years, working the phones . . . in her Georgetown home . . . , four years of endless early morning meetings, luncheons, and cross-country trips." By the time the museum opened in 1987, some $17 million had been raised, thanks largely to Mrs. Holladay's zeal. Grants were received from the National Endowment for the Arts and the National Endowment for the Humanities, and funds were made available through congressional appropriations and gifts from corporations and individuals. By 1987 the museum's membership numbered more than 67,000 persons throughout the United States and in fifteen foreign countries. In addition to its large volunteer staff recruited by Mrs. Holladay, the museum at the time of its opening had a professional staff of twenty, headed by the administrative director, Anne-Imelda Radice.

On April 7, 1987, the National Museum of Women in the Arts was officially opened by Mrs. Barbara Bush, the wife of Vice-President George Bush, with some 500 works of women's art, including the Holladays' core collection of about 300 items. As the museum's logo, reproduced on its brochures, Mrs. Holladay chose Lilla Cabot Perry's Belle Époque painting Lady With a Bowl of Violets. For its inaugural exhibition, the museum featured a collection of 124 paintings and sculptures, most of them on loan from other institutions, under the title "American Women Artists, 1830–1930," which was assembled by Professor Eleanor M. Tufts of Southern Methodist University, in cooperation with the International Exhibitions Foundation, under a grant from United Technologies Corporation. Among its highlights were several portraits by Sarah Miriam Peale of the famous family of Ameri-

can painters as well as still lifes by other female members of the Peale clan. Also featured were Mary Cassatt's Woman and Child Driving; Ellen Emmet Rand's Portrait of Henry James; Susan Macdowell Eakins' Portrait of Thomas Eakins; Louise Herreshoff's Poppies; Abby Hill's Grand Canyon; Georgia O'Keeffe's Spring and City Night; and Vinnie Ream Hoxie's marble statue Sappho. Critical opinion of the show was decidedly mixed. Robert Hughes of Time magazine (August 10, 1987) summed it up, with a few exceptions, as "a dull florilegium of derivative kitsch"; Cathleen McGuigan, writing in Newsweek (April 13, 1987), found it a "well-mannered potpourri"; and Roberta Smith reported in the New York Times (April 7, 1987) that the show had "some wonderful moments, convincing paintings by artists who today are completely unknown to the art-viewing public and specialists alike." The exhibition was scheduled later in the year to travel to Minneapolis, Hartford, San Diego, and Dallas.

Admittedly not an avowed feminist, Mrs. Holladay prefers to consider herself a "humanist." "As a person, I'm sympathetic to the feminist movement," she explained during her interview with Sarah Booth Conroy. "I'm in favor of freedom of choice and equal pay. But I believe an art museum should not be concerned with politics, abortion, or homosexuality. Art is sensitive to what's around, including the erotic movements of the day. But art museums are intended to focus on artistic creativity. Without beauty, you get sick people." Although Mrs. Holladay's contributions to art and to the interests of women have been widely commended, she has also been criticized by those who consider her approach too conservative. According to Maclean's magazine (May 18, 1987), she is viewed by some as "little more than a socialite with an elitist toy," while others have maintained that her approach would bring about a "ghettoization" of women in the arts and that she seems to avoid many of the genuine issues confronting women. To greet the opening of the National Museum of Women in the Arts, an "intentionally provocative" counterprogram was launched by the Washington Project for the Arts, featuring works by women deeply involved in feminist issues.

On the other hand, Mrs. Holladay gained substantial support within the art community. The feminist artist Judy Chicago, noting that it is "important to protect and preserve women's art," offered to make a long-term loan of one of her major works to the museum. Lowery Sims, a deputy curator with the Metropolitan Museum of Art in New York City, called the museum "an exciting and interesting venture." And Jane Livingston, the chief curator of the Corcoran Gallery of Art, suggested that the museum "could succeed as a resource center, a place to find 'lost' history." Mrs. Holladay plans to expand the scope of the museum in order to expose the public to outstanding work by women in other disciplines, including musical composition and performance, architecture, landscape design, poetry, playwriting, acting, choreography, and dance.

In addition to serving as president of the National Museum of Women in the Arts, Mrs. Holladay is president of the Holladay Foundation. She has served as board chairman of the Women's National Bank, a trustee of the Corcoran Gallery of Art, a board member of International Student House, a member of the interior design professional advisory committee at Mount Vernon College, an international board member of the American Field Service, a member of the council of friends of the Folger Library, and a patron of the Phillips Collection. She is also a member of the American Association of Museums, the American Federation of Art, Art Libraries of North America, College Art Association, Archives of American Art, the Golden Circle of the Kennedy Center, the world service council of the YWCA, the Capital Speakers Club, the Leeds Castle Foundation, the Metropolitan Museum of Art, and the Museum of Modern Art. Among honors that she received in 1987 are the Anti-Defamation League award and the Northwood Institute distinguished woman award.

Wilhelmina ("Billie") Holladay and her husband, Wallace F. Holladay, have two sons, Wallace ("Hap") Jr. and Scott Cole, and four grandchildren. Because of her full-time dedication to the National Museum of Women in the Arts, Mrs. Holladay gave up golf, tennis, and vacations. A fastidious perfectionist, she once reportedly went into shock when her cook served mayonnaise at the dining room table from its original jar. According to Sarah Booth Conroy, "Everything about her appearance as well as her personality and philosophy is exquisite. Her stole is cashmere, her brooch often diamond. She is not the sort of woman whose stockings would dare run. . . . She speaks softly, politely, as if confiding, except when she thinks questions are too personal. . . . 'Don't write about me,' she protests with some show of asperity. 'Write about the museum. It isn't an ego trip for Wally and me. We have no ambitions, social or political.'"

References: Chicago Tribune XIII p6+ F 16 '86 por, VI p4 Ap 19 '87 por; Maclean's 100:53+ My 10 '07 por; N Y Times A p8 Ag 2 '85 por, C p23 Ap 1 '87, II p1+ Ap 5 '87 por; Newsweek 99:76+ Ap 13 '87; Village Voice p89 Ap 28 '87 por; Washington Post G p1+ F 15 '87 pors; Who's Who in American Art (1986)

Holliger, Heinz

May 21, 1939- Oboist; composer; conductor.
Address: b. c/o Colbert Artists Management, 111 W. 57th St., New York City, N.Y. 10019

The oboe, which was a favorite solo instrument as well as the principal orchestral woodwind in the eighteenth century, has come into its own again in the twentieth. No one has contributed more to the restoration of the double-reeded Cinderella of wind instruments than Heinz Holliger, the Swiss player and composer who is internationally recognized as "the Paganini of the oboe." With his dazzling virtuosity, Holliger has virtually reinvented the oboe for our time and, through his compositions and more than seventy recordings, for posterity. Attracted to the oboe because it is, in his words, "the instrument closest to the human voice," with "that same direct, expressive power of declamation," he has not only thoroughly explored the traditional, chiefly baroque and early classical, repertoire but has soared beyond, executing with fluency and bright and penetrating timbre avant-garde works that extend the instrument's capabilities "via tricky tonguings, chords, and notes in the oboe stratosphere," as Barbara Jepson pointed out in the Wall Street Journal (February 1, 1984). "Others may have pioneered such effects," Miss Jepson observed, "but no living oboist equals his ability to produce them with such ease." In the opinion of many critics, as an executant composer Holliger is to the twentieth century what Liszt and Paganini were to the nineteenth.

Generally ignored by composers for more than a century and a half, the oboe has during the past quarter century accumulated a repertory of new music more important than that for the violin and other traditional solo instruments. The pantheon of contemporary composers who have been inspired to write works (a total of more than sixty) for Holliger are Hans-Werner Henze, Karlheinz Stockhausen, Ernst Krenek, and Luciano Berio. Holliger himself composes not only for the oboe but for many other instruments, including the piano, which he also plays, and for voice. Employing and extending the vocabulary of such predecessors as Anton Webern, he uses in his experimental works sounds of indefinite pitch, including explosively amplified heartbeats; multiphonics, including the playing of as many as six notes simultaneously; passages in which instrumentalists sing into or exchange their instruments; and a range of other aleatory devices and electronic effects. His most significant contribution to contemporary oboe technique is his method of "circular breathing," by which he is able simultaneously to blow into the reeds and to take in fresh air.

The son of a physician, Heinz Holliger was born in Langenthal, Switzerland, on May 21, 1939. Although his father was an amateur violinist, neither parent was very musical. Holliger began to play the recorder when he was four and the piano when he was six (at which age he also began trying his hand at composition). "I should like to have begun the oboe about then," he told Alan Blyth in an interview for the Gramophone (November 1972), "but there was nobody to teach me in my village, so I could not start until I was eleven, when I went to a teacher in Bern. I was always fascinated by the timbre of the instument, even when I heard it played badly in our local orchestra."

While attending a gymnasium in Bern, Switzerland, Holliger studied oboe (with Sándor Veress), piano, and composition at the Bern Conservatory. Subsequently he studied oboe with Pierre Pierlot and piano with Yvonne Lefébure at the National Conservatory in Paris, France. After he won first prize as an oboist in the 1959 International Music Contest in Geneva, Switzerland, he began doing solo engagements and played oboe with the Basel (Switzerland) Orchestra for three years. Worldwide recognition and increased demand for his solo appearances came with his winning the International Music Competition sponsored by the German broadcasting network in Munich in 1961. Not since the early nineteenth century had there been such a demand for a touring oboe soloist. After his marriage to the harpist Ursula Haenggi in 1962, Holliger often toured with her, as he still does.

Such early Holliger compositions as Sonata for Unaccompanied Oboe show the strong influence of the Second Viennese School, an influence that remained evident even in the 1960 composition Drei Liebeslieder for voice and orchestra. In subsequent "literary" chamber cantatas built on the richly symbolic verse of Nelly Sachs, Alexander Gwerder, and others, he developed a more individual style and a more personal musical language. As Jürg Stenzl notes in his essay on Holliger in the New Grove Dictionary of Music and Musicians (1980), in those cantatas the poetic "images—most of them nocturnal, concerning nearness to death—evoke extremely fine figurations in Holliger's settings," and "formal fragmentation is avoided through multiple serial relations, through tight constructions, sometimes with canonic features, and

through cyclic links between movements." Between 1961 and 1963 Holliger honed his compositional skills in a master class at the Basel Academy under Pierre Boulez, whom he acknowledges to be the greatest direct influence on his music.

In 1962 Holliger toured Europe and the United States as soloist with the Lucerne Festival Strings. At Carnegie Recital Hall on April 9, 1963 he was the featured player in a chamber music concert presented under the auspices of the Swiss Music Library. In that concert he performed his Mobile for Oboe and Harp (1962) with his wife, accompanied soprano Bethany Beardslee at the piano in his song cycle Dörfliche Motive (1960), and played an oboe solo sonata written for him by the contemporary Swiss composer Jürg Wyttenbach. In the Wyttenbach sonata he threw off "all kinds of sounds . . . like so many fireworks," as Raymond Erikson reported in the New York Times. Also on the program were works for oboe by J. S. Bach and Mozart and for other instruments and voice by the contemporary Swiss composers Rudolf Kelterborn and Klaus Huber.

At the World Festival of the International Society for Contemporary Music in Amsterdam in June 1963, Holliger's Erde und Himmel for tenor and five instruments (violin, viola, cello, harp, and flute), with lyrics from a poem by Alexander Gwerder, was singled out by the critic Everett Helm as the best work presented. "These three songs that form a cantata establish at once an atmosphere and maintain it; they grip the listener and hold him spellbound," Helm wrote in the Christian Science Monitor. "Using the most advanced vocabulary of modern music, Holliger creates a personal style that is as free of mannerisms as it is full of invention." When tenor Wilfred Brown and the Wigmore Ensemble gave Erde und Himmel its first British performance, at London's Queen Elizabeth Hall in January 1964, Peter J. Pirie in a review in Musical Times commented on the composition's lyrical vocal line and "the ever-changing texture of the accompaniment."

When Holliger performed Niccolò Castiglioni's new solo oboe piece Aleph in Amsterdam in 1966, Vincent McDermott, writing in Musical Quarterly, described him as "completely on top of his material, not missing a note while . . . drawing out long and frankly beautiful phrases, even through the most disruptive, pointillist passages." Holliger's engagements as a baroque and classical specialist in the 1960s included performances with the English Chamber Orchestra and the Berlin and Vienna philharmonics. Meanwhile, he was recording on the Deutsche Grammophon label, beginning in 1964, and on the Philips label, beginning in 1966. Later he also recorded on the Monitor and Vox labels.

As a composer, Holliger continued to draw much of his inspiration from poetry, even in his textless instrumental pieces. In Siebengesang for oboe, voices, and orchestra (1966–67) he interpreted the seven strophes of Georg Trakl's "Siebengesang des Todes," giving each strophe a distinct section and introducing voices in the final section. "Here, as in earlier works, a concealed, often cabalistic number symbolism determines the formal structure, the instrumentation, and the rhythmic and melodic shapes," Jürg Stenzl observes in his essay in the new *Grove Dictionary of Music and Musicians*. "The earlier Trio for Oboe, Viola, and Harp shares many structural aspects with *Siebengesang*; for instance, the fifth part of *Siebengesang* overlaps different levels of tempo and duration and grows in complexity and density, as does the first part of the final movement of the Trio. (This technique had already been used in the last part of *Glühende Ratsel*). Mobile form in the manner of Boulez' Piano Sonata no. 3 has a place in the Trio, and also in *Mobile* for oboe and harp (1962)."

Holliger began to give greater importance to sounds of indefinite pitch with the wind quintet H (1968) and especially in *Pneuma* for wind (1970), as Stenzl goes on to point out. "In H the note B (H in German nomenclature) is the center for successive expansions of the sound spectrum in the direction of noise. In *Pneuma* and the String Quartet Holliger uses breathing sounds—and in the *Cardiophonie*, heartbeats as well— . . . made audible through amplification and taken out of the control of the player. The performer and his physiological sounds are finally overpowered in a sort of theatre of the absurd. Like Holliger's earlier works, these can be heard on the largest scale as continuous expansions, reductions, or thickenings, though these formal processes may be interrupted by inserts."

Desmond Shaw-Taylor, reviewing a performance by Holliger at the Cheltenham Festival in the London *Sunday Times* (July 13, 1969), qualified his admiration with criticism of the "fierce squawks and wailing glissandos." Holliger has defended the jarring nature of some of his and other contemporary composers' works by explaining that disconcerting elements are part of "the sum total of our experience" and that the real problem is that "many people are not ready to accept reality and truth." Among the other avant-garde composers to whom he referred were André Jolivet, Karlheinz Stockhausen, and Luciano Berio, who have often been represented in his performances and those of the Holliger Ensemble, the group organized by him and his wife.

In introducing his *Discourse III* for five oboes at the December 1970 Montreux Festival, Holliger played one oboe part live on stage along with his own prerecorded tape of the other four parts. His experimental music was recorded for the first time on the album *The Spectacular Heinz Holliger* (1971), which included avante-garde pieces by Hans Huber, Luciano Berio, and Ernst Krenek in addition to his own. Also in 1971, his recording of the Mozart and Strauss oboe concertos received the Deutsche Schallplatten prize. His recording of Handel concertos was honored with the same prize the following year.

In 1973 Holliger made the first of his many tours of Japan, and during the same year eight of his works were performed at the Edinburgh Festival. With the Contemporary Chamber Ensemble at Carnegie Hall in May 1975 he performed his *Siebengesang* for oboe, orchestra, seven women's voices, and loudspeakers. Writing in the *New York Times*, Harold C. Schonberg described the composition as "well-crafted" and the performance of it "stunning," demonstrating that Holliger had "pushed technique to previously unimaginable lengths."

On five albums released in 1979, Holliger performed concertos by an array of composers, most of them baroque, ranging from Vivaldi and Haydn to Tomaso Albinoni and Johann Ludwig Krebs. "His tone is unfailingly sweet and true, without a trace of the wailing, pinched vibrato that many Continental oboists deem appropriate," Peter G. Davis wrote of the recordings in the *New York Times*, (December 2, 1979). "In technique and musical approach he conjures up the best qualities of a virtuoso singer who can spin out seamless legato phrases and execute passages of dashing virtuosity, making it all sound as natural and spontaneous as breathing."

Witold Lutoslawski's *Double Concerto* for oboe, harp, and chamber orchestra, commissioned for Holliger and his wife by the conductor Paul Sacher, was first performed by the Holligers, with Sacher conducting, at the 1981 London Promenade Concerts. When Holliger's forty-minute one-act opera for soprano and tape *Not I*, a musical adaptation of a play by Samuel Beckett, was given its American premiere at the Kennedy Center Terrace Theatre in Washington, D.C., Theodore W. Libby Jr., writing in *Musical America* (October 1981), praised the opera's "Boulez-like intensity" and the composer's skill at holding an audience in thrall through artful reiterations.

"For ease and fluency on the instrument, there is no one quite like Holliger," Marilyn Tucker wrote in the *San Francisco Chronicle* following a recital by the oboist in San Francisco in April 1985. "But he combines an effortless technique with a musicality that gives expressive dimension to the music at every turn. He can make that great-grandchild of the bagpipes do just about anything." During the 1985–86 season Holliger performed in concert with the Los Angeles Philharmonic, the San Francisco Symphony, and the Orchestre de la Suisse Romande. In the summer of 1986 he appeared with the Chicago Symphony Orchestra at the Ravinia Festival, and he performed in three concerts at the Mostly Mozart Festival in New York City. In concert with the San Francisco Symphony in October 1986 he performed Bernd Alois Zimmerman's '52 Oboe Concerto, after preparing the audience for the difficult avant-garde piece by explaining what it meant to him. "He was downright disarming . . .," Thor Eckert Jr. wrote in the *Christian Science Monitor*. "The audience was on his side. And his committed, compelling performance of this neo-Stravinskian concerto was an equally persuasive argument for new (or at least newer) music." The remainder of his 1986–87 American schedule included appearances in concert with the Cincinnati, Vancouver, and Pittsburgh symphonies and recitals in Boston and New York as well as on university campuses.

The oboe was developed from older double-reed instruments in the mid-seventeenth century, and gradual mechanical improvements since then have culminated in today's "Conservatory" model. Unlike most other contemporary oboists, who revert to the antique oboe when playing period music, Holliger uses a modern instrument of his own design (utilizing some baroque features, but essentially a Conservatory instrument) exclusively, and with it he succeeds amazingly in recreating baroque ornamentation. "He shows remarkable sympathy with works of the most varied types and periods," Jürg Stenzl observes, "and he possesses an extraordinary phrasing technique. He introduced new effects on the oboe, such as harmonics, double trills, glissandos, chords, and sounds derived from the use of a microphone within the instrument." His circular-breathing technique, in combination with fingerings derived from those proper to the baroque oboe, contributes to the ease with which he can change the color of a note according to its harmonic importance. Custom-made reeds and legato diaphragm articulation facilitate his phrasing and tonguings. Technique and mechanics, however, are in his view, secondary to imagination. "You have to search for something you want," he has said. "and then find the appropriate technique to realize it."

In a conversation with fellow oboist Frederic Palmer in 1981, Holliger said that "the great danger in the way we approach baroque music today" is that "we begin to believe everything just depends on the material things we use." "Music can only come to life through us, when we play it," he told Palmer, "and we are not psychics who can look back into time nor have we had the same experiences and education as an 18th century person. . . . To think that we can just go back to an earlier time and be happy again is very reactionary and extremely dangerous politically. Too many things have happened that can't be forgotten, and these things will always stand between us and baroque music. . . . When I approach a piece of old music I try to be as personal as I can. . . . I can never be Telemann when I play; I am still Holliger playing."

"The most fascinating music ever written for oboe," in Holliger's opinion, is that of Jan Dismas Zelenka, a Czech contemporary of J. S. Bach. Other neglected composers whose scores he has collected in his periodic sweeps of libraries include François Couperin, William Babell, Thomas Vincent Jr., Giuseppe Sammartini, and Joseph Fiala. His discography includes works by Vincenzo Bellini, Beethoven, Alessandro Marcello, Robert Schumann, Richard Strauss, and Carl Philipp Emanuel Bach and Johann Christian Bach as well as Johann Sebastian Bach. Among his recording awards are a Grand Prix du Disque and two Edison awards.

Heinz Holliger is a slender man with long, dark, thinning hair. He and his wife, Ursula, who have one daughter, live in Basel. Holliger periodically conducts orchestras in Basel and Zurich, and he has been a teacher at the Freiburg (Switzerland) Music Academy since 1965. "When he shyly comes onto the concert stage, the bespectacled and still boyish-looking Mr. Holliger seems for all the world like a precocious British schoolboy prepared to decline irregular Latin verbs," Peter G. Davis wrote in the New York Times (April 10, 1981). "When he starts to play, though, it becomes immediately clear that he is not only a master of his instrument but also a natural musician who instantly communicates with his audience. Mr. Holliger has no ready explanation of why he reaches people so effectively. 'I just try to do my best,' he explains modestly."

References: Gramophone 50:879 N '72 por; Keynote 11:18+ Je '87 pors; N Y Times C p3 Ap 10 '81 por, II p17+ Mr 7 '82 por; Wall St J p22 F 1 '84 por; Slonimsky, N. Baker's Biographical Dictionary of Musicians (1978); New Grove Dictionary of Music and Musicians (1980); Who's Who, 1986–87

Hopper, Dennis

1936– Actor; director; photographer. Address: b. c/o Michael McLean, 12725 Ventura Blvd., Studio City, Calif. 91604

When the actress Natalie Wood drowned in 1981, superstitious Hollywood gossip mavens checked off yet another victim of the "curse" on members of the cast of Rebel Without a Cause, the 1955 cult film for teenagers. Earlier, twenty-four-year-old James Dean had died in an auto accident, Nick Adams of a drug overdose, and Sal Mineo of a stabbing. Dennis Hopper, another cast member, while living dangerously, has been a surprisingly resilient survivor. In the early 1980s the multitalented Hopper, a director and photographer as well as an actor, after several career failures and decades of hard drug and alcohol abuse, succumbed to raving paranoia and was committed to the psychiatric ward of a hospital—only to come back stronger than before.

A movieland legend, Hopper was one of Hollywood's most notorious bad boys in the 1960s, wild men in the 1970s, and it appeared, burned-out cases in the mid-1980s. Studio tycoons banished the rebellious young actor in 1958, when he engaged in a monumental battle of wills with a powerful old-guard director. A decade later he emerged from obscurity as the director and costar of the immensely popular *Easy Rider* (1969), which established him as a kind of guerrilla genius among independent filmmakers and hirsute hero in the hippie counterculture. When his next picture, *The Last Movie* (1971), failed miserably, studio tycoons expelled him once again. However, in 1987, with three years of sobriety behind him, Hopper is one of the busiest actors in Hollywood. His evocation of a struggling alcoholic's pathos in *Hoosiers* (1986) and his shocking portrayal of a murderous psychopath who brutalizes a nightclub singer for his own sexual pleasure in the acclaimed *Blue Velvet* have earned accolades for Hopper and enabled him to achieve his long-sought goal of directing feature films once again.

Dennis Hopper was born in Kansas in 1936. During much of his childhood, he lived with his grandparents on their twelve-acre farm about five miles from Dodge City, where they raised alfalfa, chickens, cows, and pigs. He has recalled that there were "wheat fields all around, as far as you could see . . . no neighbors, no other kids . . . just a train that came through once a day." He used to wonder where the train "came from and where it went to." "Most of the time I spent alone, daydreaming," he told James Stevenson in an interview for a profile in the *New Yorker* (November 13, 1971). "I didn't do much; occasionally I cleaned out the chicken house."

Hopper's pivotal childhood memory is of his grandmother walking to Dodge City with him and taking him to his first movie when he was five. "Right away it hit me," he told Henry Allen of the *Washington Post* (March 30, 1987). "The places I was seeing on the screen were the places the train came from and went to! The world on the screen was the real world, and I felt as if my heart would explode I wanted so much to be part of it."

Except for his Saturday afternoons at the movies, Hopper seems to have had an unhappy childhood, full of tedium and, when he was with his parents, family discord. He lived with his grandparents throughout World War II, when his father served in Indochina with the Office of Strategic Services and his mother worked for the Red Cross and managed an outdoor swimming pool in Dodge City. "I never knew my father or my mother very well," Hopper said in the *New Yorker* interview. "I very seldom saw my father—which I resented tremendously." After the war, the father became a postal worker. Hopper's strong-willed mother was a religious fundamentalist who bitterly opposed her son's desire to become, in his words, an "artist [or] poet, [to do] something that would last." Her feeling was, in his paraphrase, "You can become an engineer, a lawyer, or a doctor. If you become an artist or an actor, you'll end up a bum."

With his parents and his brother, David, Hopper moved to Kansas City, Missouri, where, at twelve, he became interested in painting. Because his brother suffered from bronchial asthma, the family soon moved again, to San Diego, California. In high school in San Diego, Hopper played sports and, over his mother's opposition, turned to acting. He won a scholarship to the National Shakespeare Festival at San Diego's Old Globe Theatre, where he played Montano in *Othello*, Sebastian in *Twelfth Night*, and Lorenzo in *The Merchant of Venice*. Impressed by his intensity, the actress Dorothy McGuire encouraged and tutored him. After playing an epileptic in an episode of the TV series *Medic*, Hopper was courted by several movie studios. First opting for Columbia Pictures, the nervous nineteen-year-old was summoned to a meeting with Harry Cohn, the most despotic of the old studio system moguls, known as "White Fang." In an interview with Ron Rosenbaum for *Vanity Fair* (April 1987), Hopper recounted how he instructed Cohn to perform an act of intimacy with himself. "He told me I was the most naturalistic actor since Montgomery Clift. He said, 'What have you been doing?' I said, 'Playing Shakespeare.' He said, 'Oh My God. Hey, Max, give him some [money], put him in school, take all that Shakespeare out of him—I can't stand Shakespeare.' I stopped sweating and said, 'Go . . . yourself.' I was kicked out of the studio."

Impressed by his brassy defiance of Cohn, Jack Warner, the chief at Warner Brothers, signed Hopper to a seven-year contract. "I thought I was the best [young] actor in the world . . . ," Hopper told Ron Rosenbaum. "I had incredible technique, and I was very sensitive. I didn't think there was anybody to top me. Until I saw James Dean." Hopper met Dean on the set of *Rebel Without a Cause*, director Nicholas Ray's classic, moody melodrama about misunderstood teenagers. In a story that centered on the growing friendship of three soulfully inarticulate high school misfits—Jim (James Dean), Judy (Natalie Wood), and Plato (Sal Mineo)—Hopper's character, Goon, was a minor one. Awed by Dean's approach to character interpretation, an electrifying, deeply internalized style of method acting, Hopper asked Dean the secrets of his technique—how he probed so deeply into his character's psyche, how he summoned up emotions that were so real and raw, and how he improvised, playing a scene differently each time it was shot.

"That's when he started telling me to do things," Hopper told Henry Allen of the *Washington Post*. "He'd say, 'Look, just do it, don't show it. . . . If you're smoking a cigarette, just smoke the cigarette, don't act like you're smoking a cigarette.'"

Hopper worked with Dean again on *Giant* (1956), a sprawling saga about a Texas cattle-ranching family that starred Rock Hudson as the patriarch, Elizabeth Taylor as his wife, and Dean as Jett Rink, the Hudson character's nemesis, an embittered hired hand who rises to oil magnate. Hopper acquitted himself well in the part of the somberly sensitive scion of the ranching family, but Dean stole the film. The relationship between Hopper and Dean deepened, with Dean playing the role of mentor and Hopper that of hero-worshipping understudy—until Dean's sudden death on a highway on September 30, 1955, before the production of the film had been completed.

Devastated by Dean's death, Hopper never fully recovered from the sense of loss it engendered in him. He went to New York City to study with Dean's teacher, Lee Strasberg, the foremost exponent of the Stanislavski style of acting, known as the Method, in which the actor draws on the resources of his own psyche in creating a role. When Hopper returned to Hollywood, it was as the inheritor of Dean's legacy, a rebel who now had a cause: to win for himself the kind of creative freedom he had envied in such Method exemplars as Marlon Brando, Montgomery Clift, and James Dean. His pursuit of that cause was immediately frustrated, when Warners assigned him to work on *From Hell to Texas* under director Henry Hathaway, who personified the studio-dictated production values against which Hopper was reacting.

Viewing Hopper's approach to acting as a challenge to his authority, Hathaway instructed the actor to imitate the mannerisms of Marlon Brando. Hopper demurred, insisting on doing his own inner-generated line readings. The showdown between the rebellious actor and the iron-willed director came during the shooting of a ten-line scene. Balking at Hathaway's orders, Hopper did the scene eighty-six times before capitulating to the director's wishes. The word went out that Hopper was stubbornly uncooperative, and at the age of twenty-one he found himself persona non grata in the movie industry.

Moving to New York City, Hopper worked on the stage and appeared in some 140 episodes of television shows. At the same time, he wrote poetry and took up painting. He also became a professional photographer, selling some of his work to *Vogue* and *Harper's Bazaar*. Becoming familiar with the emerging Pop Art scene and its leading artists, he began buying the work of Andy Warhol, Claes Oldenburg, and others, at a time when the prices were low, amassing a collection that would ultimately be valued at more than a million dollars. Although painters considered him a photographer and actor friends like Paul Newman thought of him as both a painter and photographer, Hopper still dreamed of returning to Hollywood triumphantly. His ambi-

tion was to direct a film so transcendent that the gaudy baubles of the Tinseltown fantasy factory would be exposed once and for all as meretricious and studio-compromised. As Hopper told the *New Yorker* interviewer, he had taken up photography as "a way of learning to make movies." "I didn't crop my photographs," he said, "I was learning to work within the frame of movies."

In 1961 Hopper shocked the Hollywood elite by marrying into one of its proudest families. His bride was Brooke Hayward, the daughter of actress Margaret Sullavan and producer Leland Hayward, who intensely disliked his new son-in-law. Nevertheless, the Haywards gave Hopper entrée to the upper strata of Hollywood society. There, still haunted by the James Dean legend, he adopted the stance of revolutionary scold. His wife told Ron Rosenbaum, "We'd go to these parties where you'd have the *crème de la crème* of Hollywood, and he'd tell them that when he ran things heads were going to roll—they'd be in chains. Someday he'd make a movie and the old dinosaurs would be slain." Despite his truculence, Hopper was soon acting in films again, and even Henry Hathaway cast him in two John Wayne Westerns, *The Sons of Katie Elder* (1965) and *True Grit* (1968).

Hopper and Brooke Hayward's marriage was marred by misfortune and by his increasingly manifest proclivity for violence. In 1961 their Bel Air home was ravaged by a fire in which thousands of Hopper's poems and hundreds of his paintings were destroyed. Several years later, Hopper was about to direct the filming of a script he had written, the first version of what would later become *The Last Movie*, when the financial backing was withdrawn. According to Miss Hayward, that disappointment was the blow that plunged her husband into "the abyss."

A regular user of marijuana and hallucinogenic drugs since the 1950s, Hooper added amphetamines and LSD to his chemical intake and began to wash down the pharmacopeia with a river of hard liquor. With his grip on reality weakening, he sometimes fantasized that his radical political beliefs had made him the target of FBI surveillance, and he prowled the streets near his suburban home with a gun, searching for the elusive G-men. The holder of a Black Belt in karate, he ended one marital dispute with a bone-crushing open-fist "chop" to his wife's nose.

Several years before she divorced Hopper in 1969, Brooke Hayward introduced him to her childhood friend Peter Fonda. The two men appeared together in the low-budget biker movie *The Glory Stompers* (1966) and in Roger Corman's *The Trip* (1967), an exploitation film about a first hallucinatory "trip" on LSD. In 1968 Hopper and Fonda began work on the film that would make cinematic history and inaugurate Hopper's brief reign as a Hollywood genius.

Produced by Fonda, directed by Hopper, and costarring the two, *Easy Rider* (1969) is the story of two marijuana-smoking hippie motorcyclists, Wyatt (Fonda) and his genial, inarticulate sidekick,

Billy (Hopper). Using the proceeds from a cache of cocaine they sell in Los Angeles to fund their freedom from "straight" America, Wyatt and Billy set out through the Southwest, headed for the Mardi Gras in New Orleans. En route, they encounter the hostility of hate-filled denizens of small towns in the rural South, and in the end are murdered by a pair of gun-toting "rednecks." Although critics scoffed at the film's fatuous attempts to turn Wyatt and Billy into Christ figures, *Easy Rider* won the prize at the 1969 Cannes Film Festival for best picture by a new director, and Hopper was credited with introducing into the commercial American cinema the innovative camerawork and editing techniques of French *nouvelle vague* directors like Jean-Luc Godard and Alain Resnais.

Made for a scant $370,000, *Easy Rider* grossed more than $40 million at the box office, leading studio executives to believe that Hopper's biker saga portended a new direction in the American cinema, toward relatively inexpensive, independently produced films that could profitably address themselves to a vast new audience, the counterculture that emerged during the Vietnam war. In the aftermath of *Easy Rider*, Hopper himself was in thrall to the cant of the "New Hollywood." "We're a new kind of human being," he declared, as quoted in *Life* (June 19, 1970). "We're taking on more freedom and more risk. In a spiritual way we may be the most creative generation in the last nineteen centuries. I think we're heroes. I want to make movies about us."

With an $850,000 budget furnished by a major studio, Hopper in 1970 gathered a large cast and crew and headed for Chinchero, a remote Indian village in central Peru, to make *The Last Movie*. As Ron Rosenbaum observed, it was intended by Hopper to be "a movie that would pierce the veils of deceit that shrouded the consciousness of ordinary moviegoers and show them the emptiness of the illusions [of] ordinary movies. . . . " *The Last Movie* deals with the moral corruption of a "primitive" Indian community by an American company that films a violent, clichéd western in the community. When the crew in the film decamps, one of the stunt men, Kansas (played by Hopper), stays on. In the movie within the movie, Kansas' character had been "killed," so that the villagers now view him as a Lazarus, miraculously raised from the dead. Confusing cinematic artifice with reality, they reenact the spectacle they have witnessed in the form of a shamanist ritual, using makeshift bamboo "lights" and "cameras." Unlike professional cinema violence, theirs is real, and their pageant ends with the actual crucifixion of Kansas. Whatever narrative tension might have inhered in the unfolding of Kansas' fate was purposely undermined by Hopper, whose heavy handed use of antidramatic devices and pseudo-Pirandellian effects constantly reminded viewers that this movie about a movie was itself just a movie.

Hopper's project had begun to go sour almost as soon as he arrived in Peru, with stories being widely reported in the press about contretemps with right-wing Peruvian authorities, violence on the set, orgies, and what one writer called bouts of "drug-induced pandemonium." In addition, when Hopper returned to Taos, New Mexico, where his home had become a kind of Mecca for hippies, it took him almost a year to edit the film, a process that was not aided by Hopper's use of psychedelics to invoke his muse. Appalled by the nonlinearity of the film, studio executives ordered him to recut it, but he refused. Although *The Last Movie* (1971) won a Grand Prize for the best film at the Venice Film Festival, it opened domestically to generally dismal notices. After a brief run in New York and Los Angeles, it was hastily withdrawn from commercial release and shelved by Universal executives, and Hollywood blackballed him once again.

His credibility as a bankable filmmaker squandered, Hopper spent the next decade in a self-destructive downward spiral. He worked occasionally as an actor, most notably as the costar (with Bruno Ganz) of *The American Friend* (1976), a critically acclaimed film by the German director Wim Wenders, and as the babbling, drug-crazed journalist in *Apocalypse Now* (1979), Francis Ford Coppola's Vietnam war epic. But his major status was as premier citizen of Taos, a haven for remnants of the counterculture, where he made his home in the old Mabel Dodge Luhan house, as D. H. Lawrence once had done.

By the early 1980s Hopper was snorting cocaine totaling half an ounce every few days and consuming daily almost a gallon of rum. In 1983 he succumbed to the delusion that one of his underworld drug associates had put out a contract on his life. Fleeing Taos, he went to Los Angeles, where he began to mainline, shooting cocaine directly into his bloodstream. It was when he traveled to Mexico to appear in a film called *Jungle Fever* that Hopper was seized by what Rosenbaum termed "uncontrollable visual and aural hallucinations." Imagining that he was hearing the agonized cries of people being tortured and then cremated in his hotel, Hopper ran naked into the jungle, making his way to the town of Cuernavaca. When the police tried to get him dressed, he pleaded, "No, kill me like this."

After spending a few months in a southern California detoxification clinic for celebrities, Hopper stopped drinking alcohol but continued to use cocaine. He was well enough to portray an alcoholic father in Francis Ford Coppola's *Rumble Fish* (1983) and, when the original director was fired, to complete the direction of *Out of the Blue* (1983), about a teenaged "punk" girl who kills her abusive father (played by Hopper) and mother. By 1984 Hopper had begun again to hear "voices" and to hallucinate about torture and murder. Judged an incompetent, he was committed to the psychiatric ward of Cedars-Sinai Hospital in Los Angeles. After his release was secured by Bert Schneider (who had helped to finance *Easy Rider*), he joined Alcoholics Anonymous. As he has said, he "started working right away. And that was that."

Following parts in several minor films, Hopper made his big comeback with his roles in 1986 as an alcohol-ravaged ex-basketball star in *Hoosiers*, a portrayal that brought him an Oscar nomination for best supporting actor, and as Frank Booth in *Blue Velvet*. One of the reasons *Blue Velvet* has become the most controversial film of the 1980s is Hopper's frighteningly intense portrayal of Booth, a drug-warped, obscenity-shrieking dope dealer. According to *Blue Velvet*'s director, David Lynch, Hopper demanded that he be cast as Booth because, as he told Lynch, "I *am* Frank."

In 1987 Hopper again delivered well-received performances as a psycho drug dealer, in the film *River's Edge*, and as a drunken, irresponsible father, in the movie *The Pickup Artist*. He also directed his first feature film in sixteen years, *Colors*, starring Robert Duvall and Sean Penn. Earlier in the year, an exhibition of Hopper's photographs was mounted at the Tony Shafrazi Gallery in lower Manhattan. Some of Hopper's arresting photographs are of art world luminaries like Jasper Johns and Andy Warhol; some document civil rights marches in which Hopper took part; and some are urban street shots of flaking posters on sun-baked walls and the like, reflecting his affinity for Abstract Expressionist painting. The best of the photographs make up the book *Out of the Sixties* (Twelve-Trees Press, 1987), with text by his friend Michael McClure, the poet. According to press reports in July 1987, Hopper and a ghostwriter had begun writing his autobiography and negotiations for its publication were in progress with Dolphin/Doubleday.

From his first marriage, Hopper has a daughter, Marin. In 1971 he was briefly married to the singer/actress Michelle Phillips. By his third marriage (which also ended in divorce), to the actress Daria Halprin, he has a second daughter, Ruthana, born in 1973. Having left Taos behind, Hopper now lives outside of Los Angeles, in the beach town of Venice. He remains unapologetic about his years as a doper and drinker. "Some great moments came out of LSD," he told an interviewer for *Newsday* (October 12, 1986), "not just nightmares. . . . It's amazing I'm alive. . . . My life is wonderful." A chain smoker who now drinks copious amounts of coffee instead of rum, Hopper works constantly, taking vacations only rarely and claiming to have "no personal life at all."

References: Chicago Tribune XIII p8+ S 14 '86 por; N Y Times II p11 Jl 20 '69 por, II p11 My 10 '70 por, II p13 O 18 '70 por, II p13 Ja 7 '73, II p15 Ap 3 '83 por, C1+ Je 18 '87 pors; New Yorker 47:152+ O 9 '71; Newsday II p7 N 13 '83 pors; People 20:125+ Ja 30 '84 pors; Time 128:90 N 17 '86 pors

Houston, James A(rchibald)

June 12, 1921– Author; illustrator; designer; filmmaker. Address: 24 Main St., Stonington, Conn. 06378

Sometimes called "the neglected hero" of Canadian culture, James A. Houston has based a flourishing career as an illustrator, author, filmmaker, and glass designer on his firsthand experiences among the Inuit Eskimos of Canada's far northern territories. Houston combined his early artistic training with fourteen years that he spent living out the traditional Canadian romance with the tundra, traveling at first to the remote shores of the upper Hudson Bay on a painting expedition, and staying on to serve his own apprenticeship to the Eskimo way of life. He is credited with having introduced printmaking as a marketable skill to talented Eskimo artists during his years in the Arctic and with having become the first serious purveyor of Inuit carvings to the international art world.

Returning to "civilization" in 1962, Houston left his governmental post as the first federal civil administrator of West Baffin Island to begin an illustrious second career as a designer and consultant to Steuben Glass in New York, where he bases his intriguing crystal, metal, and Plexiglas designs on Arctic themes. Never remote from the heartbeat of Eskimo life, Houston has drawn upon his ongoing experiences with the native peoples of Canada for

more than a dozen illustrated books for children, four adult novels, a number of award-winning documentary films, and a spate of international book awards.

James Archibald Houston was born on June 12, 1921, in Toronto, Canada, the son of James Donald Houston, a clothing importer for a British yard goods company, and Gladys Maud (Barbour) Houston. Both his father and his grandfather had spent a considerable amount of time among the Indians of Canada's Pacific Northwest, where his father took advantage of his business travels to absorb as much as possible of the indigenous culture of the region. He often brought back beaded moosehide moccasins and other Indian artifacts for Jim and his sister, Barbara, amusing them with stories of his travels and regaling them with sketches he made of aboriginal Canadians and their villages.

James Houston spent his summers with Barbara and his parents at the family's cottage on Lake Simcoe, near two Indian reservations, and many of his books depict the close relationship he shared there with his sister, as well as his friendship with an aging Ojibwa Indian named Nels, who taught him Indian folkways and legends. From Nels he learned such invaluable lore as how to catch whitefish the Indian way and how to whistle to a groundhog and have him whistle right back. He later reflected that it seemed to him at the time that such experiences were the only education he could ever want. "For me the Ojibwa became a strong link with the past," he has said, in paying tribute to their influence. "They helped me shape my future."

Although he once quipped that he had been drawing madly since he was old enough to stand upright, Houston also credits his mother's artistic abilities with his decision to pursue art and writing as his career. At the age of eight, as he once told a group of Toronto grammar school students, he was recuperating from scarlet fever when his mother gave him a blank book and urged him to create his own story. At nine, he was presented with a short story by his aunt, who was president of the Canadian Authors' Association at the time, and asked by her to illustrate it in ink. "I did so with delight, and a little later I received a real check from a children's magazine for three dollars," he wrote later in an autobiographical sketch that was published in *The Fourth Book of Junior Authors and Illustrators*. "I decided at that moment that I would make my living at art."

At the age of twelve, Houston was enrolled as a student at the Toronto Art Gallery (now the Art Gallery of Ontario), where he enjoyed the company of like-minded friends, laughing, painting, and "happily hitting each other over the heads with rulers." Then Dr. Arthur Lismer, a distinguished art teacher and a member of Canada's Group of Seven, returned from a trip to the Congo to play African music in the halls of the gallery one memorable morning. "He danced among us, his face covered with a great carved mask," Houston recalls. "It shook me to the core, and I was hooked forever on the art and lives of primitive peoples. I wanted to go to all the farthest corners of the earth."

Following his high school graduation in 1939 from the John Wanless School in Toronto, Houston attended the Ontario College of Art for a year, majoring in life drawing and working as a syndicated newspaper cartoonist before his studies were disrupted by Canada's entry into World War II. In 1940 he enlisted in the Toronto Scottish Regiment of the Canadian Army, serving in both the North Atlantic and the Pacific and rising to the rank of warrant officer.

Stationed during part of his tour of duty near the villages of the Northwest Coast Indians in British Columbia, Houston traveled the coastline from Vancouver Island to Alaska, observing the methods and the milieu of the native carvers of the region. Although that tantalizing glimpse at native sculpture rekindled his childhood interest in primitive art, he had to wait several more years before he could return to pursue it in earnest. After the war, Houston went to Paris in 1947 to complete his studies in life drawing at the École Grande Chaumière.

In the following autumn Houston returned to Canada in search of "suitable people to draw." In 1948, having wearied of city life and the limitations of his small commercial art business in Grand'Mère, Quebec, he packed up his sketchbooks and traveled leisurely through Cree, Nascopi, and Chippewa Indian country, eventually arriving by train at the end of the line: an outpost called Moose Factory, where he spent a month sketching Swampy Cree Indians near James Bay. As Houston's brief vacation from the workaday world passed without offering him much hope of getting further north, his ambition to reach the eerie Arctic zones about which pilots had told him during World War II seemed impossible to realize.

On the day that he was scheduled to leave Moose Factory to return home, Houston encountered a bush pilot who was preparing to fly a regional doctor northward to treat an Eskimo child who had been attacked by a dog. Houston went along on the flight to Inukjuak, a remote Eskimo community on the eastern coast of Hudson Bay. Looking around him at what he later described as "these short, vital, oriental-looking people" whom he hoped to draw and paint, Houston made a sudden decision that was to alter the course of his life radically. "The pilot was going to leave immediately to fly the child back south," Sally B. Walker executive vice-president of Steuben Glass, has recounted. "Houston decided not to go with him. He stayed with only his sleeping bag, his sketch pad, and a can of peaches."

The Inuit Eskimos, fortunately, took Houston in, offering him food and shelter, and a painting and drawing expedition that he had originally estimated to last "a few weeks" somehow escalated into an unforgettable fourteen years. Here, at what Houston has described as "a gateway to the Eskimo world," he lived at first among an isolated, semi-nomadic tribe who were housed in snow igloos in the winter and in tents in the summer, depending for their livelihood on hunts made in whaleskin boats and sealskin kayaks. "Their remoteness in Canada had protected them from the onslaught of western civilization," Houston once wrote in an autobiographical sketch. "I became a devoted friend, as they taught me how to survive in their harsh climate."

Unable to speak their language, Houston communicated with his hosts at first by sketching them, pausing frequently as they took the pencil from his hand and drew pictures of themselves. He quickly realized the extent of their artistic ability, as he made sketches prized among the Eskimos as decorations. One day, in return for a drawing he had made of a villager and his wife, Houston was given a small sculpture of a caribou, carved from the soft soapstone exposed by Arctic ebb tides. Like other devotees of primitive art, Houston had seen ancient Eskimo carvings among museum artifacts, but hardly imagined that the craft had survived to the present day. Late in 1948 Houston headed south to Montreal to deliver a number of small ivory, bone, and soapstone sculptures to the Canadian Handicraft Guild.

"Up to then Eskimo carvings had been regarded mainly as curios that were occasionally made for interested visitors; they were not seriously considered in artistic terms," reads an entry in the 1973 supplement to the Oxford Companion to Canadian History and Literature. "The movement Houston launched changed all this. . . . " Throughout the 1950s the government set up subsidized workshops and encouraged the development of Eskimo sculpture as a cottage industry. Following his marriage, in 1949, to Alma Georgina Bardon, Houston returned with his wife to the Hudson Bay region, where from 1950 to 1952, he served as crafts officer for the Canadian Handicraft Guild, a nonprofit organization dedicated to fostering native art. During that period he brought back to Montreal a group of carvings that became the basis of the guild's permanent collection of Eskimo art. Fortunately, Houston's periodic trips to Montreal helped Inuit sculptors to develop a market for their work that made them less dependent on hunting and the declining fur industry, and provided them with a source of income that had nothing to do with traplines.

Moving ever northward in search of carvings, the Houstons had settled by 1951 in Cape Dorset, home of the Sikusalingmiut. After a stint as northern service officer for the Canadian government from 1952 to 1955, Houston became the first federal civil administrator of West Baffin Island in 1955. Raising their two sons as Inuit, the couple maintained contact with civilization through an annual supply ship that delivered official correspondence from Ottawa one year and carried back return mail the next. Houston toured his 65,000-square-mile domain by dog sled, visiting thirteen farflung camps inhabited by 343 Eskimos. The gentle kaluna (white man) whom the Eskimos called Saomik—the left-handed one, a tribute to artistic talent in Eskimo estimation—ate raw seal meat, learned to build an igloo in less than thirty minutes,

and fell through the sea ice on five harrowing occasions. During those expeditions, Houston swapped stories with hunters and carvers who told him the Eskimo legends that were to inspire his writing career a decade later.

As the demand for Eskimo sculpture increased, Houston found himself faced with a cross-cultural conundrum. Because ancient Inuit custom decreed that individual sculptors attempt a particular design only once, any type of reproduction in quantity was virtually impossible. Yet one afternoon in 1957, the carver Oshaweetuk picked up a pack of Houston's cigarettes, speculating that it must be tiresome to paint the same picture on every package. In an attempt to demonstrate the printing process by inking one of Oshaweetuk's meticulously incised walrus tusks, Houston suddenly realized that the Eskimos could be taught to make prints from their own original stone cuts. Using his accumulated leave time to travel to Japan, Houston studied for four months with the master printmaker Unichi Hiratsuka during the winter of 1958–59.

When Houston returned to Cape Dorset, a revolution in folk art was in progress. Using their own materials and tools, the Eskimos began to produce exquisite prints that eventually earned them an international reputation and gave them a profitable living. In 1959 the Inuit artists held their first exhibit and formed a cooperative that mounted increasingly successful exhibitions each year. Although he was soon to leave the Arctic, the legacy that Houston had created in both artistic and diplomatic terms was a rich one. "I think Saomik was the first man to help Eskimos," wrote the Inuit artist Pitseolak in Pitseolak: Pictures Out of My Life (1971). "Ever since he came, the Eskimo people have been able to find work. Here in Cape Dorset they call him 'The Man.'"

By 1962 James Houston had begun to feel that it was time for the Eskimos to become more autonomous—and for his sons to take advantage of educational opportunities in the "civilized" south. Having met Arthur Houghton Jr., the president of both Steuben Glass Company and the Metropolitan Museum of Art, in the Arctic that year, he left Cape Dorset to accept a position as associate director of design at Steuben Glass in New York. Not surprisingly, many of his glass designs feature an Arctic or wildlife theme, such as that of a leaping crystal trout, a blown- and cut-crystal snipe bowl, or "Aurora Borealis," a seventy-foot creation of polished prismatic spears that is now on permanent display in Calgary's Glenbow Museum.

Although he enjoyed executing his designs in challenging new media, Houston often found himself longing for the simplicity and solitude of life in the far north. Luckily for a generation of Canadian children previously exposed to little of Canada's native culture, Houston's move to Manhattan in 1962 occasioned another fortuitous meeting, with Margaret K. McElderry, then children's book editor at the publishing house of Harcourt, Brace. Before going in to his Manhattan office, Houston began writing and drawing illustrations for two hours each morning. The legends that he had heard in the Inuit igloos on long Arctic nights became the inspiration for fourteen books for children and four novels for adults, as well as four documentary films that he has produced and directed.

His first book, *Tikta'Liktak*, won the Canadian Library Association's award for the best English-language book of 1965, and Houston has gone on to win other medals and awards from the Canadian Library Association and the Canadian Authors Association. He adapted his adult novel *The White Dawn* (1971), a Book-of-the-Month Club main selection, into the screenplay for a movie released by Paramount Pictures in 1976, and has shared in twenty-six international film awards for his work as producer, director, and technical adviser for a number of documentary films.

Houston's "spare narratives," as Sheila Egoff termed his tales in *The Republic of Childhood: A Critical Guide to Canadian Children's Literature*, are frequently described as terse, stirring, vivid, and eloquent. According to her, "James Houston has not only been the most prolific spokesman for the Eskimo in children's literature, but the most artistic writer." His stories of resourcefulness and survival draw on the oral tradition to paint a non-sentimental picture of native Canadian life on its own terms, unshaded by the perceptions of more advanced cultures.

The success of *White Dawn* both as a novel and as a film was partly responsible for Houston's decision to become a consultative director of Steuben Glass in 1971, when he moved to a Rhode Island farmhouse with his second wife. Once during his nine year tenure in New York, Houston recalls that he opened the window to the familiar cry of a flock of Canada geese, flying in V-formation over East 69th Street, and moved by their call, declared, "I'm going back to Canada with them!" True to his word, the peripatetic artist journeys annually to the Canadian north and Alaska, and travels widely to give lectures about native Canadian art and culture.

"Jim" Houston, who has been described by Sally B. Walter of Steuben Glass as "a born raconteur," has black hair, hazel eyes, and a square face that resembles the countenance of "some rugged movie star." In 1967 he was divorced from his first wife and married Alice Watson, an author and editor. He has two sons, John and Sam, by his first marriage. The Houstons divide their time between a country house in Connecticut that was built long ago by a famous privateer and a writing retreat in British Columbia, where Jim Houston fishes, observes wildlife, and rises at five o'clock each morning to write in longhand. The unassuming Houston was once characterized by an admiring fifth-grader as "old in age," yet "still young at heart."

During the spring of 1987 James Houston was honored by Steuben Glass with a retrospective exhibition of forty of his crystal and metal designs, on the twenty-fifth anniversary of his career as a glass designer. Houston holds an honorary Litt. D. de-

gree from Carleton University in Ottawa and is currently a consultant on both Indian and Eskimo art in the United States and Canada. Despite his many honors, Jim Houston remains "a very shy cultural hero," in the words of Tim Harper of the *Toronto Star* (November 24, 1985). "Houston has a cult following when he really should be a household name, but he has no complaints," Harper observed. Still extraordinarily active, Houston regards his varied accomplishments with characteristic reserve. "Whatever I'm doing at the time, I tend to think that's the thing," he told Harper.

References: Oxford Companion to Canadian History and Literature (1973 supplement); Who's Who in American Art (1986); Who's Who in the East, 1974–75

Hughes, Robert (Studley Forrest)

July 28, 1938– Australian writer; art critic.
Address: b. Time Inc., Time-Life Bldg.,
Rockefeller Center, New York City, N.Y. 10020;
h. 143 Prince St., New York City, N.Y. 10012

"I've always thought of myself as a writer one of whose subjects was art," Robert Hughes said in a recent press interview. As the author of three books on art, of essays on art for magazines, particularly *Time*, of which he has been art critic since 1970, and of some thirty television documentaries on art, many of which he has also narrated, he was known to his readers and TV viewers as a writer whose only subject was art—until the appearance in 1987 of *The Fatal Shore*, his best-selling account of the settlement of his native Australia through a system of convict transportation. The title of Hughes's history of modern art, *The Shock of the New* (1980), which the art critic John Canaday pronounced "easily the best book to date on twentieth-century art," seems appropriate also to his social history of Great Britain's unprecedented, enforced colonization of an uncharted land of unique wildlife and strange human inhabitants. Applicable as well to his work as a whole is his explanation that he wrote *The Fatal Shore* for a general audience, retaining his "natural voice" while satisfying the demand of the academics for scholarly soundness. His natural voice, which has been variously heard as "arresting," "zestful," "elegant," "irreverent," "gritty," and "virile," has given him, whatever his medium, something of "the great virtue" that he once ascribed to TV, "the power to communicate enthusiasm."

A descendant of "Irish bogtrotters," to use his term, who had immigrated to Britain's penal colony in the first half of the nineteenth century, Robert Studley Forrest Hughes was born in Sydney, Australia, on July 28, 1938, to Geoffrey Eyre and Margaret Sealey (Vidal) Hughes. At a time, during the 1830s, when almost all English-speaking Australians were either prisoners or jailers, his first Australian ancestor held the post of superintendent of convicts. His grandfather, who became the first Lord Mayor of Sydney, acquired a sizable fortune, which he gave to a Roman Catholic sisterhood. "My father was a pilot in World War I," Hughes told Paul Richard of the *Washington Post* (January 10, 1981), "The first painting I can remember showed him in a biplane dueling with von Richthofen."

His strict and authoritarian Jesuit teachers at Hughes's school very likely prepared him well for the later detailed exploration of representations of the Christian doctrines of reward and punishment that he needed to write *Heaven and Hell in Western Art*. He recalled, in fact, in that book an admonitory sermon of one of his Jesuit teachers about a "demon with a great clawed foot" that would kick a transgressing boy for all eternity. Early in life he became fascinated by modern art, as he related in his introduction to *The Shock of the New* when he reflected on the motivation for that work: "Pleasure is the root of all critical appreciation of art, and there is nothing like a long, steady project to make one discover (and with luck, convey) what it was in the siren voices of our century that caught me as a boy—when I first read Roger Shattuck's translation of Apollinaire, hidden from the Jesuits in the wrapper of a Latin grammar—and has never let me go."

On his graduation in 1956 from St. Ignatius College in Riverview, Sydney, Hughes entered Sydney University, whose climate proved to be considerably less repressive. "As soon as I got to university," he recalled in the *Washington Post* interview, "—Germaine Greer was a classmate—I discovered girls and booze and atheists, and failed, failed utterly." He had intended to become an architect, but left the university before completing his training. While making architectural drafts and

renditions of buildings, he had painted abstract pictures—"Antipodean de Koonings," as he has called them—and launched his career in journalism by drawing political cartoons for local newspapers. One day in 1958 he stepped in to cover an art show for a newspaper that had just fired its regular critic. Afterward he contributed articles on art for several years to the *Nation* and the *Observer* in Sydney. In 1961 he wrote the catalogue for the exhibition "Recent Australian Painting" at the Whitechapel Art Gallery in London.

As reported in *Time* (June 17, 1985), Hughes financed his apprenticeship in art criticism through the sale of his own pictures. But after moving to Port'Ercole, Italy, in 1964, he gave up painting as a lifework. "Having been to Arezzo to see the Piero della Francesca frescoes of the *Legend of the True Cross*," he explained, "I realized that I could never in conscience give my own work a decent review." The basis for his reputation as an art critic meanwhile grew firmer with the publication of his book *The Art of Australia: A Critical Survey* (Penguin, Australia, 1966) and his catalogue "The New Generation: 1966" for the Whitechapel Art Gallery.

Although he wrote about Australian art, Hughes's move to Europe represented a dissatisfaction with his own country and its culture. "I hoped—as all juvenile expatriates do, I suppose—to leave it all behind," he admitted to Wendy Smith, who interviewed him for *Publishers Weekly* (December 12, 1986). "There was an initial Oedipal revulsion in my case from all things Australian." For the time being, he wanted a non-Australian subject. He has said that he was particularly attracted to Italian painting "from the birth of Masaccio to the death of the younger Tiepolo." But following his wide-ranging interests in art, during the mid-1960s he traveled extensively to study medieval and Renaissance painting, architecture, and sculpture not only in Italy, but in other European countries.

The intensity and scope of Hughes's research assured the scholarly integrity of *Heaven and Hell in Western Art* (Stein & Day, 1968), in which he examined the images in Western paintings, drawings, and sculptures that depicted the bliss awarded to righteous souls and the forms of torture appropriate to punishment of sinners in satisfaction of Christian moral principles. He commented interpretatively on an array of curious symbols and emblems, pointed out how and why recurrent pictorial motifs were transformed in the imagination of artists over hundreds of years, and traced the evolution of some of them, such as those relating to the paradisical garden and the devil, from their pre-Christian origins to their somewhat recent nonreligious appearances. His hundreds of illustrations include the work of renowned painters like Giotto, Bosch, Breughel, and Goya along with that of the unknown artists of mosaics, church carvings and other sculptural pieces, illuminated manuscripts, and woodcuts. Hughes also quoted abundantly from the Scriptures and classical and medieval poetry to throw some light on sources of themes or call attention to their parallel literary treatment.

Fully appreciative of the difference between medieval and modern sensibilities, Hughes knows how to make his subject absorbing to readers of a secular age whose art, as he noted, "includes no significant paintings on eschatological themes." One of the book's less enthusiastic reviewers, for the London Times Literary Supplement (January 2, 1969), found the quality of the color plates unsatisfactory and questioned the accuracy of the location of some of the illustrative material. He judged Hughes's work to be "highly entertaining but disposable art journalism" and asked, "For whom is this book intended?" As if in reply to that question, M. R. Newland described it in the New York Times Book Review (December 8, 1968) as "a rare sort of book that combines an erudite discussion of its scholarly themes with superb reproductions of great art and eye-opening excursions into exotic topics."

Heaven and Hell in Western Art helped to bring Hughes to the attention of the editors at Time, for which he then, in 1970, began to write about art. By that time he had added to his credentials as an art critic through free-lance work, mainly in England, where he had moved in 1966. He contributed dozens of reviews to the London Observer and Sunday Times and, beginning in 1965, wrote many visual arts programs for the BBC-TV. For the Australian Broadcasting Commission he made a ten-part series on Australian art, based on his book The Art of Australia, which he filmed in Australia in the mid-1970s. Later in the 1970s he made lengthy TV documentaries for the BBC on the Flemish painter Rubens, the Italian painter Caravaggio, and the Italian sculptor, architect, and painter Bernini.

Television viewers in the United States were introduced to Hughes in June 1978 when he appeared as cohost with Harold Hayes, former editor of Esquire, on the ill-starred premiere of ABC-TV's magazine series 20/20. But he more than overcame that setback with his eight-part TV series on modern art, The Shock of the New, produced by the BBC, Time-Life Films, and the German artfilm company Reiner Moritz Productions. Hughes borrowed his subtitle, A Personal View, from that of Kenneth Clark's 1969 BBC-TV series on the cultural heritage of the Western world, Civilisation. After being shown in Great Britain, The Shock of the New was seen in the United States on public television in 1981, beginning in January. Hughes's companion volume, also titled The Shock of the New (BBC, 1980; Knopf, 1981), is an outgrowth of the TV series, but has a text five times longer than his script.

Treating modern art as a confined historical period, recognized by a style of its own, The Shock of the New more or less carries on from where Civilisation ended, with "the blossoming of a sense of modernity," as Hughes phrased it, in the last quarter of the nineteenth century. His survey of the developments over the next 100 years in painting and architecture—and to a lesser extent in sculpture and photography—has a thematic, rather than a merely chronological, organization that reveals the interaction between art and society. In his opening program, or chapter, Hughes showed how western Europe's industrialization, symbolized by the Eiffel Tower, generated optimism and how the belief in the possibilities for reform and progress was linked to the formal explorations of Cubism and Futurism.

Other themes that Hughes considered in The Shock of New included the disillusionment that pervaded Europe after World War I and the response of art to dictatorship; the landscapes of pleasure created by the Fauves and Impressionists; the utopian architecture of Le Corbusier and others; the quest for freedom of the Surrealists and Abstract Expressionists; images of emotional extremes, of terror and exaltation, in Vincent van Gogh, Edvard Munch, the German Expressionists, and American Abstract Expressionists; the Pop artists of America; and the terminal condition of the avant-garde in the 1970s. As Hughes noted in the introduction to his book, his "narrative frame" did not accommodate several important artists, including Henry Moore.

"I think of this job as the best possible periscope through which to view modern Western art," Hughes once said of his post as art critic and senior writer for Time. Perhaps Christopher Lehmann-Haupt had that kind of advantage in mind when he tried to account in the New York Times (February 9, 1981) for the excellence of The Shock of the New: "[Hughes] simply knows everything there is to know about modern art and has it all available for immediate recall. This is not a far-fetched assumption, considering the refreshingly independent views that he presents of such cliché-encrusted figures as Picasso [and the many other] artists of whom we gain a new perspective."

Reviewing The Shock of the New in the New Republic (March 14, 1981), the art critic for Newsweek, Mark Stevens, found, "The great strength of the book lies in its concise portraits—usually about a page and a half—of individual artists. They are wonderfully to the point. Hughes has a way of capturing, in a phrase, not simply the look but the spirit of an artist's work." Both Lehmann-Haupt and Stevens had qualifications, as did several others who praised The Shock of the New in general. Some of the debate focused on Hughes's stern appraisal of modern architecture, in his discussions of which one critic thought him "positively exhilarating."

During the filming of The Shock of the New, Hughes traveled a quarter of a million miles, taking the viewer with him to see the buildings of the architects and the places associated with the painters whose work he was talking about. His presence on the scene helped to set the brisk pace of presentation and generate a sense of excitement. Soon after the series began, he was described in the New Yorker (January 26, 1981) as "an engagingly combustible critic, who throws off ideas and opinions like a bonfire throwing off sparks." Other observers called attention to the assuredness of his scorn for cant and sacred cows. The printed page favored his style and wit as much as the small screen: the British poet and art critic Edward Lucie-Smith called *The Shock of the New* a "swashbuckling book."

After the publication of *The Shock of the New*, Hughes continued to write about some of the conditions he deplored in his closing chapter: "the small ambitions of art" and "the appalling commercialization of the art world." In "On Art and Money" in the *New York Review of Books* (December 6, 1984) and "Careerism and Hype Amidst the Image Haze" in *Time* (June 17, 1985), he looked at the effect that art turned into "bullion," or a commodity to be valued as an investment, has had on the wares now being produced for an unprecedented sellers' market. Under the name Junius Secundus he also wrote for the *New York Review of Books* (March 19, 1984) "The SoHoiad: or, The Masque of Art—A Satire in Heroic Couplets Drawn from Life," an Alexander Popean devastation of the art gallery scene in Manhattan's SoHo district.

To work on *The Shock of the New*, Hughes took three years off from a more time-consuming project in which he became interested in 1974, when he was filming his TV series on the art of Australia. Curious about the ruins of the penitentiary he saw at Port Arthur on Tasmania, he realized that like most Australians he knew little about the convict settlers of his own country. Even though the investigations of historians of the past twenty or more years have increased Australians' awareness of their felon ancestry, studies have neglected certain human aspects of the convict system. As Australians prepared to celebrate their bicentennial, in 1988, Hughes's 700-page *The Fatal Shore* (Collins; Knopf, 1987) uncovered their colonial history perhaps more fully than some of them would have preferred.

The title *The Fatal Shore*, taken from a convict ballad, or lament, of the 1820s, reflects Hughes's desire to tell whatever he could of the story of the early settlers in their own words. "I have tried, as far as possible," he wrote in his introduction, "to see the System from below, through convicts' testimony—in letters, depositions, petitions, and memoirs—about their own experiences. Much of this material is hitherto unpublished. A total of 736 English convicts arrived on January 26, 1788, along with crews and guards, aboard the First Fleet's flotilla of eleven ships at a harbor, later to be called Sydney Harbor, on the eastern coast of an unexplored continent eventually known as Australia. They were the first white Australians, the first of some 160,000 convicts, many of whom were Irish, transported over an eighty-year period. The 1788 arrival, however, is not the beginning of Hughes's narrative, which first takes into account the horrifying economic and social conditions of Hogarthian England that swelled the ranks of the "criminal class" to the extent that the British government resorted to establishing prisons outside the country. When newly independent America ceased to be a dumping ground, Australia became "a jail of infinite space" or, as Hughes's book makes clear, a blueprint in the South Pacific for twentieth-century gulags and concentration camps.

"Parts of this book . . . are not for the squeamish," Geoffrey Wheatcroft cautioned readers of his review of *The Fatal Shore* in the *New Republic* (February 9, 1987). Details of the sadistic punishments inflicted on inmates in isolated prisons like Norfolk Island and Macquarie Harbor, prisons within the great prison, and of the perhaps even more gruesome atrocities that the Aborigines suffered at the hands of English-speaking Australians—all make up some of the most vivid, if necessarily lurid, descriptions in Hughes's story. But he does not neglect the wonders of Australia, the strange land and its shores, extraordinary mammals, birds, and plants. Records of agony are balanced by evidence of heroism, endurance, and kindness. From an unpromising beginning a distinctive national culture emerged, and the descendants of survivors of the system, as Hughes notes, "turned out to form one of the most law-abiding societies in the world," thus challenging the Georgian notion of criminality as a genetic disease.

Speculating on how his countrymen would receive his book, Hughes told Wendy Smith of *Publishers Weekly*, "Australians, particularly academics, can be quite snarky about people they regard as nonprofessionals poaching on their territory. I think there will be a certain amount of that, but a lot of Australians will want to read it." In the United States, where it was a Book-of-the-Month Club selection, it quickly became a best seller. Impressed by the factual rewards of Hughes's ten years of research, book critics also credited much of the fascination of *The Fatal Shore* to his style. "It is intelligent, colorful, urbane, and trenchant," William Boyd observed in a more-or-less representative review in the *Atlantic* (January 1987). " . . . The exact simile, the correct ironic aside, the nice sense of the absurdly humorous. . . . It is rare to read a work of historical scholarship laden with such textual pleasures."

In an effort to account for the infatuation of Americans with Australia, Hughes told Steven D. Stark in an interview for the *New York Times* (March 25, 1987): "The current American interest in Australia is due to a number of factors, but a lot of it is based on illusion. Take the idea that Australia is a frontier society. In fact, it's the most highly urbanized society in the world. Australia has sold itself as this nostalgic picture of a lost frontier, and Americans, yearning after their lost primal innocence, have bought it."

Robert Hughes has a son, Danton, by his first marriage, which ended in 1981. Later in that year he married Victoria Whistler. Meeting Hughes in January 1981 at a party in his honor at the Museum of Modern Art, a writer for the *New Yorker's* "Talk of the Town" saw him as "a solidly built Australian in his early forties with unruly blond hair, a round, ruddy face, penetrating green eyes, and a breezy manner." Among Hughes's tributes is an honorary doctorate of fine arts awarded by the School of Visual Arts in New York in 1982. According to Wendy Smith, paintings and art objects bedeck the walls and shelves of the living room of Hughes's apartment in SoHo, but "A Letter from the Publisher" in *Time* (June 17, 1985) quoted Hughes's reason for not being a serious buyer of art: "I don't think that critics should collect because then they tend to find themselves in a net of obligations to artists and dealers that may be to the detriment of their own work. Besides, it is very restful, after a hard day in museums, to come home and look at a nice blank wall."

References: Dial 2:17+ Ja '81 por; N Y Times Bk R p1+ Ja 25 '87 por; New Yorker 56:25+ Ja 26 '81; Pub W 230:38+ D 12 '86 por; Washington Post C p1+ Ja 10 '81 por, C p1+ F 8 '87 por; Contemporary Authors vol 112 (1985); Who's Who, 1986–87

Hunter-Gault, Charlayne

Feb. 27, 1942– Broadcast journalist. Address: b. The MacNeil/Lehrer NewsHour, 356 W. 58th St., New York City, N. Y. 10019

"What I have to explain to people about me," Charlayne Hunter-Gault said in a recent interview, "is that I have had a very unusual life." Indeed from the time she decided, at the age of twelve, that she wanted to be a journalist, Miss Hunter-Gault has pursued her goal with a singlemindedness and determination worthy of her childhood hero—the feisty comic-strip newswoman Brenda Starr. As the first black woman admitted to the University of Georgia, she braved taunts, vandalism, and angry mobs before earning her diploma in 1963. During a nine-year stint with the *New York Times*, from 1968 to 1977, she ran the paper's Harlem bureau and established herself as one of the most knowledgeable, hard-working, and sensitive reporters in the city. Since becoming a regular correspondent for PBS's *McNeil/Lehrer Report* (now the *McNeil/Lehrer NewsHour*) in 1978, Miss Hunter-Gault has garnered many awards for her perceptive coverage of a wide range of stories, ranging from the American invasion of Grenada to the devastating effects of apartheid on both black and white South Africans.

Charlayne Hunter-Gault was born Charlayne Hunter on February 27, 1942, in Due West, South Carolina, the oldest of the three children of Charles S. H. Hunter Jr., a Methodist chaplain in the United States Army, and his wife. In 1954 Charlayne moved with her family to Atlanta, Georgia, where her mother worked as a secretary in a real estate firm. Because her father was often posted to long tours of duty abroad, Charlayne and her two younger brothers were reared largely by their mother and a grandmother. An energetic, inquisitive woman whose formal education had ended with the third grade in grammar school, the grandmother read voraciously and traveled widely, often accompanied by her granddaughter. "She used to read three newspapers a day," Charlayne Hunter-Gault recalled, as quoted in an interview for the *Washington Journalism Review* (September 1985). "She was innately curious about the world. She was intrepid and strong. But she was also very gentle, and I think I owe a lot of my character to her."

When she was sixteen years old, Charlayne Hunter-Gault converted to Roman Catholicism, a decision that jolted her family of Protestant ministers. (One of her grandfathers was a flamboyant evangelist preacher.) She also began to prepare for a career in journalism and refused to reconsider when her guidance counselor at Henry McNeal Turner High School, which she attended from 1954 to 1959, advised her to enroll instead in the teacher-education program at Atlanta's Spelman College. An honor student, she was frequently bored and restless in class, but she found editing the student newspaper, the *Green Light*, "just exhilarating."

At the time of her high school graduation, the only college in Georgia with a school of journalism was the all-white University of Georgia. Determined to pursue her dream of becoming a reporter, Charlayne Hunter-Gault applied for admission to the school in 1959, two years after the Reverend Dr. Martin Luther King Jr. had organized the Southern

Christian Leadership Conference and a year before John Lewis and other young civil rights activists founded the Student Nonviolent Coordinating Committee. "It was just the spirit and the atmosphere of the times that you broke barriers," Miss Hunter-Gault told Claudia Dreifus, who interviewed her for *Dial* magazine (February 1987). "I did not set out with a global aim. There was something to be done—and it turned out to have monumental consequences, but it was my effort to secure for myself the type of education I needed."

Backed by a group of prominent Atlanta civil rights activists, including her family physician and Whitney M. Young Jr., who later became the head of the National Urban League, Charlayne Hunter-Gault and Hamilton Holmes, a high school friend, went to federal court to request an integration order. After two years of legal wrangling and bureaucratic delays, during which Miss Hunter-Gault attended Wayne State University in Detroit, Michigan, the court finally issued the integration order, and in January 1961 Holmes and Miss Hunter-Gault became the first black students to enter the University of Georgia in the school's 175-year history. Reflecting on the experience twenty-six years later in an article for *TV Guide* (January 17, 1987), Charlayne Hunter-Gault wrote, "At the time, I wasn't happy with the celebrity that followed because I felt that, but for the color of my skin, getting accepted to college was a fairly routine exercise."

Charlayne Hunter-Gault registered for her classes at the University of Georgia amid an atmosphere of tense expectation, but it was not until her second night on campus that the mood turned openly hostile, as groups of angry students gathered outside her dormitory, chanting, "Two, four, six, eight, we don't want to integrate" and "Nigger go home." When the demonstrators began to throw rocks, the police responded with tear gas in an effort to disperse the crowd. "I stayed in my room, unpacking my clothes, being calm, thinking to myself, 'So this is what it feels like to be in the middle of a riot,'" Miss Hunter-Gault told Claudia Dreifus. "As I was unpacking, a brick flew through the window splattering glass all over my new college clothes." In the wake of the riot, Holmes, who lived off campus, and Charlayne Hunter-Gault were suspended—allegedly for their own safety—but their lawyers intervened, and they were readmitted the next day.

Charlayne Hunter-Gault received her B.A. degree in journalism from the University of Georgia in 1963. Much of her education, however, had taken place out of the classroom. As an aspiring newspaperwoman, she observed and frequently questioned the many reporters who converged on the campus during her first weeks there. "I saw how different journalists worked and how I was treated as a story," she explained to Claudia Dreifus. "There were journalists who were sensitive and I wanted to be like them. On the other hand, there was one reporter who pulled a mob together so that he could film them—he'd missed the real riot." Because the editors of the University of Geor-

gia's campus newspaper "didn't know what to do" with her, Miss Hunter-Gault worked on weekends for the *Atlanta Inquirer*, a newspaper founded by college students from around the state (including Julian Bond, now a Georgia state legislator) who were frustrated by the failure of Atlanta's existing papers, both black and white, to cover adequately the burgeoning civil rights movement.

On her college graduation, Charlayne Hunter-Gault accepted a job as a secretary at the *New Yorker* magazine, with the understanding that she would eventually be considered for writing assignments. Promoted to staff writer a year later, she submitted "Talk of the Town" pieces and, occasionally, short stories for the next several years. She left the *New Yorker* in 1967, after winning a Russell Sage Fellowship to study social science at Washington University in St. Louis, Missouri. While there, she edited articles for *Trans-Action* magazine, which eventually sent her to Washington, D.C., to cover the Poor People's Campaign. A few months later she joined the staff of WRC-TV, the NBC affiliate in Washington, as an investigative reporter and anchorwoman of the local evening newscast.

In 1968 Miss Hunter-Gault signed on as a reporter with the metropolitan staff of the *New York Times*, where she specialized in covering the urban black community. A careful reporter with an eye for detail and a keen understanding of the aspirations and frustrations of inner-city blacks, she gave readers "a sense of being on the scene and explaining a complex story during a tense period" in the late 1960s and early 1970s, according to Arthur Gelb, then the *Times's* metropolitan desk editor, as quoted in the *Washington Journalism Review* article. In 1970 she shared with reporter Joseph Lelyveld the *New York Times* Publishers Award for an unusually vivid and disturbing account of the life and death of a twelve-year-old heroin addict. Miss Hunter-Gault subsequently won two additional Publishers Awards: in 1974, for "writing under deadline pressure" about Mayor Abraham Beame's nomination of Paul Gibson Jr. as New York City's first black deputy mayor; and in 1976, for "outstanding performance on a beat," particularly for her front-page stories on black crime and on the renaming of Harlem's Muslim Mosque for Malcolm X. She also received the National Urban Coalition Award for Distinguished Urban Reporting and, for a piece on teenage unemployment, the Lincoln University Unity Award.

Because of her longstanding involvement in the civil rights movement, Charlayne Hunter-Gault had an impressive number of contacts among black leaders on whom she could rely for information and insights that gave depth and authority to her dispatches. She also demonstrated a remarkable tenacity, which one colleague metaphorically described as a willingness "to kick down walls if she has to." In a characteristic display of courage and persistence, in the early 1970s she singlehandedly took on the *Times* editorial board, which insisted that *Times* reporters refer to Afro-Americans as

"Negroes" rather than "blacks"—the designation preferred by most civil rights activists. In a long, eloquently worded memorandum, Miss Hunter-Gault argued her case so forcefully that she managed to persuade the editors to change their policy. Except for several months in the early 1970s, when she took a leave of absence to serve as codirector of the Michele Clark Fellowship program for minority journalists at Columbia University, she remained with the *Times* for nine years.

When the producers of the *MacNeil/Lehrer Report*, PBS's weeknightly newscast, began casting around in 1978 for a third correspondent and "swing anchor" to fill in during the absences of Robert MacNeil or Jim Lehrer, Charlayne Hunter-Gault, who saw the job as a "chance to expand to a broader range of interests," auditioned for the position. After an on-the-air tryout, she was hired over eight other candidates because, according to executive producer Al Vecchione, she demonstrated an ability to handle smoothly the wide range of issues that were regularly confronted by the *MacNeil/Lehrer* news team. In 1983, when the program was expanded to sixty minutes and renamed the *MacNeil/Lehrer NewsHour*, she was named the show's national correspondent.

Originally planned to supplement the commercial networks' nightly news broadcasts, which rarely probe beneath the headlines, the *MacNeil/Lehrer NewsHour* intermixes background reports, panel discussions, interviews with experts, and filmed segments to cover a single important news story in depth. "The overriding perspective of *MacNeil/Lehrer* is to get beneath the surface and plumb the depths of a given situation," Lester M. Crystal, the program's executive producer, has explained. "We are looking at documentary reports that get all the ramifications." That determination to redefine the news has paid off in numbers. Among the most popular of PBS's regularly scheduled programs, the *MacNeil/Lehrer NewsHour* attracts a large, demographically mixed audience estimated at three million viewers nightly.

Charlayne Hunter-Gault's experiences at the University of Georgia, where she felt that people "didn't see [her] as a human being," inform her reportorial style. Finding the confrontational manner favored by some interviewers distasteful, she takes pains to avoid labeling and makes a concerted effort to get to know those she interviews as people—an approach that, coupled with her natural charm, relaxes and disarms many interviewees. Over the years, she has discussed comedy with Bill Cosby and Bill Irwin and foreign affairs with British Prime Minister Margaret Thatcher, Bishop Abel T. Muzorewa of Zimbabwe, and West German Chancellor Helmut Schmidt, and she has talked with Alfred Eisenstaedt, the photojournalist, and Soviet dissident Yuri Orlov.

Her restrained, perceptive coverage of Pope John Paul II's visit to the United States in 1979 earned Miss Hunter-Gault high praise from Robert MacNeil, who complimented her knack for "saying simple, relevant things at the right moment." Equally impressive was her four-part analysis of what she called "the Pandora's box of thorny issues" opened by the arrest of Bernhard Goetz, who in December 1984 shot four black teenagers on a crowded New York City subway car. Her report included interviews with lawyers, reporters, editors, and media critics and addressed such issues as racism, fear, the public's perception of the failure of the criminal justice system, and the role of the press in aggrandizing the "subway vigilante."

One of the first correspondents allowed into Grenada after the multinational invasion, led by the United States, of the Caribbean island on October 25, 1983, Miss Hunter-Gault won a National News and Documentary Emmy Award for her on-the-spot reports, most of which focused on the lives of the Grenadian people before and after the invasion. She returned to the island a year later to assess the long-range effects of the military action. She won another Emmy Award in 1985 for her affecting profile of Elmo Zumwalt 3d, who developed cancer after becoming contaminated by the defoliant Agent Orange while serving in Vietnam under the command of his father, Admiral Elmo Zumwalt Jr.

"Apartheid's People," Miss Hunter-Gault's insightful study of the effects of racial separatism in South Africa on whites as well as blacks, earned her a number of major journalism awards, including a 1986 George Foster Peabody Award, the prestigious prize given by the H. W. Grady School of Journalism of the University of Georgia. The compelling five-part series consisted primarily of interviews with ordinary South Africans in the black townships of Cape Town and in the white enclaves of downtown Johannesburg and the wine-growing region of Paarl. Looking back on her journey in an article for *Vogue* (March 1986), she remarked on the peculiar combination of "vulnerability and strength" that she noticed in many black South Africans, especially the wife of the imprisoned national hero Nelson Mandela, Winnie Mandela, whom she met at a press conference in Johannesburg. She also described her wrenching emotional reaction upon meeting a black woman who had been brutally beaten by the South African police. Her encounters with white South Africans, on the other hand, were "largely uneventful." The majority of Afrikaners whom she interviewed generally endorsed the government's snail-like approach to change, although one man candidly admitted that what South Africa needed was "a revolution of the heart."

Miss Hunter-Gault's stories about the underclass in the United States have been equally riveting. During one broadcast, while interviewing a group of New York City health specialists, she sparked an impassioned debate on the quality of health care for the poor. For another show, she researched and prepared a feature on the high rate of mortality among infants born to indigent black teenagers. Unlike most other *MacNeil/Lehrer* pieces, which are typically prompted by current events or recently released studies, the infant-mortality story arose directly from Miss Hunter-Gault's personal concern. "She had to sell us very hard on this," Linda Winslow, a *MacNeil/Lehrer* executive producer, told Claudia Dreifus. "This just wouldn't have happened without her."

A tall, slim woman with striking, almond-shaped, hazel eyes and close-cropped black hair, Charlayne Hunter-Gault looks much younger than her chronological age. "I have never met anyone in the world who doesn't like her," her colleague and friend Jim Lehrer said recently. "If you wanted to pick someone who was fun to be with and around, she would be the one." While she was attending the University of Georgia, she secretly married Walter Stovall, a white student. The marriage ended in divorce a few years after their daughter, Susan, was born. Since 1971 she has been married to Ronald Gault, a vice-president of the First Boston Corporation who specializes in public finance. The two live with Susan and their teenage son, Chuma, in a Manhattan cooperative apartment filled with Afro-American art and Chippendale furniture. In her spare time, Miss Hunter-Gault enjoys playing an aggressive game of tennis.

In addition to the pieces she has written for the *New Yorker*, the *New York Times*, and *Vogue*, Charlayne Hunter-Gault has contributed articles to *Ms.*, *Life*, *Essence*, *Saturday Review*, *Coronet*, the *New Leader*, and *Change*. She is a much sought-after speaker on college campuses throughout the United States, and she serves on the boards of directors of the Committee to Protect Journalists, the Center for Communication, and the Foundation for Child Development. Among her many honors are the Newswomen's Club of New York Front Page Award, the Good Housekeeping Broadcast Personality of the Year Award, the American Women in Radio and Television Award, the Atlanta Women in Communications Award for Excellence in Journalism, two awards from the Corporation for Public Broadcasting for excellence in local programming, and the Woman of Achievement Award from the New York chapter of the American Society of University Women.

References: About . . . Time 14:14+ Jl '86 pors; Dial 8:16+ F '87 por; Newsday p57 D 8 '86 por; Savvy 1:52+ Ag '80 pors; Vogue 176:488+ Mr '86; Washington, R 7:41+ S '85; O'Neill, Lois Decker, ed. The Women's Book of World Records (1979); Who's Who Among Black Americans, 1980–81

Hunthausen, Raymond G(erhardt)

Aug. 21, 1921– Roman Catholic prelate. Address: h. 907 Terry Ave., Seattle, Wash. 98104

Conscience has made a controversial international peace hero of mild-mannered Archbishop Raymond G. Hunthausen of Seattle, the highest-ranking American Roman Catholic prelate to advocate unilateral nuclear disarmament and to cross the line into civil disobedience in that cause. Hunthausen, consecrated in 1962, was an average reformist liberal bishop, quieter and shyer than most, until he was radicalized on the peace issue and made headlines around the world by announcing in 1982 that he would henceforth refuse to pay part of his income tax each year as long as the federal government continued to use the money to fuel the nuclear arms race. In keeping with Pope John Paul II's crackdown on liberal heterodoxy in the church, the Vatican in 1983 began an "apostolic investigation" of Hunthausen, a move ostensibly having nothing to do with his peace activism. In 1986 he was pressed into sharing some of his pastoral authority with a Vatican-appointed auxiliary, but his full power as archbishop was restored in May 1987.

The first of the seven children of Anthony and Edna (Tuchacherer) Hunthausen, Raymond G. Hunthausen was born on August 21, 1921, in Anaconda, Montana, a small mining city named after and controlled by the copper company of the same name. Hunthausen was strongly influenced by his father, whom he has described as "a big, powerful

man, but gentle and nonviolent," Tony Hunthausen was the proprietor of a grocery store, in which Raymond helped out, sorting potatoes, filling in behind the counter, and so forth. His childhood ambition was to become a stunt airplane pilot.

Because the income from the family store was steady, the Hunthausens were relatively secure economically, not as severely affected by local mining industry fluctuations as most of Anaconda's population. "We were isolated," Jack Morris, a fellow priest and friend of Hunthausen's who also grew up in Anaconda, has recalled. "Nobody ever locked their houses, and there was a high trust level and a lot of taking care of one another because of the periodic shutdowns of the mines. But that gives time to a boy to be a boy."

Although his parents were outgoing, Raymond Hunthausen was a shy boy. Also intelligent, deferential to authority, and diligent in his studies, he was a favorite of the nuns at St. Paul's Elementary School in Anaconda. The nuns pressed him into such extracurricular responsibilities as making welcoming speeches when the bishop of Helena and other dignitaries visited the school. Being singled out was painful to him, and he blushed throughout his speech-making, but he later came to appreciate people pushing him into "things that I should do even if I didn't want to do them." In an article in the *Chicago Tribune* (December 5, 1982), Gary Atkins quoted Jack Morris: "The interesting thing about Dutch [Hunthausen's nickname] is that he never tries to be a leader. He comes from the listening side of life and he thinks he can always learn from someone else because he doesn't think he knows that much. He's very receptive, but attached to that is a lot of guts. He responds rather than initiates, and responds in as authentically honest a way as anybody I know."

In high school Hunthausen excelled academically in science and starred extracurricularly in basketball. When he matriculated as a chemistry major at Carroll College in Helena, he was contemplating imminent service as a B-52 fighter pilot in the United States Army Air Force, but his mathematics teacher at the college, Father Bernard Toppel, persuaded him to try the priesthood. Father Toppel went on to become the bishop of Spokane and remained Hunthausen's mentor until his death in 1986.

Ambivalently, Hunthausen prepared to become a seminarian, adding philosophy and Latin to his studies at Carroll College. After taking his bachelor's degree at the college, he enrolled at St. Edward's Seminary in suburban Seattle. He was at the seminary when he heard the news of the atomic bombing of Hiroshima in August 1945. "From that moment on," he told Gary Atkins, "I never accepted the bomb; I could never accept its use again. Why couldn't we have warned them? Why couldn't we have dropped the bomb in the Pacific? We did not have to drop that on people the first time around." Being "no different from anybody else," however, he would remain silent on the issue for thirty-six years.

Hunthausen's doubts about his vocation suddenly dissolved when he became a subdeacon, and he was ordained a priest in 1948. After receiving a master's degree in science at Notre Dame University in 1953, he taught chemistry and coached football and basketball at Carroll College until 1957. He was president of the college from 1957 to 1962, and during his tenure as president he earned an

LL.D. degree at DePaul University. Pope John XXIII appointed him bishop of Helena, Montana in 1962—the same year that Pope John convened Vatican Council II, the extraordinary world synod of Roman Catholic bishops that introduced the reforms that Hunthausen, among other bishops, would try to implement.

Under the pontificate of Pope Paul VI, who tried to continue, or at least to go along with, the ecclesiastical renewal begun under John XXIII, Hunthausen was named archbishop of Seattle, and he was enthroned in St. James Cathedral there on February 25, 1975. Three years later, following the deaths in quick succession of Pope Paul VI and Pope John Paul I, the cardinals of the church elected Pope John Paul II, the former Karol Cardinal Wojtyla of Poland, a prelate steeled in the crucible of totalitarianism. Coming from a country where the Catholic deposit of faith and discipline was guarded as a precious commodity under siege by an atheistic state, Pope John Paul II assumed his duties as successor to St. Peter with no readiness to suffer gladly any toying with church tradition. Dismayed by what he viewed as the spiritual disarray of Catholicism in the West and the Third World, and believing that the liturgical experimentation and liberalized theological speculation rampant since Vatican II exceeded the bounds envisioned by the council fathers, the new pope called a halt to permissiveness and cracked down on heterodoxy. His effort to restore a conservative "balance" to the church went into high gear with his appointment in 1981 of Joseph Cardinal Ratzinger of West Germany as the prefect of the Sacred Congregation for the Doctrine of the Faith, the Vatican agency that serves as the watchdog of orthodoxy. Ratzinger, whom the pope has known since 1977, shared his concern with the church's drift toward the "fashionable" left and his view of the years since Vatican II as, in Ratzinger's words, "a period of ecclesiastical decadence in which the people who started it became incapable of stopping the avalanche."

When Cardinal Ratzinger walked into his new office in the Roman Curia, the file of letters complaining about Hunthausen, begun in 1978, was already sizable, and growing. Many of the complaints came from Erven Park, a conservative Catholic resident of Longview, Washington, and some of the 1,400 readers of Park's newsletter, *Catholic Truth*. Among Hunthausen's offenses, as the writers of the letters viewed them, were the following: he allowed Dignity, a homosexual advocacy organization, to have a special Mass in St. James Cathedral; he permitted contraceptive sterilizations in Catholic hospitals; and he authorized or ignored illicit or at least unseemly innovations in liturgy. Among the liturgical items was a festive funeral Mass at which colorful balloons were attached to the coffin. During the Mass the sister of the deceased, made up as a clown, chanted, "Today my brother and sister are together in heaven." Another, more serious item, concerned the reception of the Eucharist. Traditionally, the custom in the Roman Catholic church was to initiate believers first into confession, then Eucharistic communion. Following Vatican II, that rule was relaxed, but in 1984 the Vatican ordered a return to the old way. In Seattle, as in many other dioceses, there was a lag in conforming to the 1984 ruling.

Some American theologians place the Vatican's chief current concern with heterodoxy in the area of sexual ethics. In that area Hunthausen was accused of tacit acceptance of contraception, but he was not the only American prelate permissive on birth control, and on the more serious issue of abortion he was and remains unequivocally and vehemently "pro-life," calling abortion—after the arms race—"the other major evil of our times." Nor was he the only one who was less than strict in matters of divorce and remarriage; the reception of the sacraments by persons who might be living "in sin" because of an unresolvable marriage problem, and a whole gamut of gray moral areas. There are veteran observers of relations between the Vatican and the American church who suspect that Hunthausen's social and political stance—including not only the peace issue but also his support of sanctuary for refugees from Central America—was more than a minor factor in the Holy See's unusual interest in the conduct of his pastorate. Such observers find it difficult not to see a connection between two extraordinary facts. One is that Hunthausen was the only American liberal activist prelate of his rank who carried his activism into civil disobedience. The other is that the Vatican singled him, and him alone, out for a disciplining traditionally reserved only for bishops who have become mentally incompetent.

Although Hunthausen had added his signature to a group letter protesting the further deployment of nuclear missiles in Montana, it was not until shortly after he arrived in Seattle that his evolution as a peace activist really began. In Seattle he met Jim Douglass, a Catholic pacifist writer and activist, the author of The Nonviolent Cross and the organizer of protests against the deployment of the Trident nuclear submarine at the Navy base in Bangor, Washington, across Puget Sound from Seattle. Douglass' example shamed Hunthausen into the realization that he himself, "as a church leader had been doing . . . nothing."

Hunthausen's growth as an activist was gradual. The first step was a letter to the priests of the Seattle archdiocese, calling their attention to Douglass' activities. The second was an appearance at a protest outside the Bangor Navy base—his first of many participations there. The third was his offering a Mass at the county jail when Douglass, arrested in a demonstration, was detained there. The fourth was his call for unilateral nuclear disarmament, as a grand gesture to break the stalemate in international arms negotiations which he had come to view as "game playing."

In the spring of 1981 Hunthausen participated in a religious retreat at which another churchman suggested partial tax refusal as a significant symbolic act for drawing attention to the problem of nuclear arms. The following summer Hunthausen gave a speech at a Lutheran conference in which he uttered the words which "changed [his] life," as he recounted to Gary Atkins in an interview for a profile in the Chicago Tribune (December 5, 1982). In the talk he spoke of having a "vision" of people uniting in withholding their taxes from a "nuclear-armed Caesar." The following day the speech was headlined in the Seattle dailies and carried around the world by wire services. In the weeks following, the Seattle newspapers were flooded with letters pro and con, television talk shows vied for Hunthausen's appearance, and he received hundreds of invitations to speak around the country.

After much ambivalent soul-searching, Hunthausen committed himself personally to his "vision" in January 1982, announcing that he would henceforth withhold half of the federal tax on his personal income. He knew that his decision was a small moral gesture, not likely to do more than call attention to the issue of nuclear arms, but he believed that it counted. In a sermon in St. James Cathedral on Ash Wednesday 1982 he used the metaphor of a snowflake to describe the value of such a gesture. One snowflake weighs virtually nothing, he pointed out, but when enough flakes accumulate on a branch of a fir tree, there is a point at which just one more will break the branch. "Perhaps," he said, "there is only one person's voice lacking for peace to come about in the world."

The Vatican began its "apostolic investigation" of Hunthausen by sending Archbishop James Hickey of Washington, D.C., to Seattle in November 1983. During six days in Seattle, Hickey interviewed Hunthausen on tape for many hours, and he and two aides listened to at least sixty-seven members of the local clergy, religious, and laity. Among the negative lay witnesses was the archbishop's tireless nemesis, Erven Park, who told a reporter that he regarded Hunthausen as being in "open disobedience of the Holy Father on matters of faith and morals" and saw his advocacy of unilateral nuclear disarmament as a willingness to "surrender to atheistic Communism." Pat Cervenka, a Catholic housewife on the opposite side, later said, "A lot of us see the archbishop as a symbol of unconditional love here. The culture in the United States is different from Rome." Two hundred and fifty-two of the 280 priests in the archdiocese signed a petition supporting Hunthausen.

On September 30, 1985, Cardinal Ratzinger wrote Hunthausen a letter bringing "to a close the apostolic visitation process." Ratzinger began by commending Hunthausen's effort "to be a good bishop" and deploring the "exaggerated criticism" directed at him by his "more strident critics." He then launched into a long itemization of "areas . . . in need of correction and improvement" in the archdiocese of Seattle. The itemization ran the traditionalist gamut, but for the most part in a generalized way, speaking of "imperfect notions of the church's mission," of "faulty Christologies," and of the "role of conscience." Among the items were the special position and training of male priests ("The exclusion of women from sacred orders . . . should be explained unambiguously") and strict orthodoxy in the administration of the sacraments ("Non-Catholic Christians may be admitted . . . under specific conditions as listed in c. 844 par. 4").

In January 1986 the Holy See assigned Vatican-trained Bishop Donald Wuerl as Hunthausen's auxiliary, with the intention that Wuerl would assume authority in five or six "problem" areas, including the archdiocesan marriage tribunal, health care liturgy, and clergy formation ("to ensure that the continuing education of priests be done in ways that emphasize the bonds of the local church with the universal church"). Somehow, Hunthausen and Wuerl worked together for four and a half months before arriving at a common understanding of the special power-sharing arrangement that Rome had in mind. It was only in May 1986, when they were arguing over a homosexual rights issue, that the matter came to a head, and Wuerl spelled out his true assignment. The Vatican did not make the unusual sharing of powers official until September 4, 1986, when it announced, in a letter sent to Wuerl and made public by him, that the auxiliary was assuming authority in the "problem" areas. The next day 140 priests, nuns, and lay members of the archdiocese angrily protested "this injustice" and demanded an explanation from Rome. During the following month there was scattered support for the Vatican's action, while more than 3,000 American Catholics, including sixty bishops, wrote letters of support for Hunthausen.

Responding to the criticism of its disciplining of Hunthausen, the Vatican on October 27, 1986 sent to all bishops in the United States a detailed chronology of the events in the case. The chronology, much clearer and more detailed than previous statements, listed the charges against Hunthausen as follows: he allowed contraceptive sterilization to be performed in Catholic hospitals; misapplied ecclesiastical law regarding marriage annulments; permitted the regular use of general absolution in place of individual confession; condoned non-Catholics receiving communion at Mass and Catholics receiving communion at Protestant services; allowed church involvement with homosexual advocacy groups promoting doctrines contrary to church teaching; permitted seminary courses not grounded in church teaching; and hired laicized priests as teachers in Catholic schools and employed them in liturgical functions "contrary to the directives of the Holy See." The sorest point made in the chronology was that Hunthausen had wrongfully embarrassed the Vatican by "portraying this whole process as a one-sided affair," whereas, according to the chronology, the archbishop had more or less agreed to a power-sharing arrangement as early as September 1985.

Hunthausen said that his understanding of a number of interpretations and conclusions in the chronology differed significantly from those of the Vatican. The Rev. Michael G. Ryan, the chancellor of the Seattle archdiocese, backed Hunthausen, telling the press, "There were no alternatives. It was made clear by certain highly placed church authorities that he had to accept these conditions." Archbishop Francis Hurley of Fairbanks, Alaska, an old friend and golfing partner of Hunthausen's, described him as "the most unlikely hero for other Catholic progressives," a man who "respects the church authority" and "feels uncomfortable in this role." Hurley felt that it was "no longer a question of Hunthausen" but "a question of the state of the church." Two hundred of the 240 priests in Seattle signed a letter siding with Hunthausen.

Although a pastoral letter on economic justice was the chief item on the agenda of the National Conference of Catholic Bishops in Washington, D.C., in November 1986, the meeting was dominated by argument about the Hunthausen case. After listening to Hunthausen's apologia, the bishops debated for hours in two closed sessions and emerged with a compromise statement, expressing sympathy for and fraternity with the archbishop but affirming unreservedly their "loyalty to and unity with the Holy Father." Hunthausen expressed satisfaction with the statement but after his return to Seattle on November 13 he again questioned the "unworkable" arrangement forced on him. At the airport in Seattle a crowd of 500 greeted him festively, with cheers, flowers, and "We love you" signs. Throughout the following week the archbishop was deluged with calls, telegrams, and cables of support.

On November 25, 1986, the Seattle archdiocese released a letter from Archbishop Pio Laghi, the papal nuncio in Washington, informing Hunthausen that he had been affirmed in his post. Laghi said that Hunthausen had suffered from "exaggerated" and "mean-spirited criticism" but added that the archbishop should make himself invulnerable to such criticism by paying close attention to a number of concerns, including the needs "to present more clearly the church's teachings concerning the permanence and indissolubility of marriage" and "to insure that pastoral practice regarding the liturgy and sacramental ministry . . . is in accord with the church's universal norms."

On January 26, 1987, the Holy See appointed a three-man commission to assess the situation in Seattle and suggest a plan for resolving it. The commission was composed of Joseph Cardinal Bernadin of Chicago, John Cardinal O'Connor of New York, and Archbishop John R. Quinn of San Francisco. In the report it issued in May 1987, the commission said that despite "laudable steps" taken by Hunthausen, he was "perceived as generating or at least accepting a climate of permissiveness within which some feel themselves free to design their own policies and practices." The commission recommended that Bishop Wuerl be transferred to another see, that full faculties be restored to Hunthausen, and that the archbishop be given a coadjutor to assist him in carrying out the provisions of the letter written by Cardinal Ratzinger in September 1985. On May 26, 1987, Archbishop Pio Laghi announced the appointment of Bishop Thomas J. Murphy of Great Falls-Billings, Montana, as Hunthausen's coadjutor. Murphy was reputed to be a moderate, less conservative and more pragmatic than the departed Bishop Wuerl. In a press interview the following month Wuerl said that the "unworkable" situation in Seattle had made him an object of anger and even harassment by Hunthausen's flock and that he had had to remind himself, "They are not angry at me personally."

Raymond G. Hunthausen is frail-looking and slightly paunchy but still muscular and energetic. He has a heart condition, and he was operated on for a malignant prostate tumor in December 1986, but he was a regular skier up to the time of the operation. Soft-spoken, he is much more effective in the written word and one-on-one conversation than in the pulpit or on the podium. Simpler and more informal in his manner and lifestyle than his predecessors in the Seattle see, he is discomfited by pomp and praise, lives in a modest two-room apartment, often eats at a nearby McDonalds fast-food restaurant, and is likely to gravitate toward children before adults in mixed groups, such as those with which he participates in demonstrations at the Bangor Navy base. Shy, especially of the limelight, he refuses most of the endless speaking invitations he receives, but he is friendly, and he has a wry sense of humor. The federal tax on Hunthausen's salary is automatically withheld and forwarded to the Internal Revenue Service by the archdiocese. Beyond his salary, he makes about $10,000 a year, in fees for speeches and other such stipends. It is on that smaller, personal income that he calculates the amount he refuses to pay in taxes. He gives the money he holds back to charities and other worthy causes.

References: Chicago Tribune mag p65+ D 5 '82 pors; Economist 301:23+ N 15 '86; London Observer p8 N 23 '86 por; N Y Times A p22 O 30 '86 por, A p14 N 14 '86, A p14 N 17 '86 por, A p1+ My 27 '87; Time 122:75+ N 28 '83 por; Who's Who in America, 1986–87

Inouye, Daniel K(en)

(i-nō´ wā)

Sept. 7, 1924– United States Senator from Hawaii. Address: b. 722, Hart Senate Office Bldg., Washington, D.C. 20510; h. 469 Ena Rd., Honolulu, Hawaii 96815

NOTE: This biography supersedes the article that appeared in Current Biography in 1960.

Over the course of his twenty-eight-year career in the United States Congress, Daniel K. Inouye, the Democratic senior senator from Hawaii, has earned the esteem of his colleagues as one of the most skillful legislators on Capitol Hill. Inouye's forte is his uncommon ability to bring opposing factions together and negotiate the delicate compromises often required to turn a bill into law. The Hawaiian's preference for a behind-the-scenes role and his relatively low public profile have masked the considerable influence he wields as secretary of the Democratic Conference, the third-ranking Democratic party post in the Senate, and chairman of the Appropriations Committee's subcommittee on foreign operations, which is responsible for setting foreign aid disbursements. Inouye's judicious temperament and reputation for integrity secured him a place on the Senate select committee investigating the Watergate scandal in 1973 and, in 1986, the chairmanship of the select panel looking into the so-called Iran-Contra scandal.

The oldest of the four children of Hyotaro and Kame (Imanaga) Inouye, Daniel Ken Inouye was

born in Honolulu, Hawaii, on September 7, 1924. Hyotaro Inouye, who immigrated to Hawaii as a child from a small village in southern Japan, worked as a file clerk to support the family in what his son would later describe as "respectable poverty." As a boy, Daniel attended a special Japanese-language school as well as the neighborhood public schools. Following his graduation from Honolulu's McKinley High School in 1942, he enrolled in the premedical program at the University of Hawaii, but he dropped out of college the following year to enlist in the United States Army's newly formed 442d Regimental Combat Team. The unit was the first all-nisei combat group authorized by Congress in response to insistent pleas from young Japanese-Americans that they be allowed to prove their loyalty to the United States in frontline duty. Composed entirely of volunteers, the outfit was to become the most decorated army unit in United States history.

Commissioned a second lieutenant on the battlefield in 1944, Inouye distinguished himself as a platoon leader in Italy's Po Valley the following year. Two days before the war in Europe ended, he led an assault on a heavily defended German infantry position. Although his right arm had been shattered by a rifle grenade and he had been shot in the stomach and legs, the young officer managed to hurl a grenade into each of three enemy machine gun nests, saving his unit from almost certain destruction. For his bravery on that and other occasions, Inouye was awarded the Distinguished Service Cross (the nation's second-highest military decoration), the Bronze Star, and the Purple Heart with two oak leaf clusters, among other honors. He spent the next two years in army hospitals, recovering from his wounds and from the amputation of his right arm.

Discharged from the army with the rank of captain, Inouye returned to Hawaii in 1947 and re-enrolled at the University of Hawaii on the GI bill to study government and economics. "I had originally intended to study medicine," he has explained, "but the loss of my right arm caused me to go into the field of law; I had always been interested in politics." He obtained his B.A. degree in 1950, then continued his education at the George Washington University Law School in Washington, D.C., taking his J.D. degree in 1952. An excellent student, he served as an editor of the *George Washington Law Review* and won election to Phi Delta Phi, the professional law fraternity. While attending law school, Inouye also received some practical political training as a volunteer for the Democratic National Committee.

The young lawyer put that training to good use on his return to Honolulu in 1952. Immersing himself in territorial politics, then undergoing a sea change as nisei recently granted United States citizenship built the Hawaiian Democratic party into the dominant political force on the islands, Inouye became a protégé of John Burns, the territorial party chairman and a future governor. Inouye's steady climb up a succession of party and governmental posts began with his appointment as assistant public prosecutor of Honolulu in 1953. The following year he was elected to the territorial house of representatives, where he served as majority leader. In 1958 he moved on to the territorial senate, and when Hawaii became a state in 1959 he won election to the islands' first seat in the United States House of Representatives with the largest number of votes ever cast for a candidate in Hawaii up to that date.

As a war hero, the representative from the nation's newest state, and the first Japanese-American ever to serve in Congress, Inouye became something of an instant celebrity in Washington. Taken under the wing of Sam Rayburn, the Speaker of the House, he was assigned to the influential Banking and Currency Committee, but it was as an early supporter of the civil rights movement and a spokesman for Asian-Americans that he made his mark in the lower house. Following his reelection to Congress by an overwhelming majority in 1960, he moved to the Agriculture Committee, where he lobbied for policies favorable to Hawaii's sugar and pineapple export industries.

Inouye had originally intended to run for the United States Senate in 1959, but he stepped aside in deference to the party's elder statesmen. His patience was rewarded three years later, when he won the Democratic nomination for the Senate seat being vacated by Oren E. Long. With Long's endorsement, he trounced his conservative Republican opponent, Benjamin F. Dillingham 3d by a better than two-to-one margin. As he had done in the House of Representatives with Rayburn, Inouye forged a strong relationship with the Senate's Democratic majority leader, Mike Mansfield, who became the young legislator's mentor. A loyal Democrat, during his first term Inouye generally supported the programs and policies of Presidents John F. Kennedy and Lyndon B. Johnson. Having endured racial discrimination himself, he strongly backed the groundbreaking civil rights legislation passed during the Johnson administration, and he voted in favor of Johnson's "Great Society" social welfare programs. He also favored President Johnson's increasingly controversial Vietnam war policies.

On the Senate floor and in committee, Inouye soon proved himself to be an able parliamentarian and a natural conciliator. These recognized skills undoubtedly contributed to his being chosen for a number of leadership posts within the Senate Democratic hierarchy, including assistant majority whip and vice-chairman of the Democratic Senatorial Campaign Committee. Frequently mentioned as a possible candidate for the vice-presidential spot on a future Democratic ticket, he was tapped to deliver the keynote address at the tumultuous Democratic National Convention in 1968. His political stature enhanced by the national exposure, Inouye was reelected to the Senate a few months later with an astounding 83 percent of the vote against his Republican opponent, Wayne C. Thiessen. He was returned to office by similarly impressive margins in the general elections of 1974, 1980, and 1986.

Under Republican President Richard M. Nixon, Inouye turned against increased United States involvement in the Vietnam war. He voted in favor of the major "end-the-war" bills, including the Cooper-Church and McGovern-Hatfield amendments, and he cosponsored the historic War Powers Act of 1973, which limits the president's power to pursue an undeclared war. Domestically, too, Inouye compiled a generally liberal voting record during the Nixon years, opposing various proposed restrictions on civil liberties and favoring social welfare, education, and environmental protection programs.

Inouye marked a major milestone in his career in February 1973, when majority leader Mansfield appointed him to the Senate Select Committee on Presidential Campaign Activities, popularly known as the Senate Watergate Committee. The bipartisan seven-member panel had been set up to look into charges that Nixon administration officials had engaged in, or conspired to cover up, a number of illegal activities in behalf of Nixon's 1972 reelection campaign. Although as a relatively junior senator he had only a limited opportunity to question witnesses, Inouye earned the admiration of the public with his patient, probing interrogation of such key figures as former Attorney General John N. Mitchell and former White House aides John Dean, H. R. Haldeman, and John D. Ehrlichman. At one point during Ehrlichman's testimony, Inouye, believing his microphone was turned off, was heard to mutter, "What a liar!" Inouye later claimed that he had actually said "lawyer," not "liar," but his effort to defuse the remark failed to mollify Ehrlichman's attorney John J. Wilson, who publicly referred to the Hawaiian senator as "that little Jap." The ethnic slur sparked an outpouring of popular support for the senator. At the conclusion of the committee's public hearings in February 1974, a Gallup poll of regular viewers of the televised proceedings gave Inouye a favorable rating of 84 percent—an even higher mark than that awarded to Sam Ervin, the committee's folksy chairman.

Just four months after President Nixon's resignation, in August 1974, the New York Times detonated a new official scandal by revealing the CIA's illegal involvement in domestic intelligence operations during the Nixon administration. In the course of its investigation of the disturbing allegations, a Senate select committee, under the chairmanship of Senator Frank Church, uncovered a wide range of abuses of power by the CIA, the FBI, and other government intelligence agencies, including break-ins, warrantless wiretapping, and political sabotage at home and questionable covert operations abroad. To guard against further abuses, in May 1976 the Senate established a permanent Select Committee on Intelligence and charged it with formulating general guidelines for the various intelligence agencies and monitoring their ongoing operations. The Senate majority leader, Robert C. Byrd, picked Daniel Inouye to serve as the first chairman of the new committee, reasoning that the senator's impressive performance on the Watergate Committee and his proven patriotism might help him win the confidence of both a skeptical electorate and a demoralized intelligence community.

During Inouye's term as chairman, the Senate Intelligence Committee made considerable prog-

ress in restructuring and reforming the intelligence community. Among other things, the panel helped draft a new intelligence charter that specifically protected the fundamental rights of American citizens, laid the ground rules for the legal authorization of foreign counterintelligence investigations inside the United States, and prohibited the hiring of journalists and clergymen as covert agents. Finally, after debating measures that would have severely restricted the CIA's ability to conduct covert operations by requiring the prior notification of Congress, the Inouye committee ultimately endorsed the less stringent provisions of the Hughes-Ryan Amendment of 1974, which requires the president to certify in writing that a covert action is important to the national security and to notify Congress of such an action "in a timely fashion." Some legislators later complained that this after-the-fact arrangement turned Congress' mandated oversight role into one of impotent hindsight. To avoid developing "too close a relationship," as he put it, with the intelligence agencies, Inouye insisted on stepping down as chairman of the committee after serving for only one term. He left the panel at the close of the Ninety-Eighth Congress, in compliance with the committee rule that no member serve for more than eight years.

Inouye's overall voting record in the Senate during the administrations of President Gerald R. Ford, Jimmy Carter and Ronald Reagan inclined toward moderation, although he has consistently supported the liberal line on such divisive social issues as abortion rights, school busing to achieve racial desegregation, and gun control. The senator has also often taken positions favorable to consumers and to organized labor, backing, for example, the establishment of a Consumer Protection Agency, massive public works programs, and a major antitrust bill that allowed state attorneys general to bring antitrust lawsuits against companies on behalf of private citizens.

On defense-related issues, Inouye has been considerably more conservative. Over the past ten years, he has often voted for increases in military appropriations, particularly for the research and development of such technologically sophisticated weapons as the neutron bomb and the MX missile. He is, however, an outspoken critic of President Reagan's multibillion-dollar Strategic Defense Initiative, or "Star Wars" project, which calls for the installation of a space-based "shield" against incoming nuclear missiles. Selected to present the Democratic party's broadcast rejoinder to Reagan's televised announcement of the Star Wars program in March 1983, Inouye accused the president of exaggerating the Soviet nuclear threat not only to justify the need for the new weapons system but also to distract attention from the administration's economic failures.

Inouye has perhaps been most influential in lawmaking as the chairman or, during periods of Republican control, the ranking minority member of the Senate Appropriations Committee's subcommittee on foreign operations. In collaboration with his Republican counterpart, Robert W. Kasten Jr., he has written the majority of the Senate's foreign aid bills in recent years. He has earned the admiration of his colleagues for his habit of carefully reviewing each foreign aid proposal line by line. On the Senate floor, he has been among Israel's staunchest supporters, and he has campaigned tirelessly in favor of increased military and economic aid to that country. In keeping with his fervent anti-communism, Inouye at first backed funding for the United States-sponsored Contra guerrillas fighting the left-wing Sandinista government in Nicaragua, but following disclosures, in 1984, that the CIA had secretly mined Nicaraguan harbors to assist a Contra offensive, he voted to discontinue the aid. In the same year he brokered a compromise between the Reagan administration and Senate liberals on continued aid to El Salvador, which had roused some controversy because of the Salvadoran government's human rights violations.

Party loyalty, a talent for compromise, and mainstream political views helped Inouye rise to the post of secretary of the Democratic Conference in 1978. Since the Democrats regained control of the Senate in 1986, he has chaired, in addition to the Appropriations Committee's subcommittee on foreign operations, the communications subcommittee of the Commerce, Science and Transportation Committee, and the Select Indian Affairs Committee. Considered by many longtime observers of the Washington political scene to be a likely successor to Robert C. Byrd as Senate majority leader, Inouye, who has been reticent about his ambitions, declined to challenge his friend for the post in 1986. Although he is eminently pragmatic, he has been known to risk criticism and even his reputation in support of an unpopular position. For example, he was one of the few to defend New Jersey Senator Harrison A. Williams, a target of the FBI's controversial Abscam political corruption sting operation, during Senate expulsion proceedings in 1982.

That combination of political breadth and personal integrity, along with his past experience on the Senate Watergate and Intelligence committees, made Inouye the ideal choice for chairman of the Senate Select Committee on Secret Military Assistance to Iran and the Nicaraguan Opposition. The committee was formed in December 1986 to investigate reports that a group of Reagan administration officials, using third-party countries and private citizens as intermediaries, had secretly sold weapons to Iran and had diverted some of the profits from that sale to the Nicaraguan Contras in violation of President Reagan's declared policy and the expressed will of Congress. Serving on the committee with Inouye were five other Democrats and five Republicans, drawn mainly from the moderate-to-conservative wings of each party.

In organizing the investigative aspect of the panel's work, Inouye sought to prevent an open-ended "fishing expedition" by dividing the ten committee members into teams of one Republican and one Democratic senator and assigning each couple a specific area of inquiry. Remembering his own frustrating experience on the Watergate Committee, he decided that the primary interrogation of witnesses during the public hearings would be conducted by the pair who had researched the particular area involved, thus assuring junior senators an equal role in the proceedings. To guard against partisanship, he ruled that all decisions would be made by consensus. Finally, in an effort to avoid duplication of work and "competition for headlines," as he expressed it, Inouye broke with precedent and agreed to hold joint hearings with the House Select Committee to Investigate Covert Arms Transactions with Iran, headed by Representative Lee H. Hamilton.

The Iran-Contra hearings were convened in the spring of 1987 in an atmosphere markedly different from that of the Watergate investigation. Even before the hearings began, Inouye and other Democratic leaders, fearing that an aggressive inquiry might damage the institution of the presidency and undermine the nation's image as a world leader, indicated that they would proceed cautiously. Inouye nonetheless soon became embroiled in a dispute with Lawrence E. Walsh, the independent counsel in the Iran-Contra scandal, over the congressional committees' plans to grant limited immunity to Lieutenant Colonel Oliver L. North, a former National Security Council aide, and Rear Admiral John M. Poindexter, the former national security adviser, before Walsh had completed his criminal investigation of the ex-officials. To accommodate Walsh, Inouye and Hamilton eventually agreed to postpone the public testimony of those two key witnesses until midsummer.

During the public, nationally televised hearings, Inouye and Hamilton allowed the witnesses considerable latitude in responding to questions in order to avoid giving the impression that the panel was a prosecutorial rather than an investigative body. Critics charged that this relaxed method of inquiry encouraged witnesses to speechify rather than testify and occasionally—as, for example, in the case of the telegenic Lieutenant Colonel North—to reverse roles and put the committee members on the defensive. Some observers also faulted the panel for failing to pursue related areas of inquiry, including the potentially explosive charge that the CIA had helped the Contras smuggle large quantities of drugs into the United States.

When the public phase of the Iran-Contra hearings ended on August 3, 1987, Inouye reviewed the "chilling story" of "deceit and duplicity and the arrogant disregard for the rule of law" in his concluding remarks. He was especially disturbed by North and Poindexter's assertions that survival in what they termed a "dangerous world" sometimes required measures beyond the bounds of the law. "That is an excuse for autocracy," Inouye said, "not policy." In the senator's view, the hearings would be remembered not for uncovering facts but for exposing two radically different visions of government: one, a "shadowy," "elitist" government "accountable to not a single elected official, including the president"; the other, a "legitimate" and "balanced" governnment "accountable to the people." "For in America," he reminded his listeners, "as 200 years ago, the people still rule."

A stockily built man who stands five feet six inches tall, Daniel K. Inouye has dark-brown eyes, a broad face, and black hair that is just beginning to gray. The soft-spoken senator is relaxed and reflective in manner, "at once familiar and distant," as Lois Romano observed in the *Washington Post* (February 11, 1987). "Reserved and cautious most of the time, he'll fool you with a burst of disarming humor." Inouye is famous among his colleagues for his tastefully appointed office in the Hart Office Building, which he has furnished with Hawaiian crafts, tropical fish tanks, and luxuriant potted plants. Little inconvenienced by his handicap, in

his spare time Inouye enjoys playing one-handed piano pieces and gardening, and he is said to prefer "a good pool game to a congressional cocktail party." Inouye and his wife, the former Margaret Shinobu Awamura, whom he married on June 12, 1949, maintain homes in Bethesda, Maryland, and Honolulu, Hawaii. They have one son, Daniel Ken Jr.

References: N Y Times A p19 D 17 '86 por; Time 102:58 Ag 13 '73 por, 102:18 Ag 27 '73 por; Washington Post C p1+ F 11 '87 pors; Contemporary Authors vols 25–28 (1971); Douth, George. Leaders in Profile (1975); Inouye, Daniel K. Journey to Washington (1967); Political Profiles (1976–79); Politics in America (1986); Who's Who in America, 1986–87; Who's Who in American Politics, 1987–88

Irwin, Bill

Apr. 11, 1950– Actor; choreographer. Address: b. c/o David Williams, International Creative Management, 40 W. 57th St., New York City, N.Y. 10019

Drawing on an unlikely mixture of classical and popular art forms, ranging from commedia dell'arte to the avant-garde experiments of Jerzy Grotowski and Herbert Blau to "post-modern" dance, Bill Irwin has created a kind of "metaphysical vaudeville," as one critic put it, that almost defies description. "I'm really kind of a *grande dilettante*, if the truth be known," he told Randall Short of *New York Newsday* (April 30,

1987). "I have a lot of things that interest me in terms of performing, mostly from older stage traditions like the circus and vaudeville. My work is one long search for ways to dust them off and use them." Often compared to Charlie Chaplin and Buster Keaton, Irwin relies on his huge repertoire of skills, including juggling, tumbling, and "hat moves," to create, in his words, "interesting characters" and inventive flights of fancy, most notably *The Regard of Flight*, a tongue-in-cheek commentary on the pretensions of the so-called new theatre. Widely admired for his unique approach to performance art, in 1984 Irwin was the recipient of a Guggenheim fellowship and a five-year MacArthur foundation fellowship, popularly known as a "genius grant." He was the first active performing artist to receive a MacArthur award in the foundation's history.

William Irwin, who has always been known as Bill, was born in Santa Monica, California, on April 11, 1950, the oldest of the three children of Horace and Elizabeth (Mills) Irwin. His mother was a schoolteacher; his father, an aerospace engineer. Throughout Bill's childhood, his family moved frequently, as Horace Irwin followed jobs around the western United States. Rarely in one place for more than a year or two, the boy soon learned to be both adaptable and circumspect. "One of the lessons I learned was to wait, whether I was moving to a new city or walking into a party," Irwin recounted to Mel Gussow in an interview for a *New Yorker* (November 11, 1985) profile. "Trying to be assertive was almost always going to work against me. I have the same set of instincts in performing."

As Irwin told Mel Gussow, almost everyone in his family was, at least to some degree, stagestruck. His maternal grandfather, a teacher, staged plays and pageants in his native South Dakota, and his father designed sets for community theatre productions. Irwin himself first experienced "that peculiar performer's buzz" while giving an impersonation of the cartoon character Goofy as a reckless driver in his third-grade class in Tulsa, Oklahoma. Like most children brought up in a suburban environment in the 1950s, Irwin spent much of his free time watching cartoons, situation comedies, and variety shows on television, and he and his brother and sister, Patrick and Nan, often reenacted their favorites for their own and their parents' amusement. The family "hit" was "The Ned Bullivan Show," a spoof of the popular variety series *The Ed Sullivan Show*, with Bill playing the host and many of the guests. "Watching early television—*Amos and Andy, Sergeant Bilko*—was like learning piano by playing the scales," Irwin explained years later, as quoted in *Caught in the Act: New York Actors Face to Face* (1986). "I got a feeling for comic rhythm and structure, how long you should do something before you let it go for a while and then come back and pick it up."

Bill Irwin made his stage debut in the early 1960s, when he played the rock 'n' roll idol Conrad Birdie in a junior high school production of the musical *Bye Bye Birdie* in Woodland Hills, California. He subsequently appeared in several student productions at high schools in the United States and in Belfast, Northern Ireland, where he spent his senior year as an American Field Service exchange student. In the fall of 1968 Irwin enrolled in the theatre department at the University of California at Los Angeles, but after just two years in that rather traditional program, he transferred to the California Institute of the Arts in Valencia, the new experimental arts institution founded by Walt Disney. "I felt restless [at UCLA], confined by the realistic theatre around us," he explained to Samuel G. Freedman of the *New York Times* (October 24, 1984). "I was looking for a more physical form."

The theatre school at the California Institute of the Arts was then headed by Herbert Blau, the controversial, actor-oriented director known for his intellectual approach and his radical (some would say anarchic) experiments in "performance research." In addition to scene study and basic acting techniques, Irwin's curriculum at Cal Arts included courses in dance, mime, gymnastics, and t'ai chi. While he was a student there, Irwin also appeared in a number of campus productions, including Albert Innaurato's staging of *Escurial*, by the Belgian fantasist Michel de Ghelderode. Between classes, he earned pocket money by performing on street corners, in shopping malls, and at open-air Renaissance fairs in the San Francisco area. As he polished his routines over time, he began to create characters, among them a long-winded preacher given to malapropisms and a fire-eater billed as Carno the Magnificent Salamander.

When Blau left Cal Arts in the summer of 1971 to join the faculty of the theatre arts department at Oberlin College, in Oberlin, Ohio, Irwin and several other Blau disciples went with him. The recipient of what he has described as a "quasi quasi quasi teaching assistantship," Irwin taught a course in physical comedy at Oberlin and appeared in some conventional campus productions, most nota-

bly a comedy by Plautus, but he devoted most of his time to participating in Blau's rigorously physical experiments with a new acting technique based on what Blau called "impulse work." After months of closed-door experimentation, Blau's theatrical ensemble, named Kraken after the fabulous Norse sea monster, appeared before the public for the first time in *Seeds of Atreus*, an abstract adaptation of Aeschylus' *Oresteia*, in which Irwin played the role of Orestes, and *The Donner Party, Its Crossing*, a piece based on the experiences of a group of nineteenth-century pioneers who were driven to cannibalism after they were marooned in the Sierra Nevada by a snowstorm. Irwin credits Blau with teaching him "the meaning of using [his] own intelligence" and, perhaps more important, the conscious nature of performance, but after three years with Kraken, he began to feel stifled by the "elitism" and the "close, almost incestuous circle" of avant-garde theatre. "I wanted to open myself up to wider audiences," he explained to Janice Ross in an interview for *Dancemagazine* (June 1982).

Long fascinated by the, in his word, "surrealism" of clowning, in mid-1974 Irwin decided to attend Clown College, an intensive training school for circus performers at the winter headquarters of the Ringling Brothers and Barnum & Bailey Circus in Venice, Florida. Over the next several months, he mastered the basics of elephant riding, juggling, and acrobatics, among other skills. In the evenings he and his fellow student clowns watched films of such masters of comedy as Charlie Chaplin, Buster Keaton, W. C. Fields, and Burns and Allen. Upon his graduation from Clown College in November 1974, Irwin turned down offers of employment from Ringling Brothers and from the internationally famous Flying Gaona aerial act to work on his own as a clown.

Returning to San Francisco, Irwin answered a newspaper ad for jugglers, tumblers, and equilibrists that had been placed by Larry Pisoni, who, along with Peggy Snider, was trying to put together a small, one-ring circus. Pisoni already had more than enough clowns, but he was so impressed by Irwin's clowning that he hired him anyway. Irwin's "signature" character with the Pickle Family Circus, as Pisoni's troupe was known, was Willy the Clown, an appealing, painfully shy fellow with a shock of red hair and a bulbous red nose, but he also portrayed a variety of other characters, including Hauptman von Clown, a bumbling animal trainer. The latter's "animal" was a tap-dancing gorilla, played by Kimi Okada, a dancer and choreographer whom Irwin married in 1977.

It was through Miss Okada, who is now an associate artistic director of the Oberlin Dance Collective/San Francisco, that Irwin became interested in so-called post-modern choreography, which sees dance as pure form. Eventually, he began to incorporate some post-modern concepts, particularly its fascination with the exploration of space, into his clown routines. "I think much of the great clowns' work has to do with form," he explained to

Janice Ross. "It's really in this respect that clowning is most like ballet, and I try to push this connection by codifying certain types of movements, falls, and stumbles. So much of Keaton and Chaplin's work had to do with this kind of form."

While he was appearing with the Pickle Family Circus, Irwin supplemented his income by teaching and performing in city schools under the auspices of the San Francisco Arts Commission and by entertaining at trade shows, festivals, and private parties. In his spare time he created comedy sketches, often in collaboration with Michael O'Connor, whom he had known since his student days at Cal Arts, and Doug Skinner, a member of the Oberlin Dance Collective. In 1977 Irwin and his colleagues were invited to perform some of those short sketches in a recital with the Dance Collective. The two skits Irwin selected were Circa, in which he and O'Connor chase each other in a circle, and Murdoch and the Regard of Flight, which Irwin has described as a spoof of some then-popular performance-art pieces, such as Robert Wilson's chamber work I Was Sitting on My Patio This Guy Appeared I Thought I Was Hallucinating.

Over the next few years, Irwin invented other skits, among them Not Quite (so called because it was "not quite" a solo piece), Still Not Quite, and At the Very Least. First staged at the Intersection Theatre in San Francisco's North Beach section in 1978, At the Very Least presented Irwin as a dispirited comedian who is literally unable to take the first step toward accepting a lucrative but unfulfilling job as a disco-dancing clown in a suburban shopping mall. Irwin's increasingly frequent appearances at avant-garde theatres on the West Coast brought him an invitation to perform at the New Theatre Festival in Baltimore, Maryland. For that engagement, he combined several of his sketches into an evening-length show called The Regard of Flight, in which he appeared with his colleagues Michael O'Connor and Doug Skinner. The trio subsequently took the show to Europe for an extensive tour of Italy, France, and the Netherlands.

Upon his return to the United States, Irwin joined the Oberlin Dance Collective for a concert at the Dance Theatre Workshop in New York City. Taken by Irwin's comic inventions, David White, the Workshop's executive director, hired him to present his skits as part of a new, late-night series of performance events. That engagement not only introduced Irwin to a wider audience, but also earned him a special Obie Award for "inspired clowning" in the spring of 1981. A few months later, he was back in New York to open the Dance Theatre Workshop's two-week "new mime" series at the American Theatre Laboratory with a program entitled "Bill Irwin with Doug Skinner and Friends." The program featured several new skits, the longest and most important being Not Quite/New York—a series of challenge matches pitting Irwin, in the guise of the universal "little man," against such virtuoso performers as dancer Charles Moulton, juggler Michael Moschen, and Tommy Sellars, an accordion-playing roller skater. Try as he might, Irwin's hapless loser could not begin to equal the dazzling feats of his competitors. Defeated at every turn, he finally settled for a "safe, ordinary dance without risks, the compromise in life," as Anna Kisselgoff put it.

Miss Kisselgoff, the veteran dance critic of the New York Times, has been among Bill Irwin's champions since his first appearance in New York. In her rave review of Not Quite/New York for the Times of September 27, 1981, she contended that the "brilliance" of the piece lay in its "variation upon a stock figure" and in its "perfect" structure. "Like a good post-modern choreographer," she explained, "Mr. Irwin uses repetition, changes in speed and dynamics, and breaks in patterns to achieve his effect. Pure movement is all." Perhaps because they were accustomed to the post-modern choreographic idiom, which embraced natural "non-dance" movements, dance critics were generally more sympathetic toward Irwin's early experiments in nonverbal performance than drama critics. To the theatre critic and historian Robert Brustein, for instance, Not Quite/New York was "little more than an exercise in style." Although he conceded in his analysis for the New Republic (October 14, 1981) that Irwin was "well trained" in dance, comedy, and pantomime, Brustein thought that the performer had "not yet mastered . . . the purpose for which these techniques were invented."

Not Quite/New York gradually evolved into a new edition of The Regard of Flight, which opened at the American Place Theatre in New York City in May 1982 and went on to become the highest grossing show in that theatre's history to that date. Revised versions of the work have since been staged at the Mark Taper Forum in Los Angeles in 1983 and at the Vivian Beaumont and Mitzi E. Newhouse theatres at Lincoln Center for the Performing Arts in New York in 1987, among other arenas. The piece was also nationally televised in February 1983 by the Public Broadcasting Service as part of its Great Performances series. In recent productions, Irwin has complemented The Regard of Flight with The Clown Bagatelles, a collection of short sketches, including a send-up of minstrel shows and a two-minute version of King Lear.

In various interviews over the years, Irwin has described The Regard of Flight as "a comic surreal dream piece" about the contemporary theatre, "a clown piece," and "a rumination about the history of theatre, new and old." An actor's nightmare come to life, The Regard of Flight opens with a bewildered Irwin waking from a deep sleep to find himself onstage, with an audience watching. At first hesitantly, then with increasing temerity, he takes the opportunity to show the audience how clowning and mime techniques can be combined with avant-garde dramatic concepts to create "new theatre," which, as the audience is told, celebrates "the decline of the playwright and the rise of the actor as poet." To that end, he assumes divers personalities with the help of costumes and props retrieved from a seemingly bottomless trunk and runs through a variety of standard comic "moves," including a headfirst dive into an upturned derby hat, a demonstration of gravity-defying "lean shoes," which allow the wearer to tilt forward without toppling over, and a tap routine that ends with Irwin being pulled offstage by a powerful invisible vortex. He is constantly interrupted in his efforts by an officious commentator (played by Doug Skinner) and a hectoring, skeptical critic (portrayed by Michael O'Connor).

Commenting on the 1987 revival of *The Regard of Flight* for the *New York Times* (April 13, 1987), Mel Gussow applauded Irwin as an artist "whose name belongs alongside those of Buster Keaton and Marcel Marceau" and the piece itself as "magical." "The show is a dazzling display of physicalized wit, as the star offers doubletakes, pratfalls, hat moves, and feats of gestural wizardry (such as walking down inside a trunk as if descending a steep staircase)," Gussow wrote. "With his extraordinarily elastic body, he can sink his head into his chest and appear to lose half a foot of height, or, under a tentlike robe, he can scoot around the stage at a Toulouse-Lautrec level. His facial expressions—bemusement, innocence, surprise, rapture—are an exhibition by themselves. . . . He is one of a kind."

Although he is best known for his clowning and is, in his words, "proud to be thought of as a good clown," Irwin considers himself to be "basically an actor." Over the past five years, he has often auditioned for parts in New York theatrical productions, including Laertes in the New York Shakespeare Festival's *Hamlet*, starring Kevin Kline, and a leading role in the Broadway revival of *On Your Toes*. His recent stage credits include an aspiring Rockette in the Sandy Duncan-Don Correia musical extravaganza *Five, Six, Seven, Eight . . . Dance!* at New York's Radio City Music Hall in 1983, and Galy Gay in Brecht's *A Man's a Man* and the schoolteacher Trigorin in Chekhov's *The Seagull* at the La Jolla (California) Playhouse, an adventurous summer theatre, in 1985. His only Broadway assignment to date was the slow-witted Sergeant in the New York premiere of Dario Fo's political farce *Accidental Death of an Anarchist*, which closed just a few days after its opening, in November 1984, despite a chorus of raves for Jonathan Pryce in the central role. As for Irwin, most critics felt that his part gave him scant opportunity to display his formidable gift for physical comedy.

While he was rehearsing *Accidental Death*, Irwin was notified that he had been chosen to receive a Catherine and John D. MacArthur Foundation grant. The fellowships, which had been established expressly to "free creative people from the necessity of seeking a conventional income," provide tax-free, no-strings-attached grants ranging from $176,000 to $300,000 over a five-year period. Irwin's annual stipend was to be $36,000. Delighted as he was by the grant, Irwin initially worried that his newfound financial security might "blunt [his] competitive edge," but he gradually came to appreciate the artistic freedom it offered. "It's let me do things I couldn't otherwise afford to do . . . ," he told Richard F. Shepard in an interview for a *New York Times* (April 12, 1987) profile. "If anything, it's increased, not lessened my work because the money says, in effect, that you should be at the service of art. That means that I can take on more things that I usually couldn't afford to take."

Irwin used some of his grant money to create *The Courtroom*, which he has described as a "political cartoon" about the injudicious aspects of the judicial system. Set in a Kafkaesque courtroom, with a tap-dancing court stenographer, squabbling attorneys who literally "juggle" the evidence, and a jury comprised of smug, life-size puppets, it follows the adventures of a befuddled innocent (Irwin, in an oversized suit and shapeless hat) who wanders into the courtroom in search of a bicycle license and gets caught up in a nonsensical criminal trial. When *The Courtroom* was first presented to the public at St. Clement's Episcopal Church in May 1985, it was billed as a "work in progress," and most critics agreed that the piece had not yet jelled into a coherent work to rival *The Regard of Flight*. But in his review for the *New York Times* (May 10, 1985), Frank Rich had nothing but praise for Irwin himself: "Even if he weren't a brilliant mime and just about the most pliably rubber-limbed hoofer since Ray Bolger, Bill Irwin would still be a joy to watch. This performer is, above all, a clown—a post-modern clown, as the current lingo has it—and an uncommonly sweet and vulnerable one. . . . It is mostly the force of his lovable persona that is holding this fifty-minute outing together."

Between engagements, Irwin spends much of his time in the studio, polishing and honing existing works and creating new ones—a process he has described as "very chaotic." His most recent effort is *On and Off*, which was given its world premiere in May 1987 by New York City Tapworks as part of the Riverside Church's contemporary dance series. He also occasionally teaches workshops in physical comedy for professional performers and gives public lecture-demonstrations on clowning. Branching out into other forms of popular entertainment, he played Ham Gravy in the film *Popeye* (1980), Robert Altman's big-budget musical based on the adventures of the cartoon character of the same name, and in July 1987 he created and starred in *As Seen on TV*, the debut program in PBS's innovative *Alive From Off Center* series. In *As Seen on TV*, Irwin is physically drawn into a television set, where he finds himself an unwilling cast member in a variety of programs, ranging from *Sesame Street* to MTV music videos.

A tall, angular man, Bill Irwin has strawberry-blond hair, blue eyes, and, according to one interviewer, a "Sillyputty, Tom Sawyer face." His work is, by his own admission, his "obsession," and he rarely takes time off for leisure activities. "I have some questions about whether there is room for family or any other life . . . ," he once said, as quoted in *People* magazine (November 6, 1984). "My craft is painful, and it's painful to people around me. It combines the worst of writer's neurosis and actor's neurosis." When asked about his plans for the future in an interview in 1985, Irwin expressed a desire to act in plays that would challenge him "both as an actor and as a clown," such as Beckett's allegory *Waiting for Godot* and Goldoni's character comedy *The Servant of Two Masters*. "There's no question that I want to be involved in theatre," he told Megan Rosenfeld of the *Washington Post* (December 21, 1985). "The question is in what way. . . . After all, you can't fall down all your life." Divorced from Miss Okada in the early 1980s, Irwin lives in a cluttered apartment in New York's Greenwich Village.

References: American Way p102+ O 15 '85 pors; Ballet N 4:8 Mr '83 por; Connoisseur p140+ S '82 pors; Dance Mag 55:69+ Je '82 pors; N Y Times C p22 S 8 '81 por, II p4+ Ag 8 '82 por; New Yorker 61:51+ N 11 '85 por; People 22:43 N 6 '84 por; Washington Post E p1+ D 21 '85 por; Shewey, Don. Caught in the Act: New York Actors Face to Face (1986)

Jagger, Bianca

May 2, 1945– Actress; political activist. Address: b. c/o American Broadcasting Co., 2040 Ave. of the Stars, Los Angeles, Calif. 90067

Once the darling of New York's "glitterati" and the undisputed queen of the celebrity disco scene, Nicaraguan-born beauty Bianca Jagger, the former wife and "mirror image" of rock music superstar Mick Jagger, has since her divorce won widespread respect for her efforts to restructure her priorities and forge a new life as an actress and serious political activist who works tirelessly on behalf of leftist Central American *causes célèbres*. Her developing acting career took a back seat to a rekindled sense of social commitment in 1981, when she found herself galvanized into action by a fateful tour of Salvadoran refugee camps in Honduras. Since then, Bianca Jagger has become an outspoken champion of human rights and an effective advocate for the Sandinista revolution in her native country. Because of her political activities and the singleminded dedication with which she pursues them, Philip Norman, the rock music historian, has suggested that she "may have been misjudged." As long ago as 1973, the fashion designer Jackie Rogers was quoted in *Vogue* as saying, "Bianca is someone to watch. In the end, she'll be more important than Mick."

The oldest of three children, Bianca Jagger was born Bianca Pérez Morena de Macías (or Pérez Mora Macías, by some accounts) in Managua, Nicaragua, on May 2, 1945. Her father is listed by most sources as a well-to-do import-export merchant, but in an interview with Bob Colacello for *Vanity Fair* (November 1986), she insisted that he was "just a businessman." Apparently, reporters have occasionally confused his career with that of his brother, a "diplomat-cum-coffee-baron" who served as Nicaragua's ambassador to Cuba under the government of Anastasio Somoza. According to British journalist Philip Norman, the author of a biographical history of the Rolling Stones called *Symphony for the Devil* (1984), Bianca's father was apolitical; her mother, however, "hated Somoza passionately." As Norman recounted, Bianca herself discovered that women "were not supposed to have political convictions" when she and her brother, Carlos, took part in student demonstrations opposing Somoza's policies.

Bianca Jagger's incipient politicization began innocently enough at the School of the Immaculate Conception, the convent school in Managua where she was educated. "I was brought up very Catholic," she told Bob Colacello. "It was nothing unusual, just the way people were brought up in Nicaragua at the time. It was almost feudal: the whole idea of a girl who gets married, never goes out with anyone else before she marries her husband, the concept of virginity." The ideal was shattered, however, when her parents divorced in the early 1950s. In a country in which divorce was still a rarity, her mother was left a social outcast with poor financial prospects. To support herself and her three children, Doris Macías opened a small restaurant adjacent to her home, an act that affected her older daughter deeply. "After having an easy life, suddenly my mother had to work and suddenly my mother was treated completely differently," Bianca Jagger has explained, as quoted in the *Vanity Fair* article. "I saw the fate that women in countries like Nicaragua were condemned to have, to be second-rate citizens. I didn't want to have the same future that my mother had. I wanted to become a career woman, to have a profession, either as a politician or a diplomat."

In 1961 Bianca Jagger graduated "with unanimity"—top marks in all subjects—from the School of the Immaculate Conception. While continuing her education at the local Alliance Française, where she took advanced French courses, she managed to obtain a scholarship to the prestigious Institut d'Etudes Politiques in Paris. Despite her parents' objections, Bianca, who had never even been out in the evening unchaperoned, left her native land for France. There, as she recalled to a reporter for *People* (May 2, 1977), "I studied hard and remained a virgin till eighteen and a half." During her years at the institute, she reportedly worked for a time on the staff of the leftist newspaper *Combat*. Eventually, however, her studies in international politics were sidetracked by the Parisian social scene, and she never completed her degree.

Having "evolved into a sixties jet-set femme fatale," as Bob Colacello put it, Bianca Jagger embarked on a series of well-publicized romantic liaisons with such famous men as the British actor Michael Caine and Eddie Barclay, the French recording-industry executive. She met Mick Jagger in the late summer of 1970, at a party following the Rolling Stones's first concert in Paris. Jagger is said to have been spellbound by the sophisticated and exotic young woman, whom Philip Norman described as "an Inca princess dressed like a Dior mannequin." According to Norman, the singer saw in her face "his own perpetual reflection. . . . Narcissus looked into the pool, and was lost." Recalling their first encounter for the *People* magazine profile, Bianca Jagger told the interviewer, "I wasn't attracted to Mick for physical reasons. I found him shy, vulnerable, human—the opposite of everything I had ever imagined. It sounds silly, but it was like a bolt of lightning."

From their first meeting, the two were virtually inseparable. Bianca soon flew to Rome to join Mick for the remainder of the Rolling Stones's European tour, and at its conclusion, she accompanied him to England. By that time, news of their romance was hot copy on Fleet Street. Media interest in the couple intensified in November 1970, when Bianca began living with the singer at Stargroves, where the Stones had gone to work on a new record album, an endeavor said to have been significantly hampered by Mick's infatuation with his constant companion.

The following April the Rolling Stones moved en masse to France, apparently to escape Britain's high taxes, and once again, Bianca accompanied Mick. A little more than a month later, on May 12, 1971, the two were married in Saint Tropez at a civil ceremony in the local town hall followed by a Catholic service at the nearby Chapelle Sainte-Anne, a tiny fishermen's church. The couple exchanged their vows before a chartered planeload of guests from England, among them Queen Elizabeth II's cousin, the photographer Lord Litchfield, and former Beatles Ringo Starr and Paul McCartney. Although Mick Jagger had once told a television interviewer that he considered "the whole wedding thing" to be a pagan initiation rite, he had nonetheless informed his press agent of the details. The resulting media circus, complete with hysterical Stones fans and frequent scuffles between the paparazzi and Jagger's outnumbered bodyguards, unnerved the bride, who reportedly considered calling off the wedding. "I was really destroyed by that day—the saddest day of my life," Bianca Jagger admitted to Sonia Melchett in an interview for *Harper's Bazaar* (November 1972). "I was completely désarmée. . . . Mick tried to warn me— he's in a continuous fight with the press, and I suppose when a Rolling Stone gets married, it has to be a scandalous occasion."

Following the birth of their daughter, Jade, in Paris on October 22, 1971, the Jaggers traveled a great deal, at least partly because, as Bianca Jagger explained to Sonia Melchett, "we had this dream of an ideal place and if the place wasn't exactly like the dream, we'd leave." By the end of 1972, they had homes in the south of France, on Cheyne Walk in London's fashionable Chelsea section, and in the English countryside, although they never spent more than ninety consecutive days in Britain because of Jagger's status as a tax exile.

On her own much of the time while her husband rehearsed, recorded, or toured with the Stones, Bianca Jagger was determined to carve her own niche. "I'm not prepared to be just a part of someone's life," she told Sonia Melchett. "I will only share my life if I can keep my own identity. I would like to do something on my own, apart from Mick." At first, she asserted her independence mainly as a fashion trend-setter. The slick high-fashion magazine *Harper's Bazaar* published a profile of her in November 1972, and in February 1973 *Vogue* followed suit with a striking feature spread of photographs by the renowned Richard Avedon.

The acknowledged "queen of queens," to use Bob Colacello's phrase, at New York's most fashionable discos by the mid-1970s, Bianca Jagger numbered among her friends such high priests of the pop culture scene as Andy Warhol, Woody Allen, and Truman Capote as well as the top fashion designers Yves St. Laurent, Valentino, and Halston, at whose salons she is said to have reacted to her husband's legendary stinginess by spending a fortune. Her eclectic and highly original wardrobe, which included mannish suits, slinky evening gowns, veiled and feathered pillbox hats, and a large collection of the short swagger sticks that were her trademark, prompted Kennedy Fraser, who devoted an entire "On and Off the Avenue" column in the *New Yorker* to her "unmistakable style," to pronounce Mrs. Jagger a "female dandy."

Eventually, however, Bianca Jagger tired of being "a walking doll," as she put it. Eager to try her luck as an actress, she began taking acting and dancing lessons, and in 1975 she accepted a role as a lesbian in an Italian movie tentatively titled "Trick or Treat." She backed out of the deal after discovering that she would be required to perform several nude love scenes. A few months later, she agreed to take the part of a young widow who "falls in love like a little girl," as she put it, in François Weyergans' film *Couleur Chair*, ("Flesh Color"), which had its world premiere at the Cannes Film Festival in May 1978. Later in the year, she was a high-class prostitute in love with a married man, played by Jeff Bridges, in William Richert's *American Success*. First broadcast on cable television, the film was eventually distributed to movie houses nationwide in 1981. In her review of the "nutty but appealing" drama for the *New York Times* (January 5, 1981), Janet Maslin singled out Mrs. Jagger, who brought a "don't-rumple-my-hair demeanor to her scenes of seductive abandon," as "one of the many anomalies that keep the film perversely interesting ."

Meanwhile, the Jaggers' marriage had begun to unravel. At first, Bianca seemed to accept Mick's frequent dalliances with various music-scene groupies as part of the price of marriage to a rock superstar, but over the years she found it more and more difficult to tolerate his infidelities. On one memorable occasion, she is said to have become so enraged by his behavior that she ripped up all his shirts. Mrs. Jagger sparked rumors of extramarital flings of her own when, during her husband's absences, she appeared in public in the company of actors Ryan O'Neal and Warren Beatty, Helmut Newton, the photographer, and Jack Ford, the son of President Gerald R. Ford.

By 1977 Mick and Bianca Jagger were leading almost entirely separate lives. When Mick moved in with model Jerry Hall, Bianca started divorce proceedings in London in May 1978, although in hope of a reconciliation, she declined to serve Mick with the legal papers. Eight months later, she sued for divorce in Los Angeles Superior Court, on the grounds of her husband's admitted adultery. Her attorney, the famed "palimony" lawyer Marvin Mitchelson, tried to obtain for her half of the estimated $25 million that Jagger earned during the couple's eight-year marriage, but the suit was rejected by the court. A divorce was eventually granted in London on November 2, 1979. Under the terms of the divorce agreement, Bianca was awarded custody of Jade, then eight years old, child support, and a $1 million settlement.

Since her divorce, Bianca Jagger, who has kept her married name, has devoted some of her time to furthering her career as an actress. She has taken acting lessons from a teacher at the Royal Academy of Dramatic Art in London and from the acting coach Harold Guskin in New York, and she has appeared in several popular television series, most notably as a right-wing political assassin on *Miami Vice* and as the widow of a Latin American head of state on *Hotel*. But it has been as a spokeswoman for strife-torn Central America that she has commanded the most attention. She traces her political activism to a visit she made to Nicaragua after a devastating earthquake struck the country on December 23, 1972. "That's when I really became aware of the extent of the harm that Somoza was doing to Nicaragua," she explained to Bob Colacello. At her urging, early in 1973 the Rolling Stones staged a benefit performance that netted $280,000 for the earthquake's victims.

Her concern eventually developed into passionate commitment. While visiting her father in Nicaragua in September 1981, Bianca Jagger became interested in the plight of Salvadoran refugees fleeing the fighting in their homeland. Two months later she went to Honduras as a member of a fact-finding delegation dispatched by the Committee for the Defense of Refugees, headed by the archbishop of Cuernavaca, Mexico. During an inspection tour of a refugee camp near the border of El Salvador, she was one of a party of witnesses to the armed abduction of about forty Salvadoran refugees by "a group of military or paramilitary types," as she put it, from El Salvador. "We followed them, yelling at them and taking pictures," she recalled later, as quoted in the *New York Daily News* (December 23, 1981), "and we were successful enough that the prisoners got away." On her return to the United States, Bianca Jagger reported the incident to the House subcommittee on inter-American affairs. "Her testimony was poignant, and she proved to be very intelligent," New York Representative Robert García told a reporter for *People* magazine (March 29, 1982). "She was a damned good advocate for the refugee problem."

Over the past five years, Bianca Jagger has continued her efforts on behalf of Salvadoran refugees, mainly by working closely with several human rights organizations. She recently cohosted, with the actor Richard Gere and Charlie Clements, a left-wing activist, a press screening of the controversial PBS documentary *Witness to War*, which is sympathetic to the peasants who back the rebels in El Salvador. An eloquent and informed advocate of the Sandinista government that replaced deposed Nicaraguan strongman Somoza, she has nonetheless criticized the new regime for such heavy-handed tactics as the closing of *La Prensa*, the country's last opposition newspaper. Still, as she explained to Bob Colacello in the interview for *Vanity Fair*, "You cannot bring the standards" of the United States "to a country that for forty-three years had a dictatorship, that has never really known what democracy means. . . . The Sandinista government is not the sort of government that I would hope Nicaragua to have, but it is the best Nicaragua can have for the time being."

A stunning woman with the slender figure and chiseled bone structure of a high-fashion mannequin, Bianca Jagger has large, brooding dark eyes, a wide, full mouth, flawless *café-au-lait* skin, and a thick mane of brownish black hair. She walks with a slight limp, the result of a serious bicycle-auto collision during the summer of 1985 from which she is still recovering. Her recuperative routine includes regular workouts under the direction of a physical therapist along with yoga. Because of her admitted "obsession with health and decaying," she follows a diet comprised mainly of fresh fruits and vegetables and avoids alcohol and tobacco. Since she became involved in political and social activism, Bianca Jagger has considerably altered her lifestyle. "I can't be involved in an issue like this and go to parties," she told Carla Hall. "It's the price you pay. It's not a matter of what I like. It's a matter of what's appropriate." In her spare time, she enjoys reading in almost all subject fields. She lives with her daughter in a cooperative apartment on Manhattan's Upper West Side.

References: Harper's Bazaar 106:104+ N '72 pors; N Y Post p9 N 20 '76 pors; Newsweek 99:15 My 15 '82 por; People 7:50+ My 2 '77 pors, 17:28+ Mr 29 '82 pors; Vanity Fair 49:94+ N '86 pors; Washington Post C p1+ D 12 '81 por; Norman, Philip. Symphony for the Devil (1984)

Johns, Jasper

May 15, 1930– Artist. Address: b. c/o Leo Castelli Gallery, 420 Broadway, New York City, N.Y. 10012

NOTE: This biography supersedes the article that appeared in *Current Biography* in 1967.

In 1958 the first solo exhibition of Jasper Johns changed the course of art criticism and set the stage for the Pop and minimalist movements that dominated American art in the 1960s. The show included paintings, now acknowledged to be among the most beautiful ever produced by an American, that at the height of Abstract Expressionism reintroduced subject matter into painting with their images of flags, targets, Arabic numerals, and alphabets. Those images, chosen because they were so public that they appeared to be completely unrelated to the artist's personality, pointed to a way that lay beyond the commitment of the Abstract Expressionists to an aesthetic of self-discovery in the "arena" of the canvas.

The different meanings that Johns has said inhere in different working methods led him to sculpture in the late 1950s, and, throughout his career, to the creation of drawings that recapitulate his major motifs. In printmaking, which he began to explore in 1960, Johns has built a body of work now ranked with the greatest of the twentieth century.

In whatever medium he works in, Johns has the ability to make familiar images enigmatic. During the 1960s he incorporated words, puns, and labeled objects in his works to increase their resonance before turning in the 1970s to cross-hatching motifs that sometimes verged on abstraction. In the 1980s the artist decided to "drop the reserve" he had cultivated at the outset of his career and increasingly began to orchestrate the motifs and methods of his entire artistic cycle in single works, with such "incalculable suggestivity," in critic Max Kozloff's phrase, that seeing them became similar to seeing actual images of a mind at work. Johns's most recent work, the four-painting cycle *The Seasons* (1985–86), has been hailed by many critics as a major episode in the history of American autobiography.

Jasper Johns Jr. was born in Augusta, Georgia, on May 15, 1930, to Jasper Johns Sr., a "ne'er-do-well farmer," as his son recalls him, and Jean (Riley) Johns. Because his parents separated soon after he was born, Johns spent his early life being shunted back and forth from one relative to another around the state of South Carolina. He alternated until the end of the third grade between his grandparents and an aunt and uncle in Allendale; then he lived for a year with his mother and stepfather in Columbia. Afterwards, he moved in with his Aunt Gladys in a small lake community called the Corner, where for six years he attended a one-room school where his aunt taught all the grades. He finished high school in Sumter, while living once again with his mother and stepfather.

For as long as he could remember, even during his childhood, which he has said "wasn't specially happy," Johns had wanted to be an artist. "People would always say I was talented," he told one critic. "I knew it was good to use one's talents, but I also knew I couldn't do that where I was—there weren't any artists there—so I guess it was also a form of escape." After studying for three semesters at the University of South Carolina in Columbia, he left for New York City, where he enrolled in a commerical art school in 1949. When his money ran out in 1950, he quit, turning down a scholarship that, he was told, was offered only on the basis of need and not because his work really deserved it. He worked briefly as a messenger before being drafted into the army for a two-year tour of duty that included six months in Japan. There he developed a lifelong interest in Japanese art that later influenced his printmaking. Back in New York in 1952, Johns enrolled at Hunter College under the G.I. Bill, but dropped out after fainting from hunger at the end of his first day of classes. He then took a job at a Marboro bookstore.

While at the bookstore Johns met and began to be influenced by the thinking of the avant-garde composer John Cage. He formed other crucial friendships with the choreographer Merce Cunningham and with Robert Rauschenberg, another young Southerner who was already established as an enfant terrible in the art world. He had become known through several shows and through his erasure, with the artist's permission, of a drawing by Willem de Kooning. Impressed by Rauschenberg's complete devotion to art, Johns quit his Marboro bookstore job, and the two began earning their living by doing window displays for Tiffany & Company and for Bonwit Teller. At the height of Abstract Expressionism, they also provided each other with much-needed encouragement. They formed a kind of two-man aesthetic school to whose emergence Johns contributed collages and small constructions. In 1954, after a resemblance between his collages and those of the German Dadaist Kurt Schwitters was pointed out to him, Johns destroyed all of his works except for four that remained in the hands of friends, deciding "to stop becoming and to be an artist," as he has said.

In his new paintings Johns began to use encaustic, the translucent "skin" of pigmented, melted beeswax that has become his trademark, because, he has said, "encaustic keeps the character of each brushstroke, even in layers. . . . You can see, I think, that these ideas were the thoughts of a young person who wanted to do something worthwhile, something with some rigor to it."

Johns found the rigor for which he had been seeking in the American flag. After dreaming one night that he was painting it, he got up the next day and began, painting it strictly in two dimensions on flat cloth to which a collage of newspaper clippings had been fixed. "Using the design of the American flag took care of a great deal for me because I didn't have to design it," Johns has said. "So I went on to similar things like targets—things the mind already knows. That gave me room to work on other levels."

The first of Johns's new works to be seen in a museum exhibition was Green Target (1955), which was included in the influential "Artists of the New York School: Second Generation" exhibition, held at the Jewish Museum in 1957. The art dealer Leo Castelli saw it there and was "thunderstruck." Soon afterwards he visited Johns's studio and has recalled seeing a "complete body of work . . . ,the most incredible thing [he had] ever seen in [his] life." Castelli showed Flag (1955) in a group exhibition at his gallery in December 1957 and in the following month gave Johns his first, epoch-making one-man show.

After seeing the exhibit, one traumatized Abstract Expressionist painter declared, "If this is painting, I might as well give up." Paintings such as Flag, Flag Above White, and White Flag, all painted in 1955, scandalized some viewers by separating the American flag from its history and making it somehow inscrutable, part of a new system of signs that seemed to raise issues not of patriotism but of painting. Equally disturbing and mysterious were Target with Four Faces (1955), in which four boxes above the target display four truncated plaster casts of a face, all painted orange, and Target with Plaster Cast (1955), which is topped by nine boxes with hinged flaps that, when raised, reveal eight anatomical fragments, including a red foot, a white face, and a green penis. Much has since been written about the eerie tension between the two-dimensional targets and the three-dimensional fragments. There has also been much discussion about their laconic reply to the modernist argument that any representation of the three-dimensional pushed painting away from reality toward illusion, and about their extension of Johns's vocabulary of signs to the body.

Among the other now canonical images in the Castelli show were the twenty-seven rows of alphabets in Gray Alphabets (1956) and the eleven rows of numerals in Gray Numbers (1959). Here Johns had painted so sensuously, giving each number and its enclosing rectangle so much weight and texture that each figure had the character of "a separate passionate experience," as Harold Rosenberg observed in his book The Anxious Object (1982).

The show was a sellout. Alfred Barr bought four paintings for the Museum of Modern Art; Art News featured Target with Four Faces on the cover of its January 1958 issue; and Gray Numbers became the only American painting to win a prize at the 1958 Pittsburgh Biennial International Exhibition of Painting and Sculpture.

Despite his success a number of critics dismissed Johns's images as banal gimmicks, however gorgeously painted. Even those who lauded the paintings at first lacked a vocabulary with which to describe them. When Leo Steinberg questioned Johns directly about his aesthetic strategies, the painter responded politely, but with his now legendary courtly elusiveness, in one instance telling Steinberg that he had cut the faces in Target with Four Faces off below the eyes because they would not have otherwise fitted in their boxes.

Making their own interpretation, the editors of Art News labeled Johns's work "neo-Dada," in a reference to the radical, antirationalist art movement that flourished during and after World War I. The epithet was quickly adopted even by detractors of Johns, such as Hilton Kramer, who ridiculed the painter's style as "a kind of Grandma Moses version of Dada" in an article written for *Arts* magazine (February 1958). Unfamiliar with Dada, Johns read up on it and in the process learned about Marcel Duchamp, whose work, artistic strategies, and insistence that art incarnate ideas and not merely delight the eye confirmed some of Johns's own insights and provided him with paradigms for new ones.

In 1958 Johns began making sculptures, including a plaster and glass flashlight and a bronze light bulb. There followed the sardonic *The Critic Smiles* (1959), a sculpmetal toothbrush whose bristles were replaced by teeth, and *The Critic Sees* (1959), a sculpmetal, plaster and glass composition in which eyeglasses framed a pair of mouths. In 1960, hearing that Willem de Kooning, in a moment of irritation with Leo Castelli, had said, "You could give that son of a bitch two beer cans and he could sell them," Johns promptly made two bronze Ballantine ale cans entitled *Painted Bronze*, which Castelli sold for $1,000. Like the flashlight and the light bulb, *Painted Bronze* has been said to exemplify one of Johns's characteristic gestures: the conferring of uniqueness on mass-produced objects. *Painted Bronze* also embodied another Johns predilection: the paradox. One of the seemingly identical ale cans is taller than the other and is pierced by can-opener marks and is empty, while the other is heavy and closed. A second *Painted Bronze* of 1960, this time a bronze coffee can painted with the Savarin label and filled with paint brushes, completed the transmutation of Johns's subject, which now seemed to be bronze itself.

Meanwhile, in paintings such as *False Start* (1959), Johns struck out in a new direction by using oil paint, a looser brush stroke, and impressionistic splashes of bright color, all counterbalanced by a new strategy of mislabeling—the stenciled word "gray," for example, was applied in red to an area that is yellow. *False Start*'s black-and-white companion painting *Jubilee* (1959), also labeled with the names of bright colors, completed the paradox. *Painting with Two Balls* (1960), in which two wooden balls are wedged in a narrow gap in the painting, more openly mocked the virile approach of the Abstract Expressionists, while hinting at what Calvin Tomkins described in the *New Yorker* (August 4, 1986) as the struggle within Johns between "the thinking artist and the retinal sensualist." Tomkins felt that the sensualist won out over the thinking artist in what he described as three "incredibly beautiful" versions of the map of the United States which Johns painted between 1961 and 1963. Throughout that period, Johns continued to develop his original motifs in paintings such as *Three Flags* (1958), in which three flags of diminishing sizes, each filling a separate canvas, are superimposed so that they appear as one painting and "mislabel" each other's separate picture planes and existences.

In 1960, at the invitation of Tatyana Grossman, Johns began making prints at the Universal Limited Art Editions studio in her home in West Islip, Long Island. Almost immediately he began doing things in that medium that had never been attempted before. For his first series of prints, *0–9*, he drew the numbers 0 through 9 in two rows on the top portion of a lithographic stone, then drew a large 0 on the bottom portion. A print was pulled, the bottom 0 was erased, and a 1 was drawn in its place. The process was repeated until Johns reached the number 9. Each successive number bore some traces of those that had gone before. In addition, the top rows of numbers, although unaltered by Johns, inevitably changed as they were rubbed down in successive printings. For further transformation, each series was printed three times, with different inks and papers. Over a three-year period Johns completed sixty variations in all, each creating a kind of slow-motion record of the process of printing and—some critics feel—of change itself.

Throughout the 1960s Johns also began gradually to increase the autobiographical content of his painting by affixing such paraphernalia of his art and life as pencils, rulers, brooms, cups, and spoons to new paintings. He sometimes even left the imprint of his hands or face on his canvases. Always an aficionado of poetry, he expanded on the impulse of his elegaic grisaille painting, *Tennyson* (1958), in paintings such as *Diver* (1962) and *Periscope (Hart Crane)*, done in 1963, which refer to Hart Crane's suicide by drowning and appear to imply the paradox of a joyful dive that is also a plunge to one's death as a metaphor for the act of perception.

Johns identified two kinds of perception, that of the spy and that of the watchman, in his artistic journal, "Sketchbook Notes" (*Art and Literature 4*, Spring 1965), in which he described the spy as a deliberately invisible presence who "must remember" and the watchman as one who "falls 'into' the 'trap' of looking." Just such a fall seems to be the subject of *Watchman* (1964), which includes a cast of the watchman's lap and legs, "seated" in a chair that is inverted in the upper-right-hand corner of the painting.

The monumental *According to What* (1964), the piece that best sums up this period, includes the seated fragment of the watchman, blocks, mislabeling, gestural swatches of color spread across six joined canvases, and a portrait of Marcel Duchamp, to whom it is both a homage and rebuttal, hidden behind a hinged canvas in the lower-left corner. Like Duchamp's 1918 masterpiece *Tu m'*, on which it is based, the painting seeks to catalog the possibilities available to the medium, though with the opposite intention, for while Duchamp sought to show those possibilities could go no further after *Tu m'*, Johns's *According to What* restated them. The close of that phase of the work of Jasper Johns was marked in 1964 by two retrospectives, then almost unprecedented for an artist in mid-career, at the Jewish Museum in New York and at the Whitechapel Gallery in London.

In 1967 Johns drove past a wall in Harlem that was painted over with images of flagstones that he promptly incorporated into one panel of *Harlem Light* (1967). A similar epiphany occurred in 1972 when he glimpsed an automobile covered with marks similar to cross-hatching, a motif that came to dominate his work for more than a decade. The cross-hatching made its debut in what Mark Stevens described in *Newsweek* (October 24, 1977) as a "terrifying work," the *Untitled* of 1972. Combining oil, encaustic and collage, the painting begins with a panel of choreographed cross-hatchings in secondary colors, proceeds to two panels of flagstones in red, white and black, and ends with what one critic called a "slaughterhouse" of casts of body parts displayed on criss-crossed wooden stakes. The cross-hatchings filled the entire canvas of *Scent* (1973–1974) and subsequent paintings of the 1970s.

Johns's investigations of what he once called "the stress the image takes in different media" created a body of graphic art that flourished alongside the paintings. Working periodically after 1968 at the Gemini G.E.L. workshop in Los Angeles, he used different printing techniques "like musical instruments," according to Gerald Marzorati (*Vanity Fair*, May 1986), and produced series based on all his major motifs. A collaboration with Samuel Beckett, arranged in 1973 while Johns was in Paris designing sets and costumes for Merce Cunningham's dance troupe, resulted in 1977 in *Foraides/Fizzles*, (Whitney Museum of American Art) a book made up of five stories by Beckett and thirty-three etchings that are considered to be among Johns's greatest, all based on the 1972 *Untitled*.

In October 1977, 201 of Johns's paintings, drawings, multiples, and prints brought 4,100 visitors to the Whitney Museum in New York City for the opening of a huge retrospective that was later seen in museums in Cologne, Paris, Tokyo, and San Francisco. Some critics objected to what they saw as the "arbitrary quality" of Johns's new motifs, and Hilton Kramer declared the large paintings failures and the show a "shambles," but Thomas Hess spoke for the majority of viewers when he wrote in his *New York* article that "in wax, oil, acrylic, graphite, or ink, Johns has a wonderful way with the skin of dreams."

By the 1980s Johns's own works had become what he once had called "things the mind already knows." He unexpectedly "developed into one of the great American soliloquists," according to John Russell, the art critic of the *New York Times* (February 15, 1987). His crosshatch paintings achieved their apotheosis in 1980 with the two versions of the symphonic *Dancers on the Plane*, inspired by his work with Merce Cunningham's dance troupe, and with two versions of *Between the Clock and the Bed*, done between 1981 and 1983, that were inspired by Edvard Munch's self-portrait of the same title. In all four, Johns hid "unearthly, jewel-like colors" in the increased resonance of the cross-hatching, according to John Ashbery (*Newsweek*,

February 27, 1984). All of them were shown at a 1984 Castelli exhibit along with ten others, among them *Perilous Night* (1982), which included a page of a musical score by John Cage. They evoked "The Star Spangled Banner" and exuded "peril and menace," according to Ashbery. *Racing Thoughts* (1982), which included a portrait of Leo Castelli, the Mona Lisa, and a death's head warning against falling ice, seemed, like *Perilous Night*, almost directly to reproduce the grain of Johns's thinking and, uncharacteristically, his fears.

Full autobiography emerged with *The Seasons*, an allegorical four-painting cycle that was first exhibited at the Castelli gallery's thirtieth anniversary show in early 1987 and almost immediately acclaimed by critics as a watershed in Johns's career. The dominant image in each painting, based on a tracing of Johns's shadow, was inspired by Picasso's *The Shadow* (1953), while other motifs derive from Picasso's *Minotaur Moving His House* (1936). Johns translates Picasso's image of a Minotaur pulling a cart laden with possessions into a lapse-time transit through the classical four ages of man. In each painting Johns's shadow is juxtaposed with his possessions, including flags and cross-hatchings and a hand with a pierced palm that moves from zenith in *Spring* to nadir in *Winter*. John Russell reported in the *New York Times* (February 15, 1987) that "speculation is now rampant" about the layered meanings of Johns's allegory.

In addition to the exhibitions already mentioned, Johns has had more than fifty one-man shows, and his works are in museum collections throughout the world. He has won many awards, among them prizes at the VI and VII International Exhibition of Graphic Art in Ljubljana, Yugoslavia in 1965 and 1966, the New York City Mayor's Award of Honor for Arts and Culture in 1976, and a $100,000 Prize in Art from the Wolf Foundation in Israel in 1986. He has been artistic adviser to the Merce Cunningham Dance Company since 1967.

Jasper Johns is tall and rangy and has been compared variously to a silent movie hero, an Indian brave, and a Renaissance pope as Raphael might have painted him. He dresses in "muffled elegance," according to one reporter, and speaks with a Southern accent in the rhythms of Biblical prose. Widely read in philosophy, especially in the works of Ludwig Wittgenstein, and in contemporary poetry and prose, he used to keep his freezer full of books. Johns collects the works of Duchamp and other contemporary artists and, like Picasso, is an astute collector of his own work. He is an accomplished cook and an avid devotee of parlor games like Scrabble, backgammon, and Monopoly. He recently moved to a townhouse in Manhattan and has long had a winter home on the Caribbean island of St. Martin.

In 1980 *Three Flags*, for which he originally received $600, was sold to the Whitney for $1 million, believed at that time to be the highest price ever paid for work by a living artist. He set another record in 1986, when *Out the Window* (1959) went at auction for $3.63 million. Reached for comment on the first sale, Johns said he "felt nothing other than amusement. . . . But of course, it has nothing to do with painting."

References: New York 10:64 S 19 '77; Newsday II p4+ My 25 '86 pors; Vanity Fair 47:61+ F '84 pors; Vogue 176:194+ Ja '87 pors; Crichton, Michael. Jasper Johns (1977); Francis, Richard. Jasper Johns (1984); Steinberg, Leo. Other Criteria (1972)

Jones, Grace

May 19, 1952– Model; singer; actress. Address: b. c/o John Carmen, 148 W. 23d St., New York City, N.Y. 10011

"When I'm doing something, I have to take it to the extreme," the model, singer, and movie actress Grace Jones once said, and on another occasion she explained that her persona is "actually, . . . a lot of extremes put together, a mixture of cultures that works." The striking, Jamaican-born beauty who is known for her severely cropped and flat-topped hairstyle and her Amazonian exoticism and sensuality, first achieved international prominence in 1977, when her number-one disco hit, "I Need a Man," transformed her from a stunning fashion model into an androgynous disco diva, whose steamy stage act, with its pronounced sadomasochistic overtones brought frenzied reactions from sexually ambiguous audiences in discotheques and nightclubs. Marketed in artfully designed videos that exploited the visual language of cubism and surrealism as well as state-of-the-art commercial graphics, Grace Jones became a visual star in an aural medium, making up for what many critics called a flat and uninspired singing voice with her theatrics and physical presence.

In the 1980s Grace Jones has inched closer to what she says was her original goal, that of movie stardom, with supporting roles in Conan the Destroyer and the James Bond film A View to a Kill, and with the title role in the horror-comedy Vamp. Her bizarre image has also gained a mainstream acceptance through her appearances in magazine and television advertisements for Honda and Citröen, and even her detractors have conceded that her singing and songwriting seem to have improved with each new album. Whether viewed as an opportunistic exploiter of image or as an artist who explores an image rather than taking undue advantage of it, Grace Jones appears to be validating a boast she made in the July 1979 issue of Ebony magazine: "I am of the Eighties before my time."

Grace Jones was born, according to some sources, on May 19, 1952 in Spanishtown, Jamaica, to Robert and Marjorie P. Jones. Striking even as a child, she was nicknamed "Firefly" because of the way her bright eyes flashed against her dark skin. Her father was a Pentecostal minister, and the members of her mother's family included a great-uncle who was a bishop. In her early childhood, her father and mother moved to Syracuse, New York, where her father had a church, leaving Grace, her twin brother, Christian, and her other siblings in the care of their maternal grandparents. In that stern upbringing there was no room for television or popular music, and her knuckles were cracked when she misplayed a note in her piano lessons. "In Jamaica at that time, they believed if you spare the rod you spoil the child," she told an interviewer for the Guardian (June 8, 1985). "They certainly didn't spoil me."

Of her six brothers and sisters, Grace Jones was closest to her twin brother, Christian. She has since made the occult claim that their chemistries became "entangled at birth," accounting, she says, for her fascination with androgyny and reversed sex roles. "The way we came out, I was the big brother and he was the little sister," she told a writer for New York magazine (August 15, 1977). "I took care of him, fought for him. I played with fire and he played with dolls." She was also deeply affected by her mother, who visited her periodically from the United States. An accomplished seamstress, Marjorie Jones made and wore perfect copies of the latest Paris fashions, leaving her sheltered daughter with an enduring impression of chic glamour. Soon, according to After Dark (December 1977), her daughter Grace was "tripping off" fantasies of movie stardom.

In 1964, at the age of twelve, Grace Jones joined her parents who were now living in the middle-class, largely white Syracuse suburb of Lyncourt. Ahead of her age group in school because of her superior Jamaican education and thrown in with a group of typical American teenagers, she felt out of place, but rather than withdrawing into herself, she acted out her brazen movie star fantasies. Forbidden by her Pentecostal faith to wear slacks, she wore high-fashion gowns that showed off her breasts instead. "All the kids would laugh at me because I was the first one to wear an Afro and would wear these glamorous gowns to school at a time when the in-thing was to be casual and grubby," she recalled for a reporter for the New York Post (December 30, 1977). "I guess from the very beginning I wanted to be a movie star and started to act like it. I was very vain and still am."

In 1968 Grace Jones enrolled at Syracuse University with the intention of becoming a teacher of French, but her plans were derailed by an affair with her drama professor, a long-haired playwright with wire-rimmed glasses whose "hip" appearance fascinated her. He cast her in Joyce Kilmer and his Sister Sophocles, his absurdist musical based on the works of Geoffrey Chaucer, which had a short run in Philadelphia. Leaving the professor, the play, and Syracuse at about the same time, she embarked upon a brief "hippie" period, experimenting with drugs, living as a nudist for several months, joining a motorcycle gang for a half a year, and riding a Honda 450 to the Woodstock rock music festival in the summer of 1969. "I don't know who the hell I thought I was," she said during the After Dark interview about that phase of her life.

Encouraged by a friend who assured her that she had the high cheekbones of a fashion model, Grace Jones signed up with the Black Beauty modeling agency in New York City. Years later, in Andy Warhol's Interview magazine (November 1984), she derided her first assignment for the agency—a before and after makeover for Essence magazine—saying that she looked better "before" than "after." That reaction characterized her ambivalent attitude toward modeling throughout her career, since she resented being made over and having her image reshaped to sell a product. Modeling for Black Beauty, she told the New York Post interviewer, was "boring and restrictive." Soon she switched to the much less restrictive Wilhemina modeling agency in New York, and then moved to Paris, where models with strong personalities and bold images were more in fashion. Before leaving the United States, she played a one-line role in Gordon's War, a black exploitation film, released in 1973, about drug dealing that starred Paul Winfield. She also sampled the emerging New York City club scene that was to prove vital to her later disco success and became what rock writer Nik Cohn in New York magazine (August 15, 1977) called the "resident deity" at the the club Le Jardin.

Once arrived in Paris, Grace Jones set about systematically attracting attention to herself. She and her friends, including the fashion model Jerry Hall, who later became Mick Jagger's wife, hit the local nightclub scene with a vengeance. One night she danced in public with only a baseball cap, satin running shorts, and body glitter for a costume. She adopted the close-cropped hair that became her trademark. "It was my campaign," she recalled for After Dark. "I was really crazy . . . my God . . .

nuts. We'd go dancing and end up on the floor. And before you knew it, Elle magazine picked me off the street and did a story on me." More modeling for magazines followed, in the French and English editions of Vogue, in the German weekly Stern, even in the Russian Pravda. Eventually she graced the covers of Vogue, Harper's Bazaar, and Cosmopolitan, and she posed for such celebrated photographers as Helmut Newton, Guy Bourdin, and Hans Fuerer. Continuing to try for movie success, she appeared in the French film Attention Les Yeux and the Italian picture Calibre .38, but failed to catch on as an actress. For several years she lived the life of an international high-fashion model, gaining notoriety in avant-garde and artistic circles on both sides of the Atlantic for her audacious behavior.

During one night at the Club Sept, in Paris, Grace Jones became so inspired by the Three Degrees' recording of "Dirty Old Man" coming over the sound system that she leaped up on a table and belted out a convincing performance of the song. That incident prompted another fashion model to recommend her as a possible recording artist to her boyfriend, who happened to work for a French record company. In a short time Grace Jones signed a contract with Island Records, the company that introduced reggae, Jamaica's syncopated rock 'n' roll, to mass audiences in Europe and the United States. Her first album, Portfolio, which was released in 1977 by Island Records, included the international hit "La Vie en Rose", a French standard done to a disco beat, and "I Need a Man", which reached the number one position on the disco charts in the United States.

Riding the crest of those successes, Grace Jones went on to conquer the gay nightclub scene in New York City, where scores of gay discos and clubs flourished in the liberated ambiance of the late 1970s. "I Need a Man," as may have been deliberately intended, became a gay anthem of sorts, and her New York debut in 1977 at Les Mouches, a cavernous club near the promiscuous piers of the West Side, turned out an audience that was, in Nik Cohn's phrase, "a walking compendium of gay chic." According to Cohn, Grace Jones did not disappoint her cult followers, presenting a lascivious floor show at whose center "she was pure flame." "The celebrants blew whistles and shook tambourines, danced, popped pills, and danced again," Cohn reported. But when John Rockwell of the New York Times viewed her return engagement at Les Mouches in September of that year, he saw things differently. "Even in the context of disappointing live performances by studio-crafted disco stars, Miss Jones's singing was amateurish and awkward," he wrote. "And although she is certainly a handsome woman, she moves unsurely."

Credited by some with devising a new form of performance art called "disco theater," Grace Jones invested a great deal of thought in the lighting, costumes, scenery, and other details of her stage act. "I realized that I am more dynamic freezing than moving," she was quoted as saying in the

Guardian (June 8, 1985). "When you pose you stay in one place, you work your eyes, and you strike different attitudes. My show was like bringing a fashion photograph to life." Her songs were done as individual tableaux against stark backdrops, often with different costumes, props, and supporting casts. Her invariable show stopper was, of course, "I Need a Man," which she sang in a wedding veil, black corset, and garter belt while lightly lashing the bare buttocks of her dog-collared white male attendants with a black whip or while roughly handling some partner she had plucked from the audience.

Meanwhile, she kept striving for more outrageous effects. She made her entrance one night with a live panther on a leash and another with a motorcycle, which she drove onto the dance floor. She was able to work audiences into a frenzy, and there were many stories of wild happenings, such as the night when a crowd in Paris stripped her naked or the time when a man in a black leather face mask chained himself to her leg at a performance in New York City. Many rock critics considered her shows to be a form of hype, especially since she usually performed without a band, but sang instead to a prerecorded accompaniment. After viewing one of her performances at a Long Island nightclub, in which she seemed to be mouthing the words of her songs to a prerecorded vocal, Wayne Robins of *Newsday* (September 8, 1980) accused her of manipulating her audience and observed that there was "something about her opportunism that approaches the pathological."

After recording two more disco albums, *Fame* and *Muse*, Grace Jones, without entirely abandoning her disco roots, began to expand her repertoire with *Warm Leatherette* (Island, 1980) and *Nightclubbing* (Island, 1981). Both albums featured the extraordinary reggae rhythm section of Sly Dunbar and Robbie Shakespeare. With the other musicians on the records, they helped her to develop an amalgam of disco, reggae, and funk that won praise from the critics who had scorned her earlier efforts. The lyrics of some songs, such as the smash hit from *Nightclubbing*, "Pull Up to the Bumper," were still packed with double entendres for her gay audience, but she was also doing reputable versions of songs by established rock acts like Smokey Robinson, Tom Petty, Roxy Music, the Pretenders, Sting, and David Bowie. Robert Galano of the *Washington Post* (July 11, 1980) noted that *Warm Leatherette* added "musical depth and diversity" to her act and cited "the ease and assurance" of her improved singing, but Stephen Holden of the *New York Times* (August 8, 1981) still found Miss Jones to be "a very limited vocalist" who enjoyed the advantage of an improved backup, with its "ominous mixture of pop and reggae."

Grace Jones's act also grew more sophisticated in the early 1980s, largely under the influence of Jean-Paul Goude, a French artist-photographer who had been the art director of *Esquire* magazine and who served for a while as what a reporter for the New York *Daily News* (May 27, 1983) called

her "Svengali." It was Goude, for example, who designed the flat-topped, sculptured hairdo that became Grace Jones's trademark, and it was he who produced "A One Man Show", a visually eclectic, feature-length video that employed postmodernist imagery to present Grace Jones and her music. Writing in *American Film* (January/February 1986), Raymond Durgnat rhapsodized over "A One Man Show," comparing its "Negress cubism" to no less a milestone than Picasso's *Les Demoiselles d'Avignon*. Grace Jones and Jean-Paul Goude, who is ten years her senior, became lovers as well as artistic collaborators, and in 1980 a son, Paolo, was born of that relationship.

Her next album was *Living my Life* (Island, 1982), a record that included a number of original songs written with guitarist Barry Reynolds. By that time, she had a regular backup group including Barry Reynolds, Sly Dunbar on drums, Robbie Shakespeare on bass, and Wally Badarou on keyboards. Although she found a lack of spontaneity in both Grace Jones's stage act and recorded singing, Thulani Davis, writing in the *Village Voice* (February 8, 1983), praised much of the album by placing Miss Jones squarely in the French nightclub tradition of *sauvage* made famous by such American black entertainers as Josephine Baker, but crediting her with moving beyond the style to become an expressive artist in her own right.

When Arnold Schwarzenegger, the Austrian-born body builder turned actor, saw "A One Man Show," he was so impressed by Grace Jones's fierce appearance and rippling muscles that he had her cast as Zula, Conan's savage sidekick in *Conan the Destroyer*, a sequel to his fantasy film *Conan the Barbarian*. According to Schwarzenegger, she injured about twelve persons who were involved in filming her fight scenes, and she also made waves on the set by squabbling with the cast and crew. "Everything you see her do on video is not acting at all," Schwarzenegger informed an interviewer for the *New York Post* (July 2, 1984). "That's really her." Although critics derided the fatuous pretensions of *Conan the Destroyer*, they often singled Grace Jones out for praise, and according to the film's director, Richard Fleisher, she stole the show.

Her next film, the James Bond thriller, *A View to a Kill* (MGM/UA, 1985), paired Grace Jones with the urbane Roger Moore, who at fifty-seven was still portraying the amorous British agent. She played May Day, a villainess who is won over by Bond's charm, and once again reviewers saw her as a bright spot in an otherwise predictable rehash of James Bond clichés. Miss Jones maintains that she was given virtual control over her character's appearance and that several items of her personal wardrobe were copied for *A View to a Kill*. Her scantily clad, muscular body was placed back-to-back with the dinner-jacketed Roger Moore on the film's promotional posters. During the filming, Grace Jones overstepped the bounds of film etiquette when she suggested on British television that Roger Moore was over the hill and that her current boyfriend, Hans Lundgren, a Danish kick boxer, would make a better Bond.

In 1985 Grace Jones released two record albums. One was *Island Life*, an anthology of her work with Island Records, and the other was *Slave to Rhythm*, a compilation of eight different versions of the same song that was released by Manhattan Records, her new label. Although Stephen Holden of the *New York Times* (January 8, 1986) found *Slave to Rhythm* a "fascinating album," on which her self-styled "contralto-baritone" seemed "ominously compelling," Greg Tate of the *Village Voice* (December 31, 1985) dismissed it as "ridiculously redundant" and as nothing more than "forty minutes of James Bond themes." Nevertheless, *Inside Story*, her latest album, released by Manhattan Records early in 1987 and produced by Nile Rogers, who crafted Madonna's smash albums, was praised for the sincerity and directness with which she delivered the songs that she had written with her new collaborator, Bruce Wooley.

Returning to films in the ill-advised *Vamp* (New World Pictures, 1986), Grace Jones played a 2,000-year-old Egyptian vampire reincarnated as an exotic dancer who lures teenage boys to her lair. A combination of adolescent prurience and camped-up horror, *Vamp* failed to entice customers to the box office, and was notable chiefly for the grotesque makeup that Miss Jones wore in some scenes. Working again with Jean-Paul Goude, she produced a follow-up video to "A One Man Show" called "A State of Grace." When Stephen Holden viewed it for the first time in the spring of 1986, he conceded that "A State of Grace" was visually striking, but quipped that Miss Jones's singing on that video suggested "Ethel Merman engaging in a fit of pique."

Described by Raymond Durgnat as having "a lion's head on an antelope's body," Grace Jones impresses everyone who sees her because of her full lips, slanting eyes, and prominent cheekbones. As Andy Warhol and André Leon Talley once put it, her unique gift is for "visual originality." Although often described as six feet tall, she is actually five feet eight inches in height and weighs about 118 pounds. In the 1980s she has lived mostly in New York City in a 2,000-square-foot, loft-like, Greenwich Village apartment that commands a panoramic view of the Hudson River, with her son, Paolo, and a live-in housekeeper. Once involved romantically with Hans Lundgren, she is now being squired around town by his twin brother Dolph, who played the Russian boxer in *Rocky IV*. The former fashion model, who lifts weights to stay in shape, is still a clothes horse who owns at least thirty-five furs, including some outrageously dyed coats that she buys with what she calls the "play money" she earns from her Honda and Citröen television commercials. Like Imelda Marcos, she has a passion for shoes. In early 1987 Miss Jones opened a restaurant, La Vie en Rose, in New York City's Soho district, and she is now contemplating the possibilities of starting a cosmetics line or producing an exercise video, since she is convinced that "boredom is death."

References: *After Dark* 10:73+ D '77 pors; *Guardian* p10 Je 8 '85 por; *Ebony* 34:84+ Jl '79 pors; *New York* 10:50+ Ag 15 '77 pors; *Rolling Stone* p42 Ag 20 '81 por; *US* 2:32 Ag 8 '78 pors; *Washington Post* D p1 N 24 '81 pors

Jones, K. C.

May 25, 1932– Basketball coach. Address: b. Boston Celtics, Boston Garden, North Station, Boston, Mass. 02114

In coaching the Boston Celtics to the 1985–86 National Basketball Association championship, K. C. Jones secured an almost unprecedented twelfth world championship ring in a playing and coaching association with the NBA going back to 1958. As a play-making defensive guard, Jones helped pace the University of San Francisco basketball team to two National Collegiate Athletic Association championships in the mid-1950s, and he was a member of the Boston club that dominated the NBA from 1958 to 1966. After coaching numerous other teams on the college and professional levels for nine years, he returned to the Celtics as an assistant coach in 1977 and became head coach in 1983. During his first three years as head coach, Boston won the world championship twice and was the runner-up once. Jones and Pat Riley of the Los Angeles Lakers are the only long-term coaches in NBA history to have won more than 70 percent of their regular-season games, and they also have had the most play-off wins among active coaches.

K. C. Jones (whose forename consists only of initials) was born in Taylor, Texas, on May 25, 1932. His mother, Eula Jones, divided her time between raising her five children and working as a maid. His father and namesake was a restaurant cook and auto worker. During the Depression the Joneses moved from one Texas town to another, staying wherever the parents found work. "In the Jim Crow South . . . the odds against black people seemed as large as a mountain . . . ," Jones recounts in his autobiography, Rebound (Quinlan Press, 1986), written with Jack Warner. "Nothing was easy for us. . . . I was the oldest and I tried to do what I could to help. I'd cook, I'd clean house. . . . The cooking . . . was something I learned to love. I was the family's main cook until I went away to college."

His family's itinerancy retarded Jones's education, and he never learned to read well. Ashamed when called upon in class, he became withdrawn and extremely laconic, even at home. The only time he felt "fully free" was when he sang in church or played sports. "The first game I went for was tennis, in the third grade," he recounts in his autobiography. "But tennis couldn't be a black kid's game then. It was too expensive, and who was going to let you use their court? So I started with softball. Then football. . . . When we were living in McGregor [Texas] the girls played basketball, so I was a little suspicious of it."

When Jones was nine his father abandoned the family, and a year later Mrs. Jones moved to San Francisco with her children. "It was in San Francisco that my enthusiasm for sports really started to flow," Jones recalled in Rebound. "There were places to play and you could play with anybody—any color." Playing basketball every day at a recreation center near his home, he had developed "a really deadly set shot" by the time he entered Commerce High School in San Francisco. As a high school basketball player he broke the Triple A Prep League scoring record, was "a real bulldog on defense," and made the All Northern California All-Star team. He was also an All Star in football.

Meanwhile, his studies were, in his words, "coming in third behind basketball and part-time jobs to help support the family." Expecting nothing higher after high school than a job in the post office, he "never thought about" college, even though the University of San Francisco, a Jesuit institution, was only fifteen minutes from his home. Then "something wonderful happened" in his senior year. "Miss Mildred Smith, my history teacher . . . was a white lady who saw something in this black boy that caused her to pick up the telephone and call Phil Woolpert, the basketball coach at the University of San Francisco," he wrote in Rebound. "She didn't give up, she made more than one call. She kept after him to give me a scholarship to USF. . . . She did it because she cared. Her caring changed my life." Passing the entrance test at USF, Jones won the scholarship.

During the summer before college, Jones relates, "a strange thing happened:" he grew four inches, to six feet one inch, "which is every basketball player's dream," but at the same time he "completely lost [his] shot—which is every basket-

ball player's nightmare." In his freshman season at the University of San Francisco, he "took plenty of shots" but ended with a 5.6 scoring average. Realizing that he "would have to accept [his] new limits as a shooter and change [his] game," he decided to become "the director—the play-maker." "The team would be the talent. From now on the points I would score wouldn't show up on the box score under my name, but my teammates would score more and play better because of my efforts on the floor. Parts of the game that some more talented players paid less attention to—defense and passing—I would master." He also promised himself that he "would hustle and scrap every minute that [he] was on the floor in a basketball game."

In the autumn of 1952, when he was beginning his sophomore year at the University of San Francisco, "something happened that was to become a real directional arrow" in Jones's life: a six-foot-nine freshman named Bill Russell became his roommate, the same Bill Russell who would, twenty-eight years later, be voted the greatest player in the history of the National Basketball Association. Like Jones, Russell was a painfully shy young black man whose family had moved from the South to the Bay area. For a month the two lived together in silence, but once they started talking, the conversation never stopped. "He and I became inseparable," Jones recounted in Rebound. "We talked of everything. . . . It was like two minds working in the same direction with the same thoughts and the same goals. Often we finished one another's sentences. . . . We were always trying to determine ways to make the opponent take the shot that we wanted him to take from the place we wanted. . . . I guess by the time we graduated from USF Bill Russell and I had talked, studied, worked, practised, and played as much defensive basketball as any two people ever had." Because Jones was sidelined with a burst appendix in 1953-54, his junior year, he accrued an extra year of eligibility, and he and Russell led the USF basketball squad to two undefeated seasons and two national championships, in 1954-55 and 1955-56. Jones was also a member of the United States basketball team that won a gold medal in the 1956 Olympics.

Russell and Jones were picked by the Boston Celtics in the first and second rounds, respectively, of the 1956 collegiate draft. Russell joined the Celtics immediately, but Jones, fearing that he might not make the grade in the NBA and wanting to get his military obligation over with, joined the army for two years. While in the army, he played wide receiver on the football team at Camp Leonard Wood in Missouri, and after his discharge he was invited to try out with the Los Angeles Rams football team, in 1958. Playing defensive back in a few bruising exhibition football games convinced him that he would last longer as a basketball player, and he called Coach Red Auerbach to ask if he was still welcome with the Celtics. Informed that he was, he left the Rams without a word and began his professional basketball career.

When Jones made his first appearance in practice with the Celtics, one observer described him as "an All-American who forgot to learn how to shoot." Red Auerbach was impressed with his speed, hustle, and defensive brilliance, however, and gave him a contract. Lacking the finesse of such teammates as Bob Cousy, Bill Sharman, Sam Jones, and Bill Russell, Jones became the team's "coal miner." "The coal miner," as he explained to Thad Martin in an interview for Ebony (April 1985), complements "the delicate shooters, the elite." "He's the guy who scrapes the boards for the offensive rebounds and for the defensive rebounds. He's the first one to get the loose ball and he's great . . . in playing defense on the ball and off the ball. That means he's guarding two people. He also has to be ready to help the guy who is guarding the ball. This is the guy with no talent who has to use his brains to win."

With Jones on the squad, first as a reliever and, after Bob Cousey's retirement in 1963, as a starter, the Celtics won eight consecutive NBA championships. "I still can't put my finger on it," Red Auerbach said in retrospect of Jones's special magic on the court. "The odds were against him despite his defensive and play-making ability. However, every time I put him into a game things would turn our way."

Typical of Jones's contributions to Boston victories was his hobbling of the high-scoring guard Oscar Robertson in the 1964 semifinal series against the Cincinnati Royals. On that occasion, as Frank Deford reported in Sports Illustrated (April 20, 1964), "the whole [Cincinnati] team was upset by the successful harassment of the one key man." According to Jones, Robertson was his toughest opponent. "Tom [Satch] Sanders and I would work together when they [the Royals] would set picks," he has recounted. "Satch would take him if I couldn't get through and steer him to Russell. If I could take him, I'd do the same thing. We would then be getting a sort of triple team all the time."

After his retirement as a player, Jones was assistant basketball coach at Harvard University for a year (1967-68) and head coach at Brandeis University for four years (1968-71). He returned to the National Basketball Association as assistant coach of the Los Angeles Lakers under his former Celtics teammate Bill Sharman in 1971-72. That season the Lakers set a record by winning their first thirty-three games and went on to take the NBA championship, Jones's ninth. As head coach of the weak San Diego Conquistadors in 1972-73, he achieved a 30-54 record and a play-off spot, a feat that Phil Elderkin of the Christian Science Monitor (July 25, 1973) compared to getting "water out of a stone."

Immediately after the 1972-73 season, Jones was offered a three-year coaching contract by Abe Pollin, the owner of the NBA's Washington Bullets (then called the Capital Bullets), a team strong on offensive showboating but weak on defense. Accepting the challenge of turning the Bullets into champions, Jones confounded those who thought that he was too quiet and "nice " to bend the mile-high egos of Washington's star players to his will. Quickly winning the confidence of his players with his understanding of their particular personalities and willingness to listen to their problems, he was able to bring the several formidable egos together into a collective support system for a paralyzing team defense in addition to an exceptionally fast break. The Bullets posted a 47-35 record in 1973-74 despite many player injuries, and in 1974-75 they opened the season with a seven-game winning streak and went on to an awesome regular-season record of 60-22 before clinching the Eastern Conference Championship. Then, suddenly, they slumped, losing four straight games to the Golden State Warriors in the NBA finals.

In the closing minutes of the second game against the Warriors "something happened that seemed insignificant at the time," as Jones recounts in Rebound, but "its impact was going to rock" his life. "We were behind by two points when we called a timeout. When the team came to the bench and gathered around me I said, 'Run play C'. . . . Bernie Bickerstaff, my assistant, said, 'Should I diagram it?' I said 'sure'. . . . The television camera was zeroed in on our timeout. What people saw on their sets was a team in big trouble and Coach Jones standing silently while the players huddled around a blackboard and the assistant coach diagramed a play for them. [After] we lost the game by one point . . . a thunderstorm of criticism exploded on my head. 'Jones is a joke as a coach.' 'He does nothing.' 'His assistants run the team.' . . . The Washington papers wouldn't let [the story] go. Other sportswriters around the country played with it occasionally. . . . I was beginning to learn . . . a lesson every coach must learn—the media is part of the territory that goes with the job."

The Bullets struggled through the 1975-76 season, making the play-offs with a 48-34 record but failing to secure the Central Division championship for the first time in six years. Jones, who then had the second-best winning percentage among active coaches in the NBA (.630), was fired after the Bullets were eliminated from the play-offs in a hotly contested series with the Cleveland Cavaliers. The firing "devastated" Jones, and he "began to fall apart as a man" as the months went by with no other job offers and no answers to his calls and letters to NBA and college teams. "I was embarrassed in front of my wife and kids . . . ," he writes in Rebound. "I spent more and more time at the golf course. . . . I had never been much of a drinker. . . . Now it was different. I drank more. I was getting into the loser's habit." Then, being hired as assistant coach of the Milwaukee Bucks in the middle of the 1976-77 season only to be fired at the season's end "almost destroyed" him.

Jones was about to take a minor-league coaching job in Richmond, Virginia in 1977 when suddenly, as he recalls, "one of [his] dearest friends reached out his hand to [him] and opened a very large door." The friend was his former Celtics teammate, Satch Sanders, who had just become head coach of the Boston team. Jones went to Boston as assistant to Sanders in 1977-78, a disastrous season in which the Celtics did not even make the play-offs. He remained in Boston as assistant to two subsequent head coaches, Dave Cowens and Bill Fitch. In four seasons, Fitch coached the Celtics to 242 regular-season wins and only eighty-six losses, but the team slumped during the last half of the 1982-83 season and lost four straight games to the Milwaukee Bucks in the play-offs. "The pride was still there," Jones later told a reporter, "but it waned a bit after the All-Star break. We started losing some, and when that happens people get cross and edgy and . . . start placing blame." "I'm just sick," Larry Bird said at the end of the 1982-83 season. "Sometimes I wonder where our hearts are."

The scapegoat for the Celtics becoming, by their standards, an ordinary team, was Bill Fitch, accused by some of being a "tyrant." When Fitch resigned in the summer of 1983, Red Auerbach, who had become president of the Celtics, surprised everybody, including Jones himself, by naming Jones head coach. Charles Vincent of the *Sporting News* (November 1983), noting that "Celtic pride" had become a "a hollow old battle cry, a galling memory of what used to be," thought it most appropriate that the club should be turned over to Jones, "a man who has three decades of Celtic pride—as a player and coach—running through his veins." "There's a lot to Celtic pride," Jones told Vincent. "It started in 1958 and we went on to win eight championships in a row. What went into it was a way of players dealing with each other—player-to-player respect." Vincent commented: "Maybe Celtic pride will begin to mean something again."

Strategically, Jones gave the Celtics new defensive options, and morally, he renewed the team's pride and "made the game fun again," as center Robert Parish observed to a reporter in February 1984. That season the Celtics went 62-20 in the regular season, made their way to the final round of the play-offs, and defeated the Los Angeles Lakers to win the NBA championship "K. C. just made it all work," forward Larry Bird commented. "He understood us, every one of us." The sports commentator Tom Heinsohn, a former Celtics player and coach, described the major improvements of Jones's game plan over that of his predecessor as an emphasis on the press in defense and "a lot more switching, a lot more gambling." "He believed quickness was a major asset of [his] team," Heinsohn said of Jones, "and he wanted to capitalize on it. And you can't knock the overall success of what he's created."

In the 1984-85 season the Celtics won almost 80 percent of their games, posting a 63-19 regular-season record, but they lost the championship in a showdown with the Lakers. In 1985-86 they had a league-leading regular-season record of 67-15 and went on to dominate the play-offs and win Boston's sixteenth world championship by putting defensive straitjackets on the Houston Rockets and their versatile, seven-foot-plus "twin towers," Ralph Samson and Akeem Olajuwon. In 1986-87 the Celtics, riddled with injuries, managed to win the

NBA eastern title but again lost to the Lakers in the championship series.

The Celtics' .780 winning percentage under Jones from 1983 to 1986 was the highest in league history for a three-year period. Combined with his Washington record, his success with the Celtics made him the only coach in league history to win more than sixty games in a season with two different franchises. Jones was selected to coach the Eastern Conference All-Star team in each of his first three years as head coach of the Boston Celtics. His total All-Star record, including a game he coached while with the Washington Bullets, is 3-1.

As a player, K. C. Jones was dubbed "the man with the square eyes" by Bill Russell because of his on-court intensity and his fascination with television. Despite his shy temperament, Jones is usually lighthearted and outgoing among friends. Sam Goldpaper reported in the *New York Times* (May 28, 1986) that Jones was known in his playing days for mimicking "the way Red Auerbach walked, Bill Russell stroked his beard, and Frank Ramsey talked" in the Celtic locker room. Among Jones's favorite recreations are singing such popular songs as "Misty," "Sunny" and "You're Nobody 'Till Somebody Loves You" and dancing. He has five children by his marriage to the former Beverly Cain, which ended in divorce, and one child by his marriage to his wife since 1981, Ellen. Jones was elected to the San Francisco Bay Area Basketball Hall of Fame in 1986. His number, twenty-five, has been retired along with those of other Celtics greats and hangs with the championship banners in the rafters in Boston Garden.

References: Christian Sci Mon p14 Je 14 '83 por; Nat Observer p15 Ap 19 '75 por; Newsday C p30 F 2 '66; Sporting N 197:3 F 20 '83 por; Washington Post D p1 Je 16 '84; Jones, K. C., and Warner, Jack. Rebound (1986)

Jordan, Michael

Feb. 17, 1963- Professional basketball player. Address: b. Chicago Bulls, 980 N. Michigan Ave., Suite 1600, Chicago, Ill. 60611-4501

The Chicago Bulls, previously the dullest team in the National Basketball Association, now have one of the top gate attractions in the league—Michael Jordan, an unstoppable "big guard" and a natural showman who occasionally swings to forward, creating excitement with almost his every move, especially when a game is in the balance. As a college player at the University of North Carolina, Jordan was, in the opinion of Coach Dean Smith, the best back-court offensive rebounder he had ever coached. Jordan was twice chosen College Player of the Year and was a unanimous All-American. In addition, he was the leading scorer on the American team that won the gold medal at the Pan Amer-

Michael Jordan

his older brother Larry, who grew to be only five feet seven inches tall.

Michael's habit of sticking his tongue out when going for a shot was picked up from his father, who used to stick his tongue out when repairing the family car. James Jordan is, in Michael's words, "a go-getter," and both parents imbued their children with the work ethic, the will to strive for excellence in their chosen fields, and a sense of priorities. "In our family . . . we try to make something happen rather than waiting around for it to happen," James Jordan told Al Thomy of The Sporting News (March 26, 1984). "We believe the surest way is to work toward making it happen." As Michael has recounted, the Jordans warned their children against "the traps . . . the drugs and drink, the streets that could catch you if you got careless." Doug Collins, the coach of the Chicago Bulls since 1986, told Pete Axthelm of Newsweek (January 5, 1987): "When I met him [Michael] I wondered how, with all the distractions, he could maintain such mountains of freshness. Then I met his family and I understood. It sounds corny, but it's true—love shows."

As a youngster, Michael was, according to his father, "a happy-go-lucky, unselfish type" who "wasn't hard to please." Not a born basketball player, Michael "set goals and worked hard to achieve them," as James Jordan told Al Thomy. "His leaping didn't just happen. He worked at it. When he was thirteen, I built a backyard court and he, his brother Larry, and some other kids played almost every day." When he began playing one-on-one with Larry, Michael was the shorter of the two. That handicap only fired the more his fierce determination to win, and his hustle earned him the nickname "Rabbit."

Playing Little League baseball, Michael Jordan pitched two no-hitters. As a freshman at Laney High School in Wilmington, he was too small to make the varsity basketball team. He made the team at the beginning of his sophomore year, but barely, and he was cut from the squad soon after the season started. As a sophomore, he briefly played safety on the football team. He also ran track and played baseball. By the end of his sophomore year, he was beginning to think that perhaps baseball was "the right place" for his talent. Then he began to sprout. Between his sophomore and junior years he grew from five feet eleven inches to six feet three, and during his senior year he added three more inches, reaching his present height of six feet six inches. Already blessed with the legs of a high jumper and the shoulders of a linebacker, he was transformed by the increase in height from an all-round athlete of some promise into a potential basketball great. Following his junior season with the Laney High School basketball team, his coach, Clifton Herring, persuaded Howie Garfinkel to admit Jordan to Garfinkel's summer Five Star Basketball Camp in Pittsburgh, a training ground for big-time college prospects. Being at the camp made Jordan feel that someone had "tapped [him] on the shoulder" with "a magic wand" and

ican Games in Caracas, Venezuela, in 1983 and the cocaptain of the Olympic team that took the gold in Los Angeles in 1984.

Drafted by the Chicago Bulls in 1984, Jordan was an instant success as a professional, leading the league in scoring and earning the Rookie of the Year award. Kept out of action by a foot injury through most of the 1985–86 season, he returned to lead the NBA in scoring again in 1986–87, when he had a 37.1 point average, third highest in NBA history. Jordan, who is best known for his sensational over-the-head backhand slam dunk, electrifies the crowd with his speed and his stratospheric jumping. Playing taller than his six feet six inches, he soars above opposing forwards of greater height and seems at times to hover in the air before completing his shot. He shoots with a frequency not seen since Wilt Chamberlain, and he displays a combination of talents probably not found in a single player since Oscar Robertson. Those talents combined with his good looks and his friendly, unspoiled personality give him an unsurpassed commercial marketability. His endorsements of Nike athletic gear and other products, his royalties, and his fees for appearances bring him a supplementary income about four times greater than his annual salary as a Chicago Bull, which is reported to be approximately $800,000.

Michael Jordan describes himself as "a country boy from Wilmington, North Carolina," where he was born on February 17, 1963, to Delores Jordan, a customer-service supervisor at a bank, and James Jordan, an equipment supervisor at a General Electric plant. He has two brothers, Larry and Ronald, and two sisters, Delores and Roslyn. Both parents were only of average height, and neither was athletic. The most athletic of Michael's siblings was

said, "You must emerge as somebody—somebody to be admired, to achieve big things. But don't lose your identity."

Suddenly, Jordan became one of the most recruited high school hoopsters in the United States. Before the beginning of his senior year in high school, he accepted a scholarship from the University of North Carolina at Chapel Hill. To accelerate his development, Coach Herring, who lived a block away from the Jordans, picked Michael up every morning at six and drove him to the high school gym for an extra hour of practice throughout his senior year. The more he practiced, the more his game improved and the more confident he became in anticipating college competition.

At the University of North Carolina, Jordan majored in geography and roomed with Buzz Peterson, a white reserve player from a well-to-do business family whom he had met and become friends with when both were prep All-Americans. "What impressed me most about Michael was his love for his parents and family," Peterson told Al Thomy of The Sporting News. "And he was a fun guy to be around. All that ends when he goes on the court, though. Then he becomes deadly serious." For recreation, Peterson introduced Jordan to golf, and Jordan taught Peterson to shoot pool.

In the starting UNC lineup from the first game of 1981-82, his freshman season, Jordan played erratically, averaging only 13.5 points and four rebounds a game but coming through brilliantly in clutches, including the closing seconds of the National Collegiate Athletic Association championship game against Georgetown. On that occasion he completed a fifteen-and-a-half-foot corner jumper to give the Tarheels a one-point victory and Coach Smith his only national title in twenty-four years at UNC. Jordan was voted the Atlantic Coast Conference Rookie of the Year, and teammates and fans nicknamed him "Superman" and "Last Shot."

Under Coach Smith, Jordan learned tight all-round team play and mastered rebounding and defense, his principal weakness when he arrived at Chapel Hill. In 1982-83, his sophomore season, after a slow start he led the Atlantic Coast Conference in scoring with an average of twenty points a game, but he was proudest of his defensive improvement. As a freshman, he did not win one defensive game award. As a sophomore, he won twelve, and he was assigned not one man to guard but two. While keeping an eye on his assigned men, he free-lanced, double-teaming the ball and stealing at every opportunity. By the end of his sophomore season he already ranked second to Dudley Bradley in the UNC record book for single-season steals, with seventy-eight. In the whole course of his tenure at UNC, Smith gave such free-lancing freedom to only two other players, Bradley and Walter Davis.

Jordan was a unanimous All-American in 1982-83. When he was chosen The Sporting News College Player of the Year in March 1983, his performance on the court was described in that publi-

cation thus: "He soars through the air, he rebounds, he scores (more than 1,100 points in two years, a school record), he guards two men at once, he vacuums up loose balls, he blocks shots, he makes steals. Most important, he makes late plays that win games. Call it what you may, court sense or court presence, he has it." Maryland guard Adrian Branch described guarding Jordan as "dirty, dirty work."

During the summer of 1983 Jordan toured with various All-Star teams and starred in the Pan American Games in Caracas, where the United States basketball team won the gold medal. "There have been other gifted basketball players at Chapel Hill," Peter Alfano reported in the New York Times (December 26, 1983), "but not all have been as warmly received as Jordan. He can excite a crowd like a Sunday morning preacher and lift a team to new heights, and yet people are impressed by his unassuming nature and friendly manner. There are times when he seems too good to be real."

In 1983-84 Jordan and Sam Perkins led the Tarheels to the Atlantic Coast Conference regular-season championship, and Jordan was again chosen The Sporting News College Player of the Year. "Jordan . . . went to the top of the class because of the frequency with which he produced in clutch situations," Mike Douchant, the associate editor of The Sporting News (March 26, 1984), wrote. "In essence, Jordan is a showman under control. Sometimes Jordan spontaneously performs an electrifying high-wire act. Sometimes he puts his acrobatic assaults on hold and simply glides in for a layup or pulls up for a soft jumper. On other occasions, Jordan improvises and assumes control of a game with a crucial steal or blocked shot. Sometimes the game dictates that he temper any free-lancing and remain within the set framework of the Tarheels' offense or defense. . . . His portfolio generally consists of twenty to twenty-five points, ten-of-fifteen shooting from the floor, six rebounds, four assists, three steals, and a couple of blocked shots."

Some professional scouts remained dubious about Jordan's outside shot. Their doubts were removed in the summer of 1984, when Jordan was a member of the United States Olympic team. Under the scrutiny of Bob Knight, the Olympic coach, he became one of the most reliable of perimeter players and contributed mightily to the winning of the gold medal at the Olympiad in Los Angeles. George Raveling, the assistant Olympic coach, assessed Jordan to be "probably the best athlete playing college basketball."

In 1984 the Chicago Bulls were desperate for a superstar to move them out of the doldrums. The team had not made the National Basketball Association play-offs since 1980-81, and in only two of its previous nine seasons had it won more games than it lost. The Bulls chose Jordan third in the pro draft of college players and offered him a seven-figure five-year contract. Jordan accepted the offer and dropped out of college.

Jordan was an instant success as a pro. In 1984-85 he led the NBA in points, with 2,313, and was named Rookie of the Year, a starting All-Star, and winner of the Seagram Award for best player in the NBA. He averaged 28.2 points per game, 5.9 assists, and 2.4 steals, and he led the Bulls in rebounds, with 6.5 His highest scores were forty-five points in one game and forty-nine in another. The Bulls' home attendance increased by 87 percent, and the team led the NBA in road attendance. Ticket sales at Chicago Stadium rose from $2 million to $3.8 million.

In 1985-86 Jordan missed all but eighteen games of the season because of a foot injury. With Jordan in the lineup, Chicago won its first three games. Without him, the team lost forty-three of its next sixty-four games. When he returned to the lineup the team surged sufficiently to finish the season 30-52 and make the play-offs. In Chicago's losing play-off game against the Boston Celtics on April 20, 1986, Jordan scored sixty-three points. Larry Bird, Boston's superstar, facetiously wondered if Jordan might not be "God disguised as Michael Jordan."

In 1986-87 forward Charles Oakley was the only other member of the Chicago Bulls who approached Jordan's caliber of play. In an article in the *Christian Science Monitor* (December 8, 1986), Phil Elderkin estimated Jordan's vertical leap to be somewhere between forty and forty-four inches from a standing position. "The next thing you notice about [him] is his 'hang time'—the way his upper body appears to hover around the rim of the basket like a human helicopter while his defenders gradually drop away," Elderkin wrote. "Even though he's off the floor for only seconds, it often seems as though Michael could remain airborne indefinitely."

"He's such an easy person to like," John Paxson pointed out to Jerry Sullivan of *New York Newsday* (February 23, 1987) in explaining his backcourt mate's immense popularity with fans. "Wherever he goes, people want to touch him, say 'hi' to him. He is one of God's special children." Jordan led the fans' All-Star voting in 1986-87. In the slam-dunk championship at the NBA All-Star weekend in Seattle in February 1987, Jordan outdunked Jerome Kersey, 146-140, to claim the top prize of $12,500. Typically, he shared the prize money with his teammates, giving eleven of them $1,000 each. Jerry Sullivan described Jordan's full-court dunk: "Jordan started by marking the foul line, then began backing up little by little, planning his steps, dragging out the exercise to the delight of the crowd. Then he dribbled the length of the court, his tongue hanging from his mouth, and took off at the foul line. It is hard to say what happened from there without reviewing the film, but Jordan appeared to jump in stages. He took off at the foul line, leveled off in midair, then rose again for the dunk." Jordan, who credits much of his movement on the court to "instinct and intuition," said, "When I look back on that dunking contest, it's just unbelievable I was able to do those things."

At Chicago Stadium on April 16, 1987, Jordan scored sixty-one points in a 117-114 loss to the Atlanta Hawks. That feat made him the second player in NBA history, after Wilt Chamberlain, to surpass the 3,000 mark in a season. In the same game he scored twenty-three consecutive points, including the final seventeen of the first half, a new record. "I know records are meant to be broken . . . ," he told the press after the game. "I also know that I am the only guard in the history of basketball to have scored this many points. . . . But these records and marks meant nothing. I'd rather have had the win because it would have clinched the seventh playoff spot in the Eastern conference." The Bulls set a home attendance record in 1986-87, and they were second in the league in road attendance, surpassed only by the Boston Celtics.

ProServ, the sports management firm that represents Jordan, saw from the beginning of his professional career that he had, in the words of Donald Dell, the firm's head, "a charisma that transcends his sport" and that he belonged "in a category with Arnold Palmer or Arthur Ashe." Accordingly, they touted him as a man whose "striking good looks and fashionable wardrobe make him a natural corporate ambassador," and companies did not need much persuading. His deal to promote Nike sports apparel and "Air Jordan" basketball shoes is one of the most lucrative ever signed by an NBA player. In addition, he has endorsement contracts with McDonald's, the fast-food chain, the Wilson sporting goods company (for an autographed basketball), Coca-Cola, Chevrolet automobiles, Johnson Products (a personal-grooming line), Excelsior International ("Time Jordan" watches), and Guy LaRoche watches. In addition, he receives large fees for appearances at auto shows and other commercial events. A good portion of his off-court time is devoted to visiting schools and juvenile basketball clinics. "Michael Jordan isn't caught up in the flashy life . . . ," Jordan told Alan Steinberg in an interview for *Inside Sports* (April 1986). "He still loves kids and loves to work with kids. He knows where he came from and what it took to get him where he is right now. I haven't changed my personality at all."

When the announcer in Chicago Stadium introduces Jordan before home games, most of the introduction is impossible to hear above the roar of the 18,000 fans cheering him. Leaving the stadium after the game, on his way to his silver Corvette, he chats with maintenance and food-concession workers and signs autographs for fans. He reads as many of the fan letters he receives every day as he can, and his fan club helps him to respond to the letters with printed material and autographed photos. "He is the first athlete I've ever seen," his teammate Elston Turner has observed, "whom the fans treat like Michael Jackson. He needs a police escort to hotels; girls cry when they see him."

According to his physicians, Jordan, who weighs about 193 pounds and is physically well-proportioned, may yet grow another inch. His spiffy appearance is brightened by an effervescent smile. Jordan lives in a town house he owns in the Chicago suburb of Northbrook, where he does his own shopping and housecleaning. (According to former roommates, he is almost compulsively neat.) In his free time he watches videotapes of games, follows stock-car racing, bowls, plays pool, and listens to music (on a Walkman when he is in transit). He still often seeks the counsel of Dean Smith, his college coach, on basketball and matters in general. In his early days with the Bulls he had little social life, was shy of girls, and considered "the game [his] wife." Then, in 1985, he met his fiancée, a young woman named Juanita. The Chicago starting point guard John Paxson has ex-

plained Jordan's remarkable popularity with teammates as well as fans, by pointing out that being "the dominating force on the team" hasn't given him "an ego problem." "He could be real arrogant . . . and let all the press go to his head, but he never does. He cares about his teammates as people."

References: Chicago Tribune IV p2 Ag 17 '84; Inside Sports 8:75+ Ap '86, 9:32+ Je '87 pors; N Y Newsday p72+ F 23 '87 pors; N Y Times C p1+ D 26 '83 pors; Newsday S p11 D 4 '83 por; People 21:42+ Mr 19 '84 pors; Sporting N p2 Mr 28 '83 pors, p3 Mr 26 '84 por; Sports Illus 61:36+ D 10 '84 pors

---

Joyner-Kersee, Jackie

Mar. 3, 1962– Heptathlete. Address: b. c/o P.O. Box 21053, Long Beach, Calif. 90801

"I like the heptathlon," Jackie Joyner-Kersee once said of her seven-event sport, "because it shows you what you're made of." Although it is one of the most grueling and varied disciplines in women's athletics, the heptathlon has long been virtually ignored by the American public, and only recently has its neglect been remedied by the stellar performances of Jackie Joyner-Kersee, who in 1986 dominated the sport as no one ever had before. Her exploits that year, including the setting of two world records in twenty-six days, won her the 1986 Sullivan Award as the best athlete in the United States and began to draw the attention of the media

and the public to her sport's two-day trial by fire: a 200-meter dash, a 100-meter hurdles race, competitions in the high jump, shotput, long jump and javelin throw, and an 800-meter run. In addition to establishing her heptathlon world record of 7,161 points, Jackie Joyner-Kersee holds the American record in the long jump at twenty-three feet nine inches. In 1986 the heptathlete, who is noted for her determination as much as for her extraordinary natural ability, won a silver medal at the Los Angeles Olympics in spite of a painful hamstring injury. "People look at my marks and say 'You can't go any faster,'" she told one reporter. "I don't believe that. I believe you can go faster in the hurdles and I believe I can throw farther and jump farther." Mrs. Joyner-Kersee proved her point in spectacular fashion at the 1987 Pan American Games in Indianapolis, Indiana, when, entering the individual competition in the long jump, her first love in sports, she tied the world record in the event with a leap of twenty-four feet, five and one-half inches.

Jacqueline Joyner-Kersee was born Jacqueline Joyner in East St. Louis, Illinois, on March 3, 1962. She was named for Jacqueline Kennedy, who was then First Lady, at the insistence of her grandmother, who predicted that "someday this girl will be the first lady of something." Her siblings are Alfred Jr., Angela, and Deborah. Her parents, Alfred and Mary Joyner, were seventeen and nineteen years old respectively when she was born and had been married for three years. Their youth made family life an economic struggle, especially in East St. Louis, a depressed industrial town so crime-ridden that by the time Jackie was eleven she had seen a murder in front of her house.

That house "was little more than wallpaper and sticks," according to Kenny Moore of *Sports Illustrated* (April 21, 1987). In winter the hot water pipes froze regularly, forcing the family to heat their bath water in kettles on the kitchen stove. Rent was paid from Mary Joyner's salary as a nurse's assistant and from money Alfred Joyner Sr. earned in other cities as a construction worker. He later worked as a railroad switch operator in Springfield, Illinois, about two hours away from East St. Louis.

By that time Jackie had already begun to show her potential as an athlete, by competing at the Mayor Brown Center across from the Joyner home. "I was nine years old when I had my first track competition," she has recalled. "I finished last, but the next week in practice I could feel improvement." Her mother at first felt that track and field was inappropriate for a girl, and her father advised her to quit, but when Jackie persisted, her parents' attitude began to change. Her father told Patricia Freeman that at Jackie's second meet "she got a third, a fourth, and a second. Then the next time it was three seconds. Then she came home and said, 'I got five first places, Daddy.'" In the long jump she proved to be phenomenal, leaping over seventeen feet by the time she was twelve. Her achievements inspired her older brother Al to begin competing in track and field himself, and he eventually became a master of the triple jump.

In the classroom Jackie Joyner derived the same satisfaction from her scholastic achievements that she did from her athletic prowess. When, in the fifth grade, the teacher explained how to do long division, she did not at first understand, but she came home and worked it out by herself. She eventually got to sit at the front of the class. Less exciting for Jackie was her mother's prohibition against dating before she was eighteen. At first aghast, then resigned, she threw herself even more fervently into athletic and scholastic achievement.

Jackie Joyner first took up a multievent sport, the five-event pentathlon, when a coach at the Mayor Brown Center informed her that the quickest way to the Olympics was to master a variety of specialties. Blossoming quickly, she won the first of four consecutive National Junior Pentathlon Championships when she was fourteen, and while attending Lincoln High School, she became known as perhaps the finest athlete in the state of Illinois. She set a state high school record of twenty feet seven and a half inches in the long jump in her junior year, played volleyball, and contributed mightily to the Lincoln basketball team, which beat its opponents by an average of 52.8 points a game. After graduating in 1980 in the top 10 percent of her class, she was recruited for both basketball and the pentathlon by the University of California at Los Angeles. Opting for the basketball scholarship, she went on to star as a forward for the U.C.L.A. Bruins.

In the summer before she entered college, Jackie Joyner competed in the United States Olympic trials and bettered her personal best in the long jump by leaping twenty feet nine and three-quarters inches. When the United States pulled out of the Olympics to protest the Soviet invasion of Afghanistan, Miss Joyner, although disappointed, was buoyed by the expiration of her mother's tabu on dating and by the prospect of attending the University of California at Los Angeles. But midway through her freshman year her mother died suddenly of meningitis at the age of thirty-eight.

Although it was a tremendous blow, along with the grief there came what she has described as "a clearer sense of reality." She already knew about "setting goals and things," but now it seemed as if she had inherited some of her mother's determination. At the University of California she was discovered—and comforted—by an assistant track coach named Bob Kersee. She was concentrating on basketball and long jumping at the time, maintaining a B average and allowing her multievent skills to languish. Taken aback by this, Kersee has said that he saw "this talent walking around that everyone was blind to. No one was listening to her mild requests to do more."

Kersee went to the athletic director of U.C.L.A. and threatened to quit unless he was allowed to coach Jackie Joyner, and his ultimatum was met. He then went to Miss Joyner, tallied up her personal best performances in heptathlon events, and showed her that, even without special training, she was only 400 points behind America's then reigning heptathlete, Jane Frederick. Her sprinting ability in particular made her almost invincible in a heptathlon 200-meter dash, and Kersee lamented that although her "raw speed [was] the best," "everyone could beat her in the hurdles."

Jackie Joyner agreed to take up the heptathlon, although she rankled for some time at having to train for the 800 meters and the throws, feeling that she would spread herself too thin and compromise her long jumping and basketball training. But Bob Kersee, who has been described as "demanding and strong-willed on the track," persisted. By 1982 he could see that she would be the world record holder.

In 1983 Jackie Joyner and her brother, Al, who had excelled in the triple jump as a student at Arkansas State University, were selected to represent the United States at the track and field world championships held in Helsinki, Finland. Miss Joyner told Track and Field News (February 1987): "The Helsinki meet was the first time I ever encountered an injury [a pulled hamstring muscle] that was so bad I couldn't compete. I always felt before that I could overcome any physical problem, but Helsinki was the first time I felt my legs just couldn't go anymore. That blew me away mentally because I never had experienced anything like that before."

A year later Jackie Joyner was fully recovered mentally and physically when, along with her brother, she qualified for the United States team selected for the 1984 Los Angeles Olympics. She arrived in Los Angeles favored to win a gold medal but with a heavily taped leg because of a new hamstring injury sustained a few weeks before. Although Al Joyner Jr. was not expected to win a medal, he has recalled that both he and his sister were determined to show that there were "better things to come out of East St. Louis than just crime."

Jackie Joyner's opening day performance at Los Angeles, hampered by her pulled muscle, left her twenty points behind the leader. She expected to erase that deficit in her bread-and-butter event, the long jump, but instead on the second day she fouled on her first two long jump attempts and was forced to settle for a poor third jump of twenty feet and one-half inch. So distressed was she by the outcome that she neglected to drink enough water to keep herself performing smoothly during the rest of the competition. By early evening, the heptathlon had come down to its final event, the 800-meter run, and Al Joyner's triple jump competition was in its final stages. On the way to winning the triple jump on the strength of his first attempt—fifty-six feet seven and one-half inches, Al Joyner Jr. took time out to run beside his sister on the final leg of the 800-meter run, telling her, "Pump your arms. . . . This is it." Jackie had retaken the lead in the heptathlon by a narrow thirty-one points after the javelin competition, in which she had out-tossed her competitors by thirty feet. To maintain her lead and win the gold, she would have to stay within 2.13 seconds of the 800-meter time of her closest competitor, Australia's Glynis Nunn. With Al exhorting her, she finished the 800 in 2:13.03, missing the gold by a maddening .06 seconds.

Insult, Jackie Joyner felt, was added to the injury of loss in 1985. After giving that year's best performance in the heptathlon and setting an American record with a long jump of twenty-three feet nine inches at a Zurich meet, she was nonetheless ranked third in the heptathlon world behind the East German athlete Sabine Paetz and the American Jane Frederick. Both women had set world and American heptathlon records in 1984, but Jane Frederick had already recognized in Jackie Joyner the leader of "the next generation." "Hers was a real talent," Jane Frederick has conceded, "not a forced one. She wasn't driven to compensate for some bitterness or character failing."

After four years of a strictly mentor-protégée relationship, Miss Joyner and Bob Kersee finally became emotionally involved and were married on January 11, 1986. The marriage seems to have turned a "real talent" into a dominant force in the heptathlon. Jackie Joyner-Kersee made up her mind to prove she was just as good as Sabine Paetz and the other Europeans. As Bob Kersee told Track & Field News: "She vowed to compete against the Europeans, regardless of where she had to go to do it. She would have gone to Pluto if she had to." She was equally determined to restructure her training to eliminate the leg muscle pulls she had suffered in Helsinki and Los Angeles. And to concentrate on the heptathlon, she gave up playing on the U.C.L.A. basketball team.

The benefits of those decisions became obvious at the four meets in which she competed in 1986. Bob Kersee told Track & Field News in February 1987 that "the first one at Mt. SAC [Mt. San Antonio Junior College in Pomona, California] had the hurdles hand-timed, so the chance for any kind of official record was gone right away. That bothered her for all of about one minute. . . . I was happy with her reaction because in the past, Jackie had let things bug her in competitions." Her score of 6,910 at a meet at Mt. San Antonio Junior College was only surpassed during 1986 by her tallies at later meets. Her only lower score was at her next meet,

in Gotzis, Austria, where she won with a score of 6,841 points. She did not peak, however, until July, at the Goodwill Games in Moscow, which were organized by American broadcasting tycoon Ted Turner to promote goodwill between the United States and the Eastern bloc, which had boycotted the 1984 Olympics. The games, however, drew small crowds in the Soviet Union, were virtually ignored in America, and were marred by rule bending on the part of the Soviets.

Jackie Joyner's performance was later judged to be one of the few instances in which the games lived up to their potential. Well before the games began, Bob Kersee told Skip Myslenski (Chicago Tribune, July 8, 1986) that Jackie Joyner's heart was set on a world record and that she was "unbelievably pumped up." "She was driving me crazy in Stockholm," Kersee added. "We got there on June 29, and by July 1, I couldn't stand her anymore. I didn't want her to come [to Moscow] early, because it's such a change of atmosphere, but I was ready to send her over just to get rid of her." Of her actual performance after those weeks of anxiety, Kersee marveled that "to have an almost perfect two days like this, that's unheard of. To have two days like this, there is no accounting for that." For in those two days Miss Joyner turned in a personal best in almost every event, setting an American record 12.85 in the 100-meter hurdles and a heptathlon record of twenty-three feet in the long jump. With a time of twenty-three seconds in the 200 meters, a sixty-two inch high jump and a shot put of forty-eight feet five and a quarter inches, she was already setting a world record pace by the end of the first day, for which her point total of 4,151 itself constituted a record. In addition to making her spectacular long jump on the second day, she flung the javelin for 163 feet four inches. Well ahead of the pack, she then needed a time of 2:24.64 in the 800 to set the world record. She decided to try for 2:10, a goal that made Kersee uneasy because he thought it would make people expect too much of her for the next two years, when the World Championships and the Olympics were scheduled. Jackie Joyner had obviously won the hearts of the Russians, for when she stepped onto the track for the 800 meters the Soviet announcer declared in Russian and English over the public address system that "we all hope Jackie Joyner will make it." Miss Joyner proceeded to run exactly the 800 she had planned, clocking in at 2:10:02 and leaving the announcer exclaiming, "It's marvelous. It's magnificent." With the 964 points she earned for that performance, Joyner finished 500 points ahead of her closest competitor, the East German athlete Sabila Tile. Her 7,148 points broke the world record by 200 points and of course shattered the 7,000 point barrier. Miss Joyner was the first American woman to hold a multievent world record since Mildred ("Babe") Didrikson set a triathlon mark fifty years before, and was the first woman outside the Soviet bloc to do so in a decade.

Only twenty-six days later, "still drained from Moscow," Jackie Joyner traveled to Houston, Texas, to compete in the United States Olympic Festival. "Houston," Bob Kersee has said, "was the first time the husband and the coach in me came into conflict. I knew she was still tired and sore, but that she still was healthy and in good enough shape to go after the world record again. . . . The husband in me . . . wanted to hug her and tell her she didn't have to try for the record again. But, we all know that the softy husband gave in to the hard-line coach." Temperatures in Houston rose well above 100 degrees, but throughout the Houston meet, Jackie Joyner has said, "I just tried to block out all negative thoughts. I kept reading little books I have, books on faith that tell you to just keep exercising your faith and continuing to believe."

On the way to compiling a new record of 7,161 points, Miss Joyner broke her own heptathlon long jump record by three-quarters of an inch and finished in the hurdles, high jump, and 200 meters with marks that would have placed her in the top ten among American individual specialists in those events. Going into the 800 she needed a 2:10.55 to break her Moscow record. After pacing herself to a quick 64.5-second first lap, the heat began to tell on her, and she fell well behind the race's leader, Lana Zimmerman, and was passed by another competitor, Jolanda Jones. At about that point her brother recalls seeing "the animal come out of her [for] the first time . . . since high school." Miss Joyner looked down at the track, recalled Kersee's frequent admonition during her training runs to "go to your arms; start pumping," and closed a thirty-yard gap to beat Lana Zimmerman with a time of 2:09.69. This performance raised Jackie Joyner's average score for 1986 above 7,000 points, a barrier that continues to separate her from every other heptathlete in history. It also clinched the 1986 Sullivan Award for her, despite competition from standouts in better-known sports, such as Vinny Testaverde, football's 1986 Heisman trophy winner. Jackie Joyner was named *Track & Field News*'s "Athlete of the Year" and winner of the 1986 Jesse Owens Award.

During 1987 Jackie Joyner's momentum carried her along for another overwhelming showing. In the winter she became the women's points-standing winner of the Mobil Grand Prix track and field indoor series—in spite of having to face specialists in each event she entered because no heptathlon was included in the meet. In the spring, at the Pepsi Invitational track meet at U.C.L.A., she unofficially broke the American 100-meter hurdles record with a hand-timed 12.6-second dash. At the 1987 Pan American Games, held in August in Indianapolis, Mrs. Joyner-Kersee participated in the open long jump competition, using a slightly altered jumping technique that helped her, on her third attempt, to better her personal best by more than a foot. Her twenty-four-foot five-and-a-half-inch leap equaled the world record held by East Germany's Heike Drechsler. Not long afterwards, at the August 29-to-September 5 Rome world championships, Mrs. Joyner-Kersee easily won gold medals in both the heptathlon and the open

long jump. "Those calling her America's greatest athlete since Jim Thorpe," David Woods wrote in the *Sporting News* (September 14, 1987) " . . . might not be exaggerating." Mrs. Joyner-Kersee was awarded the 1987 McDonald's amateur sportswoman of the year award in September.

Jackie Joyner-Kersee is five feet ten inches tall and weighs about 150 pounds. She lives in Long Beach, California, with Bob Kersee, who is now women's head coach at U.C.L.A. Kersee is also the mentor of the Olympic gold medalist Valerie Brisco-Hooks, the hurdler André Phillips, and Al Joyner, who shares the Kersees' home, or "prison," as he calls it. Bob Kersee describes his personality and that of his wife as being "complementary." "I'm abrasive with promoters and coaches," he has explained. "Jackie gets along with everybody. She's happy at a banquet table. I have a fit. She's instinctive. She'll go out and lift a building and not ponder over it. I'll want to get the blueprints, find the right beam, decide on an underhand or overhand grip." Jackie Joyner-Kersee would like to pursue a career in sportscasting someday. Her more immediate goal is capturing in 1988 the gold medal that eluded her in 1984. With that in mind, she adheres to a strict training regimen that begins at 8:00 A.M. every morning, with the subsequent workout varying according to the skills that need to be strengthened. "I remember where I came from," she says, "and I keep that in mind. . . . If the young female sees the environment I grew up in and sees my dreams and goals come true, they will realize their dreams and goals might [also] come true."

References: *Chicago Tribune* IV p1 Jl 8 '86 por; *Ebony* 41:77 O '86 pors; *N Y Times* B p7 Jl 8 '86 por, C p11 Ag 4 '86 por, B p9 F 26 '87 pors, p43+ S 5 '87 pors; *Sporting N* p55 Jl 21 '86 por, p63 Ja 5 '87 pors; *Sports Illus* 65:12 Jl 21 '86 pors, 66:77 Ap 21 '87 pors, 67:18+ Ag 24 '87 pors, 67:20+ S 14 '87 pors; *Track & Field N* p42+ F '87 pors; *Women's Sports & Fitness* p38+ Ja '87 pors

---

Kainen, Jacob

Dec. 7, 1909– Artist; curator. Address: h. 27 W. Irving St., Chevy Chase, Md. 20815

As Paul Richard pointed out in the *Washington Post* (November 3, 1984), it sometimes seems that there are several Jacob Kainens: "There is Kainen the Washington Color Painter. . . . There is Kainen the printmaker. . . . And there is Kainen the museum man, the promoter of others' talents, who built the print collection of the National Museum of Art." He added that there is also Kainen the teacher, scholar, and connoisseur, whose own personal collection has been exhibited at the National Gallery. Like the layering of colors that characterizes Kainen's latest work, those many activities overlap and complement each other, ad-

Jacob Kainen

ding up to a rich contribution to the American art scene for over four decades.

In terms of style, Kainen might be considered an artistic contrarian: when the WPA artists were making murals, he was making etchings and lithographs; when the Washington color painters were doing abstract acrylics, he was painting streetscapes in oils; when figuration staged its comeback in the 1970s, he began creating serene geometric abstractions. Now retired from curatorship except when he acts as a consultant, he is devoting himself once again to his own painting and printmaking.

Jacob Kainen was born in Waterbury, Connecticut, on December 7, 1909, one of three sons of Joseph and Fannie (Levin) Kainen, both Russian-Jewish immigrants. When Jacob was ten years old, his father, a skilled mechanic, got a job in New York City as a toolmaker, and the family moved to the Bronx. "I always intended to be an artist, even when I was a child," Kainen has recalled. In grade school he borrowed library books by Howard Pyle, the great turn-of-the-century writer and illustrator, and "got a sense of pattern from his illustrations in the Art Nouveau manner, with strong black and white patterning." He also started a scrapbook, when he was twelve, of reproductions of famous paintings, which he cut out from the rotogravure section of the newspaper. By the age of thirteen, equipped with a set of oil paints he had received as a gift, and inspired by visits to museums, he was sketching and painting from nature.

Only sixteen when he graduated from high school, and too young to be admitted to Pratt Institute, he worked days as a clerk in Brentano's bookstore, and began taking evening classes with the renowned teacher of drawing, Kimon Nicolaides, at the Art Students League. The following year he

enrolled as a full-time student at Pratt, which was then a fine arts college, but which soon shifted its emphasis to commercial art. Kainen therefore found it necessary to supplement his studies. He took life drawing classes with A. J. Bogdanove at the New York Evening School of Industrial Arts, and went to Brooklyn on Sundays for private lessons with Frank Leonard Allen. He also visited the Metropolitan Museum and the Lenox Collection of the New York Public Library, where he copied works by such masters as Corot, Rembrandt, and Constable. One of the paintings he copied was Claude Lorraine's outdoor scene with landscape and figures, *The Ford.* As the art historian Harry Rand has remarked, Kainen, "in his choice of Claude, and by executing this copy, had to become aware of the wealth of material that constitutes a really good picture." Because he refused to take commercial art courses and was also an advocate of modern art, Kainen was expelled from Pratt two weeks before he was scheduled to graduate, for "consistently asserting independence in aesthetic outlook." (Twelve years later he was awarded his diploma, postdated 1930.) After leaving Pratt, Kainen continued his formal art education at New York University from 1936 to 1938; still later, between 1944 and 1946, he studied at George Washington University, in the nation's capital.

But Kainen believes that his most important artistic education came not from schools, but from associating with other artists. While he supported himself during the Depression years by drawing designs for a greeting card company and by taking a series of jobs as coffeeshop counterman, sign painter and medical draftsman, he fraternized with other artists in Greenwich Village cafeterias and visited galleries with the painter Arshile Gorky and the artist and critic John Graham. From those older artists Kainen says he learned "the importance of composing in painting, the importance of the feeling of the pigment, the importance of one edge of an area against another." Frequenting the Jumble Shop, an artists' cafe in Greenwich Village and visiting fellow artists in their studios, he expanded his friendships in the New York art world to include the sculptor David Smith and the painters Willem de Kooning, Mark Rothko, and Stuart Davis.

It was Stuart Davis who suggested that Jacob Kainen try for work with the Federal Art Project as a printmaker. At the age of eighteen, Kainen had begun experimenting with drypoint etchings, printing his first one on his mother's washing machine wringer. Davis noted that while paintings, as unique entities, were often lost or damaged by careless handling in government-sponsored projects, work produced in multiple images was salvageable. Persuaded by Davis' arguments, Kainen applied for and was accepted by the New York Graphic Arts Project of the WPA in August 1935.

His first two prints for the WPA, done in 1935, were the lithographs *Drought,* showing a dejected farmer sitting in his parched fields, and *Tenement Fire,* adapted from a painting he had made the year before. Both were part of a series of what he called his "disaster pictures." The work Kainen did with the WPA was largely inspired by observations of city life and was informed with a feeling of compassion for workers, pushcart vendors, and lonely diners in cafeterias or at luncheonette counters. Lithographs such as *Lunch* (1936) or *Night Club* (1938) make an ironic, even sardonic comment on excess and self-indulgence in a time of general distress; *Spanish Landscape with Figures* (1938) refers poignantly to the Spanish Civil War. But although Kainen's themes during that period paralleled those of the social realists, he diverged from those artists in that the terms of representation are not generalized, nor are they symbols of any political doctrine. As Harry Rand observed in his "Notes and Conversations: Jacob Kainen" in *Arts* (December 1978), "Kainen's interest was humanitarian for the particular instance, and universally sensitive without recourse to an ideological program." Also, subject matter never overcame Kainen's abiding interest in form and technique.

Jacob Kainen was one of the pioneers of color lithography as an art form, which until then had only rarely been practiced in the United States. Among his early lithograph experiments was a group of four-color prints begun, in 1937, with *Cafeteria*. In addition to his lithographs, Kainen's WPA work came to include drypoints, etchings, woodcuts, and one silkscreen, *Snowfall* (1939). This last, showing a woman rounding a street corner, buffeted by driving wind and snow, uses thirty-two separate colors and has been defined by Janet A. Flint, curator of prints and drawings at the National Collection of Fine Arts, as a "printed painting."

In 1937 Kainen joined Stuart Davis, Ben Shahn, and the critic Harold Rosenberg on the editorial board of *Art Front,* the journal of the Artists' Union. He also took part in a group show at the old A.C.A. Gallery on Eighth Street in 1938, as part of "the New York Group" of six painters, including Alice Neel and Herman Rose; a second such exhibition was held at the A.C.A. Gallery in the following year.

In 1942, with the New York Graphic Arts Project faltering, and with the need to support a wife and child, Kainen accepted a job as an aide in the division of graphic arts at the Smithsonian Institution in Washington, where he gave demonstrations of various techniques on the department's presses. With equipment readily available, he experimented with his own prints whenever he found the time, and continued to paint at night and on weekends in studio space he rented in downtown Washington. Both his prints and his paintings in the 1940s and into the early 1950s showed an interest in exploring his new city, and the older Washington buildings with their distinctive turrets and cupolas fascinated him.

In 1944 Kainen was made assistant curator of the division of graphic arts at the Smithsonian, and in 1946 he was appointed its curator, a post that he held for the next twenty years. His job involved the monumental task of building and organizing the print collection begun by the Smithsonian's first curator, Sylvester R. Koehler, but not substantially increased after his death in 1895. Although he himself produced a body of over fifty prints in various media between 1945 and the mid-1960s, Kainen decided when he became curator not to enter his own work in national print exhibitions, in order to avoid any suggestion of conflict of interest. Thus, as Janet A. Flint has pointed out, while his reputation as a scholar in the graphics field grew, his position as a printmaker in his own right became, for many years, obscured.

The move to the nation's capital, then an artistic wasteland compared to New York, was, as Kainen recalls, "like being dropped into the middle of the Gobi desert." It was not until, in 1947, he started teaching a printmaking class at the Washington Art Workshop, where his colleagues were the color-field painters Kenneth Noland and Morris Louis, that he found the kind of meeting place he had always thrived in. Noland, who taught at Catholic University in Washington, arranged for a large retrospective of Kainen's paintings there in November 1952. Kainen continued to maintain contact with his friends from New York, including Ad Reinhardt and George McNeil, who visited him in Washington in 1944.

In the early 1950s abstract expressionism exploded onto the art scene, introduced by many of Kainen's old associates in New York. Although his own work became more abstract during that period, Kainen differed from the gestural, or action, painters in that he still used figurative forms and retained his palette of subtle, muted colors. As he explained to Harry Rand, the central problem for a painter during the 1950s became "What character is the physical paint going to have?" In works such as *The Vulnerable* (1954), Kainen's paint displays a range of characteristics: dragged; wet-on-wet; crusty, thin patches; light dripping; brush streaking—showing a willingness to learn from all schools and ally himself with none.

In the early 1960s, while abstract expressionism was still the vogue in New York and hard-edge abstract acrylics were being done by Washington Color School painters, Kainen's work reflected an urgent desire to, as he stated at the time, "create noble expressive forms through the use of the figure. . . . " In a series of woodcuts and in several one-man shows of paintings (1961 at the Jefferson Place Gallery, Washington, D.C.; 1963 at the Corcoran Gallery of Art, Washington, D.C., and the Roko Gallery, New York City; 1966 at the Roko Gallery) he portrayed monumental, solitary, solid-looking figures that resembled statues.

To devote more time to his own work, Kainen resigned from his curatorship at the Smithsonian in 1966, though he was talked into working part time as curator of prints and drawings for the National Collection of Fine Arts (NCFA). He resigned that post in 1970. During the four years he spent with the NCFA, he increased its holdings from about 1,000 to 7,000 works of art, forming a collection described by Joshua G. Taylor, a former director of the museum, as displaying "an extraordinary subtlety and catholicity of taste."

While figurative painting again became the rage with his younger contemporaries from 1969 through the seventies, Kainen, ever the aesthetic independent, turned his attention to abstraction, at first retaining some suggestion of figurative forms. *Escape Artist*, one of the canvases done between 1972 and 1973, and *Elisa*, another painting of this period, are composed of geometrical shapes and angular patterns that may be read as being either animate or inanimate. In reviewing Kainen's one-man show of oil paintings at the Phillips Collection in 1973, Paul Richard of the *Washington Post* (October 5, 1973) wrote, "Many of these oils at first glimpse seem abstract . . . ,yet they all somehow seem inhabited."

In 1972 Kainen met Jack Lemon, founder of the Landfall Press in Chicago, who invited him to work in his establishment for several days. Finding it a congenial milieu, Kainen produced several black-and-white and color lithographs there that year. His later visits to the Landfall Press resulted in a large body of prints related to the direction he was taking in his painting. In a review of the show called "Three Contemporary Printmakers" at the National Collection of Fine Arts in Washington in 1973, in which Jacob Kainen exhibited along with Alber Christ-Janer and Tadeuz Lapinski, Patricia L. Raymer of the *Washington Post* (June 23, 1973) singled out "Kainen's lyrical lithographs" for special praise, calling them "candy-coated romantic playthings" that "bring to mind the playful nature of Miró or the spontaneity of the Abstract Expressionists."

In 1976 the NCFA finally acquainted the nation with Jacob Kainen the printmaker by organizing a retrospective exhibit of his prints dating back to the 1930s. Gene Baro, the consultative curator of prints and drawings at the Brooklyn Museum, wrote in *Arts* (November 1976): "The body of work is distinguished, easy and broad in conception, expert in realization. Kainen has shown himself to be formidable in woodcut, etching, and lithography. . . . The present exhibition will allow Kainen's prints to be studied for the first time and should help to win him the following he deserves."

By 1980 all remnants of the figure had vanished from Kainen's work and geometric abstraction took over. "Kainen is off in a new direction," Charles Parkhurst reported in the introduction to the catalogue of the Phillips Collection exhibit (1980–81), which included *The Way* series (1980) and the *Aegean* series (1980). "This latest manifestation of vitality is found in larger pictures with masterfully layered colors."

When another showing of Kainen's abstract paintings went on view in 1983 at the Sid Deutsch Gallery in New York, Harry Rand of *Arts* magazine (March 1983) commented: "For those who do not love painting there is nothing to look at. Underpainting peeks around edges so that forms shimmer, simple forms whose colors are so miraculously refined that they are as impossible to actively recall as subtle fragrances. In such painting, colors do not come from the tube; these tints have no name." The *Art News* reviewer (May 1983) of the same exhibition was impressed by Kainen's use of space: "Kainen plays the canvas' two dimensions off implications of a third. Each figure is obviously flat-out geometric but indicates depths in both its coloration and placement."

An exhibition of Kainen's paintings at the Middendorf Gallery in Washington in 1986 included his new "Dabrowsky" series, referring to the original surname of his mentor, Joseph Graham, and employing colors and forms inspired by his own recent visit to the Soviet Union. Most recently, Kainen has been producing abstract color woodcuts, and an exhibition of that work was scheduled for March 1987 at Washington's Hom Gallery.

Although Jacob Kainen has elected to work in many different styles and many media throughout his long career, David Tannous, in reviewing a "mini-retrospective" of Kainen's work in 1980, found certain characteristics common to his oeuvre. "What unites all these pieces—old and new, small and large, abstract and representational, paintings and prints—most fundamentally is a strong feeling of intimacy," he observed. "Kainen's works, even at their largest and most 'public,' retain always the sense of a private meditation: the artist musing about a particular corner of the world rather than trying to reshape the cosmos." Tannous also found color to be one of the unifying factors in Kainen's work. "From the earliest painting to the most recent," he noted, "his palette has remained much the same. Close-valued, refined rather than raw, the hues are velvety, subtle mixtures with an abundance of rose, lavender, smoky blue, silver-green, tawny beige. Somehow exotic, both in themselves and in their juxtapositions, the colors seem to carry a kind of built-in shimmer, as though seen through a slightly distorting scrim." Behind all of Kainen's work, Tannous detected the operation of a keen intelligence: "the hard-won balance of the composition, the unexpected combinations of distinctive colors—seems *chosen*."

In 1938 Jacob Kainen married Bertha Friedman; they had two sons, Paul and Daniel. In 1967 he separated from his wife, and the following year he obtained a divorce. At his studio home in suburban Chevy Chase, Maryland, the artist now lives with his second wife, the former Ruth Cole, whom he married in 1969. It was she who urged him to resign from his curatorship, so that he could get back to being a full-time artist. A shared love of German Expressionist prints, which Kainen had been collecting for years, originally brought them together. Their combined collection was exhibited at the National Gallery of Art in 1985 and is now promised as a future gift to the museum.

Despite his years of artistic self-effacement, Kainen has gained the respect of a wide circle of fellow curators, collectors, artists, and former students at the Washington Workshop, like Gene Davis, who has declared that Kainen "as my first teacher . . . taught me more about art than any other living person." The artist is included in Ad Reinhardt's famous newspaper cartoon *Tree of Modern American Art* (1946) on the same branch as Mark Rothko, Adolph Gottlieb, Morris Graves, and Loren MacIver. A member of the Washington Print Club, which he helped to found in 1966, and a member and director of the Print Council of America, Kainen is the author of several publications of interest to printmakers. They include: *George Clymer and the Columbian Press* (Book Club of America, 1950); *The Development of the Half-Tone Screen* (reprinted in the Smithsonian Institution's Annual Report, 1951, from an article published by Lakeside Press, Chicago); *Why Bewick Succeeded* (Smithsonian Institution Press, 1959), a study of the eighteenth-century English wood engraver Thomas Bewick; *John Baptist Jackson: 18th Century Master of the Color Woodcut* (U.S. Government Printing Office, 1962); and *The Etchings of Canaletto* (Smithsonian Institution Press, 1967).

Works by Kainen are to be found in a number of public collections in the United States and abroad, including the National Gallery of Art, the Corcoran Gallery of Art, the Phillips Collection, and the Hirshhorn Museum and Sculpture Garden in Washington, D.C.; the Metropolitan Museum of Art, the Museum of Modern Art, the Brooklyn Museum and the Brooklyn Public Library, and the Whitney Museum of American Art in New York; the Art Institute of Chicago; the Philadelphia Museum of Art; the British Museum in London; the Kunsthalle in Hamburg; and the Bezalel National Museum in Jerusalem.

Kainen's face still bears the same searching expression that it wore in his 1945 *Self-Portrait with Drypoint Needle,* with its dark, thoughtful eyes under a high, expansive forehead. His smile, like his art, is reticent, unassuming, enigmatic. His voice has been described as "gentle but defiant," and although his manner is calm, his wife, Ruth, says "underneath the surface there is a will of steel."

In assessing his overall contribution, Janet A. Flint has written, "Each phase of Kainen's work has not always been part of a steady, coherent development; he has chosen rather to follow the much harder path of a self-questioning search that has meant shifts, changes, and reexaminations. . . . What has remained constant is his total commitment."

References: Art in America 68:135 S '80; Arts 53:135+ D '78; Washington Post D p1+ N 26 '76 por, mag p32+ D 14 '80; Flint, Janet A. Jacob Kainen: Prints, a Retrospective (1976); Who's Who in America, 1986–87; Who's Who in American Art (1984)

Kalb, Marvin

June 9, 1930– Educator; journalist. Address: b. Joan Shorenstein Barone Center for the Press, Politics and Public Policy, John F. Kennedy School of Government, 79 John F. Kennedy St., Cambridge, Mass. 02138

Over the course of thirty years in journalism, primarily as the chief diplomatic correspondent for the CBS and, later, NBC network news divisions and as the moderator of NBC-TV's influential *Meet the Press*, Marvin Kalb has become one of the most respected newsmen in the United States. On June 1, 1987 the cerebral, soft-spoken Kalb embarked on a new career as an educator, becoming the first director of the Joan Shorenstein Barone Center for the Press, Politics and Public Policy at Harvard University's John F. Kennedy School of Government. Established in 1986, the center studies the impact of the media on government and of public policy on a free press. As Christopher Swan reported in the *Christian Science Monitor* of April 30, 1987, government and media insiders alike were unanimous in their praise of "the qualities of mind, spirit, and character" Kalb brought to his new post. Among the journalist's admirers was Secretary of Defense Casper W. Weinberger, who termed Kalb's appointment "a very promising, very hopeful thing."

Marvin Leonard Kalb was born on June 9, 1930, in New York City, one of the three children of Max and Bella (Portnoy) Kalb. Both his Ukrainian mother and his Polish father had immigrated to the United States to escape anti-Semitism. Max Kalb, a tailor by trade, worked for a time in garment sweatshops on Manhattan's Lower East Side before opening his own successful dry cleaning business. Marvin Kalb, his sister, Estelle, and his older brother, Bernard, received their early education in New York City public schools, and the two brothers went on to attend the highly competitive City College of New York. After earning a bachelor of social sciences degree from City College in 1951, Marvin enrolled at Harvard University. Bernard, who was by then working as a *New York Times* reporter, helped his parents pay for his brother's graduate studies. "Bernard saw potential in Marvin," Estelle told Rogers Worthington in an interview for a *Chicago Tribune* (September 23, 1981) profile. "They are very giving to each other. They're always helping each other."

After taking his M.A. degree in Chinese and Russian history at Harvard in 1953, Kalb served a two-year tour of duty in the United States Army. He returned to Harvard in 1955, intending to begin work on his doctorate. A few months later, however, he decided to accept a job as a translator in the Anglo-American Joint Press Reading Service at the American embassy in Moscow. During his tenure as a press attaché in Moscow, Kalb devoted most of his free time to researching the life of the nineteenth-century Russian educator Count Uvarov, the proposed subject of his doctoral dissertation, and to traveling around the Soviet Union. He recounted his experiences in *Eastern Exposure*, which was published by Farrar, Straus, and Cudahy in 1958 to generally favorable reviews. Among the book's admirers was Harrison Salisbury, who had himself won a Pulitzer Prize for his reporting from Moscow in 1955. "Not since Leslie Stevens' poignant *Russian Assignment*," Salisbury wrote in his review for the *New York Times* (November 2, 1958), "has so perceptive a book about Russia, the Russian people, their way of life, their patriotic aspirations, their secret longings been presented to the American public."

Returning to the United States in mid-1957, Kalb abandoned his plan to complete his doctorate in Russian history in order to join the staff of CBS News in New York. An unfriendly editor inadvertently got Kalb started on the right foot when he tried to discourage the young writer by assigning him to the midnight-to-8:00 A.M. "graveyard shift" on the sports desk. A sports enthusiast, Kalb excelled in the job and soon progressed to other assignments. In the late 1950s he took a leave of absence from the network to do graduate work in Russian and Chinese studies at Columbia University on a CBS Foundation news and public affairs fellowship. It was during Kalb's sabbatical that network officials decided to reopen CBS's news bureau in Moscow, which had been closed since the Soviet government, angered by the network's telecast of the controversial drama *The Plot to Kill Stalin* on its anthology series *Playhouse 90*, refused to allow CBS Moscow correspondent Daniel Schorr back into the country following a visit home in 1958. The CBS News executives' first choice for

the plum assignment was Larry LeSueur, but when he was denied an entry visa, they turned to Kalb, whose background and knowledge of Russian made him ideal for the post. Arriving in Moscow in the spring of 1960, he quickly established a solid reputation as a broadcast journalist. By January of the following year he was being described in the *New York Times* as "perhaps the most exciting new mind on the CBS staff," an opinion that was evidently widely shared by his peers because, three months later, in April 1961, he was honored with the first of the six Overseas Press Club Awards he was to win over the course of the next twenty-five years.

During his three years as chief of the network's Moscow bureau, Kalb contributed articles on Soviet life and culture and on East-West relations to a number of periodicals, including the *New York Times Magazine*, *Saturday Review*, and the *Reporter*. With the aid of a Ford Foundation grant, he also completed an intensive, first-hand study of the uneasy partnership between the Soviet Union and the People's Republic of China. In his *Dragon in the Kremlin* (Dutton, 1961), an analysis of the deep and widening gulf between the two nations, he predicted that the Sino-Soviet bond would "continue to function as a viable and powerful political, economic, and diplomatic force" for the immediate future but that over the long term China would gradually assume a position of dominance. In view of China's increasing importance as a world power, Kalb called for a reassessment of United States Asian policy, urging the establishment of diplomatic relations with the People's Republic and the admission of the country to the United Nations.

In mid-1963 Kalb was reassigned to the United States as the chief diplomatic correspondent in CBS's Washington bureau. Even so, he maintained his keen interest in Soviet affairs, and in 1965, after having turned down three earlier requests, the Soviet Foreign Ministry finally gave him and a four-man CBS News film crew permission to visit the cities and villages along a 150-mile stretch of the Volga River between Ulyanovsk and Kazan. Billed as "one man's report on provincial life along one of the world's great rivers," the documentary *The Volga* was telecast by CBS on January 4, 1966. American television critics generally praised both the film's visual beauty and Kalb's "tough and incisive" narration, although the *New York Times's* Jack Gould took exception to the "overtones of preachment" in the reporter's account. Incensed by what they saw as an "intentionally distorted" report, Soviet government officials protested the broadcast in the strongest terms. As outlined in a cable to Fred W. Friendly, then the president of CBS News, their particular objection was to "slanted commentary" that they considered an "insult [to] the dignity of the Soviet people." An expanded version of Kalb's script for the program was published by Macmillan in 1967 under the title *The Volga: A Political Journey Through Russia*.

While covering the diplomatic side of America's escalating involvement in the Vietnam war in the late 1960s, Kalb became increasingly interested in the history of the United States government's commitments in Asia, especially in Indochina. He and his longtime colleague Elie Abel, a former diplomatic correspondent for NBC who was then the dean of Columbia University's School of Journalism, investigated the course of American entanglement in the Far East in the book *Roots of Involvement: The U.S. in Asia, 1784-1971* (Norton, 1971), a dispassionate and painstakingly documented study. J. F. Fairbank in his review for *Book World* (April 4, 1971) hailed it as "probably both the briefest and the most comprehensive analytic account of the decision-making in America's Vietnam tragedy." Most critics shared Fairbank's view, but John Franklin Campbell, writing in the *New York Times Book Review* (April 18, 1971), wondered whether the two journalists might have been the "victims of selective 'news management' by some of the officials they have interviewed, for their account is incoherent in some places and just plain inaccurate in others."

Kalb's brand of probing, analytical journalism soon proved to be as nettling to President Richard Nixon's White House as it had been to the Kremlin. In the spring of 1973 Kalb learned that his name was included on Nixon's infamous "enemies list" and that he was among the thirteen government officials and four reporters whose telephones had been tapped by White House "plumbers" at various times between May 1969 and February 1971 in an effort to plug embarrassing leaks of secret information. "I don't know why I was selected," Kalb said, as quoted in the *New York Times* (May 17, 1973), "but what I had done in 1969 as a reporter I had done for the past fifteen years and hope to do for the next fifteen years." The wiretaps were only one aspect of what appeared to be a much wider covert surveillance operation. In the span of just three weeks in July 1973, Kalb's office in the State Department building in downtown Washington was twice ransacked. A year later, in July 1974, the reporter was publicly criticized by Bruce Herschensohn, a deputy special assistant to President Nixon, for failing to identify the anonymous "high officials" who had told him that the Watergate scandal had weakened the United States's negotiating position in its on-going strategic arms limitation talks with the Soviet Union. After being told that the unnamed source who had discussed the arms talks with Kalb and other journalists on the condition that he not be directly named was none other than Secretary of State Henry A. Kissinger, Herschensohn issued a public apology.

As CBS's chief diplomatic correspondent, Marvin Kalb accompanied Dr. Kissinger on almost all his overseas travels, including his trips to the Soviet Union, the People's Republic of China, and the Middle East. Intrigued by Kissinger's pragmatic approach to international relations and by the vital role he played in the development of foreign policy in the Nixon administration, Kalb set out to examine the man and his diplomatic achievements in *Kissinger* (Little, Brown, 1974). Written with his brother, Bernard, who had the seen the results of some of Kissinger's policies firsthand as a correspondent in Southeast Asia for the *New York Times* and CBS News, *Kissinger* was recognized by most reviewers as a detailed and, to quote James Chace, "indispensable" study of American diplomacy in the aftermath of the cold war. But as Chace went on to point out in the *New York Times Book Review* (August 25, 1974), the book was nonetheless "gravely flawed" in his view, particularly in its "omission of any extended treatment of what could be seen as Nixon's and Kissinger's failures."

Marvin Kalb took a slightly more unorthodox look at American foreign policy-making in the thriller *In the National Interest* (Simon & Schuster, 1977), which he wrote in collaboration with Ted Koppel, then ABC News's diplomatic correspondent. The story of an American secretary of state whose discovery of an explosive political secret during Mideast negotiations is known only to a star television reporter, the book grew out of the two newsmen's experiences traveling with Kissinger for thirty-three days as he practiced his now famous "shuttle diplomacy." With reviews that acknowledged its "possible popular appeal," "plausible, intelligent" scenario, and "clean," "brisk" writing, *In the National Interest* became a minor best seller in the United States and in Israel, where sales of the book were spurred by a rumor that Marvin Kalb was one of three men being seriously considered for the post of United States ambassador to Israel.

That Kalb was considering a possible career change became more evident in 1979, when he began appearing with increasing frequency at Democratic fund-raising parties in Maryland. In July he confirmed that he had been testing the state's political waters regarding a possible run for the Democratic nomination to the United States Senate in the 1980 election. "I've been watching government for a couple of years now, and the thought of being on the inside is clearly exhilarating," he admitted to Michael Weisskopf in an interview for the *Washington Post* (July 28, 1979). Commenting on charges that he was a "carpetbagger" capitalizing on his status as a television personality, Kalb told Weisskopf, "I really don't consider myself a celebrity. People are going to see me, not a face on the tube. They're going to have to deal with me, not an image." After carefully weighing his chances, he finally decided against seeking elective office.

Instead, Kalb took a new direction journalistically. On June 19, 1980, after twenty-three years with CBS News, he resigned from the network to become chief diplomatic correspondent for the rival NBC News organization. "At this point in my life . . . ," he explained, as quoted in the *New York Times* (June 20, 1980), "I wanted something new, the chance to work with people like [John] Chancellor, [Richard] Valeriani, and [David] Brinkley," referring to three veteran NBC correspondents. The "broader, richer opportunities" afforded the reporter at NBC included the chance to serve as moderator of *Meet the Press*, the network's long-running weekly public affairs program. Not unexpectedly, when Marvin Kalb left CBS for NBC, Bernard Kalb followed. "I made it clear I would not leave unless it was clear Bernie was leaving," Kalb explained to Rogers Worthington. "And he would not leave unless I was leaving, because I would not put myself into direct competition with my brother. It would be an absurd, hopeless situation and very unprofessional for both networks."

At NBC, Kalb's focus as a journalist changed, for in addition to hosting *Meet the Press*, he now began spending more time on in-depth reporting of international affairs. His controversial ninety-minute *NBC White Paper* profile of Cuban Premier Fidel Castro attracted a large audience. So, too, did an investigative report on the possible connection between Mehmet Ali Agca, the Turkish terrorist who attempted to assassinate Pope John Paul II in May 1981, and the Bulgarian secret service (and, by extension, the Soviet Union). Broadcast in September 1982, *The Man Who Shot the Pope* made headlines around the globe with its startling conclusion, in which Kalb, citing "a good deal of evidence, some of it, to be sure, circumstantial," linked the attempt on the pope's life "to the political and diplomatic needs of Red Square." The documentary earned Kalb a prestigious Peabody Prize, the television equivalent of the Pulitzer Prize.

Concurrent with his work for NBC News, Kalb continued to pursue his spare-time career as a novelist. In 1981 Little, Brown and Company published his second novel, *The Last Ambassador*, a political thriller set against the fall of Saigon to the North Vietnamese in 1975 that he wrote with his brother, who had covered the Vietnam war for CBS News. The two had originally intended to compile an historical account of the end of the war, but as Marvin Kalb explained to Rogers Worthington, "For a variety of reasons, we weren't being told the truth. . . . And we couldn't get access to the classified information. We couldn't really write a [nonfiction] book."

The Last Ambassador was seen by most critics as a *roman à clef*. According to the Kalbs, however, the two principal characters—Tony Catlett, a skeptical CIA agent, and Ambassador Hadden Walker, a career diplomat—are not fictional stand-ins for real people but the embodiments of the authors' differing views of the war. Catlett presents Bernard Kalb's case for negotiating the establishment of a coalition government; Walker proffers Marvin's argument for continued military aid to South Vietnam even as it falls. In an interview shortly after the book was published, Marvin Kalb maintained that his position, although unfashionable at the time, would eventually be adopted by a majority of Americans. That position included his "feeling that the mood of the country [the United States] is turning," as he told Daniel Southerland of the *Christian Science Monitor* (October 20, 1981), "and

that people will not look with disdain on a soldier who went to fight in Vietnam."

Kalb's regular appearances on the *NBC Nightly News With Tom Brokaw* and as anchorman of various NBC News *White Paper* documentaries on foreign affairs, his contributions to a variety of magazines and newspapers, and his efforts as a novelist kept him constantly in the public eye throughout the 1980s. The respect accorded him was reflected in his selection by the League of Women Voters as one of four questioners at the final presidential election debate between the Republican incumbent, Ronald Reagan, and his Democratic challenger, Walter F. Mondale, on October 21, 1984. The reporter's professional reputation was further enhanced in 1986, when he received two major awards, an Alfred I. Dupont-Columbia University Award for the special report *Star Wars: Defense in Space* and a Peabody Prize, his second, for the documentary *Vietnam: Lessons of a Lost War*. Kalb's long list of honors also includes an Edward M. Weintal Award for distinguished diplomatic reporting from Georgetown University and three Edwin M. Hood Awards from the National Press Club.

In March 1987 Kalb announced that he was leaving NBC News to accept the directorship of the new Joan Shorenstein Barone Center for the Press, Politics and Public Policy at Harvard University's John F. Kennedy School of Government. "The [search] committee was concerned that we find a practitioner whose interests were both broad and deep," Hale Champion, the executive dean of the Kennedy School and chairman of the committee, said in announcing Kalb's appointment, "and anyone who has seen Kalb on *Meet the Press* or gotten to know him personally will recognize his exceptional range." Long interested in the role of the media in society, Kalb numbered among his top priorities as director of the center the creation of a course on the presidency and the press and of a project devoted to the analysis of the impact that the networks' concern with profits has on their coverage of news. "Democracy cannot be sustained in this country without a healthy relationship between the press and politicians," Kalb told Christopher Swan in an interview for the *Christian Science Monitor* (April 30, 1987). "We simply have to understand each other a lot better than we do right now. We will rise together, or we will sink together."

Marvin Kalb, who stands a trim six feet four inches tall, has been described as "gravely handsome," with wavy gray hair, "kind eyes," and "a face any mother would trust." On June 1, 1958, he married the former Madeleine J. Green, a scholar and writer whose most recent book is *The Congo Cables: The Cold War in Africa From Eisenhower to Kennedy* (1982). They have two daughters, Deborah and Judith. Before accepting his post at Harvard, Kalb was an adjunct professor of press and international relations at Georgetown University. He continues to serve as a member of the senior advisory council of the School for Advanced International Studies at Johns Hopkins University.

References: *Chicago Tribune I* p15+ *S* 23 '81 *por*; *Christian Sci Mon B* p8+ *O* 20 '81 *por*; *N Y Times B* p13 *Mr* 23 '87 *por*; *Contemporary Authors*, 1st rev vols 5–8 (1969); *International Television & Video Almanac*, 1987; *Who's Who in America*, 1984–85; *Who's Who in Television and Cable* (1983)

Keneally, Thomas (Michael)

(ke-nē´lē)

Oct. 7, 1935– Australian novelist. Address: h. 24 The Serpentine, Bilgola Beach, New South Wales 2107, Australia

Thomas Keneally is the foremost Australian novelist of his generation, with an international reputation fast approaching that of Patrick White, the dean of novelists Down Under. Although there was a strong element of autobiography in some of his early works, such as *Three Cheers for the Paraclete* (1968), set in a Roman Catholic seminary, Keneally in the main applies his fictional craft to historical events, not so much to make epics of them as to trace their labyrinthine impact, often horrific, on the lives of decent, vulnerable individuals. With technical variety, he has explored subjects ranging from the colonization of Australia and Antarctic expeditions to the signing of the World War I Armistice and the American Civil War. Keneally's own favorites among his books are *Blood Red, Sister Rose* (1974), a retelling of the story of Joan of Arc; *The Chant of Jimmie Blacksmith* (1972), about racial violence in Australia at the turn of the century; and *Schindler's List* (1982), a stunning documentary novel about an unlikely hero of the Holocaust, Oskar Schindler, a Third Reich industrialist of otherwise ambiguous integrity who cunningly turned his forced-labor camp-factory into a refuge where more than a thousand Jews were saved from the Nazi death machine. Although Keneally does not regard *Schindler's List* as fiction, the novel won the 1982 Booker McConnell Prize for Fiction in England. Keneally has also won the World Society of Literature Award, the Heinemann Award for Literature, and many Australian awards. Many North Americans first became aware of his work through the motion picture versions of *The Chant of Jimmie Blacksmith* and *Schindler's List*. In addition to novels, Keneally wrote several plays early in his career.

The grandson of a blue-collar emigrant from County Cork, Ireland, and the son of a postman, Thomas Michael Keneally was born on October 7, 1935, at Wauchope on the north coast of New South Wales, Australia. "The Irish in Australia had both a great respect for books and an immense fear of them," Keneally told Michael Barber in an interview for the *Guardian* (September 1, 1976). "They looked on books and writers as mysterious entities, full of clouds and ambiguities. I think that influenced me . . . stopped me from becoming a respectable member of society—an accountant or a dentist."

During Keneally's childhood he moved with his family to Sydney, the capital of New South Wales. After graduating from a Christian Brothers' high school in the Sydney suburb of Strathfield, he entered St. Patrick's College, the diocesan seminary in New South Wales. Suffering what he has described as "a crisis of emotional suppression," he quit the seminary just six months short of his scheduled ordination to the priesthood. After working briefly as a government clerk, he taught at Waverly College, a Catholic high school in Sydney, from 1960 to 1964. During that time he wrote his first novel, *The Place at Whitton* (Cassell, 1964), a Gothic murder mystery set in a Catholic seminary and involving witchcraft. In his second novel, *The Fear* (Cassell, 1965), he told the story of a boy terrorized by his own overproductive imagination in a New South Wales coastal village during World War II, when a Japanese invasion was thought to be an imminent possibility. In *Modern Australian Prose, 1909–1975* (1980), A. Grove Day described *The Fear* as "marred by having the Catholic ethos contrasted with a villainous Communist straw man, and by a weak structure and focus of narration."

The plot dramatized in Keneally's play *Halloran's Little Boat*, first produced in Sydney in 1966, was reprised in novel form in *Bring Larks and Heroes* (Cassell, 1967). That story, set in a New South Wales penal colony two centuries ago, underscores certain enduring Irish traits as personified in its protagonists, especially the Irish soldier Phelim Halloran, a good man tainted by circumstances, who chafes at a repressive institution but cannot bring himself to quit it. The theme seems to be the need for seeking salvation within the context of one's society. A critic of the novel writing retrospectively in the London *Times Literary Supplement* (October 26, 1973) credited Keneally with writing "brilliantly," with an "abundance of ideas and facility with words" but faulted him with "self-indulgence," a lack of "austerity and discipline." "His narrative shifts in and out of character abruptly: at one moment a character is being lyrical or reflective or ironic, at the next the author is editorializing in the same or a different vein."

Keneally's earliest novels showed the strong influence of poets he admired, especially Dylan Thomas, and of the older contemporary Australian novelist Patrick White. With its crisper prose style, the well-ordered and ironic novel *Three Cheers for the Paraclete* (Angus & Robertson, 1968; Viking, 1969) signaled a major shift in technique, partly under the influence of the English Catholic novelist Evelyn Waugh. The protagonist of that novel is Father James Maitland, a young priest who teaches at a Catholic seminary in Sydney. Beset by theological doubts, Maitland runs afoul of institutional taboos and becomes the victim of institutional absurdities, but, like Halloran in *Bring Larks and Heroes*, remains loyal to the institution. Among Maitland's transgressions are the pseudonymous writing of an unorthodox book on theology—of which his archbishop asks him to write a negative review—and advising a psychotic seminarian to consult a psychiatrist. Committed to his vocation, Maitland accepts temporary suspension from his priestly duties and a later appointment to a lesser post. Reviewing *Three Cheers for the Paraclete* in *Best Sellers* (July 15, 1968), Thomas L. Vance remarked the evenhandedness of Keneally's characterization, which does not portray Maitland as "a paragon of all virtues exploited by an outdated Church" or his superiors as "vicious men." "What is refreshing about this novel," Vance wrote, "is that the priests and bishops are seen in the fullness of their humanity."

In 1968 Keneally's play *Childermass* was given its debut performance in Sydney, and four years later his play *An Awful Rose* had its premiere in the same city. From 1968 to 1970 Keneally lectured at the University of New England in Armidale, New South Wales. He made a trip to Antarctica in researching the background for his novel *The Survivor* (Angus & Robertson, 1969; Viking, 1970), about Alec Ramsey, a college teacher who is a prisoner of conscience, spending forty years trying to atone for his abandonment of a companion during an Antarctic expedition. Subsidized by one of several Commonwealth Literary Fund awards that he received, Keneally lived in Europe in 1970 and 1971.

In Keneally's symbolically complex and unnerving fable *A Dutiful Daughter* (Viking, 1971), Damien and Barbara Glover, a brother and sister in an Australian outback farm family, keep hidden from the world an horrific secret—the metamorphosis of their parents into half-human bovine, centaur-like creatures. Away at university, Damien ambivalently tries to escape the problem of his parents and his obsessive relationship to his sister. The saintly Barbara remains at home, devotedly caring for the parents while trying to comfort her brother and understand his quasi-incestuous feelings for her.

Reviewing *A Dutiful Daughter* in the *New York Times Book Review* (September 12, 1971), Angela Carter complained of a "prevailing Firbankian archness" that "sometimes effects a tinkling queasiness of tone," so that "one doesn't know whether one is cued in for a belly laugh, a nervous giggle or a shudder of horror." "The book's immense undertow of tormented sexuality," Miss Carter observed, "is often expressed in a rhetoric that puts a strain on the predominant narcissistically decorative prose. The style is in subtle conflict with the Buñuelian woes of puritanical Catholicism, pubertal disorientation, unnaturally prolonged virginity, exacerbated frustration and sexual guilt that are the monsters typified by the half-beasts Barbara hides in the byre. . . . But the novel sticks in the mind. . . . The metamorphosis itself is self-sufficient. It is authentically marvelous." In the same publication four months later (January 16, 1972), Garry Wills wrote: "He [Keneally] has built up his vision of a world 'between gods' with growing patience and economy through six novels. . . . The last [*A Dutiful Daughter*] is the best; it puts the Chiron myth to better use than Updike had, takes Joan of Arc's witchcraft more seriously than either Shakespeare or Shaw did, and details nightmare in daylight realistic style without any reliance on Kafka." Melvin Maddox of *Time* (June 7, 1971) compared the Australian nuclear-family hell depicted by Keneally to the Dublin one of James Joyce. "In the end," Maddox wrote, "Keneally looses a Jehovah-like flood on the outback and the Glovers, washing himself clean of his creation. But in the meantime, writing like an angel, he has forcefully raised an ancient question: What is the demon in man that so often makes him a monster to those condemned to love him—including himself?"

More commercially successful than Keneally's previous books in both Great Britain and the United States was *The Chant of Jimmie Blacksmith*, a tale of carnage based on events that occurred in northern New South Wales in 1900, when the murderous revolt of two aborigine brothers was answered with massacres of aborigines by whites. Keneally's Jimmie Blacksmith is a conscientious "mission halfbreed" who reacts with rage when he realizes he has been gulled into betraying his tribal heritage. Many Australian critics regarded the eponymous protagonist of *The Chant of Jimmy Blacksmith* as "the most successfully drawn of Keneally's recurrent sensitive, oppressed, ultimately self-destructive victims" and took seriously Keneally's implication "that unless white attitudes and institutions are changed, oppression of aborigines will continue."

In *Blood Red, Sister Rose* (Viking, 1974; Collins, 1974) Keneally tried to portray a Maid of Orleans more human than the saint or witch of legend and more spiritual than the earthy militant portrayed by George Bernard Shaw. In the opinion of Melvin Maddox of *Time* (February 10, 1975), he succeeded, creating a Joan of Arc—or Jehanne, as Keneally calls her—"less spectacular" but "decidedly more convincing and perhaps, at last, more moving." According to Maddox, Keneally's Joan, "part battle flag, part rebel, and part saint, adds up to a heroic surrogate for the absurd and contradictory in Everyman, 'the feel of the frayed edges of all the world's foolishness coalescing in her guts.'" Bruce Cook, who reviewed the novel for the *Washington Post* (January 26, 1975), thought that Keneally intended to reduce Joan to "recognizably human dimensions," to "expose the pettiness of war's political basis—at least that of the Hundred Years War," and "to expose war as the most vain of human vanities because the most destructive." To Cook, Keneally seemed disturbed "that the Divinity should actually have mucked about in French politics through the agency of some deluded adolescent." Neil Hepburn, writing in *The Listener* (February 6, 1975), graded the book as "an excellent historical novel—not quite in the Mary Renault class, perhaps, but a match for Helen Waddell or T. H. White." "What imprisons the book is the Keneally trademark—the use of modern, and transatlantic modern, colloquialism for dialogue," Hepburn wrote. "But you cannot help enjoying it, for all that."

In the course of his research for a World War I motion picture script, Keneally found the subject for *Gossip from the Forest* (Collins, 1975; Harcourt, 1976), one of his most exhaustively researched and most highly praised works, a runner-up for the Booker Prize. A fictional, allegorized reconstruction of the signing of the Armistice in the forest clearing at Compiègne, France, on November 11, 1918, the novel evokes the tensions of the time, the isolation of the negotiators from each other, and the vindictive and short-sighted terms that Maréchal Foch and his French attendants forced on Mathias Erzberger, the pacifist and liberal member of the Reichstag who led the German delegation. Erzberger was later assassinated by young German officers for signing the Armistice at all. "*Gossip from the Forest* is a study of the profoundly civilian and pacific sensibility beleaguered by crude power . . . ," Paul Fussell wrote in the *New York Times Book Review* (April 11, 1976). "By the end of the novel we are deeply sympathetic with Erzberger's fate and with Keneally's point, that the twentieth century will not tolerate Mathias Erzbergers. They are civilized and they are sane." Fussell characterized the book as not so much an historical novel as "a meditation on history." A television dramatization of *Gossip from the Forest* was broadcast in the United States in 1980.

In the mid-1970s Keneally was planning to continue following the somewhat experimental lines of *Blood Red, Sister Rose* and *Gossip from the Forest*, but he also planned to write some "entertainments" as a "relief from the normal grind of thinking about work in purely artistic terms and

trying to produce 'literature.'" The first of the entertainments was *A Season in Purgatory* (Collins, 1976; Harcourt, 1977), the straightforward story, grounded in fact, about a young upper-class English surgeon's gruesome experiences (relieved by operating-room humor) during World War II military service in Yugoslavia and about his ill-starred love affair with a forty-year-old partisan woman. Jonathan Yardley, writing in the *Washington Post Book World* (February 20, 1977), described the novel at its most superficial level as "a cross between *M*A*S*H* and *A Farewell to Arms*." George Steiner, who had regarded *Gossip from the Forest* as "an interesting failure," considered *A Season in Purgatory* to be a "a boring success" and wondered why an author who had previously shown "an oddly costive but unmistakable stylishness and adultness should turn out this purple tripe." Writing of Keneally in the *New Yorker* (May 23, 1977), Steiner summed him up at his best: "He is obsessed by the sensual texture of history, by the immediate impress of political and military drama on the nerve and marrow of those involved. Like Patrick White, this novelist out of a new, almost 'nonhistorical' continent is immersing himself in the dense, equivocal European past."

In *A Victim of the Aurora* (1977), Keneally reworked the plot of his earlier Antarctic novel, *The Survivor*, adding some new twists, shifting emphasis from character to action, and producing another entertainment, this one a murder mystery. The narrator of his next novel, *The Passenger* (Harcourt, 1978), is a fetus gifted with preternatural sophistication and knowledge, including genealogical memory. (One of his ancestors was an Irishman who sailed from Cork to Australia in 1799 in the hold of a convict ship.) "It may not be Keneally's best novel," Blake Morrison wrote in his review in the *New Statesman* (January 19, 1979), "but it's his wittiest and most inventive [with a] strong and original narrative voice. . . . Though it's not anti-abortionist in intention—the fetus is careful to stress that it's only his own life he wants to save—Keneally's lyrical responsiveness to the womb, with its 'rich lakes of wild and plentiful cilia, of browsing bacteria, of hearty corpuscles and of those flabbergasting denizens, the chromosomes,' makes *Passenger* a quietly effective little protection campaign for the unborn child." In the *Observer* (January 21, 1979), Hermione Lee described *The Passenger* as "a witty variant on the picaresque tradition, jauntily sustained, and versatile, in that the narrative contrivance, itself fantastical, allows . . . fantastical developments."

Keneally spent eighteen months in the United States researching his most ambitious historical novel, *The Confederates* (Harper & Row, 1980), a fictionalized account of the Civil War from the Southern point of view. Many American reviewers were amazed that a foreigner could create so realistic a portrayal of the American South, with a narrative voice that seems Southern born and bred. Reviewing the novel in the *Observer* (October 21, 1979), Stephen Vaughan wrote: "As an Australian writing about events so thronged with hosts, altars, and portents for our time but also so fervently and proprietorially American, Keneally is treading on holy ground. Dangerous ground, too, with such forerunners as Crane, Faulkner, Bierce, Sandburg, but he avoids the pitfalls of pastiche in this noble book."

Although it shambles deceptively, *The Cut-Rate Kingdom* (Wildcat Press, 1980; Allen Lane, 1984) is essentially a novel of political intrigue, set in the corridors of governmental power in Canberra in 1942, when Australia was not only threatened with military invasion by the Japanese but beginning to experience what would become a political and cultural invasion by its putative ally, the United States. Many were disappointed in the book, and some wondered if it were not a sketch of sorts for a possible movie.

Schindler's List (Simon & Schuster, 1982) was published in Great Britain as *Schindler's Ark* (Hodder & Stoughton, 1982). Keneally learned the story of Oscar Schindler through a chance meeting with Leopold Pfefferberg, one of the 1,400-odd Jews saved by Schindler from the horror of the Nazi concentration camps and gas chambers during World War II. Schindler, a Catholic German industrialist from the Sudetenland who prospered under the Hitler regime and was a bon vivant and philanderer—a man not called to goodness until he witnessed, with revulsion, the "Final Solution" being carried out. Then, with ingenuity and bluff and at great and constant personal expense and risk, he turned his factory work force in Cracow in occupied Poland into a *Gentilefrei* and kept it that way by boldly exploiting his friendship with S.S. chiefs and other high German officials. When the Soviet army advanced and the Germans made plans to kill the remaining Jewish workers in Cracow before retreating, he moved his workers to a new factory-compound in German-held Czechoslovakia.

Keneally got "quite used to having nightmares" while writing the story of Schindler, especially after interviewing "Schindler's people." (He traveled worldwide to meet fifty of the survivors.) In the novel he tried, in his words, "to avoid all fiction, since fiction would debase the record," even though he had to use "the texture and devices of the novel to tell a true story," because that was the only craft he knew. For that reason, he was at first taken aback when the book won the coveted Booker Prize "for fiction." As Jonathan Yardley pointed out in the *Washington Post Book Week*, the devices of the "new" journalism served to give *Schindler's List* a "persuasive air of authenticity" and make it "a most emphatic and powerful" act of homage. The reviewer for *Publishers Weekly* observed that Keneally's scrupulous honesty in "conveying the contradictions and ambiguities of Schindler's personality" added to "the strength of his portrayal."

In *A Family Madness* (Hodder & Stoughton, 1985; Simon & Schuster, 1986), Keneally traced the madness of a Byelorussian immigrant in Australia back to terrible events in Byelorussia in the early days of World War II, when Byelorussian patriots helped the Nazi occupation to exterminate Jews in the hope that they would be rewarded with independence. "The documentary interest of *A Family Madness* is . . . considerable," Robert Towers wrote in the *New York Times Book Review* (March 16, 1986). "Its achievement as a work of literary fiction is much less secure. Mr. Keneally's characters—and this has been true of his earlier work as well—are curiously lacking in inwardness, in the suggestion of psychological depth." Walter Clemons of *Time* (March 31, 1986) found the novel "overintricate" but nevertheless recommended it as "one of Keneally's most ambitious performances." Some of *A Family Madness* was written while Keneally was writer-in-residence at the University of California in 1984–85. Keneally's novel *The Playmaker* (Simon & Schuster, 1987) is a lusty and affectionate bicentennial commemoration, at once brutal and sentimental, of the colonizing of Australia by convicts shipped from England beginning in 1788.

As described by interviewers, Thomas Keneally is a soft-spoken and genial person, with none of the "patriarchal severity" that some of his photographs suggest. He and Judith Martin, a former nurse, were married in 1965 and have two daughters, Margaret and Jane. Because Mrs. Keneally was once a postulant nun, some people have mistakenly assumed that the couple fell in love when Keneally was a seminarian. The Keneallys live in Bigola, a beachside suburb of Sydney. For recreation together, they watch quality drama on television or go to the theatre in Sydney. Alone, Keneally enjoys spectator sports, both on television and on local playing fields, and he is the publicity officer for the Warringa Amateur Athletic Association. His favorite reading includes modern novels, nineteenth-century Australian history, and the poetry of Yeats, Auden, William Carlos Williams, the Australian poet Les Murray, and, of course, Dylan Thomas.

Now that he uses a word processor, Keneally writes faster than he used to. He writes in his study, a large room decorated with photographs, such literary trophies as the leather and gold-leaf book that comes with the Booker Prize, and other mementoes of his life and career and containing a pool table and a refrigerator stocked with beer. The morning is his optimum working time, but he continues to work through much of the afternoon, taking a break now and then to shoot some pool or go to the post office and chat with neighbors and shopkeepers. He is, as he says, "temperamentally drawn to broad and distant canvases." Those canvases are usually in the past because he finds it difficult to plan his work beforehand. In the interview with Michael Barber he quoted the Irish writer Frank O'Connor: "I have to write the bloody thing first to see what it's going to be." He explained to Barber that whereas the personal or social present is confusing, "things that you're not in the midst of, things that are finished—even parts of your own life—have a dramatic unity." For Keneally, history is not escape from the present. "History is the present . . . digested and cast up in encapsulated form."

References: *Guardian* p8 S 1 '76 por; *London Sunday Times Mag* p54 My 8 '83 por; *Newsweek* 107:70+ Mr 31 '86 por; *Contemporary Authors* new series vol 10 (1983)

Khamenei, Hojatolislam (Sayed) Ali

(kä-mä´ nä)

1939– President of the Islamic Republic of Iran; clergyman. Address: b. Office of the President, Teheran, Iran

Hojatolislam Ali Khamenei, president since 1981 of the Islamic Republic of Iran, which he helped the Ayatollah Ruholla Khomeini to establish in 1979, was described in the *New York Times* (October 6, 1981) as "the archetype of the hard-line mullahs who dominate the Islamic Republic's government, its judiciary, and parliament." A former political prisoner of the Shah, Khamenei has served as the spiritual leader of the dominant Shi'ite Moslems of Teheran and as a deputy commander of the armed forces of his country, which since 1980 has been engaged in a war with neighboring Iraq. "Our greatest problem is that our people never believed that by their actions they could determine their own fate," Khamenei said in an interview in *Newsweek* in 1982. "The old regime told us to sit and wait for everything . . . to come from abroad. We have to convince our people completely to stand on their own feet. . . . "

Hojatolislam Sayed Ali Khamenei was born in 1939 into a family of Islamic scholars in the city of Meshed, a religious center in the province of Khorasan in eastern Iran. His brother Mohammed Khamenei was wounded in 1982, apparently by opponents to the government of the Islamic Republic. A product of Iran's network of Shi'ite theological institutions, Ali Khamenei began his religious studies at the age of eighteen at An Najaf, a leading center of Shi'ite learning. At one point he reportedly received training at Palestinian camps in Lebanon and Libya. About 1958 he moved to the city of Qum to study under the Ayatollah Ruholla Khomeini, who became a major influence in his life. Like his fellow students, he sat at the feet of his master, meticulously taking notes and debating the cryptic and complex points of the Koran.

Khamenei was one of the original group of theology students in Qum who rallied to the Ayatollah Khomeini's call for religious revolution. When the ayatollah's opposition to the regime of Shah Mohammed Riza Pahlevi reached its height in the spring of 1963, Khamenei took part in massive student demonstrations against the monarchy that culminated in the storming by police of Khomeini's Madresseh Faizeh seminary, resulting in the deaths of some twenty student mullahs. After the ayatollah went into exile in 1964, Khamenei returned to Meshed, where he continued his advanced theological education for four more years and taught at the local theological college. During that period he came under the strict surveillance of SAVAK, the Shah's dreaded secret police, because of his revolutionary activities. In the decade beginning in 1964, Khamenei was arrested six times, spending a total of three years as a political prisoner. After his release from jail in 1975 he was forced to go into internal exile for a year, living in the remote town of Iranshahr in Baluchistan-Sistan under harsh climatic conditions.

As demonstrations against the Shah's regime became increasingly violent during 1977 and 1978, Khamenei took part in the street battles that preceded the departure of the Shah from Iran on January 19, 1979, and the triumphant return of the Ayatollah Khomeini from exile in France sixteen days later. With the establishment, shortly afterward, of a fourteen-member Council of the Islamic Revolution, which formed a provisional government, Khamenei became one of the first members of that body. In the government of the new Islamic republic, established by a vote of 97 percent of the Iranian electorate in a referendum on March 30 and 31, 1979, Khamenei became the council's representative in the defense ministry and headed the political-ideological bureau of the military, responsible for the indoctrination of army personnel with Islamic ideology and with keeping a close watch on the officer corps.

After the Ayatollah Khomeini formed a special militia, the Guardians of the Islamic Revolution, in May 1979, Khamenei served for a time as its commander. He was one of the founders of the Hezb-e-Jomhori-e-Islami, or Islamic Republican party

(IRP), led by clergymen described as "fanatically loyal to the Ayatollah Khomeini," which emerged as the ruling party by late 1979. Khamenei was a staunch partisan of the militant student supporters of the ayatollah who in November 1979 seized the United States embassy in Teheran and held fifty-two persons captive for 444 days in an apparent effort to obtain extradition of the Shah, who was then undergoing medical treatment in New York City. As a member of a seven-member commission dealing with the hostage question, he helped to establish conditions for their ultimate release. In December 1979 a new constitution was adopted for Iran, establishing Shi'ite Islam as the state religion, vesting supreme power in the Moslem clergy, and declaring the Ayatollah Khomeini to be national religious leader for life.

In 1980 Khamenei was elected to a four-year term in Iran's unicameral legislature, the 270-member Islamic Consultative Assembly, or Majlis-e-Shoura-e-Islami. In the same year he was appointed congregational Friday prayer leader for the Teheran mosques, a key post within the hierarchy of the Shi'ite clergy. As prayer leader, he delivered fiery weekly sermons before crowds at Teheran University or at one of the city's large mosques. He usually spoke with a rifle in his hands, emphasizing a point by thrusting its muzzle into the air while raging against the "Great Satan, America," the rulers of Iraq, and the opponents of the Ayatollah Khomeini.

In September 1980 hostilities erupted between Iran and Iraq, resulting in part from a long-standing dispute between the two nations over boundaries, notably at the Shatt-al-'Arab waterway linking the major oil ports of both countries with the Persian Gulf. Although the dispute had temporarily been settled by an agreement signed in 1975 by the Shah of Iran and the Iraqi government, the conflict flared up anew when Iraq launched an invasion of Iran's Khuzestan province, which had a substantial Arab population claimed by Iraq. A major factor in the conflict was the long-standing hostility between Iran's Shi'ite Moslem community and the Sunnite Moslems dominant in Iraq.

After the outbreak of the Iran-Iraq war, the ayatollah appointed Khamenei as a deputy defense minister and as his personal representative on the supreme defense council, established to direct military strategy. In the early stages of the war, Khamenei organized the revolutionary guard in the front-line town of Ahvaz and found himself increasingly at odds with Abolhassan Bani-Sadr, a moderate who had taken office as president of Iran in February 1980 and who favored a positive response to the Iraqi government's call for a cease-fire. "The war leads to strengthening the revolutionary understanding of the . . . values and relations which the revolution brought to society," Khamenei told an Arab journalist who was visiting the battlefront. He added that the war effort against Iraq should be seen as part of a broader "jihad," or holy war, for the sake of "building the godly structure here on earth."

Meanwhile, Bani-Sadr had come increasingly into conflict with the dominant fundamentalist Shi'ites, and in June 1981 he was stripped of his presidential powers by the Ayatollah Khomeini and went into exile in France. His removal was marked by increasing violence between the fundamentalist regime and its leftist opponents, the Mujahedeen-e-Khalq (People's Freedom Fighters). On June 27, 1981, Khamenei himself narrowly escaped death when a bomb hidden in a tape recorder exploded as he addressed a crowd at a mosque near the Teheran bazaar, severely injuring his right arm and damaging his vocal cords. On the following day a bomb explosion at the Teheran office of the IRP killed seventy-two people, including the chief justice and four cabinet members. Then, on August 30, 1981, a bomb killed Mohammed Ali Rajai, who had succeeded Bani-Sadr as president in July. Four other persons, including the prime minister and IRP secretary general, Jad Bahonar, also died in the explosion.

On September 1, 1981, Khamenei succeeded Jad Bahonar as secretary general of the ruling IRP, and about two weeks later he was designated as IRP candidate for the presidency of Iran, in the country's third national election within a twenty-one month period. Although the Ayatollah Khomeini had previously barred members of the clergy from the presidency, at this time, according to the *Christian Science Monitor* (October 7, 1981), it was "a sign of the ayatollah's present concern over the state of the republic that he has brought . . . Khamenei out of the background shadows. . . ." At first there were over forty candidates seeking the presidency, but by the time of the election the field of opponents to Khamenei had narrowed down to three, who offered only token resistance. To ensure a large turnout, the government lowered the voting age from sixteen to fifteen, scheduled the elections for the Moslem sabbath, and placed the polls in the mosques.

The election of October 2, 1981 brought Khamenei over 16 million votes, more than 95 percent of the total. Sworn in on October 13, amid cries of "Allah is Great!" and "Death to America!," Khamenei pledged "to be a custodian of the state religion, the system of government of the Islamic republic and the constitutional law," and to devote himself "to the service of the people, the grandeur of [his] country, the promotion of religion and morality, and the supporting of furtherance of justice." He declared that his election victory represented a vote of "trust for the clergy, a vote for Islam, a vote for independence, and a vote for stamping out deviation, liberalism, and American-influenced leftists."

Khamenei apparently broke a campaign promise by not nominating as his prime minister the incumbent, Ayatollah Mahdavi Kani, who had been criticized for not doing enough to stop anti-government violence. Khamenei's own choice, Dr. Ali-Akbar Velayati, a pediatrician and lay theologian, was rejected by the Majlis, mainly because there was not enough evidence that he had taken part in the struggle that led to the overthrow of the Shah. Finally, the incumbent foreign minister, Hussein Moussavi, a member of the IRP central committee and the editor of its newspaper, was agreed upon for the prime ministership.

In his first interview with an American reporter, Khamenei—designated as "the second most powerful man in Iran" and still suffering from the effects of the June 1981 bomb explosion—expressed confidence to Elaine Sciolino of *Newsweek* (February 22, 1982) that Iran would win the war with Iraq very soon. Commenting on the progress of the Iranian revolution, he asserted: "We have freed our culture to a great extent from the dependence which our enemies, especially the Americans, imposed on us. We have been born again. On the other hand . . . many imperfections still exist. Our first priority is to rescue the poor from their suffering. The second is to reexamine our government administration so that it meets our revolutionary needs. Finally, we are actively striving to establish a balanced foreign policy." Khamenei attributed Iran's economic problems, including unemployment that exceeded 25 percent of the work force and an inflation rate of some 60 percent, largely to the war and the imposition of economic sanctions. He asserted that, despite repression, large-scale arrests, and executions, Iran's system of justice was now far more equitable than it had been under the Shah. "What's important is that we will not move toward the system of justice as it is known today in the West," he declared. "Rather, we are moving in the direction of a complete establishment of justice based on Islamic laws."

In his public speeches in the months that followed, Khamenei reiterated his country's determination to bring the war with Iraq to a victorious conclusion, while denying that Iran had any designs on Iraqi territory. He continued to castigate "American mercenaries" and the "Zionist regime" of Israel, and he criticized France for granting asylum to the enemies of Khomeini. He warned Arab states in the Persian Gulf region to maintain strict neutrality in the Iran-Iraq conflict, and he asserted that Iran could easily cut off a major part of the oil supplies to the West if the United States became directly involved in the gulf war.

On the diplomatic front, Khamenei met with some success when he visited Damascus in March 1985 to conclude a secret economic and military pact with the Syrian government. He was less successful in gaining wide support for his government's formation, in 1984, of a committee to safeguard the rights of black Americans that sought to "bring the U.S. government to trial." When Khamenei visited Zimbabwe in January 1986, at the end of a six-nation African tour, he incensed his hosts by refusing, in accordance with his fundamentalist Islamic principles, to shake hands with female members of Robert Mugabe's government, and by declining to attend a state banquet to be held in his honor because wine was to be served and women were to be seated at the head table. In September of that year, at the eighth summit meeting of the nonaligned movement at Harare, Zimbabwe, Khamenei caused consternation by demanding Iraq's expulsion from the movement and the execution of its leaders as war criminals.

On the domestic front, Khamenei, who narrowly escaped another assassination attempt in March 1985, was reportedly at odds with Prime Minister Hussein Moussavi, according to an article in the London *Sunday Times* (October 27, 1985). Whereas the prime minister maintained a more radical position, insisting that priority should be given to satisfying the needs of the "dispossessed" and favoring land reforms, the confiscation of the businesses of "un-Islamic" owners, and the establishment of large state enterprises, President Khamenei represented a conservative faction that advocated a greater role for business in managing the economy and regarded socialistic reforms as contrary to true Islam. Although the conservative faction had in the past held the upper hand, more recently the reformers won increased support from the mullahs, and even from the Ayatollah Khomeini. But while in the view of some observers Khamenei had lost some of his power and was playing more and more a ceremonial role, he was easily reelected for a second term as president, with 85 percent of the vote, in November 1985.

Revelations in late 1986 and early 1987 of secret contacts between the United States and Iran, allegedly involving the trade of weapons for the release of American hostages held by pro-Iranian Shi'ites in Lebanon in what became known as the Iran-Contra affair, were greeted with scorn by Khamenei, who ruled out any prospect for reconciliation with the United States. As the gulf war heated up in the summer and fall of 1987 and the United States became increasingly involved, Khamenei continued to resist efforts to end the conflict. Addressing the United Nations General Assembly on September 22, 1987, he rejected a call for a ceasefire by the UN Security Council, which he dismissed as "a paper factory for issuing worthless and ineffective orders," and he repeatedly denounced the American "Great Satan." He charged that the United States and its "Saudi stooges" were responsible for the violence in Mecca in August, in which some 400 persons, most of them Iranian pilgrims, were killed, and he condemned a recent United States Navy attack on a mine-laying Iranian warship. On the other hand, in conversations with Secretary General Javier Pérez de Cuéllar during the UN visit, Khamenei reportedly indicated for the first time that he might agree to a ceasefire in the war with Iraq, if certain conditions were met. Meanwhile hostilities in the Persian Gulf continued, and Khamenei declared in October that from then on, Iran would attack all unfriendly vessels, regardless of what flags they might be flying.

Hojatolislam Sayed Ali Khamenei, who is married and has six children, was described by Robert D. McFadden in a profile in the *New York Times* (October 6, 1981) as "a man of sharp features and severe mien that is not softened by his black turban, thick spectacles, or dark beard." In addition to his native Farsi, he is fluent in the Turkish and Arabic languages. The author and translator of several books, Khamenei is noted for his poetry and for his writings on Islamic science, history, and literature. For recreation he indulges in traditional Persian athletics.

References: Christian Sci Mon p4 O 7 '81 por; Newsweek 99:41 F 22 '82 por; N Y Times A p12 O 6 '81; Britannica Book of the Year, 1982; Hiro, Dilip. Iran Under the Ayatollahs (1985); International Who's Who, 1987–88; Who's Who in the World, 1987–88

Kirk, Paul G(rattan), Jr.

Jan. 18, 1938– Chairman of the Democratic National Committee; lawyer. Address: b. Democratic National Committee, 430 S. Capitol St., S.E., Washington, D.C. 20003

The task of rebuilding the shattered constituency of the Democratic party after the 1984 presidential election, in which the party's ticket was buried in a forty-nine state Republican landslide, was assumed by Paul G. Kirk Jr. on February 1, 1985, when he was elected chairman of the Democratic National Committee (DNC). Because he was a former aide of the liberal Massachusetts Senator Edward M. Kennedy and had sought the chairmanship with strong backing from organized labor, Kirk's election had been opposed by some Southern and Western members of the DNC and had been achieved only after what one reporter called the "usual intramural squabbling" among the Democrats. After assuming the chairmanship,

Kirk immediately set out to put an end to such bickering, which he felt had been a factor in his party's defeats in recent presidential races.

"My memory of the 1980 and 1984 Democratic nomination contest," Kirk said in a speech at the National Press Club in Washington, D.C., on March 11, 1987, "is one of self-inflicted political wounds, of meaningless straw polls, of campaigns devoting considerable expense and effort to tearing down the opposing Democratic candidates, to trashing our traditional base constituencies, to bashing the party itself, and to bickering about nominating rules and internal procedures." Seeking to head off a repeat of that scenario at the 1988 convention, Kirk withdrew official party recognition of special interest groups, including those representing minorities; eliminated the midterm party convention, traditionally a kind of combative warm-up for the national convention; set up a commission to revise the party's nominating rules; and specifically asked labor leaders to refrain from endorsing candidates early in the 1988 race. "Those with a particular agenda," Kirk has said, "have to realize that no particular agenda is going to succeed 100 percent, and if we continue to lose elections, they are not going to succeed at all."

Paul Grattan Kirk Jr. was born on January 18, 1938, in Newton, Massachusetts, one of the five children of Paul Grattan Kirk, a lawyer who later served for ten years as an associate justice on the Supreme Judicial Court of Massachusetts, and his wife, the former Josephine E. O'Connell. Following his graduation from St. Sebastian's high school in Newton in 1956, Kirk, like his father before him, attended Harvard College, where he majored in government. Upon taking his A.B. degree in 1960, he enlisted in the United States Army and spent a year on active duty as a platoon leader before continuing his education at Harvard Law School, from which he graduated with a LL.B. degree in 1964. He remained in the army reserve until 1973, when he was discharged with the rank of captain.

After receiving his law degree, Kirk worked for a time at Hale & Dorr, a Boston law firm, then served for a year as assistant district attorney of Middlesex County in East Cambridge, Massachusetts. Between 1966 and 1969 he worked, successively, for the law firms Wardwell, Allen, McLaughlin & Skinner and Maloney, Gallagher & Kirk, both in Boston. It was while he was on the staff of Maloney, Gallagher & Kirk that he first became actively involved in politics, as a volunteer in Senator Robert F. Kennedy's campaign for the presidency in 1968. Like many of his generation, Kirk was captivated by Robert Kennedy's attempt to build on the legacy of his martyred older brother, President John F. Kennedy, and create a "post-cold war, post-New Frontier liberalism." Kennedy's assassination, on June 6, 1968, the night of his victory in the California primary, devastated Kirk, who for a time considered leaving politics. Instead, he moved to Washington in 1969 to accept a job as assistant counsel for the United States Senate Judiciary Committee's subcommittee on administrative practices and procedures. Two years later, he joined Senator Edward M. Kennedy's staff as a special assistant. He eventually became the senator's chief legislative and political strategist.

Kirk resigned from Senator Kennedy's staff in 1977 to become a partner in the law firm Sullivan & Worcester, which maintains offices in Boston and Washington, but he returned to the Kennedy camp in 1979 to become national political director of the Kennedy for President Committee. As David S. Broder observed in his column in the *Washington Post* (February 6, 1985), "In the Kennedy entourage, which was often arrogant, sometimes secretive and always protective, Kirk stood out as a man who was consistent, stable, reliable and reasonable—and who balanced his sense of personal and political loyalty to the senator with a view of the world larger than the advancement of one individual's ambitions." Robert S. Strauss, a former Democratic National Committee chairman, was equally impressed. "In 1980," he told Broder, "[Kirk] spoke for the Kennedy campaign, and I was chairman of the [Jimmy] Carter campaign. The tensions between the two groups were rather severe, but I could always talk with Paul. . . . He always kept his word." After President Carter won the party's nomination at the Democratic National Convention in August 1980, Kirk returned to his law practice at Sullivan & Worcester, where he remains a partner.

As treasurer of the Democratic National Committee, a post he held from 1983 to 1985, Kirk observed the 1984 presidential campaign, which he has since described as "too long and exhaustive," with increasing dismay. During the extended primary contests, Senator Gary Hart and the Reverend Jesse Jackson, the most powerful rivals of the party's eventual nominee, Walter F. Mondale, repeatedly attacked Mondale's programs and policies. Although they made a show of unity at the nominating convention in San Francisco in July 1984, some political damage had been done, and Mondale was faced with the task not only of taking the battle to the popular Republican incumbent, Ronald Reagan, but also of proving that "he was not the man in the portrait his opponents had painted," as one political analyst observed in a special election issue of *Newsweek* magazine (November–December, 1984). Further splintering of the party was apparent in the fact that Mondale, though backed by the labor unions, found himself struggling to retain the support of other traditional Democratic constituencies, such as blacks, who for the most part backed Jackson, Jews, many of whom distrusted Jackson because of his association with the black Muslim leader Louis Farrakhan, and feminists, who insisted that a woman be nominated as vice-president. Mondale eventually did choose a woman, New York Representative Geraldine A. Ferraro, as his running mate, but the ominous signs of a disintegrating constituency were confirmed in November 1984 by an avalanche of votes for Ronald Reagan in the general election.

After Reagan's victory, the Democratic party entered what Kirk has described as a period of "hand-wringing and soul-searching" that culminated in a hotly contested election for the chairmanship of the Democratic National Committee at the committee's semiannual meeting in Washington in January 1985. At that meeting, Kirk and his closest competitors for the post, Nancy Pelosi, the former state party chairman of California, and Terry Sanford, the former governor of North Carolina, offered analyses of what was frequently called the "devastation" of 1984 in an impassioned debate that quickly became divided along regional and racial lines. Maintaining that the new party chairman should not be "identified in the public mind with one party figure and one party faction," Nancy Pelosi condemned Kirk's long-standing association with Edward M. Kennedy and his strong support among DNC members with ties to organized labor. His election, she argued, would "send the wrong signal" to moderate and conservative voters, particularly in the West and South.

Kirk countered Mrs. Pelosi's criticisms and strengthened his chances by sponsoring a resolution requiring the new chairman to remain neutral in the 1988 presidential race. Maneuvering expertly within the party machinery, he weathered the creation of a coalition between the Pelosi and Sanford forces made possible by Mrs. Pelosi's withdrawal from the race and several procedural challenges. His election became almost inevitable when he survived a last-minute attempt to unseat twenty-five DNC voting members who supported his candidacy. A new conflict arose, however, in the wee hours of the morning before the election, when Jesse Jackson called Kirk on behalf of the party's black caucus to lobby for the selection of Mayor Richard Hatcher of Gary, Indiana, Jackson's former campaign manager, as one of the party's two vice-chairmen. Despite the threat of a possible walkout by the caucus, Kirk turned Jackson down. After his election to the party chairmanship, by a margin of 203 to 151 on a roll-call vote on February 1, 1985, Kirk refused to accept the black caucus' 32-25 endorsement of Hatcher and instead allowed Illinois State Comptroller Roland Burris, who had lost the black caucus' recommendation, to continue his pursuit of the vice-chairmanship before the entire voting membership of the DNC. When Burris was elected to the vice-chairmanship, both he and Kirk came under intense criticism from the black caucus, but Michael Barone, writing in the *Washington Post* (February 17, 1985), praised Kirk for striking "a blow at the party's whole gaggle of caucuses by reducing the power of the most visible and powerful of them." "The Democrats," Barone added, "may finally be moving away from caucuses and toward a potential majority coalition."

For many observers, however, the skirmishes surrounding Kirk's election did nothing to dispel the perception of the Democratic party as a cacophonous collection of special interests. Texas State Democratic Chairman Bob Slagle spoke for many in his region when he said of the national party, as quoted in the *Washington Post* (February 2, 1985): "We don't need their help and we don't need their interference, and we don't need them slopping things over on us. I doubt seriously that people in Texas will think electing a Kennedy chief of staff as party chairman is a moderate signal."

Kirk took pains to send moderate signals at a meeting with Southern party leaders in Atlanta, Georgia, on February 16, 1985. Although he agreed with his colleagues that the party needed to broaden its appeal by moving toward the political center, he cautioned, "We are not going to be a better party by trying to out-Republican the Republicans." As a first step in dismantling the party's image as a Noah's ark for special interests, he asked the AFL-CIO, which had been one of the major sponsors of his chairmanship, to refrain from asserting its power within the party by endorsing any candidate early in the 1988 presidential race.

Despite Kirk's efforts, some Southern and Western elected officials remained unconvinced of his sincerity, and a group of them, led by Governor Charles S. Robb of Virginia, formed a maverick "Democratic Leadership Council," which directly challenged Kirk's authority only a month after he had taken office. According to Tom Sherwood and James A. Dickinson of the *Washington Post* (February 16, 1985), the new group was designed to be "an independent policy group that will help the Democratic party project a more moderate image." As one supporter observed, the Democratic Leadership Council was "an insurance policy" for the DNC's moderate wing in the event that Kirk proved unable to reshape the party. Among its influential founding members were the 1988 presidential candidates Richard A. Gephardt, the Missouri congressman, who became its first chairman, and Governor Bruce Babbitt of Arizona.

As Roland Evans and Robert Novak noted in their syndicated column of February 15, 1985, the Democratic Leadership Council presented Kirk with "a dilemma." "If he ignored [it]," they wrote, "he risked isolation. If he [accepted its invitation and] joined it, he risked downgrading himself." Instead, he countered it by speeding up plans for the creation of a Democratic Policy Commission, whose aim would be to involve elected officials in building a coherent, centrist ideological consensus that would span the entire party. The commission would "be guided by those elected officials around the country who are sensitive to working people and minorities, but are not tied down to specific groups," Kirk told an interviewer for *U.S. News & World Report* (March 15, 1985). He added that the policy commission would allow elected officials, many of them with multiracial constituencies, to "draft ideas on subjects such as the economy, defense and trade" that would "provide a foundation for our candidates running for Congress in 1986 and . . . the presidency in 1988."

The Democratic Policy Commission convened for the first time in May 1985, under the leadership of Scott M. Matheson, the former governor of Utah. Among its eighty-odd members were many officials who also belonged to the DLC. To insure that "no Democratic official from the South [would] have to run away from the national party to get elected," Kirk told reporters in a speech at the National Press Club on May 16, 1985, the new commission planned to hold a number of regional hearings, where local Democrats could air their views on policy matters and, through the report that the commission was scheduled to release in 1986, influence the national body.

In June 1985, in its first meeting since Kirk's tumultuous election, the Democratic National Committee gave every indication of having reshaped itself in conformity with Kirk's philosophy. The ideological blood feuds of the previous winter were not in evidence, and the gathering was, on the whole, harmonious and upbeat. Kirk won quick approval for his recommendation that the party's midterm conclave, usually a contentious presidential "cattle show," be abolished, thus removing an opportunity for party members and prospective candidates to break ideological ranks prematurely. As Robin Toner observed in the *New York Times* (November 2, 1986), the tactic had the effect of "saving the Democrats from themselves."

Kirk scored another point when the black caucus staunchly backed his nominees for a new "Fairness Commission," set up to revise the party's nominating rules. Those rules were normally hammered out during what one reporter called "quadrennial battles" joined by the Democrats for that purpose. The "Fairness Commission" was a result of the 1984 battle, in which Jesse Jackson and Gary Hart had protested that the number of delegates granted them under the old rules did not correspond to the percentage of the popular vote they had won in the primaries. Although Kirk had eliminated constituency caucuses as official bodies of the DNC, he saw to it that the Fairness Commission was comprised of people from all walks of life so that the rules review would not be dominated by special interest groups or by agents of potential presidential candidates. At the same time, he reminded commission members not to tamper with the rules assuring women, blacks, and other minorities representation in party affairs according to their numbers. Insisting that the party "save [its] fight for the Republicans," Kirk urged the Fairness Commission to complete its work quickly so that the party could "get on to the issues the American people are waiting for us to focus on."

In March 1986 the new presidential nominating rules drawn up by the Fairness Commission were adopted by the entire Democratic National Committee. Kirk had by now won the support of some of those who had most ardently opposed his election, among them Texas Democratic Chairman Bob Slagle. Kirk's centrist stand, however, seemed to have alienated traditional donors to the Democratic party, who, according to Thomas B. Edsall of the *Washington Post* (November 29, 1986), "fall into what are known as 'liberal lists'—people who have strong views on such issues as abortion, civil liberties and aid to the Contras fighting the government in Nicaragua." When Kirk's fund-raising efforts fell some $2 million short of their 1986 target, the DNC's liberal wing criticized the chairman for allegedly "neglecting the party's most loyal supporters—blacks, women, labor" and, guiding the Democrats toward what one of their number called "some vaguely defined centrist/right future."

In September 1986 the Democratic Policy Commission issued a seventy-one-page centrist summa of the party that Kirk wished to build. According to E. J. Dionne of the *New York Times* (September 21, 1986), "the document contains few specific proposals and is revealing mainly in its selection of themes, many of which have already become keynotes of Democratic [off-year election] campaigns, and have been cited by polltakers as appealing." Among other things, the report condemned the creation of a "Swiss cheese" economy in which some sectors prospered while others were plunged into poverty and denounced President Reagan's military build-up as "a wild spending spree with no strategic rationale and no overall defense plan," although it endorsed the general principle of a strong military. While the report reaffirmed the Democratic party's traditional commitment to educational opportunities, job training, and economic growth, statements on domestic policy were generally moderate, and the emphasis was not on government programs but on private investment and entrepreneurship.

The results of the 1986 midterm elections, in which the Democrats regained control of the Senate despite a personal sixteen-state crusade on behalf of Republican candidates by President Reagan, were seen by many as a vindication of Kirk's instincts and of his party's political agenda. As Jacob V. Lamar Jr. noted in *Time* (November 17, 1986), "By losing the Senate, Reagan and the Republicans lost the national political momentum they had been building during the 1980s." Kirk himself declared simply, "The voters have written a foreword to a new book. . . . It's called *Election '88*." To build on the momentum gained by his party in 1986, Kirk formed a Democratic Unity Task Force in March 1987 to enforce party discipline and prevent potential intraparty squabbling by monitoring "the tone and tenor of the debate between Democratic [presidential] candidates" in 1988. Stressing that the Democratic party could begin to win back voters by showing that it had "the guts and discipline to govern [its] own business well," he requested that the party's constituent groups avoid using "narrow litmus test" issues to determine the competence of a candidate. "The question Americans want answered," he insisted, in an address to the National Press Club, on March 11, 1987, "is not 'How could the Republican party have defaulted on so many responsibilities?' Rather, 'Can the Democratic party bring us together again and restore our goodness and greatness as a people and as a nation?'"

Paul Kirk is five feet eleven inches tall, weighs 175 pounds, and has hazel eyes and brown hair. He has a reputation for being a tough negotiator who succeeds by being cool-headed, reasonable, and scrupulously honest. Like the Democratic party he envisions, he is at peace with himself. "Behind that quiet exterior," maintains one longtime Kirk associate, "is a quiet interior." Kirk and his wife, the former Gail. E. Loudermilk, whom he married on May 11, 1974, divide their time between homes in Arlington, Virginia, and Marstons Mills, Massachusetts. Kirk was a visiting lecturer at the John F. Kennedy Institute of Politics in 1971 and 1974 and at the New England Law Institute in 1977. He is a member of the Board of Directors of Harvard University and the John F. Kennedy Library Foundation.

References: N Y Times p6 F 2 '85 por; Washington Post A p19 F 6 '85; U S News 98:52 Mr 15 '85; Who's Who in America, 1986–87

Knight, Bob

Oct. 25, 1940– Basketball coach. Address: b. Dept. of Intercollegiate Athletics, Assembly Hall, Indiana University, Bloomington, Ind. 47405

Indiana University's intense and volatile Bob Knight is arguably the best active coach in basketball, amateur or professional—and the most controversial. Knight, the master of a patient but aggressive strategy based on relentless, offense-generating man-on-man defense, developed his disciplined system at Army, where he was head coach for six years before moving to Hoosier country, basketball's heartland, following the 1971 season. As coach of the Cream and Crimson, he has dominated the Big Ten and won three national championships (in 1976, 1981, and 1987), a number unequaled by any other contemporary college coach and surpassed in collegiate history only by John Wooden (ten) and Adolph Rupp (four). He is the youngest coach ever to have reached his career win mark of 468 (as against 169 defeats). In addition to his achievements in the Big Ten and the National Collegiate Athletic Association, Knight guided United States teams to gold medals in the 1979 Pan American Games in San Juan (where his hot temper almost created a virtual international—or intranational, if that is the word—incident) and the 1984 Olympics in Los Angeles. The gist of the discipline that he demands from his players is, in his words, "doing what you have to do, doing it as well as you possibly can, and doing it that way all the time."

Robert Montgomery Knight was born on October 25, 1940, in the city of Massillon, Ohio, an industrial center a few miles from the town of Orrville, Ohio, an important railroad junction, where he grew up. His parents were Carroll Knight, better known as Pat, an Oklahoma-born railroad man, and Hazel (Menthorne) Knight. He became "infatuated," as he says, with basketball as an eighth-grader. In high school in Orrville he was a three-letter varsity athlete, fair as a football end, good as a scorer in basketball, and excellent as a power hitter in baseball. His greatest hero was (and still is) Ted Williams, the defiant slugger and, later, coach. He might have gone on to a career in baseball were it not for his own defiant streak. In his senior year the baseball coach suspended him from the team for refusing to leave the field for a substitute. When reinstated, Knight chose instead to barnstorm with an all-star basketball team. "I regret that more than anything I've ever done," he told Frank Deford of Sports Illustrated (January 26, 1981).

"All Bobby ever wanted was to be a coach, in the Big Ten," Knight's ex-wife, Nancy, once said. Even in high school, Knight's long-range goal was coaching, and he spent much of his leisure time shop-talking with Bill Shunkwiler, his football coach. Despite his love for basketball, he told Frank Deford, he always thought that there was "a greater depth to football coaches." "As he should've been a baseball player," Deford commented, "so, by temperament, he would have made a better football coach." Deford's main point, however, was that Knight had seemingly been "natural-born" to coaching in general, possessed of "an almost tribal sense" of a shared "heritage and tradition." He would keep in touch with many of his schoolboy coaches and seek out as mentors or models not only great basketball coaches like Pete Newell, Clair Bee, Henry Iba, and Joe Lapchick but such football luminaries as Bear Bryant, Woody Hayes, Vince Lombardi, and Joe Paterno.

In an article he wrote for The New York Times (December 2, 1979), Knight recalled that his father, "the most honest man" he has ever known, "could never understand why a person had to get a college education just to be a coach." While Pat Knight hoped that his son would become a lawyer, "a worthwhile result of higher education," Bobby Knight "couldn't imagine anyone as honest as [his] dad wanting to have a lawyer for a son." Nevertheless, his professed aim was a career in law when he enrolled at Ohio State University, in Columbus.

At Ohio State, Knight majored in education and minored in history and government. Playing basketball alongside Jerry Lucas and John Havlicek on the Buckeye team that Fred Taylor coached to three national finals and one NCAA championship (in 1960), he gave his all and was disappointed never to rise above substitute, except in two games. His chief strength was a peculiar low-arcing shot, deadly accurate when he was free enough to get it off and especially effective against zones. "To this day," as Frank Deford observed, "no Knight team has ever set up in a zone defense [with some recent exceptions]. It's like Groucho Marx, who once said he didn't want to be part of any club that would have him as a member."

Knight the player, who fell short of his own ideal, prefigured Knight the super-achieving coach in his obsession with detail and his striving for perfection. While slow defensively, he absorbed all that Fred Taylor had to teach on defense. "It's strange," John Havlicek told Pat Putnam in an interview for Sports Illustrated (February 19, 1973). "Bobby was the worst defensive player on the team, yet his teams now are so defense-oriented. But then Bobby was quite a split personality. I can imagine why he is such a great recruiter. You have to love him after the first meeting. But until they adjust, the kids he recruits must wonder how they got there when he gets them on a basketball court. He's positively savage." Havlicek considered Knight "the smartest guy" on the Ohio State squad.

More imposing off the court than on at Ohio State, Knight was, as remembered by some who knew him there, a brash, loud prankster and self-promoter. Coach Taylor dubbed him "the brat from Orrville," and a former teammate has recalled: "To impress everybody, he claimed he was the leader of a motorcycle gang called the Dragons. . . . He tried to sugar us or bull-bleep us—whichever worked best. But most everybody liked the Dragon. He was really a nice guy. So bright. Such a wonderful storyteller. So loyal and loving. Unless you crossed him or he crossed you. In that case, he was the most disagreeable cuss he could be." Jerry Lucas told Charley Rosen in an interview for Inside Sports (July 1984): "Bobby had a lot of energy. He also had a photographic memory and his mind was always buzzing. If Bobby wasn't doing anything, then he had to be talking about doing something. . . . Ever since I've known him, Bobby's always been so vocal, so expressive, that it's hard for him to hold anything in. Either you love him or you hate him." According to Rosen, "Knight would often second-guess coach Fred Taylor's strategies [and his] teammates' misplays [and even] curse himself. Like any ordinary hooper, Bobby enjoyed rehashing the play-by-play after each ball game—but Knight also insisted on analyzing every practice session. All of his teammates knew that someday Bobby Knight would grow up to be a successful coach."

When he left Ohio State with a B.S. degree in 1962, Knight was still ostensibly considering a career in law, but he gave himself a year to decide. In 1962-63 he was assistant basketball coach at Cuyahoga Falls (Ohio) High School, where he broke a clipboard in anger during his first game. "Bobby could be very charming," Harold Andreas, the head coach at Cuyahoga Falls has recalled, "or he could be a horse's ass. But he made the decision and he did it in a split second."

When his friend Tates Locke went to the United State Military Academy at West Point as basketball coach in 1963, Knight joined him as assistant coach, and he became head coach—one of the youngest in the country—when Locke moved on to Miami of Ohio. "I had just finished a playing career during which I didn't do as well as I'd expected," Knight wrote in his *New York Times* article. "So at West Point I made up my mind to win—*gotta win*. Not at all costs. Never that. But winning was the hub of everything I was doing." He was inspired by the tough example set by the late General George S. Patton on the battlefield and by former Army football coach Colonel Red Blaik on the playing field. He tried to study everything that made Blaik a winner at West Point, reading and rereading his book *You Have to Pay the Price*, talking to his former players, going over his every move. "I patterned myself after him," Knight told Pat Putnam in the interview for *Sports Illustrated*. "Colonel Blaik was an extremely intelligent individual and he was a great organizer. The ability to prepare to win is just as important as the will to win." Knight also modeled himself after Fred Taylor, and he often sought Taylor's advice when he was at West Point. Another older football coach to whom he turned often for guidance was Clair Bee.

Like Blaik, Knight took the strict discipline the cadets were subjected to—from early rising through meals, classes, and military drills—and carried it beyond four o'clock in the afternoon, when they expected to relax, even if they were varsity athletes. "My years at West Point allowed me to develop not only an appreciation of discipline," Knight wrote in his *New York Times* article, " but also to find a way discipline could be applied to basketball and to the players I would teach."

Knowing that his Army teams were inferior to their competition in height, speed, and native scoring talent, he exacted from them their full potential through conditioning and precise compliance with his game plan. The teams won a total of 102 games and lost fifty, led the country in defense three times, were invited to the National Invitational Tournament four times, and reached the tournament finals four times. Army beat Navy, its archrival, every year, and in 1970, with a record of 22-6, the best in its history, it finished for the first time in the top twenty nationally, in sixteenth place. All the while, the academy brass was displeased with Knight's breaches of decorum, including his shouting at referees and cursing at players. Knight, for his part, felt frustrated by the hobbling effect that military decisions and congressional influence had on recruiting. Following the only losing season of his career (11-13), in 1970-71, he resigned his post at West Point to accept the position of head coach at Indiana University, in Bloomington, Indiana.

When the newly arrived Knight ordered prepractice conditioning drills in Bloomington, the players were shocked. The drills included 25-, 50-, and 75-yard dashes ending with a run up the 109 steps to the top of the stadium, Assembly Hall. When official practice began, Knight miffed the alumni who were accustomed to attending the sessions by evicting them and announcing that all practices would henceforth be closed because he wanted nothing to distract his players. At a Knight practice, the players are totally silent and fully attentive when he is speaking. "That's his classroom, and you don't talk in the classroom," Bob Hammel, the sports editor of the Bloomington *Herald-Telephone* explained to Pat Putnam. "You listen."

A key drill of Knight's was calculated to habituate the players to dive for the ball instinctively, as if it were "golden," as Steve Green, one of the players told a reporter. "Later you think, gee, that hurt," Green said. "After games we check each other for blood. We're kind of proud of how tough we are." As Charley Rosen observed in his *Inside Sports* article, it was at Bloomington that Knight first began to realize that "people are more important than numbers." "Your opponent is yourself," he would tell his players, "your own potential. That's why I coach players and why I coach against the game. It's the game that beats you. If you fool with it, it'll kill you."

In Knight's first year at Bloomington, seasoned prognosticators expected a 12-12 season at best, and he came through with seventeen victories, eight defeats, and a third-place finish in the conference. Having already begun a search for future talent, Knight went recruiting after the season ended and returned with the first of the annual batches of outstanding players that he attracted to Indiana University from high schools in Indiana, Ohio, and Illinois. (Recently he expanded the recruiting territory.) Unlike many other coaches, who allegedly offered recruits not only promises of glory but also money, automobiles, credit cards, easy academic schedules, and even, in some extreme cases, sex and drugs, Knight apparently sold, then as now, only his program. "Everybody's got goodies to offer a kid," a veteran college coach told Charley Rosen. "It all comes down to how you spread your wares. It [usually] means getting in there and snowing some eighteen-year-old kid who has a head the size of a basketball. . . . But I hear Bobby Knight is clean. . . . I hear he only sells his program."

"One of the things I learned at West Point was that you could win games with kids who were good students," Knight wrote in his *New York Times* article. "Getting this kind of athlete was to be the basis of our recruiting program in Indiana." Under Knight, 90 percent of the athletes completing four years of eligibility at Indiana University obtained their degrees, compared with a national average of less than 40 percent. Knight advocates that the athletic scholarships given to incoming freshmen should be limited to a number equal to the number of senior athletes who graduate with a degree.

In 1972-73 the Hoosiers won twenty games and lost only five, finished first in the Big Ten, and third in the National Collegiate Athletic Association. They led the Big Ten again in 1974, with a 23-5 record, and they won their first CCA championship that year. Knight was unanimously selected national Coach of the Year in 1975, when the team went undefeated until losing to Kentucky 92-90 in the regional finals. The following year Indiana capped an undefeated season with the NCAA championship, and Knight was voted Coach of the Year in the Associated Press poll. In 1977 the Hoosiers slumped, losing eleven of twenty-seven games and finishing fourth in the Big Ten. In 1978, going 21-8, they finished second. The following season they lost eleven of their first twenty-five games and then, winning eight of the remaining nine, went to the National Invitational Tournament, which they won.

In July 1979 Knight had the honor of coaching the United States men's basketball team in the Pan American Games in San Juan, Puerto Rico. His team won the gold medal, but the triumph was tarnished by several incidents involving Knight. In one, he was expelled from a game for denigrating the officials. In another, he humiliated a highly talented but young and relatively inexperienced member of his team, Isiah Thomas (later to be one of his seasoned stars) by cursing him out loudly in public for defensive faults. The most serious incident began when Knight and his team arrived for an hour's scheduled practice in a San Juan high school gym at 10:00 on the morning of Sunday, July 8. According to Mike Krzyzewski, one of Knight's assistants at the games, a "rude and arrogant" police officer gave them "a hard time" before permitting them in, and during practice, while Knight was giving his chalk talk, the officer allowed another team into the stands, creating noise. When Knight demanded quiet, to no avail, there was a confrontation in which "the policeman kept pointing his finger closer and closer to Bobby's face" and "as a reflex, Bobby swatted the policeman's arm away." Arrested on charges of aggravated assault, Knight was found guilty *in absentia* on August 22, 1979. He was fined $500 and sentenced to six months in jail, but he was never extradited. Back in the United States, he joked publicly about Puerto Rico in what many considered an offensive way.

The Indiana team finished second in the Big Ten in 1980, with a 21-8 record, and first in 1981, with 26-9. In 1981 it went on to win its second national championship, the fourth in team history. (The pre-Knight championships had been won in 1940 and 1953.) In the Final Four that year, Knight, in one of his tantrums, deposited a Louisiana State University fan in a trash barrel.

In the spring of 1981 CBS Sports offered Knight the job of directing the NCAA tournament telecasts at a salary of approximately $500,000, a figure that dwarfed his annual income as coach. According to John Feinstein, the author of *A Season on the Brink: A Year with Bob Knight and the Hoosiers* (1986), Knight was ready to sign with CBS Sports but he changed his mind when, in July 1981, his star player, Landon Turner, was in an automobile accident that paralyzed him for life. "Knight devoted most of his waking hours during the next few months to what became the Landon Turner Fund . . . ," Feinstein wrote. "Knight stayed in coaching because of Landon Turner. . . . [But] while on the surface he was the same obsessed person . . . still finding defeat unacceptable, Knight was not the same coach. This showed up most clearly in his [turning recruiting] over almost completely to his assistant coaches."

The Hoosiers went 19-10 and finished second in the Big Ten in 1982; went 24-6 and finished first in 1983; and went 22-9 and finished third in 1984. The victorious United States basketball team that Knight coached at the Olympiad in Los Angeles in the summer of 1984 gave one of the most dominant performances ever seen in the winning of an Olympic gold medal. "What we have tried to do is build a team that can do a little bit of everything well," Knight told Phil Elderkin of the *Christian Science Monitor* (August 2, 1984) during the Olympics. "Nevertheless, our overall commitment has been to learn to play tough against a variety of different defenses and . . . defense is what wins basketball games." Elderkin explained Knight's philosophy in a nutshell: "If he can stop the opposition from scoring, they usually become so preoccupied with getting their own offense back into gear that they forget about defensing yours. Bobby does this with a pressure man-to-man defense that creates as many mental problems for the opposition as it does physical ones. Knight himself prefers a motion offence."

Because his starting defense was in disarray in February 1985, Knight benched all his starters except seven-foot-two-inch senior Uwe Blab and sent in freshmen in the Big Ten Conference game against the University of Illinois—a decision that angered many Indiana fans, especially when the Hoosiers lost, 52-41. The team finished the season in seventh place, with a 19-14 record. "Although . . . Knight would never admit it, the horrific 1984-85 season changed him," John Feinstein recounts in his book. "It changed his attitude toward coaching, toward recruiting, even toward some of his cherished mind games. It reminded him how much coaching—real coaching—meant to him." In concentrating his attention on recruiting again, according to Feinstein, he began for the first tme to look for junior college talent.

Although Feinstein suggests that Knight emerged from the 1985 season with a lighter attitude, the coach did his fair share of ranting and raving during the 1986 season, when his team finished second in the Big Ten with a 21–8 record. Before the 1987 season the *Sporting News* named Knight one of the five best coaches in college basketball and ranked Indiana number one nationally. When Knight coached his team through a 30–4 season to its third national title in 1987, Paul Daugherty observed in *Newsday* (April 1, 1987: "The Hoosiers did not have the talent of North Carolina, the athleticism of UNLV [Nevada-Las Vegas], or the muscle of Iowa. But they had enough of each, and they had Knight." Daugherty and others pointed out that Knight, previously perceived as inflexibly fixed in a system that was beginning to creak, had proved himself adaptable. "In his own personal time of change—encompassing divorce, repudiation of the best-selling *A Season On the Brink*, grudging occasional use of the zone defense, and revitalization of the red sweater industry," Curry Kirkpatrick wrote in his report on the NCAA title game against Syracuse in *Sports Illustrated* (April 6, 1987), "—the most bizarre Knight move of all was injecting the dreaded [junior college] transfer into his disciplined program, in the persons of center Dean Garrett (10 points, 10 rebounds, 3 blocks and a neutralization of the Orange's Rony Seikaly) as well as the six-foot-one [Keith] Smart." On May 1, 1987 NCAA officials announced that the punishment for Knight's fist-pounding on the scorer's table during a Midwest regional game in March would be a reprimand for Knight and a fine of $10,000, to be deducted from Indiana's $1,003,375 national championship prize.

Robert Montgomery Knight is six feet five inches tall and has hazel eyes, dimpled cheeks, and, of late, a thickening neck and paunch. His handsome face bears three mementos of athletic battle: a broken nose and scars on his left cheek and eyebrow. He usually presents an informal appearance, with his tie loose, hands in pockets, and often wearing a red sweater, as if to project fierceness. On the desk in his office in Assembly Hall is a sign that reads, "The buck stops here." When he isn't stopping the buck, he likes to spend time with his teenaged son, Patrick, and his grown son, Tim, to hunt and fish, and to read the daily newspaper. It "kills" him that his countenance and personality do not adequately convey his sense of humor, which more often than not comes across as sarcastic. "I get castigated . . . and the other coach . . . he's being deified, and I know he's one of the worst cheaters in the country," he complained to Frank Deford. "Your biggest opponent isn't the other guy. It's human nature." Deford saw the conflict in Knight differently: "Knight's mind is too good to be wasted on a mere game . . . but he's personally not comfortable away from the precisely circumscribed environment in which college basketball is played." He summed Knight up as "a substance guy in a style world."

References: *Christian Sci Mon* p17+ Ag 2 '84 por; *N Y Newsday* p127+ Ap 1 '87 por; *N Y Times* V p2 D 2 '79 pors, IV p9 Jl 22 '84 por; *Sports Ill* 38:25+ F 19 '73; *Washington Post* mag p26+ Jl 22 '84 pors; Feinstein, John. *A Season on the Brink* (1986); Hammel, Bob. *Beyond the Brink with Indiana: 1987 NCAA Champions* (1987)

Knight, Gladys

May 28, 1944– Singer; actress. Address: b. c/o Sidney A. Seidenberg, 1414 Ave. of the Americas, New York City, N.Y. 10019

In a thirty-five year collaboration with her backup trio, the Pips, the pop and soul singer Gladys Knight has used her gritty contralto and masterful timing to launch twenty-four top forty hits, including such classics as "I Heard it Through the Grapevine," "If I Were Your Woman," and "Midnight Train to Georgia." She has enjoyed equal success with upbeat dance songs, soulful tearjerkers, "white" pop, and rhythm and blues standards that have resulted in more than a dozen gold records. "Miss Knight's singing is a marvel of tone and timing," wrote critic Jon Pareles of the *New York Times* (September 3, 1984). "She uses only an octave of range, but what an octave it is—deep and sultry, every note throbbing with Miss Knight's infinitely variable vibrato."

Gladys Knight has rarely stopped touring since childhood, though contract disputes with record companies have led to dry periods, and it was not until her third decade as a professional that she emerged as a superstar. "Show business is more taxing than most people could ever imagine," she has said. "But I don't think I had any choice as to what to do with my life. I feel God gave me a gift that he meant for me to use. It isn't something I rehearsed until it got better and better. I think actually I was blessed."

Gladys Knight was born on May 28, 1944 in Atlanta, Georgia, the third of the four children of Merald Knight and Elizabeth Knight. For several years her father worked simultaneously as a delivery man for a pharmacy, a postman, and gardener to support his family, but by the time Gladys entered the third grade, he had separated from his wife, leaving her to raise the children alone. By that time, Gladys Knight was a seasoned member of the Mount Moriah Baptist Church choir, which she had joined at the age of four after being encouraged to sing by her mother. From 1950 to 1953 she toured Georgia and Alabama with the Morris Brown gospel choir, standing on a soapbox so that people could see her. She performed three pop numbers, ran out and changed her dress during intermission, and returned to sing three gospel songs.

When she appeared on Ted Mack's *Amateur Hour* in 1952, the seven-year-old Gladys Knight won a $2,000 grand prize for her rendition of Nat King Cole's "Too Young" and two other songs. Later that year, on September 4, the Pips were formed at an all-day birthday party for her brother, Merald Jr, or "Bubba." To entertain guests, Gladys, Merald, their sister Brenda, and cousins William and Elenor Guest improvised a singing group. Impressed by their performance, another cousin, James ("Pip") Wood, in whose honor they named themselves, became their manager and arranged gigs for them at local clubs. When performing popular soul music they called themselves the Pips; when singing gospel they were known as the Fountaineers. Listening on the sly to the "sinful" music on the radio, Gladys Knight began to "look behind the hit, at Billie Holliday, at Sarah Vaughn," as a way of doing "research" to refine her style.

Meanwhile, as the Pips grew older, they expanded their tours and opened for major stars such as Sam Cooke and Jackie Wilson by the time Gladys Knight was thirteen. Discussing the difficulties of touring, Miss Knight told Bill O'Hallaren during an interview for *TV Guide* (July 12, 1975): "We would drive to a date in a beat-up old car and we wouldn't have any money for a motel, so we'd have to drive all the way home or on to the next date. I was too young to drive, so my job was to sit up in front and see the driver didn't go to sleep." She credits her mother with maintaining their confidence. Although she was far from being the traditional stage mother, Elizabeth Knight did provide a reservoir of support that kept her Gladys and the Pips "pushin'" for success. In 1957 the group's first single, "Whistle My Love," was released by the Brunswick recording company, but received little attention. Brenda and Elenor then left the group to get married, and Gladys, Bubba, and William were joined by their cousin Edward Patten and Langston George.

Traveling the "Chitlin' Circuit," the Pips remained "so innocent . . . they were just begging to get ripped off," to quote Sid Seidenberg, their present manager. According to an unsigned article in *Time* (July 28, 1975), a promoter in Paducah, Kentucky, once refused to pay them after a show, backing his refusal with a gun. "There was nothing we could do except leave in a hurry because we were peace-loving people," Miss Knight remembered. They brought their act to New York, where they were asked by a "friend" to help him test his recording equipment with one of the songs they were then performing. They heard nothing more about that so-called "sound check" until the single it produced, "Every Beat of My Heart," was marketed by three different record companies. Ironically, though they made no money from it at the time, it became their first hit, reaching the R&B Top Twenty in 1961 and ultimately earning a gold record.

Before that single was recorded, the Pips shared lead duties, although Gladys Knight was often the front woman after the other female singers left. According to Miss Knight, the well-known format of the Pips evolved as a result of "Every Beat of My Heart." As she explained to an interviewer for *Ebony* (November 1980): "On the first big record we had . . . I happened to be lead vocalist. So naturally, for a follow-up, they [record producers] want to continue with whatever was successful. There, again, the public dictates. It was never decided among us that, 'Well, Gladys, you're going to be the lead singer.' But with one record after another, I became the identifiable sound so far as Gladys Knight and the Pips were concerned. In doing things creatively, we added what was going to complement the lead vocal. The guys came in with [dance] routines and [backup vocals] to enhance that."

After two more recordings, including the R&B top five hit, "Letter Full of Tears," Langston George left, making the Pips a family quartet with the membership they have retained ever since. The group split temporarily when Miss Knight married at sixteen. When she returned to Atlanta to have her first baby, the male Pips sang backup for other artists. Reunited in performance after about a year, Gladys Knight and the Pips polished their act with help from the talent promoter Marguerite Mays, who upgraded their wardrobe, hired a pianist and a choreographer, and paid for their room and board.

In 1965 the group was signed by Motown, its sixth recording company, and touring with the Motown revue, Gladys Knight and the Pips began to attract a growing cross-over audience. "Just Walk In My Shoes" and "Take Me in Your Arms and Love Me" had brisk sales in Europe, and in the United States, "I Heard It Through the Grapevine" became a number two smash hit on the 1967 pop charts. Other hits, such as "I Don't Want to Do Wrong," "The End of the Road," "Friendship Train," and "If I Were Your Woman," helped to bring Gladys Knight and the Pips television exposure on Motown specials and on variety shows hosted by Ed Sullivan, Tom Jones, and others. In concert, according to Irwin Stambler's

Encyclopedia of Pop, Rock and Soul, they "played to standing-room-only crowds . . . throughout the U.S. and other nations of the world."

Despite their certified success, the Pips grew dissatisfied with their assigned position in the pecking order of the Motown hierarchy. Its president, Berry Gordy, saved the best songs for favored groups such as the Supremes, Marvin Gaye, Smokey Robinson and the Miracles, and the Temptations—who allegedly learned their dance routines by standing in the wings during Pip concerts and memorizing every move. Even after the Pips began to produce hits they were given little publicity. When their Motown contract expired in 1973, feeling they had "put too much agony into [their] work to break down and beg for bones," they switched to Buddah Records, leaving behind several unreleased recordings (which Motown later marketed) and a crossover hit, "Neither One of Us (Wants to Be the First to Say Goodbye)," which eventually occupied the number-one slot on the pop charts. There ensued a long legal battle with Motown over royalties.

In the midst of that battle, Gladys Knight and the Pips shot to the pinnacle of their success, becoming the latest supergroup to dominate the air waves. The LP *Imagination* went gold and produced three gold singles: "Midnight Train to Georgia," which reached number one in 1973; "(I've Got to Use My) Imagination," a number four hit in 1974; and "Best Thing That Ever happened to Me," which peaked at number three, also in 1974. Fans snapped up some 7.5 million Pips albums and singles in 1973, and the group, nominated for four 1974 Grammy Awards, won two, for "Neither One of Us" (Best Pop Vocal Performance by a Duo, Group, or Chorus) and for "Midnight Train to Georgia" (Best R&B Vocal Performance by a Duo, Group, or Chorus.) Within a year the Pips had another hit single, "On and On," from their recording of Curtis Mayfield's soundtrack for the film *Claudine.*

In concert, Gladys Knight and the Pips added new triumphs. Reviewing a Waldorf Astoria performance for *Newsday* (October 29, 1974), Dave Marsh praised Miss Knight's ability to bring to her audiences a "middle class, or even middle brow," but "special" warmth. "When she sings, in 'Midnight Train to Georgia,' 'I'd rather be with him in his world, than be without him in mine,' romantic love assumes a theoretical legitimacy that is rare today. . . . Cynicism has no defense against sincerity such as this."

The Pips' follow-up album to *Imagination, I Feel A Song,* lacking a "blockbuster" such as "Neither One of Us," received mixed reviews, though it did generate a new hit in Miss Knight's version of Marvin Hamlisch's nostalgic "The Way We Were." "In some ways [the album] seems like an ungainly montage of unconnected material," Dave Marsh wrote in *Rolling Stone* (January 2, 1975), "but Knight develops an identity within it. On the one hand, she is a mature woman, singing from the struggle and strife she has seen. That's what makes her 'The Way We Were' so much more interesting than Streisand's. But she is also a furious hellion, an archetypical scorned woman."

On the basis of the superstardom earned by such performances, the group was given a variety show on NBC television for the summer of 1975—with the understanding that they would be competing for a permanent slot with two similar shows, hosted respectively by singer/dancer/actor Ben Vereen and the pop duo, the Captain and Tennille. Gladys Knight later reported during an interview for an article that appeared in the *Chicago Tribune* (May 15, 1983), that her group tied in the ratings with the Captain and Tennille. "So they [NBC] had to make a choice," she recalled. "At the time we had nine gold records, two platinum albums, and one triple platinum album. The Captain and Tennille had one hit song, 'Love Will Keep Us Together.' They got the series slot. It makes you wonder."

Specifically, Gladys Knight wondered about the impact of racism throughout the entertainment industry. As she noted to Lynn Van Matre, black groups were required to have a hit on the R&B charts before the song in question would be given airplay on a top forty radio station, and that limited the kind of music black artists could record: "Suppose that our fans who aren't of color like something different from what our people do. We do all kinds of tunes—slow, fast, ballads, music with a beat. If our white fans don't get a chance to hear those songs on the radio until people of color have given them the stamp of approval, that means a lot of stuff we do won't ever be heard."

In the 1970s, however, Gladys Knight's musical fortunes continued to prosper, and a film, *Pipe Dreams* (1976), was made to take advantage of her success. Produced by Barry Hankerson, her second husband, the film featured her, Hankerson, and the gospel star James Cleveland in a romance with the unlikely setting of the Alaskan oil pipeline. Financed with the assistance of minority organizations and Buddah Records, *Pipe Dreams* was distributed by Avco-Embassy. The film failed at the box office, and Gladys Knight returned to music, but difficulties arose there also, as she and the Pips gradually began to feel that they were being victimized by Buddah Records.

On April 26, 1978, Gladys Knight filed a $23 million suit against Buddah Records, its distributor, Arista Records, and Art Kass and Clive Davis, executives of Buddah and Arista respectively. She charged that the defendants had failed to inform her of Buddah's financial insolvency—exemplified by one $100,000 check she received that, according to Robert Wallace of *Rolling Stone* (June 29, 1978), bounced twice. The suit also charged that Buddah had used Miss Knight's contract to bargain with creditors and that, with Arista, it had "maliciously and intentionally" sought to prevent her from leaving Buddah for Columbia Records. Whatever the validity of the latter charge, any such attempt had failed, for Gladys Knight signed with Columbia Records in the summer of 1978. Buddah and Arista countersued for $100 million against Gladys and CBS, Columbia Records' parent company, citing breach of contract. Another suit by those companies charged CBS with knowingly luring Gladys Knight away from Buddah Records.

While the cases were under suit, Gladys Knight and the Pips were enjoined from recording together, although they could continue to perform live. During the next two years Miss Knight cut a solo LP for Columbia, and with the permission of Buddah, the Pips recorded two albums for Casablanca. Despite those independent projects, the group did not tour separately. "We have never split," asserted Edward Patten, as quoted in Ebony (November 1980). Eventually, after several marathon meetings were held among representatives of Gladys Knight and the Pips, Arista, and Buddah, with an impetus provided by surviving feelings of friendship rather than legal expertise, the dispute was resolved outside of court for what Kass described as a "handsome settlement."

Celebrating their return to recording together, Gladys Knight and the Pips released a new album, About Love, composed and produced by Nick Ashford and Valerie Simpson, on the Columbia label in 1980. "Landlord," a single from that album, rose to number three on the R&B charts. Another album, Touch, followed in 1982. Visions (1983) introduced two solid hit singles, "Save the Overtime (For Me)" and "You're Number One." In the following years Gladys Knight and the Pips recorded the title song for The Buddy System, a film starring Richard Dreyfuss and Susan Sarandon.

By the mid-1900s Gladys Knight and the Pips were once again recording successfully and giving shows "full of energy, wit, and honest emotion," as Wayne Robins noted in Newsday (August 30, 1984). In reviewing a concert they gave at the Gershwin Theatre, David Hinckley observed in the New York Daily News (August 30, 1984) that "whereas made-for-Broadway shows sometimes come billed as soul and then get overwhelmed by Broadway gloss, this time—with a genuine soul group and genuine soul songs—the music ends up dominating."

Gladys Knight returned to television during the 1985–86 season, playing opposite Flip Wilson in the CBS sitcom Charlie and Company, which has since been canceled. Miss Knight played Wilson's wife, a schoolteacher and mother of three. The show attracted criticism as a "carbon copy" of NBC's The Cosby Show, which also features a wholesome, middle-class black family, a charge that for her, represents yet another example of the discrimination against which she has battled all her life. "The racism is very subtle but it's there," she told Michele Willens of the New York Daily News (June 1, 1986). "You've got a thousand family shows on TV and the comparisons are never there. That's the only thing that bothers me about the Cosby reference. I know where its coming from."

In additon to acting, Gladys Knight is currently developing her executive skills as a producer. In July 1986 she produced her first HBO televison special, Sisters in the Name of Love, in which she costarred with Patti La Belle and Dionne Warwick.

The show presented an intimate look at the three singers, who have been friends for over two decades, singing and sharing their ideas about having babies, relationships with men, and what they "think about being too fat and having to go out on the road." "It's like you tiptoed in on our living room, and we were letting our hair down and didn't know you were there," Miss Knight explained to Steve Schneider of the New York Times (July 6, 1986).

The mother of three children and grandmother of one, Gladys Knight has been married twice. Her first husband, Jimmy Newman, was a neighbor, schoolmate, and musician with whom she had two children. The couple divorced after six years. In 1974 Miss Knight married Barry Hankerson, a television producer, executive assistant to Detroit Mayor Coleman Young, and community youth leader. They had one son, before separating in the late 1970s. Today Miss Knight shares homes in Las Vegas and Los Angeles with her brother Bubba, with whom she runs several small music publishing and production companies. Both are now single, but Gladys told Ebony's Robert E. Johnson (November 1982), "I have somebody special."

Although she was raised as a devout Baptist, Gladys Knight converted to Roman Catholicism sometime in the early 1970s, but she is not officially affiliated with any particular church. "I changed from Baptist teachings because Catholicism was a much more peaceful religion," she explained to B. J. Mason of Ebony (June 1973). "Baptists are too distracting, hold services too long and raise too many collections. Yet I don't believe you can really make it in the world without some kind of faith." It is a tradition with the group to link hands in a prayer circle before each concert.

The act's in-church, family-oriented origins are also revealed in its studious avoidance of sexually explicit lyrics and in its priorities. Their agent, Sidney Seidenberg, once lamented: "Gladys and the Pips never work on the Fourth of July. Why? Because the family always has a picnic on the Fourth of July." He also rues a $100,000 booking that was canceled "so the family could go to Edward's daughter's graduation." Such commitment to tradition lies at the root of Gladys Knight's power over audiences and the philosophical view she takes of the vicissitudes of her career. "I've been in this business long enough to know that you're here today and gone tomorrow, and maybe back here again, if you're lucky," she told Michele Willens during the New York Daily News interview. "I never asked for caviar, so I'm not disappointed when I can't have it. Just give me my grits and eggs." Among the honors received by Gladys Knight and the Pips are four American music awards, an NAACP Image award, and Billboard and Record World awards.

References: Chicago Tribune VI p15 D 6 '81 pors, VI p5 My 15 '83 por; Ebony 28:17+ Je '73 pors, 30:33 Mr '75 pors, 35:45+ N '80 pors, 37:53+ N '82 pors; N Y Sunday News magazine p16+ O 9 '83 pors; TV Guide p20+ Jl 12 '75 por

Kraus, Alfredo

*Nov. 24, 1927– Operatic tenor. Address: b. c/o
Dean Mammel, 5420 LBJ Freeway, Suite 333,
Dallas, Tex. 75240*

Often compared with the late Tito Schipa, the
Spanish-born Alfredo Kraus has during his more
than thirty years on the international operatic stage
become one of the most celebrated lyric tenors of
his generation. Working within a relatively narrow
repertory of a couple of dozen roles in works by
Gounod, Massenet, Bellini, Donizetti, and Verdi,
he has attracted a worldwide following with a
voice acclaimed for its beauty, range, stylish and
refined musicianship, and incredible durability.
He has often been honored in his own country as
a star of films and recordings, and has given command performances before the king and queen.
"The stage," Kraus once told Rodolfo Celletti of
Opera (January 1975) "forms the artist, but ruins the
singer. And I, by profession, am a singer. To be a
singer you need a technical knowledge which you
cannot have at twenty, twenty-two, or even twenty-
five. Technique is the basis of everything. You cannot be a singer if you are not first a vocal technician, and you cannot be a good artist unless you are
also a good singer."

Alfredo Kraus was born Alfredo Kraus Trujillo
on November 24, 1927, at Las Palmas in the Canary
Islands, one of three children of a Viennese father
who had adopted Spanish nationality and a Spanish-born mother. Neither of his parents was musically inclined, although Kraus can lay claim to one
talented relative, a cousin of his maternal grandmother who was a famed tenor many years ago. Alfredo and his brother and sister started singing as
children, and his brother later had a short professional career as a baritone.

The Canary Islands have a rich legacy of folk
music, and Kraus enjoyed singing the folk songs of
his island as a child. His first experience of singing
in public came when he joined the children's choir
of his church, and he later sang in amateur opera
and madrigal programs. Friends and relatives began advising him to consider studying music and
voice training, but his immediate family felt otherwise. "My father wanted me to study something
that was safe and would assure me a living," he recalled for John Gruen in the *New York Times* (January 14, 1979). "Well, I didn't really want any of
that, but to please my father I did what he asked."
Kraus therefore prepared for a career as an industrial engineer while discreetly continuing his musical studies on the side, and not just in voice. By his
early twenties he was an accomplished pianist, and
even after Spain's compulsory military service had
interrupted his engineering studies, he went on
with his musical training.

It was while he was training as an officer in Barcelona that Alfredo Kraus met Gali Markoff, a
singer whom he described in his *New York Times*
interview as "a wonderful, mad Russian lady." He
began his first serious vocal training with her during his six months in Barcelona, and when he was
transferred to Valencia he made the acquaintance
of a teacher named Francisco Andrés. "Mind you,
I was already twenty-five," he has pointed out.
During their six months of work together, Andrés
helped Kraus enormously, and he really began to
believe in his vocal talent.

After completing his military service, Kraus returned to Las Palmas, still in some doubt as to the
desirability of pursuing a singing career. By his
own account, he "wasted" the next two years while
trying in vain to resolve his uncertainty. Finally, in
1955, he decided to go to Milan, Italy, the home of
La Scala and one of the world's major centers of
opera, "to find out whether [he] was really a good
singer or not." There he received strong encouragement from many of the people he met, despite his
relatively advanced age of twenty-seven. Most fortunate was his acquaintanceship with a Spanish
woman with the family name of Llopart, who introduced him to her sister, Mercedes Llopart, a famous soprano in Spain and Italy during the 1920s
and 1930s. Llopart, who ran her own voice school,
where one of her students was Renata Scotto,
turned out to be an ideal teacher for Kraus. Their
shared Spanish heritage made for a close personal
relationship, and her training provided him with
the musical foundation with which to perfect his
singing. Kraus began his career by entering the Geneva (Switzerland) International Competition in
January 1956, where he won the first prize, the silver medal.

On his return to Italy, Kraus was immediately
engaged by a small opera company to sing the part
of the Duke of Mantua in a touring production of
Verdi's *Rigoletto*. After making his professional
debut in that role in January 1956 on the stage of
the Theatre Royal in Cairo, Egypt, he embarked on
a series of uninterrupted successes. He made his

European debut shortly after he returned from Cairo, as Alfredo Germont in Verdi's *La Traviata* at the historic Teatro La Fenice in Venice. He also sang the role when he made his British debut at the Stoll Theatre in London in May 1957, where Renata Scotto was his Violetta.

Alfredo Kraus quickly became known for the richness, warmth, elegance, refinement, and luster of his voice, which could reach to a top D without any audible sign of strain or tension. With his light but agile tenor he found himself ideally suited to the demanding roles of such bel canto operas as Donizetti's *Don Pasquale* and Bizet's *The Pearl Fishers*. Aware from the outset of his career that his voice lacked the sheer power needed for such heavyweights in the repertory as *Madama Butterfly* or *Tosca*, he chose to restrict his roles accordingly. "A singer is like a boxer or a weight lifter," Kraus explained to John Ardoin in an interview for *Opera News* (February 3, 1979). "If you try to lift more than you can support, or you fight with someone who is heavier than you are, you will lose. If you are a little tenor like me and try a dramatic opera, after a few pages you are tired."

His role model as a singer was the late Tito Schipa. "With not one great quality," he said in his interview with John Ardoin, "he made an extraordinary career. Schipa had a small voice, no top, just a nice middle, but it is unbelievable within this range what fantastic things he could do. Perhaps he had to be an artist because of his limitations, but even with a big voice you should be an artist." His chosen repertory of the lighter works of Verdi led directly to the most celebrated performance of his early career, as Alfredo in *La Traviata* opposite the legendary diva Maria Callas at the Teatro São Carlo in Lisbon, Portugal, on March 27 and 30, 1958. The March 27 performance, in particular, became one of those moments that stand out in a veteran performer's career. Apart from the tumultuous response from those present—heightened by Maria Callas' insistence that Alfredo Kraus, and the baritone Mario Sereni, as the elder Germont, share her ovations—it was a performance that became widely known and heard. Many unauthorized tapes of that *La Traviata* surfaced over the next thirty years, in the absence of any studio recording of the work by Callas, and it became one of the most popular of all pirated opera performances. Finally, in 1980, EMI Records released an official, authorized recording. "Alfredo Kraus sings with strong incisive tone and is always alive and responsive," John Steane wrote of that long-ago performance in the British magazine *Gramophone* (October 1980).

In the years immediately following his debut, Alfredo Kraus also established himself in his native Spain as one of the most popular singers in the national operetta tradition of the "zarzuela," a form of comic musical performed, especially in Madrid, since the nineteenth century. That lighthearted musical repertory comprised the earliest of Kraus's recordings. In 1957 he was chosen by the Spanish firm of Montilla Records for the starring role of Fernando in a recording of the classic zarzuela *Doña Francisquita*, opposite the Spanish prima donna Ana María Olaria. The following year he recorded Pablo Sorozabal's *Black, El Payaso* and *La Taberna del puerto* for the Hispavox label in performances conducted by the composer. Kraus proved a popular figure on the stage and not simply because of his voice, for his finely chiseled features and dark-blond hair, coupled with an attractive physique, made him a natural for romantic musical roles.

Kraus's success on the Madrid stage in zarzuelas soon came to the attention of Spain's movie industry, and he had barely established himself as a rising young opera singer when the opportunity for an unexpected second career in films presented itself. In 1957 Sintes Films, a Spanish production company, offered him the title role in *Gayarre*, a movie biography of Julian Gayarre (1844–1890), the famous nineteenth-century Spanish tenor. The film became a box-office hit in Spain and turned Kraus almost overnight into a matinee idol. Although a soundtrack album featuring a dozen arias and songs from the film was released in the United States by Montilla Records in 1963 along with the soundtrack of Kraus's second movie, *El Vagabundo y La Estrella*, neither film has ever been released there. Warmly received by the critics, both the *Gayarre* and *El Vagabundo* albums included arias from *Rigoletto, Il Trovatore, I Puritani*, and other works upon which Kraus's later career would rest.

After making his acclaimed debut in Lisbon, Kraus returned there every year and soon added opera houses in Wiesbaden, Germany, Marseilles, France, and Edinburgh, Scotland to his schedule. He made his debut at Covent Garden in London, England, on July 10, 1959, as Edgardo in Donizetti's *Lucia di Lammermoor* opposite Joan Sutherland in the title role. Faced with such formidable competition, he sang with "taste and well-directed jets of tone," according to Harold Rosenthal, who reviewed his Covent Garden debut for the English publication *Opera* (October 1959). Kraus's debut at La Scala, in Milan, Italy, took place during the 1959–60 season in Bellini's *La Somnambula*, in which he sang the role of Elvino, a young farmer. When Kraus made his American debut, on October 31, 1962, at the Lyric Opera of Chicago, in the role of Nemorino in Donizetti's *L'Elisir d'Amore*, Roger Dettmer announced in *Opera* (January 1963) that "not since [Cesare] Valletti's American advent has a lyric tenor of such technical polish and musical persuasion been heard." He returned for the Lyric Opera's 1963 season as Count Almaviva in Rossini's *Il Barbiere di Sivigla* and as Ernesto in Donizetti's *Don Pasquale*.

The first of Kraus's recordings to be heard in America, the soundtracks to *Gayarre* and *El Vagabundo y La Estrella*, were released on the Montilla label in early 1963 and were followed by two recital discs, *Alfredo Kraus Sings Tenor Arias* and *Romanzas de Zarzuelas*. His first major releases did not appear until early in 1964, when Montilla issued a complete recording of *Marina*, by Pascual

Juan Emilio Arrieta y Correra, first produced as an opera in 1871, which starred Alfredo Kraus and Pilar Álvarez. In appraising *Marina* for the *American Record Guide* (March 1964), Jon Maclain wrote: "This is plainly Alfredo Kraus's show. From that first soaring high C in 'Costa la de Levante' to his final ringing E flat, our attention is on his every line—sung with elegance, dramatic insight, and taste. It is a rare tenor, indeed, who has such high notes *and* (sic) such intelligence!"

Later that year Kraus made his first appearance, on a major American record label, as the Duke of Mantua in a RCA Victor recording of *Rigoletto* with Anna Moffo as Gilda and Robert Merrill as Rigoletto, under the baton of Georg Solti. "Alfredo Kraus is a sterling Duke," Howard Klein reported in the *New York Times* (October 25, 1964). "He sounds young, dashing, irresistible, boyish, even likable. Mr. Kraus has a light and very bright but manly voice. Since his voice is not of an unwieldy size, he is able to indulge in many dynamic subtleties that make his phrases a joy."

Again as the Duke of Mantua, Alfredo Kraus made his Metropolitan Opera debut on February 16, 1966, and followed that up three weeks later with a performance as Don Ottavio in Mozart's *Don Giovanni*. "Mr. Kraus made a pleasing impression," wrote a critic for the *New York Times* (March 9, 1966). "His acting was fluent and natural. His voice was flexible and clear and its relatively small size was no drawback with Mozart's scoring." Kraus extended his career to the West Coast of the United States later that year, when he made his debut at the San Francisco Opera on September 20, 1966, singing the role of Lord Richard Talbot in Bellini's *I Puritani* opposite Joan Sutherland's Elvira. It was again with Joan Sutherland that Kraus returned to the Met on January 4, 1967, as Ottavio in *Don Giovanni* and for his first New York appearance as Edgardo in *Lucia di Lammermoor* on January 5. Raymond Ericson of the *New York Times* found his Edgardo "ingratiating" and his phrasing of the music characterized by "dramatic verve and suppleness."

Although Alfredo Kraus later performed with the Philadelphia Lyric Opera and with the Opera Orchestra of New York, under Eve Queler, the most important of his later American debuts may well have been his first appearance with the Dallas Civic Opera on November 17, 1972, in the title role of Massenet's *Werther*. "He not only looks the poet to perfection," John Ardoin wrote in *Opera News* (January 20, 1973), "but he sang with the elegance and cultivation needed to make the most of this brooding part." Of all the roles in Kraus's rather specialized repertory, that of Werther, the despondent and suicidal poet, was the one he came to "own" during the decade that followed. "Mr. Kraus makes the character work as few others ever could," Thor Eckert Jr. observed in the *Christian Science Monitor* (February 2, 1979) of a performance that had taken place on January 18 at the Metropolitan Opera. "Here is a dreamy poetic spirit given to expounding rapturously on ideals and unrequited love. So obsessed is Kraus's Werther with unfulfilled passion that one is aware of the inexorability of the opera's end from the very beginning." That year, Kraus also recorded *Werther* for EMI/Angel, with Tatiana Troyanos in the role of the hapless Charlotte.

By the mid-'70s Alfredo Kraus's engagements were taking him to Japan as well as to North and South America. Just as selective about the opera houses in which he performs as he is about his roles, he took a six-year absence from the Metropolitan Opera, beginning with 1972, because of the obligations that work with that company placed on his time. "For the Met you must stay a long time," he explained to John Ardoin, "one or two months. If I do this, I prefer doing it in a family theatre such as Dallas, where I am among friends and feel more comfortable. If I cannot be in a family theatre, I prefer to be in a situation such as one finds in Germany today, where you arrive, have a piano rehearsal, sing and leave." Similarly, Kraus refuses to record nearly as often as his admirers would like him to do. "It is cold," he observed of the process of making a record. "There is no audience, you cannot give a performance, they jump all around in the music, it is crazy. Then when I hear the results I never like my voice. I never buy records and I never listen to them." His more recent opera recordings include a new *La Traviata* (EMI/Angel, 1982), in which he joined forces as Alfredo with Renata Scotto's Violetta a quarter of a century after their performances at the Stoll Theatre. "His aria is done with lift and delicacy," Alan Blyth wrote in *Gramophone* (May 1982). "His contribution to both duets proves an ideal match for Scotto's . . . and like her he is a stickler for keen words. Just once or twice a rusty note shows that even Kraus cannot quite defy the years." His recent performances have ranged in similar fashion across the entire three-decade span of his career, as exemplified by his appearances in New York during the beginning of 1985. On January 11 he sang his first Metropolitan Opera performance of Offenbach's *Tales Of Hoffmann*, and followed it on February 4 at Carnegie Hall with an all-Spanish recital that reached all the way back to Arrieta's *Marina*, from the beginning of his career.

Since the late 1970s, in addition to fulfilling his opera engagements, Alfredo Kraus has been giving an increasing number of concert recitals outside Europe. He finds them more difficult than opera. "For me they are worse," he admitted to John Ardoin. "In concerts you sing many different kinds of music, there are many different characters, it takes greater concentration. If I do recitals, then I must do only recitals for a while." I cannot mix recitals and opera, for when I do something, I do it with all my force of will, my strength, my dedication."

Alfredo Kraus is a man of graceful, elegant, and patrician appearance who looks far younger than his sixty years. When not performing, he prefers to spend as much time as possible near water and the sun and returns with his family to his native Canary Islands for at least one month out of every year. When on tour, he tries to spend his free time walking in the country or visiting museums, anything to take him away from the theatre and relax him. In furtherance of his largely self-managed singing career, Kraus owns the Madrid-based Carrillon Records, for which he has recorded complete operas, among them *The Pearl Fishers*, as well as recital discs. Kraus lives in Madrid with his wife, Rosa Blanca Ley Bird. The couple have four children, three daughters and a son, and one granddaughter, and spend as much time together as his career allows. Kraus attributes his professional longevity in part to the influence of his family. "With so much youth around me, how can one grow old?" he once asked an interviewer.

References: N Y Times II p19+ Ja 14 '79; Opera 26:17+ Ja '75; Opera N 31:15 Ja 28 '67, 43:25+ F 3 '79; New Grove Dictionary Of Music and Musicians (1980)

Krim, Mathilde

July 9, 1926- Geneticist; philanthropist. Address: b. c/o American Foundation for AIDS Research, 40 W. 57th St., New York City, N.Y. 10019

"By now we all know the gruesome statistics," Dr. Mathilde Krim wrote in an August 8, 1986, *New York Times* article. "Americans in the prime of life are dying from acquired immune deficiency syndrome (AIDS) at the rate of 200 a week, and each week an even larger number of new cases is diagnosed. . . . But what we don't know or won't think about is that we need to take bold actions to provide desperately needed treatment to those who are otherwise doomed." For the purpose of taking such bold action against AIDS, Dr. Krim, a distinguished geneticist and virologist who is also a successful fund raiser and philanthropist, founded, in 1983, the AIDS Medical Foundation, later known as the American Foundation for AIDS Research. In 1986, she left New York's Sloan-Kettering Institute for Cancer Research, where she had been an associate member and a leader in interferon research from 1975 to 1985, to establish an AIDS research laboratory at the city's St. Luke's-Roosevelt Hospital Center.

In her attempt to increase funding for AIDS research, to educate the public about the nature of the disease, and to win compassion for its victims, Dr. Krim has mobilized her galaxy of social connections, including many with political power or public name recognition, and has herself made frequent television appearances. As Lindsy Van Gelder wrote in her profile of the scientist for *Ms.* magazine (January 1986), "If there's . . . a symptomatic treatment—much less a cure—for bigotry, ignorance, and business as usual, Krim is working on it."

Mathilde Krim was born Mathilde Galland on July 9, 1926, in Como, Italy, one of the four children of a Swiss father, a trained zoologist who worked as an agronomist, and a Czechoslovak mother. As her father spoke Italian and her mother German, she grew up speaking both languages at home, and she learned French at school. (She has since become fluent in English and Hebrew.) Given an easel by her paternal grandfather, a painter, when she was six years old, Mathilde soon began to show promise as an artist. An interest in science was simultaneously inspired by her maternal grandfather, a schoolteacher who instructed her in natural history. At the age of seven, after hearing the word "biologist" for the first time, she immediately decided to pursue a career in biology. As she explained to Jerry E. Bishop in an interview for *Sciquest* (September 1980), "Art was something subjective and amorphous but science was straightforward and without ambiguities (although with age I've learned there are a lot of ambiguities in science). Anyway, as a teenager you have all these uncertainties in your life and for me science was an anchor."

Science remained her anchor after Mathilde Galland moved with her family to Geneva, Switzerland, in 1932 to escape the depressed prewar economic conditions in Italy. She eventually enrolled at the University of Geneva and, though she was one of only two women in the basic sciences and was considered something of an oddball, she remained to earn a B.S. degree in genetics in 1948 and a Ph.D. in 1953. As a graduate student working in the laboratory of Jean Weigle, a physicist interested in genetics and biology, she had access to an electron microscope, "an absolutely spectacular machine," she told Bishop, "with insulators all over the place and when you turned it on there would be these big sparks shooting around like lightning; I was very impressed." Asked to see if the new microscope was powerful enough to find a gene, Mathilde Galland began examining the chromosomes of frogs' eggs a millionth of an inch at a time. After months of fruitless searching, the tedious task paid off. "I remember it was late in the evening," she recalled to Jerry Bishop, "and I was working alone with this big machine and the sparks shooting all over the place. . . . Then I switched to a new area and suddenly I saw these beautiful double threads." As far as she knows, she was the first human to see the DNA structure of chromosomes in an Electron Microscope.

Outside the laboratory, Mathilde Galland's life was, by her own account, rather conventional. Although Switzerland remained neutral during World War II, many Swiss, including the Gallands, openly admired German efficiency and culture. "My parents were sort of gently anti-Semitic," she explained to Lindsy Van Gelder, as quoted in the New York *Daily News* magazine (October 20, 1985). "I didn't question it when my parents said that Jews were dirty, or not very honest." Shortly after the end of the war, however, she saw a newsreel about the liberation of a Nazi concentration camp. "I was shocked out of my wits," she continued. "I went around crying for a week afterward. I decided right then I just didn't want to belong in the world that had done things like this."

Motivated by that experience, Mathilde Galland sought out a group of Jewish activists at the university, became involved in their politics, and eventually joined the Irgun, the Zionist underground movement. She spent several months in the south of France cleaning guns ("the girls' job") and then progressed to smuggling weapons across the border. She was given dangerous things to do, she has said, because she looked so "cherubic" and "innocent" that the police would never suspect her. At about this time, she fell in love with a young Bulgarian medical student who was also a member of the Irgun. When she announced to her family that she intended to marry him, convert to Judaism, and immigrate to Israel, they disowned her. Her father even blamed her for his subsequent heart attack. The young couple nonetheless married and, in 1953, immigrated to Israel, where Mathilde found a job as a junior scientist and eventually as a research associate in cancer research at the Weizmann Institute of Science in Rehovot. While there, she became part of the team that discovered a way to determine the sex of an unborn child through amniocentesis.

Meanwhile, realizing that they were incompatible, Mathilde and her husband divorced, and she took custody of their daughter, Daphne. For a time she continued to work at the Weizmann Institute, then, on December 7, 1958, she married Arthur B. Krim, a trustee of the institute and the chairman of United Artists. Six months later she joined her new husband in New York City and plunged into the social whirl, mixing easily with the powerful and influential people she would later mobilize in her fight against AIDS.

Quickly "bored to tears," as she put it, with life as a society hostess, in 1959 Mathilde Krim took a position as a research associate in the division of virus research at Cornell Medical College in New York. Three years later she moved across the street to the Sloan-Kettering Institute for Cancer Research to study cancer viruses. She was soon deeply involved in the investigation of mouse polyoma and SV-40 viruses. In 1970 Dr. Krim spent six months putting together a report on cancer research for a United States Senate panel. In the process, she developed an abiding interest in the protein interferon, which is produced naturally by almost all animal species and even some plants. As she explained in an interview with Bill Lawren for *Omni* (November 1985), interferon "induces the expression of certain genes and suppresses the expression of others." "My work," she went on, "led me to realize that interferon is a substance that can inhibit tumors, and modify some properties of the immune system in animals. . . . I decided right then to go into that field because, although we knew very little at the time about interferons, I was certain that a big push would come."

The "big push" seemed imminent in 1974, when the Swedish physician Hans Strander announced that interferon might have stopped the recurrence of a highly malignant bone cancer in a number of patients. Dr. Krim immediately began to press for the establishment of an interferon laboratory at the Sloan-Kettering Institute. She also lobbied for support by the National Institutes of Health and the National Cancer Institute of a nationwide research effort into interferon's effectiveness as an antitumor agent. Because interferon was at the time considered to be only an antiviral agent, Dr. Krim's ideas met with great resistance. The National Cancer Institute, however, did give her $12,000 to organize a workshop on interferon and tumors. The workshop "turned out to be a tremendous meeting," Dr. Krim told Lawren, and as a result the National Cancer Institute agreed to sponsor basic research on interferon.

Both interferon and Dr. Krim's advocacy of it were soon embroiled in controversy. Costs for the natural substance were considered prohibitive, and Strander's study was discredited, Dr. Krim was chastened by some colleagues for having sung the protein's praises. Interferon's bad press changed, however, in 1980, when Charles Weissman at the University of Zurich cloned the interferon gene, making it possible to produce the substance in large amounts. Since then, at the Interferon Evaluation Program, which Dr. Krim established at Sloan-Kettering in 1975, she and other researchers have continued to experiment with the substance in an effort to accumulate enough evidence to secure approval for its use from the Food and Drug Administration (FDA). As head of Sloan-Kettering's interferon laboratory from 1981 to 1985, Dr. Krim became known for her organizational ability as well as her research. During her tenure, she and her colleagues discovered that interferon can make leukemia cells in a kind of cancer known as hairy-cell leukemia "disappear," paving the way for FDA approval of the use of interferon in the treatment of hairy-cell leukemia.

Dr. Krim first heard about AIDS from a colleague in interferon research, Dr. Joseph Sonnabend, who had started a private practice in New York's Greenwich Village. Sonnabend's new patients included members of Greenwich Village's large homosexual community, and he soon noticed that an unusual number of them were coming down with unusual symptoms. A common condition of the patients, which seemed to open the way for both the pneumonia and the sarcoma, was an extraordinarily low count of the T-4 white blood cells that regulate the body's immune system. This collapse of the immune system, leaving the patients defenseless against even the least virulent infections, was invariably fatal. The disease was eventually found to be caused by the human immunodeficiency virus, which was being spread through fluids exchanged during sexual intercourse, through the exchange of blood, especially in the sharing of needles by intravenous drug abusers, and through fluids passed from infected pregnant women to the babies they were carrying. Dr. Krim initially became involved in AIDS research through studies of the effectiveness of interferon in treating Karposi's sarcoma, a cancer with which many of the AIDs patients were afflicted. Her involvement increased as details of the disease were gradually publicized, and AIDS, which was officially identified and named in 1981, became not "just a medical condition," as Dr. Krim once put it, but "a sociological and psychological condition."

As she learned more about AIDS, Dr. Krim became "incensed" by the fact that so many young men—"mostly sophisticated and intelligent young men"—were dying "abandoned or alone because they were afraid to contact their families." She also felt that public funding for research aimed at preventing the disease was inadequate. As a result, in 1983, she founded and became chairperson of the AIDS Medical Foundation, which awards grants, for promising AIDS research—something that, as a private organization, it was able to do more quickly than the federal government, which often takes a year or more to process grant applications. Within three months of its inception, the organization raised $650,000. In 1985 it merged with the National AIDS Research Foundation in Los Angeles to become the American Foundation for AIDS Research (AMFAR), which is cochaired by Dr. Krim and Dr. Michael Gottlieb. In building the foundation, Dr. Krim took advantage not only of her professional reputation as a prominent scientist but also of her social position as the wife of an entertainment industry executive who had once served as finance chairman of the Democratic party. She was able to "pick up the phone and get hold of anyone—from Teddy Kennedy to Barbra Streisand to the top scientist in France," according to one of her colleagues. One Hollywood celebrity, Elizabeth Taylor, became the foundation's honorary chairperson.

While research sponsored by the foundation and the government continues to seek a cure and a vaccine for AIDS, Dr. Krim feels the best way to limit the spread of the disease is through public education. In her *Omni* interview, she criticized the Reagan administration's lethargy in that direction. "The public ought to get the message that there's no need to panic at the thought of having HIV infected people and AIDS patients around us—in our cities, buses, theatres, and restaurants," she pointed out. "This is, first, because of the lack of evidence of contagion by casual contact."

Dr. Krim has taken her message to the public through numerous television appearances, in which she has stressed that the disease is transmitted mainly through sexual intercourse and that the way to prevent it is "to avoid the transmission of HIV between people" by "having sex without the exchange of bodily fluid from person to person." In the *Omni* interview, she recalled an appearance on the *Phil Donahue Show* during which she was "determined to tell people to wear condoms." "At the last minute I got embarrassed and started mumbling," she admitted to Bill Lawren. "So Donahue said to me: 'You want to say people have to wear rubbers.' And I shouted: 'Yes, yes, yes!'"

For reasons of public safety as well as of justice, Dr. Krim supports gay-rights laws. "I was very disturbed by the sociological impact of AIDS," she told Lindsy Van Gelder. "Especially when I realized that the disease was spreading partly because it was mainly affecting a stigmatized group. Gay men should be the first people to ask to be tested for evidence of infection, but as a community, they've understandably resisted that step. The test has become a marker for gayness, not just for exposure to AIDS. Since people can legally discriminate against them, they're at risk for everything from losing their insurance and their jobs to being thrown out of their apartments." Although critics charge she is spreading immorality, Dr. Krim also advocates supplying intravenous drug abusers with sterile disposable hypodermic needles. She argues that this practice would minimize the sharing of contaminated needles that is spreading HIV infection and AIDS among drug abusers and their sexual partners and, thus, to the heterosexual community. To limit the fears aroused by AIDS in the general public, she has advocated the testing of different kinds and brands of condoms for permeability to the AIDS virus, as well as personal hygene that might kill the virus.

A potential breakthrough in the treatment of AIDS occurred in 1986, when the drug azidothymidine (AZT) was shown to stop the AIDS virus from multiplying in some patients. In conjunction with the HIV, the drug's producer, the Burroughs Wellcome Company, promptly set up a rigorous "double blind" clinical trial for the drug. Two hundred and sixty patients with AIDS who had had an attack of pneumocystis carinii pneumonia within 120 days of recruitment participated in the test. Half of them were given AZT and half were given a placebo (inert substance).

Dr. Krim objected to the methodology of the test and to the restriction of AZT to a special class of AIDS sufferers. In the light of statistics for 1986 showing 10,000 Americans with the disease, 100,-000 with related illnesses, and another 1.5 million suspected of being carriers, Dr. Krim and others felt that restricting AZT to a few patients was immoral. In response to arguments that the trial was necessary because the extent of effectiveness and the potential side effects of AZT were unknown, Dr. Krim countered in an article for the *New York Times* (August 8, 1986) that "patients with cancer and other life-threatening diseases for which there is no established therapy can avail themselves of the latest, most hopeful treatments, even if they are still experimental." She also questioned the administration of placebos to patients with AIDS, whose illness was expected to worsen and probably kill them during the trials, when AZT was known to prolong life and to mitigate suffering.

The substance was approved for general use by the Food and Drug Administration in 1987. In view of the drug's toxic side effects, such as bone marrow damage in some patients, the search for an even more effective substance continues, and Dr. Krim continues to be one of the champions of that search. She has persisted in lobbying for a larger AIDS research budget in the National Institutes of Health and, through the American Foundation for AIDS Research, in providing scientists with grants of up to $60,000 a year. By July 1987, the American Foundation for AIDS Research had awarded a total of $5.3 million in three funding cycles. With projections anticipating 270,000 AIDS victims in America alone by 1990, Dr. Krim asserts that AIDS is not only a challenge to medicine and science but also to human societies and will measure "to what extent they have the right to call themselves civilized."

With her strawberry-blond hair in a schoolmarm bun and her air of maternal assurance, Mathilde Krim reminded Lindsy Van Gelder of the actress "Simone Signoret playing Madame Curie." Of her active role in battling AIDS, Dr. Krim told the reporter, "I'm personally rather shy and retiring, and I would prefer to be ensconced in a lab. This isn't necessarily the role I'd choose to play. But I use my contacts because I do feel it's my duty." Dr. Krim has written or collaborated on the preparation of seventy-three scholarly papers, and she has served on numerous educational and philanthropic organizations, including the Rockefeller Foundation, the African-American Institute, and the Institute of Society, Ethics and the Life Sciences. She has received many honors and awards. Since 1986 she has been an associate research scientist in the department of pediatrics at St. Luke's-Roosevelt Hospital Center and College of Physicians and Surgeons, Columbia University, in New York City.

References: *Ms.* 14:36+ Ja '86 por; *N Y Daily News* p6+ O 20 '85 pors; *Omni* 8:76+ N '85 por; *Sciquest* p21+ S '80

Kunin, Madeleine (May)

Sept. 28, 1933– Governor of Vermont. Address: b. Office of the Governor, Pavilion Bldg., 5th Floor, Montpelier, Vt. 05602; h. 122 Dunder Rd., Burlington, Vt. 05401

The biography of Madeleine Kunin, governor of Vermont, reads like a real-life version of the American dream. A Swiss-born refugee from Nazi persecution, she came to the United States at the age of six with her widowed mother, who instilled in her children "a limitless dream of what this country could offer," according to the Vermont governor. After pursuing a brief career in journalism, she married a Burlington, Vermont, doctor in 1959 and devoted the next decade to raising their four children. But like many women of her generation, Madeleine Kunin dreamed of combining family with career, and with the rise of the women's movement, she made that wish come true. Beginning in 1972, she won three consecutive terms as a liberal Democrat representing Burlington in the Vermont House of Representatives, and then served two terms as lieutenant governor. After losing a bid to become governor in 1982, she tried again in 1984, this time successfully, although in a very close election. She succeeded the Republican Richard Snelling as the third Democrat, the first woman, and the first Jew to become governor of Vermont.

Although she eliminated Vermont's $35 million deficit and won a key environmental battle with the entrenched interests of the powerful ski industry during her first term, Madeleine Kunin still had to fight a tough three-way race to win reelection in 1986. Vermont's personable leader combines femininity with political know-how. Ann Lewis of Americans for Democratic Action has written of

Madeleine Kunin: "She represents the new style of woman politician who views the values and experience of being a woman as positives—concerns for children, for education, for those in economic difficulty."

Madeleine (May) Kunin was born on September 28, 1933, in Zurich, Switzerland, the second child of a German-Jewish shoe importer, Ferdinand May, and his Swiss-born wife, Renée (Bloch) May. Her father died when Madeleine was three, leaving the family in straitened circumstances. Fearful of the growing Nazi threat to the Jews, her mother decided to take six-year-old Madeleine and her eleven-year-old brother, Edgar, to the United States. They left in 1940 on one of the last ships allowed to leave Italy with Jews aboard.

For Madeleine, who was much too young to understand the peril she and her family were in (five of her relatives later died in Nazi camps), the trip was only "an exciting adventure." Yet she is convinced that the Holocaust unconsciously affected her, by teaching her "that instead of being an uninvolved observer and potential victim," she wanted to be "in a position of active influence and control," as she pointed out in a 1986 interview. The Mays settled with relatives who lived in Forest Hills, in the borough of Queens, New York. Mrs. May supported her family by working as a seamstress, a French tutor, and a babysitter. "She had great expectations for her children," Madeleine Kunin recalls of her mother, with whom she was very close. When she was a teenager, the family moved to Pittsfield, Massachusetts, where she graduated from the local public high school. She then went on to the University of Massachusetts at Amherst to take a history degree with honors in 1950. To pay her college expenses, she worked as a waitress at Tanglewood, the summer home of the Boston Symphony Orchestra.

At that stage of her life, Madeleine Kunin had no political ambitions; instead she wanted to be a foreign correspondent. After taking an M.S. degree in journalism from Columbia University, she got a job with the Burlington Free Press, the only newspaper that offered her work as a general reporter instead of assigning her to the traditional woman's beat of the society page. The move to Vermont also reunited Madeleine Kunin with her brother, Edgar, himself a journalist.

While working for the Burlington Free Press, she met Arthur Kunin, a doctor specializing in kidney disease, who was affiliated with the University of Vermont Medical School. After their marriage, in 1959, she worked for another year as a writer and assistant producer for a local television station and then resigned to have her first child, Julia, in 1961. Three sons, Peter, Adam, and Daniel, followed in the next decade, and Madeleine Kunin devoted herself to being a wife and mother.

Madeleine Kunin has no regrets about interrupting her career to raise a family. "I loved having children," she told a reporter for the Vermont Sunday Magazine (March 31, 1985). "I suspect that's why I had four of them." Despite her family obliga-

tions, Mrs. Kunin remained active in community affairs, especially in her work with the League of Women Voters. In 1967 she took a second master's degree, this time in English literature at the University of Vermont. Although she did some freelance writing and public relations work, it was "just bits and pieces," she recalls. She felt that something was still missing in her life.

Then, in 1970, her family spent Arthur Kunin's sabbatical leave in Switzerland, where she met women activists who were trying to gain the vote for Swiss women. Deeply moved by their struggle, Mrs. Kunin realized that "American women really haven't fully taken advantage of the right to vote." Her old feelings of wanting her life "to make a difference" returned, and she came back to the United States primed for activism and "ready to go."

Mrs. Kunin failed in her initial effort to "make a difference" by becoming Burlington's first woman alderman in 1972, losing the race by only sixteen votes. But in the following fall she won election as a liberal Democrat to the Vermont House of Representatives, running on a platform that stressed educational, environmental, and poverty issues. For the next six years she dedicated herself to learning the basics of government. "I realized that if you are concerned about programs, you have to follow them through the budget process," she has said. In her first two-year term she got a seat on the powerful appropriations committee, and by her third term, was its chairperson.

Having served her political apprenticeship in the House of Representatives, Mrs. Kunin was ready to make a bid for statewide office, and in 1978 she ran against Peter Smith, a Republican, for the lieutenant governorship. Operating a modest, low-budget campaign out of a tiny store-front office, she mastered the art of speech-making, door-to-door canvassing, and the convivial rites of the political barbecue to defeat Peter Smith with 50.6 percent of the vote. And in 1980 she survived the Reagan sweep to win reelection with an impressive 59 percent of the vote.

As lieutenant governor in the Republican administration of Richard Snelling (in Vermont, the two officers are elected separately), Madeleine Kunin became "one of the most seasoned and familiar campaigners" in the state, in the words of the Vermont Sunday Magazine article. Turning up frequently at town meetings and public gatherings, she showed herself to be particularly adept at one-on-one politics. "I believed it was important to have personal contact with people, to show I was accessible," she has recalled of her service as lieutenant governor of Vermont.

When Richard Snelling announced that he would not run for a third term in 1982, Kunin decided to try for the governorship, but much to her dismay, after she had declared her candidacy, Snelling changed his mind and entered the race. Since incumbency is a big advantage in Vermont, and Snelling had been a popular governor, Mrs. Kunin knew that she would probably lose the election. But she was still determined to run a credible campaign, thinking that it would improve her chances for a second bid. "There are degrees of losing, and if you lose respectably in a tough race, you can emerge again," she said in an interview for *Working Woman* (July 1986).

Her confidence proved justified, for she won 44 percent of the vote, better than either of the previous Democratic candidates had done against Richard Snelling and, more important, proved that she was an adept fund raiser. In 1984 she returned to run a second, more aggressive campaign against John Easton, a former attorney general and a close associate of Snelling. Despite her impressive credentials, polls showed that Madeleine Kunin still faced prejudice against a woman candidate. Although her campaign was heavily subsidized by national women's political groups, she chose to emphasize gender-neutral issues, such as the deficit, education, and the environment.

As it turned out, Mrs. Kunin narrowly squeaked into office with 50.2 percent of the vote, only sixty votes above the 50 percent majority required by Vermont state law. She did particularly well with women voters, who preferred her to Easton by 53 percent to his 45 percent. "Madeleine was elected by women. There's no question," her pollster, Tom Kiley, has said. In her inaugural speech, Mrs. Kunin described her election as a victory not only for women but for all immigrant Americans. By choosing her, Vermont had rejected "the harsh theory of the survival of the fittest," she asserted.

As governor of Vermont, Madeleine Kunin brought a new look to the gold-domed Montpelier Statehouse in more ways than one. She redecorated the governor's office, making it lighter and more inviting, and began to hold a weekly open house there. She appointed a record number of women to state office, including two women to her five-person cabinet. And in marked contrast to Richard Snelling, who had ruled with a firm, patriarchal hand, Mrs. Kunin cultivated a more open, consensus style of government.

In the beginning, her critics wondered if the new governor could address Vermont's pressing problems with that more feminine style of leadership. From the previous administration, she had inherited a huge $35 million deficit, as well as an impending conflict with the state's powerful ski industry over new development laws, but she soon proved that she could be a tough politician. She hired as her press secretary a man who had been an outspoken critic of her timidity in office, explaining that she did not want "an executive office that sings one chorus," and then fired her first secretary of administration and finance. But her real moment of truth came when she took on the huge Killington ski resort for trying to evade Vermont's stringent environmental laws, advising it to stop "whining and crying" about having to comply. Although the ski industry called her "uninformed and insensitive," the powerful environmental lobby in Vermont applauded her firm stand.

In a similar manner, Mrs. Kunin tackled the huge deficit she had inherited from the Snelling administration. Aided by a surge of economic growth, she was able after only eighteen months in office to announce that the state budget was once again in the black. In her first term she won other legislative victories: an increase of 25 percent in the state education budget, more stringent environmental laws, creation of a new rural enterprise zone, and establishment of a state venture capital corporation.

Proving herself to be not only an effective but a popular governor, Madeleine Kunin won a 76 percent approval rating in a poll taken in December 1985. Given the incumbency advantage, her reelection in November 1986, seemed assured, but her campaign ran into an unexpected complication when Bernard Sanders, the Socialist mayor of Burlington, announced his intention to run. The prospect of facing Sanders as well as the Republican challenger, Peter Smith, increased the likelihood that Mrs. Kunin might not take the necessary 50 percent of the vote, and the election would have to be decided by the state legislature.

Both Bernard Sanders and Peter Smith ran aggressive campaigns, attacking Madeleine Kunin from the left and the right for her alleged indecisiveness. Sanders branded her style as "wishy-washy" and as "vision without substance"; Smith accused her of "hijacking" the successes of other legislators. At the polls in November, Sanders succeeded in "spoiling" the election by taking 15 percent of the vote and forcing the race into the legislature, but there Mrs. Kunin won reelection easily.

With her second term just underway, Madeleine Kunin has already won another legislative victory by having the state speed limit raised from 55 to 65 miles per hour. Her political vision is now widening to include national politics. She has been an active member of the National Governors' Association, serving on its executive committee, and is scheduled to chair the New England Governors' Conference in 1987. She was often mentioned as a possible candidate to take retiring United States Senator Robert Stafford's seat in 1988 and as a potential cabinet appointee if the Democrats take the White House in the next election. Ending months of such speculation, Mrs. Kunin announced in August 1987 that she will instead try for a third term as governor of Vermont, though she conceded that she might consider running for the Senate "at a future date."

In response to those critics who have nicknamed her "straddlin' Madeleine," Mrs. Kunin insists that "what is considered strong in leadership style—intimidation, keeping a distance from critics, talking instead of listening—may in fact be weak." Her own approach is very different. "My style is letting people know what I expect and giving them enough information to do the job," she said during the interview for *Vermont Sunday Magazine*. She added, "I don't yell, but I know how to fight for what I want."

Steeped as they are in a strong democratic tradition, Vermonters seem to like Madeleine Kunin's consensus approach. She enjoys an excellent rapport with the voters, who perceive her as a down-to-earth, unassuming person like themselves, and she is often to be seen around Montpelier eating a sandwich for lunch or doing some shopping. All over Vermont, she is called simply "Madeleine," not out of disrespect but out of affection. One observer has said: "She's like Ronald Reagan. She has a personality people like."

In politics, Madeleine Kunin seems to have found the ideal outlet for her varied assets: her intelligence, her gregariousness, and her social consciousness. She says of her vocation, "It's dynamic. It's a movable feast. It tests all your skills." By addressing substantive issues that really matter in people's lives, politics gives her the feeling that she has "some control over the uncertainties" around her. Her political interests are a natural outgrowth of her identity as a woman and a mother. "Some of my first political acts were related to my children," she mused during the *Vermont Sunday Magazine* interview, recalling a campaign to get a red light installed at a railroad crossing.

Tall and slender with graying hair, Madeleine Kunin wears feminine dresses and jewelry, eschewing the drab and severely tailored suits favored by many women in public life. Although she is sometimes accused of being too aloof, or of being "too Swiss," as one aide put it, she is incontrovertibly a warm and approachable leader. Her brother, Edgar, who is now a state senator in Vermont, attributes much of her success to "an instant empathy with people." Mrs. Kunin keeps up a punishing pace and seems to thrive on it, so long as she has one day a week to rest and gets her regular exercise by either running or swimming.

A major factor in Madeleine Kunin's success is her supportive husband, Arthur, who once even took to the streets wearing a sandwich board to help her win a campaign. As a professor at the University of Vermont Medical School, he pursues his own career and interests, which include working as a representative of the state dairy industry to publicize the health benefits of dairy products. He enjoys the different side of life that he sees as a politician's husband because he gets "to see people [he] would never run into otherwise." Since Vermont has no governor's mansion, the Kunins continue to live in the large ranch house they built in 1969, which is filled with family portraits, political memorabilia, plants, and pets.

As a working mother, Madeleine Kunin has always had to make time to be with her four children, the youngest of whom, Daniel, was only two when his mother embarked on her political career. Although they are now grown, she remembers the conflict she occasionally felt on leaving them. Once, while driving on the way to an important meeting with a carful of other politicians, she suddenly made a U-turn and rushed home, explaining that Daniel's "blankie" was in the back seat and he would never go to sleep without it.

References: People 23:102+ Ap 1 '85 por; Vermont Sun Mag p4+ Mr 31 '85 por; Working Woman 11:74+ Jl '86 por; Who's Who in America, 1986–87

Kurtz, Swoosie

Sept. 6, 1944– Actress. Address: b. c/o International Creative Management, 40 W. 57th St., New York City, N.Y. 10019

After achieving her spectacular success as the lunatic wife, Bananas, in the 1987 revival of John Guare's *House of Blue Leaves*, Swoosie Kurtz seems poised on the brink of much deserved stardom. A veteran of twenty years of acting with comedy as her forte, Miss Kurtz has paid her dues with a thorough grounding in fundamentals at the London Academy of Music and Dramatic Arts, in regional theatre in roles ranging from classic to contemporary, in film and television, and, most notably, on Broadway. Constantly in demand, she chooses her roles with care, rejecting those that she feels are not right for her. As a result, Swoosie Kurtz's collection of awards for her theatre performances attests to her taste as well as to her talent.

Swoosie Kurtz was born on September 6, 1944, in Omaha, Nebraska, the only child of Colonel Frank Kurtz, an Olympic diver and the most decorated of World War II bomber pilots, and Margo (Rogers) Kurtz, author of the autobiographical *My Rival the Sky* (1945). Her unusual name derives from the B-17 bomber that her father piloted. Patched up from old and new parts, it was nicknamed "the Swoose" after a Kay Kyser ditty: "Half swan, half goose/Alexander is a swoose." The new baby was supposed to have been named Margo after her mother, but newspapers of the time announced the arrival of "a little Swoosie." A nurse entered the name on a birth certificate and there it stayed. Although it caused her grief as a youngster, she now cherishes its individuality.

Since her father was constantly being reassigned in the Air Force, Swoosie Kurtz had little time to put down roots, and she remembers going to seventeen schools before she enrolled at Hollywood High School. Encouraged by her high school drama teacher, John Ingle, she discarded her earlier ambitions of becoming a writer or a ballerina and settled on an acting career. She was only eighteen when she played in Euripides' *Alcestis* at a drama teachers' festival in southern California, winning first prize. After studying for two years on a scholarship as a drama major at the University of Southern California, she grasped an opportunity to study at the prestigious Academy of Music and Dramatic Arts in London, from 1964 to 1966.

On her return to the United States in 1966, Swoosie Kurtz began her professional career with a season at the Cincinnati Playhouse in the Park in *Sodom and Gomorrah*, *Charlie's Aunt*, and *Skin of Our Teeth*. While working in regional theatres, she applied what she had learned during her London training. "I learned to get right on with it in rehearsal, to simply 'have a bash,'" she has said. "So that's what I do, with total commitment. And then I work backward to figure out why things happen."

In 1970, after undergoing some difficult times, Swoosie Kurtz had a breakthrough when she landed her first role in New York. Opening to mostly enthusiastic reviews on April 7 at the Off-Broadway Mercer O'Casey Theatre, Paul Zindel's *The Effect of Gamma Rays on Man-in-the-Moon Marigolds* told the story of a woman embittered by her husband's desertion who has two teenage daughters, one of whom wins a high school prize for her experiments on the effect of radiation on marigolds. As Janice Vickery, Swoosie Kurtz snared the attention of the *Newsday* (April 21, 1970) critic George Oppenheimer, who mentioned "a telling bit by Swoosie Kurtz as a rival young scientist." Although the role was such a small one that it was not even given a name in its original production in 1965 in Houston, Texas, Richard Watts of the *New York Post* (May 1, 1970) also paid her tribute with his comment that "Swoosie Kurtz, a name I cherish, is fine in her one scene as the horrible girl who tortures animals." The play went on to win the 1969–70 season's award as best American play from the New York Drama Critics Circle, was cowinner of the fifteenth annual Obie award for the best Off-Broadway play, and captured the 1971 Pulitzer Prize for drama. When it was transferred to the New Theatre, Swoosie Kurtz moved into the role of Ruth, the dumb but sexy daughter, then later into the more important assignment of Tillie, the scientific one, before the final curtain was rung down on *The Effect of Gamma Rays on Man-in-the-Moon Marigolds* in May 1972.

Moved almost intact from the Long Wharf Theater in New Haven, Connecticut, where it had played the previous winter to rapturous reviews, a revival of Eugene O'Neill's only comedy, *Ah, Wilderness!*, opened the season of Broadway's Circle in the Square on September 18, 1975. In one of the few changes in the original cast, Swoosie Kurtz took over the role of the neighbor's daughter, Muriel. Although the part was small, a reviewer for *Variety* (September 24, 1975) praised the authenticity of her performance, and Alan Rich in *New York* magazine (October 6, 1975) observed: "As Muriel, the apple of Richard's eye, Swoosie Kurtz is ingeniously cast against type, and her light comic touch almost saves the beach scene."

Although she had played bit parts in minor films of the 1970s, Swoosie Kurtz's first appearance in a major movie came with *Slap Shot*, directed by George Roy Hill and starring Paul Newman, which was released in February 1977. Of her performance as a typical hockey wife in that dark and profane comedy about the roughhouse violence endemic to the game, Swoosie Kurtz told Denise Collier, coauthor with Kathleen Beckett of *Spare Ribs; Women in the Humor Biz* (1980): "I started out with two lines and they were nothing. The first day on the set I did one line, and George said, 'Swoosie, we're going to write you into a few more scenes, okay?' They loved what I was doing—whatever it was." Although critics commented at length about Hill's ambivalence towards his theme of the public's lust for mayhem, the film's foul-mouthed language, and its mixed point of view, Swoosie Kurtz was not singled out for any special mention.

When Molière's *Tartuffe* opened at the Circle in the Square in September 1977 with John Wood in the title role, Stefan Gierasch as Orgon, the gullible man of property, and Tammy Grimes as Orgon's wife, Elmire, reviews were mixed about both the production and the acting. For Swoosie Kurtz, playing Mariane, the daughter that Orgon is bent on betrothing to the hypocritical Tartuffe, notices ranged from encomiums in *Cue* and *Newsweek* to John Simon's slashing criticism in *New York* magazine (October 10, 1977). Simon found both Swoosie Kurtz and Tammy Grimes to be "two actresses totally unsuited to these roles both histrionically and physically," and added that "their presence in the play upends virtually every scene they are in." In contrast, *Newsweek*'s Jack Kroll (October 17, 1977) discovered that "the cleanest, straightest performance is by the always delightful Swoosie Kurtz"; Allan Wallach of *Newsday* (September 27, 1977) enjoyed "Swoosie Kurtz, wide-eyed and weak-spined as Orgon's daughter"; and John Beaufort of the *Christian Science Monitor* (September 26, 1977) called her performance "engagingly foolish." Because a majority of reviewers agreed with them, Swoosie Kurtz gained her first Tony nomination.

With her career accelerating, Swoosie Kurtz next appeared in *Uncommon Women and Others* by the young playwright Wendy Wasserstein, which was produced by the Phoenix Theater at its uptown Marymount Manhattan Theater on November 21, 1977. A rueful comedy about a group of women who meet six years after their graduation from Mount Holyoke, the play used flashbacks to depict their hopes, disappointments, and conflicts as they lived through their senior year. As the witty Rita Altabel, obsessed with sexual liberation and with the conviction of her classmates' superiority, Miss Kurtz enchanted the critics and won a 1978 Obie award for her performance. Although the reviewers noted the structural weaknesses of *Uncommon Women and Others*, they singled her out for special commendation, observing that she fleshed out a role that lacked definition, seemed more in command on the stage than ever before, and "smothered her terrors in explosions of wit."

When Christopher Durang's *A History of the American Film*, a satire about the iconography of Hollywood, was given three regional productions in 1977, it received respectful attention from national publications, but when it reached Broadway on March 30, 1978, at the ANTA Theater, reviewers complained that its original mordancy had been somewhat mellowed. They did, however, admire the acting, with Douglas Watt of the New York *Daily News* (March 31, 1978) calling Miss Kurtz's performance as Bette, the tough Bette Davis-Joan Crawford type, "a valiant effort," and with Richard Eder of the *New York Times*, on the same date, observing that she "may be the only actress around who can make catatonia comical." That 1977-78 theatrical season, a banner one for Swoosie Kurtz, was capped by a Drama Desk Award for her performance in *A History of the American Film* to add to her Tony nomination for *Tartuffe* and her Obie award and Drama Desk nomination for *Uncommon Women and Others*.

Following those triumphs, Swoosie Kurtz was offered the opportunity to play a variety of roles in a new Mary Tyler Moore CBS television series called *Mary*. "Television was a total departure for me," she told an interviewer for the *New York Times* (November 24, 1978). "Two days after *American Film* closed, I got this offer. I thought, never in a million years would I dream of doing this. Television was my least favorite medium. But they kept coming back with a better offer—not just in terms of money, but also in time, in schedules and things like that." She moved to Los Angeles, but being at heart a New Yorker rather than an Angelino, she wisely kept her New York apartment, since *Mary*, broadcast for the first time on September 24, 1978, was canceled after only three weeks. When she was asked by Denise Collier what went wrong, Miss Kurtz gave a straightforward evaluation: "It wasn't any good. We did *some* good stuff. We taped eleven shows and three were shown. Through some miracle of bad taste, they chose the worst stuff we had done."

During the period that followed, television work became a principal source of income for Swoosie Kurtz. As she explained to Robert Wahls of the New York *Daily News* (September 21, 1980):

"When I did *Walking Through the Fire* for CBS, I earned more in an hour that I would have in four weeks on Broadway. Today, the pleasure is not where the money is." Another CBS movie made for TV, *The Mating Season*, was filmed for showing later in 1980, and Miss Kurtz also gained a little more pleasure, if less money, from working in regional theatres. Mike Nichols and Elaine May selected her to play Honey, the young faculty wife in *Who's Afraid of Virginia Woolf?* at New Haven's Long Wharf Theater in the spring of 1980, and also at the Long Wharf that season she joined the cast of Nancy Donohue's *Beach House*. She then returned to Off-Broadway's Hudson Guild Theater to play an Irish woman married to an older man in *Summer*, Hugh Leonard's first play to be produced after the success of his *Da*.

While still playing in *Summer*, Swoosie Kurtz was recruited as one of three replacement cast members for a Broadway production of Lanford Wilson's *Fifth of July*, which opened on November 5, 1980, at the New Apollo Theater. One of a projected five-play cycle about the Talleys, a rural Missouri family, *Fifth of July* had been a hit when staged by the Circle Repertory Company in 1978. Reverberating with Chekhovian overtones, the play centers on Kenneth Talley, a paraplegic veteran of Vietnam who is withdrawing from his responsibilities as a teacher of handicapped children and as the owner of his family homestead, which he proposes to sell. Gathered around him on that Independence Day weekend of 1977 are his family and friends, like him psychologically or physically traumatized survivors of the 1960s, including Gwen, the kooky, drug-ridden wife of a friend. It was, of course, a role virtually tailor-made for Swoosie Kurtz.

While some critics had reservations about *The Fifth of July*, they were virtually unanimous about the impact of Swoosie Kurtz's sizzling performance, and she reached another milestone of Broadway acclaim: her caricature now hung among the sketches of celebrities at Sardi's restaurant. When Christopher Reeve was replaced in the leading role of Ken by Richard Thomas in April 1981, Frank Rich of the *New York Times*, who had only grudging praise for the play when it opened in November, now felt that it had been transformed. But it was not only Thomas' performance that he lauded so extravagantly in his review of April 9, 1981. "In November, *Fifth of July* was dominated by Swoosie Kurtz's hilarious performance as the visiting Gwen, a drug-sotted copper heiress with aspirations to rock stardom," Rich wrote. "Miss Kurtz's character is now in proper perspective, and her performance is even better." Declaring that a great play had become even greater, Rex Reed wrote in the New York *Daily News* (April 17, 1981) that the new ensemble spirit of the cast had benefited Miss Kurtz: "Since she doesn't have to keep it moving with wisecracking thrust, she's finally able to relax and just play a real person." But although Swoosie Kurtz garnered the Tony for best supporting actress in addition to Drama Desk and Outer Critics Circle awards, she had not yet become a household name: a feature story about her in the *Washington Post* (July 18, 1981) misspelled her name as "Swoozie" in bold headlines.

When Tony Randall, who was hunting for a female costar for his new television situation comedy, *Love, Sidney*, saw *Fifth of July*, he was so enchanted by Swoosie Kurtz that he immediately knew that he had found the right partner. He relayed some of his enthusiasm to Douglas Bauer during an interview for *TV Guide* (March 6, 1982). "She's a marvelous craftsman, with an infallible sense of humor," Randall explained. "A great sense of timing. But mostly, there's just no one else like her." *Love, Sidney*, a half-hour prime-time series on NBC-TV, began its run on Wednesday nights on October 28, 1981. In an article written for *Glamour* magazine (May 1982) on the popular new media stereotype of American mothers as survivors, Charla Krupp analyzed the show and Swoosie Kurtz's role: "But the hippest mom the survivor on TV is Swoosie Kurtz's Laurie of *Love, Sidney*, who moves in with a middle-aged gay (played by Tony Randall) to create a makeshift family and provide her seven-year-old daughter, Patti, with a father figure." She went on to quote Miss Kurtz on her approach to the role: "My mother brought me up as an adult because my dad was away in the Air Force much of the time. When we were together, we were three people, not two parents and a child. That's kind of the way I treat Patti on the show." *Love, Sidney* turned out to be a hit, scoring in the ratings among the top-ten shows for many weeks in its first season, but when it was moved to a Saturday night slot in the following year, it slipped badly. By January 1983 NBC had temporarily suspended the show, and although the network continued to tape new episodes, *Love, Sidney* was axed after its first two seasons, despite the two Emmy nominations it had won for Swoosie Kurtz.

In a decided switch from the solicitous mother she had played in *Love, Sidney*, Miss Kurtz found time to portray a prostitute in George Roy Hill's film version of John Irving's best seller *The World According to Garp*, which opened in New York in July 1982. Although it encountered a mixed reception from the critics, she managed to make her presence felt in spite of the competition from a star-studded cast. She had another cameo role, as a good-hearted secretary working for a crooked lawyer, in *Against All Odds*, a tediously convoluted remake of the 1947 *film noir Out of the Past*. Critics who had yawned their way through most of the proceedings when *Against All Odds* was released in New York in March 1984 sat up and took notice when Swoosie Kurtz did her three-minute turn. She had a much meatier role, as a maltreated mistress, in the CBS-TV movie *Guilty Conscience*, which made its debut in April 1985 and seems destined to have a continuing life in reruns. In that novel murder mystery Anthony Hopkins, as a philandering criminal lawyer, plots to kill his wife, played by Blythe Danner, but is foiled by the two women he has most abused.

Although the end of 1985 saw Swoosie Kurtz back onstage in a Circle Rep revival of *Beach House*, in which she reprised her role as Annie, the ex-nun who rooms in the beach house of a professor of medicine, the actress soon busied herself with more film work. In 1986 two Warner Brothers film releases kept her idiosyncratic name before a wide public. *Wildcats*, which was released in February, had her playing the supportive sister of Goldie Hawn, the winning coach of an inner-city high school football team. Released in October, *True Stories* was a David Byrne vehicle about a mythical Texas town populated by oddballs. Among the flakiest was Swoosie Kurtz as Miss Rollings, the "laziest woman in the world," who spends her entire life in bed.

Swoosie Kurtz at last found another great starring role when *The House of Blue Leaves*, which won for John Guare the New York Drama Critics Circle award for best play when first produced in 1971, was revived in March 1986 at the Mitzi Newhouse Theater in Lincoln Center. An immediate success, it soon moved upstairs into the much larger Vivian Beaumont Theater to make it eligible for the eight Tony award nominations that came its way. Miss Kurtz played Bananas, the deranged wife of Artie Shaughnessy, a zookeeper, who is fearful that her husband will consign her to an institution—the House of Blue Leaves. Her fears are justified, since Artie plans to use his boyhood friendship with a movie director to run off to Hollywood with his scheming girlfriend, who lives next door, and become a writer of hit songs. At once hilarious and tragic, *The House of Blue Leaves* was defined by Harry Haun of the New York *Daily News* (October 14, 1986) as a "bizarre black comedy," in which "Swoosie Kurtz is a tragicomic tightrope-walker of the first order, specializing in eccentrics with an edge." In *Newsweek* (May 19, 1986), Jack Kroll contended that "the most difficult role is Bananas, whose flights of madness can't conceal the fact that she's the only character with a moral sense. Swoosie Kurtz brilliantly creates lunacy through a choreography of rejection."

As had been anticipated, Miss Kurtz won a Tony, along with an Obie for which she qualified because *The House of Blue Leaves* had opened at the smaller, Off-Broadway Mitzi Newhouse Theater. Characteristically, she maintained a craftsman's view, though pleased by the recognition of her peers. Harry Haun quoted her in *Horizon* (June 1987) as saying: "When I'm told this is the best thing I've done—as much as that statement thrills me—it seems like it *should* be the best thing I've ever done. It's a wonderful play and a wonderful part, and you would hope that you get better and better as you get older and more experienced."

With her agent, Sam Cohn, hoping to help her to find the film stardom that has so far eluded her, Swoosie Kurtz went to the West Coast again in the spring of 1987 to play an art thief in *Vice Versa*, a Columbia Pictures comedy. The theatre is where she has scored her greatest successes, but she has made it clear that it is not her primary goal. "My first priority is work," she told Patrice Maloney during an interview for *Cable Guide* (February 1987). "Good material. Whatever medium the good work is in is where I'll go. What's important is to seek those roles out that will be memorable so that you can say you were part of something that touched someone in some way."

Swoosie Kurtz stands five feet four inches in height and has big blue eyes that make a startling contrast to her mane of red hair. She eats garlic to ward off colds and keeps trim by observing a daily routine of fifteen minutes on a trampoline—the equivalent, she insists, of forty-five minutes of jogging. After living for twelve years in a one-room apartment on the East Side of Manhattan, she bought a six-room apartment on Central Park West where she and her menagerie of stuffed animals have a view of the Fifth Avenue skyline and the park. Swoosie Kurtz has never been married. In November 1980 she told a *New York Times* interviewer: "Once I'm out there on the stage, something magical happens. I have tunnel vision and forget about everything else. I relax. Some people get nervous on the stage. Not me. What gets me nervous is real life."

References: *Cable Guide* 6:28+ F '87 por; *East Side TV Shopper* p19 Ag 15+ '81; *Horizon* 21:42+ Ag '78 por, 30:33+ Je '87 por; *N Y Daily News* Leisure p6 S 21 '80 por, p61 N 13 '80 por, B p3+ Ja 9 '83 por; *N Y Times* C p2 N 14 '80, D p3 Jl 19 '81 por; *Newsweek* p77 My 19 '86 por; *People* 17:123+ Ap 5 '82 por; *Playbill* p108 O '81 por; *TV Guide* 30:19+ Mr 6 '82 por; Celebrity Register, 1986; Collier, Denise, and Beckett, Kathleen. *Spare Ribs: Women in the Humor Biz* (1980); Contemporary Theatre, Film and Television (1984); Who's Who in Hollywood 1900–1976 (1976); Willis, John. Theatre World, 1979–80

Lardner, Ring, Jr.

Aug. 19, 1915– Writer. Address: b. c/o Mike Marcus, Creative Artists Agency, 1888 Century Park East, Suite 1400, Los Angeles, Calif. 90067

In the late 1940s Ring Lardner Jr. was at the height of one of the most successful screenwriting careers in the history of Hollywood when he became a casualty of the domestic purges that characterized American cold war politics of the time. Five years after he won an Academy Award as coauthor of the script for the 1942 film *Woman of the Year*, Lardner, a political activist, an organizer of the Screen Writers' Guild, and a student of Marxism at the time, was subpoenaed to testify before the House Committee on Un-American Activities. Because he refused on that occasion to reveal whether he was a member of the American Communist party, he was declared to be in contempt of Congress, jailed, and blacklisted along with nine other artists popularly known as the "Hollywood Ten" or "unfriendly witnesses."

During his subsequent eighteen-year exile on the blacklist, Lardner wrote screenplays and teleplays under pseudonyms and completed *The Ecstasy of Owen Muir*, a novel that exemplified his gift for satire, deft characterization, and well-honed dialogue. In 1970 he reclaimed his position in the front rank of Hollywood writers with *M*A*S*H*, which won him a second Academy Award. His memoir, *The Lardners: My Family Remembered*, appeared in 1976. He retired from screenwriting in 1981 to concentrate on fiction writing and in 1985 published his second novel, *All for Love*. Reflecting on his experiences and his troubled times, Lardner has observed: "Now that we have devised two quite practical methods of extinguishing ourselves, nuclear war and chemical pollution, systems like capitalism and socialism have little relevance except as helps or hindrances to escaping our doom. . . . The only question . . . is whether we are capable of subordinating all the other forces within us to reason."

Ringgold Wilmer Lardner Jr. was born in Chicago, Illinois, on August 19, 1915, the third of four sons of Ring Lardner Sr., the celebrated sports journalist, short story writer, and humorist, and Ellis (Abbot) Lardner. In *The Lardners: My Family Remembered*, Ring Jr. recalled that in the Lardner family "it was a matter of course that you mastered the fundamentals of reading and writing at the age of four, and by six reading books was practically a full-time occupation."

By the time he was six, Lardner's family had moved from Chicago to Greenwich, Connecticut, and then to Long Island, where they lived next door to the newspaper executive Herbert Swope. Swope's home was a gathering place for many of the prominent literati of the day, including Heywood Broun Sr., Dorothy Parker, and Alexander Woollcott. Literary ambitions were sparked in Ring Jr. and his brothers by contact with that circle, with other friends of their parents, such as F. Scott Fitzgerald, and, of course, by the example set by their father. Although Lardner Sr. was a conservative, he seems to have communicated to Ring Jr. what, according to Heywood Broun, was concealed under his "insulation of isolation and indifference," namely "a passion against smugness and hypocrisy and the hard heart of the world."

In 1928 Ring Jr. entered Phillips Andover Academy at Andover, Massachusetts, where he joined the debating team, partly to compensate for his intermittent stutter. He won prizes for his essays and his oratory and eventually became editor in chief of the school's literary magazine. In June 1931 he delivered an impromptu speech from a bus top to promote the candidacy of Franklin D. Roosevelt— the last major party candidate that he supported or voted for until the candidacy of Senator George McGovern in 1972. In the fall of 1932, at seventeen, Lardner entered Princeton University, where he flung himself less into his studies than into his extracurricular activities, including the debating team and the bridge team. He also joined the Socialist Club and spent weekends canvassing eastern New Jersey for the Socialist party candidate, Norman Thomas.

While a Princeton undergraduate, Lardner achieved his first writing successes, when he was selected in an open competition as one of the writers of the annual Triangle Club show and was chosen, at the suggestion of Alexander Woollcott, to serve as a spokesman for his generation with an article in the inaugural issue of Esquire magazine. Those achievements made Lardner determined to launch a career as a professional writer and to stop "marking time" at Princeton. Furthermore, his father having died the previous year, he felt that his academic performance did not justify the strain that an expensive Princeton education put on his mother's income from insurance and royalties. He decided to extend his education in a different and cheaper fashion by embarking on an eight-week trip abroad in the summer of 1934, sailing third-class to Hamburg, then continuing to Leningrad by train to take advantage of the newly opened opportunity for tourist travel in the Soviet Union. He immediately cut short his itinerary in favor of remaining at the University of Moscow's Anglo-American Institute. In a New York Times (January 13, 1987) interview he told Philip Taubman, "It all seemed very simple in those days. There had been a split between Stalin and Trotsky, which Stalin won and that seemed to be a good thing because he believed in building socialism in one country. I couldn't help making the comparison to the West,

which was in the middle of the Depression. Here [in Russia] everyone seemed enthused, willing to sacrifice for the future." The positive aspects of Russian life were cast into even sharper relief by Lardner's return trip through Nazi Germany, where some of his Soviet posters were seized and he was briefly detained.

In January 1935, after his return to the United States, Lardner took a job as a reporter on the tabloid New York Daily Mirror at $25 a week. He remained there for ten months, garnering half a dozen bylines before being recommended by Herbert Swope, his former Long Island neighbor, for a job at an independent film company being launched by David O. Selznick, the son-in-law of the Metro-Goldwyn-Mayer tycoon Louis B. Mayer. In his memoirs, Lardner recalled: "It didn't become a definite offer until [Selznick's] secretary, Silvia Schulman, who became my wife fifteen months after I went to work for her boss, told him I was a good bet because she had seen me in the RKO office in New York . . . and thought I was good-looking enough to be an acting as well as a writing possibility. . . . She was embarrassed when I reported for work in Culver City and she realized it had been my brother John who had so caught her fancy in New York." Lardner failed his screen test and began work in the public relations department, receiving no screenwriting assignments for a year. Meanwhile, he filled his days and nights with "work, drinking, reading, movie-going, bridge, tennis, swimming, one sustained affair with a colleague's wife, and occasional dates, mostly with Floncy and Silvia." He was finally assigned to work with Budd Schulberg, who was then a reader in the story department, in rewriting some scenes from the original (and some critics believe the best) version of A Star is Born, the story of Vicki Lester (played by Janet Gaynor), whose rise to stardom parallels the decline into obscurity and eventual suicide of her husband, Norman Maine (portrayed by Fredric March). Lardner and Schulberg devised the now classic final scene in which Vicki Lester, newly immortalized by having her footprints preserved in concrete in the sidewalk in front of Sid Grauman's Chinese Theatre, walks up to a battery of microphones and says, "Hello, everybody, this is Mrs. Norman Maine." After completing that scene, Lardner has recalled, Selznick "decreed that [he and Schulberg] were now screenwriters." In collaboration with George Oppenheimer, on loan from MGM for that purpose, Lardner next provided an ending for Nothing Sacred, Carole Lombard's classic screwball comedy.

By that time, Lardner had been recruited by the Hollywood Communist party and was spending as many as four nights a week at Marxist study groups and similar gatherings. What he has described as primarily an intellectual attraction to Marxism-Leninism was buttressed by his belief that the people he encountered at the Marxist meetings were "brighter and more admirable and more likable than other people." In jest, he once proposed the slogan, "The most beautiful girls in Hollywood belong to the Communist party!"

In 1938, seeking more regular screenwriting assignments than he was being given by David O. Selznick's company, Lardner went to work for a time at Warner Brothers and then began a collaboration with Ian McLellan Hunter that led to his first screen credits, for *Meet Dr. Christian* (1939) and *The Courageous Dr. Christian* (1940). Both were based on Jean Hersholt's enormously popular "Dr. Christian" radio series and were faulted for their too formulaic picture of a kindly country doctor who has a knack for solving all his community's problems.

After the Dr. Christian films, partly because of his political activities, Lardner found to his consternation that "suddenly there were no jobs to be had." "In this situation," he wrote in *The Lardners*, "the only possible way to make money as a screenwriter was to create projects of my own." His fortunes were changed dramatically by one of those projects, a romantic comedy called *Woman of the Year* that he wrote with Michael Kanin. Their story concerned the relationship that develops between a hard-driving woman political commentator and an easygoing sports reporter. When it was brought to the attention of Katharine Hepburn by Kanin's brother, Garson Kanin, she was so captivated by it that "she took over the whole operation," Lardner recalls. Since the two screenwriters were as yet unknown, she removed their names from the script in order to get a higher price for it, and the price she negotiated, $100,000, turned out to be the highest ever paid for an original screenplay at the time. The completed film, released by MGM in 1942, marked the beginning of one of Hollywood's most popular pairings, that of Katharine Hepburn and Spencer Tracy, who eventually starred together in nine pictures. *Woman of the Year* also brought screenwriting Oscars for 1942 to Lardner and Kanin, and the pair negotiated a $2,000-a-week contract with MGM for work on projects of their own choosing.

Meanwhile, Lardner became even more politically involved by joining organizations such as the Hollywood Anti-Nazi League, which lasted from 1936 to 1939, and the Citizens Committee for the Defense of Mexican-American Youth, which ran an antiracism campaign in the wake of attacks by United States military personnel upon Mexican-Americans in 1943. An outgrowth of Lardner's work with the Citizens Committee was his coauthorship of the animated short film *The Brotherhood of Man* (1943), which was "one of the most notable results of this flurry" of activism in Hollywood, according to Larry Ceplair and Steven Englund in their book *The Inquisition in Hollywood: Politics in the Film Community, 1930–1960* (1979). Within the Hollywood community itself, between 1937 and 1947, Lardner served continuously on the board of the Screen Writers' Guild, in posts that included those of treasurer and vice-president, and helped to make the organization not only one of the most powerful labor unions in Hollywood but also a political nerve center and model for other talent groups in Hollywood.

Following the Japanese attack on Pearl Harbor on December 7, 1941, Lardner tried to involve himself in the American war effort but encountered considerable difficulty in securing an assignment when, after a security check, he was designated "a premature anti-fascist." The United States Army Signal Corps finally accepted him, and he worked for a time at the Astoria studios in Long Island making training films. He then returned to Hollywood and worked with Otto Preminger on an epic about the rise of the Nazi party that was never filmed. During the same period Lardner worked on *The Cross of Lorraine* (1944), a grimly powerful propaganda drama about the heroic deeds of French prisoners of war after the fall of their country. Uncredited, Lardner also worked on dialogue for what became a classic detective film, *Laura* (1944). *Tomorrow the World*, another 1944 film, cowritten by Lardner and Leopold Atlas and released by United Artists, gave a stirring account of the struggle of foster parents to change the thinking of a boy, inculcated with Nazi anti-Semitism, who arrives in the United States after the death of his parents in a concentration camp. The film won the first award granted by the Hollywood Writers Mobilization Against the War, a group of which Lardner had been a founder. The first postwar films Lardner wrote were *Cloak and Dagger*, a spy melodrama directed by Fritz Lang and released in 1946, and *Forever Amber* (1947), based on Kathleen Winsor's palpitating best seller about a young beauty who occupies various strategic beds in her climb through the levels of Restoration society until she arrives at the court of Charles II. Both films were enormous box-office successes.

After only ten years spent in plying his trade, Lardner "had one foot in the screenwriter's pantheon," according to Ceplair and Englund. It was at this point that he was subpoenaed to testify before the Committee on Un-American Activities of the United States House of Representatives. "It developed," Lardner wrote in his memoirs, "that there were nineteen of us who came to be known as 'unfriendly witnesses' as opposed to those who were willing and eager to tell the world what they knew about the Communist subversion of the movie business." For reasons never made clear, only eleven of the nineteen were actually called to testify and one of them, the influential German playwright Bertolt Brecht, was not an American citizen and promptly left the country after testifying. The remaining uncooperative witnesses, dubbed the "Hollywood Ten" by the media, were Alvah Bessie, Herbert Biberman, Lester Cole, Edward Dmytryk, John Howard Lawson, Albert Maltz, Sam Ornitz, Adrian Scott, Dalton Trumbo, and, of course, Lardner. Their legal strategy, worked out over drinks by Lardner and Dalton Trumbo, was to refuse to answer questions on First Amendment grounds. "Forced confessions, or disavowals, were what the committee was clearly demanding," Lardner later wrote, "and I felt it was an abuse of the legislative function that needed challenging."

When Lardner testified on October 30, 1947, he had a memorable confrontation with the committee chairman, Representative J. Parnell Thomas, of New Jersey. "I am not quibbling but speaking the literal truth," Lardner told Bert Andrews of the New York *Herald Tribune* (January 1, 1948), "when I say that I did not refuse to answer any question. The transcript shows that I was interrupted every time I started to speak. . . . " When Thomas asked if Lardner was a member of the Communist party, the screenwriter began a detailed answer, was interrupted twice by Thomas, and finally managed a sardonic reply: "I could answer the question exactly the way you want . . . but if I did, I would hate myself in the morning." Thomas began furiously banging his gavel and, before Lardner could continue, ordered the screenwriter to leave the witness chair. "The truth is," Lardner later wrote, " . . . the prevailing sentiment among the Hollywood Ten was that we had the better of the issue. What has to be realized now to appreciate our perspective then is that it was so much the beginning of the McCarthy era that McCarthy himself had not yet discovered the virtues of anti-Communism. . . . We didn't anticipate that our careers would be wrecked or that we would go to prison."

For a period after his brief encounter with J. Parnell Thomas, Lardner's life continued on its normal course. He was under contract at $2,000 a week to Twentieth Century-Fox and found himself in such demand that he made special arrangements to work on three screenplays in one year rather than on the two his contract allowed. Then, in November 1947, the members of the Hollywood Ten were voted in contempt of Congress. Lardner promptly lost his contract, was blacklisted from working in Hollywood, and was sentenced to one year at the Federal Correctional Institution in Danbury, Connecticut. When he began serving his sentence in July 1950 he found that he had been preceded to Danbury by his former Grand Inquisitor, J. Parnell Thomas, who had been convicted of padding his payroll.

During his nine and a half months at Danbury, Lardner began work on his first novel, *The Ecstasy of Owen Muir,* a wry tale, set in the cold war era, about a quixotic seeker after truth who at one point is jailed for his views, including his intransigent pacifism. The novel was rejected by more than six United States publishers before it was finally published in 1954, by Jonathan Cape in London and by Cameron & Kahn in New York. Although *The Ecstasy of Owen Muir* was greeted with rave reviews in England, in America it met with a dense silence broken only by an occasional review. One such notice, in the then liberal *New Republic* (April 25, 1955), praised Lardner's wit, originality, and dazzling style.

After his release from Danbury, Lardner continued to be blacklisted as a screenwriter until the 1960s, though he was able to work under pseudonyms. His last works to appear under his own name for some fifteen years were his rewrite of the dialogue for *Four Days Leave* (1950), a romantic tale of an American soldier in Switzerland, and the entire screenplay for *The Big Night* (1951), a melodrama about a troubled and rebellious teenager.

After that, until October 14, 1961, when he published "My Life on the Blacklist" under his own name in the *Saturday Evening Post,* Lardner worked pseudonymously on some seven or eight films in the United States and abroad, despite being denied a passport from 1953 to 1958. He found a major new source of income in television writing, which he undertook with Ian Hunter, another casualty of the blacklist. The two writers created a number of popular half-hour series, including *The Adventures of Robin Hood, Sir Lancelot,* and *The Pirates.*

Lardner began his rapprochement with Hollywood in the early 1960s, and his name appeared on the screen again in 1965, when *The Cincinnati Kid,* which he wrote with Terry Southern, was released by MGM. According to Joseph Gelmis of *Newsday* (October 28, 1965), the film "does for five-card stud poker what *The Hustler* did for pool—raises it to an art form."

Lardner's next project to be produced was the screenplay for *M*A*S*H* (1970), which he adapted from Richard Hooker's novel of the same title. In what film critic Judith Crist described as "brilliant" fashion, his script improved on the novel about some maverick medics who, in their struggle to care for an unremitting flood of wounded soldiers and to cope with the Korean War in general, indulge in endless pranks, japery, and black humor. *M*A*S*H* earned $23 million and helped to save the financially beleaguered Twentieth Century-Fox twenty-three years after it fired Lardner.

"The laughter [of *M*A*S*H*] is blood-soaked," Judith Crist wrote in *New York* magazine (January 26, 1970), "and the comedy cloaks a bitter and terrible truth." *M*A*S*H* brought Lardner his second Academy Award, for the best screenplay adaptation from another medium. His last produced picture before he retired to devote himself to fiction was the lukewarmly reviewed *The Greatest* (1977), which was based on the autobiography of Muhammad Ali, who played himself in the film.

When Harper & Row published *The Lardners: My Family Remembered* in 1976, Walter Clemons wrote in *Newsweek* (June 28, 1976) that "not the least of the [book's] pleasures . . . is the evidence that famous fathers' sons don't always turn out wrecks." In it, Ring Lardner Jr. chronicled the wit, fame, and alcoholic troubles of his father, the early deaths of his brothers, his mother's slow transition from optimism to pessimism, and the vicissitudes of his own career. Clemons concluded that "Ring Lardner's last surviving son has written a wonderful book." Lardner's most recent publication is a novel, *All for Love* (Franklin Watts, 1985), which deals with the seduction of a young beauty by an unprepossessing scientist who designs an aphrodisiac to encompass his ends. It was judged to be an uneven entertainment by Charles Salzberg in the *New York Times Book Review* (May 5, 1985), but Alvah Bessie, writing in the *San Francisco Chronicle* (March 31, 1985), called it "highly imaginative science fiction cum social satire."

Ring Lardner Jr. is "a tall, thin man with a weathered face," as Philip Taubman described him for his *New York Times* article. By his marriage to Silvia Schulman, which ended in divorce in 1945, Lardner has two children, Peter and Ann. He married Frances Chaney, the widow of his brother David, on September 28, 1946, and by that marriage has one child, James, and two stepchildren, Katherine and Joseph. The couple live in a pre-Revolutionary clapboard-and-shingle house in New Milford, Connecticut, where the screenwriter indulges in his favorite recreations: tennis and gardening. In discussing with Philip Taubman a return visit to Moscow in January 1987, Lardner said: "I've never regretted my association with Communism. I still think that some form of socialism is a more rational way to organize a society, but I recognize it hasn't worked anywhere yet." The first annual Ring Lardner Jr. Civil Liberties Award of the Fred R. Zimring Foundation was presented to Lardner in April 1987.

References: N Y Times C p17 Ja 13 '87 por; Sat R 234:38+ O 14 '61 pors; Froug, William. The Screenwriter Looks at the Screenwriter (1972); Lardner, Ring, Jr. The Lardners: My Family Remembered (1976)

Laredo, Ruth

Nov. 20, 1937– Concert pianist. Address: b. c/o Herbert Barrett Management, 1776 Broadway, Suite 504, New York City, N.Y. 10019

According to music critic James R. Oestreich, the diminutive American pianist Ruth Laredo "yields to no one in her willingness to explore the limits of virtuosity" but she is "willing to relent in tempo and to rein in technique where there is meaning to be found beneath the glittering surface." Ruth Laredo herself has said, "For me piano playing comes from the whole being. . . . People are always saying, 'How can you play such big music? You're only five foot one.' But it has nothing to do with your height or weight. . . . It has to do with how you use your strength, how you manage to convey certain ideas."

In the early 1970s, after being known for more than a decade primarily as the accompanist of her former husband, the violin virtuoso Jaime Laredo, Ruth Laredo discovered that her way with "certain ideas" had won her recognition as one of the great American pianists.

Her first recording, a 1967 disc for the Connoisseur Society label, offered what some critics feel are the definitive interpretations of *La Valse* and other demanding piano works by Ravel. Three years later, she helped usher in a major revival of interest in the music of the visionary Russian composer, Alexander Scriabin, by recording his complete piano works in honor of the centennial of his birth. A year later, she began work on a similar cycle to commemorate the centennial of Sergei Rachmaninoff's birth, and the C. F. Peters music publishing company was sufficiently impressed to commission her to edit a new Urtext edition of the composer's works. The first volume, *The Preludes* (Opus 23), was published in 1985.

Ruth Laredo was born Ruth Meckler on November 20, 1937, in Detroit, Michigan. Her father, Ben Meckler, a high school English teacher, and her mother, Miriam (Horowitz) Meckler, a piano teacher, took her to concerts even when she was a child, as she recalled in an autobiographical article for *Keynote* (April 1983). Like her mother's playing and teaching, the concerts inspired an early fascination with music, and at the age of two and a half she surprised her family by pounding out "God Bless America" at the piano. The crucial musical experience of her childhood, however, was a recital given by Vladimir Horowitz in the vast 4,000-seat Masonic Auditorium of Detroit. Horowitz "sat a mere five feet away from my Buster Brown shoes," she recalled in *Keynote*. He gave "an unforgettable concert. . . . The world stood on its head when I heard this man play. And he played Rachmaninoff. My love for the piano and for Rachmaninoff, Scriabin, and Chopin really began on that day in Detroit. It changed my life irrevocably. I knew then, as an eight-year-old, that I wanted to become a pianist."

Until she reached the age of ten, Ruth Laredo studied piano with her mother. When her mother decided that it was time for Ruth to begin formal musical training, she selected Edward Bredshall, who became her daughter's first mentor. In a November 1982 interview in *Clavier*, Ruth Laredo recounted that Bredshall "made the whole world change for me." He was so impressed with the precocity of her musicianship that he immediately arranged an informal audition for her before Walter Poole, the assistant conductor of the Detroit Symphony and director of its summer concert series. She made her formal concert debut in the summer of 1948 at the age of ten, performing Beethoven's Piano Concerto No. 2 with the Detroit Symphony under Poole.

Ruth Laredo's four years of study with Bredshall, from 1948 until 1952, were marked by tremendous musical and personal growth. His interdisciplinary approach to music introduced her not only to a vast range of repertory, including Stravinsky, Bartók, Prokofiev, and Debussy, but to such areas as art, drama, opera, politics, and philosophy. He also cultivated her natural enthusiasm. "[He'd] show me a difficult piece by Bartók or Stravinsky," she told Sidney Fields in an interview for the New York *Daily News* (October 4, 1976), "and say, 'I don't think you can play this,' and, of course, I'd pick up the challenge. A wonderful way to teach." The two eventually established the custom of making cash bets on her achievements. After Edward Bredshall moved to California in 1952, she continued her studies with Mischa Kottler, a Russian-born contemporary and friend of Rachmaninoff, for another year.

During the summer of 1953 Ruth Laredo attended a music camp called Indian Hill, located in Stockbridge, Massachusetts, near Tanglewood, in the Berkshires. By that time her early enthusiasm was structured into her musical personality and, as she told John Gruen in the *New York Times* (December 15, 1974), she played "anything and everything." With one of her teachers, Seymour Lipkin, who had recently won a Rachmaninoff piano competition, she soon developed a strong rapport. Lipkin helped to arrange an audition for Ruth Laredo with one of the giants of contemporary pianism, Rudolf Serkin, and she traveled to Marlboro, Vermont, where Serkin had his annual summer music festival, to perform the Beethoven Sonata Opus 101 and Chopin's A-flat Ballade for him. After hearing her perform those difficult works, Serkin said, "I can see you play like a tiger."

Ruth Laredo began formal study and a long musical relationship with Serkin in the fall of 1955, when she enrolled as one of his students at the Curtis Institute of Music in Philadelphia. In instructing her, Serkin stressed the standard German repertory, but he also encouraged her to explore her personal interests in such composers as Ravel and Chausson. She thus mastered a surprising amount of French repertory at Curtis, while still performing Bach, Beethoven, and Mozart at Serkin's summer Marlboro Festivals in Vermont.

"What Serkin imparted to me," she told John Gruen, "was something I will always have. . . . He instilled in me the understanding that there is no effort too great to make in the service of music. . . . He wanted me to play in a great big style. *How* I was to do that, I had to find out myself. Mr. Serkin would never say, 'Do this' or 'Do that.' He would say, 'The music requires such and such,' and you had to find out what that meant. I think that's the greatest thing a teacher can do for you, because that means you don't imitate him in any way, but you explore. Well, I did a lot of exploring. And, oh, the soul-searching in those practice rooms!"

While at the Curtis Institute, she met and began performing with a Bolivian-born violin prodigy three years her junior named Jaime Laredo. Laredo graduated in 1959, the same year in which he achieved international acclaim by winning Belgium's prestigious Queen Elizabeth International Music Competition. The musical partnership between the two had by that time become romantic, and they were married on June 1, 1960, after Mrs. Laredo's own graduation.

Her marriage and her husband's sudden fame had an unanticipated effect: instead of becoming established as a soloist and virtuoso in her own right—a goal toward which her training and her natural temperament seemed to have directed her—she traveled the world as accompanist to her celebrated husband. For the next fourteen years, until their divorce in November of 1974, Ruth Laredo willingly sublimated many of her own aspirations in favor of working with her husband. She pursued a career of her own only intermittently, as in her New York debut of March 28, 1963, in Carnegie Hall, with the American Symphony Orchestra under Leopold Stokowski, or her tour of Europe in 1965 with Rudolf Serkin and his son, the piano virtuoso Peter Serkin. Throughout the 1960s she was also a regular member of the roster of chamber musicians at Marlboro and its circle of internationally celebrated musicians.

On one occasion at Marlboro she was invited to take part in a private performance of some Beethoven trios with the master cellist Pablo Casals—with whom she had previously worked in master classes—and the Supreme Court Associate Justice Abe Fortas, who was an accomplished violinist. Fortas was so impressed by her playing that he helped to arrange a command performance for President and Mrs. Lyndon B. Johnson at the White House in September 1967. On that occasion, Ruth and Jaime Laredo performed at a state dinner in honor of the president of the Republic of Niger.

Despite such unexpected triumphs, Ruth Laredo's career and recitals were overshadowed by her work with her husband. But even as an accompanist, her forcefulness of spirit and musicianship occasionally manifested itself. In his *New York Times* (August 22, 1966) review of the Laredos' performance of four of Mozart's violin and piano sonatas at Philharmonic Hall, Allen Hughes called her playing "intense and self-assertive . . . much of the time louder than Mr. Laredo's violin-

playing, [and dominating] the performances."
Looking back on that period, Ruth Laredo told John
Gruen: "I did not in any way forget that I had intended and had wanted to be a pianist in my own
right. But nothing at all happened about that. I tried
out for every competition you can name, and I got
nowhere. . . . So it seemed I was to go on playing
with Jaime."

Through her careful choice of repertory, most
notably the work of Ravel, she began to attract independent attention. Reviewing her performance
of Ravel's *La Valse*, at Carnegie Recital Hall on
January 30, 1967, Miles Kastendieck of the
World-Journal-Tribune (January 31, 1967) wrote:
"Miss Laredo excelled in musical temperament. . . . Faced with bringing out the many facets
of this piece, she caught its flavor, its 'orchestral'
coloration, and its meaning both skillfully and effectively. Her performance was a tour-de-force."

La Valse, along with Ravel's *Gaspard de la Nuit*
and *Valses Nobles et Sentimentales*, were the
pieces that Ruth Laredo chose for her first solo recording, which she made for the Connoisseur Society in 1967. Reviewing the album for *High Fidelity*
(September 1968), Harris Goldsmith called it "a
most striking solo debut" and praised Ruth Laredo
as "technically a superbly accomplished pianist
with supremely even fingers, a cool, jade-like sonority and a natural rhythmic clarity. Even though
two of the works included on the disc—*Gaspard*
and Ravel's own transcription of *La Valse*—fall
into the category of compositions demanding su-
pervirtuosity . . . the present performances let
you forget the spine-chilling pyrotechnics and revel in the artist's *joie de vivre* and ebullience."

In 1969 Ruth Laredo advanced from the status of
accompanist to that of cosoloist in her professional
relationship with her husband. By 1970, in the
wake of her successful debut disc and in view of
Alexander Scriabin's centenary in 1972, she was
commissioned to record the composer's complete
piano works for the Connoisseur Society. The first
of the four Scriabin discs that she eventually recorded contained the composer's Sonata No. 5 in F-
sharp, the *Black Mass* Sonata No. 9 in F, the complete Eight Etudes Opus 42, and the *White Mass*
Sonata No. 7 in F-sharp, which, according to the pianist, is "built on a single chord" and was regarded
by Scriabin as "holy." When her recording was released in 1970 on the Connoisseur Society label, it
was an immediate success. "Making those recordings was fascinating," Ruth Laredo has said. "I
became totally immersed in each of the sonatas as
I worked on it. Some of the music is certainly neurotic, but it is all thoroughly absorbing." Lester
Trimble, in *Stereo Review* (November 1970), lauded her for her "glowing performance, all surge and
ebb, with seemingly millions of notes sparkling
forth like star-dust" on the Eight Etudes. The record was selected by the magazine as "Best of the
Month," and the *Saturday Review* named it one of
"the Best Records of the Year."

That first Scriabin disc was something of a historical event as well, since it was the first recording

of the complete etudes. A year later, on October 9
and October 31, 1971, Ruth Laredo gave two concerts at Hunter College in New York that are believed to have been the first recitals ever to
traverse Scriabin's complete ten sonatas for piano.
"Miss Laredo easily commanded the massive technique necessary to encompass the ferocious demands of the music," observed Peter G. Davis of
the *New York Times* (October 12, 1971), in reviewing the first concert. "Her tone is consistently rich
and sonorous; the clarity of her phrasing illuminates even the most densely crowded textures; she
characterizes each sonata superbly, from the rich
romantic vitality of the early works to the febrile
intensity of the late ones."

Confronted with the increasing demands of her
own burgeoning career, and partly in order to assert her separate identity within the context of that
career, Ruth Laredo ceased performing as her husband's accompanist during the early 1970s, for she
had grown less and less comfortable with the sub-
ordinate role in which their musical relationship
had placed her over the years, especially when it
seemed to become ingrained in the consciousness
of the critics. The first ego shock came after she had
played a violin and piano sonata with her husband,
and the next morning's newspapers noted: "The
accompanist was Ruth Laredo."

Her Scriabin records proved so successful that
in 1973 executives at CBS Masterworks asked Ruth
Laredo to begin work on a series of birthday centennial recordings devoted to her other great Russian specialty, Sergei Rachmaninoff. "It was an
offer I couldn't refuse," she recalled in *Keynote*,
adding, "I said yes without knowing what I was getting myself into. . . . I discovered that just to learn
the mere notes of any Rachmaninoff work is a Herculean task. I felt at first as if I were working on a
chain gang: every morning I would take out my
pick and shovel and chip away at what seemed a
mountain of material. . . . The endurance, the
speed, the power required by this music is unlike
any other piano writing I've ever encountered."
After practicing she had to have her hands mas-
saged because her entire body ached.

Her first Rachmaninoff album, containing the
Preludes (Opus 23) and *Five Pieces* (Opus 3), was
released in the spring of 1974 and was eventually
followed up by six additional discs making up the
composer's complete music for solo piano. In paying her tribute, Donal Henahan of the *New York
Times* observed that "only a pianist of Herculean
industry and virtuosic gifts would set out on such
a road, and only a keyboard musician of Ruth Laredo's quality would have a chance of finishing the
trip. . . . Miss Laredo does not manhandle (or
womanhandle) these pieces in the razzle-dazzle
style of some Rachmaninoff performers. . . .
There is a prevailing *élan*, elegance, and clarity."

Despite the opening of a bright new chapter in
her now independent career, Ruth Laredo found
that a pall of uncertainty hung over her life as a result of her divorce in 1974. "The end of a marriage,"
she told Jerry Talmer in a *New York Post* interview

(May 25, 1977), "is, you should excuse the expression, consciousness-raising. I didn't know if I could earn a living or anything, so I accepted a position as professor of music at Yale." As it turned out, her career outpaced her expectations. In December of 1974 she was honored as "Musician of the Month" by *High Fidelity/Musical America*. And on December 12, 1974, less than a month after her divorce became final, she made both her Avery Fisher Hall and New York Philharmonic debut with a performance of the Ravel Piano Concerto in G under Pierre Boulez. At the same time, her Rachmaninoff recordings established her as a specialist in yet another composer's repertory and led, unexpectedly, to a major scholarly endeavor when the music publisher C. F. Peters asked her to prepare editorially correct editions of Rachmaninoff's complete piano music.

As Ruth Laredo told David Dubal in an interview for his book *Reflections from the Keyboard: The World of the Concert Pianist* (1984), in editing the manuscripts, she had an opportunity to apply what she knew of Rachmaninoff's austere personality. "I knew immediately that the first editions that were furnished to me by Peters Publishing Company had to have been edited by someone," she explained, "as they were filled with all kinds of extraneous markings that were not characteristic of the man, and after I got some manuscript copies from the Library of Congress, I knew I was correct in my assumption. There was not an extra accent or line on any of his original manuscripts. . . . Once I saw the originals, I felt strongly that the works that I had been given to edit had to be cleaned up. I took what I call '*graffiti*' away."

Meanwhile, her performing career was flourishing. By 1976 she was giving recitals across the country, and she had made her first tour of Europe and of Japan, where the Japanese had hailed her as "the greatest of American pianists." She gave up her teaching position at Yale that year to devote herself both to touring and to her extended recording and research on Rachmaninoff. In 1980 she was named the year's "Best Keyboard Artist" in *Record World* magazine. In the same year she received a Grammy award nomination for the final recording in her Rachmaninoff cycle, devoted to the Piano Sonatas No. 1 and 2 and the *Polka on a Theme By V. R.*

Despite her acclaimed performances of Rachmaninoff, Scriabin, and Ravel, Ruth Laredo resists being labeled as a specialist who is confined to French and Russian composers. "It's amusing to me," she said during her *Clavier* interview, "because the one thing I've probably had more experience with than anything else is classical repertoire. If you study with Rudolf Serkin, you play Beethoven for him—a lot—and Mozart and Bach. It's just a matter of fate, or luck, that I was given the chance to do the Rachmaninoff; and now I'm just coming back to other repertoire that's very familiar and very much a part of me." As if to prove her point, she made that statement during the fall of 1982, a season in which she toured with programs that were largely devoted to Beethoven. She has also taken a far more active interest in the work of contemporary composers than she is often given credit for. In addition to her 1973 disc of Ned Rorem's *Day Music* and Leon Kirchner's *Sonata Concertante* for violin and piano, made with Jaime Laredo for Desto Records, her work includes a 1982 Nonesuch Records release devoted to Samuel Barber's Sonata for Piano (Opus 26), *Souvenirs* (Opus 28), and *Nocturne (Homage to John Field)* (Opus 33), for which she received another Grammy nomination.

"Ruth Laredo is about as big as a hummingbird," Donal Henahan wrote in the *New York Times* (March 9, 1973). "Her hands sometimes appear to hover over the keys, a blur to the eyes if not the ears. . . . But what hummingbird ever packed [such] power . . . ?" She lives with her daughter, Jennifer, who was born in 1969, in an apartment on New York's West Side. Her interests include art and cooking. Her most recent engagements, in addition to performances with the New York Philharmonic, Philadelphia, Cleveland, and Boston Symphony orchestras, have included regular guest appearances with the Tokyo and Cleveland quartets and recital tours with the flautist Paula Robison. She has recently become a columnist for *Keyboard Classics* magazine and has contributed another article to *Keynote* (August 1987), entitled "Artist's Life." It concludes with the observation that "the artist's life is a tough one—rigorous, demanding, but filled with the immense satisfaction of carrying on the hallowed tradition of great music. Without the performer in the flesh, the rich experience of listening to live music could never continue. 'There's nothing like the real thing, baby!' I believe that completely." In that article she also points out that because a pianist cannot carry his instrument, he faces more performance problems than other musicians and has to "take pot luck in every town he visits," forcing him to "learn to love whatever piano happens to be available, as if it were his own favorite Steinway, Baldwin, or Yamaha." "While our orchestral colleagues tootle or fiddle away backstage," she quips, "we pianists have only our love to keep us warm before a concert."

References: *Clavier* 21:10+ N '82; Hi Fi/Mus Am 24:4+ D '74; *Keyboard Classics* 6:24+ N 1 '86; *Keynote* 7:6+ Ap '83; *Music Journal* 26:52+ F '68; N Y Daily News p8 O 4 '76; N Y Times II p21+ D 15 '74; *Who's Who in America, 1986–87; Who's Who of American Women* (1979–80)

Lavin, Linda

Oct. 15, 1937– Actress; director; producer.
Address: b. c/o Sumski, Green & Co., Inc., 8380
Melrose Ave., Suite 200, Los Angeles, Calif.
90069

Actress Linda Lavin maintains that she "loved every minute"—"well, almost"—of her nine-year stint in the starring role of CBS television's *Alice*, the popular situation comedy about the plucky, hard-working single mother employed as a waitress at "Mel's Diner." Gratified that her performance in the role helped to inspire single working women and that nevertheless she had not been so typecast in the role as to hinder her in the further pursuit of her career, Miss Lavin has developed her talents in several directions since leaving the television series in 1985.

Returning in the 1986–87 theatre season to the Broadway stage where she had begun her acting career some twenty-five years earlier, Linda Lavin won a Tony award, as well as a Helen Hayes award, an Outer Critics Circle Award, and a Drama Desk Award, for her stunning performance in the role of Kate Jerome, the worn, embittered mother, in the opening run of Neil Simon's smash hit *Broadway Bound*. Branching out into directing and producing, Miss Lavin has, as she told Frank Van Riper of the New York *Daily News* (November 30, 1986), focused upon "exploring the lives of women—real women, living women or fictional women—who took, and take, chances and survive these chances."

Linda Lavin was born in Portland, Maine, on October 15, 1937. Her father, David J. Lavin, owned a flourishing furniture business, and her mother, Lucille (Potter) Lavin, was a concert singer and a local radio and television personality who once sang with Paul Whiteman's band. Miss Lavin learned to sing before she could walk, and she was encouraged by her mother in her love of music and of the theatre. "It was a very musical house to grow up in," she recalled to Frank Van Riper. "There was lots of music and the joy of performing was dominant." She made her first stage appearance at the age of five, as the White Rabbit in a production of *Alice in Wonderland*, at the Wayneflete private school in Portland. Later she studied piano and had thoughts of becoming a concert pianist, until she found out that she had to practice. She would talk to herself in the bathroom mirror, creating characters. "When I was in junior high, I lived a totally secret life!" she told Carolyn See as quoted in *McCall's* magazine (October 1978). "When I'd come home from school. . . . I'd really be sure that *nobody* was home [and] I'd sing. . . . I'd rush the whole length of the kitchen and jump up on the kitchen sink and make believe the sink was four handsome guys in tuxedoes and white socks holding me up."

Miss Lavin acted in high school and in plays produced at the local Jewish community center. By the time she graduated from Deering High School in Portland, she was ready to see more of the world. Although she had planned to attend college in Boston, after visiting a friend at the College of William and Mary in Williamsburg, Virginia, she was so intrigued with an environment that greatly differed from her native New England that she enrolled as a theatre arts major there. Among the roles in which she appeared in college theatrical productions were those of Juliet in *Romeo and Juliet*, Rosalind in *As You Like It*, and Dolly Levi in *The Matchmaker*. She also performed in 1957–58 with the Restoration Players in Williamsburg, and she acted in summer stock at the Camden County Music Circus in New Jersey and with the Edgartown Summer Theatre in Cape Cod.

After graduating from William and Mary in 1959 with a B.A. degree, Linda Lavin headed for New York City. Like thousands of show business aspirants, she was frightened and lonely while trying to "make it" in the big city, where she shared a furnished room with another aspiring actress, Olympia Dukakis. Surviving on as little as $19 a week while working at temporary clerical jobs that she obtained through the Manpower agency, she encountered the frustrating "Catch 22" of show business: she was unable to obtain an acting assignment because she did not have an agent, and she could not get an agent because she did not have a job. The only open auditions were for chorus lines, and Linda Lavin went with hundreds of other applicants to many of those. "You step out on this bare stage and sing 'What a day this has been, what a . . . ' and somebody out in the dark says, 'Thank you,' and you go home," she recalled for Bob MacKenzie in *TV Guide* (October 23, 1976). "This goes on for a while, and each time you get to sing a little more of the song, and finally there comes a day when you get a call back. And now the 100 are down to fifty people. . . . Then it's down to twenty. . . . It gets down to twelve, and everybody is desperate and terrified. . . . And then suddenly you're in the show and life is wonderful."

Linda Lavin made her Off-Broadway debut in the role of Izzy in a Gershwin revival, *Oh, Kay!*, in April 1960, in which she earned $28 a week. Her Broadway debut came at the Billy Rose Theatre in January 1962 in the musical *A Family Affair*. Although the production received less than enthusiastic reviews and closed after sixty-five performances, Miss Lavin, appearing in four small parts—listed in the program as "Wilma," "Crying Daughter," "Fifi of Paris," and "Quiet Girl"—was singled out by the critic Norman Nadel, who wrote in the New York *Herald Tribune* (January 29, 1962): "Linda Lavin . . . builds her own bright fire whenever she steps on stage."

Miss Lavin's next Broadway appearance was in the comedy *The Riot Act*, which ran for forty-four performances at the Cort Theatre, beginning March 7, 1963. As Barbara, the most sophisticated of a triumvirate of prospective brides, she drew some favorable notice from critics. After a stint as the replacement for Rose Gregorio in the role of Evelyn in the Actors Playhouse production *Kiss Mama*, beginning in October 1964, she appeared in April 1965 in the Off-Broadway revue *Wet Paint*, for which she received a Theatre World Award. Then, after performing Off Broadway in *The Game Is Up* and *Hotel Passionate*, she was featured in January 1966 in another Off-Broadway Revue, *The Mad Show*. But although by that time she was attracting increasing attention from reviewers, including Stanley Kauffmann, then with the *New York Times*, who named her "the most promising new personality," Linda Lavin was becoming more and more restive with her roles in frothy musical plays. "I started out to be a dramatic actress," she told Robert Wahls of the New York *Sunday News* (May 22, 1966). "I want to play *Macbeth*."

It was not *Macbeth* but yet another Broadway musical, *It's a Bird, It's a Plane, It's Superman*, that gave Linda Lavin what she has called her "big break." Produced by Hal Prince, it opened at the Alvin Theatre on March 29, 1966, and ran for 129 performances. Although she had originally coveted the female leading role of Lois Lane, her performance as Sydney, the girl Friday of the gossip columnist Max Mencken, enhanced her stature as an actress. But it was only gradually that she obtained more substantial roles. In the fall of 1966 she played Daisy Gamble, opposite Van Johnson, with the national touring company of *On a Clear Day You Can See Forever*, and in November 1967 she opened at the Cort Theatre, in the role of Beth Nemerov, for the 103-performance run of Carl Reiner's comedy *Something Different*.

An important landmark in Linda Lavin's acting career was her performance in the Off-Broadway revival of Jules Feiffer's black comedy *Little Murders*, which opened at the Circle in the Square in Greenwich Village in January 1969. Directed by Alan Arkin, who had been favorably impressed by Miss Lavin in *Superman*, the production met with an ambivalent response from the critics. Its fiercely comic view of the everyday violence of New York repelled some reviewers. Linda Lavin's key role as the daugher, Patsy Newquist, who is shot, randomly, on her wedding day, won her an Outer Critics Circle award and a *Saturday Review* award. Walter Kerr, writing in the *New York Times* (January 26, 1969), found her "delectable at every rough-hewn turn," and Jerry Tallmer observed in the *New York Post* (January 6, 1969): "[Linda Lavin's] wiles have always hitherto eluded me, but now I vote her for President of the world."

Although *Little Murders* went on to run for a total of 400 performances, Linda Lavin left the cast to appear in John Guare's comedy *Cop-Out* for its brief run at the Cort Theatre in April 1969. She and her costar, Ron Leibman, who had met in the summer of 1968, when the play tried out at the Eugene O'Neill Memorial Theatre in Waterford, Connecticut, were married on September 7, 1969. Projecting themselves as a theatrical partnership, they came to be dubbed "the Jewish Lunts" or "the Lunts of the 1970s."

In Neil Simon's long-running comedy *Last of the Red Hot Lovers*, about a middle-aged husband seeking extramarital liaisons to enliven the doldrums of his existence, Linda Lavin played Elaine Navazio, one of three women cast opposite James Coco. Critics differed over the merits of the typically Simonized comedy, which opened at Broadway's Eugene O'Neill Theatre on December 28, 1969, but they gave high marks to Linda Lavin's performance. Jack Kroll in *Newsweek* (January 12, 1970) applauded her "dazzling virtuoso performance," and Stanley Kauffmann in the *New Republic* (February 14, 1970) called her a "superb entertainer," though he detected too much "vaudeville" in her portrayal. In the words of Clive Barnes in the *New York Times* (December 29, 1969), "Linda Lavin, eyebrows flaunting like telegraphed messages, mouth twitching and pouting, voice dry as thunder and with a cough like electric static, is beautiful as Elaine, the sex cat feeling cooly kittenish and looking for a safe tin roof." The performance earned for Miss Lavin a nomination for a Tony award. In July 1970 she was succeeded as Elaine by Rita Moreno.

Linda Lavin herself had mixed feelings about *Last of the Red Hot Lovers*. In a feature article in *Newsday* (January 27, 1970) Jerry Parker, who interviewed her and Ron Leibman, found her "a little defensive about her solid gold Neil Simon hit, as any serious actress in a Neil Simon hit would be." He quoted her as saying: "I love the character I play. . . . I'm glad I'm not in the rest of it. But I don't think I've sold out." A stir was created by another Lavin-Leibman interview, in the *Bergen County Record*, by Emory Lewis, who quoted Miss Lavin as calling Simon "basically a playwright for the lifeless, upper-middle and middle class." Leibman later contended in an interview with Patricia Bosworth in the *New York Times* (May 31, 1970), that he and his wife had been misquoted, but the incident caused tension backstage.

During the 1970s Linda Lavin worked in the theatre from time to time and also taught acting at the Hartman Theatre in Stamford, Connecticut. In November 1970 she replaced Valerie Harper in the stage version of Paul Sills's *Story Theatre*; in 1971 she appeared in summer stock productions at Easthampton, Long Island; in January 1973 she appeared at the Bijou as Leah in the one performance of *The Enemy Is Dead*; in the summer of 1975 she played the Courtesan in Joseph Papp's New York Shakespeare Festival production of *Comedy of Errors* at the Delacorte Theatre in Central Park; in December 1975 she was Tlimpattia in *Dynamite Tonite!* at the Yale Repertory Theatre in New Haven; and in 1979 she played Sonya in a San Diego production of *Uncle Vanya*.

But Linda Lavin was dissatisfied with the range and depth of roles offered to women on the stage and was seeking other avenues to develop her talents. Since 1962 she had occasionally appeared in television productions, including a 1968 Flip Wilson special. As she traveled occasionally to the West Coast over the years she found that an "iron curtain" separated the show business establishments of the two coasts and that despite her Broadway successes she virtually had to start all over again in Hollywood. Discouraged, she tried to put together a nightclub act and was hired for two weeks at a club in Beverly Hills but was not a success. "I sat and cried a lot," she recalled of that time of her life, in an interview with Gaby Rodgers for the *Newsday* magazine (March 11, 1979). "I had to swallow all the anger and pride and start all over again."

In 1974 Linda Lavin met Danny Arnold, the producer-writer for the ABC TV *Barney Miller* show, and within a year he had developed a part especially for her, that of Detective Wentworth. Miss Lavin made five appearances in the role and was also in guest spots on the *Rhoda* and *Phyllis* shows. She made a comedy pilot, *Jerry*, which did not succeed as a series, but the CBS programming chief, Fred Silverman, was so impressed with her that he signed her to a "development agreement," placing her under contract with CBS while the studio decided how to use her talents. Then executives of Warner Brothers, which owned the hit movie *Alice Doesn't Live Here Anymore*, came to CBS with the concept of transforming the film into a television series. Linda Lavin was selected for the title part, and the series began to be shown on August 31, 1976. In the series, Alice is a thirty-five-year-old New Jersey widow who heads west with her twelve-year-old son, hoping to make a career as a professional singer. Stranded in Phoenix, Arizona, she obtains a job as a waitress in Mel's Diner. The relationship between the award-winning film and the new television series was tenuous. A critic for *Variety* (Otober 6, 1976) called the attempted merging of the two a "con job" and maintained that *Alice* was a standard "hash-house sitcom," but as such was a "reasonably good example of the genre." Miss Lavin took her role very seriously. "Comedy is just as truthful, as drama," she told Bob MacKenzie of *TV Guide* (*October 23, 1976*). "The technique should always be toward the emotional truth." She prepared for her role by visiting Phoenix and by writing to the feminist leader Gloria Steinem requesting information about single working mothers.

During its first year the show experienced a rapid turnover of producers and writers. Then, four weeks after the start of the 1977–78 season, Madalyn Davis and Bob Carroll Jr., the team that had produced the *I Love Lucy* shows, took over the production of *Alice*, placing the show on a stronger footing, which it retained until 1985. While conceding that some of the episodes of *Alice* were "silly," Linda Lavin has defended the integrity of the show and its leading character. When she told Beverly Stephen of the New York *Daily News* (February 4, 1980) that *Alice* had changed her life, she was not referring merely to her acting career. Although she had begun the series as a latent feminist, eager to portray a strong woman as well as deep friendships among women, Miss Lavin had not expected the letters she would receive from minimum-wage waitresses and single working mothers, telling her, "Thank you," for portraying their lives and giving them courage.

"*Alice* opened up a world I had no idea about," Linda Lavin told Dave Kaufman of *Variety* (April 24, 1986), "the world of women working in low-paying and non-skilled jobs, who have to fight for benefits, for a quality of life often not within their reach." After receiving the first 00 Percent Award (later called the "Alice"), for the most realistic portrayal of a working woman on television, from the National Commission on Working Women, Miss Lavin became active with that organization and began to speak publicly for the Equal Rights Amendment and the rights of American working women. On her first speaking engagement at an ERA rally, dressed as Alice, in a waitress uniform and apron, she was admittedly "very nervous."

Linda Lavin's feminist commitment was reflected in her direction and production work as well as in her acting. In addition to directing two episodes of *Alice* each year, she engaged in other film projects in which she tried to portray the type of women who could serve as role models. In October 1978 she costarred with Kristy McNichol in the CBS-TV film *Like Mom, Like Me*, about a mother-daughter relationship. Through her own production company Big Deal, Inc., she made the 1979 CBS-TV movie *The $5.20 an Hour Dream*, in which she portrayed a woman factory worker making her way on an otherwise all-male assembly line, and she developed the 1981 MTV film *A Matter of Life and Death* from a story she saw on *60 Minutes* about a remarkable nurse, Joy Ufema, and her work with the terminally ill. *Another Woman's Child*, (1983), also produced through Big Deal, Inc., presented the story of a woman who suddenly becomes a stepmother. On the lighter side, she was featured in a number of musical specials, including the *Hal Linden Special*, presented in April 1979 on ABC-TV. In November 1980 she was host of her own CBS-

TV variety special *Linda in Wonderland*, which critics found "quite delightful."

During her annual leave from *Alice* after the 1983–84 season, Linda Lavin returned to the stage and acted with Robert Brustein's American Repertory Theatre in Cambridge, Massachusetts, playing the role of the Mother in Pirandello's *Six Characters in Search of an Author*. For the same company she also starred as Lady Sneerwell in *A School for Scandal*, under the direction of Jonathan Miller. The 1984–85 season was her last as Alice, and she later told Dave Kaufman of *Variety*: "It's like a death and you grieve for it. It was a great time and a great bond. We were proud of it. . . . " Taking a year off from acting, she coproduced the CBS-TV film *A Place to Call Home*, under the aegis of Big Deal, Inc. Filmed on location, it featured Miss Lavin as an American woman with eleven children who becomes a sheep rancher in Australia.

It was while she was filming in Australia that Linda Lavin first read the script of Neil Simon's new play, *Broadway Bound*, the third of his autobiographical trilogy, following *Brighton Beach Memoirs* and *Biloxi Blues*. Returning to New York, she was the last of the performers to be cast for the play, in the role of Kate Jerome, the aspiring playwright's mother who was at that sad, empty time in her life when her husband leaves her for a more interesting, worldly woman, and her sons have grown up and are also leaving home. Miss Lavin felt a deep kinship with Kate. "She's all of us," she told Deborah Mason of *Vogue* (April 1987). "She's our history . . . , she's the women I grew up with. She's my mother, my grandmother. . . . " The scene in which Kate's husband leaves her was in her view especially poignantly stated by Simon.

After the cast began reading for the play, Simon added one more scene that became the showstopper. He decided that he wanted to show Kate at one moment when she had been happy, so he had her reenact for her grown son one night from her youth, when she was dancing at New York's Primrose Ballroom with George Raft. Leslie Bennetts, in his review in the *New York Times* (December 8, 1986) expressed the sentiment of most of the drama critics—including the minority who did not like the play as a whole—when he wrote that that scene "blazes across the stage like a shooting star, leaving a luminous trail of deeply felt emotion in its wake." Miss Lavin's triumphant return to the Broadway stage was widely hailed, but she herself, calling her Tony award-winning role as Kate "a great gift," insisted, "This is not a return; this is a birth."

After a season in *Broadway Bound*, Linda Lavin decided to move on again. In the late summer of 1987 she announced plans to go to Budapest to make a television movie, to be titled "My Hundred Children," based on a true story about a survivor of the Holocaust who returns to her native Poland after the war to rescue Jewish children left behind. Through Big Deal, Inc., she also plans to develop for CBS-TV a film based on Joy Fielding's "mystery-drama-comedy-romance" novel, *The Deep End*, as well as two television specials for children.

Linda Lavin's first marriage, to Ron Leibman, ended in divorce in 1981. She was married in August 1982 to the actor and director Kip Niven, a widower with two children, Jim and Kate. She is effusive in talking about her life, her work, and her family and is actively involved in the Stepfamily Association of America. After undergoing several years of psychoanalysis, she feels a greater self-assurance and talks candidly about her struggle to learn that acting "is a craft, not a way to get love." She serves on the board of directors of the Academy of Motion Picture Arts and Sciences, and she heads the actors peer group of the Emmy awards committee. A black-eyed brunette, Linda Lavin is under five feet tall and weighs about 100 pounds. Her petite build belies the enormous energy and radiance that she exudes.

References: *McCall's* 106:114+ O '78 por; *N Y Newsday* p75 S 4 '87 por; *Newsday* mag p23+ Mr 11 '79 pors; *Parade* p4+ Jl 24 '83 pors; *People* 9:84+ O 2 '78 pors; *TV Guide* 24:32+ O 23 '76 por; *Notable Names in American Theatre* (1976); *Who's Who in America, 1986–87*; *Who's Who in the Theatre* (1981)

Lawson, Nigel

Mar. 11, 1932– British government official. Address: b. 11 Downing St., London SW1, England

Nigel Lawson, Great Britain's chancellor of the exchequer, has been one of the chief architects of

Prime Minister Margaret Thatcher's so-called new Conservatism, a politically unpopular blend of social security cutbacks and tight money that some observers view as having more rhetoric than substance. If there is a British politician equal to the task of administering strong economic medicine to the country's ailing economy, it is Lawson, an Oxford graduate and former newspaperman with a reputation for never backing down from a political fight. His feisty impatience with the traditional niceties of partisan politics has often alienated people and alerted them to the fact that he is by no means a traditional politician. Lawson says bluntly, "I've never tried to suck up to anybody in my life."

Nigel Lawson was born on March 11, 1932, in London, England, to Ralph and Joan (Davis) Lawson. His grandfather arrived in England from Latvia around 1890, and the original family surname of "Liebson" or "Leibson" was Anglicized during World War I. Lawson told Kenneth Harris of the London Observer (March 10, 1985) that his childhood was spent in a "comfortably off, middle-class home" in the Hampstead district of north London. His father, a self-made tea merchant who had allowed his Judaism to lapse, wanted his only son to take over the family business, but Nigel had neither the inclination nor the tea-sampling palate to do so. When war began in 1939, he and his sister were evacuated from London to avoid the German blitz. He attended seven different primary schools during that disruption of his boyhood. "I didn't enjoy moving around, but it didn't give me any traumas," Lawson told Kenneth Harris.

In 1945, like his father before him, Nigel Lawson enrolled at London's historic Westminster School, where he developed a passion for mathematics and an extracurricular fondness for fencing and skiing. Convinced that the socialistic policies of Prime Minister Clement Atlee's Labour government "went totally against the grain of human nature," he also took a precocious interest in national politics. Aware that he really lacked an aptitude for mathematics, Lawson majored in philosophy, politics, and economics at Christ Church College, Oxford. Oddly enough, apart from belonging to a student Tory dinner club, Lawson showed little interest in partisan politics during his Oxford years, preferring instead to spend his spare time playing poker and acting in the student drama club.

In 1954 Lawson graduated from Oxford with first class honours, and in the following year, while serving a two-year stint in the Royal Navy, married Vanessa Salmon, the daughter of a wealthy caterer. After considering both the law and the diplomatic corps as career options, he took an Oxford counselor's advice that he try his hand at journalism. His first job was as a reporter for the Financial Times, where he worked from 1956 to 1960. Bright and talented, he soon made a name for himself, and in 1961, at the age of twenty-nine, he was appointed the first city editor of the new Sunday Telegraph. With characteristic brashness, Lawson has maintained that his editorship of the newspaper "changed the face of Sunday city journalism" in

Great Britain, but his detractors were less enthusiastic. It has been pointed out that it was while he was editing the Sunday Telegraph that he made the first of a number of serious errors of judgment that have at times thrust him into the limelight for the wrong reasons. He unwisely allowed James Slater, an executive with the British Leyland auto maker, to write a weekly investment column for the paper. Slater made a lot of money by investing in the shares he touted in his column, sometimes selling his interests just as readers were raising stock values by buying in. Although Lawson was unaware of what was happening, he was criticized for his naiveté when word of Slater's tactics became public.

His journalism career having rekindled his political interests, Lawson left the Telegraph in 1963 to accept a job as a speechwriter for Harold Macmillan, at that time the prime minister, but before he could take up his duties, Macmillan was replaced as Conservative party leader by Alec Douglas-Home. Lawson joined the new leader's staff and remained with him through the 1964 general election campaign, which was won by Labour. As it turned out, that period of backroom party work helped Lawson to sort out his own plans. "It was while working for [Douglas-Home] that I first got the idea I would like to go into politics for myself," Lawson recalled for Kenneth Harris. His intentions to seek a House of Commons seat were delayed in October 1965, when he accepted the editorship of the influential conservative weekly magazine the Spectator.

A short while after returning to journalism, Lawson again became embroiled in a controversy brought about by his lack of political acumen. Despite the fact that the Conservatives were harshly critical of government housing mortgages, Lawson took out a £20,000 mortgage on a London home that he and his wife purchased. When word of the transaction leaked out, Lawson came in for criticism from his journalistic competitors and from Labour members of Parliament.

Undaunted, Lawson was still determined to seek election. After unsuccessfully campaigning for Conservative nominations in a couple of London-area ridings, he finally won the nomination in Eton and Slough. But Lawson, an uneasy campaigner, displayed his political inexperience in the 1970 general elections when he focused on immigration quotas as his solution for many of Great Britain's economic woes. The political opposition charged him with racism, and he lost the election. Mark Linton of the New Statesman (March 15, 1985) suggested that Lawson's defeat was as much the result of what he had not done as what he had. "He does not have the ability to communicate warmth and to show respect that are normally part of every politician's armoury," Linton noted.

Lawson regarded his initial political failure as being little more than a temporary setback and immediately began looking for another Conservative nomination. He had set a deadline for himself to be elected to the House of Commons by the time he was forty, and at thirty-eight his time was running out. His efforts took on an added urgency after an election-day demand that he resign as editor of the *Spectator*. Compounding his problems were marital difficulties brought about by some bad investments that almost ruined the family financially. Lawson and his wife were forced to sell their home and move with their children into a rented house in Chelsea.

From 1970 to 1972 Lawson supported himself by working as a free-lance journalist and broadcaster. Then, in 1973, he was appointed a political adviser to Conservative leader Edward Heath, and later in the same year he secured the party's nomination in "politically safe" Blaby, a Conservative stronghold in Leicestershire. He was elected to Parliament as an MP in the 1974 general election. Lawson's outspokenness and abrasiveness won him few friends among the Conservative caucus, though his journalistic celebrity instantly marked him as one of the more high-profile new Tory MPs. His writing also kept him in the limelight, for in addition to producing a number of articles and political pamphlets, he collaborated with the veteran journalist Jock Bruce-Gardyne in 1976 on the books *The Power Game: an Examination of Decision-Making in Government* and *Britain and Canada*. In 1978 he contributed a chapter on trade unionism to a book entitled *The Coming Confrontation*. Lawson's growing political stature was reflected in his appointment in 1976 as Tory whip and in his elevation in 1977 to the party's front benches as opposition spokesman on treasury and economic affairs.

Since his austere economic theories closely paralleled those of Margaret Thatcher, following her election in 1979 as prime minister, Lawson was appointed financial secretary to the Treasury, the number-three position in that powerful and vitally important ministry. Chancellor of the Exchequer Sir Geoffrey Howe recognized Lawson's grasp of economics and began delegating more and more duties to him. Susan Crosland of the London *Sunday Times* (March 11, 1984) observed, "The medium-term financial strategy—embodying monetarism in the government's program—was Lawson's idea."

Nigel Lawson spelled out his philosophy in detail in an important speech, delivered in August 1980, that was later published as a pamphlet entitled *The New Conservatism*. He charged that British Conservatives had in recent years strayed from their historic values in favor of state interventionism. "The distinctive feature of the new Conservatism is its rejection of these false trails and its return to the mainstream," Lawson wrote. The new Thatcher government, he explained, had embarked on a form of "counter-revolution," based on a "medium-term financial strategy" grounded in monetarist theory and designed to limit price increases, curb the deficit, and reduce taxes.

Although Lawson's articulation of the "new Conservatism" and his initial political successes ensured his rapid rise through the ranks of the Conservative party under the friendly aegis of Margaret Thatcher, it was not without its price, and the long hours that he spent in tending to his official duties exacted a toll on Lawson's family life. The British media reported in sordid detail both the painful breakup of his twenty-five year marriage to Vanessa Salmon and his subsequent marriage to Thérèse Mary Maclear, a Parliamentary library researcher.

In 1981 Margaret Thatcher rewarded Lawson's service at the Treasury by bringing him into the cabinet in a junior position as secretary for energy. Despite the fact that he alienated some of his colleagues as a "know-it-all," Lawson performed more than competently in his new responsibilities. His adroit handling of government negotiations with militant coal miners and his successful sale to the private sector of the assets of the publicly owned Britoil PLC and portions of British Gas led to speculation that he had been earmarked by the prime minister to return to the Treasury as successor to Sir Geoffrey Howe in the powerful exchequer's role.

That speculation proved to be correct when on June 10, 1983, the day after her second general election victory, Margaret Thatcher announced her new cabinet. Nigel Lawson replaced Sir Geoffrey Howe, who was shifted to the Foreign Office. The new chancellor of the exchequer wasted no time in announcing his plans for the troubled economy, citing reduced inflation as one of his main goals. Then, just a few weeks later, he spelled out the details of cuts to trim half a billion pounds (then about $750 million) in public spending and to sell a like amount of government interest in the British Petroleum Company. "I see no advantage in the state owning industry," Lawson said. His tough talk continued when he rose in the House of Commons on November 17 of that year to deliver an autumn economic statement. He cautioned that a slight tax increase might be needed in 1985 to keep the deficit at about £8 billion ($12 billion), pledged to continue his denationalization program, and warned of coming cuts in government spending. Reaction to his speech was predictably mixed.

As the March 13, 1984, date of Lawson's first budget approached, there was intense lobbying both by those who wanted the government to curb its spending and by those who demanded that Lawson move to help Britain's three million unemployed. In what an *Economist* (March 17, 1984) editorial hailed as "an imaginative budget," Lawson steered a wily middle course, opting to broaden the tax base and "to stop reducing budget deficits after a sleight-of-hand showpiece this year, to accept an annual 3 to 5 percent as the target inflation rate for the rest of this Parliament and to use the small resultant leeway to introduce a budget aimed at securing the maximum possible reduction in unemployment."

Lawson's carefully planned economic strategy was upset by the controversy over the collapse in September 1984 of a London bank, by Britain's growing trade deficit, and by a sharp drop in world oil prices that led to greatly reduced income from sales of North Sea oil. The value of the pound in relation to the U.S. dollar plummeted, hitting an all-time low of $1.09 in February 1985, while unemployment reached 14 percent. A poll by the London *Sunday Times* found that four out of every five Britons felt that Lawson was mismanaging the economy. But he seemed indifferent to the polls and in a speech to the Overseas Bankers Club repeated his commitment to monetarism "for the good reason that it has achieved what it set out to achieve"—reduced inflation. He angrily blamed American economic policies and the "overvalued dollar" as the causes of Great Britain's woes.

With Margaret Thatcher's backing, Lawson responded to the crisis with his annual March budget. Clinging to a policy of fiscal restraint, he announced further cuts in the deficit and moved to spur the hiring of young, unskilled, low-income workers by reducing employer social security contributions for that group. Although the *Economist* (March 23, 1985) termed Lawson's budget a "cautious" document for "jobs and enterprise," William Keegan of the *Observer* (March 24, 1985) was less kind, calling it a "non-budget" that confirmed the death of British monetarism. By April, however, the economic crisis had eased on interest rates, and the value of the pound crept slowly upwards. The likelihood of a fourth straight year of expansion for the British economy prompted Lawson to proclaim that "the days when Britain was the 'sick old man of Europe' have gone for good." Unfortunately, the boast proved premature.

It was evident that the British government was still having serious trouble in controlling public sector wages, social security costs, and overall spending, which the London *Sunday Times* (October 20, 1985) reported was actually rising faster under Margaret Thatcher than it had under the last Labour administration. There was evidence, too, of a growing cabinet rift between Lawson and other "dries," who favored further spending cuts, and such "wets" as Secretary of State and Social Security Norman Fowler, who pressed for more social-welfare spending. As the cabinet debate intensified after a series of crushing Conservative by-election defeats, media speculation grew about a "U-turn" on the prime minister's much publicized pledge to reduce taxes.

Although he remained publicly committed to his policy of restraint, observers began noticing subtle shifts in Lawson's approach. He made no mention of tax cuts in his July speech to Oxford University Tories, and he hinted that the Treasury was ready to be more "flexible" in its attitudes. A short time later, as he moved to deregulate the stock market and implement innovative tax reforms intended to encourage employee share ownership, Lawson began touting "the virtues of the people's capitalism," a slogan coined in the 1960s by Keith Fowler, at the time the president of the New York Stock Exchange.

It was by now evident that Lawson had limited room for political maneuvering. His only means of achieving tax cuts while still maintaining vital social services was to speed up sales of Crown assets, which critics likened to "selling the family silver" for short-term gain. Lawson's annual autumn economic statement reflected the government's reluctance to commit itself to a program of accelerated denationalization. While promising a spring tax cut, to be financed by the sale of British Gas Corporation assets, the chancellor delighted Tory "wets" with a pledge of higher government spending for housing, roads, and health.

Despite a further plunge in the market price for North Sea oil in the first three months of 1986, from $29 to $15 per barrel, a drop of 7.5 percent in the pound, and a slight jump in interest rates, Great Britain's economic prospects seemed brighter. On March 18, 1986, Lawson announced a continuation of his policies in another cautious budget. In addition to promising a modest tax cut, he predicted lower than expected public sector borrowing and raised the prospect of employee profit-sharing incentives to revitalize the private sector, an idea he presented in a detailed study paper for the National Economic Development Council in May.

Meanwhile, Lawson gave further indications of his new policy initiatives in a speech he made that spring to the Lombard Association, in which he promised a more "pragmatic" approach to the economy. That pragmatism was put to the test in September 1986, when it was revealed that the country was suffering from a potentially disastrous trade imbalance, made worse by the continuing high value of the American dollar. Aware of the danger of inflation, Lawson raised interest rates slightly to prop up the pound, a strategy that seemed to satisfy the British public. And when in November of 1986 Lawson announced a £4.7 billion increase in public spending, the Conservatives surged ahead of the opposition Labour party in public opinion polls by four percentage points. While Tory "wets" were delighted with the looser purse strings, the party's right wing began grumbling that Lawson, originally viewed as too much of an economist to succeed politically, was now too much of a politician to remake Britain's stultified economy. A writer for the *Manchester Guardian* weekly (November 16, 1986) speculated that the increased level of social security spending suggested that Margaret Thatcher was already planning for a general election. An editorial in the *Economist* (November 15, 1986) chastised the government, pointing out that in spite of rhetoric, government spending in 1986 was 16.9 percent higher in real terms than it had been in 1979, when the prime minister came to power.

Taking advantage of an unexpected surplus in tax revenues of £5.5 billion, Lawson drew up for fiscal 1987-88 a "prudent and responsible" budget that called for, among other things, a cut in the basic income-tax rate from 29 to 27 percent, the introduction of measures designed to help lower-income groups, and a reduction in public borrowing. The chancellor outlined his proposals in a speech to the House of Commons on March 17,

1987. The next day, Britain's major banks, buoyed by his pledge to trim government borrowing, lowered their base lending rate by half a point, to 10 percent. Denouncing Lawson's plan as a pre-election "bribes budget," Neil Kinnock, the Labour leader, told reporters, as quoted in the *New York Times* (March 18, 1987), "It is a budget that has little to do with the general good and has everything to do with the general election."

A chunky, reddish-haired man, Nigel Lawson has been described by Ian Aitken of the *Guardian* as bearing "a striking resemblance to an old-fashioned Victorian villain." But despite his prickly political image and workaholic tendencies, there is a more genial side to him. "I have always believed private life is more important than public life, though [my wife] will never believe this now,"

Lawson told Susan Crosland of the London *Sunday Times* (March 11, 1984). Lawson is the father of six children: a son and three daughters by his first wife, who died in 1985, and a son and daughter by his present wife. Those who know him say Lawson is a warm, generous man and an engaging conversationalist with a passion for good food and drink. His friend and political colleague Cecil Parkinson has observed: "If you like him, as I do, you like him enormously. But he's not for public consumption. What is for public consumption is Nigel's competence and guts, and he's got both in enormous measure."

References: London Observer p19+ Mr 10 '85; Spec 258:8+ Mr 21 '87; International Who's Who, 1986-87; Who's Who, 1987-1988; Who's Who in the World, 1984-85

Lehrer, James (Charles)

May 19, 1934- Broadcast journalist; author. Address: b. MacNeil/Lehrer NewsHour, 3620 27th St. S., Arlington, Va. 22206

The veteran journalist Jim Lehrer is the coanchor and associate editor, together with Robert Mac-Neil, of the *MacNeil/Lehrer NewsHour*, the award-winning news program broadcast each weeknight on nationwide public television. Featuring in-depth coverage of a few selected stories, the *NewsHour*, which originated as a half-hour program in 1975, was fashioned by MacNeil and Lehrer with a view to providing a serious alternative to the news shows seen on the major networks.

Lehrer is known for his low-key, nonconfrontational style of interviewing guests and for his skill in adapting techniques of newspaper reportage to live television. Robert Wilson, who as executive vice-president of the Dallas public television station, KERA-TV, gave Lehrer his first broadcasting job almost twenty years ago, finds that success has not changed Lehrer's down-to-earth Southwestern style: "He hasn't succumbed to East Coast journalism. He doesn't go to London to buy his suits. I see Jim as a populist, a surrogate for the audience."

James Charles Lehrer was born in Wichita, Kansas, on May 19, 1934, the younger son of Harry Frederick Lehrer and Lois Catherine (Chapman) Lehrer. Lehrer's grandfather on his mother's side was a fundamentalist preacher who founded his own denomination, and his paternal grandfather was a German immigrant plumber who subscribed to the belief that America was truly a land of opportunity for hardworking people. Jim's mother taught English and Latin before going to Washington to work for the War Department, where she met Harry Lehrer when he was in the Marine Corps. Until 1946 his father worked for the Santa Fe Trailways bus company; he then formed his own independent line, Kansas Central Lines, serving passengers out of Wichita, Kansas, with three rattletrap buses: Betsy, Susie, and Lena. Jim Lehrer and his older brother, Fred, pitched in to help their father, who was endowed with energy and enthusiasm but had very little capital. The journalist has recounted the vicissitudes of that short-lived family-run enterprise in the affectionate memoir *We Were Dreamers* (Atheneum, 1975). After bankruptcy put an end to their moribund bus line, in 1947, the Lehrers moved to Beaumont, Texas, in 1948, and then to San Antonio.

Although Lehrer had once aspired to follow his father into the bus business, during World War II his journalistic ambitions were reinforced by reading such newspaper columnists as Robert Ruark and the famous war correspondent Ernie Pyle.

"Boy, that's what I wanted to be," he recalled during an interview with Van Wallach for *Continental* magazine (May, 1986). He first became involved in journalism when his high school English teacher in Beaumont, impressed by an essay he had written on Dickens' *A Tale of Two Cities,* urged him to write for the school newspaper. Lehrer decided to cover sports, since the school was sports-oriented, and not being athletic himself, he found "the best way to get around sports was to be a sports writer." Later, when his family moved to San Antonio, he edited Jefferson High School's student newspaper. Lehrer obtained an associate arts degree from Victoria College, a junior college, in 1954 and continued his higher education at the University of Missouri, from which he received his B.A. degree in journalism in 1956.

After his graduation, Lehrer enlisted in the United States Marine Corps, like his father and brother before him, and served as a Third Division infantry officer in a tour of duty that he spent largely on Okinawa. He later took charge of the camp newspaper, *The Boot,* at the Parris Island Marine training camp in South Carolina. Following his discharge from the Marine Corps as a captain in 1959, Lehrer was hired as a political reporter for the *Dallas Morning News.* Among his early stories was an investigation of alleged Communists in Texas, and his series of articles on "Barbecue Bolshevism," which demonstrated that there was little substance to the rumors, won him several awards. He also reported on the John Birch Society without any editorial interference, but encountered resistance when he submitted a series on a civil defense organization in Dallas that had become a source for dispensing right wing propaganda. Angered by the paper's refusal to run the articles, Lehrer resigned. "I literally emptied out my desk drawer," he told Van Wallach, "walked out, and never went back." The fact that he immediately got another job—on the rival paper, the *Dallas Times Herald,* led Lehrer to believe that he would, in the future, be able to stick to his ideological guns. "It planted in me the idea that I have marketable skills and that there are limits on what I have to do and not do," he said. At the *Dallas Times Herald,* Lehrer covered the courts from 1959 until 1966, when he became a political columnist. One of his pieces, which "raised a lot of hackles" in the Dallas establishment, described an imaginary secret meeting between the local Democratic and Republican party bosses. "I wrote they were going to merge," Lehrer said, "because they had become so similar and conservative."

During that period, in his spare time, Lehrer also began writing fiction. His novel *Viva Max!,* published in 1966 by Duell, Sloan and Pearce, tells how a Mexican general, Maximilian Rodríguez de Santos, decides to recapture the Alamo, triggering an international incident. "The serious overtones are few," Lehrer wrote in a brief explanatory piece that appeared in the *Library Journal* (February 1, 1966), "but basically I try to show through the Mexican general—Max—the need in all of us to be rec-

ognized for something—anything." *Viva Max!* was made into an unsuccessful movie in 1969, starring Peter Ustinov and Jonathan Winters.

In 1968 Lehrer was named city editor of the *Dallas Times Herald,* but he left the paper in 1969, hoping to devote himself full time to writing fiction, while living off the royalties from his novel and its movie sale, a decision he later came to regret. When, in 1970, he accepted an offer for a part-time position as a consultant for KERA-TV, the public television station in Dallas, he entered the field of broadcast journalism. He then served as the station's executive director of public affairs, and, with the help of a Ford Foundation grant, also edited and hosted a nightly newscast called *Newsroom.* Among the then unusual features of the program were its hiring of a black reporter and its consumer and media coverage.

Moving to Washington, D.C., in 1972, Lehrer briefly occupied a position as the first public affairs coordinator for the Public Broadcasting Service. Although he planned to advocate more public affairs programming on public television, Lehrer arrived at PBS at a time when it had come under siege by the Nixon administration, which viewed such programming as overly liberal, and which, through the offices of the Corporation for Public Broadcasting, had reduced funding for news and information programs. According to *Variety* (January 17, 1973), "the Texan [Lehrer] had high hopes of running a tough, independent operation," but his efforts to introduce controversial programming were blocked, and Lehrer resigned his position within a year.

Trying to remain in public television, Lehrer moved in 1973 to WETA-TV, the PBS station in Washington, where he became a correspondent for the PBS news service, known as the National Public Affairs Center for Television. There he became friends with another correspondent, the Canadian broadcast journalist Robert MacNeil, who had been a reporter for NBC-TV and the BBC. Replacing Sander Vanocur, Lehrer joined Robert MacNeil and Peter Kaye as one of the commentators on *America '73,* a weekly documentary with a news magazine format. "We learned a lot from each other," MacNeil told Van Wallach. "I could tell him a few things about TV technology, but . . . he did a great deal to improve my interview style. I painfully learned from Lehrer that some of the most effective questions are 'Why?' 'I don't understand,' and 'Could you say that again?' His informality has eased me up a lot."

During 1973 Lehrer and MacNeil coanchored the PBS telecasts of the Senate Watergate hearings that investigated the role of Nixon administration officials in the notorious 1972 burglary of the Democratic National Headquarters. Their unique coverage, consisting of live, uninterrupted "gavel to gavel" broadcasts of the hearings, attracted considerable attention from viewers and demonstrated conclusively the ability of public television to cover major news stories.

Robert MacNeil recalled in his memoir *The Right Place at the Right Time* (1982): "To Lehrer and me, the moment seemed supremely ripe to take what we both considered the next logical step, a nightly news program to put public television firmly in the business of regular journalism." Although at first they could not muster enough support, by 1975, WNET, the public television affiliate for metropolitan New York, offered MacNeil the opportunity to produce just such a program, and MacNeil, as executive editor, chose Lehrer as his coanchorman. Following the format of the *Huntley-Brinkley Report*, a popular NBC news program for many years, MacNeil and Lehrer coanchored the program from bases in New York and Washington, respectively. In other respects, however, MacNeil and Lehrer decided, in the former's words, "that if public television was to have its own nightly news program, it had better be as different as possible from commercial television." Instead of presenting a stream of images, MacNeil and Lehrer focused each night on a single topic, interviewing a small number of guests. The program was designed to serve as a supplement to the nightly newscasts on the major networks and was therefore scheduled to follow them. Originally called *The Robert MacNeil Report* when it made its debut in October 1975, its title was changed to *The MacNeil/Lehrer Report* when WETA in Washington began coproducing the show a year later, and Lehrer was named associate editor.

Among the early shows that attracted much attention and critical praise were interviews with the Shah of Iran in 1977, before his departure from government, and with the Ayatollah Ruholla Khomeini while he was still in exile in France. Lehrer and MacNeil also questioned General Anastasio Somoza, the president of Nicaragua, while a revolution was brewing in that country, and Anwar Sadat, then president of Egypt. Although the majority of programs focused on issues in politics, business, economics, and foreign affairs, they made several attempts at a lighter touch. One show, for example, found MacNeil and Lehrer discussing the social significance of a new brand of potato chips and another, the tastelessness of contemporary tomatoes. By 1979 the *MacNeil/Lehrer Report* had gained a national audience of about four million each week, making it the most watched show on public television. According to a Roper Poll conducted in 1978, its viewers tended to be college-educated Americans earning above average salaries, but the show also had a high percentage of blue-collar viewers with lower incomes.

The *MacNeil/Lehrer Report* won considerable critical praise. Writing in the *New York Times* (March 4, 1979), Edwin Diamond asserted that the program's hosts "have gradually created one of the best half-hours of news on television without 'visuals' at all; the major elements of the program are the interviewers themselves, always prepared with good questions, and the quality of their guests, always specialists on the night's single topic and almost always capable of speaking fresh, intelligent thoughts."

In analyzing the difference between the MacNeil/Lehrer report and network television's approach, Andrew Kopkind wrote in the *Columbia Journalism Review* (September–October 1979): "The structure of any *MacNeil/Lehrer Report* is composed of talking heads rather than explosive images, of conversation covering several points of view rather than a homogeneous statement of the world's condition, of panels of experts, proposals for policy, and the sense of incompleteness—and therefore of possibility—rather than a feeling of finality." Kopkind pointed out that the approach had its drawbacks. He noted that Gar Alperovitz, a liberal economist and political activist who appeared on the program, "felt frustrated by the format of the show, by its willful incompleteness, and by the insistence that adversaries debate, rather than project new ideas." Kopkind acknowledged that the aim of the show is to be objective, or nonpartisan, but noted, "Objectivity . . . may be illusory in a specific application."

The success of *The MacNeil/Lehrer Report* brought both men lucrative offers from the major television networks, which they declined, despite the increasingly uncertain federal funding for public television. Instead, hoping to become an alternative to network news, rather than merely a supplement, they decided to expand the format of the *MacNeil/Lehrer Report* to a full hour. In 1982 they offered PBS affiliates, whose approval was necessary for such a step, a proposal for a distinctive "truly national" hour-long program with a new format featuring several mini-documentaries in each program, as well as occasional film and book reviews. AT&T, which had underwritten the program since 1981, agreed to increase its funding to $10 million annually, so that public broadcasting channels would not be asked for additional funds. Although the PBS affiliates were wary, they finally approved the hour-long show in January 1983. Judy Woodruff and Kwame Holman were added to the team, which had already taken on Charlayne Hunter-Gault as the third anchor in 1978.

When *The MacNeil/Lehrer NewsHour*, as the show was retitled, had its premiere on September 5, 1983, it received a mixed response. In the *New York Times* (September 12, 1983) John Corry, while praising its principals as "the only two major anchors who actually practice journalism," complained that the show's content now seemed "padded." "One of its strengths is that it is not afraid to be boring; one of its weaknesses is that sometimes it *is* boring." Although the show retained its customary share of the news audience, PBS affiliates were disappointed that, as the season progressed, the hour format failed to attract the number of viewers that had been anticipated.

After suffering a heart attack in December 1983, Lehrer took leave from his broadcasting duties for several months to recover from double-bypass heart surgery. He returned to *The MacNeil/Lehrer NewsHour* in March 1984, at the same time that more than 100 PBS affiliates were agreeing to help underwrite the program for the following season. The considerable facelifting of the show's format over the following year contributed to a significant increase in the size of its audience, now estimated at twelve million viewers a week. Revising his initial assessment of the hour-long program in the *New York Times* (December 29, 1985), John Corry wrote, "They [MacNeil and Lehrer] are the best that public television currently has to offer."

During his convalescence from heart surgery, Lehrer began trying out his skills as a playwright. His friend, the well-known Mississippi novelist Eudora Welty, asked Lehrer to submit his plays to the annual "Eudora Welty New Plays Series." Subsequently, two of his plays—*Cedar Chest*, a black comedy that takes place in a Kansas City pharmacy, and *Silversides Thruliner*, which has as its background a Texas bus depot—were given readings by the New Stage Theatre in Jackson, Mississippi. Another of Lehrer's plays, *Chili Queen*, received an Off-Off-Broadway workshop performance at the Hartley House Theatre in New York by Playwright's Preview Productions in November 1986. Stephen Holden of the *New York Times* (November 26, 1986) called it "a small dark comedy that reserves its sharpest satirical jabs for the way television packages daily events while coolly manipulating the hapless participants," as well as "a reasonably well-constructed seriocomic vignette with dialogue and performances that transcend the stereotypical." *Chili Queen* was later staged at the Kennedy Center's Terrace Theater in Washington, D.C.

As a copartner with MacNeil in MacNeil-Lehrer Productions, which produces TV documentaries and special programs, Lehrer hosted two PBS specials in 1986, *My Heart, Your Heart*, a one-hour special on heart disease, which received an award from the American Heart Association as well as an Emmy and *The Heart of the Dragon*, a twelve-part series on life in today's China.

On June 4, 1960, Jim Lehrer married a schoolteacher, Kate Tom Staples, who recently has turned to writing fiction. She is the author of a novel, *Best Intentions* which was published by Little, Brown in 1987. The Lehrers have three daughters, Jamie, Lucy, and Amanda. Jim Lehrer stands five feet nine inches tall, has brown eyes and brown hair, and weighs 160 pounds. Writing about Lehrer for *TV Guide* (January 23, 1982), Paul Droesch described him as a "decidedly unblow-dried" man who "dresses in the rumpled, loosened-tie fashion of the newspaper city editor he once was." He is known to have a temper, and Robert MacNeil has called him "so emotional he can cry at a bad commercial." According to the *TV Guide* article, Lehrer and his coanchor "Robin" MacNeil are close friends off-camera. Their families take vacations together, stay at one another's homes, and share a passion for French cuisine. Lehrer enjoys tennis and boasts that he has "the finest collection of bus depot signs in America." Trailways, Greyhound, and lesser-known signs adorn the walls of his Washington office, and the basement of his home enshrines a collection of model buses, driv-

ers' badges, and other memorabilia. His brother, Fred, now a minister in Tennessee, also collects bus souvenirs, and they often swap their finds.

Over the years, *The MacNeil/Lehrer NewsHour* and its predecessor, *The MacNeil/Lehrer Report*, have been honored with more than thirty awards for broadcasting excellence, including a George Foster Peabody Award (1977), a Dupont-Columbia Award (1976–77), and the National Academy of Television Arts and Sciences Citation for Outstanding Achievement in Broadcast Journalism (1977). Lehrer himself was given the George Polk Award in 1974 for his coverage of the Watergate hearings, the Silver Gavel Certificate of Merit of the American Bar Association, the George Foster Peabody Award, and an Emmy for outstanding achievement in coverage of special events.

Jim Lehrer has lectured and taken part in symposia on the role of the media. Speaking at a symposium on the press in Austin, Texas, he decried elitism in journalistic circles. In his remarks, reprinted in Channel Thirteen's *Dial* (April 1983), he noted: "I think our major problem, our real problem is that somehow we have gotten it into our heads that we are truly the special people of this world, because we happened into journalism. . . . We became privileged people, above all laws, above all rules that the rest of society has to play by." And in an address entitled "Why Do Americans Hate the News Media?" he told a graduation forum at Brown University: "Objectivity is almost impossible. Fairness is never impossible. . . . And all that people have a right to expect is that they will be treated fairly."

References: Columbia Journalism Review p31+ S/O 1979 por; Continental p53+ My '86 por; TV Guide p11+ Ja '82 por, p16 O 3 '87 por; Washington Post D p1+ Jl 17 '87 por; Lehrer, James. We Were Dreamers (1975); Who's Who in America, 1984–85

Levi, Primo
(lâ've prē'mō)

July 31, 1919– Italian writer; chemist. Address: h. Corso Re Umberto 75, Turin 10128, Italy

BULLETIN: Primo Levi died in Turin, Italy on April 11, 1987. *Obituary:* N Y Times I p42 Ap 12 '87

The world-renowned Italian novelist Italo Calvino regarded his compatriot Primo Levi as "one of the most important and gifted writers of our time," an opinion with which another Italian literary giant, Umberto Eco, concurs. Levi's *Survival in Auschwitz*, written soon after World War II and considered a classic in Italy, charts the hell of the Holocaust, detailing with firsthand knowledge but without personal rancor, the degradation, anguish,

Primo Levi

and despair of the Nazi concentration camp. In that masterpiece and in his later work—memoirs, short stories, essays and novels, some of them witty celebrations of the joy and freedom to be found in work—Levi, a chemist, combines the close observation of a scientist with the insight of a philosopher and the imagination and verbal elegance of a poet.

Primo Levi's home in Turin, Italy, is the apartment where he was born, on July 31, 1919, to assimilated middle-class Jewish parents, Cesare Levi, a civil engineer, and Ester (Luzzati) Levi. His ancestors had settled in the Piedmont, in northern Italy, following the expulsion of the Jews from Spain in the late fifteenth century, and his more immediate older relatives spoke a jargon that combined Hebrew roots of words with Piedmontese endings and inflections. The language is seldom heard nowadays, but belongs among Levi's boyhood memories, as do his Sunday visits to his grandmother with his father: "We walked slowly down Via Po, and he stopped to caress all the cats, sniff at all the truffles, and leaf through all the secondhand books," Levi recalled in the first chapter, "Argon," of *The Periodic Table*. When his grandmother opened the door to them, his father would shout, "He's at the head of his class."

On completing his classical, or humanist, high school education, Levi enrolled in the University of Turin to study chemistry. In another essay, "Iron," of *The Periodic Table* he explained that as a student he believed "that the nobility of Man . . . lay in making himself the conqueror of matter" and that to conquer matter he must understand the universe and himself. Chemistry, moreover, counteracted "all the dogmas, all the unproved affirmations, all the imperatives" of Fascism. "Iron" celebrates Levi's "comradeship," as he terms it, with a fellow student, Sandro Delmastro. As if in preparation for what lay ahead, he learned from Sandro the skills of mountain climbing, lessons in endurance, self-discipline, and withstanding hardship. In accounting, however, for his survival in Auschwitz, Levi has said that other factors overshadowed his training in mountain climbing. Curiously, as David Denby pointed out in the *New Republic* (July 28, 1986), in the concentration camp "Levi moved through physical sensation the way a mountain climber negotiates the varied abutments and hollows of his terrain—now relaxing, now stiffening, now guarding for a fall."

Despite Mussolini's anti-Semitic laws of 1938, which barred Jews from attending institutions of higher learning, among other activities, Levi continued to study at the University of Turin, and in July 1941 he was awarded his B.S. degree *summa cum laude*. With difficulty he found a job in the laboratory of a Milan pharmaceutical factory, conducting research on a cure for diabetes. In his spare time he wrote poetry. With the collapse of Mussolini's regime in the summer of 1943 and the subsequent Nazi occupation of northern Italy, Levi fled to the mountains to join ten of his friends in forming a guerrilla band that they intended to affiliate with the resistance organization known as Giustizia e Libertà (Justice and Liberty).

Untrained, virtually unarmed, cold and hungry, the small band was an easy target of betrayal. At dawn on December 13, 1943, Levi was captured by the Fascist militia of the newly formed, Nazi-protected Republic of Saló. When he identified himself as "an Italian citizen of the Jewish race," the militia duly turned him over to the Nazi SS. In February 1944 the Nazis loaded him and some 650 other Jews onto enclosed cattle cars of a freight train and transported them slowly from the detention camp at Fossoli to the concentration camp at Auschwitz in Upper Silesia. There they were dispersed—more than 500 of them to the gas chamber and the others to Monowitz-Buna and Birkenau. Of the 650 who left Italy with Levi, only about twenty ever came back.

In that first "selection," as on similar later occasions, Levi had the advantage of physical fitness. His destination was the camp that supplied the slave labor for the I. G. Farbenindustrie synthetic rubber factory at Monowitz-Buna. The Nazi process of dehumanizing Jewish prisoners began with depriving them of their sense of identity. Levi exchanged his name for the number 174517, tattooed on his left arm, his clothes for flea-ridden "rags," and his hair for instant baldness. Habits of civilized behavior steadily diminished among the inmates, and previously accepted notions of morality yielded to the realization that a man would probably starve unless he stole his neighbor's bread.

For some months Levi was assigned to strenuous outdoor labor, mainly on the construction of the rubber factory, which, despite the countless lives it cost, never did produce a single pound of rubber. Before the onset of winter weather, however, he was transferred, on the basis of his training in chemistry, to the factory's laboratory. And it was to that relatively privileged indoor job that he has attributed in part his survival in Auschwitz. Another factor in his survival was his friendship with an Italian mason Lorenzo, who, as a "voluntary" civilian worker, had access to certain food supplies. Although his contact with a prisoner, apart from work, was illegal, every day for six months he brought Levi a container of soup to add to a daily ration that fell below the subsistence level.

Above all, Levi believes, he owed his survival to luck. By luck, or chance, he fell ill of scarlet fever in January 1944, shortly before the advance of the Red Army forced the Germans to evacuate Auschwitz. He could not, therefore, join the march in the snow of some 20,000 departing prisoners, virtually all of whom perished. Left in the infirmary to die, Levi nevertheless found the means to keep himself alive and help others until the arrival of the Russians ten days later, near the end of January. The following month he embarked on a long, roundabout journey back to Italy.

During his ten months in Auschwitz, Levi had a recurring dream, one common to prisoners there, that when he reached home and told his family and friends what had happened to him, no one paid attention. The dream was a nightmare because the determination to bear witness was sustaining his will to live. As soon as he returned to Turin he wrote out everything his memory held, in details so clear that he might have experienced them the day before. Within a few months he had completed his book Se questo è un uomo (If This Is a Man). A small Turin publishing firm, F. de Silva, accepted it in 1947, but printed only 2,500 copies. Levi's work therefore received scant notice until Giulio Einaudi Editore, after some hesitation, republished it in 1958. Since then the book has sold well over 500,000 copies in Italy, has been translated into eight languages, and has appeared under the title If This Is a Man in England (Bodley Head, 1966) and in the United States (Orion, 1959) and also in the United States under the title Survival in Auschwitz, the Nazi Assault on Humanity (Collier, 1961).

Einaudi's initial reluctance to accept Levi's memoir, as Bernard Knox suggested in the New York Review of Books (August 18, 1983), may be ascribed to its absence of hatred toward the Germans. Levi has explained that he preferred the role of witness to that of victim or avenger partly because he wanted to assure the credibility of his account—and let the reader be the judge—and partly because if he were to direct hatred against an entire ethnic or national group, he would be obeying the precepts of Nazism.

Survival in Auschwitz, in which Levi sought "to furnish documentation for a quiet study of the human mind," owes much of its distinction, in fact, among concentration camp narratives to its very tone—an absence of self-pity and personal bitterness and, for all its specificity, of indulgence in the lurid and morbid. "In some ways the book is less a memoir than a sociological and psychological

study elevated into a work of art," Fernanda Eberstadt wrote of Survival in Auschwitz in Commentary (October 1985). She praised among other qualities, Levi's "gently mocking wit, which harps upon the droll and comical aspects of human degradation as a way of making bearable an outrage too massive to endure." Regardless of certain weaknesses, she concluded, it remains "one of the finest literary works of its kind, a book whose low clear tones long echo in the reader's imagination." Denby, too, in the New Republic credited Survival in Auschwitz with "an emotional power entirely disproportionate to its size and ambition." As "a stark prose-poem on the deepest suffering of man" and "one of the most remarkable documents" he had read, Levi's book seemed to David Caute, reviewing it in the New Statesman (March 19, 1960), to belong "in a class of its own."

Resuming his work in chemistry after the war, in 1946 Levi learned the fundamentals of varnish-making in a large paint factory, DUCO-Montecatini. About a year later he began his long association with SIVA, a Turin factory specializing in paints, enamels, and synthetic resins, of which he became general manager in 1961. Although he had written poems and stories before the war, Levi has said repeatedly that he would not have become a writer if it had not been for his need to tell about Auschwitz. When the republication of Survival in Auschwitz in 1958 brought him postponed acclaim, he saw the possibility of a literary future and proceeded to write down post-Auschwitz adventures that he had been recounting to people around him for years.

Levi's sequel to Survival in Auschwitz explains how his exile from Italy became prolonged by about ten months. Written fourteen years after his first book, La tregua (The Truce) was published by Einaudi in 1963, by the Bodley Head in England in 1965 under the title The Truce: A Survivor's Journey Home from Auschwitz, and by Little, Brown in the United States in 1965 under the title The Reawakening. Summit Books reissued Survival in Auschwitz and The Reawakening in a single volume in 1985. After his release from the camp into a bomb-devastated world that, as he said, "seemed to have returned to primeval Chaos," Levi was sent first to transit camps in Poland, where he began to regain his health. Then he boarded a freight car that took him not, as he expected, south to Italy, but instead north to a White Russian village near Minsk. There he spent the summer before traveling by train for more than a month through Eastern Europe and across Austria to the Brenner Pass and home. Upbeat in mood, Levi makes his senseless, haphazard journey a metaphor of his physical and spiritual recuperation and of a battered civilization's recovery.

In his conversation with Philip Roth, published in the New York Times Book Review (October 12, 1986) and the London Review of Books (October 23, 1986), Levi noted that The Reawakening is "a more 'self-conscious' book, more methodical, more literary" than Survival in Auschwitz. "I gave emphasis to strange, exotic, cheerful episodes," he said, "—mainly to the Russians seen close up." Irving Howe called attention in the *New York Review of Books* (March 28, 1985) to a nervous tension between "the external form of the narrative and its inner vibration of memory" that contradicts in spirit the picaresque tradition that the book appears to follow.

Like Levi's first two books, *Il sistema periodico* (Einaudi, 1975; *The Periodic Table*, Schocken, 1984) is a volume of memoirs, or autobiographical reflections. His gift for the vignette, particularly the sharp character sketch, which was reflected in the anecdotal quality of his earlier work, finds ready accommodation in his collection of twenty-one prose pieces thematically unified by reference to Mendeleev's table of elements. In most of the episodes a particular incident or person in Levi's life evokes a certain element—such as zinc, gold, tin—to which he ascribes distinctive traits linking the worlds of chemistry and of man. Inevitably, Levi's elucidation of his personal experiences in terms of the periodic law of chemistry involves the sweeping historical events of his time.

The "power of joyful invention," which impressed Alvin H. Rosenfeld in his review of *The Periodic Table* for the *New York Times*, became an exhilarating force in his first novel, *La chiave a stella* (Einaudi, 1978; *The Monkey's Wrench*, Summit, 1986), winner of Italy's Strega Prize. Just as delight in the profession of chemistry motivated Levi in writing *The Periodic Table*, so does love of his work as a skilled rigger of giant derricks motivate the ebullient storyteller of *The Monkey's Wrench*. Libertini Faussone recounts his experiences on near and distant construction sites to an industrial chemist, a rigger of molecules, who is very much concerned with the art of storytelling because he is about to give up his specialization in paint manufacturing to become a full-time writer.

One of the literary projects to which Levi turned after his retirement from the Turin chemical firm in 1977 was the completion of *Lilìt e altri racconti* (Lilith and Other Stories, Einaudi, 1981), from which much of the vignettes that make up *Moments of Reprieve* (Summit, 1986) were drawn. The fifteen narratives of *Moments of Reprieve* make clear that the intervening decades had not diminished Levi's memories of the concentration camp and other scenes of the Holocaust. Some characters, such as Cesare and Lorenzo, are familiar to readers of *Survival in Auschwitz*. The mood of *Moments of Reprieve*, however, differs considerably from that of the earlier book, as Levi noted in his preface: "The scenarios . . . are hardly ever tragic. They are bizarre moments of reprieve." From the "persecuted, predestined" victims, the masses of Auschwitz, most of the men of *Moments of Reprieve* stand out because they possess, if only briefly, "the will and capacity to react."

Several of the few remarkable inmates that Levi singled out when he wrote *Moments of Reprieve* were Yiddish-speaking Eastern European Jews. Determined to test his literary ability in a book that would not be autobiographical, he decided upon a novel centering on the Ashkenazic culture, to which he had been introduced for the first time in Auschwitz. "I cherished the ambition to be the first (perhaps only) Italian writer to describe the Yiddish world," he disclosed in his interview with Roth. He also told Roth that he wanted to attack the misconception of a Jew as a meek person who declines to resist persecution.

To fulfill his three goals, Levi undertook extensive research in the traditions of Eastern European Jewry and then spent a "felicitous" year, from January 1 to December 31, 1980, writing *Se non ora, quando?* (Einaudi, 1982; *If Not Now, When?*, Summit 1985). His epic novel is a semihistorical chronicle of the journey during World War II of a defiant band of Jews from Russia to Italy, where they plan to embark for Palestine. Gathering recruits of similar purpose along the way, they risk their lives in courageous assaults on retreating German forces.

When *If Not Now, When?* won the 1982 Viareggio Prize, the eminent writer and semiotician Umberto Eco, who served on the jury, said that he ranked Levi among Italy's top writers. The novel also brought Levi the Campiello Prize. But in the United States several somewhat disappointed critics agreed, in effect, with Walter Clemons' comment in *Newsweek* (May 6, 1985), "Levi is a better memoirist than novelist." Among the many defenders of *If Not Now, When?* was Irving Howe, who wrote the introduction to the American edition. In his essay for the *New York Review of Books* Howe acknowledged that because Levi dealt with situations of which he had no direct experience, "the result cannot quite have the sensuous immediacy and abundance of many episodes of *The Reawakening*." He went on to say, "Yet it's in *If Not Now, When?* that certain of Levi's strongest literary gifts are allowed full play."

Poetry is also a literary form through which Levi has testified to the Holocaust. In the poems of a collection that has been translated into English, *Shema* (Menard, 1976), he explores the nature of human suffering. Among his books that are not available in English are the short story collections *Storie naturali* (Natural Histories, 1966) and *Vizio di forma* (Technical Error 1971), both written under a pseudonym, and compilations of letters and essays. His pieces for the Italian newspaper *La stampa* cover a variety of literary, historical, and scientific subjects.

Primo Levi and Lucia Morpurgo, a teacher, were married on September 8, 1947, and have a daughter Lisa, a biologist, and a son, Renzo, a physicist. Levi named his son after Lorenzo, who had helped to save his life at Auschwitz. In his conversation with Levi, Roth found him to be a man who "listens, and with his entire face, a precisely modeled face tipped with a white chin beard." As Roth further described him, "the Italian writer is small and slight, though not quite so delicately built as his unassuming demeanor makes him at first appear. . . . His alertness is nearly palpable, keenness trembling within him like a pilot light." Levi has recalled that he was once counted among the world's specialists in enamel coatings for insulated copper wiring. Hanging on the walls of his home are amusing animal sculptures that he has fashioned from his factory's scrap enameled wire.

References: Commentary 80:41+ O '85, 81:6+ F '86; London R of Bks p17+ O 23 '86; N Y Times p14 My 27 '85 por; N Y Times Bk R p9 D 23 '84 por, p1+ O 12 '86 pors; New Repub 195:27+ Jl 28 '86; Newsweek 105:79+ My 6 '85 por; Sat R 11:70 Jl/Ag '85 por; Contemporary Authors new rev vol 12 (1984); Hughes, H. Stuart. Prisoners of Hope: The Silver Age of the Italian Jews, 1924–1974 (1983); International Who's Who, 1986–87

Liberman, Alexander

Sept. 4, 1912– Editor; painter; photographer; sculptor. Address: b. c/o Condé Nast Publications, Inc., 350 Madison Ave., New York City, N.Y. 10017; h. 173 E. 70th St., New York City, N.Y. 10021

"In art . . . there's no point in dreaming of certain things you'd like to do. You've got to do them. Do it, risk, make a mistake, start again." Alexander Liberman's credo reflects his attitude to life, adaptability to change, and acceptance of challenges during a long career of exceptional variety and achievement. Liberman is not only the eminently successful editorial director of Condé Nast Publications, the man most responsible for the content, style, and prestige of such high-gloss magazines as Vogue, House & Garden, Mademoiselle, and

Vanity Fair, but also a talented photographer and an artist with a somewhat equivocal reputation as a painter but wide acclaim as a sculptor. Working only on weekends and during vacations—often spent in Italy or France—he has managed to paint some 2,000 pictures in a period of thirty years. In referring to Liberman's short but very deep attention span, the photographer Richard Avedon has remarked: "His efficiency is amazing. Maybe the creative force when Alex paints and sculpts also operates at a short and swift pitch, and that's how he gets so much done." Asked about his successful reconciliation of business with art, Liberman himself explained to Marie Winn during an interview for the New York Times (May 13, 1979) that he enjoys his daily job because "art is solitary and the studio is a torture area. In France, the artists go to a café when they need human contact; well, Condé Nast is my café."

Alexander Semeonovitch Liberman's life is one that can without hyperbole be termed "glamorous," since it has been played out against the background of twentieth-century political cataclysms and in the fashionable world of Manhattan's glitterati. He was the only son of parents whose lives provided him with a heritage of international culture. His father, Simon Liberman, was an economist and lumber expert who had worked for the Russian nobility but survived the revolution to become an adviser to Lenin. His mother, Henriette (Pascar) Liberman, was an actress who founded the first state theatre for children in Russia in 1919. Born in Kiev on September 4, 1912, Liberman spent his early childhood in St. Petersburg and, from 1917, in Moscow. His years of growing up seem to have reflected the chaotic conditions of Russian life during the period when communism was supplanting czarist rule. Unhappy and unruly, he was taken out of school and tutored at home. In 1921 his father was given permission to take his son to England, and there Alexander studied at St. Pirans School in Maidenhead, the first Jewish boy to be enrolled there. Eventually his father left Russia and settled with his wife in Paris, where their child joined them in 1926. When Alexander was sent to the exclusive École des Roches in Normandy, where he was again the first Jewish child enrolled, he especially enjoyed a course in industrial drafting that supplemented its classical academic curriculum. Meantime, his mother, who had always wanted her son to be an artist, encouraged him to design theatrical costumes and sets. His drawings and paintings show the pervasive influence of Russian constructivist art with which he had been brought up.

In 1930 Liberman passed his baccalaureate at the Sorbonne in philosophy and mathematics, and then enrolled in the art school conducted by the cubist painter André Lhote. Dissatisfied with what he viewed as Lhote's dogmatic approach, he transferred in the next year to the architecture section of the École des Beaux-Arts and then to the École Spéciale d'Architecture. In the meantime, because of his father's losses in the Great Depression, Liberman turned to working as a designer, of posters, window displays, and book bindings, and to writing film reviews. Eventually he obtained a job on Vu, the prototype of *Life* magazine, and rose from the post of art department assistant to its managing editor between 1933 and 1936. Vu had been founded by Lucien Vogel, the patron of the artist Alexander Iacovleff, who had been Henriette Liberman's lover, and whose niece Tatiana had been Liberman's childhood friend. Part of the fortuitous coincidences and interlocking circles that run through Alexander Liberman's life is the fact that Tatiana Iacovleff eventually became his second wife, and Lucien Vogel was the man who started him on his publishing career in America. For the time being, however, the young artist designed photomontage covers for Vu and, in his leisure time, painted realistic landscapes and portraits.

In 1936 Liberman married a German ski champion, Hilda Sturm, and lived with her in the Riviera villa that his father, who had recouped his financial losses, bought for them. Although Liberman was now able to devote all his time to painting, the quiet, retired life failed to amuse his wife, and they were divorced within a year. Returning to Paris at the start of World War II, Liberman tried to join the French army but was rejected because of a chronic ulcer condition. Tatiana Iacovleff had in the meantime married Count Bertrand du Plessix, and when he was killed at the beginning of the war, Liberman took on the responsibility for getting her and Francine, her ten-year-old daughter, out of France. They managed to escape by way of Portugal and landed in New York in 1941, joining his parents who had already arrived.

On the recommendation of Lucien Vogel, who was now working for *Glamour*, and on the strength of the work he had done for Vu and the gold medal that he had received for magazine design at the 1937 Exposition Internationale in Paris, Liberman was taken on the staff of Vogue as art director. Throughout the World War II years, Liberman, now married to Tatiana du Plessix, devoted himself largely to his work as art director of all Condé Nast magazines, which he became in 1943, doing almost no painting except for a few family portraits. Under his aegis Vogue has played a considerable role as a taste maker. From the start, Liberman commissioned artists like Marcel Duchamp and Joseph Cornell to do illustrations and saw to it that fashion photographs often included backgrounds with modern paintings. Often those photographs themselves became classics of fashion illustration, since they were done by such luminaries as Cecil Beaton, Irving Penn, and Richard Avedon. The polylingual Liberman is also considered to be a good "line" editor, and during the mid-1950s he wrote a series of articles introducing contemporary artists, including Picasso, Kandinsky, Giacometti, and Vlaminck, to Vogue's readers. Over the years, too, such respected and influential art critics as John Russell, Robert Hughes, and Barbara Rose have regularly contributed articles to the publication.

Responding to changing tastes, Vogue, like *Mademoiselle*, has evolved from its concern with haute couture to the broader interests of a mass-circulation audience. Its smaller size, adopted in 1977, new montage-like layout, and pages crowded with photographs and segments of text obviously appeal to the readership, for its circulation figures have risen considerably. In response to criticism of what he calls the magazine's new "reality," Liberman reassured a *New York Times* interviewer (June 9, 1981): "I'm not interested in the fashion magazine as masterpiece. . . . We are not making magazines to be preciously saved. I like the discardable quality of life."

The end of World War II enabled Liberman to find time again for his own art, and he embarked on a series of postimpressionist landscapes and expressionist portraits. By 1946, the year in which he was naturalized as an American citizen, he was anxious to forge a new style for himself, one that would be free of historic ties. Somewhat ironically, although he was a friend of Jackson Pollock, Mark Rothko and, especially, of Barnett Newman, he rejected their abstract expressionism because he deemed it too concerned with an old-fashioned painterly approach and too autobiographical. (Only toward the end of the 1970s, in fact, did he begin to sign his own canvases.) It can be seen, in looking back over Liberman's paintings, that style has succeeded style in a discontinuous manner and generally in complete opposition to the current trend in art. It is for that reason, and for what is perceived as his lack of a definable style of his own, that Liberman has not been considered among the "important" recent American artists. Critics have been largely lukewarm, feeling that he is too contrived, too concerned merely with effective design, and he himself has conceded that he has always been "plagued" by suspicions that he is "not quite serious."

Liberman's hiring of art critics for his magazines seems to raise questions about possible conflicts of interest if they should be called on to review his own work, and Barbara Rose, one of his contributors, has in fact written an exhaustive and indispensable study of the man and his art, *Alexander Liberman*, which was published by Abbeville Press in 1981. In defending himself against such innuendos, Liberman points out that "a review based on friendship has no meaning for the artist at all." In any event, critical rejection has not desolated him, since his creed is that art, "a call to . . . the superior qualities of human beings," transcends the venal pressures of the art market.

For twelve years, beginning in 1947, Liberman was absorbed in the project of photographing and interviewing twenty-four artists of the School of Paris in their homes and studios. The result—150 color and black-and-white photographs, winnowed down from the original amount of about 10,000 pictures—was shown to great acclaim at the Museum of Modern Art in 1959. When the photographs and their accompanying text were published as *The Artist in His Studio* in 1960 by the

Viking Press, the book was hailed as an invaluable documentary history of twentieth-century art.

Alexander Liberman has been photographing since his childhood. In 1938, in collaboration with members of the staff of the Louvre, he did one of the first color films on art, *La femme française dans l'art*, and in 1951 he edited *The Art and Technique of Color Photography* (Simon & Schuster). His own color photographs of Greece, with accompanying text by the archaeologist Iris Love, were published by Viking Press under the title *Greece, Gods and Art* in 1968. Ironically, Liberman does not consider photography an art. Using it now to record and to redirect the progress of his sculptures as they develop slowly over a period of years, he regards the camera merely as a tool for thinking.

In about 1949 Liberman began a series of hard-edge, geometrical painting that played with the theme of the circle. Meticulously drawn with a compass, or even inscribed around poker chips that he tossed onto the canvas, they exemplified a Libermanesque combination of chance and control, as in the case of *Six-Hundred and Thirty-Nine* (1959). "Circlism," as he termed it, occupied him throughout the 1950s, at a time when action painting and color field abstraction were occupying other artists. His first solo exhibition, held in 1960 at the Betty Parsons Gallery in New York, was devoted to those circle paintings, among which *Continuous on Red* (1960) was purchased for the Museum of Modern Art. On his recovery from major surgery in 1959 to relieve an ulcer condition, Liberman launched himself on a freer, more painterly style, while other artists were exploring minimalism. Inspired now by the work of Pollock, he allowed himself to splash, spatter, and then pour paint. Barbara Rose has called attention to a plausible connection between Liberman's risk-taking and the new development in his publishing career: his appointment in 1962 to the prestigious post of editorial director of Condé Nast publications.

Again, a new decade seems to have suggested a new approach to Liberman, for with the advent of the early 1970s he began to work in a wide range of heavily impastoed colors, with no hint of the geometrizing that up till then had controlled his work. Reversing himself, and ever the experimenter, he turned in 1979 to austere black-and-white abstractions. Most recently, color has returned, once again, in works that he showed at the André Emmerich Gallery in New York in the fall of 1986: tall structures made of variously shaped pieces of driftwood, combined with canvas, paper and Masonite board, painted in bright, old-Russian colors.

Liberman has speculated that his paintings may have become freer because of his work in sculpture. The persistent geometrical bent that runs through his art has found an outlet in three-dimensional work, which from the mid-1960s on became an increasingly important means of expression for him. Unlike his painting, Liberman's sculpture shows an ordered pattern of development. Beginning as far back as 1951, with shaped paintings in enamels and oils on board, designed to stand out from the wall—one example is *Sixteen Ways*, a four-panel work—he went on to do small abstract three-dimensional pieces in plexiglass and enamel on copper. Throughout the years, he has constructed larger and larger works that are meant to be exhibited in outdoor public spaces. "I love the grand scale in art in general," he once explained.

In 1959, while vacationing in France, Liberman learned welding and did *Space Cut*, his first piece of curved sections of steel welded together. Within two years he had established a studio for welded sculptures in a barn on the family farm in Connecticut, the property of his stepson-in-law, the painter Cleve Gray. Designed by Liberman but executed industrially, abstract aluminum sculptures occupied him from 1962 to 1963; like his hard-edge paintings, they are steadfastly impersonal, with their interest derived from the reflecting quality of the metal. Rejecting that precisionist approach, he turned next to assemblages of unpainted metal parts, which date from 1963 and 1964. Never publicly exhibited, they are open forms that reach out into space in spontaneous, gestural ways. Continuing to work with junk metal obtained from old boilers and gas storage tanks that he scavenged and bulldozed up from the countryside, Liberman sliced their columnar, cylindrical forms into circular or elliptical sections and welded them into abstract assemblages. From 1966 on, nearly all of his large work was painted red. Besides its attention-getting effect, it is, Barbara Rose points out, significant that the Russian word for the color red, *krasnoe*, also means "beautiful." By 1967 more linear shapes had entered his formal repertoire, and on consulting with a group of Columbia University engineers, he evolved a series of works based on cantilevered diagonals that dynamically penetrate space as they defy gravity. In Liberman's latest sculpture, work of the early 1980s, cut-out shapes in increasingly complex, baroque formations, as in the painted welded steel *Sabine Women*, 1981, have become dominant.

Liberman works with the conviction that abstract "environmental sculpture . . . is a wonderful means to choreograph public amazement," and the several colossal Liberman sculptures on view on the grounds of the Storm King Art Center in Mountainville, New York, afford ample opportunity to assess their dramatic effect. None of his outdoor pieces has been designed for a specific site, although *Prometheus* was commissioned by the architect Philip Johnson to be shown at the 1964 New York World's Fair, and Dag Hammarskjöld Plaza in New York opened, in 1971, with six of Liberman's huge constructions, among them *Odyssey*, with its mast- and sail-like forms. A year later the three-story-high *Adam*, standing outside the Corcoran Gallery in Washington, D.C., was denounced by President Richard Nixon, who ordered "this horror" to be removed. In deference to his wishes, it was eventually relocated, in 1978, outside the newly opened east wing of the National Gallery.

LICHTENSTEIN

Examples of Liberman's work in all media are to be found in important collections, including the Solomon R. Guggenheim Museum, the Whitney Museum of American Art, the Museum of Modern Art, the Corcoran, and the Tate Gallery in London. Despite the dismissive attitude of most critics, his paintings have been represented in several group exhibitions and accorded fairly frequent solo showings, most notably at the Betty Parsons Gallery and the André Emmerich Gallery, which is now his dealer. Two retrospective exhibitions of his oeuvre have been held: "Painting and Sculpture 1950–1970" at the Corcoran and the Museum of Fine Arts, Houston in 1970, and a showing at the Storm King Art Center in 1977. Liberman, who was made a chevalier of the French Legion of Honor in 1946, holds an honorary Doctor of Fine Arts degree from the Rhode Island School of Design, awarded in 1980.

Alexander Liberman and his wife still live in the Manhattan townhouse on East 70th Street that they first occupied at the time of their marriage in 1942. For many years he has also maintained a studio a few blocks away. Still trim and lithe ("wrenlike," is the adjective that *Time* critic Robert Hughes chose to describe him) as he approaches his seven-ty-fifth birthday, Liberman continues to work at an energetic pace, tempered by his old-world courtliness and charm of manner. He invariably dresses for his office in understated elegance, but once in his studio he changes to khaki work clothes, ready to hurl paint, bulldoze metal machinery, or weld steel parts. The Libermans spend their weekends in the country home they purchased in 1968 in Warren, Connecticut, and Francine du Plessix Gray, now a well-known writer, her husband, and their two sons live nearby. It is there that Liberman maintains his sculpture studio and there that, increasingly, he and his wife enjoy entertaining a small group of Russian émigré friends, who include Mikhail Baryshnikov and the poet Joseph Brodsky, so that once again a circle has been completed for Alexander Liberman, and in his American equivalent of a *dacha*, his native language and cultural ties have been revived.

References: N Y Times Mag p50+ My 13 '79 pors; New York 14:42+ O 12 '81 pors; Contemporary Artists (1983); Contemporary Photographers (1982); Rose, Barbara. Alexander Liberman (1981); Who's Who in America, 1986–87; Who's Who in American Art (1984)

Lichtenstein, Harvey

Apr. 9, 1929– President, Brooklyn Academy of Music. Address: b. Brooklyn Academy of Music, 30 Lafayette Ave., Brooklyn, N.Y. 11217

Under Harvey Lichtenstein's direction, the Brooklyn Academy of Music (BAM) has established itself as indisputedly the leading avant-garde performing arts center in the United States. A prime international showcase for innovative music, dance, and opera, its annual Next Wave Festival is especially recognized for wide-ranging modern dance and ballet programs and mixed-media performance art collaborations. BAM's inventive programming is complemented by Lichtenstein's skill in obtaining sustained financial backing and in recruiting constantly growing audiences for the avant-garde with the help of sophisticated fundraising and promotion campaigns, especially those targeted to major corporations. The Next Wave's popularity, along with an impressive program of more traditional fare that Lichtenstein presents during BAM's regular performing season, has brought Brooklyn's cultural life out from under the long shadow of Manhattan and restored lost glamour and vitality to the oldest multiple-stage performing arts facility in the United States.

Harvey Lichtenstein was born on April 9, 1929, in Brooklyn, New York, the son of Samuel and Jennie (Walodarsky) Lichtenstein. (One source gives "Meiner" as his mother's maiden name). Samuel Lichtenstein, a factory worker, immigrated to the United States from Poland at the age of seventeen,

and Jennie Lichtenstein arrived in New York from Russia as an infant. Harvey Lichtenstein grew up in the Bushwick section of Brooklyn and attended Brooklyn Technical High School, just a block from the Brooklyn Academy of Music. Much music was heard in the Lichtenstein household, for the father was an enthusiastic amateur violinist, and one of Harvey's youthful heroes was the conductor Arturo

Toscanini, then in charge of the NBC Symphony Orchestra.

Lichtenstein planned to study engineering when he enrolled at Brooklyn College, but he underwent an artistic conversion when a girlfriend introduced him to modern dance during his sophomore year. He took several dance courses at the college and after graduating in 1951 with a degree in history and English literature, won a scholarship to study at the Connecticut College School of Dance. He then studied modern dance and ballet privately with Martha Graham and Benjamin Harkarvy in New York before winning another dance scholarship to Bennington College in Vermont.

Lichtenstein reached a watershed in his artistic development when he took dance classes with Merce Cunningham at the experimental Black Mountain arts school in North Carolina for one summer in the early 1950s. "For me the worlds of painting, dance, and poetry opened all at once," he recalled for Stephen Holden of the New York Times (October 17, 1985), in referring to that mecca of the avant-garde, where he met such artists as the painters Franz Kline and Robert Rauschenberg and the composer John Cage. Lichtenstein's experience with an interdisciplinary artists' community helped to stimulate his later interest in mixed-media performance collaborations as president of the Brooklyn Academy of Music.

In the early 1950s Lichtenstein became a professional dancer with the Sophie Maslow Dance Company, which was then based at Connecticut College, and he later performed with the companies of Pearl Lang and Martha Graham. "We'd travel in a station wagon with all our equipment, playing mostly college towns," he reminisced during an interview with Jack Robbins of the New York Post (August 4, 1969). "It was a difficult life, just eking out a living." Toward the end of the decade, because he intented to marry and settle down with a "respectable job," Lichtenstein quit dancing to become a part-time fund raiser for the United Jewish Appeal, based in New York. He showed such a flair for the art of persuasion that he soon joined the staff of Brandeis University in Waltham, Massachusetts, as a full-time fund raiser.

Clad in a business suit by day, Lichtenstein still managed to don the leotard after working hours by taking classes with the Boston Ballet Company. In 1964 he found an opportunity to combine his business acumen with his love for dance through a new Ford Foundation Arts Entertainment Fellowship program to fund paid internships in cultural administration. Winning an internship with the New York City Ballet on the recommendation of the Boston Ballet director, E. Virginia Williams, he accepted a 50 percent cut below his Brandeis salary to take the post. After spending a year as an intern, during which he did everything from selling tickets to sitting in on union negotiations, he obtained a staff position with the New York City Ballet to develop and manage a ticket subscription series to help rebuild the company's declining audience. His massive direct-mail promotion campaign

backed up by newspaper advertising proved highly successful, netting 20,000 subscribers to multiple performances—twice as many as had been anticipated. That achievement led to Lichtenstein's appointment as subscription manager for the New York City Opera in 1965, a position that he held jointly with his City Ballet post.

In 1967, after working for only three years as a middle-level arts administrator, Lichtenstein was named the surprise choice to become president of the Brooklyn Academy of Music, a 106-year-old, privately governed, and city-funded Brooklyn cultural institution that had fallen into financial and artistic difficulties. Although the youngest and least experienced candidate for the post, Lichtenstein won the backing of Seth S. Faison, the BAM governing committee chairman, with his bold proposal to transform the staid, tradition-bound Academy into a national center for contemporary dance, but he faced some daunting hurdles that stood in his way to achieving his ambitious scheme. BAM could boast of its stellar past, when it attracted such luminaries as Enrico Caruso, Isadora Duncan, Sarah Bernhardt, and Edwin Booth to its stages, but it underwent a long decline beginning in the years of the Great Depression—a decline that reached its nadir in the early 1950s, when proposals were made to raze the landmark yellow-brick building at 30 Lafayette Avenue or convert it into a gymnasium. Municipal funds provided a life-support system, but they proved a poor substitute for the surrounding working- and middle-class neighborhoods that had sustained the hall until they collapsed into slums. Meanwhile, BAM's former citywide audiences had all but disappeared. When Harvey Lichtenstein took over the reins in March 1967, BAM was operating on a $600,000 budget for a largely elderly local audience and offering programming that consisted mainly of standard symphonic repertoire performed by the independently administered Brooklyn Philharmonic Orchestra, occasional theatrical works, travel films, adult education classes, and ethnic song-and-dance ensembles.

Lichtenstein's first step in resuscitating BAM was to launch a major fund-raising campaign, targeting the federal and municipal governments and such private arts patrons as the Rockefeller, Mellon, and Ferris Booth foundations. The BAM development scheme tied in with a general urban renewal plan for downtown Brooklyn, and the money was forthcoming. After refurbishing the Academy's opulent, 2,100-seat Opera House and the 1,000-seat Music Hall, since renamed the Helen Carey Playhouse, Lichtenstein mailed out 200,000 brochures to promote a subscription dance program featuring Alvin Ailey's American Dance Theater, a newly formed modern ballet troupe led by Eliot Feld, and the Merce Cunningham Dance Company. The campaign proved highly successful and helped to sustain the Merce Cunningham Dance Company for an eight-day engagement in May 1968.

His successful stratagems paved the way for Lichtenstein to inaugurate an ambitious "Festival of Dance" in October 1968, with a $100,000 grant from the Ford Foundation. The two-month program featured no fewer than five top modern dance ensembles: the Martha Graham, Paul Taylor, Anna Sokolow, Alvin Nikolais, and José Limón companies. Lichtenstein also established in-house residencies for the Ailey, Feld, and Cunningham companies to perform exclusively at BAM and to give dance classes there. He complemented that spectacular modern dance lineup with some audacious steps to develop avant-garde theatre at the Academy. He invited the experimental Chelsea Theater to take up residency rent-free at BAM and caused a sensation when he lured Julian Beck and Judith Malina's Living Theater back from Europe in October 1968, to give a sold-out engagement of its freewheeling, audience-participation play, *Paradise Now*. That autumn, BAM also sponsored the United States debut of Jerzy Grotowski's controversial Polish Laboratory Theater.

Critics were delighted with the innovative changes at the formerly sedate BAM. Clive Barnes of the *New York Times* (November 12, 1969) hailed its emergence "from its honorable position as a cultural mausoleum and social dodo," and Babette Coffey of *Dancemagazine* (June 1968) called the rejuvenated institution "Queen Victoria in a miniskirt." Despite all the lavish praise, however, Lichtenstein failed to lure the large Manhattan dance audiences he had hoped for. By the time the ten-week 1969–70 dance festival concluded to houses that were less than half-filled, it was clear that supporting the Ailey, Cunningham, and Feld residencies was no longer tenable. The companies found new homes in Manhattan, and Lichtenstein, though he still sponsored critically praised dance programs by such artists as Twyla Tharp and Maurice Béjart, began to concentrate on presenting standard and avant-garde theatre during the early and middle 1970s.

Among BAM's dramatic highlights, the Chelsea company offered provocative productions of Jean Genet's *The Screens* and LeRoi Jones's *Slave Ship*. In 1973 a newcomer named Robert Wilson stupefied audiences for twelve hours with his monumental *Life and Times of Joseph Stalin*. In 1971 Lichtenstein began a collaboration with the Royal Shakespeare Company by presenting an extended engagement of Peter Brook's controversial Broadway production of *A Midsummer Night's Dream*, and the British troupe returned in 1974, 1975, and 1976. In 1973–74 he packaged a "British Theater Season" consisting of eleven productions performed by the Royal Shakespeare Company, the Young Vic, and the Actors Company. Finally, Lichtenstein established a new in-house repertory troupe, Frank Dunlop's BAM Theater Company, that made its debut in the spring of 1977 at the variable, multidimensional Lepercq Space.

It was only to be expected that Lichtenstein's ambitious dance and theatre programs at the BAM required ever increasing outside financing, especially after both the city and state governments cut back their support during the fiscal crisis of the mid-1970s and a catastrophic flood in 1977 caused millions of dollars worth of damage to the Academy's physical plant. Although he had succeeded in more than doubling the Academy's audience and budget since becoming president, BAM's finances were still on a precarious footing when Lichtenstein decided to invest in an in-house classical repertory theatre company in 1979. With a $400,000 Ford Foundation grant as seed money, he formed a new BAM Theater Company of thirty-three actors led by David Jones, an associate director of the Royal Shakespeare Company whom Lichtenstein had met during the company's productions at the Academy. Lichtenstein entertained high hopes for the new BAM troupe. It was intended to fill a citywide need for a classic repertory company by offering a program of six plays a season that would rotate among works by Shakespeare, American dramas, and classics of the world stage. The company lasted for only two full seasons, however, before critical condemnation and minuscule audiences for its stagings of *A Midsummer Night's Dream* and Ibsen's *The Wild Duck*, among other works, drove the Jones troupe out of business. Leaving BAM with a $2 million debt, the venture ended up as the most notable failure of Lichtenstein's tenure.

In 1981 Lichtenstein rebounded rapidly with another shift in artistic direction. It came about when a member of BAM's press department hit upon the idea of creating an avant-garde subscription series. Called "the Next Wave," its aim was to sell that season's performance of works choreographed by the experimental dancers Lucinda Childs, Trisha Brown, and Laura Dean, and of minimalist compositions by Philip Glass. When Lichtenstein mounted a major promotion campaign, the series concept proved highly successful, building large audiences for the dance companies and helping to sell out all five performances of Glass's opera *Satyagraha*, which is based on the life of Mohandas Gandhi. Repeating the Next Wave series the following season, BAM scored a critical and commercial hit with the performance artist Laurie Anderson's two-part, multimedia collage *United States I-IV*. As one of BAM's fund raisers, Karen Hopkins, joked during an interview with Cathleen McGuigan for the *New York Times Magazine* (November 2, 1986): "We knew that the Next Wave had arrived opening night when someone reported that the evangelist Reverend Ike, Jacqueline Onassis, and Claus von Bülow were in the audience."

Buoyed by his success, Lichtenstein decided to concentrate Next Wave events into a fall festival beginning in 1983 and lasting for two-and-a-half months. The centerpiece of his fund-raising strategy was an aggressive corporate campaign that paid off handsomely, yielding generous contributions from such industrial giants as AT&T and the Philip Morris cigarette company, which became the Next Wave Festival's major business sponsor with a $250,000 annual pledge. He lured capital with a generous program of advertising rights for sponsors and such added patronage perquisites as free tickets and parties by invitation only. Lichtenstein also drummed up substantial ongoing support for the Next Wave from the Ford and Rockefeller foundations and the National Endowment for the Arts.

In another inspired coup, Lichtenstein hired two cultural consultants, Anne Livet and Steve Reichard, to cultivate an elite group of supporters from the worlds of Manhattan's entertainment, fashion, and visual arts, including Richard Gere, Bianca Jagger, Diane Keaton, Calvin Klein, David Salle, Julian Schnabel, and Keith Haring. His strategy succeeded in attracting the young, affluent, and trendy patrons of the Manhattan gallery and rock club scene that BAM's promoters regard as the Next Wave's natural constituency.

BAM's seemingly paradoxical success in winning broad-based acceptance and support for its avant-garde festival can be partly explained by the changing nature of the avant-garde itself, or at least that sector that Lichtenstein has chosen to stage. Critics have noted that much of today's avant-garde performing arts work, though aesthetically innovative, avoids the intentionally shocking assault on convention that helped define earlier art styles of the avant-garde. Some of the Next Wave's dance presentations, including the work by the West German choreographer Pina Bausch, recall the intensity and abrasiveness of earlier avant-garde styles, but other mixed-media festival productions might better be described as "sexy, fun and psychedelic" spectacles that resemble "intellectual rock shows," in the words of Stephen Holden of the New York Times (December 16, 1984). Loosely structured and highly visual, those performances offer spectacular high-tech effects and synthesize elements of both popular and higher culture. The slick style and easy accessibility of much of new performance art has led some critics, like Hilton Kramer, to dismiss it as a "fake avant-garde" that aims to please instead of to provoke, but others find the work as imaginative as earlier experimental styles but less judgmental and elitist. Because of BAM's superior facilities, the Next Wave Festival has played a unique role in presenting experimental works that require elaborate sets and costly multimedia equipment. Lichtenstein maintains a network of talent scouts in Manhattan, London, Stuttgart, and Paris to keep him, as he says, "on the edge of what's happening with contemporary artists."

Among the critically acclaimed and well-attended works that Lichtenstein presented during the 1984 and 1985 Next Wave Festivals were Pina Bausch's choreographed interpretation of the Kurt Weill-Bertolt Brecht theatre work The Seven Deadly Sins; Bill T. Jones/Arnie Zane and Company's pop science-fiction dance Secret Pastures; and a revival of Philip Glass and Robert Wilson's minimalist opera Einstein on the Beach. By the 1986–87 season, when BAM celebrated its 125th anniversary and Lichtenstein marked his twentieth year as Academy president, Brooklyn's premier cultural

institution was on a solid financial and artistic footing once again, thanks largely to the avant-garde festival. Lichtenstein was able to retire BAM's classical theatre debt and put the Academy back in the black with a 1986 budget of $9.2 million, one-third of which was allotted to the Next Wave.

Major Next Wave performances during the 1986–87 season included Roaratorio, a music and dance collaboration by John Cage and Merce Cunningham based on James Joyce's Finnegan's Wake; the Impossible Theater's high-tech Social Amnesia, an electronic collage of images set to computer synthesizer music that drew on the ideas and writings of Helen Keller, Black Elk, and Bertolt Brecht, among others; and the fifth act (Rome Section) of Robert Wilson's monumental opera the CIVIL warS, with a score by Philip Glass. In addition to arranging a number of collaborations by lesser-known artists, Lichtenstein and BAM also produced the Flying Karamazov Brothers' torch-juggling adaptation of Igor Stravinsky's musical theatre work The Soldier's Tale.

Although the Next Wave has monopolized most of the glamour at BAM, Lichtenstein has also scheduled stimulating music, dance, and theatre programs for its regular winter/spring performance season. For 1986–87, BAM chamber music directors Scott Nickrenz and Paula Robison organized a "Spoleto Comes to BAM" series of seven concerts running from December to May that featured young artists associated with composer Gian-Carlo Menotti's music festival in Spoleto, Italy. In February 1987 Twyla Tharp presented the premiere of her new ballet In the Upper Room, with a score by Philip Glass, and in March of the same year BAM staged a televised 125th birthday celebration with a program of music by George Gershwin. The Central Ballet of China also made a rare United States appearance at the Academy that month. Later in the year Lichtenstein opened a fourth BAM performing space at the recently renovated Majestic Theater with a typically bold and imaginative program featuring Peter Brook's English-language production of The Mahabharata, a nine-hour dramatic cycle based on the Hindu philosophical treatise Bhagavad-Gita and produced by BAM in association with the Royal Shakespeare Company. The 1987 Next Wave Festival, which began in October with The Mahabharata, concluded two months later with Peter Sellars' staging of the minimalist composer John Adams' opera Nixon in China, a coproduction of BAM, the Houston (Texas) Grand Opera, the John F. Kennedy Center for the Performing Arts, and the Netherlands Opera.

Harvey Lichtenstein is a tall, heavyset, bear-like man who looks more like a football coach than a former dancer. Among his many honors are a service award from the Association of American Dance Companies in 1980 for his work in promoting modern dance and sponsoring young choreographers and the 1986 Officer's Cross of the Order of Merit from the West German government for his contributions to furthering West German-United

States cultural relations. In January 1987 President Ronald Reagan nominated Lichtenstein to serve as a member of the National Council on the Arts, the advisory body to the National Endowment for the Arts.

Harvey Lichtenstein lives in a Gramercy Park apartment complex with his second wife, the former Phyllis Holbrook, whom he married on November 14, 1971, and twelve-year-old son, John. He has another son, Saul, from an earlier marriage that ended in divorce. For recreation, the ebullient and energetic impresario enjoys playing tennis and sailing on ponds near his summer home in Garrison, New York.

References: Dance Mag 42:47+ Je '68; N Y Daily News (Sunday's People section) p3 F 2 '86; N Y Times C p19 O 17 '85 por; N Y Times Mag p34+ N 2 '86 por; New York 10:52+ S 26 '77, 20:40 O 12 '87 por; New Yorker 46:44+ N 14 '70; Who's Who in America, 1986–87

Linden, Hal

Mar. 20, 1931– Actor. Address: b. c/o William Morris Agency, 151 El Camino, Beverly Hills, Calif. 90212; c/o Paul Tush Management, Inc., 119 W. 57th St., New York City, N.Y. 10019

Millions of Americans know Hal Linden as the actor who appeared in the title role, as the mustachioed, eternally forbearing New York City police precinct captain, in the popular television situation comedy series *Barney Miller*, presented on ABC-TV from 1975 to 1982. Television viewers have also encountered Linden as the magician-detective Alexander Blacke in the short-lived 1986 NBC drama *Blacke's Magic* and as the star of a number of variety shows and made-for-television movies. Perhaps only a minority of Linden's legion of small-screen fans are aware, however, that the actor has also had a distinguished career on the Broadway stage that includes winning a 1970–71 Tony award for his portrayal of the banking patriarch in *The Rothschilds*. A versatile performer with a range that extends from frothy farce to serious drama, Linden returned to Broadway in 1986 in the role of Nat, the feisty octogenarian park bench philosopher and protagonist of Herb Gardner's hit comedy-drama, *I'm Not Rappaport*.

Hal Linden was born Harold Lipshitz on March 20, 1931, in the Bronx, in New York City, the younger of the two sons of Charles and Frances (Rosen) Lipshitz. A Lithuanian Jew, Charles Lipshitz had immigrated to the United States in 1910 at the age of fourteen, learned the printing trade, and became a partner in a small print shop. Hal Linden's brother, Bernard, became a professor of music. The parents emphasized the cultural value of musical training, and Hal learned to play the saxophone and clarinet and attended New York City's highly selective public High School of Music and Art. He started to work as a reed man and vocalist with professional jazz big bands while still in school, and he later traveled with the Sammy Kaye, Bobby Sherwood, and Boyd Raeburn orchestras. Along the way, he adopted the name Linden, which he saw on the side of an oil tanker, off the New Jersey coast, according to one account, or on a water tower in Linden, New Jersey, according to another. As insurance against the vagaries of a musical career, he studied at Queens College and graduated with a bachelor of business administration degree from the City College of New York in 1952.

Drafted into the United States Army after his college graduation, Linden was stationed near Washington, D.C., where he was assigned to Special Services and spent much of his time organizing and starring in musical revues. His army experience reinforced his affinity for the performing arts, and after his discharge in 1954 he promptly enrolled at the American Theater Wing under the G.I. Bill to study acting for the musical theater. In addition, Linden privately studied voice in New York, with Lou McCollogh and later with John Mace, and he also received instruction in acting from Paul Mann and then from Lloyd Richards, who has remained his mentor. Linden made his theatrical debut in 1955 in the chorus of a summer stock production of *Wonderful Town* at the Cape Cod Melody Tent in Hyannis, Massachusetts. He then took the role of Charlie in the pre-Broadway tryout, at New Haven, in March 1956, of the musical *Strip for Action*, a revival of the 1942 comic salute to burlesque. But the show folded in Pittsburgh in the following month, and Linden later remembered it as the worst he had ever been in.

Hal Linden got his first major break in the theatre in November 1956, when Frances Martin, whom he had met when they both appeared in *Wonderful Town*, told him about an opening for understudy to Sydney Chaplin, the leading man in the hit Broadway musical *Bells Are Ringing*, at the Shubert Theatre, in which she was a member of the cast. Linden got the job, and in July 1958 he took over Chaplin's starring role as Jeff Moss, opposite Judy Holliday portraying Ella Peterson, in the romantic comedy about an operator for a telephone answering service who gets personally involved in the lives of her clients. Linden went with the show on national tour from March to July of 1959, and he appeared as the night club singer in the motion picture version of the musical later that year. Meanwhile, in a fitting example of life imitating art, the actor had started his own "bells ringing" by marrying fellow trouper Frances Martin on April 13, 1958.

After the success of *Bells Are Ringing*, Linden thought that he was well on his way to becoming a leading man for the 1960s, and he was disappointed to find himself still generally cast in small roles or as an understudy in a succession of mostly unsuccessful Broadway musicals. He played Matt and understudied Keith Andes as Dynamite Joe in the short-lived oil field comedy *Wildcat*, starring Lucille Ball, in 1960, and after appearing in summer stock in *Wish You Were Here* and *Bells are Ringing*, he understudied Sydney Chaplin in 1961 as Tom Bailey in *Subways Are for Sleeping*, a musical about a charming loafer in love. In 1962 Linden won the lead part of Billy Crocker in a revival of the 1934 Cole Porter classic *Anything Goes* at the Off-Broadway Orpheum Theatre, but the dated book, involving a love triangle on board a ship bound for England, failed to inspire enthusiasm in the audiences. He next appeared as the senior citizen in *Something More!* in 1964 and as standby for John Collum and Clifford Daniel in *On a Clear Day You Can See Forever*, in 1965. In 1967 he was seen as the vice overlord "No Face" in the Melina Mercouri vehicle *Ilya Darling*, based on her hit film *Never on Sunday*, and later that year he took over the role of the Devil in Mike Nichols' *The Apple Tree*. Linden supplemented those slim Broadway pickings, meanwhile, by working in summer stock and regional theatre, appearing in industrial shows and films, dubbing foreign movies, and recording voice-overs and narratives for television commercials and programming.

Linden finally won some solid notices for his performance as Yissel Fishbein in George Abbott's production of *The Education of H*y*m*a*n K*a*p*l*a*n*, which opened at the Alvin Theatre in April 1968. The Oscar Brand-Paul Nassau musical comedy was based on Leo Rosten's best-selling book, published in 1936, about a feisty Jewish immigrant who is struggling to learn English at night school and is so full of "chutzpah" that he spells his name with asterisks. The play gathered mixed reviews, but Linden won raves for his portrayal of Hyman's conceited old-country rival for the hand of the star student Rose Mitnik. "Exuding complacency out of his very pores," in the words of Clive Barnes in the *New York Times* (April 5, 1968), Linden nearly stole the show, particularly with his satirical number "Old Fashioned Husband." He followed that success with more critical praise in the role of Charlie, the imbecile third of a trio of seedy horseplayers in George Abbott's revival of the classic 1935 musical farce *Three Men on a Horse*, which opened at the Lyceum Theatre in October 1969.

It took *The Rothschilds* to make Linden a star, however. The surprise Broadway musical hit, with music and lyrics by the *Fiddler on the Roof* duo Jerry Bock and Sheldon Harnick and book by Sherman Yellen, managed to create theatre out of the world of international high finance. Based on Frederic Morton's book of the same title, *The Rothschilds*, which opened at the Lunt-Fontanne Theatre in October 1970, charted the spectacular fifty-year rise of the Jewish banking family from its obscure origins in the eighteenth-century Frankfurt ghetto to its position as the dominant financial power in Europe, controlling princes and kingdoms. Linden was cast in the leading role of the patriarch Mayer Rothschild, who starts building the family empire by trading coins of dubious authenticity in the local marketplace and then uses his ghetto base to mastermind his five sons' speculations in the money capitals of Europe, succeeding to the point of being made the special banking agent of Prince William of Hesse and a major financier of the Napoleonic Wars.

The Rothschilds' extravagant production was criticized for lacking period authenticity, and some reviewers questioned the premise of a musical that romanticized rapacity, but Linden's performance in the lead was widely praised. "Hal Linden, too long unappreciated, comes completely into his own as Mayer Rothschild," Haskel Frankel wrote in the *National Observer* (October 26, 1970). "It is a full-blown patriarch he brings to the stage, with acting of the sort one expects only in drama." Alan Bunce, writing in the *Christian Science Monitor* (October 26, 1970), concurred: "Without an actor like Hal Linden to fill the role of patriarch Mayer, the show would have been lost. He blends deep tribal resignation with irrepressible near-charlatanism." Linden's portrayal earned him the Tony award for best actor in a musical for the 1970–71 season. In 1972, after 507 Broadway performances, Linden took *The Rothschilds* on a national tour.

Linden followed up his *Rothschilds* coup with another compelling leading performance in a very different play, the musical version of *The Sign in Sidney Brustein's Window*, which opened at the Longacre Theatre in January 1972. The Lorraine Hansberry drama, originally staged on Broadway without music in 1964, is about a willfully naive idealist who finally finds himself forced to face the world on more realistic terms. "As Sidney," Clive

Barnes wrote in his *New York Times* review (January 27, 1972), "Hal Linden gives a highly charged and beautifully calculated performance, as a good and weak man who drinks too much and thinks too little. Mr. Linden is exceptionally good at conveying the moral force of Sidney, and his performance dominates the play." Less successful, in critics' eyes, was Linden's appearance as Sid Sorokin in George Abbott's revival of *The Pajama Game*, which opened at the Lunt-Fontanne Theatre in December 1973. Clive Barnes found the actor to be miscast in the proletarian boy-gets-girl musical, observing, "He sings modestly and acts with all of his considerable skill, but he is not a natural juvenile lead."

Linden's return to star status comparable to that he achieved with *The Rothschilds* came not in the theatre, but in television. The independent producer Danny Arnold who had seen him in his theatrical *tour de force*, remembered him when he was casting for an innovative police comedy series pilot in 1974. In a major career gamble, Linden turned down a starring role in a new Broadway musical, *Doctor Jazz*, to try his hand at portraying Captain Barney Miller, the harried but compassionate commander of a Greenwich Village police precinct. After several pilots were shown, and Arnold overcame initial network resistance to Linden because of his relative inexperience in television, *Barney Miller* had its premiere as a prime-time weekly series on ABC-TV on January 23, 1975.

Inauspiciously scheduled at the same time as *The Waltons*, CBS-TV's highly popular homespun drama, *Barney Miller* got off to a perilously slow start, but its ratings began to pick up in the spring, and by the summer rerun season the show was believed to have a future. A hit from the start with critics who appreciated the series' believable characterizations, realistic themes, and humor that was a cut above the usual cretinous sitcom level, *Barney Miller* built a fiercely loyal following once the show found its audience. Barney's fictional Twelfth Precinct offered a slice of New York City life at its most comically inept, pitting an ethnic grab-bag of all-too-human detectives against a slew of colorful eccentrics and petty miscreants not much different from themselves. Among the most popular detective characters were Abe Vigoda as Fish, a burned-out gumshoe of the old school, with marital problems; Jack Soo as the malevolently philosophical Japanese detective Yemana; Maxwell Gail in the role of the slow-witted, goodhearted Polish Wojo; Ron Glass as Harris, the wise-cracking, debonair black detective with literary pretensions; and two women officers played by Linda Lavin and June Gable. Finally, there was Barney, portrayed by Linden as a street-smart peacemaker, father figure, and long-suffering voice of reason that bound the disparate crew together.

By the 1977 season *Barney Miller* was one of the ten top-rated television series, and the show succeeded in holding that position for several years. Superb ensemble acting was believed to be the key

to its popularity, a blend achieved by producer Arnold's relentless demands for rehearsal and Linden's distinctly un-starlike attitude, which encouraged the other actors to develop and add to their characters. Arnold and Linden also vigorously fought network censors on such matters as depicting transvestism and prostitution to create what real New York law officers called the most realistic police series on television. *Barney Miller* won several Emmy awards for writing and directing before the show was finally "retired" in September 1982, less the victim of declining ratings than of cast fatigue and the growing difficulty in coming up with original new scripts. A spinoff of *Barney Miller*, entitled *Fish*, starring Abe Vigoda, was presented on ABC-TV in 1977–78.

To avoid being typecast as Barney Miller, Linden made other appearances on television and film during his eight years with the series. He was a frequent host and guest on serials and talk shows, and he narrated the Peabody award- and Emmy award-winning weekly children's show *Animals, Animals, Animals*, a magazine-format series examining the role of animals in human history and art that had its premiere on ABC-TV in September 1976. Linden also lent his gently authoritative presence to good effect as the host of ABC-TV's *FYI* series of commercial-length self-help tips that were spotted between daytime soap operas beginning in January 1980. Primarily aimed at a female audience, the thirty-to-forty-second spots featured the actor offering advice on such delicate subjects as preparing a daughter for menstruation and coping with children victimized by a disintegrating marriage.

Meanwhile, Linden made his feature-film acting debut in Marjoe Gortner's 1979 movie version of *When You Comin' Back, Red Ryder?*, based on the Mark Medoff play about a psychopathic young 1960s dropout who terrorizes a group of people trapped in a roadside New Mexico eatery. The film was generally panned, but Janet Maslin in her review in the *New York Times* (February 9, 1979) called the casting of Linden in the role of a pompous, cowardly, suburban husband "a sound and interesting choice."

In addition to appearing in the theatre, on television, and on film, Linden has also created his own variety nightclub and stage show, combining comedy skits, dramatic readings, song-and-dance routines, and big-band reed playing, which he introduced at Caesar's Palace in Las Vegas in 1977. His success there resulted in two well-received variety specials for ABC-TV. The first, *The Hal Linden Special*, presented in April 1979, was a wry musical summary of the ups and downs of the actor's career before *Barney Miller*. The second, *Hal Linden's Big Apple*, shown in June 1980, took the form of comedy and song-and-dance routines performed at landmark spots around New York City. Linden has continued to present his nightclub show, and in August 1986 he took it on tour with a seventeen-piece orchestra.

After retiring *Barney Miller*, Linden acted in several network and cable television movies, among them *Starflight* (ABC-TV, 1983), *I Do, I Do*, with Lee Remick, for the Arts and Entertainment channel, and *The Other Woman*, with Anne Meara, for CBS-TV. He also appeared in regional theatre, including a 1983 revival of the 1937 farce *Room Service*, at the Eisenhower Theatre in Washington, D.C. Linden turned down several television series offers in order to keep his schedule flexible, but after spending "a lot of time reading bad Broadway scripts," as he told Jerry Buck in an Associated Press interview in March 1986, he agreed to return to the small screen as the illusionist Alexander Blacke in the NBC drama series, *Blacke's Magic*. A midseason replacement, the series featured Linden as a debonair, world-famous magician who used his skills to help the Los Angeles police solve particularly baffling crimes. Linden performed much of the show's magic himself. Harry Morgan, a former star of the comedy series *M.A.S.H.*, appeared in the role of Linden's con-man father and partner. Critics praised Linden and Morgan for their solid acting but found the show's concept trivial and the writing mediocre. Viewers seemed to concur, and after several months of poor ratings *Blacke's Magic* was canceled.

Linden rebounded more than successfully on the stage in September 1986, when he replaced Judd Hirsch in one of contemporary Broadway's most original roles, as Nat, the pugnacious, iconoclastic eighty-one-year-old urban survivor in Herb Gardner's Tony award-winning comedy *I'm Not Rappaport*. Signed for a six-month engagement with costar Ossie Davis, who succeeded Cleavon Little in the role of his sidekick, Linden turned in "a magisterial performance, a little like a local 'King Lear'", in the words of Joseph Hurley in *Newsday* (September 21, 1986), as a cantakerous old Jewish socialist who refuses to conform to bourgeois society, confronting every outrage with a stout cane and acid tongue from his Central Park bench. Subduing a would-be mugger with the cane, Nat also fends off his suburban daughter's well-meaning attempt to put him in a retirement home, while "shaking things up" for the respectable citizens who cross his piece of turf, with volleys of radical rhetoric. In creating a character who is the temperamental opposite of Barney Miller, Linden explained to Joseph Hurley, "I used my own background, including my father, my uncles, and even one of my father's uncles." Linden was succeeded as Nat by Jack Klugman in June 1987.

Hal Linden is six feet one inch tall with a trim figure, gray hair, expressive brown eyes, and a handsome face. The mustache made famous by Barney Miller was joined by a full beard for *I'm Not Rappaport*. Linden has been described as a genuinely affable and even-tempered man who is easy to work with. As he recalled of his early stage experience to Marilyn Beck in the Yonkers *Herald-Statesman's TV Radio Week* (August 5, 1979), "There's nothing like having a career predicated on failure to make you put things into perspective." For recreation, Linden enjoys playing saxophone and clarinet in impromptu jam sessions, and he relaxes with games of bridge, jogging, tennis, skiing, and golf. He and his wife, the former Frances Martin, who retired as an actress and dancer to raise their family, are the parents of four grown children, Amelia Christine, Jennifer Dru, Nora Kathryn, and Ian Martin. The Lindens make their home in New York City.

References: Chicago Tribune X:8 Ap 26 '87 por; N Y Daily News (Leisure) p9 My 14 '78 pors; N Y Post p31 Jl 26 '75 por; N Y Times II p29 Je 1 '80 pors; Newsday II p7 O 22 '82 pors, II p11 S 21 '86 pors; Who's Who in America, 1984-85; Who's Who in the Theatre (1981)

Lorenzo, Frank

May 19, 1940– Airline company executive. Address: b. 4040 Capital Bank Plaza, Houston, Tex. 77002

In the era of airline deregulation that has revolutionized the domestic air travel industry since 1978, Frank Lorenzo, the chairman, president, and chief executive officer of Texas Air Corporation, has emerged as leading player in the "megaline" consolidation battles spawned by the cost-cutting strategy that he is generally credited with initiating. An acknowledged gambler in a high-stakes industry mired in debt and beset by mercurial change, Lorenzo has defied the odds against success, parlaying his business acumen into an astonishing penchant for promoting profitability. He founded the largest airline conglomerate in the United

States through shrewd manipulation of his rivals and winning industry-wide "fare wars" by offering to consumers full-service flights at low fares. Lorenzo is an astute financial strategist who capitalizes his ventures through creative operating and debt leverage. Notorious for his aggressive managerial style and his tough stance at the bargaining table, he has kept his massive fleet airborne by way of wage reductions won at the price of union enmity.

In 1972 Lorenzo purchased and rejuvenated the ailing Texas International Airlines with an infusion of the discounted "peanuts fares" that he pioneered. He won control of Continental Airlines in 1981, later filing for bankruptcy in a move that allowed him to abrogate existing union contracts, drastically reduce labor costs, and make the airline profitable. In 1982 he merged Texas International and Continental and founded New York Air. His reputation as a "union buster" caused him to lose a bid for Trans World Airlines to financier Carl Icahn in 1985, but undaunted, he then went on to acquire Eastern Airlines, in a merger hotly contested by Eastern's unions but approved by shareholders in November 1986. Lorenzo's acquisition of People Express and the assets of the bankrupt Frontier Airlines in late 1986 gave him control of an empire constituting the largest airline network in the non-Communist world, outranked only by Aeroflot, the Soviet airline.

Frank Lorenzo was born Francisco Anthony Lorenzo on May 19, 1940, in New York City to Olegario and Ana (Mateos) Lorenzo, who had both emigrated from Spain. His father, who died in 1980, was a hairdresser and the proprietor of a beauty shop in Manhattan. Frank Lorenzo grew up in the Rego Park section of the borough of Queens. At fifteen he took his first airplane trip, a Trans World Airlines flight to London, and on his return he used his savings to buy stock in that airline. Following his graduation from high school, Lorenzo studied economics at Columbia University, helping to finance his education by working as a part-time salesman at Macy's department store and driving a Coca-Cola truck as a member of the teamsters' union—a connection that he later cited as evidence that he did not deserve his antiunion reputation. As a student, and during the early years of his career, Lorenzo pored over biographies of such distinguished entrepreneurs as Andrew Carnegie and W. Averell Harriman. He graduated from Columbia with a B.A. degree in 1961 and then went on to earn an M.B.A. degree at Harvard University's Graduate School of Business Administration in 1963.

Lorenzo's first professional job, as a financial analyst for TWA from 1963 to 1965, was followed by a stint as manager of the financial analysis department at Eastern Airlines in 1965–66. During his tenure at Eastern, he met a former Harvard business school classmate, Robert J. Carney, then an employee of the investment firm of S. G. Warburg & Company, which was located across the street. In 1966 Lorenzo and Carney each invested $1,000 in a new partnership, Lorenzo, Carney & Company, an airline consulting firm, with Lorenzo as chairman, established to explore opportunities for leverage in the rapidly changing airline industry.

The partners eventually put up $35,000 between them to set up a Houston-based holding company called Jet Capital, incorporated in 1969, with Lorenzo as board chairman. Through a public stock offering Lorenzo and Carney were able to raise $1.15 million in additional operating funds. In 1971 the Chase Manhattan Bank called Jet Capital to the aid of a Texas-based regional carrier officially named Texas International Airlines, but facetiously referred to by Texans as "Tinker Toy" or "Tree Top" airways. At the time, Texas International had been losing an estimated $6 million to $7 million a year, but Jet Capital prevented almost inevitable bankruptcy by devising a $35 million recapitalization program and injecting the flagging carrier with new capital amounting to $1.5 million, of which all but $350,000 was generated by Jet Capital. In August 1972 Lorenzo became president and chief executive officer of Texas International, while Carney was named executive vice-president.

The new chief executive officer restructured the company's debt, eliminated unprofitable routes, added more lucrative flights, and purchased new planes to upgrade the efficiency of Texas International's nearly obsolete fleet, phasing out the Convair aircraft in favor of the more efficient DC-9. Throughout 1973 and 1974 Texas International steadily increased its modest profits, but a four-and-a-half-month strike in 1975 shut down the company at a critical juncture, and the airline found itself embroiled that same year in antitrust litigation, a legacy from the previous management. After settling the case, Texas International managed to right itself by 1977, when it instituted what Lorenzo referred to as "peanuts fares," offering discounts of as much as 50 percent on low-density routes. As a result, the carrier's earnings mushroomed, doubling in 1977 and nearly doubling again by mid-1978, when the company resumed paying dividends for the first time in eleven years. Texas International's half-priced fares, according to William K. Stevens, writing in the *New York Times* (November 8, 1978), "led the industry into a new competitive era." James Cook, in an article in *Forbes* (October 30, 1978), agreed. "The concept has since spread throughout the industry, radically transforming the industry's rate structure," he wrote, calling the tiny Texas International "the airline that pioneered the discount revolution in fares."

Lorenzo's reputation as a "Goliath-baiter" was confirmed after Congress passed the Airline Deregulation Act of 1978 and Civil Aeronautics Board approvals of mergers between major carriers became a viable option. In July of that year Lorenzo made headlines by announcing a proposal to take over National Airlines, a major trunk carrier three times the size of Texas International. Although he was outbid by Pan American World Airways in 1979, Lorenzo remained determined to take advantage of the expansion opportunities afforded by deregulation. By taking over one of the country's largest airlines, he reasoned, he could augment his company's existing fleet with larger aircraft, using its own smaller DC-9s to feed the hubs of the "instant markets" provided by the major carrier.

While PanAmerican World Airways had been the apparent victor in Lorenzo's first significant takeover skirmish, the struggle left Texas International with a major stake in the spoils. Lorenzo came away with about $46 million in pretax profits when he sold the company's 2.1 million shares of National stock. Emboldened, he began to buy stock in Trans World Airlines. During the summer of 1979 he invited TWA chairman L. Edwin Smart Jr. to a breakfast meeting at New York City's Carlyle Hotel. But when Lorenzo proposed buying the beleaguered carrier, which was then ten times the size of Texas International, Smart summarily dismissed the possibility and reportedly walked out. Some industry experts expressed doubts as to whether Texas International would have had the financial clout to take over TWA.

In September 1980 Lorenzo announced that his recently formed Houston-based holding company, Texas Air Corporation, of which he assumed the presidency, was establishing a subsidiary that he called New York Air. Based at LaGuardia Airport, the short-hop, shuttle carrier was founded to compete with Eastern Airlines on the busy corridor that linked New York City and Washington, D.C. On December 14, 1980, New York Air began offering $49 fares on each of ten daily business flights to Washington, as well as evening and weekend fares of $29—only 55 cents more than the Greyhound bus fare. As one writer for Time (September 22, 1980) quipped, "Lorenzo has become the flying ace in the new era of unregulated airline routes and prices."

"Texas International Airlines may rank only nineteenth among America's air carriers," Tom Nicholson wrote in Newsweek (February 23, 1981), "but chairman Frank Lorenzo likes to think big." In the previous week, Lorenzo had stepped into the ring again by announcing that Texas International had purchased a 9.5 percent interest in the stock of Continental Airlines and planned through a tender offer to attempt a takeover of the country's tenth largest carrier. According to Harry Chandis, the president of Texas International, a successful bid for the broader-based Continental would allow the airline to extend its market share beyond vacation travelers flying on unrestricted discount fares and to promote its services to the business traveler.

Business analysts speculated that Continental's fleet of DC-10s, rather than a beneficial merger of route systems, may have been the true target of Lorenzo's bid. In any case, Continental filed suit in federal court to seek an injunction against the takeover attempt, and the battle was joined. In an effort to thwart Lorenzo's bid, Continental's management devised a stock ownership plan for airline employees, many of whom were said to have bitterly opposed the merger. Pilots, in particular, were believed to have based their animosity toward Lorenzo on reputedly poor labor relations at Texas International. Lorenzo had recently purchased 48.5 percent of Continental stock when the Wall Street Journal (April 23, 1981) reported that talks between Texas International's chairman and Continental president Alvin L. Feldman had "disintegrated into a stalemate." Soon afterward, Lorenzo filed suit himself, challenging the employee stock ownership plan as a "management-entrenchment scheme."

Lorenzo won control of Continental in October 1981, after the merger was approved by the Civil Aeronautics Board, but the fallout from the bitter fight was far-reaching. Continental president Feldman helped to draft a news release announcing the takeover and then committed suicide for reasons that were in part unrelated to corporate problems. Texas International, which had purchased a 51 percent stake in the company for $100 million, found itself reporting an operating loss for Continental amounting to more than $100 million for 1981. As a result of the air traffic controllers' strike, New York Air sustained a loss of close to $12 million in the same year. A prolonged contract fight with Texas International pilots exacerbated Lorenzo's labor troubles, which were further compounded by the enmity of Continental employees after the long takeover battle.

Lorenzo merged Texas International and Continental in October 1982 under the umbrella of his Texas Air Corporation. In an effort to bring down labor costs, which had risen substantially before deregulation, and to return the company to profitability, he laid off 15 percent of the carrier's work force in March 1983. In addition, he hired hundreds of permanent replacements for striking machinists. Although Lorenzo offered employees a stock ownership plan in exchange for substantial labor-productivity concessions, the workers failed to meet his deadline for agreement. The chairman responded by announcing on September 24, 1983, that Continental was seeking reorganization under federal bankruptcy laws. Having voided extant labor contracts through the controversial move, Lorenzo then offered to hire back about one-third of the company's 12,000 employees at half pay.

After a three-day shutdown, Continental staggered to its feet and gradually began to rebuild its service and attract customers, reducing the number of cities served from seventy-eight to twenty-five, and decreasing fares while retaining the "frills" of full-service flights. Under Lorenzo's management, Continental survived a strike by pilots and flight attendants, who tried to prove that he had acted in bad faith in invoking Chapter 11 of the federal bankruptcy law. Eventually, Lorenzo won federal court approval for rejecting the labor contracts. Until the airline became profitable, Lorenzo paid himself $43,000 a year, the same reduced salary earned by his pilots. By the end of the third quarter of 1984, Continental showed a profit of $35.5 million, a dramatic improvement over the $161.3 million loss shown during the same period in the preceding year, and the number of cities it served was back up to seventy. Meanwhile, New York Air had begun to show a profit by the second quarter of 1983.

Although Lorenzo's hard-nosed image with organized labor persisted, he remained sanguine about his relations with the airline unions. "The unions are confusing the messenger with the message," he said, as quoted in *Fortune* (January 8, 1984). "The enemy isn't Frank Lorenzo, but the new competitive environment." Lorenzo has consistently refuted the "union-buster" appellation, describing himself and his management as "airline builders."

In June 1985 Lorenzo made another attempt at acquisition of the financially troubled TWA, whose management had been searching during the previous month for a takeover suitor other than the corporate raider Carl Icahn, who had already acquired almost 33 percent of TWA's stock. TWA executives agreed in principle to the merger. A report in the *New York Times* (June 16, 1985) announced the "sale" of TWA as a *fait accompli* and a "personal coup" for Lorenzo, but the declaration proved premature. Union distrust of Lorenzo caused the merger to slip through his hands once again, when Icahn reached wage accommodations with union leaders that August, and TWA's board of directors unanimously rejected Lorenzo's bids for options on the airline's assets and for a special issue of preferred stock.

In October 1985 an attempt by Lorenzo to acquire the Denver-based Frontier Airlines was rebuffed as a result of union pressure. The carrier was sold instead to People Express, whose chairman, Donald C. Burr, was a former protégé of Lorenzo and had been best man at his wedding as well as godfather to one of his children. Burr had worked for Lorenzo at Texas International from 1973 until 1980, when he resigned as its chief operating officer to found People Express. Determined to expand his operation's profitability while denying that sheer size was the goal of his repeated attempts at acquisition of a major carrier, Lorenzo finally struck gold. On February 23, 1986, executives of Eastern Airlines, the nation's third-largest air carrier, announced a tentative agreement with Lorenzo to sell the company to Texas Air Corporation for $640 million. After a month-long struggle with its unions and creditors, the management of Eastern made the move in order to avoid technical default on approximately $2.5 billion in debt and to avert threatened strikes by pilots and flight attendants. The acquisition of Eastern tripled the size of Lorenzo's enterprise, making it the nation's largest air carrier.

One major obstacle faced by Lorenzo was the strong opposition of Eastern's unions, particularly the machinists. Led by Charles E. Bryan, a member of Eastern's board of directors, the machinists had refused to join other unions in making concessions to the Eastern Airlines management, thereby precipitating the Lorenzo takeover. Although at first optimistic about his chances of being able to negotiate with Lorenzo, Bryan was snubbed when he proposed a personal audience with the Texas Air chief executive officer. From that point, the situation deteriorated rapidly. Lorenzo vowed to reduce the machinists' wages sharply and to alter union work rules that he considered counterproductive. In a letter sent in September 1986 to union members, Bryan declared "all-out war" against the new management. Meanwhile, there had been a desperate search for outside investors who might help the unions to make a counter-bid to buy the company.

After initially rejecting Lorenzo's bid for Eastern Airlines as anticompetitive, the federal transportation department approved the proposal in September 1986, once Texas Air had sold to Pan American World Airways enough takeoff and landing slots to allow Pan Am's new northeast corridor shuttle service to attain fully competitive status with Eastern. Lorenzo was named chairman of the Eastern Airlines board on October 15, 1986, in what was described in *Business Week* as "a sweeping management shakeup." At a special Eastern Airlines shareholders' meeting on November 25, the revised $676 million merger with Texas Air was approved, despite a shouting match among some shareholders and vehement protest from Bryan and spokesmen for the union coalition that had formed to attempt to purchase Eastern.

In the meantime, People Express chairman Donald C. Burr had met with Lorenzo in late June 1986, to discuss the possible sale of his struggling airline. An agreement for United Airlines to take over People Express had been reported in July, but on September 15 Lorenzo and Burr appeared together to announce Texas Air's bid to acquire People Express and the assets of its subsidiary, Frontier Airlines, recently grounded as a result of bankruptcy. Labor considerations were not believed to present an obstacle to the merger, since employees of People Express had remained non-unionized, but People's creditors still had to agree to the merger, through which Texas Air assumed the airline's staggering debt. After that approval, Texas Air's $115 million purchase of People Express went into effect on December 30, 1986. It brought the number of Texas Air's employees up to about 48,000 and its number of aircraft to 588.

Ironically, since ongoing fare wars had caused the balance of power to shift once more in the direction of consolidation in the hands of a few major carriers, government regulators had again been calling attention to the dangers of decreased competition. Some airline analysts contend that an oligopoly of the five or six large carriers with the most efficient management would be likely to survive deregulation to capture 90 percent of domestic air travel. "By its rapid maneuvers, Texas Air has emerged as the high flyer in the country's fierce merger wars," George Russell wrote in *Time* (September 29, 1986). The Texas Air-People Express takeover deal gave Lorenzo 20.1 percent of the nation's market share, far more than that controlled by any of the preregulation era industry giants. "The combination," Agis Salpukis wrote in the

New York Times (September 16, 1986), "would also create the nation's largest low-cost carrier, which could force down fares in markets dominated by such major carriers as United, American, and Delta."

In May 1987 Texas Air reported a loss of over $100 million for the first quarter, compared with $11.2 million in the previous year, but Lorenzo noted that the company's overall performance had improved in the weeks following the consolidation, on February 1, of People Express, Frontier, Texas Air, and Continental. Meanwhile, to challenge American Airlines for the title of industry cost-setter and establish Texas Air as the least expensive airline in the industry, Lorenzo introduced such innovations as a new discount fare known as "Max$aver" and incurred the wrath of the unions by announcing plans to cut labor costs at Eastern by $490 million. In July 1987 Lorenzo forced out Continental's president, Thomas J. Plaskett, and took direct control, following a second-quarter loss of $71.1 million and reports of deterioration of service. In September he announced a sweeping improvement plan for Continental.

Frank Lorenzo has been described as a shy, private man who cherishes the time he is able to spend with his wife, the former Sharon Neill Murray, a lawyer, whom he married on October 14,

1972, and their son and three daughters. According to James Cook, who called him "Lorenzo the Presumptuous" in an article in Forbes (October 30, 1978), Lorenzo is "a trim, rather boyish-looking man." To keep fit, Lorenzo runs twenty-five to thirty miles a week, and during the Continental takeover battle he spent his free time training for the New York City Marathon. At his insistence, health foods were introduced in meals served to passengers of his airlines. According to James R. Norman, writing in Business Week (July 1, 1985), critics call Lorenzo "a ruthless pragmatist whose only close friends are business associates." But colleagues have described him as "quiet," "introspective," and "cerebral." In the words of one airline executive, quoted anonymously in Newsweek (September 29, 1986), "He's a tough guy, and that's what the industry needs. He's changing the whole damn business from the bottom up."

References: Barron's 66:8+ Mr 3 '86 por; Bsns W p20+ Jl 1 '85 por, p104+ Mr 10 '86 por; Forbes 122:115+ O 30 '78 por, 123:66+ Mr 5 '79 por; Fortune 109:66+ Ja 9 '84 por, 115:68+ My 11 '87 por; N Y Times D p1+ O 4 '83 por, D p1+ Je 14 '85 por, III p1+ Mr 9 '86 por; Wall St J p1+ F 18 '82 por, II p33 S 8 '83 por; Washington Post F p1+ F 25 '86; Who's Who in America, 1986-87

Lukas, J(ay) Anthony

Apr. 25, 1933– Author; journalist. Address: b. c/o Alfred A. Knopf, Inc., 201 E. 50th St., New York City, N.Y. 10022

"I'm a reporter by trade," J. Anthony Lukas said in a recent interview. "The highfalutin' name for that is journalist, but I still think of myself as a reporter." An experienced and skilled "reporter" who specializes in plumbing the social and political currents running through contemporary American life, Lukas has twice won the Pulitzer Prize for his incisive analyses of modern urban America. In 1968 he was cited for special local reporting for his New York Times series about a grisly murder. Eight years later, his book Common Ground: A Turbulent Decade in the Lives of Three American Families, an examination of racial tensions in Boston as told through the lives of some of its citizens, won the award for general nonfiction.

Of Hungarian and German descent, Jay Anthony Lukas was born on April 25, 1933, in New York City, one of the two sons of Edwin Jay Lukas, a lawyer, and Elizabeth (Schamberg) Lukas, an actress. After his mother's death, when he was just eight years old, the boy spent more time at private boarding schools than at his father's apartment on Manhattan's East Side. From 1947 to 1951 he attended the Putney School, a coeducational prep academy in Putney, Vermont, that he has described as

"straitlaced" and "very high-minded." "I . . . spent four cloistered years at Putney—schussing the ski slopes, singing Bach cantatas, playing Hotspur and King Lear, publishing an eccentric literary magazine," he recalled to one reporter. For a time he dreamed of becoming a professional actor, but he eventually gave up that idea in favor of a career as a journalist. "If I couldn't be onstage," he told Deirdre Donahue in an interview for a *People* profile (January 13, 1986), "I pledged myself to write about the great dramatic stuff of life."

Following his graduation from the Putney School in 1951, Lukas enrolled at Harvard University, where he majored in government. While he was a student there, he served as a reporter for, and later assistant managing editor of, the *Harvard Crimson*, the campus daily newspaper. Early in 1954 he scored a major journalistic coup when he obtained an interview with Wendell H. Furry, a Harvard physics professor who had admitted in testimony before Senator Joseph R. McCarthy's Senate investigations subcommittee that he had been one of several Communists employed on a secret wartime research project. Lukas' story for the *Harvard Crimson*, in which Furry described his five years in a Communist "cell" at Harvard, was picked up by the Associated Press wire service and reprinted in newspapers all over the country. As a result, Lukas received summer job offers from several newspapers, including the *St. Louis Post-Dispatch*. During earlier college vacations, he had worked for the *Long Island Star-Journal* and the *Harrisburg* (Pennsylvania) *Patriot*. Despite the demands of daily deadlines at the *Harvard Crimson*, Lukas managed to maintain a grade-point average high enough to earn him election to Phi Beta Kappa.

A few months after he received his B.A. degree, *magna cum laude*, from Harvard in 1955, Lukas entered the Free University of Berlin for a year's graduate study as an Adenauer Fellow. He spent the summer of 1956 teaching at a seminar in American studies in Salzburg, Austria, then traveled around Eastern Europe before returning home. Shortly thereafter, he was drafted into the United States Army. Assigned to a psychological warfare unit, he spent the better part of his two-year tour of duty in Tokyo, writing fifteen-minute radio news commentaries aimed at converting the Chinese and Koreans to the "democratic way of life," as he put it.

On his discharge from the military in 1958, Lukas worked briefly as a speechwriter for Foster Furcolo, a middle-of-the-road Democrat who was running for a second term as governor of Massachusetts, then joined the staff of the *Baltimore* (Maryland) *Sun*. For the next four years, he covered a range of stories of local interest, including crime, city politics, and urban renewal. In 1962 Lukas signed on with the *New York Times*. After short stints on the *Times*'s metropolitan, Washington, and United Nations desks, he was sent to the Congo (now Zaire), with the responsibility for covering not only that strife-torn country but also the emerging nations of West Africa. In 1965 Lukas was transferred to the newspaper's India bureau. From his base in New Delhi, he reported on developments in India, Pakistan, and Ceylon (now Sri Lanka), with occasional forays into Australia, Ja-

pan, and Korea, until 1967. During his tenure there, he also contributed profiles of political personalities, such as Indira Gandhi, the prime minister of India, to the *New York Times Magazine*.

Returning to the United States after spending five years overseas, Lukas accepted an assignment on the *Times*'s metropolitan bureau. To his surprise, as he explained to Joseph Barbato in an interview for *Publishers Weekly* (September 27, 1985), he found that "there were things happening in this country which were infinitely more interesting and compelling than abroad." One of his first pieces on the social upheaval of the late 1960s was "The Two Worlds of Linda Fitzpatrick," which appeared in the *Times* on October 16, 1967. An in-depth investigation of the life and death of a well-to-do eighteen-year-old Connecticut girl who had been found beaten to death, along with her hippie boyfriend, in the boiler room of a tenement in New York City's East Village. The story focused on the striking contrast between the young woman's affluent suburban upbringing and her drug-ridden life in New York's hippie subculture. The article earned Lukas the 1968 Pulitzer Prize for special local reporting, the George Polk Memorial Award, the Page One Award from the New York Newspaper Guild, the By-line Feature Award of the Newspaper Reporters Association, and the Mike Berger Award, given annually by Columbia University's Graduate School of Journalism to New York newspapermen for distinguished reporting.

The recipient of a prestigious Nieman Fellowship, Lukas returned to Harvard for the 1968–69 academic year to study American history and literature. On completion of his studies, he rejoined the staff of the *New York Times* as a roving national correspondent, based in Chicago. The centrally located city, with its domestic unrest and increasing radicalism, particularly among the young, fascinated Lukas and provided him with the raw material for many of his most admired pieces, including the series of articles he wrote about the trial of the so-called "Chicago Seven"—a group of antiwar activists accused of conspiring to incite a riot at the 1968 Democratic National Convention.

Lukas' editors had opposed his covering the conspiracy case, and during the course of the five-month trial, he often clashed with them over how the controversial story should be handled. One bone of contention was the editors' decision to delete from a quotation the word "bullshit" and substitute in its place the euphemism "barnyard epithet." Bristling at such editorial interference, Lukas left daily reporting in 1970 to become a staff writer for the *New York Times Magazine*. Two years later, at the first A. J. Liebling Counter-Convention in New York, Lukas attacked editors in general and A. M. ("Abe") Rosenthal, then the *Times*'s managing editor, in particular. "He's a disaster," Lukas said of Rosenthal, as quoted in *Newsweek* (May 8, 1972). "I think it's because egotistical, brilliant, hard-driving reporters just make lousy editors. Editors need to put aside their egos and let the writer just write."

Lukas' assignments as a staff writer for the *Times Magazine* ranged from an analysis of racial trouble in Cairo, Illinois, to an investigation of Mc-Donald's fast-food empire and included biographical profiles of such disparate individuals as Bob Hope, sportscaster Mel Allen, Daniel Ellsberg, the antiwar activist who released to the press portions of the top secret Pentagon Papers, and Bobby Seale, a leader of the Black Panthers. In his spare time, Lukas put together two books that, in his words, "grew out of daily journalism." The first of those efforts was *The Barnyard Epithet and Other Obscenities: Notes on the Chicago Conspiracy* (Harper & Row, 1970), which the critic Richard Goldstein pronounced "the only piece of reasoned reportage to come out" of that notorious case; the second was *Don't Shoot—We Are Your Children* (Random House, 1971), in which Lukas analyzed the "generation gap" by examining in detail the lives of ten disaffected young people—Linda Fitzpatrick and her boyfriend, Jim ("Groovy") Hutchison; Sue Thrasher, a white civil rights activist; jailed draft resister Don Baty; and Don McAuliff, a disillusioned Peace Corps volunteer, among others.

As Lukas explained in his preface, *Don't Shoot—We Are Your Children* was prompted by his realization, in 1967, that "after five years abroad [he] was just as out of touch with American young people as most of the parents [he had] been talking to" for his story about the murder of Linda Fitzpatrick. Agreeing with the Freudian psychoanalyst Erik Erikson that "the younger generation makes overt what is covert in the older generation," Lukas told an interviewer for *Publishers Weekly* (March 8, 1971), "I'm just as convinced that this is going to happen to this generation, too. I can see it already. This generation, which has so scathingly exposed the hypocrisies of the older generation, is already beginning to live its own hypocrisies, and, in turn, will inflict those hypocrisies upon their children."

In his appraisal of *Don't Shoot* for the *New York Times Book Review* (April 25, 1971), the novelist Ross MacDonald commended Lukas for "his eloquence as a writer, his tenacity in research, [and] his respect for other human beings" and predicted that the book "may become a classic." Geoffrey Wolff of *Newsweek* and Richard Goldstein, a critic for the *Village Voice*, also praised the book highly, but in his review of June 24, 1971, Goldstein also chided Lukas for his "subtle detachment", and "facile reliance on detail" and for "the drab uniformity" of much of his writing.

In 1971 Lukas resigned from the staff of the *New York Times Magazine* to cofound *MORE*, a monthly journal that cast a critical eye on the news media. He was associate editor of that magazine until it folded in 1977. Concurrently, from 1973 to 1976, he was a contributing editor of the now defunct *New Times*, an "alternative" news magazine. Throughout that period, he also freelanced, submitting pieces to *Atlantic*, *Esquire*, the *New Republic*, *Rolling Stone*, *Gentlemen's Quarterly*, and *American Scholar*, among others, and he contin-

ued to contribute occasional articles to the *New York Times Magazine*, which devoted its entire issues of July 22, 1973, and January 13, 1974, to his analyses of the unraveling Watergate scandal. Lukas was at work on a third piece, focusing on the impeachment struggle, when Richard Nixon resigned the presidency in August 1974. The *Times Magazine* articles formed the backbone of his widely acclaimed book *Nightmare: The Underside of the Nixon Years* (Viking, 1976), which Mark Starr, writing in *Newsweek* (September 23, 1985), described as "arguably the best accounting yet of the Watergate chapter in U.S. history."

Even before *Nightmare* went to press, Lukas was casting around for an even more ambitious project. Despite the favorable notices accorded his three books, he felt dissatisfied. "I don't disown them; I'm happy to have written them; but they weren't my best books," he told Joseph Barbato. "They grew haphazardly out of journalistic work. . . . I was forty-one, and I thought, 'Well, life is finite, and if I'm ever going to do a book of which I am unequivocally proud, it's time to conceive a book as a book.'"

The kind of book Lukas had in mind was one based on the techniques used by Truman Capote in his "nonfiction novel" about a mass murder, *In Cold Blood*, and C. D. B. Bryan in his *Friendly Fire*, a factual account of an Iowa farm couple's efforts to learn the truth about the death of their son, who was accidentally killed by American artillery fire during the Vietnam war. "Bryan had brought a complex social issue down to the experience of a single family," Lukas explained to Barbato. "You could feel the war through the lives of this family." Lukas eventually chose as his subject the mob violence that erupted in Boston following the federal government's school desegregation order. In the *Publishers Weekly* interview, he described an antibusing rally at which Massachusetts Senator Edward M. Kennedy, who was trying to speak in favor of busing to achieve racial desegregation, was spat upon, kicked, pushed, and pelted with fruit: "I remember saying to myself, 'What is going on?'. . . . What was happening to the Irish working class, to Boston, to American liberalism? What was happening to the dream, if you will—to Martin Luther King's dream?"

In 1976, armed with a book contract and an advance from the Alfred A. Knopf publishing house, Lukas set to work on a project that he could not suspect would take him seven and one-half years to complete, instead of the two he had anticipated. To support himself during this period, he drew additional advances from his publisher, wrote a few articles and book reviews, and taught courses as an adjunct professor of journalism at Boston University, in 1977-78, and as an adjunct lecturer at Harvard's John F. Kennedy School of Government, in 1979-80. He also received fellowships from the Kennedy Institute of Politics, in 1976-77, and the Guggenheim Foundation, in 1978-79.

Lukas planned to construct his story around the experiences of three Boston families—one black, one middle-class Yankee, one working-class Irish. He interviewed scores of families before selecting the final three, but even so he was almost forced to scuttle the project after deciding that the Irish family was "not working dramatically for the book." Instead, he started over with the McGoffs, a large Irish Catholic family who lived in a dilapidated housing project in the Charlestown area of Boston. The McGoffs joined the Twymons, a black family living on welfare in a Roxbury housing project, and the Divers, upper-middle-class liberals who had moved with their two sons to a racially mixed, gentrified neighborhood in Boston's South End.

Over the course of the next few years, Lukas taped 555 hours of interviews with members of the three families and traveled to sites as diverse and far-flung as Georgia, Nova Scotia, and Ireland in order to trace their ancestries back to the eighteenth century. He also questioned the families' neighbors and friends and delved into Boston's social history. Eager to observe the Twymon and McGoff children in class at their recently desegregated school, he even persuaded initially reluctant Charlestown High School administrators to "hire" him at no salary as a part-time teacher. Feeling that he had been "massively invading their privacy" for years, Lukas asked each family to read its section of the book in manuscript and correct any "undisputed factual errors." "It is *not* a good journalistic practice, but I felt that was a very special case," he told Joseph Barbato. "To my delight, we had no real problems."

Covering the years 1968 to 1978, *Common Ground: A Turbulent Decade in the Lives of Three American Families* (Knopf, 1985) concentrates on the issues and events surrounding the implementation of court-ordered busing in the Boston public schools and its effects on the daily lives of the city's residents, but it also deals with crime, housing ills, ethnic rivalry, and other symptoms of urban blight. Over the decade, the McGoffs saw their community torn apart by the often violent opposition to the busing of black children to their local high school; the Divers, troubled by the rising crime rate in their South End neighborhood, fled to the suburbs; and the Twymons endured the indignities of being bused to a hostile school and the humiliation of seeing a son jailed for rape. Interwoven into the saga of the three families are profiles of Boston Mayor Kevin White; Louise Day Hicks, the antibusing activist; Humberto Cardinal Medeiros, the Catholic archbishop of Boston; Thomas Winship, the editor of the influential *Boston Globe*; and United States District Court Judge W. Arthur Garrity, who framed and enforced the school-desegregation plan.

After writing *Common Ground*, Lukas told a reporter for *U.S. News & World Report* (April 28, 1986) that he was "more pessimistic" about solving the country's racial problems, largely because he was "pessimistic about its sister issue of class." "The title of my book—*Common Ground*— suggests that I feel those of us who care about social justice need to think more about coalition building, more about what we have in common with some of these folks and less about what sets us apart," he went on. "Unless the privileged and the comfortable are willing to become part of the process of working out the great ideals of American life, we're going to go on seeing disasters of social policy. You put the burden on the vulnerable and the angry, and you're going to reap a whirlwind."

Admired for the force and clarity of its narrative, *Common Ground* was considered by most critics to be a landmark of social reportage. "Like a Balzac of Boston," Jack Beatty observed in his review for the *Atlantic* (September 1985), Lukas "balances thick detail with a subtle development of themes . . . , a willingness to venture interpretations, and a delicate skill in biographical portraiture." In addition to the Pulitzer Prize for general nonfiction, *Common Ground* won for Lukas the American Book Award for nonfiction, the National Book Critics Circle Award for general nonfiction, the Robert F. Kennedy Book Award, and the Political Book of the Year Award. Another tribute came in the form of an honorary doctor of letters degree from Boston's Northeastern University.

J. Anthony Lukas, who stands six feet one inch tall and weighs 185 pounds, has graying brown hair and deep-set brown eyes. By his own account "a hopelessly 1950s person" who favors "tweed jackets and buttondown shirts," Lukas is as relaxed and unpretentious as his wardrobe—"the sort of man to whom you imagine strangers . . . might very well open their hearts," according to Joseph Barbato. He and his wife, Linda Healey, an editor whom he married on September 18, 1982, live in a book-lined apartment on Manhattan's Upper West Side that is decorated with the exotic art objects he collected during his days as a foreign correspondent. A "world-class pinball player" in his bachelor days, he now lists tennis, chess, and reading as his favorite recreations. A self-described "Jewish liberal," Lukas has been an active member of the PEN American Center, the Reporters Committee for Freedom of the Press, and the Committee for Public Justice. He is currently working on a book "about democracy in a small American community."

References: *New Yorker* 51:81+ Je 30 '75; *People* 25:63+ Ja 13 '86 por; *Pub W* 199:27+ Mr 8 '71, 228:98+ S 27 '86 por; *U S News* 100:75+ Ap 28 '86; *Contemporary Authors* vols 49–52 (1975), new rev vol 2 (1981), new rev vol 19 (1986); *Dubois, Diana, ed. My Harvard, My Yale* (1982); *Who's Who in America, 1984–85*

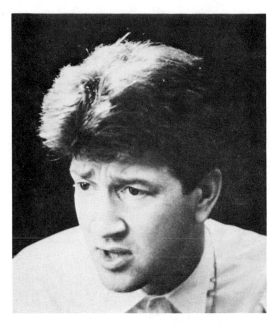

Lynch, David

Jan. 20, 1946– Filmmaker. Address: b. c/o De Laurentiis Entertainment Group, 720 Fifth Ave., New York City, N.Y. 10019

The only filmmaker who brings an avant-garde sensibility to today's commercial American cinema is the director David Lynch. A home-grown surrealist who started out as a painter, Lynch has made only four feature-length films, but he is rapidly attaining the status of *auteur*. He first achieved notoriety with *Eraserhead*, a strangely compelling, often gruesome film that gained a wide cult following on the so-called midnight movie circuit in the late 1970s. He then won critical respect with *The Elephant Man*, in which he combined the lyrical evocation of a physical monstrosity's sensitive soul with an unflinching depiction of the grim industrial landscape of Victorian England. His *Dune* was a baroque visual tapestry, and his most controversial film, *Blue Velvet*, has divided moviegoers into several camps: those who are shocked, those who are delighted and amused, and those who are repelled and enthralled at the same time. A cinematic provocateur, Lynch is noted for his obsession with stark images of vilely decaying organic matter, for his painterly vision, and for a narrative rhythm that is uniquely and quirkily his own.

David K. Lynch was born in the state university town of Missoula, Montana, on January 20, 1946. In an interview with Chris Hodenfield for *Rolling Stone* magazine (December 6, 1984), Lynch categorized his parents as "just regular people." "My dad," he recalled, "was raised on a wheat ranch in Montana and my mother is from Brooklyn, . . . so they're fairly different. They met on a nature hike in Duke University." His nature-loving father

worked for the United States Department of Agriculture as a research scientist, specializing in tree growth and the prevention of blight. His work took the family from place to place, and David spent his adolescence in placid, all-American towns like Missoula and Spokane, Washington. He also lived for a time in Idaho before his family resettled in the Washington, D.C., suburb of Alexandria, Virginia.

David Lynch insists that his obsessive interest in the hidden underside of gleaming surfaces derives from his upbringing in white-picket-fence America. "When I was little," he told Chris Hodenfield, "there were picket fences, beautiful trees . . . , Fifties cars, happiness, real quiet dreamy afternoons, real good friends, lakes, camping trips, and fires, and stuff like this. And I enjoyed all those things but there was also something else under the surface." That "something else" was fear, an almost primordial sense of dread that Lynch discovered when his mother took him to visit her parents in New York City. "I was very little," he said during an interview with the *Toronto Globe and Mail* (September 19, 1986), "I don't know how old. I went periodically [and] kept going back there, just picking up on fear. I mean, it was pleasant and everything, but I always had one eye looking somewhere else. I said to myself, 'Don't you people feel this horror? This place is unbelievable.'"

To become a painter was Lynch's consuming ambition from a very early age, but he did not know that one could make a living from art until he was thirteen and met a professional painter named Bushnell Keeler. It was, Lynch told a reporter for *Interview* magazine (March 1987), "an awakening." "I became feverish," he recalled. "I didn't want to go to school anymore. . . . High school didn't have a big hold on me. I knew I was going in a different direction." While attending Hammond High School in Alexandria, Lynch took courses at the Corcoran School of Art in Washington, D.C. After graduating in 1964, he traveled briefly in Europe, where he had an epiphany that brought him the realization that he "was seven thousand miles from McDonald's" and that he was, irreversibly, "an *American* artist," as he was quoted as saying in *Esquire* (January 1985). Back in the United States, he attended the School of the Museum of Fine Arts in Boston for a year before enrolling at the Pennsylvania Academy of Fine Arts in Philadelphia, where he studied painting from 1965 through 1969.

Influenced by *The Art Spirit*, a book by the American painter and educator Robert Henri (1865–1929), the teacher of Edward Hopper, Lynch dedicated himself to what he calls the "Art Life." What he took from Henri's book, Lynch explained in the *Esquire* interview, "was that art comes first. In the Art Life you don't get married and you don't have families and you have studios and models and you drink a lot of coffee and you smoke cigarettes and you work mostly at night. . . . You think beneath the surface of things and you live a fantastic life of ideas. And create stuff."

Later in the 1960s Lynch, who admired abstract expressionist art, began to "create stuff" by working in the medium of film, an impulse arising from his desire, he explained, "to see a painting move, . . . to do a kind of film-painting." After receiving instruction in the rudiments of operating a camera at a local Fotorama lab—which, he told Stephen Schiff of Vanity Fair (March 1987), was "a sleaze place down in Philadelphia"—Lynch made a film with one minute's worth of imagery which played on a continuous loop. He described the piece in the New York Times (October 11, 1986): "It started off with six heads and then arms and stomachs grew in. The heads caught fire and then all the heads got violently sick and then it started all over again."

It is a deep-seated fear that goads him to be creative, "the fear of being restricted—in every way," Lynch explained in the Chicago Tribune (September 25, 1986). "The fear started at art school in Philadelphia," he said, "but it's got a lot to do with the city." When he lived there, Lynch considered Philadelphia "the sleaziest, most corrupt, decadent, sick, fear-ridden, twisted city on the face of the earth." But it was there, too, that his first original ideas about art and filmmaking came to him.

For a time in Philadelphia, Lynch roomed with his brother-in-law Jack Fisk (who is now a movie director himself) next door to a morgue. Like the human ear that the young hero of Blue Velvet finds in a littered field, the morgue impelled Lynch "to go beneath the surface of things" for the first time in his life. "There were these strange vibes in the neighborhood," he told the Tribune interviewer. "You could feel it, not see it. So I probed. For me, getting invited to the morgue was a big deal, the turning point. Seeing a dead person is like proof that something can happen."

In 1970 Lynch moved to Los Angeles, where he enrolled at the American Film Institute as a fellow in the Center for Advanced Film Studies. There, in sunlit contrast to Philadelphia, he metamorphosed his ideas and disquieting experiences into art. He made a thirty-four-minute color film called The Grandmother (1970), about a lonely little boy who, abused by his parents, grows a loving grandmother from seed. They are briefly happy, then she dies, as he does shortly thereafter. In 1972 Lynch began work on Eraserhead, his nightmare vision of life on the weirder fringes of the urban American industrial wasteland, the film that would launch his career but take him more than four years to make.

Eraserhead is the numbingly slow-paced "story"—brought to the screen virtually uncensored from the lower depths of Lynch's unconscious—of Henry Spencer (played by John Nance), whose stacked hairdo and fantasy of having his head used as an eraser gives the film its title. A sensitive but spaced-out daydreamer, Henry agrees to marry his girlfriend, Mary X (portrayed by Charlotte Stewart) when she gives birth to a hideous, mewling "thing" that seems to lack an epidermis. Then nature goes awry. She gives birth to a series of strange creatures that Henry liquidates by flinging them against a wall. Eventually he kills the first and most gruesome of all his offspring in what has been called "one of the most repugnant scenes in film history." For that "crime," Henry is decapitated.

Released by the Film Institute in 1977, Eraserhead was not widely distributed until 1978, when it came to the attention of the "midnight movie" entrepreneur Ben Barenholtz. Nor did Lynch's odd, cheaply made film receive kind notices from critics. "Many film students aspire to be the next Orson Welles or Stanley Kubrick," sniffed a Variety reviewer (March 23, 1977), "but Lynch seems bent on emulating Herschell Gordon Lewis, the king of low-budget gore." In the London Observer (April 1, 1979) Philip French called Eraserhead an "old-fashioned surrealist cocktail mixing the hermetic and the emetic," but found the film "incoherent" on the whole. Nevertheless, Eraserhead ran for years as a regular weekend midnight attraction at the Waverly Theatre in Greenwich Village and recruited a large cult following in Los Angeles as well. As Stephen Schiff wrote in Vanity Fair, "Eraserhead is 'realistic' the way Kafka is realistic; it's a seducitve nightmare in black and white, but mostly black—mostly the fathomless, de Chirico black that has become a Lynch hallmark." Because of what Schiff called its "atmosphere of intense isolation and displacement, leavened by a gonzo sense of humor," Eraserhead has become one of the most successful of all midnight movies.

While making Eraserhead, Lynch suffered a series of reversals in his personal life. His first marriage broke up, and, chronically short of funds, he had to sleep most nights on the Eraserhead set, in Henry's grim "apartment." To get by, he took on a paper route, delivering the Wall Street Journal for forty-eight dollars a week. Between 1976 and 1978 he concocted the screenplay for Ronnie Rocket, about the unusual adventures of a short, red-haired scientist, a kind of postmodern Candide, who may be an alien from outer space. With Eraserhead as a dubious entry on his list of credits, Lynch tried to interest executives at established Hollywood studios in his Ronnie Rocket script, but he got nowhere.

But the comedian Mel Brooks had admired Eraserhead, and his company, Brooksfilms, was producing a version of the story of John Merrick, the so-called Elephant Man. Merrick (1863–1890) was one of the most physically repulsive men in history, but his ugliness belied a gentle, poetic soul. Exhibited as a carnival freak, Merrick had an abnormally large, disfigured head, a twisted spine, and an otiose right arm, caused by his affliction with multiple neurofibromatosis. Before dying in his sleep of possible accidental self-strangulation, Merrick was lionized by Victorian high society.

Mel Brooks was surprised when he met the director of Eraserhead. Instead of the expected "grotesque—a fat little German with fat stains running down his chin"—Lynch turned out to be a calm, quietly intense young man whom Brooks has since described as "Jimmy Stewart from Mars." Indeed, Lynch's demeanor is one of skewed normalcy, like that of the musician-auteur David Byrne. He dresses in primly new-wave combinations of black and white—tieless white shirts that are always buttoned at the collar, dark jackets and slacks, and black clodhopper shoes—and his discourse is larded with *Leave-It-to-Beaver*-land exclamations like "holy smokes," "goshamighty," and "gee whiz."

In 1978 Brooks wisely chose Lynch to direct *The Elephant Man* (1980), a critically acclaimed box-office hit that garnered eight Oscar nominations, including one for Lynch as best director. In her *New Yorker* review (October 27, 1980), Pauline Kael was impressed by the "extraordinary taste" that *Eraserhead*'s director brought to the filming of Merrick's story: "It's not the kind of taste that enervates artists—it's closer to grace. The movie shows us what the monster feels about himself and what his view of the world is and what he sees when he looks out of the single rectangular slit on his hood (which suggests an elephant's eye). . . . 'The Elephant Man' has the power and some of the dream logic of a silent film, yet there are also wrenching, pulsating sounds—the hissing of steam and the pounding of the [new] industrial age."

In a cast that included John Gielgud as the director of a London hospital, John Hurt received extravagant praise for his portrayal of the Elephant Man, and Anthony Hopkins, who played Dr. Treves, Merrick's physician-benefactor, was also acclaimed. Most critics applauded Lynch for his sensitive depiction of Merrick's inner nobility and for the power of his often dreamlike visual imagery, graphically rendered in black and white by the cinematographer Freddie Francis. But both J. Hoberman in the *Village Voice* (October 1, 1980) and David Denby in *New York* magazine (November 3, 1980) thought that, in portraying London's working classes as Merrick's cruel tormentors but members of the Victorian haute monde as his patrons and saviors, Lynch had imbued the film with an ambiguous political message. "I don't know what Lynch intended," wrote Denby, "but the movie expresses a boundless loathing for ordinary people and a rather pathetic worship of the wealthy and well-connected. Underneath the dark, visionary horror imagery there's a sweet Victorian story about an unfortunate who was treated well by the better sort of people. The confusions of the movie are finally resolved in the smuggest Victorian sentimentality."

Now regarded in Hollywood as a gifted artist and a "bankable" commodity, Lynch turned down an offer from George Lucas to direct *Return of the Jedi*, the eagerly awaited concluding chapter of Lucas' *Star Wars* trilogy. Instead, he started work on a "small" film, *Ronnie Rocket,* at director-producer Francis Ford Coppola's Zoetrope Studios, but with Zoetrope on the verge of financial ruin, Lynch was forced to suspend production early in 1981. He was therefore available when the mega-producer Dino de Laurentiis proposed that Lynch take on the monumental task of directing *Dune,* the long-anticipated screen version of the best-selling science fiction novel by the pop visionary Frank Herbert.

First published in 1965, *Dune* gained a cult following in the 1960s among the rebels of the counterculture and has attracted a worldwide readership estimated at thirty million. *Dune* is the sprawling intergalactic saga of a young nobleman named Paul Atreides, the messiah whose coming has been foretold, who in the year 10,191 leads the Fremen in a holy war against the corrupt, decadent powers that rule the universe. The Fremen, who inhabit the desert planet Arrakis, known as "Dune," are miners of "melange," a narcotic spice found only on Dune, and it is for control of the coveted consciousness-expanding, life-prolonging spice, guarded by monster worms, that the ruling families of the four advanced planets conspire against one another. Underlying the byzantine interplanetary intrigue are Herbert's quasi-mystical ideas, which meld pop mythology, messianic religion, and a political message made up of ecological utopianism, Marxism, and apocalyptic notions of a purifying *jihad,* or holy war.

The vast scope of Herbert's novel had defeated the earlier efforts of several directors to bring *Dune* to the screen, and for Lynch and de Laurentiis, *Dune* proved to be an awesome enterprise to manage as well as a serious artistic and financial risk. Produced at a cost of about $45,000,000, the film had to rake in some $200,000,000 at the box office just to break even. Moreover, Lynch himself had to compress the 500-page novel into a 120-page script, slogging his way through seven drafts before he produced one that satisfied both de Laurentiis and Frank Herbert. Then, when filming began in Mexico, he had to oversee the creation of more than seventy sets—each of *Dune*'s four planets has a completely different ecosystem—the invention of optical effects whose wizardry rivaled that of the gadget-laden films *Star Wars* and *Jaws,* and a Cecil B. De Mille-sized cast of approximately 20,000, including extras.

Released by Universal just before Christmas 1984, the two-and-one-half-hour *Dune* was greeted with mixed reviews and turned out to be a spectacular flop at the box office. Although critics praised Lynch for having created a majestic visual spectacle, they felt that he had failed to impose a coherent narrative on his leviathan. They agreed that he had been undone by the novel's bewildering array of characters and maze of subplots, and by the unfamiliar terminology of the four rudimentary new languages that Frank Herbert had dreamed up for *Dune.* According to *New York*'s David Denby (January 14, 1985), "*Dune* begins with a cartload of exposition that lasts upward of an hour—an indigestible mass of planets, emperors, dukes, wars. The movie never recovers. Thereafter, people come on, say a few solemn words, and disappear; . . . by the end, I had the vague sense that the universe had somehow been saved by a neo-fascist cult fighting for the good, but I couldn't tell for sure." And in the *Village Voice* J. Hoberman wrote that "*Dune* has the feel of a seventh-grade science project run amok [but] it's often brilliantly disgusting. The film's villains are full of tubes and implants, their faces scarred with sewn-up orifices and weird skin grafts. Lynch's favorite characters are obviously the evil [dynastic family of the] Harkonnens. . . . These baddies—who include the smirking [rock star] Sting, Jack Nance [*Eraserhead*'s star], and particularly Kenneth Mc-Millan [the Baron]—are leprously charismatic." Lynch himself feels that *Dune* was eviscerated by excessive editing and hopes that a four-hours-plus version can be released someday on videocassette.

Since the expectations for *Dune* had been as swollen as its budget—it is one of the most expensive movies ever made—the fiasco might have wrecked Lynch's career. "I learned a lot of things on *Dune*," the director told the interviewer for the *Toronto Globe and Mail*, "and I'm not totally sorry I did it. But a tremendous amount of pain was involved, and the outcome was pretty devastating. I fell in love with a lot of [Herbert's] ideas . . . , and I wanted to enter into these worlds and make them real. I needed more time. . . . But at two hours and fifteen minutes, [*Dune*] became like a garbage compacter. Things are supposed to be mysterious, not confusing."

Rather than blame his protégé for the *Dune* disaster, de Laurentiis realized that Lynch's talents might be more suited to a personal film over which the director could exercise complete control. In return for that freedom, de Laurentiis pledged to finance *Blue Velvet*, a surrealistic murder mystery that Lynch had written a few years before, so long as he would agree to work on a shoestring budget. "So I cut my salary in half, I cut the [movie's] budget down almost in half and made it," Lynch said in *Interview*. "And Dino was true to his word. He gave me total artistic control. He figured maybe he'd break even."

Produced for only $6,000,000, *Blue Velvet* had begun reaping profits within a few months of its release in the fall of 1986. One of the most-talked-about films of recent years, it is the coming-of-age story of Jeffrey Beaumont, played by Kyle Mac-Lachlan, who had starred in *Dune*. A twenty-year-old college student as earnest and innocent as the hero in a Hardy Boys adventure tale, Jeffrey returns to his normal-seeming hometown, Lumberton, when his father, the proprietor of the local hardware store, is felled by what appears to be a cerebral hemorrhage. Returning from a hospital visit with his father, Jeffrey chances upon a severed, ant-infested human ear in a field. Tantalized by the mystery of the ear, which so much resembles a seashell that when the camera enters its dark aperture the soundtrack swells with the roar of the ocean, Jeffrey launches an investigation that leads him to tunnel beneath Lumberton's placid surface and into its fetid underworld of sleazy dope dealers, official corruption, and dark sexual violence.

Jeffrey is at first assisted by Sandy (Laura Dern), a sweet, blonde-haired high school senior whose police-detective father is also investigating the mystery of the ear. (As much a comic-book character as Jeffrey is, Sandy is played as the wholesome "Betty" to his darker, more morally ambiguous "Archie.") Jeffrey's sleuthing leads him to the apartment of Dorothy Vallens (Isabella Rosellini), the chanteuse at a local nightclub and the quintessential Blue Lady. She is also the sexual slave of Frank Booth (Dennis Hopper), who has kidnapped her small son and her husband and, apparently, cut off the latter's ear.

Thanks to Hopper's disturbingly comic performance, Frank is at once terrifyingly repulsive and as mesmerizing as a serpent. He is the local drug kingpin—"Mr. Macho Sleazeball himself," to use Pauline Kael's phrase—an obscenity-spouting, drug-warped sadomasochist who brutalizes Dorothy in graphically depicted "games" of sexual bondage, and then, in a pathetic whine, calls her "Mommy." At first, Jeffrey wants only to help Dorothy, but eventually, when she begs him to strike her as a prelude to lovemaking, he complies. Thus Jeffrey learns that he is not altogether unlike the execrable Frank, who becomes his mortal enemy.

The title of *Blue Velvet* comes from the hit song of the early 1960s by the crooner Bobby Vinton, a kitschy ballad that was popular at high school proms. For his film, Lynch creates an unrelenting atmosphere of hallucinatory realism, letting the story unfold with the perverse logic of a bad dream. His Lumberton is a small, sleepy city—Anytown, U.S.A.—where the local radio station, WOOD, marks the beginning of the hour with the sound of falling timber, while the announcer boasts that Lumbertonians "*know* how much wood a wood-chuck chucks." It is a town of whiter-than-white picket fences, where the sky is indigo, and the roses are the color of burgundy, as red as blood. Although the setting is in the present, Lynch fills almost every frame with signifiers such as bric-a-brac, household furnishings, cars, and even sounds, that bespeak the last forty years of American popular culture. In short, Jeffrey "lives in an indefinite mythic present that feels like the past," to quote from Pauline Kael's ecstatic review in the *New Yorker* (September 22, 1986).

Critics acclaimed Lynch for his success in blending the real and the unreal and in merging genres and styles, such as romantic melodrama with comedy and *noir* mystery, and naiveté with purple pulp kinkiness. Pauline Kael, for example, asseverated that the director approached his material "as if he were reinventing movies," and Lynch was once again nominated for an Oscar for best director. Audiences, however, have been deeply divided in their responses to the film. As *Interview*'s Gerald L'Ecuyer observed, "*Blue Velvet* . . . has left audiences either bewildered, intoxicated or enraged—and often a murky combination of all three. . . . The amazing thing about watching the film is that some people in the audience are laughing while others are telling them to be quiet because they think it's deadly serious."

David Lynch's hypnotic visual style is achieved not by means of Martin Scorsese's languorously gliding camera or through the crisp editing of an Alfred Hitchcock, but through his painterly vision. "His technique has no lush pleasures," wrote Lloyd Rose in a lengthy analysis of Lynch's cinema for the *Atlantic* (October 1984). "We aren't swept along by Lynch's camera; we're caught by his images. Our memory of his work is likely to be a series of mysterious, iconographic compositions—as if we had been looking at an exhibition of paintings rather than at a film." So disquieting and artfully composed are Lynch's images that in one of *Blue Velvet*'s climactic scenes, for instance, Jeffrey discovers two corpses, one of them still standing, the other gagged and bound to a chair. Although bloodier and more gruesome, they compel one's attention in the manner of the "lifelike" figural sculptures by the contemporary artists Duane Hanson and Edward Kienholz.

His imagery is also notable for his obsessive concern with what Lloyd Rose calls the "obscenely organic." While in art school Lynch admits to having burned the skin off a mouse to study its inner parts, and when he delivered newspapers his route took him, he told *Interview*, "through two . . . trash areas," and he would sort through the garbage. In his review of *Dune*, Denby remarked that Lynch's "love for oozy, pullulating matter" makes him "the high priest of industrial detritus, [one] for whom the perversion of the organic becomes a fact of life both feared and shamefully admired." "Something tumorous lurks beneath the surface of his movies," wrote Rose; "the physical world is unstable, mutating, breaking apart. . . . Lynch sees the living world as a compost heap."

Much like *Blue Velvet*'s Jeffrey, David Lynch in person gives the impression of propriety gone awry. He admits that he is not articulate in a literary sense, so that creative ideas have to come to him as "a disconnected series of images and moods," as Joseph Gelmis reported in *Newsday* (September 17, 1986). "I believe that ideas come from outside us," he told Gelmis. "It's as if they are being broadcast in the air and we tune into them, like our mind is a receiver. Of course, not everybody receives the ideas as images. . . . For me, whether I'm sitting awake in a chair or dreaming, it's pictures." Lynch courts his muse with caffeine and sugar: he likes to work in cheap coffee shops, where he drinks a river of sweetened coffee and then waits for ideas and images to wash over him.

In interviews, Lynch gives the impression that for him making movies is labor, but painting is fun. His work has been exhibited in galleries in Europe, and no less an authority than the influential art dealer Leo Castelli has pronounced a recent series of Lynch watercolors "very beautiful." By his first marriage, Lynch has a daughter, Jennifer; he has a son, Austin, by his second wife. Lynch makes his home in a comparatively modest apartment in Los Angeles. Currently single, he keeps company with Isabella Rossellini, the actress-model who is the daughter of Ingrid Bergman and the late Italian film director Roberto Rossellini.

References: Chicago Tribune 13 p11+ Ap 22 '84 por; Christian Sci Mon O 9 '80; Esquire 103:105+ Ja '85; N Y Daily News p5 S 26 '83; New Yorker 63:74+ D 24 '84; Newsweek 108:102+ O 27 '86 por; Vanity Fair 50:86+ Mr '87 pors; Washington Post C p1+ D 14 '84

MacIver, Loren

Feb. 2, 1909– Artist. Address: b. c/o Pierre Matisse Gallery, 41 E. 57th St., New York City, N.Y. 10022

NOTE: This biography supersedes the article that appeared in *Current Biography* in 1953.

"This is what I would like to do with painting," Loren MacIver declared some forty years ago, "starting with simple things, to lead the eye by various manipulations of colors, objects and tensions toward a transformation and a reward. . . . " She has pursued that intention throughout a career now in its sixth decade, creating a body of work that is almost wholly independent of current art movements or aesthetic theories. Because of its very idiosyncrasy, her painting eludes stylistic classification, so that it is an oversimplification to define Loren MacIver as a "symbolist" or a "romantic" painter. Although her paintings are not completely representational, neither are they wholly abstract. Based on observed reality, they are filtered through a poet's vision and recorded in terms of an often highly personal vocabulary of signs, fulfilling her wish to "make something permanent out of the transitory, I mean at once dramatic and colloquial."

Several critics have detected a resemblance between Loren MacIver's work and Paul Klee's, without drawing any exact parallels, and one of them, Renée Arb (writing in the *Magazine of Art* in 1948), found such an affinity only in MacIver's early work and observed that even then her approach was "far more homely and realistic" than Klee's. In fact, the consensus is that it is more to the point to draw parallels between MacIver's painting and poetry, especially the imagism of Marianne Moore, who declared that "poetry is in the use that is made of experience."

Loren MacIver's visual experience has come largely from New York, the city where she was born, on February 2, 1909, and where she has lived most of her life. "No other artist," according to the art curator Robert M. Frasch, has "looked more closely at its dissimilar ingredients or translated in such fashion the many isolated and fragmentary aspects of its particular fabric." She is the daughter of Charles Augustus Paul Newman and Julia MacIver, a woman of Scots-Irish descent who preferred to use her maiden name. The artist, in turn, adopted it for her own. At the age of ten she was admitted to Saturday classes at the Art Students League. Her stint there was the only formal art education she ever had, but her inveterate museumgoing, especially to the Metropolitan Museum of Art, supplied the rest. Even in early childhood she drew and painted constantly, but she seems never to have made any conscious decision to choose art as a career. "I cannot tell you how casual it was," she has remarked. "I never intended to be a painter. I just liked to paint."

For a year or so after graduating from high school she painted in studios of friends. Then, in 1929, she married the late poet and critic Lloyd Frankenberg, and set up the first of their several Greenwich Village studio-apartments. Greenwich Village has been her home ever since. From 1931 to 1941 the couple spent their summers in North Truro, on Cape Cod, in a ten-by-twelve-foot driftwood shack on the ocean shore and even lived one winter there. *Winter Dunes* (1932), a gull's-eye (or child's-eye) view of the village and beach, with a stick-figure representation of her husband striding along the shore, prominent at the bottom center, conveys the bleakness and exhilaration of that stay. Totally different in concept, *The Shack* (1934) makes an abstract design of their house, its walls symmetrically splayed out to reveal recognizable details of the interior as if seen from high above. The painting was purchased by Alfred Barr for the Museum of Modern Art in 1935, the first of Loren MacIver's works to enter a museum. Her first representation in a group show, at the Contemporary Arts Gallery in New York in 1933 (1934?), had attracted Barr and several other private collectors.

Loren MacIver's other Cape Cod paintings are rather more conventional in design and more concerned with nature than with fantasy, as in *Beach Plum Landscape* (1933), one of the earliest of her many works devoted to observations of nature. Her later paintings, too, done in those Cape Cod years

adumbrate her abiding themes in the work to come. Although it is possible to trace the entrance of those themes in certain individual canvases, the variations that she played on them run all through her subsequent painting. Instead of her career's breaking down into a sequence of styles, it seems to have evolved of itself, with no marked breaks. Thus, her sense of wonder at the visual beauty of even mundane objects comes through in *Witchbowls* (1935): fisherman's glass floats that form a design of mysterious, glowing lights on the beach. The glass bowls around the lights marking New York subway entrances became a frequent motif, perceived and recorded with delight. As John Russell commented in the *New York Times* (April 24, 1987)—in reviewing the spring 1987 exhibition of her work at New York's Pierre Matisse Gallery that included paintings, done in 1985, of a plate of bright-colored penny candies, a display of French goat cheeses, and a birthday cake fiery with candles—her "sense of wonder . . . is still very much alive."

Back in New York, in 1935, Loren MacIver painted *Strunsky House*, which makes a flat, compartmented design of her Greenwich Village apartment house. Unlike the realistic interior of *The Shack*, the compartments contain sketchy, simplified renditions of objects that act as symbolic allusions to the tenants. A figure of a bottle, for example, is a pictograph standing for the artist's own studio.

Such private and sometimes obscure shorthand symbols became a characteristic of her work, but as John Baur pointed out in the catalogue of Loren MacIver's 1953 Whitney Museum of American Art retrospective, although her symbolism is puzzling and requires the viewer's thoughtful study, it must be interpreted eventually "or the painting achieves only half its meaning."

From 1936 to 1940 Loren MacIver was associated with the WPA Federal Art Project. She began to gain public recognition after her first solo exhibition of twenty oils, as well as gouaches and pastels, at Marian Willard's East River Gallery in 1938. Two years later she had her first showing at the Pierre Matisse Gallery, the beginnning of her long association, both personal and business, with Pierre Matisse. She spent the winter of 1939–40 in Key West in a house that was lent to her. *Moonlight* (1939) distills a magical nocturnal vision of a room in that Florida house; with its distortion of angles the composition is even slightly Picassoesque. In *Studio*, painted as recently as 1987 and conveying the same dreamy effect, the artist's palette, the dominant central motif, floats in an ambiguously angled space that is washed with soft blue light. Sketched musical notes and pictorial hints alluding to the presence of a piano in the room increase the sensation of rhythmic drifting induced by the painting's overall design. *Hopscotch* (1940) has a New York theme, and was painted in New York: the remains of chalk marks of the children's game on a sidewalk, contrasted with an area of abstract design, its impastoed surface implying the texture of blistered, cracked asphalt paving. According to Baur, *Hopscotch's* combination of suggestive design and concrete image marks the beginning of a more mature style, and it is one of her most highly regarded compositions.

From then on, New York was her major subject, with certain exceptions, as in another 1940 canvas, *The Poet*, a symbolic, even quasi-surrealist (according to some) "portrait" of Lloyd Frankenberg, in which his head becomes a vessel, from which issue bouquets, like budding poems. In *The City* (1941) Loren MacIver first used a frieze-like compositional design, making a formal pattern of city dwellers and urban objects. So, too, in the well-known companion piece, *The Violet Hour* (1943), clear representations of passersby and children playing, a pushcart, a tree, façades of houses, and a wrought-iron railing define an actual Greenwich Village street, which at the same time is taken into another realm by the frieze pattern that obviates real space between people and objects. Rows of discs, alluding to subway-kiosk lamps, make a formal border to the design. *New York* (1952) continues the "series." Over a panoramic silhouette of the nighttime city are sketched references to the city residents, who are conspicuously absent: a neon sign, a key, a shoe, a hat, and a glowing caterpillar-like object that stands for the lights of the Christopher Street subway station entrance near her home. For the most part, her evocations of the city are, like *New York* and *Hopscotch*, unpeopled. Such works as *The Ashcan* (1944), *Window Shade* (1948), *Oil Slick* (1949) or *Taxi*, a 1952 painting that captures the way raindrops on a windshield refract the blaze of neon signs and street lights, reveal the unexpected beauty to be found in some of the urban clutter.

At the same time, however, Loren MacIver delighted in noting signs of nature in the midst of the urban scene. *A Fall of Snow* (1943) reveals the crystalline structure of snowflakes as they drift in the city's lilac-hued dusk; *Tree* (1945) transforms the spring buds of a bush into candles. Her abiding love of the shape of flowers has continued to the present day, in a series of 1969 pastels and 1980 oils such as *Dogwood Blossoms* (1983) or *Garden* (1987).

From time to time over the years, Loren MacIver has turned her attention to painting the individual figure, doing portraits of people whose quixotic, contradictory personalities have appealed to her. Her earliest preserved painting, in fact, is *Sleep* (1929), an unconventional study of her husband, and another poet, e. e. cummings, was depicted by her as a disembodied head around which appears quotations from some of his poems. Notable in this genre are her portraits of circus clowns, for she has always had a special love of the theatre and of circuses. Her painting of the mime Jimmy Savo (1944) contrasts the eloquence of his hands with the wistfulness of his face, and her study of Emmett Kelly (1947) emphasizes the thinness of the boundary line that separates unbearable sadness from humor. She developed both works from quick sketches made while attending their performances.

Several commissions came her way in the 1940s. In 1941 she was invited by the Museum of Modern Art to paint backgrounds for the auditorium in which their series of four Coffee Concerts was held, and she also designed Christmas cards for the museum and for UNICEF. In 1947 she designed the dust jacket for one of Lloyd Frankenberg's books, *Pleasure Dome: On Reading Modern Poetry*, and a title page for *Steeple Bush*, a limited edition of Robert Frost's work. Her most ambitious commissioned works, however, were the murals for the *S.S. Argentina* of the Moore-McCormack Lines and for four American Export Lines ships, which occupied her in 1947-48. All those paintings are composed of exotic images that float or swim or sway.

Loren MacIver's first trip to Europe, in 1948, provided her with new motifs and inspiration for a number of paintings that she worked on only after her return home—paintings that were much larger and more varied in color than her previous canvases. As she traveled from Italy to France and then to the British Isles she captured her impressions in pencil sketches that merely place the main masses and indicate the principal lines of motion. Such "scrawls," as she terms them, sometimes filled in with crayon or watercolor, more often merely with color notations, are always used to fix her ideas, for despite the sense of immediacy in her finished work, her paintings are composed and executed with great deliberation. Among the best known of her earlier European paintings is *Venice* (1949), "perhaps the most sensuously beautiful picture she has ever painted," in John Baur's opinion. A dream memory rather than an actual description, it gives what amounts to a fish's-eye view of the golden city from across a broad expanse of iridescent blue water. *Dublin and Environs* (1950) is filled with sketchy shapes, the artist's personal, somewhat cryptic symbols of objects associated with the Irish scene. A cross stands for the prevalent stone walls; circles allude to a familiar Celtic design motif; and the ambiguous shapes at the lower right may stand for fish, or perhaps for potatoes. In 1952 she painted *Les Baux*, making of that historic site in Provence what Baur has described as "an abstract image of fantastic forms," with shafts of light bathing them in tones of icy blue.

Her trips abroad in 1953-54 and in 1960-61 took Loren MacIver back to Paris and on to Greece, Spain, and Italy, and in 1966 she returned for the fourth time, living and painting in Paris and the south of France until 1970. A considerable number of paintings were inspired by those stays, interspersed with pictures that she painted back in New York. The large and radiant *In Passsing* (1961) pays homage to the city of former years, with its familiar images of a pushcart and subway-light discs, now juxtaposed with an updating image of a TV screen. *Byzantium* (1965), which epitomizes her continuing use of larger formats and heightened luminosity, is a shimmering evocation of the mosaic surfaces of Istanbul's buildings. *Pavés et Clous* (1970), like *Hopscotch* before it, focuses on the designs traced in the texture of a city pavement. A group of paintings done during winter sojourns in Provence, canvases such as *Le Verger d'Amandes* (1967) or *Mistral, Cyprès Foncé* (1968), "look as though they had been painted with colored air," as Robert Frasch expressed it in the catalogue of Loren MacIver's Newport Harbor Art Museum exhibition, held in 1983.

The main body of Loren MacIver's work has been in oils, but pastels, drawings, and lithographs are included in what critics agree is preeminently an art of design and color, and light, an art that emphasizes the two-dimensional surface. To her, space and volume are of little concern, and texture has only occasionally been important. In general, the surfaces of her canvases are covered with soft, smoky, and mood-conveying veils of thin paint applied almost like watercolors. Her distinctive way of feathering the edges of color areas produces an aura of light that envelops shapes. Light and color emerging from darkness has always fascinated her, as in "Votive Lights" paintings of the 1940s that continued with the 1984 *Votive Lights Red and Blue*. She believes, somewhat paradoxically, that the flickering flames of the church candles actually symbolize constancy.

The artist is a member of the National Institute of Arts and Letters and an associate member of the National Academy of Design. Formal honors accorded her work include a Ford Foundation grant in 1960; the Frank A. Logan Medal of the Art Institute of Chicago in 1962; a purchase prize from the Krannert Art Museum of the University of Illinois in Urbana in 1963; a Mark Rothko Foundation award in 1972; and a Guggenheim Fellowship in 1976. Since 1940 she has been exhibiting regularly at the Pierre Matisse Gallery, and among the important retrospectives of her work are the "Loren MacIver/I. Rice Pereira" traveling exhibition mounted by the Whitney Museum in 1953; shows in 1951 and 1965 at the Phillips Collection in Washington, D.C.; an exhibition in 1958 at the Corcoran Gallery of Art in Washington; and "Loren MacIver: Five Decades" at the Newport Harbor Art Museum in Newport Beach, California, in 1983. In 1968 the Musée des Beaux-Arts in Lyons, France, sponsored "Groupe 68: Hommage à Loren MacIver," an exhibition that subsequently traveled to the Musée d'Art Moderne, Paris, and to Nice.

Her long list of group exhibition participations includes shows at the Provincetown, Massachusetts, Art Assocation in the 1930s. In 1936 she was included in MOMA's "Fantastic Art, Dada, Surrealism"; in 1938 in its "Three Centuries of American Art," shown at the Jeu de Paume, Paris; and in 1939 in "Art in Our Time." Among many other MOMA shows in which her paintings were represented were "Romantic Painting in America" (1944), "Fourteen Americans" (1946) and "Symbolism in Painting" (1947). Her work was also included in Whitney Annuals from 1944 to 1959, Corcoran Gallery Biennials between 1947 and 1959 (winning first prize at the 1957 show), the Venice Biennales of 1948 and 1962, and "U.S.A. Art

Vivant" shown in Toulouse, France, in 1966. "Women Artists: 1550-1950," which traveled across the United States in 1976-77, included her painting *Hopscotch*. Besides her substantial representation in museums in her native city (MOMA, the Whitney, the Brooklyn Museum and the Metropolitan Museum), her work hangs in public and university collections nationwide, and in the Bibliothèque Nationale, Paris.

Although she is a rather private person who prefers not to speak about herself, and only with slightly less reluctance about her work, Loren MacIver is not a difficult person to know. Her wide circle of friends has included the poets Elizabeth Bishop, Dylan Thomas, and e. e. cummings, and Alice B. Toklas, to whom she and her husband extended care and help after Gertrude Stein's death. The artist is esteemed by many Greenwich Village residents as a gentle, compassionate, and friendly neighbor. Her slight figure, usually dressed in jeans, has been a familiar sight in the area over the years. Earlier photographs show an attractive pixie-like face framed by dark straight hair cut in bangs; her wide, sensitive mouth, strongly contoured cheekbones, and contemplative gaze remain unmistakable. Despite her health problems, and even after the death of her husband in 1975, she has kept on living and working in the Perry Street apartment that has been her home since 1942, painting in an immaculate studio, bare of clutter, dominated by an easel and a grand piano.

References: Baur, John I. H. Loren MacIver/I. Rice Pereira (1953); Frasch, Robert M. Loren MacIver: Five Decades (1983); Harris, Ann Sutherland, and Nochlin, Linda. Women Artists: 1550-1950 (1977); Who's Who in America, 1986-87; Who's Who in American Art 16th ed (1984); World Artists 1950-1980 (1984);

Mandelbrot, Benoit

Nov. 20, 1924– Mathematician; scientist; educator. Address: b. PO Box 218, Yorktown Heights, N.Y. 10598

"Science would be ruined," the Polish-born mathematician Benoit Mandelbrot once wrote, "if (like sports) it were to put competition above everything else, and if it were to clarify the rules of competition by withdrawing entirely into narrowly defined specialities. The rare scholars who are nomads-by-choice are essential to the intellectual welfare of the settled disciplines." A nomad-by-choice since the early 1950s, Mandelbrot has contributed to fields as diverse as linguistics, economics, physiology, and physics. His greatest interdisciplinary contribution is fractal geometry, one of the most important developments in twentieth-century mathematics. The behavior of earthquakes, the patterns of the weather, and the distribution of gal-

Benoit Mandelbrot

axies in space are a few of the irregular, even chaotic phenomena that have begun to yield the secrets of their structures to the new geometry.

Mandelbrot's unifying theme, the concept of "scaling," refers to patterns whose large-scale ir regularities are echoed in their finer details. Its companion concept, "fractal dimension," measures the degree of irregularity and the related ability to fill space of those patterns. Mandelbrot spent much of his time during the 1960s and 1970s collecting curves and other geometric patterns that mathematicians had once considered to be "pathological" and showing them to be virtual blueprints of many natural objects. In so doing, he went beyond some limits of older theories of shape such as Euclidean geometry, which describes the natural world in terms of one-dimensional lines, two-dimensional surfaces, and three-dimensional objects such as spheres and cones.

Scientists following Mandelbrot's lead have begun to theorize about previously poorly understood phenomena whose shapes are related to their behavior. Mathematicians have found the most complex orderly object in their field in the form of the Mandelbrot set, invented by Mandelbrot in 1979 and later named in his honor. More recently, Hollywood filmmakers have made use of fractals to create alien planets for their blockbuster movies. Since 1974 Mandelbrot has been an International Business Machines fellow at the research center of the corporation. In 1985 he was awarded the Barnard Medal for Meritorious Service to Science, given by recommendation of the National Academy of Sciences once every five years to those persons whose contributions to the discipline are "beneficial to the human race."

Benoit Mandelbrot was born in Warsaw, Poland, on November 20, 1924, to Charles Mandelbrot, a clothing manufacturer, and Bella (Lurie) Mandelbrot, a physician. He learned very early that "some people live by and for the production of new mathematics" through the example of his uncle, the analytical mathematician Szolem Mandelbrojt. Tutored by another uncle, Loterman Mandelbrot, because his mother was "afraid of epidemics" and kept him at home when he should have been attending the first and second grades, Benoit began reading books and studying maps before he had mastered the entire alphabet. A precocious chess player, he was a champion in his age group, but he retired from the game in 1936 at the age of eleven, when his family moved to Paris.

At the outbreak of World War II the Mandelbrot family moved again, this time to Tulle near Clermont-Ferrand in central France. Mandelbrot told Anthony Barcellos, who interviewed him for Mathematical People: Profiles and Interviews (1985), that in 1942, after he completed the curriculum at the Lycée Edmond Perrier in Tulle, "poverty and the wish to keep away from big cities to maximize the chances of survival" forced him to dispense with higher education. "For a while, I was moving around with a younger brother," he told Barcellos, "toting around a few obsolete books and learning things my way, guessing a number of things myself, doing nothing in any rational or even half-reasonable fashion, and acquiring a great deal of independence and self-confidence."

When Paris was liberated in 1944, Mandelbrot took the grueling entrance exams at France's leading science schools, the École Normale Supérieure and the École Polytechnique, achieving scores that placed him near the top of his class in both schools. His success had little to do with any profound knowledge of analytical mathematical techniques, for he had little training in them. As he explained to Barcellos: "Faced with some complicated integral, I instantly related it to a familiar shape; usually it was exactly the shape that had motivated this integral. I knew an army of shapes I'd encountered once in some book or in some problem, and remembered forever, with their properties and peculiarities. . . . Everybody else took an exam in algebra and complicated integrals, and I managed to take an exam in translation into geometry and thinking in terms of geometric shapes."

After a brief stay at the École Normale, where geometry was out of favor, Mandelbrot switched to the École Polytechnique. Freed from a requirement to concentrate and compete in any single subject area, he read widely and voraciously and soaked up classical music "like a big dry sponge." In 1947, after receiving his degree from the École Polytechnique, he left for the California Institute of Technology, in Pasadena, where he completed the requirements for a Master of Science degree in aeronautics in 1948 and for a professional degree in aeronautics before returning to France. After serving for a year in the French air force, he enrolled at the University of Paris to work towards his Ph.D. degree.

Mandelbrot's doctoral thesis, "Mathematical Theory of Games of Communication," was inspired in part by a book review that he once had fished out of Szolem Mandelbrojt's wastepaper basket. It explained away "Zipf's law," which rules word frequencies in all languages and in the discourse of all speakers. In explaining Zipf's law, Mandelbrot made his first use of the concept of scaling, devising "lexicographic trees," each of whose branches, with their sub-branchings, replicated the entire tree on a smaller scale. The trees indicated the richness of a particular vocabulary or discourse by assigning probabilities to words corresponding to certain branch tips. In the second part of the two-part thesis Mandelbrot discussed thermodynamics. Some scholars remarked on the oddity of the combination, but Mandelbrot was granted his Ph.D. degree in 1952.

In an era of increasing specialization, Mandelbrot's interdisciplinary instincts were held in suspicion by academics, and well-meaning friends warned him to "settle down" if he wished to develop a successful career. He won a temporary reprieve from that impasse when the distinguished mathematician John von Neumann sponsored him for a fellowship to the Institute of Advanced Study in Princeton, New Jersey, for the year 1953-1954. There he met Henry McKean Jr., who introduced him to one of his major tools, the concept of Hausdorff-Besicovitch dimension. McKean had used that concept to study shapes traced by the frantic and fantastically irregular motion of fine particles suspended in a fluid known as Brownian motion. Since a particle's motion takes it all over the two-dimensional surface of the liquid, its trail becomes two-dimensional from a Hausdorff-Besicovitch perspective, though from other mathematical perspectives it remains a one-dimensional line.

That fact was a revelation to Mandelbrot. Even topology, which mathematicians had used since the nineteenth century to study objects that changed position by moving, stretching, or being twisted, would not have recognized any fundamental dimensional difference between the path of a Brownian particle and a regular line. Mandelbrot later showed that the Hausdorff-Besicovitch dimension, which he adopted on the spot, was an almost ubiquitous tool and a special example of the wider notion of fractal dimension. After his year in Princeton, Mandelbrot returned for three years to Europe, first Geneva and then France, where he taught mathematics at the University of Lille and the École Polytechnique and continued an association that he had begun in 1949 at the Centre National de la Recherche Scientifique (National Center for Scientific Research) in Paris.

Returning to the United States, Mandelbrot began a long association with IBM as a faculty adviser in the summer of 1958, and after staying on as a consultant, pursued his developing interest in economic topics. His first major conceptual breakthrough came in 1961 when IBM asked him to analyze errors caused by random noise clustering in telephone circuits—noise that the company's engineers originally thought was caused by men working somewhere in the system with screwdrivers.

The behavior of the noise characteristically reminded Mandelbrot of a shape—a diagram of the zero-crossings of Brownian motion, a dust-like pattern of points with a dimension between zero and one. Mandelbrot realized that the noise could not have been caused by workmen because it came in bursts made up of increasingly smaller bursts. It was intimately linked with the strength of the telephone signals being sent. Mandelbrot saved IBM from major waste of corporate resources by having its early noise-correcting projects called off. He and an IBM associate, Jay Berger, published "A new model for the clustering of errors on telephone circuits" in 1963, basing their model on what is now known as a "Cantor fractal dust," which can be made in its simplest form by taking a line segment and removing the middle third, then removing the middle thirds of the resulting two-line segments, and repeating the process ad infinitum. The infinite "dust" thus generated, as randomized by Berger and Mandelbrot, accounted for the pattern of noise that clung to the telephone signals.

"The full strength of scaling assumptions," as Mandelbrot puts it, became clear in the early 1960s when he applied them to the wild fluctuations of stock market prices. His model helped to disprove a then accepted method of anticipating optimum buying times and succeeded in modeling market changes on a dizzying range of time scales. Mandelbrot was able to account almost exactly for the statistical distribution of the changes in daily cotton prices over a five-year period, for fluctuations in those prices on a monthly basis, and finally for often violent price changes, involving recessions and depressions, over almost a century. Not known for his false modesty, Mandelbrot has written, "I know of no other comparably successful prediction in economics." He also hastens to say that the prediction is only statistical in nature.

Although the practitioners of the disciplines Mandelbrot encroached upon still viewed him as "a stranger who (for reasons unknown) was wandering in and out," Mandelbrot told Barcellos: "Luckily the striking (and often shocking) news I was bringing could not pass unnoticed. . . . I became very popular in many diverse departments as a visiting professor, but no major university wanted a permanent professor with such unpredictable interests." Mandelbrot became associated with Harvard University as a visiting professor of economics and a research fellow in psychology from 1962 to 1963 and a visiting professor of applied mathematics and a staff member of the Joint Committee on Biomedical Computer Science from 1962 to 1964.

Exchanges of ideas with his colleagues at Harvard made it clear to Mandelbrot that his scaling assumptions could be applied "wholesale" to the mysteries of turbulence—the violent disruptions in fluid flow and the atmosphere that are visible in waterfalls and in hurricanes and all too familiar to airline passengers who experience sudden series of bumps during flights. He prepared for his investigation by listening to amplified recordings of turbulence and by studying photographs and drawings of turbulence stretching back to the drawing known as "The Deluge" in the notebooks of Leonardo da Vinci. He concluded that one ought to study geometrically the intuitive notion that turbulence could be considered as "the superposition of eddies of many diverse sizes."

Mandelbrot next integrated a number of theories about the phenomenon, many aspects of which had baffled scientists since the nineteenth century. One theory, put forward by Lewis Fry Richardson, held that turbulent areas form when a disturbance sets off a cascade of eddies in a fluid. Mandelbrot demonstrated that such cascades "curdle" into precise fractal shapes whose dimension is greater than two. That this shape was a fractal implied a greater likelihood of intense—and, in some instances, dangerous—pockets of turbulence than had previously been realized. Mandelbrot later extended the curdling concept to the formation of galaxies. One property of fractals is that their density decreases as they grow larger. Pointing out that galactic clusters are distributed over a fractal whose dimension is less than two, Mandelbrot showed that the density of matter in the universe decreases as the volume of space increases.

Despite his wide-ranging achievements, Mandelbrot found himself in the mid-1960s still having to delete prefaces explaining the increasing unity of his insights in order to have his papers published in reputable journals. He sought and, in 1967 found a natural and concrete representation of his ideas in the form of coastlines, and in a paper published that year asked what has become his most famous question, "How long is the coast of Britain?" His answer was that it depends on the length of the ruler used to measure the coastline and its numberless promontories and bays, which can be found on all scales down to the molecular level. An extremely long ruler would fail to measure many small inlets and tiny nooks and crannies. As increasingly short rulers were selected, the coastline's measured length would grow and become infinitely long. The speed at which the coastline's length increases and becomes infinite as the ruler shrinks yields its fractal dimension. In 1973, using an algorithm supplied by Mandelbrot, Sigmund Handelman of IBM was able to make computer-generated images of coastlines that resembled those of New Zealand and the islands of the Aegean. "After seeing the coastline pictures," Mandelbrot has recalled, "everyone agreed with me that fractals were part of the stuff of nature."

That agreement led to a wider appreciation of the mathematical "monsters" that Mandelbrot had consulted and adapted in developing his models. In modeling coastlines, for instance, he had made use of the "Koch snowflake," that was invented by Helge von Koch in the early years of the twentieth century. The snowflake begins with an equilateral triangle on each of whose sides is centered an equilateral triangle one-third the size to form a Star of David. On the sides of the triangles that form the points of the star triangles one third their size are centered. Repeated until the curve starts to resemble a snowflake, the process is continued ad infinitum, so that the curve's perimeter quickly becomes infinitely long and so detailed that no straight line can be drawn to touch it at only one point. That fact caused one of Helge von Koch's colleagues to turn away "in fright and horror" when he first saw the snowflake. Between 1875 and 1925 an entire "gallery" of such monsters was created by mathematicians in an outburst that paralleled the development of atonal music and cubist painting in the arts and that was intended to prove that mathematicians could create figures totally divorced from nature.

The physicist Freeman J. Dyson has noted that Mandelbrot's triumph consists in his demonstration that "nature has played a joke on the mathematicians," since their pathological structures "turn out to be inherent in natural objects all around us." After the success of his computer-generated coastlines, Mandelbrot collaborated more and more with IBM colleagues such as Richard Voss to generate pictures of his algorithms. He also began to work on developing fractal landscapes because of their potential to drive home the persuasive power of his theory.

The fact that immensely detailed fractal shapes could be generated from relatively brief equations and the fact that so many of them suggest snails, jellyfish, and other forms of life led Mandelbrot to suspect that much of nature is created by the repetition of simple steps. The fact that a small change in the dimension of a fractal can drastically alter its shape suggested to Mandelbrot a possible way of modeling the manner in which a relatively small amount of genetic material can give rise to complex structures such as the lung and brain, and to entire organisms. By using fractals he was able to account for the biological sleight of hand that allows the blood vessels to fill every part of the human body while taking up only five percent of its volume. Such insights led to Mandelbrot's appointment to an unpaid visiting professorship in physiology at the Albert Einstein College of Medicine in 1970, a year in which he also served as a visiting professor of engineering at Yale.

Mandelbrot saw "a golden opportunity" to integrate his interests before the public when he was asked to give a talk at the Collège de France in Paris in January 1973. Unlike the prefaces he had been forced to leave unpublished over the years, the talk, he told Anthony Barcellos, "was received with much praise and no hostility at all," bringing home to him the fact that his "years in the wilderness were about to end." While consulting his son's Latin dictionary soon afterwards, he coined the word "fractal" from the Latin for broken and irregular. *Les objets fractals: forme, hasard et dimension* was published by Flammarion in Paris in 1975. A revised English version, *Fractals: Form, Chance, and Dimension* (W.H. Freeman, 1977), was followed by the full-scale "fractal manifesto," *The Fractal Ge-*

ometry of Nature (W.H. Freeman, 1982). By that time, Mandelbrot and Voss's computer imagery had become spectacular, generating realistic lunar landscapes and earth-like planets, as well as islands and unearthly mountain ranges. Fractals began to appear in motion pictures, including Star Trek II: the Wrath of Khan and Return of the Jedi.

In 1979 Mandelbrot began to investigate so-called self-inverse fractals and self-squared fractals, which led him, in the case of the self-squared fractals, to the work of Gaston Julia, whom he had encountered years before, while studying at the École Polytechnique. During World War I, Gaston Julia wrote a monumental paper referred to in Mandelbrot's school days as "the celebrated prize essay." Julia described a set that grows from a simple "mathematical seed," a number on which a certain operation is performed. In one example, the number is squared and a constant such as "one" is added to it to yield a new number, which then becomes the mathematical seed. The process is repeated indefinitely and the mathematical seeds at the heart of it are the "complex numbers"—two-part numbers involving the square root of negative one.

The result, as illustrated in Mandelbrot's computer graphics, is that "basins of attraction," appearing on the computer screen as colorful pools, form in the plane defined by the complex numbers. In the example in which the mathematical seed is squared, for instance, the general equation that defines Mandelbrot's procedure has two solutions or "roots." Many of the mathematical seeds, when used in the general equation, "converge" toward one of the roots at a certain rate. Each seed is assigned a color whose shade indicates the rate at which it converges toward a root. In this way, shade by shade, color by color, the basins of attraction form. "The result is like a glowing tapestry," Ivar Peterson observed in Science News (February 28, 1987). "And right on the convoluted boundary [of the tapestry] lie points that lead to no root." Mandelbrot named such boundaries "Julia sets." They were fractals so fantastic in shape that Mandelbrot dubbed his favorites "mathematical dragons." He created entire families of dragons and other Julia sets by allowing the constant added to his mathematical seeds to vary.

Further investigations led Mandelbrot to the set now named in his honor, which is the most complex orderly object in mathematics, with an entire Julia set associated with every one of its infinite points. The Mandelbrot set and the Julia set have since become objects of systematic study by mathematicians and computer scientists in a number of countries. Computer microscopes have discovered that, unlike self-similar fractals such as the Koch curve, the Mandelbrot set, characterized at first glance by a kind of rounded, upside-down heart shape bonded to a circular shape, reveals entire baroque landscapes of new and chimerical shapes in addition to the original one when its least detail is magnified.

Ideas that developed from the Mandelbrot set have been found to provide a good description of what happens in dynamical systems such as the human heart when they break their normal rhythm and race out of control. Together with the rest of the fractals, it is exerting a powerful influence on science in the 1980s. In some areas of physics, where the shape of a system, either in real space or so-called "phase space," accounts for much of its behavior, fractals have become crucial. In meteorology the shape of large cloud systems, and therefore the pattern, intensity, and timing of the rain that falls from them, have been found to be fractal, as is the pattern in which rainwater seeps through the soil.

The prizes have begun to flow in for Benoit Mandelbrot. After being given the Barnard Medal for Meritorious Service to Science in 1985, he received the Franklin Medal for Signal and Eminent Service in Science from the Franklin Institute of Philadelphia in 1986. He was previously the recipient of IBM's Research Division Award (1983) and Corporate Award (1984) and of a Guggenheim fellowship (1968). In 1982 he became a member of the American Academy of Arts and Sciences and in 1987 a member of the National Academy of Sciences.

Benoit Mandelbrot is blue-eyed and gray-haired and carries his 220 pounds on a large, six-foot-two-inch frame. He and his wife, the scientist Aliette Mandelbrot, were married on November 5, 1955, and they have two sons, Laurent and Didier. Mandelbrot has served as professor of the practice of mathematics at Harvard University from 1984 to 1987, but is scheduled to move to Yale University as Abraham Robinson Professor of the Mathematical Sciences. Although the isolation in which he worked for so many years has been dispelled by the growing popularity of fractals, Mandelbrot was still insisting, as recently as a 1985 interview: "I don't belong to any of the groups, and my work flies against the natural tendency of everything to divide itself into pieces."

References: N Y Times Mag p64+ D 8 '85 pors; Omni 6:64+ F '84 por; The World & I 2:162+ F '87 pors; Mandelbrot, Benoit. The Fractal Geometry of Nature (1982); Albers, Donald J., and Alexanderson, G. L. Mathematical People: Profiles and Interviews (1985); Gleick, James. Chaos: Making a New Science (1987); Who's Who in America, 1986–1987

Martens, Wilfried

Apr. 19, 1936– Prime Minister of Belgium. Address: b. 16 rue de la Loi, 1000 Brussels, Belgium; h. 24 Désiré Van Monckhovenstraat, 9000 Ghent, Belgium

Belgium's Prime Minister Wilfried Martens, who was described by Gary Yerkey in the Christian Sci-

Wilfried Martens

ence *Monitor* (July 24, 1985) as "a master of survival in a political minefield as treacherous as any in Western Europe," was a promising but still largely unknown politician when he was thrust onto the international stage in April 1979 as head of his country's government. In view of Belgium's volatile political situation and its dismal economic record, which in the previous decade had taken the country from riches to rags, not many people could have anticipated that Martens would survive to become one of Western Europe's most experienced and astute statesmen. On November 28, 1985, Martens was sworn in to head his sixth coalition government—Belgium's thirty-third since 1945.

Wilfried Martens was born on April 19, 1936, in the village of Sleidinge, Belgium, in the flatlands of the largely Dutch-speaking area known as Flanders. He came from a poor farming background, and his early life was a continual struggle. After his father's death, about 1943, his mother remarried, but her second husband died some ten years later. There was little time for Martens to be concerned with politics in the rural community in which his family lived, but since his mother was from the city of Ghent, a hotbed of trade unionism and Flemish nationalism, she followed events there closely. Wilfried Martens became politically aware by reading the newspaper *Het Volk* (The People), which was published by the Flemish Christian Democratic party. His political interests were encouraged by his teachers and by his membership in the Flemish Roman Catholic youth movement.

Following his graduation from grade school, Martens began his secondary school education at the college of Eeklo, where he soon discovered that his facility in the local Flemish dialect of his home village was not enough to see him through in his studies. As a result, he set out to learn all of Belgium's three official languages—Dutch, French, and German—as well as English. In 1954 he enrolled at the Catholic University of Louvain, from which he graduated four years later with a doctorate in law as well as degrees in notarial studies and the philosophy of Thomas Aquinas. While Martens was a student at Louvain, politics became a major influence in his life. He served as chairman of the Flemish association of Catholic university students (Katholiek Vlaams Hoogstudentenverbond) and a member of the student model parliament.

In 1960 Martens was called to the bar in Ghent, where he practiced for a time as a barrister in the local court of appeal, while remaining politically active in such organizations as the Flemish People's Movement (Vlaams Volksbeweging), the Flemish Action Committee (Vlaams Aktiekomitee), and the Young Christian People's party (Christelijke Volkspartij-Jongeren). In 1962 he became a member of the Christian People's party (Christelijke Volkspartij, or CVP), Belgium's largest and most influential political organization, a middle-of-the-road party that had been represented in coalition governments for all but five of the years since the end of World War II. In 1965 Martens was elected chairman of the CVP-Jongeren, and he remained in that post until his resignation six years later. During that time, he proved ambitious and able, using his position and influence to help bring about reforms in government structure and to define a progressive policy for the CVP. In 1965 he was enlisted as an adviser to the cabinet of CVP Prime Minister Pierre Harmel, and in 1966 he became an advisor to Harmel's successor, Paul Van Den Boeynants.

Martens' own political career began in 1968, when he joined the personal staff of Leo Tindemans, then the Flemish minister for community relations, as a chargé de mission, and he remained in that job until 1972, when the government fell. From 1972 to 1979 he served as chairman of the CVP. In 1974 he won election to the house of representatives—the lower branch of the bicameral Belgian parliament—as the representative for Ghent-Eeklo.

Over the next five years, Martens demonstrated what was described in the *Economist* as "exceptional skill as a negotiator and conciliator." In the wake of the resignation, in October 1978, of Leo Tindemans' CVP coalition government, Martens, who at the time was only forty-two years old and had no previous ministerial experience, was asked by King Baudouin to serve as chairman of the council of ministers, or prime minister. His installation, on April 3, 1979, brought to an end a six-month crisis during which Belgium had been ruled by a caretaker government headed by the former CVP Prime Minister Paul Van Den Boeynants. Marten's first administration was under a CVP-Socialist coalition with small representation from splinter parties, including a French-speaking linguistic party called the Front Démocratique des Francophones (FDF). Martens was at the time regarded by many political observers as being to the left of center, with close ties to organized labor.

Bilingualism and biculturalism have been Belgium's central historical realities for a number of years. The country of some ten million people is an association of two distinct linguistic communities, and that crucial split is always in the forefront of national affairs. Some six million Dutch-speaking Flemish, most of whom live in the north of the country, have long struggled to assert their rights in a country that until the 1920s was dominated by the minority French-speaking Walloons of Brussels and the south. Since 1960, when laws were passed providing for minority language group protection in all areas by means of bilingual administration, four distinct language areas have existed: the Flemish north, the Walloon south, the bilingual capital of Brussels, and a tiny German-speaking enclave along the country's border with West Germany. Belgium has been able to avoid fracture only because of a flexible political system that has given those federated regions an increasing authority in the central government's affairs. But although that accommodation had held Belgium together as a nation, it also had the unwanted side effect of fostering the disintegration of the three national political parties—the CVP, Liberals, and Walloon party. In their places there arose a bewildering array of splinter language parties. As a result of so many different voices seeking to be heard, the business of Belgium's parliament became ponderous and unwieldy.

During his first months in office, critics accused Martens of being indecisive and quiescent. Then, on October 2, 1979, he proved that those initial impressions were false by announcing what some observers saw as his own version of "Reaganomics," with a controversial package of economic proposals intended to reduce government borrowing for 1980 by some $720 million. Any revenue shortfall was to be made up through such measures as increased highway tolls and medical care fees, and a tightening of unemployment benefits. Just two months later Martens faced Belgium's most divisive issues—regionalism and language rights—when he attempted further implementation of the decade-old Egmont Plan, championed by his predecessor, Leo Tindemans. The essence of the proposed constitutional amendment was official recognition of Belgium's two chief linguistic groups, Dutch and French, and of the need for regional assemblies in Flanders, Wallonia, and Brussels.

It soon became apparent, however, that agreement on the plan was impossible. Nine senators from Martens' own CVP reiterated their longstanding opposition to a separate assembly for Brussels. The city, mostly French-speaking, is located in the Dutch-speaking province of Brabant, and the Flemish feared that any assembly would be French-dominated, thus giving that group control of two of the country's three regions, despite their numerical minority. Martens gambled on getting the so-called autonomy bill through on a second reading in the senate by tying it to a vote of confidence.

The bill failed, however, to get the required two-thirds majority, and Martens had no choice but to offer his resignation to a reluctant King Baudouin on April 3, 1980. After several days of hesitation and desperate eleventh-hour negotiations to resolve the crisis failed, it was accepted on April 9, and another caretaker government was installed. Frank J. Prial of the the New York Times (April 22, 1980) observed that Belgium was celebrating its 150th anniversary "in a pessimistic mood." The economy was in a shambles, unemployment was running at a postwar high of 7.6 percent, and relations between the country's two main linguistic groups were at a low ebb.

But Martens was determined to find a way out of the impasse, and political observers speculated that the king was eager to allow him to do so in order to give him a chance to press his economic austerity program. Backroom negotiations eventually proved successful, and on May 11, 1980, it was announced that the leaders of six parties—the French- and Dutch-language wings of the CVP, Liberal, and Socialist parties—had agreed to form a coalition under Martens' leadership. The key to the new accommodation was Martens' promise to the Socialists to defer a final decision on deployment of new North Atlantic Treaty Organization cruise missiles, to which Belgium had tentatively agreed at a NATO meeting in December 1979. The regional autonomy issue was resolved temporarily by giving Flanders and Wallonia their own assemblies, while a special commission was appointed to study the Brussels problem. Analyzing the situation in Current History (April 1984), Professor Pierre-Henri Laurent of Tufts University suggested that Martens had put the autonomy issue in a temporary "deep-freeze" and had "chosen to 'evade and escape' further regionalization as long as possible."

The new Martens coalition lasted just five months, before Liberal-Socialist bickering over social security cuts resulted in the government's resignation on October 7, 1980. After further negotiations, however, Martens succeeded on October 16 in patching together another CVP-Socialist coalition, giving him control of 140 of the 212 seats in the house of representatives. That uneasy alliance staggered along until March 1981, when the Socialists withdrew over Martens' proposal to ease inflation by limiting wage increases rather than allowing them to rise along with the consumer price index. Martens resigned as prime minister on March 31, 1981 and was replaced on April 6 by Mark Eyskens, his finance minister, who revived virtually the same coalition and cabinet.

Following general elections in November 1981, in which the right-wing, austerity-minded Liberals made significant gains, Eyskens stepped aside in favor of Martens, who returned to power on December 17 as head of a new center-right, CVP-Liberal coalition. Once back in office, Martens moved quickly to administer what some observers termed economic "shock treatment" to revive Belgium's ailing economy. Through a combination of cuts in government spending, major tax reform, and wage hike limitations, Martens moved to break a wage-inflation spiral that, in the words of *Business Week* (January 25, 1982), had slowly "strangled the country for a decade." On February 2, 1982, the senate gave final approval to a bill giving Martens emergency decree powers until the end of the year. In the words of the French daily *Le Monde*, Belgium had become, "like the Ottoman Empire before 1914, the sick man of Europe," and drastic measures were needed to restore the country's economic health. But Martens' attack on social security and wage indexation triggered deep emotions in some quarters. The Socialist opposition responded to Martens' program by calling a national strike on February 8, 1982. While the tactic paralyzed much of Wallonia, it was generally ineffective in other areas of the country.

One of Martens' first steps under the new emergency powers was to reduce the Value Added Tax (VAT) on construction projects, from 17 to 6 percent through the end of 1983, in an effort to spur the building industry. Then, within days, he announced that the government would allow Antwerp's debt-ridden Cockerill Yards, the giant state-owned shipyards, to go into receivership and that the Belgian franc was being devalued 8.5 percent in an effort to curb inflation and increase exports. Despite the political consequences, Martens pressed ahead, vowing to reduce the deficit at whatever cost. On August 1, 1983, he announced a budget calling for expenditures of $33.6 billion in 1984, an increase of 5.3 percent over 1983. The deficit was projected at $9.35 billion, still almost 11.5 percent of the country's gross national product. In a grim mood, Martens asserted that the entire population would be called upon to make economic sacrifices for the good of the country.

On January 13, 1984, Martens and Pierre Werner, the prime minister of Luxembourg, signed a ten-year treaty to coordinate reductions in steel production, which were being imposed by their countries' trading partners in the European Community. The two leaders agreed to a merger plan for their state-owned steel mills that involved the closing of some facilities and consolidation of output. The eventual elimination of up to 10,000 jobs in the two countries that was projected in the plan provoked protests from organized labor in view of the fact that unemployment in Belgium was already running at about 14 percent.

Amidst the uproar over Martens' economic policies, another major controversy was brewing. As the March 1985 deadline for Belgian deployment of NATO cruise missiles neared, the prime minister was under increasing pressure both from supporters and opponents of deployment, the latter including members of his own party. When the NATO foreign ministers met in Brussels on December 12 and 13, 1984, United States Secretary of State George P. Shultz held private talks with both Martens and Hans van den Broek, the prime minister of the Netherlands, in an effort to convince the two leaders to proceed with the scheduled deployment. But while Martens agreed in principle to deploy forty-eight medium-range missiles, he also abided by his position that Belgium would delay any final decision on deployment until the outcome of the Soviet-American Geneva arms reduction talks was known.

When Martens went to Washington, D.C., on a state visit in mid-January 1985, he was approached by thirteen "peace bloc" Democratic congressmen who gave him a letter asking him not to proceed with deployment of the NATO nuclear missiles. Embarrassed, Martens ignored the letter, and its existence did not become public until some weeks later. In White House talks with President Reagan, Secretary of State Shultz, and Secretary of Defense Caspar Weinberger, Martens repeated his official position and requested that State Department officials keep Belgium and other Western European allies informed of progress in Geneva. Responding to questions from a reporter for the newspaper *La Libre Belgique*, Martens said that he felt his position supported NATO while it at the same time encouraged peace by pressuring the Soviet Union to return to the bargaining table. "Alliance solidarity behind the dual-track approach is crucial to our proposals for success in the renewed negotiations," he said.

While the Geneva talks were still deadlocked, Martens made good on his promise, announcing in parliament on March 15, 1985, a cabinet decision to deploy the first NATO missiles at a Belgian air force base south of Brussels. "Postponement of the initial deployment of the missiles in our country would weaken the credibility and cohesion of the [NATO] alliance and would thereby put into question the [arms] negotiations themselves," Martens said. The decision sparked a massive street march in Brussels by an estimated 50,000 antimissile protesters and a bitter debate in parliament. Moreover, it split the CVP along linguistic lines—with most Dutch-speaking party members opposed to deployment and the French-speaking section largely in favor. Nevertheless, the government easily won support for its position by a vote of 116 to ninety-three.

Ironically, it was not the missile question, nor even Martens' austere economic policies, that set off the next major government crisis, but rather the tragic events that occurred on May 29, 1985, at Heysel Stadium in Brussels. Visiting British soccer fans went on a rampage, attacking supporters of the rival Italian team. In the ensuing melee, thirty-eight persons were killed. A parliamentary committee investigating the matter reached the conclusion that the riot was the result of serious deficiencies in police security. When the interior minister, Charles-Ferdinand Nothomb, refused to assume responsibility and resign, the French-speaking Liberals in Martens' coalition used the incident as a pretext for withdrawal of their support, and the result was the government's collapse. On July 16 Martens offered his resignation to King Baudouin, who refused to accept it. Elections originally scheduled for December were moved ahead to October 13, 1985.

Despite the fact that polls indicated that Martens was the country's most popular politician, observers predicted that the Socialists would make major electoral gains. But Martens took advantage of an opposition badly divided over the missile question, campaigning hard on his government's record of success in stabilizing unemployment, cutting spending, and reducing inflation. The electorate accepted his argument that more time was needed for his economic policies to work. Not even the efforts of left-wing terrorists to disrupt the election could prevent a victory for Martens' coalition. His own CVP gained six seats, bringing its total to forty-nine, and his four-party coalition added four, giving the government 115 seats, a majority of eighteen, in the 212-seat house. In the view of the *Economist* (October 19, 1985), the victory was Martens' own, since he had taken the center of the stage himself, dominating the campaign as no other Belgian politician had ever done.

Following installation of his new cabinet on November 28, 1985, Martens told reporters that he would continue his efforts to reduce the government's deficit. To that end, he announced that he would ask parliament to once again grant him short-term decree powers to deal with economic matters. The Socialists and their trade union allies called mass protests and public sector strikes in May 1986, in response to Martens' plan to slash government spending by some $4.25 billion. During the first week of June, a Socialist-led street demonstration in Brussels drew a quarter-million protesters, and in the next week thousands of persons, including many CVP supporters, rallied to show their displeasure with spending cuts amounting to $500 million that were planned for the Roman Catholic school system. Against this backdrop, and in the face of escalating left-wing terrorism aimed at destabilizing the country, Martens pressed ahead with his plans, while admitting that the period was "the most difficult" of his political career.

Exacerbating the political tensions in the country was the reemergence of the language question as a focus of national debate. When José Happart, the mayor of the mostly French-speaking town of Voeren, near the Dutch border, refused to comply with the law and speak Dutch in his official duties, he was dismissed on September 30, 1986, by order of the Belgian supreme court. His prompt reappointment by the town council led to angry exchanges between the country's two linguistic communities. The interior minister, Charles-Ferdinand Nothomb, resigned to show his displeasure, plunging the country into another government crisis. Faced with the possibility of a major rift in his governing coalition, Martens offered on October 15, 1986, to resign over the Voerens dispute, but the king rejected his offer. Over the next year, Martens managed to maintain an uneasy truce between Flemish-speaking and French-speaking Christian Democrats and members of the other coalition parties. The truce broke down again on October 15, 1987 over the language question, and Martens once more offered his resignation and that of his government. This time, the king accepted the resignation but kept Martens in office and instructed him to form a new government following new elections, scheduled for December 13, 1987.

Wilfried Martens and his wife, the former Lieve Verschroeven, have two daughters, Chris and Ann. In the words of the *Economist* (February 22, 1986), "hard work, patience, and adaptability are the hallmarks of his character." In 1983 Martens underwent open-heart surgery. "Since then," he has said, "my vision of life has been very calm and serene. This helps me a lot in my political life!" The bespectacled, mild-mannered Martens is a keen cyclist and a home-computer enthusiast. His religion is the Roman Catholic. "My dream is . . . that the very fact that several languages and cultures exist in Belgium should become a source of enrichment, of potential, of cooperation and collaboration," he has said, as quoted in the *New York Post* (December 10, 1986). "That is my aim and my dream."

References: Cur Hist 83:69+ Ap '84; Economist 298:34+ F 22 '86 pors; N Y Post p24 D 10 '86 por; N Y Times A p2 Ap 22 '80 por; International Who's Who, 1986–87; Who's Who in the World, 1984–85

Mason, Jackie

June 9, 1930(?)– Comedian. Address: c/o Zarem, Inc., 135 E. 55th St., New York City, N.Y. 10022

As bewildered and daunted by the world as he looks, the veteran stand-up comedian Jackie Mason has ready opinions on everything under the sun, and he expresses those opinions unhesitatingly, in free-flowing monologs that conquer the restrictions, pretensions, contradictions, hypocrisies, and clichés of our society with deadpan humor. The impact of his wry messages is enhanced by the way he delivers them, staccato, with a naturally thick Yiddish/Lower East Side accent and cadence, punctuated with finger-jabbing. A former rabbi, Mason turned his Talmudic wisdom to the purposes of comedy three decades ago, and he was one of the hottest of the ascendant young comics of the early 1960s—until the allegation by Ed Sullivan that he had used rude gestures on Sullivan's television show in 1964 unfairly branded him as, in his words, "crude and unpredictable." Although he worked constantly, stardom eluded Mason for twenty-two years thereafter, until the 1986–87 theatrical season, when his one-man show *The World According to Me!*, a legitimate-theatre translation of his club act, became an open-ended hit on Broadway. For the stage performance, he received a special Tony Award in June 1987.

Jackie Mason

Jackie Mason was born Yacov Moshe Maza in Sheboygan, Wisconsin, on June 9 in a year that he is coy about revealing—1930, by the consensus of best estimates. His father was Eli Maza, an Orthodox rabbi who had emigrated from Minsk, Russia. Jackie's three older brothers, Joseph, Gabriel, and Bernard, became rabbis, and his two younger sisters, Gail and Evelyn, married rabbis. "It was unheard of to think of anything else [but becoming a rabbi]," Mason told Ken Gross of *People* (February 23, 1987). "But I knew, from the time I'm twelve, I had to plot to get out of this, because this is not my calling. I am not so sure about God, but I knew for certain that I worshiped the young girls, and this could get me into big trouble." By his own account, Mason was "a sad, serious kid," and he is still "a sad, serious person—even shy, or at least self-conscious."

Mason grew up on Henry Street on New York City's Lower East Side, where his family moved when he was five. "As a child I was always in *shul* [temple]," he recalled in an interview for *Coronet* (July 1966). "I was in *shul* from 8:30 in the morning to 7:00 at night." He became a cantor at eighteen, and after taking a B.A. degree in psychology at the City College of New York and completing the seminary course at Yeshiva University, he was ordained a rabbi, at twenty-four.

As the rabbi of congregations in Weldon, North Carolina, and Pittston, Pennsylvania, Mason was not happy, and he stayed in the rabbinate as long as he did only out of deference to his father. After two years he began gravitating to secular jobs, ultimately to social director at Jewish resorts in the Catskill Mountains, pretending to his father that this was "kind of a hiatus." Filling in occasionally as a comedian in shows at the hotels, he knew he

had found his true métier, but at first he treated his comedy work strictly as a sideline, and he kept it secret from his father.

After his father died in 1957, Yacov Maza became Jackie Mason the full-time comedian, playing the resorts for $65 a week, or $35 and board. When the summer seasons were over, he sought nightclub work in New York City, without much success. A large proportion of the gigs he could find were in strip joints, where his accent and clean material often drew jeers. Recalling the slim pickings of his early years as a comic, he later joked, "I had to sell furniture to make a living—my own." Having second thoughts and some guilt feelings about his career change, he sought help in psychoanalysis, an experience that inspired "neurotic" jokes antedating those for which Woody Allen would become known. "When I went to a football game," he would say, "every time the players went into a huddle I thought they were talking about me." Most of the jokes were delivered, typically, in long, meandering riffs, such as: "My analyst said, What's bothering you. I said, Your $50 fee for a visit. For $50 I don't visit, I move in. He said, We have to try to find the real you. I said to myself, Why do I need him. I could call my friends. They know where I've been. And what if I find the real me and he's even worse than I am? I don't make enough for myself—I need a partner? Besides, if this is not the real me, why should I pay the $50. Collect it from the real me."

More seriously, Mason blamed much of his trouble in obtaining good engagements in the New York City area on, ironically, Jewish agents and audiences who were (and, according to him, would remain) sensitive about the Jewish image he projected with his inflection, his brash manner, and such jokes as, "Money is not the most important thing in the world. Love is. Fortunately, I love money." "Jewish audiences . . . have a problem when they see me," Mason later explained. "My accent reminds them of a background they're trying to forget." Regarding his joke about loving money, he said, as quoted by Ronald Lande Smith in *The Stars of Stand-up Comedy*: "I wasn't saying it as a Jew, I'm saying it as a person. Everybody could identify with that joke. Generally my jokes are of the opposite nature, that show up the stupidity of thinking money is everything and humanity is nothing." He went on to say, "Jews have been persecuted for so many years—it's not an illusion. But to give up your identity plays into the hands of anti-Semitism." As for him, he was "proud" of his Jewishness and would "dance with it . . . fly with it . . . make an issue of it, whether you like it or not." He viewed his "rebelliousness" as "a defiant symbolism."

In February 1960 Charley Rapp, Mason's agent at the time, secured an entrée for him at Slate Brothers, a Los Angeles comedy club frequented by show-business people. Booked for one night, he was a hit for three months at the club. After catching Mason's act at Slate Brothers, the comedian Jan Murray relayed word to Steve Allen, who went to the club and booked Mason on his popular national television show for two appearances within as many weeks. Mason's price for engagements immediately went up from $150 to $1,000 a week and opened up to him such top venues as Manhattan's Copacabana and Blue Angel nightclubs. A reviewer of a Mason engagement at the Blue Angel in October 1961 described the comedian as sounding, in his psychoanalysis routine, "like all of the Marx Brothers being analyzed at once."

From the Steve Allen show Mason moved on to other major television showcases, beginning with those of Garry Moore and Perry Como and including that of Jack Parr, then the king of late-night TV. In 1963 Mason's top-flight engagements included an appearance in Britain on BBC-TV's Sunday Night at the Palladium. His earnings from nightclub appearances, record albums, and books that year were estimated somewhere between $300,000 and $500,000. In the Catskills in 1964 he demanded $2,000 a performance, a figure that made him the most valuable property in the Borscht Belt. In 1964 Citadel Press published Mason's book of humor My Son the Candidate, with photographs by Gary Warner. Verve issued the Mason recordings I Am the Greatest Comedian in the World and I Want to Leave You with the Words of a Great Comedian.

One of Mason's most popular routines in the early 1960s was a wicked impersonation of Ed Sullivan, the host of the Sunday prime-time Ed Sullivan Show, then the pinnacle of prime-time television exposure. After seeing the impersonation on the Jack Paar Show, Sullivan booked Mason thirty times, including the fateful night of October 18, 1964, when the "finger incident" occurred. Mason had six live minutes on the show, each representing days if not weeks of perfectionist honing. Unfortunately, President Lyndon B. Johnson preempted network broadcasting just then with a televised speech. When the CBS network cut back to the Sullivan show, Mason was beyond the midpoint of his monolog and felt that he had to make every second count. When Sullivan raised two fingers to signal to him that he had only that many minutes left, he did so conspicuously, distracting the studio audience's attention from the comedian, who tried to recoup by kidding Sullivan, holding up various fingers to the audience and saying, "I've got a finger for you and a finger for you and a finger for you." The audience loved it, but Sullivan was furious.

After the historic show, Sullivan accused Mason of having made "an obscene gesture on camera," canceled a $45,000 contract for six appearances, and refused to pay him the $7,500 fee for the night's performance. According to Mason, Sullivan accused him of "insubordination" and told him, "I'll destroy you in show business." Mason initiated a libel suit, in the course of which a New York state supreme court judge declared, after viewing the kinescope, that he saw "nothing offensive" in Mason's performance. Mason dropped his suit when he and Sullivan reconciled and Sullivan let him appear on his show again, on September 11, 1966.

The reconciliation notwithstanding, the Sullivan brouhaha dealt a serious blow to Mason's career, partly because, in his view, it served to strengthen the contention of his enemies that he was not good for the Jewish image. He remained a headliner summers in the Catskills and winters in Miami Beach, Florida, where he wrote a column for the Miami Beach Sun and became a partner with hotel owner Morris Lansburgh in Mason's Basin, a boite de nuit atop the Saxony Hotel. In between he continued to play casinos in Las Vegas, and in the 1970s he had a few bookings a year at Atlantic City hotels as well. Increasingly, however, he found himself reduced to doing spots in other entertainers' shows and filling out his itinerary in dingy cocktail lounges ("the first time I ever saw dead people smoke"). That injured his morale, because he is, as he admits, "an ambitious egomaniac." Although he made "close to a million dollars some years," he did so, in his words, in "the only business in the world" where "if you make $20,000 a week, you're a pathetic failure."

Mason's morale was not helped by a series of threats to his life and limb beginning in 1966, during an engagement at the Aladdin Hotel in Las Vegas. In his act, Mason included some jokes about the difference in the ages of the veteran singer and actor Frank Sinatra and the fledgling actress Mia Farrow, who had recently married. According to a report in the New York Post (November 7, 1966), Mason received several anonymous telephone calls early in November 1966 in which he was told "We'll get ya . . . if you mention the name Frank Sinatra again." On the night of November 6, according to wire-service reports, three .22-calibre bullets were fired through a patio door into Mason's hotel room while he was on the telephone, hitting the bed on which he had been lying moments before. Mason attributed the incident not to Sinatra but to "some kook who wanted to impress Frank." Later in the same month Mason was briefly hospitalized following a head-on automobile collision, from which the woman driving the other car fled on foot. Also during the same month, Phil Greenwald, the entertainment director at the Concord Hotel in the Catskills, reported to police that he had received a score of calls of protest against booking Mason, including a death threat from an "hysterical" woman. When sitting in a parked car with a date in Miami on February 13, 1967, Mason sustained multiple face lacerations and a broken nose in a sudden attack by an unknown assailant.

In 1969 and 1970 Mason was involved in a law suit with CBS over the deletion of some of the remarks he made in a taped appearance on the TV show the Smothers Brothers Comedy Hour. The targets of the offending remarks were American policy in Vietnam and United States government officials, including President Richard Nixon ("Bobby Baker took the Fifth and they put him in jail. Nixon took the Fifth and they elected him President"). Mason contended that the cuts "tainted" him and contributed to the perpetuation of his image as "a censored comedian."

In an interview published in the New York *Daily News* on January 4, 1970, Mason said that his goal was "to become the biggest comedy actor in the world." He had never had acting lessons ("the biggest fraud in the world") but he saw himself as "a Chaplinesque character" who could, playing himself, "bring sensitivity and tenderness to a part." The main barrier to his breaking into movies or situation comedy roles on television was, in his view, as he later explained, "anti-Semitism perpetrated by Jews who run the entertainment business." "They say I'm too Jewish for the heartland. But what they mean is that I remind them of where they come from and they don't like that."

In 1969 Mason organized his own production company, JaMa Productions, Inc., in collaboration with Leon H. Charney. With Mike Mortman, Mason wrote *A Teaspoon Every Four Hours*, a good-natured comedy about a Jewish accountant, Nat Weiss, who has to take care of his two sons by himself after his wife dies. When Weiss learns that his son has a Gentile girlfriend who may be pregnant, he goes to visit the girl's mother, a black woman (he is surprised to find) who is also widowed and with whom he becomes emotionally involved. With Mason playing Nat Weiss, the play began previewing on Broadway on March 21, 1979. Responding to good rapport with preview audiences, Mason cut most of the civil rights rhetoric out of the play and began, as he said, "playing it for laughs."

A Teaspoon Every Four Hours officially opened, and closed, on June 14, 1969 after ninety-seven preview performances, a Broadway record. The critics were merciless in panning what they described as Mason's strident histrionics and self-indulgent digressions into "tasteless" and "brittle" nightclub gags. The production cost $1,200,000, and Mason personally lost $120,000 or more in the venture. Mason later commented: "The critics were waiting for me [with the question] Who is this gross Jew from the mountains, who doesn't belong on Broadway? They had to preserve their semi-homosexual atmosphere of arrogant social elegance, the Noel Coward set walking and talking in their own language, living in an Ivory Tower of 'Theatre' with all the pretentious nonsense it's supposed to represent."

The filming of a television situation-comedy pilot starring Mason, "Let's Be Honest About It," a JaMa production, was aborted by a financial dispute with an underwriting company. The JaMa motion picture *The Stoolie* (1972), written by a trio of scenarists (not including Mason), starred Mason as Roger Pitman, a New Jersey police/criminal double agent who absconds to Miami with a small fortune in hot money. While the police pursue him, he lives the high life in Miami, wining and dining a series of sexy women before finding true love with Sheila Morrison (Marcia Jean Kurtz), a suicidal legal secretary from Hempstead, Long Island. The reviewer for *Variety* (November 22, 1972) found the film to be "thin and contrived," with "marginal laughs" as a comedy-melodrama but "colorful" as a Miami travelog. The picture, which cost $1,200,000 (three-fourths of it Mason's), had limited distribution and lost half a million dollars. After *The Stoolie* flopped, Mason went back to square one and retraced his original route to popularity. From the mid-1970s into the early 1980s he did as many television guest shots as possible, worked clubs and hotels assiduously again, and even did trade shows. On the screen, he appeared in *The Jerk* (1979), a Steve Martin comedy vehicle.

Mason came to view his prolonged "semi-rut" as, at least in part, "a merchandizing problem," as he explained to Joanne Kaufman in a *Wall Street Journal* (February 17, 1987) interview: "A man can manufacture the best product, but who cares unless he can find a way to market it and sell it?" Mason's manager and former girlfriend Jyll Rosenfeld and the Emmy-winning television producer Nick Vanoff came up with the idea of presenting the comedian in a one-man theatrical show, scripted by Mason from his own material, first in Los Angeles, then on Broadway. "I didn't think it would work," Mason told Joanne Kaufman. "But people, when they come into a theatre, see you in a whole new light. It's like taking a picture from the kitchen and hanging it in a museum. In a nightclub people think of you as something that goes with a glass of liquor. If they see you in a theatre they think you have something on the ball."

During its six-month triumph in Los Angeles in 1986, *The World According to Me!* attracted to the 400-seat Canon Theatre the Who's Who of the entertainment industry, and many of the moguls and celebrities returned again and again. The playwright Neil Simon described the show as "the funniest night" he had "spent in the theatre in the last ten years." Mel Brooks said: "Nobody makes me laugh harder [than Mason]."

The World According to Me! began previews at the Brooks Atkinson Theatre in Manhattan on December 15, 1986, and opened officially a week later, on December 22, to standing ovations and reviews that "shocked the life" out of Mason, as he told Lucy Kaylin of *Gentlemen's Quarterly* in an interview at the theatre. Miss Kaylin's interview was introduced in *Gentlemen's Quarterly* in part with these words: "Jackie Mason seems a far-fetched candidate for stardom. He waddles onto a nearly barren Broadway stage, this chunky, middle-aged *schlemiel* whose hair is a shade of orange not found in nature. His props? Emphatic hands, incredulous eyebrows, a spotlight. His material? Sex, religion, the weather, politics, just like in the Catskills. . . . The audience eats it up. And no restive, polyester-clad slouches here. This is the fur-lined Manhattan crowd, and they've dubbed him the hottest act in town. And yes, the man's got style. Like a classically tailored suit, he's built to endure the caprices of a culture shaped for trends."

Referring to the bare stage on which he stood, Mason explained to the audience at the Brooks Atkinson: "There is no relationship between furniture and entertainment. . . . When you go to a furniture store, do they show you a comedian?" On sex, he quipped: "I used to think that music was more important than sex, but if I don't go to a concert for a year and a half, it won't bother me." On medicine: "That's a great profession, a doctor. Where else can you ask a woman to get undressed and then send the bill to her husband?" He brought down the house with an eight-minute impression of President Ronald Reagan trying to explain his complicity, or lack thereof, in the Iran-Contra covert operations scam then under Congressional investigation: "They say it was going on in my own basement. Why would I go to the basement? I'm the president. . . . Maybe they did it but I didn't see it, and even if I saw it I certainly didn't hear it. Maybe they told me but I wasn't listening. Besides, I don't hear on both sides. Maybe I heard it on this side, but not on that side." Mason commented: "Even when Reagan was an actor, he didn't know anything about acting, and he was doing that for thirty years. So why should he know anything about politics? This is a new field to him. But I like his attitude, which is that if it happens in this country, it's none of his business." The success of Mason's one-man Broadway show brought him numerous offers of motion picture, television, and other deals; Simon & Schuster contracted him for a book of "free-wheeling comedy essays" modeled on the show; and Warner Records released a show album that sold vigorously.

By September 1987 *The World According to Me!* had sold more than 50,000 tickets, which were being scalped for as much as $170 each. Mason planned to take a leave from Broadway, probably beginning in January 1988, in order to play a prostitutes' accountant in the Lorimar Pictures comedy "Love for Sale," based on the true story of five Queens housewives who organized their own brothel. After the shooting of the movie, *The World According to Me!* was scheduled to resume its indefinite Broadway run.

Jackie Mason is five feet seven inches tall, weighs 170 pounds, and has a puffy face with sallow complexion and prominent eyes, pouched but alert. Before he had his hair "painted," as he says, it was dark brown, and graying. He confesses that he is a "tense" person, and he looks woebegone, as if trying to make sense of a crazy world, until he goes into a monolog, for which any subject will serve as a cue. There is no essential difference between his stage persona and his real-life personality. Before an audience of one, or of 1,100 (the capacity of the Brooks Atkinson), he launches the same nervous, funny, opinionated attack on whatever issue, gesticulating constantly and turning every statement into a question with his ethnic inflection, like a Yiddish Damon Runyon character.

Mason lives in Manhattan in a luxurious Fifth Avenue apartment that is decorated and appointed expensively but sparsely, in a high-tech way, with many phones and large-screen television sets but almost no furniture or creature comforts. He lives and carries on his business in one corner of the apartment, sitting in a futuristic-looking chair with two phones beside him. Not a conspicuous spender, he does not own a car or expensive jewelry. His only indulgence is clothing, which he buys in abundance, but often off the rack, and his wardrobe is low-keyed and tasteful. While he can understand "moving your body around for health purposes," he thinks "torturing yourself" in sports is "stupid" and describes himself as "a Jewish athlete—always busy watching other people jumping and flying." He has over the years dated a long succession of women, but he is at heart a loner, vehement in his rejection of our society's emphasis on marriage as the normal adult state. "It's total hypocrisy," he told Ken Gross of *People* (February 23, 1987). "People have children but they have no time for them. Disgusting. Tell me, would you open up a store and not give it any time? That's what parents do with their children." He has always seen his act as a way of teaching people how to live in a mixed-up world by seeing through "the restrictions of conventionality." That mission of his is rooted in the Talmud, the book of Jewish religious commentaries he was bred in. "The Talmud is the study of logic," he explained to Joanne Kaufman in the *Wall Street Journal* interview. "Every time I see a contradiction or hypocrisy in somebody's behavior, I think of the Talmud and build the joke from there."

References: Gentlemen's Quarterly 57:65+ Je '87 por; N Y Daily News mag p6 Ja 4 '70 por; N Y Newsday p89 Mr 19 '87 por; N Y Post p29 O 20 '64 por; N Y Times II p4+ D 21 '86; Newsweek 109:47 Ja 12 '87 pors; People 27:90+ F 23 '87 pors; Washington Post G p1+ D 3 '86 pors; Smith, Ronald Lande. The Stars of Stand-up Comedy (1986)

M'Bow, Amadou-Mahtar

(m-bō´ ä´me-dōō mäh´tär)

Mar. 20, 1921– Director General of UNESCO. Address: b. UNESCO, 7 Place de Fontenoy, 75700 Paris, France

A member of Senegal's French-trained elite but an African traditionalist at heart, Amadou-Mahtar M'Bow served as his homeland's minister of education and of youth and cultural affairs before he joined the staff of the United Nations Educational, Scientific, and Cultural Organization (UNESCO) in Paris in 1970, as the assistant director general for education. Since he was elected to the first of two consecutive six-year terms as UNESCO's director general in 1974, M'Bow, who is said to view the agency primarily as an organization for intellectual collaboration, has been committed to the use of education and communications as tools for eradicating the adverse effects of colonialism and underdevelopment in the Third World. Widely criticized in the West for politicizing UNESCO and giving it an increasingly anti-Western bias, he left

Amadou-Mahtar M'Bow

United Nations/UNESCO/D. Roger

the agency in November 1987, after failing to win reelection to a third term.

The oldest son of Fara-N'Diaye and N'Gone (Casset) M'Bow, Amadou-Mahtar M'Bow was born on March 20, 1921, in Dakar, the capital of the then French-ruled colony of Senegal. His father, a farmer and leatherworker, was a member of the Wolof people, Senegal's largest and most influential ethnic group. A devout Moslem respected for his piety, Fara-N'Diaye M'Bow was a prominent citizen of Louga, a town of about five thousand in the semiarid peanut-growing region of the Sahel, in eastern Senegal, and it was there that young Amadou-Mahtar spent his formative years in a traditional extended family. The boy's early education came in the form of Wolof legends and fables told by his mother and aunts. Later, when he was about five, he began his religious training at a local Moslem school, where, among other things, he memorized verses from the Koran. From his father and uncles, he learned practical crafts and farming skills.

In November 1929, Amadou-Mahtar M'Bow enrolled at the French regional school in Louga. His first two years at the school coincided with the onset of the worldwide economic Depression and a severe drought that ravaged the Sahel. The deaths of tens of thousands of his countrymen from disease and starvation made a profound and lasting impression on M'Bow. "For me hunger is no rhetorical expression" he told Pierre Kalfon, who interviewed him for a *UNESCO Courier* (February 1975) profile. "One must have lived through it to understand its horror." A diligent student, M'Bow gradually overcame the language obstacle at the French school (when he entered, he spoke only Wolof) to earn a certificate of primary studies. Con-

sidered to be too old for admission to the elite Lycée Faidherbe in Saint-Louis, M'Bow, then fourteen, continued his education with a commercial course at a less prestigious higher primary school.

Upon his graduation, M'Bow obtained a job as a clerk in the governor's office in Dakar. During this period in the late 1930s, young Senegalese nationalists, in cooperation with French leftists, were campaigning for an end to forced labor, the right to form trade unions, and the granting of full citizenship rights to all Africans. M'Bow reportedly played an active role in the organization of a nationalist youth group. When World War II broke out, M'Bow, feeling that he had, as he put it, "a duty to accomplish as a free man," volunteered for military service in the French army. Soon after he arrived in France, in 1940, the country was defeated and occupied by Germany. Immediately demobilized, he returned to Senegal, which was by then under the control of newly appointed administrators, whose mismanagement led to economic and political deterioration. When that right-wing regime was overthrown by the Free French forces in November 1942, M'Bow rejoined the military. Assigned to an air force school at Agadir, Morocco, he eventually graduated at the top of his class. A specialist in aircraft electronics, he was the first black technical sergeant in the French air force.

Mustered out of the service in 1945, M'Bow remained in France, where, supported by a veterans' grant, he prepared for the *baccalauréat*, a prerequisite for admission to a university. Originally intending to study electrical engineering, he enrolled, in 1946, at the Breguet School of Electrical Engineering in Paris, but after a year there his deepening commitment to African nationalism and to socialism prompted him to transfer to the University of Paris, where he majored in geography and history, focusing on Africa. While he was a student in Paris, M'Bow helped organize the African Group for Economic and Political Research, a coalition of African students interested in reconciling Marxism with African culture. In 1948 he was elected president of the Association of African Students in Paris, and two years later he was chosen to serve as secretary-general of the Federation of Black African Students in France. The members of the last-named organization adhered to a variety of political philosophies, including Christian democracy, social democracy, Marxism-Leninism, pan-Africanism, and liberalism. M'Bow's stewardship of that polyglot group at a time when both French and African politics were in ferment proved to be first-rate on-the-job training for his later careers as a politician and civil servant.

Awarded a *licence* in geography and history and a *diplôme* in tropical geography from the University of Paris in 1951, M'Bow returned to Senegal to seek a teaching job. The French authorities in Dakar, who were trying to contain a growing nationalist movement spearheaded by returning militant students, decided to post M'Bow to Rosso College, in a remote area of Mauritania, a French colony to the north of Senegal. Although politically frustrating, the assignment gave him firsthand experience as a rural educator. As one of Senegal's few experts in that field, he was tapped, in 1953, to head the government's newly established Department of Fundamental Education, a UNESCO-sponsored agency developed to survey rural educational needs, train teachers, and formulate curricula. According to M'Bow, his four years as director of the agency were "no doubt the most inspiring and instructive" of his career because he contributed directly to raising the living standards of thousands of formerly illiterate villagers and accumulated a wealth of knowledge about Senegalese rural life.

Chastened by the loss of Vietnam and mired in a bloody war in Algeria, the French government tried to avert unrest in its African colonies by passing, in 1956, a law that granted universal adult suffrage and colonial self-government. In that new environment, the moderate, largely urban elites represented by the Senegalese Socialist party were outmaneuvered by the Senegalese Democratic Bloc (BDS), led by the poet-philosopher Léopold Senghor, in the 1956 election of delegates to the French parliament. Since 1948 the BDS had been expanding its political base by championing the interests of the rural masses and urban radicals. To strengthen the party organization in time for the March 1957 election to the territorial assembly, Senghor incorporated returned members of the African Group for Economic and Political Research and other independent Marxist groups into the BDS. Appointed associate propaganda secretary of the party, M'Bow energetically set about working for the elimination of colonialism and the modernization of Africa.

After the BDS's overwhelming victory in the territorial assembly poll, M'Bow was named minister of education and culture in Senegal's first national government during the transitional period preceding independence. In the following year, however, he resigned his post rather than support his party's decision to accept membership in the new French Community, which allowed France to retain control of economic and fiscal policy, foreign affairs, and other matters of common interest in exchange for large-scale aid. Contending that the French-led federation was just colonialism in a new guise, M'Bow and several like-minded colleagues broke with the BDS and formed the African Realignment party of Senegal, which campaigned for immediate independence and a radical reform of Senegal's socioeconomic system. But Léopold Senghor's mastery of Senegalese politics proved unassailable. In a national referendum 97.6 percent of the electorate opted for membership in the French Community.

Returning to teaching, M'Bow took a job as a history instructor at the Lycée Faidherbe in Saint-Louis, a post he held until 1964. From 1964 to 1966 he taught general education and trained secondary schoolteachers and primary school inspectors at the École Normale Supérieure in Dakar. Throughout that period he devoted much of his spare time to developing textbooks designed to enrich young Africans' appreciation of the rich cultural diversity of their continent and to publishing popular works aimed at improving Africa's image abroad. In addition, he chaired the multinational commission that revised the history and geography curricula in French-speaking African countries and Madagascar.

Since becoming president of the republic of Senegal in 1960, Léopold Senghor had effectively crippled the parliamentary opposition with his pragmatic, carrot-and-stick approach. Faced with political oblivion, M'Bow accepted Senghor's offer, in 1966, of the education ministry portfolio. As minister of education, he oversaw the "Africanization" of Dakar University, presided over the commission that developed a Senegalese alphabet from a phonetic transcription of the six Senegalese languages, and served as chairman of Senegal's national commission for UNESCO. In the last post, he led the country's delegation to UNESCO's fourteenth and fifteenth general conferences and served on the agency's executive board, where he emerged as an eloquent spokesman for Africa and the Third World, which had recently begun a vigorous campaign to make UNESCO more responsive to the needs of developing countries.

In 1968 Senegal was in the midst of an economic crisis caused largely by falling prices in the world market for peanuts, Senegal's principal export. As part of an across-the-board government austerity program, M'Bow slashed educational subsidies. To protest the cutbacks, students took to the streets in a series of strikes and demonstrations that were quelled only after considerable violence. Following widespread public criticism of his handling of the situation, M'Bow was transferred, on June 6, 1968, to the ministry for youth and cultural affairs. His domestic political career seriously compromised, for the next two years M'Bow played a more active role on UNESCO's executive board. Impressed by the African delegate's expertise, René Maheu, UNESCO's director general, asked him to join the agency's staff in 1970, as assistant director general for education. One of the first Africans to hold such a high-level position within the United Nations administration, M'Bow quickly gained a reputation as a skilled manager and a forceful but reasonable proponent of Third World needs.

When Maheu, who was ill with leukemia, announced his decision to retire on the expiration of his second term as director general in November 1974, UNESCO's African member states lobbied hard for M'Bow to succeed him. Most of the agency's 135 other member states supported their choice—as much because no black African had as yet headed a major UN agency as because of M'Bow's qualifications for the job. With the unanimous backing of UNESCO's executive board, on November 14, 1974, the organization's eighteenth general conference elected Amadou-Mahtar M'Bow as its sixth director general.

M'Bow's vaunted talent as a peacemaker was put to an immediate test when the general conference passed a series of Arab-inspired resolutions that considerably weakened Israel's position in UNESCO and barred it from participating in the agency's regional meetings. Although he was constitutionally bound to execute resolutions approved by a majority of the member states, M'Bow was acutely aware that UNESCO depended disproportionately on Western money and technological know-how. In a speech to the delegates at the final session of the general conference in Paris on November 23, 1974, he advised against "the adoption of resolutions, no matter how strong the majority behind them, that leave profound bitterness among some of us" and appealed for "tolerance and understanding" and "consensus through patient dialogue." He also emphasized that although Israel had been expelled from its regional group, it had not been excluded from UNESCO, and that he welcomed the continued participation of Israeli artists, scholars, and scientists in UNESCO activities. In spite of M'Bow's efforts to cushion the resolutions' negative impact, the United States suspended funding to UNESCO until Israel was restored to full membership in 1976. Many Western European governments also criticized UNESCO's decision, and intellectual luminaries, among them Jean-Paul Sartre and Simone de Beauvoir, sponsored protest petitions.

M'Bow's personal reputation for evenhandedness was untarnished by the acrimonious dispute over Israel's membership in UNESCO, but his commitment, which first became apparent at the agency's eighteenth general conference in 1978, to the Third World's draft resolution calling for the establishment of a "new world information and communications order" put him on a collision course with the West. Communications—"the free exchange of ideas and knowledge," as it is described in UNESCO's founding constitution—is at the heart of the agency's mandate to promote international understanding and peace. The Third World's demand for a new global information order was based on the conviction that Western news agencies, such as the Associated Press and Reuters, and multinational corporations monopolize international news and economic information. Moreover, by distorting and restricting knowledge of the Third World, they contribute to the perpetuation of the West's cultural and economic domination of underdeveloped areas. To redress the imbalance, the resolution proposed using the financial resources of the industrialized world, channeled through UNESCO, to help emerging states and regional organizations break the Western media monopoly. The motion included a recognition of the right of both UNESCO and its member states to regulate the flow of news and information in the interests of social justice and economic development. In the eyes of Western delegates, however, the most controversial proposition endorsed the government licensing of journalists on the basis of professional competence and adherence to "generally accepted" standards of journalistic ethics.

Although M'Bow and other proponents of the Third World viewpoint maintained that the establishment of a new world information order was not incompatible with freedom of the press, Western governments and media representatives remained highly skeptical. While they were prepared to contribute to the development of Third World press agencies and media systems, they were strongly opposed to any measures, such as licensing, that would "transform the press into an instrument of governments," as Cushrow Irani, the chairman of the International Press Institute and publisher of the Calcutta Statesman, put it. M'Bow tried for several years to bridge the gap between the two sides, but his efforts eventually failed, largely because of the West's refusal to commit large sums of money to Third World media development and the Third World's refusal to abandon its demand for the regulation of the international flow of information.

By late 1982, the conflict had spilled over into other areas. At a conference in November 1982 to discuss UNESCO's "medium-term" plan for 1984–89, for example, M'Bow argued that increasing inequalities among countries had pushed "vast numbers of people . . . into despair." Advances in technology had made the Third World dependent upon decisions taken by a handful of industrialized nations. Because countries had become "enmeshed in a tight and dense network of flows of all kinds," he continued, it was impossible to make a distinction between political, economic, social, and cultural activities. Consequently, he recommended that UNESCO increase its efforts in disarmament, the maintenance of peace and security, and international economics—areas that were seen by some Western delegates, including those from the United States and Great Britain, as being beyond UNESCO's purview. M'Bow also backed giving more recognition to the concept of collective as opposed to individual human rights, a move widely criticized by Westerners, many of whom felt that it would be used as a fig leaf by repressive regimes claiming to represent the popular will.

Concerned about what they viewed as the inappropriate political aims of UNESCO, many of the Western nations that contribute the lion's share of the agency's funds began demanding a greater say in its budgetary decision-making. The United States, which donated a quarter of UNESCO's budget, was especially concerned by the agency's moving into areas not covered by its charter. At a meeting in June 1983 to discuss UNESCO's proposed 1984–89 budget, Mrs. Jean Gerard, the United States ambassador to UNESCO, and Assistant Secretary of State Gregory J. Newell, warned M'Bow that the United States would not accept the proposed increase in the agency's budget. When M'Bow reportedly told the pair that they could not treat him "like an American black who has no rights," the Americans walked out of the meeting. Shortly after that, on July 28, the United States announced that President Ronald Reagan had ordered a "thorough review" of continued American participation in UNESCO, in view of "a number of controversial issues," including freedom of the press.

A the twenty-third general conference in the autumn of 1983, UNESCO delegates voted, after considerable debate, to trim the budget and to excise some of the more controversial provisions of the world information and communication program. Despite those concessions, complaints about administrative inefficiency continued to spread. A number of Western news magazines, among them the internationally respected *Economist* (August 27, 1983), published articles describing widespread discontent among UNESCO employees "trampled by a mixture of nepotism, maladministration, reverse racism, and an apparently incorrigible tilt toward the hardliners of the Third World." Among the veteran staff members who submitted their resignations was Rodolfo Stavenhagen, the head of UNESCO's social sciences division, who left the agency in 1983 because of what he called, as quoted in the *Economist*, "the atmosphere of distrust, denunciation, and a sort of bureaucratic terrorism which has led to total intellectual suffocation." Charging that his critics were orchestrating a "veritable smear campaign" against him and his administration, M'Bow eventually called for an inquiry, by a UNESCO-appointed commission, into the "untruthful allegations."

On December 28, 1983, the United States, the most critical of UNESCO's member states, announced its intention to leave the organization on December 31, 1984. Although pressure from the Western bloc throughout 1984 resulted in some administrative reforms, little progress was made in cutting the budget or in depoliticizing the agency's activities. A suspicious fire that destroyed a large part of the agency's archives on the eve of an official investigation by the United States Government Accounting Office and M'Bow's suppression of a critical report by an internal review panel, further embittered Western delegates. By the end of 1984 the governments of Great Britain and Singapore had joined the United States in withdrawing from UNESCO, and several members of the European Community had expressed reservations about continued membership if reforms were not implemented. "If one, two, three, or even ten [countries] leave, as long as the others have the will to continue to cooperate internationally, that will not affect the organization . . . ," M'Bow told John O'Leary in an interview for the London *Times Higher Education Supplement* (January 11, 1985). "I do not look at the withdrawal of the United States or the United Kingdom in terms of funds, but it raises questions about the whole UN system and international cooperation in general."

Impatient with the pace of organizational reform, twenty-six Western member nations, led by France, agreed in February 1986 to oppose the reelection of Amadou-Mahtar M'Bow to a third term as director general of UNESCO. But since M'Bow had the endorsements of the Organization of African Unity and the Arab League and the open support of many nonaligned and developing countries,

few expected the effort to succeed. Then, on October 10, 1986, M'Bow unexpectedly announced to a closed meeting of UNESCO's executive board that he would step down following the completion of his term, in November 1987. "It is necessary, whatever the cost, to get UNESCO out of the hurricane zone, while remaining faithful to its democratic principles," he explained, as quoted in the *New York Times* (October 7, 1986). He added that he hoped that his supporters would see in his decision "a wish to make a positive contribution to the consolidation of the bonds of trust that should exist between all members of the international community."

Within a few months, however, M'Bow was actively campaigning for a third term as UNESCO's director general. Formally nominated for reelection to the post on September 24, 1987, by the Organization of African Unity, M'Bow garnered most of the votes on the first four ballots cast by the fifty-member executive board, but he failed to achieve the required majority. Just before the fifth and final ballot on October 17, M'Bow withdrew his name from nomination, reportedly at the urging of the Soviet bloc delegates, who feared that his reelection might provoke other Western nations to join the United States and Britain in pulling out of UNESCO. The following day the executive board voted to nominate as M'Bow's successor Federico Mayor Zaragoza, a Spanish biochemist.

Those who know him well have described Amadou-Mahtar M'Bow as an articulate, cultured, and convivial man, although he has a reputation for what one Western reporter called "towering rages." Little is known about his private life. Married since July 27, 1951, to the former Raymonde Sylvain, who has collaborated with him on several books, he has one son, Fara-Edy, and two daughters, Awa-Martha and Marie-Amy. He lives with his family in a rent-free apartment, built for security reasons at his request in UNESCO's headquarters building in Paris. He holds scores of honorary doctorates and foreign decorations, many from Third World nations.

References: *Christian Sci Mon* p7+ D 18 '84 por; *N Y Times* p25 N 15 '74 por; *N Y Times Mag* p116 S 21 '80 por; *Times Higher Education Supplement* 636:10 Ja 11 '85 por; *U S News* 97:9 D 24 '84 por; *Unesco Courier* p14+ F '75 pors; *West Africa* p717 Ap 15 '85 por; *Africa Yearbook and Who's Who*, 1977; Colvin, Lucie G. *Historical Dictionary of Senegal* (1981); *International Who's Who*, 1987–88; *International Yearbook and Statemen's Who's Who*, 1986; *Who's Who in the World*, 1984–85

McGuane, Thomas

Dec. 11, 1939– Author; screenwriter. Address: h. McLeod, Mont. 59052

A consummate fiction stylist known for his linguistic pyrotechnics, caustic humor, quirky insights, and dazzling use of literary allusion, Thomas McGuane has discovered that his early reputation as one of the best young novelists of his generation is a difficult act to follow. Since the publication of his first novel in 1969, when Joyce Carol Oates pronounced him "at twenty-eight, that notorious and difficult creature—a writer of promise," McGuane has produced five novels, five screenplays, many essays on sports ranging from fishing to golf, and a collection of short stories. *Ninety-Two in the Shade* (1973), his most widely acclaimed novel, was nominated for a National Book Award and later made into a movie directed by McGuane himself. His novels have both impressed and irritated critics with their virtuosity, cold, gem-like precision, and sometimes self-indulgent themes of ennui and self-destruction in "Hotcakesland," the plastic and neon American wasteland of what McGuane has termed "a declining snivelization."

Discouraged by only moderate book sales and seduced by the lure of bigger money and broader acclaim, McGuane turned to screenwriting during the mid-1970s, when he temporarily abandoned the monkish seclusion of his writing regimen. For several years, headlines trumpeted McGuane's reported high life of substance abuse and sexual excess, which he shared with the coterie of writers, actors, and artists for whom his Montana ranch had allegedly become a mecca for creative inspiration and dissolute behavior. Following the publication in 1978 of his widely panned fourth novel,

Panama, two failed marriages, and a prolonged battle with both alcoholism and rejection from the critics, McGuane seems to have emerged intact, stabilized by a happy third marriage, a successful cutting-horse ranch, and a revitalized writing career.

Thomas Francis McGuane 3d was born on December 11, 1939, in Wyandotte, Michigan, the oldest of three children. His father, Thomas McGuane 2d, a New England native who majored in English at Harvard, eventually founded Tom McGuane, Inc., a successful auto parts manufacturing firm based in Detroit, and his mother, the former Alice Rita Torphy, was the daughter of a ship's chandler from Fall River, Massachusetts. His Irish Catholic forebears included judges, millworkers, and the well-known post-World War I baseball player Walter ("Red") Torphy.

McGuane spent most of his childhood in Grosse Ile, Michigan, an island suburb of Detroit, where he was steeped in the "heavy duty Irish" wit of a family of what he has called "fantastic storytellers." Although McGuane told one source that he abhorred reading as a child, he is also said to have devoured nature books at his family's summer retreat, a fishing camp in northern Michigan that resembled the setting for his first novel, *The Sporting Club.* At the age of ten, he abandoned his original career goal of becoming an ichthyologist, after collaborating with a friend on a novel that was never finished because its juvenile authors got into a fistfight over the description of a sunset.

McGuane's boyhood provided grist for what Gregory Skwira, in an article published in the *Chicago Tribune* (April 12, 1985), called "a consistent McGuane theme: unresolved business between fathers and sons." Although McGuane has fond memories of hunting and fishing with his father, who was an accomplished sportsman, the camaraderie began to pall as his father retreated increasingly into compulsive working and drinking. From 1955 to 1960 the McGuanes alternated between living in Michigan and Venice, Florida, where the father and son also spent many idyllic hours in sport fishing. "I had had this kind of never-never land," McGuane recalls. "But my dad was no longer available to go hunting or fishing by the time I was about thirteen or fourteen." In 1955, while he was a student at Cranbrook, an exclusive Michigan boarding school, he ran away to a Wyoming ranch owned by the father of a girlfriend. He returned as an avowed "sociopath." The episode was recaptured years later in his second novel, *The Bushwhacked Piano.*

Following his graduation from Cranbrook, McGuane enrolled at the University of Michigan, but rebellious and interested only in writing, he flunked out with a 0.6 grade average. He then briefly attended a small Michigan college called Olivet and finally enrolled at Michigan State, where he edited the college literary magazine, wrote compulsively, and met Portia Rebecca Crockett, a sorority girl who was a direct descendant of the frontiersman Davy Crockett. In September 1962, the year in which McGuane graduated with honors from Michigan State, he and Becky were married. Accepted by Yale Drama School, he spent the next three years halfheartedly studying to become a playwright and poring over every novel he could carry home from the Yale Library. His reading list included writers as diverse as Cervantes, Gogol, Rabelais, Faulkner, and Knut Hamsun. As he later told Thomas Collins of Newsday (April 12, 1971), the books that came to be his favorites—Robert Burton's The Anatomy of Melancholy, Thomas Nashe's The Unfortunate Traveller, and novels by Jonathan Swift, Louis-Ferdinand Céline, and D. B. Wyndham Lewis—"all had one thing in common—the comic exaggeration and excesses of language carried to an almost hallucinogenic degree." That insight was to affect the evolution of his own early novels, with their startling linguistic convolutions, their persistent themes of hip, ironic, and alienated young outsiders, their confrontations between man and his own worst nature, and with what one reviewer for Time magazine (August 6, 1973) called "the monstrous practical joke that is at the center of all his books."

During his Yale period, McGuane began work on a manuscript that would eventually become The Bushwhacked Piano. When William Styron, the novelist, submitted a second McGuane manuscript, entitled Fire Season (a precursor of The Sporting Club) to Random House, the publisher summarily rejected it. Disappointed, but not entirely discouraged, McGuane took off after receiving his M.F.A. degree in 1965, to spend a year with Becky in Spain and Italy, where they lived on $1,500 they had received as a wedding present. After spending a year at the Scuola per Stranieri in Florence, McGuane used the beginnings of another novel to win a Wallace Stegner fellowship to Stanford University. During his year at Stanford—the academic year of 1966–67, when the drug scene at Haight-Ashbury in San Francisco was in its heyday—McGuane stayed on such a straight-arrow course that he was dubbed "the White Knight" by his more adventurous friends. Applying himself feverishly, he took his work seriously enough to turn his depression around and complete The Sporting Club during a marathon six-week stretch in 1968. Jim Harrison, a poet and novelist whom McGuane had met at Michigan State, persuaded a friend's wife who worked at Simon & Schuster to show the manuscript to an editor there.

Becky McGuane, meanwhile, had given birth to a son, Thomas McGuane 4th, and the father, somewhat disconcerted by his new status as a parent and anxious about the future of his novel, had taken off on a fishing trip to Baja California, where his wife cabled to tell him that his book had been accepted by Simon & Schuster. Reviews were mixed. Some critics approached The Sporting Club with the caution often reserved for first novels, while the harshest deplored his retreat into fantasy or an "anti-novel" mode. Sara Blackburn of the Nation (April 14, 1969), however, called McGuane "one of the most original and interesting young novelists to have appeared in a long time," and Joyce Carol Oates, writing in the New York Times Book Review, (March 23, 1969), commended his "sprightly ear for dialogue," his "eye for the 'absurd,'" and his "light, fashionably cool touch that tires us only occasionally."

Shortly after publication of The Sporting Club, McGuane moved with his wife and son to Key West, Florida, to indulge his lifelong passion for sport fishing. Sometimes accused of exaggerating the superficial resemblance of his life to that of Ernest Hemingway, another Midwesterner who spent much time in Key West, McGuane discounts the criticism by explaining that he had lived in Florida as a child and liked the fishing there. Having decided against living in the West Indies because he was reluctant to lose touch with the culture that had produced him, McGuane told John Dorschner of the Miami Herald, "I didn't want to go to some exotic culture, but on the other hand, I wanted to get out on the most scrambled edge of this one."

When Hollywood offered him $75,000 for the screen rights to The Sporting Club, McGuane used the proceeds to buy a house in Key West and to make a down payment on a fourteen-acre ranch near Livingston, Montana, where he had worked one summer as a ranch hand. His second novel, The Bushwhacked Piano, published by Simon & Schuster in 1971, recounted the misadventures of Nicholas Payne, a contemporary rogue adrift in "Hotcakesland." The book elicited raves from Jonathan Yardley in the New York Times Book Review (March 14, 1971) who exulted that McGuane "has a talent of Faulknerian potential. His sheer writing talent is nothing short of amazing." Termed "slashingly inventive" by a reviewer for the National Observer (March 29, 1971), The Bushwhacked Piano won high praise, along with a measure of the sort of critical carping that was to plague McGuane increasingly in later years. "Plot, complication of character, generalizing power—forget 'em," wrote Geoffrey Wolf in Newsweek (April 19, 1971). "McGuane's game is words, and the synthetic character of words strung out in the correct and surprising sequence." McGuane, he concluded, was "a writing fool," and his second novel "a trove of pleasures."

Another trove of pleasures, however, was McGuane's Key West domicile, which had become a gathering place for a group of hard-drinking, party-loving writers and artists that included the poet Jim Harrison, the painter Russell Chatham, the photographer Guy Valdene, and the rock singer Jimmy Buffett. Both at his Montana ranch and at Key West, McGuane had become a magnet of sorts for what a writer for Time (August 6, 1973) termed "a shifting population of the lonely, itinerant, or freaked out." Although McGuane maintained that he and his family remained "everyone's straight friend," the monomaniacal intensity with which he had long been dedicated to his work seemed about to disappear.

On Thanksgiving Day, 1972, in Montana, Mc-Guane completed his third novel, *Ninety-Two in the Shade*, a fatalistic tale of two fishing guides bent on a course of mutual destruction. A month later he lost control of his Porsche on an icy road en route to the Keys, emerging unhurt but badly shaken. The close call caused him to reassess his relentless devotion to writing. "In Key West after the accident, I finally realized I could stop pedaling so insanely, get off the bike, and walk around the neighborhood," he later recalled. "The changes that came were irresistible, but it was getting unthinkable to spend another year sequestered like that, writing. I just dropped out. I quit fighting my way through marriage and the Sunday *New York Times*."

Years later McGuane insisted that reports of his temporary dissolution had been exaggerated by the media and that though it was, admittedly, "a kind of rock and roll time," he managed to accomplish a good deal of work. Published in 1973 by Farrar, Straus & Giroux, *Ninety-Two in the Shade* was acclaimed by Michael Wood in the *New York Review of Books* (December 13, 1973) as "a flippant, lucid, somber American allegory" and was nominated for the National Book Award, but like his earlier novels, it sold only moderately. When he was approached by the producer Eliot Kastner about the possibility of a film version, McGuane reviewed his options. After all, *The Bushwhacked Piano* had been awarded the prestigious Rosenthal Award of the National Institute of Letters, which is presented annually to the best novel selling the fewest copies.

McGuane wrote a screenplay of *Ninety-Two in the Shade*, and while Kastner searched for a director and financial backing, he produced a second script, for what was later to become *Rancho De Luxe*, a box-office failure about cattle rustlers on a spree that was filmed in Livingston, Montana. During its filming, one of its stars, Elizabeth Ashley, and Tom McGuane began an affair that had not yet run its course when McGuane, while working on yet another screenplay for *The Missouri Breaks*, convinced Kastner and company that he should direct *Ninety-Two in the Shade* himself. During the fall of 1974 the Canadian actress Margot Kidder auditioned for the part of Tom Skelton's girlfriend, Miranda, bewitching McGuane in the process. When Becky McGuane learned several months later that Margot Kidder was pregnant, she filed suit for a divorce that was granted the following March. When the film version of *Ninety-Two in the Shade*, completely reedited by Kastner, was released, it was damned by most critics, with the notable exception of Vincent Canby of the *New York Times*, and pulled out of theatres shortly after its release. Nine months after a daughter, Maggie, was born to Margot Kidder, her parents married, but they were divorced nine months later.

In September 1977 Thomas McGuane married his third wife, Laurie Buffett, the sister of singer Jimmy Buffett and a decidedly stabilizing force in his life. He wrote one more screenplay, *Tom Horn*, as a starring vehicle for Steve McQueen, which was released, to small critical enthusiasm, in 1979. Having recently completed his fourth work of fiction, the novella-length *Panama*, which was perceived as a tedious autobiographical howl of despair by some critics when it was published by Farrar, Straus & Giroux in 1978, McGuane began gradually to change his public persona. Becky had married the actor Peter Fonda, one of a group of McGuane's Montana neighbors that included the late novelist and poet Richard Brautigan, the writer William Hjortsberg, the controversial director Sam Peckinpah, and the character actor Warren Oates, most of whom had migrated to Montana because, as Thomas Carney observed in *Esquire* (June 6, 1978), "McGuane is the sort of placeless man who makes places wherever he goes." Peter and Mrs. Fonda bought a ranch down the road, and McGuane's son, Tom, and his daughter, Maggie, visited often.

Meanwhile, Tom McGuane had developed a far less rambunctious set of pursuits than in his hell-raising past. Raising quarter horses had become one of his many enthusiasms, and he won the team roping competition of the Gardiner, Montana, rodeo with a partner during the fall of 1977. "I've come to a point," he said in 1978, "where art is no longer as important as life."

As a serious novelist, McGuane had hardly reached the end of his tether, but he still had a few more lambastings to take from some members of the literary establishment. With the publication by Farrar, Straus & Giroux in 1978 of *Panama*, which Donald R. Katz of the *New Republic* (August 18, 1979) called "a sadly bitter book about what became of the alternate American dream," McGuane took a drubbing from those critics who failed to appreciate what they saw as his overworked rhetorical posturing. "Stomping Thomas McGuane is as rewarding to some critics as ranking him with all sorts of famous writers is to others," observed Gary L. Fisketjon of the *Village Voice* (December 11, 1978). After *Nobody's Angel*—McGuane's first novel set in Montana—was published by Random House in 1982, Jonathan Yardley of the *Washington Post* (February 2, 1982) pronounced McGuane to be "abruptly and prematurely" at "the end of the line." Among the dissenters with that verdict were Vance Bourjaily, who in the *New York Times Book Review* (March 7, 1982) called *Nobody's Angel* McGuane's "best book by far," and Jeffery Broderick, who, writing in the *National Review* (June 11, 1982), evaluated him as "a monstrous talent." In spite of the asperity of some of his critics, Tom McGuane proved he was still a formidable contender by publishing another novel, *Something to Be Desired*, with the Random House imprint, in 1985, and a collection of short stories, *To Skin a Cat*, which was issued by E. P. Dutton in 1986. For many years a contributor of articles on fishing and other sports to such magazines as *Sports Illustrated*, *Atlantic Monthly*, *Esquire*, and *Harper's*, McGuane collected his best efforts in that genre in *An Outside Chance: Essays on Sports*, published by Farrar, Straus & Giroux in 1980.

Having given up alcohol in 1981, Tom McGuane began a quieter life, reflected in his fiction by less frenetic themes, and a search for new literary forms. As Curt Suplee pointed out in the *Washington Post* (October 2, 1986), he had "a new publisher, a new book of short stories . . . a new-found imaginative breadth and empathic tone, and a radical shift from the gin-sick, belligerent self-revulsion that suffused his earlier work." In 1986 McGuane sold the 300-acre Paradise Valley ranch once referred to as "a backwoods Bloomsbury" by *People* magazine, and he now lives serenely in McLeod, Montana with his wife, Laurie, and their daughter, Anne. A tall, big-boned, rangy man with a square jaw and a broad, infectious grin, Mc-

Guane has cut off his trademark ponytail in favor of a more conventional appearance. Having inherited his father's business, which provides the family with a comfortable living, and having expended newfound energy in operating a profitable horse ranch, McGuane, in Curt Suplee's words, is "heading himself off at the past." All of his books remain in print, thanks to his loyal core of readers. As McGuane explains with his characteristically sardonic humor, "I'm not considered as illegitimate as I once was. Because in a sense I'm like lip cancer—I'm not going to go away."

References: Bul of Bibliography 35:169+ O '78; Contemporary Authors new rev vol 5 (1981); Who's Who in America, 1986–87

© Marion Ettlinger

McInerney, Jay

Jan. 13, 1955– Writer. Address: b. c/o International Creative Management, 40 W. 57th St., New York City, N.Y. 10019

The novelist Jay McInerney shot to fame with his stunning first book, *Bright Lights, Big City,* the sassily clever and funny but sobering odyssey of an angst-ridden, cocaine-snorting preppie through the purgatory of Manhattan's downtown nightlife circa 1980. The first original in Random House's Vintage Contemporaries quality paperback series, that novel, published in the fall of 1984, quickly attracted a cult readership among young, upwardly mobile urbanites, sold more than 150,000 copies within a year, sparked a general trend to trade paperback novels, and is being translated to the motion pic-

ture screen by Columbia Pictures. The film, co-written by McInerney, went into production in August 1987 and is scheduled for release early in 1988. McInerney's second novel, *Ransom* (Vintage Contemporaries, 1985), another, more conscientious tale of youthful anomie, about an American expatriate in Japan, also sold well but met with less critical success than *Bright Lights, Big City.*

The son of an international sales executive with the Scott Paper Company, Jay McInerney was born on January 13, 1955, in Hartford, Connecticut. Because his father was transferred once a year or more, McInerney grew up in a series of North American and European cities, including London, England, Vancouver, Canada, and Pittsfield, Massachusetts, and attended eighteen elementary schools before entering high school in Pittsfield. From 1972 to 1976 he did his undergraduate work at Williams College, near Pittsfield, where he majored in philosophy and minored in English. After graduation, he and a fellow student at Williams, Gary Fisketjon, bought a second-hand car and traveled around the United States. Fisketjon would later become McInerney's editor at Random House.

Aiming at a writing career but wanting to broaden his experience, McInerney worked for about a year in a wide variety of jobs, including a mink farm and the *Hunterdon County Democrat,* a New Jersey weekly newspaper. Going to Japan on a Princeton in Asia fellowship in 1977, he took Japanese courses at the Institute for International Studies outside Tokyo, taught English to aspiring future leaders of Japan at Kyoto University, and immersed himself in Samurai self-discipline for two years. After returning to the United States in 1979, he worked in New York City as a fact checker at the *New Yorker* magazine for a few months and then as a reader of unsolicited manuscripts at Random House. His friend Gary Fisketjon, by then an editor at Random House, introduced him to the poet and short story writer Raymond Carver, who was at that time teaching at Syracuse University. Carver advised him that if he wanted to concentrate on writing fiction, he ought to leave the hubbub of New York City and take refuge in a Ph.D. program at Syracuse.

Leaving behind a failed marriage to a fashion model and the nightlife that would provide grist for *Bright Lights, Big City*, McInerney went to Syracuse University on a literary fellowship in 1981. At Syracuse, he met his second wife, Merry Reymond, then a Ph.D. candidate in philosophy, who became a strong stabilizing influence in his life. "All my serious writing dates from the time I met my wife," he told Joyce Wadler when she interviewed him for a profile in the *Washington Post* (December 12, 1984).

McInerney's short story "It's Six A.M. Do You Know Where You Are?," first published in the Winter 1982 issue of the *Paris Review*, became the beginning of his first novel, *Bright Lights, Big City* (1984), which Gary Fisketjon chose to publish as the first original in the new Vintage Contemporaries trade soft-cover series that he was editing for Random House. (All of the previously published books in the series were reprints of hard covers.) Based loosely on McInerney's own experiences in New York City between 1979 and 1981, *Bright Lights, Big City* is, in his words, a picaresque story about an "almost suicidal" young man "coming to terms with failure." At the same time, it is, or at least was intended to be, "a satire about the mindless fashion-following of the 1980s," the "yuppie" trendiness in clothes, such drugs as "Bolivian marching powder," and "even nutrition" (sushi is de rigueur one week, "Tex-Mex" the next). He also felt that he was writing "a modest critique of an age" in which glitter is more important than substance, "in which getting into a [chic] nightclub is seen as a significant achievement."

The anonymous young protagonist of *Bright Lights, Big City* narrates the story in the second person singular, an unusual, challenging fictional device that somehow works in the book. That protagonist, a would-be author, is seen in the midst of a severe identity crisis. His marriage has just broken up, he is losing his job in the research department of a highbrow New York magazine (an hilarious lampoon of the *New Yorker*), and, worse, he has for a year been suppressing his bereavement over the death of his mother. The crisis is compressed into one week of cocaine-fueled Manhattan rock club-crawling, a catharsis culminating in the decision that he "will have to learn everything all over again."

Although some reviewers regarded *Bright Lights, Big City* as "sophomoric," "snotty," and "elitist," the vast majority of notices were favorable, and many were glowing. Roz Kaveney, writing in the London *Times Literary Supplement* (May 24, 1985), described the book's hero as "amoral, sentimental, charming." "What saves [the novel] from sentimentality," she wrote, "is McInerney's very precise eye and ear and his sense of the comedy that comes from character. . . . A Chandleresque palette full of urban description convinces us that there is something to this self-

wasting voice worthy of our consideration and our regard." In the same publication a year later (April 18, 1986), Galen Strawson noted that the book is "essentially plotless . . . a weakly coupled series of single scenes, stylish add-ons, and touching peripherals," but he considered it nonetheless "an impressive start: clever, fast, and emotionally plausible, an intense, witty concatenation of drug-propelled incident rapped out in short sentences."

The screen production of *Bright Lights, Big City* coincides with that of *Less Than Zero*, Bret Easton Ellis' novel about affluent, bored, and nihilistic Beverly Hills adolescents and their drug subculture. Commenting on the coincidence, John Powers wrote in *Film Comment* (December 1985): "It's tempting, and partly true, to say that these books are so hot because some place you've got to find scripts for the Brat Pack . . . that group of young men from roughly fifteen to twenty-five. . . . When Hollywood looks at McInerney and Ellis, it sees two guys who have captured the Eighties attitude—smart-talking guys on the cutting edge of the culture . . . voices of the new generation . . . poets laureate of the 'hipoisie'; both [books were promoted] with boasts that they embody a generation. Not only does McInerney choose his epigraph from *The Sun Also Rises* . . . , but the book's cover art deliberately updates the old Signet edition of *The Catcher in the Rye*."

While he found both books "facile and superficial," reading "less like novels and more like brilliant novelizations of movies you wouldn't mind missing," Powers ranked *Bright Lights, Big City* far above *Less Than Zero*. "*Bright Lights, Big City* is the more enjoyable, an extremely entertaining book in a minor key. . . . It has a pleasurable Manhattan bounce, a whooshing energy, a style that's ripe with extravagant description and wiseguy riffing about New York madness, subway grunge, the *Post*'s delirious headlines. . . . At his worst, McInerney lapses into the smug put-downs of post-*Saturday Night Live* humor; at his best, he shows a genuine eye for urban absurdity. Getting to what he saw as the book's core, Powers wrote: "For all its glitzy cover art, *Bright Lights, Big City*, is essentially conventional—a Yuppie *Bildungsroman*. As the novel begins, its protagonist is living a madly disassociated life. . . . The plot gets its force from being an adolescent's self-pitying fantasy that he is too good, too talented, too sensitive for the coarse and demeaning world around him. . . . Teenaged in its emotions, [the book] has the structure of a parental morality tale."

Danny Karlin, writing in the *New York Review of Books* (June 5, 1986), described *Bright Lights, Big City* as "the story of a young man whose carefully constructed identity cracks up in the course of a few frenetic New York days and nights," and he saw in the book the theme of "a discontent that cannot be assuaged." That same theme was more fully explored in McInerney's second novel, *Ransom* (Vintage Contemporaries, 1985), about Christopher Ransom, a young man from an affluent family who is in conflict with his father, a playwright who has turned to lucrative television work and thereby, in Christopher's view, prostituted his talent. Feeling that he has "lost his bearings spiritually" and wanting "to reclaim himself," Ransom goes to Japan and seeks to become "morally taut" through the discipline of karate, although he knows that he will not lose the sense of social alienation, of lack of community, that he carries with him. "In the scope of its ideas," Karlin wrote, "*Ransom* is definitely an advance on *Bright Lights, Big City*, but the first novel is much more adventurous in style and structure. . . . Nevertheless, though not as striking, *Ransom* is a stronger, and in the end a more disconcerting book. *Bright Lights, Big City* does not feel to have deserved the redemption, however tentative, with which it ends. Ransom's abrupt death, at the end of *Ransom*, is more convincingly the American destiny of a stranger in a strange land."

The reviewer for *Publishers Weekly* (July 19, 1985) also found "more substance" in *Ransom* than in *Bright Lights, Big City*. "This is a better novel," he wrote, "more complete, more complex and textured, with the same deft touches of wry humor and ironic insight that distinguished [the] first work. John Lownsbrough, however, writing in the Toronto *Globe and Mail* (November 16, 1985), thought that "what slight comic relief there is [in *Ransom*] tends to an over-reliance on phonetic bloopers and Japanese mangling of American colloquialisms." Galen Strawson, the reviewer for the *Times Literary Supplement*, saw *Ransom* as a bid for a stronger plot than that of *Bright Lights, Big City*. "Like so many of the best phrasemakers, McInerney is not a natural story-teller," Strawson wrote. "He is an accumulator of moments, small-scale set pieces, and he has to work hard to provide a narrative vehicle for them. He has worked hard [in *Ransom*]. He has tried to write a 'proper' novel. And in a rather stiff and formal way, he has succeeded. Unlike *Bright Lights, Big City*, which just came to a stop, *Ransom* comes to an end." Among the most scathing notices was that of David Remnick of the *Washington Post* (August 25, 1985), who dismissed both of McInerney's first two novels as "trivial" and judged *Ransom* to be the "less skilled, less felt" of the two. "Once more," Remnick wrote, "the few pleasures of McInerney's work can be found in its rather ordinary journalism, its witty feature writing."

McInerney's published short stories include "Reunion" (*Esquire*, March 1987), "Smoke" (*Atlantic*, March 1987), and "Story of My Life" (*Esquire*, August 1987). Among his nonfiction contributions to periodicals have been "Jagger-Watching: A Week Around Town With Mick" (*Esquire*, May 1985), "Sunglasses" (*Rolling Stone*, July 17, 1986), "The All-American, All-Purpose, All-Time Frug" (*Esquire*, June 1986), and the travel articles, "Old Kyoto, New Kyoto" (*New York Times Magazine*, August 18, 1985) and "Why Oh Why Do I Love Paris" (*Vogue*, April 1986). He has also done some literary criticism for the *London Review of Books* and other publications.

Talking about the theme of misplaced community that figures so prominently in his first two novels, McInerney told Hilary DeVries of the *Christian Science Monitor*: "There's a nostalgia, but also a great skepticism, among well-to-do upper-middle class Easterners for these values. The cynicism of our age comes from a sense that an awful lot of the options have been exhausted. We don't believe in anything we can't put in our wallets. I would love to find a way beyond that." For him, writing "is this kind of exploration," and "even if it becomes lonelier, it becomes more important to be a writer in this electronic age." He believes that "the writer should be a witness and an observer who ideally adds an element of conscience to his time."

Jay McInerney has curly dark-brown hair and blue eyes, and although he claims to abhor identification with trendiness, dresses in perfect preppie style, typically wearing a blazer, faded jeans, and loafers with no socks. "Garrulous yet slightly awkward, he's good-natured and instantly likable," Evelyn Renold wrote in the *New York Daily News* (September 15, 1985). "He's also irresistibly photogenic." He is quick-witted and glib, and in promoting his books and making other public appearances he handles the microphone with the assurance of a professional entertainer. McInerney and his wife, Merry, who were married in June 1984 have homes in Michigan and New York City. The author's third novel is scheduled for publication by Atlantic Monthly Press in 1988.

References: Chicago Tribune XIV p41 O 20 '85 por; Christian Sci Mon p21+ O 29 '85 por; Interview p69+ Je '85 por; Literary Review 30:107+ Fall '86; People 23:99+ O 14 '85 pors; Wall St J p26 N 2 '84; Washington Post F p1+ D 12 '84 pors; Contemporary Authors vol 116 (1986)

McLaughlin, John (Joseph)

*1927– Political commentator; broadcaster.
Address: b. National Broadcasting Co., 4001
Nebraska Ave., N.W., Washington, D.C. 20016*

With his fast-paced and brawling weekly syndicated TV round table *The McLaughlin Group*, the flamboyant John McLaughlin, an ex-Jesuit with a gusto for political polemics, has created a fresh and entertaining alternative to the traditional staid television discussion format. McLaughlin, a self-described "crypto-Republican," was the first priest ever to serve on a White House staff. As a deputy special assistant to President Richard Nixon, he wrote speeches and stumped vigorously for the President, most prominently during the Watergate scandal that drove Nixon out of office in 1974. After leaving the White House, McLaughlin forsook his sacerdotal status and function to marry Ann Dore, who joined him in running McLaughlin &

John McLaughlin

Company, a Washington consulting firm. On his television show, McLaughlin hosts a panel of four prominent print journalists, weighted to the political right, in discussions on a range of issues, from the economy to East-West relations. Believing that "there's no reason on God's planet why knowledge has to be boring," he orchestrates the panels on world affairs in a provocative slam-bang manner, so as to create "the excitement of a contest." Tim Russert, vice-president of NBC News, has called The McLaughlin Group "the Washington Gong Show . . . the best political theatre [he has] ever seen." The program, now going into its sixth year on more than 200 PBS stations and five NBC affiliates, is taped at WRC-TV in Washington, D.C., and distributed by WTTW-TV in Chicago. McLaughlin also conducts the weekly Washington TV interview show One on One. In addition to his electronic work he writes for print, chiefly as Washington editor and columnist for National Review.

According to David Remnick in Esquire (May 1986), Ann McLaughlin sees her husband's "earthly fascinations" as "rooted in denial" going back through priesthood and seminary to his New England Roman Catholic upbringing. John Joseph McLaughlin was born in Providence, Rhode Island, to second-generation Irish-American parents in the summer of 1927. In what he has described as his "rootedly Democratic" family, one uncle, Henry McLaughlin, was a long-term president of the Providence city council and another, Dr. Edward McLaughlin, was Rhode Island state health director. "My father was very interested in their careers, behind the scenes," McLaughlin told Laurence Stern of the Washington Post (June 2, 1974).

The "denial" of which his wife spoke apparently did not mean emotional or material deprivation. In an interview with Linda Charlton of the New York Times (June 2, 1974), McLaughlin recalled that he experienced "lots of affection and warmth" as a child and that when he was old enough to drive he had his own car—a mark of a certain degree of affluence for a teenager in the early 1940s. He drove the car to and from the high school he attended in Providence—LaSalle Academy, a Christian Brothers school. As a boy, he was a voracious reader of historical fiction, and he was attracted to the Jesuits, he told Linda Charlton, because they had "a gallantry, an intellectual adventurism, a style, a panache." Later, he would come to appreciate their "sophistry" as well.

McLaughlin entered the Society of Jesus when he was eighteen. He began his thirteen years of training for the priesthood in the order at Weston College, the Jesuit seminary in Weston, Massachusetts. Among the older seminarians at Weston at that time were Robert F. Drinan, who would become the first priest ever to serve as a voting member of the United States Congress, and Daniel Berrigan, the future radical peace activist. After taking his B.A. degree at Boston College, he earned master's degrees in philosophy and education there and did advanced study at Stanford University.

Slated for teaching in Jesuit high schools by his superiors, McLaughlin in the 1950s was assigned successively to the faculties of the Cranwell School, in Lenox, Massachusetts, and the Fairfield University Preparatory School, in Fairfield, Connecticut. Rejecting the role of prep-school teacher, he received permission to leave the Fairfield school and move to New York City to pursue a doctoral degree in communications at Columbia University. While earning his doctorate, he taught at Jesuit schools in New York City and began moving up the editorial ladder at America, the Manhattan-based Jesuit weekly journal of opinion. He ultimately became an assistant editor of the publication. He met his future wife, Ann (Lauenstein) Dore, a Catholic and a divorcée when, in 1968, he delivered a speech at Marymount College, in Tarrytown, New York, where Miss Dore, a Marymount alumna, was then director of alumni relations.

In the 1960s Father McLaughlin wrote, broadcast, and lectured widely on ethical and social questions. His most popular lectures, especially on college campuses, were on human sexuality. A 1969 brochure listing his available lecture repertoire included the subjects "Intimacy Before Marriage and the Swedish Experience," in four parts; "Intimacy Outside Marriage"; and "In-School Sex Education in the Seventies." Chaplain Ronald Rafferty of the University of Connecticut later told a reporter, "Father McLaughlin knows more about the Playboy ethic than most dedicated playboys." McLaughlin also conducted film seminars and served on the juries of film festivals, and he made a minidocumentary for ABC television. on the Biafran war and the suffering it was causing.

Father McLaughlin first attracted the attention of the Nixon White House with his article "Public Regulation and the News Media," published in *America* for December 13, 1969. In that article he generally supported a stinging attack that Vice-President Spiro Agnew had made on the network television news media in a speech the month before. In his article McLaughlin agreed that the "broadcasting hierarchy," dominated by "a de facto liberal ideology," had launched a "massive mobilization" against conservative forces in public life. The article was spotted and brought to the attention of President Richard Nixon by Patrick J. Buchanan, the representative of rock-ribbed conservatism on Nixon's speechwriting team. According to press reports, Buchanan, who had written the speech that Agnew delivered in November 1969, contacted McLaughlin and introduced him to the relatively leftish White House speechwriter Raymond K. Price. Another White House aide, Charles Colson, also saw White House possibilities for the Rev. McLaughlin.

Apparently there was ideological friction between Father McLaughlin and the Rev. Donald R. Campion, the editor of *America*, who later described McLaughlin as a man with a "baroque" way with words—"you don't know quite what they mean but they sort of stun you." Campion refused to discuss publicly the circumstances of McLaughlin's departure from the magazine's staff early in 1970, but others at *America* said that the parting was not amicable. Tom Stevenson of the *Washington Post* (June 28, 1974) reported one Jesuit as saying that Campion felt that "McLaughlin was a journalist who 'bought' stories from interested informants too uncritically and with insufficient checking." According to other reports, McLaughlin was often at editorial odds with his more liberal associates at *America* regarding the mandates of Vatican Council II.

Father McLaughlin voted Democratic in the presidential elections of 1960 and 1964, when John F. Kennedy and Lyndon B. Johnson were the respective successful Democratic candidates, and in 1969 he voted for John Marchi, the unsuccessful Conservative candidate for mayor of New York City. Reestablishing his residence in Rhode Island and switching to the Republican party, he mounted a challenge to John O. Pastore, the Democratic incumbent, in the race for the United States Senate in Rhode Island in 1970. In a campaign that his future wife, Ann Dore, helped to manage, McLaughlin ran as a "peace" candidate, attacking Pastore's "pro-Pentagon, pro-ABM [antiballistic missile] position," pointing out that the war in Vietnam was costing working people "an incredibly bloated expenditure" and urging that a political settlement of the war be pursued with "ruthless fury." Later, as a member of the Nixon administration, McLaughlin would defend his secular wardrobe by describing the Roman collar as "a one-inch piece of plastic." In his campaign against Pastore in a state that was 70 percent Catholic, however, his clerical regalia was an asset that bewildered and enraged Pastore, a born Catholic, nurtured in respect for and deference to the Roman cloth. "McLaughlin's driving me batty," Pastore said at the time. "How can I debate with a man my religion teaches me to call Father?" At the polls in November 1970 Pastore fared less well than he had in 1964, when his victory was 2-1, but he still roundly defeated McLaughlin, with 67.5 percent of the vote.

After his loss to Pastore, McLaughlin began writing speeches for White House special assistant Ray Price. He did so with the permission of the Rev. William G. Guindon, the provincial of the New England province of the Society of Jesus, who would say four years later: "I thought it was a good idea, but I wasn't aware what would happen in 1974." "He is very good," Ray Price said of McLaughlin. "A lot of print people can't write the spoken word. But John is excellent. He's a spoken-word man. He's made so many speeches himself on the campaign trail that he knows how to shape a sentence so that it sounds better than it reads."

Aside from his talent for speechwriting, Father McLaughlin's ecclesiastical credentials made him attractive to the men who were planning Nixon's "Southern strategy" in anticipation of the 1972 presidential elections. Over the opposition of some members of the White House staff, of Congress, and of the Roman Catholic hierarchy (including Cardinal Terence J. Cooke of New York and Cardinal John P. Cody of Chicago), McLaughlin officially joined Nixon's speechwriting team with the title of deputy special assistant to the president on July 1, 1971. He described himself as "the centrist" on the team, midway between "Pat Buchanan . . . over on the right and Ray Price . . . ideologically on the left."

In 1972 Father McLaughlin graduated from simple speechwriter to what he described as presidential "trouble shooter," "fact finder," "adviser," and "spokesman." In the spring of that year the National Security Council, the White House's secretive policy-making arm, sent him on the first of two "humanitarian" missions to Southeast Asia. After touring South Vietnam, Laos, and Cambodia, he reported that only about 10 percent of the civilians hospitalized in South Vietnam were war casualties, that bombing targets were "scrupulously and assiduously" pinpointed to minimize civilian casualties, and that the air strikes did little ecological damage. His report on his second tour of Southeast Asia, in 1973, was also for the most part positive.

In President Nixon's successful campaign for reelection in 1972 Father McLaughlin made many speeches in which he defended the "morality" of the administration's military policy in North and South Vietnam and Cambodia and asserted that "Richard Nixon has built a new structure for peace in the world that will be felt for generations to come." The Washington syndicated columnist Jack Anderson described the speeches as so "sabre rattling" as to "sometimes seem . . . to contradict the offical White House line." Anderson observed that McLaughlin appeared to disagree with White

House negotiator Henry Kissinger in warning that a Communist victory in Vietnam would result in a "blood bath" claiming a million victims in the South. McLaughlin publicly condoned the mining of Haiphong harbor and American bombing raids on the North at Christmas 1972.

During the Watergate scandal, which led to President Nixon's resignation in 1974, Father McLaughlin vigorously defended the president, more bravely than anyone else in the White House. The gist of his defense was that, sure, Nixon was not a "saint," and thank God, because a saint would be impractical in the presidency. He did, however, believe that future historians would regard Nixon as "the greatest moral leader of the last third of this century." In the general public's ken, McLaughlin, for all his speechmaking, remained an obscure Nixon administration figure until May 1974, when transcripts of taped White House conversations were released to the Senate subcommittee investigating possibly impeachable aspects of the president's conduct in office. When Hugh Scott, the Senate minority leader, echoing other Republicans in Congress, described the transcripts as portraying "deplorable, disgusting, shabby, immoral performances," McLaughlin held an extraordinary press conference in the White House, on May 8, 1974. On that occasion he dismissed the habitual use of profanity by the president and his aides as a "form of emotional drainage" with "no moral meaning." Overall, he said, "the president acquitted himself throughout those [taped] discussions with honor." Quoting St. Paul to the effect that the essence of morality is charity, he credited President Nixon with producing "a climate of charity in the international community and at home."

Reporting on the press conference in the New York Times, John Herbers described McLaughlin as speaking "passionately in the president's defense, his voice rising as if he were in a pulpit and his sentences punctuated with Latin phrases." A month later Laurence Stern of the Washington Post observed that it was the May 8 press conference that "vaulted Father McLaughlin into his current state of celebrity, a condition he clearly relishes, and [into] his problems with his Jesuit superiors, which appear to be the wages of fame."

As a White House aide, Father McLaughlin shed his clerical attire for modish secular clothes and lived independently of the Jesuit community on his $32,000 salary, sharing an apartment in the Watergate luxury complex with his pet basset hound, Oliver. In press accounts he was dubbed "the swinging celibate" and "The Brooks Brothers Jesuit." At a news conference in Boston on May 22, 1974, the Very Rev. Richard Cleary, the new provincial of the New England Jesuits, not only disassociated himself and the Society of Jesus from Father McLaughlin's defense of President Nixon's conduct in office but also told reporters that he was "puzzled" by McLaughlin's "publicly stated interpretation of his vows of poverty and obedience as well as his understanding of his status as a Jesuit priest." "I don't feel it gives very good witness to what we're trying to be," he said, "to be living in the Watergate apartments." Cleary contrasted McLaughlin's behavior with that of another political Jesuit, Father Robert F. Drinan, then a congressman, who had received Jesuit approval for his political campaigns and for all of his financial arrangements and who lived with the Jesuit community at Georgetown University, paid rent to the Jesuits, and contributed the rest of his salary to charities. Cleary asked McLaughlin to come to Boston "to pray about his situation and reflect with [Cleary] about his life." McLaughlin did so, and several days later Father Cleary issued a statement to the effect that Father McLaughlin could continue his political work with no objections from the Society of Jesus.

In an article in the Washington Post (June 28, 1974), William R. MacKaye quoted former Jesuit associates pro and con McLaughlin. Some of the pro side remembered "his wit and unpredictability." "John really needs the give and take of the Jesuit recreation room to bounce his ideas around in," one Jesuit said. "If we were still seeing a lot of each other I could tease him out of this and block him from making such an ass of himself. I really love the guy."

After President Nixon turned over the reins of presidential power to Gerald R. Ford, on August 9, 1974, McLaughlin remained on the White House staff for two months. Meanwhile, he was keeping in touch with Ann Dore, who had come to Washington as the director of communications with the Committee to Reelect the President (1971–72), had served as press secretary of the presidential inauguration committee (1972–73) and public affairs director of the Environmental Protection Agency (1973–74), and was currently a government relations executive with the Union Carbide Corporation. In the months following McLaughlin's departure from the White House in October 1974, he and Miss Dore drew closer and decided to marry, and McLaughlin petitioned Pope Paul VI for laicization. The petition was granted, but the civil marriage of McLaughlin and Miss Dore (performed before a judge in the District of Columbia court of appeals on August 23, 1975) is not recognized by the church, which has refused to annul Mrs. McLaughlin's first marriage, a sacramental one. In November 1987 Mrs. McLaughlin became Secretary of Labor in President Ronald Reagan's cabinet.

Mrs. McLaughlin joined her husband in running McLaughlin & Company, a public affairs and media relations consulting firm, with offices on K Street in Washington. In the administration of President Ronald Reagan, she served as assistant secretary for public affairs in the Department of the Treasury (1981–84) and as an undersecretary in the Department of the Interior (1984–86). Before launching The McLaughlin Group on television, John McLaughlin hosted a weekend radio talk show over WRC in Washington, on which he interviewed and argued with such guests as Barry M. Goldwater and Eugene J. McCarthy and took phone calls from the audience. "My position is that of detective, confessor, vaudevillian, advocate, and devil's advocate," he said at the time. "I joust, challenge, taunt, lay back. I sometimes even concede."

The politically conservative Edison Electric Institute financed the pilot of *The McLaughlin Group* in 1982 and remained a major funder of the show in the years following. General Electric began underwriting the show in 1986. The original "Gang of Five," as McLaughlin liked to refer to his panel, included two syndicated political columnists who have remained fixtures on the program ever since: Robert Novak, a conservative, and Jack Germond, an old-fashioned Democrat. Later, Morton Kondracke, a retooled liberal widely viewed as a "neoconservative," joined the permanent panel, and ultrarightist Pat Buchanan was a regular on the show for two years, from 1983 to 1985, when he returned to the White House as President Reagan's director of communications. Filling the rotating fourth seat on the panel have been such liberals as Hodding Carter 3d and such conservatives as Fred Barnes of the *New Republic*.

In his booming voice, McLaughlin provokes his panelists into pounding the table, hurling epithets at each other, and making brash statements they would never make in print, including risky political predictions. The result has been compared to "an opinion-makers bar brawl" and a round-table version of the situation comedy *All in the Family*. Writing in *TV Guide* (July 20, 1985), John Weisman singled out two elements that make the show unique. "The first is the speed with which McLaughlin leads his debaters through the five or six topics he's decided to cover. . . . And second, *The McLaughlin Group* is the only political show seen nationwide that favors the political right." As David Remnick observed in *Esquire*, the show "strips away the carefully layered codes of high-church print journalism—objectivity, temperance, politesse, and analysis—and replaces them with polemic, sarcasm, and bookie-parlor predictions." "I want first-rate reporting and straight opinion," McLaughlin has said, "plus energy, tempo, and bonhomie." Eleanor Clift, a reporter for *Newsweek* who is an occasional guest on the show, has said: "It's the Super Bowl of bullshit. Next to *McLaughlin*, all the rest of the shows are *Mister Rogers' Neighborhood*." During the summer of 1987 one hundred and forty independent television stations across the country began airing "Sixty Seconds," a series of one-minute spots, created by McLaughlin, in which pairs of Congressmen spoke pro and con on political issues.

John and Ann McLaughlin live in a town house they own on Capitol Hill, and they have a country place on Maryland's Eastern Shore. One friend, quoted by David Remnick in *Esquire*, has "the impression that he [McLaughlin, has] lost his faith," but the McLaughlins occasionally attend church services, Episcopal as well as Roman Catholic, according to Remnick. McLaughlin told Patti Reilly of *People* that he doesn't "miss being a priest," that "the fulfillment factor in marriage is far greater."

Even when he was wearing a Roman collar, he regarded "celibacy as a package requirement for the priesthood" to be both out of keeping with early church tradition and "obsolete," although he thought that "the state of celibacy in general is valid" for those with "more than an average need for solitude and a sense of mission." The relationship of "power to personality" has long fascinated him, along with the close alignment of the sex and power drives. On a wall in his office in the Executive Office Building next to the White House hung a portrait of Pope Innocent X, who, according to McLaughlin, "viewed power as an ego trip."

McLaughlin is a man of imposing physique, six feet two and a half inches tall, husky, and strong-featured, with a ruddy complexion and long strands of blond hair covering his widening bald spot. He admits to being "very tough on the people in the office," and some former aides and underlings have bad memories of occasions when he would "turn purple with rage." "John's a perfectionist," his wife explained to David Remnick. "He vents his emotions all the time. His blood pressure and his heart are perfect. His anger is never personal." With his wife, according to friends, he is a "pussycat." Many who know McLaughlin have remarked about his sardonic manner, his "delightful" sense of humor, his shrewdness, and his sharp intellect. "He would have made a helluva corporation president," a fellow White House staff member once suggested.

References: Esquire 105:76+ My '86 por; N Y Post p55 Ja 6 '72, p14 F 6 '74 por; N Y Times p14 O 15 '72 por, p42 Je 2 '74 por; Newsweek 83:71+ My 20 '74 por; Parade p19 Jl 7 '74 por; People 14:110+ S 22 '80 pors; Time 104:67 S 9 '74 por; U S News 76:27 Je 3 '74 por; Washington Post A p17 Ag 3 '71, A p1+ Je 2 '74 pors, B p18 Je 28 '74, mag p4 F 18 '79 por

---

McNamara, Robert S(trange)

June 9, 1916– International public servant; former United States government official. Address: h. 2412 Tracy Place, N.W., Washington, D.C. 20008

NOTE: This biography supersedes the article that appeared in *Current Biography* in 1961.

A correspondent for the *New Republic* once described Robert S. McNamara as "a planet-saver . . . a public figure with world vision, an evangelical bent, and a realization of what an endangered species mankind is." Trained in business administration, the often controversial McNamara helped to direct the planning and logistical support for American bombers duing World War II, and after the war he contributed his managerial expertise to the revitalization of the Ford Motor Company,

Robert S. McNamara

of which he became the first president from outside the Ford family. As United States secretary of
defense under presidents John F. Kennedy and
Lyndon B. Johnson, he reshaped America's armed
forces for "flexible response," asserted civilian
control of the Pentagon, and applied the latest cost-
accounting techniques and computerized systems
analysis to reduce waste in defense spending—
until Johnson's ill-starred war in Vietnam (often
also dubbed, not quite accurately, "McNamara's
war") blew his budget out of control. As president
of the World Bank (formally known as the International Bank for Reconstruction and Development)
from 1968 to 1981, McNamara tripled the bank's
loans to developing countries, focused the loans on
rural development, and led the international aid
community in recognizing that the world's poorest
populations need food and family planning more
than grandiose industrial projects. Since leaving
the bank, McNamara has been working with private foundations and as an independent lobbyist
and free-lance elder global statesman concerned
with influencing national and international policy
regarding the nuclear arms race, the population explosion, world hunger, NATO strategy, and East-
West relations.

Robert Strange McNamara was born in San
Francisco, California, on June 9, 1916, the son of
Robert James McNamara and Claranel (Strange)
McNamara. His mother was of English and Scots
descent, and his father, the sales manager for
Buckingham & Hecht, a wholesale shoe company,
was of Irish ancestry. According to McNamara's
younger sister, Margaret, the family was "normal,
middle-class." "The only thing nontypical about it
was Bob," she told Henry L. Trewhitt, the author
of the biography *McNamara: His Ordeal in the*

Pentagon (1971). "Even as a little boy my brother
was terrific. He was something special."

McNamara, who grew up in San Francisco and
in Piedmont, California, was reading at a precocious level when he entered grade school. At Piedmont High School, where he was active in student
government, he had a straight A-minus average.
He studied mathematics, economics, and philosophy at the University of California at Berkeley,
where he was elected to Phi Beta Kappa at the end
of his sophomore year and took his B.A. degree
with honors in 1937. During summer vacations he
worked as a merchant seaman on ships that plied
the waters between California and Hawaii, the Far
East, and New York.

After completing the requirements for an
M.B.A. degree at the Harvard University Graduate
School of Business in 1939, McNamara worked
briefly in the San Francisco branch of the accounting firm of Price, Waterhouse & Company before
returning to the Harvard business school as an assistant professor of accounting in 1940. Rejected for
military service because of nearsightedness at the
beginning of World War II, he remained at Harvard, helping Colonel Charles B. ("Tex") Thornton
to set up a program for training officers of the Army
Air Forces (then called the Army Air Corps) in
methods of cost-effective statistical control, and he
was an instructor in that program as well as a consultant to the Army Air Forces in their establishment of a statistical system to control the flow of
matériel, money, and personnel. Sent to England
in 1943 to set up a statistical control system for the
Eighth Air Force's B-17 bomber operations, he was
commissioned a captain within the year and was
ultimately promoted to lieutenant colonel. He
helped to direct the planning and logistical effort
supporting the operations of the long-range B-29
bomber as well as the B-17. David Halberstam in
his book *The Best and the Brightest* (1972) wrote
that McNamara put "all the infinitely complicated
pieces together, doing program analysis and operation analysis, digesting the mass of facts which
would have intimidated less disciplined minds,
less committed minds, making sure that the planes
and the crews were readied at roughly the same
time." Serving in the Far East at the end of the war,
McNamara used pioneering techniques in assessing the effects of the B-29 raids on Japan.

After the war Tex Thornton reconstituted his
"Whiz Kids," as they came to be known, into a civilian team and offered that team's managerial expertise to private industry. Hired by the financially
troubled Ford Motor Company in 1946, the ten-
member team was sent by Henry Ford 2d into every department to learn operations and make recommendations for greater efficiency and cost-
effectiveness. Replacing much of the company's
old, autocratic management, the team effected a
broad decentralization of the company, creating
divisions with well-defined areas of responsibility.

From 1946 until 1949 McNamara was the manager of the Ford Motor Company's planning and financial analysis offices. He was promoted to

comptroller in 1949, assistant general manager of the Ford automotive division in 1953, vice-president and general manager of that division in 1955, and group executive of the car and truck divisions in 1957. In 1960 he became the first president of the Ford Motor Company not a member of the Ford family.

The revitalization of Ford was one of the major success stories in postwar American industry. As a financial planner and operations manager, McNamara contributed vitally to Ford's success through the changes he wrought in administrative structure and cost-accounting practices. Perspicacious in interpreting sophisticated consumer surveys, he also supported the introduction of highly profitable new lines of vehicles, including the four-door Thunderbird (a family version of the sporty two-door model) and the compact Falcon.

While at Ford, McNamara began to consider the possibility of entering public service. Although he was a registered Republican, his maturing political outlook and social conscience were generally in accord with those of John F. Kennedy, the successful 1960 Democratic presidential candidate, for whom McNamara evidently voted. Robert Lovett, a leading New York banker and Washington power broker whom Kennedy consulted in choosing some of the top policy-makers in his incoming administration, had known McNamara in the armed forces and suggested him to the president-elect. Kennedy offered McNamara the choice of two cabinet positions, secretary of the treasury or of defense. McNamara chose defense, with the understanding that he would have absolute authority in picking his top staff. "I went to the highest categories of people," he recalled in an interview with Brock Brower for *Life* (May 10, 1968), "where there'd already been automatic selecting-out." Among those he recruited were Harold Brown, the director of the University of California's Lawrence Radiation Laboratory at Livermore, who became the Pentagon's director of research and engineering, and the economist Charles J. Hitch, a senior officer of the Rand Corporation, who became Pentagon comptroller.

Before assuming office as secretary of defense in January 1961, McNamara made clear that he would not serve as a passive mediator between the Army, Navy, and Air Force (which had become an independent service). By law, the secretaries of the three armed services were already subject to the direction, authority, and control of the president as commander in chief and of the secretary of defense. In practice, each of the services took its slice of the defense budget and went its independent way, buying, as McNamara observed, "every bright, shiny new gadget that comes along" and often leaving waste and redundancy in its wake. Centering control in his office, he set up a Pentagon budgeting system allocating funds according to function or mission rather than branch of service, coordinated the three services' supply and intelligence operations, introduced systems analysis to determine and compare the expected returns on investment of proposed new major weapons systems, and stressed "commonality" wherever possible, such as in the construction of planes adaptable for use by both Air Force and Navy.

On McNamara's recommendation, President Kennedy decided to replace the nuclear "massive retaliation" defense policy of the Eisenhower administration with one of "flexible response." Implementing the president's decision, McNamara increased American troop strength by 300,000 and made a commensurate increase in troop transport capability so as to create a strong, mobile strike force capable of meeting conventional or guerrilla challenges. He tried to persuade the countries of the North Atlantic Treaty Organization to undertake a similar conventional buildup rather than relying increasingly on nuclear weapons, which, he pointed out, are useless except as doomsday deterrents. Among nuclear weapons he favored solid fuel missiles over the liquid-fuel ICBM's because the former are less vulnerable to a first strike by the enemy and in that way provide a retaliatory "second-strike capability." If both sides have a second-strike capability, he reasoned, the pressure on either to launch a precipitate attack on the basis of misleading or ambiguous radar information is reduced. He was a strong supporter of the nuclear test-ban treaty and the strategic-arms-limitation talks.

McNamara helped to plan the blockade of Cuba following the Cuban missile crisis in 1962, and he was a charter architect of Vietnam war strategy. Vice-president Lyndon B. Johnson regarded McNamara as "the best of the lot" of Kennedy's cabinet members, and he was pleased when, after Kennedy's assassination and Johnson's assumption of the presidency in November 1963, McNamara agreed to stay on. Johnson felt he especially needed McNamara's help in coping with the war in divided Vietnam (formerly French Indochina), where the United States was assisting the non-Communist regime in Saigon in the South in its effort to crush the insurgency of the National Liberation Front (NLF) guerrillas, who were backed by the Communist regime in Hanoi in the North. McNamara made his first of many visits to South Vietnam in 1962, when the United States had more than 10,000 military "advisers" there, and he came home believing in an American combat commitment. Even after leaving government he would have little to say about the moral issues underlying that commitment. "All McNamara will say," Brock Brower wrote in *Life,* "is that the justification for the war lies in the obligation to help certain Asian nations protect themselves from various internal and external encroachments, ultimately to be traced back to a potentially expansionist China. He has talked to all the non-Communist Asian leaders and accepts their judgments over the estimates of a differing mood within the vast Asian populace."

In spite of his doubts about the stability of the Saigon government, McNamara in the beginning mistakenly predicted that American military intervention would enable that regime to stand by itself "by the end of 1965." Accordingly, in the summer of 1964 he lobbied for the Gulf of Tonkin Resolution, which Congress passed, allowing the president to send combat troops to South Vietnam without a formal declaration of war. More hesitantly, early in 1965 he joined other members of the National Security Council in approving the systematic bombing of North Vietnam. At home, he became the lightning rod for antiwar sentiment, vilified by protesters as a "baby burner"—an epithet that deeply hurt and angered him—and as the perpetrator of "McNamara's war," a phrase coined by Senator Wayne Morse. In the National Security Council, McNamara became pitted against the Joint Chiefs of Staff, who wanted unremitting and wide-ranging bombing of the North, while he deplored the bombing's lack of strategic focus and considered it to be as useless as it was inhumane.

As the American investment in the Vietnam war mounted—ultimately to more than 500,000 troops, 1,000 of whom were killed in action each month, and an expenditure of $2.5 billion a month—McNamara urged that the cost be faced realistically, but President Johnson, apparently for domestic political reasons, rejected his recommendations that taxes be raised and that the military reserves be called up. Seeing the prospect of the "stigma" of the stalemate only worsening—becoming "a 'no decision' at an even higher level"—McNamara more and more looked to a negotiated settlement. Hoping to induce the North Vietnamese to come to the peace table, he obtained Johnson's reluctant approval of a pause in the bombing of the North for thirty-seven days in December 1965 and January 1966—to no avail. With Paul Warnke and Paul Nitze he drew up the "San Antonio Formula," a peace proposal that was privately transmitted to North Vietnamese officials in August 1967, again futilely.

McNamara's relative dovishness diminished his influence with President Johnson, who, in his conviction that a decisive victory over the NFL and the North Vietnamese was within reach, favored the hawkish counsel of the Joint Chiefs of Staff and the generals in the field. In November 1967 President Johnson rejected McNamara's recommendations that he terminate the bombing of the North, freeze the level of the American military presence in the South, and return most of the ground combat to the South Vietnamese themselves.

Meanwhile, McNamara was preparing to turn his energies away from the military area, to a task consonant with his beliefs that there is an "irrefutable relationship between violence and economic backwardness" and that "security is not military hardware, though it may include it," but is, rather, "development." Since the founding of the International Bank for Reconstruction and Development in 1945, every president of that institution has been an American, nominated by the president of the United States. In April 1967 McNamara made known to President Johnson his interest in the position, which was to be vacated by the retiring George Woods on December 31, 1967.

President Johnson's nomination of McNamara to head the World Bank was ratified by the bank's executive directors in November 1967, and McNamara left the Pentagon three months later. Among those who regretted to see him go was the syndicated political columnist Mary McGrory, who mourned the departure of "the last human barrier within the government against the harsh and drastic steps recommended by the generals." Harold Johnson, the Army's chief of staff, summed up McNamara's tenure in the Pentagon by saying, "He's the only one who's ever run it." In a report in *Time* (December 8, 1967), McNamara's exit from the federal government was described as the "departure of a titan." "McNamara ruled the Defense Department longer and more efficiently than any of his seven predecessors, constructing the world's most powerful nuclear arsenal while fighting a limited war in Vietnam and a seemingly limitless conflict with hard-nosed generals and fractious legislators at home," the report read. "His administrative reforms became a model for other department chiefs while he performed a multiplicity of miscellaneous chores for the president. . . . In establishing civilian control of the Pentagon as a fact of life as well as a theory, McNamara perhaps went too far in alienating service officers. . . . On balance, nonetheless, McNamara's accomplishments must rank as historic, while his mistakes seem ephemeral by comparison."

McNamara assumed the presidency of the World Bank in April 1968, and the executive directors elected him to a second five-year term in 1972 and to a third in 1977. Founded in connection with the United Nations and the International Monetary Fund (concerned with the promotion of world trade and monetary cooperation), the World Bank is a cooperative international lending agency whose purpose is to make hard loans to help raise the standard of living in those of its 149 member nations needing such help. Originally, the loans went to European industrial countries which were rebuilding the productive power shattered by World War II. In the 1950s the loans increasingly went for the building of industrial facilities in underdeveloped nations, and the bank's affiliate, the International Finance Corporation, founded in 1956, began to provide risk capital for and to promote international investment in the private sector in such nations. Another affiliate, the International Development Association, was established in 1960 for the purpose of performing functions that could not be undertaken by the bank itself without depleting its reserve capital and jeopardizing its credit rating. Using capital contributed by the United States and seventeen other developed nations, the IDA began granting soft loans, at nominal rates of interest for fifty-year periods, to the poorest member countries, who could not afford to borrow from regular commercial sources or even from the World Bank.

Two major problems faced McNamara at the World Bank. One was the failure of loans funding industrialization and economic growth in the Third

World to filter down from the elite and affect the standard of living of the impoverished masses. The other was the growing reluctance of developed nations with economic problems of their own to continue subsidizing such loans.

While finding new sources of revenue, in, for example, the international capital markets and such oil-rich Arab states as Kuwait, McNamara enlarged the scope of the World Bank's operations and made a fundamental change in its development strategy, away from dams, power plants, steelworks, and other large civil engineering projects and toward smaller, local projects aimed at making the poorest villagers more productive and filling their basic needs for nutrition, education, health, housing, and family planning. He also pushed the funding of oil, gas, and coal exploration in developing countries, and he expedited project payments to help those countries with their balance-of-payment deficits. Under him, the World Bank more and more conditioned its granting of large project loans on the recipient governments' willingness to promote fairer distribution of income in their countries. As for the industrialized countries, McNamara in a speech in 1979 criticized the "excessive" defense expenditures of the world powers, which reduce "the resources available for other essential sectors and social services" and fuel "a futile and reactive arms race."

During McNamara's presidency, the World Bank's loans increased, in inflation-adjusted figures, from less than $1 billion to $11.5 billion annually, with 70 percent of the latter figure going for rural development. Without sacrificing the high rating of the bank's bonds in the international money markets, he succeeded in bringing what M. Narasimham, the bank's executive director for India, Bangladesh, and Sri Lanka, called "a social dimension to development." In his valedictory address before the annual joint meeting of the World Bank and the International Monetary Fund in October 1980, McNamara said that the bank had "barely begun to develop its full potential" and warned that, with the population explosion, by the year 2000 more than 600 million people were likely to be living in "absolute poverty," which he defined as a "condition of life so characterized by malnutrition, illiteracy, disease, squalid surroundings, high infant mortality, and low life expectancy as to be beneath any reasonable definition of human decency." Concluding with a call for "clear, strong, and bold vision," he echoed his late friend Robert F. Kennedy in quoting from George Bernard Shaw: "You see things and say, Why? But I dream things that never were and say, Why not?"

McNamara retired as president of the World Bank when he turned sixty-five, in 1981. Since then, he has been working a busy schedule with nonprofit organizations, including the Ford Foundation, the Brookings Institution, and the Barbara Ward Fund, as well as independently on such issues as nuclear arms, the population explosion, world hunger, East-West relations, and the antiapartheid movement in South Africa (for which he

has raised financial support). Regarding nuclear arms, the most urgent of the issues, McNamara, in a widely reprinted and condensed essay in the fall 1983 issue of Foreign Affairs, urged that we begin to reduce the high risk of nuclear war by accepting two overriding principles. "First, we must recognize that each side must maintain a stable deterrent . . . ," he wrote, according to the Newsweek version of the article. "Neither the United States nor the Soviet Union should move in a way to destabilize the other's deterrent or to provide an incentive for a preemptive strike. That's absolutely imperative. Second, we must recognize that nuclear weapons have no military value whatsoever other than to deter one's opponent from their use. All arms negotiations, military strategies, war plans, weapons development and military-force structures should be based on that principle." He fears that the Reagan administration's planned Strategic Defense Initiative, popularly known as "Star Wars," would escalate the arms race.

"I, for one, am not prepared to accept the risk that these [East-West] political rivalries will not, over a period of decades, upon occasion lead to military confrontation," McNamara told Rushworth M. Kidder of the Christian Science Monitor (December 16, 1986). Our "almost paranoic" anxiety with respect to the Soviet Union, he pointed out, "has a lot to do with a movement away from our traditional values" over the last forty years. "In order to strengthen our position vis-à-vis this 'communist threat'" the citizenry has accepted actions inconsistent with "our national heritage" of "liberty and democracy," including the support of reactionary regimes around the world, from China and Iran to the Philippines and Nicaragua. "The very heavy price for failing to deal more effectively with this East-West tension" also includes "excessive expenditure on military weapons." The goal of better East-West relations would be served, in McNamara's view, by "encouraging Europe to unify itself economically, politically, and certainly in terms of [conventional] defense."

Turning to the second major issue on his agenda, the world population problem, McNamara explained to Kidder that "the problem today is not, on a global basis, density of population," because "the carrying capacity of the world" is "greater than the world's existing population." It is rather the "imbalance of population growth rates on the one hand and social and economic advance on the other" in certain regions of the world, such as sub-Saharan Africa, where "food production growth rates—on average, per capita—have been negative for ten years."

The major policy addresses made by McNamara as secretary of defense and as president of the World Bank were collected, respectively, in The Essence of Security (Harper & Row, 1968) and The McNamara Years at the World Bank (Johns Hopkins University Press, 1981). In Blundering Into Disaster: Surviving the First Century in a Nuclear Age (Pantheon Bks., 1986), McNamara cogently and in nontechnical language laid out the issues in the Soviet-American nuclear confrontation and suggested the route forward, beginning with a freeze on the nuclear strength of the North Atlantic Treaty Organization and a buildup of NATO's conventional forces. Over the years the size of those forces has been cut to a point well below that of their Soviet counterparts with the idea that nuclear weapons would make up the difference. In other words, a first nuclear strike is part of NATO *conventional* war strategy—not a viable policy "given the tremendous devastation which those Soviet strategic forces that survived a U.S. first strike would now be able to inflict on this country."

Robert S. McNamara has three children—Margaret, Kathleen, and Robert—by the former Margaret McKinstry, whom he married in 1940 and who died in 1981. McNamara is lean of physique, even to his fingers, which are, in the words of Paul Hendrickson of the Washington Post, as "long and as straight as Macanudo cigars." According to Hendrickson, who interviewed him in his office at 1800 K Street, N.W., in Washington, he speaks in a "husky tenor" voice that "you respond to immediately," although "the body doesn't seem anxious or driving at all." A reporter for the New Republic described McNamara at the World Bank as "brisk" and "in combat-readiness: a small, taut man with a bulldog face, big-rimmed glasses, a snub nose, hair brushed back—a man in sharp focus running at full throttle [who] begins quoting figures almost immediately." McNamara is a poetry lover with wide-ranging taste, encompassing Yeats, Shelley, Kipling, and Frost. He serves on the board of directors of Royal Dutch Shell Ltd., the Washington Post Company, and the Bank of America among other corporations. His honors include the United States Medal of Freedom, the Albert Einstein Peace Prize, the Franklin D. Roosevelt Freedom From Want Medal, and numerous honorary degrees.

References: Christian Sci Mon p20 D 16 '86 por; *Interview* 13:42+ N '83 por; *New Repub* 182:2 Je 21 '80; *Newsday* II p4+ My 16 '84 por; *Washington Post* M p1+ O 12 '80 por; *International Who's Who, 1986–87;* Trewhitt, *Henry L. McNamara* (1971); *Who's Who in America, 1986–87*

Narayan, R(asipuram) K(rishnaswami)

(nä rä´yan)

Oct. 10, 1906– Indian writer. *Address:* b. c/o Wallace & Sheil Agency, Inc., 177 E. 70th St., New York City, N.Y. 10021 h. 15 Vivekananda Rd, Yadavagiri, Mysore 2, India

Although many of his Indian countrymen cannot read his works because they are written in English, R. K. Narayan is widely regarded as his country's finest living writer. The small fictional south Indian city of Malgudi, on the Sarayu River, which he first brought to life in the mid-1930s in the pages of his novel *Swami and Friends*, has come to stand, in the words of the *New York Times* critic Edwin McDowell, at the "center of India's English-language literary life." Narayan's reputation rests on more than a dozen novels and several short story collections set in Malgudi, with its Town Hall Park, Albert Mission School, and Lawley Road. In that mythical locale Narayan has created a literary microcosm that critics compare, in its accumulated richness and diversity of characterization, with William Faulkner's Yoknapatawpha county or Thomas Hardy's Wessex. Although other writers about India, like Ved Mehta and Ruth Prawer Jhabvala, may be better known, Narayan is credited with having raised the genre of the Anglo-Indian novel to its highest level of perfection. John Updike once referred to him as "the foremost Indian writer of fiction in English," and Graham Greene, who helped Narayan to publish his first novel in 1935, has called him "the novelist I most admire in the English language."

The double perspective afforded by filtering an unmistakably Indian and Brahmin sensibility through what Narayan terms the "transparent" and "adaptable" English language imbues much of his work with a gentle irony and piquancy. A limpid, casual prose that, according to Narayan, should never appear "deliberate," is the most salient characteristic of his style. Drawing his subject matter from neither the colonial experience nor the Indian aristocracy, Narayan delineates with an objectivity that does not rule out compassion or irony the everyday life of a cross-section of Indian society that includes street vendors, beggars, holy men, financial experts, tourist guides, students, and teachers. He is one of the first novelists to depict India not with the British sensibility of an E. M. Forster or a Rudyard Kipling but from the viewpoint of an insider.

R. K. Narayan was born Rasipuram Krishnaswami Narayanswami on October 10, 1906, in Madras, India, one of several children in a middle-class Brahmin family. Because his father, Krishnaswami Iyer, a headmaster in the government education service, traveled frequently, and his mother, Gnanambal, was frail and had other children to care for, Narayan was raised by a grandmother and an uncle. The grandmother supplemented his education at the Christian Mission School with after-school lessons in Tamil and with recitations of Indian tales and Vedic poetry. It was largely his grandmother who inspired in Narayan a passion for people that became central to his storytelling. "Novels may bore me, but never people," Narayan told Ved Mehta, as quoted in a New Yorker profile (September 15, 1962). "To me, all individuals are like characters in my own stories, with whom one has to live for many pages of writing, even if they stop being interesting after a while." It was largely his grandmother's world—the people who passed through her backyard to be advised on marriages, treated for scorpion bites, and have their horoscopes read—that became the subject for much of Narayan's early idyllic fiction.

When his father was transferred from Madras to Mysore, Narayan enrolled in the Maharajah's College in that city. Bored with virtually everything he read—except Rabindranath Tagore's tract fulminating against academic education—he failed his intermediate and baccalaureate examinations several times and did not receive his bachelor of arts degree until he was twenty-four, a rather mature age in India, where boys as young as fifteen or sixteen were often awarded the degree. (He later recounted his academic struggles in his 1937 novel Bachelor of Arts.)

After graduating, Narayan put in some unsuccessful stints as a teacher and as an editorial assistant before abandoning thoughts of gainful employment for a life spent at home in literary pursuits. His decision was made easy not only by a generous and indulgent father but also by the joint-family system, in which any number of relatives could live under one roof. It was during that period of unenforced idleness, in which he could savor the "pure delight of watching a novel grow . . . ," that the mythical town of Malgudi sprang into being. "On a certain day in September, selected by my grandmother for its auspiciousness, I bought an exercise book and wrote the first line of a novel," he has recalled. "As I sat in a room nibbling my pen and wondering what to write, Malgudi with its little railway station swam into view, all ready-made. . . . " For a time, Narayan wrote short stories and articles on such topics as sanitation, law cases, and scandals for the Madras newspaper Hindu and for an anti-Brahmin publication, Justice. His newspaper work provided him with a constant source of material, though it yielded him only a pittance.

The days that he spent with his grandmother, or Ammani as he called her, provided the backdrop for Narayan's first novel, Swami and Friends, which was published in 1935 by Hamish Hamilton on a recommendation from Graham Greene. That youthful work, based on Narayan's childhood recollections, is so episodic and discursive that a number of critics have commented on the modest, inauspicious beginning of his literary career. Warren French, writing in Contemporary Novelists, observed that there was little indication in Narayan's early fiction of the "work of a major artist" and called Swami and Friends "a kind of charming Indian Penrod and Sam." But William Walsh, in his book on Narayan, praised the novel for its ability to register the consciousness of a ten-year-old schoolboy who very much resembled the young Narayan. In his preface to the novel, Graham Greene remarked: "Swami is the story of a child written with complete objectivity, with a humor strange to our fiction, closer to Chekhov than to any English writer, with the same underlying sense of beauty and sadness."

Written in the tradition of Kipling and Frederick Marryat, Swami and Friends received mixed reviews, and because of its lack of commercial success the publisher turned down Narayan's second novel. But although the trilogy of his early novels, which also included The Bachelor of Arts (Nelson, 1937) and The Dark Room (Macmillan, 1938), was limited in scope, it successfully captured the complexities and tensions of Indian life as manifested in an intricate net of family relations. Furthermore, it introduced themes that were to reappear in Narayan's more mature work: the decline of tradition in a modern, predominantly urbanized, middle-class environment; an awareness of both the sad and the comic aspects of the world; and the presence of a protagonist who, in the words of William Walsh, was "usually modest, sensitive, ardent, wry about himself, and sufficiently conscious to have an active inner life and to grope towards some existence independent of the family." And, unlike some British novelists, such as E. M. Forster, who viewed India essentially as outsiders, Narayan maintained a perspective from within.

With his fourth novel, The English Teacher (Eyre and Spottiswoode, 1945), Narayan's art attained a new maturity, owing partly to the death of his wife, Rajam, of typhoid fever in 1939, after five years of marriage, and a subsequent hiatus during which Narayan wrote virtually nothing. The novel depicts a schoolteacher's attempt to find some meaning after the death of his wife, with many of the details taken directly from Narayan's life. He has explained that the work was "all about [his] life with Rajam . . . , very little part of it being fiction." In addition to ending a six-year period of literary silence, the work marked a transition from Narayan's early efforts to what Warren French called "deeper and more tightly unified work." It begins, to use French's words, "like Narayan's earlier ones, with episodic sketches of a young preparatory schoolteacher's relationships." Then it undergoes a change in density and significance as it depicts the teacher's attempts to communicate with his dead wife through séances with a spiritual medium, his eventual resignation from teaching, and finally his journey in search of "a harmonious existence." The first of his novels to be issued in the United States, *The English Teacher* was published by Michigan State University Press in 1953 under the title *Grateful to Life and Death*.

Narayan's "middle period" was characterized by three novels: *Mr. Sampath* (Eyre and Spottiswoode, 1949), *The Financial Expert* (Methuen, 1952; Michigan State Univ. Press, 1953), and *Waiting for the Mahatma* (Methuen, 1955; Michigan State Univ. Press, 1955). They seemed to demonstrate Narayan's continuing development from what William Walsh called "an enclosed, contemplative and personal art to a more strenuously imagined and external fiction." *Mr. Sampath* sums up the concerns of the three novels. It centers on Srinivas, who after a period of youthful idleness is forced by his parents to choose a profession. He establishes a newspaper but is persuaded by his printer, Sampath, to abandon it so that he can write lucrative filmscripts. When the movie-making enterprise ends in failure, Srinivas feels himself "involved in a chaos of human relationships and activities," and is plagued with a deeper sense that he betrayed some part of himself and cut himself off from his sense of tradition. Like many of Narayan's protagonists, he seeks salvation by obeying his instincts as an artist. The difficult search for "true identity" in a time of cultural disintegration might be said to be the theme that underlies all of Narayan's fiction.

The work that many critics consider to be Narayan's masterpiece is *The Guide* (Viking, 1958), an example of what William Walsh termed "serious comedy." Begun during a visit to the United States in 1956–57, the novel presents a complex series of flashbacks to narrate the rise and fall of Raju, a former food vendor turned tourist guide who, after seducing the wife of a client, gives up his profession as a guide to manage the young woman's career as a dancer. He prospers when the woman's dancing launches her into stardom, but he is eventually thrown into jail for dishonest dealings. The reader first encounters Raju sitting in an abandoned temple after his release from prison, and the novel traces his gradual discovery of his true vocation, as a mahatma or spiritual adviser in a peasant village.

Response to the novel was overwhelmingly positive. A reviewer for the *Christian Science Monitor* (April 3, 1958) wrote that "*The Guide*, like his previous novels, is a masterpiece finely spun from a few apparently inconsequential strands." And Rosanne Archer, in the *New York Post* (April 20, 1958), observed the perfection of a "graceful . . . Indo-Anglian" dialect capable of "recording the human scene with delicacy and wit" and called Narayan "a superb stylist: simple, elegant, and precise." The novel won the Sahitya Akademi award, India's highest literary honor, in 1958. A stage adaptation of *The Guide*, by Harvey Breit and Patricia Rinehart, had a brief Off-Broadway run at the Hudson Theatre in New York City in March 1968.

The novels *The Man-Eater of Malgudi* (Viking, 1961) and *The Vendor of Sweets* (Viking, 1967) expanded upon the fictional world of Malgudi and presented Narayan at what William Walsh called "the pitch of his powers," able to "fix the authentic individuality of a character and simultaneously establish it solidly in a social world." Both novels were seen by reviewers as well-crafted though somewhat flawed works. John Wain, writing in the *New York Review of Books* (June 29, 1967), remarked that the confectioner's final forsaking of the world for private contemplation struck him as "too manifestly a device." And Robin White observed in the *New York Times Book Review* (May 14, 1967) that "with deeper penetration, [*The Vendor of Sweets*] might well have been the novel of the century from the subcontinent. Its limitations make it little more than another pleasant confection from south India's greatest writer."

The Painter of Signs (Viking), Narayan's eleventh novel and his first major work of fiction in nearly a decade, was published in 1976. Its protagonist, Raman, is a meticulous sign painter and self-professed modern man who leads a placid life as an unfettered bachelor until he is commissioned to do a series of signs for a woman whose radical beliefs include vigorous support of birth control and disapproval of marriage. Raman, who is really a traditionalist at heart, enters into a disastrous marriage with her before realizing that his long established beliefs are not so easily painted away. Reviewing the novel in the *New York Times* (June 20, 1976), Anthony Thwaite remarked that "Narayan observes a deeply traditional society gradually becoming aware of change. . . . It is a world as richly human and volatile as that of Dickens, but never caricatured. . . . Funny and poignant, deftly written, *The Painter of Signs* is pure delight."

The protagonist of Narayan's next novel, *A Tiger for Malgudi* (Viking, 1983), is the tiger Raja, who narrates in "the first tiger" the efforts of his master, a holy man-hermit, or *sannyasi*, to bring him to a state of enlightenment, believing that they had been "brothers in previous lives." The book was unfavorably reviewed in the *Toronto Globe and Mail* (January 14, 1984) by Janette Turner Hospital, who argued that "animal narrators have a way of dooming a novel to the level of the cutely clever at best" and concluded that "one sorely misses the satiric edge, the off-centre perspective." But Walter Goodman, in the *New York Times* (August 8, 1983), called the book a "set of smartly linked skits" and saw it as a parable demonstrating that "true mastery resides not in dominating another creature but in controlling one's own worst impulses." Goodman concluded that "once again the skillful yarn-spinner has found enough material in our doings and undoings to produce an engaging and rewarding work."

In his thirteenth novel, *Talkative Man* (Viking, 1987), Narayan returns once again to Malgudi, this time in the guise of TM, the eponymous narrator, who must "share every experience with everyone" and relates the story of a mysterious stranger, Dr. Rann, who claims to be on a top-secret scientific UN project and promptly installs himself in TM's home. Michiko Kakutani, writing in the *New York Times* (March 14, 1987), noted the somewhat "attenuated" quality of the novel and remarked that the "storytelling process, the subjectivity and self-interest involved in any attempt to articulate the past" are issues that "never really engage the reader, so slight and glancing is this novel." Anita Desai, in the *London Review of Books* (December 4, 1986), remarked that Narayan's "recent writing has been like a drying out of his once ripe material: it . . . still bears an aroma but a drier, sharper one—it is turning into a tobacco leaf or a pinch of snuff."

Narayan's collections of short stories include *An Astrologer's Day* (Eyre and Spottiswoode, 1947), *Lawley Road* (Indian Thought Publications, 1956), *Gods, Demons and Others* (Viking, 1965), *A Horse and Two Goats and Other Stories* (Viking, 1970), and *Malgudi Days* (Viking, 1982). His *Under the Banyan Tree and Other Stories* (Viking 1985) contributes, along with his earlier collections, what Narayan called the "concentrated miniatures of human experience in all its opulence" to the slowly accumulating and resonant world of Malgudi. Alfred Kazin noted in the *New York Times Book Review* (July 21, 1985) that Narayan's stories derive their charm "from the immense calm out of which he writes." Reviewing the story "Annamalai," considered the best in the collection, Kazin remarked: "Nowhere else in this fine book does Mr. Narayan so interestingly submit to his material. . . . Though a miniature, Annamalai bursts the bonds of that predictable form, the short story. It brings a human strangeness home to us, as only a novel usually does—and that is the unexpected effect of Mr. Narayan's collection."

In discussing the differences between the novel and the short story genres, Narayan maintains that both forms are necessary for the task of bringing Malgudi to life. "The short story is the best medium for utilizing the wealth of subjects available," he wrote in his preface to *Under the Banyan Tree*. "A novel is a different proposition altogether, centralized as it is on a major theme, leaving out, necessarily, a great deal of the available material on the periphery."

Among Narayan's works of nonfiction are the volumes *Next Sunday: Sketches and Essays* (Pearl Publications, 1960), *My Dateless Diary* (Indian Thought Publications, 1960), and *My Days: A Memoir* (Viking, 1974), as well as shortened prose versions of the Indian epics *Ramayana* (Viking, 1972) and *Mahabharata* (Viking, 1978). Some of

Narayan's short stories have appeared in the *New Yorker*. Among the honors that he has received are the national prize of the Indian Literary Academy (1958), the National Association of Independent Schools award (1965), the English-Speaking Union book award (1975), and an honorary Litt.D. degree from the University of Leeds (1967). In 1964 Prime Minister Jawaharlal Nehru awarded him a Padma Bhushan for distinguished service.

R. K. Narayan was described by Ved Mehta in the *New Yorker* profile as "neither too stout nor lean," with a "sharp face," a "slightly hooked nose," and "impish, mischievous eyes" that peer out from behind the thick frames of his glasses. "Loosely, carelessly clothed," Narayan prefers informal, professorial tweeds, which he wears over a white shirt and tie. Soft-spoken, and mild-mannered, he speaks English with a lilting Indian accent. He enjoys an occasional areca or betel nut, a treat with which his grandmother sometimes spoiled him during his childhood. Since the death, in 1939, of his wife, Rajam, who bore him a daughter, Hema, Narayan has remained unmarried. He continues to live in Mysore and makes frequent visits to Europe and the United States. Although he likes to look on his work as spontaneous and unlabored, Narayan often follows his original composition with a second, a third, and even a fourth draft. He confesses that he writes best when he has "no burden" on his mind.

References: New Repub 184:24+ Ap 25 '81 por; New Yorker 38:51+ S 15 '62 por; Contemporary Authors vols 81–84 (1979); Contemporary Novelists (1986); International Who's Who, 1986–87; Twentieth Century Authors (First Supplement, 1955); Who's Who, 1987–88

Noah, Yannick

May 18, 1960– French tennis player. Address: b. c/o ProServ, Inc., 888 17th St., N.W., Washington, D.C. 20006

Blessed with what no less an authority than Arthur Ashe has called "the ideal physique for tennis," Yannick Noah is arguably the most gifted athlete playing the sport today. He is a master of the serve-and-volley game, intimidating his opponents with his imposing height, speed, agility, and acrobatic shot-making. His formidable arsenal includes an explosive serve, a deceptive, dancing drop shot, and an overhead that has been described as the "most spectacular" in men's tennis. When he won the French Open in 1983, becoming the first Frenchman to wear that coveted Grand Slam crown in thirty-seven years, Noah seemed to be on the verge of greatness, but he has yet to fulfill his promise. Troubled by personal problems and repeatedly sidelined by debilitating injuries, he did not win a single major tournament between June

Yannick Noah

1983 and May 1985, when he took the Italian Open title. Since then, he has added a clutch of Grand Prix championships to his win list and reclaimed his place among the top ten players on the international men's tour.

Yannick Simon Camille Noah was born on May 18, 1960 in Sedan, a provincial town in eastern France, the oldest of the three children of Zacharie and Marie-Claire (Perrier) Noah. His father was a professional soccer player; his mother, a teacher. When injuries ended Zac Noah's playing career two years later, he returned with his family to his native Cameroon and settled near Yaoundé, the capital city, where he opened a Renault automobile dealership. Yannick learned to play tennis from his father, who took up the game to keep fit. Although there were only a handful of courts in Yaoundé, the boy practiced whenever he could, usually with a homemade wooden racket that he had fashioned himself. To celebrate his tenth birthday, he organized a tennis tournament for his playmates. "[I] made all the other kids pay a dollar each for a trophy that I knew I would win," he told Ray Kennedy in an interview for a *Sports Illustrated* (August 15, 1983) profile. "It was my birthday present to myself."

In 1971 a group of American tennis pros on an exhibition tour of Africa gave a clinic at the tennis club in Yaoundé. One of a dozen or so local youngsters chosen to hit with the pros, Yannick Noah, then just eleven years old and still under five feet tall, found himself across the net from Arthur Ashe, a Wimbledon and United States Open champion. Seemingly unfazed, the little boy matched the pro point for point, even acing him once. Ashe was so impressed by Noah's aptitude that he telephoned Philippe Chatrier, the head of the French

Tennis Federation, which, on Ashe's advice, persuaded Zac and Marie-Claire Noah to allow their son to go to France to attend a special tennis academy in Nice.

Except for a few weeks' holiday annually, Yannick Noah spent the next five years in Nice, dividing his time between the tennis academy and a local secondary school. Lonely and homesick at first, he eventually settled down and, under the tutelage of Patrice Beust, the junior tennis coach, significantly improved his game. After his parents' divorce in the mid-1970s, he was joined in Nice by his mother and two younger sisters, Nathalie and Isabelle. Not long after their arrival, he dropped out of school, one year short of graduation in order to concentrate on tennis.

Moving to Paris, where he had access to a wider range of tennis facilities and, perhaps more important, a greater number of equally talented practice partners, Noah began working regularly with Patrice Hagelauer, the coach of the French national team. He won the French junior title in 1977 and, later in the same year, made a name for himself internationally when he reached the final of the prestigious Junior Orange Bowl tournament in Florida before falling victim to the up-and-coming Ivan Lendl, 4-6, 7-6, 6-3. The following year, his first on the professional tour, he won two minor Grand Prix tournaments, in Manila and Calcutta, and generally played well enough to boost his Association of Tennis Professionals' computer ranking from 305th to forty-ninth.

In 1979 Noah picked up three more Grand Prix tournament crowns, including back-to-back titles in Madrid and Bordeaux, where he defeated, in succession, Manuel Orantes, a former United States Open champion, and the wily Harold Solomon. He made an impressive showing in the hotly contested Grand Slam tournaments too, reaching the round of sixteen in both the French and United States Opens. In the United States Open at the National Tennis Center in Forest Hills, New York, in September, Noah impressed seasoned tennis aficionados with his cannonball serve, his polished ground strokes, and his tenacity. Hobbled by a painful cramp in his right leg during his round-of-sixteen match against the South African Johan Kriek, he gamely fought back from a two-set deficit before he was eliminated, 6-3, 7-6, 4-6, 1-6, 6-4. By the end of the year Noah was rated second in France and twenty-fifth in the world.

A badly sprained ankle and various other ailments kept Noah off the tour for several months during the winter of 1979-80, but by the late spring he was again in fighting trim. In May 1980, in the first major tournament final of his career, he met Guillermo Vilas, then near the top of the international rankings, for the Italian Open championship. Although he succumbed in straight sets to Vilas' relentless pressure from the backcourt, Noah was nonetheless buoyed by the quality of his play, particularly in the second half of the match.

A few days later Yannick Noah, the newly ranked number-one player in France, stepped onto the red clay courts of Roland Garros Stadium in Paris for his first match in the 1980 French Open, against Roberto Vizcaino of Spain. He dispatched both Vizcaino and Eliot Teltscher, his third-round opponent, in routine fashion, but he had to draw on all his strength and speed to defeat José Luis Clerc, a shrewd clay-court specialist, in the second round. During the grueling four-hour match with Clerc, he rallied after a 1-6 collapse in the fourth set to win the fifth and deciding set, 6-3. Facing the redoubtable Jimmy Connors in the round of sixteen, Noah was forced to default midway through the match, after pulling a thigh muscle diving for a return.

Sidelined for several months while recovering from his injury, Noah found himself the center of media attention after he admitted, in an interview for a French magazine in the summer of 1980, that he had occasionally smoked hashish and suggested that some players regularly used harder drugs to raise the level of their play—a practice he deplored "because you're not being beaten with the same weapons." "I thought I did my best to explain something," he told Derrick Jackson of *Newsday* (September 4, 1981). "I remember actually saying I thought it [the drug abuse among players] was *possible* but . . . the way everyone reacted, I felt that nobody wanted to hear the real thing. . . . It got to a point where I could just tell that 50 percent of the people I would meet at tournaments didn't like me."

His confidence badly shaken, Noah struggled for months to regain his old form. In 1981 he was often extended to five sets by relatively obscure players, and he won only one significant title, the WCT Championship in Richmond, Virginia, where he bested, in successive matches, Gene Mayer, Roscoe Tanner, and, in the final, Ivan Lendl. It was not until February 1982 that he racked up another major tournament victory, upsetting Lendl (to end Lendl's forty-four-match winning streak) in the final of the Congoleum Classic in La Quinta, California. Lendl avenged his defeat three months later by knocking Noah out of contention in the French Open. Noah got his own back in July, however, when he trounced Lendl to win for his country the Davis Cup contest between France and Czechoslovakia.

A tentative grass-court player, Noah won only two matches at Wimbledon in the five years ending in 1981, and he bypassed that tournament in 1982. Later in the summer his superior performance in the Mutual Benefit Life Open in South Orange, New Jersey, where he did not lose a set in five rounds of play, augured well for a good showing in the United States Open. The Open's ninth seed, he got off to a fast start, whipping Kevin Curren and Brian Gottfried in straight sets, then faltered and lost in the fourth round. Overall, Noah reached at least the semifinals in eight of the tournaments he entered in 1982 and won four titles, boosting his international ranking on the ATP computer to tenth.

After blowing two match points to lose to Manuel Orantes in the quarterfinals of a Grand Prix tournament in Monte Carlo in April 1983, Noah decided to devote himself to winning the French Open. "I was sick of being good and not great," he told Ray Kennedy. "The closer the tournament came, the harder I practiced, pushing myself when I was tired to go ten minutes more, ten minutes more. I *had* to do it. Ever since I was a boy I dreamed about winning [at] Roland Garros, and I didn't want to end my playing days without knowing that at least once in my life I had given everything I had to try to make my dream come true." Over the next few weeks, he played in three successive tournament finals, winning over Henrik Sundstrom in Madrid and José Higueras in Hamburg but losing to Mats Wilander in Lisbon.

Seeded sixteenth, Noah entered the 1983 French Open riding a wave of sixteen consecutive victories on the Grand Prix circuit. Playing with what one reporter described as "uncommon ferocity," he sailed through his first six rounds, dropping only a single set, to Ivan Lendl in the quarterfinals. Up against Mats Wilander, the defending champion, in the final, Noah immediately took charge with an aggressive, all-court game designed to unsettle the Swede, a steady baseliner. Leading two sets to none in the best-of-five match, Noah seemed to weaken in the third set as Wilander, who had never lost a match at Roland Garros, scrambled back with a succession of dazzling service returns and angled passing shots to force a tie-breaker. Quickly regaining the upper hand, Noah took the tiebreaker, 7-3, and the match, 6-2, 7-5, 7-6, when Wilander missed a forehand.

Overcome with emotion, Noah fell to his knees, then jumped to his feet and leapt into the outstretched arms of his father, who had rushed onto the court. "I am doubly happy because I didn't win this alone," he said in a post game press conference, as quoted in the *New York Post* (June 6, 1983). "It was with my family, my friends, and the French Tennis Federation. It's our victory." Ironically, two days after his historic win, Noah was fined $20,000 and suspended from competition for six weeks by the Men's International Professional Tennis Council, the sport's governing body, for having failed to appear at a scheduled competition in West Germany the previous month. Admitting he was at fault, Noah declined to appeal the suspension, although he publicly declared that the penalty was "far too great."

Heralded by the French press as the heir apparent to the legendary "Four Musketeers"—René Lacoste, Jean Borotra, Henri Cachet, and Jacques Brugnon—who dominated international tennis in the 1920s, Yannick Noah was featured on posters, celebrated in a reggae-style ballad called "Tie-breaker," and profiled in dozens of magazines. Whenever he dared to venture from his Paris apartment, he was mobbed by reporters, photographers, and adoring fans. "My life is very different [since winning the French Open]," he told Ray Kennedy in the interview for *Sports Illustrated*. "I can't go to restaurants anymore, can't go out to dance in the clubs the way I used to. Always there are eyes following you, people wanting your autograph. . . . I have the feeling that I'm losing control of my life, that I'm being pushed from all sides. I don't want to be eaten up by the star system."

After his suspension, Noah rejoined the tour in time for the 1983 United States Open. Seeded fourth on the strength of his French Open title, he played well enough, despite tendinitis in his right knee, to reach the quarterfinals, where he lost to Manuel Orantes. His respectable showing notwithstanding, some veteran observers of the game wondered publicly whether Noah had the "killer instinct" of a world-class player. Philippe Chatrier and Arthur Ashe were among those who noticed that he seemed to have lost both the confidence and the singleminded concentration needed to take Grand Slam titles. "He's out there physically, but he's not out there mentally," Ashe told one reporter.

Noah's critics' suspicions were confirmed when he tearfully announced, at a press conference in Paris on December 7, 1983, that he was moving to New York City to escape the pressures of celebrity. His life had become so "unbearable," he told reporters, that he had even contemplated suicide. "I'm French, I'm black and I wear my hair a certain way," he said, referring to his dreadlocks, a hairstyle popular among members of the mystic Rastafarian religious sect. "That means I appeal to a lot of different people, but I just can't satisfy everyone's needs. . . . I'm not happy about leaving," he added, "but I have no choice. I'm stagnating, I'm floating, and I want to play tennis. I'm ambitious and I can't practice here because I don't feel good about myself. I'm totally flipped out."

Plagued by a series of injuries and devastated by the murder of his paternal grandfather, the chief of the village of Etudi, Cameroon, in a political coup, Noah sat out most of the 1984 tour. Although he and his doubles partner, Henri Leconte, took the French Open doubles crown, Noah's best showing in singles competition was runner-up at La Quinta. He was not to win another singles title until May 1985, when he survived a seesaw battle with Miloslav Mecir to capture the Italian Open championship, 6-3, 3-6, 6-2, 7-6. Playing steady if unspectacular tennis over the next few months, Noah inched his way back up the international rankings. In July he clinched the number ten spot with his second Grand Prix tournament victory of the year, relying on his overpowering serve to defeat Jimmy Connors (for the first time in his career) and Martin Jaite in the Washington, D.C., National Bank Classic.

As he gradually regained his physical strength and mental toughness, Noah set his sights on a second French Open title. His goal seemed within reach after he beat Mats Wilander and Ivan Lendl, then ranked, respectively, second and first in the world, in successive tournaments in the late spring of 1986. Perhaps his best performance in months, however, came in the final of the Shearson Lehman Tournament of Champions in New York in May, where he simply outclassed Guillermo Vilas, who had won eight of their nine previous encounters, in straight sets. The second set, which Noah won at love, took only twenty-eight minutes.

Buoyed by the cheers of his fans at Roland Garros Stadium, Noah made it through the first three rounds of the French Open later that month, but he was clearly struggling. Just before his scheduled fourth-round match against Johan Kriek, a disappointed Noah withdrew from the tournament because of second-degree burns on his ankle, the result of laser treatments for his recurrent tendinitis. Noah lost more than three months' playing time while he recovered, yet he played well enough upon his return to the circuit to earn a berth in the Masters Tournament at year's end. His victories included the Benson & Hedges Indoor Championship at Wembley in November 1986.

Ranked fifth in the world going into 1987, Noah played impressively in the early months of the year, reaching the finals of the Australian Open, the Lyon Grand Prix (where he trounced Joakim Nystrom in straight sets for the first time since 1981), and the Shearson Lehman Tournament of Champions. In the last-named event, played on a fast Har-Tru surface that suits his aggressive ground game, Noah breezed into the final without dropping a single set, but in the deciding match, against Andrés Gómez, his usually reliable serve deserted him. Unable to gain control, he lost the match and the title, 6-4, 7-6, 7-6. In the French Open a few weeks later, Noah, who always seems to draw strength from his boisterous French fans, powered his way past Ivan Kley, Christian Bergstrom, and Michiel Schapers before he was toppled by Mats Wilander in the quarterfinals. Never comfortable on fast grass courts, Noah lost in early rounds of the Stella Artois Tournament at the Queen's Club in London, the traditional warmup to Wimbledon, and a few days later, at Wimbledon itself, where he was upset by his doubles partner, Guy Forget, 3-6, 7-6, 4-6, 6-4, 9-7. "I think I have to work more and maybe differently for my game to succeed on grass," he told reporters afterwards. "On the other hand, I lost to a friend, and I'm glad it was against him that I lost." Shortly thereafter, Noah, fearing that he was burned out, took a two-month sabbatical from the tour. He returned to the circuit in October in top form and posted a series of impressive wins as the top seed in the Swiss Indoors Tournament.

Lean and muscular, Yannick Noah is six feet four inches tall and weighs 180 pounds. He is strikingly handsome, with delicate features, large, eloquent eyes, and a gap between his front teeth that has been described as "appealing." In the past few years he has modified his Rastafarian dreadlocks, a style he originally adopted because, as he told one reporter, he likes "to dress up and play roles." In contrast to his pumped-up, aggressive on-court behavior, he is, in private, a gentle, soft-spoken, thoughtful man given to studying philosophy. He is especially fascinated by the writings of the Romanian philosopher E. M. Cioran. Gregarious by nature, in his free time Noah enjoys going to the theatre, rock concerts, and movies and visiting with friends over a meal at Guignol's, the French restaurant in New York's SoHo district that he co-owns.

Aside from his passion for classic cars (he owns several, including a 1952 Auburn), Noah appears to have little interest in material possessions, and he is on record as saying that the money earned by the top touring pros is "too much." Over the years, he has donated a portion of his estimated seven-figure income from winnings and endorsements to African famine relief agencies, and in 1980 he and his father began a tennis program for children in Cameroon, where he regularly conducts free clinics. Since 1984 Noah has made his home in a spacious loft in lower Manhattan. He also continues to maintain an apartment in Paris and a country house in Nainville-les-Roches, thirty-five miles southwest of the French capital. He shares his homes with his wife, the former Cecilia Rodhe, a Swedish model whom he married in 1984, and their two children, Joachim Simon and Tara Bianca Katharina.

References: Esquire 106:102+ S '86 por; N Y Times C p3 S 3 '79 por, C p1+ Ja 9 '84 pors; People 8:111+ N 29 '82 pors; Sport 74:54+ S '83 pors; Sports Illus 52:70+ Je 9 '80 por, 59:54+ Ag 15 '83 pors; Washington Post E p1+ Je 1 '80 por, D p1+ Je 12 '83 por

---

Olsen, Kenneth H(arry)

Feb. 20, 1926– Business executive. Address: b. Digital Equipment Corporation, Maynard, Mass. 01754; h. Weston, Rd., Lincoln, Mass. 01773

According to the editors of *Fortune*, Kenneth H. Olsen has become "arguably the most successful entrepreneur in the history of American business" since founding the Digital Equipment Corporation in 1957. With $7.6 billion in annual revenues, DEC (pronounced "deck") ranks second only to the International Business Machines Corporation (IBM) in its share of the computer market. It "is bigger today," as Peter Petre observed in the *Fortune* profile, "than Ford Motor Co. when death claimed Henry Ford," or "U.S. Steel when Andrew Carnegie sold out." As its president and guiding spirit, Olsen has fostered a climate of innovation at DEC, restructuring the company periodically from within and with it, inevitably, the computer industry. In the 1960s DEC created a new business with its PDP series of minicomputers, which brought what had been a costly, esoteric technology to the mass market. DEC next "hooked up multiple terminals to one computer," Olsen has recalled, and assembled the first extensive electronic mail service. It began linking computers in the 1970s, allowing the machines to "talk" to each other in distributed data processing networks.

In the early 1980s, when a sudden proliferation of microcomputers threatened to isolate DEC in a shrinking minicomputer market, Olsen "bet the company" on completing the development of an architecture to link large groups of computers—and to connect the increasingly overlapping computer markets as well. By 1986 he had begun to make competitive machines "the peripherals" of his new products and his aims, as expressed in DEC's annual report that year, seemed destined once more to become those of his industry: "Our goal is to connect all parts of an organization—the office, the factory floor, the laboratory, the engineering department—from the desktop to the data center. We can connect everything within a building; we can connect a group of buildings on the same site or at remote sites; we can connect an entire organization around the world. We propose to connect a company from top to bottom with a single network that includes the shipping clerk, the secretary, the manager, the vice-president, even the president."

Kenneth Harry Olsen, the second of the four children of Oswald and Svea (Nordling) Olsen, was born in Bridgeport, Connecticut, on February 20, 1926. He grew up in Stratford, Connecticut, a machine-tool manufacturing center, in a working-class community among neighbors of Norwegian, Polish, and Italian descent. Influenced by the stern discipline and religious fundamentalism of his parents, Ken was pious and, according to a boyhood friend, "down the path. He didn't do anything that would raise your eyebrows." As a youngster he preferred technical manuals to comic books and, inspired by his father, a machine tool designer who held several patents, spent much of his time in the basement tinkering with tools, inventing gadgets, and repairing the neighborhood's broken radios. "I grew up with an affection for machine tools and a love for building things," he later recalled. At fourteen, with his younger brother Stanley, Olsen put together a radio station and broke in on local broadcasts with a singing commercial about meatballs. After graduating from Stratford High School, Ken Olsen saw action during World War II in the United States Navy, from 1944 to 1946, and also obtained his first formal training in electrical engineering, learning "that the machine tool of the future was electronics." Enrolling at the Massachusetts Institute of Technology in 1947, he raced through the curriculum in three years and obtained a B.S. degree in electrical engineering in 1950.

Staying on at MIT to complete a master's degree, which he eventually received in 1952, Olsen was recruited to work on the transistor-driven Whirlwind Computer, a breakthrough machine that the school was building for the Office of Naval Research and the Air Force. An anomaly in an era of giant "number crunchers," the Whirlwind Computer was to be used for flight simulation, with applications ranging from air traffic control to guided missile warfare. Olsen's work on it introduced him to interactive computing, one of the Whirlwind's most innovative features, which is epitomized by a computer's immediate response—verging on dialogue—with instructions and incoming data.

In 1951, after the completion of the Whirlwind, the Air Defense Command assigned to MIT the development of the Semi-Automatic Ground Environment, or SAGE early-warning system. Olsen's immediate boss, Norman Taylor, had him design a small computer to test the memory device used in the Whirlwind for use in SAGE. Olsen handled the project so well that when IBM won the contract for the actual manufacturing of SAGE, Taylor sent him to Poughkeepsie, New York, to oversee the project. In an interview with Katherine Davis Fishman for her book, The Computer Establishment (1982), Norman Taylor told Miss Fishman that "Ken lived in Poughkeepsie for two and a half years, in the bowels of IBM. There was this whole new world called production that he didn't know anything about, but he was a bona fide engineer; if something didn't work he'd take his coat off and redo it himself. He could do anything." Olsen found IBM's production inefficiencies in those days "appalling" according to Taylor, and Olsen himself said that his sojourn at IBM "was like going to a Communist state," because "they knew nothing about the rest of the world, and the world knew nothing about what went on inside." He concluded, as he told Taylor, that he could "beat these guys at their own game." Back at MIT, he applied what he had learned at IBM to use in directing the building of the first transistorized research computer.

At that point, Olsen began to feel that "it wasn't really fun unless you affected the outside world." He also became rankled by the fact that the breakthroughs he and his colleagues were making and writing papers about were thought to be meaningless outside MIT "because we were just academics." Unlike the computer industry experts who "laughed or shrugged" when he presented his ideas, Olsen realized that such simple computing jobs as tracking a scientific experiment or maintaining an inventory list did not require the roomsized mainframes produced by IBM. With an MIT associate, Harlan Anderson, he began to look for backing for his idea of bringing "instant back-and-forth between man and machine" to the marketplace, in the form of a small interactive computer.

Olsen and Anderson prepared for the plunge into entrepreneurship by consulting Standard and Poor's financial data on diverse companies and books on management theory in the Lexington, Massachusetts, public library. Olsen practiced the theory by serving as superintendent of Boston's Park Street Church Sunday School. The fiery sermons of the church pastor, Harold Ockenga, "opened a broad world for us, not a narrow one," Olsen has said. Ockenga had been one of the first radio evangelists and Olsen admired his use of a technological instrument to promote fundamentalist values. Olsen's preoccupation with those values, according to his close friends, provides the "psychological key" to his later successes.

In 1957 Olsen and Anderson elucidated their ideas about computing to executives of the American Research and Development company and its president, General Georges F. Doriot, and received a now historic grant of $70,000 in seed money. Doriot advised them to make something other than computers because he felt that the idea of "two young men" competing with IBM, Burroughs, and RCA, already in the relatively new and precarious computer business, "didn't sound quite modest." Opening the Digital Equipment Corporation in one corner of a woolen mill dating back to the Civil War era, Olsen and Anderson, who were immediately joined by Olsen's brother Stan, took Doriot's advice and began producing the printed-circuit logic modules used by engineers to test equipment.

Recalling the austerity of DEC's first year of operation, in 1957, Olsen said in a New York Times article (January 14, 1979): "We did everything ourselves; we cleaned the johns and swept the floors. We did the photography in my basement; we made our printed circuit boards with real silk on wooden frames and etched them in aquarium tanks. Since I was the closest thing we had to a toolmaker, I made the tools." Some of DEC's first customers were MIT alumni, and it was nine months before Olsen hired a full-time salesman.

When he learned that DEC had made a small profit during its first year, General Doriot warned Olsen, "No one has ever succeeded this fast and ever survived in business." Bucking the fashionable tide, Olsen had set his goal as profit rather than growth. Among the other uncommon business policies he clung to as DEC prospered in the years ahead were: no government funding for research, so that DEC's emphasis would remain on manufacturing for the marketplace; no mergers or acquisitions; no leasing (even of big machines) because a reluctance to allow a product that is still producing revenue to become obsolete can grind technical development to a halt; no commissions for salesmen (who were engineers, rather than business school graduates), so that they would not be enticed into selling customers unnecessary equipment; and no dividends for shareholders, so that profits could be plowed back into development.

DEC's circuit modules, as Olsen had intended, became the building blocks of the company's first computer. It was marketed in 1960 and equipped for interactive computing with a CRT or cathode ray tube terminal similar to a television screen. Olsen called it the Programmed Data Processor or PDP-1, to help customers suspend their disbelief in a computer that sold for $120,000 instead of the then standard $1 million, and that was relatively small—the size of a small refrigerator—and did not require its own sterilized room but could be installed anywhere in an organization. The general-purpose device was well received by the engineers, scientists, and technicians at whom it was aimed. It was accepted as standard equipment after the International Telephone & Telegraph Corporation began buying it in great quantities for message-switching. DEC's next coup came in 1963, when its PDP-4 began to attract a lucrative and previously uncharted market of original equipment manufacturers (OEMs), who added their own software to the powerful machines and resold them in new markets under new names. In that way, OEMs gradually became a kind of auxiliary sales force for DEC, while saving it the enormous expense of developing new lines of software for each new group of users.

DEC became known as an "engineer's paradise" in that period, because Olsen shunned any formal corporate structure in favor of a fluid, MIT-like atmosphere in which engineers contributed to each project as their skills and ambitions dictated. Two of the engineers, Edson de Castro and Gordon Bell, joined forces to oversee the development of the $27,000 PDP-5 and of Digital's breakthrough machine, the smaller, more powerful PDP-8, which was built using a new technology: tiny integrated circuits, which were relatively cheap and faster than transistors.

Launched in 1965, the PDP-8, generally thought to be the first true minicomputer, sold for an astonishingly low basic price of $18,000 and opened up markets "we'd never been in before," DEC senior vice-president Winston Hindle told Glenn Rifkin of Computerworld (September 24, 1986). The PDP-8 gradually revolutionized the way in which industries conducted business, making it economical and practical for a technician to perform a computing job immediately on the spot, instead of having to wait to take a turn on the company mainframe. As customized by OEMs and by DEC's other customers, many of whom wrote their own software, the PDP-8 could perform in a wide variety of environments, and it turned up in machines ranging from typesetters, and medical scanners to

the scoreboard at Boston's Fenway Park. "Literally hundreds of start-ups hurried to enter" the market it created, according to Glenn Rifkin. "Most got out just as soon," he added, since they were unable to compete with an already entrenched DEC.

As sales skyrocketed, the company outgrew its free-form structure. In 1966, the year in which DEC went public, Olsen decided to "break the company into pieces" to make it more responsive to developments in the increasingly complex computer market. The "pieces" became product line groups—companies within the company, each studying and serving its own market and headed by a senior manager who worked as an entrepreneur, submitting an annual budget and product line plan to a committee of his peers that, chaired by Olsen, functioned as a kind of internal venture capital group. If his product line was "funded," the manager proceeded with research and development and "bought" services from DEC's still centralized manufacturing and sales forces. In that way, DEC gradually spawned more than thirty-one semiautonomous "companies" that jockeyed for power in what has been described as a "bubble up" or "matrix" management style. Olsen remained the company's binding force however, keeping committee meetings going until complex business problems broke down into elegant solutions and, as a former DEC vice-president told Peter Petre, constantly "flying ideas around the company" that were sometimes "like little paper airplanes aimed at a particular person" and sometimes "like leaflets from the Goodyear blimp, aimed at anyone who picks them up." The corporate culture thus created has been called both amazingly democratic—"like America"—and sternly patriarchal. It generated nearly two decades of 30 percent annual revenue and profit growth and made DEC one of the model companies regularly hymned in business magazines and included on their "best managed" lists. One of the fruits of that success (and of going public) were takeover bids from Xerox Corporation, Hewlett-Packard, and other companies. DEC also continued to battle its surviving start-up competitors, including Data Point and Data General (formed in 1968 by De Castro and other deserters from DEC).

The firm made a strong bid for some of the IBM-dominated mainframe market in 1967 when it launched its biggest machine, the PDP-10, a $400,000 computer designed for time sharing. In 1970 it reconquered the minicomputer industry with the sixteen-bit PDP-11, which became the most popular minicomputer line in history. Distributed processing networks using another innovation, DECnet software, to link PDP-11s with larger machines such as the PDP-10, became increasingly popular throughout the 1970s, monitoring such processes as the assembly of cars and the workings of oil refineries. IBM, meanwhile, was "asleep at the switch," according to one journalist, and did not enter the mini market in earnest until late 1976.

Networking on a grand scale through the linking of networks to each other as if they were individual computers, began for DEC with the Virtual Address Extension or VAX technology developed by Gordon Bell in 1974, the year in which its profits pushed DEC into the Fortune 500 category. VAX grew out of a realization by Bell and DEC's other engineers that, to remain competitive, the PDP-11 needed more of the "address space" that stores a computer's memory, and determines the size and efficiency of the networks it can support. As drafted by Bell, the VAX line was to range from thirty-two bit computers—with twice the address space of the sixteen-bit PDP-11—down to desktop-sized machines. More important, all were to have the same architecture, which would enable them to run the same software, share data bases, and communicate with ease. The first supermini in the series, the VAX-11/780, was as powerful as the IBM 370 at a quarter of the price, and was designed to accept each completed part of the VAX line as add-on equipment to make it even more powerful. Running the VMS operating system, which was developed at the same time, it had the potential of automating entire companies, and was immediately accepted as the standard against which all other minicomputers were to be measured. By 1979 the package had secured 40 percent of the worldwide minicomputer market for DEC.

Almost simultaneously with the triumph of the VAX-11/780 and the commitment of billions of DEC's dollars to the development of the rest of the VAX line, an explosion took place in the growth of the microcomputer industry at the low-priced end of the market. Attracting a horde of white-collar workers who lacked the technical expertise of DEC's traditional customers, the "user friendly" micros took Olsen and his engineers by surprise and left them in a vulnerable position in a changing industry. The "computer on a chip" at the core of the micros was soon so powerful that it began to lure away some of DEC's low-end customers while some IBM mainframes dropped in price enough to entice buyers at the high end. Belatedly in 1982, a year after IBM introduced its own best-selling micro, the PC, DEC offered a confusing selection of three such machines. Each had been built by a separate product line group of the "many-headed hydra" that, in the view of one journalist, Olsen's matrix management structure had become. Competing with established micros and with each other in a product area where DEC had neither marketing expertise nor name recognition, the computers sold sluggishly at best.

On "Black Tuesday," October 18, 1983, DEC's stock plunged twenty-one points. By the end of fiscal 1983, the company's net earnings had dropped by 32 percent. Industry analysts faulted the product line groups that had churned out the ill-fated micros and blamed Olsen's lack of hindsight and ability to run the company for DEC's fall from "excellence." Olsen was also chided, in an unsigned cover story in Business Week (November 5, 1984), for a "seeming preoccupation with an illustrious past" that might lead to an "also-ran status in the industry" for DEC.

But, in fact, Kenneth H. Olsen was once more engaged in restructuring DEC. He scrapped the product line groups—despite the consequent departure of senior managers who prized their independence—to make the company a centralized market-driven operation. As such, it would be capable of "making the new low-end desk-top products work together with DEC's bread-and-butter mini-computer line, then selling them together," according to another Business Week article (May 2, 1983).

That meant continuing to pour DEC's resources into designing the VAX machines. Olsen was again bucking one industry trend, the use of different architectures for different sizes of computers, and foreseeing another trend—a "backlash" against microcomputers by managers who, after being introduced to computing by them, would eventually want to connect them to something more powerful.

Beginning with VAX clusters in 1983, DEC marketed a series of computers "linked by a golden thread of connectivity," according to Glenn Rifkin. The VAX 8600 superminicomputer or "Venus," a small but mighty mainframe, appeared in October 1984. In May 1985 the MicroVAX II workstation, which put the classic VAX-780 on a thumb-nail-size silicon chip, was saluted as "the most important new product since the IBM PC." During the next eighteen months, seven new models in the 8000 series, in every size category, rolled out of DEC. The cycle culminated in September 1986 with the Vaxmate, an IBM-Personal Computer AT-Compatible System, and the All-in-One software package, which made it possible for IBM PC users to retrieve data instantly from any VAX computer. IBM itself was struggling to develop a networking system to link even its own machines.

In fiscal 1986, during an industry-wide recession, DEC's procession of new machines—combined with a bonus plan for its top sales people—raised company profits by 38 percent to $617.4 million. It invaded IBM's traditional markets in banking, insurance, and pharmaceuticals and pushed revenues to $7.6 billion. In the Los Angeles Times (September 22, 1986) a staff writer, Oswald Johnston, proposing superior products as a solution to the United States trade deficit, wrote: "A growing number of economists believe Digital is doing what American business must do much more frequently if it is to survive against increasingly stiff worldwide competition. . . . The trouble is that the United States does not have enough Digitals. . . . Many of the companies with Digital's potential have not taken the steps to realize it."

"As a colossus of industry," Peter Petre wrote, Kenneth Olsen "seems cast naturally for the part. He's big—two inches over six feet, with big bones, a big skull, a big determined face." The link between Olsen and computer history was reaffirmed in the mid-1970s, when he and a former MIT associate, Robert Everett, purchased the Whirlwind computer, which was about to be scrapped, and made it the first acquisition of what has become the Computer Museum. Located in a former wool warehouse in Boston, the museum also houses the other giant example of the handiwork of Olsen and his colleagues in the 1950s—the SAGE computer. Olsen's many honors include the Franklin Institute's Vermilye Medal (1980) and, in 1986, the first IEEE Engineering Leadership Award and the first IEEE Computer Society Award. Olsen annually flies his small plane to the Hudson Bay area in Canada to rough it with cronies on two-week canoeing trips. About the question of his retirement from DEC, which few employees can imagine without him, the "almost mythical father figure," as he has been called, has said, "I'm not going to disappear."

Kenneth H. Olsen married the former Eeva-Liisa Aulikki Valve on December 12, 1950 and they have four children, Ava-Lisa, Eleanor, Glenn Charles, and James Jonathan. The family live in a Boston suburb in the same modest house they moved into when DEC was founded. Olsen is a member of the board of directors of the Ford Motor Company and the Polaroid Corporation, among others, and is a deacon of the Park Street Church.

References: Bsns W p152+ S 21 '68 por, p58+ Ap 26 '76 por, p66+ My 2 '83 por, p64+ Ap 21 '86 por; Computerworld 20:14+ S 24 '86 pors; Dun's Business Month 128:28+ D '86 por; Forbes 112:22+ S 1 '73 por; Fortune 105:91+ My 3 '82 por, 114:24+ O 27 '86 por; N Y Times D p1+ My 14 '85 por, D p1+ S 4 '86 por, III p2 Jl 19 '87 por; Wall Street J p1+ Ap 3 '86; Leaders in Electronics (1979); Who's Who in America, 1984–85

Parkening, Christopher

Dec. 14, 1947– Classical guitarist. Address: b. c/o Columbia Artists Management, 165 W. 57th St., New York City, N.Y. 10019

Perhaps the best-known internationally of all the American classical guitarists is Christopher Parkening, who although not yet forty, has gained the kind of celebrity through concerts, recordings, and television appearances that most serious musicians achieve only at the apex of their long careers. A protégé and long-time personal friend of the great Andrés Segovia, Parkening has specialized—like his mentor—in the Spanish masters and in Bach, though he has increasingly addressed his attention to performing his own transcriptions of the works of the French impressionist composers.

Because of his charisma and the possession of the good looks of an all-American outdoorsman, Parkening suffered early in his career from the kind of promotional hype that publicists in the United States are wont to lavish on their most promising clients. Now his virtuosic technique, profound musicianship, extraordinary ability to achieve intimacy with an audience, and commitment to expanding the narrow limits of the classical guitar repertory have led some critics to view him as the heir apparent of Andrés Segovia, in whose career the music of Johann Sebastian Bach has also played a crucial role. And like Bach before him, Parkening believes that "the aim and final reason of all music is none other but the glory of God."

Christopher William Parkening was born on December 14, 1947, in Los Angeles, California, to Duke (Koch) Parkening, a real estate man, and Betty (Marshall) Parkening. Christopher Parkening grew up and attended school in Brentwood, a suburb of West Los Angeles. Duke Parkening, who took an early retirement, was an avid outdoorsman and hater of big cities, and father and son spent many hours together in fly-fishing for trout in northern California, Oregon, and Idaho. They became so adept that Duke Parkening won the western United States casting championship in 1967, and son Christopher followed suit in 1968.

Christopher Parkening discovered the guitar through his older cousin, Jack Marshall, a staff guitarist and composer at Metro-Goldwyn-Mayer's music department, who often visited the family's Brentwood home with his guitar. By the time he reached the age of eleven, Parkening had become fascinated with the instrument. "I wanted to learn more about the guitar, and Jack said to get the records of Andrés Segovia," he recalled in an interview with Shirley Fleming in *International Musician* (March 1975). It was Marshall who advised Parkening to study classical technique. "He told me to learn classical guitar, because from there you could do anything you wanted to," he informed Shirley Fleming. "So we called the local music store and asked the owner if he knew of any good classical teachers around. He said a Spanish family had just moved into town, and they were supposed to be very good." The Spanish family turned out to be the Romeros, among the most celebrated guitarists in the world. Parkening immediately began studying with Celedonio Romero, and later, with one of Romero's three sons, Pepe. At the end of his first year of study—in 1959—he appeared in his first public recital.

Two years after he made his recital debut, Parkening's mother helped him to take the next step in his career when she read about a competition being sponsored by the Los Angeles Young Musicians Foundation. He filed an application "just for fun," but it was returned with a note informing him that there was "no category" for guitarists. The foundation later reconsidered, however, and he was allowed to play before the judges in an unofficial demonstration of his ability. Since the distinguished panel of judges included Jascha Heifetz, Gregor Piatigorsky, Joseph Schuster, and Mario Castelnuovo-Tedesco, Parkening found performing for them to be a harrowing experience.

"I played the Bach Chaconne," he explained to Shirley Fleming. "I remember I got two or three minutes into it and a lady on the panel wanted me to stop, but Piatigorsky said 'go ahead and let him finish.' So I kept expecting to be stopped, but they let me go through to the end." Despite the "unofficial" nature of his appearance and the absence of a competitive category for his instrument, Parkening was given an opportunity to perform with an orchestra under the foundation's sponsorship. It was not the last time he would encounter a lack of official recognition for his classical guitar, nor the last time he would overcome such barriers.

In March of 1963, at the age of fifteen, Christopher Parkening made his formal concert debut under the auspices of the Young Musicians Foundation, and he later performed at other events sponsored by the organization. Despite the resulting publicity, he never considered the possibility of interrupting his high school education in order to get a head start on a career. One of the pieces he performed during that period was Mario Castelnuovo-Tedesco's Concerto in D for Guitar, which made such an impression on the composer that he sent a tape of the concert to Andrés Segovia, who was in the process of preparing his first American master classes at the University of California, at Berkeley. Invited by Segovia to join the class on a scholarship, Parkening immediately distinguished himself among the nine students from all over the world who were in attendance. In addition to receiving individual attention on a daily basis from Segovia and fulfilling constant requests to perform, Parkening was chosen as the soloist when the master class was televised later that year.

"It was a whole different galaxy," he recalled for Shirley Fleming. "I had to go home every night and refinger everything I'd learned. It was a terrific amount of work, and it was hard enough just playing for him." The two summers he spent in training with Segovia also demonstrated conclusively to Parkening how wide open the entire discipline of classical guitar study was at that time. Persuading him "that the guitar is the only instrument for which you have to be your own teacher," as Parkening told Sidney Fields in an interview for the New York Daily News (November 8, 1972), Segovia concentrated on interpretation, leaving such matters as sitting and hand positions entirely up to the student.

In 1963 Parkening made guest appearances with the Los Angeles Philharmonic Orchestra, as part of its series of young people's concerts, and in 1964 he appeared with the Pasadena Symphony Orchestra. Availing himself of the best teachers in the area, he studied interpretation with Gregor Piatigorsky, and became a student of the harpsichordist Malcolm Hamilton. He enrolled in the University of California at Los Angeles in 1964, but at Malcolm Hamilton's urging, transferred to the University of Southern California after completing his freshman year.

Since the music department of the University of Southern California had no teachers of guitar on its faculty at the time, Parkening was allowed to register as a major in cello. He studied with Gabor Rejto, the head of its string department, while continuing to learn from Piatigorsky and Hamilton, and by the end of his sophomore year was so advanced that he was asked to begin the formal teaching of guitar, which marked the beginning of the guitar department at the university. Within five years Parkening and his three assistants found themselves heading a program that included some workshops and a master class with forty students. In 1971 Parkening officially became head of the guitar department.

At the composer's invitation, Parkening presented the premiere of Castelnuovo-Tedesco's Second Guitar Concerto in 1966. It was the first work of that kind for the composer in more than a quarter-century. Parkening's concertizing and teaching continued at an accelerated pace through 1967, when a six-week interlude of ROTC training helped to precipitate an incident that carried his reputation over to Europe at the same time that it aroused a great deal of controversy among his fellow guitarists.

That incident took place during the international guitar competition that was held at Santiago de Compostela in Spain during 1968, in which Parkening was scheduled to appear. Andrés Segovia told the other judges before the contest that Parkening should win if he played well, but because Parkening had been in ROTC training at Fort Benning, Georgia for the six weeks leading up to the competition, he had been unable to practice the obligatory preliminary pieces. Segovia ruled that Parkening would be allowed to compete without submitting to the preliminary competition, a decision that so outraged the other contestants that they presented the revered guitar virtuoso with a petition of protest.

The outcry resulted in Parkening's forced withdrawal from the competition, to the embarrassment of Segovia and the smug satisfaction of the aggrieved musicians. In the final phase of the contest, however, Parkening suddenly reappeared as a member of the judges' panel, having been invited by Segovia and the other judges to join them. The contestants were so rattled that none of them was able to play well enough for the panel to award the prize.

Having signed with Columbia Artists Management that year, he prepared to embark on his first series of concert appearances throughout the United States and Canada. Also in 1968, a banner year for the young guitarist, Parkening made his recording debut with the albums In The Classic Style and In The Spanish Style for Angel Records. Released in November, both discs were immediate critical and commercial successes. Shirley Fleming, reviewing them in High Fidelity (January 1969), called them "extraordinarily beautiful" and quipped, "Move over, up there where the Big Guitarists sit, because Christopher Parkening, aged twenty, ought not to be kept waiting!" Obviously, the members of the editorial staff of Musical America agreed, because in July 1969 the magazine selected Parkening as one of the outstanding young artists of the year. Embarking on his first tour, he appeared in seventy-two concerts across the United States and Canada in addition to performing his teaching duties at the University of Southern California, and meanwhile sales of his first two albums turned out to be so brisk that Angel Records invited him back to the studio in the spring of 1969 to record his third long-playing disc, Romanza.

Although he had not yet reached the age of thirty, Parkening had already established himself as the preeminent American-born classical guitarist. With characteristic modesty, he once explained: "I just happened to start my career at precisely the moment when the guitar was reaching its peak of popularity around the world. Had I started a beat or two earlier or later, perhaps no one would have heard of me by now. But in the mid-1960s, everybody was playing the guitar, and its popularity in rock and pop music spilled over into classical music, to my very good fortune."

Not surprisingly, Parkening was especially successful at cultivating the young people who attended his college and university concerts, for the guitar had a special appeal for them. During an interview for Stereo Review (May 1974) Parkening informed William Livingstone: "At present, eighty percent of my engagements are at colleges, where the classical guitar has enormous acceptance—and not just by the classical music crowd. The audiences are not narrow stereotypes but represent the whole college."

By that time, Christopher Parkening and his classical guitar had begun to attract attention in some unexpected musical quarters. Grace Slick of the popular rock group the Jefferson Airplane invited him to play on one of their albums, and Paul Simon offered him a commission. He even turned up in the pages of Playboy magazine (September 1972) in an article that made the pronouncement: "There's no more exciting classical guitarist today than this slim, serious, twenty-four-year-old."

In 1973, a year after the release of his fourth album, Parkening Plays Bach, Angel Records issued The Christopher Parkening Album, an anthology of highlights from his earlier discs that celebrated his fifth anniversary with the label. In the same year, although he was by then performing ninety concerts annually, he found enough time to publish The Christopher Parkening Guitar Method, Volume 1 (Sherry-Brenner, Ltd.). And in July 1974 High Fidelity/Musical America honored him for a second time by naming him "Musician of the Month."

Success also brought its problems. As his touring schedule grew—in 1974 he learned from his manager that he could have a performance scheduled for every other day during the coming year—he realized that it put a severe strain not only on himself but also on the guitar's limited repertory. Because of its narrow scope, Parkening and his assistants at the University of Southern California were engaged in a constant effort to select new works for the instrument. "Transcription is a part of life for a guitarist," he explained to the author of the Stereo Review article in 1974. And selecting the music for his recordings was even more taxing. "It's extremely difficult to assemble a program that works for the guitar and is good enough to pass the New York reviewers as well as satisfy the buying public," he has pointed out. "Angel would like me to record two albums a year, but the labor of transcription is so great that I'm doing well to finish one."

By 1975 Christopher Parkening had become aware of a disquieting change in his approach to his music, his instrument, and his jet-propelled career. "In my twenties, he recalled in an article he wrote for Keynote magazine (November 1986), "I was playing about ninety concerts a year, and my approach had begun to feel mechanical. You might call some of the performances almost superficial." The career that he had begun so carefully and methodically now seemed like a whirlwind that he was trying to ride. The turning point, by his own account, came with a concert at which he arrived exhausted and feeling as if the performance were an intrusion on his travel schedule.

That experience proved so devastating that Parkening withdrew from almost all of his musical activities that year. He stopped concertizing, abandoned his recording, left the University of Southern California, and retired to his ranch in Montana with his wife, the former Barbara Colyear, a professional trainer of Arabian horses whom he had married in the summer of 1974. For the next five years, apart from some teaching at Montana State University and performing a relative handful of concerts, Parkening became what he has called "a caretaker" to his animals and his ranch, sharing responsibilities with his wife, who is as much interested in wildlife, ecology, and conservation as he. Perhaps even more important, he also discovered within himself a profound reservoir of faith in Christianity, which helped him in his gradual re-emergence. "I remembered reading in the Bible that whatever you do, you should do it all for the glory of God," he later reminisced in his *Keynote* article. "Now, I figured that there were only two things I knew how to do—fly-fishing for trout and playing the guitar—and the latter seemed the better option to pursue in order to glorify the Lord. It also provided the proper balance in my life between recreation and work." He is now a committed Christian, and is a member of Grace Community Church in southern California.

Although Parkening had interrupted his career at its peak, his five year absence proved to be surmountable, perhaps because fame had continued to follow Parkening even after his "retirement." For example, the critically well-received album *Parkening and The Guitar*, a collection of Baroque and Impressionist pieces released by Angel Records in November 1976, received a Grammy nomination as "Best Classical Recording of 1977." For his return to recording, Parkening did *Simple Gifts* (Angel), a collection of sacred music transcribed for the guitar, in 1984, his first in digital sound. He approached the Christian record market directly with a 1985 reissue of *Parkening Plays Bach* on the Word Records religious label.

During the 1984–85 season Parkening made his first joint recital appearance with the soprano Kathleen Battle at Alice Tully Hall, as part of Lincoln Center's Great Performers series. That triumph was followed by their performance together at the 1984 Ravinia Summer Festival near Chicago. Recorded by Angel and issued both on LP and on compact disc as *The Pleasure of Their Company*, the album was a Grammy nominee for the best classical recording in 1987. Parkening also made his first recording with an orchestra, the Angel release of *A Bach Celebration for Guitar and Orchestra*, with the Los Angeles Chamber Orchestra during the summer of 1984, to commemorate the tricentennial of the birth of the composer, in the following year.

During the 1986–87 season Christopher Parkening returned to his first full season of performances in over ten years. In addition to playing eighty concerts, he made appearances on NBC's *Today Show* and *Tonight Show*, on PBS's *Live From Lincoln Center*, starring Plácido Domingo, and, with Kathleen Battle, on the Grammy Awards show telecast by CBS in February 1987. His recent orchestral engagements have included performances with the Cleveland Symphony Orchestra, the Los Angeles Symphony Orchestra, and the National Symphony Orchestra at Wolf Trap. In 1987 he received the State of Montana Governor's Award for the Arts and the Outstanding Alumnus Award of 1987 from the University of Southern California "in recogni-

tion of his success in achieving our ideal of the complete musician."

Christopher Parkening is rangy, blue-eyed, and fair-haired. When he is not performing or teaching, he and his wife live at their ranch in Montana, where they spend most of their summers. While there, he teaches a master class each August at Montana State University. An ardent conservationist, he is quick to point out during interviews that even as a fisherman, he throws back most of what he catches, preferring to pursue the sport for dexterity rather than for killing.

References: Billboard 97:66 Ja 5 '85; Hi Fi/Mus Am 19:106 Ja '69, 19:MA32 Jl '69, 23:MA23 F '73; International Musician 73:6+ Mr '74; Keynote 10:28 N '86; N Y Times II 19+ F 17 '74; Stereo R 32:70+ My '74; Who's Who In America, 1985–86

Paul, Les

June 9, 1915– Musician; inventor. Address: b. Fat Tuesday's, 190 3d Ave., New York City, N.Y. 10003

No one in the history of popular music has had a greater effect on what the late critic Ralph J. Gleason called "the ultimate pop sound" than Les Paul, the self-taught pioneer electric guitarist and electronics genius. Paul emerged from the Midwest six decades ago as a blues and jazz musician and a master tinkerer with sound-delivery systems. As an inventor, he created the flat, solid-body Gibson Les Paul guitar, the first of its kind, which became the guitar of choice in the rock era, and he was the chief creator of the multitracking and overdubbing techniques that are now standard in recording. As a performer, he reached the pinnacle of his fame with the hit recordings that he made in his home studio in the 1950s with his late wife, the singer Mary Ford, including "Tennessee Waltz," "Vaya con Dios," "How High the Moon," and "The World Is Waiting for the Sunrise." Those discs, on which Mary's naturally rich, mellifluous voice harmonized with itself in front of two to twelve guitar parts laid down by Les, introduced into pop music a revolutionary new sound, multilayered, shimmering, and spatial. Outside of his partnership with Mary Ford, Paul has been best known over the years as the leader of the Les Paul Trio, a swinging modern jazz combo. Since 1984 the latest incarnation of the trio has been performing Monday nights at the Manhattan jazz club Fat Tuesday's.

Before the microchip, even before the transistor, Paul was experimenting with the electronics of the guitar, warping the notes, utilizing echo and feedback, and using the volume knob to alter the sound, and he was working acoustical magic with pre-tape turntables. "The whole idea of treating sound in a studio, bouncing it back and forth, building the track up sound-on-sound, that came from Les," Noë Goldwasser, the editor in chief of *Guitar World,* has pointed out. "And he came up with all kinds of gizmos to do it." Among Paul's inventions were a floating bridge pickup, the LP 70 electrodynamic pickup, the first guitar with two pickups, and the first with fourteen frets.

"The wizard from Waukesha," as Les Paul was known in his youth in the music business, was born Lester William Polsfuss on June 9, 1915, in Waukesha, Wisconsin, where his mother, now 100, still lives. Without any training whatsoever in electronics or music (which he still cannot read), he gravitated to both precociously. He learned music at his mother's player piano, a pump upright that he eventually electrified because, as he recounted to Chet Flippo of *Rolling Stone* (January 13, 1975), he wasn't "gonna pump this damned thing all the time." As the piano played, he watched the keys go down, "finally figured that that was C and this was D-flat," and marked the keys accordingly. By punching his own holes in the piano rolls, he took his first step in the direction of multiples, or overdubbing.

Paul's first electronic construction was a childhood crystal radio set. His first musical instrument, aside from the player piano, was the harmonica. Paul perfected his harmonica technique by listening to Sonny Terry and other blues and country musicians on WSM, the Nashville radio station. Some of those musicians were one-man bands, playing the harmonica and a string instrument simultaneously. Emulating them, Paul acquired, first, a banjo and, then, a Sears Roebuck mailorder guitar, and he invented his own "shotgun" harmonica rack, or holder, which enabled him to flip the instrument over with his chin (for backward playing). Later he would be influenced by the recordings of Carson Robison, Gene Autry, and

Nick Lucas and by the radio programs on which the crooner Bing Crosby was backed by the guitarist Eddie Lang.

A prodigy, Paul was earning money playing and singing at roadhouses and other venues in and around Waukesha, including a fast-food drive-in restaurant, when he was thirteen. To make himself more audible to the people sitting in their cars at the drive-in, he made his first experiment in guitar electrification, amplifying the sound of his acoustic Sears Roebuck instrument with a phonograph needle wired to a radio speaker. Around the same time, he improvised his first, very crude recording machine.

Paul dropped out of high school to join a cowboy band that was passing through Waukesha. With that group he traveled to Chicago, Illinois, and played on the WLS radio *Barn Dance* there. At seventeen, under the name Rhubarb Red, he was leading a country band on radio station WJJD in Chicago. At nineteen, he was being heard nationally on the NBC network, playing an electric guitar that was, in his words, his "own contraption."

Tiring of "being a hillbilly" and aspiring "to be a jazz artist," as he told Chet Flippo of *Rolling Stone,* while working on radio in Chicago he rehearsed on the side for two years with two other young musicians, bassist Ernie Newton and vocalist and rhythm guitarist Jimmy Atkins, Chet Atkins' brother. In his youthful braggadocio, Paul falsely persuaded the less sophisticated and less moneyed Newton and Atkins that he knew the famous New York-based band leader Paul Whiteman and had "a lot of pull" in New York City. In 1937 the first Les Paul Trio ventured to Manhattan, to the building now housing the Ed Sullivan Theatre, on Broadway at 53d Street. There, Whiteman's secretary slammed the door on them. Waiting for the elevator, playing and singing, they were discovered by Fred Waring, the orchestra and choral leader, whose office and studio were in the same building and who happened to be waiting for the same elevator. The first Les Paul Trio was featured on Fred Waring's show on the NBC radio network for four years. During those years Paul spent most of his nights jamming in Harlem clubs with such jazzmen as Art Tatum, Ben Webster, Louis Armstrong, Stuff Smith, and Charlie Christian. He became an especially good friend of Christian, whose slow, driving style contrasted with his own flashy, multi-noted technique.

When working in Chicago, Paul became an unpaid consultant to the Gibson guitar company, a liaison that he would maintain for decades, fieldtesting every new model that Gibson was readying for the market. The idea for a solid-bodied electric guitar came to him gradually in the late 1930s, beginning with his efforts to solve the problem of feedback by stuffing towels into the F holes of the traditional guitar and cutting a hole in the back and putting a blanket inside. He finally realized that what he wanted was nothing less than an unhollowed beam of wood. In 1941 he finished work on his first "Log," a four-by-four-inch board with strings, an attached pickup, and an Epiphone neck. When he approached the Gibson people with his design five years later, they were leery of it, and it was not until 1952 that Paul, after many attempts, came up with the multi-pickup model on which they were willing to put the Gibson name. Although Paul has modified his guitar repeatedly over the years, the Gibson Les Paul of today is essentially the same as the 1952 instrument.

In 1941 Paul disbanded his first trio and left Fred Waring's organization with the brash intention of playing with Bing Crosby in Hollywood. After a two-year detour as the musical director of radio stations WJJD and WIND in Chicago and as a member of Ben Bernie's band, he proceeded with a new trio to Los Angeles, where he impressed Crosby with what the singer described as "the greatest sound" he had ever heard. Crosby hired Paul and arranged a contract for him with Decca Records. One of the Les Paul Trio's first recordings for Decca was the hit "It's Been a Long, Long Time," with Crosby on vocals. The trio attracted the attention of jazz aficionados with their recorded renditions of such songs as "Tiger Rag" and "Little Rock Getaway."

During World War II, Paul served for a year under band leader Meredith Willson in the Armed Forces Radio Service in Hollywood, playing in programs featuring, among others, Rudy Vallee, Kate Smith, and Bing Crosby. After his army service and a stint as an NBC staff musician, he traveled with the Andrews Sisters, the most popular female singing group of the time, and later he toured with Jazz at the Philharmonic as well as his own trio. On one occasion, after performing at the London Palladium, he shuttled over to Paris to meet the legendary Gypsy guitarist Django Rinehardt, whom he had long idolized. After Rinehardt's death, his widow gave Paul his guitar, which is still in Paul's basement in Mahwah, New Jersey.

The first musician to overdub on a professional recording (an old-fashioned glass-based acetate recording) was the jazz clarinetist and saxophonist Sidney Bechet, in 1941. Long fascinated with multiple recording, Paul began doing it in 1935 privately, as background for practicing, on two disc recorders he kept in his closet. Encouraged by Bing Crosby, he stopped traveling with other musicians in 1945 to concentrate on building his own recording studio. In the first studio, in his garage in Hollywood, the disc recording machine that he constructed consisted of a flywheel from a Cadillac, dynamically balanced to serve as a turntable, a motor from a jukebox, and a linking belt purchased from a dental supply house. Breaking from the rule, rigid until then, that recording artists should be no closer than two feet from the microphone, Paul introduced what is now known as close-mike technique. He also introduced the record delay echo, by putting a playback pickup right behind the cutting head. The result was a sound that almost overnight had the industry beating a path to his garage door. Among the records cut in that garage was W.

C. Fields's famous single "My First Drink of Water"/"Talk on Temperance." Paul not only engineered that recording but lent guitar and piano background to Fields's comic monologues. In the pantheon of other stars who recorded in the studio were the singers Kay Starr, Jo Stafford, and the Andrews Sisters.

The tape recorder was invented in Nazi Germany. At the end of World War II, two of Hitler's huge tape machines were confiscated, dismantled, and brought to the United States. One was brought by Colonel Richard Ranger, who reassembled it and demonstrated its use to Bing Crosby and Les Paul. Seeing the advantage of tape over disc, Paul (who eventually hired Ranger to help engineer the sound in his television performances), followed closely the refinements of the tape recorder achieved by the Westrex and Ampex companies and began using the improved machines as the components of his multiple-track recording system (which would reach eight tracks in the early 1950s). "In the late '40s, he took eight bulky Ampex tape recorders—I've seen this thing in his garage—and stacked them up on steel shelving and figured out a way to synchronize them," Matt Umanov, a Greenwich Village guitar store owner, told Paula Span of the Washington Post (May 10, 1987). "Today this can all be done with a machine the size of a tissue box; back then the thing was eight feet high, but somehow he linked it up." Miss Span commented: "The effects Paul could wrest from his experiments—cascades of densely overdubbed guitar, rippling solo runs, an echoey ambiance that sounds as though he were recording in a basement (sometimes he was)—are now so taken for granted that any high-schooler plugging in a Stratocaster qualifies as Paul's musical heir. He never bothered to patent most of his techniques and creations, but people who care about such things know, nonetheless, what he's done." Paul did sell his eight-track design to Ampex, after it was rejected by Westrex in 1954.

Paul's first multiple-track recordings were the instrumental solos "Lover" and "Brazil," released by Capitol Records in 1948. Among his many solo hits in the years immediately following were "Nola" (number nine on the charts), "Josephine" (number twelve), "Whispering" (seven), "Tiger Rag" (six), and "Meet Mister Callaghan" (five). In tribute to the revolutionary Les Paul "sound," Capitol issued the hit album The New Sound in 1950.

In Milwaukee, Wisconsin, in 1949 Les Paul married the singer Iris Colleen Summers, who changed her name professionally to Mary Ford at his suggestion. Soon after the wedding the couple moved to the New York City area, where after a short stay in Jackson Heights, Queens, they settled in the large house in Mahwah, New Jersey, where Paul still lives and where the cluttered but sophisticated recording studio he set up has been in constant commercial use ever since.

Utilizing his innovative sound-on-sound technique, Paul multitracked his wife's vocals with his own instrumentals, so that Mary sounded like a full female trio and Les's electric guitar seemed to be supported by a large rhythm section. Their first hit together was "Tennessee Waltz," which was number one on the charts in 1950. The following year "Mockin' Bird Hill" and "The World Is Waiting for the Sunrise" were number three and "How High the Moon" was number one, as was their album *The New Sound, Volume 2.* Their second album together, *Bye Bye Blues,* was number two in 1952, and *Vaya con Dios* was number one in 1953. Among their many other hits were "I'm Sitting on Top of the World" (1953), "Whither Thou Goest" (1954), "Nuevo Laredo" (1955), and "Hummingbird" (1955). In 1956 Mary and Les switched from Capitol to Columbia Records, which released their last album, *Time to Dream,* in 1958.

In their club and stage appearances, Paul used what he calls the Les Paulverizer, a backstage electronics system controlled by dials on a small black box attached to his guitar. With that assist, the guitars (Mary also played the guitar) sounded like a full orchestra, including drums, and Mary's voice was multiplied, as on the recordings. As a reviewer for *Variety* observed in 1959, the duo's performance was enhanced by their "contagious personalities" and "naturalness," which "warmed audiences from the start." Between 1953 and 1960 Les Paul and Mary Ford did 170 television shows.

The 1960s were a trying time for Paul. His marriage to Mary Ford ended in divorce in 1964; popular musical tastes were changing; and he was beset with health problems, some of them dating back to an automobile accident in 1948, when surgeons had to reconstruct his crushed right arm. (Told that the arm would have limited mobility, he had them set it crooked, in a guitar-playing position.) In the early 1960s he underwent bone-graft surgery on his left hand and treatment for Ménière's syndrome, an inner-ear disorder.

Paul went into what he thought would be permanent retirement in 1964. In the following years he concentrated on electronics projects, including new kinds of transducers and refinements of the Les Paulverizer, the "little black box," as he calls it, which enables him to do multiples at will while walking around a stage. Originally, the box was backed by 1,100 pounds of backstage equipment. He reduced the traveling weight to less than 100 pounds. While still keeping the Les Paulverizer his personal secret, he finally, in 1967, turned over to the Gibson Company the design of the Les Paul Recording Guitar, a much more complicated instrument than the regular Les Paul guitar. The company put the sophisticated instrument on the market in 1971.

In the 1960s and 1970s the Les Paul guitar was generally regarded by musicians as the standard in the industry. It was the instrument of choice of a wide range of electric guitarists, including Wes Montgomery, Leon Russell, Eric Clapton, James Burton, George Benson, Jeff Beck, Richard Betts, Pete Townshend, Leslie West, Mick Taylor, and Greg Allman. There were close rivals on the market, some derived from the one that the country

musician Merle Travis had designed and helped to build, but the Les Paul was preferred because it had the most durable pickups and sustained sound longer. The closest rival was Leo Fender's Telecaster, and in the 1980s Fender's Stratocaster became preeminent. Many rock musicians continued to use the Les Paul, however, especially when they wanted to incorporate a blues sound.

Prodded out of retirement by a friend, a musician who said he was in desperate need of a guitarist, Paul returned to public performance, on a limited scale, in 1974. Soon Capitol Records released an album of Les Paul and Mary Ford's greatest hits, titled *The World Is (Still) Waiting for the Sunrise,* and later RCA issued *Chester & Lester,* an LP of duets by Chet Atkins and Paul, which won a Grammy in 1977. Health problems, including a heart condition that required him to undergo a quintuple bypass operation in 1980, sidelined Paul again for several years, until March 1984, when he began his current Monday night residency at Fat Tuesday's, a basement club on 3d Avenue at 17th Street in Manhattan. Originally booked at the club for a two-week trial engagement, Paul and his new trio (including Wayne Wright, and, more recently, Lou Paulo on rhythm guitar and Gary Mazzaroppi on bass) were held over indefinitely, or, as the management announced, "forever." "His (Paul's) Monday nights have become one of the liveliest shows in town," John S. Wilson reported in the *New York Times* of April 17, 1986. "[His sidemen] are now a wonderfully loose and responsive team, both musically and in projecting Mr. Paul's freewheeling humor. . . . Mr. Paul can still incorporate startling bits of invention in a solo without breaking the exuberant drive of a fast tune, and there is an exquisite gentleness in his delicate colors and phrasing for such songs as 'Summertime.'"

The Les Paul Trio's two Monday night sets attract a heterogeneous audience, including a core of devotees ranging from middle-aged couples to fledgling East Village performance artists, from doctors, accountants, and businessmen to such rock musicians as Eddie Van Halen, Jeff Beck, and Jimmy Page (who carries a framed photograph of Paul to set up on the night stands of the hotel rooms he stays in). "It's kind of a party here," one of the regulars, an antiques dealer from Long Island, told Paula Span of the *Washington Post.* "When the Les Paul Trio finally takes the stage," Miss Span wrote, "with Paul playing a supermodified reissue of the 1958 Gibson Les Paul (musicians have been walking over and eyeing it and rubbing their chins), the party swings into high gear. People laugh at Paul's jokes and call out requests ('Whispering'!) and know where to join in the corny old comic songs he sprinkles into the set. Nobody's having a better time than the guest of honor. . . . The guitar playing still glistens—old Django Reinhardt songs, jazz numbers like 'Stomping at the Savoy,' his own greatest hits. No sullen posturing rocker could get away with the eager-to-please glances that Les Paul throws his audience when he pulls off a particularly impressive guitar riff."

Les Paul is a slim man, of average height and a weight of about 140 pounds, with luminous, piercing eyes, a fluent tongue, and an open, ebullient manner. His face radiates good humor and friendliness. Except for some balding at the crown, his orange-brown head of hair is still rather full—a genetic gift from his father, he says. Two of the fingers of his right hand are hobbled by arthritis, and his right arm has been bent ever since the surgery done on it in 1948. Recently, he underwent several eardrum operations, and he learned that he has a tumor in his forehead. No matter what his physical problems, he has so far always managed to reprogram his playing technique to compensate for them.

Paul has three sons and one adopted daughter. Two of his sons play drums, and one engineers his shows at Fat Tuesday's. Between sets at the club, he limits himself to one bottle of beer, much less than his wonted intake years ago, and he no longer smokes. He drives between Fat Tuesday's and his mansion in Mahwah, New Jersey in his Jeep. The twenty-nine-room house in Mahwah has been described by a friend as "half Smithsonian, half Radio Shack." Among the items it houses are Paul's thirty-four gold records, the hundreds of guitars he has constructed and reconstructed over the years, thousands of tapes, a score of consoles and amplifiers, and miles of wiring. His studio remains very active commercially, and Paul works into the night or early morning at his inventions. In a citation from Yale University, Paul is called "the Thomas Edison of the music industry." The Gibson Company has inducted him into its Hall of Fame, and his induction into the Rock 'n' Roll Hall of Fame is almost certainly imminent. He has a lifetime contract with Gibson.

References: N Y Daily News Ex p3 Ja 15 '87; Newsday p19+ N 30 '75 por; Rolling Stone p45+ F 13 '75 pors; Washington Post G p1+ My 10 '87 pors; Kinkle, Roger D. The Complete Encyclopedia of Popular Music and Jazz 1900–1950 vol 3 (1974); Ulanov, Barry. A Handbook of Jazz (1957)

Pelikan, Jaroslav (Jan, Jr.)

Dec. 17, 1923– Historian of religion; educator. Address: Dept. of History, Yale University, 1504A Yale Station, New Haven, Conn. 06520

A dedicated student of history who aims to "fil(e) a minority report on behalf of the past," Jaroslav Pelikan has spent his life exploring the development of the Christian church as a process of "continuity and change." His five-volume history of church doctrine, The Christian Tradition, of which four volumes have been published so far, seems certain to earn him a place alongside the great church historians, in the opinion of Newsweek's Merrill Sheils, while Louise Sweeney of the Christian Science Monitor has compared Pelikan to a "medieval craftsman" who "instead of shouldering huge gray stones into place, carving trefoils, or raising flying buttresses, . . . is building . . . the print equivalent of a Salisbury Cathedral or Chartres."

Defining Christian doctrine as "(w)hat the church of Jesus Christ believes, teaches, and confesses on the basis of the word of God," Pelikan documents the gradual changes in doctrine that have taken place over time, with dogma often following in the wake of practice rather than vice versa. Avoiding both relativism and the orthodox insistence upon "statically defined truth," Pelikan seeks instead what he calls an "avenue into the authentic continuity." For Pelikan, the history of the church reflects an ongoing effort to be "catholic," to maintain its identity and universality, remaining distinct from the world while "embrac(ing) nothing less than all mankind in its vision and its appeal." In each of his works, he strives to restore tradition, "the living faith of the dead," and to avoid traditionalism, "the dead faith of the living," always bearing in mind a motto, from Goethe's Faust: "what you have as heritage,/Take now as task;/For thus you will make it your own!"

Jaroslav Jan Pelikan Jr. was born in Akron, Ohio, on December 17, 1923, the son of Jaroslav Jan Pelikan Sr., a Lutheran minister from what is now Czechoslovakia, and Anna (Buzek) Pelikan, a schoolteacher who was born in Serbia (now part of Yugoslavia). Named for an older brother who died about a year before, at the age of only ten days, Pelikan was the oldest of three children to survive infancy. As he told Gerald Melnick of the *Yale Herald* (Summer 1987), Pelikan's consciousness of his dead brother has been an underlying force in his career. "By giving me his name, which I'm told by people in pediatric psychiatry is not a good idea, I'm sure in some sense (my parents) saw me as a surrogate for him," Pelikan said. "I unconsciously took that role of fulfilling the hopes they had for him as well as for me."

Scholarship and commitment to tradition were central to Pelikan's heritage. His paternal grandfather, the first Bishop of the Slovak Lutheran Synod of North America, immigrated to the United States in 1902 to escape the Austro-Hungarian imperial policy of Magyarization that pressured Slovaks to assimilate into Hungarian culture, and a granduncle was one of the last Lutheran bishops in pre-Communist Czechoslovakia. Pelikan's mother learned English by reading Emerson. In his preface to the sesquicentennial edition of Emerson's *Nature* (Beacon, 1985), Pelikan recalled his mother's Emersonian style of speech: "the characteristic love for abstract ideals, a persistent Neo-Platonic idealism, and a chronic unsureness (which I have inherited) about 'shall' and 'will.'" It was Emerson's *Representative Men* and Gibbon's *Decline and Fall of the Roman Empire* that inspired him to become a historian. Discovering that his son had taught himself to read at the age of two but lacked enough grip to hold a pen, Jaroslav Pelikan Sr. gave the precocious boy a typewriter.

Growing up in the polyglot immigrant neighborhoods of Pittsburgh and Chicago, Pelikan developed "a quick ear for the similarities and differences among languages" that has benefited his cross-cultural research. As a small boy, he acquired a basic proficiency in English, Slovak, Serbo-Croatian, Czech, and German, the first five of the dozen or more languages he uses today. Pelikan's manifest abilities at the age of six or seven attracted the attention of a researcher from Teacher's College, Columbia University, who tested him for a study of the then prevalent theory that speaking multiple languages in childhood causes stuttering and found that Pelikan, for one, was free of that problem.

By skipping several grades in school, Pelikan entered Oliver High School in Pittsburgh at the age of nine. Pelikan told Gerald Melnick that he was "by far the youngest and smallest child" in that public high school of about 4,000 students. "Fortunately, I was adopted by a bunch of black football players who made it clear to me that I was protected," he recalled. In 1936, when his family relocated to Chicago, Pelikan began attending Concordia Junior College, a Lutheran parochial boarding school in Fort Wayne, Indiana. Modeled after the German *Gymnasium* system of education, Concordia provided a program equivalent to four years of high school and two of college, including, in Pelikan's case, instruction in Latin, Greek, Hebrew, and Syriac. At about that time, Pelikan decided to specialize in Christian history, particularly Byzantine and Slavic church history.

After graduating from Concordia Junior College in 1942, Pelikan wanted to study at Charles University in Prague, or at the University of Toronto with the Neo-Thomist philosopher and historian Étienne Gilson, but he was unable to get permission to leave the country during World War II. Instead, he enrolled in Concordia Seminary in St. Louis, although he made it clear that he did not intend to become a Lutheran pastor. "The materials I knew I wanted to work on . . . happened to be the ones that are the content of the theological curriculum," Pelikan explained to Zöe Ingalls during an interview for the *Chronicle of Higher Education* (May 4, 1984).

After studying for five semesters at the seminary, Pelikan chose Chicago as the site for his obligatory one-year internship, in order to begin graduate work at the University of Chicago. Because the professor who taught Eastern church history left Chicago that term, he concentrated on the West, using Eastern history for purposes of comparison. Returning to Concordia in the spring of 1946, he arranged to finish his work towards his bachelor's degree that semester, a year early. At the same time he wrote his doctoral dissertation, an analysis of the relationship between the Lutheran and Hussite reformations. Pelikan received his B.D. degree from Concordia in June 1946 and his Ph.D. degree from the University of Chicago in the autumn of that year, at the age of twenty-two. "If a kid wants to come now and do that, you tell him to go home and grow up," he remarked during the *Chronicle of Higher Education* interview, praising the University of Chicago of the 1940s for being "hospitable to that kind of unconventional educational pattern."

While still enrolled in graduate school, Pelikan wrote an outline for his projected comprehensive history of religious doctrine. In 1950 he expanded that outline into an eighty-four-page survey and plan of research. Since then, for nearly forty years, he has maintained what he described for a reporter from the *New Yorker* (February 2, 1981) as a "built-in filing system" in his mind, with "metaphorical boxes" to organize information that might prove to be useful for his *magnum opus*.

Pelikan's first teaching position, beginning in 1946, was at Valparaiso University in Valparaiso, Indiana, where he remained for three years, leaving in 1949 to teach at his alma mater, Concordia Seminary. In the following year he completed his first book, *From Luther to Kierkegaard* (Concordia, 1950). He accepted a teaching post at another of his alma maters, the University of Chicago, in 1953. In *Fools for Christ* (Muhlenberg, 1955), Pelikan dealt with the ideals of the true, the good, and the beautiful in the culture of Western Christendom, as exemplified by St. Paul, Martin Luther, Sören Kierkegaard, Feodor Dostoyevsky, Friedrich Nietzsche, and Johann Sebastian Bach. As James Collins pointed out in "Philosophical Problems, 1955" (*Thought*, Spring 1956), his "survey of the year's best and most representative works in philosophy," Pelikan's "unusual" decision to include Nietzsche and Bach served "a dialectical purpose." Although he at first equated the holy with the beautiful, Nietzsche ultimately rejected the beautiful in Christianity, because it conflicted with his own concept of the superman, while Bach, on the other hand, was inspired in his masterworks by Christianity and the circumambient beauty of God's world.

For his next book, *The Riddle of Roman Catholicism* (Abingdon, 1959), Pelikan drew upon church history to illustrate the common ground between Protestants and Catholics, suggesting ways in which both communions could learn from ecumenical dialogue and renewed Christian unity. Rather than artificially suppressing doctrinal differences, mutual understanding would clarify the real issues of post-Reformation theology. "Protestants must begin to study" the obstacles to reunion "and to formulate an interpretation of them that will draw the line beyond which we are not prepared to yield," Pelikan wrote. "Unconditional surrender would be easy; but . . . this would be a denial of the whole Protestant heritage and a disservice to Roman Catholicism as well. It is harder, but it is also more honest, to formulate a policy for reunion."

Selling nearly 100,000 copies amidst controversy about the presidential campaign of Roman Catholic John F. Kennedy, *The Riddle of Roman Catholicism* threw a spotlight on Pelikan as a spokesman for the movement against religious prejudice. "Christianity needs confrontation with Judaism . . . (for) whenever Christian thought loses touch with Judaism, it loses touch with a part of itself," Pelikan said in an address delivered to regional directors of the National Conference of Christians and Jews in November 1959. By the same token, "[i]t is . . . impossible to make sense of either Judaism or Roman Catholicism . . . without making reference to the major movements that have broken off from them, and, in so doing, have changed them," and Protestantism "cannot understand itself without confrontation with . . . Catholicism." At Pelikan's urging, the NCCJ opened a center for "theological dialogue" among religious leaders.

Although Pelikan received some hate mail and indignant telephone calls from both Protestants and Catholics, reviews of his book were generally favorable, except that he was criticized for overestimating the potential for reform within the Catholic church. The Vatican Council II, convened in 1962, contained a declaration upholding the continuing validity of God's covenant with the Jews and produced "greater stress on the Bible and on the laity as not just (religious) consumers but as genuine participants." Although he was invited to participate in the ecumenical council, Pelikan declined, wishing to return to his vocation as an historian. "I live in the twentieth century, it's all I've got, but it's not where I work," Pelikan said in an interview with Louise Sweeney of the *Christian Sci-*

ence Monitor (May 5, 1983). "I don't (take) an active role in contemporary church debates . . . because there ought to be somebody who speaks to the other nineteen centuries."

In *The Shape of Death* (Abingdon, 1961), Pelikan explored the "core of the Christian faith," a "pessimism about life and optimism about God, and therefore hope for life in God" as manifested in the responses of five church fathers (Tatian, Clement of Alexandria, Cyprian, Origen, and Irenaeus) to the question of death and immortality. Since few answers about the subject were available in scripture, the early Christians combined Greek and Biblical ideas, developing several conflicting theories of the origin and destiny of souls.

In 1962 Pelikan was appointed Titus Street Professor of Ecclesiastical History at Yale Divinity School. Early in his tenure he wrote *Obedient Rebels* (Harper, 1964), using Paul Tillich's idea of "Catholic substance and Protestant principle" to present Luther as a conservative reformer who "believed he was standing for the same gospel for which the church had stood before it became corrupt and condemned him." Claude Welch of *Christian Century* (February 24, 1965) found *Obedient Rebels* "strikingly successful in bringing the whole man into view," although several scholars maintained that Pelikan underestimated the degree to which Luther rejected tradition in attempting to restore the church to its ancient purity.

Focusing upon the dilemmas faced by Christian humanists, Pelikan tried "to correlate Reformation thought with contemporary problems without doing violence to either" in *The Christian Intellectual* (Harper, 1966). In his *Church History* (December 1966) review, William A. Clebsch classified the book as "intellectual autobiography" with a Christian subject, "Olympian in mode, drawing on a strikingly deep knowledge of Reformation theology and expressing itself with facility and clarity." Although he conceded that the separate essays that form *The Christian Intellectual* were interesting, a London *Times Literary Supplement* (October 12, 1967) critic expressed dissatisfaction with Pelikan's organization of his material, on the ground that "he ha(d) read notes for three good books, not matter for one."

A similar charge was leveled at *Spirit versus Structure: Luther and the Institutions of the Church* (Harper, 1968) in *The Journal of Religion* (April 1970) by John J. Ryan, who faulted Pelikan for the "negligence, eccentricity, and . . . episodic" style of "a man who is almost too familiar with Luther." But Harold J. Grimm, writing in the *American Historical Review* (April 1969), appraised the book as "a substantial contribution to our understanding of Luther" for its analysis of Luther's gradual recognition that "inherited structures . . . could and should be made effective channels for the Spirit, but only in an *ecclesia semper reformanda*." According to the *Yale Review* (March 1969), the best feature of the book is its "purely historical" picture of "how institutional practices thrust themselves all unbidden on any movement" attempting "to burst the bonds of a moribund establishment."

Pelikan's next two books sketched out issues that were becoming crucial in his monumental five-volume work-in-progress, *The Christian Tradition*. *Development of Christian Doctrine: Some Historical Prolegomena* (Yale Univ. Press, 1969) presents a critical survey of various approaches to the history of doctrine, along with case studies of doctrinal development. Those examples depict the contribution of practices, such as infant baptism, to doctrine, such as the concept of original sin. *Historical Theology: Continuity and Change in Christian Doctrine* (Westminster, 1971) is "a work in conversation with" the German Protestant theologian Adolph von Harnack, whose *History of Dogma* has dominated the field for nearly a century. Pelikan wrote that his vision of doctrinal history is "more comprehensive" than Harnack's "in that the . . . expressions of doctrine in the form of dogmatic decrees and promulgations are not isolated from other expressions of doctrine such as preaching, instruction, exegesis, liturgy, and spirituality; more restrictive in that the range and content of the doctrines considered are . . . determined . . . by the development of those doctrines themselves."

Meanwhile continuing his work on *The Christian Tradition*, Pelikan considered publishing all five volumes at once, so that he could revise earlier volumes as later research prompted changes or additions. He decided to publish the volumes one at a time after Daniel J. Boorstin, the librarian of Congress, warned him, "You will die with the biggest filing cabinet in the world, and no book." The University of Chicago Press published volume 1, *The Emergence of the Catholic Tradition* (1971); volume 2, *The Spirit of Eastern Christendom* (1974); volume 3, *The Growth of Medieval Theology* (1978); and volume 4, *Reformation of Church and Dogma* (1984). The fifth volume will carry church history from 1700 to the present day.

According to Jack Forstman, author of an article called "On the History of Christian Doctrine: A Demurral to Jaroslav Pelikan," which appeared in *Journal of Religion* (January 1975), Pelikan's "disavowal of interest in debate or conflict in favor of a demonstration of continuity" renders his work a "mere recital of beliefs" that "tells us what was believed, taught, and confessed" but "does not, with rare exception, tell us why." Forstman argues that Pelikan's "tracing of continuity" is undermined by the "same tentativeness" with which Pelikan views theological systems at any point in time and observes that by asserting the centrality of both continuity and truth in "a truly Catholic understanding of the history of Christian doctrine," Pelikan ignores the possibility of "non-Catholic" interpretations of doctrinal history and leaves unanswered the question of "what effect (this choice has) on the eyes of the historian." But the Jesuit scholar George A. Maloney, writing in 1975 in the *Review for Religious*, called Pelikan "a master at economizing words" and praised him for "letting the primary sources speak for themselves" and for

not "projecting his own conclusions." Lars Thunberg contended in the *Journal of Religion* (January 1977) that Pelikan's conception of Christian doctrine is "similar to a building, . . . continuously under construction, not because it was wrongly constructed in certain periods of history, but because it stands in the middle of its own world and history. . . . Theologizing is an act which takes place within that building, and it happens by means of *language*, . . . the very brick stones of that same building." Given that analogy, Pelikan's emphasis on the "'*what*' of theology" becomes more comprehensible for Thunberg. "Formulations, although tentative, are . . . the only means of construction available in building, and rebuilding the house."

When he was chosen, in 1984, by the National Endowment for the Humanities to deliver the twelfth annual Jefferson Lecture, Pelikan spoke on "The Vindication of Tradition." Brother Jeffrey Gros, writing in the *Review for Religious* two years later, praised Pelikan for presenting "in very readable form" the lesson "that it is impossible to relive or repeat history, but the recovery of the tradition, the rootedness and grounding of the Christian life and faith, makes organic development possible."

In *Jesus Through the Centuries* (Yale Univ. Press, 1985), Pelikan traced the images of Jesus as reflections of various cultures and their influences on them. While celebrating the Divine Jesus ("It was not merely in the name of a great teacher, not even in the name of the greatest teacher who ever lived, that Justinian built Hagia Sophia in Constantinople and Johann Sebastian Bach composed the 'Mass in B-Minor'"), he reminds us that the remembrance of the human Jesus might have mitigated anti-Semitism. "Would there have been so many pogroms, would there have been an Auschwitz, if every Christian church and every Christian home had focused its devotion . . . on icons of Christ not only as Pantocrator but as *Rabbi Jeshua bar-Joseph*?"

Over the years, Jaroslav Pelikan has written a total of twenty-two books; edited more than three dozen other volumes, including a twenty-two-volume edition of *Luther's Works* (1955–70) and the three-volume *Twentieth-Century Theology in the Making* (Collins, 1969–71); and authored countless journal articles, essays, reviews, and introductions. Since 1972 he has been the Sterling Professor of History and Religious Studies at Yale. A former chairman of Yale's medieval studies program, director of the Division of the Humanities, acting dean (1973–74), and dean (1975–78) of the Yale Graduate School, Pelikan has been the chairman of the publications committee of the Yale University Press since 1979. As DeVane lecturer (1984–86), he gave interdisciplinary courses for the public on the religious implications of such figures as Dante, Bach, and Gibbon.

Currently chairman of the first international commission promoting cultural exchange between Czechoslovakia and the United States, Pelikan has also served as president of the American Society of

Church History, the International Congress of Luther Research, and the New England Conference on Graduate Education, and in official capacities with many other scholarly associations. A founding chairman of the Council of Scholars, Library of Congress (1980–83), Pelikan was mentioned in early 1987 as a "leading candidate" for librarian of Congress, an appointment that went to James H. Billington. The recipient of many awards, fellowships, academic medals, and over twenty-five honorary degrees, Pelikan is scheduled to deliver the Gifford lectures at the University of Aberdeen, Scotland in 1992–93, an honor previously tendered to Paul Tillich, Reinhold Niebuhr, Alfred North Whitehead, and John Dewey. In Pelikan's own words, that is the "closest thing to the Nobel prize" in the disciplines of religion and "natural philosophy."

Known to his friends as "Jary," Jaroslav Pelikan "has the features of a steel mill's shop steward—thick, blunt fingers; square, furrowed face; white hair with an irrepressible tuft," according to the New Yorker interviewer, but favors the tweedy clothing style of the Ivy League academic. His "robust voice that roll(s) with assurance" bears traces of a Midwestern accent. An ordained Lutheran minister since 1946, Pelikan was a part-time

pastor at his father's church for several years. Although he sees what he terms as a "tension" between his religious training and his scholarship, his faith remains a factor in his studies. "I believe less than I used to, but what I believe, I believe more," he told Louise Sweeney.

On June 9, 1946, Jaroslav Pelikan married the former Sylvia Burica, a teacher of Latin. They have three grown children. The Pelikans live on a forested hillside in suburban Hamden, Connecticut, several miles from Yale University, where they have a collection of over 100 representations of their namesake bird, including stuffed toys and a symbolic Christian bookplate. When not working in his study, separated from the rest of the house by a small moat, Pelikan enjoys sailing on Long Island Sound, attending classical concerts, and operating the ham radio that has been in the family since he was a small boy.

References: Christian Sci Mon B p6+ My 5 '83 por; Chronicle of Higher Education p4+ My '84 por; New Yorker 56:28+ F 2 '81; Newsweek 78:62 S 6 '71 por; Yale Herald p7 Summer '87 por; Contemporary Authors new rev vol 1 (1981); Grunfield, Patrick. Theologians at Work (1967); Who's Who in America, 1986–87

Poindexter, John M(arlan)

Aug. 12, 1936– Naval officer; former national security adviser. Address: b. Dept. of Naval Operations, the Pentagon, Washington, D.C.

One of the key figures in the imbroglio created by the secret sale of American arms to Iran and diversion of at least some of the proceeds to the Nicaraguan Contras is Rear Admiral John M. Poindexter, who served as President Ronald Reagan's national security adviser from December 1985 to November 1986. Poindexter, a career Navy man who urged greater reliance on limited military force in pursuing United States foreign policy objectives, was compelled to resign his White House post when his role in managing the politically controversial and probably illegal Iran-Contra operation was revealed. Testifying before Congress in the summer of 1987, the admiral corroborated President Reagan's avowal that he was kept in the dark about the Contra diversion scheme, but many legislators doubted that Poindexter was telling the whole truth when he claimed full responsibility for the initiative. The former White House official, facing possible indictment on criminal charges for his role in the Iran-Contra affair, tendered his resignation from the Navy in September 1987, effective October 1, but he was still on active duty in the Pentagon at the beginning of November 1987.

John Marlan Poindexter was born on August 12, 1936, in Washington, Indiana, to Marlan and Ellen Poindexter. He grew up in the small Midwestern

farming community of Odon, where his father owned the town's only bank, and attended Odon High School. The academic star of his class, which graduated in 1954, Poindexter was its president and valedictorian, and he also headed the student council, worked on the school yearbook and newspaper, and acted in school plays. The United States

Navy operated a munitions storage and transshipment facility in the nearby town of Crane, a circumstance that helped influence his decision to attend the Naval Academy in Annapolis, Maryland. At Annapolis, Poindexter achieved the rare distinction of graduating at the head of his 1958 class of 899 midshipmen while also serving as brigade commander, the academy's top leadership post. After receiving his officer's commission, Poindexter went on to take a doctoral degree in nuclear physics in 1964 at the California Institute of Technology, where he studied under the Nobel laureate Rudolf Mössbauer.

As distinguished as his academic performance, Poindexter's early naval career consisted in alternate shipboard and administrative assignments as he rose rapidly up the officer ranks. He put in sea duty in the Indian and Pacific oceans as an engineering officer in the 1960s, as a commander of the guided-missile cruiser *England* from 1974 until 1976, and as a commander of a destroyer squadron from 1978 until 1980. His administrative posts included assignments at the Pentagon as staff assistant to an assistant secretary of defense from 1966 until 1969, administrative assistant to Secretary of the Navy John Warner from 1971 until 1974, and duputy chief of naval education and training from 1980 until 1981. On land and sea, Poindexter earned a reputation as a cool-headed, highly loyal, by-the-book supporting officer, whose forte lay in his exceptional organizing and managerial skills, and his ability to translate complex orders and policy initiatives into practical terms with swift efficiency.

Those attributes helped to earn Poindexter an appointment as military assistant to the national security adviser, Richard Allen, in 1981 and a promotion to the rank of rear admiral in the same year. The National Security Council (NSC) is the White House agency that is responsible for synthesizing and coordinating the daily flow of national security information to the president, conducting crisis management, advising the chief executive on foreign policy options, and mediating conflicts between different government departments involved in foreign policy and national security issues. Under Richard Allen and his successor, William P. Clark, Poindexter urged greater reliance on military force to achieve American foreign policy objectives. In opposition to the views of Secretary of Defense Caspar Weinberger and the Joint Chiefs of Staff chairman, John Vessey, for example, he favored stepping up naval bombardments and other American military actions against Lebanese Shiite guerrillas in the summer of 1983 to support the Beirut government and retaliate against terrorist attacks on the United States. In October of that year, Poindexter played the key role in the strategic planning of the American military invasion that overthrew a leftist government in the tiny Caribbean island of Grenada. The successful Grenada invasion was generally credited with helping to restore President Reagan's political popularity, which had suffered from the Lebanese fiasco.

Poindexter's role in Grenada also contributed to his promotion to the position of deputy national security adviser and head of the council's crisis-preplanning group when Robert C. McFarlane took over the helm of the National Security Council in October 1983. The admiral continued to specialize in military operations while keeping a low public profile that caused his name to be little known outside of foreign policy circles. An exception to his deliberaly cultivated reticence occurred in October 1985, when President Reagan publicly congratulated Poindexter for successfully managing the in-air interception of an Egyptian airliner carrying a group of Palestinian hijackers who had killed an American citizen aboard the cruise ship *Achille Lauro*. The Reagan administration was anxious to apprehend and punish the hijackers as part of its policy to retaliate against international terrorism. The steel-nerved admiral is said to have impressed his National Security Council colleagues by sedately eating his dinner at his desk while directing the complex and risky operation over a transcontinental secure telephone line.

In December 1985 Poindexter, now a vice admiral, succeeded Robert C. McFarlane as President Reagan's national security adviser. Although Poindexter had McFarlane's backing for the post, the admiral's appointment was at first viewed as a bureaucratic coup for the White House chief of staff Donald T. Regan, Secretary of State George P. Shultz, and Secretary of Defense Caspar W. Weinberger, all of whom wanted a National Security Council chief who would be less contentious and publicly visible than McFarlane had been. The selection of Poindexter drew fire from far-right Reagan supporters, who had lobbied for a hard-line conservative ideologue. It also generated misgivings among members of Congress and political observers who questioned the admiral's experience and training in long-term strategic planning and his grasp of broad international political issues.

In office, Poindexter proved to be something more than the colorless technocrat that many had expected, although he did not publicly attempt to assert a major policy-making role. In fact, the policy-making power of the National Security Council appeared to be generally constrained by President Reagan's cabinet-style system of government, which allowed the executive departments to develop their own policy initiatives and largely limited the president to mediating disputes among them. Reagan's governing style contrasted with that of previous presidents, such as Richard Nixon and Jimmy Carter, who preferred to develop foreign policy initiatives at the White House with the help of a powerful national security adviser and then execute that policy through the departments. Political observers credited Poindexter with exercising a reasonable amount of policy initiative during his first months in office, particularly in promoting the use of limited military force as a diplomatic tool. Poindexter, who regularly put in eighty-hour weeks on the job, was given high grades for running an efficient office and for developing good relations with the disputatious secretaries of State and Defense and the mercurial Donald T. Regan. He proved less adept at negotiating with congressional leaders over national security matters—an essential part of his job—or at promoting the administration's views through the media, whose members came to refer to their rare contacts with the admiral as "Poindexter sightings."

Among his other initiatives as National Security Council chief, Poindexter took a more confrontational approach toward the Central American revolutionary crisis than his predecessor had done. He traveled to Honduras immediately after taking office to persuade its military to continue allowing the United States to supply the Honduran-based Contras who were fighting the Sandinistas in Nicaragua. On South Africa, on the other hand, he showed that he could be somewhat flexible as he helped Secretary of State Shultz to guide American policy away from the failed strategy of pursuing reforms through "constructive engagement" with the apartheid regime and to move it toward closer ties with black leaders, including indirect contacts with the banned African National Congress. But Poindexter opposed Shultz in urging President Reagan to veto a September 1986 bill imposing economic sanctions on South Africa; Congress then voted to override the veto in a rare foreign policy setback for Reagan.

Because Poindexter had only limited experience in United States-Soviet arms control issues, he generally confined his role to providing technical data and supporting logic to back up the bargaining positions of the United States. He was criticized for failing to prepare the American press and public thoroughly and to brief President Reagan adequately on the reasons for the administration's controversial decision in mid-1986 to stop abiding by the terms of the SALT II treaty. Learning from that mistake, Poindexter spearheaded the administration's campaign that fall to convince the public that the Reykjavik superpower summit held in October had been a success, even though a proposal for sweeping cuts in offensive nuclear weapons had foundered over the United States' insistence on developing the "Star Wars" antimissile space shield.

Poindexter also played a prominent role in moving American policy toward Libya from the imposition of diplomatic and economic sanctions to military confrontation with the radical nationalist Muammar el-Qaddafi regime, which the Reagan administration had accused of sponsoring terrorist acts against American targets. In early 1986, after the bombing attacks at the Rome and Vienna airports were linked to Libya, Poindexter developed a doctrine of "proportional response" to retaliate for terrorist acts by mounting escalating attacks on Libyan military installations. In March the United States Navy tested that doctrine by staging exercises in Libyan-claimed waters in the Gulf of Sidra and exchanging fire with Libyan patrol boats and shore installations. In the following month, after the Reagan administration wrongly accused the Qaddafi regime of sponsoring a bombing attack on a West Berlin disco frequented by American servicemen, Poindexter took the lead in convincing Reagan to mount a precision United States Air Force bombing attack on Qaddafi's home in Tripoli that was evidently intended to kill the Libyan leader. When those actions failed to topple Qaddafi, Poindexter organized a covert so-called "disinformation" program in August in consultation with the State and Defense departments and the CIA that was intended to disorient the Libyan leader and make him believe he was about to be attacked again by the United States or overthrown in a domestic coup. But the program backfired spectacularly two months later when news stories revealed that the White House had apparently planted false reports in the American press as part of the disinformation campaign. The reports suggested that the United States and Libya "were on a collision course" and that Qaddafi was planning a new onslaught of terrorist actions. Although Poindexter denied that the program had deliberately set out to deceive American journalists, administration statements on Libya were met with some degree of incredulity after that.

The Libyan disinformation caper, however, quickly faded into irrelevance as the so-called Irangate scandal landed on the front pages in November 1986, engulfing the Reagan administration in its gravest political crisis to date. The fast-breaking story of devious international intrigue came to light when a Lebanese magazine reported that the Unites States had sold spare parts and ammunition for tanks and fighter planes to Iran the previous September following a secret visit to Teheran by the former national security adviser, Robert C. McFarlane. After at first denying the report, which was later corroborated by leaked American intelligence information and statements by Iranian leaders, President Reagan finally admitted in the following weeks that he had indeed authorized secret arms shipments to Iran with the aim of establishing contact with moderates in the Iranian leadership and securing Iran's help in freeing American hostages held by pro-Iranian Shiite Muslim militants in Lebanon. Administration officials later revealed that the operation was managed by the National Security Council with the assistance of the Central Intelligence Agency and a third country later identified as Israel; that the arms shipments had been underway for more than eighteen months, and that a total of some 12,000 TOW antitank and 235 Hawk antiaircraft missiles had been sold to Iran. A final twist to the puzzle came to light on November 25, when the attorney general, Edwin Meese, revealed that Poindexter's aide for Central American affairs, Lt. Col. Oliver North, had diverted millions of dollars in profits from the arms sales to a Swiss bank account held for the Contras, and that Poindexter had known of and condoned the diversion.

Those revelations raised a host of legal and political problems for the Reagan administration. The paying of ransom for hostages and the arming of

Iran, a country accused of sponsoring terrorism, contravened official United States policy, and the covert arms shipments appeared to violate the congressional reporting requirements of the Arms Export Control Act and the 1974 Hughes-Ryan covert action notification amendment. Moreover, the Contra diversion also seemed to bypass the Boland amendments, which prohibited United States military aid to the Contras in 1985 and early 1986. As shock waves reverberated through Congress and the American people, President Reagan tried to control the political damage, contending that no laws had been broken. He ordered a stop to the Iran arms sales, and, insisting that he knew nothing of the Contra diversion, fired North and accepted Poindexter's resignation as national security adviser on November 25. Reagan then appointed a panel headed by former Senator John Tower to investigate the incident and asked the Justice Department to appoint an independent special prosecutor to probe possible criminal violations. Meanwhile, Congress set about organizing its own select investigatory committees. When he was summoned to appear for preliminary questioning before the Senate and House intelligence committees in December, Poindexter invoked the Fifth Amendment and refused to testify on the "Irangate" affair, thus becoming the first active-duty admiral in American history to withhold congressional testimony on the grounds that he might incriminate himself.

In July 1987, after being granted limited immunity from prosecution—which compelled him to testify by stipulating that none of his own testimony could be used against him—Poindexter finally appeared as a witness before the Senate and House select committees holding joint televised hearings on the Iran-Contra issue. Testifying for six days with a calm detachment that contrasted sharply with North's impassioned rhetoric on the stand, Poindexter corroborated Reagan's contention that he had not known of the diversion of Iranian arms profits to the Contras. Poindexter testified that he approved of North's covert diversion idea in February 1986, and, aware of the political repercussions that would ensue if it ever became public knowledge, deliberately decided not to inform Reagan about the matter to give him "some future deniability." Although he declared that "the buck stops here with me" on the diversion issue, he insisted that he had not usurped presidential policy-making prerogatives, but had simply tried to implement Reagan's clearly expressed wish to find ways to help the Contras survive during a period when Congress had "abandoned" them. Poindexter added that he believed that Reagan would have approved of the operation had he known about it and that he himself believed the Contra supply operation did not violate the Boland amendment because the law did not apply to the National Security Council. But he acknowledged that both he and North had deliberately "withheld information" and misled congressional committees inquiring into other National Security Council efforts to solicit aid for the Contras from private donors and third countries in 1986.

In his testimony, Poindexter admitted that he had expanded the initiative that he had inherited from Robert C. McFarlane. He also revealed that he had destroyed a signed presidential "finding" authorizing a November 1985 arms shipment when the Iran-Contra scandal became public because the document showed the sale as a straight arms-for-hostages deal rather than as part of the broad diplomatic initiative that the Reagan administration contended it was. Poindexter admitted taking other possibly illegal actions to hide the program from the public, including blocking a 1986 Justice Department investigation of the Southern Air Transport company's link to the Contra supply operation and allowing North to shred scores of documents relating to the operation after the legal probe had begun.

Despite those admissions, Poindexter stoutly defended the Iran-Contra scheme and his own activities therein. He credited the arms shipments with securing the release of two hostages, the Rev. Lawrence Martin Jenco and Daniel Jacobsen, and declared that the program might well have rescued other American hostages and improved ties with Teheran had it gone on undetected. Poindexter justified the circumventing of Congress and the foreign policy departmental bureaucracies on grounds of security and expediency, adding that he believed Congress had encroached unfairly on presidential foreign policy prerogatives. At the end of his testimony Poindexter declared, "I don't have any regrets for anything I did," and remarked that he still thought his actions had been "in the long-term interests of the country."

Members of the Iran-Contra select committees from both political parties reacted to Poindexter's testimony with shock and disbelief. His lack of chagrin and bland insistence on the expediency of occasionally conducting secret foreign policy operations out of the purview of Congress or even of the president provoked testy responses from legislators who questioned his understanding of and commitment to constitutional democracy. Committee members also expressed some reservations about whether Poindexter had told the whole truth, especially in asserting that he had not sought presidential approval for North's Contra diversion scheme. Several legislators noted that keeping such a key policy initiative from the president seemed entirely out of character for a man who has been known throughout his career as a loyal and competent rulebook officer who respected authority. A suspicion that Poindexter may have played the role of "designated scapegoat" in the Irangate scandal was fueled by North's testimony that he had discussed just such a scenario with CIA director William Casey and Poindexter's own remark to the committee that "it's always the responsibility of a staff to protect their leader." Poindexter's credibility was also undermined by his many memory lapses (despite a record of Navy fitness reports commending his excellent memory for details), twists in logic and semantics, and evident reluctance to say anything at all that might reflect adversely on the president. A *New York Times*/CBS poll conducted while Poindexter was giving testimony showed that a majority of Americans believed that the admiral had not told the truth when he said the president was ignorant of the diversion. In the absence of a "smoking gun," or direct evidence linking Reagan to the diversion scheme, however, Poindexter's testimony was deemed critical in removing even the remote possibility that the president might be impeached over the Iran-Contra affair. But Poindexter's story was still considered politically damaging to Reagan since it highlighted the president's failure to exercise accountability and control over his White House subordinates.

When he left the White House, Poindexter was demoted from vice admiral, a three-star rank, to two-star rear admiral. In March 1987 he accepted a Pentagon post as strategic planner for Carlyle Trost, the chief of naval operations. He has requested retirement with three-star rank—a status being held in abeyance pending the outcome of the special prosecutor's investigation.

Meanwhile, a federal grand jury that was convoked by Lawrence E. Walsh, the Irangate special prosecutor, advised Poindexter in the summer of 1987 that he was a main target of its criminal investigation. If he is indicted, he will face several possible charges related to the diversion of the funds from the Iranian arms sales to the Nicaraguan Contras. They included conspiracy to defraud the federal government, obstruction of justice, and the making of false statements to a government agency—the Congress of the United States of America.

John Marlan Poindexter is a round-faced man of medium build with a high domed forehead. His associates characterize him as serene, reserved, highly intelligent, and "a very pleasant guy," though he also has a reputation for being aloof and abrupt with his subordinates. By all accounts, Poindexter possesses the ideal temperament to weather a sudden reversal of fortune, and he appears to have managed his personal crisis with aplomb. Since June 6, 1958 he had been married to the former Linda Anne Goodwin, a colonel's daughter who recently became an Episcopal priest. The couple has five sons: Daniel, Alan, Mark, Thomas, and Joseph. The Poindexters live in the Washington, D.C. suburb of Rockville, Maryland.

References: *Chicago Tribune* V p1+ Mr 9 '87 pors; *Insight* 2:22+ F 10 '86 pors; *N Y Times* I p24 S 23 '86 por; *Newsweek* 107:24 Ap 21 '86 por; *People* 26:34+ O 13 '86 pors; *Time* 130:9+ Jl 27 '87 pors; *U.S. News* 100:33 Je 16 '86 pors; *Who's Who in America, 1982–83*

Powell, Michael

Sept. 30, 1905– British motion picture director. Address: Lee Cottages, Avening, Tetbury, Gloucestershire, England

For fifty years Michael Powell has been one of the most distinctive and distinguished of British film directors. In collaboration with his friend and associate Emeric Pressburger, and in his own richly imaginative and individualistic films, he redefined the scope of filmmaking to embrace all the arts in a manner unique to his generation. Widely respected in the 1940s for such now-classic motion pictures as *The Life and Death of Colonel Blimp*, *A Matter of Life and Death*, and *The Red Shoes*, he has since become the revered mentor of such iconoclastic American directors as Martin Scorsese and Francis Ford Coppola.

The younger of the two sons of Thomas William and Mabel (Corbett) Powell, Michael Latham Powell was born on September 30, 1905, in Bekesbourne, a village about five miles from Canterbury, England. During World War I, his father, a hop farmer, was sent to France by the Royal Army Service Corps to help grow food for the army. At the war's end, Thomas Powell stayed on in France as the proprietor of a hotel in Cap Ferrat, on the Riviera. Throughout this period, except for occasional visits to France, Michael and his brother, John Miles, who was to die in 1918 of peritonitis, remained with their mother in England.

Michael Powell was a shy child, prone to daydreaming and interested in everything around him, from the beauty of the Kentish countryside to the architecture of Canterbury Cathedral. Having learned to read at the age of five, he devoured the

works of Louisa May Alcott, H. G. Wells, G. K. Chesterton, and Hilaire Belloc, among many other writers, as well as countless periodicals. By the time he enrolled at King's School, Canterbury in 1916, he was, in his words, a "cultivated" and "disconcerting little boy." In the dormitory late at night, he often entertained his fellow students by reciting poems or telling some of the many stories and tales that he knew by heart. "I was even then an interpreter rather than an originator," Powell wrote in his autobiography *A Life in Movies* (Heinemann, 1986; Knopf, 1987). "I was a good narrator. My mother's readings aloud had taught me the value of pause, of change of voice, of change of speed."

In 1918 Powell transferred from King's School to Dulwich College, a private secondary school in a southeastern London suburb. It was while he was a student there that he became interested in filmmaking, after reading an article about location shooting in England in the first issue of the monthly magazine *Picturegoer*. Enchanted by the new medium and the way in which it effectively combined literature, art, architecture, history, and theatre, Powell haunted the local movie houses and gradually began to develop an understanding of the film director's craft, particularly through a close scrutiny of such masterpieces as D. W. Griffith's *Intolerance*.

After his parents agreed to divorce in 1921, Powell left school without completing his degree and went to work as a clerk at a branch of the National Provincial Bank, where he remained for the next three years. Feeling that he might, in his words, be "caught for life" unless he acted quickly, on his next visit to his father in France, Powell wangled a job as a grip with a film crew working at Victorine Studios in nearby Nice, under the American director Rex Ingram (not to be confused with the black American actor Rex Ingram, who played the genie in Powell's *Thief of Bagdad*). Over the next two years, he learned virtually every practical aspect of filmmaking, from set decoration to editing. He even appeared in comic relief roles in Ingram's *The Magician* (1926) and *The Garden of Allah* (1927). He left Ingram in 1927 to accept a two-year contract with Harry Lachman, the head of Ingram's film unit, to star in and assist in the filming of a series of silent two-reel comedies called *Travelaughs*. The arrival of synchronized sound, however, forced Lachman to scrap the project after only six months of production.

Powell returned to England in January 1928 and, with Lachman's help, secured a position as a reader in the story department of British International Pictures at Elstree. Finding the story department to be, in his words, "a Sargasso Sea of hopeful scriptwriters," he escaped to the stills department, where he quickly found a niche for himself. His first assignment was to shoot the publicity stills for *Champagne* (1928), directed by Alfred Hitchcock, with whom he soon developed a close friendship. Powell's first memorable contribution to cinema came when he collaborated with Hitchcock on the script for *Blackmail* (1929). At his suggestion, Hitchcock replaced a routine chase through the streets of London with a finale atop the glass-domed roof of the British Museum Reading Room. The use of an exotic locale in the climactic sequence worked so well that it became Hitchcock's trademark.

In June of 1930 Powell was hired by the American producer Jerome Jackson, for whom he had recut a silent film the previous year, to adapt the nineteenth-century stage classic *Caste* for the screen. He ended up as the (uncredited) codirector, with Campbell Gullen, of the movie and so impressed Jackson that the producer allowed him to direct a film of his own.

The first movie to bear the credit "directed by Michael Powell" was *Two Crowded Hours* (1931), a forty-three-minute thriller about an escaped murderer's quest for revenge against his accusers. *Two Crowded Hours* was a "quota quickie," one of the scores of low-budget films produced yearly in Britain with American financing in order to meet the requirements of Britain's 1927 Cinematograph Films Act, which stipulated that a certain percentage of the pictures shown in British movie theatres be made in Britain.

Between 1931 and 1936 Powell made twenty-two quota quickies, mostly in association with Jackson, with whom he had formed a production company, Westminster Films, in 1932. With such films as *Born Lucky* (1932), *Red Ensign* (1934), and *Crown v. Stevens* (1936), he quickly developed a reputation for quality unique among poverty-row directors. His thrillers were clever and laced with unexpected humor, and all of his quota movies, whether thrillers or comedies of manners, looked like full-length feature films despite their twelve-day shooting schedules and often predictable plot lines.

Notwithstanding his success in the quota film market, by the mid-1930s Powell had begun to despair of ever moving up to major motion pictures. Then, in 1936, he managed to persuade Joe Rock, an American ex-vaudevillian for whom he had made the low-budget thriller *The Face Behind the Mask* (1936), to finance a film about depopulation and hardship in the tiny island fishing communities off the western coast of Scotland. The subject had intrigued Powell since 1930, when he had come across a newspaper account about the evacuation of St. Kilda after most of the younger citizens had deserted the desolate island in search of steady jobs on the mainland. Working with a handpicked cast and crew, Powell shot the film, from his own screenplay, on the remote island of Foula, in the Shetlands. When he completed shooting, in October 1936, he had 200,000 feet of film telling a story of tremendous power and poignancy, about simple, independent people battling each other and a changing world, and ultimately deciding to abandon the lives they had known.

Edited down to 8,000 feet (seventy-four minutes), *The Edge of the World* premiered in London in September 1937 to an enthusiastic critical response. C. A. Lejeune, writing in the London *Observer*, ranked the film "up somewhere near the top of the English classics," and Basil Wright, in his review for *Cinema*, heralded it as the first step in a new direction for British cinema, away from "vast production costs, exotic casts, and cosmopolitan scenarios." The first of Powell's films to be distributed in the United States, *The Edge of the World* opened in New York City in September 1938 to similarly favorable notices. Frank S. Nugent of the *New York Times* (September 12, 1938), for example, called the movie "one of the most beautifully photographed, most unusual and most dramatic films England has given us this year—and England has sent over a number of great ones." It was later chosen by the National Board of Review as one of the best foreign films of 1938.

On the strength of *The Edge of the World*, Alexander Korda, the founder and head of London Films, offered Michael Powell a one-year contract as a staff director. Joining the company in 1937, Powell spent most of the summer traveling in Iraq, India, and Burma scouting locations for a proposed film, tentatively called "Burmese Silver." He was called home in September, however, to direct *The Spy in Black*, a thriller intended as a vehicle for two of Korda's top stars, Conrad Veidt and Valerie Hobson. When it became clear that the book on which the script was based had no suitable roles for either performer, Powell and the assigned screenwriter, Emeric Pressburger, decided to start over with a story of their own.

Released on August 12, 1939, *The Spy in Black* became one of the top box-office attractions of the year in Britain. Its tale of German spies (albeit of World War I vintage) trying to sabotage the British fleet anchored in the Orkneys was very much of the moment in the early days of World War II. It became even more topical when a German submarine actually torpedoed a British battleship at anchor midway through the run. With its expressionistic sets, fluid camera work, and unusual blend of cynicism, eroticism, and suspense, *The Spy in Black* was the most stylistically advanced of Powell's films to that date.

Powell was released from his contract with Korda before the premiere of *The Spy in Black*, but he was soon called back to work on what was to be the grandest of all of Korda's productions, *The Thief of Bagdad*. Regarded by many moviegoers and critics alike as the finest fantasy film ever made, *The Thief of Bagdad* was officially the work of Powell, Tim Whelan, and Ludwig Berger, but the most memorable sequences—the arrival of the ship in the harbor, the bazaar in Basra, Sabu's encounter with the genie, and the love scenes between Conrad Veidt and June Duprez—were all Powell's. Released in December 1940, it was hailed by Bosley Crowther in the *New York Times* (December 6, 1940) as "next to *Fantasia* . . . the most beguiling and wondrous film of this troubled season." For its breathtaking succession of fairy-tale illustrations brought to life, *The Thief of Bagdad* earned four Academy Awards, including those for best color cinematography and best special effects.

Powell finished his work on *The Thief of Bagdad* on September 3, 1939, the day war was declared between Britain and Germany. He spent the next month rushing to complete *The Lion Has Wings*, a feature-length morale-booster about the purposeful resolve of the RAF, then rejoined Emeric Pressburger to begin work on *Contraband*, a follow-up to *The Spy in Black* that once again featured Conrad Veidt and Valerie Hobson. A suspenseful melodrama with Hitchcockian overtones, *Contraband* (1940) proved to be as commercially successful as its predecessor in both England and the United States, where it was distributed by United Artists under the title *Blackout*.

Powell's next movie, *Forty-Ninth Parallel* (1941), which was produced with the financial support of the Ministry of Information, became one of the most popular British films of the war. An epic allegory with an all-star cast, including Laurence Olivier, Leslie Howard, and Anton Walbrook, and a huge cinematic canvas, it followed a handful of German sailors, who had been stranded in hostile territory after the sinking of their submarine off the coast of eastern Canada, as they try to make their way through Canada to the safety of a still-neutral United States. According to the film historian George Perry, the thoughtful and intelligent *Forty-Ninth Parallel* greatly enhanced the prestige of British films abroad, particularly in the United States, where, under the title *The Invaders*, it won for Pressburger an Academy Award for the best original story of 1942.

With their share of the profits from *Forty-Ninth Parallel*, Powell and Pressburger decided to set up their own production company, The Archers, through which they could develop, write, direct, and produce films jointly, as equal partners. Between 1943 and 1951 The Archers' distinctive arrow-onto-target logotype and the credit "written, produced, and directed by Michael Powell and Emeric Pressburger" adorned some of the most technically accomplished and intellectually stimulating movies then being made, ranging from such large-scale, visually stunning Technicolor efforts as *The Life and Death of Colonel Blimp* (1943), a sprawling account of an archetypal British officer's career from the Boer War to World War II, to smaller, more intimate, black-and-white productions, like *I Know Where I'm Going* (1945), an enigmatic romance steeped in the mystical relationship between the British people and their land and legends. Among The Archers' other early credits were the 1943 recruiting film *The Volunteer* and a series of motion pictures that explored the moral, emotional, and psychological aspects of the war, including *A Canterbury Tale* (1944), an episodic recounting of the wartime pilgrimages of several people to the great cathedral that the critic Gavin Millar has described, in the *London Review of Books* (January 8, 1987), as "conceivably the most profoundly and self-consciously patriotic English film ever made."

The Archers' success was immediate, but not without controversy that occasionally spread outside cinematic circles. *The Life and Death of Colonel Blimp*, for example, so offended the Ministry of Information, the War Office, and, as documents discovered in 1979 revealed, Prime Minister Winston Churchill, that they tried to suppress its release. Among other things, the government objected to the film's implicit criticism of the entrenched and outmoded military establishment and to the fact that the movie's message—that total war was the only way to defeat the Nazis—was delivered by a character who was a German refugee. Although there was no official banning of *Colonel Blimp*, the Ministry of Information brought pressure upon J. Arthur Rank, the film's distributor, to block its release abroad. The dispute over *Colonel Blimp* appears to have been quickly forgotten, for in 1946 The Archers' *A Matter of Life and Death* (called *Stairway to Heaven* in the United States), a fantasy-drama about an injured airman who, while undergoing surgery, imagines that he is on trial for his life in a celestial court, became the first movie ever chosen for a Royal Command Performance.

Powell and Pressburger once again found themselves embroiled in controversy with the release, in 1947, of *Black Narcissus*, a psychological study of the physical and spiritual trials of a group of Anglican nuns running a mission school and hospital in the Himalayas. Disturbed by the unusual mix of faith, eroticism, and madness in scenes of striking visual beauty, the Catholic Legion of Decency forced the distributor to cut thirteen minutes from the film before its American release. *Black Narcissus* was subsequently awarded Oscars for art direction and color cinematography.

The Archers' work culminated in *The Red Shoes* (1948), a drama about an ambitious ballerina (played by Moira Shearer) that is also an allegory about the price of selfless dedication to art. "Here is a visual and emotional comprehension of all the grace and rhythm and power of the ballet," wrote Bosley Crowther in his review for the *New York Times* (October 23, 1948). "Here is the color and the excitement, the strange intoxication of the dancer's life. And here is the rapture and the heartbreak which only the passionate and the devoted can know." The most popular of Powell's films, during its initial release *The Red Shoes* played for more than two years at the same first-run movie theatre in New York. Among its many honors were Academy Award nominations for best picture and best original story and Oscars for color art direction and for Brian Easdale's musical score.

The Red Shoes represented a creative and commercial peak for Powell and Pressburger that they were never again able to achieve. Over the three years that followed, the postwar retrenchment in the British film industry made it increasingly difficult for the pair to secure financial backing for big-budget Technicolor extravaganzas, and two of their most ambitious projects, *The Elusive Pimpernel* (1950) and *Gone To Earth* (1950), were subjected to extensive revisions on the orders of their American coproducers, Samuel Goldwyn and David O. Selznick, respectively. Finally, in 1951,

Powell and Pressburger released *The Tales Of Hoffmann*, their long-awaited follow-up to *The Red Shoes*. A daring mix of ballet and opera, with choreography by Frederick Ashton and musical direction by Sir Thomas Beecham, *The Tales of Hoffman* reunited *Red Shoes* stars Moira Shearer, Robert Helpmann, Leonid Massine, and Ludmilla Tcherina. The initial notices were unfailingly enthusiastic, but without its illustrious predecessor's backstage melodrama, *Hoffmann* proved to be too cold and inaccessible for many moviegoers. A notorious financial flop, it marked the end of The Archers' most creative period.

The Archers ceased production for three years after the *Hoffmann* debacle, while Powell and Pressburger worked on several projects that never materialized, among them a twenty-hour film cycle developed around various works by Pablo Picasso, Igor Stravinsky, Graham Sutherland, and Dylan Thomas, for which Powell was unable to raise production funds, and a proposed film version of *The Tempest* that was to star Moira Shearer as Ariel and Sir John Gielgud as Prospero. They resumed production in 1955 with *Oh Rosalinda!!*, a curious updating of *Die Fledermaus*, complete with new lyrics, that dropped out of sight within weeks of its release. After making two more films, *The Battle of the River Plate*, a naval adventure known in the United States as *Pursuit of the Graf Spee*, and the routine wartime drama *Ill Met by Moonlight*, Powell and Pressburger dissolved The Archers in 1957.

Striking out on his own, Powell resumed directing in 1959 with the British-Spanish coproduction *Luna de Miel* (*Honeymoon*), a shapeless ballet film that was ignored in Britain despite its winning a special prize at the 1959 Cannes Film Festival. Later that year Powell and screenwriter Leo Marks collaborated on the film *Peeping Tom* (1960), a psychological thriller about a psychotic photographer who murders his models in order to film their death throes. Savaged by the critics, who denounced it as "crude," "sadistic," and "necrophilic," *Peeping Tom* was quickly withdrawn from theatres by its distributor, Anglo Amalgamated. "The controversy left my career practically in ruins," Powell said years later, as quoted in *Cinefantastique* (Spring 1980). "I was already regarded as unpredictable, and this was all it took."

His film career effectively at an end, Powell worked sporadically in television, directing episodes of various British and American series, including *Espionage*, *The Defenders*, and *The Nurses*. He also made a one-hour film of Bartók's *Bluebeard's Castle* in Yugoslavia, in association with Süddeutscher Rundfunk, and two features in Australia, *They're A Weird Mob* (1966) and *Age Of Consent* (1969), and he coproduced an espionage spoof entitled *Sebastian* (1968), starring Dirk Bogarde.

Apart from occasional stints as a visiting lecturer at film schools in Britain and the United States, by the early 1970s Powell was in semiretirement. It was the film schools and film-revival theatres, particularly in the United States, that eventually helped to rescue the director from oblivion. A new generation of filmmakers—most notably Martin Scorsese and Francis Ford Coppola—publicly credited much of their inspiration to Powell's films, and film critics and historians who had grown up with *The Thief of Bagdad* and *The Red Shoes* championed his work, giving it new commercial life. A perennial favorite in America's art houses, *The Red Shoes* climbed to twenty-second place on *Variety's* 1972 list of the seventy-five top-grossing movies of all time. In 1979 *The Thief of Bagdad* was re-released, and later in the same year, *Peeping Tom* was given its first uncut American showing at the New York Film Festival, where it scored a notable success.

In 1980 Powell was appointed senior director-in-residence at Francis Ford Coppola's Zoetrope Studios. Later in the year he and Pressburger were honored at the Museum of Modern Art in New York with a two-month retrospective of their work. A highlight of that series was the American premiere of *Return to the Edge of the World,* Powell's film of his 1978 return to Foula with the surviving cast and crew of *Edge of the World.* The MOMA retrospective was followed by similar tributes at the National Film Theatre in London, the Art Institute of Chicago, and the Athens International Film Festival. In the mid-1980s the British Film Institute, of which Powell was made a fellow in 1983, released restored editions of the director's classic films of the 1940s.

Michael Powell—"Mickey" to his friends and associates—is a short, stocky man with piercing blue eyes and a wispy moustache. He has been bald since the 1940s. Known for his wry sense of humor, he has said that his favorite recreation is "leaning on gates," but he also enjoys reading, fishing, and taking long walks in the country. Not counting an impulsive and short-lived early marriage in 1927, Powell has been married twice. From his marriage to the former Frankie Reidy, whom he wed on July 1, 1943, he has two sons, Kevin and Columba. Following her death, he married Thelma Schoonmaker, a film editor who won an Oscar for her work on Martin Scorsese's *Raging Bull,* on May 19, 1984. The Powells divide their time between homes in Avening, near Tetbury, England, and in San Quentin, California. In addition to his autobiography, Powell is the author of several books, including *200,000 Feet on Foula* (Faber & Faber, 1938), which was published in the same year in the United States by Dutton under the title *200,000 Feet: The Edge of the World, A Waiting Game* (Joseph, 1975; St. Martin's, 1976), and *The Red Shoes* (Avon, 1978).

References: Am Film 6:47+ N '80 por; Films in Review 31:415+ Ag/S '80 por; Christie, Ian. Powell, Pressburger, and Others (1978), Arrow of Desire: The Films of Michael Powell and Emeric Pressburger (1986); Who's Who, 1987–88

Price, (Edward) Reynolds

Feb. 1, 1933– Writer; educator. Address: b. c/o Harriet Wasserman Literary Agency, Inc., 230 E. 48th St., New York City, N.Y. 10014; h. 4813 Duke Station, Durham, N.C. 27706

The novelist, critic, and educator Reynolds Price once described his writing as a medium for "comprehension, control, and celebration of the urgent mysteries (the people I love, those I hate, myself, things, God) through the making of stories which transmute the lethal disorder of experience into well-formed but honest and useful public objects—mirrors, microscopes, telescopes but also shields." His "public objects" have been accepted and admired as such since the beginning of his career, although they have also been misunderstood, he feels, by literary taxonomists who immediately classified him as a regionalist and spiritual descendant of William Faulkner on the publication of his first novel, *A Long and Happy Life,* in 1962. His succeeding works of fiction, all published by Atheneum, include: *A Generous Man* (1966), *Love and Work* (1968), and *The Surface of the Earth* (1975). Like his first novel, all have been set in the American South, and have consistently divided critics, who have both praised and censured their fatalistic obsession with generational guilt and

their fusion of rhetoric with earthy wit and homely aphorism.

In the 1970s, when ironic novels without regional settings came into vogue on the American literary scene, Price's reputation, like that of Southern writing in general, seemed to go into decline, and one book reviewer, Paul Gray of *Time* magazine, perceived Price as occupying an obsolescent post—that of "Southern-writer-in-residence." Such criticisms, Price has noted, are "like complaining that all the great Victorian novels were about England." With the publication, in 1986, of his most recent novel, *Kate Vaiden*, Price seemed to have finally succeeded in discarding the regionalist label and to have forced most critics to accept Robert Penn Warren's assessment of him as "a restless craftsman, one of our finest novelists." Since 1977 Price has been the James B. Duke Professor of English at Duke University.

In an autobiographical sketch that he prepared for *World Authors 1950–1970*, Edward Reynolds Price described Macon, North Carolina, where he was born on February 1, 1933, as "a town of 227 cotton and tobacco farmers nailed to the flat red land at the pit of the Great Depression." His father, William Solomon Price, sold insurance and electrical appliances in the series of semirural North Carolina towns where Price was raised after the family lost its original home. His mother, Elizabeth (Rodwell) Price, the inspiration for his character Kate Vaiden, "wanted very much to be a man," as Price told the *Washington Post*'s Michael Specter (September 7, 1986). "She wanted to have the kinds of freedom and thrust men had. And she reached out and got as much of it as she could in the world. She was forever larking off someplace. We were terrifically poor during the Depression, but she always managed to get the $100 to have a little beat-up Ford in the backyard." Price recalls being somewhat cut off from his peers by his early interests in painting and drawing,—encouraged by an eighth grade teacher who often painted with him,—and relative lack of ability in "kid things" such as sports. Away from his art work he spent "hundreds of solitary days with books or in woods up trees." In adolescence he turned from drawing and painting to writing, feeling, as he has recalled, that his drawings were "merely copies" and that words, always available in a family that was "a ceaseless hive of oral narrative," were the best tools for "exploring the genuine mysteries and fears that had by now begun to rise [within him] in full strength and size." He wrote a play about Columbus and a string of love poems "full of Pearls, Opals, [and] Beryls" that won praise from junior high school teachers. He told Michael Specter: "Like most kids, I just kept going in the direction the praise pushed me."

Price's writing ability helped to win him an Angier Duke scholarship to Duke University in Durham, North Carolina, in 1951, after his graduation from Broughton High School in Raleigh. At Duke he wrote two of the short stories that would later appear in his collection *Names and Faces of Heroes* (1963). He met the writer he claims as his greatest influence, Eudora Welty, when she came to speak at Duke in 1955, his senior year. It was the beginning of an informal apprenticeship and a lifelong friendship. "One of the things she showed me as a writer," Price told Specter, "was that the kinds of people I had grown up with were the kinds of people one could write marvelous fiction about."

After graduating from Duke University with a B.A. degree *summa cum laude* and with membership in Phi Beta Kappa, Price went to England for three years, studying at Merton College, Oxford University, on a Rhodes scholarship. In Great Britain he continued to receive encouragement for his work from such notables as Stephen Spender and W. H. Auden. While at Oxford he wrote a thesis on the role of the chorus in John Milton's *Samson Agonistes* and continued to produce short stories, some of which Stephen Spender published in the magazine *Encounter*.

In 1958 Reynolds Price returned to Duke University and joined the faculty of its English department. Except for his visiting professorships elsewhere and his few trips abroad (including another year at Oxford in 1962), he has remained there ever since. According to one of his star students, the novelist Anne Tyler, who wrote a reminiscent article about him for *Vanity Fair* (July 1986), he became something of a romantic figure on campus, wearing a long garment tossed about his shoulders that Miss Tyler remembers as "a long black cape with a scarlet lining" and making an impact as a teacher that made him seem "older than God." Anne Tyler believes that Reynolds Price has "the great good fortune to know his place, geographically speaking . . . he has a feeling for the exact spot on earth that will properly contain him, and he has never let himself be lured away from it any longer than necessary."

In his free time, Price began a short story that at the end of two years he developed into a novel, *A Long and Happy Life* (1962), which is set among the folk and fauna of eastern North Carolina. Its title sums up the aspirations of his spunky and naive young heroine, Rosacoke Mustian, who becomes pregnant after a sexual encounter with a young man, Wesley Beavers, whom she has loved for years but who is so indifferent to her that he fails to recall her name correctly immediately after their tryst. Their marriage is brought about not, as she had hoped, by love but by the pregnancy.

The book established Reynolds Price as a precocious master of fictional technique. Granville Hicks praised his insight as "phenomenal" and went on record as saying that "to have created Rosacoke Mustian is an achievement that the most mature novelist might envy." Dorothy Parker, as paraphrased in the *New York Times* (June 25, 1963), said Price's meticulously drawn story "struck too deep to make one want to bustle around analyzing it." Published in the year of William Faulkner's death, the novel brought Price immediate fame and an unwanted reputation as the "new Faulkner." In 1962 *A Long and Happy Life* won the William Faulkner Foundation Award for a notable first novel and the Sir Walter Raleigh Award as well.

At Oxford in the following year, Price completed a collection of short stories, *The Names and Faces of Heroes* (1963). Rosacoke Mustian appears again, at a younger age, in the story "A Chain of Love," which is generally judged to be the high point of the collection. Although some of the critics found a few of the stories too slight in content, the majority agreed that the collection affirmed Price's talent. William Barrett, writing in the *Atlantic* (July 1963), singled out Price's "gift for writing from inside his people." That gift, according to Anne Tyler, has the effect that "any North Carolinian, reading one of [Price's books], must stop at least once per page to nod at the rightness of something a character says . . . [its] startling, almost incongruous eloquence."

Price's second novel, *A Generous Man* (1966), concerns the sexual coming of age of Rosacoke Mustian's brother, Milo, through his courtship of Lois, whom he meets at a fair. The courtship is worked out in the course of a hunt through the North Carolina backwoods for Milo's retarded brother, his dog, and an escaped python named Death, which belongs to Lois's aunt. Granville Hicks detected "the seeds of greatness" in the book, and Elizabeth Janeway observed in the *New York Times Book Review* (March 27, 1966) that "myth and fiction . . . mesh so intimately [in *A Generous Man*] that no strain is felt. . . . Fiction is badly in need of writers who can find a sort of symbology that reverberates in the ear of the common reader. . . . Mr. Price [has] proved himself to be such a writer." A number of critics, however, complained that Price's style had become mannered, and his characters and his novels too peopled with generic Southerners. Once more raising an unwelcome specter, John Wain wrote in the *New Republic* (May 14, 1966), that "perhaps it is not too late to remind [Price] that Faulkner's books have already been written." Price rebutted such criticisms in an essay for the *Virginia Quarterly Review*, 44 (Autumn, 1968), by asserting that *A Generous Man* was in part, "a coffin [he] was building for the great Southern hunt."

Price shifted his scene from the North Carolina backwoods to a university campus in his next novel, *Love and Work* (Atheneum, 1968). His protagonist, Thomas Eborn, is a writer and teacher so absorbed in his work—which, he believes, begets freedom—that he refuses to accept a phone call from his seriously ill mother, and when he finally drives to her house, he finds her dead. He then tries to reconstruct her life and his father's and to examine his own ability to love by writing a novel. With its clipped sentences and low-keyed mood, *Love and Work* disappointed some Price aficionados, who missed what one called the "lyrical style and exquisite mosaic structure" of his earlier work. But Peter Wolfe, in reviewing it for *Book World* (June 23, 1963) found that *Love and Work* was "more flowing, melodic, and conventionally told than Price's first two novels" and that it made "you feel that you are living through an experience, not reading a book."

Love and Work was followed by two books of poetry—*Late Warning: Four Poems* (1968) and *Torso of an Archaic Apollo—After Rilke* (1969), both published by Albondocani Press—and then by a book of short stories, *Permanent Errors* (1970). In his preface to *Permanent Errors*, Price articulated a goal that could well apply to all his fiction, explaining that he sought to "isolate in a number of lives the central error of act, will, understanding, which, once made, has been permanent, incurable, but whose diagnosis and palliation are the hope of continuance." Critics disagreed over the merits of his technique. Some complained that his rich, convoluted prose impeded the flow of the narrative, but many were mesmerized. John Wain, appraising *Permanent Errors* for the *Southern Review* (Winter 1973), noted that "the fingers of Reynolds Price creep steadily, evenly over people, things, and properties of existence. . . . They are like the fingers of the blind, ruthlessly gentle, respectfully demanding. . . . "

Price's next book, *Things Themselves: Essays and Scenes* (1972), included essays on William Faulkner, Eudora Welty, John Milton, and Rembrandt. It presented his probing but somewhat controversial views of art and what he felt to be the secondary role of criticism. It was followed by *Presence and Absence: Versions from the Bible* (Bruccoli Clark, 1933) and by one of the novels Price considers to be his best, *The Surface of the Earth* (1975), which he has called the book he was "born to write" and which won the Lillian Smith Award in 1976. Describing the process of writing it in somewhat mystical terms, he told Lindsay Miller of the *New York Post* (September 6, 1975) that it had been dictated by his unconscious mind and that he would "just wake up each morning with one or two pages worth of material." The novel refined from those pages is a visionary chronicle of forty-one years in the lives of two families intertwined through marriage, the Mayfields and the Kendals. Price's longest work, weighing in at almost 500 pages, it evoked a mixed response from the critics. Anne Hobson Freeman maintained in the *Virginia Quarterly Review* (Autumn 1975) that it met "the supreme test of the novel: it manages to recreate a world and people it with characters as complex and stubbornly mysterious as those in life, and it draws the reader into that world," while Price's longtime champion, Eudora Welty, called it a book for all readers who "are able to accept the reality of other people, living and dead, who have spoken and acted and dreamed out of their own lifetimes."

But Peter S. Prescott groused in *Newsweek* (July 7, 1975) that the book was a "slablike vestige" of the Southern Gothic, though he conceded that "any given part of this novel is impressive." Stephen Koch acknowledged in the *Saturday Review* (July 26, 1975) that "Price's gifts . . . are so very considerable that no reviewer should presume to pronounce himself on the book's ultimate prospects for fulfilling [its] high designs. . . . Certain images in it obsess the mind after one reads it, just as they must have driven and obsessed Price's mind as he wrote it. . . . [But] penance and prophecy must impinge on *something*." Phoebe-Lou Adams, who dismissed the novel as "unconvincing" in the *Atlantic Monthly* (August, 1975), sardonically observed that it contained "the largest number of deaths in childbirth ever packed into a single novel."

The theme of death in childbirth has, in fact, been a frequent one in Price's fiction, but not all critics have reacted to it as negatively as Phoebe-Lou Adams. Rosellen Brown, writing in the *New York Times Book Review* (June 29, 1986), saw it as the anchor of Price's vision, noting that many of his novels are shaped around the experience of children whose mothers have died in giving birth to them, "children, that is, who feel or are treated as if they are guilty from their first breath." Price himself has said that the deaths in childbirth in his novels reflect the frequency of its occurrence in the early decades of the twentieth century. "My mother nearly died when I was born," he has explained. "Or, as I saw it, I nearly killed her. A man felt he risked killing a woman everytime he had sex with her." Along with the guilt, Price's orphaned characters often experience a sense of permanent abandonment. His mother's parents had died when she was young, and she "saw herself to the day of her death as an orphan," he once said. "She impressed upon me constantly the terrors of orphanhood, so much so that the force of parental abandonment became one of my own central concerns."

In 1977 Price brought out a volume of poems, *Lessons Learned: Seven Poems* (Albondocani Press), and a play—a dramatization of his *A Long and Happy Life*—called *Early Dark*, which was performed the following year at New York City's WPA Theater. The *New York Post* drama critic Clive Barnes praised the play's "softly dramatic" writing, comparing it favorably to the plays of William Inge. Those works were followed in 1978 by a privately printed volume of poems, *Christ Child's Song at the End of Night*, and by *A Palpable God: Thirty Stories Translated from the Bible with an Essay on the Origins and Life of Narrative* (1978), which was nominated for a National Book Award for translation in 1979. *The Source of Light* (1981), Price's sequel to *The Surface of the Earth*, met with a reception similar to that accorded its predecessor, with many critics finding Price's undeniable novelistic powers undermined by an unwieldy plot.

In the summer of 1983 Price began work on *Kate Vaiden*, but in June 1984, after completing about one-third of the novel, he was diagnosed as having cancer of the spine. After undergoing an operation he was not expected to survive, followed by a series of painful radium treatments, he found himself permanently disabled. "During the twelve months it took me to realize I was becoming a paraplegic," Price told Michael Specter, "I wrote more than two-thirds of 'Kate Vaiden,' a trilogy of plays, completed a volume of poems and a book of essays. I kept wondering if this was one of those great au-

tumnal bursts of energy that precede death. And of course it might be."

Kate Vaiden, Price's only novel written in the first person, was published in 1986. His choice of a female narrator partly resulted from his desire to confront "the compartmentalization of male and female sensibilities" that he feels "has followed upon the otherwise rewarding movement for women's rights" and partly from his "long curiosity about the life of [his] mother before [his] birth." In *Kate Vaiden*, the "terrors of orphanhood" his mother described to him are concentrated in a scene in which Kate's father inexplicably kills her mother and then himself, leaving the eleven-year-old orphan in the care of an aunt and uncle. After Kate's young lover dies in a freak accident, or possible suicide, a few years later, she shuns any deep commitment to other human beings, fearing that she will bring about their destruction or that they will desert her. Finally she abandons her infant son. Decades later, she discovers that she has cancer and sets out to find him again. "She begins to hear death rattling toward her," Price told Specter, "and she is attempting to make some consecutive sense out of the whole thing."

Critical response to *Kate Vaiden* was overwhelmingly positive. Michiko Kakutani, in her review for the *New York Times* (June 24, 1986), called it a "fierce validation" of Price's original promise as a writer and a novel that "glows with the fine, burnished fire of mature ambition." Robert Wilson wrote in a *New Republic* article (October 13, 1986) that "Kate's speech, which is almost exhaustingly rich in perfect homely metaphors, is . . . the high point in Price's evolving literary style." Other critics congratulated Price on his ability to capture the female sensibility. *Kate Vaiden* won the 1986 National Book Critcs Circle Award for fiction.

According to Anne Tyler, the face of Reynolds Price is "round and serene and gravely trusting," while Michael Specter characterized him as "a dandy still," who wears "designer jeans and a polo shirt" and speaks in a voice as "soft as mist yet strong as bourbon." Price has been a Guggenheim fellow (1964–65) and a National Endowment of the Arts fellow (1967–68) and the recipient of a National Institute of Arts and Letters award (1971), a Bellamann Foundation Award (1972) and, on four occasions (1962, 1976, 1981, 1984), the Sir Walter Raleigh Award.

His disability and confinement to a wheelchair have had a relatively minor impact on Price's lifestyle. For twenty-nine years he has lived in Durham, North Carolina, in a house surrounded by a pond, pine trees, and forty acres of land. For half a year he continues to teach courses on writing and on John Milton. He has scheduled a new book of poems for publication in 1987, and has completed a book of essays and a new novel, "Good Hearts," in which the story of Rosacoke Mustian and Wesley Beavers is taken up again when they are forty-eight and fifty years old, respectively. "I don't write with a conscious sense of the hangman at my door,"

Price has said. "But I am a tremendously driven person, and I have gotten more so since sitting down. Words just come out of me the way my beard comes out. Who could stop it?"

References: N Y Times Mag p60 S 20 '87 por; Vanity Fair 49:82+ Jl 86 por; Washington Post G p1+ S 7 '86 pors; Contemporary Authors vol 1–4 (1967); Dictionary of Literary Biography vol 2 (1978); World Authors 1950–1970 (1975)

Prigogine, Ilya
(prē-gō´-jēn)

Jan. 25, 1917– Chemist; author. Address: Ave. Fond'Roy 67, 1180 Brussels, Belgium

When, in 1977, Ilya Prigogine was awarded the Nobel Prize in Chemistry, a spokesman for the Nobel committee cited him for having "revitalized science" with theories making possible "the study of the most varied problems," such as city traffic congestion, the stability of insect communities, the development of ordered biological structures, and the multiplication of cancer cells. Prigogine, who was born in Russia but reared in Belgium, has been called "the poet of thermodynamics" because of his conceptual daring and elegant mathematical reasoning. His theories, centered on the idea that under certain conditions the second law of thermodynamics, as traditionally viewed, can seem to be broken, have entered the scientific vernacular after decades of controversy. The second law traditionally predicts the relentless increase of disorder and incoherence—entropy—within a given system, whether that system be a steam engine or a universe. Prigogine's reinterpretation was revolutionary because the "terrible" second law was long thought to doom the universe to a long slide into equilibrium or "heat death," in which all useful energy would be lost in random motion. He proposed that in conditions that are sufficiently far from equilibrium, fluctuations of order in a random system could suddenly stabilize. The resulting "dissipative structures"—the most dramatic of which is life itself—would last indefinitely, taking energy out of their chaotic environments and "dissipating" entropy back into them. Prigogine's international best seller, Order out of Chaos, which he wrote with the chemist, philosopher, and scientific historian Isabelle Stengers and which expounds his theories for the layman, was published in paperback in an English translation by Bantam Books in 1984 and distributed in hardcover by Random House.

Ilya Prigogine, the second son of Roman Prigogine, a chemical engineer and factory owner, and Julia (Wichman) Prigogine, a former student at the conservatory of music in Moscow, was born in Moscow on January 25, 1917, nine months before the outbreak of the Russian Revolution. In 1921 his family left Moscow to escape the restrictions on private enterprise imposed by the new Soviet government, and the Prigogines spent a year in Lithuania before moving on to Berlin. Ilya Prigogine's childhood coincided with the disastrous inflation and national despair that Germany suffered between the world wars, but despite the disruptive historical changes of the period and the growing violence in the streets, Julia Prigogine did all she could to give him and his brother the same kind of cultural upbringing she had enjoyed. She taught them music, and before he could read books, Ilya Prigogine was beginning to read piano scores. He eventually learned to play Bach, Mozart, Schumann, and Debussy. After trying and failing to start several businesses, his father, alarmed by the first stirrings of Nazism, fled Berlin for Brussels, where Ilya enrolled at the Athénée, a public secondary school noted for its rigorous classical curriculum. Although he continued to play music and dreamed of becoming a concert pianist, he also became absorbed in the classics, which he read voraciously, along with books on archaeology, literature, and philosophy. A lasting influence was the thinking of Henri Bergson on the differences between time as conceived in the theories of science and time as it is experienced in everyday life. In an article that appeared in Quest (December 15, 1980) Mary Lukas noted that in Brussels as in Germany, Prigogine "was an oddity, a little Jewish boy from somewhere in the East, fallen into homogeneously bourgeois Catholic Belgium, handicapped by a thick German accent. . . . He became a master of surface conformity." When he was seventeen, his family decided that he should pursue a legal career, and he agreed. Deciding that the first step in studying law would be to understand the mental makeup of a criminal, he began looking around for a book on criminal psychology and discovered a book on the chemical composition of the brain instead. Thoughts of the law as a career quickly gave way to a passionate interest in chemistry, and he entered the Free University of Brussels with that science as his prospective specialty. Bringing to its study his already extensive background in humanistic thought in which the role of history—whether human or cosmological—is central, he was puzzled by the relegation of time in science to the status of a convenient parameter. "The fact that in chemistry and physics, past and present could play the same role," Prigogine told an interviewer for The Omni Interviews (Ticknor & Fields, 1984), "I found, well, a little strange. . . . Everyone knows that tomorrow is not the same as today. Yet they described a universe where present and past were identical, timeless, and reversible."

As he has since explained, the roots of that emphasis on reversible time can be traced to "one of the greatest dates in the history of mankind—" April 28, 1686—when Sir Isaac Newton presented part of the manuscript of his Principia to the Royal Society of London. In the three books of that work, published in 1687, Newton formulated the fundamental laws of motion, or dynamics, so profoundly that he seemed to have made the workings of the universe as comprehensible (and reversible) as those of a clock. A potential contradiction of that view emerged during the Industrial Revolution, when the spread of the British steam engine focused the attention of scientists on the mechanical uses of heat. Thermodynamics, or the "science of heat," that emerged from their investigations, was formulated in terms of three basic laws. The second and most famous law was based, as Prigogine and Stengers note in Order out of Chaos, on the fact that "fuel used by the steam engine disappears forever." Within the engine there is a gradual wearing down, or increase of entropy, that eventually brings all of its functioning to a dead stop. That increase of entropy embodies what was later to be described by Sir Arthur Eddington as "the arrow of time," the irreversible trajectory of which is apparent in the dramatic difference in a machine on the day it is bought and the day that it is junked. A major step in understanding the trajectory of entropy was taken when the great Austrian physicist Ludwig Boltzmann described the entropy of systems of molecules, such as those that compose gases, in terms of the probability of changes in the entire system rather than in terms of changes in specific trajectories traditionally measured in Newtonian mechanics. He found that the molecular systems were "attracted" to an equilibrium state in which all interactions and structures became improbable and only a kind of insipid broth of random motions remained. That type of "natural selection" was in stark contrast to that outlined by Charles Darwin, a contemporary of Boltzmann, who was propounding his theory of evolution. Prigogine and Stengers explain that the contradiction raised a still vexing question: "How . . . could Darwinian evolution— the statistical selection of rare events—be reconciled with the statistical disappearance of all peculiarities, of all rare configurations, described by Boltzmann?" One of Prigogine's mentors at the University of Brussels, Theodore De Donder, was among those who investigated that question.

Prigogine began studying thermodynamics under De Donder in 1939, his fourth year at the University of Brussels. In that same year, continuing his interest in the humanistic aspect of time, he entered an academic music competition and won with his performance of several Schumann piano pieces. In the laboratory his work eventually enabled him to predict a number of new phenomena, among them the low-temperature separation of mixtures of helium isotopes and the effects of entropy in polymer solutions near equilibrium. The most valuable product of those investigations, the law of minimum entropy production, explained the stability of near-equilibrium structures. Prigogine's interests, however, developed in the direction away from equilibrium, where the irreversible effects of "the arrow of time" were indisputable. In 1946 he began for the first time to theorize that the irreversibility of those reactions, far from being a kind of irrelevant "buying of time" before solutions returned to equilibrium, was actually a source of new structures—durable watersheds against disorder. Prigogine has recalled that he was "very, very happy to have this idea, which has never left [him]. Perhaps in science, at some point, there is a close relationship between who you are and what you try to do."

Despite the difficulties of the war years in Brussels (the first classes that Prigogine gave after receiving his Ph.D. degree in 1941 were held in halls and church basements), he remained an inveterate optimist committed to confronting his time and proving its grim implications wrong. In his interview for The Omni Interviews Prigogine asserted that "the attitude of Einstein toward science, for example, was to go beyond the reality of the moment . . . [for him] time was an imperfection, and science, a way to get away . . . from the turmoil, from the wars. He wanted to find some kind of safe harbor in eternity. . . . My own attitude is very different, because I want to feel the evolution of things. I don't believe in transcending, but in being embedded in a reality that is temporal." In propounding that reality, Prigogine at first met with great resistance, for the reaction of well-known scientists to his ideas was uniformly negative.

Prigogine nonetheless forged ahead, publishing his Ph.D. thesis, The Thermodynamic Study of Irreversible Phenomena in French, and with a Japanese translation, in 1947. When he succeeded De Donder as the guiding spirit of thermodynamics at the University of Brussels, he gathered a group of loyal coworkers from a number of fields around him, including the university's outstanding biology department. At one point his future collaborator, Isabelle Stengers, was a member of that group.

In 1954 Prigogine published his seminal Introduction to Thermodynamics of Irreversible Processes (John Wiley, 1962), in which he advanced the idea that thermodynamic equilibrium is actually relatively rare in nature. More important both to science and to everyday life, he proposed, were far-from-equilibrium structures such as cells, towns or whirlpools, which survive in a delicate balance with their less-organized surroundings. In that same year he was awarded the Franqui Prize for his ideas and their growing influence on the scientific community. Three years later he documented his investigation of near-equilibrium helium and polymer solutions in *The Molecular Theory of Solutions* (North Holland, 1957), on which he collaborated with A. Bellemans and V. Mathot. Seeking out the exact mechanism of irreversibility, he continued to plumb deeply into the secrets of far-from-equilibrium structures, notably into the reaction that originally inspired his insights, the Benard instability, which occurs when certain fluids are heated from below to create a "temperature gradient" that causes the solution to reach a moment of choice, or bifurcation. There follows "a spectacular phenomenon," in the view of Prigogine and Stengers: "Millions of molecules move coherently, forming hexagonal convection cells of a characteristic size." The implication for Prigogine, who has described systems at equilibrium as "blind," was not only that the Benard instability suggested a means by which life might have originated, but that the ability of "sighted" far-from-equilibrium structures to make "choices," to bifurcate, introduced a kind of free will into the basic fabric of the universe.

Such speculations about the "profoundly optimistic" implications of the "broken time symmetry," or irreversible distinction of past and future embodied by the convection cells, continued to be doubted by many scientists, and Prigogine continued to seek precise mathematical formulations for them. That led him to create models for biochemical examples of self-organization even more complex and "lifelike" than the Benard instability, and this eventually resulted in "the Brusselator," a mathematical model for so-called auto-catalytic cycles, such as those involved in chemical clocks and chemical waves and in more patently inanimate phenomena such as explosions. In those cycles a substance—or a fireball—in effect generates itself. The Brusselator was devised by Prigogine and one of his students, Réné Lefever, between 1965, when Prigogine won Belgium's E. J. Solvay Prize, and 1967, during a grueling study of the metabolic sugar cycle in living things. "From that time on," observed Mary Lukas, "Prigogine no longer had to stand on lecture platforms generalizing about the relationship between living systems and dead chemical reactions. He had equations to show how such systems might work." It was at about that time, at the Institut de la Vie in Paris, that he dubbed the phenomena he had been studying "dissipative structures."

When, at about the time the Brusselator was completed, news arrived from the Soviet Union of the Belousov-Zhabotinski reaction, in which a mixture of malonic acid, bromate, and cerium ions in sulfuric acid bifurcated at certain temperatures and formed complex structures, Prigogine's ideas received accidental but definitive proof. The Belousov-Zhabotinski reaction is sufficiently dramatic, in fact, to have prompted the query, in John P. Briggs and F. David Peat's book *The Looking Glass Universe*, as to whether it was "a chemical reaction as a life form." In 1968 one of Prigogine's colleagues repeated the Belousov-Zhabotinski reaction in Oregon and devised the "oregonator," a mathematical descendant of the Brusselator, that described it exactly. With the importance of his ideas now beyond dispute, the size of Prigogine's group at the University of Brussels mushroomed to sixty scientists from a variety of disciplines, and the concept of the dissipative structure was applied to evolution, embryology, sociology, city planning, and even, under the aegis of the United States Department of Transportation, the prevention of traffic jams. Prigogine began to envision the opening of a "new era in the history of time" in which all disciplines worked with the knowledge that "we live in a pluralistic universe in which reversible and irreversible processes coexist, all embedded in the expanding universe." A steady stream of honors culminating in the 1977 Nobel Prize, the first for a Belgian chemist, was for Prigogine, according to one of his colleagues at the University of Brussels, "in the normal course of things." The University of Texas at Austin, with which Prigogine had been associated since 1967, commemorated the occasion by renaming the center where he had worked for three months out of a year, the Ilya Prigogine Center for Studies in Statistical Mechanics. Symposia at which leading scientists discussed and presented papers on the application to their fields of the irreversible arrow of time and the dissipative structure were held both in Europe and the United States.

Meanwhile, Prigogine began to think of opening a dialogue with the general public about the optimistic revolution implied by his insights. To that end, he and Isabelle Stengers published the French edition of *Order out of Chaos, La Nouvelle alliance—métamorphose de la science*, in Paris in 1979 under the imprint of Gallimard. An international best-seller, the book was hailed by Italo Calvino as "a passionate meditation on Man and the Universe." *Order Out of Chaos* traces the scientific and philosophic ancestry of dissipative structures from the time of Aristotle to the "clash of doctrines" represented by the disagreement of Prigogine's thermodynamics, not only with Newton's predictions about the universe but also with the views of his contemporaries in the "hard sciences"—especially quantum and relativistic physics—for whom time remains reversible.

In their preface to the revised English edition, which was published by Bantam Books in 1984 with the full title, *Order out of Chaos: Man's New Dialogue with Nature*, Prigogine and Stengers propose nothing less than the "reconceptualization of physics." To achieve that, they propose not only a new dialogue among sciences but also a new dialogue between the sciences and the humanities, and they take care to couch their thermodynamical concepts in humanistic terms. Referring to the works of such philosophers as Kant, Whitehead, and Bergson, they present time as a "construction" that confers an ethical responsibility. Finally Ilya Prigogine and Isabelle Stengers propose a "renewal of nature," to be carried out by means of carefully orchestrated bifurcations, whether in the earth's climate and food supply, in the field of disease control and bioengineering or in global scientific and political reorganization. (In 1982 Prigogine had founded the Committee for the Development of European Science and Technology to help coordinate scientific activity in the different European nations.)

The critical reception of *Order out of Chaos* seemed to establish something of the dialogue with humanists that Prigogine had hoped for. In a review for *Choice* (January 1985), P. D. Skiff observed that "belying its sensational appearance and a dreadful introduction by Alvin Toffler, the work is accurate, sensible and significant." Stephen Strauss warned readers of the *Toronto Globe and Mail* (July 28, 1984) of a sometimes difficult but ultimately rewarding plough through "stony, mathematical acres." When the French government awarded Prigogine the medal and the title of Commandeur de l'Ordre des Arts et Lettres for *Order out of Chaos*, he noted with satisfaction that the title and medal usually honor achievement in the arts.

The existence of an internal time, or history, within each entity—whether human, subatomic or stellar—is a key concept in Prigogine's recent work. He told philosopher Renée Weber, in an interview for her book *Dialogues with Scientists and Sages* (Routledge & Kegan Paul, 1986) that internal time is "freer," like musical time, than the complementary "external" time that is measured by watches. Like music, internal time is complex enough to be almost a structure in itself, and it meets Prigogine's standards of irreversibility because even if a part of it recurs, like a repeated musical phrase, it will be distinguished by being familiar and will produce a new effect. The similarity of that type of cumulative "time evolution" to the time of everyday experience, of course, brings Prigogine full circle, back to his original concept of time.

Renée Weber has described Ilya Prigogine as giving an impression of "sheer dynamic energy compressed into a man" and as "a muscular man with a powerful stocky frame that supports a leonine head." She also noted his "lively brown eyes and sudden smiles." He divides his time between Austin, Texas, and Brussels, Belgium, where he lives with his second wife, Marina, an engineer, and his son, Pascal. His many distinctions include a dozen honorary degrees, medals, and other honors from nineteen countries, Belgium's Van Laar Prize and A. Wetrems Prize (1951), and membership in twenty scientific academies. He won the 1983 Honda Award with its honorarium of ten million yen (about $40,000) for his applications of his

ideas to ecotechnology, the study of the harmonious positioning of technology in nature. His numerous publications include *Kinetic Theory of Traffic* (Elsevier, 1971), cowritten with R. Herman, *Thermodynamic Theory of Structure, Stability and Fluctuations*, cowritten with G. Glansdorff (John Wiley, 1971), and *From Being to Becoming—Time and Complexity in the Physical Sciences* (W. H. Freeman and Company, 1980), which is aimed, like *Order out of Chaos*, at a lay audience. Prigogine's wide-ranging interests continue to include the piano, which he no longer plays as often as he would like, art, and archaeology. He collects pre-Columbian statuary and ancient jade. In his books, mathematical investigations, and interdisciplinary collaborations, Prigogine continues to lay the groundwork for what he believes will be a new science of irreversibility that might well break the grim symmetry of the world's problems. "Now we know," he told Mary Lukas, "that we are not merely prisoners of circumstances."

References: Newsweek 90:87 O 24 '77 por; Quest 4:15+ D '80 pors; International Who's Who (1986–87); Weber, Renée. Dialogues with Scientists and Sages (1986); Weintraub, Pamela. The Omni Interviews (1984)

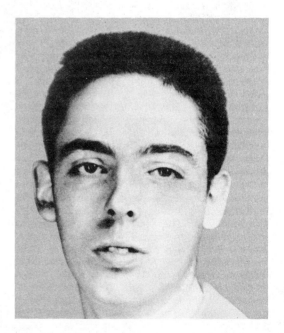

Pynchon, Thomas
(pĭn´chen)

May 8, 1937– Writer. Address: b. c/o Little, Brown & Co., 34 Beacon St., Boston, Mass. 02106

The novelist and short story writer Thomas Pynchon is considered to be among the best contemporary American authors by some critics, who rank him with such literary heavyweights as Saul Bellow, Joseph Heller, Norman Mailer, Isaac Bashevis Singer, and Kurt Vonnegut. Like other reclusive novelists, such as J. D. Salinger, he shuns publicity, wishing to be known only through his writing. His novels, V. (1963), The Crying of Lot 49 (1966), and Gravity's Rainbow (1973), show an extraordinary command of the English language, an encyclopedic knowledge of world literature, a strong background in science and history, and a striking command of popular culture.

According to the editors of the New York Times Book Review (December 3, 1973), who chose Gravity's Rainbow as one of the three most significant books of the year, "Pynchon is capable of the most intricate literary structures—plots and counterplots and symbols and facts that twist in time and space. In his universe, the characters become mechanical men whose trajectory toward death is touched by a manic and comic impulse or a vague free-floating anguish. For all its power and intelligence, Pynchon's novel is a magnificent ruined necropolis, but its teetering structure towers above the surrounding literary shacks and hovels."

Thomas Ruggles Pynchon Jr. was born on May 8, 1937, in Glen Cove, Long Island, New York, the oldest of the three children of Thomas Ruggles Pynchon Sr. and Katherine Frances (Bennett) Pynchon. He has a sister, Judith, and a brother, John. His father, an industrial surveyor, presided over the local Republican club and was town supervisor of Oyster Bay. Literary authorities often stress that Thomas Pynchon is a member of a noted family whose earliest recorded member had gone to England from Normandy in the eleventh century with William the Conqueror. The first American to bear the family name was William Pynchon, who in 1630 emigrated from England to the Massachusetts Bay Colony. His theological tract The Meritorious Price of Our Redemption, published in England in 1650, was condemned by the Puritan authorities. In 1851 Nathaniel Hawthorne was surprised to hear from two members of the family who were upset by his use of the name "Pyncheon" in The House of the Seven Gables. One of them, the Reverend Thomas Ruggles Pynchon (1823–1904), was a great-grand-uncle of Thomas Pynchon, the novelist.

As a high school student, Pynchon wrote a column for his school newspaper entitled "The Voice of the Hamster," in the form of letters by one Roscoe Stein of the fictitious Hamster High to his friend Sam in Oyster Bay. Here Pynchon used the kind of bizarre names that he later favored in his fiction and showed a wry sense of humor as well as an interest in collective behavior and in human misfits. In 1953 he graduated from Oyster Bay High School, where he was class salutatorian and the recipient of the Julia L. Thurston award as the senior with the highest average in English.

In the fall of 1953 Pynchon entered Cornell University on a scholarship, with a major in engineering physics. He adamantly refused at the time to submit his photograph to the freshman register, and to date there seem to be no more than two published photographs of him. At Cornell, Pynchon received straight A's in his engineering and physics courses, and although he later changed his major to English, physics remained one of his cardinal interests. According to Frank D. McConnell, writing in Contemporary Novelists, "one of his former teachers still wonderingly remembers his apparently voracious appetite for the complexities of elementary particle theory." Jules Siegel, a former fellow student at Cornell, recalled in an article in Playboy (March 1977): "Tom Pynchon was quiet and neat and did his homework faithfully. He went to Mass and confessed, though to what would be a mystery. He got $25 a week spending money and managed it perfectly, did not cut class and always got grades in the high 90s. He was disappointed not to have been pledged to a fraternity, but he lacked the crude sociability required for that. . . . He was, if anything, a very private person."

At the end of his sophomore year, Pynchon left Cornell for a two-year hitch in the United States Navy, some of it at the naval base in Norfolk, Virginia. During that period, Pynchon kept company with Anne Cotton, a young woman who worked for an intelligence agency in Washington, D.C. He introduced her to jazz at Washington nightclubs, and she stimulated his interest in opera, which later was to play such a significant role in his writing.

In the fall of 1957 Pynchon returned to Cornell, where he took a course with Vladimir Nabokov and, according to Mathew Winston's essay about him in Mindful Pleasures (1976), was "a constant reader—the type to read books on mathematics for fun. . . ." Although he had an opportunity to take part in the honors program, he passed it up, reportedly because he was too modest. During his junior and senior years, he served on the editorial staff of the undergraduate literary magazine Cornell Writer, which published several poems and stories by his close friend, the late writer, folk singer, and self-styled revolutionary Richard Fariña, to whom he later dedicated his novel Gravity's Rainbow. It was during his last years at Cornell that Pynchon wrote five of his six published stories: "Mortality and Mercy in Vienna" (Epoch, Spring 1959), an involved tale larded with allusions to T. S. Eliot, Shakespeare, and Joseph Conrad; "The Small Rain" (Cornell Writer, March 1959), which deals with conflict between officers and men; "Lowlands" (New World Writing, 1960), about a middle-class man trying to escape the ennui of his existence; "Entropy" (Kenyon Review, Spring 1960), which contrasts chaos with a well-ordered existence; and "Under the Rose" (Noble Savage, May 1961), a "spy story," which evolved into a chapter in the novel V. The last four stories mentioned were later included in the volume Slow Learner.

On obtaining his B.A. degree from Cornell in 1959, with distinction in all subjects, Pynchon had a choice of several fellowships, including the Woodrow Wilson, and was also offered a job teaching creative writing at the university. Deciding to devote himself to his own literary career, he began work on his first novel, V., while staying with friends in Greenwich Village in New York City. He then moved to Seattle, where he worked for the Boeing Company from February 1960 to September 1962 as an engineering aide and technical writer, with top security clearance. As a member of the Minuteman Logistics Support Program, he wrote for the intramural *Minuteman Field Service News*, and he also had the article "Togetherness" published in the magazine *Aerospace Safety* for December 1960. According to Walter Bailey, a fellow employee at Boeing, who was quoted by David Cowart in his book *Thomas Pynchon: The Art of Allusion* (1980), Pynchon was a "taciturn and withdrawn young man whose apparent misanthropy did not make him particularly well liked." Bailey was one of the few co-workers with whom Pynchon communicated on a personal level, partly because not many of the other people in the office shared his interest in literature. After leaving Boeing, Pynchon went to California, and then on to Mexico, where he completed V. It was published in 1963 by the J. B. Lippincott Company, which already had acquired an option on the novel through his agent, Candida Donadio. From that time on, biographical information about Pynchon has been scant, and his life has become almost coextensive with his writings.

An encyclopedic work, V. combines two plots. One, set in the United States in the mid-1950s, is about an Italian-Jewish drifter named Benny Profane, who is determined to perfect his "schlemielhood"—the state of being a victim. His friends, known as the "Whole Sick Crew," symbolize the decadence of Western civilization. In one of his adventures, Profane takes part in an alligator hunt in the labyrinthine sewers of New York City. The other plot, skeletal, nonlinear, and more fragmentary, focuses on crises, from the Fashoda incident in Egypt in 1898 to World War II. It concerns the quest of an adventurer named Herbert Stencil to track down V., a mysterious and corrupt woman, described by David Cowart as a "kind of Nazi Venus, a nightmare vision of the eternal feminine," whose initial recurs in the memoirs of his father, a British foreign office official, and who reappears under various names and guises in such diverse places as New York, Paris, Alexandria, Florence, Malta, and South Africa. Filled with bizarre incidents and a cast of bohemian characters, V. became a cult book of the 1960s. Its style reminded critics, variously, of Nathanael West, William Faulkner, Lawrence Durrell, and Vladimir Nabokov. Others found that its experimental approach and bizarre humor recalled the work of such authors as Joseph Heller, William Burroughs, John Barth, and Kurt Vonnegut.

In an excess of enthusiasm, Richard Poirier called V. "the most masterful first novel in the history of literature." To Charles G. Gros, writing in *Best Sellers* (April 1, 1963), it seemed that "reading V. is like listening to a scholarly but erratic documentation of Hell by a disinterested onlooker while verbal sewage and vignettes of all that is most disgusting in mankind alternate with sociological asides, sardonic and blasphemous attacks on Christianity, Freudian tidbits. . . . " George Plimpton, in the *New York Times Book Review* (April 21, 1963), found V. "as complicated and varied as a Hieronymus Bosch triptych" and credited Pynchon with "a vigorous and imaginative style, a robust humor, a tremendous reservoir of information . . . and, above all, a sense of how to use and balance these talents." And the critic for *Newsweek* (April 1, 1963) asserted that "this splendid first novel is simply a picture of life, as first-rate novels always are, reflecting a creative force of great originality, complexity, and breadth." V. earned for Pynchon the William Faulkner Award as the best first novel of 1963.

While working on a new novel, Pynchon wrote his sixth, and to date his last, short story, "The Secret Integration," which was published in the *Saturday Evening Post* (December 19, 1964), about children in a Massachusetts town who create a fantasy world in which racial distinctions are eliminated. He then wrote the article "A Journey into the Mind of Watts," a study of the 1965 racial riots in a black section of Los Angeles, which appeared in the *New York Times Magazine* (June 12, 1966). In it, he concluded that "far from a sickness, violence may be an attempt to communicate, or to be who you really are." Remarking on how some people in Watts seemed to believe in great surprises in life, he wrote: "Their world and their scene cannot accept the possibility that there may be, after all, no surprise." In his *Pynchon: A Collection of Critical Essays* (1978), Joseph W. Slade described the article as "a skillful piece of journalism" that "traces the ironies of black life in a prosperous white city."

Pynchon's second novel, *The Crying of Lot 49* (Lippincott, 1966), segments of which had previously been published in *Esquire* and in *Cavalier*, was more accessible to the general reader than its predecessor, perhaps because of its strong and unified plot and its length of fewer than 200 pages. It centers upon Oedipa Maas, a California housewife who, as executrix of the will of her lover, the real estate mogul Pierce Inverarity, gets involved in what appears to be a conspiracy directed by a mysterious, ubiquitous, and centuries-old postal service, the Tristero. In the novel, Pynchon uses the Second Law of Thermodynamics, describing entropy, or energy loss, as a metaphor for a deteriorating civilization.

In his book *The Grim Phoenix; Reconstructing Thomas Pynchon* (1978), William M. Plater noted that *The Crying of Lot 49* had "a tightly controlled plot based on the highly successful movie formula, an economy of dialogue, plausible fantasy, and characters that are at least imaginable." Those characters included rock 'n' roll singers, right-wing extremists, and other denizens of the subculture of southern California. But to Arthur Gold, in *Book Week* (April 24, 1966), *The Crying of Lot 49* seemed "a curiously dead novel." Nevertheless, Pynchon received the Rosenthal Foundation Award of the National Institute of Arts and Letters for it.

Seven years elapsed before the publication of Pynchon's next major work, the novel *Gravity's Rainbow* (Viking, 1973). Impossible to summarize because of its complexity, *Gravity's Rainbow* interweaves at least five major stories. The ostensible protagonist, or antihero, is Tyrone Slothrop, an American lieutenant stationed in London during the blitz, whose phallic erections indicate the targets of German V-2 rockets and who eventually deserts to avoid becoming a mere manipulated object. The novel follows his adventures from London to the Casino Hermann Goering in the south of France, and on a journey across Germany. In the end, he tends to lose his personhood, becoming "Rocketman." According to the editors of the *New York Times Book Review*, who were quoted by Peter Kihss in the *New York Times* (May 8, 1974), the V-2 rocket is seen as a symbol of "sexual love and death," which in Pynchon's view is "the driving paranoid force behind modern history."

Michael Wood, in assessing the novel for the *New York Review of Books* (March 22, 1973), saw *Gravity's Rainbow* as "a tortured cadenza of lurid imaginings and total recall that goes on longer than you can quite believe. Its people, like the characters in *V.*, are marginal people, layabouts, dropouts, gangsters, failed scientists, despairing spiritualists, spies, SS men, dancing girls, faded movie stars. A number of old friends from *V.* crop up. . . . The mythical population of the book runs from King Kong to Dillinger to Fu Manchu to Tannhäuser, with lyrics by Rilke and T. S. Eliot, and there are plenty of songs . . . and limericks and gags. . . ." Wood noted that Pynchon could "intuit huge canvases from small details, whole cultures from a fragment of stone. . . ."

Richard Locke, in the *New York Times Book Review* (March 11, 1973), called *Gravity's Rainbow* the "longest, most difficult and most ambitious novel" to appear in the United States since Nabokov's *Ada*, and Walter Clemons, who noted in *Newsweek* (March 19, 1973) that "it isn't plausible to call a novel great the week it's published," classified it as "at the very least, tremendous." Lawrence Wolfley, in an essay in PMLA (October 1977), saw *Gravity's Rainbow* as "shot through with the particular Freudian thinking" represented by the classical scholar and philosopher Norman O. Brown, who equated repression of sexuality with death and destruction. For Wolfley, who considered Pynchon's novel "one of the greatest of our time," *Gravity's Rainbow* "dramatizes the perpetual struggle of life against death" by "joyfully embracing and celebrating all the death instincts of Western man in a style of unmediated euphoria."

Praise for *Gravity's Rainbow* was not unanimous, however. John Gardner, in his book *On Moral Fiction* (1978), criticized its subversion of moral values, and Robert Alter, in the *New York Times Book Review* (August 10, 1980), called its brand of apocalypticism juvenile and disapproved of its excessive use of sex and scatology. In the opinion of George P. Elliott, writing in *Harper's* magazine (July 1980), the novel projects rather than analyzes paranoia.

In 1974 the three judges of the Pulitzer Prize committee unanimously selected *Gravity's Rainbow* as the best novel of 1973, but the fourteen-member Pulitzer advisory board overruled them, branding the huge novel as "obscene" and "unreadable." Consequently, no Pulitzer Prize for fiction was awarded that year. Also in 1974, *Gravity's Rainbow* shared the National Book Award in fiction with Isaac Bashevis Singer's *A Crown of Feathers and Other Stories*. But the award ceremony, arranged by Thomas Guinzburg of Viking Press and featuring readings by Jessica Tandy and Hume Cronyn from the winning novels, was not attended by Pynchon, who sent the stand-up comedian and self-styled "world's greatest expert on everything," Professor Irwin Corey, to accept the $1,000 prize for him.

In 1975 Pynchon was designated the winner of the Howells Medal of the American Academy and Institute of Arts and Letters for *Gravity's Rainbow*, which was judged the best novel of the past five years, but he turned it down. "I don't want it," he wrote to the academy. "Please don't impose on me something I don't want. . . . I know I should behave with more class, but there appears to be only one way to say no, and that's no." Instead, William Styron was presented the medal in the reclusive author's name, and it was kept at the academy in the event that Pynchon should want to claim it in the future.

For about a decade, Pynchon published virtually nothing. In 1983 he wrote an introduction for the Penguin reprint of Richard Farina's *Been Down So Long It Looks Like Up to Me*, which was reprinted in the *Cornell Alumni News*. In his brief but notable essay, "Is It O. K. to Be a Luddite?" published in the *New York Times Book Review* (October 28, 1984), Pynchon used C. P. Snow's celebrated lecture "The Two Cultures" as a jumping-off point for understanding the Luddite tradition in art and history and discussed regimentation, revolt, and anarchy.

Apparently because his short stories had been circulating for years in pirated pamphlet editions, Pynchon decided to publish five of the six stories—including "The Secret Integration" but excluding "Mortality and Mercy in Vienna"—in the volume *Slow Learner* (Little, Brown, 1984), along with a twenty-three-page introduction, in which he criticized what he considered the inadequacies of his own early attempts at fiction. Peter S. Prescott, in *Newsweek* (April 9, 1984), pronounced the book a "minor disaster," but Christopher Lehmann-Haupt, in the *New York Times* (March 29, 1984), praised the stories for their "unusual narrative vigor and inventiveness." Although, in an article that she wrote about Pynchon for the *Chicago Tribune* (April 8, 1984), Helen Dudar felt that the stories were "flabby and only marginally interesting," she viewed *Slow Learner* as "a fascinating display of the feeling for style and imagined event this greatly talented and intelligent man had by the time he was twenty-one."

Over the years, Thomas Pynchon has inevitably become something of a cult figure, and a number of wild rumors have circulated about him, including the preposterous one, in the 1970s, that he was actually J. D. Salinger. Since 1979, a newsletter, *Pynchon Notes,* has been published at Wesleyan University in Middletown, Connecticut. To date, four collections of essays on Pynchon have been published, and there are about a dozen monographs about him.

According to unsubstantiated rumors, Thomas Pynchon is said to have been briefly married during his college years. In the *Chicago Tribune* article by Helen Dudar, who interviewed some of his acquaintances, Pynchon emerges as "a restless, rootless man who lives, as unencumbered as possible, from place to place and coast to coast in borrowed or sublet quarters. He seems to walk in and out of people's lives as if they were rest stops on a transcontinental highway. . . . He is good company and a fairly accomplished cook, tending toward vegetarianism. . . . His friends are expected to honor his lust for anonymity, introducing him to

their friends by whatever fake name he is using." Irving Goodman, the former head of Viking Press, who lunched with Pynchon in the spring of 1984, described him to Helen Dudar as being neatly dressed in a sports shirt and jeans, as standing over six feet tall and as lean, with graying black hair and a mustache. Goodman was surprised by the "ease and comfort" of their meeting. In 1984 Pynchon was reported to be working on a new novel and was quoted as saying that it was "closer to the end than to the beginning."

References: Book World p3 Ap 22 '84; Chicago Tribune XIV p36+ Ap 8 '84 por; Confrontation 30/31:44+ N '85; N Y Rev of Bks 20:22+ Mr 22 '73; N Y Times Bk R p 1+ Mr 11 '73; New Times 11:59+ O 16 '78; Newsweek 103:100+ Ap 9 '84 por; Playboy 24:97+ Mr '77; Clerc, Charles, ed. Approaches to "Gravity's Rainbow" (1983); Contemporary Authors 1st rev vols 17–20 (1976); Contemporary Novelists (1986); Levine, George, and Leverenz, David, eds. Mindful Pleasures: Essays on Thomas Pynchon (1976); Pearce, Richard, ed. Critical Essays on Thomas Pynchon (1981); World Authors 1950–70 (1975)

Randi, James

Aug. 7, 1928– Magician; author; educator.
Address: b. Fifi Oscard Associates, Inc., 19 W. 44th St., New York City, N.Y. 10036; c/o Prometheus Books, 700 E. Amherst St., Buffalo, N.Y. 14215; h. 5901 N.W. 12th Ct., Sunrise, Fla. 33313

"The uncritical, worldwide acceptance of supernatural, paranormal and occult claims has entirely changed the direction of my life in recent years," the renowned conjurer James ("The Amazing") Randi has said. Beginning in the mid-1960s, when he was still known mainly as a brilliant magician and escape artist, Randi established himself as the scourge of spurious or dishonest psychics and sloppy parapsychological researchers and became what one observer has called "the standard bearer of the rationalists." In 1964 Randi offered $10,000, an amount that has yet to be earned, for proof of paranormal abilities under his rigorous testing. He has since used his skills to duplicate and expose the tricks of figures such as Uri Geller, who in the 1970s gained some scientific backing for his claims of supernatural powers.

At the lectern and in such books as *The Truth About Uri Geller* (1982) and *Flim-Flam! Psychics, ESP, Unicorns and Other Delusions* (1980), both published by Prometheus Books, Randi has broadened his effort to help the public separate what is "worth believing in" from what is not. Such reputable figures as Isaac Asimov, B. F. Skinner, and Carl Sagan were drafted into his camp when he helped to organize the Committee for the Scientific Investigation of Claims of the Paranormal (CSICOP) in 1976. Three years later he began handing out "Uri Awards" on April Fool's Day to psychics and to scientists, journalists, and organizations, including, on one occasion, the Pentagon, which he feels are taken in by them. Randi has most recently joined battle with faith healers who claim such powers as the ability to perform "psychic surgery" and sometimes cozen members of their congregations into abandoning much-needed medical treatment in favor of what Randi calls "the latest miracles." For his latest achievement, in particular, Randi was tapped in 1986 by the John D. and Catherine T. MacArthur Foundation to receive one of its annual fellowships, widely known as "genius awards," that are normally bestowed on overachievers in the arts and sciences.

James Randi was born Randall James Hamilton Zwinge on August 7, 1928, in Toronto, Ontario, Canada, one of the three children of George Randall and Marie Alice (Paradis) Zwinge. His father was a telephone company executive and his mother "a plain old housewife." A child prodigy with an I.Q. of 168, James was too small for boyhood sports and was bored and disruptive in school. Nicknamed "the professor" by his classmates, he habitually corrected his teachers, and as his sister, Angela, has recalled, told them "everything they were teaching was wrong." A shy and lonely child, he found a haven in the Toronto Public Library, where his self-education included learning how to read hieroglyphics.

At the age of twelve, after being mesmerized by a performance of the magician Harry Blackstone Sr., James Randi began to frequent Toronto's Arcade Novelty and Magic Shop. Blackstone, to whom he later paid tribute in Flim-Flam! as "not only the world's greatest magician" but "also a towering inspiration," became his mentor. His knowledge of magic progressed to the point where he quickly recognized its use when at fifteen he visited a local spiritualist church whose pastor specialized in reading the contents of sealed envelopes. Rushing on stage, the incensed adolescent demonstrated how the trick worked and was arrested for disrupting a religious meeting. The four hours that Randi spent "seething" in a police station while waiting to be picked up by his father, he has recalled, were "the worst four hours the world's 'psychics' ever spent, although they didn't know it at the time."

When he was seventeen, Randi adopted the pseudonym Zo-ran and, as an experiment, wrote an astrology column for a newspaper started by two of his friends. "I went out and bought an astrology magazine, clipped a few pages of daily forecasts at random, mixed them in a hat, and pasted them up in any old fashion," he recalled in Flim-Flam! Chagrined at the delighted reactions to his column, Zo-ran "hung up his scissors, put away the paste pot, and went out of business."

After attending the Oakwood Collegiate Institute in Toronto from 1940 to 1945, Randi was offered college scholarships in chemistry, physics, and mathematics. However, he was weary of "being taught what to think, not how to think," as he has recalled, and he abandoned his formal education just a few days short of his high school graduation. Joining a traveling carnival as a magician, the seventeen-year-old, who still sometimes stammered when meeting strangers, "figured [he] would] do the thing [he] feared most, which was getting up in front of people." "The first three

weeks were pure hell," he recalled in an interview for People (August 11, 1986), "but I wouldn't have given up that experience for anything."

Naming himself "Prince Ibis" and "The Great Randall, Telepath," Randall Zwinge, complete with goatee and turban, perfected a mentalist act. The Toronto Evening Telegram of August 14, 1950, described him as "a slim, bespectacled young man with a receding hairline, Extra Sensory Perception and a PSI capacity" and took note of the fact that he had correctly prophesied the outcome of the 1949 World Series. To his dismay, many persons took his routines so seriously that they tried to enlist his aid in finding lost children or choosing horses at the race track. Unable to convince them that his psychic powers were derived from trickery, Randi decided he "couldn't live that kind of lie" and went back to his rabbits and handkerchiefs.

Now billing himself as "The Amazing Randi," the magician worked up a nightclub act in Montreal. In the manner of Harry Houdini, his idol, he drummed up audiences by escaping from the local jail. His career moved forward full tilt in the 1950s after he appeared on American television, and by the mid-1960s, he was able to assert, "I've broken out of jails in twenty-seven different cities of the world, from Copenhagen to Tokyo." Extricating himself from knotted ropes, locked safes, and straitjackets, he practiced his escape artistry on children's shows such as Wonderama, on frequent visits to the Mike Douglas Show and The Tonight Show, and on his own television specials in the United States, Canada, Europe, Japan, and Australia. In 1974 he was even invited to the White House by President Gerald R. Ford and his wife, Betty. That year he escaped from a straitjacket while hanging suspended over a Manhattan street, and on another occasion he made a similar escape while suspended over Niagara Falls. In 1975 he toured briefly with the rock star Alice Cooper as an executioner who simulated a guillotining of the singer during each performance.

Randi's interest in exposing parapsychological fakery had its origins in a radio show on Manhattan's WOR that he hosted for two years beginning in 1964, leading discussions from midnight until five in the morning on issues ranging from interracial marriage to unwed motherhood. Drawing listeners from all over the country, the program elicited as many as 150 letters a day. Alarmed by the numbers who phoned in with enthusiastic reports of self-declared clairvoyants and faith healers and by the fact that the press was publishing such claims, Randi took up the cudgels against charlatans. During a panel discussion in 1964, Randi was challenged by a parapsychologist to "put your money where your mouth is," and he promptly offered to pay $10,000 "to any person who demonstrates a paranormal power under satisfactory observational conditions." He carries a check around with him at all times, and he has stipulated in his will that the same offer will be made by his estate. By the time that Flim-Flam! was published in 1982, there had been more than 600 claimants, of which number only fifty-four had survived Randi's preliminaries. "The money was never safer," Randi still affirms. (His stint as a talk-show host ended when he "stepped on a couple of sacred cows.")

Increasingly, Randi's work as a debunker of parapsychology began to vie with his career as an entertainer, but in spite of his methodical investigations of psychics, he found it difficult to gain recognition for anything but his sleight-of-hand stunts. "I complained loudly," Randi said during an interview for Newsday (August 2, 1986), "and no one took me seriously until I began touring and giving lectures at colleges." On the college and university circuit during the 1970s he discovered that his debunking of paranormal phenomena by duplicating such "psychic" marvels as spoon-bending, telepathy, and clairvoyance was beginning to draw bigger audiences than his magic act.

His resistance to what he saw as an engulfing tide of irrationality in the United States intensified when Uri Geller, a charismatic young Israeli who claimed to have psychic powers, arrived in December 1972 to be tested at a prestigious Menlo Park, California "think tank" called the Stanford Research Institute. Geller convinced the prominent laser specialists Harold E. Puthoff and Russell Targ, who conducted the SRI research, that he could use psychic energy to foretell events, read minds, advance time on clocks, and even bend solid metallic objects such as spoons and keys. The test results appeared in the October 18, 1974, issue of Nature, one of the world's most prestigious science magazines, with an editorial stressing that publication was not intended as an endorsement of the results but as an example of the kind of research being done in the "arguable field" of parapsychology. Geller became a media darling and folk hero in short order and had "the U.S. almost under [his] spell," according to a Time magazine senior editor, Leon Jaroff, who wrote the foreword for Randi's The Truth About Uri Geller, which updated The Magic of Uri Geller (Ballantine, 1975).

On February 6, 1973, James Randi began a painstaking two-year unraveling of that spell, always allowing for the possibility that it might be cast by genuine powers. Fresh from his triumph at SRI, Geller arrived in the offices of Time magazine on that day to give the editors a demonstration of his psychic feats. Posing as a staff member, Randi was witness to "a perfectly transparent sleight-of-hand performance," which he duplicated after Geller left. As a result, Time published the first negative story on the psychic's extravagant claims. Shortly after that, Uri Geller made an embarrassing appearance on Johnny Carson's Tonight Show because he had been denied access to any of the test materials before the telecast began and because Carson's staff had sought advice from Randi on how best to safeguard the props from tampering. Although he failed with Johnny Carson, Geller did manage to deceive both Mike Douglas and Barbara Walters. When Randi appeared on Barbara Walters' syndicated Not for Women Only show, he dis-

enchanted the newswoman, who, according to Randi, confessed that "she had based the whole past year of her life on the reality of Geller's tricks."

Before delivering the manuscript of The Magic of Uri Geller to the printer, Randi sent Geller a registered letter offering him the opportunity of a private talk as "a way out that would not only make him a hero and a prince of hoaxers, but also pave the way for him to step into legitimate show business as an established conjuror." Randi was ready to accept a statement from Geller "to the effect that he had performed his deceptions in order to show that scientists are easily fooled" and that the media are inclined to be gullible about paranormal claims. Geller responded with the threat of a libel suit, but he never filed. When The Magic of Uri Geller was published, it was adjudged to be "sensible, well-informed, witty, compassionate, and utterly devastating" by Martin Gardner in the New York Review of Books (October 30, 1975).

In July 1975 James Randi traveled to England to demonstrate Geller's methods before a group of prominent scientists, including Maurice Wilkins, the Nobel Prize recipient credited with the co-discovery of the DNA molecule structure, at the Biophysical Laboratory of King's College, London. In a letter reprinted in the appendix of The Truth About Uri Geller, the members of the committee stated: "We believe that in investigating phenomena of apparently paranormal nature a qualified conjuror must be closely involved." Next, in a successful imposture carried out under the name of "Zwinge," Randi wangled an interview with the weekly Psychic News and was featured on its front page on July 24, 1975, as an overnight psychic discovery. Wryly, Randi observed that, with his conjuring ability, he himself could have launched a career "as a genuine psychic marvel."

In 1976, partly because of criticism from some quarters of his lack of academic credentials, James Randi helped to found the Committee for the Scientific Investigation of Claims of the Paranormal (CSICOP), a group of twenty-five scholars, scientists, authors, and "one lone conjuror," at a symposium sponsored by the American Humanist Association titled "The New Irrationalism: Antiscience and Pseudoscience." As its principal consultant, investigator, and "hit-man," Randi has contributed regularly to its journal, The Skeptical Inquirer, as well as to The Humanist, Technology Review, Science et Vie, Omni, Discover, Free Inquiry, New Scientist, and other periodicals. Echoing the objectives of the CSICOP, Randi maintained in Flim-Flam!: "I cannot prove that [paranormal] powers do not exist; I can only show that the evidence for them does not hold up under examination."

When CSICOP refused to implement member Martin Gardner's idea for the annual Uri Awards because "it's not dignified," the impish Randi personally took on the responsibility for dispensing the award, beginning in 1979. As specified by Randi in Flim-Flam!, the four categories for the award, "a tastefully bent stainless-steel spoon with a very transparent, very flimsy base," are: (1) "the Scientist who says or does the silliest thing relating to parapsychology in the preceding twelve months"; (2) "the Funding Organization that supports the most useless parapsychological study during the year"; (3) "the Media outlet that reports as fact the most outrageous paranormal claim"; (4) "the Psychic performer who fools the greatest number of people with the least effort."

The winner for 1979 in the second division was the McDonnell Foundation, which donated $500,-000 to Washington University in St. Louis for a psychic research lab to study "spoon-bending children." Early in 1978 James Randi had launched Project Alpha, an experiment in which two teenage magicians, Steven Shaw and Michael Edwards, infiltrated the lab and, for a total of 160 hours over the next three and one-half years, bamboozled researchers into believing they had paranormal powers. Randi did not reveal the hoax, which was instrumental in subsequently closing the lab, until a press conference in 1983. The payoff came when the Parapsychological Association, the official organization of psychic researchers, advised its members that it would be wise to use an experienced conjuror to police certain experiments.

In recent years Randi's prime targets have been American faith healers. During a 1984 Regents lectureship at the University of California at Los Angeles, he demonstrated one of the faith healers' most dramatic techniques by performing "psychic surgery" on a volunteer. According to Michelle Markel of the Los Angeles Times (March 14, 1984), Randi "plunged his hands into [the] volunteer's stomach, ferreted out what appeared to be bloody tissue and closed the wound without a trace of a scar." "Faith healers," Randi has said, "are the same thing as Geller, but they are much more dangerous. They each make millions preying on innocent victims." In an interview with Scot Morris of Omni (April 1980), Randi cited as an extreme example of the "irrational belief" fostered by faith healers the suicides in 1978 of almost the entire population of the Guyanese religious commune of Jonestown at the command of its leader, the Reverend Jim Jones. While he concedes that most faith healers do not want to establish death cults, he told Scot Morris that at first Jones "just wanted to be worshipped like a god and have people give him everything they owned. And there are lots more like him." Randi's campaign against faith healers has brought about the cancellation of some of their programs by several television and radio stations.

Such activities have brought Randi a lot of hate mail and a number of threats, and one faith healer even reminded him of a Biblical account of a magician who had been struck blind by a vengeful God. "That's all I need," Randi is reported to have said. To protect himself, he has installed a burglar alarm in his house and now includes in the letters that he sends to faith healers under his investigation a warning that duplicate letters have been sent to the FBI. When attending their meetings to gather facts, he wears a bulletproof vest and brings along his "bully boys." Occasionally he is recognized and pointed out to congregations as a representative of Satan, which prompts him to bow and wave.

"The Hydra of the paranormal grows heads faster than one can lop them off. But one tries," Randi wrote in The Truth About Uri Geller. His effort, involving considerable sums expended in travel and research, was officially honored in August 1986 when he was awarded a MacArthur Fellowship for his "dedication to educating the public." A physician who sits on the MacArthur foundation's fifteen-member selection committee, which especially cited Randi's work against faith healers, remarked that "Randi may save more lives than most doctors." The $272,000 grant, to be distributed over a five-year period free of taxes, with no strings attached, moved Randi to declare: "Now I can do battle against fakes from a charger, in a suit of armor, instead of naked on a mule." He plans to computerize his office files, hire a full-time assistant, and endow a college scholarship for future debunkers. For his lecture "Science and the Chimera," Randi was awarded the Blackstone Cup of the International Platform Association in 1983, and in 1987 he received a special award from the Magic Castle in Hollywood. Additional books by James Randi are Test Your ESP Potential: A Complete Kit with Instructions, Scorecards, and Apparatus (Dover, 1982) and, with Bert Randolph Sugar, Harry Houdini: His Life and Art (Grosset & Dunlap, 1976). His latest book, The Faith Healers, was published by Prometheus Books in October 1987.

James Randi is five feet seven inches in height, slight of build, green-eyed, and bald, with a magician's domed forehead, fringe of white hair, white beard, and Mephistophelean white eyebrows. He has held forth on the devious ways of tricksters at many institutions, including the American Association for the Advancement of Science, the Royal Institution of Great Britain, and—surprisingly enough—at the American Parapsychological Association. He compared his presence at the last-named organization to "Martin Luther walking into the Vatican for lunch."

In addition to replicating the feats of psychics and faith healers, Randi has continued to perform his own magic, although he renounced his more strenuous performances after escaping from a straightjacket while suspended from a helicopter over Tokyo, Japan, in 1985. He has contemplated writing a book on the subtleties of trickery and the mechanics of the art of escape that he has absorbed over the years, but now deems it "a wiser and more satisfying plan" to teach his skills to the sorcerer's apprentices who seek him out. During his long career he has sheltered and taught a number of young magicians, feeling that he is amply rewarded when "they go out and represent the trade well." He has also supported several foster children.

James Randi attributes his bachelor status to "being an escape artist." Since 1985 he has lived in Sunrise, Florida, where the brass knocker announces a "Charlatan." An amateur astronomer and archaeologist, he dug up his own collection of pre-Columbian artifacts in Peru. In the *Omni* interview, Randi identified himself as an agnostic who "adhere[s] to the tenets of the Unitarians," although in *Who's Who in America* he classifies himself as an atheist. Pressed about the possible threat to religious belief posed by his debunking, Randi told the story of a Unitarian man who was about to dress a burn on his son's finger with ointment. The son asked if the ointment would sting. After some hesitation, the father replied, "Son, if I were sure of anything, I wouldn't be a Unitarian." Randi wishes that he "could sell something like that" to religious believers. "They think that not believing . . . must take the joy out of life. Not at all." In the epilogue to *Flim-Flam!* he elaborated: "To know that you are an individual not put here for some mysterious reason by some supernatural means, and that you are not protected by unknown powers or beings; to know that you are a product of millions of experiments in the evolutionary process and not the result of a seed thrown on this planet by extraterrestrials—that, to me, is very exciting."

References: Discover 4:10+ Mr '83 por, 8:50+ N '87 pors; Los Angeles Times V p1+ Mr 14 '84 por, II p1+ My 11 '86, I p2+ S 14 '86 por; Money 15:114+ S '86 pors; NJ Monthly 5:46+ Jl '81 por, 10:26 F '85 por; N Y Times XI p2 Jl 5 '81 pors, C p3 F 15 '83 por, A p15 Jl 15 '86 por; Newsday II p3 Ag 2 '86 por; Omni 2:77+ Ap '80 por; People 15:57+ Ap 20 '81 por, 26:96+ Ag 11 '86 pors; Contemporary Authors vol 117 (1986); Encyclopedia of Occultism and Parapsychology (1985); Who's Who in America, 1986–87

Rau, Johannes
(rou)

Jan. 16, 1931– West German political leader. Address: b. Harold Strasse 2, D-4000 Düsseldorf 1, Federal Republic of Germany; h. Katernberger Strasse 171, D-5600 Wuppertal 1, Federal Republic of Germany

Campaigning under the election slogan "conciliation instead of division," Johannes Rau, a middle-of-the-road Social Democrat, was his party's standard-bearer in its attempt to recapture the government of the Federal Republic of Germany from the Christian Democratic Chancellor Helmut Kohl in January 1987. A protégé of the late statesman and Protestant lay theologian Gustav Heinemann, who served as West Germany's president from 1969 to 1974, Rau joined the Social Democratic party in 1957 and rose rapidly in its ranks. As minister president, since 1978, of his native North Rhine-Westphalia, West Germany's most heavily populated state, Rau promoted a comprehensive program for the modernization and revitalization of its troubled industrial economy and the protection of its environment. Although his bid for the chancellorship in the 1987 elections was unsuccessful, Rau remains one of his country's most personable and popular political leaders.

Johannes Rau was born on January 16, 1931 in Wuppertal-Barmen, in what is now North Rhine-Westphalia, to the Reverend Ewald and Helene (Hartmann) Rau. His father, a Protestant minister and evangelist, inculcated in him a profound religious humanism. As a student at a Gymnasium in his home city, Rau became active in the Bekennende Kirche (Confessing Church), which during the Hitler era had insisted on the independence of religion from state authority.

In 1949 Rau left the Gymnasium without taking his *Abitur* (school-leaving examination) and after serving a two-year apprenticeship in publishing and book selling in Wuppertal he attended a special school in Cologne for training in the book trade. In 1952 he went on the road as a traveling representative of a church-owned publishing house in Wuppertal that specialized in publications for Protestant youth. He remained with the firm until 1967, becoming its business manager in 1954, a member of its executive board in 1962, and managing director in 1965.

Meanwhile, in the early 1950s, Rau had met and made friends with Gustav Heinemann, who had resigned in 1950 as minister of the interior from the cabinet of Konrad Adenauer in protest against plans for the rearmament of West Germany. In

1952 Rau helped Heinemann, who had left the dominant Christian Democratic Union (CDU), to establish the All-German People's party (Gesamtdeutsche Volkspartei, or GVP), which favored a unified Germany as a neutral third force between East and West. Rau organized a youth group within the GVP, and in 1954 he became a member of the editorial board of the party's publication *Gesamtdeutsche Rundschau*.

When as a result of lack of popular support Heinemann dissolved the GVP in the spring of 1957, Rau followed him into the Social Democratic party of Germany (Sozialdemokratische Partei Deutschlands, or SPD). Although at first Rau did not feel quite comfortable in the SPD, with its emphasis on lofty theorizing, he soon became a leading member of its North Rhine-Westphalia organization. In 1958 he was elected on the SPD ticket as representative of a Wuppertal constituency in the North Rhine-Westphalia Landtag, or state legislature, where he became a member, and later chairman, of committees dealing with youth and cultural affairs. In 1962 he obtained a seat on the executive committee of the SPD faction in the Landtag, and in 1967 he became the committee's chairman.

In addition, from 1958 to 1962 Rau served as chairman of the SPD's youth organization, the Young Socialists (Jungsozialisten), in Wuppertal. Concurrently, from 1959 to 1962 he was a member of the executive of the regional SPD organization in Wuppertal, and from 1962 to 1968 he was its deputy chairman. From 1964 to 1978 Rau served on the Wuppertal city council, and he was also for three years, until 1967, chairman of its SPD faction. On the national level, Rau became a member of the executive of the federal SPD organization in 1968 and was elected to a seat on its presidium ten years later.

As Oberbürgermeister, or chief mayor, of Wuppertal during 1969–70, Rau was noted for his farsighted administration, and for his energetic promotion of educational and cultural life in the city. After the state elections of July 1970 confirmed North Rhine-Westphalia's governing coalition of the SPD and the Free Democratic party (FDP), he was appointed by Minister President Heinz Kühn to the newly established cabinet office of minister for science and research, in which he served until 1978. During his tenure he founded new institutions of higher learning, at Duisburg, Essen, Paderborn, Siegen, and Wuppertal in 1972, and established West Germany's first correspondence university, at Hagen, in 1974.

In June 1977 a state party conference at Duisburg elected Rau by a narrow margin as chairman of the North Rhine-Westphalia SPD, the Federal Republic's largest Social Democratic regional organization, with some 300,000 members. Although he was known as a middle-of-the-roader with no marked left-wing sympathies, it was the radical Young Socialists who helped him to get elected, because they felt that his opponent, the Labor Minister Friedhelm Farthmann, an orthodox trade unionist and law professor, stood too far to the right.

When Minister President Heinz Kühn retired in September 1978, Rau was chosen as his successor, defeating his rival, the Finance Minister Diether Posser, by a vote of 161 to 150 at a special state SPD conference. At the time of his election, a political writer for the *Kölner Stadt-Anzeiger* was quoted in the *German Tribune* (October 1, 1978) as saying, "The man who in his twenty-year political career has managed to steer clear of scandal . . . has also managed not to make any enemies. . . . There is no doubt that he is capable of stabilizing the ship of government, heeling badly in the last year." Taking office at Düsseldorf, the state capital, on September 20, 1978, Rau indicated that he would govern in a fair and unconditional partnership with the FDP and consult with the CDU opposition in dealing with problems. He relinquished all commitments that he felt might interfere with his duties as minister president, including his seat on the administrative council of the Westdeutsche Rundfunk, but he retained his chairmanship of the state SPD organization. At a conference at Herne in June 1979 he was reelected state party chairman with 293 of the 307 delegate votes.

The SPD won a major victory in North Rhine-Westphalia's state elections on May 11, 1980, receiving 48.8 percent of the popular vote and an absolute majority of the Landtag seats. The outcome was attributed to Rau's personal popularity, enhanced by his direct contacts with the citizens of his state during the campaign. Despite his own modest assessment that the extent of his victory was "undeserved," the election augmented his stature within the national SPD organization. Since the FDP received slightly less than the 5 percent of the popular vote it needed for parliamentary representation, Rau was now able to govern with an all-SPD cabinet.

For West Germany's general election of October 1980, Rau mobilized SPD support in North Rhine-Westphalia to help ensure the reelection of Helmut Schmidt as chancellor of the Federal Republic. In October 1981 he visited Moscow, where he engaged in frank discussions with Soviet officials about the Schmidt government's defense policies. The esteem in which he was held within the national party was again confirmed when at the SPD party congress in April 1982 he was elected to succeed Hans-Jürgen Wischnewski as a deputy chairman of the SPD national executive, becoming one of party chairman Willy Brandt's chief aides.

After exercising power for some thirteen years in the Federal Republic of Germany, the SPD was forced into opposition on the national scene on October 1, 1982, when Helmut Schmidt was defeated in the Bundestag by a vote of no confidence. He was succeeded as chancellor by CDU chairman Helmut Kohl, who formed a new coalition with his party's Bavarian affiliate, the Christian Social Union (CSU), and the FDP. In the national elections of March 6, 1983, the SPD, with Hans-Jochen Vogel as its candidate for chancellor, failed to regain power, receiving 38.2 percent of the vote, as compared with the 42.9 percent that it had obtained in 1980.

Meanwhile, in North Rhine-Westphalia, Rau confronted some grave problems. The state's budget deficit was steadily mounting, and the restructuring of the coal, steel, and chemical industries was bringing about large-scale unemployment, exceeding 10 percent of the working population. Although his moderate, centrist policies were popular, as was also his practice of "leadership by discussion" rather than by authoritarian directives, he came increasingly under fire, not only from the opposition, but from his own party as well. He managed to recoup his losses somewhat when in 1983 he launched a comprehensive environmental protection program and introduced a future-oriented "high tech" modernization plan for industry. He also gained some favorable publicity with his trips abroad, including a visit, in August 1983, to the People's Republic of China. In January 1985 he visited the German Democratic Republic for discussions with Communist party leader Erich Honecker, and in the following month he went to Washington, D.C., for political talks with American officials, including Vice-President George Bush.

As the state elections of May 12, 1985, approached, Rau was in an optimistic mood. He conducted an energetic reelection campaign, sidestepping partisan politics while appealing to a broad spectrum of voters and bringing his attractive young family into the limelight. Although he emphasized his party's policy of "ecological modernization of the economy, he rejected the prospect of an alliance with the environmentalist and countercultural Green party. The election resulted in a landslide victory for the SPD, which won 52.1 percent of the popular vote and more than two-thirds of the Landtag seats.

The North Rhine-Westphalia election represented a severe setback for Chancellor Helmut Kohl, whose protégé Bernhard Worms was soundly defeated by Rau in his bid to capture the post of minister president for the CDU. Rau's victory placed him in the forefront of likely candidates for the federal chancellorship, along with Hans-Jochen Vogel, the leader of the opposition in the Bundestag, and Oskar Lafontaine, the new minister president of the Saarland. Although at the time Rau denied any aspirations for the chancellorship, public opinion polls taken in the summer of 1985 confirmed his popularity among the voters.

On September 16, 1985, following his return from a visit to Moscow, where Soviet leader Mikhail Gorbachev had conveyed to him a proposal for a Central European zone free from nuclear weapons, Rau was informally nominated by SPD leaders as the party's candidate for chancellor, pending formal approval by a party congress. He affirmed his candidacy on December 16, 1985, at a special SPD meeting in the Westphalian mining town of Ahlen. Declaring his intention to be a "chancellor of all citizens," he called for a consensus of the divergent elements of society and introduced his campaign slogan—"conciliation instead of division." He reiterated his commitment to "ecological renewal of our industrial society" and depicted the Kohl government as a champion of the privileged and as "the greatest obstacle to an effective campaign against mass unemployment." Calling for a more equitable distribution of economic benefits and social obligations, he proposed a number of reforms to improve the quality of life for Germans with low and moderate incomes.

On the international level, Rau affirmed West Germany's commitment to the Western alliance and to friendship with the United States. He called for an end to the armaments race and advocated negotiations aimed at the removal of American and Soviet strategic weapons from Europe, the strengthening of economic and cultural relations between East and West, and a determined struggle for universal human rights, including freedom from hunger and want. At the end of his speech, Rau received a standing ovation and was given an unqualified endorsement by party chairman Willy Brandt.

Although a national economic upswing late in 1985 bolstered the hopes of Kohl's governing coalition for the 1987 national elections, public opinion polls placed Rau well ahead of the incumbent chancellor in terms of popularity, political style, and other aspects of his persona. In February 1986 Rau visited Washington, D.C., once more, and during a half-hour meeting he and President Ronald Reagan discussed East-West relations and human rights, but only vaguely broached the Reagan administration's Strategic Defense Initiative, or "star wars" program, which Rau and his party strongly opposed. In April Rau was welcomed as an old friend in Israel, which he had visited some fifteen times over a twenty-five year period. He went to the USSR again in July 1986 to open a North Rhine-Westphalia industrial exhibition, and during two hours of talks with Gorbachev he assured the Soviet leader that he would initiate a "second phase of a policy of détente" if elected chancellor.

At a pre-election party congress, held at Nuremberg for five days, beginning on August 25, 1986, the SPD's election campaign was formally launched. The segment of the election platform that dealt with foreign affairs and security policy clearly bore the mark of the party's left wing. It called, among other things, for repudiation of West Germany's agreement with the United States for cooperation on space weapons research and for withdrawal of NATO's American-made medium-range missiles from West Germany. It also demanded limitation of the country's military establishment, to make it incapable of attacking the Soviet Union, and it called for rejection of a Kohl government measure to extend military service for draftees from fifteen to eighteen months. While pledging to continue West German membership in NATO, the party called for a renewal of détente with the USSR and insisted that "the self-assertion of Europe should be one of the main goals of Bonn's policies." In the wake of the Soviet nuclear disaster at Chernobyl in April 1986, the party demanded the phasing out of nuclear power in West Germany within ten years.

In his ninety-minute speech to the Nuremberg congress, Rau often echoed the party platform on questions involving defense and foreign policy. Turning to domestic issues, he castigated the Kohl government for neglecting the plight of the nation's 2.2 million unemployed and pledged to make the battle against unemployment the party's "most important task." He called on his fellow party members to fight for an absolute SPD majority in the Bundestag and, to that end, to "seek out people who have up to now voted conservative or Green." Although Rau drew some criticism from both the left and right, Willy Brandt and Helmut Schmidt called on the party to unite behind him. The Nuremberg congress formally nominated Rau as condidate for chancellor by a vote of 425 to one, with three abstentions.

During the final months of 1986, the SPD's hopes for victory dimmed in the wake of unfavorable state election results. Rau's insistence on an absolute majority for his party and his continued rejection of an alliance with the Greens was generally considered by political observers to be unrealistic. In the Bavarian state elections on October 12, 1986, the SPD received only 27.5 percent of the popular vote, as compared with the 55.8 percent garnered by Franz Josef Strauss's CSU. Then, in the city-state elections held on November 9 in Hamburg, long a Social Democratic stronghold, the SPD lost power for the first time in some thirty years, its vote reduced to 41.8 percent from the 51.3 percent that it had received in 1982. The party's poor showing prompted Wolfgang Clement, a leading SPD spokesman, to resign as Rau's campaign manager. Despite last-ditch efforts by Rau to rally the SPD out of its mood of defeatism, on the eve of the national elections few observers held much hope for an SPD victory.

In the national elections of January 25, 1987, Kohl retained power, although his CDU-CSU faction's share of the popular vote was reduced to 44.3 percent from the 48.8 percent it had received in 1983. The SPD came in as a poor second, with 37 percent of the vote, slightly less than the 38.2 percent that it had received in the previous national elections. The FDP, which remained the junior partner in the governing coalition, increased its share of the vote to 9.1 percent from 7 percent, while the Green party won 8.3 percent of the vote, as compared with 5.6 percent in 1983.

Following the elections, Rau renounced any claim to succeed Willy Brandt as party chairman. He declared that he intended to remain a deputy party chairman and to concentrate his efforts on his position as minister president of North Rhine-Westphalia. On March 23, 1987, Rau announced Brandt's resignation, following a controversial appointment, in order to spare the SPD inner strife as it faced a series of difficult state elections. Brandt was succeeded as party chairman by Hans-Jochen Vogel.

Rau is a member of the synod of the Protestant Church in the Rhineland and a deputy member of its governing body. He is a trustee of the Friedrich-Ebert-Stiftung, an honorary member of the Ring Bildender Künstler and, since 1962, a member of West Germany's Education and Science Employees' Union. Among the honors that he has received are the Federal Republic's Grand Cross of Merit (Grosses Bundesverdienstkreuz) with star and sash, Belgium's Grand Cross of the Order of Leopold II, Brazil's Order of Rio Branco, and the rank of grand officier in France's Ordre National du Mérite. In 1982-83 he served in the largely honorary post of president of West Germany's Bundesrat, the upper house of Parliament. Rau's publications include Die neue Fernuniversität (The New Correspondence University, 1974) and Lebensqualität? (Quality of Life?, 1974). Since 1985 he has served on the board of the Protestant monthly Evangelische Kommentare (Evangelical Commentary).

Affectionately known to his friends and constituents as "Brother Johannes," Rau is an adept at quoting the Bible, and he is also a master story-teller who enjoys an occasional tankard of beer and a game of skat at his tavern hangout in Wuppertal. His favorite hobby is collecting stamps, especially those of Israel. Henri de Bresson, quoted in the Le Monde section of the Manchester Guardian weekly (June 9, 1985), referred to his "square jaw, easy laugh, impressive appetite, and a readiness to give the shirt off his back." Long considered a confirmed bachelor, Johannes Rau was married on August 22, 1982, to Christine Delius, a granddaughter of Gustav Heinemann. She is twenty-six years younger than he and holds a doctorate in political science. Their children are Anna Christina, Philip-Immanuel, and Laura-Helene. Klaus Bölling, a former spokesman for the SPD, criticized Rau in a book about the Bonn political scene, published in 1986, for having insisted repeatedly that his family was an important to him as politics. But Rau asserts, "I can only stand politics if I stay what I am."

References: Aufbau p1+ S 27 '85 por; Christian Sci Mon p7+ Ag 8 '86 pors; Der Spiegel 39:24+ D 23 '85 por; German Tribune p4+ My 26 '85 por; Manchester Guardian W p12 Je 9 '85 por; N Y Times A p4 D 9 '86 por; Vorwärts p5+ D 21 '85 pors; International Who's Who, 1986-87; Wer ist Wer? (1986)

Rauschenberg, Robert

Oct. 22, 1925– Artist. Address: b. c/o Leo Castelli Gallery, 420 West Broadway, New York City, N.Y. 10012

NOTE: This biography supersedes the article that appeared in Current Biography in 1965.

Robert Rauschenberg

For more than thirty years Robert Rauschenberg has remained one of the most influential American artists of the second half of the twentieth century. A survivor of the many stylistic trends that came after abstract expressionism, "he still comes off," according to a *New York Times* art critic, Grace Glueck, "as a kind of Wunderkind who might be up to something very new next week." Usually credited, with his friend and former collaborator, Jasper Johns, as being a forerunner of pop art, Rauschenberg can also be said to have anticipated minimalism and conceptualism, and even the recent return to figurative painting. His career has embraced not only painting, three-dimensional constructions, the graphic arts, and photography, but work in dance and theatre, both as a performer and as a designer.

Whatever his chosen art form, Rauschenberg is convinced that it has to be involved with life. His own much-quoted dictum is: "Painting relates to both art and life. Neither can be made. I try to act in the gap between the two." That would also seem to relate to what is the central characteristic of Rauschenberg's art—the collaborative gesture that is at once method and medium, and form itself. As he has acknowledged, "I always like to collaborate; it's a device to fight ego." Rauschenberg views the imposition of a personal style on the world as a handicap that tends to slow it down. In fact, he conceives of his work as being "a conversation that goes on with people I don't have the opportunity to meet."

The gigantic multimedia construction *One Quarter Mile or 2 Furlong Piece*, begun in 1981 and still in progress, is a dazzling epitome of Rauschenberg's convictions and of the art they have produced. As installed in the new Lila Acheson Wallace Wing of the Metropolitan Museum of Art, in an "edited" 388-foot-long version, it provides a one-work retrospective of Rauschenberg's enormous productivity. There are allusions to his collaboration with the urban environment (three-dimensional pieces made from highway construction signs, cardboard boxes, discarded public library books), and to his collaborative work as graphic artist and man of the theatre. The visual mélange records his various styles from the all-white paintings of the 1950s to his transfer prints on fabrics. Throughout are collages of silk-screened fragments of photographs and the printed word reverberating with allusions to events of our times so that viewers shape messages for themselves as they pass through what the *New York Times*'s chief art critic, John Russell, has called a "thinking man's Epcot."

Robert Rauschenberg was born Milton Rauschenberg in Port Arthur, Texas, on October 22, 1925, the only son of Ernest Rauschenberg, a utilities company employee, and Dora (Matson) Rauschenberg. According to Calvin Tomkins' book *Off the Wall: Robert Rauschenberg and the Art World of Our Time* (1980), Ernest Rauschenberg both raised and trained the finest bird dogs in the entire state of Texas, and was a prodigious duck hunter. So nearsighted that he was unable to hit anything with a gun, his son, Robert, became a collector rather than a hunter of animals and at one time owned a private menagerie of two hunting dogs, some goldfish, a bantam rooster, a goat, and a horned frog.

The reading disability of dyslexia so hampered Robert Rauschenberg in school that he "excelled in poor grades," as he reported in *Autobiography,* the seventeen-foot-long lithograph of 1968 in which he combined visual images with a written text. The difficulties brought on by his handicap were mitigated by drawing, which he began to do at the age of ten and which he continued during his years at Jefferson High School. After graduating in 1942, he enrolled at the University of Texas in Austin in the fall of that year. There he studied pharmacy until he was expelled, in 1943, for refusing to dissect a frog. Shortly after that, he was drafted into the United States Navy. After completing boot camp, Rauschenberg announced to his chief petty officer that since he had no intention of killing anyone, he should not be given a gun. Consequently, he was assigned to the hospital corps and finally to Camp Pendleton near San Diego, where he worked as a neuropsychiatric technician. Although while in service he amused himself and his fellow enlisted men by doing portrait sketches, it was a visit to the Huntington Library in San Marino, California, that provided his first real encounter with art. Struck with its portraits by such British masters as Gainsborough, Reynolds, and Lawrence, he decided that he would pursue his new interest after the war. A friend persuaded him to enroll in the Kansas City Art Institute, and from 1946 to 1947 he studied there under the G.I. Bill, earning extra money by doing store window displays. It was at that juncture that he discarded the name "Milton" in favor of "Robert," feeling that his given name was not altogether suitable for an artist. Then another idea struck him—that artists should study in Paris—and he therefore left for France to enroll at the Académie Julian, but his lack of adequate technical preparation and inability to understand French well enough to profit from criticism led him and his friend Susan Weil, another American student (who in 1950 was to become his wife), to leave the school. In 1948, having read that the Bauhaus master Josef Albers, then teaching at Black Mountain College in North Carolina, offered courses that stressed a disciplined approach to painting, Rauschenberg decided that this was precisely what he needed. He and Susan Weil thereupon became members of that avant-garde academic community. Despite Albers' poor opinion of his ability, Rauschenberg considers him "the most important teacher" he has ever had. Of equal importance to the development of his ideas and modes of expression was his fortunate meeting at Black Mountain College with the composer John Cage and the dancer Merce Cunningham.

Established in a New York studio, Rauschenberg then studied (1949–50) at the Art Students League with Morris Kantor and Vaclav Vytacil and with the noted abstract expressionists Franz Kline, Robert Motherwell, and Jack Tworkov. Between 1949 and 1951 he embarked on his first collaborative project, when he and Susan Weil started making photo images of their own bodies on light-sensitive blueprint paper, which they used because it was relatively affordable. Only one of that series survives: Female Figure (Blueprint) of about 1949. Proceeding to make prints of miscellaneous objects dropped on to blueprint paper, the Rauschenbergs used them for window decorations commissioned by the Bonwit Teller department store. Their work was featured in a Life magazine "Speaking of Pictures" spread in April 1951.

Taking a bold approach, the young artist, unannounced, brought some of his work to the noted New York art dealer Betty Parsons. Hoping for acceptance but expecting rejection, he was agreeably surprised when she scheduled an exhibition at her gallery in May 1951. Among the best known of the works shown in that first exhibition was The Lily White (1949/50), an all-white oil painting except for the black numbers scrawled over its surface. Rauschenberg then painted a series of proto-minimal completely white canvases, enlivened only by shadowy reflections of the viewer, who thus "collaborates" in creating the effect; next, a group of all-black paintings, composed of torn and crumpled newsprint painted on to the canvas backing; and finally, a series of all-red paintings.

After his divorce, in 1952, Rauschenberg went to Italy, Spain, and North Africa with the American painter Cy Twombly. During a trip of several months he worked on constructions composed of bits of wood and stones, which he placed in boxes, something on the order of Marcel Duchamp's ready-mades. Those pieces, which in 1953 were exhibited in galleries in Florence and Rome, no longer exist, for on the advice of an Italian art critic,

Rauschenberg jettisoned them in the river Arno before returning to New York. There he lived in great poverty in a studio on Fulton Street.

In those constructions of wood and stones, however, lay the germ of what Rauschenberg, in 1955, began to call his "combine paintings." Sometimes pretentiously labeled by critics as neo-Dadaist, they were influenced, as he acknowledges, by the paintings of Leonardo, in which trees, rocks, and the figure of the Virgin are all of equal importance, by the collages of the Dadaist Kurt Schwitters, and by the work of Duchamp. Beginning to elaborate on that mode, Rauschenberg won his reputation as an enfant terrible of the avant-garde with such works as a "painting" made from a box of earth planted with grass and birdseed (1953); Erased de Kooning. Robert Rasuchenberg. 1953, exactly that: an abstract expressionist drawing given him by Willem de Kooning, which, in a reverse sort of collaborative gesture, he obliterated; and Bed, created one day in 1955 when he found himself without canvas, and dribbled paint over his own patchwork quilt, stretched on a frame. Exhibited in 1958 at the first of many subsequent one-man shows at his dealer, the Leo Castelli Gallery, Bed aroused much controversy: the paint dribbles suggested murder or rape to some observers. Later in the year Bed was banned from exhibition at the Festival of Two Worlds at Spoleto, Italy.

Additional excitement was stirred by Curfew (1958), a semiabstract canvas through which the artist cut a hole and inserted four Coca-Cola bottles. Writing in 1964, a Life magazine reporter called Curfew the first pop art painting. And then there was the notorious Monogram, consisting of a stuffed Angora goat found by Rauschenberg in a taxidermist's shop. Encircled by an automobile tire, its muzzle painted with a smear of colors, it stands on a collaged base that incorporates a tennis ball, a shirtsleeve, a rubber heel, and footprints. Monogram, on which Rauschenberg worked from about 1955 to 1959, derives its title, according to Robert Hughes, the art critic of Time magazine, from its personal significance. The goat alludes to a pet that the artist had as a child, and Hughes postulates that the piece can also be read as an icon of male homosexuality. In 1959 Rauschenberg added another sensory dimension to his combines. Broadcast includes three radios tuned to different stations, and Canyon incorporates a mirror that reflects the viewer and the world outside the picture. A pillow dangling from the canvas calls attention to the space into which a stuffed eagle, also attached to the picture, might soar.

Between 1955 and 1962 Rauschenberg lived in a succession of lower Manhattan studios with another Southern-born artist, Jasper Johns. While the two men, by working together, exchanging ideas, and encouraging one another, were changing the course of modern art, their day-to-day existence depended on the brilliantly realistic window displays they did for Tiffany & Company and Bonwit Teller under the collaborative name of "Matson Jones." Despite the bitterness of his eventual break with Johns, Rauschenberg's art, unlike Johns's hermetic and enigmatic paintings, became more and more life-affirming. According to Calvin Tomkins in his *Off the Wall*, Rauschenberg proceeded to turn "outward to the world at large, trying to annex as much of it as possible into his work."

In other innovations, Rauschenberg contributed to the art of drawing by working out a frottage process that resulted in a one-dimensional equivalent of the combines. By sprinkling such solvents as lighter fluid on collages made up of fragments of printed images or lines of text, over which he drew penciled marks, he was able to transfer images to underlying sheets of paper. Among the most important of such drawings are the thirty-four that illustrate Dante's *Inferno*, one for each canto and each a kaleidoscope of allusive, contemporary images seen through a blizzard of pencil strokes. Done between 1959 and 1960 and owned by the Museum of Modern Art, the drawings were published in a limited edition by Harry N. Abrams in 1964. A retrospective exhibition of all of Rauschenberg's drawings, dating from 1958 to 1968, was shown at Acquavella Contemporary Art, Inc., in New York in 1986.

Another one-dimensional equivalent of the combine paintings were the silkscreen paintings that succeeded them in the early 1960s. A stenciling technique allowed pictures, photographs (including the artist's own), and texts to be transferred, with changes of scale, on to canvas, cloth, or cardboard. As in *Barge* (1962), the fragments, juxtaposed or overlapping one another in seemingly haphazard relationships, induce a sort of reverie, and the effect of veiling introduces not only a spatial but a temporal quality. *Axle* (1964), in which photos of President John F. Kennedy reappear as a leitmotif, created a sensation at the 1964 Kassel Documenta exhibition and won the gold medal at the 1965 Corcoran Gallery of Art (Washington, D.C.) biennial. Rauschenberg's international reputation was, in fact, made secure in 1964 by a series of European shows, among them one at London's Whitechapel Art Gallery and the Venice Biennale, in which he won first prize in painting, becoming, with James Abbott McNeill Whistler and Mark Tobey, only the third American artist to be thus honored.

It was in 1964 also that Rauschenberg toured Europe and the Orient with the Merce Cunningham Dance Company, with which he had been associated over the past decade as a designer of costumes, sets, and lighting, as stage manager and, on occasion, dancer. Throughout the rest of the 1960s Rauschenberg often participated in "happenings" and other multimedia events, and he sometimes danced with other companies as well. In 1963 he choreographed his own work, *Pelican*, in which, to the accompaniment of a taped collage of sounds, he performed on roller skates, wearing a stylized parachute and helmet of his own design.

In the context of that type of allusion to technology, and the repertoire of urban debris that went into the making of his combines, there can be

placed another of Rauschenberg's collaborations, this time with Billy Klüver, a scientist at Bell Telephone Laboratories. In 1966 the two men set up E.A.T. (Experiments in Art and Technology), a nonprofit foundation "to function as a catalyst for the inevitable fusing" of industry, technology, and the arts. The venture lasted until about 1970, when corporate financial support began to fall away and Rauschenberg felt other demands on his time, such as his establishment that year of Change, Inc., a foundation to help needy artists. Always a champion of liberal causes, he has lobbied for legislation to guarantee artists royalties on resales of their work.

Eventually, Rauschenberg's frenetic activity of the 1960s gave way to a lull in his work in the 1970s. In 1971 he left New York to live on Captiva Island, off Florida's Gulf Coast, where he devoted most of his attention to printmaking. He had started doing lithographs in 1962 at Tatyana Grosman's press, Universal Limited Art Editions in West Islip, New York, and in about 1965 began a long relationship with the Gemini G.E.L. workshop in Los Angeles. Among the best known of his lithographs are the 1970 *Stoned Moon* series, with its references to the first moon landing in 1969, and the *Hoarfrost* series of 1974-75, with its transparent, veiled images. Of the latter series the artist has commented that it was "done on silk, cotton or cheesecloth, presenting the imagery in the ambiguity of freezing into focus or melting from view."

In 1975, in a continuing search for new materials and new sources of inspiration, Rauschenberg and a group of assistants, under Gemini G.E.L. sponsorship, went to the Gandhi Ashram at Ahmedabad, India, where he worked on constructions composed of bits of sari cloth, pieces of folded paper, sticks of bamboo, and mud. At that time of new ventures Rauschenberg was accorded the first major retrospective of his work that had been held since the 1963 showing at New York's Jewish Museum and the 1965 exhibition of his paintings at the Walker Art Center in Minneapolis. Between 1977 and 1978 an exhibition of 157 of his works, acclaimed by John Russell as "some of the finest art that has been made in our lifetime," traveled from the National Collection of Fine Arts in Washington to the Museum of Modern Art, the San Francisco Museum of Modern Art, the Albright-Knox Art Gallery in Buffalo, and the Art Institute of Chicago.

In 1981 two exhibitions, one at the Centre Georges Pompidou at the Place Beaubourg in Paris, the other at Boston's Institute of Contemporary Art, gave viewers the opportunity to become acquainted with Rauschenberg the photographer, whose flat-patterned prints frequently parallel the ambiguities of scale and perspective characteristic of his silkscreen paintings. Selections from the Paris show were published in *Robert Rauschenberg Photographs* (New York, Pantheon, 1981), with a text-interview that explains his feelings for the medium. In 1979 a commission to make an arrangement of 600 of his slides to be projected as a backdrop for *Glacial Decoy*, a dance devised by the choreographer Trisha Brown, had reawakened his long-dormant interest in photography. At Black Mountain College, Rauschenberg had studied with the noted photographer Harry Callahan, and one of his earliest ambitions, soon abandoned, was to photograph the entire United States, step by step. Parenthetically, the first Rauschenberg work ever acquired by a museum was a photograph of an old buggy, purchased by Edward Steichen for the Museum of Modern Art in 1952. In 1987 Rauschenberg received an award from the International Center of Photography in New York for creative use of the camera in connection with his art.

In 1982 Rauschenberg and an entourage took off for China, where they set up a workshop at an ancient paper mill in Anhui province. Their project was the making of assemblages of present-day Chinese poster images, covered over with specially made translucent paper and collaged on to sheets of mulberry fiber. Going on to Japan, Rauschenberg worked at a ceramics factory, producing such works as *Dirt Shrine: South* (1982), a kind of combine on which images relating to Japanese life, mostly derived from photographs, were fired into the glaze.

His collaborations with native Japanese artisans and source-specific materials were the precursors of ROCI, or the Rauschenberg Overseas Cultural Interchange (a word-play, also, on the name of the artist's pet turtle, Rocky). ROCI will take Rauschenberg on a five-year round of visits, beginning in 1985, to some twenty-two countries, where he will collaborate with local artists, using and elaborating on traditional methods and imagery. An attempt to promote international understanding, the mammoth enterprise is privately funded, with coordinating headquarters at the University of South Florida. As ROCI proceeds, its tangible results will, somewhat like a mammoth artistic chain letter, be shown in each host country, incorporating works from different stops along the way. Examples will be left behind as gifts to the people, while other works will be sent on to the National Gallery of Art in Washington for a major windup exhibition that has been planned for 1990. Local writers will contribute texts for the catalogues of the ongoing shows, and Rauschenberg's own photographs will document the entire project. In 1985, 230 pieces done in Mexico were exhibited in Mexico City; in 1986 ROCI/Japan opened in Tokyo.

Over the years, since 1951, the roster of Rauschenberg's one-man shows in galleries and museums in the United States and Europe has taken on impressive length. Among his many significant group exhibitions are: "Sixteen Americans," MOMA, 1959; "Artists of the New York School: Second Generation," the Jewish Museum, 1958; "Art of Assemblage," MOMA, 1961; "Dada, Surrealism, and Their Heritage," MOMA, 1968; and "New York Painting and Sculpture: 1940–1970," the Metropolitan Museum of Art, 1969–70. In addition to the holdings of the artist's works in major American museums, at London's Tate Gallery, and in collections in Amsterdam, Zurich, Cologne,

Düsseldorf, and Stockholm, there will now, as a result of ROCI, be Rauschenberg pieces or Rauschenberg-inspired collaborations in museums around the world. The holder of several major art prizes and honorary university degrees, Rauschenberg is also a member of both the American Academy and Institute of Arts and Letters and the Royal Academy of Fine Arts of Stockholm.

Although he has described himself as being unable to sustain a close emotional relationship, Rauschenberg has always been friendly and gregarious. When not traveling, he lives on his thirty-acre Captiva estate, a compound including houses, studio space, and a graphics workshop, Untitled Press, Inc. He often visits New York, where he maintains a five-story home in downtown Manhattan. He retains old ties with his former wife, now a close friend and printmaking collaborator, and their son Christopher, born in 1951, who is an artist-photographer. Robert Rauschenberg's tanned, lithe, and youthful appearance reflects his active outdoor life. His penetrating gaze and characteristic smile affirm his much-quoted avowal: "I'm for 'yes.' 'No' excludes. I'm for inclusion." Commenting on his 1977 retrospective exhibition, a *Village Voice* critic described it as "jammed with enough major works to flesh out a dozen careers," and compared Rauschenberg's creative pace to Picasso's. Ten years later, both comments still held true.

References: Contemporary Artists (1983); Forge, Andrew. Rauschenberg (1972); National Collection of Fine Arts. Robert Rauschenberg (1976); Tomkins, Calvin. Off the Wall: Robert Rauschenberg and the Art World of Our Time (1980); Who's Who in America 1986–87; Who's Who in American Art (1984); World Artists 1950–1980 (1984)

Richards, Lloyd

1922 (?)– Theatrical director; actor; educator. Address: b. Yale University School of Drama, 222 York St., New Haven, Conn. 06520

Equally dedicated to giving a dramatic voice to the black experience in America and to creating a viable academic forum for the development of new plays, the veteran stage actor and director Lloyd Richards hopes to foster "a national sense of theater" through his work as a founding member of the regional theatre movement. The first black director ever to stage a Broadway play—the acclaimed 1959 production of Lorraine Hansberry's *A Raisin in the Sun*—Richards went on ten years later to become artistic director of the National Playwrights Conference of the Eugene O'Neill Theater Center, the prestigious birthplace for new American plays that are developed each summer in Waterford, Connecticut.

Lloyd Richards

In 1979 Lloyd Richards replaced Robert Brustein as dean of the Yale University School of Drama and artistic director of the Yale Repertory Theatre. There, he has developed a reputation for vision, sensitivity, and enterprise, establishing the theatre's annual Winterfest of works by new playwrights and creating a noncommercial atmosphere of excellence that has spawned a number of eventual Broadway successes. Through his professional relationships with the playwrights Athol Fugard and August Wilson, Richards has presided over the development of important new plays with racial themes. Ironically, both in spite of and because of his focus on the text of the play rather than on its production, such works as Fugard's *Master Harold and the Boys* and Wilson's *Fences* have gone on to achieve major commercial coups on the "Great White Way," whose color barrier he played such a vital role in hurdling.

Lloyd George Richards was born about 1921 or 1922 in Toronto, Canada, the son of Albert George Richards, a carpenter, and the former Rose Isabella Coote. Little has been written about his youth, other than that he immigrated to the United States with his parents in 1923 and graduated from Northwestern High School in Detroit, Michigan. He obtained a B.A. degree in theatre arts from Wayne University, which is also in Detroit, in 1944 and served for a year with the United States Army Air Force during World War II, attaining the rank of cadet pilot.

Richards began his theatrical career in radio. He did some broadcasting for the Wayne University Radio Guild and eventually found work as an announcer and disc jockey on Detroit radio station WJLB. Among his radio credits was a stint as narrator for a program entitled *Little Church on the Air*

on Detroit's station WWJ. In 1948, eager to try his luck on Broadway, he moved to New York, where he studied acting at Paul Mann Actors Workshop from 1949 to 1952. He made his New York acting debut in 1948, when he appeared as Pee Wee in an Equity Library Theatre production of *Plant in the Sun*. His early professional assignments, according to John P. Shanley in the *New York Times* (January 17, 1960), "were neither entirely discouraging nor financially rewarding. Mr. Richards appeared in off-Broadway productions of *Stevedore* and other plays, usually portraying old men, although he was then in his twenties. His pay was a little as $7 a week."

His chance at commercial success finally arrived in 1950, when he played his first Broadway role as Oz in the short-lived run of *Freight* at the Fulton Theater. He later appeared as Iago in a stage reading of *Othello* and as Carr in the Equity Library Theatre production of *Winterset*. He performed in radio dramas, including *Hotel for Pets*, *Front Page Drama*, and *Murder by Experts*, and acted in television programs ranging from soap operas to the prestigious *Hallmark Hall of Fame*.

Although his off-Broadway roles and television assignments kept him at least intermittently busy, Richards still had to support himself by working as an assistant chef and waiter in the executive dining room of the Paramount Building on Times Square. Meanwhile, he was gradually acquiring a reputation as a fledgling director and educator. During his tenure as assistant director and teacher at the Paul Mann Actors Workshop from 1952 to 1962, he also served, in 1954, as resident director of the Great Lakes Drama Festival. From 1955 to 1958 he was resident director at the Northland Playhouse in Detroit, and in 1957 he returned to Broadway, to appear as Perry Hall, a Communist, in the three-week run of Molly Kazan's *The Egghead*. Among the critics who highly praised his performance was Walter Kerr of the New York *Herald Tribune* (October 10, 1957), who reported that Richards "bares his teeth and plunges into a passionate condemnation of American racism that is bitter, brutal, and wholly comprehensible in its hammer-stroke of power."

Richards would later use his maturing, uncanny flair for pinpoint accuracy of characterization to even fuller advantage in directing other actors and in collaborating with playwrights. His pivotal role in *The Egghead* represented a breakthrough in terms of what it presaged for the future of black stage artists victimized by racial discrimination and stereotyping. "There was a time, not long ago," said Richards in an interview for an article that appeared in the Manchester *Guardian* (July 13, 1959) "when Negro actors and actresses couldn't get anything better to play than chauffeurs and maids and other servants. But the situation has changed. I'm optimistic about the future."

His optimism was vindicated when the music publisher Philip Rose, who had optioned the black playwright Lorraine Hansberry's *A Raisin in the Sun*, selected him to direct the ground-breaking production of the first play by a black woman writer and the first staged by a black director ever to reach Broadway. The seven New York drama critics accorded *Raisin in the Sun* unanimous raves after its opening night, including high praise for Lloyd Richards from Walter Kerr of the New York *Herald Tribune* (March 12, 1959), who lauded him for having directed the play with "a fluid, quick-tempered grace that permits no moment—and no shade of desperation—to pass unexamined." The following month the production was voted by the New York Drama Critics Circle as the best American play of 1959.

Raisin in the Sun met with a less hospitable reception from London critics when it opened there in July 1959. The Manchester *Guardian* interviewer noted that Richards nevertheless appeared confident that there would be more and more plays with blacks in them, without their being necessarily "problem plays." "Involvement in the theatrical situation transcends racial differences," Richards concluded. Although his Broadway success marked a turning point in his directorial career, opening the doors to opportunities to direct plays without racial themes, Richards never forgets his own connections with a heritage similar to that depicted by Lorraine Hansberry and by August Wilson. As Eric Pace observed in the the *New York Times* (January 11, 1981): "In the American theatre, as well as in his own life, *A Raisin in the Sun* was a milestone: it was the first serious black play on Broadway, and it made black domestic life a fit subject for the Great White Way."

After *Raisin in the Sun*, Richards received a succession of directing assignments for Broadway plays, summer stock productions, films, and television dramas, interspersed with engagements at university theatres and "try-out" runs of potential Broadway material. The ill-fated *The Moon Besieged*, a play about the American abolitionist John Brown, whose theme Richards compared to the plight of the Freedom Riders of the civil rights era, closed on Broadway on December 5, 1962 after only one performance. The Coney Island musical, *I Had A Ball*, of 1964, played to mixed reviews, while the much-anticipated production, in 1965, of *The Yearling*, from which Richards resigned as director before opening night, was roundly panned by critics.

In spite of those minor setbacks, Lloyd Richards' academic and professional career continued to flourish. By 1962 he had founded his own acting studio in New York, where he taught for ten years. From 1966 through 1972 he headed the actor-training program at New York University School of the Arts, and was also involved as a teacher with the Connecticut Commission on the Arts training program, the Negro Ensemble Company, Rhode Island University, and Boston University.

His Broadway success with *Raisin in the Sun* led the organizers of the Eugene O'Neill Memorial Theater Foundation to tap Lloyd Richards to direct new plays at the O'Neill Theater Center's National Playwrights' Conference in the summer of 1966,

the second year of its existence. The annual three-week forum offers professional playwrights an opportunity to see newly created plays presented by a professional director and cast, to quote George C. White 3d, the founder of the conference, as "technically perfect staged readings." Each summer, selected playwrights receive feedback and analysis from critics who make evaluations "within the process," as Richards explained in an interview for the *New York Times* (August 7, 1973), rather than issuing one-time, opening-night pronunciamentos.

His commitment to the process of developing new work to ensure the survival of American drama was apparent from the outset of Richard's involvement with the National Playwrights' conference. "I feel I have a personal stake in the conference," he told an interviewer for the *National Observer* (August 7, 1967), "in that my work as a director or actor exists only after a play has been written." Following the 1968 session, Richards was named the annual artistic director of the National Playwrights' Conference. Once branded as "Tryout Town, USA"—the legacy of its early years, when producers and agents often descended on the town of Waterford to scout potential commercial "properties"—the conference, under Richards' direction, soon earned a warranted reputation as one of the country's foremost noncommercial forums for the development of new playwrights.

Throughout the 1970s Lloyd Richards continued to teach in the department of cinema and theatre at Hunter College and at the National Theatre Institute—positions that he continues to hold. In 1971 he created the American Shakespeare Festival's theatre demonstration programs, based in Stratford, Connecticut, which he directed through 1974. Toward the close of the 1970s his noteworthy directorial assignments proliferated. Even the highly controversial 1977–78 Broadway drama *Paul Robeson*, by Phillip Hayes Dean, which was denounced as a superficial treatment of its subject by Robeson's son and a host of distinguished black signatories of a two-page ad in the trade publication *Variety*, brought Richards praise for his sensitive staging. His selection as director of two 1979 television specials—a segment of the phenomenally successful *Roots: The Next Generation* and a PBS documentary made for *Bill Moyers' Journal*—enhanced his growing national acclaim.

In December 1978, when Yale University decided not to renew the contract of Robert Brustein, who had for thirteen years been dean of the Yale School of Drama and artistic director of the Yale Repertory Theatre, Lloyd Richards was appointed his successor for a five-year term beginning on July 1, 1979. The new dean was immediately called upon to respond to allegations that his appointment was part of a move to "deprofessionalize" Yale's drama program. Richards began his ongoing tenure at Yale in the face of such pointed criticism as that of Erika Munk, who in the *Village Voice* (January 22, 1979) called Richards' attitude toward the ideas of theatre "so bland it is alarming." She went on to assert that, based on what she considered to be "the overwhelming philistinism of the O'Neill [Center's] discourse . . . [it] looks as though the promise of social concern, openness, and diversity will be contained in the embrace of a soothing anti-intellectualism." She qualified her criticism, however, by conceding that "oil on troubled waters is Lloyd Richards' specialty, statesmanlike formulations his genius." Other observers were more charitable, including Leo Seligsohn of Newsday (August 19, 1979), who predicted that Richards' appointment was certain to strengthen the already mutually beneficial bond that linked the Yale Drama School to the O'Neill Theater Center, only forty-five minutes away in distance, but, in spirit, "a lot closer than that."

Richards lost no time in setting about to prove his critics wrong. He expanded the Yale Repertory Theatre's scope by opening the theatre's doors to both the university and the ghetto in which it is located. During his first season at Yale, he staged the American premiere of the South African playwright Athol Fugard's A Lesson From Aloes, a coup that a critic of the New York Times (April 6, 1980), Mel Gussow, said "honors the theatre and, by itself, validates Mr. Richards' first year at Yale. . . . Particularly under the pressure of marshaling an initial season in very short time, Mr. Richards has performed with remarkable agility, and . . . with an aloe-like stubbornness that augurs well for the continuing independence of the Yale Rep." By the end of his second season at Yale, Richards was being applauded for his venturesome style and uncompromising aesthetic standards.

Convinced that without the impetus that comes from the development of new plays, "there is no theater except the theater of the past," Richards began in January 1981 to offer his audiences a sampling of contemporary drama. The occasion was the inaugural season at Yale of Richards' so-called Winterfest of new American plays, a three-week mini-repertory of four two-act works by both professional and student playwrights. In his search for what he has termed "a unique voice for the theater," Richards has created in effect what Mel Gussow has called "a next step of theatrical nurturing," between the new play's original staged reading and the often premature leap to production on the commercial stage.

In 1982 the Yale Repertory Theatre presented the world premiere of Master Harold and the Boys by Athol Fugard. It was the result of a creative partnership between the playwright and Lloyd Richards, who not only provided artistic guidance and inspiration during the rewriting process but went on to collaborate with Fugard on subsequent plays. After staging a Yale Rep revival of A Raisin in the Sun in 1983, in celebration of its twenty-fifth anniversary, Richards directed the successful Broadway production of Ma Rainey's Black Bottom by the new black playwright August Wilson. First given a staged reading at the Eugene O'Neill Theater in 1982 and presented by the Yale Rep in April 1984, the Broadway production, which opened at the Cort Theater on October 11, 1984 for a run of 275 performances, won praise for both its cast and its director. Partly because Richards had "handled the play with the sensitivity and drive of a theatrical Duke Ellington," as Jack Kroll of Newsweek (October 22, 1984) put it, Ma Rainey's Black Bottom went on to win the New York Drama Critics Award and garnered several Tony nominations. Another, even more successful collaboration between Richards and Wilson was the Pulitzer Prize-winning drama Fences, which opened at the 46th Street Theater on March 26, 1987, after preliminary stagings at the Yale Rep, the Goodman Theatre in Chicago, and the Seattle Repertory Theatre and in Carole Shorenstein Hays's production in San Francisco over a four-year period.

When Richards was appointed to the National Council for the Arts in 1985 by President Ronald Reagan, it established a precedent, since it was the first time that a representative from the noncommercial theatre had been named to that rank. Among his many other honors are the Connecticut Arts Award (1982); the Artist Award from the Greater New Haven Arts Commission (1983); the New England Theatre Conference's award for "outstanding creative achievement in the American theatre" (1984); and the Evelyn F. Burkey Award from the Writers Guild of America for "one whose contribution to the writing community has brought honor and dignity to writers everywhere."

Short, rotund, and bustlingly energetic, Lloyd Richards has wiry gray hair and a grizzled beard that makes him resemble what some have described as "a Santa Claus of theater." He was a founding member of two off-Broadway theatres, These 20 People and the Greenwich Mews Theater. Before his Yale appointment, he served as an American theatre specialist for the United States State Department, for which he conducted a theatre survey of several African nations. He was awarded an honorary doctorate by Yale University in 1979. Since October 11, 1957, Richards has been married to the former Barbara Davenport, a writer and member of the Yale Rep staff. Their two sons, Scott and Thomas, both of whom graduated from Yale, are actors.

Committed to the promotion of cooperative efforts among regional, nonprofit theatres, Richards continues to foster a national awareness of theatre, through both the Winterfest and his participation in the O'Neill playwrights' conference. Looking ahead to his eventual retirement, Richards said in a recent New York Times interview (January 26, 1986) that he is trying to establish an endowment to ensure that new plays continue to be produced through Winterfest. Deeply concerned over the ultimate fate of theatre and its related art forms, Richards recently contrasted television's manipulation of reality with the live interaction that is such an essential element of theatre. "I don't think that [we] have devised anything to replace that [kind of communication]," he was quoted as saying in an interview with Rushworth M. Kidder of the *Christian Science Monitor* (November 4, 1986). "I think that as long as that exists we will have theater. We will have people telling stories and . . . having conversations. And the theater is a conversation."

References: *Directory of Blacks in the Performing Arts (1978); Notable Names in American Theatre (1976); Who's Who Among Black Americans, 1985; Who's Who in America, 1986-87; Who's Who in the East, 1986-87*

Ringwald, Molly

Feb. 18, 1968– Actress. Address: b. c/o Guttman and Pam Ltd., 120 El Camino Dr., Beverly Hills, Calif. 90212

Molly Ringwald, who is perhaps the most publicized member of the group of teenaged actors who came into prominence in the mid-1980s as the result of a rash of movies aimed at adolescents, has earned high marks from critics for her portrayals of the travails of growing up in John Hughes's *Sixteen Candles, The Breakfast Club,* and *Pretty in Pink*—the so-called Molly trilogy. A performer since the age of four, Miss Ringwald appeared in stage productions and television series before turning, in 1982, to motion pictures, with a supporting role in *Tempest.* In the opinion of John Hughes, who has directed her in two films, she stands "alone among young actors." Her performances are "flawless," he has said. "Molly is a real, legitimate, world-class actress."

Molly Ringwald was born in Roseville, just north of Sacramento, California, on February 18, 1968, the youngest of the three children of Bob and Adele Ringwald. Her father, who has been blind since childhood, is a pianist who leads the Great Pacific Jazz Band. Molly soon learned the tunes for many of the songs in the band's repertoire and sang along while her father practiced. "I was singing before I can remember, to the cats, to the swings," she recalled for Susan Toepfer in an interview for a New York *Daily News* magazine (May 6, 1984) profile. "My mother says I used to sing to my feet. So they started teaching me lyrics. I'd go with my father to festivals and sing jazz and blues. I did Bessie Smith songs—but they had to change the words."

By the time she was four years old, Molly Ringwald was appearing regularly with the Great Pacific Jazz Band, belting out such favorites as "Oh Daddy," "I Wanna Be Loved By You," and "You Gotta See Momma Every Night or You Won't See Momma at All." Some of those numbers were included on *Molly Sings,* the album that she recorded with the band in 1974. Dreaming of a career as a vocalist, Molly idolized the great blues stylists Billie Holiday and Ella Fitzgerald. Once assigned by her second-grade teacher to impersonate a famous American for a class show-and-tell period, Molly chose Bessie Smith. "When I was a little kid," she explained, as quoted in *Time* (May 26, 1986) magazine, "I thought I would grow up to be black and sing jazz in nightclubs."

Recognizing Molly's precocity, the Ringwalds enrolled her in singing, dancing, and acting classes when she was five. Shortly after that, the child joined her brother, Kelly, and sister, Beth, in amateur productions at a local community theatre. Among her roles were the dormouse in *Alice in Wonderland* and the preacher's daughter in Truman Capote's fantasy *The Grass Harp.* Rarely assigned a speaking part, Molly often amused herself by memorizing the lines of all the other actors.

Molly Ringwald made her first professional television appearance in 1977, as a guest on ABC's *New Mickey Mouse Club* and her professional stage debut in 1978, as Kate in the West Coast production of the hit musical *Annie.* While she was performing in *Annie* in Los Angeles, the Ringwald family moved to that city, at least partly to advance Molly's career. A few months later, the girl was hired to play Molly in *The Facts of Life,* a sitcom set in a girls' boarding school that had its premiere on NBC in the fall of 1979, but after just one season, her character was written out of the script. "I was devastated," she told the interviewer for *Time.* "But my mom kept saying it was for the best, and she was right. I didn't work for a year, which gave me a chance to grow up a lot."

In answer to an open casting call, Miss Ringwald auditioned for the role of Miranda in Paul Mazursky's film *Tempest,* an offbeat, contemporary retelling of Shakespeare's *The Tempest.* She was, in Mazursky's words, "immediately interesting." "She was unafraid of me," the director told Hillary Johnson in a conversation for *Rolling Stone* (March 28, 1985). "And she seemed real. . . . She was *not* like an actress." Taken by her unaffected spontaneity, Mazursky hired Molly Ringwald to play the feisty young daughter of his modern-day Prospero, a burned-out architect who flees New York for self-imposed exile on an isolated Greek island. To help her prepare for her part as a street-wise city kid who is suddenly uprooted and transplanted to the Greek countryside, the director installed the actress and her parents in a flat in New York's Greenwich Village, where for three months she worked on improvisational technique with costars John Cassavetes and Gena Rowlands, who portrayed her father and his estranged wife.

When *Tempest* opened in the summer of 1982, the critics were generally unimpressed, most of them agreeing with Vincent Canby, who, in his review for the *New York Times* (August 13, 1982), belittled the film as "an overblown, fancified freak" that was "amusing in isolated moments but, finally, exhausting." Miss Ringwald, however, won virtually unanimous praise for her freshness, believability, and "obvious potential." In Pauline Kael's view, she and Susan Sarandon, as Aretha (Mazursky's Ariel), were "the two best reasons for seeing the film." Miss Ringwald's performance earned her a Golden Globe nomination as the best new actress of 1982.

The young actress was less fortunate in her next assignment: the role of the orphaned waif Niki in Lamont Johnson's 3-D extravaganza *Spacehunter: Adventures in the Forbidden Zone* (1983). Asked to play a nebulously defined character who functions both as the possible love interest and as the matey sidekick—a kind of "*Star Trek* Tonto," in Harry Haun's description—of Peter Strauss's laconic intergalactic bounty hunter, Molly Ringwald seemed to most critics to have settled for an "abrasive brat portrayal" that eventually became "obnoxious," as a reviewer for *Variety* (May 18, 1983) put it.

Molly Ringwald's budding acting career took a turn for the better in 1984, when she appeared in *Sixteen Candles*, the first of three extremely successful youth-market movies written by John Hughes, the screenwriter responsible for the hit comedies *Mr. Mom* and *National Lampoon's Vacation*. Impressed by Miss Ringwald's performance in *Tempest*, Hughes had created Samantha Baker, the central character in *Sixteen Candles*, with her in mind. (He is said to have written the script with an eight-by-ten-inch glossy photograph of the actress taped above his word processor.) "I'm not like her now, but when I was fifteen I was identical to the character," Miss Ringwald told Rex Morgan in an interview for *Cable Guide* (June 1985). "Back then she and I were exactly the same. We had a lot of the same emotions and questioning of self-worth. The movie hits right at home."

The plot of *Sixteen Candles* revolves around Samantha's efforts to survive her sixteenth birthday, which her family, caught up in last-minute preparations for her older sister's wedding, seems to have forgotten. A shy and insecure high school sophomore, she suffers a series of humiliations,

ranging from the unwanted attentions of an awkward freshman known only as Geek to the temporary commandeering of her bedroom by her visiting grandparents, before she is finally noticed at a school dance by the handsome senior she adores. A smash hit with young moviegoers, *Sixteen Candles* also enchanted the majority of adult critics, who appreciated Hughes's gentle, "deliciously silly" humor and accurate eye for the vagaries of American adolescent behavior. Under his direction, Miss Ringwald turned in a credible and thoroughly engaging performance. Pauline Kael, writing in the *New Yorker* (May 28, 1984), especially admired her "offbeat candor." Her artless acting "gives the picture a lyric quality," Miss Kael continued. "The tilt of Samantha's head suggests a guileless sort of yearning, and there's something lovely about the slight gaucheness of her restless, long arms."

In *The Breakfast Club* (1985), the second of the Hughes-Ringwald collaborations, Molly Ringwald played Claire Standish, one of five unruly students who are ordered to spend a Saturday in detention in the library of their suburban high school. Assigned to write essays about themselves, the five classmates—"a brain, an athlete, a basket case, a princess, and a criminal," as one of them puts it—hold an impromptu group therapy session and discover that despite their outward differences they share the same fears, dreams, embarrassments, and pressures. Some reviewers, among them the *Washington Post*'s Paul Attanasio, complained that Molly Ringwald's performance as the social-climbing Claire, was, like the film itself, "all surface." In her assessment for the *New Yorker* (April 8, 1985), Pauline Kael conceded that Claire seemed less appealing than the heroine of *Sixteen Candles*, but she maintained that Miss Ringwald, who "[slipped] into the well-heeled Miss Popularity languor without any unnecessary fuss," had offered a valid characterization.

Returning briefly to television, Molly Ringwald played an emotionally ravaged adolescent in *Surviving*, a wrenching made-for-television movie about teenage suicide that was first broadcast on ABC-TV on February 10, 1985. Her insightful portrayal of the troubled Lonnie as "a lost lamb looking for help," to quote the *New York Times*'s John Corry, touched most critics, but perhaps the highest praise came from the veteran actress Ellen Burstyn, who took the part of the mother of Lonnie's boyfriend. "She has a huge talent," Miss Burstyn said of her younger colleague, as quoted by Hillary Johnson in his piece for *Rolling Stone*. "I was just amazed at her natural ability. She seems to understand intuitively what's needed in a scene, and she produces it. I haven't been so impressed by a young actor in a long time, if ever, and I think she's going to be an absolutely major actress—and a star." Miss Ringwald's recent television credits also include the "Johnny Appleseed" episode of *Faerie Tale Theatre* and the telefeatures *P.K. and the Kid* and *Packin' It In*.

Pretty in Pink, which was released in February 1986, was the third panel in the Hughes-Ringwald movie triptych. The story of a sensitive young girl's struggle for identity, it starred Molly Ringwald as the spunky Andie Walsh, a senior from the wrong side of the tracks trying to make her way in an affluent high school, Andrew McCarthy as her rich preppie boyfriend, and Harry Dean Stanton as her unemployed father. An immediate hit with its targeted teenage audience, *Pretty in Pink* grossed $12.4 million in the first ten days of its release despite a generally apathetic critical response. For many reviewers, the one redeeming feature of the otherwise "slight" and "vapid" soap opera was Molly Ringwald's "charismatic normality," as Pauline Kael, who is perhaps the actress' staunchest admirer among the critics, put it. "When the picture was shot, she hadn't yet turned eighteen," Miss Kael wrote in her *New Yorker* review of April 7, 1986, "but she looks completely free of self-consciousness or affectation. The poise with which she plunks herself in front of the camera is uncanny. And this redheaded goddess of the ordinary carries the movie, though she has nothing particularly arresting to do or say."

After an absence of more than ten years, Molly Ringwald returned to the stage in November 1986 to play the title role in the New York premiere of *Lily Dale*, the third play, chronologically, in Horton Foote's Robedaux family cycle. Set in turn-of-the-century Texas, *Lily Dale* explores the relationship between an estranged brother and sister who meet again after many years. In the opinion of most observers, Molly Ringwald, as the spoiled sister, seemed unable to reconcile the disparate aspects of her character. Lily "is both an hysterical child and a calculating witch ," Sylviane Gold wrote in her review of the short-lived production for the *Wall Street Journal* (December 10, 1986), "and it's up to the actress to let us know when she's being honest, when she's lying, and when she's lying to herself. Such nuances are well beyond Ms. Ringwald's abilities at the moment, and she can only smirk when she gets her way and pout when she doesn't."

Until her graduation in 1986, Miss Ringwald attended the Lycée Français, a prestigious, bilingual private school in Los Angeles. When she was making a film, she took her lessons on the set from a private tutor. After leaving school, the actress has completed work on her sixth motion picture, *The Pickup Artist*, (1987), James Toback's romantic comedy about a lecherous schoolteacher in pursuit of a spirited museum guide. The actor-producer Warren Beatty, the film's executive producer, had been trying to persuade Miss Ringwald to appear in one of his films ever since he saw her in *Tempest*. Beatty has been her "loyal friend" and mentor for the past several years, advising her on her career and on Hollywood politics. The pair have also discussed the possibility of making a film adaptation of Jean Stein's best-selling *Edie; an American Biography* (1982), about the life of Edie Sedgwick, the Andy Warhol "superstar" who died of a drug overdose.

Standing five feet eight inches tall, Molly Ringwald has fair, freckled skin, large brown eyes, "waxed-candy" lips, and tousled, henna-rinsed reddish-brown hair. Her penchant for what has been described as "designer-junk shop couture" has been widely copied by her young fans. In her spare time, she enjoys shopping in neighborhood malls, listening to rock music (she is especially fond of the Rave-Ups, a Los Angeles-based group), and singing with her father's band. According to Hillary Johnson, her singing voice is "sassy and petulant, generous and warm, whatever the song requires." She lives with her parents in the San Fernando Valley, northwest of Los Angeles, California.

References: *Cable Guide* 4:38+ Je '85 pors; *N Y Daily News* mag p7+ My 6 '84 pors; *People* 25:12+ Mr 24 '86 pors; *Rolling Stone* p39+ Mr 28 '85 por; *Time* 127:67+ My 26 '86 pors

---

Rivers, Joan

June 8, 1933– Comedienne. Address: c/o Bill Sammeth Organization, 9200 Sunset Blvd., Suite 431, Los Angeles, Calif. 90069; c/o Richard Grant & Associates, 300 Mercer St., Suite 10-L, New York City, N.Y. 10003

NOTE: This biography supersedes the article that appeared in *Current Biography* in 1970.

Joan Rivers, thought by many to be the funniest comedienne in America, is one of the first women to establish herself in the tradition of taboo-flouting, insult-laced humor long considered the sole province of male comedians. Asking "the questions that truly obsess America," in the phrase of the critic James Wolcott, Miss Rivers directs rapid-fire ridicule at the flaws of celebrities as well as her own and the nation's neuroses, especially those touching on physical appearance, lifestyle, and sexuality. "Can we talk?," her signature phrase, suggests an invitation to gossip that makes the members of her audiences feel like intimates. That invitation, backed by a 40,000-joke arsenal, guarantees sellout crowds for her nightclub appearances, high ratings for her television projects, and best-seller status for her books and records.

In 1986, for a guaranteed $10 million over three years, Miss Rivers signed with the fledgling Fox Broadcasting Company network to host *The Late Show Starring Joan Rivers*, thus entering into direct competition with *The Tonight Show Starring Johnny Carson*, on which she got her first big break in 1965 and of which she had been permanent substitute host since 1983. When accused of being an "ingrate" in Carson's regard, she typically turned personal distress into quip, countering, in an allusion to Carson's divorces and alimony problems, that she was "the only woman in the history of the world who left Johnny Carson and didn't ask him for money."

The younger of two daughters of Dr. Meyer Molinsky, a general practitioner of medicine, and Beatrice (Grushman) Molinsky, Joan Rivers was born Joan Alexandra Molinsky in Brooklyn, New York. According to school records, the date of her birth was June 8, 1933. Less reliable published sources yield years ranging from 1935 through 1939. Both of her parents were Russian-Jewish refugees who were, in her words, "almost pathologically terrified of poverty." Beatrice Molinsky in particular pined for the luxurious lifestyle of her childhood before the Russian Revolution, when her family had supplied the Czar with furs, beef, and brick. Her husband, working to pay for maids, governesses, and progressively better addresses, could never make enough money to recapture her lost lifestyle and this sparked what James Brady described in the New York *Daily News* (July 27, 1986) as "a domestic civil war that would have reduced Clint Eastwood to stuttering."

Joan took some comfort in her father's gift for telling jokes and doing comic impersonations of his patients. She herself began to be attracted to performing while playing a kitten in a prekindergarten play at the Brooklyn Ethical Culture school. By the time she was eleven she had sent a photograph of herself to MGM in Hollywood and had succeeded at making her father's visiting colleagues laugh. She had also developed a fear of being fat and unattractive that, in adulthood, would inspire continuous dieting, minor plastic surgery, and jokes about a body whose photograph was shown to men on death row "to take their minds off women," a body that had been large enough to occupy "the whole front row" in one class picture. Meanwhile she was being groomed to enter upperclass society by her mother, who saw to it that she had elocution, piano, and violin lessons and was enrolled in the best private schools.

While attending the Adelphi Academy preparatory school in Brooklyn, Miss Rivers participated in the drama program, founded the school newspaper, and placed second in a *Photoplay* acting contest. Not long after her graduation she landed a small role in the 1951 movie, *Mr. Universe*, earning $15.56 a day. Then, "playing by [her] mother's book," despite her desire to act full time, she attended Connecticut College for Women and later Barnard College in New York City. She studied English and anthropology at Barnard and graduated with membership in Phi Beta Kappa in 1954. Passing up a summer acting apprenticeship at the Westport County Playhouse in Connecticut, she entered the business world, beginning in the publicity department at Lord and Taylor before moving on to the Bond clothing stores as fashion coordinator for the entire national chain. In 1957 she married Jimmy Sanger, the son of the Bond stores' merchandiser, but her desire to continue working, and even to try her hand at performing again, resulted in conflicts that led to the annulment of the marriage in 1958. Within six months she had abandoned her parents' ambitions for her and, cut off temporarily from all financial and emotional support, set out to launch a career as an actress.

Miss Rivers' seven initial years of struggle to establish herself in show business are chronicled in detail in her best-selling autobiography, *Enter Talking* (Delacorte Press, 1986), written with Richard Meryman. At first she supported herself as an office temporary worker while finding little acting work beyond Off-Off Broadway plays that closed after brief runs. She turned to comedy in 1960 with the initial aim of earning easy money to support her acting. She found herself working a grim itinerary of strip joints, Catskill resorts, and grimy, often Mafia-run clubs. She was fired regularly from those clubs, but she gradually began to see herself primarily as a comic. Minor breakthroughs came when she was cast in a dramatic role in the Broadway revue and talent search, *Talent '60*, and in dramatic and comedic roles in *Talent '61*. She also gained some exposure in the 1960 USO show, *Broadway USA*, and her *Talent '60* performance led to two potentially landmark bookings on NBC-TV's *Tonight Show*, then hosted by Jack Paar. Unfortunately, Paar disliked her act when she first appeared, and her performance was disrupted by news flashes about a plane crash on the second occasion.

In September 1961 Miss Rivers auditioned successfully for the Chicago-based improvisational acting troupe Second City. The experience of the group's stream-of-consciousness comedy technique set her on the path to her mature routines. As she recounts in her autobiography, learning "to short circuit thought and hitch impulses directly to [her] tongue," she felt "a comedy ego beginning to grow, which gave [her] the courage to begin tentatively looking" into herself for material.

After inventing two important Second City characters, including a man-hungry prototype of her later stage persona, Miss Rivers returned to New York City in 1962. Disappointed in her job expectations, she settled into performing gratis at a circuit of small Greenwich Village clubs, especially the Showplace. At one of his Village Vanguard performances she discovered Lenny Bruce, who embodied and confirmed for her the virtues of using personal pain and insight to generate comedic material. At the Showplace she began similarly speaking "directly and personally to the audience," in a style already wild and picaresque. "The way my mother sees things," she told one audience, "she has two daughters that aren't, as the expression goes, moving. She is so desperate to get me married that if a murderer called, she'd say, 'So, he has a temper.' When a boy does come to the house, to impress him she puts out intellectual magazines like *Partisan Review* and the *Atlantic Monthly*. She even leaves a Bible open on the coffee table and writes 'true' in the margin."

In 1963 Miss Rivers teamed up for a time with Jim Connell and Jake Holmes in a relatively conventional song and comedy team, "Jim, Jake, and Joan," which toured with moderate success, earning money and bringing her an unprecedented amount of recognition. She soon tired of the "sophomore humor" of the trio's material, and of Jim and Jake as well. She quit the group in 1964 and pinned her survival on a long-term solo engagement at a Sheridan Square club called the Duplex. Jan Wallman, the club owner, has described her at that time as being "untried, a little raw—brilliant, though. And she had the *fastest* comedy mind I'd ever seen. . . . If she was stopped in one direction, she moved in another. She just wouldn't take no for an answer." Roy Silver, an agent known at the time for having helped to launch Bill Cosby's career, offered to manage Miss Rivers immediately after seeing one of her shows at the Duplex. While working with her to hone her material, he repeatedly tried to book her on the *Tonight Show* with Johnny Carson, but was told each time that she was "not right" for the show or for television.

Meanwhile, through director Jorn Winther, Miss Rivers secured television work as a writer for CBS-TV's *Candid Camera*. This added to credits she had already gained collaborating with Michael McWhinney on scripts for the Topo, the puppet mouse, segment on the *Ed Sullivan* show and writing material for Phyllis Diller and Zsa Zsa Gabor. Her own material and career, however, seemed to be becalmed at the Duplex, and in 1965 Irving Arthur, an agent, told her she was "too old," had been seen and passed over by too many people, and would never make it as a solo comic. A week later Roy Silver finally secured a booking for her on the *Tonight Show*.

Because another comic, her friend Milt Kamen, was booked for the same night, Miss Rivers appeared on the February 15, 1965, program billed as a comedy writer who would discuss her life and craft with Carson. The two established an immediate rapport and "struck gleeful gold," according to critic Jack O'Brien, as Miss Rivers detailed her

mother's struggle to get her married; an accident involving a motorist who ran over her wig and apologized for killing her dog; and the life and times of Mr. Phyllis, her hairdresser, whose mother had wanted a girl—and gotten one. Carson pronounced her a future star at the end of the interview and his viewers set the *Tonight Show's* switchboard blinking with inquiries about the funny lady.

Having scaled "the Everest of comedy" as Lee Israel described the *Tonight Show* in *Ms.* magazine (October 1984), Miss Rivers became the darling of the nightclub circuit and was booked into all the choice comedy spots, including Mister Kelly's in Chicago and the hungry i in San Francisco. In September 1965 she was put under contract by NBC and late in the year she recorded the album *Joan Rivers Presents Mr. Phyllis and Other Funny Stories* for Warner Brothers. She also began what became a five-year engagement at the comedy club Upstairs at the Downstairs in Greenwich Village. She had a dramatic cameo role in the Columbia picture *The Swimmer* (1968), and in the fall of 1968 NBC created the program *That Show* for her. Airing every weekday morning, the half-hour program consisted of an opening monologue followed by ad-lib conversation with the audience and guests. It lasted for 260 segments, the last of which was broadcast in 1971.

Joan Rivers continued to be seen regularly on NBC throughout the 1970s as a guest host on the *Tonight Show* and in 1971 became the first woman to serve as a guest host for the show for a full week. With mixed results, she also embarked on writing or cowriting and sometimes producing a series of stage, film, and television projects. Among them were the coolly received Broadway comedy *Fun City* (1971), which she cowrote and in which she acted, and the enormously successful ABC made-for-television movie *The Girl Most Likely To* (1973), a black comedy. Said to derive in part from Miss Rivers' view that comedy can be a medium for revenge, it tells the story of a woman made beautiful—and unrecognizable—by plastic surgery, who hunts down and kills the men who once rejected her. It became the highest-rated made-for-television movie in history when it had its premiere and has since established a record for most repeat airings. Also financially successful, though damned by the critics, was Joan Rivers' debut as a movie director, *Rabbit Test* (Avco Embassy, 1978), which she also financed and which emboldened her to set up her own loan-out corporation, Shafta Productions.

In other media Miss Rivers was equally—and sometimes even more—successful. From 1973 to 1976 she wrote a nationally syndicated thrice-weekly column for the *Chicago Tribune*. In the same period she completed a kind of humorous A-to-Z catalogue of gynecological anxieties called *Having a Baby Can Be a Scream* (Hawthorn, 1975), which has sold over 1.5 million hardcover copies and 2.5 million copies as an Avon paperback.

On the nightclub circuit and on the *Tonight Show* the fast-talking comedienne continued to prove that, if necessary, she "could drill most comics before they even got a joke out of their holsters,"as Larry Kart observed in the *Chicago Tribune* (June 13, 1982). By the early 1980s Mr. Phyllis and the dead wig were being pushed into the background of Miss Rivers' routines by new jokes about celebrities such as Elizabeth Taylor, regarding whose weight problem at the time, Miss Rivers joked, "Mosquitos see her and scream 'Buffet!'" Additional commentary was offered on most of the celebrities gossiped about in the *National Enquirer*, which Miss Rivers mined—and continues to mine—for source material. Her audience could now expect updates on the wardrobe of Queen Elizabeth II of England ("gowns by Helen Keller"), Nancy Reagan's "bulletproof" hair ("if they ever combed it, they'd find Jimmy Hoffa"), and, as before, her own supposed physical decline ("a Peeping Tom looked in [her] window and pulled down the shade"). Although some critics accused Miss Rivers of being masochistic and trivial as well as cruel—"a fly buzzing around Liz Taylor's cottage cheese," as David Hinkley put it in the New York *Daily News* (August 14, 1983)—no one denied her wit. James Wolcott, writing in *New York* (January 24, 1983), observed that she was insinuating herself "into the wrinkles of our national worries," namely "money, popularity, flab [and] aging."

Those themes were all in evidence in 1981 and 1982, when Joan Rivers went on an enormously successful tour with her antithesis, the mild-mannered and squeaky-clean David Brenner, and in 1983, when she embarked on a sold-out, twelve-city tour that included a February 4 appearance at Carnegie Hall. After completing the tour Miss Rivers was a guest host on *Saturday Night Live* and released a hit comedy album, *What Becomes a Semi-legend Most?* (Geffen Records), which sold over 500,000 copies by the end of the year and was nominated for a Grammy Award.

Joan Rivers reached another career milestone in August 1983, when NBC, recognizing that she sometimes outdrew Johnny Carson in ratings when she presided over his show, made her the first and only permanent guest host of that program, a position she maintained until 1986. By filling in for Carson during his extensive vacations of eight or nine weeks a year, she achieved a degree of national exposure that put the finishing touches on her new superstardom. She began to appear on many magazine covers and commanded $200,000 for five nights in Las Vegas. In October 1983 she was chosen to cohost, with comic and actor Eddie Murphy, NBC's thirty-fifth Annual Emmy Awards show. In August 1984 she addressed the National Federation of Republican Women at the 1984 Republican convention. Although Ray Kerrison later complained in the *New York Post* (May 13, 1985) that "it is in this era of anything goes that Joan Rivers became a star," most observers seemed to share the assessment made by Jerry Adler in *Newsweek* (October 10, 1983) that Miss Rivers was popular because she had been accepted as "the little girl who points out to everyone that the empress is wearing no clothes." On the *Tonight Show,* Adler observed, she did that regularly, "cutting through the blather about a guest's terrific relationship with his or her new spouse to demand to know what went wrong with the first marriage." Adler pointed out that she has "a style very different from Carson's masterful technique of giving the guests enough conversational rope to hang themselves"—that she "ties it around something vital and gives a yank."

In 1984 Joan Rivers published *The Life and Hard Times of Heidi Abromowitz* (Delacorte Press), the story of her fictitious "former best, best friend," a fallen woman with the reputation of being "the most renowned tramp since Charlie Chaplin" and of having "been in more motel rooms than the Bible." The book spent eighteen weeks on the *New York Times* best-seller list and its first hardcover printing sold half a million copies. Moreover, it was only the second book of humor to have the honor of being chosen as an alternate selection by the Literary Guild. A salute to Heidi, broadcast on cable TV's *Showtime* in June 1985, was hailed by Marvin Kitman of *Newsday* (June 13, 1985) as "the comedy hit of the summer." Another 1984 triumph for Miss Rivers was her appearance on London Weekend Television's *Audience With,* which scored one of the highest ratings for that program. That appearance eventually led to the BBC's signing her for a series of six one-hour specials entitled *Joan Rivers: Can We Talk?,* which aired in April 1986 and secured unusually high ratings.

Despite her now confirmed status as the hottest comedienne in America, Miss Rivers has admitted to waking up every morning wondering, "Do I still have it? Are they still going to like me?" After a slow night in Las Vegas, she would "want to kill [herself] afterwards in the dressing room." Instead, she continued to "work at it" every night, to write her jokes, and to "go into little tiny clubs in Los Angeles and . . . work out."

In *Enter Talking,* Miss Rivers traces her insecurity back to her childhood and her early failures in tiny clubs. Though the book was considered "whiningly downbeat" by some critics when it was published, the disarmingly candid autobiography was judged a "terrific book" by others, who liked its honesty, its wealth of detail, and its vivid depiction of the sleazy underbelly of show business. It reached number four on the *New York Times* nonfiction best-seller list in only two weeks.

In October 1986 Miss Rivers began hosting *The Late Show Starring Joan Rivers,* spearheading the media baron Rupert Murdoch's bid to make his Fox Broadcasting Company the fourth major television network in America. Johnny Carson, who apparently viewed her competitive move as treacherous, hung up on her when she phoned him to explain her plans, but Miss Rivers professed to continue to "love Johnny." She revealed that she accepted the Murdoch offer after learning that she was not on NBC's list of possible replacements for

Carson, who is expected to retire towards the end of the decade. The opprobrium heaped on Miss Rivers in some press quarters, David Richards observed in the *Washington Post* (June 11, 1986), "might even have something to do with the persistence of sexism." When a male television anchor "jumps stations for bigger bucks and better billing," Richards pointed out, he is not treacherous but "going for it."

The October 9, 1986, premiere of *The Late Show Starring Joan Rivers* had a solid A.C. Nielsen rating of 4.2. While the show increased viewership for Fox Broadcasting on 70 percent of the stations in the nation's top-fifty markets, it soon began to decline steadily in the ratings, and by March it was down to 2.0. The downward spiral was attributed by many observers to Miss Rivers' abandonment of the acerbic, backbiting style for which she is best known, as well as to what one observer described as Fox Broadcasting's "Mickey Mouse" programming strategies. "It was a shock to see [Joan Rivers] on this show," Marvin Kitman wrote in *Newsday* (May 26, 1987). "She was too kind to her guests. . . . She was embracing all these swine celebrities. It was almost as if this was the price she paid to get them on the show. . . . It was the Joan Rivers show without Joan Rivers." In May 1987 Fox Broadcasting ended Miss Rivers' tenure as permanent host of the show, shortened the program's title to *The Late Show*, and brought in rotating guest hosts.

Joan Rivers, a five-foot-two, 110-pound, brown-eyed woman with blonde-colored hair, lives in Bel Air, California. She has an eighteen-year-old daughter, Melissa, who is a University of Pennsylvania student. Intimates stress the dramatic contrast between the public and private personas of Miss Rivers, describing her as a devoted family woman, shy, introverted, and bookish once away from the stage and the rigors of "the career," as she and her late husband, Edgar Rosenberg, the behind-the-scenes architect of a number of her successes, referred to her professional life. Rosenberg, whom Miss Rivers married on July 15, 1965, was the executive producer of *The Late Show Starring Joan Rivers*. Depressed over the failure of the show as well as by his own failing health, Rosenberg committed suicide on August 14, 1987. "I don't know why I am being tested in this way," Joan Rivers told Richard Meryman in *People* magazine (August 31, 1987), "but I have to go on because of my daughter." Deciding to make hard work her grief therapy, she agreed to appear as a presenter on the 1987 Emmy Awards program, made plans to perform in Las Vegas, and signed on as a regular with ABC's *Hollywood Squares* television program. "I don't want sympathy audiences," she told Meryman. "It's my job to make them laugh, and I'm a professional, and my husband was a professional. I don't want to turn my career into anything maudlin or sentimental. Besides, I'm too short to be a tragic figure."

Joan Rivers maintains a staff of servants and collects French and Russian antiques. "If Louis XIV hasn't touched it," she once quipped, "I don't want it." Miss Rivers has been the national chairman of the Cystic Fibrosis Society since 1982, and she was the first major entertainer to headline fund raisers for AIDS. She was named Woman of the Year by the Harvard Hasty Pudding Society in 1984, and she is a former Hadassah Woman of the Year. She has received the Georgie from the American Guild of Variety Artists for best comedienne and the award for nightclub performer of the year from the New York Friars Club. She has twice been named the Las Vegas Comedienne of the Year and has won two Cleo awards (1976, 1982) for her work in television commercials. The comedienne continues to appear regularly on the nightclub circuit, has just come out with a Mattel VCR game, a parody of a soap opera, and has agreed to appear in a movie to be entitled, "Hot to Trot."

References: Ms. 13:108+ O '84 pors; N Y Daily News Mag p2+ Ja 23 '83 pors; New York 16:4+ Ja 24 '83 por; Newsweek 102:58+ O 10 '83 pors; People 9:33+ Ag 31 '87 pors; Time 121:85+ Ap 11 '83 por; Vanity Fair 48:22+ My '85 por; Washington Post B p1+ Je 11 '86 pors; Rivers, Joan, and Meryman, Richard. *Enter Talking* (1986)

Robertson, Pat

Mar. 22, 1930– Religious broadcaster; television executive. Address: b. CBN Center, 1000 Centerville Turnpike, Virginia Beach, Va. 23463

There is political fire in the gut of "Bible conservatives," the Christian Pentecostal, Fundamentalist, and other evangelical voters who for decades have felt dispossessed by the hegemony of liberal secular humanism in American government, buttressed by the mass media. Formerly predominantly Democratic, those voters (or, more precisely, some 80 percent of them) helped to elect Republican Ronald Reagan president in 1980 and 1984. The growing importance of evangelicals in the Republican party is now dramatized in the candidacy for the 1988 Republican presidential nomination of the religious broadcaster and television entrepreneur Pat Robertson, a former Democrat and a charismatic in both the religious and secular senses of the word. Robertson is the founder of an international communications and education empire centered in the Christian Broadcasting Network (CBN), one of the world's largest satellite-to-cable television systems, with thirty million subscribers in the United States alone, and he gained a wide national following as the amiable and prepossessing host of that network's flagship daily talk show, The 700 Club, which has a Nielsen-rated cumulative audience of 7.3 million households with twelve million viewers. CBN reported revenues of $600 million and expenses of $500 million between 1979 and 1984 and a net worth of $112 million in 1985. After scoring stunningly in early caucuses in Michigan and South Carolina, Robertson resigned from the ministry and from his broadcasting posts, in September 1987, and formally declared his political candidacy, in October.

Robertson espouses the "traditional values" of the Reagan mandate, and he believes that he may be "called" to continue the realization of that mandate. "The primary characteristic of a president is the ability to lead," he has said, "and I am perceived—give or take my shortcomings—as a strong leader who has vision and gets things done. . . . From what I've seen, [the other potential Republican presidential nominees do not have] either the national charisma or the television ability, the telegenic qualities, [to win]." He views his constituency not as right wing but as "the new center" of the Republican party, which wants "the government off our backs and out of our pockets." Robertson's "agenda for public action" includes an "historic interpretation of the Constitution," "individual freedom," a free market economy, the teaching of "religiously based morality" in public schools, and the questioning of the judiciary's assumption of preeminence in the federal system. In his book "Pat Robertson: A Personal, Religious, and Political Portrait," scheduled for publication by Harper & Row in November 1987, David Edwin Harrow claims, according to the publisher, that Robertson is essentially an old-fashioned Southern populist and that he is the first American to give conservative Christians a secular forum.

The younger of two sons in an old Southern family with long traditions in politics and religion, Pat Robertson was born Marion Gordon Robertson in Lexington, Virginia, on March 22, 1930. His father, Absalom Willis Robertson, served in Congress thir-

ty-four years, first in the House of Representatives and later in the Senate, where he was chairman of the Banking and Commerce Committee. Both Senator Robertson and his wife, the former Gladys Churchill Willis, were children of Baptist clergymen. More distant relatives included a chaplain to the Jamestown colony, presidents William Henry Harrison and Benjamin Harrison, and, very distantly, Sir Winston Churchill. It was A. Willis Robertson Jr., better known as Taddy, the older son in the family, who gave his younger brother the nickname Pat, which stuck.

According to old friends of the Robertson family, the mother, following a "born again" experience, was an intensely religious woman who prayed and read the Bible ceaselessly, placed little value on her husband's success in politics, and urged Pat to surrender his life to Jesus Christ. At the same time, Pat was also strongly influenced by his father. "I learned the words 'constituent' shortly after I learned the words 'mama' and 'daddy,'" he told Doug Hill for a profile in TV Guide (March 15, 1986). "Wherever I would go, I would be under careful scrutiny. So I was always aware of that, and it has stood me in good stead." What influenced him most, he said, were his father's "integrity," his antipathy to "government intervention in the affairs of people," and his "sense of the history of this country"—a history that included "the persecution of Baptists."

A Democrat of the "old-school South," ready with a Biblical quotation for almost all occasions, A. Willis Robertson was an anti-New Deal hardliner in the House of Representatives, beginning in 1933. In the Senate, from 1947 to 1967, he was one of the fiercest and most eloquent conservatives in the Southern caucus. During his last term as a senator, he quoted Jesus ("The poor ye shall always have with you") in denouncing what he regarded as the hubris and futility of President Lyndon B. Johnson's declaration of a "war on poverty," and when the Supreme Court outlawed official prayer in the public schools he warned that the continued application of the First Amendment to the religious affairs of the states would "undoubtedly sweep us down the broad and easy highway of secularism."

Garrett Epps, a novelist and newspaper columnist with an intimate knowledge of Virginia politics, has pointed out that Pat Robertson cannot be understood by any analyst who overlooks the fact that Robertson "is very much his father's son." In an article in the Washington Post (October 19, 1986), Epps wrote: "Robertson's critics often depict the evangelist-broadcaster as a political extremist with bizarre beliefs. But it may make more sense to view him as the last old-school Southern politician. Like his father . . . , Pat holds an old-fashioned Southern view of the Constitution. Like his father, he is highly conservative on . . . social issues, fiercely anti-Communist and pro-military [although critical of Pentagon prodigality] and critical of deficit spending and welfare programs. And like his father, he sees nothing wrong with invoking the Bible and religious values in political debate."

Robertson prepared for college at the elite McCallie School in Chattanooga, Tennessee. While attending Washington and Lee University in Lexington, Virginia he did farm work summers. His extracurricular activities in college included wrestling, soccer, and membership in the Sigma Alpha Epsilon fraternity. He was elected to Phi Beta Kappa in his junior year, and he graduated *magna cum laude* in 1950. After briefly studying economics at the University of London, he served in the Marine Corps for two years, becoming a lieutenant. (In October 1986 Robertson filed libel suits against United States Representative Andrew Jacobs Jr. and former Representative Paul McCloskey Jr. in response to their allegation that he used his father's influence to avoid combat duty in the Korean war. "Not only did I not use influence to avoid combat in Korea," Robertson said, "the record is clear that I served in the combat zone.") At some point Robertson boxed in Golden Gloves competition.

While studying law at the Yale University Law School, Robertson accompanied his father to the Democratic National Convention, in 1952, and worked on the staff of the Senate Appropriations Committee, during the summer of 1953. He took his J.D. degree at Yale in 1955, but by that time he had become disillusioned with law, because of its lack of moral absolutes. Studying desultorily, he failed to pass the New York bar exam. After spending a year as a financial analyst and management trainee at W.R. Grace Company in New York City, he became a partner in the Curry Sound Corporation, an audio components firm. Having married when at Yale, he settled with his growing family on Staten Island in New York City, where he was chairman of the Richmond County Adlai Stevenson for President Committee in 1956.

Fellow students at Yale remember Robertson as having been as worldly as any of them, and Robertson recounts in his autobiography *Shout It From the Housetops* (Logos International, 1972) that in New York City he "was beginning to enjoy some of the social life, the Stork Club, Le Pavillion and trying to cut a little bit of a figure in the Big Apple." There was, however, "a God-shaped vacuum" in his life. "I was so burdened with the futility of life," he wrote, "that at one point I had actually contemplated suicide." Meanwhile, his mother, described by him as "a powerful prayer warrior," was besieging heaven in his behalf and mailing him religious tracts. Finally, she arranged for him to meet Cornelius Vanderbreggen, a Baptist missionary she knew, for dinner in Philadelphia. The meeting catalyzed a profound religious experience. "I began to examine my life. And I believed Jesus Christ died for the sins of the world and for my sins, too, and it was like a light went on! I entered a whole new world." The following day he was sitting at his desk in his office when he leaned back in his chair and "burst out laughing" at the realization that he "had been saved." The new world that he entered was one in which "the gifts of the Spirit" were operative. Those paranormal gifts include miraculous healing through faith, "speaking in tongues," and divinely inspired "discernment" of God's will.

The "born again" Robertson enrolled in New York Theological Seminary, and as a seminarian he did charitable work in the Bedford-Stuyvesant section of Brooklyn, a black ghetto. He received his master of divinity degree in 1959 and was ordained a Southern Baptist clergyman two years later. The ordination took place at the Freemason Baptist Church in Norfolk, Virginia. At first Robertson planned to found a mission in Beford-Stuyvesant, but God "led" him, as he puts it, on a different path, back to his native Tidewater. Informed by his mother that a run-down UHF television station in Portsmouth, Virginia, was up for sale, he was inspired with the idea of developing a Christian ministry that would make full utilization of the electronic media. With seventy dollars in his pocket, he returned to Virginia with his family, raised $37,000 in loans, and acquired the TV station along with its sister radio facility, an FM station. In 1960 he incorporated the Christian Broadcasting Network and made the first license application in FCC history for a TV facility that would devote more than half of its schedule to religious programming.

The first CBN stations went on the air in 1961. Calculating that he needed $7,000 a month from his Tidewater audience, in the fall of 1963 Robertson ran a telethon appealing for 700 people to pledge $10 a month each. The show offered a variety of talk and music, and telephone lines were open for prayer and guidance as well as for pledges. The response from the Tidewater viewers was such that Robertson made *The 700 Club* a continuing regular production. In asking viewers to call in and share their problems and pray with telephone counselors, *The 700 Club* pioneered "two-way television."

During the 1960s and early 1970s the donations from viewers were supplemented by income from other sources, including the sale of $7.3 million in notes to investors in twenty-seven states. CBN acquired three additional television stations (including one in Lebanon that reached much of the Middle East) and five additional radio stations as its annual budget rose into the tens of millions. Robertson was still far short of his dream—a true network, capable of challenging and offering an alternative to the sex, violence, and secular values of CBS, NBC, and ABC. Approaching other station owners, he found ninety TV and 120 radio outlets interested in becoming part of a network. In August 1977 the Christian Broadcasting Network began bouncing its programs off the RCA SATCOM II satellite to receiving dishes in the sixty top markets in the United States. Within weeks, CBN was the largest American syndicator of programs via satellite, a position it held until Ted Turner developed his Atlanta-based "Super Station that serves the nation." Today, CBN stands approximately fourth in the satellite/cable ranking.

In 1977 Robertson founded CBN University and began building the CBN Center, a $20 million complex on a 187-acre site in Virginia Beach. Upon completion of the center, all CBN operations, including the university, were moved there. CBN University is a fully accredited institution with five graduate schools, offering advanced degrees in subjects ranging from journalism to religion, and a law school. The current student body numbers about 800.

In January 1978 CBN held its first live coast-to-coast telethon, which brought in $750,000 in donations in one week. By mid-1978, The 700 Club was being received in all the states in the union and some thirteen foreign countries. More than 100 television stations carried it, and several thousand communities received it via cable-TV and radio. On the show, Robertson and his assistant, Ben Kinchlow, would present guests, both celebrities and unknowns, who had tales to tell of personal experiences with conversion, miraculous events (including healing), and the fight against such evils as abortion, sexual deviation, the occult, and pornography. Listening to a guest, Robertson and Kinchlow would contribute a "Praise God!" or other encouraging exclamations at appropriate intervals. They did little protracted preaching of their own, although Robertson was forthright in his comments on such issues as public education ("attempting . . . to take children away from parents and educate them in a philosophy that is amoral, anti-Christian, and humanistic"), abortion (Three Supreme Court justices "have on their hands the blood of seventeen million aborted babies"), and women's rights ("Now this may be unpalatable to some of us . . . but . . . the ultimate authority needs to be the husband").

In addition to the interviews with guests, each program offered news and news analysis of interest to Christians and live or taped music. "The show has demonstrated that a hot message can be communicated effectively on a cool medium," William Martin observed in the Washington Post Magazine (June 4, 1978). "Though he sometimes gets worked up to a fair intensity, Robertson's style and the format of The 700 Club remind one less of Billy Graham or Rex Humbard or Oral Roberts than of Johnny Carson or, more aptly, Merv Griffin." According to Martin, in 1977 counselors at CBN headquarters handled over a million phone calls. In addition, hundreds of thousands of calls came into sixty local centers staffed by volunteers across the United States. For five years, from 1977 to 1982, Robertson wrote and mailed to members of the club Pat Robertson's Perspective, described by his office as "a geopolitical newsletter" devoted to such "macro-economic issues" as investment philosophy, monetary trends, foreign trade, and the Federal Reserve Board and federal fiscal policy. In the letter he repeatedly assailed federal deficit spending for the ever heavier burden it put upon posterity.

In 1978 Robertson started Operation Blessing, described by his office as "one of America's largest private organizations serving the poor and needy." That relief organization claims to have helped five million needy Americans in 1984 alone. According to reports in Newsweek (October 14, 1985)

Sojourners (October 1985), and Christianity Today (November 8, 1985), Operation Blessing also spent $2 million on nonmilitary supplies for the anti-Communist Nicaraguan Contras. To combat functional illiteracy in urban American ghettos, Robertson started another service, Operation Heads Up, in 1985.

The Christian Broadcasting Network was from the beginning a nonprofit, tax-exempt organization, and it remains so on the federal level. (It pays taxes locally, in Virginia Beach.) In 1979 Robertson founded the CBN Continental Broadcasting Network, a for-profit tax-paying corporation, for the purpose of handling CBN's commercial side, including the sale of advertising time in the network's nonreligious programming. In 1980 he bought, for a relative song, the rights to such old black-and-white television series as The Rifleman, Flipper, Father Knows Best, I Married Joan, and Wagon Train—programs which, while not religious, had a wholesomeness that, in his view, is no longer available on the secular TV networks. CBN viewership tripled after reruns of those shows were introduced into the network's schedule in 1981. Also introduced were an evening newscast, World Class Wrestling, and the CBN-produced Christian soap opera Another Life. Ultimately, CBN would gross $230 million annually.

In keeping with his interest in relating Biblical prophecy and ethics to public policy, Robertson in 1981 cofounded the Freedom Council, a tax-exempt grassroots foundation with regional chapters whose purpose was to recruit evangelical Christians for political action and to promote a conservative social agenda. Both the Freedom Council, which attracted 45,000 dues-paying members, and the National Perspectives Institute, a think tank, were once subsidized by CBN but are now independent. Another political-action group founded by Robertson, the Committee for Freedom, raised $500,000 for candidates it backed around the country. "I have always thought that Christians should get involved in public life," Robertson told Kenneth R. Clark of the Chicago Tribune (June 26, 1985). "I don't think being a Christian means just spending time within the confines of the church, behind stained-glass windows, singing hymns and reading a book of Old English. I think there's life and dynamism in the Christian message, and we have a role to play in every phase of life. The way you lead is from service. If we serve the people with knowledge and compassion and with care, that's the way we ought to take over leadership."

Robertson began contemplating a possible run for the Republican nomination for president of the United States in the summer of 1985. In an interview with Jon Margolis and Bruce Buursma of the Chicago Tribune (November 3, 1985), he said that he was "talking to wise counselors" and "listening for circumstances" indicating whether or not it was God's will that he run. Should he run, he said, his political base would be "a coalition of evangelical Christians on the one hand and those in America who favor traditional values on the other." Already, he said, he had found in that constituency "a degree of enthusiasm . . . like nothing [he had] ever seen."

Margolis and Buursma reported that Republican political strategists in Washington viewed a possible Robertson campaign "with decidedly mixed emotions." "He's dynamite on television . . . ," one told them, "but I don't know about that faith-healing stuff, or claiming to have prayed the hurricane [Gloria] away from Virginia. I don't think that goes over too well with a lot of voters we need." Perhaps to offset such criticism, Robertson had begun to play down the more controversial aspects of his charismatic ministry. Distinguishing himself from the right wing of the evangelical movement, he told the two reporters that he wanted a government of "compassion to the poor and the needy," that he thought $60 billion could be trimmed from the Pentagon's budget, and that he opposed the right-wing dictatorships of the "rich oligarchies" as well as the Communists in Latin America. Margolis and Buursma added: "Unlike some of his fellow evangelicals, he has no history of segregationist sympathies (cohost Kinchlow is black) or of anti-Catholic or anti-Jewish statements."

In the 1986 Michigan primary anticipating the 1988 Republican National Convention, Robertson won a presentable share of delegates, putting him in a second-place contest with Representative Jack Kemp, behind Vice-President George Bush, the favorite of the party regulars. According to his campaign workers, he also showed considerable strength in Iowa and in western states and in the South, not only among evangelicals but also among "baby-boomers" and blue-collar workers. As he crisscrossed the country in his company's BAC One-Eleven jet, he turned over much of the day-to-day management of CBN to his son Tim. He also cut back The 700 Club from ninety minutes to an hour and left the show increasingly in Ben Kinchlow's hands, limiting himself to guest appearances.

At a nationally televised rally on September 17, 1986, Robertson said that he would officially announce his candidacy for the Republican presidential nomination if he could raise three million signatures of people pledging to support his candidacy. Ten months later he told the press that he was still "about two million short" of the goal and that he would accept verbal pledges of support over the telephone in lieu of written signatures. At the South Carolina Republican convention in the spring of 1987, Robertson supporters took about 40 percent of the state party delegate seats despite fast maneuvering by party regulars. In the fifteen months ending October 1987, Robertson's campaign raised $11.7 million, second among Republicans only to the $12.7 raised by Vice-President George Bush.

The firm stance that Robertson takes on such issues as school prayer, homosexuality, and abortion makes him a prime alternative for social conservatives dissatisfied with Bush and Kemp. Economic conservatives are prepared to look beyond Robertson's religion because of his intelligence, "toughness," and "grasp of the facts." They appreciate his advocacy of a flat tax and the cuts in both defense and domestic spending that he believes necessary to reduce the federal deficit. The Harvard University economist John Exter, a former vice-president of the Federal Reserve, has said, "I am the kind of person who can swallow all that religion when I see his understanding of economics." At the fifty-fifth annual conference of United States mayors in Nashville in June 1987, Robertson proposed replacing most federal urban-aid programs with a voluntary system that would give tax credits to corporations and individuals who contribute to local government projects. He pointed out that the proposal would increase citizen participation because taxpayers would have to write checks specifically supporting local programs to qualify for the credit.

On October 1, 1987, Robertson formally declared his candidacy for the Republican presidential nomination. Five days later his campaign was shaken by the disclosure in the Wall Street Journal that Robertson, who had been celebrating his wedding anniversary on March 22, was actually married on August 27, 1954, when his wife was nearly seven months pregnant. Mrs. Robertson is the former Adelia Elmer, better known as Dede, an erstwhile teacher of nursing. She and Robertson have four grown children, Timothy, Elizabeth, Gordon, and Ann, and three grandchildren. The Robertsons live at the CBN Center in Virginia Beach, on a CBN-owned estate that includes a stable housing Robertson's four horses. Horseback riding is his favorite recreation.

Robinson donates his CBN salary (reported to be $70,307 in 1984) to his own and other ministries and lives on other income, much of it from his books, which have enjoyed total sales of over a million. In addition to Shout It From the Housetops, he has written My Prayer for You (Fleming H. Revell, 1977), The Secret Kingdom (Thomas Nelson, 1982), Beyond Reason (William Morrow, 1984), Answers to 200 of Life's Most Probing Questions (CBN University Press, 1985), and America's Date with Destiny (Thomas Nelson, 1986). In the last mentioned, in the publisher's words, he "reminds us of the brave heritage we can't afford to forget and focuses our attention on the crucial choices that will shape our nation's future."

At six foot one, Pat Robertson is considerably taller than he looks next to the still taller Ben Kinchlow on television. Having a smile, chuckle, and low-keyed demeanor that puts him in a "communicator" class with President Ronald Reagan, he is more moderate in tone than most television evangelists. The soft-spoken, elegantly dressed broadcaster reminded Susan Page of Newsday (June 27, 1986) of "the prosperous, Ivy League-educated lawyer he once seemed destined to become." Dick Dabney, writing in Harper's (August 1980) described Robertson's eyes, despite their "good-old-boy droop" and "ingratiating friendliness," as having "the afterglow of fierceness in them—a fire banked by time and policy."

Robertson keeps in shape with exercise and a low-fat diet including chicken, fish, fruit, grains, and vegetables. Rising at dawn, he spends an hour at Bible study and prayer and jogs two miles before beginning his day's work.

References: Chicago Tribune II p1+ Je 26 '85 pors; Christianity Today 29:48+ N 8 '85 pors, 30:34+ Ja 17 '86 pors; Conservative Digest 11:1+ Ag '85 pors; Harper's 261:33+ Ag '80 por; New Repub 195:14+ O 13 '86; New York 19:22+ Ag 18 '86 por; Newsday II p1+ Je 27 '86 pors; Newsweek 106:77 O 14 '85 por; People 26:26+ Ag 11 '86 pors; Sat Eve Post 257:50+ Mr '85 pors, 258:61+ S '86 pors; Time 127:62+ F 17 '86 pors; U S News 101:24+ Jl 14 '86 pors; Wall St J p1+ O 17 '85 por, p44 Jl 18 '86 por, p32 Jl 3 '87 por; Washington Post D p1+ O 18 '85 pors, A p19 Je 3 '86 por, H p1+ O 19 '86; Contemporary Authors vol 111 (1984); Robertson, Pat. Shout it From the Housetops (1972); Who's Who in America, 1986-87

Roderick, David M(ilton)

May 3, 1924– Corporation executive. Address: b. USX Corporation, 600 Grant St., Pittsburgh, Pa. 15230

Since becoming chairman and chief executive officer of the United States Steel Corporation in 1979, David Roderick has ended the era when "Big Steel" was the backbone of American industry by steering it away from the steel market into the oil, chemical, and energy markets. Its transformation was acknowledged when it was renamed the USX Corporation in 1986. Unlike the steel production men who traditionally ran U.S. Steel, Roderick came up through the ranks of the company's finance division, and his devotion to the balance sheet has set a precedent for a new breed of chief executive officers throughout the industry.

After assuming control in 1979, when U.S. Steel was what one industry analyst called an "unmitigated disaster," Roderick set out to stream-line the behemoth company, simplify its byzantine management structure, and make it less dependent on the cyclical and intensely competitive steel market. In 1982 he acquired the Marathon Oil Company and in 1986 the Texas Oil & Gas Corporation. At the same time he sold off peripheral holdings in timberland, coal, and other areas and shut down or idled six steel plants and 139 steel-related facilities, thus eliminating some 100,000 jobs and "turning many mill communities in western Pennsylvania, Ohio, and South Chicago into industrial ghost towns," according to Business Week (February 25, 1985). Roderick modernized remaining plants and brought them within the restrictions of the United States Environmental Protection Agency, but U.S. Steel became primarily an energy company, deriving less than a third of its revenues from steel sales.

His cutbacks and antiunion stance helped to set off the longest strike in the history of the steel industry in 1986 and 1987. Other troubles sprang from the $5 billion debt he had incurred in acquiring the energy companies and the unpropitious timing of the Marathon acquisition, just before a plunge in oil prices. Not unexpectedly, USX became a take-over target, and in 1986 Carl C. Icahn made an ominous $8 billion take-over proposal. Forced into a rapid restructuring of his company, Roderick managed to outmaneuver Icahn by erecting what one reporter called "a wall of debt" around USX. As one expert observer of the corporate world has pointed out, Roderick is "hard-nosed enough to do things other people don't have the nerve to do," and Roderick himself has said that he learned a long time ago not to flinch "when someone says they're going to hit you."

David Milton Roderick, the son of Milton S. Roderick, a postman, and Anna (Baskin) Roderick, was born on May 3, 1924, in Pittsburgh, Pennsylvania. He grew up on the city's North Side in an Irish-Catholic working-class neighborhood, where he gained a reputation as a fearsome boxer. His first contact with big business came when he went to work as a messenger for the Gulf Oil Company, at the age of seventeen. After graduating from high school in 1942, he joined the United States Marines, serving first as a rifle instructor, then as a platoon sergeant in the South Pacific. He returned to Gulf Oil after his discharge from the Marines, working as a clerk while attending night school at the Robert Morris Junior College and at the University of Pittsburgh. It took him ten years to obtain his degree in economics and finance.

In 1959, after serving a stint as assistant comptroller of the Bessemer and Lake Erie Railroad Company and the Union Railroad Company, Roderick began working for U.S. Steel as assistant to the director of statistics in the New York office. In January 1962 he was appointed accounting consultant for international projects, and he and his family moved to Paris. Two years later, he was made vice-president-accounting, international, and given the task of overseeing all of U.S. Steel's overseas markets. When appointed, he joked that his family might not see much of him in the future because he planned "to travel extensively." His achievements in that period, among them a plan that enabled a struggling manganese operation in Gabon to turn a profit, led to his promotion to vice-president, international, in 1967. He became chairman of the finance committee and a director of U.S. Steel in 1973. Roderick maintains that he was "absolutely surprised" by the latter appointment, which, he says, marked the beginning of his dream of becoming chief executive officer.

David M. Roderick was elected president of U.S. Steel on August 1, 1975, at a time when the American steel industry was slumping badly in the face of intense competition from low-priced imports that arrived in the United States from state-of-the-art foreign mills. The industry was also under pressure from the United States government to bring its antiquated furnaces into conformity with environmental quality standards. Working under U.S. Steel's chief executive officer, Edgar B. Speer, Roderick went on the offensive, living up to his corporation's "tough guy" managerial image.

To prevent foreign competitors from selling steel in America at fire-sale prices sometimes lower than their cost of producing it, U.S. Steel filed "antidumping" suits. The steel industry as a whole sent up a distress signal, combining mass layoffs and shutdowns with a lobbying crusade, that, according to Agis Salpukas of the New York Times (January 8, 1978), "brought together the United Steelworkers of America, officials from communities with heavy layoffs, and a 'Steel Caucus' of 170 Congressmen." In 1978 President Jimmy Carter's administration responded by setting a minimum trigger price below which steel products could not be imported without setting off a federal investigation. Although the trigger price system promised to raise earnings in the American steel industry by $900 million a year, Roderick called it "a drop in the bucket," noting that to modernize their mills and remain competitive, American companies would have to spend $5 billion a year.

By that time, Roderick was becoming known as an astute analyst of figures who also took into account the wider political and economic aspects of large-scale business enterprise. When Edgar B. Speer, because of illness, stepped down as chairman of the board and chief executive officer of U.S. Steel in April 1979, Roderick was named to re-

place him by a board that had been looking for "someone who was willing to take tough actions." Roderick quickly broke with U.S. Steel tradition by appointing an outsider, William R. Roesch, to improve efficiency in the steel division. Like Speer, Roesch was a production man, with twenty-five years of steel-making experience. Roderick also stepped up a program of diversification into the petrochemical business begun under Speer.

That move drew fire from analysts and investors who felt that it was a mistake to invest in a business with a relatively slow growth rate (though still double that of steel's) and with a dependency on an oil market then dominated by OPEC, but Roderick insisted that long-term prospects for the chemical industry were good and that the decline in earnings in the chemical division (from $216 million in 1974 to $21 million in 1978) was temporary. His sanguinity was seemingly vindicated when chemical sales rose to almost a billion dollars in 1979.

In November 1979 Roderick announced the closing of fifteen antiquated plants and mills in eight states, an action that led to job losses for 13,000 employees, or 8 percent of U.S. Steel's work force, in one of the largest shutdowns in the nation's economic history. Roderick's decision was applauded by many steel industry analysts on Wall Street who believed that the company ran too many marginal plants, but steelworkers were bitter. The layoffs, with the resulting loss of production and costs of compensation for jobless workers, resulted in a fourth quarter loss at U.S. Steel that, at $516.7 million, was the largest in corporate history.

At a news conference held not long after the plant closings were announced, Roderick was confronted with the charge, which he vigorously denied, that the closings were rooted in the past sins of U.S.S. management. For decades that management, controlling the lion's share of the steel market, had been known for accepting narrow profit margins and low product quality and for high-handed treatment of customers and labor, as well as for its secretive, slow-motion decision-making process. The closing of one of the plants, for instance, had originally been announced in 1945. Roderick, who had begun to move to make the company more efficient and to democratize its autocratic structure, attributed the closings to a failure by the federal government to enforce the antidumping trigger price of 1977. At a candid meeting with industry analysts in December Roderick injected a note of humor into the grim discussion when asked what he would have changed if given a chance to modify past decisions. "I sort of regret we didn't buy an oil company five years ago," he said. In 1980 Roderick jeopardized his popularity with rival steel companies and with the Carter administration by filing antidumping suits against virtually the entire range of imports from the steel makers of West Germany, France, Great Britain, Italy, Belgium, the Netherlands, and Luxembourg. Nevertheless, Roderick's strategies since taking office seemed to pay off that year, for the company recovered from its $293 million loss in 1979 with a $504 million profit on overall sales of $12.5 billion. That seemed "a monumental achievement" to Charles A. Bradford, an industry analyst, who said that U.S. Steel had gone "from a bad company to an average company."

Meanwhile, Roderick pursued his diversification program. He sold a considerable number of U.S. Steel interests, including a cement business, California real estate, and its own corporate headquarters. Moreover, he accumulated a cash reserve of $1.5 billion to make new acquisitions. In 1981 he borrowed some $3 billion and made a $5.93 billion bid for Marathon Oil Company, which U.S. Steel acquired in March 1982 for $5.93 billion, after outmaneuvering Mobil Corporation. Although Roderick intended to resist the temptation to use Marathon's significant cash flow to bolster his steel business, U.S. Steel could expect significant tax benefits from the acquisition. Furthermore, Marathon, with its 49 percent stake in the richest oil reservoir in the continental United States, had excellent long-term prospects. Theodore Levitt, the Edward W. Carter Professor of Business Administration at the Harvard Business School, speculated that the acquisition "may be the shrewdest thing done since U.S. Steel was organized by J. P. Morgan and Andrew Carnegie in 1901." The *Wall Street Transcript* gave David M. Roderick a silver award as top CEO in the steel industry, citing his aggressive diversification program as having saved the corporation.

Others were skeptical of Roderick's dependence on oil, an industry subject to the same downturns in the business cycle at the same time as steel, and they questioned the decision to acquire Marathon during a national recession when interest rates were high. Some analysts rated U.S. Steel as one of the "riskiest steel stocks." "Their problems are formidable," declared Joseph Wyman, an analyst for Shearson/American Express, "from time to time it looks like they made a horrible mistake." Diversification also raised the question of a shirking of economic responsibilities. A lawyer who had fought the closing of U.S. Steel's Youngstown, Ohio, plant said, "It's not as if the United States were able to do without steel, or as if U.S. Steel was investing in something that would replace steel." Roderick himself admitted that the recession was deeper than he had realized and that an oil industry slump had pushed Marathon's market value below the price he had paid for it, but insisted that "what we're doing is for the long term. . . . We're looking at where we want to be in the year 2000."

But for the time being, U.S. Steel was "reeling" from its $5 billion debt, according to Leslie Wayne (*New York Times,* July 10, 1983), and it lost $361 million on its revenue of $18.91 billion in 1982. Roderick was forced into some dexterous strategems. U.S. Steel issued perferred stock on two occasions in 1983 and continued to sell its peripheral assets and to reduce its staff. In April 1983 Roderick, who that year was chairman of the American Iron and Steel Institute, was asked to appear before the Congressional Steel Caucus after making a bombshell proposal to cut production costs by importing 3.5 million tons of unfinished steel slabs a year from the British Steel Corporation. The deal eventually fell through, but not before it confirmed Roderick's image as the industry's most controversial figure. Although it was endorsed by Wall Street analysts, it was widely viewed as a betrayal of the protectionist stance exemplified by Roderick's antidumping suits and his lobbying for federal aid for steel and other basic industries, and it rankled some of his peers in the steel industry.

To steelworkers the plan seemed especially onerous because it called for the elimination of between 1,000 and 3,000 jobs. They found it even more galling because it was announced only a few days after the conclusion of contract negotiations in which they made major wage concessions in the interest of job security. It indicated to them and to others that Roderick had not eliminated all of the old arrogance and insensitivity from the management of U.S. Steel, but the imperturbable Roderick said that he was willing to "take some heat," because he thought he was "accomplishing something." He persisted in his program to make U.S. Steel a company that would derive 40 percent of its revenues from steel, 40 percent from oil and gas, and 20 percent from chemicals and other activities.

In a move praised by economists, but deplored by labor, Roderick announced the closing of an additional three obsolescent plants as of April 1984, thereby reducing the company's steelmaking capacity by 16 percent and eliminating 15,430 jobs. At the same time U.S. Steel reopened a modernized Fairfield, Alabama, mill where Roderick had obtained cost-saving concessions from workers, and 1,600 new jobs were created. Roderick justified the closings by noting that while his company had lost $1.16 billion in 1983, largely because of losses in its steel division, it earned $493 million in 1984, largely on the strength of Marathon's $10.2 billion in overall revenues.

In 1985 an attempt to bolster the steel division by merging with the nation's seventh-largest steel maker, National Steel Corporation, fell through because of what Roderick dismissed as rigidly mathematical, "schoolboy" antitrust restrictions. He then sought a "third leg" for U.S. Steel by acquiring the Texas Oil & Gas Corporation in a $3.6 billion stock transaction. That move made U.S. Steel essentially an energy company, with a steel division that provided only about one third of its revenues by 1986. The new acquisition, like the Marathon merger, would cushion U.S. Steel against heavy write-offs in its steel sector and, according to one of its executives, would enable the corporation to weather a lengthy strike "without any meaningful financial damage."

A significant restructuring took place in 1986, when U.S. Steel became USX, a parent company with four operating units: USS of Pittsburgh; U.S. Diversified Group of Pittsburgh; Texas Oil & Gas of Dallas; and Marathon Oil of Findlay, Ohio. The X added to the company logo had been U.S. Steel's symbol on the New York Stock Exchange since 1924. Meanwhile, labor relations, always poor, took a turn for the worse, and on August 1, 1986, a strike by 22,000 workers began, which became the longest in the nation's history. It helped to push losses in steel to $1.4 billion before it was finally settled in January 1987 with the steelworkers' union accepting a loss of 1,346 jobs.

The oil recession, low steel prices, the financial strain of diversifying, and the record length of the strike combined to push USX stock to a ten-year low of $15 a share. It led to rumors of a takeover that set off a trading frenzy in which fifty million shares of USX stock changed hands in one week in October 1986. Possible suitors were the Australian investor Robert Holmes à Court, T. Boone Pickens Jr., Carl C. Icahn, and Irwin Jacobs, all of whom bought significant holdings of USX stock. The corporate raiders speculated that the value of USX broken into its components parts was between $30 and $40 a share because of the oil companies. The New York investor Carl C. Icahn, who had previously taken over and turned around Trans World Airlines, emerged as the most ardent wooer. In October he made a "friendly" proposal of $31 per share or $8 billion for USX stock.

To prevent a shareholder revolt, Roderick was now forced to develop a strategy for restructuring USX that would raise its stock—which take-over speculation pushed to $27 a share in late 1986—above $31 dollars a share. Although he entered into complex negotiations with Icahn, Roderick made clear that he "would not be rushed" into a restructuring. Betting that Icahn would not press his bid before seeing the restructuring plan, Roderick stalled, retiring for "judicious" study of the details of Icahn's proposal with bankers at First Boston Corporation and Goldman, Sachs & Company. The restructuring plan, to be drawn up by the bankers from options ranging from making a new acquisition to dismembering the company, was still unfinished when Icahn's October 22 deadline came around. Roderick meanwhile bought time. He raised $1 billion in cash by selling off USX assets, including its chemicals business. He also placed USX's West Texas Yates oilfield—its "crown jewel"—out of the reach of the raiders by tying it to $850 million in bank loans that would have to be paid back from oilfield revenues if USX were taken over. He guarded USX as a whole with a total of $3 billion in debt that would become due if the company changed hands. Thwarted, Icahn retracted his $8 billion bid on January 8, 1987.

Roderick used the money he had borrowed for further restructuring of USX, including elimination of almost 27 percent of its remaining steelmaking capacity. In July 1987, with oil prices on the rise, USX reported second quarter earnings of $149 million, or more than ten times the earnings of its 1986 second quarter. Its steel division reversed a $59 million 1985 loss by posting a $37 million profit. Roderick called the results "gratifying." "Although

we experienced post-strike start-up costs," he said, "the decision to operate only our most efficient facilities combined with benefits of a competitive labor agreement are beginning to show up in our steel results."

David Roderick is five feet ten and a half inches tall, weighs 165 pounds, and has hazel eyes. His most important guide, in business as in his personal life, is, he says, the Bible. Roderick is chairman of the American Iron and Steel Institute, which in 1984 awarded him the Gary Medal, its highest award. In that year he also received the Americanism Award, the highest honor of the Anti-Defamation League of B'nai B'rith. Roderick takes a strong interest in civic affairs in Pittsburgh. He sits on the boards of directors of many companies and organizations, including Texas Instruments, Inc., the Advisory Council on Japan-U.S. Economic Relations, and the National Action Council for Minorities in Engineering.

On January 31, 1948, Milton D. Roderick married the former Elizabeth J. Costello. They have two sons, Daniel Milton and Thomas Kevin, and one daughter, Patricia Anne. The Rodericks divide their time between Fox Chapel, a wealthy Pittsburgh suburb and a sixty-acre farm in western Pennsylvania. In early summer they like to travel to Canada to fish for Atlantic salmon. Roderick also enjoys golf and is still an excellent marksman who goes off on hunting trips for duck and game.

References: Christian Sci Mon p21+ Mr 5 '85 por; Bsns W p50+ F 25 '85 pors, p32 F 2 '87 pors; Fortune 116:64 Ag 3 '87; London Observer p16 Ag 1 '82 por; N Y Times D p5+ F 19 '81 pors, III p3+ Jl 10 '83 pors; Wall St J p1+ F 1 '83 por; International Who's Who, 1986-87; Who's Who in America, 1986-87

Rubik, Erno

July 13, 1944- Inventor; designer; architectural engineer. Address: Magyar Iparmuveszeti Foiskola, 1121 Budapest, Zugligeti ut 11/25, Hungary

In the early 1980s an Hungarian architecture and design professor named Erno Rubik became one of the few self-made millionaires in the Communist bloc when he marketed an inexpensive puzzle, Rubik's cube, that boggled the minds of millions and racked up sales of more than 100 million authorized copies. When taken from its package, the cube is uniformly but differently colored on each side and is made from twenty-six smaller "cubies" that rotate on a central axis. Nine "cubie" faces, in the pattern of a tic-tac-toe diagram, are fitted to form each side of the cube, and when the cube is twisted, the cubies—and the colors—are scrambled. The person doing the twisting then has the monumental task of returning it to its original for-

Erno Rubik

mation, after somehow bypassing its more than 43 quintillion wrong configurations. For its aficionados, the cube represented everything from a source of headaches to a fount of pleasure, to a kind of mobile sculpture of the way subatomic particles behave. Other Hungarians viewed it as a scale model of limited capitalism.

To Rubik himself, the cube seemed a virtual philosopher's stone. "It has something of the laws of the universe in it," he once said. "It is simple in form but complicated in solution. It addresses questions of order and chaos, of harmony and discord. One must search within oneself for one's own answer. It becomes a deeply personal thing." In the aftermath of the cube craze, which lasted for about two years, Rubik gained permission from the Hungarian government to open his own design firm, which in 1986 marketed a new puzzle, Rubik's Magic, in anticipation of another international frenzy. On a promotional tour, Rubik announced that his new puzzle had an even greater number of possible configurations than the cube. "On the way to the solution," Rubik told Martin Gottlieb for a *New York Times* article (August 3, 1986), "you can have wonderful discoveries because you have wonderful shapes. The cube was very intellectual. This item could be more fun and more pleasurable—it is beautiful and changeable."

Erno Rubik was born on July 13, 1944, in the air raid shelter of a Budapest hospital. His mother, Magdolna Szanto Rubik, was a published poet, and his father, Erno Rubik Sr., after achieving a reputation as an outstanding aircraft engineer, started his own glider company, which is today considered perhaps the finest in Hungary. The younger Erno Rubik's fascination with shapes began in childhood and although he did well in school, he liked

drawing more than study. As an art student, he felt "somewhat out of place" among his classmates, convinced that he could not be as bohemian as they were. After receiving his degree in sculpture at the Technical University in Budapest, he studied architecture at the Academy of Applied Arts and Design in that city and then stayed on as a professor of design, eventually earning his now famous salary of approximately $150 a month.

At home in a room in his mother's apartment (his parents had divorced while he was in college), Rubik's combined interests in sculpture, design, and geometry resulted in a room crowded with cardboard and wooden models of his geometric flights of fancy. One of them, the prototype of his now famous cube, was constructed from twenty-seven smaller wooden blocks during several weeks in 1974. "It just happened in the back of my mind," Rubik recalled for a reporter from *People* magazine (September 28, 1981). According to John Tierney, writing in *Discover* magazine (March 1986), Rubik's "real interest was the structural problem—how could the blocks move independently without falling apart?" Elastic bands at first solved the problem, and Rubik began twisting the cubes to investigate the motion of the individual blocks. When the elastic broke, he hit on the idea of having the cubes hold themselves together, and he sanded and shaped them painstakingly until they interlocked. After labeling each side with adhesive paper in different colors, Rubik began to twist. "It was wonderful," he has written in a kind of fractured English in an unpublished autobiography, "to see how, after only a few turns, the colors became mixed, apparently in random fashion. It was tremendously satisfying to watch the color parade. . . . After a while I decided it was time to go home, let us put the cubes back in order. And it was at that moment that I came face to face with the Big Challenge: What *is* the way home?"

Enthralled but at the same time bedeviled by the problem he set himself, Rubik did not know if it were possible in one lifetime to sift through the configurations and return the cube to its pristine state. (It was later calculated that Rubik's cube was capable of keeping every person on earth busy with finding its solution for three centuries.) For Rubik it was like "staring at a piece of writing written in a secret code." "But for me," he told Tierney, "it was a code I myself had invented! Yet I could not read it." After a month full of effort, he discovered certain sequences of moves that promised to reorder the cube, and when he finally recovered the pristine configuration he felt "a euphoric feeling of freedom." Then it occurred to him that "if that reaction could be provoked in [him], perhaps it could be provoked in others." He did some research to see if the cube might have already been invented, but except for two similar and nearly simultaneous inspirations—one in Japan and one in America—about which Rubik had no way of knowing, there turned out to be nothing resembling the cube anywhere.

In January 1975 Rubik applied for a patent, and in 1977 Konsumex, the overbureaucratized Hungarian state trading company, began production of the cube. Although the cube appeared in stores at the end of the year, the international craze was still several years away, and the first cube owners that Rubik observed were therefore members of an advance guard of as-yet-unsuspected millions of purchasers. The first, as Rubik has described him, was "an eight-year-old street urchin, barefooted, shirt torn, covered in bruises, broken and chewed nails, badly in need of a good wash—a small Oliver Twisting." The second was "a still youthful mother in her thirties who must have just emerged from the beauty salon. She was sitting on a bench and cast only an occasional glance at her baby in the pram, so thoroughly was she immersed in the cube. It was astounding to catch on the faces of these diametrically opposite people—the very same expression."

Sales of the cube remained sluggish until Tibor Laczi, a Hungarian businessman living in Vienna, saw it for the first time while on a business trip to Hungary. He bought it on the spot from a restaurant waiter who was struggling with it and the next day went to Konsumex's offices to ask permission to market it in the West. When the officials to whom he talked claimed to have displayed the cube to no avail in a number of international toy fairs and had canceled half their order of ten thousand cubes, he asked them how they had displayed it. As he recalled for John Tierney, "They said it was on a shelf with hundreds of other toys. Was it taken out of the box? They didn't know. How many people working at the booth could demonstrate how to solve the puzzle? None of them." Finally, Laczi visited Rubik, who taught him to solve it and asked him, a little wistfully, if he thought it possible to sell "30,000 pieces." Laczi responded that if he thought sales would stop at 30,000, he "wouldn't touch" the cube. At the Nuremberg toy fair in 1979 Laczi walked around touting the cube, and, to quote John Tierney, "gathering crowds like a carnival barker." Several months after the Nuremberg toy fair, the Ideal Toy company, based in the United States, ordered one million cubes and, because its marketing schedule did not allow enough time to apply for patents outside Hungary, christened the puzzle, previously called Buvos Kocka (the Magic Cube), "Rubik's Cube," allowing the company at least to patent the name.

Accompanied by Laczi, Rubik made his first visit to the West on a promotional tour to Vienna. Married by then, and with a child, Rubik so disliked being away from his family that he spent most of his time in his hotel room. "He was always that way," Laczi informed Tierney, "even after the money started. . . . The only thing he did was start smoking better cigarettes. . . . He was always in another world." "The money started" in earnest in 1980, when 4.5 million cubes were purchased worldwide. According to Fred Hauptfuhrer of People magazine (September 2, 1981), the cube, in infiltrating so many homes, "laid waste to the nerves of the civilized world," if not to the pockets of Erno Rubik or the coffers of the Ideal Toy company. Bureaucratic difficulties kept Konsumex and Hungary from providing an adequate supply of cubes at the height of the craze and from reaping the profit they should have made, with cubes sometimes being bought three or four at a time by eager citizens when they appeared in Hungarian stores. In all, some twenty million cubes were sold worldwide in 1981. To diminish the impact of his success on his lifestyle, Rubik continued to live, as he had for several years, in a two-bedroom apartment on top of his father's house with his wife, Rozsa, an architect whom he had married in 1977, and their daughter Anna. By September 1981 they had moved into a house Rubik had designed in Budapest's Hill of Roses district, where his neighbors were doctors, lawyers, and Communist party officials. He continued his habit, as his wife has reported, of "always drawing and making models of anything that [came] into his mind, [bringing] it to the table, [staying] up all night upon occasion. It [superseded] all else."

Meanwhile, the "Mondrian-colored" cube, continued its astonishing spiral of sales. Fortunes were made by manufacturers of pirated cubes, who sold an eventual total of 50 million. Reports appeared in the press of divorces caused by the neglect of a spouse by his or her cube-owning partner, and "Rubik's thumb," "a tendonitis brought on by protracted Cube twisting," according to Hauptfuhrer, was identified in England. By 1982 there were reports of the cube being flung from moving vehicles, deliberately crushed under wheels, stuffed into trash compactors, and hammered into forty-three quintillion pieces. Nevertheless the craze continued. One executive of the Ideal Toy Company, who was quoted in an April 19, 1982 article in Newsweek, said, "Every month we pinch ourselves and say it won't last, but the cube is still selling like nothing else." The high tide of user frustration led to some fifty published books—guides for the perplexed that explained everything from solutions to the cube to the aesthetic appeal of various configurations on the way to the solution. Therapeutic T-shirts were manufactured that read "Rubik's cube cures sanity," and in November 1981 no fewer than three guidebooks to the Rubik cube occupied slots on American lists of best-sellers. Their titles ranged from the reassuring (You Can Do the Cube) to the enticing (The New Challenge! Cube Games: 92 Puzzles and Solutions). Written by thirteen-year-old Patrick Bossert, an English schoolboy who discovered the cube while recuperating from a broken arm, You Can Do the Cube became an international best-seller. A similar work, The Simple Solution to Rubik's Cube, sold more than seven million copies and was the fastest-selling selection in the history of Bantam Books. The hopelessly addicted could purchase You Can Kick the Cube and 101 Uses for a Dead Cube.

In a more serious vein, the cube was found, by Rubik and others, to be a fine teaching tool for group theory, the part of mathematics that can map what Sir Arthur Eddington once called the "structure of a set of operations." The cube, of course, embodies in plastic the structure of a set of 43 quintillion operations, each twist being an operation. Because each twist uncovers a new arrangement of the parts of the cube without changing their actual relationship to the whole, the Rubik cube is quintessentially a "group." Seeking the shortest path to an unscrambled cube, mathematicians dubbed it "God's algorithm." Some physicists used the cube as a model of relationships among the building blocks of matter, twisting it to demonstrate possible ways in which up-, down-, and antiquarks combine to make up subatomic particles such as protons. Internationally, cube-racing clubs were formed, using "racing cubes" whose hinges had been oiled, and at an official competition held in 1982 in Budapest, a Vietnamese high school student solved the cube in 22.95 seconds, less than half the time it would have taken Rubik to solve it.

In the United States and elsewhere the cube spawned spinoffs such as Rubik's Revenge, a cube with sixteen tiles on each face instead of nine, Rubik's Pocket Cube, a scaled-down version for children, and Rubik's World, a globe made from twenty-six twistable sections. What a writer for Newsweek (April 19, 1982) described as a "heyday for masochists" also featured Rubik's Game for several participants and the Calendar Cube, which required the owner to solve it each day to find the date. Rubik's Snake, a less nerve-wracking offering, could be shaped into a thousand geometric forms. It sent what the Wall Street Journal (September 23, 1981) described as "shivers of excitement through the toy world" and sold briskly. Rubik admitted that he did not have the time to spend the money he was earning ($30,000 a month after taxes) and that anyway "only the creation matters."

In Hungary, production of the Rubik Cube continued to be so slow that at one point one million cubes manufactured elsewhere had to be imported into the country to satisfy shoppers who eventually cleared the shelves of almost two million cubes. Mezei Andras, who wrote a play about the impact of the cube on Hungary, told John Tierney, "Everyone made money off the Cube except the Hungarians, but . . . it taught people that our way of centrally directing the economy has to change." In an August 3, 1986, article that appeared in the New York Times, Martin Gottlieb reported that "fledgling entrepreneurship has emerged as a key component in the Hungarian economy." After the cube craze ended in 1982, the Hungarian government allowed the inventor to open Rubik Studio, a firm that designs everything from buildings to flow charts to new puzzles. When, after years of development, the company put Rubik's Magic on the market in August 1986, anticipatory shivers of excitement once more traversed a slumping toy industry. When Rubik arrived with his puzzle at the 1986 Nuremberg Toy Fair, he was mobbed by potential manufacturers. David C. W. Yeh, chairman of Universal Matchbox, which eventually won the

account, told Martin Gottlieb in the interview for the August 3, 1986, New York Times article, "We hope we can create a craze." Universal Matchbox, known primarily for its manufacture of toy cars, is not a household name like Matel or Hasbro, but it might achieve that status if it engineered another "Rubikmania." It therefore augured well for Erno Rubik and for Universal Matchbox when, at the premiere of Rubik's Magic at a toy fair in Budapest, fights broke out between shoppers who took home 35,000 puzzles in ten days.

Each Rubik Magic puzzle consists of two rows of four plastic squares on whose black surfaces three rainbow-colored rings appear. The object is to rearrange the squares on their filament-like hinge until the rings are intertwined. After seeing the new puzzle, Rick Anguilla, the editor of Toy and Hobby World magazine, said that "unlike a movie sequel, this is better than the original. It is derivative in that it has the same obsessive quality as the Cube, but it is less mathematical, more imaginative. . . . You sort of expected a lot of [Rubik] after the Cube, and I think he delivered." But even Anguilla entertained some doubts and decided that "the question is, does the consumer want it? Is it what the country [America] wants? There are so many factors. It's like the fashion industry." According to a representative of Markham/Novell Communications, which promotes Rubik's Magic, the puzzle sold three million copies in America during the first three months it was on sale.

To prevent the mass introduction of pirated copies that had reduced his profits on the Cube, Rubik patented the design for Magic in forty countries, including China, where the puzzle is manufactured by 2,000 workers in a Canton factory. He also began writing a book about his philosophy and the solution to the puzzle, which, as with the Cube, are intertwined. He was quoted by Robert Cross, in an article that appeared in the Chicago Tribune (November 4, 1986) as saying, "The puzzle is something like a tanagram, a very old toy from the Far East. A tanagram is a square divided into five triangles . . . and you can arrange the shapes to form different kinds of shadow pictures. Rubik's Magic is somewhat like that, but in three dimensions. The most exciting thing for me is structures. Nature itself is a structure, a complicated one. It contains elements, and they are connected. Rubik's Magic is a special construction. You can open it a different way than you close it. . . . One of the things I'm interested in most is applying new types of constructions. . . . To make possible what seems impossible."

Before Rubik, who was busy on a promotional tour, could complete his book, two University of Pennsylvania students, Ashwin Belur and Blair Whitaker, had written one of their own. According to Belur, when he learned from a radio show in August 1986 that a new Rubik puzzle was on the way, he "knew somebody was going to write a book and somebody was going to have a best seller. [Belur] figured it might as well be [he]." Whitaker and he started a frantic hunt for a copy of the puzzle, and on September 22 they finally received a promotional copy. Interrupted only by a few hours of sleep and homework assignments, they worked on the puzzle continuously for fifty hours until Belur cracked it at two in the morning of September 25. The two students quickly sold their book about the solution to the puzzle to Dell Publishing Company, and 500,000 copies were printed but not shipped because on hearing of the book, Rubik was "disappointed and surprised that the authors didn't contact" him and declared his intention to file suit for patent infringement. He later dropped the suit, applauded the students' cleverness, and agreed to write an introduction for their book, which was shipped to bookstores under the title, *A Practical Solution to Rubik's Magic* at $2.95 a copy. Meanwhile, Rubik continued his promotional tour and filmed television commercials for Universal Matchbox.

When Laczi first saw Rubik, he "looked like a beggar . . . terribly dressed [with] a cheap Hungarian cigarette hanging out of his mouth." During his promotional tour, he was described by Robert Cross as "the fulfillment of a press agent's dream. . . . Strangers might have sized him up the other morning as an exceptionally bright, small man with sandy hair and sharp features. But nooo. His publicity people . . . insist the inventor is 'a cross between Julio Iglesias and Carl Sagan' and that his wardrobe 'is more Miami Vice than Iron Curtain.'"

Erno Rubik is known in Budapest as "a taciturn, suspicious loner," according to John Tierney. In 1985 he married his second wife, Agnes, and they live with the son and daughter from his previous marriage in his newly renovated house, with its Western-style three-car garage and basement sauna and swimming pool. Rubik, who took a leave of absence from his post as lecturer and then director of postgraduate studies at Budapest's Institute of Crafts and Design during the cube craze, took another sabbatical to promote Rubik's Magic. He won the Toy of the Year award for 1981–82 in the United Kingdom, the Federal Republic of Germany, Italy, Sweden, Finland, France, and the United States. He is a member of the Hungarian Peace Council, and he has received the Labor Order of Merit Gold Medal of the Hungarian People's Republic for his contribution to the Hungarian economy, and that country's State Prize (1983). Rubik is coauthor and editor of *A buvos kocka* (The Magic Cube, 1981), which remains untranslated. He enjoys swimming, skiing, sailing, and solving chess problems. Someday he would like to write a "general theory of structures." He and Universal Matchbox plan more complex forms of Rubik's Magic, together with competitions, if a full-scale craze should develop. "Our whole life is solving puzzles," he told Tierney. "If you are hungry, you have to find something to eat. But everyday problems are very mixed—they're not clear. A good puzzle, it's a fair thing. Nobody is lying. It's very clear, and the problem depends just on you."

References: *Chicago Tribune* p3+ N 4 '86 *pors*; *Discover* p81+ Mr '86 *pors*; *N Y Times* F p6 Ag 3 '86 *por*, C p 18 O 20 '86 *por*; *People* p31+ S 28 '81 *pors*; *Wall St J* p1+ S 23 '81

Salerno-Sonnenberg, Nadja

Jan. 10, 1961 Violinist. Address: b. c/o Ronald A. Wilford, Columbia Artists Management, 165 W. 57th St., New York City, N.Y. 10019

Since her sudden emergence as a star of the concert stage in 1981, Nadja Salerno-Sonnenberg has become a much-publicized figure among the world's violin virtuosi. In a field where musicians often do not approach their peak until their late forties or early fifties, she mowed down a dozen seasoned and well-known violinists in her first competition, which she entered at the age of twenty. Her talent has been called "so intense and original that it is positively frightening" by Tim Page, a music critic for the *New York Times*, and in only her mid-twenties, she may be on her way to reaching the stratospheric heights inhabited by such figures as Itzhak Perlman, Jascha Heifetz, and Isaac Stern.

Nadja Salerno-Sonnenberg was born on January 10, 1961, in Rome, Italy, the second of two children of the former Josephine Salerno and a Russian father who abandoned the family shortly after her birth. Her mother later remarried, and it is from her stepfather, who later also left the family, that Nadja Salerno-Sonnenberg gets the second half of her double-barreled last name. The Salerno household in Rome was highly musical, thanks largely to her older brother Eric, who as a boy was a promising singer as well as an aspiring trumpeter, cellist, and pianist. Josephine Salerno often accompanied his singing at the piano, while Nadja spent her early childhood in his musical shadow. "My brother was the talent in the family," she told Charles Passy in an interview for *Ovation* (April 1987) of those years. "He chose not to pursue music as a career, but as far as raw talent is concerned, I'm nothing in comparison to him."

When Nadja was five, a family friend suggested that she be given her own opportunity to make music, and her mother bought her a forty-dollar violin. She demonstrated an instant affinity for the instrument, although not for the practicing it demanded. Over the next three years she studied first with the friend who had suggested the violin and then with Antonio Marchetti, a member of the Italian Radio Orchestra. Both teachers recognized her unusual talent and potential, and Marchetti urged her mother to take her to the United States for further musical training. As a result, at the age of eight, Nadja, along with her brother, mother, and her maternal grandparents moved to Cherry Hill, New Jersey. "We carted the whole family over," she recalled of that move, in an interview with Judith Wyatt for *The Instrumentalist* (January 1987). "I'm still feeling the guilt."

To support the family, her mother worked as a teacher in the Philadelphia public school system. Meanwhile, Nadja grew up as a self-described "regular neighborhood kid," approaching both her new language and such American cultural icons as *Star Trek*, baseball, and Godzilla with tomboyish enthusiasm. Her other indelible memory of growing up in New Jersey was her taking advantage of the local garage sales. "That's a way of life for me," she recalled for Joseph McLellan in the *Washington Post* (July 8, 1983). "Until I was eighteen or nineteen I wore only garage sale clothes. My mother would go every Saturday, every Sunday—I wore garage sale gowns, dresses, everything. We're not very rich, and that's a good way to handle it."

Meanwhile she began developing her musical technique, again largely with the help of her mother, who imposed a daily ritual of practice. "I am forever indebted to her," she says of her mother's influence and sacrifices for her. She started elementary school in Cherry Hill at the age of eight, but soon entered the Curtis Institute of Music in Philadelphia, where she was the youngest student ever admitted into its precollege division. She began studying with Jascha Brodsky and quickly found herself surrounded by fellow students who were twice her age and size. "Here I was," she recalled in *The Instrumentalist*, "with all these twenty-year-olds. I came up to everybody's knees." Although she dedicated long hours to practice at the Curtis Institute, she admits to also having had a propensity for cutting classes and for playing pranks.

Such diversions aside, Nadja quickly acquired an impressive reputation at the Curtis Institute. On July 28, 1971, having made an audition the previous spring, she made her orchestral debut with the Philadelphia Orchestra at the age of ten, in a performance of the first movement of Bach's Concerto for Violin in A Minor at an outdoor children's concert conducted by William Smith. It was then that she first displayed her informality in the concert hall—a characteristic of her adult career as well—by excitedly waving from the stage to a group of friends who were seated in the front row.

If Miss Salerno-Sonnenberg was happy as an emerging star at the Curtis Institute of Music, she was less so at the Philadelphia inner-city high-school that she attended. "The kids beat me up," she told Leslie Rubinstein, in an interview for *Stagebill* that accompanied the program of a February 1987 Carnegie Hall performance. "It was my wimpy stage, until I showed them I was good at sports." After having spent six years there, she left the Curtis Institute in 1975 and transferred to the precollege division of Manhattan's Juilliard School of Music. Upon her acceptance, she was presented with a $15,000 violin by the New Jersey violin maker Sergio Presson, which had been paid for by an anonymous admirer.

At Juilliard, Miss Salerno-Sonnenberg became a student of Dorothy DeLay, the celebrated teacher who had earlier taught such luminaries as Itzhak Perlman. She failed to distinguish herself musically, however, at Juilliard because her arrival there coincided with a troubled period in her personal life in which she found it difficult to dedicate herself to the practice and study that the school demanded. And she became known as a rebel for her casual attitude toward such matters as dress. "[People would] tell me, 'You don't want to come to Juilliard wearing pants with holes in them,'" she recalled during her interview for the *Washington Post*, "which I never really thought a very serious matter." By 1979 Nadja Salerno-Sonnenberg had developed a reputation as a fiercely independent and talented, but thoroughly undisciplined musician, a reputation that was not helped by a seven-month period during which she stopped practicing and playing altogether. "I just didn't want to work at all," she has said of that hiatus. "The only time I picked up the fiddle was to play a gig with some pit orchestra to pay the rent."

Finally, in 1980, Miss Salerno-Sonnenberg had a confrontation with Dorothy DeLay over her increasingly erratic musicianship. Her mentor for the previous five years, Miss DeLay warned her that she would drop her as one of her students unless she began taking both her music and herself seriously again. It marked a turning point for her music and her life. Her response to that ultimatum was to rise to an even greater and wholly unexpected challenge: the Walter W. Naumburg Foundation's International Competition. Widely recognized as the most prestigious annual musical competition in the United States, its previous winners included the pianists Adele Marcus and Jorge Bolet and the cellist Nathaniel Rosen. But the Naumburg is also a week-long event that requires greater discipline and concentration than she had shown in her five years at Juilliard with Dorothy DeLay. Three months before the opening of the competition, she began a crash program of practice, refining and reshaping both her approach to music and her playing.

"I decided to get dedicated," she told Leslie Kandell in the New York Times (May 24, 1987), in explaining her sudden turnaround. For twelve weeks she lived in almost complete isolation, except for her visits to Dorothy DeLay and her ventures out to do her laundry, surviving on a diet of sausages, Coca-Cola, and ice cream as she devoted herself to practice. "It was a sick time," she has said of her impassioned ritual, which she had originally hoped would get her as far as the final round. Instead, she won, edging out such established performers as Ida Kafavian of Peter Serkin's Tashi during the weeklong competition that was held from May 25 to May 29 in 1981 at New York's Abraham Goodman House.

The fact that at the age of twenty she was the youngest performer ever to win the Naumburg competition made Nadja Salerno-Sonnenberg famous overnight, and she immediately left Juilliard without graduating in order to avail herself of the perquisites of the career at hand. In addition to a cash prize of $3,000, the Naumburg victory carried with it performances with the Chicago and Detroit symphony orchestras, a recording contract, and two fully subsidized recitals at Alice Tully Hall in Lincoln Center. Even before she gave her first award recital, she availed herself of the opportunity afforded her by the recording contract with the Musical Heritage Society by recording the first violin sonatas of Gabriel Fauré and Serge Prokofiev. The album was released by Musical Heritage in 1981.

Nadja Salerno-Sonnenberg made her major New York debut on January 24, 1982, with the American Symphony Orchestra at Carnegie Hall. Reviewing her performance of the Tchaikovsky Violin Concerto in the New York Times (January 27, 1982), Bernard Holland praised her "ability to make her instrument speak in very personal ways." Two weeks later her first Naumburg award recital took place at Alice Tully Hall, on February 6, 1982, with Sandra Rivers at the piano, in a program that included the Bach Sonata No. 5 in F-minor, Fauré's Sonata in A-minor, the Prokofiev Sonata No. 1 in F-minor, and Pablo de Sarasate's Carmen Fantasy. Once again, Bernard Holland applauded her in the New York Times (February 8, 1982) as "a talented young player with powerful technique." He was especially enthusiastic over her performance of the Prokofiev sonata, remarking on her "animal spirits and tension [and] real elegance in the Andante."

Those early performances also engendered a certain amount of controversy, principally owing to Nadja Salerno-Sonnenberg's youth and the nature of her sudden emergence as a professional musician. Although Bernard Holland took a charitable view of her lack of experience and of the youthful brio and exuberance that dominated her playing,

other critics were harsher. Harrison Goldsmith, in evaluating her first award recital in Musical America (May 1982), for example, complimented her for her "raw temperament, big altoish sonority, and mostly excellent intonation," but described her playing as "studentish" and considered her winning of the Naumburg Award "premature."

But Miss Salerno-Sonnenberg persevered through the crucial year that followed her debut recital and began to establish a reputation outside student musical circles. She was profiled as part of a CBS News special entitled Juilliard and Beyond: A Life In Music, broadcast on July 24, 1982. And she started winning over more critics, as her experience in the concert hall allowed her to focus her musicianship more carefully. Assessing her second award recital that took place at Alice Tully Hall on February 22, 1983, John Rockwell of the New York Times (February 23, 1983) hailed her performance as "a model of refined violinistic poetry." The popular press was even more florid in its praise, with Harriett Johnson of the New York Post (February 24, 1983), for example, describing her playing at the same recital as "inflamed as if by ancient demons, strangely, spiritually impassioned."

What followed for Nadja Salerno-Sonnenberg was a whirlwind of touring, with between forty and fifty concerts a year throughout the United States. In addition to appearing with the Chicago, Detroit, and Buffalo Philharmonic symphonies, she performed with the Los Angeles Chamber Orchestra and the Aspen Festival Orchestra in 1982, and gave a recital at the Library of Congress, in Washington, D.C. More recently, she has performed regularly in New York's annual summer Mostly Mozart Festival and played with the Cleveland Orchestra, the Philadelphia Orchestra, the Pittsburgh Symphony, and the Houston, Cincinnati, and Montreal symphonies.

Audiences and critics alike have been galvanized by the mix of passion and musical eloquence in Miss Salerno-Sonnenberg's performances that seem to resemble grueling athletic events, complete with wrenching facial expressions. "Her musicianship is so tightly wound that one worries for her," Tim Page observed in the New York Times (July 21, 1986) of her performance of Mozart's Violin Concerto No. 3 in G (K. 216) at New York's Mostly Mozart Festival on July 19, 1986. "She plays with fury and conviction, and if some of the pouting and fidgeting of her onstage manner finds its way into her music making, her performances are never less than technically impeccable."

In the mid-1980s Nadja Salerno-Sonnenberg became a "hot" interview subject, both in print and on television. Beginning with her appearance on the CBS News special Juilliard and Beyond, she enchanted viewers, journalists, and talk-show hosts with her candor, earthiness, and ready willingness to talk about her passions outside of music, which include baseball and auto racing. She appeared as a frequent guest on The Tonight Show with Johnny Carson and was the subject of a segment of CBS's news-magazine show 60 Minutes on December 7, 1986.

But the very qualities of her stage deportment and personality that made Nadja Salerno-Sonnenberg such good copy also made her controversial. From the outset of her career, at the announcement of her Naumburg victory at Carnegie Hall on May 29, 1981—when she ran a half-mile to Juilliard at Lincoln Center to tell her teacher— she defied the mandarins of the classical music establishment. Critics occasionally focused on the clothes she wore at her recitals, which included electric-blue pantsuits, slacks, and dresses that—in the words of Joseph McLellan of the *Washington Post*—"looked as if [they'd] been purchased at a garage sale." Peter G. Davis went so far as to call her "an S&M punkette" in *New York* magazine (July 27, 1987). Her willingness to discuss baseball and car racing during interviews also distressed some conservative critics who were already repelled by her disdain for the virtuoso's time-hallowed devotion to constant practice. In an otherwise favorable review of one of her performances at the Mostly Mozart Festival, Allen Hughes of the *New York Times* (August 16, 1985) wrote: "Attired in a purple jump suit, she indulged in attention-getting histrionics. Was she being funny on purpose . . . or is she merely lacking in stage discipline?"

Miss Salerno-Sonnenberg denies that her public persona is a contrivance. "Everybody wants me to go around as though I were made of porcelain," she complained to Joseph McLellan during her *Washington Post* interview, "but I couldn't. I've had my hair cut because of complaints about how it was always in the way. Just recently, I went and bought a gown at Saks, which to me is such a waste of money: $255 for a gown and I could buy it for $5 at a garage sale. I could have bought a Yankees subscription with that."

Her recent performances have included recitals in Vienna, Munich, Stuttgart, Frankfurt, Geneva, Rotterdam, and Lisbon, and her schedule for the 1987–88 season features appearances with the London Philharmonic Orchestra and the Pittsburgh Symphony and recitals in New York, Chicago, and Los Angeles. She has also made her second recording, the Mendelssohn Violin Concerto, for EMI/Angel Records, which is slated for release in early 1988.

Nadja Salerno-Sonnenberg is a small, slender woman with dark hair and incandescent Mediterranean facial features. Her hobbies, apart from baseball and auto racing, include listening to pop music and jazz, and watching old movies. She lives with her cat in New York, in an apartment overlooking Central Park, whose furnishings include a huge projection television screen, an Art Deco pinball machine, and a considerable amount of Godzilla memorabilia.

References: Elle 2:6 p38+ F '87 por; Instrumentalist 41:6 Ja '87 por; N Y Times II p19 Je 14 '81, II p13 My 24 '87; Ovation 8:20+ Ap '87 por; Stagebill p7+ F '87 por; Washington Post C p1 Jl 8 '83 pors

Salinger, Pierre (Emil George)
(sal´in-jer)

June 14, 1925– Broadcast journalist; author.
Address: b. c/o ABC Public Relations Office,
1330 Ave. of the Americas, New York City, N.Y.
10019; h. 248 rue de Rivoli, Paris 75001, France

NOTE: This biography supersedes the article that appeared in *Current Biography* in 1961.

The proverbial "American in Paris" to millions of American television viewers and to millions of French men and women from all walks of life, Pierre Salinger played many career roles on both sides of the Atlantic before becoming an award-winning reporter for ABC News in 1978 and, finally, in 1983, ABC's chief foreign correspondent. Salinger's previous post of greatest public prominence dates back to the early 1960s, when he served as White House press secretary in John F. Kennedy's administration. In the interim period, he has been a United States senator, a political speechwriter, a business executive, and a magazine columnist, remaining always the "bon vivant," the lover of good wine, good food, and good cigars.

Pierre Emil George Salinger was born on June 14, 1925 in San Francisco, California, one of four sons of Herbert and Jehanne (Bietry) Salinger. His father, a Jewish-American, was a mining engineer and a talented musician who was one of the founders of the San Francisco Symphony children's concerts. His mother, who was of French-Catholic background, had been a journalist and writer. Farther back in his dual heritage, his paternal grandparents were accomplished pianists, while his maternal grandfather, Pierre Bietry, was a member of the French Chamber of Deputies. Pierre Salinger was baptized in the cathedral of Notre Dame in Paris, and French was his first language at home.

A piano prodigy as a child, Pierre Salinger was giving major piano recitals by the time he was eight, but his concert career ended at twelve, after his parents decided that his solitary daily practice schedule was making him too shy and introverted. Endowed with an I.Q. of 140, he shone academically, and was allowed to enter high school at the age of eleven. After graduating in 1941, when he was just fifteen, he entered San Francisco State College, where he edited the college newspaper. He supported himself by working nights as a copyboy with the *San Francisco Chronicle*.

Interrupting his studies in 1942 to enlist in the United States Navy, Salinger was sent to the Pacific as the third officer on a submarine chaser. By the time he was nineteen, he had been made captain of the ship, with a crew of twenty-five men, all of them older than he. It was then that he started smoking cigars, perhaps to appear more mature and authoritative. Following the Japanese surrender, the ship was converted into a minesweeper, and Salinger was awarded the Navy and Marine Corps Medal for helping to save the lives of fourteen seamen who were stranded on a sand bar during an Okinawa typhoon.

After the war, Salinger resumed his studies at the University of San Francisco, majoring in history and working nights as a cub reporter with the *Chronicle*. Following his graduation with a B.S. degree in 1947, he became a full-time reporter. In 1950 he was promoted to night city editor. An interest in investigative reporting led him to some firsthand experiences of the seamier side of San Francisco life when, in the course of writing a story, he disguised himself as a vagrant drunk and was incarcerated in the county jail. Salinger wrote a seventeen-part exposé of jail conditions, for which he won the Edward V. McQuade Memorial Award in 1953 and a commendation from Earl Warren, then governor of California. He also wrote a series of articles that led to a statewide cleanup of illegal practices in California's bail-bond system.

In 1954 Salinger took a leave of absence from the *San Francisco Chronicle* to manage the unsuccessful California gubernatorial campaign of the Democratic candidate, Richard P. Graves, against Goodwin J. Knight. He also took an active part in the local and statewide Democratic presidential campaigns of Adlai E. Stevenson in 1952 and 1956 as Stevenson's press director and speechwriter. From 1950 to 1955 Salinger was a guest lecturer in journalism at Mills College in Oakland, California.

In 1955 Salinger left the *San Francisco Chronicle* to become the West Coast editor of *Collier's* weekly magazine. Having been assigned to write a series of articles on Dave Beck, the boss of the corruption-ridden Teamsters union, he went to Washington, D.C., where he met Robert F. Kennedy, who was soon to be appointed counsel to the Senate subcommittee charged with investigating labor racketeering. Although *Collier's* ceased publication before Salinger's exposé could be published, Kennedy used Salinger's research material in the Senate probe and in February 1957 hired him as the first staff investigator of the Senate's newly formed Select Committee on Improper Activities in the Labor or Management Field, popularly known as the Senate rackets committee.

It was through his work on that committee that Salinger met John F. Kennedy, then a senator from Massachusetts and one of the committee's leading members. When Kennedy decided to run for the presidency in 1959, Robert F. Kennedy recommended Salinger as press aide to his brother, and on November 10, 1960, President-elect Kennedy appointed Salinger as his press secretary.

The youngest press secretary in the history of the White House, Pierre Salinger revitalized presidential press relations with an easygoing informality appropriate to the new openness of the "Camelot" years. Writing in *Harper's* (April 1961), William S. White compared the White House press office under James C. Hagerty, President Dwight D. Eisenhower's press secretary, to an army orderly room, whereas under Salinger it resembled a newspaper city room—"essentially lighthearted, however aware it may be of man's manifold trials upon Earth." Salinger introduced more open and more frequent presidential press conferences, which for the first time were covered live by the television networks. Much of the success of President Kennedy's press talks has been credited to Salinger who, at an informal meeting before each conference, briefed the president on topics likely to be discussed and summed up the background of some of the important issues.

It was in 1961, as a representative of John F. Kennedy, that Salinger returned to France for the first time since his infant baptism. His mission was to set up a meeting between President Kennedy and French President Charles de Gaulle. Salinger instantly fell in love with Paris, and the French he had spoken as a child came back to him with such ease that he soon charmed the country by giving press conferences in that language. A more sobering trip was the one that he took to Moscow in 1962 to meet Soviet Premier Nikita S. Khrushchev and attempt to arrange a televised Kennedy-Khrushchev debate. *Time* magazine's report (June 1, 1962) made much of the fact that Salinger returned four pounds heavier, having dined on caviar and indulged in vodka, but the idea for an exchange of views on television went nowhere, and within a few months the Cold War had intensified again because of the Cuban missile crisis.

That agonizing crisis would have jangled the nerves of any White House press secretary, but Salinger came through it admired and respected by the White House press corps for having proved that he could be calm and orderly in times of emergency, despite his usual casualness and unbuttoned informality. The White House never seemed the same to Salinger after the assassination of President Kennedy in 1963, and though he stayed on for a while as press secretary to President Lyndon B. Johnson, it was only a matter of time before he decided to leave.

Many years later, in a discussion with the *Chicago Tribune* reporter Cheryl Lavin (February 18, 1979), Salinger looked back on the Kennedy era as the best years of his life: "What could be better than getting up in the morning, going to the White House, working with a man like John Kennedy, having the feeling that you're contributing to decisions affecting your country. It was incredible." In 1966 Doubleday published Salinger's memoir of those years, *With Kennedy*. In reviewing it for the *New York Times Book Review* (September 11, 1966), Tom Wicker sensed the paradox not only of the book, but of Pierre Salinger himself in that critical time: "This air of likable fun is the major trouble with Mr. Salinger's book, just as it was one of his major troubles as press secretary. It was too difficult to take him seriously, to make the mental connection between the *bon vivant* of the poker table, the piano bar and the golf course, and the shrewd, often knowledgeable spokesman for President Kennedy."

That problem of not being taken seriously plagued Salinger when he decided to run for political office. In early 1964 it became apparent that Clair Engle, the Democratic senator from California, was dying of brain cancer, leaving the Democratic primary open. Longing to leave the Johnson White House, Salinger quit his post as press secretary and filed his name in the primary only two hours before the deadline. The magic of the Kennedy aura carried him to a primary victory over Alan Cranston, who was then state controller, and when Clair Engle died in July 1964, California Governor Edmund G. ("Pat") Brown appointed Salinger to complete the last few months of Engle's term. But Salinger was defeated at the polls in November by the Republican candidate, George Murphy. Salinger recaptured that experience for Cheryl Lavin in the following words: "It was not one of my great moments. My wife left me, I lost the election, and I was $300,000 in debt. I had to start from scratch."

For Salinger, that meant occupying a variety of posts in private business, including the vice-presidency of National General Corporation and then of Continental Airlines, a $50,000-a-year position that he left in January 1968 in order to work for Robert F. Kennedy's presidential campaign. He was standing only ten yards away from Robert Kennedy when he was shot, and, finding it hard to recover from the trauma of that assassination, he decided to leave the country. At that point, Salinger was serving as chairman of Great America Management and Research Company International (GRAMCO), a Nassau-based mutual fund, and he moved to Paris to direct its operations in Europe and the Middle East.

Because Salinger never really thought of himself as a businessman, he continued to be involved in journalism and politics. He covered Richard Nixon's election to the presidency for European radio and television, for example, and did a commentary on Nixon's inauguration for ABC-TV in Washington. He also wrote a novel, *On Instructions of My Government* (Doubleday, 1971), a suspense story loosely based on the Cuban missile crisis. Reviewers disagreed on its merits, but all of them found the book disquieting, disturbing, and, above all, authentic.

In 1972 Salinger returned to the United States to work as cochairman of the National Citizens for McGovern Committee. In that capacity he traveled across the country and gave as many as twelve to fourteen speeches a day. When McGovern suffered his disastrous defeat at the polls, Salinger made up his mind not to attempt another return to politics. On his return to France, he was hired by the popular French newsweekly *L'Express* as a kind of Gallic Alistair Cooke to interpret and report on the American scene for the benefit of the French. When the Watergate scandal broke, Salinger's columns were eagerly read throughout France by politicians and taxi drivers alike, and he became so well-known a figure that he was more readily recognized in France than in the United States as the "American in Paris," the archetypal "Yankee." He extended his activities to include radio and television journalism, highly paid lectures, and the writing of books, including his autobiography, *Je suis un Américain* (*I Am an American*, Stock, 1975), which was reviewed on the front page of the Paris daily *Le Monde*.

When she was chief European correspondent for the *New York Times*, Flora Lewis said of Salinger, as quoted by Cheryl Lavin: "In Paris he's Mr. America. The French are not aware that he's not the most important man in the United States. When people want an American to make a speech, appear on television or radio, or judge a beauty contest, music contest, art contest, or toothbrush contest, he's the one they turn to." Salinger himself admitted to Cheryl Lavin: "It's incredible how many people stopped me and congratulated me on Jimmy Carter's election. They can't imagine that an American president could be elected without my help."

Meanwhile, Salinger kept *au courant* about the United States by reading a dozen American newspapers and magazines each week and by returning there for visits eight to ten times a year. In 1976 Roone Arledge, the president of ABC News and Sports and a personal friend of Salinger's, persuaded him to do a few human-interest spots for ABC as part of the network's coverage of the Winter Olympic Games in Innsbruck, Austria, and in January 1978 the network hired him as a consultant. By September of that year he had become a full-time correspondent. Salinger luxuriated in his role despite the difficulties he encountered in adjusting to television, such as working under the direction of men half his age and having to compress complex stories into two minutes of air time. As ABC correspondent Greg Dobbs commented in an interview for *TV Guide* (January 25, 1986): "All of us at ABC were aware that this household name,

Pierre Salinger, had become one of our peers, and we wondered how quickly he would rise and on whose coattails he would ride. But in fact he had to rise on his merits and rode nobody's coattails, because he was put on the same bloody stakeouts as the rest of us."

Salinger rose on his own merits, for in 1979 he was made head of the Paris bureau of ABC News. His first big scoop came on December 1 of that year, when he received a phone call from François Cheron, the lawyer for the Iranian government. Cheron wanted to know if Salinger could help him and his law partner, Christian Bourguet, contact the American government to begin negotiations for the release of the sixty-six American hostages, then in their twenty-eighth day of captivity in the U.S. embassy in Teheran. "In less than thirty seconds Cheron had won my undivided attention," Salinger recalled later, in his *America Held Hostage: The Secret Negotiations* (Doubleday, 1981). He immediately telephoned his friend Arthur Hartman, then the United States ambassador to France, to get the process rolling. Both sides agreed that Salinger would be kept abreast of all developments, provided that he not yet make anything public.

Salinger already knew many of the leading players in the cast of characters in the Iranian hostage drama. He had met the Shah of Iran—once, when he was President Kennedy's press secretary, and again when, as a reporter for *L'Express*, he covered President Jimmy Carter's 1977 visit to Iran. Before the fall of the Shah, many of the leading figures of the Iranian opposition movement had lived in exile in France, and Salinger knew both the Iranian Foreign Minister Sadegh Ghotbzadeh and President Abolhassan Bani-Sadr. Salinger began work on a documentary about the ongoing negotiations, a project so secret it was given its own code name, "Tango Delta." He carried a locked briefcase and set up a working headquarters in a suite in New York City's Plaza Hotel, from which a microwave dish, placed in the hotel window, beamed the material by laser ten blocks north to the ABC News offices and the select few there who knew of the project. The veil of secrecy was finally lifted on January 20, 1981, when the hostages were released. Salinger's three-hour documentary, *America Held Hostage: The Secret Negotiations*, was broadcast to high ratings and much critical acclaim only two days later. It won many awards, including the George Foster Peabody Award, the Gold Hugo Award, the Cornelius Ryan Award from the Overseas Press Club, and the George Polk Award.

Salinger's spinoff book of the same title was similarly widely acclaimed. In it he tells some stunning "inside" stories, including an account of the October 19, 1979 foreign policy breakfast at which President Carter's advisers urged him to allow the Shah to enter the United States for medical treatment. According to Salinger's account, Carter was at first reluctant, but he finally yielded with the prophetic comment: "What are you guys going to recommend that we do when they take our embassy and hold our people hostage?"

In addition to contributing his exclusive story on the hostage negotiations, Salinger broke several other major international stories for ABC News. In 1981, for example, he revealed that Israel was secretly selling arms to Iran, and in 1982 he was the first to report that the $1.4 billion missing from the Banco Ambrosiano in Milan had been secretly funneled to right-wing political leaders in Latin America. Salinger also reported that a division of I.T.T. shipped materials to Iran during the hostage crisis despite an embargo imposed by President Jimmy Carter. His work made him so respected at ABC that in 1983 he inherited Peter Jennings' old job of chief foreign correspondent.

In 1983 and 1984 Salinger covered President Ronald Reagan's trips to Japan, England, and France, and he reported on the fortieth anniversary of D-Day. He also filed a two-part "Special Assignment" report on Norwegian spying for *World News Tonight* and contributed a segment on espionage to its ten-part series "U.S./U.S.S.R: A Balance of Powers." Aired in November 1983, the series won an Emmy Award, a National Headliners Award, and the Alfred I. DuPont-Columbia University Award. In 1983 Salinger also served as the correspondent for two "Closeup" documentaries: an investigation of the international banking crisis, titled "On Borrowed Time," and a piece on art thievery called "Alias A. John Blake." He somehow also managed to find the time to coauthor two books: *The Dossier*, a thriller written with Leonard Gross, and *Above Paris*, written with Robert Cameron. Both books were published by Doubleday in 1984. Salinger's most recent effort is the thriller *Mortal Games*, scheduled for publication by Doubleday in February 1988, in which and Leonard Gross resurrected the hero of *The Dossier*—the American foreign correspondent André Kohl.

In 1985 Salinger covered President Reagan's trip to Europe, which included a visit to the Bergen-Belsen concentration camp and the controversial excursion to Bitburg cemetery. Later in the year he reported on the TWA Flight 847 hijacking. Among the many stories he handled during 1986 were the Reagan-Gorbachev summit meeting in Geneva, the Gorbachev-Mitterrand summit meeting in Paris, and the Tokyo economic conference.

The other television networks are aware that they cannot hope to match Salinger's knowledge of the French scene. NBC's Paris correspondent, Paul Miller, remarked to Roderick Townley in an article for *TV Guide* (January 25, 1986): "We're not even in the same league with the guy. . . . If he wants to know what the president of France thinks, he can call him up. I'd end up, if I'm real lucky, talking to one of the president's higher-up press people."

Pierre Salinger lives in a spacious apartment on the rue de Rivoli that commands a panoramic view of the Tuileries gardens, the Eiffel Tower, and the Left Bank. Two hours away, in the French countryside, he owns a seven-bedroom Renaissance chateau, to which he repairs frequently for peace and relaxation. He counts many of the rich and famous among his close friends, and those who have signed the guest book at his chateau include the president of France, Jacqueline and Aristotle Onassis, and several ambassadors, as well as superstars from the world of music and entertainment.

On June 18, 1965, Salinger married Nicole Hélène Gillman, a French journalist whom he met when she came to interview him in California. He was previously married to Renée Laboure, in 1947, and Nancy Brook Joy, in 1957. By his third wife, Salinger has one son, Gregory. He also has two children, Suzanne and Stephen, from his first marriage. His bushy eyebrows and jowly face, together with his cigar, have been Salinger's trademarks in the public eye for over a quarter of a century. Although he is known for his brashness, the reporter admitted to Cheryl Lavin: "I've always been a relatively insecure person. . . . I'm also very timid,

which is the total opposite of my public personality." Fine food and wine continue to count among Salinger's greatest pleasures in life, and in 1986 he hosted the thirteen-week PBS series *Dining in France*. Salinger is one of the few American members of the French Legion of Honor. He is chairman of the board of trustees of the American College of Paris, which has bestowed on him an honorary doctorate.

References: Chicago Tribune I p12+ N 12 '81 por; Chicago Tribune Mag p14+ F 18 '79 pors; N Y Times p2 Ja 13 '69 por; TV Guide p19+ Ja 25 '85 por; Contemporary Authors, new rev vol 14 (1985); International Who's Who, 1987–88; Salinger, Pierre. With Kennedy (1966); Who's Who in America, 1986–87

Sarah, Duchess of York

Oct. 15, 1959– Address: Buckingham Palace, London SW 1, England

Sarah Ferguson, known to her friends and to thousands of admirers around the world as "Fergie," brought the plot of a romantic novel to life when, in 1986, she married Prince Andrew, the second son of Queen Elizabeth II, and Britain's most eligible bachelor. An upper-class working girl with impeccable connections, Miss Ferguson, who is on the editorial staff of a graphic arts publisher, charmed the royal family and her countrymen with her good nature and friendly, outgoing manner, in-

spiring in them " the same kind of cozy warmth as does the Queen herself," as one observer put it. A few hours before the marriage ceremony, the Queen conferred upon Andrew the titles Duke of York, Earl of Inverness and Baron Killyleagh, thus making her new daughter-in-law Her Royal Highness the Duchess of York.

Through her paternal grandmother, Lady Elmhirst, who is a member of the family of the Duke of Buccleuch, the Duchess of York can trace her ancestry back to the Royal House of Stuart. Her grandmother is a cousin of Princess Alice, Duchess of Gloucester, an aunt, by marriage, to Queen Elizabeth II. The Duchess of York was born Sarah Margaret Ferguson on October 15, 1959, in London, England, the younger of the two daughters of Major Ronald Ferguson, an officer in the Life Guards, and his wife, the former Susan Fitzherbert Wright. During the course of his twenty-year career in the military, Major Ferguson served for a time as commander of the Sovereign's Escort of the Household Cavalry. Since his retirement from the service in 1968, he has been deputy chairman of the Guards Polo Club at Windsor and polo manager for the Prince of Wales.

Miss Ferguson and her older sister, Jane, spent their early years in Sunninghill, a village near Ascot, about thirty miles southwest of London. In the late 1960s the two girls moved with their parents to Dummer Down House, a Georgian manor set in 800 acres of farmland in rural Hampshire that Ronald Ferguson had inherited, and it was there that young Sarah took up riding. Fearless and hotly competitive, she became an accomplished equestrienne before she reached her teens. When Sarah was thirteen years old, her parents divorced, and her mother left England to become the wife of Hector Barrantes, an Argentinian polo player. "It was a trauma," Major Ferguson told an interviewer for *People* (April 7, 1986), "a bit of a fright, to put it mildly, for everyone. It meant that at that vulnerable age they didn't have Mother, so Father took over and did his best." Three years later, Ronald Ferguson also remarried. "It says much for Fergie's big heart that she welcomed me with great enthusiasm as her stepmother," Susan (Deptford) Ferguson has remarked, as quoted in the same *People* interview. "She was very close to her real mother, but she went out of her way to make me feel welcome." Miss Ferguson is also said to be close to her stepbrother and her two stepsisters.

After obtaining her elementary education at the Daneshill School, in nearby Basingstoke, Sarah Ferguson attended Hurst Lodge, a boarding school for girls in Ascot. An average student, she was better known for high spirits than high marks, but she excelled at sports, especially swimming and tennis, and she was popular enough among her classmates to be chosen "head girl" in her last year. Following her graduation from Hurst Lodge at the age of sixteen, Miss Ferguson enrolled at Queen's Secretarial College in London. Records there describe her as "bright" and "bouncy," if "a bit slapdash," with "initiative and personality which she will use to her advantage when she gets older." On the completion of the two-year program, Miss Ferguson and a friend, Charlotte McGowan, took a four-month jaunt through the New World by bus, using the Barrantes' ranch near Buenos Aires as a starting point.

Returning to England, Miss Ferguson settled in an apartment in the Clapham section of South London and took the first in a series of secretarial jobs. Over the next several years, she worked for a trendy Covent Garden art gallery and two public relations firms before landing a position as editorial "directrice" in the London office of a Swiss-based graphic arts publisher. In her spare time, Miss Ferguson maintained an active social life that included frequent visits to the late-night haunts favored by the so-called "Sloane Rangers," the upwardly mobile and well-connected young professionals whose lives revolved around parties and shopping in London's fashionable Sloane Square area. Her social set included Lady Diana Spencer, who, following her marriage to Prince Charles in the summer of 1981, became the Princess of Wales. The two women had known each other since childhood, but it was not until they were both living and working in London that they became close friends. Their bond of friendship grew even stronger after Diana's wedding. As the daughter of Prince Charles's polo manager and a cousin of Robert Fellowes, an assistant secretary to the Queen and Diana's brother-in-law, Miss Ferguson was one of the very few to be accepted as a suitable companion for the new princess. Indeed, she was the only guest, other than members of the royal family itself, at Diana's twenty-first birthday luncheon at Kensington Palace in 1982.

At Diana's request the Queen added Sarah Ferguson's name to the guest list for the annual festivities at Windsor Castle during Royal Ascot Week in June 1985. In the traditional royal procession around the track preceding the opening race, Miss Ferguson shared an open carriage with Prince Andrew, the Queen's second son—also reportedly at Diana's suggestion. Seated together at lunch, the two playfully pelted each other with profiteroles after Andrew apparently tried to force the rich pastries on his companion, who protested that she was "meant to be on a diet." Reporters, who ordinarily pounced each time Prince Andrew—nicknamed "Randy Andy" by the tabloid press—so much as looked at a woman, virtually ignored the incident. Perhaps because of her father's royal connections, Miss Ferguson was assumed to be simply an old friend of the family. In fact, although Andrew and Sarah had met as children, probably at polo matches, they lived very different lives and moved in different circles. But whatever the reason for the media's uncharacteristic hesitancy about predicting a new royal romance, it gave the couple the chance to become better acquainted in private.

Prince Andrew, a pilot in the Royal Navy, was often away on duty, and Miss Ferguson was busy with her publishing job, but they met fairly regularly over the next several months. The Princess of Wales frequently invited her friend and her brother-in-law to dinners at her home in Kensington Palace and encouraged other family members to extend invitations to the pair. Toward the end of the year, the Queen asked Miss Ferguson to join the royal family for its annual New Year's gathering at Sandringham, her private country house in Norfolk. It was during that holiday week that an enterprising photographer spotted Andrew and Sarah holding hands. From the moment that she was identified as a possible serious love interest of the eligible bachelor prince, Miss Ferguson was hounded by newsmen, as her friend Diana had been six years earlier, and her background was thoroughly investigated. Among other things, her former romantic liaisons soon became public knowledge. According to most press accounts, Miss Ferguson had had a number of boyfriends over the years and had been seriously involved with two men—Kim Smith-Bingham, a stockbroker, and Paddy McNally, a wealthy motor-racing consultant some twenty years her senior. Her three-year relationship with McNally ended in 1985, reportedly after she gave him an ultimatum that they either marry or break up.

Like Diana, Miss Ferguson survived the ordeal of press scrutiny with grace and good humor, chiefly by following the princess' advice to "keep smiling." Her visit, with other members of the royal family, to Andrew's ship, HMS *Brazen*, while it was docked in London in February 1986 fueled public speculation that the prince's playboy days might soon be coming to an end. Rumors about her relationship with Prince Andrew increased the following week, when Miss Ferguson accompanied Charles and Diana on a skiing trip to Klosters, Switzerland. Badgered by reporters about an impending engagement to Andrew, she cracked, in good-natured imitation of a popular British television character, "Cor blimey, darling, you must be joking."

Toward the end of February, Prince Andrew, who had a forty-eight-hour pass, and Miss Ferguson traveled separately to Scotland to spend a weekend at Floors Castle, the home of the Duke and Duchess of Roxburghe. The prince later confessed that it was there that he had gone down on both knees to propose marriage to Sarah Ferguson. "She told me that when I woke up the next morning I could tell her it was all a huge joke," he said later, as quoted by Douglas Keay in *Good Housekeeping* (August 1986). "I didn't." For a number of reasons, however, including the absence of the Queen and Prince Philip, who were on a tour of Australia and New Zealand, the official public announcement was not made until the morning of March 19, 1986, when an engagement notice was posted, by tradition, on the gates of Buckingham Palace.

In a brief interview with the press later on the same day, Miss Ferguson displayed for the first time her ruby and diamond engagement ring, reportedly designed by Prince Andrew himself, and the pair revealed that they were planning a summer wedding. The bride-to-be's compatriots were delighted by the news. As Jilly Cooper, the usually waspish columnist, told a reporter for the New York *Daily News* (June 6, 1986), "It is no small achievement that by being her lovely, larky, unaffected self, she has captured the heart not only of the most eligible man in the country but also the entire nation."

Shortly after that, Miss Ferguson moved from her Clapham flat into a suite of rooms in Buckingham Palace, where she was taught the details of royal conduct that would now govern her life. Meanwhile, the media frenzy intensified, as reporters vied with each other to uncover tidbits about her background. The sleepy rural village of Dummer was invaded by scores of journalists bent on interviewing anyone who could provide a personal glimpse of Miss Ferguson's life, from her former headmistress to the local postman. In London, vendors hawked a wide variety of souvenirs, ranging from postcards and T-shirts to Wedgwood plates, but despite the public's genuine interest in the young couple, sales of Andrew and Sarah souvenirs failed to keep pace with the continuing sales of mementos of Prince Charles's wedding five years earlier. "The difference" one souvenir vendor told James Revson of *Newsday* (July 22, 1986), "is that Charles will be king and Andrew will be a flier."

Over the next few months, Miss Ferguson's days were occupied with wedding preparations, fittings for her bridal gown, which was being created by the relatively unknown West End designer Lindka Cierach, prenuptial parties, and a smattering of official public appearances, but despite her crowded schedule the irrepressible young woman found time to plan an elaborate practical joke, which she intended to play on Prince Andrew on the night of his bachelor party. Disguised as policewomen, Miss Ferguson and the Princess of Wales set out to crash the prince's stag party. Realizing that reporters had discovered the location of Andrew's bash,

they went instead to Annabel's, a chic London nightspot, where they giggled and sipped champagne until astonished patrons began to recognize them. "You have to have a good laugh sometimes," Diana explained later.

On the morning of July 23, 1986, more than 1,800 guests assembled at Westminster Abbey for the marriage of Sarah Ferguson and Prince Andrew. Although no foreign heads of state had been invited, the list of celebrities in attendance included First Lady Nancy Reagan, Estée Lauder, Prince Albert of Monaco, and pop singer Elton John as well as British Prime Minister Margaret Thatcher. Outside the abbey, hundreds of thousands of Britons and tourists from around the world stood ten deep along the parade route, cheering and waving as gilded horsedrawn carriages bearing various members of the bridal party passed by. To guard against a possible terrorist attack, armed security experts, masquerading as costumed footmen, accompanied each royal coach, and hundreds of uniformed police officers lined the streets. According to some reports, the bride and groom, the Prince and Princess of Wales, and Prince Edward, who acted as his brother Andrew's best man, had been briefed by the SAS, an elite antiterrorist squadron, on how to behave if they were kidnapped.

As their families and friends and an estimated 300 million television viewers worldwide looked on, Miss Ferguson and Prince Andrew took their matrimonial vows before The Most Reverend Robert Runcie, Archbishop of Canterbury. To the distaste of many feminists, who had applauded her determination to continue with her career after marriage, Miss Ferguson chose the traditional Anglican ceremony, in which the bride promises to "obey" her husband. "I was thinking of obeying in moral terms, as opposed to physically obeying," she explained, as quoted in *People* magazine (August 4, 1986). "I am not the sort of woman who is going to meekly trot along behind her husband." Following a wedding breakfast at Buckingham Palace and the customary public appearance on the palace balcony, the new duke and duchess departed in an open carriage for the grounds of the Royal Hospital in Chelsea, where they boarded a helicopter that ferried them to Heathrow Airport for a flight to the Azores.

After a honeymoon cruise on the royal yacht, *Britannia*, the young couple returned to London and took up residence in Buckingham Palace. Andrew resumed his advanced weapons-training course at Yeovilton, in Somerset, and Sarah, true to her word, went back to her publishing job, although for security reasons, she agreed to work from an office in the palace. Her first assignment was to complete a book about the Palace of Westminster, the seat of Parliament. An earlier effort, a coffee-table book on impressionist art that she helped to produce before her marriage, has reportedly sold a remarkable 165,000 copies. Apart from her career, Sarah has assumed her share of royal duties, such as attending charity galas, opening special exhibitions, visiting schools and hospitals, and accompanying her husband on official visits abroad.

Described by her husband as a "vivacious, cheerful, outgoing, [and] vibrant" woman, the red-haired, blue-eyed Duchess of York stands five feet seven inches tall and weighs about 140 pounds. Her Rubenesque figure and "frumpy" fashion sense were once the subjects of widespread ridicule in the international press, but she soon learned to ignore the criticism. "I'm quite pleased with the way I am," she said in a television interview shortly before her wedding. "I haven't dieted and I don't intend to. When I buy a dress, it is because I like it and I will jolly well wear it again if I wish. . . . At first I made the mistake of reading some of the hurtful things that were written. Now I've smartened up and I don't read any of it anymore." Nevertheless, royal watchers have noticed that the duchess has lost weight since her marriage, apparently by following a diet and exercise program that includes a daily swim in the palace pool.

Fond of outdoor sports, Sarah enjoys swimming, riding, and playing tennis, and she is said to be a "brilliant and fearless" downhill skier. So that she could, in her words, "take an interest" in her husband's career, the duchess has learned to fly, and she recently took up carriage driving, a favorite hobby of her father-in-law, Prince Philip. Her preferred sedentary recreations include reading spy novels, listening to music, and playing the popular board game Trivial Pursuit. The Duke and Duchess of York share an eight-room apartment in Buckingham Palace, but they are reported to be looking for a house near Andrew's navy base at Portsmouth. They also have a country house, Chidcock Manor, in Dorset.

References: Good H 203:102+ Ag 19 '86 pors, 204:130+ Ap '87 pors; Ladies Home J 103: 48+ Jl '86 pors, 104:114+ F '87 pors; McCalls 113:39+ Je '86 por; N Y Times C p1+ Mr 20 '86 pors; People 25:4+ Ja 27 '86 pors, 25:14+ Ap 7 '86 pors, 26:23+ Ag 4 '86 pors, 28:25+ Jl 20 '87 pors; Vanity Fair 49:56+ Je '86 por; Washington Post C p1+ Jl 22 '86 pors

Schindler, Alexander M(oshe)

Oct. 4, 1925– Reform Jewish leader; organization official. Address: b. c/o Union of American Hebrew Congregations, 838 5th Ave., New York City, N.Y. 10021

Rabbi Alexander M. Schindler, president, since 1973, of the Union of American Hebrew Congregations, the central body of Reform Judaism in the United States and Canada, is recognized at home and abroad as a leading spokesman for the American Jewish community. A champion of liberal causes, in particular of freedom of speech and separation of church and state, Schindler is also a leader in the efforts to achieve a more prominent status for Reform Judaism in Israel and to reinvigorate the Jewish tradition in the United States. "Never before in recent history has there been a greater yearning for those ideas and ideals which the synagogue enshrines," Schindler has said. "Let us reach out and embrace all who hunger after truth and who come to us to find it. We believe that Judaism is a living faith, constantly evolving."

Also known as Liberal or Progressive Judaism, Reform Judaism originated in Germany in the early nineteenth century. It focuses on a need for change when dictated by contemporary conditions and treats *halakhah*, the Jewish law that Orthodox Jews believe emanates from divine authority, as a guideline to be interpreted by the judgment of man. Central to all Judaism is the belief in one God. Unlike Orthodoxy, however, Reform Judaism does not subscribe to a personal Messiah to lead the Jews of the Diaspora back to the Holy Land, but considers their countries of residence as their permanent homes rather than as places of temporary exile.

The Union of American Hebrew Congregations, founded in 1873 in Cincinnati, was the first national organization of Jewish congregations in the United States, with an initial membership of thirty-four traditional and Reform synagogues in twenty-eight Western and Southern cities. It was established by Rabbi Isaac Mayer Wise, the prime mover of American Reform Judaism, who in 1875 set up a rabbinical seminary, Hebrew Union College

(HUC), also in Cincinnati, as "the first institution of Jewish higher learning in America." HUC merged with the Jewish Institute of Religion (JIR), in New York City, in 1950. The UAHC had become a Reform Jewish organization when a number of Conservative members withdrew to form their own school, the Jewish Theological Seminary in New York, in 1886.

Alexander Moshe Schindler was born on October 4, 1925, in Munich, Germany, to Eliezer and Sali (Hoyda) Schindler. He has a sister, Mrs. Eva (Schindler) Oles. From his father, a writer of both religious and romantic poetry and an outspoken critic of the Nazis, he inherited a love for literature. The Schindlers left Germany in 1932, going first to Italy and France and then, in 1938, to the United States. Alexander Schindler was naturalized as a United States citizen in 1943.

Schindler's studies at the City College of New York in the early 1940s were interrupted by World War II. He served from 1944 to 1946 in the United States Army's Tenth Mountain Division ski troops, taking part in three European campaigns and earning a Bronze Star and a Purple Heart. His war experiences helped to influence him to become a rabbi, and family circumstances may also have contributed to his decision. His uncle Rabbi Eleazar Steinberg had been his first teacher, and another uncle, Dr. Jacob Neubauer, was dean of the rabbinical seminary of Amsterdam. Those uncles and other relatives perished in Nazi death camps.

After the war, Schindler continued his college studies, receiving his bachelor of social science degree from CCNY in 1950, with honors in history for his paper "From Discrimination to Extermination," a study of the evolution of the Nazi government's anti-Jewish policies from 1933 to 1945, which he completed in 1949. From Hebrew Union College-Jewish Institute of Religion (HUC-JIR), the seminary for Reform rabbis and cantors, Schindler received his bachelor of Hebrew literature degree in 1951, his master of Hebrew literature in 1952, and his ordination as a rabbi in 1953. As a student rabbi he gained experience working with congregations in Logan and Williamson, West Virginia, and in Petoskey, Michigan, and he was for a time Jewish chaplain at the Longview Hospital for the mentally ill in Cincinnati, Ohio.

Following his ordination, Schindler served from 1953 to 1956 as assistant rabbi and from 1956 to 1959 as associate rabbi of Temple Emanuel in Worcester, Massachusetts, where he also directed the activities of the B'nai B'rith Hillel Foundation at Clark University and at the Worcester Polytechnic Institute. From 1959 to 1963 Schindler was council director of the Federation of Reform Temples of the Union of American Hebrew Congregations (UAHC) for the six-state New England region. During the same period he was literary editor of the CCAR Journal, the publication of the Central Conference of American Rabbis, which forms the third branch of the American Reform Jewish movement. From 1963 to 1967 he was director of education for the UAHC at its New York City

headquarters and professional leader of the Joint Commission on Jewish Education of the UAHC and the CCAR. As head of the UAHC's publications department, Schindler was founding editor, in 1966, of Dimensions, a Reform Jewish quarterly magazine for religious thought. He also was editor from 1963 to 1967 of Reform Judaism's pioneering series of graded textbooks. As vice-president of the UAHC from 1967 to 1973, Rabbi Schindler ranked second to the president, Rabbi Maurice N. Eisendrath, who had headed the organization since 1943.

Rabbi Alexander M. Schindler assumed the presidency of the Union of American Hebrew Congregations on November 12, 1973, three days after Rabbi Eisendrath died of a coronary attack as he was about to deliver his retirement address to 3,500 members gathered in New York City for their biennial meeting and centennial celebration. Rabbi Schindler had already been scheduled to succeed Rabbi Eisendrath as the head of the UAHC, which as the central body of Reform Judaism in North America has some 800 affiliated synagogues and 1.25 million members. George Dugan, in a New York Times profile (November 12, 1973) of the new president, who at forty-seven was one of the youngest men ever to head a major American religious organization, noted that "the mantle of leadership . . . falls snugly and easily on the shoulders of Rabbi Alexander Moshe Schindler," succeeding to Reform Judaism's "most influential and prestigious post." Schindler declared his intention to carry on Rabbi Eisendrath's religious and social mission and his mandate that "we involve ourselves in the great issues that confront us, not only as Jews, but as human beings." Reflecting his lifelong literary interest, Schindler wrote his consecration speech as UAHC president in blank verse.

At the time when Schindler became president of the UAHC, Judaism in the United States had been undergoing some drastic changes, notably with regard to the role of women. In the preceding year, for example, Sally J. Preisand, a graduate of HUC-JIR, was ordained as the first woman rabbi in the United States. Although he endorsed such innovations in Jewish life, Schindler also concerned himself with enriching Reform Judaism through the restoration of some of the tradition, emotion, and ritual that had been lost when early Reform Jews reacted against them and their successors did little to reincorporate them. A tangible sign of change was the publication in the 1970s of more traditional prayerbooks for Reform services.

An executive board member, since 1967, of the Conference of Presidents of Major American Jewish Organizations, Schindler was the first Reform Jewish leader to be elected as its chairman, a post in which he served from January 1976 to June 1978. The conference is an "umbrella group" comprising forty-four national Jewish religious and secular bodies that deal with the rights of Jews in foreign lands and represent a "Jewish voice" in Washington, D.C., and in other world capitals. To help achieve its goals, the organization's members meet with some of the world's outstanding political leaders. In 1978 Rabbi Schindler became the first American Jewish leader to receive an invitation from the Egyptian president, Anwar Sadat, to discuss the prospects of peace in the Middle East.

A major concern of Rabbi Schindler has been the status of Reform Judaism and religious pluralism in Israel, where Orthodoxy has ruled in all religious questions, notably in matters of marriage and divorce. Although Reform and Conservative rabbis have been permitted to perform those functions there, final approval by an Orthodox rabbi has been legally required. Shortly after taking office as president of the UAHC, Schindler told reporters at a news conference that Reform Judaism was "going to assert its rights and not accept a second-class status" in Israel. While denying that he was attacking Orthodox Judaism, Schindler criticized what he called "the entrenched hierarchy of the rabbinate," which in his view "does not truly serve the cause of Orthodoxy" but with its "primary concern with the retaining of political and economic power actually drives Jews away from Orthodox Judaism." In keeping with Schindler's objectives, the Association of Reform Zionists in America, an affiliate of the UAHC, was formed in 1977 to interest Reform Jews in the United States in supporting Progressive Judaism and religious equality in Israel. By the mid-1980s there were eighteen Reform Jewish congregations in the country. Among ARZA's projects are Yahel, Reform Judaism's first kibbutz, established in 1977, and Lotan, a second one, founded in 1983.

Rabbi Schindler has devoted much of his effort to defending the authenticity of the Reform Jewish movement to Orthodox leaders both in the United States and abroad. At the heart of the controversy is the Law of Return, which came into being in Israel on July 7, 1950, to allow every Jew the right to immigrate to Israel, except for such obvious reasons as criminality or contagious illness. Some members of the Jewish community raised the question as to who is a Jew, whether it is a person who conforms to the halakhic definition, that is, born of a Jewish mother or converted to Judaism. The Israeli Supreme Court has decided that a Jew is "anyone who in good faith identified himself as a Jew." In fact, the law does not specify what kind of conversion—Orthodox, Conservative, or Reform—is necessary. The Orthodox, who wanted to control all Israeli legislation, especially the Law of Return, threatened not to recognize conversions by Conservative and Reform rabbis. Reform Jewish authorities added to the controversy by adopting a resolution in 1983 to accept patrilineal descent on an equal basis with matrilineal descent in determining one's Jewish status. They even went one step further than biological origin in requiring a child of either a Jewish mother or father to demonstrate identity with the Jewish people and to perform mitzvot, or religious deeds.

In the spring of 1987 Rabbi Schindler joined with twenty other leaders of Reform and Conservative Jewish organizations in responding to another attempt by the Orthodox to nullify the Law of Return. They signed a telegram that read: "We are profoundly disturbed by news reports that a political deal is being made to give the Orthodox rabbinate the power to decide the legitimacy of conversions made abroad." Earlier in 1987 Shoshana Miller, an American non-Jew who converted to Reform Judaism, was at first refused an identity card to live in Israel. When she finally received it, Schindler commented that the ruling in her behalf "was a great victory for Jewish pluralism."

Another major concern of the Reform Jewish community has been a loss of members through assimilation and intermarriage and, even more significantly, through apathy. As quoted in the New York Times (December 3, 1978), Rabbi Schindler rejected the notion that Jews do not proselytize. "That may have been true for the last four centuries, but not for the 4,000 years before that," he said. Outreach, the official UAHC proselytizing program, is primarily directed at non-Jews married to Reform Jewish spouses to try to encourage them to raise Jewish families. Although mixed marriages are neither encouraged nor officially sanctioned, Reform Judaism will not penalize or reject those who intermarry. Schindler also aims Outreach at Americans who are "unchurched" and seeking roots in religion. His approach is to provide knowledge to those who seek it voluntarily and not to "strive to wean people from religions of their choice . . . with the boast that ours is the only true and valid faith." Those who convert are called "Jews by choice."

During the 1980s Rabbi Schindler has been in the forefront, along with other liberal Jews as well as Christians, in seeking to uphold the precepts of the First Amendment of the Constitution of the United States and to defend American pluralism against attack by such sectors of the radical religious right as the Rev. Jerry Falwell's Moral Majority. In Schindler's view, the separation of church and state is a "gut issue" for American Jews. In an article in Newsweek (September 17, 1984) he explained: "Everywhere else in our wanderings we suffered persecution; never here. In all other countries there was an established faith; here there is none. That is why we prize the First Amendment as the very cornerstone of our liberties. And this is why we are worried by the manipulation of theology to serve partisan ends."

A major objective of the UAHC, as stated in a resolution adopted by its trustees at a meeting in Secaucus, New Jersey, in May 1984, has been the restoration of a "coalition of conscience" that had long made Jews and blacks "natural allies in the struggle for social justice in America," despite recent strains in that relationship. "Our commonality far outweighs our differences," Rabbi Schindler said in his address to the meeting. "Our agendas for America, if not identical, are felicitously congruous. . . . We cannot permit the stresses and strains of the hour to divert us from our historic pursuit of social justice and human decency."

The phenomenon of acquired immune deficiency syndrome (AIDS) has been another recent concern of the UAHC, which claims to be the first American Jewish group to deal with that tragic illness by providing educational and counseling materials to its members. "The challenge of our Jewish tradition is clear," Rabbi Schindler said in 1986. "Where there is illness and suffering we must seek to comfort. Where there is fear and prejudice, we must seek to dispel it."

An urgent matter to Schindler during 1986 and 1987 has been Israel's role as a supplier of arms to South Africa, about which he has said: "Is not apartheid a first cousin to the Nuremberg laws? . . . Can a state that calls itself Jewish align itself with a racist state? Can we as Jews stand silent while it does?" Although sharply critical of the repression of Jews in the Soviet Union, Schindler believes that efforts for peace between the world's two superpowers and avoidance of nuclear confrontation should not be abandoned "in the name of protest." In a speech before a physicians' conference in Moscow in June 1987, he warned against falling "into the trap of joining the shrill voices of those who wish to sink the Soviet Union and America into incendiary rhetoric and reciprocal military confrontation." At the UAHC convention in Chicago in November 1987, Schindler called on Israel to seek the establishment of an international "umbrella" for direct negotiations with Jordan and other Arab states to settle the dispute over the status of the Israeli-occupied Gaza Strip and the West Bank.

On September 1, 1987, Schindler was one of a delegation of Jewish leaders who met with Pope John Paul II at Castel Gandolfo, Italy to discuss such concerns of the Jewish community as the Roman Catholic Church's role with regard to the Holocaust, the Vatican's continued lack of diplomatic recognition of Israel, the general question of anti-Semitism, and the Pope's audience, in June 1987, with Austrian President Kurt Waldheim, who had allegedly been implicated in war crimes during his World War II service in the German army. In Schindler's view, it was essential for Jews and Catholics to establish a dialogue and try to repair their relationship. Although that meeting, and a subsequent one later that month in Miami, Florida, during the Pope's visit to the United States, failed to resolve outstanding differences, the discussions tended to ease somewhat the discord between Jewish leaders and the Holy See.

Schindler received an honorary D.D. degree from HUC-JIR in 1977 and an honorary D.H.L. from the University of South Carolina in 1987. At ceremonies on Mount Scopus on July 3, 1978, the Hebrew University of Jerusalem awarded him the Solomon Bublick Prize as the person who during the preceding two years made "the most significant contribution to the progress and development of Eretz Yisrael." Among previous recipients of the award had been David Ben-Gurion and Harry S. Truman. Later that same year Schindler was presented with the Townsend Harris Medal of the City College of New York for his "exemplary contribution to his chosen field of endeavor." He has also been honored by the Hebrew University in Jerusalem for his creative and imaginative labors, throughout his career, "to extend and deepen the process of Jewish education."

A vice-president of the World Jewish Congress and of the World Union for Progressive Judaism, Schindler is also a past president of the American Federation of Polish Jews and chairman of the Commission on the Holocaust of the Memorial Foundation for Jewish Culture. He has served on the executive boards of the HUC-JIR, the CCAR, the American Association for Jewish Education, and the American section of the World Zionist Organization. Other organizations with which he is affiliated include the Synagogue Council of America, the America-Israel Public Affairs Committee, United Israel Appeal, the United Nations Association of the United States of America, the American Joint Distribution Committee, the Jewish Agency for Israel, and the National Jewish Community Relations Advisory Council.

Rabbi Alexander M. Schindler lives in Westport, Connecticut, where he is affiliated with Temple Israel. He was married on September 29, 1956, to Rhea Rosenblum, a teacher. Their children are Elisa Ruth, Debra Lee, Joshua Michael, Judith Rachel, and Jonathan David. A distinguished-looking man with white hair and brown eyes, Schindler is five feet nine and a half inches tall and weighs about 180 pounds. His recreations include reading, listening to opera, skiing, and playing tennis.

References: N Y Times p35 N 12 '73; American Jewish Biographies (1982); Encyclopedia Judaica Yearbook, 1974; Who's Who in America, 1986–87; Who's Who in American Jewry, 1980; Who's Who in Religion (1985); Who's Who in World Jewry (1987)

Scowcroft, Brent
(skō´kroft)

Mar. 19, 1925– Business executive; consultant. Address: b. Suite 440, 1875 I St., N.W., Washington, D.C. 20006

Few Washington insiders were surprised when, in November 1986, President Ronald Reagan appointed Brent Scowcroft to the three-member investigative panel charged with conducting a "prompt and thorough" study of the role of the president's National Security Council in the so-called Iran-Contra scandal, which involved the covert sale of weapons to Iran and the secret diversion of some of the profits from that sale to the Nicaraguan rebels, or Contras. Scowcroft had himself served as head of the National Security Council during President Gerald R. Ford's administration in the mid-1970s, and, as more than

Brent Scowcroft

sor in the department of social sciences at West Point, where he taught Russian history for the next four years. In 1958 he continued his own studies at Georgetown University's School of Languages and Linguistics. A specialist in Slavic languages, Scowcroft put his linguistic skills to concrete use the following year as the assistant air attaché at the United States embassy in Belgrade, Yugoslavia, a post he held until 1961.

Returning to the United States, Scowcroft joined the faculty of the United States Air Force Academy in Colorado Springs, Colorado, in 1962 as an associate professor of political science. A year later he was promoted to full professor and named head of the political science department. After the 1963–64 academic year, he left the Air Force Academy to serve on the staff of the long-range planning division of the plans and operations section at Air Force headquarters in Washington, D.C. Scowcroft, who received his Ph.D. degree in international relations from Columbia University in 1967, returned briefly to teaching later in the same year, when he became an instructor at the National War College, which offers courses in military strategy and the formulation and implementation of national security policy for senior military officers and government officials.

Beginning in 1968 Scowcroft served successively in a series of national security posts in the Department of Defense, among them staff assistant for the Western hemisphere region in the office of the assistant secretary of defense for international security affairs; deputy assistant director of plans for national security matters in the office of the deputy chief of staff for plans and operations; and special assistant to the director of staff of the Joint Chiefs of Staff, General John W. Vogt. According to one of his associates, during his tenure at the Pentagon, Scowcroft was "deeply concerned" about the welfare of enlisted men.

In November 1971 Scowcroft, who had by that time attained the rank of colonel, was tapped to succeed General J. D. Hughes as military aide to President Richard Nixon. Three months later, he accompanied the president on his historic trip to the People's Republic of China. He was the highest ranking United States military officer to visit China in a quarter of a century. Promoted to brigadier general upon his return, Scowcroft headed the twenty-four-member advance party to Moscow that laid the groundwork for Nixon's visit to the Soviet Union in May 1972. As a reporter for the New York Times (April 21, 1972) pointed out, the assignment was a touchy one, in view of the renewed American bombing of North Vietnam, a Soviet ally, but Scowcroft's experience in planning positions and his fluency in Russian made him the ideal choice for the job.

Impressed by Scowcroft's demonstrated ability as an administrator and by his straightforward, forceful manner, Dr. Henry A. Kissinger, the head of the National Security Council, chose him to replace General Alexander M. Haig, who had been named vice-chief of staff of the Army, as deputy

one wag observed, he knew where the skeletons might be buried. Although he has held many government posts, both throughout his twenty-eight-year career as a United States Air Force officer and afterwards, Scowcroft has nonetheless remained a relatively obscure figure, his preference for working quietly in the background militating against instant name recognition by the American people. A moderate Republican respected by conservatives and liberals alike, he is especially admired for his grasp of complicated national security and foreign policy issues. For the past five years, Scowcroft has been vice-chairman of Kissinger Associates, Inc., a Washington-based international consulting firm specializing in strategic issues.

Brent Scowcroft was born in Ogden, Utah, on March 19, 1925, the son of James and Lucile (Ballantyne) Scowcroft. He obtained his elementary and secondary education in the local public schools, then enrolled in the United States Military Academy at West Point, New York. After receiving his B.S. degree from the academy in 1947, he was commissioned as a second lieutenant in the United States Air Force. He earned his fighter pilot wings the following year. Several months later, Scowcroft, who had hoped to become a career military pilot, was seriously injured when his disabled plane crashed. Assuming he would never be able to fly again, he began investigating other Air Force career options.

Between 1948 and 1953 Scowcroft held a succession of operational and administrative Air Force staff positions. At some point during this period, he resumed his education as a graduate student in international relations at Columbia University. Upon receiving his M.A. degree from Columbia in 1953, he accepted an appointment as an assistant profes-

assistant to the president for national security affairs. Assuming his new post in January 1973, the self-effacing Scowcroft—who, as more than one observer has remarked, had been trained to serve his superiors loyally—eventually became one of Kissinger's most trusted aides. The first White House staffer to brief the president each morning, with a fifteen-minute intelligence report on the latest international political and military developments, he regularly put in eighteen-hour days in his cramped, cable-strewn cubbyhole adjoining Kissinger's quarters. Largely because he always worked in Kissinger's shadow and never gave a "for the record" interview to any news correspondent, Scowcroft was dismissed by some as a "paper shuffler" or as "Kissinger's errand boy," but Dr. Kissinger himself has praised his deputy as "one of the two or three best officers [he'd] ever encountered."

During his tenure as deputy assistant, Scowcroft was often called upon to take charge of the National Security Council while Kissinger was on the road in his capacity as secretary of state. When Kissinger resigned from the NSC in 1975 to devote all his time and energy to his State Department post, Scowcroft was the obvious choice to succeed him as head of the NSC in Gerald R. Ford's administration. In order to accept the promotion, Scowcroft resigned his commission as a lieutenant general in the Air Force. Although his tenure as national security adviser was, perhaps, overshadowed by Kissinger's powerful presence, Scowcroft did not hesitate to set his own direction. As Peter Rodman, then a member of the State Department policy planning council, later told a reporter for *Business Week* (April 11, 1983), "Henry was in charge of foreign policy, but Brent kept things running. He was the coordinator, the organizer."

According to some Ford administration officials, Scowcroft played as important a role as Dr. Kissinger in the orchestration of the interim SALT II pact, which was approved by President Ford in 1974. He was also the chief behind-the-scenes planner of the evacuation of United States personnel from a besieged Saigon in April 1975 and the military response to the Cambodians' seizure of the American-owned merchant freighter *S.S. Mayaguez* a month later. Scowcroft left the National Security Council in January 1977, upon Jimmy Carter's inauguration as president of the United States, but he continued to serve the government throughout the Carter administration as a member of the president's general advisory committee on arms control. Among other things, the committee helped formulate the SALT II treaty that was signed by Carter and his Soviet counterpart, Leonid Brezhnev, in June 1979.

Largely because of his association with the policy of détente practiced by the Nixon and Ford administrations and his involvement in the development of the SALT II agreement, which many conservatives regarded as a sell-out to the Soviets, Scowcroft was not offered a policy-making post in the administration of Ronald Reagan, who

became president in January 1981. As a recognized expert in the areas of weapons development and military strategy, however, he was soon appointed to a governmental committee charged with evaluating the various options for the deployment of the MX missile, an experimental multiple-warhead missile. He also frequently participated in nongovernmental conferences and symposia on national security matters.

At one such symposium on strategic nuclear policies, weapons, and command control sponsored by the United States Air Force's electronic systems division and the Mitre Corporation, an Air Force think tank, in October 1981, Scowcroft focused on the need to "communicate with the enemy" after a nuclear war had begun. High-level communication, he argued, was essential to arranging a cease-fire as quickly as possible, and yet, strategically, the initial American strike would most likely be aimed at the enemy's headquarters and communications systems. "There's a real dilemma here," Scowcroft explained, as quoted in the *Washington Post* (July 22, 1982). "The kinds of controlled nuclear options to which we are moving presume communications with the Soviet Union; and yet, from a military point of view, one of the most efficient kinds of attack is against leadership and command and control systems. It's much easier than trying to take out each and every bit of the enemy's offensive forces."

Recognizing Scowcroft's skill as a military strategist and his reputation as a nonideological consensus builder, in January 1983 President Reagan chose the former national security adviser to head the new bipartisan Commission on Strategic Forces, which had been set up at the request of Congress to reevaluate the many different proposals for deploying the MX missile. Scowcroft accepted the appointment with some reluctance, as he later admitted in the interview for *Business Week*: "I was not enthusiastic about becoming chairman of the president's commission. . . . I questioned whether we could reach a consensus in proposing constructive solutions to the MX issue and the problems of shaping our future strategic missile forces. . . . Our report will have to be politically and militarily acceptable first to the president, then to the Defense Department, the State Department, the Joint Chiefs of Staff, and then to the Senate and the House. That's a tall order."

The fact that a consensus was indeed reached within three months was attributed by many panel members to Scowcroft's leadership. Taking into account the widely divergent views of the commissioners (who included among their number four former secretaries of defense and two former secretaries of state), Scowcroft prepared a 10,000-word report that, in his words, offered "new directions both in ICBM forces and in arms control." Disputing President Reagan's repeated warnings about the growing vulnerability of fixed land-based missiles to Soviet attack, the commission proposed deploying 100 multi-warhead MX missiles in existing Minuteman silos. To supplement the MX arsenal and, at the same time, improve the "stability of the strategic balance" by halting the disturbing trend toward dependence on multiple-warhead weapons, the panel also recommended the development of an unspecified number of small, mobile, single-warhead intercontinental ballistic missiles. "The objective for the United States," as the commissioners saw it, "should be to have an overall program that will so confound, complicate, and frustrate the efforts of Soviet strategic war planners that, even in moments of stress, they could not believe they could attack our ICBM forces effectively." The commission further suggested a shift in arms control goals from limiting the number of delivery vehicles to limiting the number of warheads.

Inevitably, the Scowcroft commission's report had its critics, both within the government and without. As word of the report leaked to the press just before its release to the public, the *New York Times* (April 7, 1983) editorialized: "The commission was given the opportunity to step free of past dogma and find a fresh approach. Having interviewed a mountain of witnesses, it has labored mightily—and now seems likely to produce a mouse." Rather than recommending the deployment of the MX, the *Times* went on, "the Scowcroft commission would have done better to urge a moratorium of the flight-testing of new land-based missiles by both sides" to allow time "for negotiating the reductions that both sides have proposed." Congressional reaction to the report ranged from qualified support to unreserved denunciation. Nevertheless, the report proved to be the first step toward winning Congressional approval for MX funding.

Nearly a year later, on March 23, 1984, the Commission on Strategic Forces issued a final report reaffirming its earlier positions and warning the Reagan administration to proceed with "extreme caution" in order to avoid jeopardizing the Anti-Ballistic Missile Treaty of 1972. Some administration officials interpreted the warning as a criticism of the president's controversial Strategic Defense Initiative—the so-called Star Wars program—but the commission was equally hard on those who favor a nuclear freeze, which would, according to the report, do "nothing to increase stability." In conclusion, the panel advocated following a careful, step-by-step approach in arms control negotiations, contending that strategic stability, "if it can be achieved at all, will come only after extended and sustained effort over many years."

Scowcroft himself was becoming increasingly pessimistic about the prospects for an arms control agreement. In Moscow in March 1984 with a group of American foreign policy experts who met for informal talks with their Soviet counterparts, Scowcroft attempted to deliver a personal message from President Reagan to Konstantin Chernenko, the general secretary of the Communist party, but Chernenko declined to receive him. On his return to the United States, Scowcroft described his assessment of the Soviet mood as "very, very negative." "There are not too many options in dealing with the Soviet Union," he explained to Seth Mydans in an interview for the *New York Times* (April 18, 1984). "We are going to have a basically antagonistic relationship as far into the future as any of us can reasonably see. And the question is how best to manage this relationship. . . . We do have mutual interests which should help, once we start talking."

Over the next several years, Reagan administration officials frequently sought Scowcroft's advice, especially in national security matters. It was only natural, then, that the president turned once again to Scowcroft when, on November 26, 1986, he appointed a special commission, formally known as the President's Special Review Board, to examine the role of the National Security Council "in the development, coordination, oversight, and conduct of foreign and national security policy," especially in regard to the Iran-Contra affair. As the only member of the three-man commission, which was headed by former Senator John G. Tower, to have served on the NSC, Scowcroft oversaw the commission's study of the NSC's performance in twelve historical crises, dating back to the administration of Harry S. Truman. To that end, the commissioners contacted three former presidents, three former vice-presidents, and every former secretary of state, secretary of defense, and national security adviser.

Issued on February 26, 1987, the Tower commission's report was a scathing indictment of Reagan administration policy in the Iran-Contra affair. "Primary responsibility for the chaos" was laid at the feet of Donald T. Regan, then the White House chief of staff, but President Reagan himself was directly criticized for not monitoring more closely the actions of his subordinates and for failing to "insist upon accountability and performance review." Because the NSC had generally performed effectively in the past, the commission declined to give any "radical prescription for wholesale change." Scowcroft provided perhaps the best summary of the panel's findings at the news conference following the release of the study: "The problem, at the heart, was one of people, not of process. It was not that the structure was faulty. It is that the structure was not used."

A slightly built man, Brent Scowcroft stands five feet eight inches tall and weighs 130 pounds. He has kept trim and fit throughout his life by skiing, swimming, and playing golf, tennis, and squash. He is also an excellent marksman and has won several medals in shooting competitions. A Mormon, he neither smokes nor drinks alcoholic beverages. Friends have described him as modest and unassuming, but Scowcroft himself recently insisted to one interviewer that he was not "a shy, shrinking violet." "I think 'quiet' describes me O.K.," he said, as quoted in the *New York Times* (February 27, 1987). "And 'comfortable out of the limelight.' I'm more interested in the substance than in the atmosphere." Scowcroft and his wife, the former Marian Horner, who have been married since

September 17, 1951, have a daughter, Karen. His many honors include the Legion of Merit (with oak leaf cluster), the Air Force Commendation Medal, and the National Security Medal.

References: Bsns W p111+ Ap 11 '83 por; N Y Times p8 Ap 21 '72, A p15 Ja 4 '83, A p14 F 27 '87 por; Newsweek 86:44 N 17 '75 por; Time 106:26 N 17 '75 por; International Who's Who, 1986–87; Political Profiles: the Nixon/Ford Years (1979); Who's Who in America, 1986–87

Shatner, William

Mar. 22, 1931– Actor. Address: b. c/o William Morris Agency, 151 El Camino, Beverly Hills, Calif. 90212

William Shatner, whose distinguished career in theatre, motion pictures, and television spans more than three decades, was described by the critic Gary Arnold in the Washington Post (June 2, 1984) as an actor who "suggests a home-grown version of Richard Burton and has proved considerably more durable." Since the 1960s Shatner has gained international recognition and a place in contemporary pop culture as a television archetype for his portrayal of Captain James T. Kirk in the legendary science fiction adventure series Star Trek. First labeled a theatrical wunderkind in his native Canada, where he served his apprenticeship with the Stratford (Ontario) Shakespeare Festival and won the Tyrone Guthrie Award as the most promising actor in 1956, he went to New York City and appeared in a number of television showcases during that medium's "golden age" of live drama. On

Broadway he earned the Theatre World Award as best actor for his starring performance in the hit play The World of Suzie Wong (1958), and in Hollywood he was featured in such acclaimed film productions as The Brothers Karamazov (1958) and Judgment at Nuremberg (1961).

Ever since appearing from 1966 to 1969 as the lead in NBC-TV's Star Trek—which afterwards went into what appeared to be perpetual rerun on syndicated television—Shatner became inextricably linked in the public's imagination with Kirk, the heroic and resourceful commander of the USS Enterprise, and he has in recent years re-created the role in Paramount's ongoing, successful blockbuster feature films based on the series. "Of course no actor wants to be tied to one part," Shatner told Iain Blair of the Chicago Tribune (November 30, 1986), "but despite everything else I've ever done, . . . it's the role they always remember . . . and I may as well face the fact that, for better or worse, I am Captain Kirk."

The only son in an upper-middle-class Jewish family, William Shatner was born in Montreal, Canada, on March 22, 1931, to Joseph and Anne Shatner. His father headed a successful clothing manufacturing firm called Admiration Clothes, which William Shatner was expected some day to join. Recalling his childhood in his autobiography Shatner: Where No Man . . . (Tempo Bks., 1979), he told his coauthors, Sondra Marshak and Myrna Culbreath, "I always had the best. I never wanted for anything. My parents were not particularly well-off [but] my father . . . provided us with everything we needed." At summer camp, usually on a French-Canadian farm, he excelled in athletics and developed a lifelong fondness for the outdoors. Later he served as a camp counselor. It was while performing in a camp play when he was six years old, in the role of a Jewish boy in Nazi Germany, that he first experienced the thrill of acting. "When the performance was over it was kind of—a little awesome . . . ," he explained to his collaborators. "I felt good about getting the kudos and the approval and the affection from the audience, including my parents, as a result of having performed well." When he was a little older, he made his public debut at Montreal's Children's Theatre, in the title role of Tom Sawyer, in a play based on the Mark Twain classic.

As a student at West Hill High School in Montreal, Shatner divided his extracurricular activities between playing on the school football team and acting in student plays, a seeming contradiction not lost on his teammates, who would often tease him as he left the playing field for the rehearsal hall. He also became an avid reader of science fiction. Soon after entering McGill University's college of commerce in 1948, Shatner phased out his scholastic and athletic endeavors to immerse himself in the theatre. As he told his coauthors, he spent "eighteen hours a day producing, directing, and writing college musicals." He also served as president of the radio club, and he acted in plays outside of the university. Shatner was still being groomed as a successor to his father in the family business when, in his third year at McGill, he decided to embark upon a theatrical career. "For weeks father argued with me," he recounted to Ben Gross in an interview in the New York *Sunday News* (December 31, 1968), "but I refused to become discouraged and finally he gave in. Later, while I was struggling in Toronto, he asked me to come back, but I refused."

On graduating from McGill in 1952 with a B.A. degree, Shatner put in a brief stint as business manager of an acting company. In 1952 and 1953 he appeared in summer stock with the Montreal Playhouse, and during the 1952-53 and 1953-54 seasons he played juvenile roles on tour with the Canadian National Repertory Theatre based in Ottawa. In 1954 he was one of the first Canadian actors invited to join the newly established Stratford (Ontario) Shakespeare Festival, whose founder, the renowned English director Tyrone Guthrie, helped to nurture the young protégé among such acting luminaries as Sir Alec Guinness, James Mason, Anthony Quayle, and Irene Worth. Shatner worked his way up from bit parts to featured status during his three seasons with the festival, mastering about 100 roles in some sixty plays, including those of Lucentio in *The Taming of the Shrew*, Lucius in *Julius Caesar*, Gratiano in *The Merchant of Venice*, and the Duke of Gloucester in *Henry V*.

Shatner made his Broadway debut in January 1956 at the Winter Garden, playing Usumcasane in the Canadian Stratford Festival's critically acclaimed short-run revival of Christopher Marlowe's *Tamburlaine the Great*, starring Anthony Quayle. Although his part required little more than carrying a sedan chair he attracted some favorable notice. A Twentieth Century-Fox studio representative who spotted him offered him a seven-year motion picture contract at a starting salary of $500 a week, as compared with the $80 he earned with the Stratford Festival. But he turned the contract down, later explaining his reasons to Michael Fessier Jr. in a *TV Guide* interview (October 15, 1966): "I wanted to be independent, to choose my own roles. I thought there was nothing to be gained from signing and everything to lose. *Mainly my youth.*"

Shatner returned to Toronto that spring to star in a Canadian Broadcasting Corporation production of *Dreams*, a teleplay he had written, and to finish his third and final year with the Stratford Festival. After receiving the festival's Tyrone Guthrie Award as the most promising actor, he decided to use the accompanying $750 scholarship to return to New York and try to make his way in television and the theatre. By that time he was already something of a television celebrity in Canada, where, as Barbara Moon noted in a *Maclean's* magazine profile (October 26, 1957), "the grin, the charm and the look of rude young vigor had made Shatner one of the CBC's few matinee idols, with his own fan clubs." In New York Shatner soon became one of the busiest young stars of American television, which was then in its heyday of live drama. He won critical accolades for memorable showcase performances, including the *Studio One* shows "The Defenders," with Ralph Bellamy, and "No Deadly Medicine," with Lee J. Cobb; the NBC-TV *Goodyear Playhouse* production of "All Summer Long," with Raymond Massey; and the *Playhouse 90* presentation of Rod Serling's drama "A Town Has Turned to Dust," starring Rod Steiger.

While visiting Hollywood in April 1957 to appear in a television show and to make routine exploratory visits to the top-five film studios, Shatner landed a lucrative contract with MGM and was immediately cast by producer Pandro Berman in his first motion picture role, as Alexey, the saintly youngest brother, in MGM's epic adaptation of Dostoevsky's *The Brothers Karamazov* (1958), starring Yul Brynner and Richard Basehart. In view of the generally favorable opinions that his performance evoked from the critics, Shatner considered settling permanently on the West Coast and pursuing his dream of movie stardom. He was lured back to Broadway, however, giving up his MGM contract to play the romantic lead in what he believed was a "beautiful, poetic play"—Joshua Logan's lavish new production of *The World of Suzie Wong*. Paul Osborn's stage adaptation of Richard Mason's novel, set in Hong Kong, was about a love affair between Robert Lomax, a Canadian writer, and a young Chinese prostitute, played by France Nuyen. When it opened on October 14, 1958, at the Broadhurst Theatre, the play earned less than sympathetic reviews. "Its manly hero . . . ," Walter Kerr wrote in the New York *Herald Tribune* (October 26, 1958) of Shatner's performance as Lomax, "[is] played with an oddly melodramatic gloss and many a deepseated sigh by the normally interesting Canadian actor." Nevertheless, the play went on to become a commerical hit, running for 508 performances, and it won for Shatner the Theatre World Award for best actor in 1958. Shatner next appeared on Broadway as Paul Sevigne in *A Shot in the Dark*, Harry Kurnitz' version of Marcel Achard's courtroom farce. Starring Walter Matthau and Julie Harris, the play opened on October 18, 1961, at the Booth Theatre and ran for 389 performances to critical acclaim.

While shuttling back and forth between coasts and among his stage, screen, and television careers, Shatner added to his list of credits performances in Hollywood feature films that had, in his view, "something to say." In Stanley Kramer's *Judgment at Nuremberg* (1961), a disturbing courtroom drama about Nazi war crimes, he performed in a supporting role as an American aide-de-camp to the presiding judge, played by Spencer Tracy; in the low-budgeted, but nevertheless seriously intended *The Explosive Generation* (1961), his performance as an enlightened schoolteacher embroiled in a scandal over sex education in the classroom earned him sympathetic, if tepid, reviews; in Roger and Gene Corman's low-budget feature *The Intruder* (1962), he starred as a young hate-mongering demagogue—based on the real-life racist John Kasper—who incites racial violence in a Southern town; and in *The Outrage* (1964), an adaptation of the Japanese classic *Rashomon*, he appeared with Paul Newman, Claire Bloom, and Edward G. Robinson, in the supporting role of a clergyman. But after the "critical" dust had settled, Shatner—already disenchanted by the more commercial aspects of the Broadway theatre—began to feel that his dream of movie stardom had grown somewhat hollow. "All the things I thought went along with it—good parts, money and acclaim—weren't happening," he told Robert Higgins in a *TV Guide* interview (June 22, 1968). "As a star, I was one step down from Paul Newman—a good actor but not popular enough to bring in big audiences."

With the help of producer Herbert Brodkin, whom he described as "my mentor in those days," Shatner continued to be productive in television. By 1966 he had appeared in an estimated 100 live dramatic shows. He rejected a number of offers to star in television series, including the successful *Dr. Kildare* and *The Defenders*, before he overcame his concern over being typecast and agreed to try out for a projected ABC series, *Alexander the Great*, based on the life of the Macedonian conqueror. He spent a year preparing for the part, rebuilding his body and learning how to fence and ride bareback, but the 1963 pilot film failed to attract a series sponsor. Shatner obtained his first series lead in Herbert Brodkin's CBS-TV production of *For the People*, in which he played an all-too-human assistant district attorney in New York. The 1965 dramatic series was well received by the critics, but it had the misfortune of playing at the same time as the hit *Bonanza* series, and it was canceled after a disappointing thirteen weeks.

Shortly afterward, in the spring of 1965, the producer and writer Gene Roddenberry offered Shatner the lead in a second pilot film for the science fiction adventure series *Star Trek*, after the first pilot—"The Cage," starring the late Jeffrey Hunter as Captain Christopher Pike—was rejected by NBC as being too cerebral for its prime-time audience. The second pilot, entitled "Where No Man Has Gone Before," costarring Leonard Nimoy as Mr. Spock and DeForest Kelly as Dr. Leonard ("Bones") McCoy, succeeded where the first pilot had failed. The series had its premiere on September 8, 1966, with Shatner at the helm as the newly designated Captain James T. Kirk.

Set in the twenty-second century, *Star Trek* presented the adventures of the USS *Enterprise* crew on its five-year mission to encounter and befriend unknown civilizations in outer space. At the outset, after the program fell to fifty-second place in the network ratings, it seemed that neither the public nor the reviewers would buy it. One critic for *Variety* (September 14, 1966) wrote that the new series "obviously solicits all-out suspension of disbelief, but it won't work." Eventually, however, the critics were won over, and there emerged an ardent core of fans, known as "Trekkies," whose unprecedented letter-writing campaign, mounted from Los Angeles, brought a half-million pieces of correspondence to NBC and kept the series from

being canceled midway through its second season. In September 1969, after its third season on NBC, *Star Trek* was taken off network television and went into syndication. Broadcasting on 150 independent stations and in sixty foreign countries, *Star Trek*'s seventy-nine one-hour episodes gained new life, and the series was transformed from a mere cult phenomenon into one of television's most popular and enduring series.

The respected and prolific science fiction writer Isaac Asimov, in an article for *Cue* magazine (December 29, 1975), suggested that *Star Trek*'s appeal lay in its believable characters. "We could expect Captain Kirk to make hard decisions and to temper his forcefulness with humor," Asimov wrote. "We were always ready for First Officer Spock's cool calm, his rationality and his sense of ethics. We could count on Dr. McCoy's dedication, emotionality, and short temper. Every other regular had quirks that grew familiar. Most of all there was a consistent streak of humor . . . and an obvious affection of the characters for each other." For whatever reason, the humanitarian and intergalactic exploits of the *Enterprise* crew managed to touch a nerve in cynical, Vietnam-era America. Shatner's own characterization of Kirk reflected his striving to embody a personal ideal. "I gave myself guidelines, as I would have wanted to be," he told Sandra Marshak and Myrna Culbreath. "I acted Captain Kirk in the manner that I wished that I could behave—as the way it really would be." An animated cartoon version of *Star Trek*, with the voices of the original cast members, was presented on NBC-TV from 1973 to 1975.

In the wake of *Star Trek*'s demise from network television, the future of Shatner's career appeared uncertain. Personal traumas, including his father's death in 1967 and a separation from his first wife, left him searching for the meaning of his life. "That isn't as sophomoric as it sounds," he confided to Robert Higgins of *TV Guide*. "Working as I did—not a day off in three years—I never realized how dependent I was on my wife and children. It brought on a whole new sense of aloneness." Nevertheless, throughout the 1970s Shatner remained highly visible, in demand at *Star Trek* conventions and at game and talk shows and appearing in television commercials. He toured with regional theatre productions, including *There's a Girl in My Soup* (1969), *Tricks of the Trade* (1977), and *Deathtrap* (1982), and he directed a Los Angeles production of *Cat on a Hot Tin Roof* in 1981. He also made occasional dramatic appearances in television films, such as the 1969 PBS-TV drama *The Andersonville Trial*, in which his starring role as the prosecuting attorney won him critical acclaim.

Shatner served as host for the syndicated underwater television documentary *Inner Space* (1974). He received critical praise for his performance in the controversial CBS-TV drama *The Tenth Level* (1976), as a psychology professor who, while haunted by the Nazi Holocaust, conducts experiments on the threshold of human pain. In the short-lived

ABC series *The Barbary Coast* (1975–76) he co-starred as one of two undercover operators in gold-rush San Francisco. He was also seen as Dr. Benjamin Rush in an episode of *The Statesman* (1975), a CBS-TV miniseries about Benjamin Franklin, and as Paul Revere in the miniseries *The Bastard/Kent Family Chronicles* (1978). In addition, he appeared in the NBC-TV miniseries *Little Women* (1978), the ABC television film *Disaster on the Coastliner* (1979), and the Canadian feature film *Visiting Hours* (1981). In the popular police action series *T. J. Hooker*, presented on ABC-TV beginning in 1981 and later shifted to CBS-TV, Shatner was featured as a tough law-and-order cop, a role that helped to loosen the grip of typecasting that Captain Kirk had on his career.

Categorized by that time chiefly as a television actor, Shatner was compelled to accept roles in feature films that were, in his view, of "lesser quality," among them the notorious *Big Bad Mama* (1974), in which he appeared with costar Angie Dickinson in some steamy love scenes; the horror-thrillers *The Devil's Rain* (1975) and *Kingdom of the Spiders* (1977); and the suspense picture *Kidnapping of the President* (1980).

Capitalizing on the popularity of such science fiction action films as George Lucas' *Star Wars*, Paramount Pictures released the first installment in its blockbuster feature film series based on *Star Trek*, entitled *Star Trek: The Motion Picture* (1979). Produced by Gene Roddenberry and directed by Robert Wise, the long-awaited appearance on the screen of the original *Enterprise* crew, featuring Shatner as James Kirk—now holding the rank of admiral—was deemed an honorable failure by most critics, a judgment to which Shatner himself later subscribed. Heavily laden with flashy special effects, the film managed to bring in record-breaking prerelease revenue and eventually more than recouped its staggering cost of $43 million by earning $175 million at the box office.

In contrast to its somber predecessor, *Star Trek II: The Wrath of Khan* (1982) won raves from critics who cited its "the gang's-all-here" spirit. After it broke all first-weekend box-office records, Shatner was prompted to remark to Gail Buchalter in a *People* magazine interview (July 5, 1982), "I am the fulcrum, and I really wanted this popular validation. I always knew there was a large audience that wanted to see me." Directed by Nicholas Meyer, the film featured the death of Mr. Spock, setting the stage for the next installment in the series, entitled *Star Trek III: The Search for Spock* (1984), in which Spock is brought back to life by an enigmatic Vulcan process called a 'mindmeld.' Supervised by Leonard Nimoy in his debut as director, the performances of the series regulars were applauded by the critics. Even more successful was the next installment, *Star Trek IV: The Voyage Home* (1986), directed once again, with a comic touch, by Nimoy. This time the *Enterprise* crew was time-traveling back to the 1980s on an earth mission to save an endangered species. The lighthearted chemistry between Shatner's Kirk and Nimoy's Spock ensured

the film's popularity. "It's really developed over the years," Shatner told Iain Blair, "and I think there's a warmth and fondness there that we both feel for each other in real life, that can't be faked on the screen." In the summer of 1987 Shatner was at work as director and star of a fifth installment of the *Star Trek* feature film series, and in October 1987 he was host of the CBS-TV documentary *Top Flight*, celebrating the fortieth anniversary of the United States Air Force. Meanwhile, a new *Star Trek* television series, subtitled "The Next Generation," with an entirely new cast of actors, went into production at Paramount TV in April 1987.

In addition to working in theatre, film, and television, Shatner has gone on tour with his own one-man shows, presenting readings from science fiction classics against a background of symphonic music, and he has recorded several LP albums, including *William Shatner–Live*. He narrated the Academy Award-nominated NASA documentary film *Universe*, and he was nominated for a Grammy award as narrator of the Isaac Asimov recording *Foundations*. He and the producer Aaron Spelling have been working on a theatrical play about the late actress Vivien Leigh.

William Shatner stands five feet eleven inches tall, weighs 165 pounds, and has brown hair and brown eyes. Respected among his colleagues for his professionalism, he has a reputation for having a "galaxy-sized ego" tempered with a sense of humor and has been described by his long-time friend Leonard Nimoy as "a bundle of energy, a blur of motion." He is an avid outdoorsman whose passions over the years have included archery, golf, scuba diving, water and snow skiing, motorcycling, car racing, canoeing, flying, and breeding Dobermans. A horse enthusiast, Shatner breeds and raises quarter horses and American Saddlebreds and often competes in world-class shows. His horse "Kentucky Dream" won the National Horse Show in 1986, and he owns the world champion "Sultan's Great Day." He also works in his spare time to rehabilitate handicapped children, using horseback riding as therapy. Shatner was first married on August 12, 1956, to Gloria Rand, a Canadian actress. From that marriage, which ended in divorce in March 1969, he has three daughters, Leslie Carol, Lisabeth Mary, and Melanie Ann. With his second wife, the actress Marcy Lafferty, whom he wed on October 20, 1973, Shatner divides his time between his ranch in Malibu, California and his blue-grass farm, 'Belle Rêve,' at Versailles, near Lexington, Kentucky.

References: Chicago Tribune p6+ N 30 '86 por; *Cue* 44:61+ D 29 '75 por; *Maclean's* 70:31+ O 26 '57 pors; *N Y Post* p33 My 4 '68 por; *N Y Times* p15 N 8 '86 por; *People* 18:50+ Jl 5 '82 pors; *Starlog* p45+ N '81 por; *TV Guide* 16:12+ Je 22 '68 por, 30:18+ Ag 14 '82 por; Shatner, William, Marshak, Sondra, and Culbreath, Myrna. *Shatner: Where No Man . . .* (1979); *Who's Who in America, 1986–87; Who's Who in Canada, 1986; Who's Who in the Theatre* (1981)

Shcharansky, Anatoly

(shä-rän´ skē)

Jan. 20, 1948– Expatriate Soviet dissident; Zionist activist. Address: b. c/o Random House, 201 E. 50th St., New York City, N.Y. 10022

On February 11, 1986, the internationally renowned Soviet-Jewish dissident Anatoly Shcharansky walked across a bridge to West Berlin and freedom, following years of imprisonment. A founding member of the Moscow Helsinki Watch, a group devoted to monitoring Soviet violations of human rights, Shcharansky was jailed by Soviet authorities in 1977 for his outspoken criticisms of his country's repressive policies on Jewish emigration and political dissent. Combining liberal political convictions with a strong Jewish identity, Shcharansky provided a link between the two previously separate strands of dissent in the Soviet Union—the Jewish emigration movement and the broader human rights movement.

Thanks to the tireless efforts of his wife, Avital, and his brother Leonid, Shcharansky's fate became an international cause célèbre. Finally, in February 1986, apparently as part of an effort to improve relations with the United States, the regime of Mikhail Gorbachev released Shcharansky in an East-West prisoner exchange, and he was allowed to join his wife in Israel. Since gaining his freedom, he has visited the United States to press the cause of Soviet Jews and political prisoners. For many, Shcharansky's great courage and strong convictions have made him a "hero of our time."

Anatoly Shcharansky was born on January 20, 1948, in Donetsk, a Ukrainian coal mining town near the Black Sea. He was the second of two sons born to Boris Shcharansky, a filmwriter and jour-

nalist, and his wife, Ida Milgrom, an economist. Anatoly received a gold medal for scholarship when he graduated from high school and, having played chess since he was eight, became his city's chess champion when he was just fourteen. Growing up in an assimilated Jewish family, he learned little about Judaism and, because of his parents' protectiveness, remained unaware of the widespread anti-Semitism of post-Stalinist Russia.

Shcharansky's awareness of his Jewish identity began to grow during his student years in Moscow, where he went in 1966 to attend a special mathematics school. His first brush with anti-Semitism came on a hiking trip with his best friend, who during an argument called him a "Yid." He later told an American reporter, "I think it was then that I decided [the Soviet Union] was no place for me."

But it was the dramatic Six-Day War of 1967, in which tiny Israel defeated a strong coalition of Arab enemies, that brought Shcharansky, along with many Soviet Jews, to a new consciousness of his Jewish heritage. In the late 1960s and early 1970s, the "Jews of Silence," as Elie Wiesel once termed them, began to find their voice: to organize classes in Hebrew language and Jewish culture, to memorialize the victims of the Holocaust, and above all, to dream of going to Israel.

In April 1973, a year after graduating from the prestigious Moscow Physical-Technical Institute with a specialty in cybernetics and taking a job as a computer specialist with the Moscow Research Institute for Oil and Gas, Shcharansky applied for an exit visa to go to Israel. His request was rejected, on the grounds that his work had given him "access to classified materials," though none of the work he had done at the Moscow Physical-Technical Institute had been of a military nature. His thesis was on programming computers to play chess, and the institute where he worked was classified as an "open" institution, not involved in secret work.

Now branded as a "refusenik"—a Jew denied an exit visa—Shcharansky was subject to special harassment by the authorities. Angered by that state of affairs, he joined the Jewish dissident movement which, starting in the late 1960s, had begun to challenge the government's restrictive emigration policy. Those who protested too openly or tried to escape were given harsh prison sentences. As the numbers of the imprisoned grew, other Jews, among them the twenty-five-year-old Shcharansky, began to organize public protests in their behalf.

It was at one such public protest in October 1973, that the young activist met Natalia Shtiglits (or Stieglitz), an ardent Zionist, whose "refusenik" brother was serving a brief prison term for his political activities. The young couple began to live together soon after and, having decided to marry the following spring, both applied for exit visas to go to Israel. In June 1974, while Shcharansky was serving his first prison term as part of the "suspicious and subversive element" that was hidden from view during President Richard Nixon's second visit to the Soviet Union, Natalia learned that her visa had been granted. Believing that Anatoly's visa would soon follow, they were married the day he was released from prison, on July 4, 1974, and on the following day Natalia, now using her Hebrew name, Avital, left for Israel.

But Shcharansky's visa never came. That second refusal, coupled with separation from his wife, redoubled his commitment to the dissident movement. He became part of a team, closely watched by the KGB, that traveled to outlying towns and provinces during October and November 1974, collecting information on the experiences of the "refuseniks" and was one of nine signatories to a letter to President Gerald Ford that detailed many cases of abuse and harassment that they had discovered on their journeys. The letter was dated November 18, 1974, five days before Ford flew to Vladivostok to meet with Soviet leader Leonid I. Brezhnev. As a result of a compromise negotiated by Henry A. Kissinger during those talks, the United States Senate in 1974 passed the Jackson Amendment to the Trade Reform Act of 1972, linking East-West trade to the easing of Soviet emigration restrictions. A further amendment to the act, introduced by Senator Adlai Stevenson 3d, set a $300 million limit on United States banking credits to the Soviet Union, making Soviet-Jewish emigration one of the conditions for any increase in those credits. The amended Trade Reform Act was signed by President Ford on January 3, 1975, but Soviet authorities, irate over the amendment, canceled the agreement seven days later. With others who had pinned their hopes on the Jackson Amendment, Shcharansky now took part in new letter-writing campaigns and protest demonstrations, including a rally on the steps of Moscow's Lenin Library on February 24, 1975. Two of the organizers were arrested, tried, and sentenced to five years of exile in Siberia.

In August 1975, even as reprisals against the "refuseniks" increased, the Soviet government signed the Helsinki accords, which recognized Soviet hegemony over Eastern Europe in exchange for a guarantee of human rights, including the right of emigration. Shcharansky later observed in an interview in the *Washington Post* (May 4, 1986) that the agreement was meaningless: "The moment they signed it, they started to take steps to discourage people from using it." Nevertheless, the Helsinki accords gave Soviet dissidents a new platform around which to organize. In May 1976, led by the physicist Yuri Orlov, a small group of activists, among them Anatoly Shcharansky, founded the Moscow Helsinki Watch to monitor Soviet compliance with its human rights provisions. In the following months, the group collected information on a wide range of abuses and published regular reports that were distributed to the embassies of the nations that had signed the Helsinki accords, as well as to the press.

Because of his central role in the Helsinki group, Shcharansky lost his job and was subjected to constant surveillance and threats. Then he was accused in *Izvestia* of spying for the CIA, and on

March 15, 1977, he was arrested and charged under the Soviet penal code with "treasonable espionage" and with anti-Soviet agitation and propaganda.

Despite the fact that his former roommate, Sanya Lipavsky, named him as a CIA agent, Shcharansky insisted that he was not a spy. Even President Jimmy Carter came to his defense by issuing a statement that the Jewish activist had no links with the United States intelligence agency. Western observers agreed that the spy charge was a trumped-up cover for Shcharansky's real "crime," his prominent role in the dissident movement. The authorities intended to make an example of him, to frighten other dissidents.

Shcharansky's trial began on July 10, 1978, two days before the start of United States-Soviet Strategic Arms Limitation Talks (SALT) in Geneva. Western observers and supporters of Shcharansky were barred from the courtroom, but his brother Leonid was allowed to attend (except for a secret session on July 11 and 12, which met to consider classified material that Shcharansky was alleged to have passed to foreign agents) and he conveyed information about the proceedings to about 150 supporters and journalists outside the courtroom. The prosecution charged Shcharansky with passing classified documents to agents posing as journalists, in particular to Robert Toth, a reporter for the *Los Angeles Times*, who was accused by Soviet authorities of working for the CIA. Conducting his own defense, Shcharansky rejected the charges as "absurd." Denied permission to call witnesses for his defense and restricted by the judge in his questioning of prosecution witnesses, Shcharansky was convicted on July 14 and sentenced to three years in prison, to be followed by ten years in a labor camp.

Then began almost a decade of nightmarish imprisonment. Shcharansky spent the first three years at Chistopol prison in solitary confinement. To keep his sanity, he did mental exercises: playing imaginary chess games with himself (which he always won, as he once jokingly told a reporter), outlining a book that he wanted to write, and singing Hebrew songs as loudly as he could. "I was sure that my people and my friends hadn't forgotten me," Shcharansky recalled, as quoted in the *Washington Post* (May 4, 1986), and that gave him the strength to resist the KGB's continued efforts to break his will.

Indeed, his family and friends had not forgotten him, and after the immediate protests over his imprisonment died down, they worked ceaselessly to keep his memory alive. His mother and his brother Leonid kept petitioning the Soviet authorities in his behalf and met regularly with Western journalists in Mosow. Those activities cost Leonid his job. Because he was considered a security risk, he was fired in 1982 from his position as a computer programmer for a Moscow industrial firm. Meanwhile, in Jerusalem, Avital founded the Association for the Release of Anatoly Shcharansky. With the support of international Jewish organizations, she took his case to Western heads of state, embarrassing the Kremlin with her outspoken condemnation of her husband's treatment.

Shcharansky remained optimistic and good-humored in his imprisonment. Moved to Perm 35, a labor camp for political prisoners, where he was assigned to work as a welder, he had more access to the outside world. His reading was heavily censored, but occasionally the camp authorities slipped up; an anti-Zionist magazine that they once gave him to read included a facsimile of a letter from Ronald Reagan to his wife, Avital. Shcharansky's spirit of resistance remained strong. Since he refused to work unless he was allowed to keep prayer books and candles, he was often sent to the "punishment cells." Accused of being a "bad influence" on other prisoners, he was sent back in January 1981 to Chistopol prison to serve a three-year sentence. In February 1982 he began a four-month hunger strike to protest the confiscation of his mail, during which he was forcibly fed.

Although his emotional stamina was exceptional, Shcharansky's physical health was poor. As a result of his severely restricted diet, his weight dropped at one point to less than 110 pounds. He suffered from chronic heart and blood pressure problems, and lack of medical attention for his eyes left him nearly blind. Fearing for her husband's life, Avital became increasingly outspoken in her public appeals in his behalf. Ignoring hints from the Soviet leader Yuri Andropov that Shcharansky might be released if she stopped her "noisy campaign," she went to the United States in 1984 for a White House ceremony on human rights and unexpectedly asked for a private interview with President Ronald Reagan. His administration later used every opportunity to tell Soviet authorities that the United States would regard the release of Shcharansky and his fellow "prisoner of conscience," Andrei Sakharov, as an important sign of their willingness to work for better East-West relations.

With Mikhail Gorbachev's accession to power, the Soviet Union became more receptive to the idea of freeing Shcharansky as a way to help thaw Soviet-American negotiations. Although the precise details were never revealed, Reagan and Gorbachev evidently reached an agreement on his release at the Geneva summit conference in November 1985. After some unexplained delays on the Soviet side, final plans were made to include the activist in an East-West exchange of captured intelligence operatives. To underline their insistence that Shcharansky had never been a spy, the United States authorities insisted that he be released before the other prisoners. As hundreds of journalists watched, along with the United States ambassador to Bonn and West German officials, Anatoly Shcharansky walked across the Glienicke Bridge from Potsdam into West Berlin on February 11, 1986, and at long last became a free man. Shcharansky immediately flew to Frankfurt, where he met Avital and, demonstrating his usual wit, greeted her with the words, "I'm sorry I'm late." That same day, nine years after their wedding, husband and wife finally realized their dream to go to Israel together. At Jerusalem airport, where they were met by Prime Minister Shimon Peres and a joyful crowd, Shcharansky said that it was the "happiest day of our life" and added, "I am not going to forget those whom I left in the camps, in prisons, who are still in exile or who still continue their struggle for the right to emigrate and for their human rights."

Physically and emotionally exhausted, Shcharansky went into seclusion for a few months to prepare for a trip to the United States, which he planned and financed himself, to thank his American supporters. He arrived in New York City on May 7, 1986, to a hero's welcome. Four days later he was the guest of honor at the annual Solidarity Parade in behalf of Soviet Jews, which culminated in a rally at Dag Hammarskjöld Plaza that drew an estimated 300,000 people. The following day, in the office of Random House publisher Robert Bernstein, who is chairman of the United States Helsinki Watch Committee, Shcharansky met for the first time in a decade with Yelena Bonner, another founder of the Moscow Helsinki Watch, who had been sentenced, along with her husband, the Nobel Prize-winning Soviet physicist Andrei D. Sakharov, to internal exile in Gorky for "anti-Soviet slander," but was in the United States on medical leave. Shcharansky then flew to Washington, D.C., where on May 13 he received the key to the city from the mayor and was awarded the Congressional Gold Medal, at a reception in the Capitol Rotunda. On the same day, he met with President Reagan, Vice-President George Bush, Secretary of State George P. Shultz, national security affairs adviser John M. Poindexter, and White House chief of staff Donald T. Regan, in a closed forty-minute conference in the Oval office, but the details of that conference were not released because of the administration's emphasis on "quiet diplomacy." During the next two days he met individually with leaders of the Senate and the House of Representatives and testified at hearings before the congressional committee that monitors compliance with the Helsinki accords.

During his visit, Shcharansky repeated the same message at every opportunity. While acknowledging that "quiet diplomacy" had helped to gain his release, he urged the United States to continue putting public pressure on the Soviet Union to release the estimated 400,000 Jews still awaiting exit visas and to moderate its policies on human rights in general. He told reporters that the United States "must leave no doubt with the Soviet authorities that the human rights problem is not a propaganda issue but a question of principle on which all the structure of the relationships between East and West can be built." Describing his release as a "cosmetic" gesture, Shcharansky expressed the view that the Soviet regime would not change markedly under Gorbachev unless it was subject to relentless pressure, including economic sanctions. "Just the fact that Gorbachev understands things better than his predecessors gives some reason for optimism," Shcharansky told Francis X. Clines in an interview for the *New York Times* (February 8, 1987). He added, however: "The West must not be deceived by his campaign of gestures and must be firm. . . ."

Shcharansky, who now uses his Hebrew given name "Natan" and has changed the spelling of his surname to Sharansky, continued to face some difficult challenges in his new homeland. Although he tried to steer clear of Israel's bitter factional politics, he has on occasion become embroiled in controversy. In the late summer of 1986 he came under fire for insisting that arms controls talks with the Soviet Union be tied to human rights issues and for opposing a meeting between Israeli and Soviet negotiators to reopen diplomatic relations between their two countries. Asked how he felt about the criticism, Shcharansky replied, "That's the beauty of democracy."

But in November 1986 the activist became embroiled in a more embarrassing controversy by meeting with two Palestinians, who asked him to investigate alleged human rights violations by Israeli authorities on the West Bank—in particular, the expulsion of a Palestinian newspaper editor. Rightist spokesmen maintained that the two men had connections with the Palestine Liberation Organization and bitterly attacked Shcharansky for listening to them. He issued an apology, explaining that he had been ignorant of their PLO ties and affirming that Israeli efforts to suppress the PLO "birds of prey" could never be considered a violation of human rights.

In the midst of his turbulent new life, Shcharansky's family has been a special source of joy. Honoring a commitment made at the time of his release, the Soviet Union allowed his brother Leonid, along with his wife and their two sons, and his mother, to immigrate to Israel in August 1986. Then, in November, Shcharansky's wife presented him with their first child, a girl. Asked how he and his wife were getting along after their long separation, Shcharansky replied that he had always felt spiritually close to her in their years apart. "But I was surprised," he admitted, "how we started understanding one another from the very first moment" after his release, and added that he was very proud of the political prominence she had acquired in his absence. Avital Shcharansky, a convert to Orthodox Judaism, is religiously more observant than her husband and has been identified with the religious right.

Described by Richard Grenier in *Insight* (March 17, 1986) as an "awesomely cheerful little man" who is "amiable, intelligent, even amusing," Anatoly Shcharansky is five feet two inches tall, stocky, and bald. After reading his moving letters from prison, which are quoted at length in Martin Gilbert's biography *Shcharansky: Hero of Our Time* (Viking, 1986), reviewers were eagerly awaiting his memoirs, scheduled to be published by Random House. On November 1, 1981 a flight of steps opposite the United Nations building in New York City was named the "Shcharansky Steps" at a ceremony sponsored by the Greater New York Conference on Soviet Jewry, the Student Struggle for Soviet Jewry, and Mayor Edward Koch of New York City. An honorary degree, conferred by Yeshiva University, was accepted for him by his wife in 1984.

References: Insight 2:32+ F 2 '86 por; N Y Rev of Bks 33:13+ S 25 '86 por; Newsday II 4+ My 19 '86 por; Washington Post C p1+ My 17 '86 por; Gilbert, Martin. Shcharansky: Hero of Our Time (1986). International Who's Who, 1986–87

Shepherd, Cybill

1950– Actress. Address: b. c/o Picturemaker Productions, 20th Century-Fox Television, 10201 W. Pico Blvd., Bldg. 38, Los Angeles, Calif. 90035

With the adulation she has received for her portrayal of Maddie Hayes, an ex-model turned private eye on the hit TV show *Moonlighting*, Cybill Shepherd has made a comeback worthy of comparison to the dreamlike plot of a Frank Capra movie. In 1970, when she herself was a well-known cover girl, she was "discovered" by Peter Bogdanovich, a gifted young filmmaker who cast her in *The Last Picture Show*, became her lover and mentor, and helped to make her a star. But in the mid-1970s, when her films stopped making money, the dream turned sour. A predatory, celebrity-hungry press turned her into "the most clobbered actress in Hollywood" and studio tycoons drove her from the film capital. Chastened but undefeated, Cybill Shepherd returned to her hometown and began to rebuild her career. After several years of performing in regional theatre and of singing in small nightclubs, she went back to Hollywood, where she found work in television. And now Cybill Shepherd, once dismissed as "a no-talent dame with . . . a toothpaste smile and all the star quality of a dead hamster," is being hailed as the Carole Lombard of the 1980s.

Named for her grandfather, Cy, and father, Bill, Cybill Shepherd was born in 1950 and raised in Memphis, Tennessee. Her father, William Jennings Shepherd, managed the family's home-appliance distributorship, and her mother, Patty (Shobe) Shepherd, was a housewife who has been described by her daughter as "a Southern lady who plays bridge in the afternoon." Miss Shepherd was the middle child in a family of three children. Her older sister, Terri, is a nurse, and her younger brother, Bill, is a producer of commercials in Memphis. In 1968 Miss Shepherd's parents were divorced after twenty-five years of marriage.

Tall, with a large frame and remarkably broad shoulders, Cybill Shepherd seems to have inherited the physique of her father, a former football player. A tomboy during her adolescence, she was a good student and an exceptional athlete at Memphis' East High School, where she competed in swimming, softball, track, and basketball. Although she was voted the most attractive girl in her senior class, Cybill Shepherd feels that her looks did not mature into striking beauty until she turned nineteen. Nevertheless, at sixteen she won the Miss Teenage Memphis title after relatives entered her in the competition. At the Miss Teenage America pageant, she failed to place among the seven finalists but won the congeniality award. In 1968 she took first place in the Fashion Model of the Year contest, a nationally televised event sponsored by CBS-TV. Whisked away to Manhattan, she became an overnight cover-girl sensation when discovered by Glamour magazine and the trend-setting fashion photographer Bert Stern.

With her golden hair, peach-pink complexion, heavy-lidded blue eyes, and all-American cheerleader looks, Cybill Shepherd was more than just another photogenic face. With her 130 pounds distributed over her five-foot-eight-and-one-half-inch-tall body, she represented a radical departure from the "standard of near anorexic daintiness that reigned among models of the . . . Sixties," to quote from Hillary Johnson's profile of Miss Shepherd in Rolling Stone (October 9, 1986). As Ruth Whitney, the editor of Glamour, has remarked, "Cybill has a strong, open face. There's nothing cute or kewpie doll about her."

By 1970 Cybill Shepherd was earning $500 a day and could have battened on her $80,000-a-year income but for her desire to obtain an education in art history and modern literature. Dividing her time between modeling assignments and taking courses in those two fields of study, she enrolled first at Hunter College and then at the College of New Rochelle, when she lived for a time in Westchester County. It was in 1970, when she had returned to Manhattan and was attending New York

University, that Peter Bogdanovich came into her life.

At that time, the thirty-one-year-old Bogdanovich was one of Hollywood's most ambitious and promising young directors. A film critic turned moviemaker, he had recently completed his first film, the low-budget but well-received Targets, and had begun work on The Last Picture Show, which he adapted from Larry McMurtry's poetically bleak novel about a young man's coming of age in a small north Texas town in 1951. While shopping one day at a California supermarket, Bogdanovich saw Cybill Shepherd's face on the cover of Glamour and said to himself, "That's Jacy!" He was referring to one of the characters crucial to his film: Jacy Farrow, a spoiled teenager who victimizes men in her singleminded quest for a financially secure marriage.

Bogdanovich lost no time in flying to New York to audition Miss Shepherd for the role, despite her lack of theatrical training. In an interview with Newsday (March 2, 1975), he recalled his first encounter with his future ingenue: "Cybill was toying with the flowers in a vase, and there was something so casually destructive about it, it seemed to imply the kind of woman who doesn't mean to be cruel to men, but who is." Certain that she was perfect for the part of Jacy, Bogdanovich overcame Miss Shepherd's initial reluctance to play a nude scene by promising to film the brief erotic sequence tastefully.

Released in the fall of 1971, The Last Picture Show (Columbia) was proclaimed the best American film of the year by many of the most demanding critics. In Newsweek (October 11, 1971) Paul D. Zimmerman called it "the most impressive work by a young American director since 'Citizen Kane.'" He also congratulated Bogdanovich for casting "an untried fashion model" as Jacy and "artfully draw[ing] from her a performance that embodies every crummy value in [the fictitious town of Anarene]—duplicity, hard ambition, rote obedience to every local shibboleth." In his Washington Post review (December 25, 1971), Gary Arnold ventured his opinion that "Cybill Shepherd . . . makes Jacy the most memorable figure in the film—and the most convincing movie incarnation of a bitch in quite some time."

It was during the filming of The Last Picture Show that Cybill Shepherd and her director became lovers, and although Bogdanovich was the married father of two young girls, a very public affair ensued. By 1972 Miss Shepherd had left behind her modeling career in New York to become a Hollywood actress, and she and Bogdanovich were living together in a Bel Air mansion that had previously belonged to Clark Gable's widow. While Bogdanovich's divorce was pending, he and Miss Shepherd held interviews in which they seemed to scorn the institution of marriage. More than once, Cybill Shepherd declared that marriage seemed valid only when a couple decided to have children. Such statements reinforced Bogdanovich's growing reputation for intellectual arrogance, and Miss Shepherd's for being insouciantly glib.

Cybill Shepherd and Peter Bogdanovich conducted their affair as if they expected the film industry to love them for living out the classic Hollywood fantasy: a golden girl is discovered serendipitously by a precocious director, who molds her, makes her his lover, and engineers her astonishing rise to the top. But instead of comparing them to Josef von Sternberg and Marlene Dietrich, Hollywood insiders whispered that Bogdanovich was a would-be Svengali and Miss Shepherd his short-on-talent Trilby. Moreover, Bogdanovich came under fire for having left Polly Platt—his wife of almost ten years—a talented set designer who had made significant contributions to her husband's first two career-making films—when he met Miss Shepherd.

Cybill Shepherd and her friend attributed much of the hostility they encountered to envy, for after The Last Picture Show, Bogdanovich made two successive hit films, What's Up Doc? and Paper Moon, and Miss Shepherd's was a star-turn performance in the popular Heartbreak Kid (Palomar Pictures, 1972). Scripted by Neil Simon and directed by Elaine May, The Heartbreak Kid is a comedy about Lenny (Charles Grodin) a charming but guileful young man, who jettisons his wife (Jeannie Berlin) on their honeymoon when he meets Kelly (Miss Shepherd). A cool WASP beauty, she is the sexual apotheosis of Lenny's tainted American dream, and he doggedly pursues her to the altar. "As the object of [Lenny's] unreasonable passion," Vincent Canby wrote in the New York Times (December 18, 1972), "Miss Shepherd succeeds in the fairly unusual feat of being lovely, bitchy and funny, all more or less simultaneously. . . . "

As Hillary Johnson worded it in Rolling Stone, Cybill Shepherd's Hollywood "fall from grace was steep and rocky," and it was accelerated by her next two films, both conceived as star-making vehicles for her by Bogdanovich. The director said that he cast her as the Henry James heroine Daisy Miller, a spirited, nouveau-riche girl from Schenectady, who innocently flouts Old World social customs in the Europe of 1878, because "there was a tremendous similarity between Daisy and Cybill. Cybill flirts reflexively. Daisy was a relentless flirt. But Cybill, like Daisy, was often misunderstood. . . . There was an innocence behind Daisy and Cybill which was at odds with the flirting."

Daisy Miller (Paramount, 1974) turned out to be a box-office dud and, despite a few mildly favorable reviews, was considered a handsomely mounted bore by most critics. Although in Newsweek (May 27, 1974) Jack Kroll called Miss Shepherd's performance "the most incandescent and affecting one . . . in the film," the failure of Daisy Miller began the Cybill-and-Peter bashing that the media gleefully engaged in during the mid-1970s. In Time (June 3, 1974) Jay Cocks wrote that Cybill Shepherd "has a home-fried hauteur good enough for the one-dimensional roles she played in The Last Picture Show and The Heartbreak Kid. . . . But she has no resources as an actress. She runs short of breath in the middle of lines, and gives no appearance of understanding the words she blurts out in little hiccups. Daisy is supposed to be unspoiled . . . and callow. . . . [Cybill] Shepherd projects instead a taunting sexual hostility that turns Daisy into a little bitch goddess on a pedestal."

Also in 1974, Bogdanovich imprudently encouraged Miss Shepherd to record, and Paramount Pictures to underwrite, an album of Cole Porter songs. Coyly titled Cybill Does It . . . To Cole Porter (Paramount), the LP raised the question, "What did Porter ever do to her?" In a savage review in Newsday (May 24, 1974) of both the album and Daisy Miller, Joseph Gelmis wrote, "Filmmaker Peter Bogdanovich is trying to do with Cybill Shepherd what Citizen Kane did with his no-talent protégée—foist her on the public in a lavish setting. . . . Bogdanovich and his lady love Cybill Shepherd are the Bonnie and Clyde of movies and records, getting away with murder in public. Cybill not only can't act or sing, she can't even talk. Whenever she opens her mouth in 'Daisy Miller,' she rattles away like a ventriloquist's dummy."

A more resounding failure than either the Cole Porter album or Daisy Miller was Bogdanovich and Cybill Shepherd's next movie, At Long Last Love (Twentieth Century-Fox), a six-and-a-half-million-dollar box-office disaster that regularly heads critics' lists of the worst films of 1975. At Long Last Love was a misguided attempt by Bogdanovich—who directed, produced, and wrote the script—to make a lighthearted musical comedy in the romantic, Art Deco style of 1930s Paramount productions. The score featured sixteen Cole Porter tunes, and the movie's unlikely leads were Burt Reynolds and Cybill Shepherd, neither of whom is an accomplished singer or dancer. In Esquire (June 1975) the acidulous critic John Simon shredded Miss Shepherd's performance: "[She] plays a poor little snotty rich girl with a notion of sophistication that is underpassed only by her acting ability. (I will not sully my pen by making it describe her singing and dancing.) If it weren't for an asinine superciliousness radiating from her, Miss Shepherd would actually be pitiable, rather like a kid from an orphanage trying to play Noel Coward." A decade later, in People magazine (November 4, 1985), Bogdanovich recalled that "Cybill took the heat for the film and our relationship. It was unfair. People like to put her down."

When Bogdanovich tried to put his inamorata in his 1976 movie Nickelodeon, producer David Begelman ruled that if Cybill Shepherd were included in the cast, the film would not be made. Worse, the Hollywood powers-that-be had by now concluded that Miss Shepherd spelled box-office poison for any film in which she was starred. In the New Yorker (March 24, 1975) Pauline Kael analyzed Cybill Shepherd's inability to project celluloid warmth. According to her, Bogdanovich's would-be Galatea aroused feelings of "vindictive masculinity" in male viewers. "Men wanted to get at her to wipe the jeering smile off her face. Bog-danovich engendered these ambivalent feelings toward her: an overgrown baton twirler, she was a projection of men's resentment of the bitch-princesses they're drawn to. . . . She's an object, not a star; people don't feel for her and don't iden-tify with her."

It was decreed by Hollywood's major studios that henceforth Cybill Shepherd would be cast only in supporting roles as an aloof and unobtain-able ice queen. She embodied that stereotype ad-mirably in *Taxi Driver* (Columbia, 1976), the powerful and unsettling Martin Scorsese film that starred Robert De Niro, in which she played an al-luring campaign worker for a liberal presidential candidate. "Cybill Shepherd is just right in image and behavior as Betsy, the frosted flower of the metropolitan bourgeoisie," wrote Jack Kroll in *Newsweek* (March 1, 1976). And in her *New Yorker* review (February 9, 1976), Pauline Kael ob-served that "Cybill Shepherd has never been bet-ter: you don't see her trying to act. She may actually be doing her least acting here, yet she doesn't have that schoolgirl model's blankness; her face is ex-pressive and womanly."

One of Cybill Shepherd's last starring roles was in *Special Delivery* (1976), a B-movie distributed by American International Pictures. In that light-weight comedy about a bank heist masterminded by a Vietnam vet (Bo Svenson), she acquitted her-self well as a recent divorcée who becomes Sven-son's love interest. The movie, however, was dead on arrival at the box office and failed to restore the actress's credibility with Hollywood moguls. In *Silver Bears* (Columbia, 1978), a caper film about a group of international swindlers and con men, Miss Shepherd was cast as a married screwball who beds down with the movie's star, Michael Caine. Although her comic performance was wide-ly praised, the film suffered from convoluted plot-ting and lackluster direction by Ivan Passer. When *Silver Bears* also failed at the box office, Cybill Shepherd's Hollywood career had reached the end of a cul-de-sac.

By 1978 Cybill Shepherd's love affair of some eight years with Peter Bogdanovich was over, and with good roles coming her way no more, Tinsel-town's blonde pariah went home to Memphis. There she met David Ford, a Memphis State Col-lege dropout three years her junior, who was em-ployed as an auto-parts manager for a local Mercedes-Benz dealership. While filming a bland remake of Alfred Hitchcock's classic *The Lady Vanishes*, she married Ford in a ceremony held in a thirteenth-century Gloucestershire church late in the autumn of 1978.

Despite a cast headed by Elliott Gould, Angela Lansbury, and Cybill Shepherd, *The Lady Vanishes* (Hammer Films, 1979) failed to enchant audiences and critics alike. Cast in the leading role of the heroine, Amanda Kelly, Cybill Shepherd made "a hateful spectacle of herself all over again," in the opinion of reviewer Gary Arnold of the *Washington Post* (March 18, 1980). In 1980 she ap-peared in *The Alien's Return*, a film so deservedly obscure that Miss Shepherd does not even list it on her official résumé. Released under the title *Earthright*, it was according to one critic, an abys-mal "ripoff" of Steven Spielberg's *Close Encoun-ters of the Third Kind*. The title was changed to *The Alien's Return* when it was interred in the late-night TV movie graveyard.

With her film career in shambles, Cybill Shep-herd now tried to carve out a niche for herself as a nightclub chanteuse. Having studied voice with an opera coach for about three years when she first moved to southern California, she put together a jazz band called the Memphis All-Stars, with her husband on guitar, cut an album called *Vanilla* (1979), and took her act on the road. Reviewing one of her sets with the Memphis All-Stars at a Green-wich Village night spot, Wayne Robins of *Newsday* (December 15, 1979) wrote, "Her pitch and phras-ing were not remarkable, but they were adequate. Occasionally, her voice lost a little control in the lower registers, but for the most part, she sounded capable. . . . The band's playing was perfuncto-ry. . . . But the All-Stars . . . couldn't quite erase the taste of dilettantism that pervaded the show."

Cybill Shepherd's climb back to the top began inauspiciously, when, on the advice of her friend Orson Welles, she started doing regional theatre in relatively small venues in the Midwest, South, and Southwest. "I really came alive as an actress," she told *People* (November 4, 1985), "but I was barely breaking even financially." In 1982 she ended her marriage to David Ford—"We outgrew each other," she laconically explained in the *Rolling Stone* interview—and returned to Hollywood. Her former agent, the power broker Sue Mengers, in-formed her: "Cybill, you've been in Memphis for four years. You might as well be dead." After doing a guest spot on the TV show *Fantasy Island*, she landed the leading role in *The Yellow Rose*, a prime-time soap opera that made its debut on the NBC-TV network in the fall of 1983. A contempo-rary Western with Miss Shepherd playing the em-battled owner of a Texas ranch, *The Yellow Rose* lasted just one season, but it afforded her an ample opportunity to prove that she had grown as an ac-tress. "I looked great," she told *People*. "I had confi-dence. For the first time people in the business saw that I was standing on my own two feet, and I was no longer Peter Bogdanovich's girlfriend."

In 1984 a young television writer, Glen Gordon Caron, sold the idea for an offbeat detective series to ABC-TV, the premise of which was that a rich fashion model named Maddie Hayes has been swindled by her business manager, leaving her with little but money-losing businesses. One of those tax-shelter investments is a faltering detec-tive agency mismanaged by David Addison, an au-thority-flouting, womanizing wiseacre whose boss she now becomes. When Caron was about halfway through the first draft of his script for the series' pi-lot episode, "Cybill Shepherd's face simply sprang off the page," as he recalled in *TV Guide* (Decem-ber 7, 1985). "I wanted," Caron explained, "a cool blonde heroine in the Alfred Hitchcock mold—a Vera Miles, a Grace Kelly, if you will. I wanted a classy lady capable of handling, and not handling, the crazy guy who ran the detective agency—with the wit of the Tracy-Hepburn and Cary Grant–Rosalind Russell confrontations in the old movies."

Inspired more by films of the screwball comedy genre like *Bringing Up Baby* and *His Girl Friday* than by TV private eye fare like *Hart to Hart,* Caron fashioned a fast-paced adult *talk* show that features some of the sassiest, sauciest repartee in prime-time history. With Cybill Shepherd set to play Maddie Hayes, Caron and his staff had to audition some 3,000 actors before finding one who could play, as a writer for *Newsweek* (September 8, 1986) observed, the hard-partying macho Punk to her Prom Queen, one who could achieve at least a stand-off against Cybill Shepherd in Caron's 1980s video version of the battle of the sexes. That actor was a young unknown, a part-time Manhattan bartender named Bruce Willis.

Moonlighting's debut came late in the 1984–85 television season, in March. But despite mostly glowing reviews, it did not creep into the top twenty of the Nielsen ratings until more than halfway through the 1985–86 season. When *Newsweek* featured Cybill Shepherd and Bruce Willis on one of its covers, Harry F. Waters attributed the show's appeal to its "wit, style, . . . snap," and a "sexual chemistry" between the Hayes and Addison characters "potent enough to curl plexiglass." "Cybill Shepherd," wrote Waters, "both plays off and sends up her own ice-maiden, ex-cover girl image. Gorgeous, petulant, spunky, haughtily sarcastic and very much her own boss, her Maddie Hayes may be the most formidable female ever to ignite the tube."

Although *Moonlighting* is considered the tube's hippest, most innovative series to appear since the premiere of of NBC's *Miami Vice,* even its champions have complained that sometimes "the show strains so hard to be madcap that it comes down with the cutes," as Waters once groused in *Newsweek*. However, no critic has faulted Cybill Shepherd. She subverts the stereotype of cold, spoiled brat that made her the disliked bitch goddess of the 1970s, and with Willis to give her comeuppance for moments of callous soullessness, the subtext of *Moonlighting* is, as Caron says, "the taming of the shrew." With her now finely honed sense of comic timing and natural-seeming penchant for physical comedy, Miss Shepherd exhibits more control over her acting, and exercises it with a minimum of theatricality. "Maddie is a million miles from the ice bitches I tend to play," she said in the interview with *People*. "And I can't believe I'm finally funny. Lombard pulled off being beautiful and funny. And that's not easy."

In March 1987 Miss Shepherd married Bruce Oppenheim, a Los Angeles chiropractor, and seven months later she gave birth to twins, Ariel and Zachariah, fathered by Oppenheim. Miss Shepherd also has an older daughter, Clementine, from her marriage to David Ford. Among her friends is the novelist Larry McMurty, who reputedly based the heroine of his novel *Lonesome Dove* on her.

Although often compared to Carole Lombard, Cybill Shepherd told the interviewer for *TV Guide* that she yearns to be "the Mae West of the 1980s." She explained: "I'm kind of a sexy broad, you know. I have a really dirty sense of humor. I love double-entendre. I love to say shocking things. I admired Mae West for her longevity, and also because she believed nobody had enough sex and it didn't matter with whom you had it as long as you enjoyed yourself." Cybill Shepherd maintains the 130-thirty-pound weight of her youth by means of a regimen of swimming and, during breaks on the *Moonlighting* set, race-walking. Although she makes a weekly salary that hovers in the neighborhood of $50,000, she is thrifty. In 1986 she was still driving a seven-year-old Cadillac she had bought in Memphis, choosing to invest most of her money in real estate. She has always been an avid reader of modern fiction, and she is an outspoken proponent of women's rights.

Although she favors elegant clothing, she is often photographed wearing an evening gown and tennis shoes, because the latter are more comfortable than conventional women's footwear. At the 1986 Emmy Awards ceremony, with *Moonlighting* having received sixteen nominations, including one for Miss Shepherd as best actress in a dramatic series, she startled the audience by appearing onstage in a black strapless gown and orange Reebok sneakers.

References: *N Y Daily News* p1+ D 14 '79 por; *N Y Daily News Mag* p11 Ap 20 '86 pors; *N Y Post* p15+ N 6 '71 por; *N Y Times* II p29 Mr 10 '85; *People* 11:48+ F 5 '79 pors, 13:94 Ja 28 '80 pors; *TV Guide* 32:30+ Ja 28 '84 por; *Washington Post* L p5 O 14 '73 por, B p1+ Mr 11 '75 por, B p3 D 20 '76 por

Singh, Giani Zail

(sing gē-ä´nē zāl)

May 5, 1916– Former president of India.
Address: Sandhwan, Punjab, India

Giani Zail Singh, who served as India's seventh president for a five-year term ending in July 1987, was the first member of the nation's Sikh community to occupy that largely ceremonial but prestigious office. A veteran of the struggle for Indian independence, Singh served as a cabinet minister and as chief minister in his native state of Punjab and was for two years minister for home affairs in India's national government. Singh had been chosen for the presidency in 1982 primarily because of his loyalty to the late Prime Minister Indira Gandhi, but after her death in 1984 he occasionally clashed with her son and successor, Rajiv Gandhi.

Giani Zail Singh

Unlike many of his more militant coreligionists, Singh is a moderate who believes that the tenets of the Sikh religion are secular and based on principles of universal brotherhood.

Giani Zail Singh, the son of Sardar Kishan Singh and his wife, Ind Kaur, was born on May 15, 1916, in a mud hut in the village of Sandhwan, in the Faridkot district of Punjab, then a province of British India. (The name "Singh," meaning "lion," is carried by virtually all mature male Sikhs; "Giani," meaning "learned one," is an appellation that Zail Singh acquired after he became versed in the Sikh scriptures.) His father, a religous-minded nationalist and a descendant of artisans who later went into agriculture, owned about sixty-five acres of farmland. As a boy, Zail Singh gained insight into the aspirations of the common people of India through his contacts with the laborers and farmhands who worked on the family's property. When he was six, his father died, and his mother became the major influence in his life. "She was not only my creator in the physical sense, but also the architect of my political and public career," Singh told his biographers, B. K. and Shashi Ahluwalia, as quoted in their book *Our President Giani Zail Singh* (1983).

Although Singh was at first a somewhat indifferent student, he chose, after completing his early schooling, to become a professional reader of the Sikh scriptures, and he also familiarized himself with the sacred works of other religions, including the Koran, the Bhagavad-Gita, and the Ramayana. When the Indian independence movement under Mohandas K. Gandhi reached his home district, Singh turned his attention to politics and decided to devote himself to the freedom struggle. In April 1938 he organized a branch of Gandhi's All-India Congress party in Faridkot and in the same year became founder-president of the Praja Mandal movement in his state, actions that so enraged the ruling rajah of Faridkot that Singh was imprisoned for a five-year term, much of it under hard labor or solitary confinement. "It was an animal's existence," he has recalled.

After his release from prison in 1943, Singh went to Amritsar, where he worked as a Sikh missionary and edited the Punjabi weekly *Khalsa Sewak*. Meanwhile, he continued his involvement in the national independence movement. Returning to his home district in 1946, he defied the ruling rajah by launching the state's national flag movement that helped to pave the way for independence in the following year, when British India was divided into the sovereign nations of India and Pakistan. Singh's activities eventually came to the attention of Jawaharlal Nehru, who visited Faridkot and personally hoisted the new Indian tricolor flag there. Singh has said that he owed his political career to both Nehru and Maulana Abul Kalam Azad (one of the early Congress party stalwarts), who became his mentors when he was a lowly party worker. Over the years, he kept up his friendship with Nehru and his daughter, Indira Gandhi.

After independent India was established under Prime Minister Jawaharlal Nehru in August 1947, some princely rulers, including the rajah of Faridkot, held out against the new government for a time. In 1948, with the help of some 1,000 volunteers, Singh established a parallel government in Faridkot, which merged later that year, along with other princely states, into the newly established Patalia and East Punjab States Union (PEPSU). That in turn was integrated in November 1956 into the state of Punjab. Within the PEPSU government, Singh served in 1948–49 as revenue minister and in 1951–52 as minister for public works and agriculture. In 1955–56 he was president of the PEPSU provincial Congress committee. As a state cabinet minister, Singh was credited with the abolition of injustices against agricultural laborers, small landowners, and tenant farmers, and with helping to establish PEPSU as the first Indian state to abolish the "right of superior ownership" of agricultural land. Proprietary rights were thus granted to tillers, and absentee ownership was eliminated.

From 1956 to 1962 Giani Zail Singh served in the Rajya Sabha, the upper house of the Indian national parliament, and in 1956 he also became senior vice-president of the Punjab Pradesh Congress committee. Elected to the Punjab assembly in 1962, he was appointed a minister of state in the Punjab government of chief minister Pratap Singh Kairon, but he resigned when the government was streamlined under a reorganization scheme known as the Kamaraj plan that was instituted by Prime Minister Nehru in 1963, in the wake of border hostilities between India and the People's Republic of China. From 1966 to 1972 Singh was president of the Punjab Pradesh Congress committee.

In March 1972 Singh was elected by the unanimous vote of the Congress party faction in the Punjab assembly to head the state government as chief minister. During his five years and three months in office the state of Punjab made steady progress in agricultural and industrial development, in higher education, the construction of roads and hospitals, and women's rights. He promoted the so-called green revolution for the production of high-yielding grain in what was known as the "wheat bowl" of India, and he also fostered a "white revolution" to stimulate increased production of milk and dairy products.

Meanwhile, Indira Gandhi, who had been serving as prime minister since 1966, had come increasingly under fire from her critics for her purported authoritarian policies and alleged corruption. In the national elections of May 1977 she was swept from power in a tidal wave of public discontent and succeeded as prime minister by Morarji Desai, the head of the new Janata coalition. Giani Zail Singh, whose government in Punjab was among the Congress party adminstrations in several states that were also defeated, retired to his native village in 1977 to take over the presidency of the Punjab Cooperative Union while supporting Mrs. Gandhi in her effort to return to power. In a subsequent investigation of allegations of corruption and abuse of office during Singh's chief ministership in the Punjab, an inquiry commission in 1980 cleared him of most charges and ruled against him in only one minor administrative case.

In the national elections of January 1980 that returned Mrs. Gandhi to power with an increased majority for her new Indian National Congress-I ("I" for Indira) party, Singh won the seat for Hoshiarpur in the Lok Sabha—the lower house of the national parliament. As a reward for his loyalty, Mrs. Gandhi took him into her cabinet as home affairs minister, a post that also placed him at the head of the national intelligence bureau. As home minister, Singh defended the national security bill, approved in December 1980, which allowed detention of individuals without trial for up to three months, and he assured the opposition that Mrs. Gandhi would not use the measure for a vendetta against her political enemies. He met with some success in reducing India's crime rate and in bringing contending factions to the negotiating table.

On the other hand, opposition spokesmen maintained that Singh did very little to prevent the breakdown of law and order in northern India, that he failed to curb the unrest that had erupted in Assam over the immigration of Bengalis into that state, and that he was unsuccessful in putting down a revolt in his home state by militant Sikh separatists. Often given to making controversial statements, Singh drew fire for his proposal, in November 1981, that members of the "untouchable" caste, known as harijans, be armed for self-defense against attacks by upper-caste Hindus. His praise, in a parliamentary speech he delivered in early 1982, of Adolf Hitler's abilities as a national unifier so embarrassed Congress party leaders that they forced him to withdraw the remarks, which were eventually expunged from the record.

Although Singh was extolled in the Asian Recorder as a home minister who "earned wide respect for his broadness of outlook and patience in dealing with difficult problems," and his admiring biographers, B. K. and Shashi Ahluwalia, went so far as to hail him as "an Indian version of Abraham Lincoln," detached observers held more negative views. In the Economist (June 26, 1982) he was called "probably the least effective" home minister that India ever had. Darryl D'Monte, in the New Leader (August 9-23, 1982), referred to his "frequent faux pas" that "made him something of a laughing stock," and in the Indian Express he was compared to "Caligula's horse"—a reference to the Roman emperor who appointed his horse as a consul.

On June 22, 1982 Singh resigned his home office portfolio following his nomination, by Indira Gandhi and ten of her cabinet members, which was seconded by eleven members of parliament, to succeed N. Sanjiva Reddy, who was retiring as India's president at the end of a five-year term. Although traditionally the president of India remained aloof from partisan politics, Singh was nominated for the post primarily because of his unflagging loyalty to Mrs. Gandhi, and also because his election would assure the six million members of the Sikh community that they were being represented nationally. "If my leader had said that I should pick up a broom and be a sweeper, I should have done that," Singh said after he was nominated. "She chose me to be president." When asked whether he might ever take a stand against Mrs. Gandhi and her Congress-I party, Singh answered: "There will never be any such situation. Why should I think of such unpleasant things? Indira Gandhi in the true sense is a great woman and is the greatest democrat in the country—she will never let such a situation arise." His worshipful comments prompted Chandra Shekhar, a spokesman for the opposition, to ask: "Can such a mind guide, advise, and help the prime minister?"

Mrs. Gandhi had rejected a proposal advanced by the opposition parties that the president should be chosen by a consensus. She made it clear that she had selected Singh because she wanted to avert possible confrontations between the prime minister and the president on crucial issues. Singh's opponent in the election was Hans Raj Khanna, a respected former supreme court justice, who was chosen by the combined opposition after the original candidate, Hirendra Nath Mukerjee of the pro-Moscow Communist party of India, was disqualified because he was not a registered voter. Khanna acknowledged during his campaign that Singh, as the candidate of the dominant Congress party, had more votes on his side. He asserted that he was contesting the election to combat corruption and end what he saw as a decline in moral values. His appeal to legislators to vote "according to their conscience" and for "the better man" incensed Mrs. Gandhi, who accused Khanna of trying to engineer defections from the Congress party.

In the presidential election, which ended on July 15, 1982, Zail Singh won 72.7 percent of the votes of the electoral college, consisting of the members of the two houses of the national parliament and of the state legislatures. Khanna's share of the vote was 27.3 percent. Sworn in ten days later, Singh took office, following a twenty-one-gun salute, for a five-year term as India's seventh president. In his address to the nation he called for "greater discipline in national life"; the creation of a congenial climate for "social and economic emancipation of the weak, the undernourished, and the downtrodden"; the achievement of "unity of minds and hearts amongst peoples of different states, religions, castes, and . . . languages"; and "peaceful means of settlement of all disputes." Congratulating him on his victory, Mrs. Gandhi called Singh a veteran freedom fighter whose "origins were humble," but whose achievements were impressive. In December 1983 India's supreme court unanimously upheld Singh's election as president, rejecting a challenge by the opposition that he was "not a suitable person" to hold the office.

Although the president of India is legally bound to follow the advice of the prime minister, he has constitutional powers that enable him to act as a stabilizing force in the nation's politics and to make crucial decisions in times of crisis. In addition to exercising such ceremonial functions as receiving foreign dignitaries, making state visits abroad, officiating at festive events, and addressing an annual joint session of parliament, the president is also nominal supreme commander of the armed forces. He is authorized to sign or to reject legislation and ordinances, and he may impose presidential rule in areas where state and local government have become ineffective. In some circumstances he is even empowered, in theory at least, to dismiss a prime minister or to dissolve the parliament.

Among other ceremonial activities, in October 1983 Singh launched "Project Impact," a program to benefit the disabled that was sponsored by India's ministry of health and social welfare in cooperation with UNICEF and WHO. In the same month he inaugurated Gandhi University and the Pontifical Oriental Institute in Kerala. Singh also presided over such events as the inauguration of the Valmiki World Poetry Festival in New Delhi in March 1985, and he announced the publication of important literary works, including a Punjabi translation of the Bible. In 1982 he went to the United States for cardiac bypass surgery at the Texas Heart Institute and was made an honorary citizen of Dallas.

Singh's duties as president took him to Mauritius, Yemen, Bahrain, Hong Kong, and Nepal. In the spring of 1984 he traveled to Mexico, Argentina, and Peru on the first state visit ever made by an Indian president to Latin America. In his presidential residence, the Rashtrapati Bhavan in New Delhi, Singh received, among many others, United States Vice-President George Bush, President Mohammad Zia ul-Haq of Pakistan, Soviet leader Mikhail

S. Gorbachev, and the president of the African National Congress, Dr. Oliver Tambo. He also met with Queen Elizabeth II of Great Britain and with Pope John Paul II.

In the wake of continuing violence by Sikh militant separatists in Punjab in October 1983, Singh suspended the legislature and imposed presidential rule in his home state on recommendation of Prime Minister Indira Gandhi, and in February 1984 he opened a joint session of parliament with an appeal to the people of Punjab to restore peace. In May 1984 he imposed central rule in the northeastern state of Sikkim, whose chief minister, following a dispute with Mrs. Gandhi, had refused her order to resign. The conflict between the central government and Sikh militants in Punjab reached its height when in June 1984, acting on orders of Indira Gandhi, the army raided the Golden Temple in Amritsar, the Sikhs' most sacred shrine, at the cost of over 600 lives. At an officially banned Sikh convention at Amritsar in September, Zail Singh was formally censured by the five Sikh high priests for failing to take steps to prevent the army's assault, but the censure was reversed when Singh visited the Golden Temple shortly afterward and apologized for the army's action.

In apparent retaliation for the raid on the Golden Temple, Indira Gandhi was gunned down at her official residence in New Delhi on October 31, 1984, by two Sikh members of her security guard. According to press reports, Singh was also believed by intelligence officials to be an intended target of militant Sikh assassins. Within hours of the assassination, Singh cut short a state visit to North Yemen and flew back to New Delhi to swear in Mrs. Gandhi's son Rajiv as head of the government, even though he could have appointed an interim prime minister from among members of the outgoing cabinet pending formal election of a new party leader. Addressing parliament in January 1985, amid continuing Hindu-Sikh violence, Singh declared that Indira Gandhi had "joined the ranks of the immortals of world history" and that the unprecedented mandate received by Rajiv Gandhi showed "the overwhelming concern" of the people "for the unity and integrity of the nation and their desire for a strong and stable government."

Although relations between President Singh and Prime Minister Rajiv Gandhi were at first harmonious, friction soon developed. According to press reports in the spring of 1985, the prime minister consistently ignored the convention of reporting regularly to the president and of meeting with him following his trips abroad. Gandhi was also said to have criticized Singh for not having done enough to curb Sikh violence during his tenure as home minister. In a letter by Singh published in the *Indian Express* in March 1987, the president accused the prime minister of failing to inform him of important affairs of state and of canceling foreign trips that he had planned. In mid-1987 Singh thwarted Gandhi by refusing to sign legislation that permitted government security forces to intercept mail. He was even reported to have threatened to dismiss Rajiv Gandhi as prime minister but failed to gain enough support from party rebels for such a move. At the end of his five-year term, on July 24, 1987, Giani Zail Singh was succeeded as president of India by Ramaswamy Venkataraman, a former lawyer and legislator who had been serving as India's vice-president since 1984. He was elected by an overwhelming majority on July 16 as the presidential candidate of the Congress party.

Giani Zail Singh and his wife, Pradhan Kaur, have a son who manages the family farm in Sandhwan, and three daughters, two of whom are doctors. Tall, handsome, and somewhat portly, Singh was described in the *Economist* (June 26, 1982) as "bluff and genial," with an "earthy, homespun personality" and "no intellectual pretensions." According to Sanjoy Hazarika, writing in the *New York Times* (July 16, 1982), Singh "prides himself on being a fastidious dresser and often wears the traditional Indian long coat and tight trousers." In keeping with Sikh religious practice he wears a turban and a beard. Singh likes to quote humorous Urdu-Punjabi couplets, often to put down a political opponent.

References: Asian Recorder 28:16739+ Ag 13–19 '82; Economist 283:42 Je 26 '82 por; India News 21:1+ Jl 19 '82 por; London Times p7 Je 23 '82 por; N Y Times A p3 Jl 16 '82; New Leader 65:7+ Ag 9 '23 '82 por; Ahluwalia, B. K. and Shashi. Our President Giani Zail Singh (1983); Hindustan Yearbook and Who's Who, 1986; International Who's Who, 1986–87; Who's Who in the World, 1987–88

1985 © Fred W. McDarrah

Smith, Liz

Feb. 2, 1923– Journalist; author. Address: b. New York Daily News, 220 E. 42d St., New York City, N.Y. 10017

In becoming America's most popular gossip columnist over the course of the past twelve years, Liz Smith has redefined her craft and, in the words of Gloria Steinem, "transcended a whole art form." Miss Smith, whose lively daily column is published in the New York *Daily News* and some sixty-five other newspapers serviced by the Chicago Tribune Syndicate, describes herself as a "chronicler of the ways and means and social mores of the celebrities of our time," and she is affectionately known in the fourth estate as gossip's "godmother" or "good ole gal." In a profession too often identified with either savage scandal-mongering or crass promotion of show business personalities, Miss Smith is as well liked as she is well read, known for a daily ration of tattle that is honest but fair and free of malice and delivered with a common touch and a droll sense of humor. Her columns are miscellanies, each beginning with a pithy, wise, or witty quotation, often culled from her wide reading, and offering, amidst the trivia, regular scoops in the fields of publishing and politics as well as show business. In addition to her work in print journalism, Liz Smith does a twice-weekly spot on *Live at Five*, NBC's local early-evening news telecast in New York City.

Liz Smith was born Mary Elizabeth Smith in Fort Worth, Texas, on February 2, 1923, the lone daughter among the three children of Sloan Smith, a cotton broker, and Sarah Elizabeth (McCall) Smith. In *The Mother Book* (1978), the giant compendium of "trivia and grandeur" about mothers and motherhood that she compiled, Miss Smith warmly recalled her childhood in Forth Worth, where she, her younger brother, Bobby, and her older brother, James, were reared with the help of a black nanny, Dott Burns. They were raised in the fundamentalist faith of their paternal grandmother, Martha Tipton Smith, who is described in *The Mother Book* as a "narrow-minded" West Texas Southern Baptist of Irish heritage "who disapproved of almost everything." Their gentler, Mississippi-bred maternal grandmother, Sallie (Ball) McCall, was a "picture-book woman" who traced her Ball ancestors back to George Washington's mother. Both grandmothers lived for years with the family, and each had a strong influence on Liz, who has described her childhood in Forth Worth as bounded on one side by the Travis Avenue Baptist Church and on the other by the Tivoli motion picture theatre. She sometimes wrote fan letters to her favorite movie stars, including Tom Mix and Ginger Rogers.

"Even as a kid, I was making up newspapers," Miss Smith told Sherrye Henry during an interview for the syndicated Sunday newspaper supplement *Parade* (February 1, 1987). "So naturally, I enrolled in the journalism department at the University of Texas." At the university, she was an associate editor of the campus literary magazine and a columnist for the student newspaper. When she wrote a story for the magazine about the movie star Zachary Scott, an alumnus of the university, Scott was so impressed that he offered to get her a job if ever she needed one.

Miss Smith took her degree at the University of Texas in 1948. The following year she moved to New York City, leaving behind her failed four-year marriage to a football player. In New York she supported herself by working as a typist while looking for a job in journalism or publishing. When she read in a newspaper that Zachary Scott was living in the city, she called him up. "Right away, he sent me to the editor of *Modern Screen* magazine, who said I had a virile style," she recalled in her interview with Sherrye Henry. "I didn't know what that meant and was too afraid to look it up, but he hired me on the spot for $50 a week." To supplement her salary sufficiently to enable her to attend the theatre regularly, she did proofreading for *Newsweek* magazine nights and on weekends. At some point in her career she also worked as a publicist for the singer and comedienne Kaye Ballard.

Between 1953 and the early 1960s Liz Smith was, successively, an associate producer of the broadcasts that Mike Wallace, the news commentator and interviewer, was then doing on CBS radio in New York; an associate producer of *Wide, Wide World* on NBC television; and a ghostwriter for Igor Cassini's "Cholly Knickerbocker" gossip column in the New York *Journal-American*. She was entertainment editor of *Cosmopolitan* from 1964 to 1966, when she became film editor of that magazine. Quotations from her *Cosmopolitan* reviews in movie ads made her name a familiar one in the entertainment industry in the late 1960s and early 1970s. In addition, as a staff writer for *Sports Illustrated* (1966–67) and as a free-lance contributor to *New York, Ladies' Home Journal, American Home, Vogue, Esquire, Today's Health,* and other magazines, she wrote on a variety of subjects including boating, nudist cults, the psychology of fashion, the "fabulous Ford women," Elizabeth Taylor's trove of jewelry, and the travails and triumphs of Jacqueline Kennedy Onassis and her children and stepchildren.

When the editors at the New York *Daily News* and its syndicate (now the Chicago Tribune Syndicate) in 1975 decided to introduce a new column, they looked for someone with a friendly tone that would cut across demographic lines. Passing over some better-known writers, they were attracted to Liz Smith chiefly because of her easy and comfortable style and her sense of humor. "I'd had enough of those bitchy and brittle columnists," one of the editors later explained. "I wanted fresh air."

When offered the job, Miss Smith wondered if gossip wasn't "a washed-up genre" and part of her "recoiled at the idea of doing such a column." "Part of me still does," she confessed to Harry Stein, a contributing editor of *Esquire* (August 1979). "God knows, it had never been my ambition to be a gossip columnist. I mean, I was never particularly intrigued by show business celebrities. . . . I really want most of them to leave me alone, so I can go talk to writers, which is what I really enjoy. Writers are madmen—they're all secretly in the closet, jerking off their egos—but there's something rewarding and vulnerable about them."

In the end she "just couldn't resist getting such an important forum in America's largest newspaper and best tabloid." Also, as she confessed to Harry Stein, she "would make more money than [she had] ever imagined making" and she "knew it would be the last chance for [her] professionally" because "after all, [she was] not a kid anymore." "Properly scared to death" when she wrote her first columns because she was not sure that the editors were right in bringing back "a real old-fashioned gossip column to a newspaper that once had Bob Sylvester, Danton Walker, Hedda Hopper, and Ed Sullivan writing for it at one time," she was elated when "people responded instantly well" to the column.

The first column appeared in February 1976. The problem in the beginning was a relative paucity of sources, as she recounted in a retrospective article in the *Daily News* on the column's tenth anniversary. She had "a few highly placed friends who might give [her] a tip or two," but she wondered "whence would come the needed grist for this mill of gossip, which would grind inexorably if successful?" Writing the column was like "riding a tiger; one is afraid to get off!" Recalling how "the good souls" in the fundamentalist religion in which she had grown up used to say that "the Lord will provide," she wrote: "He did, along with many press agents, tipsters, and the people Carl Bernstein dubbed 'the truthsayers.' A routine developed—many phone calls, lots of background reading, too much going out looking for news and happenings." The paper promoted her column with a huge blowup of her face on its delivery trucks and a caption suggesting that she *had* to be read. As readership grew, many readers themselves became tipsters of sorts, mailing in suggestions for items or quotations.

While she wanted her column to be "the most inexpensive and lively entertainment in town," Liz Smith also wanted, when possible, to offer her readers harder news, scoops in the tradition of Dorothy Kilgallen, without using her column as a base for power-punditry and ego-aggrandizement in the way that Walter Winchell and some others of Miss Kilgallen's era had used theirs. In March 1976 she broke sensational prepublication details from *The Final Days,* Bob Woodward and Carl Bernstein's book about the twilight of President Richard Nixon's administration, just before the book was excerpted in *Newsweek.* Six months later, after sources at the National Broadcasting Company leaked information to her about troubles brewing in the executive suite there, she published that information. Her editor yanked the NBC story after the first edition of the *Daily News* that day, but the column went out over the syndication wire and received wide reaction around the country. Through Jack Martin, her legman in Los Angeles, meanwhile, she was regularly scooping the Hollywood press on news breaks in its own yard (not one of the sixty markets in which she was then syndicated).

In February 1977 Miss Smith's appearances in the *Daily News* were increased from three to six per week. At that time David Gelman, writing in *Newsweek* (February 28, 1977), credited her with bringing "fresh vigor and even a touch of compunction" to a "shameless old genre." "Smith has scruples about reporting the seamier doings of the celebrity demi-monde . . . but she laces her niceness with just enough bitchiness to keep the franchise." While granting that "inevitably, Smith has detractors," Gelman quoted in her favor such colleagues as the journalist James Brady ("Liz just doesn't have that killer instinct. She's really a good ole gal"). Gelman described Miss Smith spending two hours on the phone trying to check out a rumor about the imminent demotion of a prominent theatre critic. Worried that the critic would be "hurt" by the story, which she did not succeed in verifying, she agonized overnight before deciding to use a muted version of it. Miss Smith described herself to Gelman as "a typically puritan hedonist."

In an interview with Kitty Hanson, a colleague of hers on the *Daily News* (May 14, 1978), Liz Smith said that while people have always been interested in the doings of others, especially celebrities, gossip journalism owed its current surge in popularity, in her opinion, to our being "in a period of soft news." "We're not in a war," she explained. "The student unrest, the time of assassinations—that's over. There's only the normal amount of political malfeasance in office. And the country, thank God, is not in the grip of terrorists and revolt. So people turn to trivia." Laughing, the columnist told Miss Hanson: "I'll never get a Pulitzer. I don't like to take it [her column] seriously. I'm always surprised when other people do. On the other hand, I've had some good scoops and I like staying ahead of the competition."

One of the scoops, if it may be called that (there had been some previous press exposure), was the story of the high-echelon embezzlement at Columbia Pictures in 1977 and the temporarily successful effort of the board of directors of Columbia's parent company to cover it up. In his book on the subject, *Indecent Exposure* (1982), David McClintock acknowledged that "one of the most important catalysts" in bringing the scandal into the "focus of a major media onslaught" was the story by Liz Smith titled "And Now Folks, 'Hollywoodgate,'" published on January 12, 1978. "The scandal at Columbia Pictures was not certified as major news until it was addressed at length by Liz Smith," McClintock wrote. "By devoting the bulk of her col-

umn to the subject [she] drew more attention to it than the combined enterprise of [such giants as] the *Wall Street Journal* [and] the *Washington Post*." She remained on the "Hollywoodgate" story in subsequent columns, including one based on an exclusive two-hour interview with the actor Cliff Robertson, a victim of the embezzlement and a key figure in its disclosure, who told her that after discovering that someone had forged and cashed a $10,000 Columbia Pictures official check in his name he came to fear for his life and for the safety of his wife and daughter.

In 1978 Miss Smith began doing her twice-weekly news commentary on WNBC-TV in New York City. Barbara Costikyan, writing in *Cosmopolitan* (September 1981), described a broadcast in which Liz, beginning a discussion of the prime-time soap opera *Dallas*, decided to add some local color. "In mid-sentence, she suddenly stopped short. 'Oops,' she drawled. 'Forgot mah hat.' Reaching under the table, she pulled out a fancy Stetson, plunked it atop her head, lowered the brim so the whites of her eyes hardly showed, and finished the item Texas-style." Miss Costikyan went on to generalize: "Clowning around, making people laugh, is Liz Smith's way with the news. She does it on camera and she does it in print. All sorts of people feel comfortable with her; she's everybody's neighbor, no matter what the neighborhood. To the smart set on both coasts, she's a sophisticated journalist plugged in at the highest level. To the people who live and work in between, her common sense and self-deprecating humor are on their wave-length. 'She's my kind of gal,' says an Illinois housewife. 'I could just love her.'"

In her 1978 interview with Kitty Hanson, Miss Smith described herself as "an information magpie, a writer-collector" who can't let go "of a scrap of information, an interesting observation, or just a lone little fact in search of publication." Inspired by her friend the theatrical director Burt Shevelove's dinner-table tales about his mother, she began collecting proverbs and other sayings, anecdotes, memoirs—everything she heard or read about mothers and motherhood. Over a period of five years she collected a huge mass of material from which she culled *The Mother Book*, a lively potpourri of "facts, fancies, overblown sentimentalities, sociological speculations . . . literature, pieties, profundities, and curiosities." Published by Doubleday in May 1978, the book was in its third printing by June, and a Bantam paperback edition was issued the following year. While critical of an occasional "breezy flippancy that is sometimes annoying, sometimes tasteless," Margo Jefferson of *Newsweek* (May 22, 1978) found the book to be similar to Miss Smith's "best columns and articles . . . a shrewd mix of frivolity, seriousness, chit-chat and social commentary" that was "instructive, informative, and entertaining." Barbara Grizzuti Harrison, the reviewer for the *Saturday Review* (May 13, 1978), found some "chaff" in the book but thought that in her own memoir about her mother Miss Smith was "close to first rate—honest, tough-minded, sweet, and enormously likable."

Because of her relative benignity by the standards of her craft, Liz Smith is *persona grata* with most celebrities. A notable exception is the singer and actor Frank Sinatra. When the writer and radio disc jockey Jonathan Schwartz suddenly went on a premature sabbatical from station WNEW-AM in New York City in 1980, many persons close to the situation knew that Sinatra, a friend of the board chairman of Metromedia, the owner of the station, had been furious over Schwartz's on-air handling of one of his recordings, and they were convinced that he was a causal agent in Schwartz's sudden departure. When Liz Smith gave their side of the story in her column, asking, "Who the hell does Frank Sinatra think he is?," Sinatra sent her a scathing telegram (which she published) and proceeded for some time to attack her verbally virtually everwhere he appeared, including the stage of Carnegie Hall. Miss Smith, who seems able to maintain her dignity in any storm, responded by observing, as quoted in *People* (May 5, 1980), "He [Sinatra] is terribly spoiled and powerful, and he doesn't react well to criticism."

Miss Smith, who began her column at a salary of $50,000, had a gross annual income of $100,000 by the early 1980s. On the way to and from Greece in the summer of 1981, her itinerary included, typically, the royal palace in Monaco and Franco Zeffirelli's villa in Positano, Italy. "She gets invited to parties that have dash, zip, names," Barbara Costikyan reported in her *Cosmopolitan* article, enumerating: "Barbara Walters' small Christmas do; Zeffirelli's lavish party at Hisae's, a health-food restaurant that draws the glitterati . . . ; [and] the surrealistic benefit given by Allan Carr for the Variety Clubs International production . . . at Lincoln Center. . . . Liz's night life makes good copy because she can reduce awesome action and heady celebrity to down-home talk." Miss Costikyan quoted Liz Smith regarding Elaine's restaurant, the Manhattan mecca for some of the biggest names in literature and journalism (including *New York Times* reporters, who are among her most important tipsters) as well as show business: "I could rip out my telephone and just go to Elaine's for my messages."

When Miss Costikyan visited her high-rise apartment in the Murray Hill section of Manhattan, Miss Smith was dressed in "her standard preppie work clothes of freshly pressed chinos and pastel Oxford shirt," sitting hunched over the word processor with video display on which she composes her copy and transmits it directly to the *Daily News* and the Chicago Tribune Syndicate, "mumbling to herself the words she is putting down, her shoulder-length hair bobbing with each stroke of the keys." "As Liz works, the telephones jangle without mercy and her pet cats doze in the letter baskets," Miss Costikyan wrote. "She is so absorbed that when she breaks for lunch at one o'clock, she collides with the office door and doesn't even realize it." According to Miss Costikyan, Liz Smith's telephone bill was $600 a month and her restaurant bills were "astronomical."

Among her other expenses was the salary of her assistant, St. Clair Pugh, known as Saint, who takes her calls, checks facts, and proofreads and edits her copy, helping with a phrase here and there and fine-tuning her innuendoes.

When Literacy Volunteers, a nonprofit educational organization that tutors adults and teenagers in reading and writing, lost its federal funding because of Reagan administration cutbacks, Miss Smith contributed time, energy, and column space to fund-raising for the group. For her contribution to that cause she was the guest of honor at an all-star benefit production at the Shubert Theatre on Broadway on January 13, 1983. Among those who performed or otherwise participated was Claudette Colbert, who called Miss Smith "one of the kindest people" she had ever met. "More than anyone else, Liz has made things happen for us," Dianne Kangisser, the executive director of Literacy Volunteers, said. "The majority of New Yorkers have not been aware that one out of five English-speaking adults in the city lacks critical reading and writing skills."

At the elite Manhattan nightclub Studio 54 on February 11, 1986, Liz Smith was subjected to a "roast" for the benefit of the Women's Action Alliance, a nonprofit national group that promotes full equality for women. Among those taking part were Iris Love ("Liz resembles my favorite person, the dolphin. Like him, she is intelligent, curious, willing to learn, and ready to save everyone and everything") and Gloria Steinem ("Only Liz has turned gossip into kindness and support for justice and humor"). In her turn at the microphone, Miss Smith said that "a roast is a piece of cake" for someone like her, whose craft requires her daily to "tell the truth and be entertaining, and not be sued." Among Miss Smith's other causes have been the New York Public Library and an information center in Manhattan for poets and writers.

Liz Smith rises at about nine each morning, except on the two days a week when Vincent Roppatte, her hairdresser, comes to her apartment, when she gets up at seven. After pouring herself a cup of coffee, she feeds her dog and cats and goes into her office, a converted bedroom that is filled with mail, magazines, and books. A page from *Newsweek* with the headline "Gossip's Good Ole Gal" is framed on one wall. Pugh reports to her on phone calls and luncheon and other invitations, and reminds her of her commitments for the day, and begins going over with her the breaking news items and other grist for the column that will be published the following morning. After telephone conversations with such friends as Nora Ephron and Marie Brenner, Miss Smith works first on her column and then on her television script. After a lunch break, she answers mail, returns calls, and perhaps works on a special Sunday *Daily News* article or a free-lance piece for *Vogue*, *Cosmopolitan*, or *Interview*, until it is time to go to the NBC studio where the early-evening local newscast *Live at Five* is televised. Another person besides Pugh who helps her get her work done is

Denis Ferrara. "He [Ferrara] started writing us anonymous letters about Elizabeth Taylor," Pugh explained to Chris Chase, an interviewer for *Cosmopolitan* (June 1985). "He was the foremost authority on everything she [Miss Taylor] was doing." Ferrara told Chase: "Liz was one of the few journalists that Elizabeth Taylor would actually sit down and speak to."

Blue-eyed Liz Smith says that she inherited her Irish face from her grandmother. Miss Smith's second marriage, to a New York travel agent, was no more successful than her first had been. She describes both George Beeman and Fred Lister as "terrific guys," and she facetiously attributes her divorces to her own immaturity and inability to live up to the image of perfection she saw in Myrna Loy's conjugal screen portrayals. Psychoanalysis has helped her come to terms with herself and her success. "Listen," she has said, "if I didn't have this column, I would fade from sight and memory faster than Pia Zadora's last movie."

References: *Cosmopolitan* 191:240+ S '81 por, 198:228+ Je '85 por; *Celebrity Register* (1986); *Contemporary Authors* vols 65-68 (1977); *Who's Who in America*, 1986-87

Sprinkel, Beryl (Wayne)

Nov. 20, 1923- Economist; United States government official. Address: b. White House Old Executive Office Building, Washington, D.C. 20500; h. 1705 Brookwood Dr., Flossmoor, Ill. 60422

As undersecretary of the treasury for monetary affairs during the first Reagan administration (1981-85), Beryl Sprinkel was one of the chief architects of the president's controversial economic policies. Since 1985, when he became chairman of the Council of Economic Advisers, he has taken on a less abrasive if perhaps less influential role as a "team player" and cheerleader for the administration's policies. Sprinkel was widely considered to be a leading candidate for successor to Paul A. Volcker as chairman of the Federal Reserve Board, which governs the United States central bank and determines the nation's monetary policy. The prospect of his getting that job—which he surely must have coveted—were reduced, however, by the departure from the White House of his political mentor, presidential chief of staff Donald Regan, in the wake of the Iran-Contra affair. In June 1987 President Ronald Reagan chose Alan Greenspan to succeed Volcker.

A farmer's son, Beryl Wayne Sprinkel was born on November 20, 1923 to Clarence and Emma (Schooley) Sprinkel in Richmond, Missouri, a completely different milieu from the corporate boardrooms and international conference halls that he was later to frequent. A professional singer early in his career, he entered Northwest Missouri State University, in Maryville, Missouri, in 1941 with the intention of becoming a music major. After spending two years there, a year at the University of Oregon, in Eugene, Oregon, and two years in the United States Army, where he served as a tank gunner in World War II, Sprinkel enrolled at the University of Missouri, in Columbia, Missouri. He graduated in 1947 with a degree in public administration.

Sprinkel then embarked on his graduate studies at the University of Chicago, where he came under the influence of Milton Friedman, who was to win the 1976 Nobel Prize in Economics. Friedman subscribes to the theory that the money supply—and only the money supply—determines the rate of economic growth and inflation. Although Sprinkel is often considered to be a monetarist disciple of Friedman, the future Nobel laureate had not in fact fully evolved his theory at that time, and Sprinkel's convictions on the overriding importance of the money supply owe much to Harry Gunnison Brown, a University of Missouri professor who was one of the pioneering researchers on the subject.

In 1948 Sprinkel received a master's degree in business administration from the University of Chicago, and in 1952 he earned a Ph.D. degree in economics from the same institution. He then left academic life to join the staff of the Harris Trust and Savings Bank, one of Chicago's largest. During his twenty-eight-year career at the bank he became its director of research and eventually rose to the rank of executive vice-president. He wrote *Money* and Stock Prices (Irwin, 1964), Money and Markets: A Monetarist View (Dow Jones-Irwin, 1971), and with R. J. Genetski, collaborated on Winning With Money: A Guide for Your Future (Dow Jones-Irwin, 1977). In the articles that he contributed to professional journals he was often an outspoken critic of Federal Reserve Board policies.

Several of the themes that were later adopted by the Reagan administration were foreshadowed by Sprinkel in a U S News & World Report interview (July 30, 1979). In the course of it, he said he favored a tax cut, provided that it was accompanied by restraint in federal spending to hold down the deficit, which was forecast at $28.7 billion for fiscal 1980. In order to encourage savings and investment, Sprinkel recommended a reduction in the progressivity of the income tax system—a goal that was achieved in 1986, when the new tax law established only two basic rates—15 percent and 28 percent of taxable income.

In 1981 Sprinkel was appointed undersecretary of the treasury for monetary affairs by the incoming United States secretary of the treasury, Donald T. Regan, who explained, "I wanted the best monetarist I could get." In keeping with his monetarist principles, Sprinkel urged the Federal Reserve Board to tackle double-digit inflation by restricting the money supply. That is achieved chiefly by two means: by selling government securities on the open market, thereby reducing bank reserves and thus the ability of the banking system to create deposits, and by raising the required reserve ratio—the percentage of deposits that banks must maintain on reserve at the banks of the Federal Reserve system.

That policy was in fact being pursued by Paul A. Volcker and the other governors of the Federal Reserve Board when the Reagan administration took office, and it continued through 1981, producing the highest interest rates since the Civil War. The prime rate, the annual interest rate that banks charge their best corporate customers, was as high as 20.5 percent in 1981, and as a result of the difficulty of borrowing money, a deep recession developed in October 1981 that lasted for more than a year and raised the rate of unemployment to a level not seen since the Great Depression. The consumer price index, however, which rose 12.4 percent in 1980, increased by only 8.9 percent in 1981 and 3.9 percent in 1982. The inflationary spiral was broken, and in the view of economists like Sprinkel, economic suffering was necessary to reestablish stable prices.

The policy of tight money did not please the "supply-siders" within the Reagan administration—those who, like Sprinkel, supported the tax cut that was enacted in 1981 but opposed the tight-money policy that raised interest rates. Sprinkel also antagonized Wall Street by his frequent and highly vocal criticism of the Federal Reserve Board even when it seemed to be doing almost exactly what the Treasury Department wanted it to do. The points he was trying to make prodded the board into adopting a new accounting system that gives it tighter control over bank reserves.

Sprinkel was also unpopular abroad, where he spent much of his time trying to sell American policy to skeptical European central bankers who complained that high interest rates in the United States were driving up the dollar and forcing them to raise their own interest rates in order to maintain the value of their own currencies. In no uncertain terms, Sprinkel rejected the idea that the United States Treasury should intervene in foreign-exchange markets to keep the dollar from rising. Sprinkel's no-nonsense views won him the epithet "Beryl the Peril" among his detractors—although his friends explained that the proper pronunciation, Midwestern style, sounding like "Burl," would make it more appropriate to call him "Beryl the Pearl."

It was during that period that Beryl Sprinkel volunteered a succinct definition of monetarism, which was to his critics a sample of his intellectual arrogance, when he said in a speech, "Only money matters. Control the money supply and everything else falls into place. Thank you, and good night." His statement was shorthand for the monetarist creed: insure a steady but slow (to avoid inflation) growth of the money supply in order to modulate economic growth; let the marketplace establish interest rates and currency values; and avoid tinkering with fiscal policy by increasing or cutting taxes and by raising or lowering government expenditures to deal with particular situations. Interviewed by Desirée French for Forbes magazine (November 9, 1981), Sprinkel said, "The beauty of looking at money as an explanation is that it works for all times and people."

In a speech he delivered before the International Law Institute on December 17, 1981, Sprinkel called the turn for the next few years. "We are now in a period of decelerating inflation," he said, "and investors have begun to sell their tangible assets [like houses, antiques, and gold] and put their money in financial assets [such as stocks and bonds]. . . . The result of this change in investment decisions is an increase in the supply of credit available for investment in financial assets, and therefore, lower interest rates. . . . Therefore, if monetary growth remains under control and inflationary expectations continue to abate, rising deficits will not be translated into rising interest rates." And, in fact, the prime had dropped to 11 percent by the end of 1982 in spite of the growing federal deficit, while the Dow Jones index for the New York Stock Exchange broke through the 1,000 barrier, heralding the impending bull market.

Sprinkel continued to nettle foreign bankers, however. At the annual joint meeting of the International Monetary Fund and World Bank in Toronto, Canada, on September 8, 1982, he urged the two international lending agencies to be chary of extending new loans to debtor nations in spite of the growing crisis enveloping nations such as Mexico. Declaring that the lending agencies had been too lenient in the past, he said, "It's not our job to make sure that no bank loses capital. . . . We do not want to throw good money after bad."

By early 1983 Sprinkel was becoming too outspoken even for Regan's taste. At a conference of the International Monetary Fund held in Paris in January 1983, Sprinkel was quoted as saying that in order to deal with the world debt crisis, other Western nations and Japan would have to join with the United States in stimulating their economies, giving rise to the impression that Washington was shifting its priority from fighting inflation to stimulating growth. That impression was not, in fact, mistaken, but Sprinkel had upstaged Regan, who was en route to Paris, and he was reprimanded by his superior. According to a colleague who was quoted in *Newsweek* (March 4, 1985), "Beryl learned the headlines were for Donald, and he has remained pretty much under wraps ever since."

With inflation seemingly vanquished and the 1984 election campaign underway, Regan and Sprinkel sniped at the Federal Reserve Board for not, in their estimation, relaxing monetary controls. After the departure of Martin Feldstein, the chairman of the Council of Economic Advisers, who had antagonized the Reagan administration by repeatedly calling for a tax hike to reduce the deficit, Sprinkel was tapped to act as a general spokesman for economic policy. Just before the election, he averaged about three speeches a week, some of which were arranged by the Reagan-Bush campaign committee.

In early 1985 Donald T. Regan traded jobs with the White House chief of staff, James A. Baker, and on February 21 Beryl Sprinkel was nominated chairman of the Council of Economic Advisers. That body, which provides economic advice for the president and issues an annual report to Congress, rarely ventures into the formulation of policies. Instead it provides the analytical support for current policies or for policies that the administration might adopt later. The Council of Economic Advisers had been moribund since Feldstein's resignation in 1984, and Reagan had even raised the possibility that it would be abolished. Beryl Sprinkel downplayed his new role. "The president is his own chief economic adviser," he told William Gruber of the *Chicago Tribune* (October 13, 1985). "He has a degree in economics, you know, and his grasp of situations is amazing."

Under Sprinkel, the Council of Economic Advisers erred on the side of optimism in making its predictions for 1985 and 1986. For 1985 the Council predicted 4 percent economic growth. Although the actual pace lagged sharply in the first half of the year, Sprinkel predicted a 5 percent growth rate for the second half of the year. The actual growth rate for 1985 turned out to be 2.3 percent. For 1986 the Council again predicted a 4 percent growth rate, but the actual figure was barely above 2 percent.

To fuel greater economic activity, Sprinkel had been expecting a rapid growth in the money supply, and in early 1986 the Council criticized the Federal Reserve Board for allowing a key component of the money supply to grow by 12 percent in 1985. But any fear of inflation was dispelled when

1986 saw the smallest increase in the cost of living since 1961, mainly because of lower oil prices. The Federal Reserve Board cut the discount rate (the rate at which member banks borrow from the system) four times in 1986, reducing it to the lowest level in nine years.

In July 1986 Sprinkel conceded that the new forms of money created by financial deregulation in the late 1970s and early 1980s, particularly interest on bank checking account deposits and new forms of economic behavior during the low-inflation 1980s, had made monetarism difficult to apply. Because of lower inflation and declining interest rates, Americans were less anxious to buy something today on the ground that it would cost more tomorrow, and they were keeping money in checking accounts longer because they were less worried about losing interest. In other words, the most "active" money supply (M-1, cash plus checking account deposits) was proving larger than expected but lacked "velocity"—that is, it was being spent at a slower rate. Because the Federal Reserve Board had come to the same conclusion, in July 1986 it abandoned setting an official target for M-1. In December, Sprinkel declared reassuringly, "We have no concern about present monetary policy." His forecast of a real annual growth of 3.2 percent for 1987 seemed to be holding up through the first half of the year.

Despite the popular perception of him, Sprinkel once said during an interview granted to the *New York Times* (July 21, 1980). "I never looked upon myself as an ideological monetarist." In fact, he deeply resents the opinion that he is an ideologue. "I guess that's the thing that blows my fuse the fastest," he told Art Pine of the *Wall Street Journal* (June 13, 1982), "because it implies that I don't look at the evidence. But the fact is, I do." Lawrence Kudlow, the chief economist with the Wall Street brokerage firm of Bear, Stearns, & Company, has said: "Beryl has softened his views quite a bit, and he has done so honestly."

Although his recent flexibility may have boosted Sprinkel's stock within the administration, where supply-siders remain influential, the departure of Donald T. Regan from the White House was a serious blow. According to Alex Brummer in the *Manchester Guardian* weekly (January 25, 1987), Regan had let it be known that Sprinkel was the "odds on" favorite to take over the helm of the Federal Reserve Board when Volcker's term expired in August 1987. Sprinkel lost another round politically when Ronald Reagan decided to back a health-insurance plan to deal with catastrophic illness that Sprinkel had called "inconsistent with the administration's policies to . . . use private-sector solutions whenever possible."

Perhaps because he was disappointed that he was not chosen to succeed Volcker, Sprinkel submitted his resignation on September 14, 1987, to become effective in November. As factors behind his decision, he cited "personal reasons" and a desire to return to private life. But when, on October 29, Reagan refused to accept his resignation and raised his post of chief economic adviser to cabinet-level, Sprinkel agreed to stay on for an "indefinite" period. He mentioned the recent Wall Street meltdown and the uncertain economic future of the country as two of the reasons that prompted his decision.

Beryl Sprinkel is a short, stocky, and somewhat bald man whose exposure to the cosmopolitanism of the world's capitals has left no noticeable mark on him. According to a Treasury aide, "On trips abroad he never changes money because he never has time to spend it. He goes to his dinners, he goes to his meetings, and he goes to his hotel to sleep." In Washington he has been known to appear in his office in checked suit and Western boots instead of the standard banking official's uniform of pinstripes and wingtips. Murray Weidenbaum, Reagan's first chairman of the Council of Economic Advisers, shared an apartment in Washington with Beryl Sprinkel during the first seven months of the Reagan administration, while they awaited the ar-

rivals of their wives. "I think of him as a plain-speaking Missouri farm boy," Weidenbaum told Peter T. Kilborn of the New York Times (February 22, 1985). "Beryl doesn't lie because he doesn't know how to. He appears gruff and plain because he doesn't know how not to. He's also a caring and considerate good guy."

By his first marriage, to Esther Pollard, on September 7, 1947, Beryl Sprinkel has two children: Gary and Kevin. By his second, to Barbara Angus Pipher, on May 31, 1970, he has two stepchildren, Debra and Pamela. The Sprinkels currently live in McLean, Virginia, where they go bicycle riding and play tennis and golf in their rare leisure time. Sprinkel's other avocational interests include singing and lecturing. He is a Baptist and a Republican.

References: N Y Times D p1+ F 22 '85 por, p12 Ag 9 '85 por, D p1+ Jl 3 '86 por; Wall St J p54 Jl 13 '82 por; Contemporary Authors 1st rev vols 11–12 (1974); Who's Who in America, 1986–87

Stone, Oliver

Sept. 15, 1946– Motion picture director; screenwriter. Address: b. 9025 Wilshire Blvd., Suite 301, Beverly Hills, Calif. 90211; b. c/o M/S Billings Publicity, Ltd., 250 W. 57th St., New York City, N.Y. 10107

The enormous critical and popular success of Oliver Stone's Vietnam war drama Platoon has propelled the young writer and director to the front rank of independent filmmakers in the United States. A searing portrait of jungle warfare and mo-

ral betrayal as seen through the eyes of a combat infantryman, Platoon, which Stone had based on his own wartime experiences in Vietnam, captured eight Academy Award nominations and four Oscars, including those for best director and best picture of 1986, and an Orson Welles Motion Picture Directorial Achievement Award as the best writer-director of an English-language film. In the same year, Stone also earned two Academy Award nominations for Salvador, a semidocumentary about civil unrest in Central America. The multiple honors augured a remarkable career turnaround for the director, whose reputation had until then rested almost entirely on his lurid screenplays for such controversial films as Midnight Express and Scarface.

The only child of Louis and Jacqueline (Goddet) Stone, Oliver Stone was born in New York City, on September 15, 1946. A successful stockbroker, Louis Stone was also the author and publisher of a monthly investors' newsletter on economics and politics written in a style that his son later described as "right-wing Walter Lippmann." Oliver Stone's boyhood, which was divided between homes in Manhattan and Connecticut, was one of wealth and privilege. He attended Trinity School, an elite day school on Manhattan's Upper East Side, then the Hill School, a college prep academy in Pottstown, Pennsylvania, and he regularly spent his summer vacations with his maternal grandparents in France. By his own account, he was an unruly youth—a temperamental cross between his ebullient, sociable mother and his reserved, pessimistic father. Stone's sheltered world collapsed during his junior year at the Hill School, when his parents divorced and he discovered that his father was deeply in debt. That traumatic turn of events, Stone later explained in an interview for a Time (January 26, 1987) profile, forced him to confront the values and way of life that he had taken for granted and eventually caused him to "break out of the mold" that was shaping him into an "East Coast socioeconomic product."

Inspired by Joseph Conrad's exotic tropical novel *Lord Jim*, he left Yale University after his freshman year, in 1965, to accept a job teaching English and history at the Free Pacific Institute, a Chinese School in Cholon, the ethnic Chinese district of what was then Saigon, South Vietnam. His arrival in Vietnam coincided with the first large-scale commitment of American ground troops to the escalating Indochinese conflict. "There were guys walking around with pistols, no curfews, shoot-outs in the streets," Stone recalled in the *Time* magazine interview. "The place was like Dodge City." After six months in that chaotic environment, Stone signed on as a merchant seaman on a tanker bound for the United States, then traveled on to Guadalajara, Mexico, where he began to work on a novel, tentatively titled "A Child's Night Dream," based on his adventures in Southeast Asia. Returning to Yale the following year, he devoted so much time to completing his novel that he neglected his courses. He finally dropped out of college a second time to concentrate on his writing. Unable to interest publishers in his mammoth Joycean opus, the despairing young author ended up throwing half of the manuscript into the East River.

At loose ends and seeking, in his words, "total anonymity," Stone enlisted in the United States Army in 1967 and specifically requested combat duty in Vietnam. Assigned to the 25th Infantry Division, he was initially "very gung-ho" about fighting Communism, but "about a day" after he joined his combat unit in the jungles near the Cambodian border, he realized that he had made a terrible mistake. "Nobody was motivated, except to get out," he recalled to the *Time* interviewer. "Survival was the key. It wasn't very romantic." Two weeks into his fifteen-month tour of duty, Stone was shot in the neck during a night ambush, and he later sustained several shrapnel wounds. For extraordinary acts of courage under fire (he once wiped out a Viet Cong machine-gun nest with a hand grenade), he was awarded a Bronze Star and a Purple Heart with Oak Leaf Cluster. During his months in the field, he also personally witnessed some of the atrocities committed against Vietnamese civilians by American soldiers that he was to re-create so chillingly in *Platoon*. "We killed a lot of innocents," he told the *Time* correspondent.

Discharged from the Army in 1968, Stone experienced the feelings of anger, guilt, and alienation common to many Vietnam combat veterans. "Vietnam completely deadened me and sickened me . . . ," he explained to Paul Attanasio in an interview for the *Washington Post* (January 11, 1987). "I came back very mixed up, very paranoid and very alienated." At the same time, Stone added, surviving the war "in a sort of paradoxical way did keep me optimistic. I did try to keep that faith, that I had made it out of there, and I had to try to do something with my life." He eventually decided to enroll at New York University's film school under the G.I. Bill. A hotbed of experimental filmmaking in the late 1960s, the NYU program offered the young veteran a new creative outlet and the opportunity to study with Martin Scorcese, the maverick motion picture director whom Stone has credited with helping him to "channel [his] rage." While at the university, Stone made two short films: *Last Year in Vietnam*, about a veteran wandering the New York streets, and *Michael and Marie*, a take-off on the gangster film genre.

After graduating from NYU with a bachelor of fine arts degree in 1971, Stone began writing screenplays. Two years later he sold his first effort, a horror story about a fantasy writer whose creations come to life, to a Canadian production company, which also awarded him the job of directing the movie on a miniscule $150,000 budget. Described by a reviewer for *Variety* (November 20, 1974) as "stylishly filmed but murkily plotted," *Seizure* (1974) was seen by most critics as a creditable debut. Nevertheless, Stone lapsed into what he has since called a "hibernative" period that lasted several years. During that time he consumed ample amounts of marijuana and the hallucinogen LSD and supported himself by working variously as a taxi driver, messenger, and photocopy-machine operator. In his spare time he managed to write eleven scripts, but failed to sell a single one. Finally, as the United States celebrated its Bicentennial in the summer of 1976, he "came out of this spin," as he put it, and settled down to the long-deferred task of exorcising his Vietnam war demons by drafting a foot soldier's view of that conflict.

The finished script, which was essentially the same one that he was to film ten years later as *Platoon*, became Stone's calling card when he moved to Hollywood in 1976, but with the Vietnam trauma still fresh in the nation's memory, motion picture producers unanimously rejected the grim narrative as a certain commercial failure. Some executives at Columbia Pictures, however, were sufficiently impressed by Stone's skill as a scenarist to hire him to write the script for *Midnight Express*, a low-budget drama based on the harrowing real-life experiences of a vacationing American college student, Billy Hayes, who escaped from a hellish Turkish prison after being jailed in the early 1970s for attempting to smuggle hashish out of the country. When it was released in 1978, the film, which was directed by Alan Parker and starred Brad Davis, aroused considerable controversy. Some critics, among them *Newsweek*'s David Ansen, who praised the movie as a "stirring document of human endurance," felt that the graphic violence, occasionally heavyhanded narrative, and deliberately exaggerated characters played an important part in the creation of a nightmarish world of systematic brutalization that reduced all human relationships to those of power and fear. Others, however, argued that *Midnight Express* was sensationalistic, racist, and gratuitously violent. Pauline Kael, for example, in her December 4, 1978 review for the *New Yorker*, complained that the film was little more than a "sadomasochistic revel," and the *Washington Post*'s Gary Arnold, in his review of October 28, 1978, accused the picture of setting "a new standard of shamelessness." Angered by the film's portrayal of Turkish officials as uniformly evil or corrupt, the Turkish government issued an official protest statement.

All the controversy helped make *Midnight Express* a commercial success and undoubtedly contributed to its five major Academy Award nominations. The sole winner among those five nominees, Oliver Stone collected the Oscar for best screenplay adaptation of 1978. His script also earned him Golden Globe and Writer's Guild awards. Suddenly in demand as a screenwriter, Stone, who was still determined to tell a realistic story about the Vietnam conflict, wrote a film adaptation of *Born on the Fourth of July*, a memoir by Ron Kovic, a paraplegic Vietnam war veteran, that was to star Al Pacino. Forced to drop the project when his financial backing fell through, he then contracted with Orion Productions to write and direct *The Hand* (1981), a suspense-horror hybrid based on Marc Brandel's novel *The Lizard's Tail* and starring Michael Caine as a cartoonist who, after losing his drawing hand in a freak accident, becomes obsessed by the idea that the severed extremity is stalking and killing his enemies. Critics were generally intrigued by the film's imaginative play between the psychological thriller and horror genres, but that ambiguity baffled audiences and contributed to *The Hand*'s disappointing performance at the box office. "I went from being very hot to being very cold," Stone recalled to Paul Attanasio. For the next four years, he was, by his own account, "unemployable" as a director.

Stone responded to this abrupt reversal of fortune with a dramatic change in his lifestyle. After penning the script for John Milius' pulp adventure-fantasy *Conan the Barbarian* (1982), which featured body-builder Arnold Schwarzenegger in the title role, he moved to Paris to shake off his growing drug dependency and escape the temptations of Hollywood's party scene. There, he began working on the screenplay for Brian de Palma's proposed remake of *Scarface*, Howard Hawks's classic 1932 gangster film. Updated to the 1980s, Stone's story, which he has described as his "farewell to drugs," centered around Tony Montana, a Cuban refugee who realizes his "American dream" by ruthlessly working his way to the top of the cocaine-smuggling industry in Florida before being destroyed by his own greed. With Al Pacino as Tony Montana, *Scarface* was released late in 1983. Because of its many explicit scenes of slaughter, it had barely escaped an "X" rating for excessive violence, but the resulting notoriety and generally unfavorable reviews proved to be a bonus at the box office, as viewers lined up to see what the fuss was about. Most critics agreed with Stanley Kauffmann of the *New Republic* (January 9, 1984) that the film was "overblown, banal, and vulgar," although a few sided with Vincent Canby, who, in his review

for the *New York Times* (December 9, 1983), judged *Scarface* to be "the most stylish and provocative—and maybe the most vicious—serious film about the American underworld" since *The Godfather*.

After completing *Scarface*, Stone struck a deal with producer Dino De Laurentiis to script, from a novel by Robert Daly, Michael Cimino's *Year of the Dragon* in exchange for De Laurentiis' promise to make *Platoon*. The Cimino film, about an obsessive white detective's one-man crusade to wipe out New York City's so-called "Chinese mafia" and its international drug-dealing network, was mauled by critics (the *New Yorker*'s Pauline Kael, for one, called it "hysterical, rabble-rousing pulp") and was boycotted by many Chinese-Americans, who denounced it as racist. A box-office flop, *Year of the Dragon* disappeared from movie theatres shortly after its release in mid-1985. Compounding Stone's disappointment, De Laurentiis reneged on his pledge to produce *Platoon* after failing to come up with an American distributor for the film.

Stone fared no better with his next project, *Eight Million Ways to Die* (1986), the film version of Lawrence Block's mystery novel about a former narcotics detective trying to retrieve his personal honor. After Stone submitted his script, Hal Ashby, the director, switched the setting from New York City to Los Angeles, changed key characters, and hired David Lee Henry to rewrite much of the dialogue. "I never saw the movie until it came out," Stone told Paul Attanasio. "I saw twenty minutes, I couldn't take it. I really shouldn't have my name on it. But my name was such trash anyway it doesn't matter."

Frustrated by these successive failures and eager to shed his image as a pulp writer, Stone set up shop as an independent writer-director. He found his first vehicle in some sketches his friend Richard Boyle, a free-lance journalist and photographer, had written about his experiences covering the civil war in El Salvador during the early 1980s. The semidocumentary script that Stone wrote in collaboration with Boyle followed the photojournalist on a kind of road trip to moral discovery, as he evolved from a cynical, pill-popping "war junkie" into an outspoken partisan willing to risk his life to expose human-rights abuses by security forces and by right-wing death squads linked to the United States-backed government. Stone's angry indictment of American policy in El Salvador found no support in Hollywood. "When I tried to sell it, my script was not just turned down—it was *hated*," the director recalled to Mike McGrady of *Newsday* (December 14, 1986). "People felt it was anti-American." Undaunted, Stone mortgaged his house and set out to produce the film himself. Eventually, however, he got the financial aid he needed from the British producer John Daly and Daly's Hemdale Film Corporation by offering to direct the movie for free.

Filmed on location in Mexico for under $5 million (an unusually low budget by Hollywood standards), *Salvador* (1986) starred James Woods in the role of Richard Boyle and Jim Belushi as his sleazy sidekick, Dr. Rock. Rapid pacing, abrupt editing, and hand-held camera work gave the film a tension-filled immediacy, and its occasionally savage humor served as an effective foil for its convincing re-creations of right-wing terrorist attacks, including the assassination of Archbishop Oscar Arnulfo Romero and the murders of four American churchwomen in 1980. Despite generally enthusiastic reviews, *Salvador*'s audience was limited at first by Hemdale's inability to secure the services of a major American distributor, but following the huge success of *Platoon*, it was rereleased to a wider range of movie theatres.

In the interview with Mike McGrady, Stone described *Salvador* as "one of those movies [he'd] go to [his] grave and be proud of." To conservative critics who accused him of manipulating the facts to suit a liberal political agenda, the director replied, as quoted by Mark Brennan in the London *Sunday Times* (January 18, 1987), "I may have juggled the facts because I had three years of tumult to cover in two hours, but in doing so, I don't believe that I violated the spirit of those three years in Salvadoran history." With regard to United States policy in Central America, he added, "It seems that we've completely betrayed the principles of the American Revolution, which called for a right to self-determination and, certainly, the right to revolution. We seem to have come down on the side of oppression."

On the merits of *Salvador*, Hemdale Film Corporation agreed to produce *Platoon*. Working fast lest his dream evaporate once again, Stone began filming *Platoon* in the Philippines immediately after completing *Salvador* and finished shooting in only fifty-four days. Although he was denied logistical and material cooperation by the United States Army because his script was deemed antimilitary, Stone went to great lengths to give his film detailed authenticity. He even subjected his young actors to a grueling, two-week jungle boot camp run by a former Marine drill instructor. As the first Vietnam combat veteran to direct a film about that war, Stone was intent on capturing the physical discomforts of heat, insects, and mud, the fatigue, and the soul-deadening boredom that made up so much of the infantryman's world. Other Vietnam veterans who viewed the finished film credited the director with an extraordinarily precise command of details, down to the way the men wore their dog tags and "customized" their uniforms.

Drawing heavily on his own wartime experiences for *Platoon*'s plot, Stone constructed his story around Chris Taylor, a college dropout who had volunteered for the Army to get a taste of "real life." Like Stone, Taylor quickly discovers that war is more than he bargained for. His first sight on arriving in Vietnam is of neat rows of body bags surrounded by a unit of haggard veterans. Shortly thereafter, on his first night patrol with his unit, he freezes with fear at the sight of the enemy and barely escapes death. Months later, Taylor participates in a "search and destroy" mission against a

village whose inhabitants are suspected of harboring Viet Cong guerrillas. In one of the film's most harrowing sequences, the American soldiers, maddened by the frustration of fighting a wily and all-but-invisible enemy, lash out at the civilians, club an old woman to death, and burn the entire village to the ground.

That brutal episode sets up a violent confrontation between two veteran platoon leaders— Sergeant Barnes (Tom Berenger), a grotesquely scarred Army "lifer" who has survived by turning himself into an invincible killing machine, and Sergeant Elias (Willem Dafoe), the romantic, resourceful renegade who is the conscience of the company. Taylor feels as if these two strong and charismatic leaders are "fighting for possession" of his soul, and his attraction to each is graphically illustrated during the village assault, when he angrily fires his rifle at the feet of a petrified villager, but later stops his comrades from gang-raping some Vietnamese girls. (Both episodes were drawn from Stone's own experience.) The moral conflict, embodied in the characters of Barnes and Elias, reaches its deadly resolution as the Americans fight both the Vietnamese and each other in the chaotic nighttime battle that is the climax of the film.

"*Platoon* is the first real Vietnam film and one of the greatest war movies of all time," David Halberstam, who won a Pulitzer Prize for his coverage of the Vietnam war, observed, as quoted in the *Time* magazine cover story about the film. "The other Hollywood Vietnam films have been a rape of history. But *Platoon* is historically and politically accurate. . . . I think the film will become an American classic. Thirty years from now, people will think of the Vietnam war as *Platoon*." Film critics praised the movie for its brilliant ensemble acting and for its technical expertise, particularly its brilliance in capturing the fear-drenched silences and blindingly swift assaults characteristic of guerrilla warfare. Those who disliked the picture tended to object most to Taylor's "stupefying" and "redundant" voice-over narration and to the "haranguing righteousness" and "simpleminded moral schemata" of the film as a whole.

Platoon's impact on the general public went far beyond its merits or demerits as a film to take on a broad political significance. Within two months of its release in December 1986, *Platoon* was the top-grossing film in the country. As several political commentators observed, with the passions of Vietnam fading and the Central American conflicts heating up, Americans appeared to be ready to confront a realistic movie that raised basic questions about counterinsurgency war. *Platoon*'s unexpected success suggested to some that "Rambomania"—the public's fascination with the cartoonishly indestructible hero of a series of Vietnam revenge-fantasies starring Sylvester Stallone—could not be seen as an endorsement of military adventurism in real life. The original screenplays of *Platoon* and *Salvador* were published by Vintage in 1987 under the title *Oliver Stone's Platoon and Salvador*.

After picking up his Oscars for *Platoon*, Stone turned his attention to the takeover battles and merger wars in the high-stakes world of corporate finance. Tentatively titled "Wall Street," the film, which Stone coauthored with Stanley Weiser, stars Michael Douglas as a successful trader who has a corrupting influence on his protégé, played by Charlie Sheen. "I'm interested in contrasting the old ethics with the new ones," Stone explained, as quoted in the trade paper *Variety* (February 11, 1987). The film, shot on location in New York, was scheduled for release in December 1987.

Oliver Stone is a broad-shouldered, powerfully built man of medium height with a ruggedly handsome face, receding black hair, and a broad, gap-toothed grin. Feisty and energetic, he is said to thrive on creative arguments, and he has a reputation for being brutally honest on the set. According to his wife, the former Elizabeth Cox, his assistant on *The Hand* whom he married on June 7, 1981, Stone is a "compulsive worker, always reading or writing." "He simply loves ideas," she said, as quoted in the *Time* article. "He's filled with them, and he's thrilled with them." Stone's first marriage, to Najwa Sarkis, a Lebanese national, ended in divorce. The Stones live with their son, Sean, in a spacious house in Santa Monica, California.

References: London Sunday Times p49 Ja 18 '87 por; N Y Times III p8 My 15 '81 por, C p13 Ap 13 '87 por; Newsday II p9+ D 14 '86 pors; Rolling Stone p23+ Ja 29 '87 por; Time 129:59+ Ja 26 '87 pors; Washington Post H p1+ Ja 11 '87 por; Who's Who in America, 1986-87

Stone, Robert (Anthony)

Aug. 21, 1937– Writer. Address: b. c/o Candida Donadio & Associates, 111 W. 57th St., New York City, N.Y. 10017; c/o Alfred A. Knopf, 201 E. 50th St., New York City, N.Y. 10022

While Robert Stone's locale keeps changing from novel to novel, as he targets New Orleans, Vietnam and California, Central America, and Hollywood on location in Mexico, his theme and moral concern abide—what is happening to America today. Regardless of their settings, his four novels, *A Hall of Mirrors* (1967), *Dog Soldiers* (1974), *A Flag for Sunrise* (1981), and *Children of Light* (1986), all create an appalling, drug-ridden world of brutality, violence, and despair, where decency has only a slim chance of survival. *Newsweek*'s literary critic, Walter Clemons, regards Stone as "the strongest novelist of the post-Vietnam era," and Joseph Epstein in a *Commentary* analysis justifies so high an evaluation of Stone's work: "His prose has what Marianne Moore once called fiber: it is strong and flexible. He does landscapes and cityscapes with great artistry. He has keen ventriloquial qualities and can speak out of the mouths and minds of a vast range of characters. . . . He has a novelist's gift of sympathetic imagination, especially for the down and out. . . . And he can persuasively describe the world for us as it is seen through a drug-induced perspective."

Robert Anthony Stone was born on August 21, 1937, in south Brooklyn, New York City, to C. Homer and Gladys Catherine (Grant) Stone. When, many years later, he learned from his mother that she and his father had not been married, he thought of their relationship as having been "very romantic." He had never known his father, who escaped from domestic responsibilities in his son's infancy. Robert's early life, therefore, was principally affected by his mother and her family of Scottish Presbyterians and Irish Catholics who earned their living as tugboat workers in New York's harbor.

Stone's mother was a teacher in an elementary school, but lost her job because of schizophrenia. When able to, she worked as a chambermaid in Manhattan's Savoy Plaza Hotel and made a home for her son in cheap rooming houses and welfare hotels. For a few years, beginning at the age of five or six, he lived in an orphanage. But despite the uncertainty of his environment and his sense of its being different from that of other boys, Stone has said that his childhood was not unhappy. He attended a parochial school in Manhattan and the Archbishop Malloy High School. "One thing the Catholic school system did for me was to really teach me how to read and write thoroughly and grammatically," he told Charles Ruas in an interview that appears in Ruas' *Conversations with American Writers* (1984).

As early as the age of ten, Stone has recalled, he learned a lesson about prose style from reading Thomas Carlyle's *The French Revolution*. His teachers, later on, in the art of fiction included Joseph Conrad, John Dos Passos, Ernest Hemingway, F. Scott Fitzgerald, and Nathanael West. "Always kind of in love with language," to quote his phrase, he tried to give narrative form to his experiences in order to make sense out of them. One of his short stories won a contest for high school students, but his adolescent years seem to have been otherwise unpraiseworthy. He clashed with the Marist Brothers and had to quit school before graduation, having disgraced himself by drinking too much beer and being "militantly atheistic."

In 1955 Stone enlisted in the United States Navy, where he served first as a radioman and then as a journalist for the United Force Press Service. He reported on an expedition to Antarctica, among other events. On leaving the Navy in 1958, he enrolled in New York University, but soon gave up studying to take a job as an editorial assistant for the New York *Daily News*. After a year or two he moved on to New Orleans, yielding to a "romantic" impression he had of that city as a colorful haven for oddballs. There he wrote poetry, which he read to jazz accompaniment in the French Quarter, and worked at various jobs—in a coffee factory, on the piers for the Merchant Marine, and as an actor on the radio. He also learned much about the different sections of the city and their inhabitants by helping to take the New Orleans census in 1960.

On the merits of the first chapters of a projected novel that he began to write on his return to New York in 1962, Stone was awarded a Stegner fellowship in the creative writing program at Stanford University. Living in Menlo Park, California, he succumbed—momentairly, at least—as readily to the lifestyle of Ken Kesey's "acid-dropping" Merry Pranksters as he had to that of the alcoholic, marijuana-smoking beatniks he had known in New Orleans. He became acquainted with such counterculture spokesmen as Neal Cassady, Jack Kerouac, and Allen Ginsberg, and he was aboard the Merry Pranksters bus on the 1964 cross-country trip recounted by Tom Wolfe in *The Electric Kool-Aid Acid Test* (1968).

"As far as I'm concerned, what was going on was a lot of extremely pleasant goofing. It was just a crazy time," Stone reminisced in a talk with Eric James Schroeder that was published in *Modern Fiction Studies* (Spring 1984). Through his own experimentation with drugs in the early 1960s, however, he came to confront his deep-rooted religious sensibility. Curt Suplee, who interviewed him for the *Washington Post* (November 15, 1981), quoted him as saying, "I discovered that my way of seeing the world was always going to be religious—not intellectual or political—viewing everything as a mystic process."

It was, moreover, during that period of involvement in the drug culture that Stone reached a greater clarification of his vision of America, which he was to make the subject of his books. Rheinhardt, the protagonist of his first novel, *A Hall of Mirrors* (Houghton, 1967), is a broadcaster for a right-wing radio station, a misfit and a drifter who missed his chance to become an excellent musician. Freaked out, as usual, on alcohol and marijuana, he makes a statement at a political rally that Joseph Epstein, writing in *Commentary* (March 1982), pinpointed as the theme of all Stone's novels: "The American way is innocence. In all situations we must and shall display an innocence so vast and awesome that the entire world will be reduced by it. American innocence shall rise in mighty clouds of vapor to the scent of heaven and confound the nations!"

For the setting of *A Hall of Mirrors*, and for his metaphor of America, Stone chose New Orleans because it seemed to him that conditions of life throughout the country reached their extremity in that city. Arriving in New Oreleans in the spring of 1962, Rheinhardt falls in with two other young newcomers, Geraldine, a rural Southern girl whose face has been scarred by her psychotic former boyfriend, and Rainey, a misguided, faith-hungry social worker. All three are outcasts, lost souls who become the dupes and tools of a power-grabbing racist and superpatriot in staging a demonstration that explodes into a catastrophe.

Critical reception of *A Hall of Mirrors* corresponded to the selection of Stone as winner in 1968 of the William Faulkner Foundation Award for a "notable first novel." Many reviewers admired the author's narrative skill and language facility, and Emile Capouya in *Commonweal* (April 5, 1968) called attention to the strength of characterization in developing what he found to be "the unspoken theme" of the novel: "The relation between the prosperous official society and its necessary underworld of drop-outs and cast-offs." In his comments for the *New York Times Book Review* (September 24, 1967) Ivan Gold credited Stone with "an ear which encompasses the dictions of hippies, and senators, and a good portion of the worlds in between; which seems incapable of producing or reproducing a line of dialogue which does not ring true." A film adaptation of *A Hall of Mirrors* was released by Paramount Pictures in 1970 with the title *WUSA*. Stone wrote the script, but had no control over the finished product, which, despite the efforts of its star, Paul Newman, who considered it his "most significant film and the best," was not a success.

Partly with the help of a Guggenheim fellowship, Stone went to London in 1971 resolving to work there on his second novel. But inasmuch as his intended subject was America, he became aware that he should see for himself what was going on in Vietnam, where United States troops were deeply involved. The London biweekly *Ink*, a newly founded imitation of the *Village Voice*, supplied him accreditation as a correspondent. During his two months in Vietnam he witnessed little actual combat, but he has said that what he found out about the drug trade in Saigon was as disturbing to him as anything on the firing line. His reports on Vietnam appeared in the summer of 1971 in the Manchester *Guardian*, instead of *Ink*, which had proved to be short-lived.

Returning to the United States later in 1971, Stone observed with a heightened perspective the corrupting impact of the Vietnam War on American society. The changes he discerned together with his knowledge of the Saigon drug scene decided the content of *Dog Soldiers* (Houghton, 1974). Stone's years as a seafarer and later as a wanderer may be reflected in his use of a journey, or journeys, in the narrative progress of his novels. That journey is sometimes analogous to the "trip" induced by drugs, to the extent that both may have as their ultimate goal some transcendent flash, an assurance, however fleeting, of the presence of God. More often the end turns out to be death.

In *Dog Soldiers*, accordingly, a journey begins when John Converse, an ineffectual American journalist in Vietnam, gets his friend, Ray Hicks, formerly of the Marine Corps, to smuggle three kilos of pure heroin into the United States and deliver them to his wife, Marge Converse, in Berkeley. She, in turn, plans to sell the heroin to certain prospective buyers. Federal "regulatory agents," however, who are themselves drug dealers, upset the scheme and pursue Hicks and Marge on a wild drive down through Southern California as they flee with their cache of heroin. Together with Converse, on whose return they have kidnapped and tortured, the agents catch up with the desperate, dope-surfeited pair in the mountains near the Mexican border.

Stone took the epigraph for *Dog Soldiers* from a passage in Conrad's *Heart of Darkness*: "I've seen the devil of violence and the devil of greed and the devil of hot desire; but, by all the stars! these were strong, lusty, red-eyed devils that swayed and drove men—men, I tell you. But as I stood on that hillside, I foresaw that in the blinding sunshine of that land, I would become acquainted with a flabby, pretending weak-eyed devil of a rapacious and pitiless folly." Paul Gray of *Time* (November 11, 1974) called *Dog Soldiers* "a harrowing allegory." Other critics used terms like "shocking" and "stunning" to characterize Stone's depiction of depravity in a world traumatized by Vietnam. Like Stone's other novels, *Dog Soldiers* has no heroes. Some of his men and women are psychopaths or near-psychopaths, but generally they are made morally responsible for their behavior. If they are out of control, it is by their own choosing. As unlikeable and blameworthy as Converse and Hicks are, they are not so inhuman that Stone's readers cannot recognize something of themselves in their failings.

The winner of the National Book Award for 1974, *Dog Soldiers* established Stone as one of the most important American novelists of the decade. Again he tried to adapt his work for Hollywood, collaborating with Judith Rascoe on the script for *Dog Soldiers*, which United Artists released in

1978 as *Who'll Stop the Rain?* Stone objected to changes both in the title and in the character of Marge, who was portrayed by Tuesday Weld, co-starring with Nick Nolte.

"I wanted Vietnam almost literally in the background of the mind's eye while the rest of the story happened," Stone said of *Dog Soldiers* during his conversation with Schroeder. The same intention may well extend to *A Flag for Sunrise* (Knopf, 1981), a cautionary novel about the United States presence in Latin America. The book grew in part out of three visits that Stone made to Central America in the mid-1970s. Its setting is Tecan, a fictional, but representative Central American country whose poverty-stricken inhabitants are being driven to the verge of revolution by a cruel and greedy government, a site ripening for a clash between American economic interests and Marxist influence.

One of the story's two principal journeys, which will converge in Tecan, begins with the departure from New York of Holliwell, a well-meaning, skeptical, alcoholic anthropologist scheduled to lecture at a Central American university. He rejects a request that he repeat the kind of assignment he once undertook for the CIA in Vietnam and check out a Roman Catholic mission on the shores of Tecan. But curiosity leads him eventually to the small, bleak mission of Canadian Father Egan, a whiskey-saturated Gnostic, and Sister Justin, a beautiful American nun who has diverted her religious fervor to the revolutionary effort. Another American destined for the shores of Tecan, Pablo is a Coast Guard deserter, a dope-addict, and a demented killer who joins a band of gunrunners supplying arms to the revolutionaries. In the words of Stone, as quoted in *Modern Fiction Studies*, "Pablo is a real little rat who is almost ennobled by his addled mysticism."

Not all reviewers cared for Stone's moral and philosophical preoccupations in *A Flag for Sunrise*. Jonathan Yardley, for example, complained in the *Washington Post* (November 1, 1981), "His rhetoric is tiresome." For others, Stone's questions about the purpose of existence and the nature of evil and his despairing tone called to mind Conrad, Graham Greene, Jerzy Kosinski, and Norman Mailer. "But Stone is his own man, indentured to nobody in his ability to play on our nerves in a contemporary way," Walter Clemons wrote in his tribute to Stone in *Newsweek* (October 26, 1981). Neither a religious nor a political tract, *A Flag for Sunrise* is a novel of adventure in the tropics, of fast-paced action and suspense, and a thriller with a profoundly alarming theme.

Equally nightmarish is the journey in the ironically titled *Children of Light* (Knopf, 1986) of Gordon Walker, a strung-out screenwriter and occasional actor. Dejected after his wife's desertion, he seeks a reunion with an old flame, Lu Anne Bourgeois, known to the public as the superb actress Lee Verger. On location in Bahía Honda, Mexico, Lu Anne is starring in a film adaptation of Kate Chopin's 1899 novel, *The Awakening*, for which Walker had written the script a decade earlier. Her dedication to her role leads her to give up the pills she takes for schizophrenia because they interfere with expressive acting. When Walker arrives, bearing booze and cocaine, she is in the company of winged "Long Friends," as she calls her hallucinations.

The background for the tormented lovers in their self-destructive pursuit of nirvana is Hollywood in Bahía Honda, including a set that has been made to look exactly like Louisiana. Victimization in *Children of Light*'s power struggle, one of the recurrent themes of Stone's novels, takes the form of an unconscionable squandering of the talents of performers, directors, designers, photographers, and others who make up the motion picture industry. Stone is a firsthand witness to that exploitation, but he denies that his novel is his revenge on Hollywood.

Although probably no more excessive than in Stone's other novels, the vast consumption of drugs and alcohol in *Children of Light* drew noticeable negative critical reaction. Jeff Danziger, for instance, argued in the *Christian Science Monitor* (March 17, 1986), "The literary experience suffers when the drug takes over the thought and speech of the character. When cocaine becomes the greatest force and symbol in the plot, then it becomes for the reader what it has evidently become for the characters: a sad and boring misery." Intoxication is nevertheless essential to Stone's Hollywood scene with its brilliantly delineated cast of studio types, writers, and hangers-on—predatory, coldhearted, pretentious, and foolish. "Stone's voice here is fresh and piercing," Whitney Balliett commented in the *New Yorker* (June 2, 1986) article. " . . . He should stifle his tendency toward godly musings and carryings on, and let his comic ear go where it will."

In his review of *Children of Light* for the *New York Review of Books* (April 10, 1986), A. Alvarez regretted that Stone had "sacrificed the intricate, gallows-humor detachment that has made him, in his previous books, one of the most impressive novelists of his generation." Despite certain reservations, Alvarez counted *Children of Light* as a contribution to Stone's "world and style and tone of voice of great originality and authority" and to his recognition as "one of the few writers who are at once culturally sophisticated—full of sly quotes and literary references, strong on moral ambiguities—and streetwise."

Among Stone's honors are the John Dos Passos prize for literature and an award in literature from the American Academy and Institute, both in 1982. He is a member of the executive board of PEN. Since 1971, when he was appointed writer-in-residence at Princeton, he has followed an itinerant academic career. He was on the faculty of Amherst College from 1972 to 1975 and in 1977–78, of Stanford University in 1979, the University of Hawaii in 1979–80, Harvard University in 1981, the University of California at Irvine in 1982, New York University in 1983, and Princeton University in 1985.

Teaching is a part of what Stone calls his "embourgeoisement." He was quoted in *Newsweek* (October 26, 1981) as saying, "The people in my books are alternates for me—they go through all that horrendous stuff so I don't have to." Nowadays, a considerable part of his recourse to drugs and alcohol would also seem to be vicarious, through his characters. Feeling "unhealthy, dissipated, hung over, strung out, whatever word you want to use" would interfere with the creative process, he once remarked in a *Washington Post* interview. He retains a tie, however, with his Merry Pranksters days through his friendship with Ken Kesey. A dialogue between the two on shocks that have befallen the male psyche since World War II appeared in a special issue of *Esquire* (June 1986), "The American Man: 1946-1986."

Also conducive to the continuing process of *embourgeoisement* is Robert Stone's stable home life in a small New England town. While attending New York University in 1958–59, he met Janice G. Burr, whom he married on December 11, 1959. They have a daughter, Deirdre M., and a son, Ian A. Mrs. Stone is a social worker. Ruas' introduction of Stone to the readers of *Conversations with American Writers* included a description: "Robert Stone is of medium height and build, with the ruddy complexion of the country life. His thinning red-brown hair and free growing beard give the impression of an academician, or of an outdoorsman in town for the day. This is reinforced by his reserve and shyness. He is soft-spoken and precise in his choice of words, and has a wonderful speaking voice." Stone enjoys snorkling on his holidays, a recreation shared by Holliwell of *A Flag for Sunrise*, whose diving adventure is fraught with drama and metaphysical speculation.

References: Modern Fiction Studies 30:135+ Spring '84; *N Y Post* p35 Ja 4 '75 por; *N Y Rev of Bks* 33:23+ Ap 10 '86 por; *N Y Times Bk R* p1+ Mr 16 '86 por; *Newsweek* 98:88+ O 26 '81 por; *People* 17:95+ F 22 '82 pors; *Washington Post* G p1+ N 15 '81 por, B p1+ Ap 3 '86 pors; *Contemporary Authors* vols 85–88 (1980); Ruas, Charles. *Conversations with American Writers* (1984); *Who's Who in America, 1984-85; World Authors 1975-80* (1985)

Strauss, Franz Josef

Sept. 6, 1915– Minister President of Bavaria; West German political leader. Address: b. Bayerische Staatskanzlei, Prinzregentenstrasse 7, Munich 22, Federal Republic of Germany

NOTE: This biography supersedes the article that appeared in *Current Biography* in 1957.

Franz Josef Strauss, the minister president of Bavaria since 1978, is one of the most enduring and

Franz Josef Strauss

controversial personalities in West German politics. Elected to the first Bundestag—the lower house of the parliament of the Federal Republic of Germany—after World War II, Strauss has had a political career spanning four decades, including service as defense minister and minister of finance. In 1980 he made an unsuccessful bid for the federal chancellorship. Although Strauss has had his share of notoriety, especially for his role in the *Der Spiegel* affair of 1962, as the leader of Bavaria's Christian Social Union, he remains an influential leader of West Germany's conservative movement.

Franz Josef Strauss was born on September 6, 1915, in Munich, Germany, the son of Franz Josef Strauss, a butcher, and Walburga (Schiessl) Strauss. Growing up under the ill-fated Weimar Republic, he was a youthful witness to the rise of the Third Reich. The elder Strauss bought his poultry from a breeder named Heinrich Himmler, and Adolf Hitler often visited a nearby photographic shop. Nevertheless, butcher Strauss resisted pressure to join the Nazi party and kept his family from getting involved. According to *Time* (October 29, 1956), "Catching his son distributing Nazi propaganda one day, . . . [he] gave the boy a thrashing right there in the Schellingstrasse," which the future Bavarian minister president remembered as his "first experience in politics."

Strauss attended a Gymnasium to prepare for a career as a teacher, studying history, classical languages, and economics, and passed his Abitur. As a member of a Roman Catholic student organization, he sometimes clashed with young Nazis. The outbreak of World War II in 1939 interrupted his education, and he joined the artillery of the German army, rising through the ranks to a lieutenan-

cy, although he was once almost courtmartialed for ridiculing his uniform. He saw action in Poland, France, and Russia and led a platoon in the Battle of Stalingrad. Eventually declared unfit for combat as a result of a severe case of frostbite, he spent the last months of the war as an instructor in an antiaircraft gunnery school in southern Bavaria, where he was taken prisoner by the United States Third Army.

Untainted by membership in the Nazi party, Strauss came to the attention of American authorities while still a prisoner of war. Returning to civilian life in 1945, he served for a time as an interpreter and adviser to the American military government and was appointed deputy district councilor of Schongau, the first of his several local government jobs. Discovering a talent for political oratory, he abandoned plans for a career in teaching or law and devoted himself to politics. In 1945 he helped to found the Christian Social Union (CSU), the Bavarian affiliate of the right-of-center Christian Democratic Union (CDU), West Germany's dominant political party. In 1948 he became general secretary of the CDU, and in the same year he was appointed director of the youth bureau of the Bavarian ministry of the interior and served as a delegate to the economic parliament in Frankfurt, where he supported the free market economy favored by Dr. Ludwig Erhard.

Following approval of the provisional constitution of the Federal Republic of Germany, Strauss was elected on August 14, 1949 as representative of the Weilheim district in the first postwar Bundestag—the lower house of the West German parliament. As a leading spokesman for the ruling CDU/ CSU conservative coalition, he was formidable in parliamentary debate, overcoming opponents with his earthy humor and the sheer volume of his voice. Gifted with "political flair and sharp elbows," as David Hotham commented in the *New York Times Magazine* (March 23, 1969), he advanced rapidly, even earning the regard of the West German Chancellor, Konrad Adenauer.

Observers were therefore not surprised when after the general elections of September 1953, Adenauer brought Strauss into his cabinet as minister for special tasks. In 1955, after West Germany obtained its sovereignty, Strauss was appointed minister for atomic affairs and deputy chairman of the West German defense council. Charged with the task of creating the atomic affairs ministry, he successfully turned it into a vehicle for the growth of a nuclear industry under civilian control and organized an advisory atomic energy commission, as well as an interministerial committee on atomic energy. He negotiated with the Western Allies for the provision of nuclear materials and helped to draft laws to permit private ownership of nuclear fuels under government regulation.

Convinced that Germany could never again be an independent military power, Strauss envisioned his country's future as part of a United States of Europe. As Anthony Sampson wrote in the *London Observer* (December 22, 1968), Strauss urged the unification of Europe in order to "create a European architecture into which Germany's ambitions can be integrated." Since, in his view, it was doubtful whether the United States government would in the long run risk atomic warfare for the sake of protecting West Germany, Strauss called for the strengthening of the Federal Republic's armed forces, in numbers as well as in technology and professionalism. The most controversial aspect of the program was Strauss's insistence that the new West German army would have to be equipped with nuclear weapons as part of a proposed European nuclear force. Those views on the part of Strauss were disturbing to his foes at home and abroad, who viewed him as a potential strongman of a resurgent Germany looking for a new way to dominate Europe.

In October 1956 Adenauer named Strauss minister of defense, to replace Theodor Blank, a critic of the military establishment. Strauss immediately took the popular step of reducing West Germany's commitment to the North Atlantic Treaty Organization, cutting the need for military conscription. He rebuilt the armed forces, using highly trained professional volunteers, and earned the title "father of the modern German army." At the same time, he insisted that West Germany should be an equal partner in NATO.

Strauss alarmed many of his critics with his right-wing rhetoric and his talk of military strength. His commitment to parliamentary democracy was suspect, and he was called by some "a Bavarian bull in a political china shop." For example, in a widely quoted speech he delivered just after the Hungarian crisis in the fall of 1956, Strauss asserted that the Western alliance was in a position to "wipe the Soviet empire from the map." Strauss's foes in parliament even went so far as to label him "the most dangerous man in Europe."

Foremost among Strauss's adversaries in public life was Rudolf Augstein, the publisher of the liberal weekly Der Spiegel, who regarded him as a potential dictator and insisted that he had to be prevented at all costs from ever attaining the chancellorship. The magazine combined its attacks on Strauss's politics with accusations of personal corruption, alleging that he had taken a bribe in connection with his recommendation of a firm of German architects to construct barracks for American troops in West Germany. Strauss immediately filed suit for libel, but the case was not settled until years later, long after irretrievable damage had been done to his reputation. Other reports accused Strauss of public drunkenness, carousing in lowclass night spots, and having an affair with the late American film actress and sex symbol Jayne Mansfield. In one widely publicized incident, Strauss, on his way to a cabinet meeting, had his car delayed by a policeman and was reported to have declared furiously: "As a cabinet minister, I expect to be treated differently from a washerwoman." As David Hotham reported in the New York Times Magazine, the end result was that "the policeman became famous and got a much better job, and

Strauss was held to be bad-tempered, uncontrolled, lacking in the proper attitude toward legal forms."

Then came the "Der Spiegel affair," considered the most serious public crisis in West German history since World War II. After a critical article about a NATO training exercise, written by Conrad Ahlers, was published in Der Spiegel in October 1962, the government brought charges that it betrayed state secrets, and Augstein was arrested, along with two associates. The magazine's offices in Hamburg were searched, and Ahlers was arrested by Generalissimo Francisco Franco's police while on vacation in Spain, and returned to Germany. Defense Minister Strauss, who was generally believed responsible for the raid and the arrests, which were compared to Nazi tactics, finally had to resign in order to resolve a governmental crisis that threatened to topple the Adenauer government.

It might have seemed to many that Strauss's political career was finished as he returned to Bavaria in disgrace, but it was there that his strength really lay. In the two years that followed the "Der Spiegel affair" he consolidated his power base and refurbished his image. In January 1963 he was named parliamentary chairman of the CSU and deputy chairman of the CDU/CSU faction in the Bundestag. Renouncing the rambunctious behavior for which he was notorious in the past, he engineered a comeback, and by 1964 his political fortunes seemed well on their way to recovery.

In the fall of 1966 the West German government, headed by Ludwig Erhard, who had succeeded Adenauer as chancellor three years earlier, faced a serious crisis. Erhard's insistence on increasing taxes to meet a budget deficit led to the resignation from the cabinet of the four members of the Free Democratic party (FDP), which had held the balance of power in the coalition with the CDU/CSU. Left with the first minority government in the history of the Federal Republic, Erhard resigned. Meanwhile, Strauss, reportedly working with Adenauer behind the scenes to bring down the government, took on the role of "kingmaker." Using his influence, he had Erhard replaced by Kurt-Georg Kiesinger, who took office on December 1, 1966, as head of a "grand coalition" that brought the Social Democrats (SPD) into the government for the first time with the still dominant CDU/CSU.

Kiesinger, in turn, appointed Strauss finance minister in the new government. During his three years in that office, Strauss instituted important financial reforms and brought expenditures in the previously chaotic budget in line with revenues. On the international level he insisted that West Germany be treated as the economic power she had become rather than as a second-rate nation, and resisted foreign pressure to revalue the West German mark as a means of helping to resolve French balance of payments problems.

In October 1969 the SPD and the FDP were able to present the Social Democratic leader Willy Brandt with a slim parliamentary majority, and the

CDU/CSU alliance went into opposition for the first time since 1949. As Harry Ellis reported in the *Christian Science Monitor* (October 24, 1969), that respite provided a valuable opportunity for Strauss, who was "expected to use the next four years on the opposition benches to lever himself to the top of the CDU-CSU heap." He was regarded by many as the likely CDU/CSU candidate in 1973, but he needed an issue that he could use to rally support in Protestant northern Germany and widen his political base. Hoping to capitalize on fears inspired by the sweeping changes sponsored by the Brandt government, Strauss spoke out vehemently against the ruling coalition. He was quoted by Hella Pick in the *Guardian* (November 15, 1972) as saying, "I want . . . to rescue Germany from Willy Brandt, who is destroying the economic miracle, is turning the Federal Republic into a Marxist state and whose Ostpolitik [rapprochement with Eastern Europe] seems designed to put Germany under a *pax sovietica.*"

Popular though such incendiary rhetoric might be in rural Bavaria, it created problems for the leadership of the CDU. Strauss's votes would be needed if the conservatives were to regain power, but his far-right positions were objectionable to many in the moderate north. CDU leaders Rainer Barzel and Helmut Kohl had to struggle to distance themselves from Strauss, who seemed determined to pull the alliance rightward or to destroy it.

Strauss was indeed in a position to threaten the CDU/CSU alliance. His standing in his party had never been stronger. In October 1974 the CSU, which, in the words of John Goshko in the *Guardian* (November 26, 1974), was "a party totally under Strauss's domination," won 62 percent of the vote in the Bavarian state elections, the largest margin it had received since the war. As the relationship between the CDU and the CSU began to deteriorate, Strauss threatened to use the loyalty of his constituents to cancel the agreement that had defined the relationship between the two parties. The more conservative CSU had always confined itself to Bavaria, leaving the other nine West German states to the CDU. While the two "sister parties" had remained independent of each other, they had always formed a joint parliamentary caucus and had, in national elections, united behind a single candidate.

The CDU/CSU coalition held through two more national elections, as Rainer Barzel was defeated by Brandt in his bid for the chancellorship in November 1972 and Helmut Kohl unsuccessfully ran against SPD candidate Helmut Schmidt in October 1976. The split, exacerbated by personal animosity between Kohl and Strauss, came one month after the second defeat. On November 19, 1976, the CSU parliamentary delegation met secretly in Kreuth, Bavaria, and voted to end the twenty-seven year alliance. At odds with Kohl's tactics, Strauss felt, according to Craig R. Whitney, writing in the *New York Times* (November 28, 1976), that "the now defunct 'union' had made a mistake in two national elections, . . . not pushing opposition to détente

hard enough." To fill what he perceived as a gap on the right, Strauss was apparently planning to make his party a "national force" rather than a "regional group," with the hope that such a tactic would result in enough additional votes to restore the conservatives to power in 1980.

According to an editorial in the *New York Times* (November 20, 1976), Strauss's dissolution of the CDU/CSU alliance was "widely interpreted as a last desperate bid to salvage whatever chance he may have to become chancellor," since he had thus far been unable to put himself at the head of a unified CDU/CSU ticket. According to political analysts, in view of the popularity of Helmut Schmidt it hardly seemed likely that a national CSU on the far right would gain extra votes for the conservatives. On a national level, it appeared that Strauss would be taking votes not from the Social Democrats, but from the CDU.

Such prospects prompted Strauss and Kohl to come to terms three weeks after the dissolution of the CDU/CSU alliance, but the relationship between the two parties remained rocky. It was not until the spring of 1979 that the proposal for the CSU to become a nationwide party was finally tabled because it could not find organizations or individuals able to lead the party to a substantial share of the vote outside of Bavaria. Meanwhile, in November 1978, Strauss became minister president, or head of the state government, of Bavaria.

The underlying current of hostility between Kohl and Strauss surfaced again in May 1979, when the latter declared publicly his availability to serve as chancellor. Accepted by a joint CDU/CSU parliamentary caucus on July 2, 1979, Strauss's candidacy superseded Kohl's nomination of Ernst Albrecht, the politically moderate minister president of Lower Saxony. According to the *Economist*, cynics believed that Strauss's non-admirers acquiesced in his candidacy because they hoped that his likely defeat "would dispose of the Strauss problem once and for all," ending the perennial threat of a separate national CSU ticket. A more positive argument was that "the Christian Democratic opposition needed a better chancellor-candidate" than it had in Kohl and that Strauss could after all "turn out to be the man for the moment in 1980."

Strauss's campaign was shaky from the start. After functioning for so long as a regional politician, or junior partner, he seemed to some observers to lack competence on the national stage for the role of spokesman for the opposition as a whole. Struggling to put together a national election team, he found that many leading CDU members were unwilling to work with him. In search of a national image "he stopped being a party polemical politician and became a moderate, sensible statesman," according to Siegfried Buschschluter, writing in the *Guardian* (March 17, 1980). Those confusing signals troubled his supporters while failing to convince moderates, who still thought of Strauss as a potentially dangerous right-winger. The *"Der Spiegel* affair," as well as more recent, unsubstantiated charges that Strauss had been receiving pay-offs from Lockheed Aircraft Corporation in connection with West German purchases of Star-fighter planes were dug up by Schmidt supporters in what was described in *Time* (September 1, 1980) as "a vicious war of character assassination, bor-derline libel, slanderous posters, films and cam-paign buttons." A polemical documentary film hostile to Strauss, entitled *Der Kandidat* and di-rected by Volker Schlöndorff and others, was re-leased in 1980.

The nomination of Strauss represented "a last vain bid to achieve the impossible and regain pow-er in Bonn singlehandedly," according to Bernd Stadelmann's article in the daily *Stuttgarter Nachrichten*, quoted in the *German Tribune* (Oc-tober 19, 1980). In the elections of October 5, 1980, many CDU voters supported the centrist Free Democrats. The CDU/CSU representation in the 498-member Bundestag dropped from 243 to 226, while Helmut Schmidt's SPD/FDP coalition gar-nered 271 seats, giving it a majority of forty-five.

Despite the CDU/CSU defeat, the election re-sulted in a personal victory for Helmut Kohl, to whom the conservative bloc turned after Strauss's failure at the polls. Pulling the alliance back to-ward the center, Kohl was in a position to attract the support of the Free Democrats and bring down the government of Helmut Schmidt with a no-confidence vote, and to form a new coalition gov-ernment with the FDP, following the national elec-tions of March 6, 1983. The increased influence of the Free Democrats at the expense of the CSU frus-trated Strauss, who launched personal diplomatic initiatives in the early and mid-1980s that were aimed, according to some observers, at gaining en-trance into Kohl's cabinet as foreign minister, a post held since 1974 by FDP chairman Hans-Dietrich Genscher.

In view of his perfervid anti-Communism and his persistently scornful attitude toward negotia-tions with the Eastern bloc, the most startling of Strauss's diplomatic efforts were in behalf of Com-munist East Germany. His reported arrangement of a $397 million private bank loan to the German Democratic Republic in July 1983 was followed up by several meetings with East German Communist party leader Erich Honecker. Strauss also made visits to Albania, Poland, Syria, Japan, China, Gre-nada, and Gabon, ostensibly to enhance Bavaria's stature on the international stage. Although the trips seemed to have been designed, in part at least, to upstage and embarrass Kohl, the chancellor ap-peared to have attained a strong enough position in his own right to resist any challenges posed by Strauss.

For the national elections of January 25, 1987, Strauss made what some political observers viewed as probably a final bid to share in the lead-ership of the Bonn government and to steer its for-eign and domestic policies to the right. Campaigning vigorously, he called on his compa-triots to come out of the "shadow of the Third Reich" and once more take pride in being Ger-

mans. But although Kohl's CDU/CSU-FDP coali-tion defeated the SPD opposition in the elections, its share of the vote was diminished and Strauss's CSU suffered a substantial reduction in its strength. On the other hand, the FDP did compara-tively well, thus precluding the prospect that Strauss might displace Genscher as foreign minis-ter.

Among the many honors that Strauss has re-ceived are several honorary doctorates from Amer-ican universities. His published works include *Gebote der Freiheit* (Demands of Freedom, 1980) and *Verantwortung vor der Geschichte* (Responsi-bility Before History, 1985). Several biographical works have been written about him, including *Franz Josef Strauss—Der Mensch and Staatsmann* (1984), by Walter Schöll. A *Festschrift* honoring his seventieth birthday, *Franz Josef Strauss—Erkenntnisse, Standpunkte*, with a preface by Ronald Reagan and contributions by Margaret Thatcher, Shimon Peres, and Helmut Schmidt, among others, was published in 1985. In 1983-84 Strauss served in the largely honorary post of presi-dent of the Bundesrat, the upper house of the fed-eral parliament.

Franz Josef Strauss was married on June 4, 1957, to Marianne Zwicknagel, the daughter of a party colleague. She died in an automobile accident in 1984. Their children are Max-Josef, a lawyer, Franz-Georg, a businessman, and Monika (Mrs. Michael Hohlmeier). Strauss is about five feet nine inches tall, weighs some 200 pounds, and has brown hair and blue eyes. Roswin Finkenzeller, in an article in the *Frankfurter Allgemeine Zeitung* reprinted in the *German Tribune* (September 22, 1985), called him "admired, feared, respected, and suspected," as well as as "extremely intelligent, en-tertaining, and quick-witted man." A champion cy-clist in his youth, Strauss also enjoys reading, swimming, hunting, and flying. He qualified as a jet pilot at the age of sixty-nine.

References: German Tribune p5 S 22 '85 por, p3 Ag 30 '87 por; N Y Times p2 D 1 '66 por; N Y Times Mag p37 Mr 23 '69 pors; International Who's Who, 1987-88; Wer ist Wer? (1986); Who's Who, 1987-88

Swaggart, Jimmy (Lee)

1935– Evangelist; gospel singer. Address: b. c/o Linda Westbrook, P.O. Box 2550, Baton Rouge, La. 70821

The most watched television evangelist in the United States today is Jimmy Swaggart, a Southern populist Pentecostal whose daily and Sunday broadcasts reach a total of about two million Amer-ican homes and who claims to have a worldwide following of 200 million. Swaggart is also one of the most controversial of the electronic preachers,

Jimmy Swaggart

blunt and incendiary in expressing his fundamentalist scorn for Roman Catholics ("poor, pitiful individuals who think they have enriched themselves spiritually by kissing the Pope's ring"), modernist Protestants, and such agents of "secular humanism" as liberal national legislators and Supreme Court justices. His espousal of conservative political views, including anti-abortion, has made him a leader of the increasingly powerful Christian right wing.

Swaggart has described his ministry as the "old sawdust trail, sort of upgraded." Jimmy Swaggart Ministries, as his organization is offically called, grosses about $141 million in donations and other income annually. The organization is based in Baton Rouge, Louisiana, where Swaggart is pastor of a local congregation of 4,300, and has a headquarters, sprawling over 270 acres, that includes a Bible college, a printing and mailing plant, a television production center, and a music recording studio. (In addition to preaching, Swaggart sings gospel, partly to his own piano accompaniment. His records have sold at least fifteen million copies.) From his base in Baton Rouge, he regularly embarks on preaching tours across the United States and in many foreign countries, especially South America, where he has an enormous following. Those crusades are televised Sundays in the two-hour program called *Jimmy Swaggart*. The preacher's daily broadcast is the shorter, more subdued Biblical discussion show *A Study in the Word.* "Not since Billy Sunday has a soul-saver done more swaggering about the podium, waving the Good Book, flailing his arms, perspiring, shouting, and telling a tearful audience, with hurtin' in his voice, that they will all go straight to perdition if they don't get right with Jesus," Martin Gardner wrote of Swaggart in the

New York Review of Books (August 13, 1987). "Between exhortations he pummels a piano, bouncing his right leg to his band's pounding Nashville beat and belting out hymns that often make him cry."

Jimmy Lee Swaggart was born in 1935 in Ferriday, Louisiana, a small backwoods town near Natchez where gambling, carousing, and brawling were as rife as hallelujahs. Like Jerry Lee Lewis, the rock 'n' roll star, his first cousin, Swaggart derived his middle name from his uncle Lee Calhoun, a well-to-do landowner who, although not religious himself, had paid for the construction of the frame Assemblies of God Church in Ferriday. The largest Pentecostal organization in the United States, the Assemblies of God was founded in Arkansas in 1914 and became part of "a vast evangelical movement that swept most of the South and Midwest during the roaring twenties and Depression thirties," as Swaggart noted in his autobiography, *To Cross a River* (Logos International, 1977), written with Robert Paul Lamb. Assemblies of God worshipers subscribe to the sixteen basic tenets of Pentecostalism, including baptism with the Holy Ghost as evidenced in the charismatic "gifts" of miraculous healing, glossolalia, or "speaking in tongues," the "discernment" of religious truth, and the power of prophecy. Believing in direct divine inspiration, Pentecostals reject the concept of a sacerdotal elite fostered by Catholicism and some of the other mainstream Christian denominations. Along with a wide spectrum of fundamentalists, they hold to the literal inerrancy of the Bible as the Word of God and to premillennialism, the belief that Jesus Christ will come, not at the end of the world, but in time to reign with his saints during the final period of peace and righteousness on earth.

Swaggart's father, a grocer, was a strict disciplinarian and an occasional preacher in the local Assemblies of God Church, and eventually both parents became evangelists. As a young boy, Swaggart was also influenced by his grandmother, who, according to him, "studied the Bible incessantly." It was in her presence at a prayer meeting in a "little house" in Ferriday that nine-year-old Swaggart felt "called" to the ministry. "I still see myself sitting on the floor," he has recounted, "leaning on the couch with my back up against it. And there was an utterance in tongues that was given. I don't remember who gave it. There was an interpretation to those tongues and I don't remember who gave that. But it said something that had been dealing with my little nine-year-old heart for months. 'You will preach My Gospel all over the world. You will take it even to Africa'—I remember that distinctly. And I knew the Holy Ghost was talking about this poor, pitiful, now preacher, then child. I knew it. I had no doubt about it."

If Jimmy Swaggart represents the God-fearing side of a Faulknerian clan, Jerry Lee Lewis represents the clan's Snopesian side. Born in the same year and living near each other, Lewis and Swaggart grew up inseparable from each other and from another cousin, Mickey Gilley, the country-and-western singer and founder of Gilley's, the famous Houston honky-tonk that inspired the 1980 film *Urban Cowboy.* "There was constant rivalry," Swaggart told a writer for *People* (October 27, 1986), "but we loved each other very much." The three engaged in mischief together; learned to play on their uncle Lee Calhoun's piano and honed their skills on a Stark upright Lewis' father bought for him; and became surreptitious auditors at Haney's Big House, a black music club in Ferriday that their parents had declared off limits, where they would listen to the barrelhouse piano players perform boogie-woogie.

When Gilley was in his late teens, he moved to Houston with his parents. Meanwhile, both Swaggart and Lewis had dropped out of school. In 1953 Swaggart stopped his backsliding and, remembering his "calling" at age nine, decided to follow his parents into evangelism. Lewis, the "bad seed," expelled from a Bible college for blasphemously pounding out a boogie version of "My God Is Real," moved on to nightclubs and Memphis recording studios. He became one of the legends of early rock 'n' roll, but his stardom was soon eclipsed by his notoriety. "Man, I got the Devil in me," he shouted orgiastically at the historic recording session that produced his first massive hits, "Great Balls of Fire" and "Whole Lotta Shakin' Goin' On." In the years since, he has often been hospitalized for drug and alcohol addiction; has entered into one disastrous marriage after another; has been accused of criminal violence on several occasions; and has suffered such tragedies as the death of two sons in accidents. In his autobiography, Jimmy Swaggart has written: "I will not be satisfied until I know Jerry Lee has entered the kingdom of God."

Swaggart began preaching on street corners and at rural meetings, at which he would lead congregations in song while playing the piano or the accordion. If he was tempted by his cousin's worldly success to stray from the path of the righteous, he had an experience in 1957 that steeled his Christian resolve. According to him, it was an encounter with a hellish creature. "He had the body of a bear," he recounted in his autobiography, "and the face of a man. The expression on his face was the grisliest I had ever seen. The beast was the picture of evil." He defeated the beast, he said, by invoking the name of Jesus. On New Year's Day 1958, Swaggart dedicated himself to preaching full time and quit his regular jobs, even though he had a wife and two-year-old son to support. Nonetheless, he and his wife began traveling what one writer called "the tree-stump Southern circuit," preaching to the "biscuit and syrup kind of folk" in frame churches along one-lane country roads.

Swaggart insists that his ministry has taken shape through direct intercession on the part of Jesus Christ. And in the early 1960s, as Jerry Lee's career scraped bottom, that of his preacher cousin advanced. At about that time, the Lord, according to Swaggart, gave him "permission" to record gospel albums, and through exposure on Christian radio stations, his country-and-western-inflected

brand of gospel music began to attract a following. Crowds flocked to his Bible-thumping revival meetings and religious crusades throughout the Deep South. In 1969, in obedience to the Lord, who had instructed him to take to the airwaves, he launched *The Camp Meeting Hour,* a radio showcase for hymn-singing and hortatory preaching that was broadcast over hundreds of stations. His *This Is Just What Heaven Means To Me* and *There Is a River* were the best-selling gospel albums of 1971 and 1972. In *To Cross a River* Swaggart explained that a royalty arrangement had been negotiated with the Lord years before. "Now about these record albums," the Almighty said. "Father," Swaggart asked, "would you take ninety per cent and let me have ten per cent?"

It was not until 1973, however, that Swaggart began to achieve prominence on video. Aided by the boom in cable television, he became in just one decade, the most popular electronic evangelist in America. His video congregation is no longer confined to the fundamentalist South and small towns in the conservative Midwest: more than 200 stations beam *The Jimmy Swaggart Telecast* into some 1,880,000 households every week. Surprisingly, Los Angeles and New York, the American Sodom and Gomorrah, provide the largest TV markets for what he calls "that old-fashioned gospel Holy Ghost message." Approximately fifteen million of Swaggart's gospel albums have been sold, and his monthly magazine, *The Evangelist,* has a readership of 800,000.

In the opinion of Dan Rather, Jimmy Swaggart is "the most effective speaker in the country" perhaps because he is the most histrionic of the current crop of televangelists. He opens his crusades by welcoming the multitude to "an old-fashioned, heartfelt, Holy Ghost, heaven-sent, Devil-chasin', sin-killing, true-blue, red-hot, blood-bought, God-given, Jesus-lovin' indoor camp meeting!" Addressing the faithful in rolling Louisiana cadences, he prowls the stage like a vigilant bear, whipping his crowds into emotional crescendos with the fervor of Bruce Springsteen. "He can speak for hours without notes," a writer for *Newsweek* observed, "shouting, crying, whispering into the microphone as if it were the ear of Lazarus." His orotund baritone voice quavers as he castigates the secular world for its wretched sinfulness, modulates into rejoicing as he proclaims, "Devil, you gettin' a black eye tonight!" And finally chokes with passion as he invokes the sweet, redemptive love of Jesus. "Communism may pass away," Swaggart shouts, his sweaty forehead glistening beneath high-intensity lights. "Socialism may pass away. Evolution will pass away. Secular humanism will pass away." Holding his Bible aloft, he then intones the supreme promise: "But my Word shall stand forever. Amen!" The crowd sways in rapture and resonates with cries of "amen" and "hallelujah" as Brother Swaggart calls forth the lambs who have gone astray to "make a stand for Jesus." The spectacle is recorded for posterity by the neutral gaze of strategically positioned television cameras.

Like Jerry Falwell, the fundamentalist founder of the Moral Majority, Swaggart is one of the most influential Christian exponents of right-wing populism in America. The United States Supreme Court and the Congress are, he believes, "institutions damned by God." In addressing the question of organic evolution, he has said: "The most asinine, idiotic, stupid, illiterate lie that's ever been told is . . . that ten billion years ago you wiggled out of a primordial ooze." In his sermons he bitterly denounces "the media" and "the intelligentsia," regarding them as institutions that "are philosophically committed to imposing . . . a system of atheistic socialism where all decisions are imposed by this small, elite, superior intellectual class who do the thinking for all common people."

Jimmy Swaggart is the only celebrity "televangelist" thus far to endorse the Reverend Pat Robertson in his bid to win the 1988 Republican nomination for the presidency, since he views the founder of the Christian Broadcast Network and the host of the talk show the 700 Club, as "one of us." He has held White House parleys with both President Ronald Reagan and Vice-President George Bush, and he repudiates the concept that the constitutional separation of church and state implies any division between "God and state." As for Pat Robertson's presidential aspirations, Swaggart told a Washington Post reporter (September 29, 1986): "Politics is ugly because good Christians have not gotten involved like they ought to. The scuffling will be clean. Won't be lying and cheating and bribes and kickbacks and payoffs involved." If Robertson is elected, the "First Amendment will be guaranteed," Swaggart contends, "because true Christians believe in the freedom of others that are outside our faith more than anyone else."

Despite his lack of formal theological instruction, Swaggart holds in contempt many of the traditions that prevail in both Roman Catholicism and mainline Protestantism. He views the Roman Catholic mass as a "liturgical religious monstrosity" and, in condemning Catholicism itself as "a false cult" based upon the "doctrines of devils," has beseeched born-again Catholics to leave the church. Indeed, Swaggart has suggested that even Mother Teresa of Calcutta has no promise of salvation, apparently because she emphasizes good works at the expense of spreading the Word of God through the interpretation of Scripture. In The Evangelist Swaggart once wrote that Roman Catholics are "poor pitiful individuals who think they have enriched themselves spiritually by kissing the pope's ring. . . . I would be thrilled and pleased if the pope suddenly announced that he is not the vicar of Christ on earth."

However, Swaggart has also assailed Christian Science as "neither 'Christian' nor 'scientific'"; called the Mormon faith "contrary to the Word of God"; and criticized the "faith healing" practices of fellow evangelicals like Oral Roberts. Although Swaggart is, like many fundamentalists, a militant supporter of the State of Israel and says that he

"loves the Jewish people," he has seemed to suggest that European Jewry brought the Holocaust on itself because of the Jews' refusal to accept Christ as their redeemer. "There's nothing in the world any greater than to be a Jew," Swaggart told the Washington Post, "and nothing in the world any worse than being an atheistic Jew. That's what you call the paradox of all paradoxes."

In the spring of 1987 Swaggart found himself embroiled in the lurid sex-and-bribery scandal that brought about the downfall of the husband-and-wife televangelist team of Jim and Tammy Bakker. A fellow member of the Assemblies of God clergy, Bakker was the mainstay of PTL (Praise the Lord or People That Love), until it was revealed that in 1980 he had committed adultery with a young church secretary and then arranged to purchase her silence with cash gifts. Bakker explained away his resignation from PTL not by citing his own transgressions but by accusing Swaggart of hatching a "diabolical plot" to take over the multimillion dollar PTL empire, whose holdings include a satellite TV network and a Christian theme park, Heritage USA. Swaggart scoffed at the idea of "stealing" PTL and called the Bakker affair "a cancer that needed to be excised from the Body of Christ." In fact, Swaggart had informed Assemblies of God officials of the adulterous activities of two clergymen, Bakker and a New Orleans TV preacher named Marvin Gorman, in an attempt to force the denomination to undertake internal housecleaning. When Gorman sued Swaggart for $90 million, claiming that he had been accused of several illicit affairs when he had really engaged in adultery only once, Swaggart said, "I think I'm more of a victim than anything else."

In the aftermath of the Bakker scandal, Swaggart launched an assault against what he fears is a growing trend towards "doctrinal deviation" on the part of many Assemblies of God ministers. In recent years the denomination has become tolerant of diverse Christian teachings, some of which have only superficial affinities with Pentecostalism, and Swaggart is especially offended by ministers who promote what he views as a "man-centered," Satan-devised philosophy that obscures the central tenets of biblical prophecy. "In Swaggart's view," wrote Lloyd Grove in the Washington Post (April 8, 1987), "the world is rapidly accelerating into 'moral and spiritual dissolution,' the church is 'falling away,' and the Second Coming is imminent: Jesus will soon 'rapture' all believers into Heaven, setting the stage for the reign of the Antichrist, the Battle of Armageddon and 'the terrifying Great Tribulation.'" Swaggart wants most to purge the church of so-called Kingdom Age, or charismatic, teachings, which hold that the church is getting stronger and that Christ will not return until the Kingdom of God has been built on earth. He has denounced the charismatics for embracing such allegedly "occultist" and "shamanist" practices as "the power of positive thinking" and "internal healing" as the means of creating this earthly Christian utopia. In The Evangelist Swaggart answered the moderate Assemblies of God pastors who have accused him of launching an inquisition that might split the sect, irrevocably dividing Pentecostals and charismatics. "Today," he wrote, "if anyone preaches the unadulterated Word and reproves and rebukes, he is accused of 'dividing the Body.' As a consequence, we now have puppets instead of prophets. Today we wallow in conformity. . . . We are living in an age of compromise."

Anthony Podesta, the president of People For the American Way, an organization formed by the liberal activist Norman Lear that opposes the evangelical right, sees Swaggart as "an equal opportunity bigot" because of the "hateful things" he has said "about Catholics, Jews, Baptists," and other groups. But Swaggart believes it his evangelical duty "to make you squirm." "It's my business to make you kind of hot where you're sitting," he explained in the Toronto Globe and Mail (June 17, 1986). "It's my business to keep you up at night, to make you toss and tumble, unable to sleep." Swaggart's associates insist that there is a profound difference between the fulminating scold in the pulpit and the considerate, roguishly charming man who is their friend. "I believe people fail to understand Jimmy's heart and spirit," the Reverend J. Don George told Lloyd Grove. "They develop in their minds a caricature

of the man. . . . Many people feel that he is an angry man, a man with a God complex. . . . He is neither of those. He's a gracious, kind gentleman who is incensed . . . by the froth and the fluff that exists in the Body of Christ. There is a rage in his heart against things which aren't pure."

Jimmy Swaggart is a muscular, six-foot-tall man with ginger-colored hair and a mellifluous speaking voice. His Jimmy Swaggart Ministries owns several gospel radio stations, and the complex in Baton Rouge includes a 7,000-seat Family Worship Center. Five hundred students are enrolled in the Jimmy Swaggart Bible College. Much of the Jimmy Swaggart Ministries' income is spent on charity, chiefly the Assemblies of God foreign missions programs, but by far the largest expenditure is for television air time and production. The business side of the Swaggart ministry is run by his wife, Frances, and his son, Donnie. "Even though it takes business sense and many of the tactics used by the Fortune 500," Swaggart has said, "it's the Holy Spirit that is guiding us."

References: Newsday Mag p8+ Ap 29 '84 pors; Newsweek 103:65 Ja 9 '84 por; Time 129:60+ Ap 6 '87 pors; Washington Post C p1+ S 29 '86, C p1 Mr 26 '87, A p4 Mr 29 '87; Marshall, Richard. Encyclopedia of Country & Western Music (1985)

Tambo, Oliver

Oct. 27, 1917– South African political activist; lawyer; Address: b. c/o African National Congress, PO Box 31791, Lusaka, Zambia

"The most peculiar thing about South Africa is that you have twenty-eight or twenty-nine million people living in the same country—and twenty-four or twenty-five million don't exist! They're virtually foreigners in South Africa, without any rights. . . . This must end." That ultimatum came from Oliver Tambo, the president of South Africa's most influential liberation organization, the African National Congress, in a 1982 interview. The soft-spoken Tambo has for many years been targeted as the "public enemy number one" of his country's white minority government, having campaigned throughout the world to isolate that regime, both economically and politically, ever since he first established a foreign base for the outlawed ANC in Lusaka, Zambia, in 1964. His diplomatic successes since then include the securing of long-term financial backing for the ANC from Scandinavian and other Western countries; the garnering of weapons and other types of aid from the Soviet Union and the Eastern bloc, and the winning of acceptance as a de facto head of state in the nonaligned countries.

In January 1987, after decades during which the ANC had been ignored by the American government, Tambo achieved another significant diplomatic triumph when he met with United States

Carl T. Gossett/NYT Pictures

Secretary of State George P. Shultz in Washington, D.C. That meeting—and its tacit acknowledgment that the ANC's prestige among South African blacks made it a powerful player in that country's politics—infuriated American conservatives and South African government officials because of what they perceived as the ANC's links to communism and terrorism. A significant amount of crossmembership exists between the ANC and the pro-Moscow South African Communist party (SACP), and the organization has resorted not only to mass demonstrations and boycotts but also, in recent years, to hit-and-run violence in its attempts to dislodge the white South African regime and its policy of apartheid, or legalized racial discrimination. Tambo has dismissed complaints about SACP connections as attempts to foster "tribalism" and has echoed the American Declaration of Independence by declaring that "in the face of systematic tyranny it becomes a duty and a right to take up arms."

Oliver Tambo, one of seven children, was born on October 27, 1917, to peasant subsistence farmers of the Pondo tribe in the Transkei village of Bizania, near Johannesburg. During what he has described as a politically "sheltered" childhood, he attended Anglican and Methodist mission schools, took part in intervillage horse races, and was an outrider in the equestrian section of a tribal chief's entourage. After graduating from the Anglican-run St. Peter's School in Johannesburg with an impressive first-class pass in 1938, he received a scholarship to Fort Hare University (some sources call it University College at Fort Hare), where he studied science and education. When an assault on a black woman dining-room employee by a white male superior went unpunished, Tambo, previously known mainly as a brilliant student, found himself "playing quite the leading role" in a student protest. After obtaining his B.S. degree in 1941, he stayed on at Fort Hare to work towards a diploma in education. "I didn't really want to be a teacher," he has said, "but there was nothing else I could be. . . . It was just the racial restriction on Africans." He was expelled from Fort Hare—and thoroughly politicized—in 1942 when he led a large student protest against arbitrary restrictions on the use of a tennis court.

Ignoring his expulsion, St. Peter's promptly hired Tambo as an instructor of science and mathematics, a post that he held until 1947. In addition to teaching at St. Peter's, Tambo composed music and conducted the school's choir on occasion. He also seriously considered entering the Anglican ministry, but began to find his true vocation in the black protest movement. In 1944 he became a founding member, with Nelson Mandela, his former schoolmate at Fort Hare, several of his fellow teachers at St. Peter's, and others, of the Youth League of the African National Congress.

"We were never really young," Tambo has said of that period. "There were no dances, hardly a cinema, but meetings, discussions, every night, every weekend." The discussions covered topics that ranged from the ineffectiveness of the genteel ANC parent body to the overlapping membership, then hotly opposed by Tambo, of the ANC and the South African Communist party. The Youth League that emerged from those bull sessions declared its intention to "galvanize" the ANC by becoming "the brain-trust and power-station" of the struggling black liberation movement.

As the Youth League hammered out its policies, Tambo became increasingly interested in law and was apprenticed to a Johannesburg law firm through Walter Sisulu, another Youth League member, who had already performed a similar service for Nelson Mandela. The law books that Tambo pored over began to change in 1948, when the Afrikaaner Nationalist party, which came to power that year, began to codify and elaborate existing repressions under its new apartheid policy. Laws were passed limiting, among other things, the education, freedom of movement, and choice of dwelling place of blacks, who also continued to be denied the franchise.

In 1949 Oliver Tambo and Nelson Mandela were elected to the ANC executive body. It was at their insistence and that of their supporters, that the Youth League's carefully orchestrated "Programme of Action," calling for boycotts, strikes, civil disobedience, and general defiance of the laws of apartheid, was adopted by the ANC as a whole. The Programme of Action was launched in 1952 with a massive "defiance campaign" that for months brought tens of thousands of demonstrators into the streets of South Africa and pushed membership in the ANC from 7,000 to 100,000. In 1955, in Kliptown near Johannesburg, a multiracial "Congress of the People" convened and adopted the Freedom Charter, the seminal document of the South African liberation movement and the embodiment of the vision of Tambo and the rest of the new ANC leadership. It opened with the promulgation of the ANC's keynote concept: "South Africa belongs to all who live in it, black and white."

Tambo and Mandela simultaneously battled apartheid in the courts, beginning in 1952 when they opened the first black law firm in Johannesburg in defiance of official orders to relocate to a township. Tambo still wistfully recalls the way his name and Nelson Mandela's appeared in "the gold lettering on the glass" of the law firm door. "To reach our desks each morning," he wrote in his introduction to Mandela's *No Easy Walk to Freedom* (1965), "Nelson and I ran the gauntlet of patient queues of people overflowing from the chairs in the waiting-room into the corridors." "South Africa," he added, "has the dubious reputation of boasting one of the highest prison populations in the world. . . . To be unemployed is a crime. . . . To be landless can be a crime, and weekly we interviewed the delegations of grizzled, weatherworn peasants from the countryside who came to tell us how many generations their families had worked a little piece of land from which they were now being ejected. . . . Our buff office files carried thousands of these stories and if, when we started our law partnership, we had not been rebels against apartheid, our experience in our offices would have remedied the deficiency." He and Mandela, sometimes handling seven cases a day, "had risen to professional status in our community," Tambo continued, "but every case in court, every visit to the prison to interview clients, reminded us of the humiliation and suffering burning into our people."

In 1956 Tambo and Mandela were themselves arrested along with 154 others and charged with treason. Tambo had recently been accepted as a candidate for ordination in the Anglican church, but the treason charge forced him to abandon all thoughts of entering the clergy. When not in court for the long preparatory session for the treason trial, he and Mandela practiced law as best they could. The treason trial finally opened officially in August 1958. The prosecution set out to establish, under South Africa's sweeping anticommunist legislation, that the Youth League Programme of Action, the ANC's Freedom Charter, and other documents in effect declared the ANC's intention to found a communist state. Evidence was flimsy, and charges against Tambo were dropped almost immediately. All defendants were found not guilty in March 1960.

At that time Tambo still believed that the ANC would never "have to go for violence as opposed to nonviolence." In March 1960 in Sharpeville, a town forty miles from Johannesburg, police opened fire on unarmed persons in a demonstration sponsored by the Pan Africanist Congress, an ANC splinter group, killing sixty-nine people and wounding 181. "It is hard to overstate the impact that Sharpeville made on us," Tambo once said. "We were unarmed, we were peaceful, and they shot us down in the street." At that point Tambo "knew that nonviolence had become meaningless." "We couldn't take it any further," he added. Anticipating a crackdown by the government, the ANC executive decided that Tambo should prepare to flee the country and establish a foreign base.

Two days after the now historic Sharpeville massacre, the ANC was banned. Its members went underground, and after forty-eight years of nonviolence, began building an armed wing, Umkhonto we Sizwe (Spear of the Nation). A state of emergency was declared, and Tambo left South Africa for Botswana to begin the establishment of the foreign headquarters. According to Peter Godwin of the London Sunday Times (June 29, 1986), his "escape, however, was very nearly undone when masked South African agents tried to kidnap him by drugging him with chloroform, but locals spotted them and reported their presence. It was only the first of a string of threats against Tambo's life." Another reporter noted that Tambo's life after that became, of necessity, one of "secret itineraries and meetings in anonymous offices behind heavily padlocked doors." In June 1960 he traveled to the United States in search of funds and political support, but American officials, pressured by South Africa, hesitated to give him a visa. His request for aid "received no real response," he has said.

Meanwhile, Umkhonto we Sizwe carried out sabotage attacks against government buildings that it felt symbolized apartheid until 1962, when Mandela and his colleagues were betrayed by an informer and rounded up, tried, and given life

sentences almost to a man. In 1963 Tambo traveled to the Soviet Union in quest of the funds and arms he had failed to obtain in the United States and succeeded in his mission. The Soviet Union later became the ANC's main supplier of arms and even provided some academic scholarships for ANC recruits.

While Mandela was serving his life sentence and taking on mythical proportions in the minds of the majority of South Africa's people, Tambo remained "incredibly self-effacing," in the view of Bishop Trevor Huddlestone of South Africa. He assumed the role of "the workaholic who [made] all the difficult decisions" that held the ANC together in exile and won new financial support for it, especially from the Scandinavian countries, during a number of years when its prominence in the South African black community was replaced by a more radical black-consciousness movement. This movement grew in influence until 1976, when, in the township of Soweto, government security forces fired upon unarmed students demonstrating against a number of newly imposed restrictions on education for blacks. There followed a sixteen-month explosion of unrest in the townships during which 700 people were killed by the authorities. The importance of Tambo's work in establishing the ANC outside South Africa now became obvious, as thousands of young blacks poured across the border to join the ANC and Umkhonto we Sizwe, which represented the only surviving organized resistance to the government.

The immediate problem that Tambo and the other ANC leaders faced with those new recruits was to convince them, as one ANC official explained, that "there is more to this than simply grabbing a gun and going back to kill the people who have been stepping on them." A more subtle and lingering problem, as Tambo discovered in subsequent years, was South African security's use of informers to infiltrate the steady stream of ANC recruits. Tambo told the American journalist Joseph Lelyveld, in an interview for Lelyveld's 1985 book, Move Your Shadow, that on one occasion "there was a group of ten [recruits], and only one was genuine." Despite careful screening, it became "awkward to have large groups because you can't be sure when they just come." The first waves of recruits after Soweto, however, enormously bolstered the strength and effectiveness of the ANC and those that followed eventually gave it an effective fighting force of 10,000 men. By using hit-and-run guerrilla tactics, they tried to gain political leverage against a regime backed by a vastly superior defense force of 400,000 men who were supported by a yearly budget of $3 billion and some of the world's most sophisticated weapons.

By 1981 the government's Terrorism Research Center was reporting an ANC military strike every 53.2 hours. Employing Soviet-made explosives, Umkhonto we Sizwe struck against what it felt to be symbols of South African repression, including police stations, pass records offices, military headquarters, and such economic pillars of apartheid as the SASOL oil refinery and, in 1982, the Koeberg nuclear power plant.

The government in Pretoria viewed the ANC attacks and the presence on the thirty-member ANC executive body of members of the South African Communist party as evidence of an indirect but "total onslaught" against South Africa by the Soviet Union. It followed up its rhetoric by attacking the ANC directly, staging reprisal raids against suspected ANC headquarters in the neighboring "front-line" states. In 1981 a bombing raid against a suspected ANC base in Lesotho, a country surrounded by South African territory, resulted in the deaths of fifty-four civilians who were "asleep in their beds," according to Mark Uhlig. Another attack and two parcel bombs accounted for the deaths of fifteen ANC members in other front-line states. Tambo declared that "our violence compared to the regime's violence, physically, is minimal—minimal. Sharpeville, Soweto, hangings, shootings by the police—the number of people they have killed!" He also noted that Angola, Mozambique, and Zimbabwe had all won independence by fighting "serious armed struggles, while we were looking for economic targets."

In its first attack that resulted in civilian deaths, the ANC exploded a car bomb in May 1983 outside the South African Air Force headquarters close to the center of Pretoria, killing eighteen people, including eight blacks, and wounding some 200. Pretoria cited the attack as new evidence of ANC links to "international terrorism," and it helped Pieter W. Botha, South Africa's prime minister since 1978, to perpetuate the ANC's pariah status in the United States and Great Britain. Within Africa, Pretoria exerted so much economic and military pressure on three long-time ANC supporters, Mozambique, Lesotho, and Swaziland, that those countries closed their borders to the ANC.

In February 1985, through the nightly broadcasts of the ANC's Lusaka, Zambia-based "Radio Freedom" and through ANC agents within South Africa, Tambo exhorted blacks to make their townships "ungovernable." A new government policy that took effect in January 1985 and allowed Asians and coloreds, or mixed-race South Africans, token representation in Parliament but denied it to blacks, accomplished that goal for him by setting off demonstrations and riots on an unprecedented scale. The Botha government declared two states of emergency, one in July 1985 and the other in June 1986, during which 22,000 blacks, including small children, were imprisoned, many without charges. Some 2,300 blacks were killed between September 1984 and June 1986, the great majority struck down by South African security forces. Scores died as a result of power struggles, mob justice, and raw frustration within the black community itself. As the death toll rose, Tambo announced in 1985 that Umkhonto we Sizwe would attempt to force the violence into the insulated and oblivious white areas—still striking at inanimate military and government targets but now also attacking military personnel and abandoning special efforts to limit the casualties that might result among nearby civilians. As rioting in the townships and international pressure for the South African government to make reforms steadily intensified, in September 1985 a group of prominent South African businessmen traveled to Lusaka to meet with Tambo and other senior ANC leaders. Tambo assured them of the ANC's nonracialism and insisted that black and white sit side by side, not face to face at the conference table, "because we are all South Africans."

The ANC economic program, calling for the nationalization of banks, mines, and monopoly industry to create a mixed economy and thus facilitate South Africa's incontrovertible need for a redistribution of wealth, has been compared to that of the British Labour party. Although it troubled some of the businessmen, others felt that a mutually acceptable solution was within the range of negotiation. Pretoria condemned the meeting, but subsequent "pilgrimages to Lusaka," as one journalist called them, were made by clergymen and by members of the South African Parliament's white opposition party.

In September 1986 Tambo traveled to London for exploratory talks with Sir Geoffrey Howe, the British foreign secretary, and, separately, with Chester H. Crocker, the American assistant secretary of state for African affairs. That grudging recognition of the ANC by both governments came in the wake of indisputable evidence of ANC influence within South Africa, including clenched-fist salutes to Tambo and Mandela and ANC banners flown at mass funerals for many of the blacks killed by the South African security forces; the adoption of the goals of the ANC Freedom Charter by the umbrella opposition group, the United Democratic Front; and polls showing strong support for the ANC among millions of blacks despite the presence of a growing number of young radicals who, seeming to disregard all authority, including the ANC, often set up their own tribunals, and meted out justice with the "necklace"—a gasoline-soaked tire in which a "collaborator" or an "informer" was burned to death.

Abroad and in South Africa, the ANC began increasingly to be seen as an indispensable factor in averting a bloodbath, and one former South African police spy complained that "the ANC's real weapon isn't the AK-47. It is the ability to popularize and politicize discontent." Realizing that fact, the South African government narrowed press freedoms to the vanishing point throughout its two emergencies, but what journalists managed to report was enough to inspire the United States Congress to impose limited economic sanctions on South Africa in October 1986, over the objections of the Reagan administration. In December 1986 the South African government prohibited journalists from photographing "visible signs" of unrest such as corpses, or even from being "at a place within sight of any unrest, restricted gathering, or security action."

In January 1987 Tambo traveled to the United States to meet with Secretary of State George

Shultz not long after celebrating the ANC's seventy-fifth anniversary with a speech in which he invited South Africa's whites into a "massive democratic coalition" with blacks. In the same speech he exhorted blacks to spread the unrest of their townships to white areas. Tambo continued to walk that rhetorical tightrope in the United States, where conservatives expressed outrage at his meeting with Shultz in newspaper ads. The North Carolina Senator Jesse Helms, the former U.N. ambassador Jeane Kirkpatrick, and many others called on Shultz to cancel the meeting. The fifty-minute meeting with Shultz took place behind closed doors on January 28, 1987, while conservatives staged a protest outside.

Tambo pressed, unsuccessfully, for a "total break," both economic and political, between Washington and Pretoria and for special aid to the front-line states that Pretoria tries to intimidate and destabilize. When Tambo was questioned by Shultz and by journalists on the issue of ANC terrorism, he responded that the South African regime practiced the worst terrorism in all of Africa, apartheid being in itself an act of violence. Throughout his visit, the issues that Tambo wished to discuss were pushed into the background by questions of the influence on ANC policy of its pro-Moscow Communist members and of the Soviet Union itself. "I dominate the ANC," Tambo assured one reporter. At a Washington, D.C., church

he drew an analogy familiar to Americans. "We are like the Jews in Hitler's concentration camps," he said. "When they looked among themselves, who cared what the next person believed or did not believe? Who cared among the Allies whether the Soviet Union was a socialist state? . . . The overriding issue was the destruction of the Nazi system. The issue today is destruction of a Nazi system."

Oliver Tambo is a small, professorial-looking man, with a greying walrus mustache. His owlish appearance is reinforced by his spectacles. He and his wife, Adelaide, a nurse, were married in 1956. They have three children who live with Mrs. Tambo in London. Living with them, Peter Godwin reported, "would have signed [Tambo's] death warrant." His own address is kept secret. Tambo relaxes by listening to classical music on a pocket tape recorder before going to bed. He continues to write his own music, including what Godwin described as "the haunting melodies sung by the ANC choirs in beautiful harmony."

References: Chicago Tribune IV p1+ F 1 '87 por; London Sunday Times p29 Je 29 '86 por; N Y Daily News p1+ F 1 '87 pors; N Y Rev of Bks 31:27+ F 2 '84 por; N Y Times IV p13 F 7 '82 por; Newsweek 109:35+ F 2 '87 pors; Time 127:40 Je 2 '86 por; Washington Post G p1+ Ja 29 '87 pors; Benson, Mary. Nelson Mandela: The Man and the Movement (1986)

Tange, Kenzo

Sept. 4, 1913– Japanese architect; urban planner; educator. Address: b. Kenzo Tange Associates, 7-2-21 Akasaka, Minato-ku, Tokyo, Japan; h. 1702, 2-3-34 Mita, Minato-ku, Tokyo 108, Japan

In a career that parallels his country's spectacular rebirth and recovery from the destruction of World War II, Kenzo Tange has earned the title of the dean of modern Japanese architecture. His landmark buildings, which include major office towers, cultural centers, sports facilities, and government headquarters, reflect his creative blending of Japan's rich architectural tradition with the innovations of modernist design. With major architectural and urban planning projects on five continents to his credit, Tange has also distinguished himself abroad. A guiding theme in Tange's work is his search for an architecture appropriate to the Information Age—an architecture that would transcend impersonal functionalism by facilitating communication and by creating "a dynamic balance between technology and human existence." In 1987 Tange's half-century of architectural achievement was recognized with the Pritziker Prize, the premier international award in his field.

Kenzo Tange was born on September 4, 1913, in the town of Imabari, Ehime Prefecture, on the is-

land of Shikoku, Japan. The only child of Tokiyo Tange, a bank manager, and Tei (Kowaki) Tange, Kenzo had three half siblings much older than he by his father's previous marriage. He spent several years as a small boy in Hankow and Shanghai, China, after his father was transferred there with the Sumimoto Bank, and then attended the local Imabari schools after the family returned to Japan. Adept at mathematics, Kenzo enrolled as a boarding student at Hiroshima High School in 1930 at seventeen with the vague intention of becoming an astronomer, but he soon found himself drawn to literature and the arts instead. While reading an art magazine one day, he chanced upon some design drawings by the revolutionary French modernist architect Le Corbusier for a Palace of Soviets in the Soviet Union. Tange was so struck by Le Corbusier's rendering of industrially inspired forms that magnified structural elements but were "nonetheless awe-inspiringly beautiful" that he promptly settled on architecture as a career that could synthesize his interest in both science and the arts.

Tange's aesthetic dabblings left him ill-trained in the technical requirements for his chosen field, however, and he failed the entrance examinations for Tokyo University after graduating with the third-lowest record in his high school science class. Although he enrolled in the film school division of Nihon University to avoid Japan's military draft, he spent much of the next two years leading a bohemian life in Tokyo's literary cafes and bars, where he and other ronin (lapsed students) argued about the latest European novels and philosophy. When Tange finally gained admission to Tokyo University's architecture program on his third attempt, in the spring of 1935, he decided to specialize in design. His studies deepened his admiration for Le Corbusier but increased his dislike for the soulless "white sanitary-porcelain boxes" of much contemporary functionalist architecture. Tange judged Le Corbusier to be unique in shaping works that spoke to the mind and spirit while retaining the modernist love of clean lines and the austere rejection of excess ornamentation. His prize-winning graduation design for a "Château d'Art" in 1938 was greatly indebted to the French master and helped him to get a job in the Tokyo office of Corbusier-trained Kunio Mayekawa, one of Japan's leading architects.

Although Tange succeeded in designing several wooden buildings during the three years that he worked with Mayekawa, he actually spent much of his time on theoretical and historical research projects, including a comparison of the work of Michelangelo and Corbusier. When the outbreak of World War II ended nonmilitary building, he returned to Tokyo University for graduate studies and extended his research to traditional Japanese architecture and urban planning in ancient Greece and Rome. He made his professional reputation during the war years by winning three major design competitions with proposals that successfully blended ancient Japanese shrine elements, like raised floors and gabled roofs, with modernist forms in large-scale, modern buildings. When he was appointed a professor of architecture at Tokyo

University in 1946, Tange quickly organized the Tanken Team, a talented group of research students from Tokyo and other universities who contributed to the rebuilding of war-devastated Japan. For the following three decades, Tange continued to teach at Tokyo University while heading his independent architectural design and urban planning studio. He received a doctoral degree from the university in 1959 after submitting a dissertation on "The Structure of Tokyo City."

His first major postwar project in 1946 was helping to plan the reconstruction of Hiroshima, which had been flattened by the atomic bomb attack by the United States on August 6, 1945. Tange's high-school memories of that city, along with the tragic coincidence that his own mother was killed by an incendiary bomb in Imabari on the same day that Hiroshima was destroyed, prompted him to volunteer for the on-site job despite radiation danger. Most of his land-use plan for the city was accepted, and in 1949 he won an open competition to design a Peace Center to be built at the epicenter of the atomic blast. Completed in 1955, the Hiroshima Peace Memorial Museum brought Tange international recognition for the first time. A long, narrow, one-story, concrete-and-glass building raised twenty feet off the ground on stilts, the museum is not only indebted for its design to both Le Corbusier and the International Style's "weightless box" concept, but also recalls the Japanese tradition with its slat-like concrete window partitions set in repetitive vertical frames. The building's austerity and elevated structure reflect Tange's interest in architectural symbolism, representing peace as a condition that must be actively created by mankind and always hangs in a delicate balance. The Peace Center also includes Tange's designs for a children's library shaped like a concrete trumpet bell and a Memorial for the Dead that lists the names of Hiroshima residents who were killed in the nuclear attack.

A series of other major public commissions in the 1950s allowed Tange to experiment with new architectural vocabularies that incorporated traditional Japanese features. Among his best-known structures of that period are the Tokyo and Kurashiki city halls and the Kagawa prefectural office. All three buildings adapted the recessed ground pillars, post-and-beam superstructure, and open peripheral spaces common to traditional wooden construction, but differed dramatically in how they applied those elements. In the Tokyo building, for example, Tange used a slender steel exterior grid frame that only hinted at the post-and-beam style, while he made the connection forcefully in the Kagawa office, using exposed, crisscrossed concrete beams that suggested an outsized timber teahouse. The fortress-like Kurashiki hall, finally, recalls the solid peasant construction tradition with its massive, stacked blocks of raw concrete and narrow, horizontal recesses for windows.

While exploring contemporary applications of traditional Japanese architecture, Tange also intensified his criticism of functionalism during that period and engaged in innovative theoretical work in urban planning. He judged the functionalist theory to be unsatisfactory in that it failed to unify and order the many different functions a typical office building must perform and did not take into account future functional changes. To remedy that defect, he adopted a method he called the "typification of functions," by means of which he tried to identify the "most human, essential, and future-oriented" uses of a building and to make them the determining factors in its design. Beyond typification, Tange saw the need to create generally coherent spatial structures to unify disparate functional elements in both buildings and cities.

Foreseeing the advent of the postindustrial service economy in advanced capitalist societies, Tange identified the primary architectural and urban planning structure required for the Information Age as that of facilitating communication. Because communication is fundamentally subjective and interpersonal, he reasoned, contemporary architecture and urban planning should go beyond industrialism's emphasis on material functions and efficiency in favor of designs that speak more directly to the spiritual aspirations and existential needs of human beings. As Tange defined the issue in a 1960 address, "Architects and designers are the only people who stand in the middle ground between technology and humanity, and it is therefore essential that with the advance of science they manifest more and more creativity."

Tange set out to apply his structuralist urban development principles on a citywide scale when he presented his *Plan for Tokyo 1960* at the first World Design Conference, which was held in Japan that year. That visionary $50 billion scheme called for extending the badly congested Tokyo city center across the middle of Tokyo Bay by means of a narrow bridge of landfill that the architect termed a "civic axis." The strip would support a vast complex of office towers along with rapid transit and communications facilities, and it would serve as the urban core for an array of residential housing units constructed on floating platforms and connected by highways and pedestrian causeways to either side of the axis. Tange envisioned the civic axis as the urban design of the future, allowing infinite, uncongested growth along an "open" linear system of interconnected hubs unlike the "closed" structure of contemporary cities built concentrically around a single focal point.

Although it was ridiculed as wildly extravagant and visionary in 1960, Tange's Tokyo Bay scheme has gained new respectability in recent years as stratospheric land prices and crushing population density in downtown Tokyo make development of the shallow waterway increasingly attractive. He has responded to that reawakened interest with a substantially modified *Plan for Tokyo 1986,* which proposes developing a huge new coastal city of Tokyo on underused waterfront land and linking it with a high-speed transportation and communications axis to a new Tokyo Bay City built entirely on a series of artificial islands extending across the bay. Tange's ambitious plans for Tokyo Bay City foresee a working population of one and a half million and a resident population of more than two and a half million.

His growing interest in large-scale urban planning in the 1960s led Tange to organize a major new design group called Urtec. A contraction of the English words "urbanists" and "architects," the name was changed to Kenzo Tange Associates in 1985. Urtec undertook a number of important city development projects in Japan and abroad during that decade, including the reconstruction of the earthquake-devastated city center of Skopje, Yugoslavia in 1965-66.

During those years, Tange applied the structuralist method to design some of the outstanding buildings of his career. The two National Gymnasiums that he created for the Tokyo Olympics in 1964 are widely regarded as his masterworks and were hailed by the Pritzker jury as "among the most beautiful buildings of the twentieth century." Because the massively graceful structures brilliantly synthesize traditional Japanese architectural forms and state-of-the-art tensile steel construction design, they achieve both practical and spiritual effects. Viewed from above, the sweepingly arched roof of the 15,000-seat main gymnasium resembles two commas or yin-and-yang symbols out of alignment at each end. The building stands in dynamic balance with its smaller sister gymnasium sited nearby, which is shaped something like a spiraled snail's shell. The roofs of both gymnasiums are suspension structures of welded steel plates supported by steel cables that require no internal supports and provide a minimum volume of unused space. Besides imparting a sense of openness, the soaring lines inside the gymnasia are intended to inspire and spiritually unify the contestants and spectators.

His National Gymnasiums elevated Tange to the front rank of world architects, and he further enhanced his reputation in 1964 with a stunningly dramatic design for the Cathedral of St. Mary in Tokyo. A sculpted fusion of soaring stainless steel and concrete wings, the building is illuminated by a cruciform skylight and so successfully conveyed his symbolic ideal that he received a congratulatory letter from Pope Paul VI. Around the same time, Tange began exploring a radically different architectural style based on so-called Metabolist principles. The Metabolist concern with designing buildings to accommodate growth and change is best realized in the sprawling Yamanashi Communications Center that Tange built in the city of Kofu near Mount Fuji from 1961 to 1967. Dispensing with the central structural and service core that is commonly used in office buildings, Tange designed sixteen dispersed cylindrical shafts that support and carry services to four basic building blocks—an arrangement that increased the building's structural strength in an earthquake-prone area and allowed much longer floor spans. The structurally independent building blocks also offer great space flexibility, allowing floor sections to be added, expanded, or removed, while the dispersed service cores permit building functions to interconnect or proceed separately, as required.

The Yamanashi building became the prototype for Tange's Shizuoka Press and Broadcasting Center in the Ginza district of Tokyo. Consisting of a single 190-foot-tall aluminum service cylinder with cantilevered glass office boxes plugged irregularly into its sides, it was enthusiastically hailed by *Architectural Forum* magazine (March 1968) as "one of the most astonishing tours de force put up anywhere since New York's Flatiron Building was constructed in 1902."

Although his individual buildings were widely admired, Tange aroused controversy with some of his urban planning schemes in the late 1960s and early 1970s. His master plan for the Expo '70 World's Fair held in Osaka, adhering to his "civic axis" concept by grouping the exhibition areas around a long central axis with a "theme" pavilion, was criticized as being boring and predictable. Two ambitious proposals to redevelop inner-city districts in San Francisco and Baltimore foundered over environmental concerns, and his bid to build a sports complex in New York City's Flushing Meadows was killed for cost considerations.

But Tange fared somewhat better with his scheme, proposed in 1975, to develop the Fiera District Center in Bologna, Italy. The large-scale office complex located on the outskirts of the historic city, which has been under construction for a decade, is intended to serve as a business and governmental subcenter. Although Tange has tried to integrate such traditional Bolognese architectural forms as piazzas, porticoes, and towers into his work, the project's stark concrete high-rises built with multiple cylindrical cores and joist slabs clash jarringly with the city's many medieval and Renaissance buildings.

In the late 1970s and early 1980s Tange undertook large-scale, glamorous government projects for oil-producing countries glutted with "petrodollars." He designed an enormous royal palace for King Khalid in Jeddah, Saudi Arabia, built the King Faisal Foundation Complex, a government office, business, and residential center in the Saudi capital of Riyadh, and completed an international airport for Kuwait in 1979. Among his other ambitious recent projects are the University of Oran in Algeria and the Arabian Gulf University in the Persian Gulf sheikhdom of Bahrain, both of which are currently under construction. His firm was also entrusted with two vast urban planning projects, the designs for new federal capitals for Nigeria and Malaysia. The Nigerian project, commissioned in 1979, involves the planning of the central civic axis and several buildings for the new city of Abuja in the country's interior, in an attempt to overcome tribal regionalism and relieve congestion in the current capital of Lagos. In Malaysia, Tange is carrying out plans for a new federal twin capital to be built in the pristine hills of Pahang state just thirty kilometers from the current over-populated capital of Kuala Lumpur. The design scheme, begun in 1983, proposes the linking of the new city to Kuala Lumpur along a civic axis that would ultimately extend across the Malay Peninsula and promote development in the interior and along the east coast.

More recently, Kenzo Tange has turned to designing landmark skyscrapers in Japan, Singapore, and Australia. Since 1980 an outcropping of Tange towers, including the 900-foot-tall Overseas Union Bank and the City Telecommunications Centre, the tallest telecommunications building in the world, have helped to vitalize Singapore's previously nondescript skyline. In Sydney, Australia, Tange Associates is building World Square, a four-tower complex with a large central atrium that will house offices, apartment buildings, and a shopping center. The slope-roofed towers will stand at right angles to one another and rise in height in a clockwise direction, giving an impression of openness and upward spiral movement from the atrium.

In Japan, Tange designed the Aksaka Prince Hotel high-rise, which was completed in 1982. Multiple folding wings that extend forward from either side of the building greet visitors with a welcoming embrace, making the hotel resemble a huge handheld fan. Its ultramodern interior is designed to create an impression of serene spaciousness in one of Tokyo's busiest districts. Tange's current major project in Japan is the mammoth new Tokyo City Hall Complex, for which he won the design competition in 1986. Located in the western district of Shinjuku, it is to include two huge office buildings, an assembly hall, and an outdoor plaza shaped like a half-moon. The larger office building will be distinguished by its Notre Dame-like twin towers, the tallest in Japan. Another outstanding feature of Tange's design is the variegated, concrete-framed fenestration that suggests the post-and-beam architectural style.

The Tokyo City Hall project is Tange's most visible signature to date in his home city, and he hopes to follow it up eventually with similar works in New York and Paris, his favorite international cities. He has submitted a proposal, still pending, to redevelop the Place d'Italie in Paris, but his competed work in the United States has been limited so far to designing a 1975 expansion of the Minneapolis Art Museum. Americans may become more familiar with Tange if his recent proposals to develop Chicago Park and Pacific Rim Plaza in Los Angeles reach fruition.

In addition to contributing articles to professional publications, Tange has collaborated with others on books on traditional Japanese architecture, both secular and religious. He has been showered with honors from Japan and abroad, including gold medals from the Royal Institute of British Architects (1965) and the American Institute of Architects (1966), an associate membership in the prestigious Académie des Beaux-Arts of the Institut de France (1984), and the $100,000 Pritzker Architecture Prize in 1987. Although he relinquished his professorship in 1974, the septuagenarian

Tange has lost none of his professional vigor, and remains the revered father figure, creative leader, and final authority for the talented young staff of ninety-two architects and urbanists at Tange Associates. "It's very hard to be satisfied by past work," the Japanese master remarked to Newsday's Joanna L. Krotz (March 26, 1987) shortly after receiving the Pritziker award. "I'll only retire when I die."

Kenzo Tange is five feet five inches tall and has a wiry, deceptively frail-looking frame. He combs his graying black hair straight back from his brow, and his bushy eyebrows, perched high above bright, dark eyes, give him a slightly bemused expression. The soft-spoken architect has been described as the "world's champion listener," with a leader's knack for disguising his decisions as suggestions, but he is also known for his tenacious will when he finds it necessary to press his point of view. Since 1971 Tange has been married to Takako Iwata (he was previously married in 1949, to Toshiko Kato) and is the father of two children, Michiko and Noritaka. He makes his home in Tokyo.

References: Am Institute of Architects 45:82+ Je '66 por, 48:44+ O '67; Architectural Rec 123:127+ Jl '58; Horizon 4:58+ S '61 por; Japan Architect 51: whole issue Ag–S '76, 54: whole issue Jl–Ag '79, 60:7+ Ap '85 pors, 60:6+ My '85, 60:6+ Jl '85 pors, 60:6 Ag '85 por, 60:6+ S '85 pors, 60:8+ N–D '85 pors, 61:6+ Ja '86 por, 61:8+ F '86 por; Los Angeles Herald Examiner VI p2 Ap 5 '87; N Y Newsday III p4 Mr 26 '87; Read Digest 94:155+ F '69; Time 74:78+ N 30 '59; 130:68+ S 21 '87 pors; UNESCO Courier 38:4+ Mr '85; Washington Post C p1+ Ag 30 '86, C p1+ Mr 19 '87; Bognar, Botond. Contemporary Japanese Architecture (1985); Boyd, Robin G. P. Kenzo Tange (1962), New Directions in Japanese Architecture (1968); Contemporary Architects (1980); International Who's Who, 1986–87; Kultermann, Udo, ed. Kenzo Tange: 1946–1969 (1970); Macmillan Encyclopedia of Architects (1982); Riani, Paolo. Kenzo Tange (1970); Who's Who in Architecture (1977)

Tartikoff, Brandon

Jan. 13, 1949– Broadcasting executive. Address: b. NBC, 30 Rockefeller Plaza, New York City, N.Y. 10020; NBC, 3000 Alameda Blvd., Burbank, Calif. 91523

When NBC overtook CBS in April 1986 to become the premier network in television's all-important Nielsen ratings for the first time in three decades, much of the credit went to Brandon Tartikoff, the young president of NBC Entertainment. Since he was named to that post in 1980, Tartikoff has labored to establish NBC as the acknowledged champion of literate and innovative programming, even at the risk of losing some viewers. His gamble began paying off in the mid-1980s, as NBC's roster of sophisticated, urban-flavored series, including Hill Street Blues, Family Ties, The Cosby Show, and Miami Vice, reaped bushels of awards and eventually outdrew the competition in key upscale, urban markets. In recognition of his achievement, Tartikoff was honored as Broadcaster of the Year in 1986 by the Television, Radio, and Advertising Club of Philadelphia.

The son of Jordan and Enid Tartikoff, Brandon Tartikoff was born on January 13, 1949 in Freeport, Long Island, a bedroom suburb of New York City. His father is in the fabric business; his mother works for a cruise company. A child who, in his words, always "had to be doing ten different things," Brandon focused most of his abundant energy on sports, especially baseball, and television. He even went so far as to feign illness so that he could stay home from school and watch daytime reruns of such shows as My Little Margie, I Married Joan, and Burns and Allen. Unlike many other members of the so-called television generation, however, Tartikoff watched the small screen with a critical and perceptive eye. After viewing the premiere episode of the situation comedy Dennis the Menace in 1959, for instance, he turned to his parents and said, "They could have made that show much better." He also demonstrated an uncanny knack for predicting which new programs would become hits.

When he was about thirteen years old, Tartikoff drifted into a group of rowdy adolescents and began to neglect his schoolwork. Recognizing that their son would never achieve his potential unless he was challenged by his peers, his parents decided to send him to Lawrenceville, the well-known preparatory school near Princeton, New Jersey. In his first year there, he went out for three sports, joined six extracurricular organizations, including the chess and French clubs, served as feature editor of the yearbook, and still managed to earn academic honors. An accomplished swordsman, he won the New Jersey state fencing championship in his senior year.

Following his graduation from Lawrenceville in 1966, Tartikoff enrolled at Yale University, where he continued to participate in many extracurricular activities. Among other things, he played varsity baseball, captained the fencing team, coedited (with Garry Trudeau, the cartoonist who later created the syndicated comic strip "Doonesbury") the campus humor magazine, and headed the students' social committee. Originally an economics major, he eventually switched to English and set his sights on becoming a writer. His first efforts were hardly promising. As part of a creative writing course taught by the novelist and poet Robert Penn Warren, Tartikoff wrote "The Long Novella," whose protagonist, improbably named Saliva Schwartz, tries to track down Siamese twins who are spreading a sexually transmitted disease across the United States.

On receiving his B.A. degree, with honors, from Yale in 1970, Tartikoff took a job with a New Haven, Connecticut, advertising agency. Two years later he signed on as director of advertising and promotion for WTNH-TV, the ABC affiliate in New Haven, where he got, as he put it, "a liberal-arts education in television." In 1973 he landed a similar job at WLS-TV, the ABC-owned station in Chicago, Illinois. Brimming with self-confidence, he spent every vacation in Los Angeles looking for a job in network television—until a personal crisis forced him to reorder his priorities. Shaken by the sudden death of a close friend, Tartikoff made an appointment for a routine physical examination and was diagnosed as having Hodgkin's disease, a form of lymphatic cancer. Over the next several months, he underwent regular chemotherapy and radiation treatments. He lost most of his hair, and his weight dropped from 170 to 135 pounds, but in defiance of his doctor, who repeatedly stressed the debilitating nature of the disease, Tartikoff went to work every day and continued to play basketball three times a week. "When I got cancer and was faced with at least an understanding of my mortality, nothing was a given anymore," he told an interviewer for People (November 12, 1984). "It helped me channel my energies. A lot of my cockiness disappeared. I really hadn't been arrogant, but I had always felt I was owed something, and then just getting better was such a gift."

Tartikoff began to attract the attention of his superiors at WLS when, in January 1976, he substantially boosted the ratings for the station's late afternoon movie by taking from the film vault a handful of low-budget horror movies and packaging them under the promotional banner "Not for the Weak Week." He followed up with "Gorilla My Dreams" and "Thrilla Gorilla" weeks, featuring King Kong and other "ape" movies. Impressed by the surge in afternoon ratings at WLS, Fred Silverman, then head of ABC's programming division, hired Tartikoff in 1976 as the network's director of dramatic development. Tartikoff remained with ABC only until September 1977, when he left to become director of comedy programming at NBC. "ABC was so successful at the time that I was like a third-string quarterback on a championship team," he explained to Tony Schwartz in an interview for New York (April 24, 1980). In contrast, NBC had been mired in third place, behind CBS and ABC, in the Nielsen ratings since 1976.

In June 1978 Fred Silverman, who had been credited with lifting ABC from its status as a perennial loser in the ratings race, was also lured to NBC. Silverman quickly drew Tartikoff into his inner circle, making him vice-president of West Coast programming on June 29. Eighteen months later, on January 15, 1980, the thirty-one-year-old Tartikoff became the youngest division chief in the network's history when Silverman named him president of NBC Entertainment. Charged with overseeing sixty-nine hours of network programming—that is, everything except news and sports—each week, he was also expected to select independently produced shows for broadcast, to negotiate with producers about themes for individual episodes or entire series, and to administer an annual budget of some $800 million.

Tartikoff enthusiastically embraced his broad mandate, but it was Silverman—widely known in the industry as a man reluctant to delegate responsibility—who actually crafted NBC's prime-time schedule. Desperate for a hit during the dismal 1980–81 season, Silverman hastily scheduled several poorly conceived new shows, then just as quickly jettisoned them when they failed to attract an audience. As NBC's ratings—and profits—plummeted, Tartikoff remained Silverman's most visible lieutenant, loyally defending such low-calibre shows as The Misadventures of Sheriff Lobo, B. J. and the Bear, and the rabble-rousing Speak Up, America so often that one Hollywood producer called him "Silverman's Charlie McCarthy." In the midst of that ill-starred season, in December 1980, Tartikoff was named one of the ten outstanding young men in America by the Junior Chamber of Commerce.

When Grant Tinker succeeded Fred Silverman as president of NBC on July 1, 1981, Tartikoff, to the surprise of many television insiders, was asked to stay on the job. Moreover, in marked contrast to Silverman and his aggressively hands-on management style, Tinker immediately made known his intention to give Tartikoff considerable autonomy. "I knew that Fred had been calling all the shots," Tinker explained to Harry F. Waters, the television critic of Newsweek (May 16, 1983). "Brandon hadn't yet been up to bat. What struck me was his excellent sense of this town. He recognized who the best people were and he was willing to let them do their work without meddling. Too many network programmers try to produce the producers."

In September 1982 Tartikoff introduced the first prime-time schedule bearing his signature. It included four ambitious new series: *Family Ties*, a generation-gap situation comedy about two 1960s liberals raising conservative children; *Cheers*, a broadly satirical comedy set entirely in a Boston bar; *St. Elsewhere*, an often bleak drama about life and death in an inner-city hospital; and the sophisticated crime drama *Remington Steele*. Despite favorable reviews, none of those shows was an immediate hit, but all four remained on the air. Tinker and Tartikoff agreed that talented independent producers would be more likely to offer their shows to NBC if they knew that the network gave blue-ribbon series a reasonable opportunity to develop an audience.

Ironically, of all the new programs introduced by NBC during the 1982-83 season, the one that fared best in the ratings was the decidedly lowbrow action-adventure series *The A-Team*. A midseason replacement that Tartikoff concocted after meeting the hulking Mr. T at a boxing match, *The A-Team* follows the exploits of a band of resourceful mercenaries. The series, which Tartikoff has described as "*The Magnificent Seven*, *The Dirty Dozen*, *Mission Impossible*, and *Road Warrior* all rolled into one," became an unqualified hit, inspiring a line of related toys and other products and considerably boosting NBC's profits. In December 1982 NBC reaffirmed its commitment to Tartikoff by giving him a three-year contract to continue as president of its entertainment division and raising his salary to a reported $300,000 annually.

The A-Team, *Family Ties*, *Cheers*, *St. Elsewhere*, and *Remington Steele* were all prominently featured in NBC's 1983 fall lineup. Another holdover was *Hill Street Blues*, a gritty police drama that garnered a record eight Emmy Awards eight months after its midseason debut, in January 1981. Nonetheless, 1983-84 marked the ninth straight season that NBC trailed CBS and ABC in the Nielsen ratings. Even more sobering for Tartikoff, all nine of the new shows that he added to the prime-time program roster in September 1983 flopped. Among these quickly discarded disappointments were *Mr. Smith*, a sophomoric comedy featuring an orangutan with an I.Q. of 256; *Bay City Blues*, a *Hill Street Blues* imitation about a baseball team; *The Yellow Rose*, a family saga set on a 200,000-acre cattle ranch; and *Buffalo Bill*, a comedy starring Dabney Coleman as an egomaniacal talk-show host.

Referring to *Buffalo Bill* and *Bay City Blues* as "high-risk shows" that needed "twenty-five minutes to explain the concept," Tartikoff decided to concentrate instead on simpler, more down-to-earth audience-pleasers. That new sensibility was reflected in NBC's schedule for the 1984-85 television season—the season that so clearly signaled the network's resurgence and forged Tartikoff's repu-

tation for programming wizardry. The schedule had its genesis early in 1984, when Tartikoff decided to purchase a new situation comedy series, recently rejected by ABC, starring Bill Cosby as the middle-aged father of five children. Focusing on everyday family problems, *The Cosby Show* made its debut on September 20, 1984, and quickly became one of the most popular comedies in television history. Scheduled on Thursday nights at 8:00, *The Cosby Show*, which attracts an estimated sixty million viewers weekly, provided a strong lead-in for the shows that followed—*Family Ties*, *Cheers*, and *Night Court*—and contributed significantly to their increased ratings. Although it was never a runaway hit by ratings standards, *Hill Street Blues*, which completed NBC's formidable Thursday night prime-time lineup, was nonetheless a moneymaker for NBC because, like *St. Elsewhere*, it appealed to well-educated, affluent, eighteen-to-forty-nine-year-old urban viewers, the most important demographic group to advertisers.

September 1984 also saw the debuts of *Highway to Heaven*, featuring Michael Landon as a probationary angel being tested for his worthiness, the action-adventure series *Hunter*, and *Miami Vice*, a police show that achieved hit status on the strength of its dynamic stars, Don Johnson and Philip Michael Thomas, pulsating rock score, and glossy visual style. Acknowledging the visceral appeal of those shows, Tartikoff told a reporter for the trade weekly *Variety* (June 4, 1986) that he would not be doing his job if he let his own artistic preferences dictate NBC's entire schedule. "I always push for a balanced menu," he said.

Buoyed by the success of its Thursday-night comedies and by the continued popularity of such holdovers as *The A-Team*, NBC pulled ahead of ABC in the prime-time ratings in October 1984 and began to challenge CBS for the lead. The network's position was strengthened by its solid late-night lineup and by a string of critically and commercially successful made-for-television movies, including *The Burning Bed*, starring Farrah Fawcett as a battered wife; *Adam*, a powerful drama about a missing child; and *Fatal Vision*, based on Joe McGinniss' best-selling account of the bizarre case of Dr. Jeffrey R. MacDonald, who was convicted in 1979 of murdering his pregnant wife and two young daughters. With such powerful contenders, NBC earned more Emmy nominations than ABC and CBS combined. More important, for the first time in a decade, the network finished the season in second place.

Reluctant to tamper with a winning roster, Tartikoff introduced only four new hours of series programming in the fall of 1985, the smallest number in years. In what was widely considered to be a programming coup, he signed Steven Spielberg, the phenomenally successful motion picture director and producer, to mastermind a suspense anthology series called *Amazing Stories*. Spielberg, who had been wooed by all the networks, decided to go with NBC because of its willingness to commit itself to forty-four episodes, or two years on the program schedule. Despite a lavish budget that allowed for some spectacular special effects, *Amazing Stories* left most viewers cold. On the other hand, *The Golden Girls*, a show developed from a concept by Tartikoff, more than lived up to its enthusiastic advance publicity. A snappy comedy about three middle-aged women sharing a home with a tart-tongued octogenarian, *The Golden Girls* benefited from its crisp dialogue and the accomplished ensemble acting of its cast of veteran actresses.

After experiencing thirty-one years as an also-ran, NBC wrested the prime-time ratings lead from CBS in April 1986. To Tartikoff, the victory seemed especially sweet, and in June 1986, amid rumors that he would leave the network to accept a top executive position with a major film studio, he extended his commitment to NBC to 1990. Few details of Tartikoff's lucrative long-term contract were made public, but according to most reports, the network agreed to his request that NBC enter the motion picture production business. "As the [film] studios become more and more like networks, we have to become more and more like studios," Tartikoff explained, as quoted in the *Washington Post* (October 27, 1986). Under Tartikoff's supervision, NBC Productions, the unit that makes some of the network's television movies and miniseries, will produce as many as five theatrical films a year. One of its first efforts was *Square Dance*, which was released in February 1987.

As the 1986–87 television season got underway, Tartikoff basked in the glow of the public's warm response to many of his new programming choices. A key entry, *L.A. Law*, which was developed by Steven Bochco, the creator of *Hill Street Blues*, quickly found a niche near the top of the Nielsen charts. Television viewers also responded favorably to *Matlock*, starring Andy Griffith as a wily, homespun attorney, and *Amen*, featuring Sherman Hemsley as the overbearing and pompous deacon of a Philadelphia church. Capping a year in which almost nothing went wrong, NBC garnered nineteen of the thirty-one prime-time Emmy awards presented in 1986.

A tall, slim man with an ingenuous manner and a self-deprecating sense of humor, Brandon Tartikoff has a boyishly round, open face crowned by a helmet of brown hair. "Perversely unfashionable," as Tony Schwartz observed, he favors jeans, crew-neck sweaters, and novelty T-shirts, and he never wears a watch. Tartikoff and his wife, the former Lilly Samuels, a dancer with the New York City Ballet whom he married in 1982, live in an unpretentious three-bedroom house in Coldwater Canyon, California, with their daughter, Calla Lianne. In his extremely limited spare time, Tartikoff shoots baskets on his home court and plays third base in a weekend softball league.

References: N Y Daily News mag p6+ O 13 '85 pors; N Y Times C p25 Ap 24 '80 por; New York 18:42+ S 30 '85 pors; Newsweek 101:84 My 16 '83

por; People 22:103+ N 12 '84 pors; Time 127:74 D 3 '84 por, 126:64+ S 16 '85 por; Washington Post B p1+ Jl 18 '85 por; Levinson, Richard and Link, William. Conversations with the Makers of Prime Time Television (1986); Who's Who in America, 1986–87

Taylor, Peter (Hillsman)

Jan. 8, 1917– Writer. Address: h. 1841 Wayside Place, Charlottesville, Va. 22903

Although relatively unknown, at least until recently, except to readers of the *New Yorker* and aficionados of Southern fiction, Peter Taylor is, in the words of Robert Penn Warren, one of the twentieth century's "real, and probably enduring, masters of the short story." Taylor's stories are distilled, artfully rambling and digressive fictional memoirs about a genteel and circumscribed world that has all but vanished—that of the middle and upper classes carrying the burden of old manners, mores, and morals with them as they are displaced from country to city in the changing upper South. Despite their suggestion of mystery in human motivation, they are stories in the realist mode, exact in their observation of the minute details of class behavior while gentle and understated—often with ironic humor—in their treatment of the terrible tensions involved in social displacement and family dissolution. Unlike the fiction of most other twentieth-century Southern writers, they elicit pathos without morbidity or terror.

Taylor, who began contributing to literary reviews and magazines almost half a century ago, is the author of seven collections of short stories, including *The Collected Stories of Peter Taylor* (1969). In addition, he has written the novella *A Woman of Means* (1950), the novel *A Summons to Memphis* (1986), and many experimental one-act plays. *A Summons to Memphis* won Pulitzer and Ritz-Hemingway prizes in 1987. Taylor cannot be considered a stereotypical regional writer for two reasons: his distrust of the Southern past and his universality of tone and message.

Peter Hillsman Taylor was born on January 8, 1917, in Trenton, Tennessee, which becomes Chatham or Thornton in his fiction. His father was Matthew Hillsman Taylor, a lawyer who was for some years the president of an insurance company in Saint Louis, Missouri. His mother was Katherine Baird Taylor (her maiden name as well as her married name). While his father was the dominant personality in the household, it was largely from his mother that Taylor acquired his passion for listening to and telling stories. The family history was rich in grist for saga. The maternal grandfather, Robert L. Taylor, was a United States congressman, a governor of Tennessee, and a United States senator, and two of his own sons fought him tooth and nail in the 1886 Tennessee gubernatorial campaign.

Moving from Trenton when Peter was seven, the Taylors lived in Nashville, Tennessee, from 1924 to 1926, in Saint Louis, Missouri, from 1926 to 1932, and in Memphis, Tennessee, from 1932 to 1937. Rather than creating a sense of instability and impermanence, the moves gave Taylor the opportunity to observe at first hand the effects of urbanization and industrialization on the lives of middle- and upper-middle-class families transplanted from small rural Southern towns still linked to the antebellum past. The clash of cultures that occurs when a family's history and traditional values come into question in a modern and indifferent or even hostile setting is a constant theme in Taylor's work. He pursued it without resentment of the new conditions or undue wistfulness for an imagined arcadian paradise. His characters are drawn willy-nilly from life, as he told Michael Kernan of the *Washington Post* (March 4, 1985): "You can't make them up, incredible as they are. But . . . you have to change people. I'll make use of a figure . . . but I'll change it, combine it with other people. As you do this your understanding of people changes too. I think that writing fiction is a way of learning what you think." Just as William Faulkner's grandmother provided the raw material for Faulkner's fiction about Yoknapatawpha County, Mississippi, Taylor's mother was the source of much of the material that he transmutes in his stories about Chatham and Thornton, Tennessee. At first Mrs. Taylor tended to bowdlerize the family history, but as she told the same stories again and again, Taylor recounted to Kernan, "the censorship broke down . . . and she would reveal scandalous things that she had buried," such as her father's divorce.

Knowing that he had writing talent, Taylor resisted his father's wish that he become a lawyer and enrolled at Vanderbilt University in Nashville in the fall of 1936 to study literature and creative writing with the poet and critic John Crowe Ransom. Vanderbilt was the base of the group of Southern poets known as the Fugitives, who represented the most important movement in American letters since Transcendentalism and spearheaded the Southern literary renaissance. Ransom, Allen Tate, and Robert Penn Warren were among the original contributors to the *Fugitive* poetry magazine, published in Nashville between 1922 and 1925, and Andrew Lytle and Cleanth Brooks later became closely associated with the group. The Fugitives were essentially conservative, committed to the traditional Southern agrarian ideal in the midst of encroaching industrialization. They brought to an end the perception of the South as a cultural backwater and launched the New Criticism, a formal aesthetic focusing on the autonomous verbal structure of a poem or other literary text apart from its social context and other extrinsic considerations. That method of literary analysis gradually permeated and ultimately transformed the teaching and study of literature in universities throughout the United States and, in varying degrees, abroad.

When Ransom moved to Kenyon (Gambier, Ohio) College in 1937, Taylor transferred to Southwestern College in Memphis, where Tate was then on the faculty, for a year, and then finished his undergraduate work under Ransom at Kenyon. "It was my great luck to have come along at the time when those people were in the part of the world I was growing up in . . . " Taylor told Jean W. Ross in an interview for *Contemporary Authors* (1983). "Allen Tate was the person who really influenced me the most, I suppose, and next John Crowe Ransom. Tate was simply my [composition] teacher, and at once he liked my writing, and he gave me the feeling that writing was important. . . . And then he and I became great friends. I learned more from him as a friend than formerly as a teacher. . . . Ransom, too, . . . had a real influence on the form my writing has taken. He made me write poetry and discouraged me from writing fiction. I think that made my fiction more compressed and made me turn to short stories more than to novels." Taylor also "had to write poetry to get any attention" from the poets Randall Jarrell and Robert Lowell, fellow students of his at Kenyon College. One of Taylor's poems was published in the *Kenyon Review* (Spring 1940), the literary magazine founded at the college by John Crowe Ransom.

After taking his B.A. degree at Kenyon College in 1940, Taylor did graduate work for a year under Cleanth Brooks and Robert Penn Warren at Louisiana State University. During that year three of his short stories were published in the *Southern Review*. (Later he would contribute stories to the *Sewanee Review*, the *Kenyon Review*, the *Partisan Review*, the *Virginia Quarterly Review*, *Shenandoah*, *Harper's Bazaar*, and *McCall's*, among other publications. He would become best known for his contributions to the *New Yorker*.)

Taylor served with the United States army in England during World War II. After the war he joined the faculty of the University of North Carolina at Greensboro, where he taught intermittently until 1967.

In his introduction to Taylor's first collection of short stories, *A Long Fourth and Other Stories* (Harcourt, 1948), Robert Penn Warren described the author's style as traditional, having the "atmosphere of family tale-telling," and his sensibility as an "ironic" one that discovers extraordinary significance in the "small collisions" of ordinary middle- and upper-middle-class life in the new urban upper South, where family life and old loyalties, mores, and values were breaking down and characters raised in one set of circumstances were finding themselves in another. In the title story Taylor subtly examined the disappointment and stress experienced by characters unable to accommodate their idealization of the past to present reality. Reviewing the collection in the *Saturday Review of Literature* (March 27, 1948), Marjorie Brace said: "Mr. Taylor writes with limpid sobriety of undramatic incidents. . . . On the surface, his material is not very complex. . . . What [he] is really doing, with honesty and sureness and beauty, is to experiment, both technically and psychologically, with very difficult approaches to extremely difficult definitions. [He] is inquiring into those relations through which things take on their meaning, and he makes his inquiry . . . through connections so unfamiliar that he shakes the reader into emotional insecurity. . . . The strangeness and the remarkable effectiveness of Mr. Taylor's writing comes, never from the distortion of reality, but from considered and questioning rearrangement. His is a thoughtfully unpretentious and original talent." The reviewer for the *New Yorker* (March 13, 1948) found the collection to be "particularly notable for a vein of unobtrusive humor and for a complete lack of the regional chauvinism that Southern authors so frequently exhibit when writing about their own."

The book regarded by many critics as Taylor's finest work is the 30,000-word novella *A Woman of Means* (Harcourt, 1950). Set in Saint Louis in the mid-1920s, that work is a retrospective first-person account by an adolescent boy of the disintegration of his widowed father's second marriage and of his loving but troubled stepmother's final descent into madness. The father is a traveling salesman who, in the process of satisfying his wealthy new wife's longing for a son (the narrator, Quint Dudley), creates in her mind the nagging suspicion that he has married her only for her fortune. Some reviewers complained at the time that the stepmother's sudden, terrible breakdown, "too feebly foreshadowed" in the boy's earlier, pleasant recollections, was an "incredible" melodramatic trick, but others were left "breathless with admiration" for the "subtle" and "beautiful" study of "the death of aristocracy"—and the latter is the critical assessment that has prevailed. The book displays all of the narrative skills that readers have come to asso-

ciate with Taylor: the gentle irony intended, as Victor A. Kramer observes in the *Dictionary of Literary Biography* (1981), "to reflect the involutions of human experience"; the digressive but always forward-moving memoir of things seen and heard, but now lost; and, perhaps most important, the use of a narrator made untrustworthy and suspect by the very specificity of his limited and prejudiced point of view. Taylor's subtle handling of the tensions between urban and rural forces, masculinity and feminity, and childhood innocence and the pain and loneliness of coming-of-age makes for a narrative of power and authenticity.

The collection *The Widows of Thornton* (Harcourt, 1954) contained the one-act play *Death of a Kinsman* in addition to nine short stories about several families living in Thornton, Tennessee. In those seemingly simple but psychologically complex stories set in the region he knows best, Taylor wove, without didacticism, the common thread of a universal theme: that the bedrock of a healthy humanity is the sanctity of the home. The title story in *The Widows of Thornton* is more than a mere narrative about the woes of women who have lost their husbands; it is a long, hard look at the dependent, subservient roles to which women are consigned in a patriarchal, male-dominated society.

In the later short story "Promise of Rain," which is set in Nashville, the narrator is a father who ruminates on the fact that his and his son's perceptions of the city are so different that they are virtually living in two different places. "Promise of Rain" was one of the ten stories in the collection *Happy Families Are All Alike*, the title of which is an allusion to the first line in Tolstoy's *Anna Karenina* ("Happy families are all alike; every unhappy family is unhappy in its own way"). Most of the stories in the collection blend joy and sadness in such a way that, as Jeremy Brooks observed in the *New Statesman* (August 6, 1960), "it would be hazardous to guess openly whether Mr. Taylor imagines he is writing about happy families or unhappy ones." Ruth Blackman pointed out in her review in the *Christian Science Monitor* (December 24, 1959) that the layers of meaning are so complex that "items that seemed like trivia on the first reading are apt to turn up as clues on the second." Other reviewers noted that the stories seemed even more effective in one volume than when they had appeared separately because when read together they more forcefully convey a sense of the sustained "patrician serenity" and "balanced" world view of the author.

Taylor's short story "Venus, Cupid, Folly and Time," which won an O. Henry Award in 1959, is about two people who cannot escape the past. They are an eccentric old brother and sister, both unmarried, who are socially prominent in their small town but who socialize with other townsfolk only at an exclusive party that they host once a year. After a stranger crashes the event and dredges up a hint of incest, the two become totally reclusive. "Venus, Cupid, Folly and Time" was included in the collection *Miss Leonora When Last Seen and*

Fifteen Other Stories (Obelensky, 1963). Among the other stories were the title piece, about an old woman who returns after a long disappearance, and "What You Hear from 'Em?," in which the past is glimpsed through the memory of an old black woman, Aunt Munsie, who has raised two white boys only to see them go off to Memphis and Nashville and who dreams of their returning to live in Thornton again. While an acute sense of place, community, and shared history helps many of Taylor's characters to adapt to new surroundings and social orders, that sense does not guarantee security or success, and the adaptation is often fraught with danger. The past in Taylor's world always intrudes into the present, often in ways not pleasant or helpful.

In 1967 Farrar, Straus published *Randall Jarrell, 1914-1965* edited by Peter Taylor, Robert Lowell, and Robert Penn Warren, and two years later the same publisher issued *The Collected Short Stories of Peter Taylor*. "The new stories of the *Collected Stories* are not startlingly different from many early ones," Victor A. Kramer pointed out in his essay on Taylor in the *Dictionary of Literary Biography*. "What is evident, however, is Taylor's gradual refinement of technique. Over the years he seems to have become more attentive to the complexity of fictional situations and especially to the intricacies of the individual psyche and how language reveals this complexity."

Viewing the short story as essentially a dramatic medium, the mature Taylor naturally turned more frequently to the experimental one-act play to probe the complex and often subconscious motivations of his characters. While some of the plays have been produced, they are for the most part "closet dramas," as Victor A. Kramer observed. The play *A Stand in the Mountains*, published in the *Kenyon Review* in 1965, was first produced in Abingdon, Virginia in 1971. Seven other dramatic pieces—*A Father and a Son, Missing Person, A Voice Through the Door, Arson, Two Images, The Whistler*, and *Sweethearts*—were collected in *Presences* (Houghton, 1973). As in his short stories, differing interpretations of events is a common subject in the plays, and a ghost or person representing an earlier time is often present. "When Taylor transfers his technique to a stage production" J. William Broadway once noted in the *Atlanta Constitution*, "the effect is mesmerizing." Regarding *A Stand in the Mountains*, Broadway wrote: "This play could stand as the most unsettling of all Taylor's works because of its display of psychological and physical violence. Yet its very real power of presentation will make it unforgettable. . . . *A Stand in the Mountains* will prove that Peter Taylor has matched the works of his beloved Chekhov in more ways than one."

Meanwhile, Taylor had been experimenting with free-verse narratives, written in what he describes as "broken-line prose." He did so because he was seeking compression, as he explained to Jean W. Ross for *Contemporary Authors*: "Short stories are not just short novels. They're much more intense, and the words have to do a lot more work. . . . The advantage [in broken-line prose] is that you get the two kinds of syntax and, most important, you get . . . the impact at the end of the line." As is evident in the broken-prose stories included in *In the Miro District and Other Stories* (Knopf, 1977), another result is greater intimacy with the narrator and his involvement in the storytelling itself. Whereas much of the emphasis in Taylor's earlier stories was on women and their preservation of the sanctity of the home, the stress in that collection was on men, masculinity, and the male rite of passage. In the title story the narrator is a young man who openly tells of having sex with his girlfriend, in defiance of his grandfather's code of social ethics—that of the Old South—in which the Southern woman's honor demanded that such a relationship be kept absolutely private. Writing of *In the Miro District and Other Stories* in the *Virginia Quarterly Review* (Spring 1978), Jane Barnes Casey noted that Taylor has always been concerned with the conflict or tension between order and disorder, "whether the disorder is sexual, drunken, or natural." "Originally," she wrote, "Mr. Taylor seemed to give himself to Southern society, even though it was doomed, but his loyalty has undergone a transformation. While he continues to regard marriage as central, the conditions for its survival are more mythic than regional. What is interesting is that what appears to have made the reaffirmation of marriage possible is an avowal of sex as part of love; more importantly, this avowal is synonymous with an affirmation of masculinity. . . . Until this collection, Mr. Taylor has written more from the female point of view, using it as a screen through which he has observed disorder. Almost without exception, disorder has been associated with men trampling the social restraints enforced or represented by women." Writing in *Shenandoah* (Fall 1978), Alan Williamson identified the opposing forces seeking resolution in Taylor's fiction as narrow "self-love," with its compelling archaic demands, and "the wider eros," which directs men outward, toward social, ethical, and spiritual relationships.

The title story in *The Old Forest and Other Stories* (Dial Press/Doubleday, 1985), set in Memphis in 1937, is about a young man whose plans for an upper-class marriage are suspended under social pressure after he is involved in an automobile accident with a woman of lower class (who disappears from the accident scene). Reviewing *The Old Forest and Other Stories* in the *New York Times* (February 14, 1986), Robert Towers wrote: "Peter Taylor's stories are like miniature novels. . . . His narrative method is to hover over the action, to digress from it, to explore byways and relationships, to speculate on alternative possibilities—in short, to defy the convention of brevity and concentration that we usually associate with the genre. What results is often a thickly populated microcosm of an entire society, with its assumptions, virtues, loyalties, and snobberies revealed." The people in that isolated society, Paul Gray observed in *Time* (August 23, 1985), cherish restrictive customs and at the same time "sense that they should not be too content with their restrictions."

Philip Carver, the narrator of Taylor's novel *A Summons to Memphis*, (Knopf, 1986), is a middle-aged New York editor and book dealer who regards as the key, crucially unfortunate incident in his family's history its move from Nashville to Memphis, Tennessee, in 1931, when he was thirteen. A return to Memphis occasioned by the intended (but never realized) marriage of his widowed octogenarian lawyer father to a much younger woman (and the threatened disinheriting of Philip and his spinster sister) takes him on an odyssey into his past that is related with humor as well as pathos, along with considerable power. "It provides yet another avenue by which we can approach that particular Southern province that Taylor has made so distinctly his own," Robert Towers wrote in his review of *A Summons to Memphis* in the *New York Review of Books* (September 25, 1986).

In the spring of 1986 the judges of PEN, the elite literary society, voted *The Old Forest and Other Stories* the best work of fiction of the previous year. On April 6, 1987, Taylor won the $50,000 Ritz-Hemingway award, the world's most lucrative novelism prize, for *A Summons to Memphis*. Ten days later the same novel brought him the Pulitzer Prize in fiction. Taylor's other honors and awards have included a Guggenheim fellowship (1950), a grant from the National Institute of Arts and Letters (1952), a Fulbright fellowship (1955), the O. Henry Memorial Award (1959), a Ford Foundation fellowship (1960), a Rockefeller Foundation grant (1966), and memberships in the National Institute of Arts and Letters and the American Academy of Arts and Sciences.

After resigning his post as professor of English literature at the University of North Carolina in 1967, Taylor directed the creative writing program at the University of Virginia in Charlottesville for two decades. Over the years he has been a visiting lecturer at several other universities, including Oxford, Harvard, and the University of Chicago.

Peter Taylor is a slightly built man who speaks with a courtly Southern accent. He and the former Eleanor Lilly Ross, a poet, were married on June 4, 1953 and have two children, Katherine Baird and Peter Ross. The Taylors, who enjoy restoring old houses, live in Charlottesville and maintain vacation residences in Monteagle, Tennessee, and Gainesville, Florida. They often travel abroad, especially to France and Italy. Taylor is incommunicado, even to his wife, from about eight in the morning until one in the afternoon, when he does his writing. He writes his initial draft or drafts in longhand, discarding 100 pages for every ten he keeps, and types the final draft. Much of his prose begins as verse, because the slow process of writing poetry forces him to find the *mot juste*.

References: *N Y Times C* p19 My 7 86; *Shenandoah* (special Taylor issue) vol 28 Winter '77; *Washington Post mag* p23+ N 24 '68 pors; *Contemporary Authors* new rev vol 9 (1983); *Dictionary of Literary Biography, 1981*; Griffith, Albert J. *Peter Taylor* (1970); *Twentieth Century Authors* (First Supplement, 1955)

Tebbit, Norman (Beresford)

Mar. 29, 1931– British political leader. Address: b. House of Commons, Westminister, London SW1A OAA, England

Since he was first elected to Parliament in 1970, Norman Tebbit has been the spokesman for what one political commentator has called "the rising voice of lower-middle-class Toryism." A populist with an instinctive understanding of the concerns of the ordinary man, Tebbit has come to personify the brand of Conservative ideology that has become known as "Thatcherism." A self-described "unashamedly partisan" politician, he earned a reputation among his fellow MPs for aggressiveness (some would say ruthlessness), but his undeniable skill as a political tactician impressed even his enemies. For years one of Prime Minister Margaret Thatcher's closest advisers, he has served her government in several cabinet-level posts, including secretary of state for employment and secretary of state for trade and industry, and as chairman of the Conservative party. Tebbit resigned his post as Conservative party chairman on November 3, 1987.

The second of the two sons of Leonard and Edith Tebbit, Norman Beresford Tebbit was born on March 29, 1931, in Enfield, a working-class section of north London, England. Some sources say that his father was a jobbing builder; others, that he managed a pawnshop. Tebbit received his early education at the local primary school, then, after spending most of the war years as an evacuee in Wales, he went on to the Edmonton County Grammar School, where he was enrolled in a general academic curriculum. It was while he was a student there that Tebbit became interested in the Conservative party's philosophy. "I liked the concept of social mobility and a free market economy, and the opposite struck me as rigid and restrained," he explained, as quoted in a London *Observer* (October 7, 1984) profile. "I felt you should be able to make your own fortune; you should be the master of your fate."

When he was sixteen (the age at which British teenagers complete their compulsory education), Tebbit, who hoped to become a journalist, left school to take an entry-level job at the *Financial Times*, one of Britain's most prestigious newspapers. He remained on the newspaper's staff for two years, but because he lacked a university degree, he was not promoted to a higher position. In 1949 Tebbit resigned from the *Financial Times* to fulfill his National Service obligation. Enlisting in the Royal Air Force, he was eventually commissioned as a pilot. At one point during his military career, he nearly lost his life when his Meteor fighter suddenly burst into flames. To escape the fire, he broke the impact-resistant cockpit canopy—a feat requiring almost superhuman strength. Since that first brush with death, he has felt that he has been "playing with the casino's money," as he once put it. Following the completion of his two-year tour of duty, Tebbit served for four years on the County of Middlesex Squadron of the Royal Auxiliary Air Force.

On leaving military service in 1951, Tebbit applied unsuccessfully for a series of what he has called "slightly way-out jobs," including piloting seaplanes in the Falkland Islands and managing a tea plantation in northern India. For a time he sold advertising space in trade magazines, but he found both the job and the daily commuting to the office so tedious that in 1953 he decided to join the British Overseas Airways Corporation (BOAC) as a pilot. He remained with the airline for seventeen years. A labor activist, he joined BALPA, the British airline pilots' association, in two strikes against BOAC and blacklegged in a third and, as a member of the 707 pilots' council, took part in contract negotiations with BOAC executives. Discussing his role as a union negotiator in an interview for the *Manchester Guardian* weekly (April, 10, 1983), Tebbit told John Torode, "It colored my attitudes, and it certainly didn't persuade me that the management was necessarily always right. Or, indeed, that the union was."

Tebbitt found piloting commercial aircraft to be, in his words, an "enormously satisfying and challenging" profession, but as he approached the age of forty, he began to investigate other careers, at least partly because "pilots retire relatively young." With the encouragement of Iain Macleod,

the longtime Conservative MP for Enfield West, Tebbit, who had been active in local party organizations since 1946, decided to run for Parliament, as the Conservative candidate for Epping, a lower-middle-class urban district just a few miles northeast of London, in the 1970 general election. When the voters went to the polls on June 18, they turned out the ruling Labour party of Prime Minister Harold Wilson in favor of a new Conservative government headed by Edward Heath. Tebbit was among the freshman MPs swept into Parliament on the Conservative tide.

In his maiden speech on the floor of the House of Commons a few weeks later, Norman Tebbit characteristically broke with tradition by addressing controversial issues, and for the next nine years, he was one of the most consistently outspoken Tory backbenchers. In 1972 he was named parliamentary private secretary to the minister of state for employment, but he resigned from that post less than a year later so that he could freely speak out on industrial affairs. Following a redistribution of seats, Tebbit was returned to the Commons in October 1974, as the MP for Chingford, in northeast London. He has held that seat, by steadily increasing margins of victory, ever since. While he was a backbencher, Tebbit served as a member of the select committee on science and technology, secretary of the all-party new towns members group, vice-chairman of the Conservative housing committee, and chairman of the Conservative parliamentary aviation committee. Until the 1979 general election, he supplemented his income as an MP by working for a multinational computer company and as the assistant director of information of the National Federation of Building Employers.

When Margaret Thatcher assumed the prime ministership in May 1979, Tebbit was appointed parliamentary undersecretary of state at the Department of Trade. Twenty months later he was named a minister of state at the Department of Industry, a post he held until his elevation to full cabinet rank, as secretary of state for employment, in September 1981. He was created a privy counselor at the same time. Charged with implementing Mrs. Thatcher's program for curbing the power of the trade unions, he began his crusade with a tough speech at the Conservative party conference a few weeks later. Digressing from his prepared text, he recalled how his father had reacted to the loss of his job during the Depression of the 1930s: "He did not riot. He got on his bike and looked for work." According to Julian Haviland, a political correspondent for the London *Times*, Tebbit's aside established him as a Conservative hero, but it also earned him the enmity of organized labor, which interpreted his remarks as a rebuke to Britain's unemployed.

In Tebbit's view, the unions had contributed to the country's unemployment problem by authorizing a series of crippling strikes during a period of worldwide economic recession. As a result, he told the delegates at the Conservative party's annual conference in Brighton in October 1982, the "most privileged trades union movement in the world, commanding a huge conscript army in the closed shop, has failed its members. It has left them near the bottom of the productivity league, condemned to see the big pay rises wiped out by inflation." To help prevent future strikes, Tebbit insisted on including in the 1982 Employment Act a provision allowing unions to be sued for organizing illegal industrial actions. Although some Tories thought that Tebbit had gone too far, the secretary himself saw his plan as a way to "[give] the unions back to their members," as he put it.

Reappointed to his post in the wake of the Conservative party's decisive victory in June 1983, Tebbit continued his efforts to "provide for greater democracy" in the trade union movement by introducing in the Commons a bill designed to give rank-and-file members more of a voice in union organization. Among other things, the measure included proposals for the use of secret ballots to elect union officials and to decide on possible strike actions and for a regular poll of the membership to determine political contributions. (Historically, the unions have been a major source of funding for the Labour party.) Len Murray, the general secretary of the Trades Union Council (TUC), condemned the government's proposals as "irrelevant" and "dangerous" propositions that, if implemented, would "constitute an unwarranted interference with trade union democracy." Nevertheless, the TUC, at its annual meeting in September 1983, voted to hold talks with Tebbit on a variety of issues of common interest.

When Cecil Parkinson, the secretary of state for trade and industry in Prime Minister Thatcher's second cabinet, resigned in October 1983 following the revelation of his extramarital affair, Tebbit was appointed to succeed his longtime friend and colleague in the post. As minister for trade and industry, Tebbit played a key role in developing Britain's international trading relationships and in promoting business investments at home. One of his first acts was to sign an agreement with Japan's Nissan Motor Company that allowed Nissan to construct and operate an automobile manufacturing plant in Britain. Although the project would create hundreds of jobs, it was nonetheless criticized by union representatives and by some MPs, both Conservative and Labour, as a threat to the country's domestic auto industry. Perhaps in an effort to boost that industry, Tebbit supported BL PLC (formerly British Leyland), the state-owned car manufacturer, in its attempt to retain 25 percent of the shares in Jaguar, its luxury sports car subsidiary, which was being sold to private investors under the government's privatization program.

Although he occasionally favored continued government aid for strategic industries, such as volume car-making, Tebbit soon became the Thatcher cabinet's point man for the privatization of nationalized industries. He outlined his views on the subject in a Disraeli lecture at St. Stephen's Constitutional Club, a Conservative social organization in London, in November 1985. "State owner-

ship, state monopolies, state regulation, and state planning, through the centralization of economic power, inevitably lead to economic failure," he warned the members. "They inevitably increase both the temptation and the scope for abuses of political power until freedom itself is threatened. . . . The fruits of centralized economic planning are corruption, poverty, and servility."

Of his political views in general, Tebbit told John Torode, in the interview for the *Manchester Guardian* weekly, "On social issues, I suppose I am to some extent a paternalist, whereas on economic issues I tend to be a liberal. I think there is a general lack of discipline in society, and I think that is a great pity." He attributed his popularity among his constituents to his intuitive grasp of their hopes and fears: "Ordinary people hear me saying things they say, and they feel that I understand what they have been talking about for a number of years. They may disagree with me about all sorts of things, perhaps about my analyses and how to put things right. But I think they, at least, have the feeling that I do understand what they may feel."

Long one of Mrs. Thatcher's closest advisers, Tebbit was for some time one of the so-called "Gang of Four" that helped her prepare for prime minister's question time in the Commons. He also counseled her on strictly political matters. By all accounts, it was Tebbit who, sensing a Conservative landslide, urged Mrs. Thatcher to call a general election in June 1983. As a member of the cabinet, he increasingly came to serve as a sounding board for the prime minister's policies. "I look at things openly and do not pretend that things are other than they are," he explained to John Torode. "People standing in the pub bar have talked of the reasons for our problems for years. They knew. But nobody in government dared say what was wrong. The electors are not to be regarded as stupid."

By late 1984 Tebbit was being touted in the press as a possible successor to Mrs. Thatcher as Tory leader. Although his abrasive style worried some party regulars, many analysts predicted that Tebbit's political stock would rise considerably at the 1984 Conservative party conference in Brighton, where he was scheduled to deliver a major address on privatization and political liberty. The conference was interrupted by an explosion that ripped through the Grand Hotel in the early morning hours of October 12, killing four persons and wounding thirty-two, among them Tebbit and his wife, Margaret. Responsibility for the bombing—the most serious assault against the upper echelons of the British government since Guy Fawkes and a group of English Catholics conspired to blow up parliament and King James I in 1605—was claimed by the Provisional Irish Republican Army.

Tebbit plunged two stories after the upper floors of the hotel collapsed and lay buried beneath the rubble for nearly four hours while a team of firefighters labored to dig him out. He had sustained several broken ribs, a broken leg, a broken shoulder, crushed vertebrae, and numerous cuts and bruises; his wife had suffered severe spinal injuries, which have left her paralyzed. Tebbit's rescue was broadcast live on television, and his courage and fortitude throughout the ordeal won him the admiration of his countrymen. Three months after the bombing, the minister was back on the job. "[Work] is better than alcohol," he told reporters, as quoted in the London *Times* (February 25, 1986). "Through work you can avoid that tendency to brood about what might have been, or how hard life has been on you."

In an attempt to reverse a sharp downturn in the Tory party's political fortunes, in September 1985 Margaret Thatcher appointed Norman Tebbit to succeed John Selwyn Gummer, who had taken much of the blame for the party's poor showing in that year's by-elections, as chairman of the Conservative party organization. At the same time, he was named to the Cabinet-level post of chancellor of the Duchy of Lancaster. Some political observers questioned whether Tebbit's aggressive manner and confrontational approach made him a suitable architect of electoral strategy in a three-party race. The sniping increased after a series of local election losses in the spring of 1986. Peregrine Worsthorne, the editor of the London *Sunday Telegraph*, went so far as to suggest that Tebbit lacked "that desirable touch of class" generally associated with Tory politicians. Within the party, too, the chairman came under fire from some Conservatives who thought that his "raucous" style was damaging to the Conservative cause.

By the summer of 1986, political prognosticators were openly discussing likely candidates to succeed Tebbit as party chairman. Fueling the speculation were reports of his occasional quarrels with Margaret Thatcher over policy matters, such as British support of the United States bombing raid on Libya in April 1986, the drafting of a platform for the upcoming Conservative party conference, and his no-holds-barred campaign against alleged anti-Tory bias in the media, especially the BBC. That campaign escalated on October 30, 1986, when the Conservative Central Office released a report charging that the BBC's coverage of the American bombing of Libya had been little more than "alarmist hyperbole"—"a mixture of news, views, speculation, error and uncritical carriage of Libyan propaganda." To prevent such "lamentable lapses" in judgment in the future, Tebbit recommended a review of "managerial and editorial standards" at the BBC. A week later, the BBC responded with a line-by-line rebuttal of Tebbit's accusations and a strongly worded letter, signed by Marmaduke Hussey, the newly appointed chairman of the BBC's board of governors, defending the corporation's independence. Most Britons agreed that Tebbit had overstepped his authority. In a poll commissioned by the London *Times*, fully 88 percent stated that it was wrong for the Conservatives to try to influence the BBC.

Although he was viewed in the press as a politician on the decline, Tebbit was nonetheless the first choice of Conservative voters to succeed Margaret Thatcher as party leader. According to a na-

tionwide poll conducted by Market Opinion Research International in January 1987, he received 38 percent of the votes, more than twice as many as his closest competitor, Sir Geoffrey Howe, the foreign minister. As the date for a general election approached, the Conservatives, under Tebbit's supervision, stepped up their campaign against the centrist Alliance of Liberals and Social Democrats. At a Conservative Central Council meeting in Torquay on March 20, 1987, Tebbit warned, "The voters will not give [Labour leader Neil] Kinnock the front door key" to the prime minister's residence, "but a Lib-Lab [Liberal-Labour] pact could give him the ladder to climb in through the back window."

The close working relationship between Tebbit and Margaret Thatcher reportedly deteriorated in the waning days of the campaign, as the prime minister began to rely more and more on her inner cabinet for advice. In the general election on June 11, 1987, the voters returned Mrs. Thatcher and the Conservatives to power for a third consecutive time, although the Tory majority in Parliament fell from 144 seats to 101. Two days later Tebbit resigned his cabinet post as chancellor of the Duchy of Lancaster and retired to the back benches of the House of Commons. He retained his position as party chairman until November when, following controversy and delay over the choice of a successor, the prime minister accepted his resignation. As more than one political commentator pointed out, Tebbit's resignation effectively ended his chances of becoming leader of the party, although others saw in it a carefully contrived scheme to advance his eventual claim to succeed Mrs. Thatcher. Tebbit has kept his own counsel, but has branched out into business by becoming a nonexecutive director of British Telecom PLC, Blue Arrow PLC, the British stores company Sears Group PLC, and the service and publishing group BET PLC.

In announcing his resignation, Tebbit cited his desire to spend more time with his wife, who had recently been released from the hospital after nearly two years of medical treatments for the injuries she sustained in the Brighton bombing. "I am sure there will be mornings when I shall think 'What are they doing, what are they up to? I wish I was there,'" he told Colin Brown of the London *Independent* (June 15, 1987). "But I hope there will be mornings when I am sitting on my terrace watching the butterflies, seeing the flowers open, perhaps enjoying a glass of Sancerre or something, when I shall chuckle to myself and say, 'I bet they wish they were here.'"

Tall and gaunt, with a receding hairline and deep-set, watchful eyes, Norman Tebbit has been described by a former cabinet colleague as "a man full of paradoxes." He is, by his own admission, "brusque" in public, but according to John Torode, his "carefully crafted image" conceals "an easygoing manner and a self-deprecating sense of humor." A workaholic by nature, he once gave as his hobbies "peace and quiet." In reality, he enjoys watching cricket matches and gardening, and since his wife's incapacity, he has become, in his words, "not a bad cook." Tebbit and his wife, the former Margaret Elizabeth Daines, have been married since 1956. They have three children, Alison, John, and William, and four grandchildren. The Tebbits divide their time between a house in west London and a cottage in Devon. Both have been specially adapted for Margaret Tebbit's wheelchair.

References: London Observer p7 O 7 '84; London Sunday Telegraph mag p9 O 21 '84; Manchester Guardian W p5 Ap 10 '83 por; Spectator 256:9+ My 24 '86; Times p12 O 10 '85 por; International Who's Who, 1987–88; Who's Who, 1987–88

Terra, Daniel J(ames)

June 1911– Art collector; United States diplomat; chemist; industrialist. Address: b. Terra Museum of American Art, 666 N. Michigan Ave., Chicago, Ill. 60611; United States Department of State, 2201 C St., N.W., Washington, D.C. 20520

The Terra Museum of American Art in Chicago, a moderate-sized but important regional art facility, is the centerpiece of the several grand accomplishments of Daniel J. Terra, the self-made Illinois multimillionaire industrialist who has been United States ambassador at large for cultural affairs since the beginning of the administration of President Ronald Reagan, in 1980. Trained as a chemical engineer, Terra in the mid-1930s developed a printing chemical that made today's high-speed offset publishing possible. In 1940 he founded Lawter International, Inc., a leading manufacturer of spe-

cialized chemicals of which he remains chairman and chief executive officer (temporarily unsalaried). He began collecting American art as an avocation almost half a century ago, concentrated on American art beginning in the mid-1950s, and opened his collection to the public in 1980. His museum, envisioned by him as "a center for American art in the Midwest" and first housed in an intimate little gallery in Evanston, Illinois, moved with much fanfare into a two-building, multilevel structure on bustling and prestigious North Michigan Avenue, Chicago's "magnificent mile," in April 1987. The small museum in Evanston remains in use, as a satellite to the new facility.

The State Department post of cultural ambassador was created expressly for Terra as a reward for his work as finance chairman of the 1980 Reagan-for-President campaign. As ambassador, he has no set functional responsibility other than to advise on and facilitate—and ceremonially represent the United States in—cultural exchanges with other countries, including projects that will advance the appreciation of American art. In keeping with his special deep commitment to American art of historical importance, his museum's exhibitions, including those on loan from other collections, cover the range of the national experience, from the colonial era on. The greatest strength of the museum's $100 million permanent collection of more than 800 works is the genre art, impressionism, and postimpressionism done by Americans in the nineteenth and early twentieth centuries—work that was snobbishly undervalued until Terra began amassing it. Among the collection's prized items are Mary Cassatt's genteel watercolor Summertime: Woman and Child in a Rowboat (c. 1894), Charles Courtney Curran's lush oil Lotus Lilies (1888), William Merritt Chase's familial pastel The Hallway at "Shinnecock" (1893), Charles Sheeler's sunny canvas Bucks County Barn (1940), Ammi Phillips' naive painting Portrait of a Girl in a Red Dress (no date), and Charles Demuth's modernist Paris scene Rue du Singe qui pêche (1921).

Daniel James Terra was born in June 1911, in a suburb of Philadelphia, Pennsylvania. According to Who's Who in America, his day of birth was June 8. Other sources say it was June 9. He grew up in Philadelphia, where his father, Louis J. Terra, an immigrant from Italy, managed a lithography plant. His mother, Mary (DeLuca) Terra, a dancer, taught him ballroom, tap, and soft-shoe dancing. He entered Pennsylvania State University with the intention of studying theatre arts but changed his major to chemical engineering. While studying at Penn State, he worked part time at his father's plant, where he became acquainted with the problems of processing printer's chemicals—the subject of his college thesis. Unable immediately to find a job as a chemist when he took his B.S. degree in 1931, he worked professionally as a song-and-dance man for two years, doing vaudeville-style routines in what he remembers as "the better speakeasies" in Philadelphia and singing on radio station WCAU there. As a singer, he continued to perform occasionally, at weddings and other such opportunites, until he was in his forties, and he is today ranked among Washington's superior ballroom dancers.

In 1933 Terra found employment with the Philadelphia plant of the Columbian Carbon Corporation, where he was assigned the task of scanning the scientific literature for developments in chemical research, especially in Germany. Much of his work involved translating from the German, in which he had minored in college. In the course of reading technical journals for his job, he came across a patent for fractioning kerosene that he thought could be applied to printing chemicals. Persuading Columbian Carbon to buy the patent from its Boston inventor for $1,500 he supervised the development of a chemical vehicle for printer's ink that accelerated the speed at which magazine presses could print. Within eighteen months the *Saturday Evening Post* was being printed by the new process, and in 1936 the process contributed to the creation of *Life,* the picture news weekly magazine. Hired by the *Life* printers, R. R. Donnelly & Sons, Terra literally lived for six weeks in the Donnelly plant in Chicago as a consultant before and during the press run of the first issue of the magazine.

Borrowing $2,500 from a rich friend, John H. Lawson, Terra in 1940 founded Lawter Chemicals Inc. (now Lawter International, Inc.), devoted to making specialty chemicals for printer's ink and other purposes. Terra shut down the firm while he served in the Navy during World War II and reopened it in 1945. During the following ten years, his success as an industrialist was modest; in 1955, when he was offered a job at $37,000 a year by the Union Carbide Corporation, he was making $6,000 at Lawter. On the advice of a management consultant, who told him that he was trying to do too much by himself, he borrowed money from relatives and hired a research director and financial, marketing, and advertising executives. By 1960 the company was netting enough profit to go public. Still headquartered in Northbrook, Illinois, it today has twenty-two branches or subsidiaries in twelve countries.

Meanwhile, Terra had been fund-raising for the Illinois Republican party since 1939. As for art collecting, his interest in that was quickened by his first wife, the late Adeline Evans Richards, an art history graduate of Northwestern University whom he married in 1937. "She has the great eye," he once explained to an interviewer, "and I have the courage to buy." In the beginning the Terras were electic in their purchases. The first painting they bought was a nineteenth-century English landscape for which they paid forty dollars at Marshall Field's, the Chicago department store, and which still hangs over Terra's mantel. They subsequently purchased more British landscapes as well as works by French impressionists and old masters.

It was not until 1955, when he visited a New York City apartment filled with early twentieth-century American paintings, that Terra decided to specialize in American art. During the 1960s and 1970s he bought a large number of American impressionist and nineteenth-century genre paintings, including works by John Singer Sargent, Childe Hassam, and Ernest Lawson, at a fraction of what they would cost today. The William Merritt Chase landscape *The Olive Grove,* for which he paid $800, for example, is now appraised at $650,-000. An aggressive, competitive collector, Terra boasts about his acquisitions of those years "much like a general recounting his great battles," according to Michael Kilian in the *Chicago Tribune Magazine* (April 19, 1987). He likes to tell how he acquired James Abbott McNeill Whistler's oil on paper *Note in Red: The Siesta* (one of his fifteen Whistler works on paper), which was then in a contested estate, by negotiating separately with both contending heirs, and how he spent fifteen years talking the previous owner into selling him one of Winslow Homer's croquet paintings, and he gloats that his portrait of Claude Monet by Theodore Robinson is "a painting that really makes the saliva come out of museum directors."

As the value of the works he sought appreciated, so did the purses Terra was willing to put up for them, and he made headlines with his purchase in 1979 of John Caleb Bingham's 1848 oil *The Jolly Flatboatmen, No. 2* for $1 million. By that time it was clear that the Terra collection was too valuable, and would incur too great an estate tax, to remain strictly private. Negotiations were undertaken with several potential recipient museums, among them the Art Institute of Chicago, but no museum would promise him the control over his collection that he demanded. He did not think of starting his own museum until someone pointed out to him that there was no museum of American art within 400 miles of Chicago. "And that was that," Terra recounted to Avis Berman when she interviewed him for *Modern Maturity* (June/July 1987). "It was unthinkable that Chicago had no center for American art."

The first Terra Museum of American Art opened in May 1980, not in Chicago but in a former greenhouse and florist's shop in the Chicago suburb of Evanston that had room for the display of approximately 100 works. The location was characterized by Franz Schulze in *Art News* (December 1980) as "twelve miles and a lifestyle" away from the downtown Chicago art scene. "He [Terra] ran the [Evanston] museum like his own little toy," one former staff member told Meg Cox of the *Wall Street Journal* (April 21, 1987). "The good side was that after a weekend, you could come back to find three new paintings. In a regular museum, paintings don't just appear out of the trunk of somebody's car." Cox quoted David Sokol, former curator of the Evanston museum: "He [Terra] was mercurial. . . . I realize that his vision will last, but day to day, it's hard for any human being to survive under that."

The Evanston museum quickly became popular however, attracting an average of 100,000 visitors a year and hundreds to the educational symposia it held at Northwestern University. Thematic loan exhibitions were mounted, and the Terra collection itself grew in the meantime, increasing tenfold in five years. In 1982 the museum's reputation took a quantum leap with Terra's purchase of Samuel F. B. Morse's *The Gallery of the Louvre* for $3.25 million, $750,000 more than had been paid previously for any painting by an American. Done in 1831–33, the six-by-nine-foot painting depicts the *salon carré* (square gallery) of the Louvre Museum in Paris, complete with strikingly clear and accurate scaled-down copies of thirty-eight masterpieces therein, including paintings by Leonardo da Vinci, Raphael, Titian, Rembrandt, Rubens, and Caravaggio. Terra had first seen a reproduction of *The Gallery of the Louvre* when, as a student not very interested in art, he was researching Morse in connection with a physics experiment with electromagnetic forces and was surprised to learn that the inventor of the telegraph was also an artist. When his wife saw the Morse painting, she ranked it an "icon of American art," and Terra was determined to acquire it. After persuading the owner—Syracuse University, where it was languishing in a basement storeroom—to sell it, he nervously waited out the Metropolitan Museum of Art's ninety-day first option and bought the painting within ten minutes after the Met's option expired.

Terra also acquired works by George Inness, Edward Hopper, Arthur Dove, Charles Demuth, George Bellows, John Marin, Martin Johnson Heade, Charles Burchfield, Fitz Hugh Lane, Andrew Wyeth, Rockwell Kent, Reginald Marsh, Lyonel Feininger, and Thomas Eakins, among others. He paid a Swiss collector $5 million for major early modernist works by Stuart Davis, Patrick Henry Bruce, and Marsden Hartley. With the exception of a portrait by John Singleton Copley, Terra generally ruled himself out of the fierce, astronomical bidding for outstanding eighteenth-century works. His monotypes by Maurice Prendergast were lent to the National Gallery of Art in Washington, D.C. for an exhibition there in 1985 and 1986. After a domestic tour the monotypes are scheduled for exhibition in China.

While building his art collection and presiding over Lawter International Inc., Terra continued his involvement in politics, in which he found "an emotion . . . that doesn't exist in business." From 1973 to 1979 he was chairman of the Illinois United Republican Fund, an organization principally supporting conservative candidates. After Ronald Reagan asked him to serve as finance chairman for his presidential campaign in 1979, he, a long-time Reagan admirer, crisscrossed the country for fifteen months, traveling 500,000 miles and raising $21 million. Following Reagan's election in November 1980, he was offered several high diplomatic posts, including the ambassadorship to Great Britain. When he turned them down, because a protracted stay abroad would cut him off from his business and art interests, the post of ambassador at large for cultural affairs was created for him. To accept the $70,000-a-year position he gave up his

annual salary of $750,000 at Lawter International Inc.

In his unique, unprecedented diplomatic post, Terra is America's representative in international cultural exchange. He also sees himself as a "catalyst" for such exchange and as a go-between who "brings people together" to that end. Out of his office came the idea for the American "Art in Embassies" program and the support for "Festival of India," an exhibit of Indian crafts that toured ninety-one American cities. More recently, his office has been abetting the upcoming "New Sweden '88." Looking to the future, Terra told Jo Ann Lewis in an interview for the *Washington Post* (April 21, 1987) that "the big focus is on what's happening between us and the U.S.S.R." As a speaker who is much in demand across the United States, Terra uses his enhanced position to urge greater private funding, both corporate and individual, for American art.

For the new headquarters for his art collection, Terra bought four buildings on North Michigan Avenue at Erie Street in Chicago. At a cost of $35 million, architect Laurence Booth and his associates transformed two of the buildings (one eleven stories tall and the other five) into the first wing of the new Terra Museum of American Art, which has triple the Evanston exhibition space. According to Terra's plan, the two other buildings, adjacent to the north and south, would later be incorporated as the second and third wings of the museum, at a total cost of at least $75 million. Retail stores and other commercial enterprises were allowed to remain on the ground floors, but the rents were raised so high in new leases as to threaten the existence of a bookstore run by Stuart Brent and long treasured by Chicago literati. The outrage voiced in the Chicago press was intense, and Terra capitulated, extending Brent's old lease.

With a legion of Washington notables and rich Chicagoans in attendance, the Terra Museum of American Art on North Michigan Avenue opened on April 21, 1987, and the inaugural was followed by a week of black-tie dinners and forty nights of fund-raising receptions. In a preview article in the *Chicago Tribune* (April 19, 1987), the architecture critic Paul Gapp described the new museum as "an architecturally tasteful, finely detailed, and stylishly appointed collection of spaces" but thought that it "may be the most strangely laid out small museum in the nation." "Booth appears to have done his best, but the incongruity of the two buildings and their basic unfitness for art exhibition venues defeated even his considerable talent," Gapp observed. "Most first-time visitors will find the museum's layout confusing." Robert C. Morgan wrote in the *Village Voice* (August 18, 1987): "While not an architectural tour de force, the building which houses the Terra collection is appropriately modest in scale and expediently designed. It's easy to move from one floor to another. [The] works on display are, for the most part, lesser-known paintings by many recognizable and some not so recognizable names in the history of American regionalist art."

Terra has budgeted the annual operating expenses of his museum at $4 million, of which one-fifth will go to educational programs (because he believes that "the public doesn't know American art"). He hopes that the money will come from the foundation he has set up, from memberships, from admission charges, and from the rents for the ground floor retail stores. "Meanwhile," he told Jo Ann Lewis in the Washington Post interview, "I'll have to carry it until it begins to carry itself." Some close observers believe that it will not "carry itself" until Terra is gone, because rich donors are loath to contribute to another's "personal monument."

Although Terra leaves the day-to-day fine-arts operations of his museum to his curatorial staff, he keeps a close tab on those operations and makes all major decisions, especially about the buying and selling of art. Terra's critics have faulted the museum as a "vanity operation" that is "autocratically" run by an "egomaniac" whose taste leans to "salon art" that is "pretty" or "anodyne," but even many of them grudgingly admire his drive and shrewdness—and his success. "He wanted to have a great museum, his museum. Damn it, he's done it and done it first rate," Lewis Manilow, an art collector who helped to found Chicago's Museum of Contemporary Art, has said. "I don't believe it has to be done with modesty. There will be decades to institutionalize it." Answering those who would dimiss the Terra museum as, at best, "a good provincial museum," Alan G. Artner, the art critic for the Chicago Tribune (April 19, 1987) wrote: "Whatever one thinks of . . . the pieties this institution is attempting to serve . . . the new Terra museum represents an artistic gift to Chicago that is without parallel in our century. No one else, living or dead, has realized quite as much completely on their own terms."

"Ronald Reagan has said that I've done more for American art than any other man in the history of the country," Terra has been quoted as saying. "And it's absolutely true." Terra sits on several international cultural boards, including those of Arts International, and the Woodrow Wilson Center for Scholars, and he is a member of the president's committee on the arts, which reviews domestic arts policy. Among the beneficiaries of his philanthropy are the Chicago Lyric Opera, the Chicago Symphony, and the Art Institute of Chicago. As a businessman, Terra has invested widely, and he is a director of the Stewart-Warner Corporation. He has received several honorary degrees and has been named commander of the Order of Arts and Literature of the French Empire.

Ambassador Terra, whose first wife died in 1982, married Judith Banks in 1986. With his wife, Terra hosts some of the most elegant dinners and parties in Washington, including an annual reception for the winners of the presidential National Medal of the Arts, held in the State Department's sumptuous diplomatic reception rooms. In addition to their apartment in one of northwest Washington's more fashionable neighborhoods, the Terras retain the home in the Chicago suburb of Kenil-

worth that the ambassador bought years ago. By his first wife, Terra had a daughter, Penny Jane, who is deceased, and a son, James D., who is in the electronics business, owns a horse farm, and is an art collector in his own right.

Daniel J. Terra is short, white-haired, dapper, agile, raspy-voiced, and by his own description, "scrappy," although probably less so than before he suffered a heart attack in 1986. (Since the heart attack, he has added a three-mile walk to his daily routine.) "The diplomatic life seems made for Terra, an enthusiast, a promoter, a born meeter-and-greeter, and an unabashed booster sporting an upbeat manner," Avis Berman wrote in Modern Maturity. "He's chipper and alert, with a fund of stories and anecdotes at the ready. He's candid about his aims and beliefs, although skilled enough at sidestepping questions to avoid any personal secrets." In the Chicago Tribune Magazine Michael Kilian described him as "a worldly sophisticate with a hearty laugh" who "is as warm and friendly as a kindly uncle." "He is," Kilian wrote, "in the truest sense, a gentle man." Terra, whose net worth has been estimated at more than $300 million, lives by the philosophy, "Money is fleeting. Art is forever."

References: Chicago Tribune VII p5+ Jl 2 '86 por, mag p8+ Ap 19 '87 pors; Modern Maturity 30:48+ Je/Jl '87 por; Wall St J p1+ Ap 21 '87 por; Washington Post p1+ Ap 21 '87 por; Who's Who in America, 1986–87

Thicke, Alan

1948 (?)- Television performer; producer; writer.
Address: b. American Broadcasting Company,
2040 Ave. of the Stars, Century City, Calif. 90067

The situation comedy Growing Pains, a surprise hit of the 1985–86 television season, continued to earn top-twenty A. C. Nielsen ratings in 1986–87. Canadian-born Alan Thicke stars in that ABC series as Dr. Jason Seaver, a psychiatrist who practices at home and minds the children, two boys and a girl, so that his wife can pursue a career in journalism. Thicke, a multitalented, compulsive achiever, has been working both sides of the border as a TV writer, producer, and performer for two decades. During the 1970s he wrote for a long list of comedy and musical series and specials, including The Lohman and Barkley Comedy Show, Saturday Night Live, and vehicles for Flip Wilson, Paul Lynde, Anne Murray, Olivia Newton-John, Bobby Darin, Mac Davis, Tony Orlando, and Bobby Vinton, and he produced as well as wrote for the mock talk shows Fernwood 2-Night and America 2-Night. In the early 1980s he hosted two genuine talk/variety shows: The Alan Thicke Show, a Canadian hit, and Thicke of the Night, an American flop. Thicke has also done some professional singing, and he has

Alan Thicke

written more than thirty compositions for television, including the themes for the situation comedies *Diff'rent Strokes* and *Facts of Life.*

Alan Thicke was born Alan Jeffery to William Jeffery and his wife in the small mining town of Kirkland Lake, Ontario, Canada, in on about 1948. After his parents divorced, when he was six years old, his mother married a physician whose surname was adopted by Alan and his brother Todd, who is now a TV producer and director. Thicke told Glenn Esterly in an interview for *TV Guide* (April 9, 1986) that his stepfather taught him "a lot about drive and ambition." Growing up in the succession of towns where his stepfather practiced medicine, Alan became a good hockey player and developed verbal and musical skills as well. He entertained schoolmates with imitations of the Beatles, and he shone as an orator. "I gave sermons in the local United Church of Canada at the same time that I was president of Catholic Youth Organization," he recounted in the interview with Esterly. Briefly, he considered entering the ministry.

In deference to the wishes of his stepfather, Thicke took premedical courses at the University of Western Ontario. More interested in sportswriting and popular communications in general than in medicine, he never entered medical school. Instead, he auditioned with the Canadian Broadcasting Corporation in Toronto, singing to his own guitar accompaniment as well as doing a comic monologue. He went to work for the CBC as a "gofer," and while chauffeuring radio and television personalities and fetching coffee for crews, he began contributing material to television shows. Among his credits in the late 1960s were *The Good Company Show, The Tommy Hunter Show,* and

a Johnny Cash special. He also sang and danced on a country-and-western music show, and he hosted a radio program.

After arriving in Los Angeles in 1970, at the age of twenty-two, Thicke attended hockey games at the Los Angeles Forum, the home of the Los Angeles Kings. He had known some of the players back in Canada, and they introduced him to showbusiness people they knew. Those connections, along with those of his wife, the actress Gloria Loring, facilitated his entry into American television.

Thicke's first major American credits as a television writer were comedy specials for Flip Wilson, the comedian, broadcast on the NBC network in 1974 and 1975. Subsequently he contributed material to network specials starring Sammy Davis Jr., Sandy Duncan, and Glen Campbell and composed the theme music for the game shows *Celebrity Sweepstakes* (which he also produced), *The Joker's Wild, Blank Check,* and *Wheel of Fortune.* He was one of the writers of Richard Pryor's first TV special, on NBC in 1977, and he was a member of the writing teams that won Emmy awards for a Barry Manilow special in 1977 and the *Saturday Night Live* comedy-variety-music series the following year.

A major turning point in Thicke's television career came in 1977, when he was hired by Norman Lear to produce a new syndicated nightly thirty-minute series, *Fernwood 2-Night,* a parody talk show spun off from Lear's mock soap opera *Mary Hartman, Mary Hartman.* (Mary Hartman's fictional hometown was Fernwood, Ohio.) Running as a summer replacement from July to September 1977, *Fernwood 2-Night* was presided over by a character named Barth Gimble, a fugitive from a Miami sex scandal. Barth Gimble was played by Martin Mull, the wry ad-libber who had performed in *Mary Hartman, Mary Hartman* as Barth's brother, Garth Gimble, an unsavory character whose death—by impalement on a Christmas tree he was decorating—was greeted with universal jubilation. Garth Gimble's second banana on *Fernwood 2-Night* was Fred Willard (Jerry Hubbard), a dunce who got the job through nepotism. The four-man house band, the Mirth Makers—who deliberately played off tempo and off key—was conducted by Happy Kyne (Frank DeVol), who ran a chain of eateries called Bun 'n' Run on the side. The guests were mostly fictional, interspersed with occasional real-life celebrities.

The off-the-wall humor on *Fernwood 2-Night* ranged from the whimsical to the heavy-handed and deliberately offensive. Typical were a "guest" trying to prove that leisure suits cause cancer; a visiting pianist playing Mozart sonatas while hanging upside down in an iron lung; a shameless mock Vietnamese refugee coming on the show to plug his autobiography, *Yankee Doodle Gook*; and the male principal of Fernwood High School demonstrating correct corporal punishment on the buttocks of a nubile cheerleader. "We will offend the sensitivities of a number of Americans, for which we apologize out front," Thicke said at the outset.

"But we're not being discriminatory in our satire, we're offending everybody, regardless of race, creed, color, or income level." "If *Mary Hartman* skirmished around the boundaries of good taste as defined by those craven geese in the network censorship offices," Bill Mann wrote in the Toronto *Globe and Mail* (August 20, 1977), "*Fernwood 2-Night* is a declaration of all-out war." Commercially, the show was marginally successful.

From April to August 1978 Thicke produced episodes of *America 2-Night*, created at Lear's Tandem Productions studios with the same cast as its predecessor and essentially the same concept but set in the town of Alta Coma, California, "the unfinished-furniture capital of the world." Throughout the 1970s Thicke commuted to Canada to produce and/or write for numerous shows on the CBC and CTV networks, including *The Hart and Lorne Terrific Hour, Sunday Morning, The Al Hamel Comedy Bag, Weekend, The Bobby Vinton Show*, a René Simard special, and several Anne Murray specials. He became known throughout Canada as the host of the CTV game show *First Impressions*, and his popularity soared with his hosting of *The Alan Thicke Show*, a talk/variety program. Although the latter was, according to Jerry Gladman, the television critic for the Toronto *Sun*, "fairly bland . . . like Canadian Merv Griffin . . . no killer show," it had the highest ratings of any program in the history of Canadian daytime television. "I still feel Canadian," Thicke told Bill Mann in the Toronto *Globe and Mail* interview, "and am certainly going to keep my citizenship. It keeps me in touch with my CBC friends [and] my parents . . . [who] still live in Bramalea, Ontario."

In the autumn of 1982 the American television producer Fred Silverman offered Thicke the opportunity to host a new late-night variety show to be syndicated by MGM/United Artists. A few months later the coming debut of *Thicke of the Night* was announced and a $1 million advertising campaign was launched to tout Alan Thicke as an unknown threat from Canada who would make Johnny Carson, NBC's king of late-night tube talk, "move over." The campaign embarrassed Thicke, who correctly sensed that the hype would backfire.

Thicke of the Night, a pretaped ninety-minute show, was produced at KTTV in Los Angeles by Metromedia Television and Silverman's Inter-Media Entertainment Company for distribution five nights a week to more than 120 stations, including the seven owned by Metromedia. Many of the stations scheduled the show for 11:00 and 11:30 in the evening, directly opposite *The Tonight Show Starring Johnny Carson*, which ran for an hour beginning at 11:30. Besides its incumbency in late-night leadership, the Carson show had the advantage of late-breaking topicality, because it was taped on the day of broadcast. *Thicke of the Night* had a lag of several days to a week, and some portions of some shows were taped weeks or even months in advance.

Thicke of the Night was planned as a variety show aimed at a younger audience than Carson's and emphasizing music and comedy over talk. "It will be alternative programming," Thicke told Kay Gardella of the New York *Daily News* (February 6, 1983) after he had begun taping some segments of the show. "For instance, we interviewed a Kenny Rogers look-alike instead of Kenny Rogers. We fabricate interviews where everything goes wrong. We even took a camera and interviewed Eric Estrada while he was doing his daily run around. . . . They [the production crew] will be real characters playing themselves . . . as part of the show. . . . I'll be the consistent persona . . . the central focus point. I don't appear to be a threat, so there isn't a segment of the audience that will be left out—grandmothers and college students can relate to me. They trust me. Basically I'm Everyman." Miss Gardella agreed, describing Thicke as "good-looking, facile, and funny, with an image that should be equally acceptable in Indiana and New York." Later Thicke said that if the audience accepted him as a "middle-of-the-road Everyman," then he could "lead them to the lunatic fringe."

Previewing the tapes of the first few *Thicke of the Night* programs, Harry F. Waters of *Newsweek* (September 5, 1983) described the show as "an almost schizoid mélange of manic inspiration and just plain silliness." Waters reported that the show's six-member comic repertory company (including the hip stand-up comedian Richard Belzer) seemed "perfectly in sync with Thicke's outrageous style." He found "hilarious" a sendup of Ted Koppel's *Nightline* in which the interviewee was the operator of an artificial-insemination clinic specializing in hatching full-grown humans, but at other moments he thought that Thicke's "willingness to pander to teeny-bopper libidos" was "unseemly."

Thicke of the Night made its debut on August 29, 1983. Reviewing the first program, George Maksian of the New York *Daily News* (August 30, 1983) described it as "a mishmash of songs, comedy, skits, interviews, what-have-you." He found some of the mixture "good" but "most of it . . . boring." "Thicke himself is personable enough and good looking, but [he makes] Merv Griffin [a talk show host graded low by Maksian] look good. . . . The show is busy, with too many clowns adding their two cents." Writing in *TV Guide* for October 29, 1983, Robert MacKenzie described Thicke singing a pop song with the house band à la Rick Springfield, with his sleeves rolled up, displaying an ease in interviewing, and "sitting around with a few of his house comics, trying funny lines." Averse to "improv," MacKenzie said he would have liked the sketches better had they been written. "When Thicke gets away from all this backup and wings his way through a real situation, he's charming." In November 1983 Thicke spoke on the air about being homesick for Kirkland Lake, Ontario, and looking for a United States town that resembled his birthplace. Many towns across the country offered to make him an honorary citizen; accepting the offer that came from Boone, Iowa, he traveled to

Boone for a tongue-in-cheek honorary ceremony. Despite such demonstrations of popularity, the show was losing the ratings war.

In midseason, the format of *Thicke of The Night* was altered in favor of more talk, to no avail in the ratings, and the show was canceled at the end of the season. After the cancellation, Thicke worked the celebrity banquet circuit, wrote television specials for Frank Mills and Anne Murray, recorded the single "Thicke of the Night" (the show's theme song, composed by him), and studied acting. During the 1984–85 television season he had roles in an episode of *The Love Boat* series and the television movie *The Calendar Girl Murders*, both on ABC. The ABC Circle Films producer Ilene Berg and the ABC casting director John Crosby, impressed with Thicke's acting and his ability to ad-lib, recommended him to the executive producer Michael Sullivan, who was looking for an actor to play the lead in a new ABC situation comedy, *Growing Pains*, a sort of white version of *The Cosby Show*. Thicke successfully auditioned for the part, that of Dr. Jason Seaver, a psychiatrist/father who moves his office into his home so that he can keep house and care for his three children after his wife, Maggie (Joanna Kerns), goes to work as a reporter.

Almost from the moment it made its first appearance on the ABC network in the fall of 1985, *Growing Pains* ranked in the top twenty in the Nielsen ratings. The initial critical reaction generally ran counter to the public's affirmative reception of the show, with reviewers using such adjectives as "harmless," "infantile," and "aggressively mediocre." Among the dissenters from the negative critical consensus was Don Merrill of *TV Guide*, who thought the show was "funny" and "thoroughly entertaining." "The youngsters are amusing without being obnoxious," Merrill wrote, "and Thicke has found a form that suits his talents, which are considerable." Joanna Kerns told Glenn Esterly, the *TV Guide* interviewer: "The strange thing is that Alan is much more like himself playing this fictional part than he ever seemed to be on *Thicke of the Night*. He's a much more caring, sensitive man than I would have guessed from watching that show." The producer of Thicke's Canadian talk show said, "Boy, it's good to see the old Alan back." Thicke himself explained to Glenn Esterly, "I was expected to be funny all the time on *Thicke of the Night*. I'm not funny all the time." By February 1987 *Growing Pains* was the tenth most popular series on the air, with a 23.0 rating and a 34 percent share of the viewing audience. In its 8:30 P.M. Tuesday time slot it was number one.

Alan Thicke is a slightly built man who prefers to dress informally, in Reebok sneakers, for example, and who drives a Porsche. He has more than his fair share of insecurities. "I worry about things like, 'Am I handsome enough? Smart enough? Witty enough?,'" he has confessed. "And that's just for a dinner date, much less putting yourself in front of a national audience." According to Gloria Loring, the television actress who was married to

Thicke for nearly fourteen years, until 1984, living with him was "like being on an endless est seminar." His brother, Todd, told Glenn Esterly, the writer of the *TV Guide* article: "Before *Thicke of the Night* and before his divorce he was a golden boy; he'd always been successful at whatever he'd been interested in. Then everything crashed down on him. So before *Growing Pains* came along, he had a rough rebuilding year. He had to deal with being tarnished." Thicke's friend David Foster, the Grammy-winning composer and producer, remembering that Thicke had always been a compulsive worker, said: "Alan went through a lot of soul-searching and came out of it with considerably more perspective. If you had known him before the talk-show troubles and before the divorce, you'd like him a lot better now. He's still a very hard worker, but he's a lot calmer."

Some of the ideas for *Growing Pains* come from Thicke's home life with his sons Brennan, twelve, and Robin, ten, of whom he shares custody with his ex-wife. "As a father," Todd Thicke told Glenn Esterly, "if Alan errs, it's in being too indulgent, just like Jason Seaver [the father in *Growing Pains*]. Alan wants the kids to have everything and do everything. He's not too much of a disciplinarian." With his sons, Thicke shares a house on an acre of land on Toluca Lake in the San Fernando Valley. For recreation, he plays hockey with a team in the North Hollywood League, and he sometimes works out with the Edmonton Oilers. Wayne Gretzky, the star of the Oilers, is a close friend of his. His favorite charity is the Juvenile Diabetes Foundation, a cause to which he became devoted after his son Brennan was diagnosed as having the disease.

References: Chicago Tribune TV Week p1+ Ap 27 '86 pors; N Y Daily News L p5 F 6 '83 por, p58 Jl 8 '85; Newsday II p3 S 4 '83 pors, II p20 Jl 6 '85 por; Newsweek 102:71 S 5 '83 por, 107:73 Ap 14 '87 por; People 25:14+ Ap 7 '86 por; Toronto Globe and Mail mag p16+ Ag 20 '77 por; TV Guide 32:40+ N 3 '84 por, 36:26+ Ag 9 '86 por

---

Thiebaud, Wayne

(thē bō)

Nov. 15, 1920– Artist; educator. Address: c/o Dept. of Art, University of California, Davis, Calif. 95616; Allan Stone Gallery, 48 E. 86th St., New York, N.Y. 10028

For more than three decades the realist painter Wayne Thiebaud has been engaged in a basic inquiry into light and structure, into what he once called the means of "taking color to its full strength and intensity," and into the mysteries of "shadow itself . . . the difference between shadow and substance, if there is a difference." Freely using a vocabulary of influences that ranged from the impressionists and Fauves to old masters such as Ver-

Wayne Thiebaud

meer and Ingres and to such contemporaries as Richard Diebenkorn and William de Kooning, Thiebaud painted bakery counter confections beginning in the early 1960s before expanding his subject matter to include the human figure and landscape. The cakes and pies, despite the lovingly sculpted impastoes with which they were rendered, gave Thiebaud a reputation as a slick and talented painter of pop art—a style whose concerns are actually directly opposed to his own. In the 1970s and 1980s a vertiginous series of San Francisco cityscapes brought unmistakably into the foreground the "suspension of disbelief about space" that, as Thiebaud once said, he tries to create with each of his paintings. A teacher as well as a practitioner, Thiebaud has been a professor of art at the Davis campus of the University of California since 1960. In 1985 a retrospective of his work, mounted at the San Francisco Museum of Modern Art by the curator Karen Tsjimoto, who also wrote the catalogue, proved for some critics that Thiebaud is entitled to membership in the ranks of American masters.

Morton Wayne Thiebaud was born in Mesa, Arizona on November 15, 1920, the son of Morton J. and Alice Eugenia (LeBaron) Thiebaud, both devout Mormons, who were active in church affairs. In 1921 the family moved from Arizona to Long Beach, California; in 1931 to Utah and then back to Long Beach two years later. The artist's father, an inventor and engineer who built the world's largest electric truck, worked during the Depression as a machine shop foreman, a Utah rancher, and a real estate salesman. The Thiebauds found room for art in their peripatetic household. During her pregnancy, the artist's mother tried to influence the course of his future development by attending

cultural events, and during his childhood, she gave him art projects to occupy his enforced leisure on rainy days. His uncle, a talented amateur cartoonist, entertained him with his drawings.

At Long Beach Polytechnic High School, which he attended from 1936 to 1938, Thiebaud took part in sports and debating. He sang to his own guitar accompaniment—sometimes on local radio—joined the Sea Scouts, and worked on a school stage crew. Because that activity behind the scenes involved elaborate backdrops and lighting effects, it gave the young Thiebaud insights that surfaced years later in such hallmarks of his style as the dramatic spotlighting of objects and figures to isolate them from their backgrounds and to enlarge and deepen their shadows.

After injuring his back during a sporting event in his first year at Long Beach High School, Thiebaud concentrated on drawing and cartooning. While still a student, he landed a job at the Walt Disney Studios in Los Angeles, where he was paid fourteen dollars for an exhaustingly long work week. Employed as a so-called in-betweener, he filled in the frames between the first and final frames drawn by the animators. In 1937 he was fired from the job for taking part in a studio strike.

For two years following his high school graduation, Thiebaud worked at a variety of jobs: as a free-lance cartoonist, stage technician, shipfitter, and poster artist for neighborhood movie houses. In 1942 he joined the United States Army Air Force and was assigned to what is now Mather Air Force Base near Sacramento as a cartoonist for the service newspaper *Wing Tips*. In 1945 he was transferred to the Air Force Motion Picture Unit at Culver City, California, where he designed scale map models of Japan and worked on documentary and training films. Discharged later that year, he undertook a succession of cartooning and commercial art jobs with advertising and publishing firms in Los Angeles and New York. Back once more in California, he painted backgrounds for publicity stills at Universal International Studios, until he was once again fired for his union sympathies.

For the next three years (1946–49) Thiebaud worked as a layout designer for the Rexall Drug Company and as a cartoonist for their house organ. Despite what he considered to be the banal imagery of the layouts—lipstick, hot water bottles, and brassieres—the actual process of learning design inevitably led Thiebaud to those examples of fine art from which the designs derived, including Mondrian, Degas, and Matisse. He recalls that he was "transfixed" by the revelation. Other revelations reached Thiebaud through his friendship with his coworker, the sculptor Robert Mallary, who introduced him to the world of ideas through the works of Marx and Shakespeare, and who inspired him to study art history and aesthetics, and to paint seriously. Thiebaud began to work in a cubist-expressionist style, and within a year he was given his first exhibition at the 1948 "Artists of Los Angeles and Vicinity" annual of the Los Angeles County Museum.

Now aged twenty-nine, and married, with a child, Thiebaud returned to school under the G.I. Bill to study painting. In 1951 he received his B.A. degree, and in 1953 his M.A. degree, from California State College in Sacramento. Immediately upon his graduation in 1951 he embarked upon the teaching of art, which has remained a vital part of his career, beginning as an instructor at Sacramento Junior College, now known as Sacramento City College. Throughout his years of teaching, Thiebaud has focused on setting forth the basics of art, working on exercises that explore problems of color, light, scale, and composition. The discipline that is so central to his approach, is, he contends, "not a restriction but an aid to freedom. It prepares an artist to choose his own limitations."

During his first nine years in Sacramento, Thiebaud was one of the founding fathers of the local art community. He designed sets for local theaters, created public murals and sculptures, arranged art exhibitions for the annual California state fairs, cofounded the Artists Cooperative Gallery, now the Artists Contemporary Gallery, and formed a small film company in his own home that from 1954 to 1959 produced art education films for junior high schools. Meanwhile, he kept abreast of happenings on the East Coast by making yearly trips with his students and faculty colleagues and visiting galleries, museums, and artists' studios. A sabbatical leave in 1956–57 provided him with a more indepth exposure to the New York art world, where he met and fell under the influence of the abstract expressionist painters of the Tenth Street school, such as Willem de Kooning, Franz Kline, and Barnett Newman. During that year he supported himself by taking jobs as art director for advertising agencies.

Thiebaud now regards much of the painting he did before 1959, even though it was often exhibited, as student work. As early as 1953 he had started to do pictures of food counter displays (for example, the 1955 Hors d'Oeuvres), presaging his much more widely known canvases of the 1960s, that document what he has referred to as "tattletale signs" of our culture. Paintings done during his New York sojourn and immediately after his return to California, show the influence of the gestural abstract painting to which he had been exposed, as in Ribbon Shop (1957) or The Sea Rolls In (1958). At the time, Thiebaud was embarrassed by the fact that "there was subject matter in there"—the ribbons and the sea—and he tried to "cover it up with arty strokes." His continued research in the history of art led him to the work of late nineteenth-century realists such as the Italian group known as I Macchiaioli (the "splash" painters) and the Spanish painter Joaquín Sorolla y Bastida. Balancing those influences from the past were his contacts with contemporary Bay Area figurative painters, especially Richard Diebenkorn, artists whose way of handling paint particularly fascinated him. Combining those sources, he developed the first phase of his mature painting: the delineation of totally representative images by means of expressionist applications of rich layers of paint.

The year 1960, which marked that stylistic turning point, was also the year in which he was appointed assistant professor in the department of art at the University of California at Davis. He was subsequently an associate professor from 1963 to 1967, and has been a full professor there since 1967. With a lighter teaching load and more time for his own art, he began a series of still-life paintings. The images he chose, such as cakes and pies, lollipops, candy machines, lipsticks, and ice-cream cones, were painted from memory and rooted ultimately in his childhood fascination with Long Beach boardwalk candy-dispensing machines and the colorful store window displays he once described as "the last refuge of the Byzantine tradition." His interest in them had reemerged after a trip to Mexico when, upon entering the United States, he found that what struck him most were the fauvist colors of hamburger stands and dime stores.

After he finished painting his first arrangement of pies, he recalls that he sat laughing in relief because for once he felt really free aesthetically, even while he suspected that it might be the end of him professionally. Indeed, patrons did drop him after a show of those new canvases in 1961 at the Artists Cooperative Gallery in Sacramento. But the Allan Stone Gallery in New York, now his dealer, proved more receptive. "Wayne Thiebaud: Recent Paintings," his first one-man show in the city, was held at the gallery in 1962 and was a triumphant success. Works were purchased by the Museum of Modern Art, the Wadsworth Atheneum, and private collectors. Thiebaud, according to Robert Hughes (Time, October 28, 1985), was "misunderstood into fame" by reviewers who hailed him as a bright light in the pop art firmament. That misalignment has dogged Thiebaud's reputation ever since.

"Of course, you're thankful when anyone ever calls you anything," Thiebaud once remarked, "so you don't mind even being called a Pop artist. But I never felt much a part of it. I must say I never really liked Pop art very much. . . . " While the Pop artists produced icons of irony and detachment with a mass-produced appearance, Thiebaud luxuriated in painting, being drawn, as he once admitted, by "moments of attractiveness. . . . that primitive issuance of desire that makes you want to touch wet paint."

On canvas those moments have most often been rendered as still lifes. Thiebaud has continued to do them, with evolving stylistic nuances, into the 1980s. Characteristic of his earlier still lifes are Penny Machines (1961), Pies, Pies, Pies (also 1961), Window Cakes (1963), Three Lipsticks (1965), and Tie Pile (1969). Among the most acclaimed of all his works are the cake paintings, continued with such canvases as Heart Cakes/Valentine Cakes (1976) and Various Cakes (1981), in which Thiebaud's desire to make "the relationship between paint and subject matter as close as [he could] get it," to make paint "'become' frosting," is embodied in orchestrations of light and structure set down in brilliant colors. Writing in *New York* (August 8, 1977), Thomas B. Hess noted the shimmer of a "Platonist ideal" in Thiebaud's work. "He dreams of the perfect triangle, cube, and sphere," Hess wrote, "and they appear as a wedge of Swiss cheese, a helping of layer cake, a scoop of orange ice."

Another characteristic of Thiebaud's paintings is the subtle halo of color that surrounds each image and that derives from his interest in the "halation" that is caused by the imperfect merging of images in binocular vision and seen as vibrations around the edges of objects when they are stared at fixedly. Thiebaud renders the halation, he has said, to "give a little bit of vibration, so the eye will accept the form as not being so pasted on." When the halation works, as Robert Hughes has said, it lends Thiebaud's images "an apparitional flicker." More often than not, the apparitions seem almost edible, bathed in fluorescent light, and casting strong, chromatic shadows—references to the impressionists and Fauves—that anchor them to their hygienically white and featureless backgrounds.

A fellowship that was awarded to Thiebaud in 1964 by the Creative Research Foundation of the University of California gave him the chance to spend a year working on almost life-size paintings of human figures. Relying at first, as with his still lifes, on visual memory, Thiebaud soon felt the need to use live models; because of the difficulty he experienced in drawing from the model, however, he has continued since 1976 to devote one day a week to life-drawing sessions with a group of Bay Area artist friends. Works such as *Bikini* (1964) and *Woman in Tub* (1965) are among many paintings for which his second wife posed. Those paintings and others, like *Girl with Pink Hat* (1973–76) or *Man Reading* (1963), though less well received, are not unlike the still lifes in purpose and effect. By no means portraits, devoid of emotive overtones, and thus enigmatic, they are ultimately studies of form, and so become, as Karen Tsujimoto suggests, virtual abstractions. *Toweling Off* (1968), one of a group of paintings of that year's Wimbledon tennis matches that was commissioned by *Sports Illustrated,* has indeed been termed as much a picture of the towel that covers the young woman's face as of the woman herself. The style in those figure paintings remained much the same, too, as that of the still lifes, with clear, assured draftsmanship, a product of his commercial art training, and the use of dramatic lighting to isolate the object, now become a figure.

In 1966 Thiebaud shifted to yet another subject and began a series of country and urban landscape paintings. Often perceived by critics as abrupt and dramatic, those changes of theme are regarded by the artist himself merely as cyclic, a "tightrope walk," to use his phrase, between the development of a convention that for a time answers his artistic demands, and the calcification of a convention becoming a formula. Thus, even while embarked on his landscape/cityscape work, Thiebaud went on painting still lifes and in the 1980s introduced a new approach to that subject matter. Instead of presenting strongly lit objects against light backgrounds, he now painted cakes, candy apples, rows of shoes, a lipstick, a single rose in a box,—a reversal of his 1965 painting, *Woman in Tub,*—that seem to glow with light of their own against dark backgrounds.

With the landscape paintings came also a radical change of medium: from impastoed oils to pastels, watercolors, or gouaches; thinly stained acrylics, as in *Cliffs* (1968); or combinations of oils and charcoal, as in *Corner Apartments/Down 18th Street* (1980). Beginning the new series of work with paintings, drawings, or pastel sketches of the Sacramento Valley, he went on to oil paintings of the Grand Canyon or of Yosemite. One example is *Half Dome and Cloud* (1975), which was commissioned for the United States Department of the Interior's Bicentennial exhibition. Again, the challenge for him was the solution of formal problems; not interested merely in rendering the pictorial aspects of Western scenery, Thiebaud was trying instead "in some way to manage it, manipulate it, or see what [he could] turn it into." The quick on-site sketches he did in conjunction with those paintings, drawings that he calls "visual hunches," enabled him to liberate himself from the tyranny of exact visual fact; as he worked them up into the finished paintings he added to them from memory, rearranged certain elements, and allowed for a degree of expression and interpretation. Thus the landscape paintings become less a type of strict recording and more a contemplation of reality.

In the 1970s the rural landscape began to be replaced for the most part by San Francisco cityscapes painted with the aid of a telescope from his second-floor pied-à-terre on Portrero Hill, which rises above the busiest industrial section of the city. They were inspired, Thiebaud told Grace Glueck (*New York Times,* July 22, 1977), by drives among plunging streets, where "you can't feel where you're at in terms of space." In paintings such as *Apartment Hill* (1981) he explored that abrupt "loss of position" by painting, as sturdily as the structure of any layer cake, the angular, interlocked patterns of vertiginous hills. He trained his eye with the telescope and its tendency to flatten what it enlarged, and employed the conventions of Asian isometric perspective. Those conventions have the effect, according to Karen Tsujimoto, of projecting the center of vision "beyond human perspective," allowing lines to converge in the foreground and placing background objects progressively higher in the composition in a manner contradictory to Western conventions and habits of seeing. He extended his experiments by combining several viewpoints in one painting, as in *Curved Intersection* (1979), and developing in that and in other works such as *California Street* (1978), *Urban Freeways* (1979–80) or *Urban Downgrade, 20th and Noe* (1981), a way of conveying spatial shock and tension. Typical of his nonnarrative approach, the roller coaster streets are devoid of habitants, in the same way that the figure paintings are devoid of revelations of personality and that his food paintings, since they are unaccompanied by images of utensils, are devoid of any suggestion of the act of eating. The critical reaction was overwhelming. According to Robert Hughes, "Everything seems to be on the point of falling, flaking or sliding into the Pacific, and the city becomes a meticulously ordered metaphor of anxiety." Like Hughes, Alan G. Artner of the *Chicago Tribune* (April 27, 1986) felt that after seeing the cityscapes, "a traveler could not approach the city again without having it appear drastically altered."

Over the years Thiebaud has explored many media other than painting. Since the 1960s he has worked on intaglio prints, etchings, lithographs, linocuts, and silk screens and has published several editions of his prints, including *Seven Still Lifes and a Rabbit* (Parasol Press, 1971) and *Thiebaud Graphics: 1964–1971* (Whitney Museum of Modern Art, 1971). In 1983 he traveled to Japan under the auspices of the Oakland-based Crown Point Press to collaborate with traditional woodblock artists on the print *Dark Cake.*

Many academic honors have been awarded Thiebaud. Since 1967 he has been a visiting professor or artist-in-residence at institutions all over the United States and in Canada. He won the Chicago Golden Reel Award and first prize at the Art Film Festival at the California State Fair for "Space" in 1956. His other films include "Works of Wayne Thiebaud" (1965) and "Wayne Thiebaud" (1971). He has contributed articles and reviews to *Time,* the *Nation, ARTnews,* and other magazines. A doyen among West Coast painters, Thiebaud was cited by the College Art Association of America as Most Distinguished Studio Teacher of the Year, in 1981; and holds honorary doctorates from the California College of Arts and Crafts in Oakland, and from Dickinson College in Carlisle, Pennsylvania.

The listing of solo and group showings of Thiebaud's work, in museums and galleries in the United States and abroad, fills twenty pages in Karen Tsujimoto's catalogue: beginning with his first solo exhibition, "Influences on a Young Painter," held in 1951 at the E.B. Crocker Art Gallery (now the Crocker Art Museum) in Sacramento, and including the important show that introduced pop art, "New Realists," held at the Sidney Janis Gallery in New York in 1962. His first European showing was at the Galleria Schwarz in Milan, in 1963; subsequently he represented the United States at the 1966 São Paulo Bienal and the 1977 Kassel Documenta. Thiebauds paintings and prints are found in a substantial number of American and European collections, public and private, including the Museum of Modern Art, the Metropolitan Museum of Art, and the Whitney Museum of American Art in New York; the Albright-Knox Art Gallery in Buffalo; the Chicago Art Institute; and the San Francisco Museum of Modern Art.

A thoroughly Western type in appearance, Wayne Thiebaud was once described by *ARTnews* correspondent Thomas Albright as "tall, rawboned, athletic, with craggy but finely chiseled features, [and] deep-set brown eyes." His unassuming,

relaxed manner only partly masks his alert and searching intelligence. Thiebaud was married to Patricia Patterson in 1943. Two years later their daughter Twinka was born; Mallary Ann was born in 1952. After his divorce in 1959 he married Betty Jean Carr, a filmmaker; their son Paul LeBaron was born in 1960. The artist continues to live in Sacramento, commuting regularly to his San Francisco pied-à-terre. Thiebaud plays in senior tennis tournaments and still enjoys guitar playing. In painting he continues to approach observation as "a kind of eternal proposition," as he expressed it to Thomas Albright. "And the whole question that you're left with is: can any of us ever understand our impressions?"

References: ARTnews 77:82+ F '78 pors; Quest 4:78+ D '80 pors; Contemporary Artists (1983); Contemporary Authors vol 45–48 (1974); Tsujimoto, Karen. Wayne Thiebaud (1985) pors; Who's Who in America, 1984-85; Who's Who in American Art (1984); World Artists 1950 to 1980 (1984)

Tisch, Laurence A(lan)

Mar. 5, 1923– Business executive. Address: b. Loews Corp., 666 Fifth Ave., New York City, N.Y. 10019

A self-made billionaire and "conglomerateur," Laurence A. Tisch has a record of buying into failing or troubled corporations, revamping their management, and turning them into profitable enterprises. Having made his fortune in real estate and his reputation as head of the Loews Corporation, he achieved his latest coup by blocking a hostile take-over of CBS by purchasing for $750 million almost 25 percent of its stock and becoming its chairman and chief executive officer. Dubbed a "white knight" by Wall Street investors, he has begun to rescue the broadcasting corporation from its falling ratings, its sluggish profits, and its tarnished image.

Laurence Alan Tisch was born on March 5, 1923, in Bensonhurst, Brooklyn, into a supportive, close-knit family of achievers. His father, Al Tisch, a former All-American basketball player at the City College of New York, owned a garment-manufacturing business and then bought two summer camps in New Jersey, which his wife, Sadye (Brenner) Tisch, helped him to operate. Mrs. Tisch encouraged Larry and his younger brother, Preston Robert ("Bob") Tisch, to work together from an early age, instilling in them a strong feeling for family.

Swift-moving and decisive even in his youth, Tisch went through both high school and college in only five years, graduating cum laude from New York University at the age of eighteen. By the time he was nineteen he had obtained a master's degree in industrial engineering from the Wharton School of Finance and Commerce of the University of Pennsylvania. He then spent three years in the United States Army, making up secret codes for the Office of Strategic Services, the precursor of the CIA, during World War II.

In 1946, after sampling Harvard Law School for one semester, Tisch followed his father into the hotel business, purchasing a sleepy Lakewood, New Jersey, resort hotel named Laurel-in-the-Pines with $125,000 from his father and a $50,000 investment from a friend of the family. To lure more customers, the Tisches installed an indoor swimming pool and outdoor skating rink, and in the first year made enough to buy out their partner. In 1948, after graduating from the University of Michigan with a degree in economics, Bob Tisch joined his brother in the enterprise. That year the Tisch brothers made such a success of their first joint venture that they acquired another property, the Grand Hotel, a summer resort in New York's Catskill Mountains. Building their hotel empire as if they were playing a game of Monopoly, in 1950 they bought the landmark Traymore Hotel in Atlantic City, New Jersey, which had been running at a loss. By trimming expenses, improving its food and facilities, and modernizing its decor, they turned it into a million-dollar-a-year operation. They then embarked on two more Atlantic City ventures, leasing the Ambassador Hotel in 1951, at first as a tax write-off but improving it to such a degree that in two years it was averaging an annual net income of $750,000, and buying the rickety Brighton Hotel in 1954, which they redid four years later as the bustling 275-room Colony Motel.

Applying their success formula to Manhattan real estate, the Tisch brothers leased and renovated two New York City hotels: the McAlpin, which was sold to the Sheraton chain in 1954 for $9 million, and the Belmont-Plaza, where they invested $1 million, recovered their investment in two years, and sold their lease at a $1.7 million profit. The first hotel they built from the ground up was the luxurious Americana in Bal Harbour, Florida, which they constructed in 1955 at a cost of $1.7 million without a mortgage. Specializing in convention catering, the 780-room hotel did approximately $12 million worth of business a year at the outset, in what a writer for the Miami Herald (February 20, 1962) called "one of the most profitable business enterprises in the state."

Equipped with $65 million in profits from their thriving hotels, the Tisch brothers started buying into the Loews Corporation in 1959, taking advantage of the fact that an antitrust decree had forced the separation of Loews Theatres, Inc., from its movie-making parent. In September 1959, Larry Tisch won a seat on Loews's board and became chairman of its powerful finance committee, while his brother Bob was made head of its executive committee. In 1960 the Tisches consolidated their control by buying up 25 percent of Loews's 2,668,-000 shares. At a stockholders meeting on January 24, 1961, Larry Tisch gained total control of Loews and ousted its then president and chief operating officer, Eugene Picker, in a policy dispute over diversification.

Moving quickly to rid themselves of some of Loews's unprofitable movie theatres, the Tisches steered the corporation into the hotel and motel business. As their pilot project, they replaced an old movie house at Fifty-first Street and Lexington Avenue with the Summit, the first new hotel to be built in Manhattan in thirty years. In a bid for the city's lucrative convention business, Loews Hotels also built the 2,000-room, fifty-story Americana, which was the world's tallest hotel when it was completed in 1962. With its ballrooms, exhibition space, private meeting rooms, shopping promenade, and a 350-car parking garage, it made a formidable bid for conventioneers. Today the Loews hotels in New York City also include the Howard Johnson Motor Lodge, the Ramada Motor Inn, and the Regency. In addition, Loews owns a total of some nine hotels elsewhere in the United States and in Canada, Europe, and the Bahamas. With brother Bob in charge of the hotel subsidiary, Larry handled Loews's stock portfolio and remained on the lookout for possible acquisitions.

Using Loews, of which he and other insiders control about 40 percent, as a base, Larry Tisch acquired Lorillard, the fifth-largest cigarette company in the United States, in a friendly take-over in 1968. He immediately trimmed away one whole level of top management and rid the company of its losing candy and cat-food businesses to boost its profit margins. In 1974 he gained control of CNA Financial Corporation, a Chicago-based insurance company when its earnings were severely depressed and turned that company around as well. Bringing in the insurance professional Edward J.

Noha from Allstate to head CNA's insurance operations and cutting CNA's employment from 12,000 to 10,500, he transformed CNA from a nearly insolvent company to one with an A-plus rating in the industry and with $16.5 billion in assets.

The Bulova Watch Company, the fourth subsidiary of Loews, was acquired in March 1979 at a time when the Japanese were making considerable inroads into the American watch business. Some analysts questioned the wisdom of that investment, but in the first year of Tisch control, the producer of Bulova, Caravelle, and Accutron watches had a net income of $8.3 million, as opposed to a $2.5 million loss the year before. With those judicious acquisitions, Tisch built Loews's revenues from a little over $100 million in 1970 to over $3 billion a decade later.

Writing in *Fortune* magazine (May 1971), Charles G. Burck attributed much of the success story of Loews to the teamwork of the brothers Tisch and the "natural division of labor" between them. "Where Larry's intuition allows him to grasp immediately the board outline of a situation," he observed, "Bob can cut his way through to a clear understanding of its minute operating complexities and commit the important details to a total-recall memory." Laurence, low-key and unassuming, has been described as the "private man" who handles investment strategy; Bob, the more gregarious of the two, as the "public man" adept at overseeing day-to-day operations. Until Bob moved to Washington, D.C., in August 1986 to take on his new job as postmaster-general, the brothers were known to socialize with their families together, go to Temple together, play tennis together, and even commute to work together. "Larry frowns and Bob smiles," the financial adviser to Loews has said. The brothers have always respected each other's abilities and, according to an associate, are "still as close as peanut butter and jelly."

Even Wall Street experts sometimes make mistakes, and Laurence Tisch is no exception. Perhaps his biggest miscalculation was buying up almost half a million shares of Equity Funding stock the week before the company fell apart in a massive fraud scandal. As Tisch told Charles Elia, the reporter for the *Wall Street Journal* (April 25, 1973), "There's no way of adjusting for massive fraud in analyzing a stock."

In general, however, Laurence Tisch's investment strategy has been one of playing it safe, rather than getting involved in highly speculative ventures. "We're bottom dwellers," one of his sons has said, meaning those who invest in undervalued properties and then wait for a turnaround. The Tisches also cover their bets. Even in deals that failed, such as their attempted take-over of Commercial Credit, Laurence Tisch came out ahead, selling the marked-up stock he had purchased to reap a profit of $28 million. When the brothers sold the Traymore Hotel in 1956 for $15 million, they retained control of its management and also retained a parcel of its land, so they were able to cash in on the subsequent Atlantic City casino boom. Recent-

ly, Laurence Tisch purchased a fleet of oil tankers, figuring that if the oil business does not rebound, he will still be able to sell the boats for the scrap metal. CBS was another no-lose proposition, since it could be seen either as a long-term investment or a short-term arbitrage deal, considering that he purchased the stock at only $127 a share, far below its estimated $200 value.

The move by Laurence Tisch to control CBS came at a time when a variety of problems beset the communications conglomerate. Its chairman and chief executive officer, Thomas H. Wyman, had led CBS into the precarious movie industry and got it to invest in the toy business with the purchase of Ideal Toys Corporation, for about $57 million. The latter venture lost money, and CBS had to sell the operation. When Wyman bought a number of specialty magazines from the Ziff-Davis Publishing Company for $362.5 million, he drew criticism that he had overpaid. The ratings of CBS were low, while NBC had risen to first place in prime-time viewership, and its advertising revenues were dwindling. There had also been dissatisfaction, expressed by Bill Moyers and others, that the network that had once provided a rostrum for such outstanding journalists as Edward R. Murrow, Eric Sevareid, and Walter Cronkite was now substituting "show business" for hard news.

In additon, the network was the target of several takeover bids during 1985, including attempts by Ted Turner, the cable television entrepreneur and owner of the Atlanta Braves, who based his bid on a package of high-risk securities; Marvin Davis, the Denver oilman, investor, and recent owner of Twentieth Century-Fox; and conservative Senator Jesse A. Helms, who was tempted by the possibility of being "Dan Rather's boss." Determined to keep the network independent, CBS repurchased 21 percent of its own stock, taking on $1 billion in long-term debt.

To deter hostile raids, CBS sought the aid of Laurence Tisch. By mid-August of 1986 his stake in the company had grown to 24.9 percent. It was kept at that figure because, according to a "golden parachute" clause in Wyman's contract, if anyone acquired 25 percent or more of CBS stock, the chairman could bail himself out with about $2 million worth of stock as his severance pay.

After a tense eleven-hour board meeting on September 10, 1986, at "Black Rock," the CBS corporate headquarters, Wyman was asked to resign. A major factor in his ouster was his revelation to the board that he had been negotiating to sell the network to the Coca-Cola Corporation. As the company's largest shareholder, Laurence Tisch became its acting chief executive, to serve until a new chairman and chief executive officer were selected. In addition, William S. Paley, the company's eighty-six-year-old founder and holder of an 8.1 percent stake, became acting chairman. Harold Brown, a board member, was asked to head a six-member executive search committee to find a permanent chief executive.

The Tisch management style has been described as "Spartan." One writer once noted that "the spare furnishings and beige industrial carpet" of Laurence Tisch's corner office at Loews headquarters, were "reminiscent of a Howard Johnson's motor inn." Personnel is kept to the bare minimum, with a supervisory staff of only sixty persons to oversee a corporate empire of 22,000 employees. Tisch does not believe in such perquisites as limousines and executive dining rooms for himself or anybody else and thinks that writing memos is a waste of time and money.

The austere "Tisch touch" is already in evidence at CBS, according to an article in the *Wall Street Journal* (October 3, 1986). During his first three weeks as top administrator, Laurence Tisch instituted major staff reductions and, with an eye for detail, banned messenger and courier services except in emergencies, prohibited the use of rented typewriters, put purchases of new furniture on hold, restricted first-class airline travel, and eliminated limousine service. In addition, he hired management consultants from Coopers and Lybrand "to assist in a review of systems and procedures within CBS," including "paperwork flows, financial systems, data processing functions, reports, forms, and organizational structures."

A management shakeup at CBS began within the first month of the new Tisch dispensation. On September 11, the day after Tisch took over, Van Gordon Sauter, the president of CBS News, resigned, and in the first week of October Neil E. Derrough, president of CBS-owned television stations, follow suit. On October 17, 1986, the *New York Times* announced that Peter A. Derow, president of the CBS Publishing Group, was leaving, along with fourteen members of his staff. "I think that Larry feels the entire corporation is overstaffed," Derow commented. On October 24, 1986, CBS announced its first divestitures since Tisch became acting chief executive. CBS Educational and Professional Publishing, which includes the textbook publisher Holt, Rinehart & Winston and W. B. Saunders, the world's largest medical publisher, would be sold to Harcourt Brace Jovanovich, Inc., for $500 million, and CBS Songs, the music-publishing wing of CBS, would be sold to three entrepreneurs for $100 million. The *New York Times* (October 25, 1986) reported that CBS was also considering selling its magazine publishing business, which includes *Woman's Day, Field and Stream,* and *Yachting.*

To assure both CBS employees and the public that he would balance the demands of public service and the bottom line, Laurence Tisch said during an interview for *Time* magazine (September 22, 1986): "I'm really wearing two hats. My first obligation is to do what's best for the network and ensure quality programming. My secondary role is as a businessman to manage the company in a way that is right for the employees and shareholders." Although Laurence Tisch has been exercising more and more operational control at the network, he is not considered to have legal control. The FCC, acting on a complaint by Fairness in Media, ruled on October 16, 1986, that Tisch's appointment does not constitute a "take-over" because he is only one of thirteen members of the board and can be countermanded at any time.

Originally viewed as a transitional figure, Laurence Tisch soon emerged as the front-running candidate to become permanent chief executive officer at CBS. Walt Disney Company chairman and chief executive officer Michael D. Eisner and Robert A. Daly, the chairman and chief executive of Warner Brothers, were approached by the search committee, of which Tisch is a member, but both turned down the job. Tisch, who had indicated his willingness to assume the position if no other candidates were found, was unanimously elected president and chief executive officer at the network's monthly board meeting on January 14, 1987. Before receiving the board's approval, Tisch reportedly agreed not to try to sell the company's major assets, including the records and magazine publishing divisions.

Tisch immediately set to work to streamline the operations of CBS News, whose budget had grown by almost 250 percent since 1978. In March he approved plans to trim the news budget by some $50 million, or 17 percent, by shuttering some national and overseas news bureaus and by dismissing more than 200 employees, among them the veteran CBS reporters Ike Pappas and Jane Bryant Quinn. At the time, Tisch was widely criticized within CBS News, but in the fall of the of the year he regained a measure of support when he penciled into the prime-time schedule a regular weekly documentary series—the network's first since the cancellation of the highly regarded *CBS Reports* in 1971. In another restructuring move, Tisch approved the sale of CBS Magazines to a group led by Peter G. Diamandis, that division's president, for $650 million. CBS was expected to plow the proceeds of the sale into its broadcasting and records businesses.

Despite his ever-increasing business responsibilities, Laurence Tisch still finds the time and energy to be involved with many civic, cultural, religious, and philanthropic organizations. Proud of his heritage, he is a past president of the United Jewish Appeal of New York and is a trustee of the Federation of Jewish Philanthropies. A prominent art patron and collector, he is a former trustee of the Whitney Museum of Art, and he is currently a trustee of the Metropolitan Museum of Art, to which he and his brother recently donated $10 million for the construction of new galleries for major international loan exhibitions. He is a trustee of the New York Public Library and a director of the Legal Aid Society, as well as chairman of the board of trustees of New York University, his undergraduate alma mater, where a $2 million donation from the brothers helped pay for the building of Tisch Hall, in honor of their late father. In 1982 the Tisch brothers gave $7.5 million to the university for its School of the Arts.

Friends note that in moving into the management of CBS, Tisch has found a way to combine his dollars-and-cents investment strategies with his *pro bono* agenda. The *New York Times* (September 11, 1986) quoted a source close to Tisch as saying: "This is no longer a financial investment for him. He believes that this is an investment he made for history, for his children, for financial reasons, and out of the desire to become a corporate statesman." He explained his stance to Ken Auletta in an article for the *New York Times* (June 8, 1986): "My only desire is to keep CBS as a first-class independent network. It's very important for the country. CBS and the other two networks mold, in large part, some of the thinking of the country. It's a serious obligation. It's not a toy."

In 1948 Laurence Tisch married Wilma ("Billie") Stein. They have four sons, three of whom, following in the family tradition, work with their father. Andrew is a Loews director and president of Bulova; Dan is a managing director of Salomon Brothers investment firm (he allegedly alerted his father to the fact there was a bargain to be had in CBS stock); James is vice-president of finance for Loews; and Tom is a private investor.

For relaxation, Laurence Tisch plays bridge once a week, and one friend has remarked that he plays it much the same way he runs a company—"He bids slams on solid assets, and he

doesn't like a void." He plays tennis as much for its social aspect as for the exercise, and his long-term tennis partners include Leonard Goldenson, the chairman of ABC, and investment bankers Bernard Stein and James D. Wolfensohn.

Considering the fact that the total personal worth of the Tisch brothers is estimated to be around $1.7 billion, Larry Tisch and his wife live without ostentation. They spend most of the week in a modestly furnished Fifth Avenue apartment and their weekends in their home in Rye, New York. "Your standard of living doesn't change after the first million," Larry remarks. "I don't want to become possessed by my possessions." The Tisches entertain generously but not lavishly, preferring small dinner parties and movie screenings for their guests. Tisch usually drinks nothing but ginger ale at cocktail parties and, although he owns a tobacco company, he does not smoke.

References: Fortune 61:132–4+ Ja '60 por, 83:158+ My '71 por; New York 19:36+ S 1 '86; N Y Times p59 S 6 '68 por; N Y Times Mag p34+ Je 8 '86 pors; Newsweek 108:46+ S 15 '86 por; Washington Post K p1+ N 10 '85 por; American Jewish Biographies (1982); Who's Who in America, 1986–87; Who's Who in Finance and Industry, 1985–86

Truman, (Mary) Margaret

Feb. 17, 1924– Writer. Address: c/o Scott Meredith Literary Agency, Inc., 845 3d Ave., New York City, N.Y. 10022

NOTE: This biography supersedes the article that appeared in *Current Biography* in 1950.

Being the daughter of an American president proved both an advantage and a disadvantage to Margaret Truman, the only child of Harry S. Truman and the wife of the former *New York Times* managing editor Clifton Daniel. While she enjoyed being a White House debutante, she struggled at the same time to become a personality in her own right. In her early twenties she tried a career as a concert singer, then she was for a time a radio and television interviewer, and in recent years she has met with some success as a published author. Miss Truman has disclosed information about her famous family in several nonfiction books, including her autobiography, *Souvenir,* as well as *Letters from Father* and the biographies of her parents, *Harry S. Truman* and *Bess W. Truman.* Using her firsthand knowledge of the Washington scene, she has also written well-crafted mysteries set in the nation's capital, of which several, including *Murder in the White House, Murder in the Supreme Court* and *Murder in Georgetown,* reached the best-seller list.

At the time Mary Margaret Truman was born, on February 17, 1924, in Independence, Missouri, her father, Harry S. Truman, was a county judge. Starting as an ambitious farmer, he had after a nine-year courtship, in which he tried to prove himself financially worthy, married Elizabeth Virginia (Bess) Wallace, the reigning social queen of Independence. After serving as a captain in the field artillery in World War I, Harry Truman became part owner of a Kansas City haberdashery and entered politics as a protégé of Thomas J. Pendergast, the boss of the Kansas City Democratic machine. Margaret's birthplace and childhood home in Independence was built before the Civil War by her mother's great-grandfather, a prominent flour miller, and it was maintained by Harry S. Truman as his home base throughout his White House years.

An only child, but part of a large, close-knit, extended family, Margaret recalls being spoiled by her father, disciplined by her mother, taught manners by her grandmother, Mrs. David W. Wallace, and pampered by doting aunts and uncles. She was also within shouting distance of many girlfriends of her age, and together they took over a chicken coop in the Truman backyard, and turned it into a clubhouse, where they put out a newspaper, "The Henhouse Gazette," that featured family anecdotes among other items.

After Harry S. Truman was elected a United States senator in 1934, the family spent half of each year in Independence, where Margaret went to public school, and the remainder of the year in Washington, D.C., where she attended Gunston Hall, a girls' boarding school. There she won prizes for her achievements in Spanish and English, was included on the honor roll, and performed in school productions of Shakespeare. In 1942 she entered George Washington University, where she excelled in her major subjects of history and international relations. She sang in the university glee club, joined the Pi Beta Phi sorority, and was active in the Canterbury Club, an Episcopalian organization.

Margaret Truman was twenty-one years old when her father, who had become vice-president eighty-three days earlier, succeeded to the presidency on April 12, 1945, following the sudden death of Franklin D. Roosevelt. She soon discovered that among the positive features of living in the White House was the chance to meet a variety of interesting people. "The opportunity to associate with great men and women who rise to the top in a democracy is the most superb advantage," she wrote in Souvenir. Another advantage was that as a confirmed movie buff she was able to "command" whatever films she wished to see. The main disadvantage of public life was its lack of privacy. Margaret Truman felt the pressures of the goldfish-bowl existence in her social life and vowed never to marry while she was still in the White House.

Influenced by her piano-playing father and bolstered by his constant encouragement, Margaret Truman had begun to take voice and piano lessons as a child and sang in the choir of Trinity Episcopal Church in Independence. She was encouraged in her musical aspirations by the noted vocal coach Estelle Liebling, and she received intensive voice training from Mrs. Thomas J. Strickler, a family friend who had once served as an assistant to the teacher of Amelita Galli-Curci.

After obtaining her B.A. degree from George Washington University in 1946, Margaret Truman went to New York to prepare for a concert career. She made her professional singing debut as a coloratura soloist with the Detroit Symphony under Karl Krueger on March 16, 1947, on its weekly network radio program. In August of that year she made her first appearance on the concert stage with Eugene Ormandy and the Hollywood Bowl Symphony, a performance that brought her seven curtain calls. During the next three months she toured more than thirty cities across the United States, presenting a program of operatic arias, *lieder,* and light classics. Her reviews were mostly kind, although some critics tactfully suggested she needed further training.

Because of her family's prominence, Miss Truman found it difficult to assess her voice in terms of critical opinion. As she wrote in *Letters from Father,* "Because of my father, I was more easily able to obtain important engagements. But I also received more attention by first-string critics and more demanding audiences, who felt that because my father was the President, I had to be not better than average but better than the best in order to justify my appearing on the stage."

During 1948, Margaret Truman took a sabbatical from her singing career to help her father with his campaign for reelection, in which he defeated the Republican challenger Thomas E. Dewey, notwithstanding predictions by political pundits and the media to the contrary. Coached by her fellow Missourian Helen Traubel, she resumed her singing career in 1949, appearing in radio and television concerts. That year she signed long-term contracts with NBC and with RCA-Victor records.

The legendary exchange between President Truman and the *Washington Post* music critic Paul Hume, may be regarded as the beginning of the end of Margaret Truman's music career. In his review of her performance in a concert in Washington, D.C., on December 5, 1950, Hume praised her personality but commented that she "cannot sing very well," that "she is flat a good deal of the time," and that she has no "professional finish." The President wrote in huffy response: "I have just read your lousy review. . . . I never met you, but if I do you'll need a new nose. . . ."

After she abandoned her singing career in the 1950s, Margaret Truman conducted her own radio show, *Authors in the News,* for seven years and also did some acting in summer stock. In 1955 she was cohost of a radio show, *Weekday,* with Mike Wallace. Allen Ludden, the show's producer, recalls, "She was a joy to work with, a nice, dignified, kind of square lady who was very good on the show." In 1965 Miss Truman was the television hostess of the *CBS International Hour,* presented on five CBS stations, introducing music and dance programs from around the world.

On April 21, 1956, Margaret Truman married Clifton Daniel, then a foreign correspondent for the *New York Times*, who later became its managing editor. Shortly after their engagement, Miss Truman wrote her first book, *Souvenir; Margaret Truman's Own Story* (McGraw-Hill, 1956), in collaboration with Margaret Cousins. In her words, she wrote it "in self-defense" when she heard that someone else was planning a book about her life. "Maybe I was still trying to please my father, though, and fulfill his prophecy," she remarked. "He wrote me at the end of 1946 that 'you write interestingly and perhaps when you arrive [at a certain age] and your good voice cracks, you can be a great storywriter. . . .'"

N. L. Browning, reviewing it in the *Chicago Sunday Tribune* (May 27, 1956) called *Souvenir* "a fascinating chronicle of Margaret Truman's life from early childhood to the present." Josephine Ripley observed in the *Christian Science Monitor* (May 24, 1956) that the author "is as well-behaved in print as she is in public. . . . Here is . . . a rollicking running account of the life of a spontaneously natural little girl from the Midwest who slid down a rabbit hole and found herself at 1600 Pennsylvania Avenue."

Although Margaret Truman's *White House Pets* (McKay, 1969), generously illustrated with photographs, qualified as an eligible coffee-table item, it was ignored by most of the major media. It was rather unreliably assessed in *Kirkus Reviews* (October 15, 1969) as "an anecdotal splatter of pet tales" and summed up as "tame, but name-plated for salability." *Publishers Weekly* (October 20, 1969) announced that "Miss Truman has come up with some "lightly entertaining material. . . . "Disingenuous but pleasant." *White House Pets* was excerpted in the January 1970 issue of the *Ladies Home Journal*.

In *Souvenir*, Margaret Truman had modestly written, "I have had no thought of writing history. The best I could hope to write would be a footnote to history. As the only child of the President of a great world power in a cataclysmic time, I will certainly be expected to make some comment on this man who will belong to history—to evoke him in special ways, available only to a daughter." Assisted in her research by the historian Thomas Fleming, Miss Truman fulfilled that expectation in 1972 with her biography *Harry S. Truman* (Morrow, 1972), which was chosen as the Book-of-the-Month Club's special midwinter 1973 selection.

"No chancelleries are going to topple, no certainties become unhinged, because of any revelations made here," Cabell Phillips wrote in his review in the *New Republic* (January 6/13, 1973). As for her evaluation of her father's place in history, W. C. McWilliams commented in his review in the *New York Times* (October 24, 1972), "Her political portrait of her father is unbelievable because it presents him as faultless." The reviewer went on to say, however, "It is the personal, familial side of her biography that makes it valuable—every anecdote adds dimension to the Trumans as a family and to Harry as a man."

A distaff counterpart of John F. Kennedy's *Profiles in Courage* (1964), Margaret Truman's fourth book, *Women of Courage* (Morrow, 1976), written with the help of Alice and Tom Fleming, contains biographies of twelve American heroines. As the *New York Times* reviewer Letitia Baldrige (November 28, 1976) pointed out, "This is not a book by an accomplished historian. . . . It is rather a simple narrative by an admitted patriot. . . . " Although the book included heroines from the eighteenth and nineteenth centuries, such as Dolley Madison and Dr. Elizabeth Blackwell, the reviewer felt that Miss Truman wrote best when describing women she had known personally—Dr. Frances Kelsey, Senator Margaret Chase Smith, and Marian Anderson. Since it was a timely addition to the then relatively untapped field of women's history, the reviewer recommended: "This is a book to give your daughter to read—and your son, too."

The major media paid little attention to *Letters from Father; The Truman Family's Personal Correspondence* (Arbor House, 1981), which was edited and annotated by Margaret Truman. Appraising the book for *Library Journal* (August 1981), William Thomas Miller wrote: "While affording an intimate glimpse of the Trumans, this collection offers scant new information or insights."

Margaret Truman's memorial to her mother, who died in 1982 at the age of ninety-seven was a biography, *Bess W. Truman* (Macmillan, 1986). "Refreshing, real and touching," was Helen Thomas' evaluation of the book in the *New York Times Book Review* (April 3, 1986). "Far from being a 'Mommy Dearest' or even an uncomplimentary autobiographical novel like 'Home Front' by Patti Davis, . . . *Bess W. Truman* is primarily about love. . . . " Robert F. Nardini in *Library Journal* (April 1, 1986) found the work disappointing, however, and noted that "the author fails to show that Bess Truman was an interesting figure in her own right, and worthy of a separate biography."

Writing murder mysteries was not an improbable departure for Margaret Truman. For many years she had been an avid mystery reader, an interest that she shared with her father. The first in her series of Washington-based mystery novels was *Murder in the White House* (1980). According to Don Fine, the editor and publisher of Arbor House, which published *Murder in the White House* as well as her subsequent mystery novels, it was not ghostwritten, like so many other celebrity books. It was Don Fine who mapped the marketing strategy for the book. "The fact that Margaret has instant recognition is a great plus," he said, "but she doesn't have instant recognition as a novelist." The publisher placed some 50,000 copies in chain bookstores before publication and arranged for the stores to help finance an advertising campaign. "We wanted to build interest in the book on its own terms so that it wouldn't be hostage to a terrible review somewhere," Fine explained. The plan worked, and when a *New York Times* review of the book came out it was already in its third printing, with 71,000 copies in circulation, and on the best-seller list for several weeks. Dick Clark Cinema Productions purchased the movie rights; the Book-of-the-Month Club designated the novel as an àlternate feature selection; and Fawcett Books acquired the paperback rights for $215,000.

To guarantee authenticity, Miss Truman scrutinized the floor plans of the White House. She denied that she had based her characters on real persons, but as Douglas Martin observed in the *Chicago Tribune*, "The unmarried secretary of state's penchant for pretty girls is at least vaguely reminiscent of one recent German-accented occupant of that office. And the strong-willed White House chief of staff bears a passing resemblance to H. R. Haldeman." The President also has a daughter about the age Margaret was when her father entered the White House. She "is clearly very different from Margaret Truman," William French noted in the Toronto *Globe and Mail* (June 26, 1980) "but we can feel through her some of the frustration that Miss Truman must have felt in her social life."

It turned out to be fortunate that Arbor House did not count on the critics to boost sales. Although reviewers conceded that *Murder in the White House* contained some elements of a fine mystery novel, they felt that it suffered from lack of polish. Chris Chase, for example, wrote in the *Chicago Tribune* (July 6, 1980): "There's nothing terrible about *Murder in the White House*; there's nothing terrific either. Truman is no master of suspense, her characters are thinner than tissue paper, and as a writer she is fairly careless." As William French noted in his *Globe and Mail* review, "Miss Truman seems to have studied Agatha Christie on how to introduce false leads, point to the wrong suspect and generally confuse the issue. She does this with a certain amount of technical dexterity, but it's too mechanical and juiceless." The Canadian reviewer felt that the attitudes revealed by Miss Truman were more interesting than her prose: "She is cynical about politics and politicians, and not just because her secretary of state is a satyr. . . . Most of the politicians who make an appearance are incompetent or corrupt. . . ."

Nor were the critics rhapsodic about the writing style in Margaret Truman's second mystery novel, *Murder on Capitol Hill* (1981). Jean M. White of the *Washington Post* (July 19, 1981) noted that she "writes entertainingly about the Washington scene and not without a touch of gentle amusement," but criticized her "uninspired" prose and complained that she "clutters her plot and cast of characters."

Her next contribution to the mystery genre, *Murder in the Supreme Court* (1982), was chosen as a Book-of-the-Month Club alternate selection. James Kaufman of the *Christian Science Monitor* (November 3, 1982) observed: "It's easy to overlook the sometimes slight characterizations here, because the plot clips along and provides good intrigue by an adept writer." High praise came, too, from the mystery maven who writes under the pseudonym of Newgate Callender, who noted in the *New York Times* (November 7, 1982): "Her distaste for chicanery and hypocrisy in high office is apparent, and her real indignation when confronted with moral dishonesty is one of the bonuses of the book."

Praise for *Murder in the Smithsonian* (1983) was much more subdued. Reviewing the novel for the *New York Times* (June 24, 1983), Anatole Broyard wrote: "Margaret Truman is intelligent and observant, but she is not a natural writer, and in reading *Murder in the Smithsonian*, one realizes what an enormous difference there is between talent and contrivance. One feels Miss Truman bravely, stubbornly standing behind each of her sentences, holding them up, as it were." And Dan McCoubrey, writing in the *Washington Post* (June 27, 1983), noted that "however accurately expressed, the writing is very self-conscious and the characters, except for a few, are stock despite nice touches now and then." McCoubrey went on to say that she failed to tie up loose ends at the conclusion, but acknowledged that *Murder in the Smithsonian* "is a good light read—it is probably not coincidental that the publication comes just in time for the beach and swimming pool trade."

Margaret Truman's next attempt to cash in on her knowledge of the capital city, *Murder on Embassy Row* (1984), was described in *Kirkus Reviews* (June 1, 1984) as "another mild, talky Washington D.C. mystery." The reviewer found it "slow but likable, with some faint attempts at Nick-and-Noraish repartee from the lover/sleuths—and sure to reach a sizable, sedate mystery-readership." Les Whitten, writing in the *Washington Post* (July 15, 1984), pointed out some strangely coincidental similarities between Margaret Truman's *Murder on Embassy Row* and Elliott Roosevelt's *Murder and the First Lady*, both of which were published in 1984. "Consider," he wrote, "the authors are both children of successive Democratic presidents. Both novels' locales are upper-crust Washington. Both murders in the title are perpetrated with poison. Both principal villains are British. Both books use the British embassy and the White House for crucial scenes. Both center on transatlantic smuggling." But the reviewer went on to comment, "There, alas for Margaret Truman, these chance affinities cease. For Elliott Roosevelt's book is an urbanely mellow (if gory) yarn of merit, while Truman's is meretricious."

Margaret Truman's sixth suspense novel, *Murder at the FBI* (1985), begins on the FBI firing range, where a horde of tourists watches a marksman shoot a target that turns out to be the body of agent George Pritchard. "It's a corker of an opener," Jean M. White wrote in the *Washington Post* (August 18, 1985). "Truman writes a lively Washington scene with the sure hand of one who knows her way around the streets, institutions, restaurants, watering holes, people and politics. Her characters have more substance than those in previous books. . . . But the prose still lacks style and verve and can turn turgid."

According to *Kirkus Reviews* (June 15, 1986), Margaret Truman's seventh mystery, *Murder in Georgetown* (1986), "keeps the action reasonably lively" and is "filled out with nice romance . . . and musings on journalism ethics." The reviewer for *Publishers Weekly* (June 6, 1986) suggested that "it may be deemed the best of Truman's bestsellers." *Murder in Georgetown* was chosen as a Mystery Guild selection and as a Literary Guild alternate, as was Miss Truman's next work *Murder in the CIA* (1987), about the killing of a literary agent and its solution by her friend, an agent for the Central Intelligence Agency. According to a reviewer for *Publishers Weekly* (October 9, 1987), with this book the author demonstrated "a deepening knowledge of her craft, topping her previous bestsellers."

Margaret Truman and her husband, Clifton Daniel, who although retired from the *New York Times* continues to lecture and write, make their home on Park Avenue in New York City, in a triplex furnished with Truman family antiques and possessions that belonged to Daniel while he was based in London. They also have a weekend house on Fire Island. Miss Truman prefers New York to Washington, which she calls "a company town." The Daniels have four grown sons, Clifton Truman, William Wallace, Harrison Gates, and Thomas Washington.

Described as more attractive in person than she is in her photographs, Margaret Truman has large blue-green eyes, ash-blonde hair, a flawless complexion, and a dimpled smile. She is five feet five inches tall and usually wears classically styled couturier clothes, most of them designed by Fontana of Rome. Admitting that domestic science is not her forte, Miss Truman has generally hired a housekeeper and had a nursemaid for her children when they were small. She confesses that her husband is a better cook than she is. She loves to dance and retains a lively interest in the theatre. A trustee of the Harry S. Truman Institute and of George Washington University, Miss Truman also serves as a director of Riggs National Bank and Seabury Press, and she is secretary of the Harry S. Truman Scholarship Foundation. She holds honorary degrees from George Washington University, Wake Forest University, and Rockhurst College.

References: *Biog N* p475 Ap '74 por; *Book-of-the-Month Club N* '72 por; *N Y Post* p37 Jl 21 '67 por; *Parade* p4+ Ja 9 '77 pors; *People* p92+ Je 16 '80 por; *Contemporary Authors* vol 105 (1982); Quinn, Sandra L., and Kantor, Sanford. *America's Royalty: All the Presidents' Children* (1983); Truman, Margaret. *Souvenir* (1956); *Who's Who in America*, 1986–87

Vollenweider, Andreas

(fōl´ en-vī-der)

1953– Swiss harpist. Address: b. c/o CBS Records, 51 W. 52d St., New York City, N.Y. 10019

Although he disavows the label, the Swiss electric harpist and latter-day flower child Andreas Vollenweider is "new age" music's brightest star. Vollenweider, a self-taught improvisatory master of many instruments, began to concentrate on the harp in the late 1970s, when he customized what he calls his "electracoustic modified pedal harp," broadening the percussive and rhythmic possibilities of the instrument and making it amenable to his consciousness-expanding music and his relaxed, adventurous way of playing it. In 1981 he formed a harp-oriented ensemble for the performance of what he terms his "aural paintings," freely rendered atmospheric compositions in which "natural sounds" are processed with electronic subtlety to open the listener to the personal peace that he believes is a prerequisite for peace in the world. Touring and recording with the band, he attracted a cult following that grew to include some of the mainstream audience, first in Europe and later in North America. On his tours of the United States he now regularly sells out venues as large as Radio City Music Hall, and he is even more popular in Europe, where his song "Pace Verde" has be-

come the theme of the pro-ecology Greenpeace movement. He thinks of himself as "a channel" in the "movement of awareness" of nuclear danger and environmental pollution, problems that are personally real to him if for no other reason than the fact that in his garden at home in Switzerland "the trees are dying; the cucumbers this year didn't show up." He is an optimistic channel, determined "to make things brighter."

With his ensemble, Vollenweider has recorded four albums—Behind the Gardens, Caverna Magica, White Winds, and Down to the Moon—with total sales of nearly three million, a phenomenal figure for an eclectic music that eludes conventional classification. Some would dismiss new-age music in general as "high tech Muzak." Barney Cohen, writing in Esquire (October 1985), offered a shrewder assessment: "The rhythms and melodies are slightly more sophisticated than pop-rock and the improvisational trips are a little more accessible than jazz, but mainly what has been discovered here for the umpteenth time in history is the chant. New age music is instrumental chanting. Like Zen or tribal or Gregorian chanting, it engages a part of the mind so completely that the rest of the mind is loosed to float free. White Winds is as clear a delineation of this sensibility as has been recorded. . . . Vollenweider is good music. As for the rest [of the new-age musicians], caveat emptor."

The son of Hans Vollenweider, a prominent Zurich cathedral organist, pianist, and composer, Andreas Vollenweider was born in Zurich, Switzerland, in 1953. "I grew up in a family of musicians and painters and designers," he recounted in an interview published in the Detroit Free Press (October 24, 1984). "There was always creativity around me. I was never forced to do anything I didn't want to." He was, in his words, a "stubborn" enfant sauvage, a "kind of a wild animal" who "never had enough discipline to actually learn an instrument in school" and insisted on going his "own way." While his father, after trying in vain to coach him, encouraged his maverick talent, his mother, taking him on long walks in the countryside around Zurich, imbued in him a pantheistic love of nature as well as what he calls an "instinctual anthropomorphic way of thinking."

By trial and error, and with a minimum of formal instruction in musical theory, Vollenweider in childhood taught himself to play a range of instruments, including the piano, the flute, the saxophone, and the guitar. Hearing a friend of his father's play the harp, he was early riveted by the sound of that instrument, although he did not like the "tenseful" playing of harpists trained in classical and baroque traditions. Apparently the only harpist who influenced him to any degree was the late Harpo Marx, of Marx brothers movie fame. "Harpo could groove," he has explained. "He was the first [to] play . . . the harp rhythmically and . . . in a fun way. And that was the key for me . . . his sense of humor. So . . . he helped me to open up and express myself physically with this instrument." Unable to afford a larger model, he experimented with a small, Celtic-style harp, but he would not make the instrument peculiarly his own until adulthood.

In his late teens Vollenweider began scoring motion pictures and television shows, and he earned the bulk of his livelihood in that way for eight years. Because he was temperamentally indisposed to writing dark, brooding, or threatening music, most of the films that he scored were nature documentaries. During the same period, from 1972 to 1978, he played flute, piano, guitar, and saxophone with a Swiss group called Poetry and Music, which combined recited poetry with mood music. With that group he performed all over Europe, toured the United States (in 1975), and cut three albums. The strong visual imagery and narrative leanings of many of his compositions are traceable in large measure to his work with the Poetry and Music group.

Vollenweider arrived at a sense of his own musical identity when he went back to the harp in 1977. "I'd been experimenting with the zither, recording it on two-track home equipment, and that led me to the harp," he told Stephen Holden of the New York Times (October 19, 1984). "[When] I discovered my own way of doing rhythm [on the harp] I was shaking—my entire body began to sweat." His "making music with the harp" was "more of a development" than "a question of decision," he explained to Alan Niester of the Toronto Globe and Mail (April 20, 1985). "I had played many other instruments and was looking for something that really suited me. Eventually I came to the harp. As I played, it dawned on me that this was the instrument with which I could express most what I felt." The harp "was not difficult to master," he said. "It is played instinctively, the melodies slipped upon by chance. There's a lot of improvising."

Modifying the harp to suit himself, Vollenweider began making his own strings, using thick, silver-wound steel to deepen the sound of the bass strings and various other metals as well as silk and nylon for the other strings. He amplified the sound by putting a small electronic pickup on each of the forty-seven strings, and he added a damper, operated by his left knee, to enable him to shorten at will the instrument's otherwise prolonged pattern of note decay and further broaden its percussive and rhythmic possibilities. Thus altered, the harp suited his relaxed manner of playing it in what he calls the "South American" way, strumming and plucking as the spirit moves him.

Recruiting boyhood musician friends to play drums, keyboards, and other instruments, Vollenweider formed an ensemble around his harp. Beginning with an enthusiastic reception at the Montreaux Jazz Festival in 1981, "Vollenweider and Friends" concertized throughout Europe in the early 1980s, winning a wide following—especially in the Low Countries, West Germany, and Scandinavia—with their partly improvisatory renditions of Vollenweider's compositions, fantasies in sound intended by the composer to become "three-dimensional landscapes" in performance.

In the four years beginning 1981 Vollenweider and his sidemen recorded three albums of his music that comprised a sort of thematic trilogy. American release of the albums lagged as long as two years behind the initial European releases, apparently because CBS Records was slow in recognizing the potential international appeal of Vollenweider's music. The first of the recordings was *Behind the Gardens*, a set of nature tone poems chiefly inspired by his Zurich surroundings. The LP included the cuts "Pyramid/In the Wood/In the Bright Light," "Micro-Macro," "Skin and Skin," "Moonlight Wrapped Around Us," "Lion and Sheep," "Sunday," "Afternoon," and "Hands and Clouds." On that album Vollenweider did vocals and played woodwinds, soprano saxophone, synthesizer, electric and acoustic guitars, and accordion in addition to the harp. Pedro Haldemann and John Otis were on percussion, and Walter Keiser was on drums. A critic for *Stereo Review* characterized the album as "elaborate" and "busy" and described Vollenweider as being "as close to a one-man electronic band as one would care to get." "The tone paintings he had devised have much more in common with a Maxfield Parrish than with a Renoir," the reviewer wrote. "Vollenweider's musical palette, like Parrish's, is heavy on peachy and sky-blue colors, with an occasional red tossed in for effect. This is a middlebrow Fantasyland with a Teutonic accent."

The second LP was *Caverna Magica* (1982), a best seller in Europe and the choice for West German pop album of the year in a poll conducted by the magazine *Audio*. Among the cuts were "Lunar Pond" and "Pace Verde" (Green Peace), which, along with the title track, evoked visual associations with fairy tales; "Huiziopochtli," featuring chanting to sitar accompaniment; "Angoh!," in which the harp was complemented by steel drums and accordion; and "Belladonna" and "Schajah Satetosh," which combined samba rhythms with Caribbean *solkattu* singing. When that album was later released as a CBS Masterworks compact disc in the United States, a reviewer for *High Fidelity* described it as "a lacy amalgam of melodic pop and chamber music" manifesting "singular instrumental vision" and observed how the "gently rhythmic, spare arrangements" served to showcase the "shimmering timbres" of Vollenweider's harp along with the nuanced sound of plucked guitars, synthesized flutes, and "otherworldly" steel drums and vocals by Corinna Curschillas. "Though it sounds almost insufferably saccharine on paper, *Caverna Magica* is very nearly irresistible" the reviewer wrote. "[The compact disc is] dotted with dreamy stereo panning effects, surreal murmurs both vocal and instrumental, and, of course, the rich tonal colors of the various instruments, playfully camouflaged. [It] preserves the analog version's detail and grace, exploiting the utter absence of surface noise and tape hiss in the bargain." Others pointed out that the soothing songs swirled and undulated resonantly each into the next, forming "dreamscapes" in which the listener could escape this troubled world and, as Vollenweider intended, find peace and spiritual nourishment.

"They are records of exquisitely improvised melodies, vigorous yet trancelike rhythms, and sound effects that make one feel transported to lunar caves and tropical jungles," Wayne Robbins wrote of *Behind the Gardens* and *Caverna Magica* in *Newsday* (October 20, 1984). The two recordings together sold a million copies in Europe in the early 1980s. Scantily promoted in the United States and not fitting into convenient classical or popular pigeonholes for radio air play, they became known to American ears only gradually, at first mostly by word of mouth, especially the recommendation of such early American admirers as the pop music stars Paul Simon and Carly Simon (no relation), the rock musician Peter Wolf, the choreographer Alvin Ailey, the pioneer new-age pianist George Winston, and John Brancotti, the manager of the record department in the Rizzoli International Bookstore in New York City. When Brancotti played Vollenweider's music over the speaker system in the store, browsers who heard it bought 15,000 copies. "I first heard it [Vollenweider's music] a few years ago while browsing through a bookstore, and I instantly loved it," George Winston told an interviewer in 1985. "Andreas is just wonderful at creating textures and composing incredibly beautiful melodies. And the amazing thing is, every time I hear his music, I hear something new. There are so many hidden things in it to enjoy each time you listen." As Winston observed, Vollenweider is that rare musician who uses electronics in a warm, "very human" way.

When Carly Simon, a songwriter and guitarist as well as a singer, first heard Vollenweider's harp, when shopping in a boutique in the SoHo section of Manhattan in 1983, it sounded to her like "the most perfect guitar [she] had ever heard." "It was one of those times in your life where a light bulb goes off in your head," she told Wayne Robbins of *Newsday*. "It was like I'd known his music from another life, another universe, another dream. I immediately bought forty copies and gave them to everybody I knew, and felt like a fool." Miss Simon finally called CBS Records, obtained Vollenweider's telephone number in Switzerland, and called him to convey her admiration. "It was a very positive shock," Vollenweider later said. "She has some spiritual things in her music that are the same as mine. But maybe she is too shy to develop them."

Miss Simon and Vollenweider met face to face for the first time in October 1984, when the harpist made his New York City debut in a concert produced by the singer at the Beacon Theatre, an early stop on a successful twelve-city American tour. On the tour Vollenweider was accompanied by Pedro Haldemann on percussion, Walter Keiser on drums, Jorg-Peter Siebert on reeds, and Christof Stiefel on synthesizer. To drum up interest in the tour, CBS Records hired a topflight publicity firm otherwise noted for its promotion of rock acts and released a three-cut extended play single and the video "Pace Verde," which was shown on both HBO and Showtime cable television. Vollenweider wrote and directed the video, designed its sets, and created its visual effects.

The rapport between Vollenweider and his sidemen is such that the band easily improvises as much as two-thirds of each performance. Covering the tour that began in the fall of 1984 for *Down Beat* (March 1985), Bill Milkowski reported that Stiefel joined Vollenweider on melody lines, "creating a shimmering effect," that Keiser took his "insistent" drumming "beyond the ethereal realms of ambient music into the rock arena," that Siebert "added some jazz flavor" in his improvisations on the saxophone, and that Haldemann "added an Afro-Cuban flair" on conga, shekere, talking drum, and assorted gongs. "The music touched all bases and crossed all barriers," Milkowski wrote. "Vollenweider laid down bass lines with his left hand while running single-note flurries with his right, at times plucking octaves or strumming ferociously with his long fingernails. The effect was light years away from the 'heavenly music' sounds usually associated with the harp, which is precisely what Vollenweider is aiming for."

Vollenweider began receiving at least as much fan mail from Americans as from Europeans; his first two recordings climbed onto American charts across the board, in the classical, pop, and jazz categories; and his third album, *White Winds*, (1985) was on *Billboard*'s Top Pop chart for several months, reached high rank on jazz listings, and ultimately went gold in North America. *White Winds* (1985) was even more eclectic than *Caverna Magica*, drawing its inspiration from sources ranging from classical to Afro-Cuban, rock, and jazz. Critics pointed out that it was a more mature effort, one in which Vollenweider introduced some quite discordant harmonics and shaded the sweetness and light of innocence with a touch of the introspective pathos and apprehensiveness that comes with experience. "Moving from harp to winds to Japanese koto [a banjo-like string instrument] and back, Vollenweider weaves a spell of variations upon a single, brief, almost haphazard melody that rolls on like winds produced by softly controlled substances," Barney Cohen wrote of *White Winds* in his *Esquire* article. "If this be 'space music' [so labeled by its only regular outlet, National Public Radio), then we are talking about the 'space' between your right ear and your left. The process draws heavily on musical memory. Recall the crescendos never quite reached by Phil Spector's rock. Add the repetitious minimalism of Philip Glass, the guitar glissandi of Led Zeppelin's 'Stairway to Heaven,' and a jazzy riff by Jean-Luc Ponty. Mix the songs of the whales and the occasional SFX, and shoot it all full of the unlamented lilt of Rod McKuen; cook slowly with all-natural ingredients."

In the spring of 1985 Vollenweider and his band (including, on that occasion, the guitarist Max Lässer) made a second North American tour that drew full houses in thirty-nine cities. Reporting on one of the engagements in the tour, a reviewer for *Variety* wrote: "Tuned percussion, jousting with synthesizer, harp pizzicati merging with chimes, breathy Peruvian flutes and the jazzy contrast of saxophones, all heighten the effect of [the] performance, offering a jeweled setting for the harpist's virtuoso flights."

In 1986 Vollenweider gave a benefit performance for Greenpeace and Amnesty International in Switzerland, toured Europe, and then embarked on his third North American tour, a two-month itinerary. Early in the last-mentioned tour he and his band sold out Radio City Music Hall in New York City. "Mr. Vollenweider's Radio City Music Hall concert blended innovative, impressionistic, harp-oriented music with much more conventional Latin-flavored pop-jazz in which the harp became the equivalent of a rhythm guitar," Stephen Holden of the *New York Times* (August 21, 1986) reported. "As defined by Mr. Vollenweider, 'new age' music is really old-fashioned mood music with new instrumentation." According to Wayne Robins, writing in *Newsday* on the same date, "the hypnotic grooves, heartbeat rhythms, and ethereal melodies" were so spellbinding that "there wasn't a whit of conversation" while Vollenweider played, and after the finale "the audience was too stunned to move for ten seconds" before it broke into "an explosion of rapturous applause."

Whereas Vollenweider's initial trilogy of recordings generally explored fragments of fantasy, *Down to the Moon* (1986) had a unifying narrative. "The influence of the moon may not be perceptible," Vollenweider said of that album's central, allegorical image, "yet this apparently calm sphere arcing across the night sky is the force behind such mighty events as the tides of the seas. Similarly, music has a force capable of crossing realms—from imagination to reality. It can touch the flow of moods, and propel the tides of change. I hope my music can take us to a more peaceful place."

In performance, Vollenweider surrenders himself to his music, eyes closed, tossing his reddish-brown mane, the picture of total absorption. "With other instruments I always have to think about technique," he has said. "But with the harp . . . it just flows." Welcoming participation by the audience, he tries to create a "space" in which people can "make music for themselves rather than relying on a substitute, the pushing of a button and hearing something that is prefabricated." To facilitate his fingering of the harp, he wears long artificial nails on the fingers of his right hand. Tape is wrapped around the two fingers of his left hand with which he produces the low bass tones. Between numbers, he talks to the audience about Eastern religions, ecology, universal brotherhood, inner and outer peace, love, nature, and other elemental forces, often using mystical imagery. Wishing to submerge his playing into the "oneness" of his band, he eschews solos.

With his diminutive stature, long, frizzy hair, lively eyes, beatific, whimsical smile, and all-white attire, Vollenweider looks like a cross between an angelic urchin and a throwback to the hippies of the 1960s. He and his wife, Beata, who is now a kindergarten teacher, were married in 1971. They live in a country house on the outskirts of Zurich with a large garden, tended mostly by Beata, and a view of the Lake of Zurich. Fortified by one cup of coffee ("so I'm half awake and half asleep and so my mind isn't bothering me too much"), he composes in the early morning hours, looking out at the garden and lake as his fingers roam his harp. Composing, as he says, "by chance," he "hears every note [as if] for the first time." In addition to composing and playing music, he sculpts and paints. In all of his work he tries, as he has told interviewers, to contribute to our knowing "more and more about our hidden wishes and thoughts so that we can control them"

and "live in a world where human beings can finally understand themselves as being part of nature instead of seeing nature as an enemy."

References: Chicago Tribune 13 p14+ My 12 '85 por; Christian Sci Mon p24 S 29 '86 por; N Y Daily News p42 O 17 '84 por; N Y Times C p25 O 19 '84 por; Newsday II p15+ O 20 '84 por, II p13 Ag 21 '86 por; People 24:107+ Ag 5 '85 pors; Sat R 11:5 Ja/F '85 por; Toronto Globe and Mail E p4 Ap 20 '85 por; Wall St J p30 O 24 '84

Waldheim, Kurt
(vält´hīm)

Dec. 21, 1918– President of Austria. Address: Ballhausplatz 2, 1010 Vienna, Austria

NOTE: This biography supersedes the article that appeared in Current Biography in 1972.

On June 8, 1986, Kurt Waldheim, a career diplomat who had served as secretary general of the United Nations from 1972 to 1982, won election as president of Austria after a bitter controversy over his World War II service in the German army. During the election campaign, evidence surfaced that, contrary to his two books of memoirs and his official UN biography, Waldheim had served in the Balkans with a German army unit that had committed brutal reprisals against Yugoslav partisans and arranged mass deportations of Greek Jews to death camps. After the war, the Yugoslav war crimes commission listed Waldheim as a war criminal, but, for reasons unknown, never prosecuted him.

Confronted with that evidence, the former secretary general admitted that he had served with the German army in the Balkans, but not in any decision-making capacity. After combing archives for evidence, the World Jewish Congress and other groups revealed that Waldheim had in fact been an intelligence and ordnance officer and alleged that he had a direct role in the Nazi atrocities. Far from hurting Waldheim, the accusations apparently helped him to defeat his Socialist opponent in a runoff contest for the largely ceremonial presidency being vacated by the retiring Rudolf Kirchschlager. But the bitter controversy over their new president revived a "half-buried national past" that many Austrians would prefer to forget.

Like most Austrians of his generation, Kurt Waldheim grew up in an era that forced uncommonly hard choices on its young people. He was born on December 21, 1918, in St. Andrä-Wördern, a village near Vienna, the oldest child of Walther and Josefine (Petrasch) Waldheim. A conservative Roman Catholic school inspector of modest means, Walther Waldheim sacrificed to educate his three children for more promising careers. But his ambitions for them were soon disarranged by political upheaval.

Struggling to overcome the economic depression resulting from the devastating loss of its empire in World War I, Austria succumbed to civil war and the growing domination of the Nazi regime to the north. In March 1938 a German army marched into Austria and declared an Anschluss, or union of the two nations. Because of his openly anti-Nazi views, Walther Waldheim was jailed briefly and forced to resign his post.

At the time of the Anschluss, Kurt Waldheim was a student at the University of Vienna, pursuing legal and diplomatic training. Although in his later career he denied having belonged to any Nazi-affiliated organizations, the recent investigations indicated that on April 1, 1938, three weeks after the Anschluss, he joined the Nazi student union, and on November 18, 1938, shortly after the Kristallnacht, when anti-Semitic violence reached its height, he joined the mounted unit of the Nazis' paramilitary Sturm-Abteilung, or S.A., also known as the "brownshirts."

When war broke out in 1939, Waldheim was drafted into the German army with the rank of lieutenant. In the spring of 1941 he was sent to the Eastern Front, and he was wounded in the ankle the following December. According to his autobiographies, *The Challenge of Peace* (Rawson, 1980) and *In the Eye of the Storm* (Adler & Adler, 1986), that wound ended his active service. On his return to Vienna, he was allowed to resume his studies toward his law doctorate, which he received in 1944, after completing a dissertation on the nineteenth-century political theorist Konstantin Frantz, who proposed the creation of a central European federation that would dominate the continent. But photographs and documents show that concurrently Waldheim remained an officer in the German army from 1942 to 1945, a fact he had concealed for over forty years. According to the historian Gordon A. Craig, who analyzed Waldheim's doctoral dissertation in the *New York Review of Books* (October 9, 1986), the work was "a summary rather than an analysis of Frantz's thought" and was "largely accomplished, in all probability, during the three months of leave that followed Waldheim's service in Bosnia."

It was Waldheim's military service in the Balkans that became the focus of the recent controversy. In March 1942 he returned to active duty, assigned as an intelligence officer to the staff of General Alexander Löhr, an Austrian who was executed as a war criminal in 1947. Under Löhr's command, the German Army Group E engaged in brutal campaigns against the Yugoslav partisans led by Marshal Tito, burning whole villages and slaughtering their inhabitants. Löhr's forces also helped arrange the deportation of some 40,000 Greek Jews from Salonika to Auschwitz.

The extent of Waldheim's knowledge of and participation in these atrocities has remained unclear. Researchers have uncovered army daybooks written by Waldheim and intelligence reports apparently initialed by him that strongly suggest that he had detailed knowledge of the partisan campaigns and the deportations of Jews. Moreover, in July 1942, he received the Order of the Crown of King Zvonimir from the Nazi puppet state of Croatia, honoring him for his service "under fire" and "heroic bravery in the battle against the insurgents in the spring and summer of 1942."

Waldheim told reporters in 1986 that his duties on Löhr's staff were primarily those of an interpreter and clerk. He admitted to having known of the partisan campaigns but swore he had no part in the interrogation of suspects or military actions against the guerrillas. While at first he categorically denied receiving the Zvonimir medal, he later told the Associated Press that the decoration was routinely handed out "like chocolates" to all staff officers, regardless of their service. He denied having any awareness of the Jewish deportations although, as Gordon Craig and others pointed out, all Jews had to wear yellow stars, and it would have been difficult not to notice the disappearance of one-fifth of the population of Salonika.

Whatever his own recollections, evidence of Waldheim's complicity in the brutal work of Army Group E was strong enough to warrant his inclusion on lists of Nazi war criminals compiled after the war. In December 1947 the Yugoslav war crimes commission forwarded a four-page report on Waldheim to the Allied war crimes commission, seeking extradition rights to try him for the murder of Yugoslav partisans. The charges were based on the testimony of three witnesses who said that Waldheim had supervised the destruction of three partisan villages in October 1944.

Reviewing the evidence, the Allied war crimes commission gave Waldheim an "A" ranking, denoting a suspect who should be subject to trial as a war criminal. But the Yugoslavs never followed up on the charges, and Waldheim's file, along with those of some 40,000 other suspects who were never tried, was sealed and given to the United Nations for safekeeping. Waldheim has refuted the testimony of the three witnesses, whom he described on the CBS-TV program *60 Minutes* in 1986 as desperate men trying to "save their skins" by naming others. "I was never involved in anything that would justify a feeling of guilt," he said as quoted in *U.S. News & World Report* (April 28, 1986).

In the turbulent aftermath of World War II, Waldheim's wartime service never became a public issue. Because Austria had been "invaded" by Germany in 1938, the Allies declared it the "first victim" of Hitler's regime and excused it from the reparations imposed on Germany. Despite the enthusiasm many Austrians had shown for Nazism, including its anti-Semitic excesses, the nation never went through the kind of collective self-examination and public remorse experienced by the Germans. Like Kurt Waldheim, many Austrians were eager simply to forget their wartime complicity with the Nazis.

In postwar Austria, the talented and ambitious Waldheim advanced rapidly. He entered the Austrian foreign service as soon as the war ended. After clearance by the Office of Strategic Services he became the personal secretary of Karl Gruber, the Austrian foreign minister, and quickly rose through the diplomatic ranks. When Austria regained its sovereignty in 1955, Waldheim went as its delegate to the United Nations, and he then served from 1956 to 1960 as Austria's ambassador to Canada. In 1960 he returned to the ministry of foreign affairs, where he was head of the Western political department from 1960 to 1962 and director general for political affairs from 1962 to 1964. In 1964 Waldheim returned to the UN for a four-year term as Austria's permanent representative, serving also as chairman of the Committee on Peaceful Uses of Outer Space from 1965 to 1968 and as chairman of the Special Committee on the Definition of Aggression in 1967.

In a cabinet reshuffle in 1968, Austria's chancellor and leader of the ruling People's party, Josef Klaus, named Waldheim as his minister of foreign affairs. One of the first crises that Waldheim had to deal with in that post was the Soviet invasion of Austria's neighbor, Czechoslovakia. In *Eye of the*

Storm he wrote, "The Austrian media were practically unanimous in condemning the Soviet attitude, and Moscow became very concerned about this reaction. The Austrian government had to tread something of a tightrope in order . . . to respect its commitment to neutrality." A document made public by the World Jewish Congress in October 1986 alleged that Waldheim was responsible for ordering his country's embassy in Prague to turn away Czech citizens seeking asylum. But the Austrian ambassador in Prague, according to the document, ignored the directive and issued more than 5,000 visas a day, enabling Czechs to leave the country.

When the Klaus party lost the elections in 1970, Waldheim resumed his post as ambassador to the UN. He then took leave to stand for election as president of Austria but lost to the incumbent Socialist, Franz Jonas, and returned to the UN, where he became chairman of the safeguards committee of the International Atomic Energy Agency. When, in the fall of 1971, UN Secretary General U Thant of Burma announced his intention not to run for a third term, Waldheim emerged as his likely successor. His polished, nonideological style was acceptable to both superpowers, but the People's Republic of China, newly admitted to the UN in Taiwan's place, at first blocked his appointment. After three closed sessions of the Security Council, Waldheim finally won the nomination and took office in January 1972. He won a second term in 1976, and only narrowly missed taking an unprecedented third term in 1981 because the Chinese insisted on a Third World candidate. In none of those elections did Waldheim's war record arise as an issue.

During Waldheim's tenure at the UN, the organization's political character changed dramatically. The admission of the People's Republic of China and the addition of many former colonies to membership increased the power of the Third World or "nonaligned" nations. The old East-West divisions of the 1960s gave way to much more complex political alignments, in which the Western nations were often outvoted. As secretary general, Waldheim faced the almost impossible task of reconciling American, Soviet, and Third World interests. Aware that several of his predecessors had lost their effectiveness by pursuing their own political visions too vigorously, Waldheim sought to lead by consensus. Despite the many obstacles he faced, Waldheim was generally recognized as a dedicated and active secretary general. One of his first goals was to put the UN back on a sound financial basis by reducing operating costs and persuading recalcitrant members to pay their assessments. He then turned his energies to peace-keeping efforts in Cyprus, Vietnam, and the Middle East.

Perhaps Waldheim's finest hour as secretary general came during the 1973 Middle Eastern war when he helped to bring Israel and Egypt to the negotiating table. But he soon drew upon himself the ire of Israel and the American Jewish community. In 1975 the UN General Assembly passed a resolution condemning Zionism as a form of racism, an action for which many Israelis blamed Waldheim, even though the secretary general had no power to influence the assembly vote. Then, in 1976, the secretary general condemned Israel's raid to rescue hostages held on a hijacked plane at the Entebbe airfield in Uganda as "a serious violation of the national sovereignty of a United Nations member state."

In his second term as secretary general, Waldheim faced other serious challenges to world peace: Israel's occupation of southern Lebanon; the war in Afghanistan; the Iran-Iraq conflict; and the Iranian hostage crisis. "Waldheim was not lucky in what was tossed his way, during his ten years as secretary general," the Irish diplomat and former UN official Conor Cruise O'Brien wrote in the *Times Literary Supplement* (January 17, 1986). "He got pretty hopeless stuff . . . where there was nothing much the UN could do. . . . " O'Brien, who had the opportunity to work closely with Waldheim, described his *modus operandi*: "the discreet and effaced style; the accurate assessment of restricted possibilities; the setting of modest objectives; and the patient and even crafty pursuit of the same."

According to some sources, Communist bloc officials who had known of Waldheim's war record allegedly used it to blackmail him. A report in the *Washington Post* in late October 1986, quoted Anton Kolendic, a former Yugoslav intelligence officer, as saying that he was "absolutely certain" that Soviet officials had approached Waldheim in the early postwar years and tried to pressure him to become an agent for them, using their knowledge of his activities in the Balkans as a threat. His statement was corroborated by another, unidentified, Yugoslav intelligence officer. An editorial in the *New Republic* (June 30, 1986), evaluating those reports, listed Waldheim's pro-Soviet actions during the postwar years and noted, "In 1971, when he first ran for secretary general of the UN, Waldheim was stoutly supported by the Soviet Union, and that support never wavered throughout his tenure. . . . " But interviews conducted in June 1986 by *New York Times* reporter Elaine Sciolino with both Western and Eastern-bloc UN officials, seemed to reveal no pattern favoring either East or West. Some pointed to times when on issues involving Vietnam and Cambodia he appeared to bow to American pressure. Officials on both sides expressed the view that his extraordinary ambition made him susceptible to pressure by various missions at different times.

After losing his bid for a third term as secretary general to Javier Pérez de Cuéllar of Peru, Waldheim was a visiting professor of diplomacy at Georgetown University in Washington, D.C., from May 1982 to July 1984. In 1985 he announced his intention to run as the conservative People's party candidate for president of Austria, a post that the Socialists had held for sixteen years. The People's party hoped to capitalize on growing concern about nuclear power, scandals involving the adulteration of wine, and government corruption, to break the Socialists' long monopoly on high office.

In the course of what had been a quiet, almost lackluster campaign, the revelations about Waldheim's war record came as a bombshell in early March 1986. The Austrian news magazine *Profil* and the World Jewish Congress produced documents revealing his membership in the Nazi organizations and his military service in the Balkans. In an interview with *New York Times* reporter John Tagliabue (March 4, 1986), Waldheim admitted the authenticity of the documents but denied that he had committed any war crimes. Asked to explain his affiliation with the Nazi organizations, he insisted that he had no political sympathies with the Nazis but joined the groups only so that he and his family would be spared persecution. He told the interviewer that he regarded the youth groups as "harmless" and justified his membership by saying, "If I ever had the idea of finishing my studies, I had to have some protection."

The documents and Waldheim's admission of their authenticity touched off an international uproar. As the World Jewish Congress continued to dredge up material on Waldheim's wartime service, authorities in Israel, Austria, and the United States asked to see the confidential file on Waldheim compiled by the Allied war crimes commission contained in the UN archives.

Within Austria, however, the charges created sympathy for Waldheim, who before the controversy started had been having difficulty in establishing rapport with the average voter. Angry at what they perceived to be foreign interference in their domestic politics, many Austrian voters accepted Waldheim's portrayal of himself as the unfortunate victim of a smear campaign. Affixing a sticker that read "Now More than Ever" to his original campaign poster, which said "The Man the World Trusts," Waldheim lashed out against his accusers. "We were not doing anything but our duty as decent soldiers. We were not criminals but decent men who faced a terrible fate," he said in one campaign speech reported in the *New York Times* (May 1, 1986).

The voters apparently responded to his argument, because Waldheim's standing in the opinion polls steadily rose. But the campaign unleashed an ugly wave of anti-Semitism. Austria's small Jewish population was deluged with hate mail, and there were angry street demonstrations. Despite warnings from Socialist leaders that Waldheim's election would cause dissension, voters gave him 49.6 percent of the vote in the election of May 4, 1986, as compared to 43.7 received by his Socialist opponent, the former health minister Kurt Steyrer. Having failed to win a clear majority, Waldheim faced Steyrer in a run-off election on June 8, 1986, which he won with 53.9 percent of the vote. Waldheim was inaugurated for a six-year term as President of Austria on July 8, 1986 in what United States Senator Daniel P. Moynihan of New York termed "a symbolic amnesty for the Holocaust."

Waldheim's election did not end the controversy, however. Israel boycotted the inauguration and immediately recalled its ambassador to Austria. In London, a senior government official said that it was unlikely that Waldheim would be invited to make an official visit, and there were indications that the new president would not be welcome in other countries such as Yugoslavia, Greece, and Holland. In the United States, after reviewing the evidence, Neal Sher, the director of the Justice Department's office of special investigations, recommended to Attorney General Edwin Meese 3d in late April 1986 that Waldheim be barred from the country as a suspected war criminal. The State Department, according to an article in the *New York Times* (May 16, 1986), informed Edgar M. Bronfman, the president of the World Jewish Congress, that it was launching its own investigation. But in December 1986, amid objections, Waldheim was invited by the UN office in Vienna to be a guest of honor at a ceremony scheduled for January 1987, commemorating the first UN secretary general, Trygve Lie.

The United States Justice Department for the first time branded the head of state of a friendly country an undesirable alien when in April 1987 it formally placed Kurt Waldheim on a list of persons barred from entering the United States, citing evidence that established a "prima facie" case that Waldheim had "assisted or otherwise participated in" activities that amounted to persecution of Jews and others in Greece and Yugoslavia during World War II. The Austrian president called the American decision "incomprehensible" and insisted that he had a clear conscience.

Meanwhile, Waldheim remained under fire both at home and abroad. Invitations from other European countries were not forthcoming, and Austria's ruling Socialist party went so far as to ask him to resign the presidency. Waldheim's audience with Pope John Paul II in June 1987, his first official trip abroad since his election as president, provoked anger among Jewish spokesmen which was only partially mitigated by a pastoral letter written by the Pope in August that addressed Jewish suffering in the Holocaust and by a meeting of the Pontiff and American Jewish leaders in Miami, Florida in September 1987.

Kurt Waldheim has been described, in retrospect, by some former aides at the UN as a tyrant to his subordinates and obsequious to higher-ups. Such organizations as the World Jewish Congress have continued to hold to the belief that Waldheim was a war criminal, but many commentators seemed to concur with the view of Simon Wiesenthal, the veteran hunter of Nazi war criminals, who considered him "an opportunist" but not a war criminal. Similarly, according to Linda-Marie Deloff, writing in *Christian Century* (August 27–September 3, 1986), Professor Fritz Fellner, a distinguished political scientist at the University of Salzburg, regarded Waldheim as "an inveterate opportunist who has always known how to advance himself in any given situation," but who "was at too low a level of responsibility to know automatically what was going on around him. . . . "

The debate over his past has taken its toll on the tall, angular, gray-haired Waldheim whose smile, during the election campaign seemed forced and who often appeared drawn and anxious throughout the controversy. His mainstay has been his wife, the former Elisabeth Ritschel, known as "Cissy," whom he married in 1944, and who has admitted to having once been a member of the Nazi party. The Waldheims have two daughters, Liselotte and Christa, and a son, Gerhard, a lawyer, who has traveled to the United States to present the legal case for his father's innocence to the Justice Department. Waldheim's published books, in English, include *The Austrian Example* (Macmillan, 1971), *Building the Future Order* (Macmillan, 1980), and his now partly discredited two volumes of memoirs.

References: *Christian Sci Mon* p1+ Ap 9 '86 por; *N Y Times Mag* p38+ S 13 '81 pors; *Newsweek* 107:30+ Je 9 '86 por; *U S News* 100:37+ Ap 28 '86 por; *Contemporary Authors* vols 89–92 (1980); *International Who's Who, 1986–87; Worldmark Encyclopedia of the Nations* vol 1 (1984)

Wang, An

Feb. 7, 1920– Business executive; inventor.
Address: b. *Wang Laboratories, Inc., 1 Industrial Ave., Lowell, Mass. 01851*

A "technological visionary," the soft-spoken but steel-willed An Wang combines uncanny prescience in anticipating market changes with a flair for making the innovations those changes mandate. As a result, his Wang Laboratories have for decades held at bay or handed out market defeats to such giant competitors as the International Business Machines corporation (IBM). With an average annual growth rate of 42 percent since its inception in 1951, Wang Labs has moved under the benevolent dictatorship of its founder from one crest of emerging technology to another—supplying electronic calculators in the 1960s, word processors in the 1970s, and, in its 1980s incarnation, office auto-

mation systems. An emigrant from China who completed his education at Harvard, Wang invented the magnetic core memory, a key component in the evolution of the modern computer, in 1948. Commenting on his business success in his 1986 autobiography, *Lessons*, written with Eugene Linden and published by Addison-Wesley, Wang credited a combination of Confucian values, American entrepreneurial daring, and an ability to "go for a long time without shooting [oneself] in the foot."

An Wang, whose name means "Peaceful King," grew up in a period of civil strife in China known as "the Age of Confusion," which he has described in *Lessons* as "the struggle for the soul of China after centuries of medieval rule. The blood shed in that struggle, followed by the Japanese invasion, disrupted his childhood. . . . During those upheavals, he lost his parents and one sister." Wang believes that his innovative, no-nonsense view of things was shaped by those events. In *Lessons* he observed that "confidence is sometimes rooted in the unpleasant, harsh aspects of life, and not in warmth and safety. It is an intangible quality, but it has its own momentum. The longer you are able to survive and succeed, the better you are able to further survive and succeed."

The oldest of the five children of Yin Lu and Zen Wan (Chien) Wang, An Wang was born in Shanghai, China, on February 7, 1920. Until he was twenty-one, he lived either in Shanghai or about thirty miles away, in Kun San, which had been the home of his father's ancestors for 600 years. An Wang's father taught English in a private elementary school in Kun San but turned to the practice of traditional Chinese medicine whenever the school was disrupted by the surrounding bloodshed. He started teaching his son English when Wang was four years old, and because the elementary school had no first or second grades, Wang began his formal education in the third grade at the age of six. When he was only sixteen, he entered Shanghai's Chiao Tung University, "the MIT of China," and began his studies in an atmosphere of fear caused by Japanese acts of aggression against China that had already included the bombing of Shanghai. His mother died during his freshman year, her health broken by "years of fear and conflict." Wang immersed himself in electrical engineering, with an emphasis on communications, and his English skills were gradually developed by American textbooks. As editor of a kind of scientific digest, he translated articles of general interest from American magazines such as *Popular Mechanics* and *Popular Science* into Chinese. In 1937, before the beginning of Wang's sophomore year, Japan seized Peking, and war broke out. Wang recalls that at the university "the war was close by, but it was not there, and that made all the difference in the world."

After his graduation with a B.S. degree in 1940, An Wang signed on as a teaching assistant in electrical engineering at the university. In the summer of 1941 he volunteered for a project in the interior of China that involved the designing and building of transmitters and radios for government troops. As an engineer for the Central Radio Works located in Kweilin (1941-45), An Wang was in charge of what he has described as a "seat-of-the-pants operation" exemplified by one project in which his group improvised a generator from scavenged parts. Their labors were punctuated by weekly Japanese bombing raids that the team waited out in a cave over games of contract bridge. After three years, the group was evacuated to Chungking for the final year of the war.

In 1945, in a program sponsored by the Nationalist government as part of China's postwar reconstruction, An Wang was sent with several hundred other engineers to the United States as a technical observer, but when he landed in Newport News, Virginia, in June for a two-year American visit, he decided that graduate study would teach him more than an apprenticeship as an observer, and he enrolled at Harvard. Beginning classes in September 1945, he sailed through the work because of his practical experience and was granted an M.S. degree in 1946. He then spent three tedious months in a mostly clerical stint for the Chinese government supply agency in Ottawa, Canada, before returning to Harvard in February 1947 to enter the Ph.D. program in applied physics. By that time, the ruling Nationalist party in China was embroiled in a civil war with Communist forces led by Mao Tsetung, and before the year was over it became apparent that the Chinese Nationalists would be crushed. Wang decided not to return to his homeland. "I . . . knew myself well enough to know that I could not thrive under a totalitarian Communist system," he has explained in *Lessons*. "I had long been independent, and I wanted to continue to make my own decisions about my life." In the spring of 1948 Wang was ready to defend his Harvard thesis on nonlinear mechanics. Except for courses in digital electronic circuitry, which ultimately proved to be basic to his computer innovations, An Wang's graduate studies had nothing to do with computer science, then in its infancy.

As a research fellow in the Harvard Computation Laboratory from 1948 to 1951, Wang worked under Howard Aiken, who handed him a seemingly impossible problem in data storage. Aiken and his colleagues had designed the first binary computer in the United States to be operated by electricity. Introduced in 1944, that Automatic Sequence Controlled Calculator, nicknamed the Mark I, was a noisy, cumbersome machine, fifty-one feet long and eight feet high, with thousands of mechanical relays. An Wang's task was, in his words, "to find a way to record and read magnetically stored information without mechanical motion" within the computer. He already knew that information could be stored in the form of "magnetic flux" without mechanical motion by magnetizing a material in either a positive or negative magnetic direction. The material would hold that magnetic direction or "flux" indefinitely and, depending on the weather, it was positive that the flux could be "read" as either a one or a zero in the binary language of computers. The problem, as was obvious to Wang, stemmed from the fact that reading such a text reversed the direction of the flux and destroyed the information it stored. In a matter of weeks, the solution came to him in a flash, "not as the logical conclusion of a conscious train of thought," as he was strolling through Harvard Yard. He recalled in *Lessons*: "It did not matter whether or not I destroyed the information while reading it. . . . I could simply *rewrite* the data immediately afterward. Moreover, since magnetic flux could be changed in a few thousandths of a second, I could do this without any real sacrifice of speed." That concept of rewriting information is the primary feature of Wang's memory device. It took him longer to hit upon the most suitable materials to execute his design of the individual magnetic cores, and the use of a nickel-iron alloy with the trade name Deltamax was eventually superseded by materials based on metal composites called ferrites. An Wang's arrays of magnetic cores, tiny, doughnut-shaped data storage elements, were to be commonly used as a stable medium for computer memory—a means of rapid access to data—for the next twenty years.

Wang patented his invention and, after working on Mark IV with Aiken, left the lab when Harvard began to phase out basic computer research. Now recognized as an expert in digital electronics, An Wang decided to manufacture and sell memory cores and to seek contracts for special projects in his field. With a capital of $600 in savings, he rented 200 square feet of office space at about seventy dollars a month in a loft on Columbus Avenue at the South End of Boston. On the first day of business on June 30, 1951, the sole proprietor of Wang Laboratories had no orders or contracts and no office furniture. Wang, his wife Lorraine, and the patent attorney Martin Kirkpatrick made up the board of directors, and the staff consisted of one part-time assistant.

An Wang concentrated his efforts on devising a variety of small-scale commercial applications of his memory cores, involving the counting, storing, and displaying of data. The electronic scoreboard at New York's Shea Stadium was one of his early successes. As business increased, Wang moved the company to Cambridge, Massachusetts, in 1954, and on June 30, 1955, it officially became a corporation, with Wang as its first president and treasurer. He was then in the midst of complex negotiations for the sale of his memory core patent—negotiations he credits with giving him a privileged view of IBM's "hardball" business style and somewhat cumbersome decision-making process that served him well in later confrontations. On March 6, 1956, at a time when his annual business income was about $10,000, he settled with IBM for $400,000 and became suddenly wealthy.

The company relocated to Natick, near Boston, then to Tewksbury, near Lowell, Massachusetts, as its offerings expanded to include electronic counters, machine tool controls, block-type readers, encoders, and telecoder generators. An Wang for a long time personally designed those products, including the first electronic justifying typesetter system, a boon to newspaper productivity, the LINASEC, in 1962; Wang Labs' first electronic scientific desk calculator, called LOCI, followed in 1964. With a keyboard resembling that of an adding machine, LOCI (an acronym for logarithmic calculating instrument) could not only add, subtract, multiply, divide, and compute roots, but also provided the unique feature of generating exponential values with a single keystroke. At a base price of $6,500, a fraction of that of a mainframe, LOCI was easier to operate than a computer. A transitional product intended primarily for scientists and engineers, LOCI was followed by the Model 300 desktop calculator, which was even simpler to use and one-quarter the cost, and with it, An Wang took his mission of making jobs easier through digital electronics "into the ordinary workplace." With his company constructing timesaving applications for particular markets, such as users interested in computing mortgage payments or discounting bonds, An Wang continued to be motivated "by the idea that people do not want technology; they want solutions to problems."

With Wang Labs owning the calculator market and filling the gap between the slide rule and the minicomputer, sales exploded, reaching $2.5 million in fiscal 1965, $3.8 million in 1966, and, by the end of the next fiscal year, $6.9 million. An international division was established, with the first offices in the United Kingdom, Belgium, and Taiwan. In 1967 the small, energetic firm went public and proved to be the hottest of that year's "hot" stocks, shooting from twelve dollars to thirty-seven dollars on the first day and leveling out at a total value of what one reporter called "an awesome $79 million."

The next move of Wang Laboratories was an attempt to build its first minicomputer, converting the 700 model into a programmable calculator in 1968 to beat rivals to the punch. The 700 series was the last successful entry to use magnetic core memory for data storage. Wang Labs then became the first customer to purchase semiconductor-based random access memory (RAM) chips (which held 2,000 bits of memory) from Intel Corporation and put them into their 600 series of calculators. Initially shipped in 1972, the System 2200, first referred to as a computing calculator, was a true general-purpose minicomputer that signaled the firm's entry into the data processing market. A version was still on the market in the mid-1980s.

As the new decade set in, An Wang began to realize that business offices needed products to handle both word processing, the technology for creating and editing documents, and data processing, the technology that helps to manipulate structured data such as the columns of numbers in a financial report. Despite spirited debate within the financially conservative firm, An Wang intrepidly set its course for a market sector largely dominated by IBM, and in 1972 Wang Labs rolled out the 1200 Word Processing System, a "thinking typewriter" with an electronically controlled dual cassette. The WCS (Wang Computer System) series, priced below IBM's machines and with more peripheral options, appeared in 1975. In that year, Wang moved to secure permanent control of his company and to retain the authority to make controversial policy decisions such as the one to challenge IBM, which might have resulted in his being overruled or removed by a powerful board of stockholders. He took his company's stock from the New York Stock Exchange and transferred it to the American Stock Exchange, created a separate, limited voting-class of stock (Class B common), and eventually fixed 70 percent of Wang stock under family control. In the following year Wang Labs launched the WPS, a cathode-ray tube (CRT)-based word processing system, in which the user could manipulate text by moving words on a full-size, television-like screen that was then unprecedented in the office automation industry. With this revolutionary piece of equipment that included a high-speed printer, the company established a "beachhead" in the Fortune 1,000 list. The media now labeled Wang Laboratories "the word processing company."

An Wang's knack for sensing the emerging thrust of the market helped to hoist Wang Labs to second place after IBM in the small-business computer market and to third place in word processing. Phenomenal growth made another relocation, which bestowed economic rebirth on Lowell, a factory town twenty-five miles northwest of Boston, necessary. Among a raft of new products, in 1977 Wang submitted the VS line of computers, which permitted programs of a length normally feasible on mainframe computers to be run on the lower-cost Wang machines.

Two years later, with his company in the midst of a string of what would be twenty-six record growth quarters, Wang once again identified a major potential market and launched the Office Information Systems (OIS) series, a linking of word processing and data processing that could be upgraded according to the needs of the user. Continued success hinged on the development of image processing, audio processing, and networking functions so that professionals and managers could garner the same benefits as secretaries. In 1981 Alliance, a third generation of the Wang OIS product lines that united all the key technologies, was unveiled, and WangNet, a broadband-based local network affording the concurrent transmission of all types of office information, including text, voice, and video, was also announced. Wang Labs, which earned $100 million on revenues approaching $1 billion in fiscal 1981 after five years of 55 percent annual growth, had to confront a serious threat when the Goliath companies IBM, AT & T, Hewlett-Packard, and Digital Equipment Corporation invaded the office automation market. IBM's popular Personal Computer outsold the Wang Professional Computer, introduced nine months later in 1982. The first Professional Image Computer (PIC), which can store photographic images of documents, maps, and charts was added to Wang's arsenal in 1982, but it has yet to receive the same market response as other Wang products. Analysts found WangNet to be ahead of its time, since they discovered that it was very "engineering-driven rather than marketing-driven."

As Wang's slice of the office automation market began to slip, weaknesses in the company's infrastructure became apparent. Wang admitted, "Since we are growing so fast, our organization is weaker than it should be. Paperwork procedures and systems are always behind." "The Doctor," as he is affectionately tagged by employees, in 1981 relinquished his one-man rule to a management committee that included his two most likely successors, vice-presidents Frederick A. Wang, his son, and John F. Cunningham, a top-notch marketing man. The five-member group, which included An Wang, still the chairman and chief executive, took over formal strategic planning with decisions by consensus and practiced delegation of duties. As noted in a *Business Week* article (May 17, 1982), some observers questioned whether the committee could "replace the doctor's entrepreneurial genius and ability to inspire messianic zeal and loyalty."

In January 1983 An Wang conferred the title of president and chief operating officer on John F. Cunningham. Despite its delivery problems with fourteen new products announced in October 1983, *Dun's Business Month* (December 1984) singled out Wang Labs as one of "the five best-managed companies" of 1984 for continuing "to turn state-of-the-art strategy and technology into phenomenal financial growth." But rising revenues of $2.2 billion and earnings of $210 million in 1984 were followed in 1985 by a drop in earnings to $15.5 million despite revenues of $2.4 billion. In response, Wang Labs laid off 1,600 workers and instituted a cost-reduction regime. Revenue and earnings for fiscal 1986 were $2.6 billion and $50.9 million, respectively.

With the resignation of John F. Cunningham in June 1985, An Wang came out of semiretirement in July 1985 to take charge again, as president, of day-to-day operations in the midst of an industry-wide computer depression. Despite his aversion to traveling, he embarked on an odyssey worthy of a campaigning politician, visiting more than fifty American and eight foreign company sales offices. The complaints he heard from customers concerned delayed deliveries, inadequate servicing and support, unavailability of good software, and incompatibility with IBM and other brands of machines. Restoring confidence in the beleaguered company, An Wang personally set in motion solutions to those problems. In April 1986 Wang's second-in-command, executive vice-president J. Carl Masi, left when An Wang took total control of sales and marketing.

In January 1986 Wang Labs landed the biggest contract in its history, a $480 million minicomputer sale to the United States Air Force. While reducing management layers and emphasizing a synergistic relationship between research and development and sales, the company introduced enhanced products in the VS minicomputer family that offset lessened demand for OIS systems. Announced in April, the Wang Integrated Office Solution, combining voice and data communications, provided Wang Labs with a headstart on the competition. With the acquisition of InteCom, a Texas-based communications switching manufacturer, Wang Labs jointly developed the Keystone, a teleworkstation. The company's goal under its new president, Frederick. Wang, who was named in November 1986, is to become a $5 billion company by 1990.

The dapper, bright-eyed An Wang is slight in build. Although usually shy of the press, he is known to be a charismatic if sometimes volatile leader. He maintains a patriarchal status among his employees by virtue of his "astounding" intellect, his policy of leading "by example rather than dictate," his generous package of employee benefits, and his "skip-level communication" policy that allows employees with problems or bright ideas to go a level or more above managers who will not listen to them. Despite a $1.6 billion net worth that made him the fifth-richest man in the United States, Wang lives a quiet, family-oriented life and owns only two suits at any one time. He and his wife, the former Lorraine Chiu, have been married since July 10, 1949, and have three children, Frederick, Courtney, and Juliette. A noted philanthropist who seeks in charity, as in technology, to "find a need and fill it," Wang rescued Boston's foundering main performing arts theatre (now named the Wang Center) with a $4 million gift in 1983. Other gifts have built an outpatient clinic at Massachusetts General Hospital and funded student exchanges between the United States and China through Harvard University, the Massachusetts Institute of Technology, and "the Doctor's" own Wang Institute of Graduate Studies. Founded in 1979 to train recruits Wang "could use," the last-named offers an interdisciplinary program in computer science and hard-nosed business management and is only one of three schools in the United States to award a master's degree in software engineering. In 1985 Wang donated a computer network to New York City's shelter for the homeless and built a $15 million computer assembly plant to provide jobs in Boston's Chinatown. His determination to return to the world more than he has taken from it has been recognized by the American Electronics Association, which awarded him its Medal of Achievement in 1984 for his contributions to the advancement of electronics, and by the United States Government, which awarded him the Medal of Liberty as one of twelve outstanding naturalized citizens at the relighting of the Statue of Liberty on July 3, 1986.

References: Bsns W p102+ N 13 '71 por, p144+

Mr 21 '77 por, p100+ Je 4 '79 por, p84+ D 15 '80, p100+ My 17 '82 pors, p222 Ap 18 '86 por; Dun's Business Month p48+ D '84 por; Forbes 118:103+ O 15 '76 por, 125:170 Ja 17 '80 por, 129:36+ F 15 '82 por; Fortune 113:106+ F 3 '86 pors; N Y Times III p3 F 24 '80 por, I p1+ My 5 '84 por, III p4 O 14 '84; Sales and Marketing Management 117:1, 51+ S 13 '76 por, 128:19 Ja 18 '82 por; Time 116:81 N 17 '80 por; American Men and Women of Science (1982); Leaders in Electronics (1979); Wang, An, with Eugene Linden. Lessons: An Autobiography (1986); Who's Who in America, 1986–87

Webb, James H(enry), Jr.

Feb. 9, 1946– United States Secretary of the Navy. Address: b. Department of the Navy, The Pentagon, Washington, D.C. 20350

"In my mind, I am a writer. In my heart I am a soldier, and I always will be," United States Secretary of the Navy James H. Webb Jr. once said. Appointed by President Ronald Reagan, Webb succeeded John F. Lehman Jr. in April 1987 as the civilian overseer of some 584,000 naval personnel and 199,000 marines. In the decade and a half following his return from Vietnam as a wounded and highly decorated Marine Corps officer, Webb wrote three novels and one nonfiction book on military strategy and served in several defense-related government posts. Although his frank and forthright comments on a number of issues have at times involved him in controversy, the new secretary of the navy immediately established rapport with top-ranking of-

ficers who had frequently clashed with his predecessor, and he has begun to deal with the major problems confronting his department, notably the maintenance of naval strength and the restoration of public confidence in the recently crisis-ridden Marine Corps.

James Henry Webb Jr. was born on February 9, 1946, in St. Joseph, Missouri, to James Henry and Vera Webb. His father was a colonel in the United States Air Force, and members of the family had fought in the Revolution and in every subsequent American war. Webb remembers that at the age of five he was required, with his brother and two sisters, to stand at attention while his father conducted a military-style inspection of his room. "Did you ever see The Great Santini?" Webb once asked an interviewer, with reference to the 1979 film about a military man who has difficulty adjusting to civilian life. "I grew up with the Great Santini."

Webb lived the peripatetic life of a military youngster, attending eight different schools from the sixth to the tenth grades. After graduating from high school he received a naval ROTC scholarship to attend the University of Southern California, but he soon switched to the United States Naval Academy. At Annapolis, Webb earned distinction as a boxer, but on one occasion he lost the brigade championship to a classmate and future fellow Reagan aide, Oliver North. Although not an outstanding student, Webb was one of eighteen graduates in the class of 1968 to receive a letter of commendation from the superintendent of the academy for outstanding leadership contributions.

Exercising an option available to graduates of Annapolis, Webb chose to be commissioned a second lieutenant in the United States Marine Corps. He then attended the marine officers basic school, where he became the honor graduate in his class of 243. Webb's next assignment was in Vietnam, where he served as a platoon leader and company commander with the first battalion of the Fifth Marine Regiment, later rising to the rank of captain.

In the course of his nine-month service in Vietnam, Webb saw considerable action, earning the Navy Cross, a Silver Star, two Bronze Star medals, and two Purple Hearts. During one eight-week period, in the An Hoa basin, his rifle platoon suffered fifty-six casualties. The severity of the injuries that Webb sustained in combat led to his evacuation from the combat zone and, after several operations, his medical discharge.

Webb's final military assignment brought him to Washington, D.C., where he spent a year in the White House liaison office of the secretary of the navy. Leaving the military service in 1972, Webb remained in the District of Columbia to study at the law center of Georgetown University, where he earned his J.D. degree in 1975 and won the Horan competition for excellence in legal writing.

As a student at Georgetown, Webb became involved in a study of American strategy in the Pacific, particularly the role to be played by Micronesia. He spent July 1973 doing research for the territorial planning commission in Guam, and he returned to that island during the following summer as an adviser to the local government. Before his graduation from law school, Webb outlined his findings in his book *Micronesia and U.S. Pacific Strategy: A Blueprint for the 1980s* (Praeger Pubs., 1974). As a starting point, Webb endorsed the Nixon doctrine under which the United States would provide a nuclear shield for its allies but would expect them to provide for their own defenses in conventional wars. The gradual withdrawal of American forces from their "forward positions" in Japan and on the Asian mainland could eventually lead to a concentration of United States Pacific defenses on the string of islands from Guam to Tinian in the Marianas. If that were to happen, Webb warned, Americans would have to take great care to minimize the impact of the military on the people of the area in order to win their cooperation.

After earning his law degree, Webb wrote his novel *Fields of Fire* (Prentice-Hall, 1978). The book focuses on the experiences of the fictional Lieutenant Robert E. Lee Hodges Jr. of Kentucky and one squad in his platoon of Marines during several months in the An Hoa basin. *Fields of Fire* is considered by many, and especially by veterans, to be one of the finest and most realistic in the genre of Vietnam combat novels. Initially rejected by nine publishers, the book was eventually nominated for a Pulitzer Prize and sold a million copies.

The title *Fields of Fire* derives from the military term referring to the area that a soldier is responsible for covering with his weapon. Within the context of the novel, however, the title also alludes to the role of the battlefield as a test of human mettle, and it suggests the moral ambiguity of the conflict in Vietnam, where the absence of a traditionally defined "front" obscured the relevance of the term.

Although the book contains unsympathetic descriptions of antiwar demonstrators, its primary concern is not the politics of the Vietnam conflict. Its attention is, instead, focused on the ways in which the various soldiers of the unit meet their destinies and pursue their duties. In some respects, *Fields of Fire* is fatalistic and cynical. Almost every sympathetic character is killed or maimed or resigns from the service. On the other hand, malingerers escape with minor wounds, some of which

are self-inflicted; careerist soldiers receive medals and promotions for senseless commands that cost the lives of those under them; and the Vietnamese—on both sides—are portrayed as being trapped in an imbroglio that they did not control.

The message of *Fields of Fire* concerns the dignity of men doing their duty in battle. Hodges comments that "it was the fight, not the cause that mattered." The novel ends on a somewhat hopeful note with the redemption of Will Goodrich, a Harvard dropout who ended up at An Hoa after joining the marines in the false expectation of being assigned to the Corps's band. His lack of nerve and his qualms about killing make Goodrich at least indirectly responsible for the deaths of some of his fellow marines on several occasions, but in the end he finds his courage. Reviewing *Fields of Fire* in the *New Republic* (October 21, 1978), Raphael Sagalyn noted that while it was not "the most powerful war novel in a generation," it deserved to be read "as a vivid reminder of what it was like to live through the war most everyone would now like to forget."

In 1977 and 1978 Webb worked as assistant minority counsel for the Committee on Veterans Affairs of the House of Representatives, and from 1979 to 1981 he was its minority counsel. He also served in 1979 as visiting writer and professor of literature at the United States Naval Academy, teaching courses on poetry and the novel. Outside of Congress, Webb, who was national cochairman of Vietnam Veterans for Gerald Ford in 1976, organized support among veterans' groups for conservative political candidates. Known for his proclivity for controversial statements, Webb charged on one occasion that antiwar demonstrators had cost 10,000 American lives and remarked of the actress Jane Fonda, who visited Hanoi during the fighting, "I wouldn't pay to see her cut her wrists. Although I might." In November 1981 he resigned from the national sponsoring committee for the Vietnam Veterans Memorial because he felt that the design resembled a "mass grave" and could become a "wailing wall for future antidraft and antinuclear demonstrators." He nevertheless remained active with the project and was the principle advocate for the addition of a sculpture and a flag to the original design.

When Ronald Reagan became president in 1981, the new Republican administration considered appointing Webb as head of the Veterans Administration, but Webb became involved in a dispute over the agency's budget with David Stockman, the president's director of the Office of Management and Budget, and withdrew his name from the list of potential nominees. Later, in an interview on network television, Webb disparaged Stockman's avoidance of military service during the Vietnam conflict. He noted that Stockman chose to remain in divinity school until his draft lottery number was high enough to guarantee that he would not be drafted.

After leaving government service, Webb remained in Washington and resumed his career as a novelist. His decision reflected, in part, his frustration with the legislative process and with the prevailing attitude that elaborate programs provide solutions. Convinced that aid to veterans was a problem of society rather than one of legislation, he noted that "in writing, you can affect people's emotions and attitudes," and added that he thought that literature "touches people more deeply than veterans' programs." For Webb, novels allow a treatment of ethics that he found impossible in politics. In his view, the characters about whom he writes "face situations where morality is not clearly defined." In that respect their experience is that of all Americans during the past quarter century as well as of those who served in Vietnam. "But politics is the art of taking ambiguities and boiling them down simply enough so you can say 'yes' or 'no,'" Webb has argued. "It is the opposite of writing. In writing you take these ambiguities and you expand them. You flesh them out. You deal with them."

Webb's second novel, *A Sense of Honor* (Prentice-Hall, 1981), focuses on the United States Naval Academy. Set in 1968, the book involves first classman "Wild Bill" Fogarty, an athlete and leader determined to make a successful career as a Marine Corps officer, and plebe John Dean, who is academically brilliant but lacking in military aptitude. Fogarty is determined to make or break Dean by subjecting him, despite the academy's ban on hazing, to difficult and dangerous physical exploits. Other important characters are Captain Ted Lenahan, who dislikes hazing but recognizes its role in separating leaders from losers, and a civilian professor concerned about civil rights, who pushes the situation to its inevitable conclusion as each participant in the drama follows his own sense of honor. The book sold some 250,000 copies, and Peter Braestrup, writing in the conservative *American Spectator* (September 1981), noted "its special value as a timely, unfashionable reminder that schooling, testing, developing future military commanders is no ordinary educational task."

A Sense of Honor created a stir when the officer in charge of the midshipman store at the naval academy directed the bookstore to cancel a prepublication order for the novel and to make it available only in response to direct requests. The officer was quoted in the *New York Times* as saying that "in the opinion of most people who read it, there's a large amount of vulgarity and a less-than-accurate picture of the officers, midshipmen, and faculty of the academy." Webb was offended and angered by the academy's reaction. "I don't believe I have to create a fairy tale in order to show that I'm proud to have attended the naval academy," he remarked, as quoted in *Publishers Weekly* (March 20, 1981). "I think it's a disservice to the institution to try and paint it like something out of a '30s movie called 'Men of Annapolis.'"

Webb also felt that the action taken against *A Sense of Honor* was a retaliation for an article that he had published after serving as writer-in-residence at the naval academy in 1979. Entitled "Women Can't Fight," the essay appeared in the *Washingtonian* magazine. In it Webb criticized a congressional decision in 1975 to open the military academies to females, who are barred by law from combat. He argued that the traditional role of the service academies as producers of combat leaders had been weakened, and he even suggested that the government might close the service academies in favor of expanded ROTC programs at civilian universities. After the article appeared. Webb recalled, officials at the academy "had me barred from the buildings, refused to allow me to show someone around the premises—which is the right of *all* graduates—that kind of thing."

In 1983 Doubleday published Webb's third novel, *A Country Such as This.* The book traces the lives of three naval academy roommates, Judd Smith, Red Lesczynski, and Joe Dingenfelder, from their graduation in 1951 to 1976. Smith wins a Navy Cross for heroism with the marines in Korea and eventually becomes a congressman. Lesczynski, a naval aviator, is shot down over Vietnam and becomes a prisoner of war. Dingenfelder becomes involved with the American missile program, first as an air force officer and then as a civilian. An important part of the tension in the novel derives from the confrontation between Smith and Dingenfelder's feminist ex-wife, Dorothy, who has left her husband in protest against his involvement with the production of armaments and has become a member of Congress. The reviewer for the *Wall Street Journal* (November 16, 1983) found *A Country Such as This* a refreshing exploration of moral and social dilemmas. He praised Webb's "fine eye for narrative detail" and his ability to refrain "from any kind of polemical attack." The critic for the *Chicago Tribune* (January 8, 1984) was less sympathetic. He termed the book "a stilted polemic" and described the clashes between two opposing members of Congress as "dishonestly staged."

In 1983 Webb went to Beirut, Lebanon, in behalf of PBS's *MacNeil/Lehrer NewsHour,* just prior to the terrorist bombing of a United States Marine barracks there that took 241 lives. After returning from that assignment, he argued, in an interview in *People* magazine (November 7, 1983), that the United States had to maintain a presence in the area, lest the Soviet-influenced Syrians provoke a war with Israel by attempting to take over Lebanon. He contended, however, that the marines had too many men in the zone just to show the flag and too few to conduct effective military operations, and that terrorists would not have been able to blow up the Marine headquarters in Beirut had there been enough soldiers available to maintain an "aggressive defense." Webb's coverage won an Emmy Award from the National Academy of Television Arts and Sciences.

Webb returned to government service in February 1984, when President Reagan, named him the first assistant secretary of defense for reserve affairs. To honor his retired father, Webb asked him to administer the oath of office, and he also included in the ceremony six veterans, some of them disabled, who had served with him in Vietnam. As assistant secretary, Webb was in charge of implementing the new "total force doctrine" that, in reaction to a decision to rely on volunteer active forces, changed the missions of the National Guard and the Reserve forces.

Webb's three-year tenure as assistant secretary, which earned him a Distinguished Public Service Medal, was noncontroversial for the most part, although his defense of the use of Honduras as a training ground for National Guard and reserve units disturbed some state governors. While serving in that post, which carried with it the equivalent of four-star rank, he was twice invited to the United States Naval Academy, where he lectured midshipmen on courage and honor.

On February 18, 1987, after John F. Lehman Jr. declared his intention to resign as secretary of the navy, President Reagan announced that he would nominate Webb for the post. At Webb's confirmation hearing before the Senate Armed Services Committee on April 6, in which much of the questioning focused on his attitude toward women in the military, Webb gave measured and conciliatory responses. The nominee, whose mother-in-law had served in the marines during World War II and whose present wife had been an army nurse for five years, restated his opposition to committing women to combat but added that he accepted the change in the academies. On April 9, 1987, after the twenty committee members present voted unanimously in favor of Webb, the Senate approved his appointment, by voice vote and he was sworn in as the sixty-sixth secretary of the navy on the following day. At his own request, Webb was sworn in for a second time, on May 1, 1987, at the United States Naval Academy, with Secretary of Defense Caspar W. Weinberger administering the oath.

Navy brass welcomed Webb's assumption of the post of secretary. Although they had supported Lehman's successful advocacy of a 600-ship fleet, many were unhappy with his efforts to reshape the service according to his own priorities and maintained that he had interfered with promotions and had assumed power at the expense of the uniformed leadership. Webb, who has said, "unlike my predecessor, I grew up in the military," immediately sought to distance himself from those actions and called in 500 top-ranking officers to state his priorities and to assure them that he would consult them on policy matters.

On April 14, 1987, Webb announced that the Navy would no longer make special accommodations for officers who wanted to take part in professional sports. His action affected Ensign Napoleon McCallum, who had played on weekends for the NFL's Los Angeles Raiders, and Midshipman David Robinson of the National Basketball Association's San Antonio team. That same month, Webb reversed another Lehman decision by reinstating a list of officers recommended by a board of admirals for advancement to the rank of captain. The former secretary had disbanded the promotion board on the ground that it was promoting too many submarine officers. The inspector general of the Department of Defense had earlier concluded that Lehman, although responding to advice from the chief of naval personnel, had "exceeded his authority."

In keeping with his promise to draw on the expertise of the uniformed leadership. Webb, on April 16, 1987, directed senior navy admirals and marine generals to assess within sixty days the current status of their services and their prospects for the next ten years. In particular, he asked for suggestions regarding competition in submarine warfare with the Soviet Union, a solution to the Marine Corps's "serious identity crisis," and answers to the navy's shortages of medical personnel and facilities.

Perhaps the most difficult problems immediately facing Webb concerned the Marine Corps, which had been shaken by charges that four of its enlisted men, assigned as guards at the United States embassy in Moscow, had allowed KGB agents to gain access to the premises. Webb refused to condone the conduct of those accused, but he also complained that Arthur A. Hartman, the American ambassador to the USSR between 1981 and 1987, should be held accountable for setting a permissive tone at the embassy.

Other problems confronting Webb in his early months as secretary of the navy involved the United States presence along the oil routes of the Persian Gulf, where an Iraqi attack in May 1987 on the frigate USS *Stark* resulted in the deaths of thirty-seven American sailors; the involvement of Marine Lieutenant Colonel Oliver North, a former key presidential aide, in the Iran-Contra scandal; and reports that Soviet submarines in mid-1987 outnumbered those of the United States, 280 to ninety-six. Webb was also concerned about the immediate need for the production of two new aircraft carriers to replace outdated ones, and the possibility that the Marine Corps might lose its mobility by weighing itself down with too much heavy equipment.

James H. Webb Jr. is married to the former JoAnn Krukar, whom he met in 1979. They have three children, Jimmy, Sarah, and Julia. Webb's daughter Amy also lives with them in their Falls Church, Virginia, home. She is the only child from Webb's first marriage, in 1968, to Barbara DuCote, a lawyer, which ended in divorce. Webb is handsome, with a full head of curly dark hair and a boyish, all-American appearance. He has an eagle and the letters "USMC" tattooed on his left arm. He enjoys H. Upmann cigars, and he works out with a heavy punching bag to stay fit. The official Soviet newspaper *Pravda* has termed Webb a combination of the American pop-culture heroes Rocky, Rambo, and American Samurai and has described him as "a troubadour of chauvinism, jingoism, aggression, and violence."

References: Cong Q 45:676+ Ap 11 '87 por; N Y Times Biog Service 14:1014 Ag '83 por; Newsweek 109:6 My '87 por; Parade p4+ Jl 5 '87 pors; People 25:81+ My 5 '86 pors; Contemporary

Authors vols 81-84 (1979); Who's Who in America, 1986-87

Westheimer, (Karola) Ruth

1928– Psychologist; author; broadcaster; family and sex counselor. Address: b. c/o Metromedia, 205 E. 67th St., New York City, N.Y. 10021

Dr. Ruth Westheimer, a flamboyant, middle-aged New York psychologist, broadcaster, and writer who is popularly known as "Grandma Freud" or simply "Dr. Ruth," "doles out sexual advice like good hot chicken soup" every Sunday night on Sexually Speaking, her phenomenally popular two-hour syndicated radio phone-in show. The diminutive former German-Jewish refugee, who sometimes exhorts her listeners to "Have Good Sex," has parlayed a talent for demystifying discussion of human sexuality into international celebrity and fortune. Dr. Westheimer's is a classic American success story in every sense of the term. "I came to this country with absolutely nothing," she told Patricia Bosworth of Ladies Home Journal (February 1986). "I've worked hard to get where I am, but—if you'll excuse the cliché—what's happened to me could only have happened in America."

Dr. Ruth Westheimer was born Karola Ruth Siegel in Frankfurt, Germany, in 1928, the only child of Orthodox Jewish parents. Her father was a successful notions wholesaler, and Ruth Westheimer's childhood was comfortably middle class. Possessed of an insatiable energy and inquisitive mind, she learned about sex early by sneaking into her father's library to read his books. But there

were soon things other than childhood curiosity about which to be concerned; with the coming of the Nazis into power, in 1933, wide-scale, violent anti-Semitism became an increasingly ugly fact of life for Germany's Jews. Fearing the worst, in 1939 the Siegels decided to flee. When Ruth Westheimer's aged grandmother refused to accompany the family, the decision was made to send young Ruth away to the safety of a Swiss school for six months, until the trouble "blew over" or until arrangements could be made to immigrate to what was then Palestine. Ruth Westheimer never saw her family again. She now believes that they died in the concentration camp at Auschwitz.

The Swiss school to which the Siegels sent their daughter thus became a kind of an orphanage, where Ruth and 100 other Jewish refugee girls waited out the war. Her memories of that period of her life are not happy ones; compounding her misery was the school directress' low opinion of her. Regarded as a "welfare case," she was trained only as a maid. One of her teachers noted disapprovingly on a report card that she was "very intelligent, very lively, and doesn't let anybody else talk." She did nothing to improve bad opinions when, as a sign of things to come, she began sharing some of the knowledge she had furtively acquired in her father's library. "I taught all the other girls about menstruation," she recalled in an interview with New York Daily News reporter Jonathan Mandall (April 10, 1983). "And I got into trouble with the directress. She told me to shut up."

Following the war, Ruth Westheimer immigrated to Palestine, where she shed both her Germanic-sounding first name—Karola—and her Orthodox Judaism on becoming a staunch Zionist. By 1948, when she was twenty, she had become a member of the Haganah, the Jewish underground movement fighting for creation of a Jewish homeland. Although trained as a sniper, she never actually fired a gun except in target practice. Her closest encounter with death came during an artillery bombardment of the kibbutz where she was teaching kindergarten, when she narrowly missed having her feet blown off by a big explosive shell. Fortunately, she survived intact. "Otherwise, I might have been even shorter," she once quipped.

Despite her apparent ebullience, at that stage in her life Ruth Westheimer desperately sought romance and a sense of direction. She dreamed of becoming a doctor, but without family support and money, she despaired of her chances of doing so. And, acutely aware of her four feet seven inches of height and convinced of her own physical limitations, she lamented in her diary, "Nobody is going to want me because I'm short and ugly." When, in 1950, a young Israeli soldier proposed marriage to her, she accepted immediately. "I married the first man who asked me," she later admitted. The newlyweds moved to Paris, where her husband studied medicine and Ruth Westheimer earned a degree in psychology from the Sorbonne, despite the fact that she never graduated from high school. The marriage did not survive the strains of student life and ended in divorce after five years. When her husband returned to Israel, she remained behind, living contentedly in a third-floor walk-up with a shared, ground-floor toilet. Ruth Westheimer told a *McCall's* magazine interviewer (October 1983), "Everybody around me didn't have money. We went to cafés and had one cup of coffee all day long. Everybody."

In the midst of a love affair with a young Frenchman, she married him to legalize a pregnancy that she says she wanted, and, at her insistence, moved with him to New York City in 1956. Despite the birth of a daughter whom the couple named Miriam, the second marriage was no more successful than the first. "Intellectually, it was just not tenable," she has explained. "I had always to think, what can I talk to him about next?" Ruth Westheimer now supported herself and her daughter by working as a dollar-per-hour housemaid (ironically, her Swiss school training paid off) while she learned English and attended evening classes for a masters degree at the New School for Social Research. Following her 1959 graduation, she found work as a research assistant at Columbia University's School of Public Health.

While on a ski trip to the Catskill Mountains of northern New York in 1961 she met and fell in love with her third husband, Manfred ("Fred") Westheimer. "I went up the mountain with my boyfriend, Hans. He was six foot. We were very uncomfortable because a T-bar pushes us up. So, when the bar was on my behind, it was on Hans's ankle," she told a *People* magazine interviewer (April 15, 1985). "On top, somebody introduced me to Fred Westheimer. And I told Hans, 'I'm going up the mountain with that short one.'" As it turned out, it was soon apparent to Ruth Westheimer that she and the five-foot-five-inch Fred Westheimer, an easy-going German-Jewish refugee who sometimes calls her "my little skiing accident," had a lot more in common than their lack of height. They were married nine months later and in 1964 became the parents of a son they named Joel.

Meanwhile, Ruth Westheimer continued both her working life and her education. She applied for a job at a Planned Parenthood clinic in Harlem, and in 1967 was appointed its project director. She spent her days at the clinic for the next three years and her evenings at Columbia University, working towards her doctorate in family counseling, and also taking courses in sex counseling. After submitting a thesis on the interdisciplinary study of the family, she received her doctorate in education from Columbia in 1970. In the early 1970s she began teaching as an associate professor in the department of sex counseling at Lehman College in the Bronx. When, in 1977, budget cutbacks led to her layoff, she found another teaching job at Brooklyn College. That association ended abruptly, when Dr. Westheimer was fired for reasons she has not revealed. She has said that the blow devastated her emotionally. "It made me feel as I did when I got kicked out of Germany. Angry, helpless, rejected. As it turns out, it was my big break," she told the interviewer for *People* magazine.

Not long afterwards, she gave a lecture to a group of New York broadcasters about the need for more sex education programming to promote what she calls "sexual literacy." It happened that Betty Elam, then the community affairs manager of New York radio station WYNY-FM, was in the audience. Intrigued by what Dr. Westheimer had said, she invited her to be a guest on the NBC affiliate's Sunday morning public affairs show. When that appearance went well, in late 1980 Betty Elam offered Dr. Westheimer twenty-five dollars a week to do *Sexually Speaking*, her own fifteen-minute, taped show shortly after midnight on Sundays. "At first, the station manager was not thrilled about the idea. But I promised him that it would work, and with Ruth it worked," Betty Elam said. The show's instant success was readily apparent when the station offered listeners a promotional "Sex on Sunday" T-shirt. Susan Brown, the producer of *Sexually Speaking*, anticipated a few hundred requests, but got more than 3,500.

By September of 1981, what has been termed by *Newsweek* as Dr. Westheimer's "effervescent blend of candor, humor and common-sense practicality," had attracted such a large and loyal audience that the show was given an expanded one-hour time slot, from ten to eleven each Sunday evening, and its format was changed to that of a live phone-in show. Listeners were invited to call and talk on the air with "Dr. Ruth" about their sexual problems; so many called that on an average night WYNY's switchboards were jammed by an estimated 4,000 calls. Susan Brown prescreened all callers who got through, allowing thirty or so of the most insistent, urgent, and interesting to go on the air. Ratings in the summer of 1983 indicated that "Dr. Ruth's" show was attracting a quarter-million listeners weekly, thus making it the top-rated radio show in the New York City area for its time period.

Dr. Westheimer was as surprised as anyone by the show's instant popularity. "All I'm doing on radio is educating," she insists. Many observers agreed. *Newsweek* (May 3, 1982) writer George Hackett noted that Dr. Westheimer was only one of a growing number of "media therapists" offering free advice over the airwaves, perpetuating a trend begun in 1975 in Los Angeles, when the popular psychologist Dr. Toni Grant began answering listener questions on radio station KABC. Within a decade, an estimated 25 million listeners weekly were tuning-in to the fifty "radio shrinks" being heard on stations around the country. *Sexually Speaking* was therefore by no means unique, but "once you've talked sex with Dr. Ruth," as Tom Shales asked rhetorically in the *New York Post* (June 4, 1985), "can it ever be as good with anyone else?"

Dr. Ruth has attributed her success to her accent, entertaining commentary, short stature, and willingness to call the parts of the body by their proper names. Moreover, she is convinced of the real need for a show like *Sexually Speaking*. D. Keith Mano noted in his *National Review* (May 13, 1983) profile of "Dr. Huth Vestheimer" that "[her German-Jewish] accent relieves all sense of impropriety. European women are allowed to talk-about-that." It is true that when talking about "that" Dr. Westheimer is nonjudgmental towards her audience, espousing the theory that just about any nonviolent sexual activity between consenting adults is a normal, healthy part of life. ("There's nothing wrong with new uses for peanut butter or onion rings as long as you have a relationship," she told one male caller to her show.) But she is no libertine; in fact, she often proudly refers to herself as "an old-fashioned square." Mano added that she "and responsible people like her are go-betweens: they allow an entire social stratum to console and teach each other."

Dr. Ruth Westheimer is a firm believer in marriage and the family. She declines to offer "on-air" advice to anyone under the age of sixteen, preferring instead to have young people write to her. But she incurs the wrath of both religious and political conservatives because of the explicitness of her answers to questions about such topics as orgasm ("just a reflex, like a sneeze"), homosexuality ("one or two homosexual experiences does not mean you are a homosexual"), and premature ejaculation ("sometimes the man is under terrific pressure to perform"). Her vehement advocacy of sex education, contraception, and a limited right to abortion have also aroused their hostility.

"Her message is just indulge yourself," charges Father Edwin O'Brien, former secretary to the late Terence Cardinal Cooke. "Whatever feels good is good. There's no higher law or overriding morality and there's no responsibility." Other critics have taken exception to what they view as Dr. Westheimer's "hot chicken soup" approach to what they feel are serious human problems; New York psychiatrist Dr. Benjamin Saddock, for example, calls *Sexually Speaking* "voyeurism of the ear." Still other critics dislike what has been termed her emphasis "on plumbing" at the expense of "humanism and personality."

Although she takes such criticism into serious consideration, Dr. Westheimer dismisses some of her detractors as simply being envious of her success. She defends herself and her program to others by emphasizing that she gives "good information in an entertaining way because that's what a good professor does. It's not therapy; it's basic information. It's good advice . . . I dispense common sense with a smile, based on good scientific knowledge." To those who accuse her of stressing the physical aspect of sex, she points out that she often does talk about relationships. "Sex is not just intercourse. Sex is a smile, sex is holding hands, sex is a relationship," she says.

Not surprisingly, Dr. Westheimer also has many admirers. Her colleague and former mentor, Dr. Helen Singer Kaplan, says: "She takes complex technical information and translates it into simple terms for people who really need it. She is very warm and caring about people, and that comes across. And she has tremendous energy." Frank Osborne, the WYNY-FM station manager, agrees.

"She's just so right. Once you finish talking to her you know exactly what to do," he says. The general public evidently agrees, since her popularity has grown steadily since her 1980 radio debut. By late 1982, in addition to her radio show, she was writing a monthly *Playgirl* magazine column and was touring the same professional lecture circuit as Henry Kissinger, earning as much as $10,000 for her appearances on college campuses, where she has a wide following. Dr. Westheimer began capitalizing on her radio success when she launched the *Dr. Ruth* television show on New York's Channel 5. Although the show lasted for just thirteen weeks, it convinced her that her potential audience was much larger than she had ever imagined. She found, too, that she enjoyed the celebrity that came with being a television personality, though she remained acutely aware of the danger of getting caught up in the glamour and excitement of the medium. "So far, this has been a glorious adventure," Dr. Westheimer said. "But I'm ready to enjoy what happens after the excitement dies down. I mean it."

That relish she takes in her work may be one of the reasons Dr. Westheimer has not abandoned her private practice as a psychologist and family counselor. She somehow still finds time to spend fifty minutes or an hour with each private patient, to be affiliated with the Human Sexuality Program at the New York Hospital-Cornell Medical Center, to do sex therapy in the Department of Geriatric Medicine at Bellevue Hospital Center, and even to teach a course at West Point Military Academy. "I'm the shortest instructor ever to teach there," she once joked.

In May 1983 Dr. Westheimer moved in another career direction when Warner Books published her first book, a paperback entitled *Dr. Ruth's Guide to Good Sex*. It eventually sold more than 169,000 copies and was translated into three languages: German, Spanish, and Japanese. Buoyed by her success, she returned to television on August 27, 1984, with a nationally televised show on the Lifetime cable network. The thirty-minute *Good Sex With Dr. Westheimer* aired nightly, except Sundays, and featured actors relating problem situations that were discussed by the doctor. There were also, of course, the inevitable questions posed in "man-on-the-street" interviews done on New York's busy Sixth Avenue. The show's producers set up a camera with a sign, "Ask Dr. Ruth." "People came right up and talked about [their] problems," Dr. Westheimer said. "We got 126 situations and I answered them in the studio later." Each Thursday the show expanded to an hour and reverted to the familiar phone-in format.

Within a week of the debut of her new TV show, Dr. Westheimer could also be heard nationally on NBC radio, which on September 2, 1984, began syndicating her Sunday night WYNY show. "I read very carefully the Practices and Standards book, and there is nothing I could disagree with," she told Martin Burden of the *New York Post* (August 3, 1984). Media watchers who said that Dr. Westheimer's appeal might not carry over to a national audience were proved wrong. The Lifetime cable TV show, available in two million homes, helped to boost the ailing network's ratings while, at the same time, the radio show was drawing ever-larger audiences. Fears that *Sexually Speaking* would offend listeners in more conservative areas proved largely groundless, and only one radio station, in Atlanta, canceled the show as a result of listener complaints.

The public's appetite for Dr. Westheimer seemed insatiable. In September 1985 her television show was renamed *The Dr. Ruth Show* and more than sixty radio stations in the United States and Canada joined the network for *Sexually Speaking*. In addition, she began to make guest appearances on the David Letterman and Johnny Carson late-night talk shows and to do television commercials. There was a $7,000-per-couple Dr. Westheimer-led tour of India's "ancient sensual sites," and even a *Good Sex* board game and a television video. Tom Shales dubbed Dr. Westheimer "our first true superstar sex therapist," pointing out that she was by now so successful that she had incorporated herself as Karola, Inc., and hired the publicist Pierre Lehu to tend to her interests.

A publicist's skills were needed in the wake of an error in a new Dr. Westheimer book, a paperback called *First Love: A Young People's Guide to Sexual Information*, which was published by Warner Books in October 1985. In explaining the rhythm method of birth control, Dr. Westheimer incorrectly informed her teenaged readers that "the *safe* times [for sexual intercourse] are the week before and the week of ovulation." The sentence should have read "*unsafe* times." The typographical error, ferreted out by a sharp-eyed New Jersey librarian, prompted a hurried recall of 115,000 copies of the book. An embarrassed Dr. Westheimer could only explain sheepishly, "Even big shot people like myself make mistakes."

If the foul-up cost Dr. Westheimer anything more than embarrassment, it was not apparent in reduced ratings for either her radio or television shows: the former began its third season in the fall of 1986, while the latter was by then syndicated to ninety-three radio stations. Meanwhile, her third book, *Dr. Ruth's Guide for Married Lovers*, was in book stores, and she made her acting debut in the film *One Woman or Two*, starring Gérard Depardieu and Sigourney Weaver. In October she signed a contract with King Features Entertainment for a syndicated television show called *Ask Dr. Ruth*. The new half-hour program, intended eventually to replace her *Lifetime* show, hit the airwaves in January 1987, five nights a week on more than seventy stations. By August the program had run into difficulties, drawing "pint-sized audiences," according to *TV Guide* (August 1, 1987), and Lifetime was seeking to lure Dr. Westheimer back to a late-night slot without the censorship restrictions of non-cable programming.

The ash-blonde, blue-eyed Ruth Westheimer, who has been described as having "a voice that be-

longs in a birdcage" and "an energy level higher than that of a charged particle," is said to sleep very little. She lives with her husband, Fred, an engineer, in an apartment building in the Washington Heights area of New York City. Her daughter, Miriam, is completing a doctorate at Columbia and her son, Joel, is a student at Princeton.

Dr. Westheimer's autobiography, *All in a Lifetime*, written with Ben Yagoda and published by Warner Books in October 1987 includes an account of her traumatic childhood experiences. Dr. Westheimer suffered from writer's block while attempting to set down those experiences, as she told Georgia Dullea in an interview for the *New York Times* (October 26, 1987), and she was forced temporarily to undergo psychoanalysis in order to complete the book. "I tell everybody, 'Go for help,' right?" she said in the interview. "And here I was, holding back painful experiences, not wanting to look at them, maybe because I was scared I would get so sad that I wouldn't be able to do the things I needed to do as 'Dr. Ruth.'" On the rare occasions when Ruth Westheimer relaxes, her pastimes include skiing, dining out, tending to her doll collection, and spending weekends at the family's country home in Peekskill, New York.

References: Ladies' Home J p82+ F '86 por; McCall's p76+ O '83 pors; Newsday p14+ Ag 14 '83 pors; N Y Times B p8 O 26 '87 por; People p109 Ap 15 '85 pors; Vogue p275+ Mr '83

Wharton, Clifton R(eginald) Jr.

Sept. 13, 1926– Pension system administrator; educator; economist; development expert. Address: b. Teachers Insurance Annuity Association and College Retirement Equities Fund, 730 Third Ave., New York City, N.Y. 10017

When Clifton R. Wharton Jr. became chairman and chief executive officer of the Teacher Insurance Annuity Association and College Retirement Equities Fund on February 1, 1987, he moved from the top of the nation's largest university system to the top of its largest private pension system. Dr. Wharton is accustomed to top jobs and large challenges. As chancellor of the State University of New York (SUNY) for eight years, he earned a reputation as an able administrator who brought a sense of cohesion and "family" to the 360,000-student, sixty-four-campus university system. Before he became chancellor at SUNY, he was president of Michigan State University, where he was the first black to fill the top job at a predominantly white major university. Wharton began making momentous decisions while working for John D. Rockefeller 3d at the Agricultural Development Council, a foundation that assists developing countries. An economist and international affairs expert

Clifton R. Wharton Jr.

who has earned degrees from Harvard College, the Johns Hopkins University, and the University of Chicago, Wharton directed the council's operations in Cambodia, Laos, Malaysia, Thailand, and Vietnam, from 1958 to 1964.

Clifton Reginald Wharton Jr. was born on September 13, 1926, in Boston, Massachusetts. His mother, the former Harriet Banks, was a chemistry professor and social worker, and his father, Clifton Wharton, was a lawyer and the first black career ambassador in the United States. The senior Clifton Wharton moved up through the diplomatic ranks after an initial assignment in Monrovia, Liberia, and eventually served as minister to Romania and as ambassador to Norway before retiring from the service in 1964. His father's foreign postings, interspersed with occasional home leaves, had a profound impact on the education and upbringing of young Clifton, his two brothers and a sister. Wharton began his education while his father was serving as United States Consul in the Canary Islands, a Spanish possession. Since there were no American schools, his mother took on responsibility for his education, tutoring him with the aid of books from a correspondence school in Baltimore. "She was a superb teacher," Wharton told George R. Metcalf, author of *Up From Within: Today's New Black Leaders* (McGraw-Hill, 1971). "She took me certain afternoons to a French school, operated by White Russians, where I had my first exposure to French. I picked up Spanish at the same time I learned English, so I was trilingual from the beginning."

After spending six years abroad, Wharton was sent back to Boston, where he attended the prestigious Boston Latin School and lived with his maternal grandmother, a woman he once described as "something of a martinet." At Boston Latin, the nation's first public school and a competitive institution with a reputation for graduating many outstanding students, Wharton became a part of the educational elite and carried forward a family tradition of scholarship.

While attending Boston Latin, Wharton worked in a spool factory in Boston. The job came at his father's insistence, in the belief that it would build his son's character. Wharton also took up track, a sport he would pursue at Harvard, which he entered at age sixteen. In his junior year at college, he pulled a muscle in the high hurdles and never ran again. There were other undergraduate activities that appealed to him, however. Wharton was the first black to join the Harvard radio station; he also helped to found the National Student Association and served as its first national secretary. Meanwhile, he studied hard enough to graduate *cum laude* in 1947 with a B.A. degree in history. Not yet twenty when he graduated, he went to Tuskegee, Alabama, in 1945, where black Air Force pilots were trained during World War II. His military service was brief and with the war over, he turned his attention to beginning a professional career.

Wharton's first impulse was to follow his father into the foreign service. He was accepted at the School of Advanced International Studies of the Johns Hopkins University, where he obtained an M.A. degree in international affairs in 1948. Thinking over his career choice, though, he had a change of heart. The idea that whatever he achieved in the foreign service might be attributed to or compared with his father's accomplishment prompted him to abandon plans for a diplomatic career. "I really decided I wanted to do something on my own," he told Stephen Frank, in an interview for an article that appeared in the Albany, New York, *Times-Union* (September 14, 1986).

Wharton chose to enter a related field—that of international economic development. From 1948 to 1953 he worked for Nelson A. Rockefeller's American International Association for Economic and Social Development, an organization that dealt primarily with Latin American countries. Having decided, after spending five years with the Rockefeller group, that to advance his career in international development he would need a Ph.D. degree, Wharton enrolled in 1953 in the graduate school of economics at the University of Chicago. Wharton looks back upon his Chicago years, when he studied with such esteemed economists as Theodore W. Schultz, as the most intellectually demanding of his career. "They didn't care who you were," he told Stephen Frank. "You had to meet those standards. It was as rigorous as could be." Wharton was granted his Ph.D. degree in 1958 after writing a thesis about capital and technology in the agricultural development of Minas Gerais, Brazil. He had already accepted an offer to join the Agricultural Development Council (ADC), a nonprofit organization established by John D. Rockefeller 3d, to work in the field of agricultural and economic development, especially in Asia. From 1958 to 1964

Wharton directed council programs in Vietnam, Laos, Thailand, and Cambodia. During his tenure in Malaysia, according to an unsigned article in *Ebony* (July 1970), Wharton "used to tramp around sun-drenched Southeast Asia rice fields talking to peasants in Vietnamese about crop yields and prices, hearing of their problems that—as he warned the U.S. State Department—would later tend to help the Viet Cong gain influence in Vietnam's rural areas." Such knowledge later proved invaluable when he faced student protests against the Vietnam War as a university president. Also a visiting professor of economics at the University of Malaysia during that period, Wharton was gradually "Oriented" to Asian civilization. "I would have to say that the experience of living and working in Asia was a very, very significant influence on us," he told Stephen Frank. "The gentility and courteousness of most Asian cultures is quite remarkable. You can go to the poorest village in Southeast Asia. They don't have enough to feed themselves, but they will treat you with gentility and courtesy."

In 1964 Wharton returned to the United States to spend a sabbatical year at Stanford University teaching economic development. From Stanford he moved to New York as director of the ADC's Universities Research Program, which focused on the problems of agriculture in the Third World. Wharton became the ADC's executive director in 1966 and a year later was named its vice-president. His association with the Rockefellers and his rise within the ranks of the organization catapulted him into the nation's corporate boardrooms. In 1969 he became a director of the Equitable Life Assurance Society of the United States, and he later joined the boards of the Ford Motor Company, Federated Department Stores, Inc., Time, Inc. and Burroughs.

Wharton has told interviewers that he responds to "creative opportunities." Such an opportunity presented itself in 1969, when he was named president and professor of economics at Michigan State University in East Lansing. The opportunity was also a challenge. Wharton replaced John A. Hannah, who had left to become administrator of the United States Agency for International Development, at a time when campuses across the country were rocked by student demands for an end to American involvement in the Vietnam war and for changes in various domestic policies. His early years at Michigan State were marked by demonstrations, sit-ins, and riots. Soon after he arrived on campus, in 1970, four students were killed at Kent State University in a protest over American military activity in Cambodia. To keep his campus calm, Wharton appeared on closed-circuit television, assuring students that "perhaps I feel the frustrations and anxieties even more acutely than many of you, since I have been personally involved with Asians and Asia for many years." He later suspended classes for a day of teach-ins on Indochina, ROTC, police policy, and tools of effective protest. Wharton's actions earned him "a reputation as a fair and affable administrator who sought to defuse confrontations through diplomacy and quiet

reasoning," according to Lorenzo Middleton in an article that appeared in the *Chronicle of Higher Education* (March 9, 1981). His actions also evinced his desire to serve as a conciliator and consensus-builder, a trait that has characterized his administrative style throughout his career. He told an unidentified interviewer for *Ebony* (July 1970) that as an individual he was "firmly convinced" that expansion of the Vietnam War was "a serious error and miscalculation," but as head of Michigan State University he said he offered to take any university community petitions—for or against American policy—to Michigan's congressional delegation in Washington.

Much attention focused on the fact that Wharton was the first black president of a major American university when he was tapped to head Michigan State. But by 1978, when he left East Lansing to assume the chancellorship of the State University of New York, his race was receiving relatively little press attention. "People soon realized," Wharton told Middleton, "that I was there to handle all issues across the board, not just to focus on a narrow band in the spectrum." Wharton arrived in Albany after a period of dramatic growth for SUNY in which $3.3 billion of new construction in less than two decades had caused the thirty-year-old system to mushroom from a cluster of thirty-two colleges to a vast network of research, technical, medical, and liberal arts institutions and community colleges. Wharton's incumbency began in the midst of a fiscal retrenchment that had already required the layoff of 246 faculty members at the system's twenty-nine state-operated campuses. In that atmosphere, with the physical plant and the academic program in place, the new chancellor faced important decisions about whether, and in what areas, SUNY should undertake a climb into the top ranks of American higher education. He promptly undertook a tour of the entire system and announced that he would move it "toward its great potential for excellence," especially in subject areas that would benefit its patron, New York State. Most of the early years of his tenure, though, were devoted to keeping SUNY financially stable from year to year through politicking, persuading, and administrative maneuvering with his board of trustees, the governor, and the state legislature.

Early on, Wharton developed a reputation as a leader "who could run anything," board of trustees chairman Donald M. Blinken told Lorenzo Middleton. "He has a very, very vivid sense of priorities, and always seems to know where we should be going and how we should get there." Wharton began to move his system out of the shadow of the Northeast's prestigious private colleges and universities, which had been attracting New York's best students long before SUNY existed, by lobbying for an increase in SUNY's share of public funds and public recognition. In the process, his penchant for conciliation could sometimes give way to skirmishing and attack, as in 1982, when the New York legislature enacted a law requiring the registration and monitoring of lobbyists for the state's public universities and colleges. Wharton was among a number of public educators who felt the legislature had targeted them at the behest of private institutions, which were already monitored. As a result he unleashed, in a memorandum to SUNY campus presidents, what Gene I. Maeroff described in the *New York Times* (July 6, 1982) as "a salvo of accusations at the private sector of higher education." He argued that free lobbying by public institutions should not be restricted since theirs was the considerable task of making "higher education opportunities accessible to a broad spectrum of students, from the less gifted to the exceptional," while "private institutions still may practice any degree of elitism they choose." Fighting that and other battles earned Wharton a reputation, according to Samuel Weiss (*New York Times*, October 16, 1986), for being "an articulate spokesman for public higher education in a period of tight fiscal constraints and at a time when the sprawling 64-campus system no longer appeared to attract the high level of political support it received" during the boom years of the 1960s and early 1970s. In 1983, SUNY's thirty-fifth anniversary year, however, Wharton could report that the system's major centers were increasingly holding their own against private institutions. "The evidence," he observed, "suggests that New York's best and brightest students find SUNY more appealing each year. . . . Competition for entry into programs at some SUNY campuses has grown as fierce as at almost any private institution." Recognition of that fact by the state legislature, of course, would generate funds to help SUNY improve in other areas. Those areas were identified by an independent commission of educators and business and political leaders appointed by Wharton in February 1984. It reported in January 1985 that the two principal problems still facing SUNY were red tape, which prevented the timely allocation of funds for necessities as basic as roof repair, and the low national standing of its research, graduate, and professional schools. To remedy the criticism about red tape, Wharton tenaciously lobbied Governor Mario Cuomo and the legislature for reform legislation. The result was a law, enacted in June 1985, that gave the system's campus administrators and presidents more flexibility in deciding how to spend their money and whom to hire. Extra funds, for instance, could be allocated to perfect already outstanding university centers such as those at Stony Brook and Buffalo.

Wharton, who on October 16, 1986, announced his intention to resign as chancellor, has said that he considers the flexibility legislation one of the major achievements of his nine-year tenure. His announcement came at a time when the larger task of upgrading SUNY's graduate programs was just beginning, and late in October, the university announced plans to bolster its graduate programs, an initiative that Wharton said he regretted he would not be there to see realized.

Throughout his career as an academic administrator, Wharton has pursued a parallel career as an economist and international affairs expert through serving on many boards and institutes. In June 1982 he was elected chairman of the board of trustees of the Rockefeller Foundation, succeeding Father Theodore M. Hesburgh. He is a trustee of the Aspen Institute for Humanistic Studies, the Council on Foreign Relations, the Foreign Policy Association, and the Council for Financial Aid to Education. He is also deputy chairman of the Federal Reserve Bank of New York. In 1983 he was appointed cochairman of the Commission on Security and Economic Assistance by Secretary of State George P. Shultz. From 1976 to 1983 he served as chairman of the United States State Department's Board for International Food and Agricultural Development, to which he was appointed by President Ford and reappointed by President Carter. He is also a past chairman of the National Association of State Universities and Land-Grant Colleges.

In February 1987 Wharton became chairman and chief executive officer of the Teachers Insurance Annuity Association and College Retirement Equities Fund, which, with its $54 billion in assets, is the nation's largest private pension system. Wharton, who received a salary of $89,250 as chancellor, will be paid $500,000 a year to run the fund, according to a report in the *New York Times* (October 16, 1986). He is the first university president to oversee the fund, which had been criticized by higher education officials as inflexible and out of step with the current financial scene. Those officials almost universally applauded the choice of Dr. Wharton, whose "enormous prestige," Robert Atwell, president of the American Council on Education, observed, promised to be invaluable, because "T.I.A.A.-C.R.E.F. at this time in its life needs the kind of visibility and attention [Wharton will bring] to its external activities." Of his decision to take on the new job, Wharton said he was "particularly attracted by the challenge" of running the pension system in an economic "environment of great flux and change."

Dr. Wharton is an athletically built six-footer, who now has a slight paunch. He is an elegant and gracious man, patrician in manner but with a ready laugh. In 1950 he married the former Dolores Duncan, who is now president of the Fund for Corporate Initiatives, Inc., and author of a book on contemporary Malaysian artists. They have two sons, Clifton 3d and Bruce. In 1977 Dr. Wharton received the Joseph C. Wilson Award in recognition of his service in Southeast Asia during the 1960s, and in 1983 he was selected to be in the first group of recipients of the President's Award on World Hunger. Dr. Wharton has published extensively on the problem of development, and his many writings include *Continuity and Change; Academic Greatness Under Stress* (East Lansing, 1971); *Subsistence Agriculture and Economic Development* (Aldine Publishing Company, 1969), of which he was editor; and *Patterns for Lifelong Learning* (Jossey-Bass, 1973), cowritten with Theodore M. Hesburgh.

References: *Chronicle of Higher Education* p1+ O 22 '86 por; *Ebony* 25:58+ Jl 1970 pors; *Newsday* mag p21+ D 17 '78 pors; *N Y Times* C p1+ Jl 6 '82 por, C p1+ Ag 30 '83, B p6 O 16 '86; Metcalf, George. *Up From Within: Today's New Black Leaders* (1979)

White, Betty

Jan. 17, 1922- Actress. Address: b. c/o William Morris Agency, 151 El Camino Dr., Beverly Hills, Calif. 90212

"My greatest talent is being able to be natural in front of the cameras," the vivacious television actress Betty White said in an interview some thirty years ago. At that time, she was already a television veteran, having starred in two television comedy series and served as a host for two talk shows, but it was not until the mid-1970s that she scored her first big success, as Sue Ann Nivens, the catty, man-hungry "Happy Homemaker" on the now legendary *Mary Tyler Moore Show*. Her mastery of "the field of sugary malice," to use the television critic Tom Shales's phrase, brought her two Emmy awards. She recently earned her fourth, for best actress in a comedy series, for her portrayal of Rose, the slow-witted innocent in the top-rated sitcom *The Golden Girls*.

An only child, Betty White was born on January 17, 1922, in Oak Park, Illinois, a suburb of Chicago. Her father was an electrical engineer; her mother, a housewife. Shortly thereafter, the Whites moved with their daughter to Los Angeles, California, where Betty attended the local public schools. It was while she was a student at Beverly Hills High

School that she first became interested in acting. During her years there, she appeared in a number of high school dramatic productions and wrote several plays, including her class's graduation play. For a time, she considered becoming a writer, but she eventually decided to devote herself to acting instead.

Following her graduation from high school, Betty White made her professional stage debut at the Bliss Hayden Little Theatre in Beverly Hills. Over the next few years, she played leading roles in many of the theatre's productions. She also performed occasionally in bit parts in some of the most popular radio shows of the day, among them *Blondie*, *This is Your FBI*, and *The Great Gildersleeve*. In the late 1940s Miss White found increasing opportunities for employment in the burgeoning television industry. Her credits for those years include frequent appearances on such local television shows as *Tom, Dick, and Harry*, the *Dick Haynes Joke Shop*, *Grab Your Phone*, and Al Jarvis' *Hollywood on Television*. After several years as Jarvis' on-air sidekick, she succeeded him as host of the show in the early 1950s.

Betty White landed her first starring role on national television in 1953, when she was cast as Elizabeth White, a comically perfect housewife in *Life with Elizabeth*, a situation comedy built around such flimsy plot lines as "Elizabeth's biscuits not turning out," according to the actress. "We didn't worry about relevance in the early days," she told Tom Shales in an interview for the *Washington Post* (September 11, 1977). "We were trying to be funny. We were more two-dimensional cartoon characters than three-dimensional real people." Although the series survived for only one season, Miss White, whose bubbly personality and all-American good looks charmed the television audience, was voted the "female personality viewers would most like to invite into their homes" in a *Tele-Views* popularity poll.

Her personal popularity notwithstanding, none of the television shows in which she starred during the 1950s was a ratings hit. *The Betty White Show*, a daytime talk show that she hosted in 1954, was axed by NBC after just eleven months on the air despite its Emmy nomination as the best daytime program of the year. Miss White struck out twice in the 1957-58 season—first with *A Date With the Angels*, a contrived domestic comedy about a newly married couple, Vickie and Gus Angel, that ABC canceled in midseason, then with a second edition of *The Betty White Show*. Recast as a comedy-variety program, *The Betty White Show*, which replaced *A Date With the Angels* in ABC's prime-time schedule in February 1958, was bumped from the roster after only a three-month run.

Disappointed by a string of flops, Betty White decided to avoid series television for awhile and concentrate instead on her developing career as a free-lance guest artist. Over the next dozen years, she was a frequent celebrity panelist on a number of popular game shows, including *To Tell the Truth*, *I've Got a Secret*, *The Match Game*,

Password, and the durable What's My Line? "It's like stealing money," she said of her game-show appearances, as quoted in TV Guide (July 28, 1974). "You sit down and play games with nice people." From 1959 to 1962 she also appeared regularly on The Jack Paar Show, a late-night favorite with viewers, and on Girl Talk, a syndicated program devoted to women's issues, and during the late 1960s she hosted a daily CBS radio feature called "Ask Betty White," in which she answered readers' questions on a variety of subjects.

Throughout that period Betty White often spent the summers performing in theatrical productions on the straw-hat circuit. It was during an engagement in a stock company staging of Critic's Choice, in the summer of 1962, that she and her costar, Allen Ludden, the host of Password, became romantically involved. By her own account "militantly single" since her divorce, in 1949, from Lane Allen, Miss White at first resisted Ludden's campaign to persuade her to marry him, but after a year, she capitulated. "It's true, I always said on the Tonight show and everywhere else that I'd never get married again," she told Bob Williams in an interview for the New York Post (April 12, 1963). "But Allen out-numbered me. He started in, and the children [Ludden, a widower, had three teenage children] joined—and even the two poodles got in the act. And I surrendered—willingly." In a joint interview six months after their wedding, on June 14, 1963, the pair talked about the enthusiastic response of the viewing public to the news of their marriage. Thousands of Password fans had written to voice their approval and offer their congratulations. "Apparently all over America, people had picked Betty for me and me for Betty," Ludden said, as quoted in the New York Post (December 8, 1963).

Betty White and Allen Ludden continued to play opposite one another in summer stock presentations of such plays as Brigadoon, Any Wednesday, and Guys and Dolls for several years, and Miss White carried on as a frequent panelist on television game shows, including Password. In 1971 she returned to regularly scheduled weekly television as the host of the syndicated half-hour program The Pet Set, an offbeat talk show featuring celebrity guests and their pets as well as experts in such areas as pet care, ecology, and wildlife preservation. Commenting on her years as a talk- and game-show regular, she told Jerry Buck, who interviewed her for the New York Post (October 31, 1977), "Once you get into the talk routine, producers won't trust you as an actress. They forget you started out as an actress."

One producer, however, did not forget. During a preproduction brainstorming session to discuss possible story lines for the fourth season of The Mary Tyler Moore Show, the top-rated CBS sitcom about Mary Richards (Miss Moore), the assistant producer of a daily newscast at a Minneapolis television station, Ed Weinberger, the series' line producer, proposed introducing a new character—a "Betty White type"—who would have an affair with the unseen husband of Phyllis Lindstrom,

Mary's tart-tongued landlady. Ironically, because Miss White was a long-time friend of Miss Moore's, the producers at first declined to offer her the part, fearing that she might prove to be unsuitable. But after auditioning ten actresses without success, they decided to take a chance and cast Miss White without a reading.

Betty White joined The Mary Tyler Moore Show in the fall of 1973, as Sue Ann Nivens, the star of "The Happy Homemaker" cooking show at the fictional station WJM-TV. On camera, Sue Ann was the cloyingly sweet epitome of frilly femininity; off camera, she was a sex-obsessed man hunter "after anything in pants," to use the actress' words. After years of playing what she has described as the "icky sweet girl," Miss White relished the opportunity to portray the calculating and predatory Sue Ann Nivens. "So many people [knew] me as that nice lady," she said, as quoted in TV Guide (July 20, 1974). "It was great fun for them to see that nice ladies sometimes have claws. For me, it was like being born again." Betty White made such a hit with viewers that she quickly became a series regular. Before the show ended its seven-year run, she had collected back-to-back Emmys, for the 1974-75 and 1975-76 seasons, for outstanding continuing performance by a supporting actress in a comedy series.

When The Mary Tyler Moore Show went off the air in 1977, its producer, MTM Enterprises, Inc., approached Betty White about doing a series of her own. "We all agreed it should not be the Sue Ann character again," she told Tom Shales. "She's a good hit-and-runner, not a sustainer." They eventually settled on Joyce Whitman, the temperamental star of a second-rate television police series called "Undercover Woman." "The new character I play has overtones of Sue Ann but not quite as much promiscuity," Miss White went on. "There's bitchiness, but with the new character, she doesn't strike first. She waits until somebody else strikes and then she lets 'em have it." More often than not, that "somebody" was Joyce Whitman's estranged husband (John Hillerman), with whom she hoped to reconcile although he insisted that they were incompatible.

The Betty White Show bowed on CBS on September 12, 1977, to mostly favorable reviews. Among its supporters was TV Guide's Robert MacKenzie, who appreciated the series for "recognizing that middle-aged people have sexual relations" and for "having the nerve to satirize the television business." As for its star, he continued in his review of November 19, 1977, "Miss White is a funny lady indeed and the mistress of a certain comedic territory. . . . Her way of delivering a sarcastic slice with a sunny smile is a lesson in comedy technique." Scheduled opposite the NBC Monday Night Movie and ABC's Monday Night Football, both of which finished the season among the top twenty, The Betty White Show never had the chance to develop a following. Trailing badly in the ratings, it was abruptly canceled in January 1978. "There is sadness in me I can't ignore—and a lot of embarrassment, too," Miss White admitted to Joel Kotkin of the *Washington Post* (January 9, 1978). "You feel you promised so much and delivered so little."

Although she was no longer associated with a weekly series, Betty White remained before the viewing public with frequent appearances on game shows, in miniseries such as *The Best Place To Be* (1979), and in made-for-television movies, among them *With This Ring* (1978), *Before and After* (1979), and *The Gossip Columnist* (1980). She also played a recurring role in the short-lived NBC comedy series *Mama's Family*, a spinoff of one of the running skits on *The Carol Burnett Show* starring Vicki Lawrence as the irascible matriarch of a large and contentious family. In January 1983 she made her debut as the host of *Just Men!*, a daytime game show in which female contestants tried to predict the answers male celebrities would give to an assortment of questions. "Everything about it is strictly from yuck . . . ," Tom Shales wrote in his evaluation of *Just Men!* for the *Washington Post* (January 4, 1983). "[It] is the litmus test for people who think the TV show that can make them physically ill hasn't been invented." Although Shales and other critics felt that Miss White was, in Shales's words, "terribly demeaned" by her role, her skill as a moderator earned her an Emmy award as the outstanding host of a game or audience participation show during the 1982–83 season.

In 1985 Betty White signed on for a leading role in *The Golden Girls*, a sassy situation comedy about four older women, all widowed or divorced, who share a house in Miami. Originally considered for the part of Blanche, the sexy Southern belle, Miss White ended up in the role of Rose, the gentle and naïve widow who is, as the actress put it, "just a little off-center." The key to the character "is her innocence," she explained to Dusty Saunders in an interview for the New York *Daily News* (May 26, 1986). "There's really nothing pretentious or conniving about her. . . . To Rose, life is a romantic musical, and she's waiting around to see how it all turns out. Meanwhile, she's humming her way through life." The other "golden girls" are Blanche (Rue McClanahan), Dorothy (Bea Arthur), an acerbic divorcée, and Sophia (Estelle Getty), Dorothy's intractable, outspoken mother.

A marked departure from conventional situation comedies, *The Golden Girls* set out to prove that "you don't self-destruct" after the age of fifty-five. "You have the same virtues and faults and joys and sorrows as anybody else . . . ," Betty White explained, as quoted in the syndicated newspaper supplement *USA Weekend* (September 15, 1985). "So it isn't the stereotypical aged person, it's just ladies who are all struggling to cope, and hopefully in a humorous way. But we let the scar tissue show every once in a while." One of the series' most popular episodes to date was "In a Bed of Rose's," in which Rose had to deal with the death—in her bedroom—of her married lover. Another revolved around her efforts to end a relationship with a midget she has been dating only to have him break with her first because she isn't Jewish.

Slotted into NBC's Saturday night schedule, *The Golden Girls* made its network debut in September 1985. To the surprise of many television insiders, who felt that Saturday was an unlikely night for adult comedy, the premiere ranked number one in the weekly Nielsen ratings, attracting an astonishing 43 percent share of the audience. In their reviews of the new series over the next few months, some critics complained about its "adolescent ribaldry," jokes that were "as obvious . . . as a broken arm," and occasionally "farfetched" plot lines, but no one could fault the superb ensemble playing of its four leading actresses. "[They] are the Marx Brothers or Sisters of TV sitcoms today," Marvin Kitman wrote in his television column for *Newsday* (September 16, 1985). "They can do 'the look,' the double-take, the throwaway line. They know how to squeeze the juice out of every line and situation." All four were nominated for Emmy awards, but it was Betty White who walked off with the honor. In her acceptance speech, she said, as quoted in *Parade* (October 26, 1986), "It was really for all four of us. We're a matched set. You can't split us up."

A trim five feet four inches tall, Betty White has short, curly blond hair, bright blue eyes, and a heart-shaped face, but as Helen Dudar observed more than twenty years ago, in a profile of the actress for the *New York Post* (December 8, 1963), "her most flamboyant features are the pair of perfect dimples that stamp her forever a girl born to promote the nutritional benefits of orange juice." In her leisure, she enjoys doing needlepoint and crewel embroidery. Since Alan Ludden's death in 1981, Miss White has shared her rustic home in Brentwood, California, and her seaside retreat up the coast in Carmel with two dogs and a cat. "I believe it's important to have only as many pets as you can relate to, one on one," she told Alan Carter of the New York *Daily News* (February 8, 1987). "Frankly, I don't know how I would exist without my 'kids.' When I come home at night, no matter how bad my day, I'm the most important thing in the world to them."

By her own account, Miss White has a special fondness for all creatures with "a leg on each corner," and she has for many years devoted time, energy, and money to animal welfare organizations, among them the Fund For Animals, the American Humane Association, and Pet Pride, a national humane society for cats. She was for three years president of the Morris Animal Foundation, which funds research on the diseases and health problems of domestic and zoo animals, and she is a long-time member of the board of directors of the Los Angeles Zoo. While on a promotional tour for *Betty White's Pet Love: How Pets Take Care of Us*, (Morrow, 1983), a book about the therapeutic effects of animals that she wrote with Thomas J. Watson, she set up a pet therapy program at Children's Hospital in Oakland, California. "Animals are her real work," one of her three stepchildren has said. "Acting is just a hobby." Miss White discussed acting, animals, marriage, and a variety of other topics in her book of reflections *Betty White in Person* (Doubleday, 1987).

References: *Ladies Home J* 103:30+ F '86 pors; *N Y Daily News* p27 F 8 '87 por; *Parade* p18 Je 22 '86 por; *People* 25:55+ Ja 6 '86 pors; *T V Guide* 22:10+ Jl 20 '74 por; *USA Weekend* p11+ S 15 '85 por; *Who's Who in America, 1986–87*

Willis, Bruce

Mar. 19, 1955– Actor. Address: b. c/o Picturemaker Productions, 20th Century-Fox Television, 10201 W. Pico Blvd., Bldg. 38, Los Angeles, Calif. 90035

Less than three years ago, Bruce Willis was a denizen of the New York City actors' ghetto, struggling to make ends meet between an occasional stage or television part by tending bar at a trendy Manhattan dance club. But after being cast as the ultra-hip private eye David Addison on *Moonlighting*, one of the ABC-TV network's few prime-time hit shows, the Emmy award-winning Willis has become one of Hollywood's hottest and most promising commodities. His comedic acting blends such unlikely styles as Cary Grant-like urbanity and Three Stooges silliness. To quote Harry Waters, a *Newsweek* critic, "There's never been a TV leading man like his David Addison, a loosey-goosey, finger-poppin', doo-woppin' wise guy with the fastest mouth in prime time."

Willis and his costar Cybill Shepherd, who plays private detective Maddie Hayes, have become the Nick and Nora Charles—without wedding bands—of the weaned-on-the-tube baby boom generation. With their sassy repartee and high-voltage sexual electricity, the thus-far-platonic Addison and Hayes teased the nation's television audience for two years with the question: "When will Maddie and David ever 'get horizontal,'" as Bruce Willis himself has put it. Moreover, along with Don Johnson of the hit TV show *Miami Vice*, Willis is considered an avatar of the New Machismo of the 1980s, the new-wave video masculinity that unites postfeminist vulnerability and the hardboiled suavity of old-fashioned tough guys like Humphrey Bogart and John Garfield.

Bruce Willis was born on March 19, 1955, in Germany, where his father, David Willis, a serviceman with the United States Army, was stationed. In 1957 the Willis family returned to the United States, settling in the small town of Carneys Point, New Jersey, where David Willis, who was descended from what his son called "a long line of welders and mechanics," found work at the Camden Shipyard, and in his spare time operated a machine repair shop with one of his brothers. He and his German-born wife, Marlene, reared a family of three boys and one girl, with Bruce being the oldest sibling.

Carneys Point is situated on the Delaware River in southern New Jersey, not far from the Pennsylvania and Delaware state lines and seventy miles inland from Freehold, the hometown of Bruce Springsteen. Ringed by the slightly larger municipality of Penns Grove, Carneys Point, like its encircling twin, is a blue-collar community whose economic life subsists on factories and chemical plants, especially those owned by E. I. du Pont Nemours & Company, Inc., the chief employer for the towns' predominantly ethnic population. As Bruce Willis recalled in an interview with *Newsweek* (September 8, 1986), "When I was growing up, I thought everyone was Italian."

At Penns Grove High School, Willis was an irrepressible cutup, precisely the kind of devil-may-care prankster his TV alter ego, David Addison, might have been as a teenager. Although Willis' shenanigans endeared him to his fellow students, who elected him president of the student council, his teachers regarded him as a troublemaking "bad boy." And when racial discord at Penns Grove High flared into violence, Willis was one of the students singled out as an instigator and expelled. For the remainder of the academic year, policemen with guard dogs patrolled the corridors, and Willis' father was forced to hire an attorney to appeal to the school board on behalf of his son. As Bruce Willis recounted in an interview with Fred Schruers for *Rolling Stone* (March 27, 1986), " . . . This lawyer was like Perry . . . Mason. Very soft-spoken, . . . he went to each teacher and said, 'Did you actually see Bruce?' They said, 'No, I . . . ' And he said, 'Thank you very much.' They reinstated me, and I graduated." It was in high school that Willis earned the sobriquet of "Bruno," an affectionate nickname that persisted through his years as a New York bartender and is still used by his closest friends. And although he had been afflicted by a stutter since the age of about eight, he was active in Penns Grove's drama club. Portending his future, Willis' stammer would vanish any time an audience assembled before him.

After graduating, Willis took a job with the du Pont plant in nearby Deepwaters, New Jersey, where his father, no longer self-employed, still works. In charge of ferrying a work crew around the plant in a truck, Willis lasted at du Pont until a fellow driver was killed while motoring past a building that exploded while chemicals were being mixed inside. "They found parts of him all over the place," Willis told *Rolling Stone*. "I wasn't that shook by it, but I saw how the older guys, guys there for ten or twenty years, took it. They were gone, just white. I quit about a week later."

For a time, Willis hung out in bars and, as a lover of soul music who had taken up the mouth harp in high school, played harmonica for a local blues band called "Loose Goose." He soon found work as a night security guard at a nuclear generating station then under construction, and eventually enrolled at Montclair State College, where tuition fees for state residents were low and the theatre curriculum was outstanding. There Willis excelled as Brick in Tennessee Williams' *Cat on a Hot Tin Roof* and began cutting classes to travel to Manhattan to audition for parts in Off Broadway productions. One of his Montclair State professors, Jerry Rockwood, told Fred Schruers that he had instructed other young actors with as much talent as Willis, but "what they didn't have was Bruce's aggression."

When in January 1977 he was cast in an Off Broadway play called *Heaven and Earth,* Willis quit school and moved to Manhattan. There he lived in a long and narrow "railroad" apartment on West Forty-ninth Street and resolved to work at the actor's trade for as many years as it would take him to break into show business. He chose New York over Hollywood, where he might have used his charm or sheer force of personality to win television roles, because he wanted to learn his craft by "working, onstage and Off Broadway, . . . just working in front of a house," as he explained in the *Rolling Stone* interview.

In the summer of 1979 he began to get regular exposure before a live audience when he was admitted to the six-member performing cast of Barbara Contardi's First Amendment Comedy Theatre, a workshop-repertory group on West Twenty-second Street, where Willis had been taking classes. Two years later he landed the part of a Robber Baron-era railroad magnate in a play called *Railroad Bill,* which was staged at the Labor Theatre. Shortly after that, Willis got his first Off Broadway lead, in *Bayside Boys,* receiving critical praise for his portrayal of a domineering construction worker whose marriage is falling apart.

Throughout his years in New York, Willis supported himself by working as a bartender, including a long stint in the early 1980s at the Cafe Central, a popular Upper West Side hangout for hip show business celebrities. "He was

outrageous," one of his fellow bartenders told Harry Waters, who wrote about Willis in *Gentlemen's Quarterly* (October 1986). "He used to roller-skate into the place dressed in huge parachute pants, headbands and ripped T-shirts. . . . He was into punk years before its time." One of Willis' women friends from New York told Waters that "what used to most crack [her] up was seeing him suddenly stop wiping glasses and break into a rhythm-and-blues number." "He was always singing, or being funny, or playing his harmonica," she said. "And he was no lech. You could tell he genuinely liked women because he really talked to them. He knew he had something, but he never tried to push it. Maybe he was preparing himself for not being snowed by fame." The brash and self-confident Willis was not cowed by the Hollywood superstars whom he met, and charmed, while working at Cafe Central. "I would [shoot the bull] with them and . . . crack jokes," he told Harry Waters. "One night Sam Shepard and I talked about cars for like two or three hours. And so there was never any pressure on me to say, 'Oh, God, these people are the icons of the business.' To me, they were just real people."

In the meantime, Willis aggressively pursued his career in the intensely competitive world of acting in Manhattan. "Even when the notice said, 'Don't phone, don't come by,' I would do it anyway," Willis told *Rolling Stone*. "Find some clever way, or sometimes not so clever. Just blunt, crash in the door and say, 'Look, here's the picture, let me read.' The most important thing is getting the job." His tenacity paid off in the form of roles in B movies like *In Search of the Guru* and a television commercial for Levi Strauss's 501 blue jeans. In 1984 his career received a boost when he succeeded his friend Will Patton in the leading role of Eddie in *Fool for Love,* a hit play by Sam Shepard that had been enjoying a long Off Broadway run. It was while he was tending bar at a trendy downtown disco, Kamikaze, that Willis got his first significant television part. While starring in *Fool for Love,* he had impressed Bonnie Timmerman, the casting director for *Miami Vice,* NBC's crime and suspense show. In 1985 she and *Miami Vice*'s executive producer, Michael Mann, featured him as a vicious, wife-beating weapons smuggler with CIA connections in an episode called "No Exit."

After being rejected for the part of Madonna's musician boyfriend in the film *Desperately Seeking Susan,* Willis was one of the last of the 3,000 actors to read for the part of David Addison in *Moonlighting*. He showed up for the audition wearing khaki fatigues, an earring, and a spiky-punk haircut, but his affinity for the Addison character, whom he thought of as "a guy on the edge who's horsing around out there where the air's real thin," was obvious. As *Moonlighting*'s creator and executive producer, Glenn Gordon Caron, told *Gentleman's Quarterly,* when he conceived the Addison character he had explained to the curious: "'Jeez, there are no men on television.' I meant there were a lot of boys on television, and a lot of white wine being consumed, and a lot of breathy conversations, but not a whole lot of real male behavior. I wanted a guy who plants his feet and speaks his mind and deals with women as he deals with men." Caron instantly recognized that Willis had exactly the right attitude for Addison, a wisecracking chatterbox whose charm is poised between cool aloofness and impudent narcissism, between quick-thinking resourcefulness and boyish impetuosity. And when Willis did a screen test with Cybill Shepherd, who had already been cast as Maddie Hayes, Caron knew that *Moonlighting* would have what *Newsweek* called "potent sexual chemistry." "The first time Bruce and I were in a room together," Miss Shepherd has recalled, "there was a reaction. Sparks flew. . . . It's chemistry, baby. Either you got it or you don't, and David and Maddie have it."

Although Caron cast Willis as Addison over the objections of network executives, who felt the young and comparatively unknown actor simply did not look like a leading man, *Moonlighting* made its prime-time debut in the spring of 1985. It took a full season for the show to become more than a cult favorite, but within one year *Moonlighting* became ABC's only regular entry in the Nielsen Top Ten ratings and had received a record sixteen Emmy nominations, including one for Willis as Best Actor in a weekly dramatic series. The reasons for its success are varied. Basing the show to some extent on film classics of the screwball comedy genre such as *Bringing Up Baby* and *The Philadelphia Story*, Caron and his staff of writers have updated the perennial battle-of-the-sexes for TV in the mid-1980s. Moreover, *Moonlighting* is a refreshing departure from TV's typical cut-to-the-car-chase fare, insofar as the show's producers have fashioned an adult *talk* show, with some of the randiest banter ever heard on the tube. (For example, David playfully embraces Maddie, who exclaims: "Be serious!" "I just had my hand on your behind," he ripostes. "If I get any more serious, they'll move us to cable." Or, she: "David, you're in my seat." He: "Please, Maddie. There are children watching.") Breaking again with prime-time predictability, *Moonlighting* can be as moody as a Miles Davis trumpet solo one week, and as madcap as the Keystone Cops in the following one. But Glenn Gordon Caron believes that the show's appeal basically lies in its placing of David and Maddie in "emotional rather than physical jeopardy." He elaborated on his theory in *Newsweek*: "It's, 'If I care for you, and I suspect that maybe you don't care as much for me, what do I do?' I think the audience sees this and says, 'OK, *now* something is at stake here. Your heart is on the table.' There's always a little ache running underneath everything."

Moonlighting is popular, too, for the way it reflects "an intriguing reversal in the psychic direction of our cathode heroes," to quote *Newsweek*'s Harry Waters. In the 1970s some of TV's most popular leading men—talk-show host Phil Donahue, *MASH*'s Alan Alda, and Daniel J. Travanti of *Hill Street Blues*—were sensitive exemplars of feminist consciousness-raising. But in the postfeminist 1980s it is the soulful machismo of actors like Don Johnson and Bruce Willis that has sauntered back to center stage. In the New York *Daily News Magazine* (September 14, 1986), Roger Director, one of *Moonlighting*'s writers, discussed the advent of the *New* New Man, as exemplified by the David Addison character: "This is not Alan Alda. This guy isn't afraid to be a sexist. But what you really have between David . . . and Maddie . . . is two very different people who engage in sexual sparring because they're attracted to each other. There's nothing new about that at all. The main difference is that there's a certain political and social consciousness from Addison's side, which is a necessary part of the whole social equation today."

Emulating his character in *Moonlighting*—who routinely breaks into song—Willis recorded *Bruce Willis: The Return of Bruno* (Motown, 1987), an album of soul and rhythm and blues songs. The album sold 500,000 copies and spawned a hit single ("Respect Yourself") and HBO television musical special, but many critics panned Willis as a poseur with a nondescript voice. Also in 1987, Willis made his motion picture debut in *Blind Date* (Tri-Star Pictures,) a fairly well-received comedy directed by Blake Edwards. In the fall of 1987 Willis received the Emmy award for best actor in a drama series.

Although his *Moonlighting* persona is loquacious, Willis himself only rarely grants interviews to journalists, so that his reluctance to confess to *TV Guide* the sins of his womanizing past or play the part of a jovial talking head on the *Tonight Show* had fueled the perception in some Hollywood circles that Willis is as arrogant as the character he plays on TV. But, as Willis told Fred Schruers, in refraining from talk-show accessibility, he has been unfairly characterized as a "snob." "When the show first happened," he said, "there was a lot of stuff goin' on inside me that I had to figure out. . . . And I really didn't feel I had that much to say. I don't get that—because you are all of a sudden highly visible, do your opinions carry more weight? . . . I want to keep my private life private."

To ensure his privacy, Willis lives in exclusive Hollywood Hills, in a large house equipped with a swimming pool and surrounded by a six-foot-high wall. Nevertheless, Willis seems not to have "gone Hollywood." His closest friends are still those who were part of his Manhattan gang, and among the few concessions he has made to sudden wealth have been his acquisition of a black 1966 Corvette and an expensive wardrobe. Willis refuses to talk about his love life, but he is often seen in public in the company of Sherry Rivera, the ex-wife of the broadcast journalist Geraldo Rivera and has been linked romantically to the actress Demi Moore. Willis has explained that he especially likes Italian women, because he grew up among them in Carneys Point.

Those who work with Willis feel that his future in acting is unlimited, and according to Glenn Gordon Caron, the public has seen "only about ten percent" of what he is capable of doing. One of the show's producers, Jay Daniel, attributes the improvisational texture of Willis' performance to the actor's untrammeled concentration and his capacity for hard work. "I've been on TV shows," Daniels told *Gentlemen's Quarterly* "where the actors come in, hit their marks and then ask, 'When will we wrap for lunch?' That's just not in Bruce. We'll be on the set at 8 P.M., everyone exhausted, and he'll still be trying to attack a line he's already done six times in a new way." "He's attractive *and* he's funny, which not too many people have had," Cybill Shepherd said of her costar. "Cary Grant epitomize[d] it, maybe William Powell, but Bruce has a different quality from anyone I've ever seen."

IIis "different quality" appealed so much to Edgar Bronfman Jr., the young president of the House of Seagram, that Willis was signed to a multiyear contract, worth between five and seven million dollars, to promote Seagram Golden Wine Cooler, which is being targeted for the young urban professional market. "Bruce is more than just hip," Bronfman has said. "His overriding quality is charm. He can be irreverent, funny, and serious. He can do all those things but do them in a fashion as to be infinitely appealing. That twinkle in his eye lets him get away with a lot."

Although Willis is at work on "Sunset," his second feature film, he told *Rolling Stone* that his chief desire is "to go back to New York and do something onstage." "I miss that control," he said. "You're the master, it's your performance, and there's no take two." He says that his acting style is based on the work of some of Hollywood's wackiest comedians: Bob Hope, Jerry Lewis, and, especially, Curly of the Three Stooges. "People look at me kind of weird when I tell them this," Willis remarked in the *Gentlemen's Quarterly* interview, "but the Stooges' humor has never been duplicated. . . . No one has even attempted it."

References: Newsday II p9 Je 2 '86; por; Newsweek 106:75 O 28 '85 pors, 108:46+ S 8 '86 pors; Rolling Stone p46+ Mr 27 '86 pors

Wilson, August

1945– Writer. Address; b. c/o New American Library, 1633 Broadway, New York City, N.Y. 10019

When August Wilson learned at his home in St. Paul, Minnesota, that *Fences*, then running on Broadway, had won the 1907 Pulitzer Prize for drama, his reaction was one of gratification that his play about a black American family in the 1950s had touched a general audience. Because of the humanity of his drama of domestic and social clash, people of widely different backgrounds had been able to recognize something of themselves. Like *Ma Rainey's Black Bottom*, which had introduced Wilson to Broadway theatregoers in 1984, *Fences* belongs to a projected cycle of ten plays in which Wilson proposes to look at a central issue confronting blacks in each decade of the twentieth century and question the choices that they have made and the directions that they have taken. With their metaphorical language and their rhythm and intonation of dialogue, his plays draw much of their emotional impact from skills acquired in many years of writing poetry. New American Library published *Ma Rainey's Black Bottom* in 1985 and *Fences* in 1986.

August Wilson was born in 1945 in Pittsburgh, Pennsylvania, and grew up in a family of six children in that city's Hill district, a black slum community. He has said that the "cultural environment" of *Fences*, which is set in a black neighborhood of an industrial city like Pittsburgh, stems from his own life. The father-son relationship depicted in that play was not part of his actual

experience, however, since he barely knew his father, August Wilson, an irresponsible white man, a baker of German origin who did not live with the family. But some traits of the fictional father in *Fences* may have been borrowed from Wilson's black stepfather, David Bedford, who figured in his adolescent years.

By means of welfare checks and then wages from a cleaning job, August's mother, Daisy Wilson, who had moved to Pittsburgh from North Carolina, raised her children in a two-room cold-water apartment. A reader since the age of four, August Wilson recalls that he was always fascinated with words themselves, how they are formed and what they mean. How they sound also became important. On entering high school, however, he proved to be a disappointing student. In an article on Wilson in the *New York Times Magazine* (March 15, 1987), Samuel G. Freedman suggests some reasons why: "bricks through the window when the family tried moving into mostly white Hazelwood; 'Nigger, go home' notes on his desk at an overwhelmingly white parochial high school; accusations of cheating when a term paper on Napoleon seemed a bit too good to have been done by a black boy."

Napoleon, indeed, whom Wilson conceived of as a great hero of history with a strong will to power, seems to have been a sustaining inspiration after he dropped out of the ninth grade at fifteen. The public library apparently had become his preferred classroom at about the age of twelve, when he began to read the work of Ralph Ellison, Richard Wright, Langston Hughes, and other black writers. In his late teens he further explored in books the life of blacks in America, seeking out its values and a place for himself. Preparing to become a writer too, he began to observe the behavior and listen to the speech of people around him, on the street corners of Pittsburgh and in the jobs he held as a cook in coffee shops and as a stock clerk.

April 1, 1965, in August Wilson's book of days, is his birthdate as a poet. It is the day he bought his first typewriter, with $20 that his sister, Freda Wilson, a student at Fordham University, sent him for writing a term paper for her, "Two Violent Poets— Robert Frost and Carl Sandburg." Wilson's reading of a range of American poets, including John Berryman and Imamu Amiri Baraka, and of the Welsh poet Dylan Thomas, noticeably influenced his own early poetry. Some of his poems were published in little magazines like *Black World* and *Black Lines* (Summer 1971 and September 1972). Freedman pointed out in his *New York Times Magazine* article, "He is one part Dylan Thomas and one part Malcolm X, a lyric poet fired in the kiln of black nationalism"—a description that Wilson himself regards as accurate.

"I became involved in the Black Power movement in the late '60s, early '70s," Wilson told Charlayne Hunter-Gault, who interviewed him for public television's *MacNeil/Lehrer NewsHour* on April 30, 1987. "I called myself a Black Nationalist then, and I still consider myself a Black Nationalist." It was as a medium to express his political beliefs that he first became attracted to the theatre. His playwriting had developed from hard work on the dialogue of his short stories in an effort to make the words of his characters ring true.

Together with the playwright and teacher Rob Penny, during the 1960s Wilson founded a black activist theatre company, Black Horizon on the Hill, which produced his early plays and various cultural programs. His purpose in the theatre then was to "politicize the community and raise consciousness." Regardless of his concern with the causes of black nationalism, propaganda in his plays by no means excluded the literary claims of poetry and drama. "I think black theatre of the '60s, was angry, didactic, and a pushing outward," Hillary DeVries quoted him as saying in the *Christian Science Monitor* (October 16, 1984). "What I try to do is an inward examination. . . . I think the black Americans have the most dramatic story of all mankind to tell."

In 1978 Wilson went to St. Paul to visit his friend Claude Purdy, who had worked in the theatre in Pittsburgh before becoming director of Penumbra, a black theatre in St. Paul. Drawn to the comparatively more relaxed atmosphere of St. Paul, Wilson decided to make his home there and took a job with the Science Museum of Minnesota writing scripts for short theatrical pieces to accompany its exhibitions. He also became involved in the work of the Playwrights Center in Minneapolis.

Once away from Pittsburgh, Wilson began to hear as if for the first time the speech of the blacks of his old neighborhood. Its rhythm and modulation were echoed in the words of his characters in the plays that he wrote at the urging of Purdy. *Jitney*, a realistic drama set in a Pittsburgh gypsy-cab station, was produced at the Allegheny Repertory Theater in Pittsburgh in 1982. He tried his emerging voice as a playwright also on a script with a town-versus-country theme, *Fullerton Street*, named after a Pittsburgh street no longer in existence.

When asked in an interview for *New York Newsday* (April 20, 1987) about his primary literary influences, Wilson replied, "The blues would be the first. . . . I see the blues as a book of literature and it influences everything I do. . . . Blacks' cultural response to the world is contained in blues." He was profoundly stirred in 1965 by a recording of the legendary blues singer Bessie Smith, who had taken lessons from the pioneering Gertrude (Ma) Rainey. The music of a Ma Rainey album that he bought in 1976 fused with the idea of exploitation that preoccupied him at the time to germinate *Ma Rainey's Black Bottom*.

Because Wilson's intention was to depict an imaginary incident in the career of Ma Rainey, not to write a biography, he avoided the extensive study of her life that might have had a "straightjacket" effect on his portrait. His interest was in what lay behind the blues, music that he believes represents the total experience of blacks in the earlier South. In the play Ma Rainey herself reflects on the nature of the blues: "White folks don't understand about the blues. They hear it come out, but they don't know how it got there. They don't understand that's life's way of talking. You don't sing to feel better. You sing 'cause that's a way of understanding life."

"Ma Rainey's Black Bottom," which refers to a black clog dance popular in the 1920s, is the name of one of the songs that Ma Rainey and her back-up band are recording in a dingy Chicago studio one afternoon in March 1927. A massive, bejeweled and befeathered, regal figure, Ma Rainey behaves contemptuously toward her white manager and the white record company owner, indulging outrageously in temperamental whims. After all, she, the Mother of the Blues, is the one who fattens their coffers with sales of her records. But her garish borrowings from white stardom do not lead her into self-deception about her "place": "When I've finished recording, it's just like I'd been some whore, and they roll over and put their pants on."

The dramatic focus of *Ma Rainey's Black Bottom,* however, is not on the title character, but on the young trumpet player, Levee, one of her four talented accompanists, who joke and reminisce among themselves in the studio before and after Ma Rainey sings her songs. While making each musician representative of a different point of view in coping with racism, Wilson keeps to his aim as a playwright "to unmask the stereotypes, to uncover the humanness behind that." Brash, ambitious, and rebellious, Levee wants to substitute his own "swinging" version of "Ma Rainey's Black Bottom" for the old-fashioned one Ma insists upon singing. He moves on a current of change that he hopes will bring him fame as a jazz composer and band leader, rejecting the past with its indignities and enraging memories, especially of his witnessing in boyhood the rape of his mother by a gang of white men. His bitter protest, "The white man's god takes the nigger's prayers and throws them in the garbage pail," forebodes a more violent eruption and tragic outcome.

Completing *Ma Rainey's Black Bottom* in December 1981, Wilson submitted it for consideration to the National Playwrights Conference, which gave it a staged reading the following year at the Eugene O'Neill Theater in Waterford, Connecticut. The conference's artistic director, Lloyd Richards, who is also artistic director of the Yale Repertory Theater in New Haven and dean of the Yale School of Drama, staged a production of the play at the Yale Repertory Theater in April 1984. After a brief run at the University of Pennsylvania's Annenberg Center in Philadelphia, *Ma Rainey's Black Bottom* opened at the Cort Theater on Broadway on October 11, 1984. It closed the following June, completing 275 performances and winning the New York Drama Critics Circle Award and several Tony nominations.

"In *Ma Rainey's Black Bottom,* the writer August Wilson sends the entire history of black America crashing down upon our heads," Frank Rich commented in the *New York Times* (October 12, 1984). "The play is a searing inside account of what white racism does to its victims—and it floats on the same authentic artistry as the blues music it celebrates. Harrowing as *Ma Rainey's* can be, it is also funny, salty, carnal, and lyrical." Many other critics gave the play equally warm reviews, especially praising Wilson's sure command of characterization and dialogue. But some complained of "talkiness," a flawed structure, a contrived and melodramatic ending, and an inappropriate,

though catchy, title. *Ma Rainey's,* however, left even its more severe critics, like Stanley Kauffmann of the *Saturday Review* and Paul Berman of the *Nation,* with abundant hopes and expectations of Wilson as a playwright.

While New Yorkers were applauding *Ma Rainey's Black Bottom,* Wilson's *Fences* was progressing on its four-year journey from its staged reading at the Eugene O'Neill Center's 1983 National Playwrights Conference to its New York opening at the 46th Street Theater on March 26, 1987. Along the way Richards, its director, Wilson, and the cast had shaped and polished the play in presentations at the Yale Repertory Theater, the Goodman Theater in Chicago, and the Seattle Repertory Theater, and in Carole Shorenstein Hays's production in San Francisco.

James Earl Jones, who had earned stardom twenty years earlier in another powerful drama of black American life, Howard Sackler's *The Great White Hope,* headed the cast of *Fences* as Troy Maxson, a garbage collector and an embittered former baseball player in the Negro Leagues of the 1950s, when blacks had not yet been admitted to the major leagues en masse. Among the few significant careers open to blacks have been those in music and sports, but in instances of what Wilson has called "missed possibilities," those are the endeavors that frustrate the protagonists of both *Ma Rainey's* and *Fences.*

In contrast to the prevailing stereotype of a black male, Wilson has explained, he wanted to present a positive image of responsibility, and he began *Fences* with a mental picture of a man standing with a baby in his arms. His fallible, perverse hero, Troy, is a dominating father who prides himself on working hard to provide for his family. Yet he alienates his son by opposing his athletic career, either because of jealousy or because of a desire to protect the teenager from his own disappointment in baseball. He then destroys his marriage by betraying his gentle, patient wife in an adulterous affair and appeals to her to raise his infant when his girlfriend dies in childbirth. Also compelling him to self-justification is his treatment of his brother, mentally disabled by a war injury, whose government compensation he highhandedly appropriates to build his own house.

Besides the 1987 Pulitzer Prize for drama, *Fences* won the New York Drama Critics Circle Award for best play and four Tony awards, including one for best play of the 1986–87 Broadway season. Reviewers compared *Fences* to Arthur Miller's *Death of a Salesman* and Lorraine Hansberry's *A Raisin in the Sun,* among other notable American plays. In the opinion of William A. Henry 3d, drama critic of *Time* (April 6, 1987), "Wilson's greatest gift is his ability to make sense of anger; he writes naturalistic scenes of genial humor turning into an explosive violence that flows from his characters and from the warping effect racism has had upon them. . . . In craftsmanship, poignance and lingering impact, *Fences* represents a major step forward for Wilson."

From time to time in *Fences*, Troy works on a fence he is building around his yard at the request of his wife. As his friend remarks, "Some people build fences to keep people out, . . . and some build fences to keep people in." The deliberately ambiguous title involves choices, underscoring Wilson's concern with the theme of responsibility. Repeatedly in press interviews he has discussed his exploration in his plays of the likelihood that in the past blacks collectively have made choices not in accordance with their cultural values and best interests. "By not developing their own tradition, a more African response to the world, they lost their sense of identity," he once observed, as quoted in the *Chicago Tribune* (September 16, 1984).

The move of blacks from the agrarian South to the industrial North is a choice that can be rife with hardships, as some of Wilson's migrants find in *Joe Turner's Come and Gone*. Its setting is a boardinghouse in Pittsburgh in 1911, when sons and daughters of former slaves were trying to find new homes. After laboring for seven years in forced servitude to Joe Turner, the bounty hunter of the title, Herald Loomis arrives at the boardinghouse with his young daughter, looking for his wife. But his search is really a metaphysical quest for self-knowledge, spiritual roots toward which black music and ancient African myths offer him guidance.

On the first lap of its tour of regional theatres, *Joe Turner's Come and Gone* had its premiere in May 1986 at the Yale Repertory Theater, a production on which Wilson again collaborated with Richards. In his review for the *New York Times* (May 6, 1986), Frank Rich found it to be "potentially its author's finest achievement yet . . . as rich in religious feeling as in historical detail." A forthcoming play in Wilson's cycle, *The Piano Lesson*, which is set in the 1930s, also deals with choices. At issue, as the author explained in a *Chicago Tribune* interview, is "what do you do with your legacy? There's 130 years of family history in the piano that you see on stage. What does the family do with it?"

After moving to St. Paul, August Wilson married Judy Oliver, a social worker. By a previous marriage he has a daughter, Sakina Ansari. In his many interviews and public appearances since *Ma Rainey's* brought him celebrity, he has impressed others as a reflective, articulate man of "quiet affability and almost old-world politeness," to quote the description of one journalist. Wilson's artistic mentor is the black painter Romare Bearden, who, he has said, "illuminates black life with a humanity and richness and fullness." The qualities that Lloyd Richards sees in Wilson himself are much like Bearden's: "wit and wisdom and great respect for life."

References: *Chicago Tribune* 13 p13+ S 16 '84 por, 13 p12+ F 9 '86 por, 5 p7 Ap 10 '87 por; *Christian Sci Mon* p29+ O 16 '84 por, p1+ Mr 27 '87 por; *Essence* p51+ Ag '87 por; *N Y Newsday* II p11+ Mr 27 '87 por, p47 Ap 20 '87 por; *N Y Times* C p12 O 22 '84 por; *N Y Times Mag* p36+ Mr 15 '87 pors; *Newsday* II p4+ O 7 '84; *Washington Post* F p1+ O 4 '87 por; *Contemporary Authors* vol 115 (1985); *Contemporary Literary Criticism* vol 39 (1985)

Winfrey, Oprah

Jan. 29, 1954– Talk show hostess; actress. Address: b. WLS-TV, 190 N. State St., Chicago, Ill. 60601

Since 1984 Oprah Winfrey, who in the view of the *Newsday* columnist Marvin Kitman, is "a real person in the fake world of TV," has become one of the most watched television talk show hosts in the United States, as well as one of the most promising of the new generation of film actresses. Her Chicago-based *Oprah Winfrey Show* has been credited by some observers with having dethroned the monarch of the daytime talk shows, Phil Donahue, in the city where he had reigned for almost two decades. *The Oprah Winfrey Show*, which in the opinion of Liam Lacey of the Toronto *Globe and Mail*, resembles "a combination of cabaret revue and group therapy session," was launched on 138 television stations in September 1986 by King World Productions with projected earnings that would make it the largest-grossing program in the history of first-run syndication.

Oprah Winfrey's screen debut in Steven Spielberg's *The Color Purple* in 1985 was honored with nominations for both Academy and Golden Globe awards, and she was immediately cast in another film, *Native Son*, released in 1986. Miss Winfrey attributes her success to her tendency to follow her own instincts. "Dishing the dirt and meddling in other folks's business is what I do best," she has explained. "In acting you lose your personality in favor of the character you're playing, but you use it to provide energy for your character. The same way on my show. I lose it and use it to concentrate on bringing the most out of my guests." In February 1987 the *Oprah Winfrey Show* won an Emmy Award for television's best talk show, and Miss Winfrey received an Emmy for best talk-show host.

The daughter of Vernita Lee and Vernon Winfrey, Oprah Gail Winfrey was born on a farm in Kosciusko, Mississippi, on January 29, 1954. Her parents had intended to name her Orpah, after Ruth's sister-in-law in the Bible, but the midwife transposed the name's second and third letters on the birth certificate, and she became Oprah. Her unmarried parents separated and Miss Winfrey spent her earliest years on an isolated farm with her maternal grandmother, a harsh disciplinarian. There she became her "own entertainment," as she put it, "play-acting" with a corncob doll, chickens, and the cows she took to pasture every morning. Instructed by her grandmother, she learned to read at the age of two and a half, and, even earlier, had blossomed as a public speaker at the age of two, when she addressed the congregation of a rural church on the topic "Jesus rose on Easter Day." When she was enrolled in kindergarten, she promptly wrote a note that pointed out in no uncertain terms that she belonged in the first grade, and her astonished teacher had her promoted. After completing that academic year, she skipped directly to the third grade.

At the age of six, Oprah Winfrey was sent north to join her mother and two half brothers in the Milwaukee ghetto. Deprived of the farm animals she once had played with, and without the money to buy a dog, she kept cockroaches in a jar as substitute pets. Because of her precocious elocutionary skills, she was invited to recite poetry at black social clubs and church teas, where she became known as "the little speaker." At twelve, during a visit to her father in Nashville, she earned $500 for a speech she delivered at a church. That evening she announced that she knew what she wanted to do for a living—be "paid to talk."

Back in Milwaukee, she discovered that her mother was still absorbed in trying to make ends meet by supplementing her fifty-dollar-a-month domestic's salary with whatever welfare was available, and she found comparatively little time to devote to Oprah. In the absence of continual parental attention, acts of sexual abuse by a series of trusted men, which had begun when Oprah was nine, resumed. Each incident left her guilty, confused, and afraid to report the offense.

She began staging dramatic, if minor, acts of delinquency. When her mother refused to replace a pair of butterfly-framed glasses that Oprah thought were not fashionable enough for the all-white school she was being bused to, she faked a robbery by smashing the glasses, ransacking the house, and feigning amnesia. During that period she also stole from her mother's purse and once flung her moth-

er's jewelry out of a window. On one occasion she spotted Aretha Franklin getting out of a limousine and told her such a convincing story about being abandoned that the singer gave her a hundred dollars "to get home to Ohio." Oprah Winfrey then promptly holed up at a Milwaukee hotel. When, after three days, she returned home penniless and in the custody of her minister, her mother dragged her to a detention center, only to find there were no beds. At that point, the beleaguered mother had Vernon Winfrey take his daughter to live in Nashville with him and his wife Zelma.

"My father saved my life," Oprah Winfrey told Randy Banner of the *New York Daily News* (September 7, 1986). A barber who became a member of the Nashville city council, he was a strict disciplinarian who provided her with guidance, late-night discussions, and books. He refused to let her have dinner unless she added five new words to her vocabulary every day, and he demanded a weekly book report. Under his stern regimen, she began to excel in school, both in and out of the classroom. She presided over the high school council, joined the drama club, and distinguished herself in oratory and debate. When she was sixteen she won an Elks Club oratorical contest that guaranteed her a full scholarship to Tennessee State University after her graduation, and in the following year she was invited to a White House Conference on Youth. While still in high school she was crowned Miss Fire Prevention by WVOL, a local radio station. In addition to awarding her the title and a Longines watch, the station hired her to read newscasts and for a few months before her high school graduation, she headed for work each day as soon as classes ended, to become, every half hour on the hour, the voice of WVOL.

During her freshman year at Tennessee State University, Oprah Winfrey became Miss Black Nashville and Miss Tennessee, relying on her poise and talent to compensate for what she has described as her "fudge brownie" skin color, which, she thought, might conceivably handicap her in competition with "gingerbreads" and "vanilla creams." In 1971 she was also a contestant in the Miss Black America Pageant. When the local CBS television station offered her a job she turned it down twice, but as a nineteen-year-old sophomore, when her speech teacher reminded her that job offers from CBS were the reason "people go to college," she accepted a position with WTVF-TV, becoming Nashville's first black woman to serve as coanchor on the evening news. "Sure I was a token," she told Judy Markey during an interview for *Cosmopolitan* (September 1986), for she was also the first woman in that job. "But honey, I was one happy token."

Because of her father's continued strictness, Oprah Winfrey was "the only news anchor in the country who had to be home by midnight," as she told Gary Ballard in an interview for an article that appeared in *Drama-Logue* (March 20–26, 1986), although she was earning $15,000 a year while still a junior in college. After graduating in 1976, she leaped at the chance to escape the curfew by accepting a job offer from WJZ-TV, the ABC affiliate in Baltimore, Maryland. As a reporter and co-anchor on the six o'clock news, she found that she had "to fight back tears" when reporting a story that was "too sad." When the station management threatened to discharge her if she failed to question a woman at the scene of a fire in which she had lost her family, Miss Winfrey complied, but apologized later during the live news broadcast.

Her difficulites were compounded, Oprah Winfrey told Cheryl Lavin in an interview for an article that appeared in the Chicago Tribune (December 19, 1985), when the assistant news director at WJZ-TV tried to make her "Puerto Rican." "Your hair's too thick, your nose is too wide, and your chin's too big," he told her. Terrified, she let the station send her to New York beauticians and hair salons, with the result that a botched permanent left her completely but temporarily bald. On camera she tried desperately to cover her scalp with a scarf. Although she cried "constantly," she found in the ordeal an opportunity for self-discovery. "You learn a lot about yourself when you're bald," she told Joan Bartel of Ms. magazine (August 1986). For solace Miss Winfrey turned to food, and the weight problem that has become part of Oprah Winfrey folklore began. In 1977 the station switched her first to doing 7:25 A.M. "cut-ins"—updates on local news—on ABC's Good Morning America, and then to the morning talk show Baltimore is Talking as cohost with Richard Sher. After her first day with the latter program she concluded: "This is what I was born to do. This is like breathing."

For the next seven years Oprah Winfrey and Richard Sher tackled every topic from divorce to child rearing, the Ku Klux Klan, and Siamese twins. Then Dennis Swanson, the general manager of WLS-TV, an ABC affiliate in Chicago, spotted Miss Winfrey on an audition tape that had been sent to his station by Debra DiMaio, her producer. Recognizing her special talent and impressed by her Baltimore ratings, which were even better than those of Phil Donahue, Swanson hired both Oprah Winfrey and her producer. Unheralded and unpromoted, Miss Winfrey moved to Chicago in January 1984 to become the latest in a series of anchors to take over A.M. Chicago, a lackluster morning show that was consistently last in the ratings for its time slot. Aware when she arrived in Chicago of the city's reputation for racial polarization, she expected pickets to show up in front of the building housing WLS-TV, but no such protest materialized. Instead she was confronted by what she perceived as the triviality of A.M. Chicago when she first watched it on a television set in her hotel room. She promptly changed what one journalist described as the program's "mascara and cooking" emphasis in favor of subject matter that was more topical and more controversial. When she took over, the Phil Donahue Show had dominated the local talk show scene for more than sixteen seasons.

One month after Oprah Winfrey arrived in the city, A.M. Chicago drew even with Donahue in the ratings, and after three months it nosed ahead. By September 1985 the program had been expanded to an hour and had been renamed The Oprah Winfrey Show. Perhaps wisely, Phil Donahue departed for New York to be with his wife, the actress Marlo Thomas. "They said I was one of the reasons he moved his program to New York, but I don't flatter myself," Oprah Winfrey told one journalist. "I know it was Marlo Thomas." At a farewell luncheon, Donahue made his only public comment on his rival, wishing her well, but "just not in [his] time slot." For her part, Miss Winfrey credits Donahue with having "paved the way" for shows like hers by proving that "women were interested in more than mascara" and by setting "the standards."

Among the changes that led to Miss Winfrey's victory in the ratings was her wish, which was granted by management after a halting interview with the actor Tom Selleck, to abandon prepared scripts and cue cards and just "wing it." That allowed for the emergence of what Alan Richman described in People magazine (January 12, 1987) as "a mind as quick as any in television, yes, Carson and Letterman included." Added to that was a rare combination of fearlessness, down-home charisma, ebullience, and vulnerability that caused viewers, many of them housewives, to think of Oprah as "a real good friend," according to Debra DiMaio.

In her quest for novelty, Oprah Winfrey chose guests who ranged from a sex surrogate on one day to Marie and Donny Osmond on the next. When she was asked how she could manage to remain so calm while listening to Klansmen espouse their racist views, she replied: "Because I know when this hour is up, they will still be members of the Klan, and I'm going home to my apartment. I don't try to change people. I try to expose them for what they are."

Taking her commitment to exposure literally, a group of nudists titillated the studio audience by appearing naked while the cameras focused only on their faces. Another program featured an actual birth on the air. But it was Oprah Winfrey herself as "Everywoman" who provided some of the most riveting subject matter of her show. One of her popular topics, with which many viewers empathize, is her unrelenting struggle with her weight, which hovers usually between 180 and 190 pounds, and with her self-image. Some of her devotees have worried that becoming thin would drastically change her personality, but she has given them the reassurance, "Honey, it ain't in my thighs." The vicissitudes of her love life also crop up at times on her show's agenda. During one lull in her romances, she announced that "Mr. Right" was on the way, but was "in Africa, walking."

"We go to the heart of the matter," Oprah Winfrey likes to say. "We go for the absolute gut." She once asked a porn star, "Don't you ever get sore?"—and she is equally frank with celebrity guests such as Dudley Moore, Geraldine Ferraro, and Barbara Walters, the model she used for her broadcasting style in Baltimore. When she asked

Jesse Jackson whether he had been nervous meeting Mikhail Gorbachev, he replied: "I was more nervous when I met you. You're more unpredictable." Her unpredictability can shock audiences and reviewers alike, as when she announced, during a serious discussion of penis size, "Bring a big one home to Mama!"

If at such times her program has taken on what was described in TV Guide (August 30, 1986) as "a Marx Brothers quality," more often Oprah Winfrey's spontaneity, empathy, and ability to be herself before the cameras has elicited some remarkable disclosures from "ordinary" people. On one show an elderly black man, in tears, described a lynching he had witnessed in the South. When treating such harrowing topics, she has been known to hold the hand of the person she was questioning throughout the interview. "If Donahue intellectualizes (or pseudo-intellectualizes) the problems he discusses," Steve Sonsky observed in the Miami Herald (September 7, 1986), "Oprah feels them—if she hasn't outright lived them."

One dramatic example occurred on a program about incest, when a guest revealed that she had borne an autistic child after being raped by her own father. Oprah Winfrey burst into tears, hugged her, and called for a break after which she revealed the abuse that she herself had suffered, beginning at the age of nine, when she was raped by a nineteen-year-old cousin who bribed her to keep silent with an ice cream cone and a trip to the zoo. Learning "where babies come from" not long after the rape, she had gone through the fifth grade excusing herself whenever she had a stomach ache in order to go to the bathroom, "have the baby there and not tell anyone." Indeed, she did not tell "a soul" about being abused until she was twenty-two. Her on-the-air disclosure drew 879 telephone calls, and people began coming up to her on the street, weeping and thanking her because they too had been molested as children and had been suffering in silence.

In 1985 the composer and producer Quincy Jones, on a six-hour visit to Chicago, "discovered" Oprah Winfrey as a potential motion picture actress after coming across her program while watching television in his hotel room. Although she had only one acting credit at the time, for a one-woman show, The History of Black Women Through Drama and Song, which she had presented at a Black theater festival in 1978, she was cast, through Quincy Jones, in a big-budget film adaptation of her favorite book, Alice Walker's The Color Purple. In the film, which Steven Spielberg directed and Quincy Jones coproduced, Oprah Winfrey played Sofia, a proud, assertive woman who serves as a kind of foil for the main character, Celie, with whom the movie deals both as an abused child and later as a battered wife. Both characters struck responsive chords in Miss Winfrey, "who came from a broken home, and who has seen so many Celies and Sophies in her life. "I've known all these women," she once said.

When Warner Brothers released The Color Purple in December 1985, Oprah Winfrey was hailed for a debut that was called "shockingly good" by movie critic Gene Siskel in the Chicago Tribune (December 20, 1985) and "spectacular" by Steven Watson, writing in Newsday (January 22, 1986). In addition to receiving Oscar and Golden Globe nominations for her performance, she was named a Woman of Achievement by the National Organization of Women in June 1986. On the strength of her contribution to The Color Purple she was cast in the 1986 film version of Richard Wright's novel Native Son. In the film, released by Cinecom pictures and directed by Jerrold Freedman, Miss Winfrey portrays the mother of Bigger Thomas, a black youth who accidentally kills a white heiress. She admitted to being somewhat nervous about playing a mother, since she did not even "have goldfish," and there were artistic differences and problems on the set, but at the time the film was released she merely said, diplomatically, "Nothing could ever beat The Color Purple for me." Her portrayal of Bigger Thomas' mother was judged to be overly sentimental by some critics.

But Oprah Winfrey's mastery on television remained beyond dispute as her program, already drawing twice the size of the Chicago audience of the Phil Donahue Show in November 1985, skyrocketed in popularity in the wake of her Color Purple Oscar nomination. On September 8, 1986, King World put her show into syndication in a record 138 cities, with unprecedented projected earnings of $125 million for the 1987–88 season and $150 million for the 1988–89 season. Although the distribution deal left her still short of Donahue's 200 stations, when her show aired nationwide, Oprah Winfrey won her time slot by a wide margin, drawing 31 percent of all those watching television at the time and carrying each of the country's top ten markets. John Dempsey reported in Variety (December 31, 1986) that, with a guaranteed 25 percent of gross earnings "right off the top," Miss Winfrey was likely to earn at least $31 million in 1987–88, which made her the highest-paid performer in show business. She signed a five-year contract with King World, her distributor, in late December 1986.

On January 23, 1987, WLS-TV and the Chicago Sun-Times launched a yearlong anti-drug campaign with Miss Winfrey as host of their flagship program, Say No. While interviewing a panel of reformed drug abusers and superstar athletes who had never used drugs, she created the intensity of a "tent-meeting," according to a critic for Variety (January 21, 1987), and proved "excellent in drawing out the pain of the ex-addicts and leading them back to their feelings, ranging from self-hate and disgust to their eventual triumph over addiction." The following month Miss Winfrey taped a segment of her show before an all-white audience in Forsyth County, Georgia, where no blacks have lived since 1912. Three weeks previously, on the anniversary of Martin Luther King Jr.'s birthday,

20,000 people had marched in Forsyth County in a protest against racism after a previous civil rights march had been broken up by Ku Klux Klan members and their supporters. According to a report in *Newsweek* (February 23, 1987), that program was punctuated with progressive statements as well as racist outbursts from the audience and Miss Winfrey "left satisfied that she had encouraged whites to begin discussing race on their own."

The dynamic Oprah Winfrey is just under five feet tall. She lives in an $800,000 condominium on Chicago's Gold Coast and indulges a taste for fine furs and designer clothes. Success, reportedly, has not changed her, for she spends four nights a week lecturing, often gratis, at churches, shelters, and youth organizations, and spends two Saturdays a month with the Little Sisters program she set up at Chicago's notorious Cabrini-Green housing project.

In April 1986 Oprah Winfrey received a special award from the Chicago Academy for the Arts for her unique contributions to the city's artistic community, and in August 1986 she formed Harpo, Inc., ("Oprah" spelled backwards) to produce "things [she] really [wants] to do," namely films, videos, and television movies of social importance. "When I look at the future," she has said, "it's so bright it burns my eyes."

References: *Chicago Tribune* II p1+ D 19 '85 pors; *Ebony* 25:100 Ap '85 pors; *Miami Herald* K p1 S 7 '86 pors; *N Y Daily News* p12+ S 7 '86 pors; *Newsweek* 109:67 F 23 '87 pors; *People* 27:48 Ja 12 '87 pors; *Toronto Globe and Mail* C p2 O 25 '86 pors; *Variety* 325:1+ D 31 '86; *Washington Post* D p4+ O 21 '86 pors; Waldron, Robert. *Oprah!* (1987)

Winter, Paul

Aug. 31, 1939– Musician; composer. Address: b. c/o Living Music Records, 215 W. Standley St., Ukiah, Calif. 95482; h. Norfolk Rd., Litchfield, Conn. 06759

Whether it be called jazz, "new age" music, "earth" music, "healing" music, or "living" music, one feature of the innovative Paul Winter Consort remains constant: a combination of jazz, folk, ethnic, and classical music elements with the living sounds of our endangered environment, including the screams of eagles, the howls of the timber wolf, and the songs of the humpback whale. In the inter-

est not only of making music but also of bringing people together in social harmony and preserving wildlife everywhere, Winter has sailed the seas, rafted down the Colorado River, and explored the forests of Siberia and its Lake Baikal. According to Winter, who is a jazz-trained soprano saxophonist and the founder, in 1980, of Living Music Records, "through music the diverse cultures of the world find common ground; Living Music, as the name implies, is a vital medium through which the cultural and natural environments unite." Winter, whose own definition of his music is "earth jazz," is an artist-in-residence at the Cathedral of St. John the Divine in New York City, which he calls "Grand Canyon East."

Paul Theodore Winter was born on August 31, 1939 in Altoona, Pennsylvania, the son of Paul Theodore and Beulah (Harnish) Winter. He came to music naturally—perhaps inevitably—since his grandfather, who at seventeen had been the youngest bandleader in the American Civil War, owned the local music store, and his great-aunts and great-uncles had belonged to a vaudeville troupe that introduced the saxophone to the United States. Winter's father, a piano tuner, helped to run the music store with his brother.

Winter began playing the drums at the age of five, the piano at six, and the clarinet at eight, under the direction of a strict and demanding teacher of classical music. He studied for ten years, but only under protest. He once told John S. Wilson, the jazz critic of the *New York Times* (July 27, 1969): "As a kid I was stultified . . . bored by every piano piece. I had to practice. Then I picked up on Benny Goodman and Stan Kenton and Miles Davis and be-bop." By the time he was twelve, Winter had chosen the saxophone as his prime instrument and had organized his first band. He also played in the local symphony and, at seventeen, made his first tour, with the Ringling Brothers Circus Band.

In keeping with what was to become his lifelong protest against the academic aspects of music, Winter majored in English composition, not in music, at Northwestern University, from which he obtained his B.A. degree in 1961. Instead of studying jazz formally, since he was convinced that was not the way to learn, he frequented jazz clubs in nearby Chicago, where he listened to such great jazz musicians as John Coltrane. In 1961 he formed the Paul Winter Sextet, recruited from college students in the Chicago area, which after winning first prize in an intercollegiate jazz competition, was signed to a contract with Columbia Records by the celebrated jazz impresario John Hammond. After recording their first album, The Paul Winter Sextet (1962), they went on a tour of Latin America under the sponsorship of the State Department, as the first student jazz group sent abroad under the cultural exchange program.

The tour proved to be a watershed in Paul Winter's career. During a six-month period, the sextet performed some 160 concerts to an estimated 250,000 people in sixty-one cities in twenty-three countries. The Paul Winter Sextet became one of the first groups to assimilate the syncopations of the bossa nova of Brazil, which was soon to become a big hit in the United States, like the samba that it so strongly resembled. A lasting influence on Winter was the softer Brazilian instrumentation: gentler horns, and the use of guitar in place of the piano. Before the tour, the Paul Winter Sextet even played their pop ballads fortissimo. The tour was also a liberating experience in other ways. The integrated sextet, composed of three whites and three blacks, discovered that its music could unify widely diversified audiences, the proof being that rich and poor, black and white, and young and old, sat side by side beating time with their feet. "In Latin America," Winter explained to Lee Underwood during an interview for Down Beat (May 4, 1978), "I felt like I had rejoined the human race. Before that, my only experience had been that of our urban, tight, cold social world here in America . . . probably the most lonely, most alienated nation on earth."

Setting yet another precedent, on November 19, 1962, the Paul Winter Sextet followed up its Latin-American tour by performing the first jazz concert ever held at the White House—a program for young people presided over by Jacqueline Kennedy. (Jazz groups had previously performed there for private dances and receptions, but only as background.) Although Winter was accepted for admission to the University of Virginia Law School at about that time, he scrapped his plans for a career as a lawyer. Instead, he led his sextet on two more tours of Latin America and appeared with it at jazz festivals and on television shows, including Today. Between 1962 and 1965 the Paul Winter Sextet cut seven albums for Columbia Records.

When sales of its recordings proved disappointing, Columbia Records executives dropped the Paul Winter Sextet from their roster, and the group disbanded. Winter told Lee Underwood: "I thought it was tragic that a lot of young musicians would get discouraged from making music their lives because they felt that New York was the big challenge, and if they didn't make it there, they'd better give up." But the enterprising Winter discovered that "you'd write a letter, maybe play a few pieces for free, and then the next time you'd get a hundred bucks and the next time maybe more."

Working out of his rented stone cottage in West Redding, in rural Connecticut, he formed, in 1967, the Paul Winter Consort, an eclectic ensemble that combined classical, rock, jazz, folk, Brazilian, and African elements in its music. "I wanted a broader texture of sounds," he explained to Lee Underwood, "the warmth of the classical guitar, the variety of Latin/African percussive instruments, and some of my favorite symphonic instruments." The Paul Winter Consort recorded three albums for A&M Records between 1967 and 1971. Although a cassette of Road (1971) was taken to the moon on Apollo 15 and left there by the astronauts, who named two lunar craters after a couple of its songs, Winter felt that his new fusion of musical elements had failed, and that he was, as he put it, "graduating from eclecticism." And unimpressed by the fact that George Martin, the former producer for the Beatles, called the consort's Icarus (1972) for Epic Records "the finest album [had] ever made," Winter dissolved the group.

Paul Winter did not record commercially for five more years, perhaps because his albums were so eclectic that the major record companies were at a loss as to how to market them. Meanwhile, he continued to maintain his enthusiasm for the music of Charles Ives, who once lived in West Redding, Connecticut, and with whose relatives he had struck up a friendship. By working with the music of Ives, Winter began to define his own musical identity after having gone through so many musical phases. In order to keep himself and his reconstructed five-member Consort active and to liquidate a burden of debt, he organized special musical events, such as Charles Ives festivals, and celebrations of the winter and summer solstices at the Cathedral of St. John the Divine in Manhattan, the biggest Gothic cathedral in the world. It has become a favorite performing and recording site for Winter ever since his first encounter with that majestic and all-enveloping space. As he recalled during an interview with Les Line for Audubon magazine (November 1982): "The sounds floated and hovered and seemed to glow with a richness I had never known. It was mesmerizing."

The seed of Paul Winter's "earth music" was planted in 1968, when he first heard a recording of the sounds made by humpback whales. "They changed my life," he told Linda Witt of People magazine (October 2, 1978). "Listening to the long complex songs the whales repeat, I was amazed by their musical intelligence, and I was shocked to learn that these extraordinary creatures were rapidly being hunted to extinction." His fascination with those remarkable sounds impelled him, over the course of three years, to sail to the shores of

Newfoundland, British Columbia, Baja California, El Salvador, and the Inner Hebrides, playing his saxophone to various species of sea mammals.

It was around the same time that Winter first developed his abiding interest in timber wolves. "I saw a wolf that was brought through my town in Connecticut as part of a traveling program sponsored by conservationists," he recounted to Sara Terry of the *Christian Science Monitor* (August 10, 1978). "I was completely taken. Wolves are not the vicious creatures they're made out to be. They're very gentle, intelligent, admirable creatures." In 1973, in Minnesota, he visited the last wild population of timber wolves in the lower forty-eight states. In 1975, at a wildlife research center in California's Sierra Nevada mountains, he played his saxophone to captive wolves and discovered that they howled back their answers, just as he had been able to call whales to his raft off Baja California. In the wailing of wolves, which Winter interprets as a kind of celebration, he hears the blues cadences and intonations of the late pioneering jazz saxophonist Charlie Parker.

In 1977 A&M Records released *Common Ground*, the first Paul Winter album that mixed the actual voices of animals and the sounds of nature into his compositions, including musical improvisations based on the cry of an African fish eagle, the song of a whale, and the howl of a wolf. In *Callings* (1980), the voices of thirteen different sea mammals were woven into the music tracks. His musical meditations on whale sounds culminated in *Whales Alive* (1987), with ten of the eleven pieces on the album derived from melodies "composed" by the whales themselves, that were culled from the vast library of whale recordings collected by Dr. Roger Payne, the director of the Long Term Research Institute, who pioneered in the recording of the sounds of whales. Royalties from the album *Whales Alive* were donated to the World Wildlife Fund.

In 1980 Paul Winter was named artist in residence at the Cathedral of St. John the Divine. Invited by its dean, the Rev. James Parks Morton, to write an ecumenical mass for life on earth, he had his Consort record partly at the cathedral and partly at the Grand Canyon, which Winter regards as a natural "cathedral of the earth." "Both have the same sense of majesty, the same seven-second reverberation," he told Stephen Trimble of *Sierra* magazine (March/April 1986). The resulting *Missa Gaia/Earth Mass* (1982) included such sounds as the song of a canyon wren, the overpowering rush of river waters, and the beating of a ceremonial drum accompanying the voices.

Released by Living Music Records in 1985, *Canyon* is the result of Paul Winter's decade-long visits to the Grand Canyon in northern Arizona and his trips with his Consort down the Colorado River. "I felt put back together on the river," he explained to Stephen Trimble, "and I wanted to make music from that place. I wanted to make music of the canyon rather than just about it." *Canyon* reached fourth place on *Billboard*'s jazz LP chart

and also crossed over to the Top Pop LP chart, on which Winter had not appeared since 1962. In January 1987 *Canyon* was nominated for a Grammy award in the newly created "Best New Age Album" category. A film documentary, *Canyon Consort*, was also released in 1985, featuring as one of its highlights a "Howlelujah Chorus," in which the audience wails in response to a wolf.

Their use of outdoor sites has changed the musical configuration of the Paul Winter Consort considerably. In the mid-1970s its members traveled around with a tractor-trailer full of instruments, but near the end of the decade Winter simplified the instrumentation, which now usually consists of a cello, a piano or organ, sometimes a guitar, often another wind instrument, and a percussion instrument or two. Because its sound carries better outdoors, Winter now usually plays a soprano saxophone instead of his former alto instrument. Whenever feasible, the Paul Winter Consort plays acoustically, without a sound system, but Winter has made one concession to high technology: a twenty-four-track recording studio in a converted barn on his seventy-seven-acre farm near Litchfield, Connecticut.

Balking at the "new age" label sometimes applied to the music of the Paul Winter Consort, Winter made his position clear during an interview with Mairi N. Morrison of the *Washington Post* (May 6, 1987). "New Age, that's just another marketing ploy," he said. "In my twenty-five years of playing jazz, I've heard about ten different labels for our music, from progressive to fusion, to world, to whole earth." If his work must carry a tag, Winter prefers "earth music," "earth jazz," or "living music."

Living Music's early releases put the fledgling record company into six-figure debt, but it has since achieved solvency under the astute direction of Richard Perl, a young alumnus of Columbia's law and business schools who also manages Winter's career. "Paul does not like the words 'deadline' or 'budget,'" Perl has said. "And he's a perfectionist. He wrote ten drafts of the *Canyon* liner notes. That can drive me batty." Perl soon discovered that his Thoreauvian client "just was not grounded in doing business traditionally. He needed someone who found the business end as much of an art form as he finds the music."

In 1983 Living Music Records, whose recordings are now distributed by Windham Hill Records and A&M Records, Inc., through the RCA distribution system, released Winter's *Sun Singer*, which was named jazz album of the year by the National Association of Independent Record Distributors. On June 5, 1985, the Paul Winter Consort recorded live in the United Nations General Assembly on World Environment Day their album *Concert for the Earth*. On that occasion, Winter was given a World Environment Day award in recognition of the many benefit concerts he has played for such environmentalist groups as the Sierra Club, the Wilderness Society, and Greenpeace, as well as for the ceremonial environmental observances of the

United Nations. Among Winter's other honors is a Joseph Wood Krutch award.

In the summer of 1984 Paul Winter undertook the first of several trips to the wilderness areas of the Soviet Union in preparation for a series of albums to be made over a period of seven to ten years that will have the collective title *A Song of Russia.* By mid-1985 he had made three more trips to eastern Siberia, attracted particularly to Lake Baikal, the world's deepest freshwater lake. On his first trip to the Soviet Union, in July 1984, Winter had met the celebrated Russian poet Yevgeny ("Genya") Yevtushenko, and in June of 1985 the Paul Winter Consort and Yevtushenko toured the United States together on a national "Concert of the Earth," with the poet reading his work to the improvised music of the Consort. By producing his Russian albums, Winter hopes to "show that the people of the Soviet Union love their earth as much as we love ours and *that* just may be a common ground for peace, spoken through the universal language of music."

Paul Winter is lanky, bearded, and somewhat bald. He often spends an entire week alone on his farm, awakening before dawn and beginning his day with yoga and Zen meditation before hiking or cross-country skiing. A teetotaler and vegetarian, he usually thrives on a macrobiotic diet. Winter somehow manages to survive without television and has not seen a Hollywood movie in years. No recluse, however, he gives week-long summer workshops on his farm for which previous musical experience is not required. He is unmarried. According to Winter, music is not a *part* of life or nature; it *is* life and nature. To him, music is an expression of the natural rhythm that binds the universe together. "When people make music, they're more integrated, more whole, more connected with each other and to the earth than from any other activity," he once said. "Music is one of the great hopes for the human species."

References: Audubon 80:88+ Jl '78 por, 84:5 N '82; Down Beat 45:18+ My 4 '78 por; People 10:96+ O 2 '78 pors, 26:117+ O 6 '86 pors; Sierra 71:59+ Mr/Ap '86; Soviet Life 6:31+ Je '87 pors; Who's Who in America, 1986-87

Yarborough, Cale

Mar. 23, 1939– Racing car driver. Address: b. c/o National Association of Stock Car Auto Racing, 1801 Volusia Ave., Daytona Beach, Fla. 32015

"It's called being a hard charger," the stock car racer Cale Yarborough, the only five-time Southern 500 winner, asserts of his nervy, foot-to-the-floor driving style, "and there's only one other type of driver, and that's an also-ran." For three decades Yarborough has been thrilling stock car fans throughout the United States and outmaneuvering or even angering other drivers with his surgically precise, canny, and ruthless charging. He has won the Daytona 500 four times (second only to Richard Petty's mark) and once set a record qualifying time of 205.109 miles an hour for that race. Between 1976 and 1978 Yarborough won a record three consecutive Winston Cup championships. His eighty-three career wins (third on the all-time list) have made him a folk hero in his native South. In his 1986 autobiography, *Cale: The Hazardous Life and Times of the World's Greatest Stock Car Driver,* written with William Neely and published by Times Books, Yarborough traces his achievements back to the South Carolina countryside where he grew up and where he still makes his home. In reviewing his career, which has proved that fortunes can be made in stock car racing, he also provides a history of the rise of the National Association for Stock Car Auto Racing to prominence.

William Caleb Yarborough was born in Timmonsville, South Carolina, on March 23, 1939, the oldest of the three sons of Julian Yarborough, a cotton and tobacco farmer and general store owner,

and Annie Mae Yarborough. By the time he was five, Cale had begun to work in the family tobacco fields. In the prologue to his autobiography, he confesses that he "had [his] fill of fighting the land for survival by the time [he] got to ninth-grade civics."

In 1950, at the age of ten, Yarborough discovered the racing world when he and his father designed and built a Soap Box race car together. His first race took place fifteen minutes away from Timmonsville, in Darlington, where they were finishing the first super-speedway ever designed especially for stock cars. Although his Soap Box race did not go well, he was bitten by the racing bug. When Labor Day came around that year, he and his father listened to the radio broadcast of the first Southern 500, which was to become the South's Indianapolis 500, World Series, and Kentucky Derby "all wrapped up into one," according to Yarborough.

In 1951 Yarborough's father was killed when his private plane went down in the unpredictable air currents above Timmonsville. Feeling as if his "heart was going to tear out of [his] chest," the eleven-year-old Yarborough became "the man of the house," at least ceremonially. In practice, his mother "took over everything," running the general store, the cotton gin, and the farm, and still managed to fuss over her sons "like an old mother hen." Yarborough found some relief when the new Soap Box season began, and he plunged into racing again, once more with little success. By the time he was fifteen he had graduated to a 1935 Ford, rebuilt with the help of some of his friends, which he had driven to a first place finish on a dirt track in Sumter, South Carolina. Away from the race track, in high school, Yarborough took little interest in academic subjects but excelled in athletics, making the all-state team as a fullback and twice winning the South Carolina Golden Gloves welterweight boxing championship. He also indulged in less organized recreations, such as wrestling an alligator and catching poisonous snakes. While considering several college football scholarships and a tryout offer from the Washington Redskins, he drove a bus for his high school and spent time cutting timber, harvesting tobacco, and helping out on his family's 500-acre farm.

After graduating from high school, Yarborough began racing full time, intent on qualifying for the NASCAR circuit. Explaining the increasingly broad-based appeal of the association and of stock car racing in general, he recalled in his autobiography that "life in our part of the country was gray and drab, and sort of like a black-and-white movie, with nothing but cotton mills and farms and hard work. But that was starting to change, and stock car racing—the sport that was once frowned upon—was part of the reason for the change. . . . It was like a traveling circus, going from small track to small track and leaving behind it a little hope. And a lot of pleasure."

In 1957 Yarborough, aged seventeen, obtained his NASCAR license by using a fake birth certificate. NASCAR officials discovered his ruse just before his first race at Darlington, on September 2, 1957, but after sneaking out onto the track and competing with his idols, Yarborough himself realized that as yet "he didn't belong out there with the big boys, anyway." He completed 42.6 miles of the race and won $100 in prize money. Yarborough turned to semipro football to make his living and also helped to start a flying circus complete with a ground show of daredevil car-rolling and ramp-leaping, but a near-fatal jumping accident convinced him, after a brief stint in the rodeo, to return to auto racing. From 1957 to 1961 he made one Grand National drive a year at Darlington, earning a total of $535. The rest of the racing season he spent in perfecting his "loose car" driving skills in races on the dirt tracks so abundant in the Carolinas, competing against such future luminaries as Lee Roy Yarbrough and Tiny Lund.

In 1961 Cale Yarborough married Betty Jo Thigpen, a former high school cheerleader whom he had met at his uncle's drugstore in Olanton, South Carolina, where she worked behind the soda fountain. He began to think of ending his hand-to-mouth existence as a racer in order to have a stable home life, but a two-year venture into turkey farming wiped out the couple's combined life savings of $30,000. Yarborough then returned to the racing world by accepting a job as a handyman with Holman-Moody Racing, one of NASCAR's premier race shops, where he swept floors, operated a forklift, and helped to keep the place clean in the hope of being on hand when racing opportunities arose. To generate extra income, he entered the races of the main NASCAR circuit whenever he could persuade a car owner to let him drive. In 1963 he managed to drive in eighteen Grand National races, posting three finishes in the top five. In 1964 he started in twenty-four Grand National races and ended with two top-five finishes.

In 1965 Holman and Moody officially made Yarborough the driver for a year-old race car they had been thinking of selling. Yarborough knew that he "would have to drive well, maybe even over [his] head." He drove in all fifty-four races on the Grand National circuit in 1965 and won his first NASCAR race at Valdosta, Georgia, besting such legendary figures as A.J. Foyt and Junior Johnson. At that point he realized that his "long, tough apprenticeship was over."

In that journeyman year, Yarborough learned how mistakes can be greatly amplified at 150-mile-per-hour or 200-mile-per-hour speeds. At the 1965 Southern 500, deep into turn number one, he nudged fellow racer Sam McQuagg's car while trying to pass. His own car lifted into the air above the three-story-high bank of the curve. In his autobiography he recalls feeling "like one of those astronauts" and doing everything he could think of that might help "land the car." "It doesn't do any good to mash the brakes when you're in the air, but [he] did." He continued to steer while he was upside down, though that too was useless. The car's jarring touchdown fortunately left him unharmed, though more wary of passing on tight curves.

After sitting out much of the following season because Ford, for which he was again racing, boycotted NASCAR, Yarborough began a period of dominance of the Grand National circuit in 1967 when he won the Atlanta 500 on April 3 before a record crowd of 80,000. Driving at an average speed of 131.078 mph, Yarborough fought off challenges by Mario Andretti and Richard Petty to drive his 1967 Ford to victory and pocket $20,315 in prize money. Gaining his first victory on the NA-

SCAR circuit for the year, Yarborough led for 302 out of 334 laps. Later in the year he took his second major race, the Firecracker 400, at Daytona Beach, Florida. In 1968 Yarborough continued his winning ways by defeating Lee Roy Yarbrough on February 26 in the Daytona 500 by a second to earn $47,250 for 3 hours, 23 minutes and 44 seconds over the 2.5 mile oval speedway. His average speed was 143.251 miles per hour, slower than the 154.334 miles per hour record set four years previously by Richard Petty. On July 2, on the Daytona International Speedway, Yarborough drove the fastest long-distance automobile race ever run, and won his second Firecracker 400. His average speed of 167.247 miles per hour not only beat the Firecracker 400 record of 153.813 miles per hour set by Sam McQuagg in 1966, but also the Daytona 500 record of 154.334 and the Indianapolis 500 mark of 152.882. The victory, which was worth $18,050, including $2,650 in lap money, brought his season's earnings to $126,066, tops in the NASCAR's Grand National circuit for big-bore stock cars.

Yarborough's fourth victory in super-speedway events for the year and the most important of all to him was the Southern 500 stock car racing classic, in which he earned a $102,000 purse. Its special significance stemmed from the fact that it would be Yarborough's last chance to win on the "old" Darlington Raceway track, which, with a small ripple or "stripe" that could send cars flipping end over end, was known as "the track nobody could tame." (It was repaved in 1969.) Yarborough does not claim to have tamed it, but admits that he "sure got its attention." He took command of the race for eighty-eight laps from the finish, but the record crowd watched in excitement as David ("the Fox") Pearson closed a twenty-five-second gap to almost pull out a win. Yarborough's victory upped his season earnings to $126,066, the highest on NASCAR's Grand National Circuit for big-bore stock cars. He was becoming known as "the master of the 2.5 mile track."

In the following year Yarborough narrowly escaped death when he hit an iron wall at 200 miles per hour in a race in Texas and suffered several injuries, including a shattered bone in his back, but he recovered, and when Ford, his sponsor, withdrew its support from NASCAR, he also left and joined an Indy car team owned by a Firestone tire dealer, Gene White of Atlanta, Georgia. The time he spent on the Indy circuit was disappointing, mainly because Yarborough was the team's second driver, the first being the veteran Lloyd Ruby. In four Indy 500s, Yarborough finished only once, and that in tenth place in the 1972 race.

In 1973 Junior Johnson, made famous by the film The Last American Hero, hired Yarborough to replace Bobby Allison, thus beginning what was to become one of the most successful driver-owner relationships in stock car racing history. During their partnership, which lasted until 1980, the Yarborough/Johnson combination dominated NASCAR, winning forty-nine Grand National events, three consecutive Winston Cup championships, and $3 million in earnings. Yarborough's biggest year during his association with Junior Johnson came in 1977 when he won his second Winston Cup Championship and achieved something that no one in the history of NASCAR's Grand National program had ever done. He earned a record $431,576 in a single season and finished all thirty of his races in the Winston Cup Series, winning nine of them.

The achievement earned Yarborough $10,000 and the prestigious Olsonite Driver of the Year award, an honor to which he had come close twice before. In 1974 he had tied with Bobby Unser but lost on a tie-breaking vote, and two years later David Pearson edged him out for the award. To win, Yarborough outpolled A.J. Foyt, the first man to win the Indianapolis 500 a fourth time. In accepting the award, Yarborough said: "I don't know how the other guys feel about the award. To me it's the best single award a driver can receive. It means he's been judged the best among drivers of my kind from any organization. The money's nice, but this is an award that really means more than money to me."

Yarborough continued to be on a roll in 1978. In finishing first in the grueling American 500 at Rockingham, North Carolina, in November, he clinched his third straight national stock car championship, a feat that no other stock car driver had ever achieved. It was the most lopsided victory of the season on the Grand National circuit's big tracks, since Yarborough finished more than two miles ahead of runner-up Bobby Allison to sew up the fifty-ninth victory of his career. In an interview excerpted four years earlier in Newsday (February 18, 1974), Yarborough summed up the physical and mental battle involved in such achievements: "You're driving at an average 200 miles an hour bumper to bumper around in a tight circle. The temperature inside the car is 150 degrees and you've been driving almost five hours. . . . You are strung out on tension, continuously controlling your fear, thereby turning it into what some might call courage. On one front, you're fighting the track, watching every ripple, every angle. On another, you're listening to the scream of your engine, hearing noises that aren't there, and praying to God you'll hear noises that are. All this against a psychological race with the man in front: What will he do when you pass? Is he wearing down? You run a different race with the man behind and the one coming up on your side: What are they thinking and how do they feel?"

At the end of the 1980 season, Yarborough announced his intention of reducing his racing schedule by half because on one of his rare days at home he realized that his "kids were growing up without knowing their daddy." He told Junior Johnson, who wanted him to work a full schedule, to look for another driver for the 1981 season and signed up instead with Georgia businessman M. C. Anderson under a contract that allowed him to spend more time at home.

In 1981 and 1982, racing for Anderson, Yarborough scored five wins in all. Yarborough refused an Anderson offer of "a million dollar deal" to return to the thirty-race schedule and announced in November 1982 his intention of leaving the Anderson team and teaming up with the Kentucky industrialist Harry Rainer and Hardee's food system to run a sixteen-race schedule.

Yarborough won his third Daytona 500 in February 1983. He made history on the first of two qualifying laps available to him, breaking the 200 miles-per-hour barrier at 200.503 and becoming the all-time stock car speed record holder. On the second qualifying lap, however, Yarborough's Chevrolet Monte Carlo spun out of control and flipped twice before being demolished. His backup car, a year-old Pontiac Grand Prix, was sent from Charlotte for the race itself, in which he could not claim the pole position because the pole setter must start the race in the car he qualifies. As the race reached its climax, Yarborough was in second place, "drafting" a foot behind the bumper of Buddy Baker's car. Yarborough has explained in his autobiography that at such close quarters the trailing car enters an air pocket of "slipstream" opened by the lead car. The teardrop-shaped slipstream stretches over both vehicles, and both are swept along at a higher speed while using less power. When the rear car swings out of the slipstream, a last aerodynamic push "slingshots" it into the lead. Buddy Baker was therefore a "sitting duck" with Yarborough behind him for the last ten and one-half laps. Yarborough made his move on the last lap, slingshotting past Baker and knowing he "had to take the third car with" him in *his* slipstream, but gambling that if he could make Baker and the third car race side by side, he "had it made." The successful timing brought him in under the checkered flag in five hours, twelve minutes and twenty seconds, with an average speed of 155.979 miles per hour. He pocketed a record-winner's purse of $119,000.

By the end of 1983 Yarborough had four wins for the season and was approaching $4 million in his total career earnings. Like 1983, the 1984 season began with Yarborough winning his fourth Daytona 500 in February, once more zipping from second place to victory by eight-car lengths on the final lap, and becoming only the second driver to defend his Daytona title successfully. Richard Petty had done it in 1973 and 1974. Yarborough's pace was 150.944 miles per hour, slightly less than his winning speed in 1983 and the slowest winning speed since 1979. That victory was the seventy-ninth of his career, moving him into a second place tie on NASCAR's all-time win list. He had additional wins in 1984 at Pocono and Talledega.

The 1985 season started off on a disappointing note, as Yarborough's team suffered seven mechanical failures and enjoyed just three top-five finishes through the first eleven races, but by the end of the year, Yarborough had notched victories at the Talledega 500 and the Charlotte Motor Speedway and a pair of second place finishes at Atlanta and Darlington. In 1986 he had his worst season in fourteen years, but several top-five and top-ten finishes brought him $137,010. In 1987 he began fielding his own team—the Race Hill Farms organization—for the first time in his career.

When not racing, Cale Yarborough lives on his 1,300-acre farm in Sardis, South Carolina, with his wife and three children. Yarborough has shrewdly invested the more than $4.5 million he has won in auto racing in a small business empire that includes ownership of a Honda/Mazda dealership in Florence, South Carolina; a Goodyear tire dealership in Timmonsville, South Carolina; a Honda dealership in Savannah, Georgia; seven Hardee restaurants; three dry-cleaning establishments; and a company that makes satellite television dishes.

In 1972 Yarborough ran as a Republican for a seat on the Florence County Council and won. He was reelected in 1976 as a Democrat, having joined that party so that he could support Jimmy Carter's presidential bid. He served until January 1, 1977, when he relinquished the job because he had moved out of the county. In his autobiography he maintains that he "got enough of politics at the county level to last [him] a lifetime."

Ruddy-complexioned, with thinning blond hair, Yarborough is five feet seven inches tall and weighs 185 pounds. He has no firm plans to retire, only suggesting that he will begin selling "cars and hamburgers" when he fails a test of reflexes he gives himself in the shower—squeezing a bar of soap until it pops out of his hand and then catching it "on the way up."

References: Newsday p58 F 18 '74 por; Sporting News p63 D 15 '86 por; Sports Illus 46:10+ F 28 '77 pors 49:99+ N 6 '78 pors; Yarborough, Cale, and Neely, William. Cale: The Hazardous Life and Times of the World's Greatest Stock Car Driver (1986)

Yeager, Jeana

1952 (?)– Test pilot. Address: b. c/o Voyager Aircraft, Inc., Hangar 77, Mojave, Calif. 93501

On Tuesday, December 23, 1986, at 8:05 in the morning, the aircraft *Voyager* descended out of the clear desert sky and touched ground at Edwards Air Force Base, California. Tens of thousands of spectators lined the dry desert lake bed to watch the historic landing, and millions more watched on television as its pilot, Dick Rutan, and copilot, Jeana Yeager, emerged from the cockpit, the first persons to fly around the world without stopping or refueling. Jeana Yeager and Dick Rutan thus added their names to aviation history in what was a triumph of will, vision, and determination, as well as of skill. Their nine-day flight had been rough and dangerous, and Jeana Yeager emerged bruised and tired, but exhilarated. Her goal, she had said just

Jeana Yeager

before the flight began, was "to take a step into the future."

Unaccustomed to the spotlight, Jeana Yeager is extremely reticent about her personal life, although it has been established that she was thirty-four years old at the time of the milestone *Voyager* flight. "The gutsy little Texan," as Edwards Park once described her in his article for *Smithsonian* magazine (February 1985), is not related to the famous test pilot Chuck Yeager. She grew up in Texas and once trained horses, but after moving to California took up engineering design. She worked as a draftsman on Operation Free Enterprise, a project of the retired United States Navy captain Robert Truax, whose goal it was to build a commercial rocket. Dissatisfied with a sedentary life, she took up skydiving in her spare time and then decided to graduate to helicopter flying. Having been advised that she would be better off if she learned to start with a fixed-wing plane, she began flying one at twenty-four. At an air show in 1980 she met Richard Rutan, a heavily decorated former fighter pilot, who was there to perform grandstanding stunts.

Invited by Rutan to return with him to Mojave, where he worked as chief test pilot for the Rutan Aircraft Factory, Jeana Yeager was soon shattering speed records with the specially designed Rutan planes. By the time she copiloted the *Voyager*, in 1986, she had been flying for ten years and had established nine aviation speed and endurance records. In March 1981 Dick Rutan decided to quit as chief test pilot of the Rutan Aircraft Factory, owned by his brother Burt, and he and Jeana Yeager discussed several ideas about possible businesses or ventures, all of them connected, in one way or another, with flying. One day the Rutan

brothers were having lunch with Jeana Yeager at the Mojave Inn, canvassing the possibility of Jeana and Dick's setting up their own aircraft-sales outfit and searching for a concept that would capture public attention and launch their venture in a big way. When Burt Rutan predicted that the newly available aircraft building materials, light in weight and high in strength, would render existing aviation distance records obsolete, Jeana Yeager suggested that she and Dick try to break the existing record for a flight with no stops or refueling. That record, set in 1962 by a B-52 bomber, stood at 12,532 miles. Burt assured her that he could design and build a plane that could go twice that far—26,-000 miles, around the world—and he sketched his idea on a restaurant napkin.

It took five years for the trio to get from the first, tentative, and preliminary drawing on the restaurant napkin to the finished plane on the tarmac. During those years the plane, soon christened the *Voyager*, became the obsessive center of the lives and thoughts of Jeana Yeager and the Rutan brothers. In order to build the plane, they rented a shed at Mojave Airport, Hangar 77, for $65 a month, and in the meantime Miss Yeager moved in with Dick Rutan and his mother. All of their time and money were invested in the *Voyager*.

From the first, it was very much a family affair. Built by the Rutans, Miss Yeager, and their friends and volunteers, it took shape in the years 1982 and 1983. By 1984 the airframe was basically finished, and Jeana Yeager and Dick Rutan formed Voyager Aircraft, Inc., selling souvenirs and accepting cash donations from aircraft buffs and inquisitive visitors. Because Burt Rutan was well known in aviation circles and had won international acclaim for his aircraft designs and innovations, he was able to obtain donations of expensive aircraft equipment, including the magnamite graphite fiber that composed 90 percent of the plane's body, from Hercules Corporation; the insulation sandwiched between the graphite layers, from Hexcel, Inc.; and the rear engine, from Teledyne Continental. In describing the craft in the *New York Times* (December 24, 1906), Malcolm W. Browne wrote: "Like the Wright brothers' Flyer, the *Voyager* incorporates a pioneering aeronautical design and some of the most advanced structural materials of its day. But in other respects the *Voyager* is as crude as any airplane that ever flew, and its flight into the record books had less to do with space-age technology than with the personal sacrifices, improvisations and dedication of its impecunious creators."

The problem that Burt Rutan confronted in designing and building the *Voyager* was to build a light airplane that could carry a very heavy load, namely, all the fuel needed for a round-the-world flight. The unorthodox, H-shaped design that he hit upon for the *Voyager* as his solution continued the hallmark of the Rutan planes, a design called the "canard" configuration, in which the main wing is at the rear and the horizontal stabilizer is near the nose. (That was also the configuration used by the Wright brothers.) The configuration creates a strong airframe with very efficient wings, and the wingspan itself is 111 feet, longer than that of a 727 jetliner. The only metal in the plane is that of the engines, fasteners, cables, and fittings, and the frame itself, stronger than steel, consists of a "sandwich" of magnamite graphite fiber and the honeycomb insulation material.

Those materials were fused together in the Mojave Airport hangar in a homemade oven that was constructed from corrugated house siding together with parts from a home furnace. When completed, the plane weighed just 938 pounds, without the engines, and was ready to carry up to five times its total weight of 1,860 pounds. At its takeoff for the round-the-world flight, it was holding 9,400 pounds of 100-octane gas. William Marbach and Peter McAlevey, writing in Newsweek (September 22, 1986), called it "essentially a fuel tank that flies." Two engines powered the craft: a rear-mounted, 110-horsepower engine, permitting speeds of 80–100 miles per hour, and a somewhat more powerful engine in front for use during takeoff and landing, as well as for special maneuvers.

By 1986 the Voyager was ready for flight. In mid-July Dick Rutan and Jeana Yeager took their first extended trip, a four-and-a-half day flight that broke world records for distance and endurance. Travelling in laps up and down the California coast, they went 11,600 miles, and learned some of the problems of surviving for days in the small cockpit quarters that Rutan characterized as "a little cocoon home." Seven and a half feet long by about three feet wide, the cockpit permitted the pilot to sit up at the controls, while, alternately, Dick Rutan and Jeana Yeager would take turns stretching out alongside. Before the flight, they had planned to shift positions and responsibilities on set schedules, but by the third day they adapted themselves to more natural rhythms, and would spell each other at the controls when the one who was piloting felt tired.

Acting out, in that one respect, a perhaps traditional nurturing female role, Jeana Yeager made sure throughout the flight that Dick Rutan took the right amount of food and water, but neither of them monitored their own eating habits that closely. As a consequence, she became dehydrated, for eating and drinking required a real physical effort in such cramped quarters, and she sometimes failed to make the effort. She consumed less than a gallon of water throughout the flight, and fainted at the news conference held soon after they landed. Nonetheless, Jeana Yeager had an upbeat assessment of the whole experience. "It was not the mental torment we were told it was going to be," she said. "As we got into it, everything fell into place very nicely. It was fairly comfortable."

That extended test flight enabled Dick and Burt Rutan and Jeana Yeager to iron out some of their most bothersome problems before attempting to go around the globe. For example, the noise in the cockpit was so great that both of them suffered a temporary hearing loss after the July flight, and doctors estimated that they would suffer perma-

nent hearing damage of 30 percent during a flight of twelve days. But word of the Voyager was spreading, and one day a representative from Bose Corporation, the audio manufacturer, came, unsolicited, to Voyager headquarters with a specially designed set of headphones, electronically controlled to emit a muted tone that would cancel the engine noise. Other personal details, such as bedding and the waste management system, were also improved after the July flight. Although Voyager Inc., remained $300,000 in debt, with no single corporate backer or government sponsor, Jeana Yeager remained optimistic. She remarked to Kathy Sawyer of the Washington Post (December 14, 1986): "The money will come. It always has. We're going to do it anyway and worry about the bills later."

The world flight of the Voyager was originally scheduled for mid-September, a time when global weather conditions would be best for flying, but continued problems caused cancellations and delays. During the fifty-fourth test flight in late September, part of the front propeller was lost, necessitating the mounting of new propellers, as well as retooling the engines and retesting the plane. Burt Rutan was now warning against a certain rush on the part of Miss Yeager and his brother to get on with the flight, but they did not want to postpone it until spring, and besides the "weather window" of reasonable flying conditions was quickly closing. On December 4, Dick Rutan and Jeana Yeager had their sixty-fifth test flight, on an almost full fuel tank, but before the global flight itself took place, the Voyager had never taken off fully fueled.

The big day arrived on Sunday, December 14, 1986. Jeana Yeager and Dick Rutan climbed into the cockpit (with Rutan at the controls for takeoff) at Edwards Air Force Base, some eighty miles northeast of Los Angeles. The flight ran into trouble from the very start. The wings, weighted down with the load of fuel, scraped the runway on takeoff, damaging the winglets, small structures on top of the wing tips, but Rutan was able to shake off the damaged winglets early in the flight, thus averting the potential risk of dislodging and rupturing a fuel tank. The Voyager headed out over the Pacific, but near the Philippines it ran into Typhoon Marge with its eighty-mile-per-hour winds. As the more experienced pilot, Rutan remained at the controls and managed to make his way around the storm. Jeana Yeager later remarked that she failed to realize what they were going through at the time. "I was never terrified until after the worst moments were behind us," she recalled.

The morale of both pilots remained high as the Voyager picked up speed and, riding on the typhoon tailwinds, reached a velocity of 147 miles per hour. They fed on precooked dinners and bland food supplements, and exercised with the help of a five-foot rubber band, but sleep came fitfully to them both, in two- or three-hour stretches. Their route had been carefully planned, taking into consideration the hazards of both weather and politics, including the danger of traveling through hostile air space, although they found they had to make several changes in their plans because of unexpected severe storms. From Malaysia virtually all across the continent of Africa, the Voyager had to climb to less fuel-efficient altitudes, sometimes using both engines, to avoid storm turbulence. Word reached the Voyager ground team that the crew was being tossed about and that Jeana Yeager in particular was badly bruised.

The mood of the two pilots was as unstable as the weather. Burt Rutan reported to the press that they seemed to be on an emotional seesaw, in good spirits one moment and at other times "fatigued almost to the point of incapacitation." One high point was the half-way mark of their trip, on December 18, over the Indian Ocean, which roughly coincided with breaking the record for distance flight. Jeana Yeager was at that time described by Lee Herron, a ground crew spokesman, as being "very bubbly and up."

Crossing the continent of Africa turned out to be an ordeal, what with its turbulent skies and high mountain ranges that forced the Voyager to climb to an altitude of 20,000 feet, using extra fuel in the process. Both Jeana Yeager and Dick Rutan were overjoyed and relieved to leave Africa behind and begin the home stretch across the Atlantic, but their euphoria was short-lived for that crossing too was harrowing. An unexpected storm near the Equator caught them by surprise, and Rutan, who was then at the controls, momentarily lost control of the craft. That same day, the rear engine overheated when both pilots, fatigued to the point of forgetfulness, forgot to check the oil level.

The final leg of the trip took the Voyager across Central America and up the Pacific coast towards California. Jeana Yeager piloted the plane for part of that stretch, although she had flown the aircraft only 15 percent of the total time. She radioed back to "mission control" (the Voyager ground team adopted the terminology of space flight) that "everything" was "hard," but that although bruised and exhausted, she was in good spirits. Burt Rutan told the press on the final day; "One minute they are so high, and the next it's hard for them even to get words out."

Although the grinding fatigue and the hazards, and the suspense lasted until the final day, the Voyager crew achieved a near-perfect landing on December 23, 1986, a full day ahead of schedule. Dick Rutan served as pilot for the landing, while Jeana Yeager cranked down the landing gear by hand. A member of the ground team radioed to Rutan, "I really like your little main gear motor, Dick," whereupon Rutan, in a rare personal reference to his copilot, radioed back, "Yeah, she's a real cutie. It's that Yeager pilot." Smiling, the two climbed out of the Voyager and sat on top of it for a few minutes, answering questions. Then, leaning on friends and relatives, they walked a few feet to waiting ambulances that took them to the base hospital for checkups. Later that day they held a news conference. Although Jeana Yeager played down

the bruises and injuries she had received, she admitted that the two pilots "got rest, but not a lot of sleep" and that "it was a lot more difficult than we ever imagined." She concluded: "No telling what we'll do next."

A week later Jeana Yeager and Dick and Burt Rutan were awarded the Presidential Citizens Medal by President Ronald Reagan, an honor established by Richard Nixon for Americans who "have performed exemplary deeds of service for their country or their fellow citizens." Miss Yeager spoke only briefly at the ceremony, for as she admitted afterwards, she was somewhat exhausted from the barrage of publicity and did not quite know what to make of it all. But she soon learned as the public appearances and television talk show interviews piled up. Miss Yeager and Dick Rutan hired Peter Riva, a New York publicist, to manage their appearances, talks, and relations with the corporations that were now asking for product endorsements from the Voyager crew. Riva stated quite frankly: "The job is to see that Dick and Jeana get recompensed for six years of no food in the refrigerator and working twelve hours a day," although, he added sardonically, some of the offers were being rejected, such as the sponsorship of decorated underwear and the marketing of a cuddly Jeana doll. A ghostwriter named Phil Patton was hired to marshal their thoughts for a book. Entitled Voyager, it was published by Alfred A. Knopf in October 1987.

The Voyager itself was flown back from Edwards Air Force Base to Mojave Airport, to be displayed for six months at the hangar where it was assembled, after which it was to take its place in the National Air and Space Museum in Washington, D.C., alongside Charles Lindbergh's Spirit of St. Louis. Dr. Bruce Holmes, of NASA's Langley Research Center, commented that "just having done this opens new doors where we didn't even know doors existed," and the Pentagon was reported to be interested in the Voyager's design, including its extraordinary range and resistance to radar, for potential use in reconnaissance missions.

Jeana Yeager and Dick Rutan live together in a gray, single-story home in Mojave, California, that is decorated inside with several medals, a model helicopter, and a rendering of the Voyager. A close friend informed Michael Specter of the Washington Post (December 24, 1986) that "they have a very complicated relationship. They are both intensely private people, and neither is interested in having anybody they don't know reading about their habits." Their close comradeship is evident. Badgered by questions at the postflight news conference on the difficulty of being with someone in such close quarters for so long a time, Rutan replied: "We support each other very nicely. I would fly around the world with her again." Jeana Yeager merely smiled.

References: Newsweek 108:86+ S 22 '86 por, 108:34+ D 29 '86 por; Smithsonian 15:72+ F '85 por; Time 128:10+ D 29 '86 por; Washington Post

A p1+ D 24 '86 pors; Lomax, Judy. *Women of the Air* (1987)

Photo Credits

OBITUARIES

ABEL, I(ORWITH) W(ILBUR) Aug. 11, 1908–Aug. 10, 1987 Labor union official; president of United Steelworkers of America (1965–77); pioneer steel mill organizer; went to work as mill hand in Canton, Ohio in 1926; began organizing mills in 1936; was secretary-treasurer of United Steelworkers from 1953 to 1965; believed that benefit of workers, employers, and public is mutual and that organized labor should play role in all aspects of civic life; as president, oversaw addition of some 500,000 members, successfully lobbied for more federal protection for workers, coordinated bargaining with leading steel companies, reached productivity agreements, and initiated separate bargaining for other metals unions; when foreign steel imports threatened jobs in early 1970s, signed Experimental Negotiating Agreement with companies ("a better way," in his words) and won sizable wage and benefit increases without a strike; died in Malvern, Ohio. See *Current Biography* (November) 1965.

Obituary *N Y Times* D p3 Ag 11 '87

ADAMS, JOHN CRANFORD Oct. 11, 1903–Nov. 24, 1986 President emeritus of Hofstra University; Elizabethan stagecraft scholar; during his tenure (1944–64), Hofstra grew from tiny liberal arts college with enrollment of 367 to 9,000-student university; was the principal founder of Hofstra's annual Shakespeare festival; designed three-level stage used at festival, a replica of that in the Globe Playhouse; wrote *The Globe Playhouse: Its Design and Equipment* (1942); died in Ithaca, New York. See *Current Biography* (September) 1958.

Obituary *N Y Times* B p18 N 27 '86

ADAMS, SHERMAN Jan. 8, 1899–Oct. 27, 1986 Former Republican government official; as America's powerful "assistant president" in administration of President Dwight D. Eisenhower, established prototype for recent strong presidential chiefs of staff; directed day-to-day White House operations from 1953 until 1958, when he resigned under fire following House subcommittee revelations that he had accepted expensive gifts, including vicuña overcoat, from textile manufacturer seeking federal favors; had previously been forester, lumber company executive, and New Hampshire state legislator, congressman, and governor; later developed ski resort in his home state; wrote memoir *Firsthand Report: The Story of the Eisenhower Administration* (1961); died in Hanover, New Hampshire. See *Current Biography* (November)

1952.

Obituary N Y Times D p28 O 28 '86

ANOUILH, JEAN June 23, 1910–Oct. 3, 1987 Playwright; one of France's most distinguished theatrical craftsmen; wrote plays that ranged from grim drama to such sophisticated comedies as *The Waltz of the Toreadors* (1952); was noted for contemporary treatment of classical or historical themes, in such plays as *Antigone* (1942), *Oreste* (1945), and *Medée* (1946); won success on Broadway stage with *The Lark* (1953), an historical drama about Joan of Arc; received Tony award for *Becket*, as most distinguished play of 1961; also wrote film scenarios, including *Monsieur Vincent* (1947); adapted and translated works of Shakespeare and Oscar Wilde; died in Lausanne, Switzerland. See *Current Biography* (April) 1954.

Obituary N Y Times D p13 O 5 '87

ARNAZ, DESI Mar. 2, 1917–Dec. 2, 1986 Cuban-born television and film actor; musician; bandleader; producer; with Lucille Ball, whom he married in 1940, created battle-of-the-sexes situation comedy *I Love Lucy* (1951–61, and still in syndication worldwide in 1987), then the most popular program on television; on that show, played Ricky Ricardo, heavy-accented second-banana husband of wacky Lucy (Miss Ball); for the show, helped originate television's now standard three-camera film technique; with wife, formed the media conglomerate Desilu Productions, which produced such hit series as *Our Miss Brooks*, *The Untouchables*, and *The Danny Thomas Show*; was divorced from Miss Ball in 1960; sold his Desilu stock to her for $3 million in 1962; died at his home in Del Mar, California. See *Current Biography* (September) 1952.

Obituary N Y Times D p26 D 3 '86

ASTAIRE, FRED May 10, 1899–June 22, 1987 Dancer, singer, and actor whose debonair manner, skill, and seemingly effortless style made him enormously popular internationally; began to dance professionally as a child with his sister, Adele; performed in vaudeville and in such Broadway musicals as *Lady Be Good* (1925) and *The Band Wagon* (1931); appeared in over thirty Hollywood film musicals, ten of them with Ginger Rogers as his dance partner, including *The Gay Divorcee* (1934), *Roberta* (1935), and *The Story of Vernon and Irene Castle* (1939); costarred with Rita Hayworth, in *You'll Never Get Rich* (1941), with Judy Garland, in *Easter Parade* (1948), and with Cyd Charisse, in *Silk Stockings* (1957), among others; also played dramatic roles, including that of a scientist in *On the Beach* (1959); starred in 1957 television special, which won nine Emmy awards; received Life Achievement Award from American Film Institute in 1981; died in Los Angeles. See *Current Biography* (April) 1964.

Obituary N Y Times A p1+ Je 23 '87

ASTOR, MARY May 3, 1906–Sept. 25, 1987 Motion picture actress; best known for splendid portrayals of sophisticated, perfidious beauties and, later, loving mothers; in forty-five year career, starred or was featured in some 100 films, beginning with silents and ending with the Guignolesque thriller *Hush,*

Hush . . . Sweet Charlotte (1964); reached her pinnacle playing villainesses in *The Maltese Falcon* (1941) and *The Great Lie* (1941); for her role in latter, won Academy Award for best supporting actress; was central figure in Hollywood scandal in 1936, when her alleged amorous diary was made public; wrote autobiography *My Story* (1959), movie-making memoir *A Life on Film* (1971), and five fairly well-received novels; died in Woodland Hills, California. See *Current Biography* (November) 1961.

Obituary N Y Times p34 S 26 '87

AWOLOWO, OBAFEMI Mar. 6, 1909–May 9, 1987 Nigerian statesman; laywer; educator; publisher; author; a founding father of Nigerian nationalism; was chief of Yoruba tribe and leader of Unity party; under British colonial rule, served as prime minister of Western Nigeria (1954–59); after independence, led opposition in federal Nigerian parliament (1960–63); was chancellor of universities of Ife (1967–75) and Ahmadu Bello (since 1975); ran unsuccessfully for president of Nigeria in 1979 and 1983; retired from politics following military coup in 1983; died in Ikenne, Nigeria. See *Current Biography* (July) 1957.

Obituary N Y Times D p11 My 11 '87

BACON, PEGGY May 2, 1895–Jan. 4, 1987 Artist; author; famed in 1920s and 1930s for skillful, wittily captioned caricatures of well-known personages, her affectionately satirical pictorial diaries of her everyday encounters, and her pastels of New York City alley cats; wrote and illustrated sixty books, including *Lion-hearted Kitten* (1927), *The Good American Witch* (1957), and *The Magic Touch* (1968); won 1980 American Academy and Institute of Arts and Letters' Gold Medal for graphic art; died in Kennebunk, Maine. See *Current Biography* (January–February) 1940.

Obituary N Y Times A p20 Ja 7 '87

BAIRD, BIL Aug. 15, 1904–Mar. 18, 1987 Puppeteer; in the half-century following his founding of Bil Baird's Marionettes in 1934, enchanted successive generations with some 3,000 hand-manipulated characters, many made in collaboration with his late wife, Cora; numbered among his stage credits his contribution to *The Ziegfeld Follies of 1941*, among other Broadway musicals, and such all-puppet shows as his production of Igor Stravinsky's performance piece *L'Histoire du Soldat* (1982); created dancing goats for film *The Sound of Music* (1965); was nominated for Emmy award for television production *Art Carney Meets Peter and the Wolf* (1958); had numerous other television credits, including hundreds of commercials; passed his craft on to many protégés, including Muppets' creator Jim Henson; wrote classic manual *The Art of the Puppet* (1966); See *Current Biography* (March) 1954.

Obituary N Y Times B p6 Mr 20 '87

BALDRIGE, (HOWARD) MALCOLM Oct. 4, 1922–July 25, 1987 United States secretary of commerce since 1981; while advocating free trade, knew that fair trade is "the bedrock on which free trade stands"; was chief force behind Reagan administration's reluctant toughening of its policy vis-à-vis unfair practices of international trading partners; previously, was chief executive officer and chairman of Scovill, Inc.; transformed that sluggish Connecticut brass-milling firm into diversified, multinational company with annual sales of approximately $1 billion; died in rodeo accident in Walnut Creek, Calif. See *Current Biography* (August) 1982.

Obituary *N Y Times* A p1+ Jl 27 '87

BARROW, ERROL W(ALTON) Jan. 21, 1920–June 1, 1987 Prime minister of Barbados; founded Democratic Labor party in 1961; led country to independence from Britain in 1966; was premier from 1961 to 1976 and from May 1986 until his death; died in Bridgetown, Barbados. See *Current Biography* (September) 1968.

Obituary *N Y Times* B p10 Je 3 '87

BAUR, JOHN I(RELAND) H(OWE) Aug. 9, 1909–May 15, 1987 Museum director; authority on American art; supervisor of education (1934–36) and curator of painting and sculpture (1936–52) at Brooklyn Museum; curator (1952–58), associate director (1958–68), and director (1968–74) of Whitney Museum of American Art; author of *Revolution and Tradition in American Art* (1951), *American Painting in the Nineteenth Century* (1954), and other books; died in New York City. See *Current Biography* (December) 1969.

Obituary *N Y Times* p10 My 16 '87

BEAU, LUCAS VICTOR Aug. 3, 1895–Oct. 22, 1986 Retired Air Force major general; headed Civil Air Patrol (1947–55), Air Force's civilian auxiliary; was pilot in France during World War I; commanded Mediterranean Air Transport Service during World War II; organized European Air Transport Service during occupation of Germany; was awarded Legion of Merit in 1952; died in Washington, D.C. See *Current Biography* (June) 1954.

Obituary *N Y Times* B p9 O 24 '86

BENNETT, MICHAEL Apr. 8, 1943–July 2, 1987 Choreographer; theatrical director; master of the backstage musical; creator of quick and seamless movement that revealed character and advanced story; began career as a chorus performer—the unsung breed whose dedication and love of dance he celebrated in *A Chorus Line* (1975), the longest-running show in Broadway history, conceived, directed, choreographed, and coproduced by him; received Tony nomination for every one of his solo choreographed efforts, including the first, *A Joyful Noise* (1966); won eight Tonys, beginning with his choreography for *Follies* (1971) and including that for *Dream Girls* (1981) as well as for the multi-honored *A Chorus Line*, for which he also shared the Pulitzer Prize for drama; died in Tucson, Arizona of AIDS-related cancer. See *Current Biography* (March) 1981.

Obituary *N Y Times* A p1+ Jl 3 '87

BISHOP, JIM Nov. 21, 1907–July 26, 1987 Author; journalist; feature writer; early in career, rose from rewrite desk at New York *Daily Mirror* to high editorial positions with *Collier's, Liberty,* and *Catholic Digest* magazines; wrote twenty-one books, including best sellers *The Day Lincoln Was Shot* (1955), *The Day Christ Died* (1957), and other terse but melodramatic hour-by-hour pop retellings of great historical events; from 1956 to 1983 wrote newspaper column "Jim Bishop: Reporter" for King Features Syndicate; died in Delray Beach, Calif. See *Current Biography* (June) 1969.

Obituary *N Y Times* B p6 Jl 28 '87

BOLGER, RAY(MOND WALLACE) Jan. 10, 1904–Jan. 15, 1987 Eccentric dancer; comedian; began career as comic and song-and-dance man on legitimate theatre and vaudeville circuits; had first substantial Broadway role in *George White's Scandals of 1931*; later starred in *On Your Toes* (1936), *By Jupiter* (1942), and *Where's Charley?* (1948; film version, 1952), among other musicals; as Hollywood's leading specialty dancer, achieved his most memorable success as the rubber-legged Scarecrow in the classic musical film *The Wizard of Oz* (1939); among other television credits, played straight dramatic role as dour Roman Catholic prelate in *The Runner Stumbles* (1979); died in Chevi-ot Hills, California. See *Current Biography* (August) 1942.

Obituary *N Y Times* D p19 Ja 16 '87

BOLZ, LOTHAR Sept. 3, 1903–Dec. 29, 1986 Former East German government official; during Nazi regime, fled via Poland to Soviet Union, returned to Soviet-occupied zone of Germany in 1946 and became head of East German National Democratic party of Germany two years later; served as building minister (1949–53), foreign minister (1953–65) and deputy prime minister (1950–67). See *Current Biography* (September) 1959.

Obituary *N Y Times* B p8 D 30 '86

BRATTAIN, WALTER H(OUSER) Feb. 10, 1902–Oct. 13, 1987 Research physicist; with two colleagues at Bell Laboratories in Murray Hill, New Jersey, in 1947, invented the transitor, making electronics miniaturization possible; for that invention, shared 1956 Nobel Prize in physics; died in Seattle, Washington. See *Current Biography* (September) 1957.

Obituary *N Y Times* B p12 O 14 '87

BRENAN, (EDWARD FITZ-)GERALD Apr. 7, 1894–Jan. 16, 1987 British writer; arguably the most authoritative and definitive contemporary scholar and observer writing in English on the culture, literature, and history of Spain, where he lived for much of his life, in province of Málaga, Andalusia; wrote, among other books, *The Spanish Labyrinth* (1943), a history of Spain from 1874 to the Civil War of 1936–39 (with an epilogue about the war), *The Face of Spain* (1951), a travel narrative, *The Literature of the Spanish People* (1951), *South from Granada* (1953), containing retrospective observations on the Spanish temper and peasant folkways and beliefs, and the autobiographies *A Life of One's Own* (1962) and *Personal Record, 1920–1972* (1974); died in Alhaurín el Grande, Málaga. See *Current Biography* (July) 1986.

Obituary *N Y Times* p9 Ja 24 '87

BROGLIE, LOUIS (VICTOR PIERRE RAYMOND) DE Aug. 15, 1892–Mar. 19, 1987 French physicist; member of Académie Française; permanent secretary of

Académie des Sciences; in early 1920s worked out mathematical description of the electron (traditionally perceived as particle-like) as a wave motion; for that contribution to the development of quantum wave mechanics, was awarded Nobel Prize in 1929; later, as professor at University of Paris, concentrated on study of photon; founded center for studies in applied mathematics at university's Poincaré Institute in 1943; as government adviser beginning in 1945, pushed for development of nuclear energy; wrote more than twenty books; had successive inherited titles of prince and duke; died in Paris. See *Current Biography* (September) 1955.

Obituary *N Y Times* B p6 Mr 20 '87

BROWN, HARRISON (SCOTT) Sept. 26, 1917–Dec. 8, 1986 Geochemist; former professor, California Institute of Technology; editor in chief of *Bulletin of the Atomic Scientists* since 1985; was a key developer of plutonium production process for atom bomb during World War II; later became prominent in the scientific community's campaign against further nuclear weapons development; was widely honored for his work on world hunger, population control, and resource allocation projects as well as his scientific planetary studies; wrote *Must Destruction Be Our Destiny?* (1946), *The Challenge of Man's Future* (1954), *Learning How to Live in a Technological Society* (1979), among other books; died in Albuquerque, New Mexico. See *Current Biography* (July) 1955.

Obituary *N Y Times* B p18 D 9 '86

BURKE, MICHAEL Aug. 6, 1916–Feb. 5, 1987 Former sports, show business, and broadcasting executive; as Office of Strategic Services agent in World War II, executed missions behind enemy lines in Europe that were recounted in Corey Ford and Alistair MacBain's story of the OSS, *Cloak and Dagger* (1946), and film of same name (1946); after war, became, successively, Hollywood writer, adviser to United States High Commissioner in Germany, manager of Ringling Brothers and Barnum and Bailey circus, and vice-president of Columbia Broadcasting System; as president of New York Yankees baseball team (1966–73), oversaw radical renovation of Yankee Stadium; was later president of Madison Square Garden, until 1981; died in Ireland, where he had been living on his farm in Aughrim, Galway, since his retirement. See *Current Biography* (April) 1972.

Obituary *N Y Times* p10 F 7 '87

BURNS, ARTHUR F(RANK) Apr. 27, 1904–June 26, 1987; U.S. government official; economist; as adviser to presidents, beginning with Dwight D. Eisenhower in 1953, played key role in shaping U.S. economic policy for over three decades; was a pragmatic conservative whose concern over dangers of inflation was tempered by his commitment to the role of the government in promoting prosperity; taught economics at Rutgers, Columbia, and Georgetown universities; served as chairman of Federal Reserve Board (1970–78), distinguished scholar in residence at American Enterprise Institute (1978–81), and U.S. ambassador to Federal Republic of Germany (1981–85); was author of *Prosperity without Inflation* (1957) and other books; died in Baltimore, Maryland. See *Current*

Biography (August) 1976.

Obituary *N Y Times* p1+ Je 27 '87

CALDERONE, FRANK A(NTHONY) Mar. 10, 1901–Feb. 10, 1987 Physician; former public health official; authority on preventive medicine; was first deputy health commissioner of New York City from 1943 to 1946; in 1948, helped to organize United Nations' World Health Organization and became medical director of its headquarters; from 1951 to 1954 directed UN Secretariat's health service; after leaving UN, was executive with Long Island theatre chain that his father had founded; died in New York City. See *Current Biography* (July) 1952.

Obituary *N Y Times* A p25 F 24 '87

CALDWELL, ERSKINE Dec. 17, 1903–Apr. 11, 1987 Novelist; won early fame—and notoriety—with his frank and sometimes humorous tales of dirt-poor, lusty, and often degenerate white sharecroppers and mill hands in Georgia; was hailed as great proletarian chronicler by some and as unduly "melodramatic" and gratuitously "dirty" by others who were unfamiliar with the milieu that he described; was best known for *Tobacco Road* (1932), a best seller that went on to break Broadway and Hollywood records in its stage and screen adaptations, and *God's Little Acre* (1933)— both of which were widely banned; wrote a total of some fifty books, including the autobiography *Call It Experience* (1951); died in Paradise Valley, Arizona. See *Current Biography* (October) 1940.

Obituary *N Y Times* A p1 Ap 13 '87

CARLSON, FRANK Jan. 23, 1893–May 30, 1987 Governor of Kansas (1947–51); U.S. representative (1935–46) and U.S. senator (1951–69); a middle-of-the-road Republican; adviser to President Dwight D. Eisenhower; member of Hoover Commission on governmental reorganization; sponsored farm legislation and measure calling for national system of water control; favored simplified federal income tax laws and helped to devise tax withholding system; served as chairman of International Council of Christian Leadership and as international president of Christian Laymen; died in Concordia, Kansas. See *Current Biography* (April) 1949.

Obituary *N Y Times* p32 My 31 '87

CARROLL, MADELEINE Feb. 26, 1906–Oct. 2, 1987 Actress; the first British-born motion picture leading lady to become a star in both England and North America; remembered for her fragile blonde beauty and gentle, well-bred manner; began stage career in England in 1927; beginning in 1928, had leading roles in some eighteen British films, including Alfred Hitchcock's classics *The Thirty-Nine Steps* (1935) and *Secret Agent* (1936); in Hollywood made another score of films, including spy thriller *The General Died at Dawn* (1936) and comedy *My Favorite Blonde* (1942); after retiring from screen, in 1949, continued to act for several years on stage, radio, and television; died in Marbella, Spain, her home for more than fifteen years. See *Current Biography* (April) 1949.

Obituary *N Y Times* p33 O 3 '87

CASEY, WILLIAM J(OSEPH) Mar. 13, 1913–May 6, 1987 U.S. government official; lawyer; director of Central Intelligence Agency from 1981 until his retirement for health reasons in February 1987; chairman of Securities and Exchange Commission (1971–73); undersecretary of state for economic affairs (1973–74); president and chairman of Export-Import Bank (1974–75); member of foreign intelligence advisory board (1976); manager of Ronald Reagan's presidential campaign (1980); was under investigation, at time of death, for alleged role in sale of U.S. arms to Iran in exchange for funds to support Nicaraguan contra rebels; died in Glen Cove, New York. See Current Biography (March) 1972.

Obituary N Y Times A p1 My 7 '87

CASPARY, VERA 1904–June 6, 1987 Novelist; playwright; screenwriter; wrote best-selling stories about working-women heroines striving for independence; was best known for murder mysteries Laura (1943) and The Weeping and the Laughter (1950) and for the screen adaptation of Laura (1944); wrote eighteen novels (including the book on which screen musical Les Girls was based), ten screenplays, and four stage plays; died in New York City. See Current Biography (Yearbook) 1947.

Obituary N Y Times B p11 Je 11 '87

CHAMOUN, CAMILLE N(IMER) 1900–Aug. 7, 1987 Lebanese Maronite Christian politician, government official; diplomat; namesake of the "Chamounists," catchall name for those opposed to left-of-center, largely Muslim "Chehabists"; was president of Lebanon from 1952 to 1958; in 1958, founded National Liberal party; during civil war of 1975–76, cofounded, with Pierre Gemayal and others, the Lebanese Front, a Christian coalition; at time of his death was minister of finance in caretaker cabinet; died in Beirut. See Current Biography (July) 1956.

Obituary N Y Times p32 Ag 8 '87

CHASINS, ABRAM Aug. 17, 1903–June 21, 1987 Composer; pianist; a protégé of Josef Hofmann; taught at Curtis Institute in Philadelphia (1926–35) and at Berkshire Music Center in Tanglewood (1940); joined New York City radio station WQXR as music consultant (1941); as musical director of WQXR (1943–65), made it into one of most distinguished AM-FM classical music stations; was musician in residence at University of Southern California (1972–77) and artistic director of its radio station KUSC (1973–77); composed over 100 works, including Three Chinese Pieces (1925) and Twenty-four Preludes for Piano (1928); wrote Music at the Crossroads (1972), among other books; received many honors, including a Peabody Award; died in New York City. See Current Biography (February) 1960.

Obituary N Y Times D p32 Je 23 '87

CHUTE, (BEATRICE) JOY Jan. 3, 1913–Sept. 6, 1987 Writer; wrote about adolescent boys in stories published in popular magazines and in such novels as Shattuck Cadet (1940) and Camp Hero (1942); wrote adult fiction, including romantic novel Greenwillow (1956), which was made into a Broadway musical in

1960; also published the books The Fields Are White (1950), The Blue Cup and Other Stories (1957), The Story of a Small Life (1971), Katie: An Impertinent Fairy Tale (1978), and The Good Woman (1986); taught English and creative writing at Barnard College; served as director of Books Across the Sea and was a past president of PEN American Center; died in New York City. See Current Biography (Yearbook) 1950.

Obituary N Y Times D p35 S 15 '87

CLAGUE, EWAN Dec. 27, 1896–Apr. 12, 1987 U.S. government official; economist; statistician; educator; joined bureau of research and statistics of Social Security Board as associate director in 1936; became director of bureau's research branch in 1937; served as commissioner of labor statistics for Department of Labor in both Democratic and Republican administrations from 1946 to 1965; later taught labor statistics at University of California at Los Angeles and other institutions; died in Bethesda, Maryland. See Current Biography (July) 1956.

Obituary N Y Times B p5 Ap 15 '87

COCO, JAMES Mar. 21, 1929–Feb. 25, 1987 Actor; self-described "fat character actor"; worked on stage for two decades before Terrence McNally wrote, with him and his rotund physique in mind, Next (1968), his vehicle to Off Broadway stardom; became Broadway star in Last of the Red Hot Lovers (1968–69), written for him by Neil Simon, who viewed him as "an acting comedian" typifying a "loser" with ability "to play the foibles" of others; later appeared in several Simon movies, including Only When I Laugh (1981), among other films; was frequent television talk show guest; won Emmy in 1983 for guest role in TV dramatic series St. Elsewhere; starred in short-lived television situation comedies Calucci's Department (1973) and The Dumplings (1976); wrote The James Coco Diet Book (1984); died in New York City. See Current Biography (May) 1974.

Obituary N Y Times D p19 F 27 '87

COHEN, ARTHUR A(LLEN) June 25, 1928–Oct. 31, 1986 Author; ecumenical Jewish scholar; publisher; founder and president of Meridian Books (1955–60); later held high editorial positions at Holt, Rinehart & Winston and Viking Press; with scores of published essays on modern currents and cross-currents in religious thought, made important contribution to interfaith dialogue; wrote Martin Buber (1958) and The Natural and Supernatural Jew (1963), among other books of nonfiction; drew heavily from philosophy and Jewish theology in his five novels, including An Admirable Woman (1983), inspired by personality and intellectual career of his friend Hannah Arendt; died in New York City. See Current Biography (September) 1960.

Obituary N Y Times p14 N 1 '86

COHEN, WILBUR J(OSEPH) June 10, 1913–May 18, 1987 Former government official; social reformer; went to Washington as first employee of Social Security Administration in 1934; helped draft New Deal's Social Security Act, and most of the major social welfare legislation of the Kennedy and Johnson administrations, in the 1960s; was assistant secretary of Health, Education, and Welfare under President Kennedy and secretary of HEW under President Johnson; later taught at universities of Michigan and Texas, headed American Public Welfare Association, and founded Save Our Security (SOS), a coalition that blocked many proposed cuts in welfare programs; died in Seoul, South Korea, where he was to speak at conference on welfare for the aging. See *Current Biography* (September) 1968.

Obituary *N Y Times* D p30 My 19 '87

COLE, W(ILLIAM) STERLING Aug. 18, 1904–Mar. 15, 1987 Former Republican U.S. representative from up-state New York (1935–1957); was first director of International Atomic Energy Agency (1957–1961), set up to promote the building of nuclear reactors worldwide; as congressman, was strong voice for government frugality, decentralization, and a nuclear arsenal to match that of the Soviet Union; died in Washington, D.C. See *Current Biography* (March) 1954.

Obituary *N Y Times* B p6 Mr 17 '87

COLLINS, J(OSEPH) LAWTON May 1, 1896–Sept. 12, 1987 United States Army officer; was known as "Lightning Joe" when he commanded a division on Guadalcanal in early phases of World War II; led seventh army corps in D-Day landing at Normandy (1944) and commanded troops in campaigns in France, Belgium, and Germany, earning designation by General Omar Bradley as one of "outstanding field commanders"; after war, served as deputy commanding general and chief of staff of army ground forces; succeeded General Bradley as army chief of staff (1949–53); served as special envoy to Vietnam before his retirement in 1956; became vice-chairman of board of Pfizer International subsidiaries in 1957. See *Current Biography* (November) 1959.

Obituary *N Y Times* B p16 S 14 '87

DANGERFIELD, GEORGE (BUBB) Oct. 28, 1904–Dec. 27, 1906 Historian; over course of fifty-year career as author and lecturer, wrote many books on variety of historical subjects, ranging from *Bengal Mutiny: the Story of the Sepoy Rebellion* (1933) to *Victoria's Heir: the Education of a Prince* (1941) to *Interpreting American History* (1970); won both Bancroft Prize and Pulitzer Prize for *The Era of Good Feelings* (1952), which describes the transition from Jeffersonian to Jacksonian democracy; died in Santa Barbara, California. See *Current Biography* (September) 1953.

Obituary *N Y Times* D p22 Ja 6 '87

DENEBRINK, FRANCIS C(OMPTON) June 22, 1896–Apr. 8, 1987 Former U.S. naval officer; served in both world wars and in Korean conflict; was officer in charge of Navy Department press section (1926–28); served briefly as White House naval aide during Calvin Coolidge administration; as commander of cruiser USS *Brooklyn* during World War II, oversaw rescue on September 3, 1942 of all 1,500 men aboard the burning transport ship USS *Wakefield*; commanded Pacific fleet service force (1949–52) and Military Sea Transportation Service (1952–56); died in San Francisco, California. See *Current Biography* (February) 1956.

Obituary *N Y Times* B p6 Ap 17 '87

DOISY, E(DWARD) A(DELBERT) Nov. 13, 1893–Oct. 23, 1986 Biochemist; chairman emeritus, department of biochemistry, St. Louis University School of Medicine; for isolating vitamin K, a factor in blood coagulation, shared 1943 Nobel Prize with Henrik Dam; also isolated and identified female sex hormones estrone and estradiol; died in St Louis, Missouri. See *Current Biography* (March) 1949.

Obituary *N Y Times* p9 O 25 '86

DONNER, FREDERIC G(ARRETT) Oct. 4, 1902–Feb. 28, 1987 Former corporation executive; trained in economics, joined General Motors Corp. as accountant in 1926; working his way up corporate ladder, became chairman and chief executive officer of General Motors in 1958; under his nine-year chairmanship, corporation set new records in domestic and international sales, earnings, and dividend payments; remained a company director for total of thirty-two years; died in Greenwich, Connecticut. See *Current Biography* (January) 1959.

Obituary *N Y Times* I p40 Mr 1 '87

DRAPER, CHARLES STARK Oct. 2, 1901–July 25, 1987 Aeronautical engineer; founder and director of Charles Stark Draper Laboratory, which was originally attached to Massachusetts Institute of Technology but is now independent; a pioneer in application of gyroscopic principles to advanced military, aeronautical and astronautical guidance instrumentation; began working with gyroscopes at M.I.T. in 1920s; invented gyroscope-stabilized gunsights used by U.S. in World War II, Korea, and Vietnam; directed development of guidance technology for jet fighter planes, nuclear submarines and missiles, the Atlas and Titan rockets, and the Apollo spacecraft that took American astronauts to moon; died in Cambridge, Massachusetes. See *Current Biography* (December) 1965.

Obituary *N Y Times* A p16 Jl 27 '87

DUNTON, A(RNOLD) DAVIDSON July 4, 1912–Feb. 7, 1987 Former Canadian journalist; educator; in 1930s, was reporter and associate editor with *Montreal Star* and editor of *Montreal Standard*; chaired board of governors of Canadian Broadcasting Corporation from 1945 to 1958, when he became president of Carleton University in Ottawa; remained on university's board of directors after his retirement as president in 1972; died in Ottawa. See *Current Biography* (January) 1959.

Obituary *N Y Times* B p11 F 9 '87

DU PRÉ, JACQUELINE Jan. 25, 1945–Oct. 19, 1987 British-born cellist; one of world's premier instrumentalists of twentieth century, noted for her flawless technique and her sensitive interpretations, especially of the sonatas of Brahms and the concertos of Haydn, Boccherini, Schumann, Dvorak, Saint-Seëns, Delius, and Elgar; began to play at age of five and won her first competition at eleven; toured extensively with her husband, the Israeli pianist Daniel Barenboim, whom she married in 1967, until she was incapacitated by multiple sclerosis in mid-1970s; died in London, from effects of the disease. See *Current Biography* (May) 1970.

Obituary *N Y Times* B p5 O 20 '87

EAKER, IRA C(LARENCE) Apr. 13, 1896–Aug. 6, 1987 U. S. Air Force general, retired; became officer in Army Air Corps in 1918; between world wars, served in Philippines and in Department of War in Washington, among other posts; commanded the American bomber fleet in Europe in World War II; after war, helped to plan establishment of Air Force as separate military service; following retirement from Air Force in 1947, was executive with Hughes and Douglas aircraft companies; with General H. H. ("Hap") Arnold, wrote three books on military flying and aviation industry; also wrote syndicated newspaper column on military affairs; died at Andrews Air Force Base in Camp Springs, Maryland. See *Current Biography* (October) 1942.

Obituary *N Y Times* p32 Ag 8 '87

EURICH, ALVIN C(HRISTIAN) June 14, 1902–May 27, 1987 Educator; as first president of State University of New York (1949–51), was responsible for bringing together thirty-two state-supported colleges under one university system; vice-president of Ford Fund for the Advancement of Education (1951–64); executive director of Ford Foundation educational division (1958–64); vice-president (1944–48) and acting president (1948) of Stanford University; president of Aspen Institute for Humanistic Studies (1963–72); founder and chairman (1961–87) of Academy for Educational Development; died in New York City. See *Current Biography* (June) 1949.

Obituary *N Y Times* B p6 My 29 '87

FIELDING, GABRIEL Mar. 25, 1916–Nov. 27, 1986 Novelist; physician; educator; although trained as physician, practiced only part time after establishing career as writer with publication of *The Frog Prince and Other Poems* in 1952; wrote more than a dozen books, most recently *The Women of Guinea Lane* (1986), but is perhaps best known for Blaydon family trilogy: *Brotherly Love* (1954), *In the Time of Greenbloom* (1956), and *Through Streets Broad and Narrow* (1960); left native England in 1966 to join faculty of Washington State University as professor of English, a post he held until his retirement in 1981; died in Bellevue, Washington. See *Current Biography* (February) 1962.

Obituary *N Y Times* p8 Ja 3 '87

FINGESTEN, PETER Mar. 20, 1916–Sept. 9, 1987 German-born symbolist sculptor; educator; immigrated to United States in 1939; won acclaim for his idealized, seemingly gravity-defying expressionist sculptures, often constructed of concrete mixed with pigments and other materials; founded art department at Pace University in New York City in 1950 and served as its chairman until 1986; established university art gallery in 1956; author of *East is East* (1956), *The Eclipse of Symbolism* (1970), and *Dynamics of Creativity* (1987); died in New York City. See *Current Biography* (October) 1954.

Obituary *N Y Times* B p8 S 11 '87

FLEMING, DONALD M(ETHUEN) May 23, 1905–Dec. 31, 1986 Canadian government official; lawyer; served in various municipal government posts in Toronto before election to Parliament in 1945 on Progressive Conservative ticket; as M.P. for Eglinton-Toronto riding (1945–63), specialized in financial problems; served as finance minister (1957–62) and justice minister (1962–63) in John G. Diefenbaker's cabinet; appointed governor of World Bank and International Monetary Fund (1957–63); wrote numerous articles on legal subjects and two-volume political memoir *So Very Near* (1960); died in Toronto, Canada. See *Current Biography* (February) 1959.

Obituary *N Y Times* p8 Ja 3 '87

FORD, HENRY II Sept. 4, 1917–Sept. 29, 1987 Industrialist; beginning in 1940, learned automobile manufacturing from bottom up in company founded by his grandfather and namesake; as president (1945–60) and chairman (1960–80), reversed Ford Motor Company's downward trend and rebuilt it into second leading autom maker in United States and world industrial giant; died in Detroit, Michigan. See *Current Biography* (June) 1978.

Obituary *N Y Times* A p1+ S 30 '87

FOSSE, BOB June 23, 1927–Sept. 23, 1987 Choreographer; theatrical and film director; began career as musical comedy dancer; won Tony awards for choreographing Broadway hit musicals *Pajama Game* (1956) and *Damn Yankees* (1957); as director, won Tony awards for *Redhead* (1958) and *Sweet Charity* (1966), both starring his third wife, Gwen Verdon; received Oscar award as best director for film *Cabaret* (1972); directed stage productions of *How to Succeed in Business Without Really Trying* (1961), *Pippin* (1972), and *Chicago* (1975) and films *Lenny* (1974) and *All That Jazz* (1979), among others; also appeared as dancer and actor in several films; died in Washington, D.C. See *Current Biography* (June) 1972.

Obituary *N Y Times* D p23 S 24 '87

GERHARDSEN, EINAR May 10, 1897–Sept. 19, 1987 Prime minister of Norway (1945–51, 1955–65); leader of Labor party until his retirement in 1972; played key role in development of Norwegian welfare state and promulgated "binding cooperation with the Western democracies"; died in Oslo, Norway. See *Current Biography* (March) 1949.

Obituary *N Y Times* L p60 S 20 '87

GIMBEL, PETER (ROBIN) Feb. 14, 1928–July 12, 1987 Explorer; filmmaker; scion of Gimbel Brothers, Inc.; began career in investment banking on Wall Street in 1952 but abandoned it in 1960 to pursue his paramount interests full time; released *Blue Water, White Death*, his poetic motion picture account of encounters with white sharks off Australia, in 1971; for nearly three decades, explored and photographed sunken Italian luxury liner *Andrea Doria* and made two television documentaries about it, released in 1976 and 1984; explored previously uncharted Vilcabamba Range in Peruvian Andes in 1963; died in New York City. See *Current Biography* (January) 1982.

Obituary *N Y Times* D p10 Jl 13 '87

GINGOLD, HERMIONE (FERDINANDA) Dec. 12, 1897–May 24, 1987 British-born actress; an irrepressible comedienne, spirited and sharp-tongued, with throaty, mirthful voice; in England, acted in Shakespeare at Old Vic, appeared in such films as *The Pickwick Papers,* and performed in many revues, including *Sweet and Low* and *Sweeter and Lower,* the productions that introduced her to American servicemen during World War II; in United States, became popular guest on *The Jack Paar Show* and other CBS television programs; on American screen, was perhaps best known as superannuated French courtesan in musical comedy *Gigi;* had several Broadway roles, including Madame Armfeldt in musical *A Little Night Music;* wrote memoir *The World Is Square* (1945) and cowrote several of her stage vehicles; died in New York City. See *Current Biography* (October) 1958.

Obituary *N Y Times* A p37 My 25 '87

GLEASON, JACKIE Feb. 26, 1916–June 24, 1987 Actor; comedian; musician; television producer; corpulent master showman; after early career in cabarets, carnivals, and summer stock, on radio, and in minor film roles, broke into television as star of comedy series *The Life of Riley* (1949–50); portrayed comic characters on *Jackie Gleason Show* (1952–70); attained height of popularity as Brooklyn bus driver Ralph Kramden in series *The Honeymooners* (1955–71); won Tony award for Broadway performance as Uncle Sid in *Take Me Along* (1959); was featured in some fifteen motion pictures; was nominated for Oscars for performance as Minnesota Fats in *The Hustler* (1961) and Chaplinesque portrayal of mute janitor in *Gigot* (1963); composed and recorded mood music; was elected to Television Hall of Fame (1985); died in Fort Lauderdale, Florida. See *Current Biography* (October) 1955.

Obituary *N Y Times* B p4+ Je 26 '87

GOODELL, CHARLES E(LLSWORTH, JR.) Mar. 16, 1926–Jan. 21, 1987 Former U.S. senator from New York; lawyer; elected to House of Representatives in 1958, established reputation as moderate Republican with liberal record in civil rights; appointed to Senate in 1968 to fill unexpired term of the assassinated Robert F. Kennedy; an outspoken critic of Vietnam war, became favorite target of Nixon administration hatchet men; after losing 1970 election, practiced law and served as board chairman of DGA International, Inc., a public relations firm; died in Washington, D.C. See *Current Biography* (December) 1968.

Obituary *N Y Times* B p20 Ja 22 '87

GOODRICH, LLOYD July 10, 1897–Mar. 27, 1987 Former museum director; author; helped widen appreciation of indigenous American art; joined Whitney Museum of American Art at its founding in 1930; became director in 1958; was instrumental in building the Whitney's core collection and guiding the museum's evolution from largely private to public institution; wrote numerous books on American art and artists, including *Pioneers of Modern Art in America: The Decade of the Armory Show, 1910–1920* (1960); strove throughout his career to raise rewards earned by artists to a level commensurate with their value to society; was founding member of National Council on the Arts and Government; died in New York City. See *Current Biography* (May) 1967.

Obituary *N Y Times* p32 Mr 28 '87

GRANT, CARY Jan. 18, 1904–Nov. 29, 1986 British-born motion picture actor; developing superb timing and a style as crisp and clipped as his distinctive cosmopolitan accent, created dashing and debonair public persona, the American cinema's epitome of sophisticated aplomb; maintained that devil-may-care persona with good humor, artful ease, and seeming agelessness through screen career numbering thirty-four years and seventy-two films, ranging from the funny and sexy melodrama *She Done Him Wrong* (1933) and the classic comedy *Mr. Blandings Builds His Dream House* (1948) to the comedy-thriller *North by Northwest* (1959) and the black farce *Charade* (1963); at his peak, was most identified with light romantic leading roles in such comedies as *The Awful Truth* (1937) and *Once Upon a Honeymoon* (1942); brought a rascal's aloofness to romantic roles and was charming even when sinister, as in *Notorious* (1946); nominated for Academy Award for realistic dramatic performance in *None But the Lonely Heart* (1944); received special 1970 Oscar "for his mastery of the art of film acting"; died in Davenport, Iowa. See *Current Biography* (November) 1965.

Obituary *N Y Times* A p1+ D 1 '86

GREEN, EDITH S(TARRETT) Jan. 17, 1910–Apr. 21, 1987 U.S. Democratic representative from Oregon (1954–74); one of the most powerful women ever to serve in Congress; as second-ranking member of House Education and Labor Committee and head of its subcommittee on higher education, helped to win passage of legislation creating first federal scholarships for college undergraduates; championed legislation aimed at providing women with equal pay for equal work; played crucial behind-scenes role in passage, in 1967, of President Lyndon B. Johnson's key antipoverty legislation while vigorously opposing his Vietnam war policy; died in Tualatin, Oregon. See *Current Biography* (May) 1956.

Obituary *N Y Times* D p31 Ap 23 '87

GREENE, HUGH CARLETON Nov. 15, 1910–Feb. 19, 1987 Former British broadcasting executive; brother of novelist Graham Greene; was foreign correspondent for London *Daily Telegraph* (1934–40) before joining British Broadcasting Corporation as director of its wartime propaganda broadcasts to Germany; later served at BBC as assistant controller of overseas services (1952–55) and news director (1958–59); as director-general (1959–69), revolutionized previously stodgy BBC television and radio programming and met competition from independent television networks with frank, lively programs sometimes satirizing such sacrosanct British institutions as Royal Family; was knighted in 1964; died in London. See *Current Biography* (September) 1963.

Obituary *N Y Times* p9 F 21 '87

GREENE, LORNE Feb. 12, 1915–Sept. 11, 1987 Actor; best known as firm but benevolent patriarch of Ponderosa ranch in highly successful NBC-TV series

Bonanza (1959-73); during World War II, was Canada's leading radio newscaster; appeared on Broadway stage in *The Prescott Proposals* (1953-54) and other plays, and in Hollywood films, including *The Silver Chalice* (1951), *Peyton Place* (1957), and *The Buccaneer* (1958); on television, played in dozens of dramas, in such series as *Griff* (1973-74) and *Battlestar Galactica* (1978-79), and in the miniseries *Roots* (1977); also made recordings of stories set to music; died in Santa Monica, California. See *Current Biography* (January) 1967.

Obituary N Y *Times* p36 S 12 '87

GREENWOOD, JOAN Mar. 4, 1921-Feb. 1987 British actress; made first professional stage appearance in London as Louisa in *Le Malade Imaginaire* in 1938; later played Ellie Dunn in *Heartbreak House*, Ophelia in *Hamlet*, Nora in *A Doll's House*, and Celia in *Volpone*, among many other roles; made Broadway debut as Lucasta in *The Confidential Clerk* in 1954; on screen, was best known for comedic parts especially those with Alec Guinness in *Kind Hearts and Coronets* (1950) and *The Man in the White Suit* (1951); enjoyed latter-day revival of career in roles in several British television series; was found dead at her home in London on February 28. See *Current Biography* (May) 1954.

Obituary N Y *Times* D p21 Mr 3 '87

GROSS, H(AROLD) R(OYCE) June 30, 1899-Sept. 22, 1987 United States conservative Republican representative from Iowa for twenty-six years, beginning in 1949; was tenaciously economy-minded and isolationist in his voting; in pursuing his commitment "to save this country from bankruptcy," questioned necessity or size of virtually every proposed federal expenditure, large or small, especially for such internationalist projects as the United Nations, the Marshall Plan, and the Peace Corps; died in Washington, D.C. See *Current Biography* (January) 1964.

Obituary N Y *Times* D p23 S 24 '87

GRZIMEK, BERNHARD Apr. 24, 1909-Mar. 13, 1987 West German zoologist; zoo director; wildlife conservationist; after World War II, rebuilt devastated Zoological Garden in Frankfurt into state-of-the-art institution closely duplicating animals' natural habitats; in his concern for endangered species, made numerous expeditions, conducted popular television show, and wrote many books, including *Serengeti Shall Not Die*, an eloquent plea for saving the last of Africa's great game preserves; made documentary film of same name about Serengeti that won an Oscar in 1960; edited monumental *Grzimek's Animal Life Encyclopedia*; died in Frankfurt. See *Current Biography* (March) 1973.

Obituary N Y *Times* D p11 Mr 16 '87

HALEY, SIR WILLIAM JOHN May 24, 1901-Sept. 6, 1987 British journalist; broadcasting executive; began career with London *Times* (1921); joined staff of Manchester *Evening News* (1922); became its chief subeditor in 1925 and managing editor in 1930; led fight among editors against appeasement of fascism during Munich crisis in 1938; joint editor of Manchester

Guardian and Evening News Ltd. as well as director of Press Association and of Reuters news agency (1939-43); restored public confidence in BBC with his reputation for erudition and his "fervently democratic editorializing" as its editor in chief (1943) and director-general (1944-52); instituted BBC's third radio channel in 1946; as editor in chief of London *Times* (1952-66), replaced front page death and marriage notices with hard news and made paper less automatically supportive of government; editor in chief of *Encyclopedia Britannica* (1967-69); died on island of Jersey in English Channel. See *Current Biography* (April) 1948.

Obituary N Y *Times* D p27 S 9 '87

HAMMOND, E(DWARD) CUYLER June 14, 1912-Nov. 3, 1986 Biologist; director of statistical research (1946-66) and vice-president for epidemiology and statistics (1966-77) with American Cancer Society; with help of as many as 60,000 trained volunteers across country, conducted complex large-group studies into causes of cancer; in early 1950s, made public first data linking cigarette smoking to lung cancer; later in same decade, published facts and figures indicating higher risk of death from all causes faced by cigarette smokers; still later, produced statistics regarding health hazards of asbestos and pollutants in workplace; died in New York City. See *Current Biography* (June) 1957.

Obituary N Y *Times* B p14 N 5 '86

HAMMOND, JOHN (HENRY, JR.) Dec. 15, 1910-July 10, 1987 Record producer; jazz and blues impresario, music critic; civil rights champion; a key figure in bringing "race" music into mainstream; discovered or brought to wide public attention scores of artists of calibre of Lionel Hampton, Teddy Wilson, Charlie Christian, Billie Holiday, Count Basie, Bob Dylan, Bruce Springsteen, and Aretha Franklin; catalyzed formation of Benny Goodman band in 1934; promoted such historic events as the *Spirituals to Swing* concerts of late 1930s; contributed from 1930s on to such diverse publications as *New Masses*, the *Nation*, *Gramophone*, *Melody Maker*, *Downbeat*; and the *New York Times*; retired as vice-president in charge of talent acquisition at Columbia Records in 1975; died in New York City. See *Current Biography* (July) 1979.

Obituary N Y *Times* p1+ Jl 11 '87

HARRISON, WILLIAM K(ELLY) JR. Sept. 7, 1895-May 25, 1987 Retired lieutenant general, U. S. Army; a direct descendant of President William Henry Harrison; was field commander in France in both world wars; after World War II, served under General Douglas MacArthur in occupation of Japan; was tough, laconic senior UN negotiator in 1951-52 truce talks ending Korean conflict; died in Bryn Mawr Terrace, Pennsylvania. See *Current Biography* (July) 1952.

Obituary N Y *Times* B p6 My 29 '87

HASS, H(ENRY) B(OHN) Jan. 25, 1902-Feb. 13, 1987 Chemist; was a discoverer of gas chromatography, a key analytical tool in contemporary chemistry; chaired Purdue University chemistry department (1932-49); made wide-ranging contributions to organic chemistry, including study of nitration that helped launch nitroparaffin industry; as member of Manhattan Project (1942–46), helped develop atomic bomb; managed research and development at General Aniline and Film Corporation (1949–52); was president of Sugar Research Foundation (1952–60); directed chemical research at M.W. Kellogg Company. (1961–70); died in Manhasset, New York. See *Current Biography* (April) 1956.

Obituary *N Y Times* p15 F 14 '87

HAUGHTON, DANIEL J(EREMIAH) Sept. 7, 1911–July 5, 1987 Corporation executive; rose through ranks from systems analyst (1939) to board chairman of Lockheed Aircraft Corporation (1967–76); presided over production of U-2 and SR-71 Blackbird reconnaissance planes as well as problem-plagued production of C-5A supertransport plane, Cheyenne high-speed helicopter, and L-1011 TriStar commercial jetliner; through arrangements with banks and with British and U.S. governments, narrowly averted bankrupty after cost overruns had brought Lockheed into financial difficulties; stepped down as chairman in 1976 amid charges that Lockheed had won some contracts through bribery; died in Marietta, Georgia. See *Current Biography* (September) 1974.

Obituary *N Y Times* D p27 Jl 7 '87

HAYES, WOODY Feb. 14 1913–Mar. 11, 1987 Football coach; at Ohio State University from 1951 to 1978, coached Buckeyes to thirteen Big Ten titles and four national championships; in career spanning twenty-nine years, had 238-72-10 record, fourth best in major-college history; used knowledge of military tactics in developing Ohio State's ground attack; was named top college coach in 1957 and 1975; had legendary temper, which was finally his undoing; was dismissed as head coach after he punched opposing player who had intercepted Buckeye pass; died in Upper Arlington, Ohio. See *Current Biography* (February) 1975.

Obituary *N Y Times* B p6 Mr 13 '87

HAYWORTH, RITA Oct. 17, 1918–May 14, 1987 Actress; known as the "great American love goddess"; epitomized Hollywood glamour of 1940s and 1950s; appeared in over forty motion pictures, including *Only Angels Have Wings* (1939), *Strawberry Blonde* (1941), *My Gal Sal* (1942), *Cover Girl* (1944), *Miss Sadie Thompson* (1953), and *Pal Joey* (1957); attained star status as dancing partner of Fred Astaire in *You'll Never Get Rich* (1941); also won wide attention in *Gilda* (1946) and in the thriller *The Lady From Shanghai* (1949), directed by Orson Welles, the second of her five husbands; was under care of her second daughter, Princess Yasmin Aga Khan, since 1981, after being stricken by Alzheimer's disease; died in New York City. See *Current Biography* (May) 1960.

Obituary *N Y Times* p10 My 16 '87

HEINZ, H(ENRY) J(OHN) July 10, 1908–Feb. 23, 1987 Business executive; grandson of the founder of the H.J. Heinz Company; in 1935, while serving as assistant to his father, the company's chief executive officer, established manufacturing plant in Australia that became the largest food processor there; later established Heinz subsidiaries in Venezuela, Japan, Italy, and Portugal; tenure as CEO (1941–66) was distinguished by acquisitions of high-performance companies, including Star-Kist Foods, Inc.; chaired United States Council of the International Chamber of Commerce (1948–51) and other economic and public service organizations; died in Hobe Sound, Florida. See *Current Biography* (June) 1947.

Obituary *N Y Times* A p25 F 24 '87

HELLER, WALTER W(OLFGANG) Aug. 27, 1915–June 15, 1987 Economist; chairman, White House Council of Economic Advisers (1961–64); except for period of government service, was professor at University of Minnesota from 1946 until 1986; was known as liberal Democratic "demystifier of the dismal science" and its jargon; developed theory, based on Keynesianism, for fine-tuning economy, chiefly through tax policy; introduced idea that recovery from national recession requires going beyond prerecession gross national product; persuaded President John F. Kennedy to use tax cuts and some deficit spending to stimulate inflation-free growth of economy; later, when cost of Vietnam war began to spark inflationary trend, failed, woefully, to persuade President Lyndon B. Johnson to raise taxes; died at vacation home near Seattle, Washington. See *Current Biography* (September 1961).

Obituary *N Y Times* A p1+ Je 17 '87

HEMINGWAY, MARY (WELSH) Apr. 5, 1908–Nov. 26, 1986 Writer; widow of Ernest Hemingway, her third husband, whom she met in 1944, and whose life she shared during their often turbulent marriage, from 1946 until his suicide in 1961; began her career as a journalist in Chicago in 1930; worked as war correspondent for *Time* and *Life* magazines in London (1940–45); in recent years, aided young writers financially through Ernest Hemingway Foundation; author of autobiography, *How It Was* (1976); died in New York City. See *Current Biography* (September) 1968.

Obituary *N Y Times* D p9 N 28 '86

HENDERSON, LEON May 26, 1895–Oct. 19, 1986 Economist; played key role in New Deal's transition from Depression recovery programs to massive economic mobilization for World War II; using analyses of consumption, was canny prognosticator of economic trends, beginning when he was pro-consumer director of remedial loan division of private Russell Sage Foundation (1925–34); after serving at high levels in several other Washington agencies, including National Recovery Administration, became in 1941 first director of Office of Price Administration, set up to ration goods as well as to curb wartime inflation through price ceilings; after retirement from O.P.A. post in 1942, worked as economic consultant and commentator; died in Oceanside, California. See *Current Biography* (July) 1940.

Obituary *N Y Times* D p31 O 21 '86

HERZOG PAUL M(AX) Aug. 21, 1906–Nov. 23, 1986 Lawyer; educator; industrial relations expert; chairman of National Labor Relations Board (1945–53); had previously chaired New York State Labor Relations Board; taught government and economics at Harvard

University and was acting dean of Graduate School of Public Administration there from 1953 to 1957; was president of Salzburg Seminar in American Studies, promoting European understanding of American affairs, from 1965 to 1971; died in New York City. See Current Biography (July 1945).

Obituary N Y Times D p27 N 25 '86

HESS, RUDOLF Apr. 26, 1894–Aug. 17, 1987 German government official and Nazi party functionary; joined Adolf Hitler's National Socialist party in 1921; was arrested after abortive "beer-hall putsch" (1923) and confined to Landsberg prison, where he transcribed Mein Kampf to Hitler's dictation; was named head of political section of Nazi party (1932), minister without portfolio in cabinet council (1934), and deputy party leader, second in line of succession, after Hermann Goering (1939); parachuted into estate near Glasgow, Scotland, on May 10, 1941, after flying twin-engine plane from Augsburg, Germany, ostensibly to negotiate peace agreement between Germany and Great Britain, and was taken prisoner of war; after Nuremberg war crimes trial (1946), served life term as sole inmate of Berlin's Spandau prison; committed suicide in West Berlin. See Current Biography (November) 1941.

Obituary N Y Times A p1+ Ag 18 '87

HIGHTOWER, JOHN M(ARMANN) Sept. 17, 1909–Feb. 9, 1987 Journalist; known for painstaking and cool-headed analytical reporting; joined Associated Press in Nashville in 1933; was assigned to AP's Washington bureau from 1936 to 1971; in 1951, predicted course of Korean war truce negotiations and predicted dismissal of General Douglas MacArthur; in 1952, became first journalist to win in one year a Pulitzer Prize, the Raymond Clapper Memorial Award, and an award from the journalistic fraternity Sigma Delta Chi; later taught journalism at University of New Mexico and wrote column for Santa Fe New Mexican; died in Santa Fe, New Mexico. See Current Biography (November) 1952.

Obituary N Y Times B p18 F 10 '87

HIGLEY, HARVEY V(AN ZANDT) Oct. 26, 1892–Oct. 15, 1986 Former government official; chemical engineer, business executive; headed Veterans Administration from 1953 to 1957; was previously president and chairman of board of Ansul Chemical Company; died in Marinette, Wisconsin. See Current Biography (October) 1956.

Obituary N Y Times B p20 O 16 '86

HOLT, A(NDREW) D(AVID) Dec. 4, 1904–Aug. 7, 1987 Educator; professor of education; as president of University of Tennessee from 1959 to 1970, oversaw tripling of enrollment and quadrupling of state funding; previously, was vice-president of the university, from 1953 to 1959; earlier in career, had been elementary and high school teacher, principal, director of teacher training at West Tennessee State College, supervisor of schools in the West Tennessee area, editor of The Tennessee Teacher, and executive secretary-treasurer of Tennessee Education Association; was president of National Education Association in 1949

and 1950; died in Knoxville, Tennessee. See Current Biography (November) 1949.

Obituary N Y Times I p34 Ag 9 '87

HUSTED, MARJORIE CHILD 1892–Dec. 23, 1986 Home economics executive; was director of home service program of General Mills, the food corporation, from 1928 until 1946; in 1948 became executive-level company consultant; for General Mills, developed the character Betty Crocker, a synthetic public image offering advice on cooking and homemaking; was voice of that character in series of radio interview shows; helped to research and edit The Betty Crocker Picture Cookbook (1950), a perennial best seller; died in Minneapolis, Minnesota. See Current Biography (June) 1949.

Obituary N Y Times p28 D 28 '86

HUSTON, JOHN Aug. 5, 1906–Aug. 28, 1987 Motion picture director; scenarist; actor; directed forty-one films, including such classics as The Maltese Falcon (1941), The Red Badge of Courage (1951), and The African Queen (1952); won Academy Awards as best writer and director for Treasure of the Sierra Madre (1948), which earned an Oscar as best supporting actor for his father, Walter Huston; directed his daughter Anjelica Huston in her Oscar-winning performance in Prizzi's Honor (1985); acted in some twenty films, among them The Cardinal (1963), The Bible (1966), Chinatown (1974), and Winter Kills (1979); received a number of career-achievement awards, including those of American Film Institute and Film Society of Lincoln Center; died in Middletown, Rhode Island. See Current Biography (March) 1981.

Obituary N Y Times p1+ Ag 29 '87

IMPELLITTERI, VINCENT R(ICHARD) Feb. 4, 1900–Jan. 29, 1987 Sicilian-born former mayor of New York City (1950–1953); lawyer; as city council president, became acting mayor when William O'Dwyer resigned under fire in 1950; later that year, defying Tammany Hall Democratic political machine, which refused him its nomination, won mayoralty in his own right, becoming first independent to do so; later served as New York special sessions court judge (1953–1965); died in Bridgeport, Connecticut. See Current Biography (February) 1951.

Obituary N Y Times B p8 Ja 30 '87

JENNINGS, PAUL (JOSEPH) Mar. 19, 1918–Sept. 7, 1987 Labor union official; helped to found International Union of Electrical Workers (later the International Union of Electronic Workers) with James B. Carey in 1949, to supplant the allegedly Communist-dominated United Electrical Workers; challenged Carey for leadership in 1964, after union membership had begun to decline, and won presidency following recount of disputed vote; introduced "coalition" bargaining in negotiations of IUE and twelve other unions with General Electric in 1966; campaigned against reelection of Richard M. Nixon in 1972 and was included on Nixon White House list of "political opponents"; died in West Hempstead, New York. See Current Biography (December) 1969.

Obituary N Y Times p27 S 10 '87

KARAMI, RASHID Dec. 30, 1921–June 1, 1987 Lebanese statesman; lawyer; a leader of Sunni Moslems; member of Lebanese parliament from 1951 until his death; since 1955, served ten times as Lebanese prime minister, most recently as head of national unity government (1984–87); was known as an independent Arab nationalist who supported Syria's position as major power broker in Lebanon's twelve-year-old civil war; was killed by bomb explosion on board military helicopter carrying him from Tripoli to Beirut. See *Current Biography* (November) 1959.

Obituary *N Y Times* A p1+ Je 2 '87

KAYE, DANNY Jan. 18, 1913–Mar. 3, 1987 Comedian; actor; a protean, manic clown, nimble and easily improvisatory in his exaggerated dancing, singing, mimicry, pantomime, mugging, rapid patter, character changes, and such physical antics as comic symphony orchestra-leading; began career on borscht circuit; after several years in vaudeville and nightclubs, became Broadway sensation with breakneck rendition of novelty song "Tchaikovsky" in musical *Lady in the Dark* (1941); often appeared on radio and television variety shows, including his own network TV show in mid-1960s; starred in eighteen movies, including *The Secret Life of Walter Mitty* (1947) and *The Court Jester* (1956); won special Oscar in 1954; performed before juvenile audiences around world for UNICEF, his favorite charity; died in Los Angeles. See *Current Biography* (November) 1952.

Obituary *N Y Times* A p1+ Mr 4 '87

KAYE, NORA 1920–Apr. 30. 1987 Ballerina; widely regarded as foremost dramatic ballerina of her day; as charter member of Ballet Theatre in New York City in 1940s and 1950s brought new expressiveness to dance-drama under guidance of choreographer Anthony Tudor; served as associate artistic director of American Ballet Theatre from 1977 to 1983; was executive producer of motion picture *The Turning Point* (1977), melodrama about aging ballerina that was directed by her husband, Herbert Ross; died in Los Angeles. See *Current Biography* (January) 1953.

Obituary *N Y Times* p40 Mr 1 '87

KEYSERLING, LEON H. Jan. 22, 1908–Aug. 9, 1987 Economist; lawyer; government official; advocate of federal economic policy directed toward full national employment; as Senate adviser, helped to draft much of the New Deal legislation in 1930s; suggested the policies that became law in Employment Act of 1946, which mandated establishment of a presidential Council of Economic Advisers; as an original member (1946–53) and chairman (1949–53) of that council, was force for continuation of Rooseveltian liberalism in administration of President Harry S. Truman; after leaving government, was private consultant and lawyer, mostly for public employees unions and foreign governments; founded Conference on Economic Progress, a nonprofit public-interest organization; died in Washington, D.C. See *Current Biography* (January) 1947.

Obituary *N Y Times* D p22 Ag 11 '87

KISHI, NOBUSUKE Nov. 13, 1896–Aug. 7, 1987 Former foreign minister (1956) and prime minister (1956–60) of Japan; career government official; a leader of ruling Liberal Democratic party; served as minister of state and vice-minister of munitions during World War II; was jailed without trial for three years during postwar American occupation; resigned as prime minister because of massive street protests against new security treaty he signed with U.S. in 1960; died in Tokyo. See *Current Biography* (June) 1957.

Obituary *N Y Times* p32 Ag 8 '87

KRAUS, LILI Mar. 4, 1903–Nov. 6, 1986 Hungarian-born pianist; was most celebrated for her renditions of music of Mozart; during World War II was interned as prisoner of war by Japanese; from 1966 on, lived in United States while continuing to tour internationally; died in Asheville, North Carolina. See *Current Biography* (October) 1975.

Obituary *N Y Times* D p18 N 7 '86

KUEKES, EDWARD D(ANIEL) Feb. 2, 1901–Jan. 13, 1987 Newspaper artist; editorial cartoonist; worked at Cleveland Plain Dealer from 1922 until he retired in 1966; won four Freedom Foundation awards (1949, 1950, 1951, 1952) for cartoons promoting American way of life; received Pulitzer Prize in 1953 for editorial cartoon on irony of soldiers fighting in Korea being too young to vote, died in Oklahoma City, Oklahoma. See *Current Biography* (March) 1954.

Obituary *N Y Times* p15 Ja 17 '87

LABOUISSE, HENRY R(ICHARDSON) Feb. 11, 1904–Mar. 25, 1987 Former U.S. government official; former United Nations official; headed UN Children's Fund (UNICEF) from 1965 to 1979; began his long career in international public service as a State Department liaison in 1940s; directed UN Relief and Works Agency for Palestine Refugees from 1954 to 1958; became a World Bank consultant in 1959; was special adviser to UN Secretary General Dag Hammarskjöld during Congo crisis of 1960; directed International Cooperation Administration in 1961 and 1962; was American ambassador to Greece from 1962 to 1965; under him, UNICEF provided relief for both sides in Nigerian civil war in 1968 and famine relief for Cambodia in 1979; died in New York City. See *Current Biography* (October) 1961.

Obituary *N Y Times* D p18 Mr 27 '87

LANCHESTER, ELSA Oct. 28, 1902–Dec. 26, 1986 British-born character actress; pixieish comedienne; widow of the actor Charles Laughton; performed in more than eighty-five plays and films; began career as dancer and singer; after becoming darling of British stage and screen, settled in Hollywood, where she was principal comedienne at Turnabout Theatre while earning wider fame in dotty film roles that often failed to exploit to full advantage her eccentric comedic talent; is perhaps best remembered for *The Bride of Frankenstein* (1935) in which she played both Mary Shelley and the woman monster; among numerous other roles, portrayed Anne of Cleves in *The Life of Henry VIII* (1933) and one of the lunatic sisters in

Ladies in Retirement (1941); wrote autobiographies *Charles Laughton and I* (1938) and *Elsa Lancaster, Herself* (1983); died in Woodland Hills, California. See *Current Biography* (May) 1950.

Obituary *N Y Times* p16 D 27 '86

LANDON, ALF(RED MOSSMAN) Sept. 9, 1887–Oct. 12, 1987 Republican governor of Kansas for two terms (1933–37); met with success as oil producer before entering politics; as Republican presidential candidate in 1936, was defeated in landslide vote by Franklin D. Roosevelt; represented liberal wing of Republican party and supported many of Roosevelt administration's New Deal measures; after 1936 defeat did not run for public office again but became respected elder statesman; was father of Republican Senator Nancy Landon Kassenbaum of Kansas; died in Kansas. See *Current Biography* (February) 1944.

Obituary *N Y Times* B p7 O 13 '87

LASH, JOSEPH P. Dec. 2, 1909–Aug. 22, 1987 Author; journalist; as result of twenty-three-year friendship with Eleanor Roosevelt, was chosen by her son Franklin D. Roosevelt Jr., after her death in 1962, to write the official biography, *Eleanor and Franklin* (1971), based on her private papers, and won a Pulitzer Prize, a National Book Award, and the Francis Parkman Prize for it; also earned acclaim for its sequel, *Eleanor; The Years Alone* (1972); during 1930s, served as officer of Student League for International Democracy and American Student Union; became disillusioned with radical left after Stalin-Hitler pact of 1939, but remained strong liberal; reporter, editorial writer, and columnist with the then liberal *New York Post* (1950–66); author of biographical studies of Dag Hammarskjöld, Helen Keller, and Felix Frankfurter, among other books; died in Boston. See *Current Biography* (December) 1972.

Obituary *N Y Times* I p40 Ag 23 '87

LAY, JAMES S(ELDEN) JR. Aug. 24, 1911–June 28, 1987 U.S. government official; assistant executive secretary (1947–50) and executive secretary (1950–61) of National Security Council; deputy assistant to director of central intelligence Allan W. Dulles (1961–64); executive secretary of U.S. intelligence board (1962–71); consultant to president's foreign intelligence advisory board (1971–77); died at Perry Point, Maryland. See *Current Biography* (March) 1950.

Obituary *N Y Times* D p23 Jl 1 '87

LEVI, PRIMO July 31, 1919–Apr. 11, 1987 Italian writer; chemist; in his powerful books, drew on his travail as World War II anti-Nazi partisan and concentration camp inmate as well as joy he found in work; wrote with the elegance of a poet, the detail of a scientist, and a wit that precluded bitterness; best known for *Survival in Aushchwitz*—the first volume in an autobiographical trilogy—written just after the war and considered a classic in Italy; in addition to memoirs, wrote novels, short stories, essays, and poetry; worked as a chemist and sometime general manager at SIVA, a Turin paint factory, from 1947 until 1977; died in Turin, Italy, reportedly a suicide. See *Current Biography* (March) 1987.

Obituary *N Y Times* I p42 Ap 12 '87

LEVINE, JOSEPH E(DWARD) Sept. 9, 1905–July 31, 1987 Motion picture producer; was small-time New England exhibitor and distributor until late 1950s, when he began buying up foreign films, mostly Italian "spear and sandal" spectaculars and releasing them in U.S. with saturation booking and promotional pizzazz; later financed some more prestigious productions; produced or presented some 500 films, including *Godzilla, Hercules, Two Women, The Easy Life, 8½, The Producers, The Lion in Winter, The Graduate, Carnal Knowledge,* and *A Bridge Too Far*; died in Greenwich, Connecticut. See *Current Biography* (October) 1979.

Obituary *N Y Times* p36 Ag 1 '87

LEVINE, PHILIP Aug. 10 1900–Oct. 18, 1987 Physician; serologist; bacteriologist; identified Rh factor in human blood in early 1940s and showed that Rh positive blood in fetus of an Rh negative mother triggered hemolytic disease, in which antibodies transmitted from mother destroyed blood of the fetus and newborn; cleared way for virtual elimination of deadly effects of this disorder through blood transfusion shortly after birth; codiscovered blood factors, M, N, and P in 1928, while working under Nobel laureat Dr. Karl Landsteiner at Rockefeller Institute for Medical Research; instructor at University of Wisconsin medical school (1932–35); bacteriologist and immunologist at Beth Israel Hospital in Newark, New Jersey (1935–44); sponsored laws in Wisconsin and New Jersey, in 1935 and 1939 respectively, that authorized courts to determine paternity by blood test; directed Ortho Research Foundation in Raritan, New Jersey, later named the Philip Levine Laboratories, from 1944 to 1965; died in New York City. See *Current Biography* (May) 1947

Obituary *N Y Times* B p4 O 20 '87

LIBERACE May 16, 1919–Feb. 4, 1987 Pianist; a flamboyant and self-parodying showman of the keyboard who was as well known for his androgynous persona as for his floridly romantic execution of popular songs, old parlor favorites, and abridged, up-tempo versions of the more accessible classics of such composers as Beethoven and Chopin; was household synonym for kitsch pianism since 1950s, when television exposure made him the top draw on the pop concert circuit; became a stellar attraction in Las Vegas, where he lived in sybaritic opulence, surrounded by his glittering multimillion-dollar wardrobe, his custom-designed pianos, with candelabra, and his other collections of memorabilia and expensive curiosa, including vintage automobiles; through 1986, broke attendance records at such enormous theatres as Radio City Music Hall; died at his vacation home in Palm Springs, California "of an opportunistic disease caused by acquired immune deficiency syndrome," according to the Riverside County coroner. See *Current Biography* (March) 1986.

Obituary *N Y Times* B p6 F 5 '87

LIPTON, SEYMOUR Nov. 6, 1903–Dec. 5, 1986 Sculptor; self-taught creator of metaphoric metal sculptures with images of suffering, continuity, and rebirth; did *Archangel* (1964), considered his masterpiece, for Lincoln Center's Philharmonic Hall; created other commissioned works for synagogues, corporations, and public buildings; frequently drew on themes from his Jewish religious heritage; taught art at Cooper Union, the New School for Social Research, and Yale University; exhibited widely abroad as well as in leading U.S. museums; died in Glen Cove, Long Island. See *Current Biography* (November) 1964.

Obituary *N Y Times* B p14 D 8 '86

LUBELL, SAMUEL Nov. 3, 1911–Aug. 16, 1987 Public opinion analyst; writer; by means of door-to-door opinion polls, predicted election results and political trends in United States during 1950s and 1960s with high degree of success, while avoiding strict statistical approach; had previously worked on editorial staffs of *Washington Post* and *Richmond Times-Dispatch* and as free-lance writer for *Saturday Evening Post*; during World War II, served as aide to Bernard Baruch at Office of War Information and to James F. Byrnes at Office of Economic Stabilization; author of syndicated column "The People Speak" (1958–68) and of several books, including *The Future of American Politics* (1952); died in Los Angeles. See *Current Biography* (November) 1956.

Obituary *N Y Times* p33 Ag 22 '87

LUCE, CLARE BOOTHE Apr. 10, 1903–Oct. 9, 1987 Writer; socialite; wife of late Time-Life cofounder and publisher Henry R. Luce; United States Republican representative from Connecticut (1943–47); ambassador to Italy (1953–57); associate editor of *Vogue* magazine (1930); associate editor (1931–32) and managing editor (1933–34) of *Vanity Fair*; author of several plays, including the hits *The Women* (1936) and *Kiss the Boys Goodbye* (1938); converted to Roman Catholicism in 1946; member of editorial board of *Encyclopedia Britannica* (1974); member of President Ronald Reagan's foreign intelligence advisory board (from 1982); received Presidential Medal of Freedom (1983) and other honors; was noted for her sharptongued repartee; died in Washington, D.C. See *Current Biography* (April) 1953.

Obituary *N Y Times* p1+ O 10 '87

LUDLAM, CHARLES Apr. 12, 1943–May 28, 1987 Theatrical entrepreneur; cofounder and resident all-around genius of Ridiculous Theatrical Company, gender-bending Greenwich Village repertory troupe devoted to staging his gleefully lurid farces, parodic reinventions exploiting the conscious artifice and broad physicality of such varying melodramatic traditions as vaudeville, burlesque, silent movies, and opera; wrote, produced, directed, designed, and starred in more than thirty productions, including *The Mystery of Irma Vep*, a lampoon of the Gothic dime novel in which he and Everett Quinton, his real-life lover, played all of the roles (including female), and *The Artificial Jungle*, a send-up of the film noir; won four Obie awards for Off-Off-Broadway achievement; died in Manhattan of pneumonia brought on by AIDS. See *Current Biography* (August) 1986.

Obituary *N Y Times* A p1+ My 29 '87

LYNCH, J(OHN) JOSEPH Dec. 6, 1894–May 14, 1987 British-born Jesuit priest; seismologist; educator; joined staff of seismic observatory at Fordham University, New York City, in 1920; at Fordham, taught seismology and mathematics from 1950 to 1967 and directed the observatory from 1962 until failing health forced his retirement in 1983; died at the university. See *Current Biography* (October) 1946.

Obituary *N Y Times* D p14 My 18 '87

MacDONALD, JOHN D(ANN) July 24, 1916–Dec. 28, 1986 Novelist; wrote some seventy books, most of them detective and mystery novels or collections of short stories in the thriller genre, which sold a total of eighty million copies; was best known as creator of Travis McGee, a contemporary knight errant featured in twenty-one books, and as author of several novels that became motion pictures, including *The Executioners* and *Condominium*; died in Milwaukee, Wisconsin. See *Current Biography* (October) 1986.

Obituary *N Y Times* B p15 D 29 '86

MACHEL, SAMORA MOISES Sept. 29, 1933–Oct. 19, 1986 First president of People's Republic of Mozambique; commanded guerilla forces during nine years leading up to Mozambique's independence from Portugal in 1975; unified country partly by strength of his personality and his reputation for integrity; a nondoctrinaire Marxist, sought pragmatic solutions to nation's economic and other problems, including insurgency by South African-backed rebels; signed nonaggression treaty with South Africa in 1984; died in plane crash near Mozambique-South Africa border. See *Current Biography* (March) 1984

Obituary *N Y Times* A p1+ O 21 '86

MACMILLAN, (MAURICE) HAROLD Feb. 10, 1894–Dec. 29, 1986 British statesman; former Conservative prime minister (1957–63); book-publishing heir, was first elected to Parliament in 1924; served in succession of cabinet posts, including secretary for air (1945) and foreign secretary (1955); as Conservative leader, helped Britain to adapt to end of colonialism and more limited role in world affairs; as prime minister, exhorted Britons to recognize and accept force of "wind of change" in African nationalism and dealt with British withdrawal from Suez and Nigeria; also tried to be "honest broker" between Washington and Moscow; after retirement from politics, was chairman of Macmillan & Company (1963–67) and chairman (1963–74) and president of Macmillan Ltd. (since 1974); became Earl of Stockton in 1984; died in Sussex, England. See *Current Biography* (January) 1955.

Obituary *N Y Times* A p1+ D 30 '86

MACY, JOHN W(ILLIAMS), JR. Apr. 6, 1917–Dec. 22, 1986 Former U.S. government official; began career as intern with National Institute of Public Affairs and for next fifteen years served in various administrative positions with Social Security Board, War Department, and Atomic Energy Commission; as executive director (1953–58) and chairman (1961–69) of Civil Service Commission, upgraded civil service to attract best people; later served as first president of Corporation for Public Broadcasting (1969–72) and director of Federal Emergency Management Agency (1979–81); was author of *America's Unelected Government* (1984), among other books; died in McLean, Virginia. See

Current Biography (January) 1962.

Obituary N Y Times p44 D 25 '86

MADDEN, RAY J(OHN) Feb. 25, 1892–Sept. 28, 1987 Former Democratic United States representative from Indiana; lawyer; was elected comptroller of Gary, Indiana in 1935 and treasurer of surrounding Lake County in 1938; during thirty-four-year tenure in Congress, beginning in 1942, served as chairman of Democratic Congressional campaign committee, Democratic steering and policy committee, House Rules Committee, and committee investigating 1939–40 Katyn Forest Massacre in Poland; died in Washington, D.C. See Current Biography (April) 1953.

Obituary N Y Times D p34 S 29 '87

MARTIN, JOHN BARTLOW Aug. 4, 1915–Jan. 3, 1987 Journalist; liberal Democratic political speechwriter for Adlai E. Stevenson, John F. and Robert F. Kennedy, and Hubert H. Humphrey; in his prolific contributions to mass-circulation magazines on such subjects as crime, the criminal mind, and prison reform in the 1940s and 1950s, prefigured "new journalism"; was ambassador of Dominican Republic from 1962 to 1964; wrote fifteen books, including The Life of Adlai E. Stevenson (1952), Break Down the Walls (1954), and his memoirs, It Seemed Like Only Yesterday (1986); died in Highland Park, Illinois. See Current Biography (Yearbook) 1956.

Obituary N Y Times B p4 Ja 5 '87

MARVIN, LEE Feb. 19, 1924–Aug. 29, 1987 Actor; prototypical "tough guy" of Hollywood movies; appeared in fifty-six films, beginning with You're in the Navy Now (1950) and including The Wild One (1953), Bad Day at Black Rock (1955), The Man Who Shot Liberty Valance (1962), The Killers (1964), Ship of Fools (1965), The Dirty Dozen (1967), Prime Cut (1972), and Gorky Park (1985); won Academy Award as best actor in dual role, as villainous outlaw and as rum-soaked but goodhearted gunfighter, in western spoof Cat Ballou (1965); also appeared on stage and in television dramas, including police series M Squad (1957–60); was respondent in landmark "palimony" case involving reciprocal property rights of unmarried couples (1979); died in Tucson, Arizona. See Current Biography (September) 1966.

Obituary N Y Times A p17 Ag 31 '87

MATTHEWS, H(ARRISON) FREEMAN May 26, 1899–Oct. 19, 1986 Diplomat; former deputy under secretary of state (1950–53); during World War II, was American liaison with France's Vichy government (1940–41), political adviser to General Eisenhower in planning invasion of North Africa (1942), and key adviser at Yalta and Cairo conferences; later served successively as ambassador to Sweden, the Netherlands, and Austria and as cochairman of Permanent Joint Board on Defense for the United States and Canada; died in Washington, D.C. See Current Biography (March) 1945.

Obituary N Y Times D p31 O 21 '86

McCARTHY, FRANK June 8, 1912–Dec. 1, 1986 Motion picture producer; retired brigadier general; former government official; joined War Department in 1941 as military secretary to Army chief of staff George C. Marshall; during World War II served as secretary of department's general staff and as assistant secretary of state for administration; began motion picture career as technical adviser on film Brother Rat (1938); produced Decision Before Dawn (1951), the Academy Award blockbuster Patton (1970), and MacArthur (1977), among other pictures; died in Los Angeles. See Current Biography (September) 1945.

Obituary N Y Times B p26 D 4 '86

McKENNA, SIOBHAN May 24, 1923(?)–Nov. 16, 1986 Irish actress; alumna of all-Gaelic An Taibhdhearc Theatre in Galway and Abbey Theatre in Dublin; made London debut as Nora Fintry in The White Steed in 1947; brought powerful, lilting voice to portrayals ranging from Shakespearean roles to Pegeen in Playboy of the Western World, the title part in Héloïse, and Miss Madrigal in The Chalk Garden; was best known in United States for her vigorous and incandescent Broadway performance as Joan of Arc in Bernard Shaw's Saint Joan (1956) and her one-woman readings from Irish writers Here Are Ladies (1971) and Dubliners, Exiles, Epiphanies (1982); died in Dublin. See Current Biography (November) 1956.

Obituary N Y Times B p8 N 17 '86

MEDAWAR, PETER BRIAN Feb. 28, 1915–Oct. 2, 1987 Brazilian-born British zoologist; shared 1960 Nobel Prize in Medicine and Physiology for his part in formulating and proving theory of acquired immunological tolerance, which paved way for modern skin and organ transplant surgery; taught at University of Birmingham and University of London's University College; directed National Institute of Medical Research from 1962 to 1971; wrote eleven books; was knighted in 1965; died in London. See Current Biography (April) 1961.

Obituary N Y Times D p13 O 5 '87

MOLOTOV, VIACHESLAV M(IKHAILOVICH) Mar. 9, 1890–Nov. 8, 1986 Soviet Communist party leader and government official; one of leading figures in regime of Joseph Stalin; played important role in helping to prepare November 1917 revolution; member of Politburo of Soviet Communist party's Central Committee (1926–53); chairman of Council of People's Commissars (1930–41); deputy chairman of Council of Ministers (1941–57); minister of foreign affairs (1939–49, 1953–56); negotiated Soviet-German nonaggression treaty (1939) and World War II alliances with Great Britain and U.S. (1941–42); was expelled from Communist party in 1962 under Nikita S. Khrushchev's de-Stalinization policy but was reinstated in 1984. See Current Biography (June) 1954.

Obituary N Y Times A p1+ N 11 '86

MONROE, LUCY Oct. 23, 1906–Oct. 13, 1987 Singer; official soloist for American Legion and Veterans of Foreign Wars; specialized in singing "Star Spangled Banner," which she performed 5,000 times by her own estimate; began career as an operatic soprano in 1932 and later sang as a soloist with New York Philharmonic and Metropolitan Opera and with companies in other cities; during 1930s, was featured on radio programs, including *American Album of Familiar Music*; sang national anthem for three presidents, and at New York World's Fair, USO shows, war bond rallies, and New York Yankees baseball games; died in New York City. See *Current Biography* (August) 1942.

Obituary *N Y Times* B p5 O 16 '87

MOORE, GERALD July 30, 1899–Mar. 13, 1987 English pianist; through his fine and sensitive performance of lieder and art songs and his witty lectures and writings on the art of accompaniment, contributed more than any other single individual to the elevation of that art from auxiliary status to its present public stature; made first major public appearances in London in 1925, accompanying his mentor, the tenor John Coates; in hundreds of subsequent concert and recording collaborations with almost all the major soloists of the day covered vast repertory and displayed chameleonic keyboard sense in supporting a wide variety of sensibilities; wrote, among other books, the autobiography *Am I too Loud?* (1962); won Grand Prix du Disque four times; died in Buckinghamshire, England. See *Current Biography* (October) 1967.

Obituary *N Y Times* B p8 Mr 17 '87

MULLIKEN, ROBERT S(ANDERSON) June 7, 1896–Oct. 31, 1986 Physical chemist; beginning in 1928, elaborated molecular orbital theory, explaining chemical bond that holds atoms together when they combine to form a molecule; pictured molecule not as sum of its atomic parts but as new entity, defined by orbit of outermost electrons not around nuclei of individual atoms but around whole molecule; for that quantum-mechanical breakthrough, received Nobel Prize in 1966; was on faculty of University of Chicago for fifty-eight years, until spring of 1986; died in Arlington, Virginia. See *Current Biography* (September) 1967.

Obituary *N Y Times* D p15 N 3 '86

MYRDAL, (KARL) GUNNAR Dec. 6, 1898–May 17, 1987 Swedish economist; social reformer; professor at Stockholm University; head of Stockholm Peace Research Institute; shared 1974 Nobel Prize in Economics for his "pioneering analysis of the interdependence of economic, social, and institutional phenomena"; through such books as *Crisis in the Population Question* (1934), written with his wife, and his membership on government commissions, helped shape Swedish welfare state and influence welfare policy in Scandinavia generally; "lecturing us like a Dutch uncle, because he loves us" (as his American economist friend Paul A. Samuelson said), wrote two-volume classic *An American Dilemma* (1944), which influenced landmark 1954 U.S. Supreme Court ruling against "separate but equal" racial policy in education; wrote exhaustively on world poverty and its solution through land reform, lessening of social inequities, and international aid in three-volume *Asian Drama*, among other books; was Swedish secretary of commerce (1945–47); headed numerous international commissions, including UN Economic Commission for Europe (1947) and International Commission of Inquiry into U.S. War Crimes in Indochina; died in Sweden. See *Current Biography* (March) 1975.

Obituary *N Y Times* A p1+ My 18 '87

NAKIAN, REUBEN Aug. 10, 1897–Dec. 4, 1986 Sculptor; in his quasi-abstract art, used heroic subject matter drawn from Greek and Roman mythology; was first known for realistic portrait sculpture, including life-size studies of President Franklin D. Roosevelt and members of his cabinet; later, influenced by Arshile Gorky, turned to expressionism; in 1943 did bust of Marcel Duchamp that is considered one of his masterpieces; received many public commissions; is widely represented in American museums, including Museum of Modern Art, which owns his nine-foot-high bronze *Hiroshima*; died in Stamford, Connecticut. See *Current Biography* (February) 1985.

Obituary *N Y Times* D p20 D 5 '86

NORTHROP, JOHN HOWARD July 5, 1891–May 27, 1987 Biochemist; cowinner of 1946 Nobel chemistry prize for his work on purification and crystallization of enzymes, which "opened an important road to the investigation of protein constitution and the chemistry of digestion"; was life member of Rockefeller Institute for Medical Research (now Rockefeller University); later taught bacteriology and biophysics at University of California at Berkeley; died in Wickenberg, Arizona. See *Current Biography* (June) 1947.

Obituary *N Y Times* D p22 Jl 22 '87

OBOLER, ARCH Dec. 1909–Mar. 19, 1987 Writer; in 1930s and 1940s was radio's most prolific dramatist, turning out hundreds of original scripts for several dramatic series, the most popular of which was the suspense/horror program *Lights Out*; was the chief developer of radio drama's stream-of-consciousness monolog; for motion picture screen, wrote, among other films, 3-D movie *Bwana Devil* (1952), which he also produced and directed; for Broadway, wrote science fiction drama *Night of the Auk* (1956); later headed and wrote stage, screen, and radio pieces for Oboler Productions; died in Westlake, California. See *Current Biography* (March) 1940.

Obituary *N Y Times* I p36 Mr 22 '87

O'BOYLE, PATRICK (ALOYSIUS) CARDINAL July 18, 1896–Aug. 10, 1987 Roman Catholic prelate; archbishop of Washington, D.C. (1948–73); a doctrinal hard-liner, created bitter ecclesiastical controversy in 1968 by invoking canonical sanctions against more than forty defiant D.C. priests, who had refused to recant their permissive interpretation of church's teaching on artificial contraception; a champion of "social justice," desegregated D.C. parochial schools in 1951, three years before racial integration of public schools became law of the land; also lobbied for more liberal immigration and social welfare policies and endorsed 1972 iceberg lettuce boycott in solidarity with "pitifully" exploited migrant farm workers; was hailed by supporters as "progressive" social "reformer" and denounced by enemies as an exponent of "lingering paternalism" who "still believes in charity rather than changing institutions"; died in Washington, D.C. See *Current Biography* (July) 1973.

Obituary *N Y Times* D p23 Ag 11 '87

O'KONSKI, ALVIN E(DWARD) May 26, 1904–July 8, 1987 U.S. Republican representative from Wisconsin;

considered himself "a New Deal Democrat domestically"; in foreign affairs, was a staunch opponent of Soviet Union; directed World League to Stop Communism (1947-48); cowrote G.I. Bill of Rights and backed such measures as those establishing farm price supports and the Fair Employment Practices Commission; published Hurley, Wisconsin, newspaper *Iron County Miner*; owned and operated local radio and television stations; died in Kewaunee, Wisconsin. See *Current Biography* (November) 1955.

Obituary *N Y Times* A p25 Jl 9 '87

PAGE, GERALDINE Nov. 22, 1924-June 13, 1987 Actress; intuitive and unconventional but controlled in her often fluttery and florid characterizations, was a superb exponent of "the Method"; with Rip Torn, her husband, founded Sanctuary Theatre, a repertory company; began acting in stock in early 1940s; in 1950s and early 1960s, was best known for portrayals of neurotic Tennessee Williams heroines, especially in stage and screen productions of *Summer and Smoke* and *Sweet Bird of Youth*; later ranged in roles from comic mother in movie *You're a Big Boy Now* to vengeful one in Sam Shepard's play *Lie of the Mind*; was nominated for eight Academy awards; finally won Oscar for best actress in 1986 for her poignant performance in *The Trip to Bountiful*; on television, won Emmys for roles in *A Christmas Memory* and *Thanksgiving Visitor*, adaptations of stories by Truman Capote; was nominated for Tony for her role in Broadway revival of *Blithe Spirit*, in which she was still a cast member at the time of her death; died at her home in New York City. See *Current Biography* (November) 1953.

Obituary *N Y Times* B p14 Je 15 '87

PANTALEONI, HELENKA (TRADEUSA ADAMOWSKI) Nov. 22, 1900-Jan. 5, 1987 Organization official; presided over American committee to the United Nations International Children's Emergency Fund (UNICEF) for more than twenty-five years, beginning in 1955; was previously secretary of theatre department of Association of Junior Leagues of America; founded Paderewski Fund for Polish Relief (1941) and helped found Women United for the United Nations (1946); died in New York City. See *Current Biography* (November) 1956.

Obituary *N Y Times* A p20 Ja 7 '87

PLAZA (LASSO), GALO Feb. 17, 1906-Jan. 28, 1987 Ecuadorian statesman; landed agriculturalist; former president of Ecuador (1948-1952) and secretary general of the Organization of American States (1968-1975); after serving as minister of national defense (1939-1940) and ambassador to the United States (1944-1946), was a leader of movement instrumental in deposition of dictator Jose María Velasco Ibarra; in 1950s and 1960s served UN and other international bodies as expert on Latin American economic affairs and as troubleshooter in Lebanon, Cyprus, the Congo, and Haiti; lectured and wrote on Latin American problems; died in Quito, Ecuador. See *Current Biography* (April) 1969.

Obituary *N Y Times* B p8 Ja 30 '87

POAGE, W(ILLIAM) R(OBERT) Dec. 28, 1899-Jan. 3, 1987 Former U.S. representative from Texas; lawyer; after serving twelve years in state legislature, won election to House of Representatives from Texas' Eleventh Congressional District in 1936; for next forty-two years—thirty-four of them on the House Agriculture Committee—championed cause of small farmer and defended high price supports and subsidies for cotton and other commodities; chaired Agriculture Committee from 1967 until deposed by fellow Democrats in general housecleaning following Watergate revelations in 1974; died in Temple, Texas. See *Current Biography* (December) 1969.

Obituary *N Y Times* B p4 Ja 5 '87

PRESTON, ROBERT June 8, 1918-Mar. 21, 1987 Actor; began career with small Shakespearean troupe; was discovered by Hollywood talent scout when performing at Pasadena Playhouse; on screen, had, in his words, "the best role in every B picture and the second-best in the A pictures"; won Tony for starring portrayal of the fast-talking Midwestern flimflam man Professor Harold Hill in musical *The Music Man*; reprised that outstanding performance in movie of same name (1962); died in Santa Barbara, California. See *Current Biography* (December) 1958.

Obituary *N Y Times* B p7 Mr 23 '87

RAU, DHANVANTHI (HANDOO) RAMA May 10, 1893-July 19, 1987 Indian organization official; social worker; a leader of world family planning movement; known as the "Margaret Sanger of India"; was president of All-India Women's Conference (1946); founded Family Planning Association of India (1949) and organized first All-India Family Planning Conference; chaired Indian government's Social and Moral Hygiene Enquiry Committee (1955); was member of Central Social Welfare Board (1956-61); served as president (1963-71) and then president emeritus of International Planned Parenthood Federation; received Padma Bhushan award, among other honors; wrote autobiographical *An Inheritance* (1977); acquired title Lady Rama Rau when her husband, Sir Benegal Rama Rau, was knighted in 1939; died in Bombay. See *Current Biography* (April) 1954.

Obituary *N Y Times* D p12 Jl 20 '87

RAY, GORDON N(ORTON) Sept. 8, 1915-Dec. 15, 1986 Literary scholar; bibliophile; university professor; president of John Simon Guggenheim Memorial Foundation (1961-85); noted for his authoritative biographical studies of Thackeray and H.G. Wells; at University of Illinois, headed English department (1950-57) and was provost and vice-president (1957-60); from 1962 to 1980 was professor of English at New York University; out of his work in the Wells literary archives at Illinois, distilled such books as *Henry James and H.G. Wells* (1958, with Leon Edel), *H.G. Wells and Rebecca West* (1974), and new editions of Wells's fiction; died in New York City. See *Current Biography* (March) 1968.

Obituary *N Y Times* B p18 D 16 '86

RICH, BUDDY June 30, 1917-Apr. 2, 1987 Drummer; orchestra leader; known for his dynamic style, blistering speed, and impeccable technique in rendering complex jazz rhythms; began career as toddler ("Baby Traps") in vaudeville; played for big bands of Artie Shaw, Tommy Dorsey, and Harry James; toured with Jazz at the Philharmonic; in addition to his small jazz combos, led own orchestra briefly in swing era; formed second, more enduring Buddy Rich Big Band in 1966; away from traps, was man of strong opinions, which he voiced hotly and abrasively in frequent television talk show appearances; died in Los Angeles. See *Current Biography* (June) 1973.

Obituary *N Y Times* B p5 Ap 3 '87

ROGERS, CARL R(ANSOM) Jan. 8, 1902–Feb. 4, 1987 Psychologist; former professor, universities of Chicago and Wisconsin; a founder of humanistic psychology, an alternative to psychoanalysis and behaviorism that dwells not on past but on potential for lifelong "self-actualization"; during 1950s, originated "client-centered" psychotherapy, in which therapist seeks to be only a catalyst in client's "self-correction"; became architect of encounter group technique for person-to-person therapy and for training leaders in business, education, politics, and other fields; published, among some dozen works, *On Becoming a Person* (1961), a bible of humanistic psychology; founded Center for Studies of the Person in La Jolla, California, in 1963; conducted workshops and seminars there and elsewhere, in the United States and abroad, for the rest of his life; died in La Jolla. See *Current Biography* (December) 1962.

Obituary *N Y Times* D p16 F 6 '87

ROWAN, DAN July 2, 1922–Sept. 22, 1987 Comedian; as straight man in nightclub comedy team of Rowan and Martin, formed in 1952, was astute foil for buffoonery of Dick Martin; with Martin, made two motion-picture comedies, guested on television, and coproduced and cohosted wacky NBC weekly hour of "cartoon humor" *Rowan and Martin's Laugh-In* (1968–73), a hit throughout most of its run and the most popular television show in the United States from 1968 to 1970, a free-form, rapid-fire montage of schtick and slapstick by Rowan, martin, and a resident troupe of fresh young comics, including Goldie Hawn and Lily Tomlin, died in Englewood, Florida. See *Current Biography* (September) 1969.

Obituary *N Y Times* D p31 S 23 '87

RUSTIN, BAYARD Mar. 17, 1910–Aug. 24, 1987 Social activist; organization official; champion of civil rights and pacifism; favored nonviolent "progressive change" with support of liberals, organized labor, and Jewish community, but was often criticized by black militants; was imprisoned as conscientious objector during World War II; served as race relations director of Fellowship of Reconciliation (1941–53), field secretary of Congress of Racial Equality (1941), executive secretary of War Resisters League (1953–55), and special assistant to Rev. Martin Luther King Jr. (1955–60); organized March on Washington for Jobs and Freedom (1963); president (1966–79) and cochairman (from 1979) of A. Philip Randolph Institute; died in New York City. See *Current Biography* (June) 1967.

Obituary *N Y Times* A p1+ Ag 25 '87

SAUNDERS, STUART T(HOMAS) July 16, 1909–Feb. 7, 1987 Railroad executive; lawyer; worked his way up to presidency (1958–63) of Norfolk & Western Railway; arranged merger of Norfolk & Western with Virginian Railway and, later, with Wabash and Nickle Plate railroads; as president of Pennsylvania Railroad, beginning in 1964, was instrumental in merger with New York Central Railroad that resulted in creation of the mammoth Penn Central Railroad; served as chairman of Penn Central until 1970, when it filed for bankruptcy; after returning to private law practice and hiring himself out as financial consultant, refused to give interviews; broke silence in privately published and circulated autobiography; died in Richmond, Virginia. See *Current Biography* (April) 1966.

Obituary *N Y Times* B p11 F 9 '87

SCHRAM, EMIL Nov. 23, 1893–Sept. 18 1987 Financier; farmer; chairman of Reconstruction Finance Corporation in administration of President Franklin D. Roosevelt (1939–41); president of New York Stock Exchange (1941–51); president of United Service Organizations (1953–57); operated farms in Peru, Indiana and Hillview, Illinois; died in Peru, Indiana. See *Current Biography* (May) 1953.

Obituary *N Y Times* p37 S 19 '87

SCHWARZHAUPT, ELISABETH Jan. 7, 1901–Oct. 29, 1986 Former West German minister of health (1961–66); first woman cabinet member in her country's history; lawyer; lecturer on women's rights and family problems; because of her opposition to Nazis, was dismissed from early post as assistant district judge in 1933; as counsel to Evangelical church, helped that institution to resist Nazi encroachments on religious freedom and to reconstruct some of its facilities after World War II; took seat as Christian Democratic representative in Bundestag in 1953; was reelected through 1969; died in Frankfurt. See *Current Biography* (January) 1967.

Obituary *N Y Times* A p20 O 31 '86

SEGOVIA, ANDRÉS Feb. 21, 1893(?)–June 2, 1987 Spanish guitarist; one of foremost concert artists of his time; established guitar, previously considered suitable mainly for flamenco or folk music, as classical instrument; adapted works of Bach, Haydn, Mozart, and other classical composers to guitar; inspired modern composers, including Villa-Lobos and Castelnuovo-Tedesco, to compose works for him or his disciples, among them Julian Bream and John Williams; made concert debut in Granada in 1909 and won world fame in subsequent years through international tours and recordings; taught at Santiago de Compostela in Spain, and Accademia Chigiana in Siena, Italy, among other institutions; author of *Andrés Segovia: An Autobiography of the Years 1893–1920* (1976); died in Madrid. See *Current Biography* (June) 1964.

Obituary *N Y Times* A p1+ Je 4 '87

SOAMES, (ARTHUR) CHRISTOPHER (JOHN), BARON of FLETCHING Oct. 12, 1920–Sept. 16, 1987 British statesman; diplomat; protégé and son-in-law of Sir Winston Churchill; Conservative member of House of Commons (1950–66); secretary of state for war

(1958-60); minister of agriculture, fisheries and food (1960-64); as ambassador to France (1968-72), played key role in promoting Great Britain's entry into European Economic Community; as last governor of Rhodesia, presided over transformation of that former British colony into independent Republic of Zimbabwe; leader of House of Lords (1979-81); was knighted in 1973 and created a life peer in 1978; died at his family home in Hampshire, England. See *Current Biography* (August) 1981.

Obituary *N Y Times* B p14 S 17 '87

SOSS, WILMA (PORTER) Mar. 13, 1900-Oct. 10, 1986 Founder (1947) and president of Federation of Women Shareholders in American Business; with background in public relations, was colorful crusader for rights of small stockholders and for election of women to corporate boards; died in New York City. See *Current Biography* (March) 1965.

Obituary *N Y Times* B p20 O 16 '86

STOESSEL, WALTER J(OHN), JR. Jan. 24, 1920-Dec. 9, 1986 Diplomat; was key, multilingual State Department specialist in Communist affairs and East-West relations; entered Foreign Service in 1942; while ambassador to Poland (1968-72), helped to arrange meetings between U.S. and Chinese Communist officials that led to normalization of relations between the two countries; as ambassador to Soviet Union (1974-76), helped to usher in era of U.S.-Soviet détente; appointed ambassador to West Germany (1976-81); became under secretary of state for political affairs in 1981 and appointed deputy secretary of state in 1982; died in Washington, D.C. See *Current Biography* (June) 1970.

Obituary *N Y Times* D p35 D 11 '86

STOKES, ANSON PHELPS, JR. Jan. 11, 1905-Nov. 7, 1986 Retired Episcopal bishop of Massachusetts (1956-70); previously served in parishes, including St. Bartholomew's in New York City, where he was rector from 1950 to 1954; during his episcopacy, chaired Massachusetts Council of Churches' commission on church and race; an ecumenicist, called for enlightened Protestant attitude toward presidential candidacy of John F. Kennedy, a Roman Catholic, in 1960; was early opponent of war in Vietnam. See *Current Biography* (July) 1962.

Obituary *N Y Times* p44 N 9 '86

STREIBERT, THEODORE C(UYLER) Aug. 29, 1899-Jan. 18, 1987 Broadcasting executive; former United States government official; as president of radio station WOR in New York City in 1940s helped to bring into existence Mutual Broadcasting System, which he chaired from 1949 to 1951; headed newly formed United States Information Agency from 1953 to 1957; after leaving government, was vice-president of Time-Life Broadcasting Inc. and president of Free Europe Fund; died in Syosset, Long Island. See *Current Biography* (February) 1955.

Obituary *N Y Times* B p20 Ja 22 '87

SUSSKIND, DAVID Dec. 19, 1920-Feb. 1987 Producer; television talk show host; began career as press and talent agent; won forty-seven Emmys as TV producer,

beginning in Golden Age of television drama in 1950s; moderated issue-oriented discussion programs *Open End* (beginning in 1958) and *David Susskind Show* (1967-86); produced five Broadway shows, including *Rashomon* (1959), and thirteen motion pictures, including *Raisin in the Sun* and *Requiem for a Heavyweight* (both 1961); finished career with four television specials on world leaders in 1986 and 1987; was found dead in his hotel room in New York City on February 22. See *Current Biography* (May) 1960.

Obituary *N Y Times* A p1+ F 23 '87

SWIGERT, ERNEST G(OODNOUGH) Aug. 4, 1892-Nov. 30, 1986 Manufacturing executive; former president of National Association of Manufacturers (1957-58); founded Hyster Company, manufacturers of lift trucks, tractor cranes, and similar heavy equipment, in 1929; headed company until his retirement in 1971; died at his home in Portland, Oregon. See *Current Biography* (October) 1957.

Obituary *N Y Times* B p14 D 8 '86

SZENT-GYÖRGYI, ALBERT (VON NAGYRAPOLT) Sept. 16, 1893-Oct. 22, 1986 Hungarian-born biochemist; expert in muscular physiology; promulgator of bioelectronic theory of cancer; won Nobel Prize in 1937 for his isolation of vitamin C and his discovery of role it plays in metabolism; received 1954 Albert Lasker Award for his research in heart muscle contraction; was also disarmament advocate; in addition to purely scientific works, wrote *Science, Ethics, and Politics* (1963), *The Crazy Ape: Written by a Biologist for the Young* (1970), *What Next?!* (1971); was associated with Marine Biological Laboratory in Woods Hole, Massachusetts since 1947; died in Woods Hole. See *Current Biography* (January) 1955.

Obituary *N Y Times* p9 O 25 '86

TAYLOR, MAXWELL D(AVENPORT) Aug. 26, 1901-Apr. 19, 1987 U.S. army general; helped to shape post-World War II American military policy of flexible response; participated heroically in Allied campaigns in Sicily and Italy (1943); as commander of 101st Airborne division (1944-45), played key role in Normandy invasion, Netherlands campaign, and Battle of the Bulge; was superintendent of U.S. Military Academy at West Point (1945-49), commander of Eighth Army and UN forces in Korea (1953), commander in chief of U.S. Army Far East and UN command (1955), and U.S. Army chief of staff (1955-59); as military representative of president (1961), visited Southeast Asia to assess U.S. position; served as chairman of joint chiefs of staff (1962-64); wrote *The Uncertain Trumpet* (1959) which influenced military policies of John F. Kennedy; died in Washington, D.C. See *Current Biography* (December) 1961.

Obituary *N Y Times* A p1+ Ap 21 '87

TOMÁS, AMÉRICO (DEUS RODRIGUES) Nov. 1894-Sept. 18, 1987 Portugese statesman; rear admiral; president of Portugal (1958-74); hand-picked for the presidency by the right-wing dictator Antonio Salazar, remained titular head of state under Salazar's successor, Marcello Caetano, whose liberal proposals he opposed; along with Caetano, was ousted in leftist military coup; died in Cascais, Portugal. See *Current Biography* (December) 1958.

Obituary *N Y Times* p37 S 19 '87

TRAPP, MARIA AUGUSTA Jan. 26, 1905–Mar. 28, 1987 Singer; musician; writer; lecturer; guiding light of Trapp Family Singers; was governess to seven children of widowed Baron Georg von Trapp, whom she married in 1927, and with whom she later had three more children; organized Trapp family choir, which won choral competition at Salzburg Festival (1936); fled with family to U.S. in 1938 to escape Nazi takeover of Austria; performed with family ensemble in Europe, U.S., Latin America, and Pacific (1938–56); founded and taught at Trapp Family Music Camp at Stowe, Vermont (1951–56); was immortalized as leading character in Rodgers-Hammerstein musical play *The Sound of Music* starring Mary Martin on Broadway (1959) and Julie Andrews in film (1965); died in Morrisville, Vermont. See *Current Biography* (May) 1968.

Obituary *N Y Times* B p6 Mr 30 '87

TUDOR, ANTHONY Apr. 4, 1909–Apr. 20, 1987 Dancer; one of leading choreographers of his time; revolutionized classical ballet with introduction of penetrating psychological insight and exploration of emotional conflict in his choreography of such works as *Jardin aux Lilas* (1936), *Dark Elegies* (1937), *Romeo and Juliet* (1942), *Pillar of Fire* (1942), and *Undertow* (1945); principal ballet dancer with various companies (1930–50); choreographer of Ballet Rambert in London (1930–38); choreographer (1939–80), associate director (1974–80), and choreographer emeritus (1980–87) of American Ballet Theatre; died in New York City. See *Current Biography* (November) 1945.

Obituary *N Y Times* A p21 Ap 21 '87

ULLMAN, AL(BERT CONRAD) Mar. 9, 1914–Oct. 11, 1986 Former U.S. Democratic representative from Oregon (1957–81); chairman of House Ways and Means Committee (1975–81); was sponsor of sweeping 1975 tax-cut legislation; died in Arlington, Virginia. See *Current Biography* (August) 1975.

Obituary *N Y Times* D p35 O 14 '86

UNRUH, JESSE M(ARVIN) Sept. 30, 1922–Aug. 4, 1987 California Democratic party leader; in state assembly, was cagey and blunt-spoken cloakroom manipulator, with nationwide political connections; as speaker of state assembly (1961–69), quietly and persistently opposed conservative policies of Governor Ronald Reagan; played role in presidential candidacies of John F. and Robert F. Kennedy; was elected state treasurer in 1974; died in Marina del Rey, California. See *Current Biography* (October) 1969.

Obituary *N Y Times* B p6 Ag 6 '87

VILA, GEORGE R(AYMOND) Mar. 12, 1909–July 8, 1987 Rubber company executive; joined staff of United States Rubber Company in 1937; as a research chemist with its Naugatuck division, helped to spur growth of rubber industry with work, in early 1940s, on GR-S synthetic rubbers; served during World War II on technical industrial intelligence committee of U.S. Joint Chiefs of Staff; visited Germany in 1945 for studies leading to American development of new form of synthetic rubber; was vice-president (1957–60), president (from 1960), chief executive officer (1961–65), and chairman of board and executive committee (1965–75) of United States Rubber Company (renamed Uniroyal in 1967); encouraged rubber industry's diversification from tires to chemicals, plastics, and other goods; died in New York City. See *Current Biography* (March) 1963.

Obituary *N Y Times* D p19 Jl 10 '87

WARHOL, ANDY Aug. 6, 1928(?)–Feb. 22, 1987 Artist; a founder of Pop art, of which he was the most famous exponent; drew his painted and printed images directly from America's popular culture and mass-producing consumer economy, replicating icons of movie stars and other celebrities, dollar bills, soup cans, and other commerical and social artifacts; made *Eat*, *Haircut*, *Sleep* and other minimalist, deliberately boring underground experimental films; published *Interview*, gossip and fashion magazine for the New York-based sybaritic set of "beautiful people" who lionized him; died in New York City. See *Current Biography* (July) 1986.

Obituary *N Y Times* A p1+ F 23 '87

WESLEY, CHARLES H(ARRIS) Dec. 2, 1891–Aug. 16, 1987 Historian; educator; helped to shape modern approach to black history, emphasizing black contributions to American success; author of over a dozen books, including *Negro Labor in the United States, 1850–1925* (1927), *Collapse of the Confederacy* (1937), and *Neglected History* (1965); championed educational reform in numerous articles; edited *International Library on Negro Life and History*, and *Negro History Bulletin*; professor and chairman of history department at Howard University (1920–42); president of Wilberforce University in Ohio (1942–47); helped to found Ohio's Central State University in 1947 and remained as its president for eighteen years; came out of retirement in 1974 to direct Afro-American Historical and Cultural Museum in Philadelphia; died in Washington, D.C. See *Current Biography* (March) 1944.

Obituary *N Y Times* B p6 S 2 '87

WILLIAMS, EMLYN Nov. 26, 1905–Sept. 25, 1987 Welsh playwright; actor; producer; wrote over two dozen plays, including *Night Must Fall* (1935) and the autobiographical *The Corn Is Green* (1938) in which he played the leading male roles in the original London productions; among many other roles, appeared as Richard III, as Pope Pius XII in *The Deputy*, and as Sir Thomas More in *a Man for All Seasons*; performed in a number of films, including *The Citadel* (1938), *Jamaica Inn* (1939), and *Major Barbara* (1941); beginning in 1951, toured internationally with one-man show *Emlyn Williams as Charles Dickens*, also wrote memoirs, screenplays, and fiction; died in London. See *Current Biography* (April) 1952.

Obituaries Manchester Guardian W 137:14 O 4 '87; *N Y Times* p35 S 26 '87

WILLIS, PAUL S. Nov. 8, 1890-June 5, 1987 Trade association executive; as president of Grocery Manufacturers of America (1932-65), formulated policies for food industry; served on government committees concerned with distribution, conservation, and unfair practices in food trade; during World War II, served on Food Industry War Committee and coordinated food supplies sent to U.S. troops in Europe, but opposed President Franklin D. Roosevelt's food subsidies policy; promoted his trade association's public stand, in 1944, favoring use of surplus food for foreign relief; was member of Citizens Food Committee (1947); served as chairman of American Food-for-Peace Council and as executive committee member of U.S. Freedom From Hunger Foundation; died in New Rochelle, New York. See Current Biography (January) 1951.

Obituary N Y Times B p7 Je 8 '87

YOUNG, PHILIP May 9, 1910-Jan. 15, 1987 Former U.S. government official; economist; educator; spent early years of career as economist and administrator with several federal agencies; after brief tenure (1948-53) as dean of Columbia University's Graduate School of Business, returned to government as chairman of Civil Service Commission (1953-57); subsequently served as U.S. ambassador to the Netherlands (1957-60) before returning to private sector as executive director of International Chamber of Commerce (1960-65); died in Arlington, Virginia. See Current Biography (December) 1951.

Obituary N Y Times D p8 Ja 19 '87

BIOGRAPHICAL REFERENCES

Almanac of American Politics, 1986

American Architects Directory, 1970

American Catholic Who's Who, 1978

American Medical Directory, 1979

American Men and Women of Science (1986)

American Songwriters (1987)

Asia Who's Who (1960)

Biographical Directory of the American Congress, 1774–1971 (1971)

Biographical Directory of the USSR (1958)

Biographical Encyclopaedia & Who's Who of the American Theatre (1966)

Biographical Encyclopedia of Pakistan, 1971–72

Biographical Encyclopedia of Scientists (1981)

Burke's Peerage, Baronetage, and Knightage, 1970

Canadian Almanac & Directory, 1987

Canadian Who's Who, 1982

Celebrity Register (1986)

Chi è? (1961)

China Yearbook, 1982

Chujoy, A., and Manchester, P. W., eds. Dance Encyclopedia (1967)

Columbia Dictionary of Modern European Literature (1980)

Concise Biographical Dictionary of Singers (1969)

Concise Oxford Dictionary of Ballet (1982)

Congressional Directory, 1960–1986

Congressional Quarterly Almanac, 1960–1986

Contemporary Artists (1983)

Contemporary Authors (1962–87)

Contemporary Dramatists (1986)

Contemporary Foreign Language Writers (1985)

Contemporary Literary Criticism, 1973–87

Contemporary Literary Critics (1982)

Contemporary Novelists (1986)

Contemporary Poets (1986)

Contemporary Poets of the English Language (1970)

Contemporary Theatre, Film, and Television (1986)

Debrett's Peerage and Baronetage (1985)

Dictionary of Contemporary American Artists (1982)

Dictionary of International Biography (1975–84)

Dictionary of Latin American and Caribbean Biography (1971)

Dictionary of National Biography, 1971–1980 (1986)

Dictionnaire de biographie française (1972)

Dictionnaire des écrivains français (1971)

Directory of American Scholars (1982)

Directory of British Scientists, 1966–67

Directory of Medical Specialists (1985)

Encyclopedia of Pop, Rock and Soul (1977)

Ewen, D., ed, Composers of Today (1936); Living Musicians (1940; First Supplement 1957); Men and Women Who Make Music (1949); American Composers (1982); European Composers Today (1954); The New Book of Modern Composers (1961); Composers Since 1900 (1969); Musicians Since 1900 (1978)

Far East and Australasia, 1986

Feather, L. Encyclopedia of Jazz (1984); Encyclopedia of Jazz in the Sixties (1967)

Filmgoer's Companion (1978)

Football Register, 1984

Foremost Women in Communications (1970)

Grove's Dictionary of Music and Musicians (1955)

Hindustan Year Book and Who's Who, 1963

Hvem er Hvem? 1973

International Authors and Writers Who's Who, 1982

International Motion Picture Almanac, 1987

International Television Almanac, 1987

International Who's Who, 1987–88

International Who's Who in Art and Antiques, 1976

International Who's Who in Music and Musicians Directory (1985)

International Who's Who in Poetry, 1977

International Who's Who of the Arab World (1984)

International Year Book and Statesmen's Who's Who, 1986

Japan Biographical Encyclopedia & Who's Who, 1964–65

Katz, E. Film Encyclopedia (1982)

Kelly's Handbook to the Titled, Landed and Official Classes, 1964

Kleine Slavische Biographie (1958)

Kraks Bla Bog, 1964

Kürschners Deutscher Gelehrten-Kalender, 1970

Leaders in Education (1974)

Leaders in Electronics (1979)

Leaders in Profile (1975)

Martindale-Hubbell Law Directory, 1979

McGraw-Hill Encyclopedia of World Biography (1973)

McGraw-Hill Encyclopedia of World Drama (1984)

McGraw-Hill Modern Scientists and Engineers (1980)

Middle East and North Africa, 1984–85

National Cyclopaedia of American Biography (1926–84)

New Century Cyclopedia of Names (1954)

New Grove Dictionary of Music and Musicians (1980)

Nobel Prize Winners (1987)

Nordness, L., ed. Art USA Now (1963)

Notable Australians (1978)

Notable Names in American Theatre (1976)

Nouveau Dictionnaire National des Contemporains (1968)

Official Baseball Register, 1984

Official Catholic Directory, 1976

Oxford Companion to American Theatre (1984)

Oxford Companion to Film (1976)

Oxford Companion to the Theatre (1983)

Panorama Biografico degli Italiani d'Oggi (1956)

Political Profiles (1976–79)

Politics in America (1986)

Poor's Register of Corporations, Directors and Executives, 1985

Prominent Personalities in the USSR (1968)

Quién es Quién en la Argentina, 1968–69

Quién es Quién en Venezuela, Panama, Ecuador, Colombia, 1956

Robinson, D. 100 Most Important People in the World Today (1972)

Slonimsky, N. Baker's Biographical Dictionary of Musicians (1978)

Something About the Author (1971–86)

Thomas, S. Men of Space (1960–68)

Thompson, K. A. Dictionary of Twentieth-Century Composers (1973)

Thompson, O., ed. International Cyclopedia of Music and Musicians, 1985

Thomson, D. Biographical Dictionary of Film (1981)

Twentieth Century Authors (1942; First Supplement, 1955)

Two Hundred Contemporary Authors (1969)

Vem är Det, 1973

Webster's Biographical Dictionary (1971)

Wer ist Wer? (1984)

Who is Who in Music (1951)

Who's Who, 1987–88

Who's Who among Black Americans, 1985

Who's Who in Advertising (1963)

Who's Who in Africa, 1973

Who's Who in America, 1986–87

Who's Who in American Art (1986)

Who's Who in American Education, 1967–68

Who's Who in American Politics, 1987–88

Who's Who in Art (1986)

Who's Who in Australia, 1985

Who's Who in Austria, 1983

Who's Who in Baseball, 1971

Who's Who in Belgium (1962)

Who's Who in California, 1985

Who's Who in Canada, 1984–85

Who's Who in Chicago and Illinois (1950)

Who's Who in Colored America, 1950

Who's Who in Communist China (1969)

Who's Who in Economics (1986)

Who's Who in Engineering, 1982

Who's Who in Finance and Industry, 1983–84

Who's Who in France, 1983–84

Who's Who in France (Paris), 1953–54

Who's Who in Germany (1980)

Who's Who in Hollywood, 1900–1976

Who's Who in Israel, 1985–86

Who's Who in Italy, 1957–58

Who's Who in Labor, 1976

Who's Who in Latin America (1971)

Who's Who in Library and Information Services (1982)

Who's Who in Malaysia and Singapore, 1983

Who's Who in Music, 1969

Who's Who in New York State, 1982

Who's Who in New Zealand (1968)

Who's Who in Opera, 1976

Who's Who in Philosophy (1969)

Who's Who in Professional Baseball (1973)

Who's Who in Publishing (1971)

Who's Who in Railroading in North America (1959)

Who's Who in Rock Music (1982)

Who's Who in Saudi Arabia, 1984

Who's Who in Space, 1966–67

Who's Who in Spain, 1965

Who's Who in Switzerland, 1982–83

Who's Who in the Arab World, 1986–87

Who's Who in the East, 1985–86

Who's Who in the Midwest, 1986–87

Who's Who in the Netherlands, 1962–63

Who's Who in the People's Republic of China (1987)

Who's Who in the South and Southwest (1986)

Who's Who in the Soviet Union (1984)

Who's Who in the Theatre (1981)

Who's Who in TV and Cable (1983)

Who's Who in the United Nations (1975)

Who's Who in the West, 1984–85

Who's Who in Western Europe (1981)

Who's Who in the World, 1984–85

Who's Who in World Aviation and Astronautics (1958)

Who's Who in World Jewry (1978)

Who's Who of American Women, 1986–87

Who's Who of British Engineers, 1980

Who's Who of British Scientists, 1980–81

Who's Who of Jazz (1985)

Who's Who of Rhodesia, Mauritius, Central and East Africa, 1965

Who's Who of Southern Africa, 1982

Who's Who on Television (1983)

Wie is Dat? (1956)

World Artists 1950–1980 (1984)

World Authors 1950–1970 (1975)

World Authors 1970–75 (1980)

World Authors 1975–80 (1985)

World Biography (1954)

World Film Directors 1890–1945 (1987)

World Film Directors 1945–1985 (1988)

World Who's Who in Science (1968)

World's Who's Who of Women, 1982

Writers Directory (1986–88)

PERIODICALS AND NEWSPAPERS CONSULTED

ALA Bul—American Library Association Bulletin
After Dark (disc.)
Am Artist—American Artist
Am Libs—American Libraries
Am Scholar—American Scholar
Am Sociol R—American Sociological Review
America
Américas
Arch Rec—Architectural Record
Archaeology
Art & Artists
Artforum
Artnews
Arts
Arts & Arch—Arts & Architecture
Atlan—Atlantic Monthly

Ballet N—Ballet News (disc.)
Barron's
Biog N—Biography News (disc.)
Book-of-the-Month Club N —Book-of-the-Month Club News
Book World
Broadcasting
Bsns W—Business Week

Cath World—Catholic World
Chicago Tribune
Christian Sci Mon—Christian Science Monitor
Columbia J R—Columbia Journalism Review
Commonweal
Cong Digest—Congressional Digest
Cong Q—Congressional Quarterly Weekly Report
Cosmo—Cosmopolitan
Cue (now incorporated into New York)
Cur Hist—Current History
Cur World Leaders—Current World Leaders

Dance & Dancers
Dance Mag—Dance Magazine
Discover

Ebony
Economist
Ed & Pub—Editor & Publisher
Encounter
Esquire

Facts on File
Films & Filming
For Affairs—Foreign Affairs
For Policy Bul—Foreign Policy Bulletin
Forbes
Fortune

Gentlemen's Q—Gentlemen's Quarterly
German Tribune
Good H—Good Housekeeping
Guardian

Harper's
Hi Fi—High Fidelity
Hi Fi/Stereo R—Hi/Fi Stereo Review
Horizon

Illus Lond N—Illustrated London News
India News
Inside Sports
International Herald Tribune

Keynote

Ladies Home J—Ladies' Home Journal
Le Monde
Lib J—Library Journal
Life
London Observer
London R of Bks—London Review of Books
Los Angeles Times

Manchester Guardian W —Manchester Guardian Weekly
McCall's
Maclean's
Mlle—Mademoiselle
Modern Maturity
Ms—Ms.
Mus Am—Musical America
Mus Mod Art—Museum of Modern Art Bulletin

N Y Daily News
N Y Herald Tribune Bk R —New York Herald Tribune Book Review (disc.)
N Y Newsday New York Newsday
N Y Post
N Y Rev of Bks—New York Review of Books
N Y Sunday News
N Y Times
N Y Times Bk R—New York Times Book Review
N Y Times Mag—New York Times Magazine
N Y World-Telegram—New York World-Telegram and Sun (disc.)
N Y World Journal Tribune (disc.)
Nat Geog Mag—National Geographic Magazine
Nat R—National Review
Nation
Nations Bsns—Nation's Business

Nature
New Leader
New Repub—New Republic
New Statesm—New Statesman
New York
New Yorker
Newsweek

Omni
Opera N—Opera News
Ovation

Parade
Penthouse
People
Philadelphia Inquirer
Playbill
Playboy
Plays & Players
Pub W—Publishers Weekly

Read Digest—Reader's Digest
Redbook
Rolling Stone

Sat Eve Post—Saturday Evening Post
Sat R—Saturday Review
Scala (English edition)
Sci Am—Scientific American
Sci Mo—Scientific Monthly
Sci N L—Science News Letter
Science
Smithsonian
Spec—Spectator
Spiegel—Der Spiegel
Sport
Sporting N—Sporting News
Sports Illus—Sports Illustrated

Time
Times—London Times
Times Lit Sup—London Times Literary Supplement
Toronto Globe and Mail
TV Guide

U N Rev—United Nations Review
U S News—U.S. News & World Report

Vanity Fair
Variety
Village Voice
Vogue

Wall St J—Wall Street Journal
Washington J R—Washington Journalism Review
Washington M—Washington Monthly
Washington Post
Wilson Lib Bul—Wilson Library Bulletin
World Press R—World Press Review

Yale R—Yale Review

CLASSIFICATION BY PROFESSION—1987

ARCHITECTURE
Gehry, Frank O.
Tange, Kenzo

ART
Haacke, Hans
Holladay, Wilhelmina
Hopper, Dennis
Houston, James A.
Hughes, Robert
Johns, Jasper
Kainen, Jacob
Liberman, Alexander
Lynch, David
MacIver, Loren
Rauschenberg, Robert
Terra, Daniel J.
Thiebaud, Wayne

AVIATION
Lorenzo, Frank
Yeager, Jeana

BUSINESS
Bernstein, Robert L.
Buffett, Warren E.
Clark, Dick
Conner, Dennis
Eisner, Michael D.
Gottlieb, Robert A.
Haig, Alexander Meigs, Jr.
Hodel, Donald P.
Holladay, Wilhelmina
Lorenzo, Frank
McNamara, Robert S.
Olsen, Kenneth H.
Robertson, Pat
Roderick, David M.
Rubik, Erno
Scowcroft, Brent
Terra, Daniel J.
Tisch, Laurence A.
Wang, An

DANCE
Danilova, Alexandra
Irwin, Bill
Lichtenstein, Harvey

DIPLOMACY
Shcharansky, Anatoly
Waldheim, Kurt

EDUCATION
Bloom, Harold
Coetzee J. M.
Curran, Charles E.
Elkin, Stanley
Friendly, Fred W.
Gaddis, William
Kainen, Jacob
Kalb, Marvin
M'Bow, Amadou-Mahtar
Pelikan, Jaroslav
Price, Reynolds
Richards, Lloyd
Rubik, Erno
Scowcroft, Brent
Tange, Kenzo
Thiebaud, Wayne
Westheimer, Ruth
Wharton, Clifton R., Jr.

FINANCE
Buffett, Warren E.
McNamara, Robert S.
Tisch, Laurence A.

GOVERNMENT AND
POLITICS, FOREIGN
Arias Sánchez, Oscar
Calero, Adolfo
Cerezo, Vinicio
Finnbogadóttir, Vigdis
Habré, Hissène
Khamenei, Hojatolislam Ali
Lawson, Nigel
Martens, Wilfried
M'Bow, Amadou-Mahtar

Rau, Johannes
Shcharansky, Anatoly
Singh, Giani Zail
Strauss, Franz Josef
Tambo, Oliver
Tebbit, Norman
Waldheim, Kurt

GOVERNMENT AND
POLITICS, U.S.
Babbitt, Bruce E.
Baker, Howard
Barry, Marion S.
Biden, Joseph R., Jr.
Boland, Edward P.
Cisneros, Henry G.
Dole, Robert J.
Gephardt, Richard
Gore, Albert, Jr.
Haig, Alexander Meigs, Jr.
Hodel, Donald P.
Inouye, Daniel K.
Kirk, Paul G., Jr.
Kunin, Madeleine
McLaughlin, John
McNamara, Robert S.
Poindexter, John M.
Salinger, Pierre
Scowcroft, Brent
Sprinkel, Beryl
Terra, Daniel J.
Webb, James H., Jr.

INDUSTRY
McNamara, Robert S.
Roderick, David M.
Terra, Daniel J.

INTERNATIONAL
RELATIONS
M'Bow, Amadou-Mahtar
McNamara, Robert S.
Salinger, Pierre
Shcharansky, Anatoly
Waldheim, Kurt

JOURNALISM
Brinkley, David
Donaldson, Sam
Frankel, Max
Friendly, Fred W.
Hughes, Robert
Hunter-Gault, Charlayne
Kalb, Marvin
Lawson, Nigel
Lehrer, James
Lukas, J. Anthony
Salinger, Pierre
Smith, Liz

LABOR
Diller, Moe

LAW
Babbitt, Bruce E.
Gephardt, Richard
Hodel, Donald P.
Inouye, Daniel K.
Kirk, Paul G., Jr.
Tambo, Oliver

LITERATURE
Amis, Kingsley
Astor, Brooke
Bloom, Harold
Coetzee J. M.
Elkin, Stanley
Gaddis, William
Ginsberg, Allen
Houston, James A.
Keneally, Thomas
Lardner, Ring, Jr.
Levi, Primo
McGuane, Thomas
McInerney, Jay
Narayan, R. K.
Price, Reynolds
Pynchon, Thomas
Salinger, Pierre
Stone, Robert
Taylor, Peter
Truman, Margaret
Webb, James H., Jr.
Wilson, August

MATHEMATICS
Mandelbrot, Benoit

MEDICINE
Bonner, Yelena
Gale, Robert
Goldstein, Joseph L.

MILITARY
Andrew, Duke of York
Haig, Alexander Meigs, Jr.
McNamara, Robert S.
Poindexter, John M.
Scowcroft, Brent
Strauss, Franz Josef

MOTION PICTURES
Allen, Debbie
Ashcroft, Peggy
Bogosian, Eric
Broderick, Matthew
Carter, Benny
Chamberlain, Richard
Clark, Dick
Cruise, Tom
Crystal, Billy
Danilova, Alexandra
Depardieu, Gérard
Douglas, Michael
Eisner, Michael D.
Fox, Michael J.
Friedkin, William
Hogan, Paul
Hopper, Dennis
Houston, James A.
Jagger, Bianca
Jones, Grace
Keneally, Thomas
Kurtz, Swoosie
Lardner, Ring, Jr.
Linden, Hal
Lynch, David
Mason, Jackie
Powell, Michael
Ringwald, Molly
Rivers, Joan
Shatner, William
Shepherd, Cybill
Stone, Oliver
Winfrey, Oprah

MUSIC
Carter, Benny
Clapton, Eric
Clark, Dick
Dutoit, Charles

Eldridge, Roy
Hoiby, Lee
Holliger, Heinz
Jones, Grace
Knight, Gladys
Kraus, Alfredo
Laredo, Ruth
Lichtenstein, Harvey
Parkening, Christopher
Paul, Les
Salerno-Sonnenberg, Nadja
Swaggart, Jimmy
Truman, Margaret
Vollenweider, Andreas
Winter, Paul

NONFICTION
Amis, Kingsley
Astor, Brooke
Curran, Charles E.
FitzGerald, Frances
Friendly, Fred W.
Ginsberg, Allen
Houston, James A.
Hughes, Robert
Kalb, Marvin
Lukas, J. Anthony
McGuane, Thomas
Narayan, R. K.
Pelikan, Jaroslav
Prigogine, Ilya
Randi, James
Rivers, Joan
Salinger, Pierre
Smith, Liz
Truman, Margaret
Wang, An
Westheimer, Ruth

ORGANIZATIONS
Kirk, Paul G., Jr.
McNamara, Robert S.
Schindler, Alexander M.

OTHER CLASSIFICATIONS
Sarah, Duchess of York

PHILANTHROPY
Astor, Brooke
Holladay, Wilhelmina

PHOTOGRAPHY
Hopper, Dennis

PSYCHOLOGY
Westheimer, Ruth

PUBLISHING
Bernstein, Robert L.
Doubleday, Nelson
Gottlieb, Robert A.
Lehrer, James
Liberman, Alexander

RADIO
Randi, James
Westheimer, Ruth
White, Betty

RELIGION
Curran, Charles E.
Hunthausen, Raymond G.
Khamenei, Hojatolislam Ali
Pelikan, Jaroslav
McLaughlin, John
Robertson, Pat
Schindler, Alexander M.
Swaggart, Jimmy

SCIENCE
Gale, Robert
Goldstein, Joseph L.
Guth, Alan H.
Krim, Mathilde
Mandelbrot, Benoit
Olsen, Kenneth H.
Prigogine, Ilya
Randi, James
Wang, An
Westheimer, Ruth
Yeager, Jeana

SOCIAL ACTIVISM
Bernstein, Robert L.
Bonner, Yelena
Ginsberg, Allen
Jagger, Bianca
Shcharansky, Anatoly
Tambo, Oliver

SOCIAL SCIENCES
Sprinkel, Beryl
Wharton, Clifton R., Jr.

SPORTS
Becker, Boris
Conner, Dennis
Ditka, Mike
Doubleday, Nelson
Jones, K.C.
Jordan, Michael
Joyner-Kersee, Jackie
Knight, Bob
Noah, Yannick
Yarborough, Cale

TECHNOLOGY
Olsen, Kenneth H.
Rubik, Erno
Wang, An
Yeager, Jeana

TELEVISION
Allen, Debbie
Ashcroft, Peggy
Bogosian, Eric
Brenner, David
Brinkley, David
Broderick, Matthew
Carter, Benny
Chamberlain, Richard
Clark, Dick
Crystal, Billy
Donaldson, Sam
Douglas, Michael
Eisner, Michael D.
Fox, Michael J.
Friendly, Fred W.
Hogan, Paul
Hopper, Dennis
Hughes, Robert
Hunter-Gault, Charlayne
Irwin, Bill
Jagger, Bianca
Jones, Grace
Kalb, Marvin
Knight, Gladys
Kurtz, Swoosie
Lardner, Ring, Jr.
Lavin, Linda
Lehrer, James
Linden, Hal

Mason, Jackie
McLaughlin, John
Randi, James
Richards, Lloyd
Ringwald, Molly
Rivers, Joan
Robertson, Pat
Salinger, Pierre
Shatner, William
Shepherd, Cybill
Smith, Liz
Swaggart, Jimmy
Tartikoff, Brandon
Thicke, Alan
Tisch, Laurence A.
Westheimer, Ruth
White, Betty
Willis, Bruce
Winfrey, Oprah

THEATRE
Allen, Debbie
Ashcroft, Peggy
Bogosian, Eric
Broderick, Matthew
Chamberlain, Richard
Depardieu, Gérard
Douglas, Michael
Durang, Christopher
Fichandler, Zelda
Finnbogadóttir, Vigdis
Hopper, Dennis
Irwin, Bill
Keneally, Thomas
Kurtz, Swoosie
Lavin, Linda
Lichtenstein, Harvey
Linden, Hal
Mason, Jackie
Richards, Lloyd
Ringwald, Molly
Shatner, William
White, Betty
Willis, Bruce
Wilson, August

CUMULATED INDEX—1981-1987

For the index to 1940-1985 biographies, see
Current Biography Cumulative Index 1940-1985.

Barzini, Luigi (Giorgio, Jr.) obit
May 84
Basie, Count obit Jun 84
Basie, William See Basie,
Count obit
Battle, Kathleen Nov 84
Baur, John I(reland) H(owe)
obit Jul 87
Bausch, Pina Sep 86
Baxter, Anne obit Feb 86
Bayar, (Mahmut) Celal obit
Oct 86
Beard, Charles E(dmund) obit
Oct 82
Beard, James (Andrews) obit
Mar 85
Beatrix, Queen of the Nether-
lands May 81
Beattie, Ann Oct 85
Beau, Lucas Victor obit Jan 87
Beauvoir, Simone (Bertrand)
de obit Jun 86
Becker, Boris Feb 87
Behrens, Hildegard Jan 85
Bell, Elliott V(allance) obit
Mar 83
Belushi, John obit Apr 82
Benchley, Nathaniel (God-
dard) obit Feb 82
Benelli, Giovanni Cardinal
obit Jan 83
Benn, Anthony (Neil) Wedg-
wood See Benn, Tony
Benn, Tony Nov 82
Bennett, Michael Mar 81 obit
Aug 87
Bennett, Robert Russell obit
Oct 81
Bennett, William J(ohn) Sep 85
Bergen, John J(oseph) obit Feb
81
Berger, Peter L(udwig) Mar 83
Bergman, (Ernst) Ingmar Oct
81
Bergman, Ingrid obit Oct 82
Berlinguer, Enrico obit Aug 84
Berman, Emile Zola obit Aug
81
Bernardin, Joseph L(ouis) Oct
82
Bernbach, William obit Nov
82
Bernstein, Philip S(idney) obit
Feb 86
Bernstein, Robert L(ouis) Jul
87
Berri, Nabih Nov 85
Berry, Wendell (Erdman) May
86
Betancourt, Rómulo obit Nov
81
Betancur (Cuartas), Belisario
Apr 85
Betjeman, Sir John obit Jul 84
Bettis, Valerie obit Nov 82
Beuys, Joseph obit Mar 86
Bhave, Vinoba obit Jan 83
Bhutto, Benazir Jul 86
Biaggi, Mario Jan 86

Bidault, Georges obit Mar 83
Biddle, Katherine Garrison
Chapin obit Jan 84
Biden, Joseph (Robinette), Jr.
Jan 87
Bieber, Owen F(rederick) Apr
86
Biller, Moe Jun 87
Bingham, Jonathan B(rewster)
obit Aug 86
Binns, Joseph Patterson obit
Mar 81
Bird, Larry June 82
Bird, Rose E(lizabeth) May 84
Bishop, Jim obit Sep 87
Black, William obit May 83
Blackwell, Betsy Talbot obit
Apr 85
Blades, Rubén May 86
Blake, Eubie obit Apr 83
Blake, Eugene Carson obit Oct
85
Blanding, Sarah Gibson obit
Apr 85
Bliss, Ray C(harles) obit Oct 81
Bloch, Felix obit Nov 83
Block, John R(usling) Apr 82
Bloom, Harold Apr 87
Blough, Roger M(iles) obit Jan
86
Bluford, Guion S(tewart), Jr.
Sep 84
Bly, Robert (Elwood) Mar 84
Boesak, Allan (Aubrey) Nov 86
Bogosian, Eric Sep 87
Böhm, Karl obit Oct 81
Boland, Edward P(atrick) Oct
87
Boland, Frederick H(enry) obit
Feb 86
Boles, Paul Darcy obit Jun 84
Bolger, Ray(mond Wallace)
obit Mar 87
Böll, Heinrich (Theodor) obit
Sep 85
Bolotowsky, Ilya obit Jan 82
Bolz, Lothar obit Apr 87
Bonner, Elena See Bonner,
Yelena
Bonner, Yelena Apr 87
Bonynge, Richard Feb 81
Boone, Richard obit Mar 81
Boorstin, Daniel J(oseph) Jan
84
Borges, Jorge Luis obit Aug 86
Borofsky, Jonathan Jul 85
Bossy, Mike Jun 81
Botha, Roelof F(rederik) May
84
Boult, Sir Adrian (Cedric) obit
Apr 83
Bourgeois, Louise Oct 83
Bowen, Otis R(ay) Nov 86
Bowles, Chester (Bliss) obit Jul
86
Boyer, Ken(ton Lloyd) obit Oct
82
Boyer, M(arion) W(illard) obit
Jan 83

Boy George Oct 85
Boyle, W(illiam) A(nthony) obit
Jul 85
Boylston, Helen Dore obit Nov
84
Bradbury, Ray Jul 82
Bradford, Robert F(iske) obit
May 83
Bradley, Bill Sep 82
Bradley, Omar N(elson) obit
May 81
Bradley, William W(arren) See
Bradley, Bill
Bradshaw, Thornton
F(rederick) Jun 82
Brady, William T(homas) obit
Jul 84
Brandt, Bill Aug 81 obit Feb
84
Brattain, Walter H(ouser) obit
Nov 87
Braudel, Fernand (Paul) Apr
85 obit Jan 86
Brenan, (Edward Fitz-)Gerald
Jul 86 obit Mar 87
Brenner, David Mar 87
Brett, George Jul 81
Brett, George P(latt), Jr. obit
May 84
Breuer, Marcel (Lajos) obit
Aug 81
Breytenbach, Breyten Jun 86
Brezhnev, Leonid I(lyich) obit
Jan 83
Bricker, John W(illiam) obit
May 86
Brinkley, David (McClure) Sep
87
Brinton, Howard H(aines) obit
Yrbk 84 (died Apr 73)
Bristow, Gwen obit Yrbk 84
(died Aug 80)
Broderick, Matthew May 87
Brodsky, Joseph (Alexan-
drovich) Jul 82
Brody, Jane E(llen) Feb 86
Broglie, Louis (Victor Pierre
Raymond) de obit May 87
Brokaw, Tom May 81
Bromley, Dorothy Dunbar obit
Feb 86
Brooks, Louise Apr 84 obit Oct
85
Brower, Charles (Hendrickson)
obit Nov 84
Brown, Charles L(ee, Jr.) Sep
81
Brown, George obit Jul 85
Brown, Harrison (Scott) obit
Feb 87
Brown, Rita Mae Sep 86
Brown, Sterling (Allen) Aug 82
Bruhn, Erik (Belton Evers) obit
May 86
Brundtland, Gro Harlem Nov
81
Bruner, Jerome (Seymour) Oct
84

Bryant, Paul W(illiam) obit Mar 83
Brynner, Yul obit Nov 85
Buchanan, Patrick J(oseph) Aug 85
Buchanan, Wiley T(homas), Jr. obit Mar 86
Buckley, William F(rank), Jr. Oct 82
Buckmaster, Henrietta obit Jun 83
Buffett, Warren E(dward) Nov 87
Bugas, John S(tephen) obit Feb 83
Bunker, Ellsworth obit Nov 84
Buñuel, Luis obit Sep 83
Burke, Michael obit Mar 87
Burnet, Sir (Frank) Macfarlane obit Oct 85
Burnham, (Linden) Forbes (Sampson) obit Oct 85
Burns, Arthur F(rank) obit Aug 87
Burns, Eveline M(abel) obit Jan 86
Burr, Donald C(alvin) Sep 86
Burrows, Abe obit Jul 85
Burton, Richard obit Sep 84
Buscaglia, (Felice) Leo(nardo) Oct 83
Bush, George (Herbert Walker) Sep 83
Buthelezi, Mangosuthu G(atsha) Oct 86
Butler, Richard Austen See Butler of Saffron Walden, R.A.B., Baron obit
Butler of Saffron Walden, Richard Austen Butler, Baron obit May 82
Byrne, David Jun 85
Byrne, John Keyes See Leonard, Hugh
Byrnes, John W(illiam) obit Mar 85

Cabot, John M(oors) obit Apr 81
Caetano, Marcello (José) obit Jan 81
Cagney, James obit May 86
Calder, Nigel (David Ritchie) Jun 86
Calder, (Peter) Ritchie obit May 86
Calderone, Frank A(nthony) obit Apr 87
Caldicott, Helen Oct 83
Caldwell, Erskine obit May 87
Caldwell, Millard F(illmore) obit Feb 85
Caldwell, Taylor obit Oct 85
Calero (Portocarrero), Adolfo Oct 87
Callahan, Harry M(orey) Nov 84

Calvino, Italo Feb 84 obit Nov 85
Calvo Sotelo (y Bustelo), Leopoldo Aug 81
Campbell, Earl Apr 83
Campbell, Joseph Jun 84
Cámpora, Héctor José obit Feb 81
Canady, John (Edwin) obit Sep 85
Canetti, Elias Jan 83
Canfield, Cass obit May 86
Canham, Erwin D(ain) obit Feb 82
Capote, Truman obit Oct 84
Carlino, Lewis John May 83
Carlisle, Kitty See Hart, Kitty Carlisle
Carlson, Frank obit Jul 87
Carlucci, Frank (Charles 3d) Oct 81
Carmichael, Hoagy obit Feb 82
Caro, Anthony Nov 81
Caro, Robert A. Jan 84
Carroll, John A(lbert) obit Oct 83
Carroll, Madeleine obit Nov 87
Carroll, Vinnette Sep 83
Carson, Johnny Apr 82
Carter, Benny Jul 87
Carter, (Bessie) Lillian obit Jan 84
Carter, Betty Mar 82
Carter, (William) Hodding, 3d Aug 81
Carver, Raymond Feb 84
Cary, William L(ucius) obit Apr 83
Case, Clifford P(hilip) obit Apr 82
Casey, William J(oseph) obit Jun 87
Caspary, Vera obit Aug 87
Castelli, Leo Aug 84
Catledge, Turner obit Jul 83
Caudill, Rebecca obit Jan 86
Celler, Emanuel obit Mar 81
Cerezo (Arévalo), (Marco) Vinicio Mar 87
Chagall, Marc obit May 85
Chagla, Mahomed Ali Currim obit Jan 84
Chaikin, Joseph Jul 81
Chamberlain, Richard Nov 87
Chamoun, Camille N(imer) obit Sep 87
Chandrasekhar, Subrahmanyan Mar 86
Chapin, Katherine Garrison See Biddle, K. G. C. obit
Chapman, Albert K(inkade) obit Yrbk 84
Chapman, Charles F(rederic) obit Yrbk 84 (died Mar 76)
Charles, Prince of Belgium obit Jul 83

Charles, (Mary) Eugenia Oct 86
Charlot, Jean obit Yrbk 84 (died Mar 79)
Charlotte, Grand Duchess of Luxembourg obit Aug 85
Chase, Lucia obit Mar 86
Chase, Mary (Coyle) obit Jan 82
Chase, Stuart obit Jan 86
Chasins, Abram obit Aug 87
Chayefsky, Paddy obit Sep 81
Cheever, John obit Aug 82
Chernenko, Konstantin U(stinovich) Aug 84 obit May 85
Chicago, Judy Feb 81
Childs, Lucinda Apr 84
Chillida, Eduardo Sep 85
Christopher, Warren M(inor) Jun 81
Chuikov, Vasili (Ivanovitch) obit May 82
Chun Doo Hwan Mar 81
Church, Frank (Forrester) obit May 84
Church, Sam(uel Morgan), Jr. Oct 81
Churchill, Caryl Jun 85
Churchill, Sarah obit Jan 83
Chute, (Beatrice) Joy obit Oct 87
Ciardi, John (Anthony) obit May 86
Cimino, Michael Jan 81
Cisneros, Henry G(abriel) Aug 87
Citrine of Wembley, Walter McLennan Citrine, 1st Baron obit Apr 83
Clague, Ewan obit Jun 87
Clair, René obit May 81
Claire, Ina obit Apr 85
Clapton, Eric Jun 87
Clark, Dick Jan 87
Clark, Lord Kenneth (Mackenzie) obit Jul 83
Clark, Mark W(ayne) obit Jun 84
Clark, William P(atrick) Jul 82
Clausen, A(lden) W(inship) Nov 81
Clavell, James Oct 81
Cleese, John Jan 84
Clements, Earle C. obit May 85
Cleveland, James Aug 85
Clinchy, Everett R(oss) obit Mar 86
Close, Charles See Close, Chuck
Close, Chuck Jul 83
Close, Glenn Nov 84
Coco, James obit Apr 87
Cody, John Patrick Cardinal obit Jun 82
Coetzee, J(ohn) M. Jan 87
Cohen, Arthur A(llen) obit Jan 87

Cohen, Benjamin V(ictor) obit Oct 83
Cohen, Wilbur J(oseph) obit Jul 87
Cohen, William S(ebastian) Apr 82
Cole, Sterling W(illiam) obit May 87
Coleman, Lonnie (William) obit Oct 82
Collingwood, Charles (Cummings) obit Nov 85
Collins, Joan Jan 84
Collins, J(oseph) Lawton obit Oct 87
Collins, Martha Layne Jan 86
Collins, Marva Nov 86
Collins, Phil Nov 86
Colville, Alex Mar 85
Conable, Barber B., Jr. Jul 84
Conley, Eugene obit Feb 82
Connelly, Marc obit Feb 81
Conner, Dennis Nov 87
Conti, Tom Jun 85
Conway, Tim Apr 81
Cook, Donald C(larence) obit Feb 82
Cooke, Terence J(ames) Cardinal obit Nov 83
Coon, Carleton S(tevens) obit Jul 81
Cooper, Irving S(pencer) obit Jan 86
Corcoran, Thomas Gardiner obit Feb 82
Cori, Carl F(erdinand) obit Feb 85
Corman, Roger Feb 83
Corson, Fred Pierce obit Apr 85
Cortázar, Julio obit Apr 84
Cosby, Bill Oct 86
Cossiga, Francesco Jan 81
Costello, Elvis Sep 83
Cotrubas, Ileana Oct 81
Cousins, Frank obit Jul 86
Cowles, Gardner, Jr. obit Aug 85
Cowles, John obit Apr 83
Cowles, Virginia (Spencer) obit Nov 83
Cox, Allyn obit Jan 83
Cox, William Trevor See Trevor, William
Craft, Robert Mar 84
Craig, Walter E(arly) obit Sep 86
Crawford, Broderick obit Jun 86
Crawford, Cheryl obit Nov 86
Craxi, Bettino Feb 84
Crenshaw, Ben Sep 85
Crick, Francis Mar 83
Crisler, Herbert Orin obit Oct 82
Cronin, A(rchibald) J(oseph) obit Mar 81
Cronin, Joe obit Nov 84
Crosby, John (O'Hea) Nov 81

Cross, Ben Aug 84
Crossley, Archibald M(addock) obit Jul 85
Crowther, (F.) Bosley obit Apr 81
Cruise, Tom Apr 87
Cruyff, Johan Nov 81
Cruz, Celia Jul 83
Crystal, Billy Feb 87
Cukor, George obit Mar 83
Cullberg, Birgit Nov 82
Cunningham, Sir Alan (Gordon) obit Apr 83
Cunningham, Mary (Elizabeth) Nov 84
Cuomo, Mario (Matthew) Aug 83
Curran, Charles E(dward) Jan 87
Curran, Joseph E(dwin) obit Oct 81
Curzon, Clifford obit Oct 82
Cushman, Robert E(verton), Jr. obit Apr 85

Dacre of Glanton, Baron, See Trevor-Roper, H. R.
Dahlberg, Edwin T(heodore) obit Oct 86
Dalai Lama Jun 82
Dale, Jim Jul 81
D'Amato, Alfonse Sep 83
Dangerfield, George (Bubb) obit Mar 87
Daniels, Jonathan (Worth) obit Jan 82
Danilova, Alexandra Jul 87
Dannay, Frederic obit Oct 82
Danner, Blythe Jan 81
Dart, Justin W(hitlock) obit Mar 84
Dassault, Marcel (Bloch) obit Jun 86
D'Aubuisson, Roberto Jul 83
Dausset, Jean May 81
Davis, Al(len) Jul 85
Davis, Andrew May 83
Davis, James C(urran) obit Feb 82
Davis, Patti Nov 86
Davis, Peter (Frank) Feb 83
Day, Dorothy obit Jan 81
Dayan, Moshe obit Jan 82
Dean, William F(rishe) obit Oct 81
Debray, (Jules) Régis Jun 82
Debus, Kurt H(einrich) obit Nov 83
Decker, Mary Oct 83
Decter, Midge Apr 82
Defferre, Gaston obit Jun 86
Deighton, Len Sep 84
de Kiewiet, Cornelis W(illem) obit Apr 86
de Kiewit, Cornelis W(illem) See de Kiewiet, C. W. obit
De Kooning, Elaine (Marie Catharine) Jul 82

De Kooning, Willem Sep 84
De La Madrid (Hurtado), Miguel Apr 83
Del Tredici, David Mar 83
De Mille, Agnes Jan 85
Demme, Jonathan Apr 85
De Montebello, (Guy-)Philippe (Lannes) Apr 81
Dempsey, Jack obit Jul 83
Dempsey, William Harrison See Dempsey, Jack obit
Denebrink, Francis C(ompton) obit Jun 87
Densen-Gerber, Judianne Nov 83
Denton, Jeremiah A(ndrew), Jr. May 82
De Palma, Brian Sep 82
Depardieu, Gérard Oct 87
De Rochemont, Richard (Guertis) obit Sept 82
Dershowitz, Alan M(orton) Sep 86
Deukmejian, (Courken) George, Jr. Jun 83
DeVries, William C(astle) Jan 85
Dewey, Charles S(chuveldt) obit Feb 81
Dial, Morse G(rant) obit Jan 83
Diamond, Neil May 81
Diana, Princess of Wales Jan 83
Dickinson, Angie Feb 81
Dietz, David obit Apr 85
Dietz, Howard obit Sep 83
Dillard, Annie Jan 83
Diller, Barry (Charles) Apr 86
Dillon, Matt May 85
Dingell, John D(avid), Jr. Aug 83
DiSalle, Michael V(incent) obit Nov 81
Ditka, Mike Oct 87
Dodds, Harold W(illis) obit Jan 81
Dodge, Cleveland E(arl) obit Feb 83
Doe, Samuel K(anyon) May 81
Doenitz, Karl obit Feb 81
Dohnányi, Christoph von Oct 85
Doisy, E(dward) A(delbert) obit Jan 87
Dole, Elizabeth Hanford Jun 83
Dole, Robert J(oseph) Oct 87
Dolin, Anton obit Jan 84
Domenici, Pete V(ichi) Jun 82
Donaldson, Sam Sep 87
Donner, Frederic G(arrett) obit Apr 87
Donovan, Raymond J(ames) Jan 82
Dorticós (Torrado), Osvaldo obit Aug 83
Doubleday, Nelson May 87
Douglas, Donald W(ills) obit Mar 81

Douglas, Melvyn obit Sep 81
Douglas, Michael Apr 87
Douglas, Thomas C(lement) obit Apr 86
Downey, Morton obit Jan 86
Drabble, Margaret May 81
Draper, Charles Stark obit Sep 87
Drew, George A(lexander) obit May 84
Druckman, Jacob May 81
Drummond, (James) Roscoe obit Nov 83
Duarte (Fuentes), José Napoleón Sep 81
Dubinsky, David obit Jan 83
Dubos, René J(ules) obit Apr 82
Dubuffet, Jean obit Jul 85
Dunne, John Gregory Jun 83
Dunton, A(rnold) Davidson obit Apr 87
Du Pré, Jacqueline obit Nov 87
Durang, Christopher Jun 87
Durant, Will(iam James) obit Jan 82
Duras, Marguerite Nov 85
Durrell, Gerald May 85
Dutoit, Charles Feb 87

Eaker, Ira C(larence) obit Sep 87
Eastland, James O(liver) obit Apr 86
Eckstein, Gustav obit Nov 81
Eckstein, Otto obit May 84
Eco, Umberto Apr 85
Edwards, Blake Jan 83
Edwards, James B(urrows) Nov 82
Edwards, Joan obit Oct 81
Edwards, (W.) Don(lon) Mar 83
Egan, William Allen obit Jul 84
Ehricke, Krafft A. obit Feb 85
Eisenhower, Milton S(tover) obit Jul 85
Eisner, Michael D(ammann) Nov 87
Eldridge, Roy Mar 87
Eliade, Mircea Nov 85 obit Jun 86
Elizabeth, Queen Mother of Great Britain Aug 81
Elkin, Stanley (Lawrence) Jul 87
Ellerbee, Linda Oct 86
Ellis, Perry Jan 86 obit Jul 86
Emerson, Faye obit May 83
Enders, John F(ranklin) obit Jan 86
Engstrom, E(lmer) W(illiam) obit Feb 85
Erlander, Tage (Fritiof) obit Aug 85
Ernst, Jimmy obit Apr 84

Ershad, Hussain Muhammad Nov 84
Ervin, Sam(uel) J(ames), Jr. obit Jun 85
Estes, Simon Aug 86
Ethridge, Mark (Foster) obit Jun 81
Eurich, Alvin C(hristian) obit Aug 87
Evans, Harold (Matthew) Apr 85
Evans, Linda Mar 86
Evans, Luther H(arris) obit Feb 82
Evren, Kenan Apr 84

Fabius, Laurent Feb 85
Fagerholm, Karl-August obit Jul 84
Fagg, Fred D(ow), Jr. obit Jan 82
Falwell, Jerry Jan 81
Farrar, Margaret (Pether-bridge) obit Aug 84
Farrington, (Mary) Elizabeth Pruett obit Sep 84
Fassbinder, Rainer Werner obit Aug 82
Feinsinger, Nathan P(aul) obit Jan 84
Feld, Irvin obit Nov 84
Feldstein, Martin (Stuart) May 83
Ferguson, Homer obit Mar 83
Ferraro, Geraldine A(nne) Sep 84
Feynman, Richard P(hillips) Nov 86
Fichandler, Zelda Jun 87
Field, Henry obit Mar 86
Fielding, Gabriel obit Apr 87
Fielding, Temple (Hornaday) obit Jul 83
Fierstein, Harvey Feb 84
Fingesten, Peter obit Oct 87
Finnbogadóttir, Vigdis May 87
Fischl, Eric Jun 86
Fishback, Margaret obit Nov 85
Fisher, M(ary) F(rances) K(ennedy) Sep 83
Fisher, Welthy (Blakesley Honsinger) obit Feb 81
Fisk, James Brown obit Oct 81
Fitzgerald, Albert J. obit Jul 82
Fitzgerald, Ed obit Jun 82
FitzGerald, Frances Jun 87
FitzGerald, Garret Aug 84
Fitzgerald, Robert (Stuart) obit Mar 85
Fitzsimmons, Frank E(dward) obit Jul 81
Fleming, Lady Amalia obit Apr 86
Fleming, Donald M(ethuen) obit Mar 87
Flesch, Rudolf (Franz) obit Nov 86

Florinsky, Michael T(imofe-evich) obit Jan 82
Flory, Paul J(ohn) obit Nov 85
Flutie, Doug Oct 85
Fo, Dario Nov 86
Folon, Jean-Michel Feb 81
Fonda, Henry obit Sep 82
Fonda, Jane Jun 86
Fontanne, Lynn obit Sep 83
Foot, Michael (Mackintosh) May 81
Foote, Horton Aug 86
Ford, Frederick W(ayne) obit Sep 86
Ford, Harrison Sep 84
Ford, Henry, II obit Nov 87
Forsyth, Frederick May 86
Fortas, Abe obit May 82
Fosse, Bob obit Nov 87
Fossey, Dian May 85 obit Feb 86
Foster, Jodie Jun 81
Fowler, Mark S(tapleton) Mar 86
Fox, Carol obit Sep 81
Fox, Michael J. Nov 87
Fox, Robert J(ohn) obit Jun 84
Fox, Virgil (Keel) obit Jan 81
Francis, Clarence obit Mar 86
Francis, Dick Aug 81
Frankel, Max Apr 87
Fraser of North Cape, Bruce Austin Fraser, 1st Baron obit Apr 81
Frayn, Michael Jan 85
Frederika (Louise), Consort of Paul I, King of the Hellenes obit Apr 81
Freehafer, Edward G(eier) obit Feb 86
Frei (Montalva), Eduardo obit Mar 82
Freud, Anna obit Mar 83
Friedkin, William Jun 87
Friendly, Fred W. Aug 87
Frings, Ketti (Hartley) obit Apr 81
Frisch, Karl von obit Yrbk 83 (died Jun 82)
Frye, (Herman) Northrop Aug 83
Fujiyama, Aiichiro obit May 85
Fuller, R(ichard) Buckminster, (Jr.) obit Aug 83
Futter, Ellen V(ictoria) Oct 85

Gaddis, William Nov 87
Gajdusek, D(aniel) Carleton Jun 81
Gale, Robert (Peter) Jan 87
Gallo, Robert C(harles) Oct 86
Gallup, George (Horace) obit Sep 84
Galtieri, Leopoldo (Fortunato) Aug 82
Gandhi, Indira (Priyadarshini Nehru) obit Yrbk 84 Jan 85

Gandhi, Rajiv (Ratna) Apr 85
García Pérez, Alan Nov 85
Gardner, John (Champlin, Jr.) obit Nov 82
Garn, Edwin (Jacob) See Garn, J.
Garn, Jake Aug 85
Garroway, Dave obit Sep 82
Garth, David Jan 81
Gass, William H(oward) Apr 86
Gates, Thomas S(overeign), Jr. obit May 83
Gay, Peter (Jack) Feb 86
Gayle, Crystal Mar 86
Gehry, Frank O(wen) Jun 87
Geldof, Bob Mar 86
Gemayel, Amin Mar 83
Genet, Jean obit Jun 86
George, Boy See Boy George
George-Brown, Baron See Brown, G. obit
Gephardt, Richard (Andrew) Oct 87
Gerbner, George Aug 83
Gerhardsen, Einar obit Nov 87
Gernreich, Rudi obit Jun 85
Gershwin, Ira obit Oct 83
Gerstenmaier, (Karl Albrecht) Eugen obit May 86
Getty, Gordon P(eter) Feb 85
Geyer, Georgie Anne Aug 86
Giauque, William F(rancis) obit May 82
Gibb, Barry Sep 81
Gibson, Mel Apr 84
Gibson, William Jul 83
Gideonse, Harry David obit May 85
Gielgud, John Feb 84
Gilder, George Oct 81
Gilder, Rosamond obit Oct 86
Gilels, Emil G(rigoryevich) obit Jan 86
Giles, Barney McKinney obit Aug 84
Gimbel, Peter (Robin) Jan 82 obit Aug 87
Gingold, Hermione (Ferdinanda) obit Jul 87
Ginsberg, Allen Apr 87
Giroux, Robert Nov 82
Glass, Philip Mar 81
Glasser, Ira Jan 86
Gleason, Jackie obit Aug 87
Glemp, Jozef Sep 82
Glubb, Sir John Bagot obit May 86
Gmeiner, Hermann obit Jun 86
Gobbi, Tito obit May 84
Godfrey, Arthur obit May 83
Godunov, Alexander Feb 83
Goldberg, Whoopi Mar 85
Golden, Harry (Lewis) obit Nov 81
Goldmann, Nahum obit Oct 82
Goldstein, Israel obit Jun 86

Goldstein, Joseph L(eonard) Jul 87
Golub, Leon (Albert) Aug 84
Gomulka, Wladyslaw obit Oct 82
Goode, W(illie) Wilson Oct 85
Goodell, Charles E(llsworth, Jr.) obit Mar 87
Gooden, Dwight (Eugene) Apr 86
Goodman, Benny obit Aug 86
Goodrich, Frances obit Apr 84
Goodrich, Lloyd obit May 87
Gorbachev, Mikhail (Sergeyevich) Aug 85
Gordon, Mary (Catherine) Nov 81
Gordon, Ruth obit Oct 85
Gore, Albert, Jr. Jun 87
Gorin, Igor obit Jun 82
Gorsuch, Anne (McGill) Sep 82
Gosden, Freeman F(isher) obit Feb 83
Gossage, Rich Aug 84
Gottlieb, Robert A(dams) Sep 87
Goudge, Elizabeth obit Aug 84
Gould, Chester obit Jul 85
Gould, Glenn obit Nov 82
Gould, Stephen Jay Sep 82
Grace, Princess of Monaco obit Nov 82
Graham, Bob Jul 86
Graham, (Daniel) Robert See Graham, Bob
Gramm, Donald obit Jul 83
Gramm, (William) Phil(ip) May 86
Grant, Cary obit Jan 87
Grass, Günter (Wilhelm) Jul 83
Grasso, Ella T(ambussi) obit Mar 81
Graves, Nancy (Stevenson) May 81
Graves, Robert (Ranke) obit Feb 86
Gray, Gordon obit Feb 83
Gray, Simon (James Holliday) Jun 83
Gray, Spalding Sep 86
Greeley, Dana McLean obit Aug 86
Green, Edith S(tarrett) obit Jun 87
Greenberg, Hank obit Oct 86
Greene, Harold H(erman) Aug 85
Greene, Hugh Carleton obit Apr 87
Greene, Lorne obit Oct 87
Greenwood, Joan obit Apr 87
Gregorian, Vartan Oct 85
Gretzky, Wayne, Feb 82
Grey, J(ames) D(avid) obit Sep 85
Gribble, Harry Wagstaff (Graham-) obit Apr 81

Griffin, (Samuel) Marvin obit Aug 82
Grillo, Frank Raúl See Machito
Gross, H(arold) R(oyce) obit Oct 87
Gross, Paul Magnus obit Jun 86
Grosvenor, Melville Bell obit Jun 82
Gruenther, Alfred M(aximilian) obit Jul 83
Grumman, Leroy R(andle) obit Jan 83
Grzimek, Bernhard obit May 87
Guare, John Aug 82
Guinness, Alec Mar 81
Gumbel, Bryant Jul 86
Gurney, A(lbert) R(amsdell), Jr. Jul 86
Guth, Alan H(arvey) Sep 87
Guthrie, Arlo Feb 82

Haacke, Hans (Christoph) Jul 87
Habib, Philip C(harles) Sep 81
Habré, Hissène Aug 87
Haddon, William, Jr. obit Apr 85
Hagegard, Hakan May 85
Hagerty, James C. obit Jun 81
Haig, Alexander Meigs, Jr. Sep 87
Hale, Clara Jul 85
Haley, Sir William John obit Oct 87
Hall, Donald (Andrew) May 84
Hall, Joyce C(lyde) obit Jan 83
Halleck, Charles A(braham) obit Apr 86
Hallstein, Walter obit May 82
Hamilton, Margaret obit Jul 85
Hamilton, Scott Apr 85
Hammond, E(dward) Cuyler obit Jan 87
Hammond, John (Henry, Jr.) obit Aug 87
Hancock, Joy B(right) obit Oct 86
Handler, Philip obit Feb 82
Handy, Thomas T(roy) obit Jun 82
Hanfmann, George M(axim) A(nossov) obit May 86
Hanks, Nancy obit Mar 83
Hanna, William Jul 83
Hanson, Duane (Elwood) Oct 83
Hanson, Howard obit Apr 81
Harburg, E(dgar) Y(ipsel) obit Apr 81
Harden, Cecil M(urray) obit Feb 85
Hardwick, Elizabeth Feb 81
Hare, David Aug 83
Haring, Keith Aug 86

Harkness, Rebekah (West) obit
Sep 82
Harlech, Fifth Baron See
Ormsby-Gore, (W.) D. obit
Harrar, J(acob) George obit
Jun 82
Harrell, Lynn Feb 83
Harriman, W(illiam) Averill
obit Sep 86
Harris, Sir Arthur Travers obit
May 84
Harris, Patricia Roberts obit
May 85
Harrison, William K(elly), Jr.
obit Aug 87
Harrison, Rex Feb 86
Harrison, Wallace K(irkman)
obit Jan 82
Harry, Debbie Nov 81
Hart, Kitty Carlisle Oct 82
Hartman, David Jun 81
Harvey, Paul Mar 86
Hass, H(enry) B(ohn) obit Apr
87
Hatch, Orrin G(rant) Aug 82
Hatfield, Mark O(dom) Mar 84
Hauge, Gabriel (Sylfest) obit
Sep 81
Haughey, Charles J(ames) Feb
81
Haughton, Daniel J(eremiah)
obit Aug 87
Hauser, (Benjamin) Gayelord
Feb 85
Havel, Václav Mar 85
Hawke, Bob Aug 83
Hawke, Robert James Lee See
Hawke, Bob
Hawking, Stephen W(illiam)
May 84
Hawkins, Augustus F(reeman)
Feb 83
Hawkins, Paula (Fickes) Sep
85
Hayden, Sterling obit Jul 86
Hayes, Woody obit May 87
Hays, (Lawrence) Brooks obit
Jan 82
Hayworth, Rita obit Jul 87
Head, Edith obit Jan 82
Heaney, Seamus (Justin) Jan
82
Hearns, Thomas Mar 83
Hearst, Patricia (Campbell)
Aug 82
Hecht, Anthony May 86
Heckler, Margaret M(ary
O'Shaughnessy) Aug 83
Hedden, Worth Tuttle obit Jan
86
Hefner, Christie (Ann) Oct 86
Heimlich, Henry J(ay) Oct 86
Heinz, H(enry) J(ohn) obit Apr
87
Heinz, (Henry) John, (3d) Apr
81
Held, Al Jan 86
Heller, Walter W(olfgang) obit
Aug 87

Hellman, Lillian obit Aug 84
Helmsley, Harry B(rakmann)
Jun 85
Helpmann, Robert obit Nov 86
Helstein, Ralph obit May 85
Hemingway, Mary (Welsh)
obit Jan 87
Henderson, Leon obit Jan 87
Henderson, Loy W(esley) obit
May 86
Henley, Beth Feb 83
Hentoff, Nat Aug 86
Herbster, Ben M(ohr) obit Mar
85
Hersh, Seymour (Myron) Mar
84
Herzog, Paul M(ax) obit Jan 87
Hesburgh, Theodore M(artin)
Jul 82
Heseltine, Michael (Ray Dib-
din) Jun 85
Hess, Rudolf obit Oct 87
Heston, Charlton Jul 86
Hicks, Granville obit Aug 82
Hightower, John M(armann)
obit Apr 87
Higley, Harvey V(an Zandt)
obit Jan 87
Hildebrand, Joel H(enry) obit
Jul 83
Hill, Abram obit Nov 86
Hill, Benny Feb 83
Hill, Lister obit Feb 85
Hillenkoetter, Roscoe H(enry)
obit Aug 82
Himmelfarb, Gertrude May 85
Hines, Earl (Kenneth) obit Jun
83
Hines, Fatha See Hines, Earl
(Kenneth) obit
Hines, Gregory Jul 85
Hirsch, John (Stephen) Apr 84
Hirsch, Judd Mar 84
Hirshhorn, Joseph H(erman)
obit Oct 81
Hoagland, Edward (Morley)
Sept 82
Hobson, Laura Z(ametkin) obit
Apr 86
Hodel, Donald P(aul) Jun 87
Hoffa, James R(iddle) obit Mar
83
Hoffer, Eric obit Jul 83
Hoffman, Abbie Apr 81
Hoffman, Anna M(arie) Ro-
senberg obit Jul 83
Hogan, Paul Aug 87
Hogben, Lancelot (Thomas)
obit Jan 84
Hogwood, Christopher Jul 85
Hoiby, Lee Mar 87
Holden, William obit Jan 82
Holladay, Wilhelmina (Cole)
Oct 87
Holliday, Jennifer Jun 83
Holliger, Heinz Jan 87
Hollings, Ernest F(rederick) Jul
82

Hollomon, J(ohn) Herbert obit
Aug 85
Holloway, Stanley obit Mar 82
Holmes, Larry Aug 81
Holt, A(ndrew) D(avid) obit
Sep 87
Holt, John (Caldwell) Jun 81
obit Nov 85
Holyoake, Keith J(acka) obit
Feb 84
Hope, Stanley C. obit Oct 82
Hopper, Dennis Aug 87
Horne, John E(lmer) obit Apr
85
Horne, Lena Nov 85
Horner, H(orace) Mansfield
obit Jul 83
Horrocks, Sir B(rian) G(wynne)
obit Mar 85
Hosmer, (Chester) Craig obit
Mar 83
Houghton, Amory obit Apr 81
Houseman, John Apr 84
Houston, James A(rchibald) Jul
87
Houston, Whitney Nov 86
Howard, Elston (Gene) obit
Feb 81
Hoxha, Enver obit Jun 85
Hu Yaobang Nov 83
Hudson, Rock obit Nov 85
Hughes, Barnard Sep 81
Hughes, Emmet John obit Nov
82
Hughes, Robert (Studley For-
rest) May 87
Hughes, Sarah T(ilghman) obit
Jul 85
Hunsaker, Jerome C(larke)
obit Nov 84
Hunter, Alberta obit Jan 85
Hunter-Gault, Charlayne Apr
87
Hunthausen, Raymond
G(erhardt) Aug 87
Huppert, Isabelle Nov 81
Hurd, Peter obit Sep 84
Hurt, John Jan 82
Hurt, William May 86
Hussein, Ahmed obit Feb 85
Hussein, King of Jordan Apr
86
Hussein, Saddam (al-Tikriti)
Sep 81
Hussein Ibn Talal See Hus-
sein, King of Jordan
Husted, Marjorie Child obit
Feb 87
Huston, John Mar 81 obit Oct
87
Hynek, J(osef) Allen obit Jun
86

Icahn, Carl C. Apr 86
Idris Senussi I, King of Libya
obit Jul 83

Idriss Senussi I, King of Libya
See Idris Senussi I, King of
Libya obit
Iglesias, Julio Jun 84
Ilg, Frances L(illian) obit Sep
81
Illia, Arturo (Umberto) obit
Mar 83
Impellitteri, Vincent R(ichard)
obit Mar 87
Ingersoll, Ralph (McAllister)
obit May 85
Inouye, Daniel K(en) Sep 87
Irons, Jeremy Aug 84
Irwin, Bill Oct 87
Isherwood, Christopher (William) obit Feb 86
Ivory, James Jul 81

Jackson, Henry M(artin) obit
Oct 83
Jackson, Jesse (Louis) Jan 86
Jackson, Michael Nov 83
Jacob, John E(dward) Feb 86
Jacobi, Derek May 81
Jagger, Bianca Apr 87
James, Clive (Vivian Leopold)
Nov 84
James, Harry obit Aug 83
Jarrett, Keith May 85
Jaruzelski, Wojciech (Witold)
Mar 82
Jarvik, Robert K(offler) Jul 85
Jarvis, Howard (Arnold) obit
Sep 86
Javits, Jacob K(oppel) obit Apr
86
Jaworski, Leon obit Feb 83
Jayewardene, J(unius)
R(ichard) Jan 84
Jenkins, Ray H(oward) obit
Feb 81
Jenkins, Roy (Harris) Oct 82
Jenner, William E(zra) obit
May 85
Jennings, Paul (Joseph) obit
Oct 87
Jennings, Peter (Charles) Nov
83
Jennings, Waylon Apr 82
Jensen, Jackie obit Oct 82
Jessel, George (Albert) obit Jul
81
Jessup, Philip C(aryl) obit Mar
86
Jobs, Steven (Paul) Mar 83
Johanson, Donald C(arl) Feb
84
John, Tommy Oct 81
Johns, Jasper May 87
Johnson, Crockett obit Jan 84
Johnson, Don Apr 86
Johnson, Earvin Jan 82
Johnson, Harold K(eith) obit
Nov 83
Johnson, Magic See Johnson,
Earvin

Johnson, Pamela Hansford
obit Aug 81
Johnson, Sonia Feb 85
Johnson, (Thomas) Walter obit
Sep 85
Johnson, Virginia May 85
Jones, Carolyn obit Sep 83
Jones, David C(harles) Jul 82
Jones, Grace Sep 87
Jones, James R(obert) Oct 81
Jones, K. C. Feb 87
Jones, Marvin obit Jan 84
Jordan, Michael Sep 87
Joyner-Kersee, Jackie Jul 87
Julia, Raul Sep 82

Kahn, Herman obit Aug 83
Kainen, Jacob Feb 87
Kaiser, Edgar F(osburgh) obit
Feb 82
Kalb, Marvin Jul 87
Kampelman, Max M. Jul 86
Kane, Harnett T(homas) obit
Yrbk 84
Kane, Joseph Nathan Nov 85
Kania, Stanislaw Jun 81
Kapitsa, Pyotr L(eonidovich)
obit May 84
Kapitza, Peter L(eonidovich)
See Kapitsa, P. L. obit
Karajan, Herbert von Sep 86
Karami, Rashid obit Jul 87
Karmal, Babrak Mar 81
Kasparov, Gary Apr 86
Kassebaum, Nancy Landon
Feb 82
Kastler, Alfred obit Mar 84
Kaufman, Henry Aug 81
Kay, Hershy obit Feb 82
Kaye, Danny obit Apr 87
Kaye, Nora obit Apr 87
Kean, Thomas H(oward) Jul 85
Keighley, William obit Aug 84
Keillor, Garrison Aug 85
Kekkonen, Urho K(aleva) obit
Oct 86
Kelly, E(verett) Lowell obit
Apr 86
Kelly, Grace See Grace, Princess of Monaco obit
Kelly, John B(renden), Jr. obit
Apr 85
Kelly, Petra (Karin) Mar 84
Kelman, Charles D(avid) Jun
84
Kemper, James S(cott) obit
Nov 81
Keneally, Thomas (Michael)
Jun 87
Kennedy, Donald Jul 84
Kennedy, William May 85
Kent, Corita obit Nov 86
Kertész, André obit Nov 85
Keyserling, Leon H. obit Sep
87
Keyworth, George A(lbert), 2d
Mar 86

Khalid, King of Saudi Arabia
obit Aug 82
Khamenei, Hojatolislam
(Sayed) Ali Nov 87
Khashoggi, Adnan (Mohamed)
Mar 86
Kieran, John (Francis) obit Feb
82
Kiewiet, Cornelis W(illem) de
See de Kiewiet, C. W. obit
Kim Dae Jung Sep 85
Kimball, Spencer W(oolley)
obit Jan 86
King, Don Jun 84
King, Larry May 85
King, Stephen Oct 81
Kingman, Dave Mar 82
Kingsley, Ben Nov 83
Kinnell, Galway Aug 86
Kinnock, Neil (Gordon) Apr 84
Kinski, Nastassja Jun 84
Kintner, Robert E(dmonds)
obit Feb 81
Kirk, Paul G(rattan), Jr. Aug 87
Kirkpatrick, Jeane (Duane)
J(ordan) Jul 81
Kirkpatrick, Ralph obit Aug 84
Kishi, Nobusuke obit Sep 87
Kistiakowsky, George B(ogdan)
obit Feb 83
Kitaj, R(onald) B(rooks) Apr 82
Kitchell, Iva obit Jan 84
Klein, Edward E(lkan) obit
Sep 85
Klein, Julius obit May 84
Kline, Kevin Jul 86
Kline, Nathan S(chellenberg)
obit May 83
Knight, Bob May 87
Knight, Gladys Feb 87
Knight, John S(hively) obit
Aug 81
Knopf, Alfred A. obit Oct 84
Koestler, Arthur obit Apr 83
Koivisto, Mauno (Henrik) Sep
82
Kolar, Jiri Apr 86
Kolff, Willem Johan May 83
Kolvenbach, Peter-Hans May
84
Komar, Vitaly, and Melamid,
Aleksandr Oct 84
Koo, V(i) K(yuin) Wellington
obit Jan 86
Koop, C(harles) Everett Sep 83
Koppel, Ted Jul 84
Korda, Michael (Vincent) Aug
85
Kosygin, Aleksei
N(ikolayevich) obit Feb 81
Kotschnig, Walter M(aria) obit
Sep 85
Kozol, Jonathan Jan 86
Krantz, Judith May 82
Krasna, Norman obit Feb 85
Krasner, Lee obit Aug 84
Kraus, Alfredo Jun 87
Kraus, Lili obit Jan 87
Krebs, Sir Hans obit Feb 82

Kremer, Gidon Mar 85
Krim, Mathilde Aug 87
Krishnamurti, Jiddu obit Apr 86
Kroc, Ray(mond) A. obit Mar 84
Kucuk, Fazil See Kutchuk, (M.) F. obit
Kuekes, Edward D(aniel) obit Mar 87
Kundera, Milan Mar 83
Kunin, Madeleine (May) Jul 87
Kuralt, Charles Jul 81
Kurtz, Swoosie Oct 87
Kutchuk, (Mustafa) Fazil obit Mar 84
Kuznets, Simon obit Sep 85
Kylian, Jiri Sep 82
Kyser, Kay obit Sep 85

LaBelle, Patti Jul 86
Labouisse, Henry R(ichardson) obit May 87
Ladurie, Emmanuel Le Roy See Le Roy Ladurie, E.
Laeri, J(ohn) Howard obit Aug 86
Laffer, Arthur (Betz) Feb 82
Lagerfeld, Karl Jan 82
Lainc, Cleo Feb 86
LaMarsh, Judy obit Jan 81
Lamm, Richard D(ouglas) May 85
Lancaster, Burt Apr 86
Lancaster, Osbert obit Sep 86
Lanchester, Elsa obit Feb 87
Land, Edwin H(erbert) Mar 81
Landon, Alf(red Mossman) obit Nov 87
Lang, Jack Aug 83
Lange, David Sep 85
Lange, Jessica May 83
Langer, Susanne K(atherina Knauth) obit Sep 85
Lansing, Sherry (Lee) May 81
Lardner, Ring, Jr. Jul 87
Laredo, Ruth Oct 87
Larkin, Philip (Arthur) Jan 85 obit Feb 86
Lasch, Christopher Mar 85
Lash, Joseph P. obit Oct 87
Lauder, Estée Jul 86
Laughlin, James May 82
Lauper, Cyndi Aug 85
Laurents, Arthur Nov 84
Lavin, Linda Nov 87
Lawe, John (Edward) Jan 84
Lawson, Nigel Mar 87
Lay, James S(elden), Jr. obit Aug 87
Leakey, Mary (Douglas) Apr 85
Lebowitz, Fran(ces Ann) Mar 82
Leboyer, Frédérick Jul 82
Lee, Doris (Emrick) obit Jan 86
Léger, Jules obit Jan 81

Le Guin, Ursula K(roeber) Jan 83
Lehman, John F(rancis), Jr. Nov 85
Lehrer, James (Charles) Jan 87
Lehrer, Tom Jul 82
Lelouch, Claude Nov 82
Lem, Stanislaw Oct 86
Lendl, Ivan Sep 84
Lengyel, Emil obit Apr 85
Lennon, John obit Feb 81
Lennox-Boyd, Lord Alan T(indal) obit May 83
Lenya, Lotte obit Jan 82
Leonard, Elmore Sep 85
Leonard, Hugh Apr 83
Leonard, Ray See Leonard, Sugar Ray
Leonard, Sugar Ray Feb 81
Leopold III, King of the Belgians obit Nov 83
Lerner, Alan Jay obit Aug 86
Le Roy Ladurie, Emmanuel (Bernard) Jul 84
Lesage, Jean obit Feb 81
Leser, Tina obit Mar 86
LeSourd, Catherine Marshall See Marshall, S.C.W. obit
Levi, Julian (Edwin) obit Apr 82
Levi, Primo Mar 87 obit May 87
Levin, Meyer obit Sep 81
Levine, Joseph E(dward) obit Sep 87
Levine, Philip obit Nov 87
Lewis, Carl Nov 84
Lewis, Drew Feb 82
LeWitt, Sol Jul 86
Liberace Mar 86 obit Mar 87
Liberman, Alexander May 87
Liberman, Evsei (Grigorevich) obit May 83
Lichtenstein, Harvey May 87
Liebman, Max obit Sep 81
Lilienthal, David E(li) obit Mar 81
Limann, Hilla Jun 81
Linden, Hal Jan 87
Link, Edwin (Albert) obit Yrbk 83 (died Sep 81)
Lipmann, Fritz (Albert) obit Sep 86
Lipton, Seymour obit Feb 87
Littlejohn, Robert McG(owan) obit Jul 82
Little Richard Sep 86
Livingston, M(ilton) Stanley obit Nov 86
Llewellyn, Richard obit Jan 84
Lloyd Webber, Andrew Jun 82
Lockridge, Richard obit Oct 82
Lodge, Henry Cabot, (Jr.) obit Apr 85
Lodge, John Davis obit Jan 86
Loeb, William obit Nov 81
Loewy, Raymond (Fernand) obit Sep 86
Lon Nol obit Jan 86

London, George obit Jun 85
Lonergan, Bernard J(oseph) F(rancis) obit Feb 85
Longo, Luigi obit Jan 81
Loos, Anita obit Oct 81
López Bravo, Gregorio obit Apr 85
Loquasto, Santo Jun 81
Lorenzo, Frank Feb 87
Loring, Eugene obit Oct 82
Lortel, Lucille Feb 85
Losey, Joseph obit Aug 84
Loudon, Dorothy Jun 84
Louganis, Greg Oct 84
Louis, Joe obit Jun 81
Love, Iris (Cornelia) Aug 82
Lovett, Robert A(bercrombie) obit Jun 86
Lowery, Joseph E. Nov 82
Lubell, Samuel obit Oct 87
Lucas, Martha B. See Pate, M. B. L. obit
Luce, Clare Boothe obit Nov 87
Ludlam, Charles Aug 86 obit Jul 87
Ludlum, Robert Nov 82
Lukas, J(ay) Anthony Jan 87
Luns, Joseph M(arie) A(ntoine) H(ubert) Apr 82
Lurie, Alison Feb 86
Lustiger, Jean-Marie Feb 84
Lynch, David May 87
Lynch, J(ohn) Joseph obit Aug 87
Lynd, Staughton (Craig) May 83
Lynde, Paul (Edward) obit Feb 82
Lyng, Richard E(dmund) Sep 86
Lyons, Eugene obit Mar 85

Ma, Yo-Yo Jul 82
MacDermot, Galt Jul 84
Macdonald, Dwight obit Mar 83
MacDonald, John D(ann) Oct 86 obit Feb 87
MacDonald, Malcolm (John) obit Mar 81
Macdonald, Ross obit Sep 83
MacEachen, Allan J(oseph) Apr 83
Machel, Samora Moises Mar 84 obit Jan 87
Machito Feb 83 obit Jun 84
MacInnes, Helen (Clark) obit Nov 85
MacIver, Loren Nov 87
Mackay, John A(lexander) obit Aug 83
Mackerras, Sir Charles Feb 85
MacLeish, Archibald obit Jun 82
Macmillan, (Maurice) Harold obit Feb 87

Macy, John W(illiams), Jr. obit Apr 87
Madden, John Aug 85
Madden, Ray J(ohn) obit Nov 87
Madonna May 86
Mahon, George (Herman) obit Jan 86
Malamud, Bernard obit May 86
Malik, Adam obit Nov 84
Malone, Moses Jun 86
Maltz, Albert obit Jul 85
Mandela, Nelson (Rolihlahla) Jan 84
Mandela, (Nomzamo) Winnie Jan 86
Mandelbrot, Benoit Jun 87
Mandlikova, Hana Jan 86
Mandrell, Barbara Aug 82
Maris, Roger (Eugene) obit Feb 86
Marjolin, Robert (Ernest) obit Jun 86
Markham, Beryl obit Oct 86
Marriott, J. Willard obit Oct 85
Marsalis, Wynton Oct 84
Marshall, E. G. Jun 86
Marshall, (Sarah) Catherine (Wood) obit May 83
Martens, Wilfried Feb 87
Martin, John Bartlow obit Mar 87
Martin, Judith Jun 86
Marton, Eva Apr 85
Marvin, Lee obit Oct 87
Mason, Jackie Jul 87
Mason, James obit Sep 84
Mason, Marsha Apr 81
Massey, Raymond obit Sep 83
Masursky, Harold Aug 86
Matthews, H(arrison) Freeman obit Jan 87
Mauroy, Pierre Jun 82
Maynard, Robert C(lyve) Jun 86
Mayr, Ernst Nov 84
Mays, Benjamin E(lijah) obit May 84
Mazey, Emil obit Nov 83
M'Bow, Amadou-Mahtar May 87
McBride, Lloyd obit Jan 84
McCabe, Thomas B(ayard) obit Jul 82
McCain, John S(idney), Jr. obit Jun 81
McCall, Tom (Lawson) obit Mar 83
McCarthy, Frank obit Feb 87
McCartney, Paul Jan 86
McClintock, Barbara Mar 84
McColough, C(harles) Peter Jan 81
McCormack, John W(illiam) obit Jan 81
McCullough, Colleen Apr 82
McEwen, Terence A(lexander) Jul 85

McFadden, Mary Apr 83
McFarland, Ernest W(illiam) obit Aug 84
McFarlane, Robert C(arl) May 84
McGannon, Donald H(enry) obit Jul 84
McGinniss, Joe Jan 84
McGuane, Thomas Nov 87
McInerney, Jay Nov 87
McKellen, Ian Jan 84
McKenna, Siobhan obit Jan 87
McKinley, Chuck obit Sep 86
McLaughlin, John (Joseph) Jul 87
McLean, Robert obit Feb 81
McLuhan, (Herbert) Marshall obit Feb 81
McMurtry, Larry (Jeff) Jun 84
McNamara, Robert S(trange) Mar 87
McPhee, John (Angus) Oct 82
McQueen, Steve obit Jan 81
McRae, Carmen Apr 83
Mearns, David C(hambers) obit Jul 81
Medawar, Peter Brian obit Nov 87
Medeiros, Humberto S(ousa) obit Nov 83
Médici, Emílio Garrastazú obit Jan 86
Medvedev, Roy (Aleksandr) Sep 84
Meese, Edwin, 3d Sep 81
Meier, Richard Jan 85
Melamid, Aleksandr See Komar, V.
Mendès-France, Pierre obit Jan 83
Mengistu Haile Mariam Jul 81
Mennin, Peter obit Aug 83
Menon, K(umara) P(admanbha) S(ivasankara) obit Yrbk 83 (died Nov 82)
Mercer, Mabel obit Jun 84
Merman, Ethel obit Apr 84
Merrifield, R(obert) Bruce Mar 85
Merrill, James (Ingram) Aug 81
Michals, Duane (Steven) Apr 81
Michel, Robert H(enry) Sep 81
Mifune, Toshiro Jun 81
Mikulski, Barbara A(nn) Nov 85
Milgram, Stanley obit Mar 85
Milland, Ray obit Apr 86
Millar, Kenneth See Macdonald, R. obit
Miller, Arnold (Ray) obit Sep 85
Miller, Irving obit Feb 81
Miller, James C(lifford), 3d May 86
Miller, Jonathan (Wolfe) Nov 86
Miller, Merle obit Jul 86

Miller, Roger Sep 86
Miller, William E(dward) obit Aug 83
Milosz, Czeslaw Oct 81
Miner, Worthington (C.) obit Mar 83
Minnelli, Vincente obit Sep 86
Mintoff, Dom Mar 84
Miró, Joan obit Feb 84
Mitchell, Joan Mar 86
Mitterrand, François (Maurice) Oct 82
Moch, Jules (Salvador) obit Nov 85
Molotov, Viacheslav M(ikhailovich) obit Jan 87
Monaco, Mario del obit Jan 83
Monk, Meredith Feb 85
Monk, Thelonious obit Apr 82
Monroe, Lucy obit Nov 87
Montagu, Ewen (Edward Samuel) obit Sep 85
Montale, Eugenio obit Nov 81
Montana, Joe Sep 83
Montebello, (Guy-)Philippe (Lannes) de See De Montebello, Philippe
Montgomery, Robert obit Nov 81
Moody, Joseph E(ugene) obit Jul 84
Moon, Sun Myung Mar 83
Moore, Brian Jan 86
Moore, Dudley Jun 82
Moore, Gerald obit May 87
Moore, Henry (Spencer) obit Oct 86
Moreno, Rita Sep 85
Morgan, Joe Sep 84
Morganfield, McKinley See Waters, Muddy
Morgenthau, Robert M(orris) Jan 86
Morley, Malcolm A. Jun 84
Morris, James Jul 86
Morris, Jan Jun 86
Morris, Wright (Marion) May 82
Morrison, Philip Jul 81
Morse, Philip M(cCord) obit Nov 85
Mortimer, John (Clifford) Apr 83
Morton, Thruston B(allard) obit Oct 82
Moses, Edwin Nov 86
Moses, Robert obit Sep 81
Mosley, Sir Oswald (Ernald) obit Feb 81
Motley, Arthur H(arrison) obit Jul 84
Mowat, Farley (McGill) Feb 86
Moynihan, Daniel Patrick Feb 86
Mubarak, (Mohamed) Hosni Apr 82
Mudd, Roger (Harrison) Jan 81
Mueller, R(euben) H(erbert) obit Sep 82

Mulliken, Robert S(anderson) obit Jan 87
Mulroney, (Martin) Brian Apr 84
Mumford, L(awrence) Quincy obit Jan 83
Murphy, Charles S(prings) obit Oct 83
Murphy, Eddie Nov 83
Murray, Anne Jan 82
Murray, Bill Jan 85
Murray, Charles (Alan) Jul 86
Myer, Dillon S(eymour) obit Jan 83
Myrdal, Mrs. Alva obit Mar 86
Myrdal, Mrs. Gunnar See Myrdal, Mrs. A. obit
Myrdal, (Karl) Gunnar obit Jul 87

Nader, Ralph Apr 86
Naisbitt, John Nov 84
Nakasone, Yasuhiro Jun 83
Nakian, Reuben Feb 85 obit Feb 87
Narayan, R(asipuram) K(rishnaswami) Sep 87
Navasky, Victor (Saul) May 86
Navon, Yitzhak May 82
Neagle, Anna obit Jul 86
Neagle, Dame Anna See Neagle, Anna obit
Nearing, Scott obit Oct 83
Neel, Alice (Hartley) obit Jan 85
Nelligan, Kate Jul 83
Nesbitt, Cathleen (Mary) obit Sep 82
Nettles, Graig Jul 84
Neuharth, Allen H(arold) Apr 86
Neumann, Emanuel obit Jan 81
Newell, Homer E(dward), Jr. obit Sep 83
Newman, Paul May 85
Newman, Randy Oct 82
Nicholson, Ben obit Apr 82
Nicolson, Marjorie Hope obit Jun 81
Niemöller, (Friedrich Gustav Emil) Martin obit May 84
Niven, David obit Sep 83
Noah, Yannick Aug 87
Noel-Baker, Philip J(ohn) obit Mar 83
Nofziger, Lyn Jan 83
Nolan, Lloyd obit Nov 85
Norman, Marsha May 84
North, John Ringling obit Jul 85
Northrop, John Howard obit Sep 87
Northrop, John K(nudsen) obit Apr 81
Novak, Michael Feb 85
Nozick, Robert Jun 82

Oboler, Arch obit May 87
Obote, (Apollo) Milton Apr 81
O'Boyle, Patrick (Aloysius) Cardinal obit Sep 87
Obraztsova, Elena Feb 83
O'Brien, Leo W(illiam) obit Jul 82
O'Brien, Pat obit Jan 84
Ochsner, (Edward William) Alton obit Nov 81
O'Connor, John J(oseph) Jun 84
O'Connor, Sandra Day Jan 82
Odishaw, Hugh obit Jun 84
O'Dowd, George A. See Boy George
O'Hara, Mary obit Jan 81
O'Keeffe, Georgia obit Apr 86
O'Konski, Alvin E(dward) obit Aug 87
Oliver, James A(rthur) obit May 82
Olsen, Kenneth H(arry) Mar 87
Olson, Harry F(erdinand) obit Jun 82
O'Neil, James F(rancis) obit Sep 81
O'Neill, William A(tchison) Feb 85
Opel, John R(oberts) Mar 86
Orff, Carl obit May 82
Ormandy, Eugene obit May 85
Ormsby-Gore, (William) David obit Mar 85
Ortega, Daniel Oct 84
Osborn, Frederick (Henry) obit Mar 81
O'Shea, Milo Jun 82
Ovandia Candia, Alfredo obit Mar 82
Owings, Nathaniel A(lexander) obit Aug 84
Oz, Amos Jul 83
Özal, Turgut Jun 85
Ozick, Cynthia Aug 83

Packwood, Bob Jan 81
Padover, Saul K(ussiel) obit Apr 81
Page, Geraldine obit Aug 87
Paige, Leroy (Robert) obit Aug 82
Paik, Nam June Mar 83
Paisley, Ian (Richard Kyle) Jun 86
Paley, Grace Mar 86
Palme, (Sven) Olof (Joachim) obit Apr 86
Palmer, Lilli obit Mar 86
Pantaleoni, Helenka (Tradeusa Adamowski) obit Mar 87
Papandreou, Andreas (George) Apr 83
Parkening, Christopher Apr 87
Parker, Buddy obit Jun 82
Parsons, Harriet (Oettinger) obit Mar 83

Parsons, Rose Peabody obit Jun 85
Parsons, Mrs. William Barclay See Parsons, R. P. obit
Partch, Virgil F(ranklin) obit Oct 84
Pastora (Gómez), Edén Jul 86
Pate, Martha B. Lucas obit Jul 83
Paterno, Joe Feb 84
Paul, Les Aug 87
Pauley, Edwin W(endell) obit Sep 81
Paxton, Tom Sep 82
Payne, (Pierre Stephen) Robert obit Apr 83
Payton, Walter Nov 85
Pears, Peter obit May 86
Peckinpah, Sam obit Feb 85
Peerce, Jan obit Feb 85
Pelikan, Jaroslav (Jan, Jr.) Sep 87
Pella, Giuseppe obit Aug 81
Pelletier, Wilfrid obit Jun 82
Pelli, Cesar Apr 83
Peltz, Mary Ellis (Opdycke) obit Jan 82
Pendleton, Clarence M(cLane), Jr. Sep 84
Penniman, Richard Wayne See Little Richard
Penzias, Arno A(llan) Sep 85
Pepper, Claude (Denson) Jan 83
Perahia, Murray Mar 82
Pereira, William L(eonard) obit Jan 86
Pérez de Cuéllar, Javier Aug 82
Pérez Esquivel, Adolfo Mar 81
Perkins, Carl D(ewey) obit Sep 84
Perkins, Dexter obit Jul 84
Perkins, R(ichard) Marlin obit Aug 86
Perlman, Alfred E(dward) obit Jul 83
Perry, Gaylord Nov 82
Pertschuk, Michael Sep 86
Peters, Bernadette Sep 84
Peterson, (Frederick) Val(demar Erastus) obit Jan 84
Peterson, Oscar Oct 83
Petrillo, James Caesar obit Jan 85
Phillips, William Oct 84
Picasso, Paloma Apr 86
Pickens, T(homas) Boone, (Jr.) Jul 85
Pidgeon, Walter obit Nov 84
Pierce, Samuel Riley, Jr. Nov 82
Piñero, Miguel Nov 83
Piniella, Lou Aug 86
Plaza (Lasso), Galo obit Mar 87
Plunkett, Jim Feb 82

Poage, W(illiam) R(obert) obit Mar 87
Podgorny, Nikolai (Viktorovich) obit Mar 83
Poindexter, John M(arlan) Nov 87
Pollack, Jack H(arrison) obit Feb 85
Pollack, Sydney Sep 86
Ponnamperuma, Cyril (Andrew) Apr 84
Ponnelle, Jean-Pierre Mar 83
Popkin, Zelda obit Jul 83
Potok, Chaim May 83
Potvin, Denis Oct 86
Powell, Michael Aug 87
Powell, William obit May 84
Prebisch, Raúl obit Jul 86
Preminger, Otto (Ludwig) obit Jun 86
Presser, Jackie Sep 83
Pressler, Larry Oct 83
Preston, Robert obit May 87
Prestopino, Gregorio obit Apr 85
Price, Byron obit Sep 81
Price, (Edward) Reynolds Apr 87
Price, George (Cadle) Aug 84
Price, Gwilym A(lexander) obit Aug 85
Price, Margaret Aug 86
Priestley, J(ohn) B(oynton) obit Oct 84
Prigogine, Ilya Feb 87
Primrose, William obit July 82
Prince Feb 86
Pusey, Merlo J(ohn) obit Jan 86
Putnam, Ashley Mar 82
Pym, Francis (Leslie) Sep 82
Pynchon, Thomas Oct 87

Quay, Jan Eduard de obit Aug 85
Quennell, Peter (Courtney) May 84
Quimby, Edith H(inkley) obit Mar 83

Rafferty, Max(well Lewis, Jr.) obit Aug 82
Rahner, Karl obit May 84
Rainey, Homer P(rice) obit Feb 86
Ram, Jagjivan obit Aug 86
Rambert, Marie Feb 81 obit Aug 82
Ramey, Samuel Jul 81
Rand, Ayn May 82 obit May 82
Randi, The Amazing See Randi, James
Randi, James May 87
Rangel, Charles B(ernard) Mar 84
Raskin, Judith obit Feb 85

Ratzinger, Joseph Cardinal Apr 86
Rau, Dhanvanthi (Handoo) Rama obit Sep 87
Rau, Johannes Mar 87
Rauschenberg, Robert Oct 87
Rauschning, Hermann obit Apr 83
Rawlings, Jerry (John) Jun 82
Rawls, Lou Mar 84
Ray, Gordon N(orton) obit Feb 87
Reagan, Nancy May 82
Reagan, Patricia Ann See Davis, Patti
Reagan, Ronald (Wilson) Nov 82
Reddy, N(eelam) Sanjiva Mar 81
Redford, Robert Mar 82
Redgrave, Sir Michael obit May 85
Redpath, Jean Feb 84
Reed, Ishmael Oct 86
Reed, John S(hepard) Jan 85
Reeve, Christopher May 82
Regan, Donald T(homas) Nov 81
Reich, Steve Apr 86
Reichelderfer, F(rancis) W(ilton) obit Mar 83
Reid, Kate Mar 85
Renault, Mary obit Feb 84
Retton, Mary Lou Feb 86
Rexroth, Kenneth Apr 81 obit Aug 82
Rich, Buddy obit May 87
Richards, Lloyd Oct 87
Richardson, Sir Ralph obit Nov 83
Richie, Lionel Jul 84
Richter, Charles Francis obit Nov 85
Rickover, Hyman G(eorge) obit Aug 86
Riddleberger, James W(illiams) obit Jan 83
Ride, Sally K(risten) Oct 83
Riegle, Donald W(ayne), Jr. Oct 86
Rifkin, Jeremy Feb 86
Riley, Bridget (Louise) Sep 81
Ringwald, Molly May 87
Ríos Montt, José Efraín May 83
Ritchie-Calder, Baron of Balmashannar See Calder, (Peter) Ritchie obit
Ritter, Bruce Jun 83
Rivera, Chita Oct 84
Rivers, Joan Mar 87
Rivlin, Alice M(itchell) Oct 82
Roa (y García), Raúl obit Sep 82
Roach, Max Jul 86
Robarts, John P(armenter) obit Jan 83
Robertson, Marion Gordon See Robertson, Pat

Robertson, Pat Sep 87
Robinson, John (Arthur Thomas) obit Feb 84
Robinson, M(aurice) R(ichard) obit May 82
Robison, Paula May 82
Robitzek, Edward H(einrich) obit May 84
Robson, Dame Flora obit Sep 84
Rochberg, George Sep 85
Rock, John obit Jan 85
Roderick, David M(ilton) Apr 87
Rodgers, Bill Aug 82
Rogers, Bernard W(illiam) Oct 84
Rogers, Carl R(ansom) obit Mar 87
Rogers, Kenny Jan 81
Rogers, Roy Oct 83
Rogge, O(etje) John obit Jun 81
Romano, Emanuel obit Feb 85
Romano, Umberto obit Nov 82
Romulo, Carlos P(ena) obit Feb 86
Rooney, Andy Jul 82
Root, Waverley (Lewis) obit Jan 83
Rose, George Sep 84
Rose, Leonard obit Jan 85
Rose, William C(umming) obit Jan 86
Rosen, Samuel obit Jan 82
Rosenberg, Anna M(arie) See Hoffman, A. M. R.
Rosenstock, Joseph obit Jan 86
Ross, Nancy Wilson obit May 86
Rostenkowski, Dan(iel D.) Jan 82
Roszak, Theodore [artist] obit Oct 81
Roszak, Theodore [historian] Apr 82
Roth, William V(ictor), Jr. Apr 83
Rotha, Paul obit May 84
Rothenberg, Susan Mar 85
Rothschild, Louis S(amuel) obit Oct 84
Rouse, James W(ilson) Feb 82
Rowan, Dan obit Nov 87
Roy, Maurice obit Jan 86
Rubbia, Carlo Jun 85
Rubik, Erno Feb 87
Rubin, William (Stanley) Nov 86
Rubinstein, Artur obit Mar 83
Ruffing, Charles H(erbert) obit Apr 86
Ruffing, Red See Ruffing, C. H. obit
Rukeyser, Louis Feb 83
Rushdie, (Ahmed) Salman Nov 86
Russell, Donald J(oseph) obit Feb 86
Russell, Mark Mar 81

Rustin, Bayard obit Oct 87
Ryan, T(ubal) Claude obit Nov 82
Ryle, Sir Martin obit Jan 85

Sabato, Ernesto Oct 85
Sacks, Oliver (Wolf) Feb 85
Sadat, Anwar (el-) obit Nov 81
Sadat, Jihan Aug 86
Sade Sep 86
St. George, Katharine (Delano Price Collier) obit Jul 83
Salazar, Alberto May 83
Salerno-Sonnenberg, Nadja Nov 87
Salinger, Pierre (Emil George) Mar 87
Salisbury, Harrison E(vans) Jan 82
Salle, David Sep 86
Sananikone, Phoui obit Feb 84
Sanders, Harland obit Feb 81
Sanders, Marlene Feb 81
Sanger, Frederick Jul 81
Santmyer, Helen Hooven Feb 85 obit Apr 86
Sarah, Duchess of York Mar 87
Sargeant, Howland H(ill) obit Apr 84
Sarkis, Elias obit Aug 85
Sarney, José Mar 86
Saroyan, William obit Jul 81
Sarton, May May 82
Saunders, Stuart T(homas) obit Mar 87
Sauvé, Jeanne Aug 84
Saville, Curtis (Lloyd) and Kathleen Jan 86
Saville, Kathleen (McNally) See Saville, C. and K.
Savimbi, Jonas (Malheiro) Aug 86
Savitch, Jessica Jan 83 obit Mar 84
Sawyer, Diane Oct 85
Sayles, John Feb 84
Scalia, Antonin Nov 86
Scargill, Arthur Jan 85
Scavullo, Francesco May 85
Schacht, Al(exander) obit Sep 84
Schaller, George B(eals) Aug 85
Schapiro, Meyer Jul 84
Schaufuss, Peter May 82
Schillebeeckx, Edward Jun 83
Schindler, Alexander M(oshe) Sep 87
Schlamme, Martha obit Jan 86
Schlauch, Margaret obit Sep 86
Schlöndorff, Volker Aug 83
Schmidt, Benno C(harles), Jr. Aug 86
Schnabel, Julian Nov 83
Schneerson, Menachem Mendel Sep 83

Schneider, Alan obit Jun 84
Schneider, Romy obit Jul 82
Scholder, Fritz Apr 85
Schrader, Paul Aug 81
Schram, Emil obit Nov 87
Schreyer, Edward Richard Feb 81
Schwartz, Arthur obit Oct 84
Schwartz, Tony Jul 85
Schwarz, Gerard Apr 86
Schwarzhaupt, Elisabeth obit Jan 87
Schygulla, Hanna Jul 84
Scott, Hazel (Dorothy) obit Nov 81
Scott, Michael (Guthrie) obit Apr 85
Scourby, Alexander obit Apr 85
Scowcroft, Brent Jul 87
Scull, Robert C. obit Feb 86
Seaga, Edward (Phillip George) Apr 81
Seghers, Anna obit Jul 83
Segovia, Andrés obit Jul 87
Seifert, Elizabeth obit Oct 83
Sellars, Peter Jan 86
Selleck, Tom Nov 83
Selye, Hans (Hugo Bruno) Jan 81 obit Jan 83
Serkin, Peter Jun 86
Serra, Richard (Antony) Jan 85
Sert, José Luis obit May 83
Sert, Josep Lluis See Sert, José Luis obit
Sessions, Roger obit May 85
Seymour, Whitney North obit Jul 83
Shamir, Yitzhak Feb 83
Sharansky, Natan See Shcharansky, Anatoly
Sharon, Ariel Apr 81
Shatner, William Jul 87
Shaw, Irwin obit Jul 84
Shawn, Wallace Jun 86
Shcharansky, Anatoly Feb 87
Sheed, Frank (Joseph) Sep 81 obit Jan 82
Sheed, Wilfrid Aug 81
Shehan, Lawrence (Joseph), Cardinal obit Oct 84
Shehu, Mehmet obit Feb 82
Shepherd, Cybill Mar 87
Shepherd, Jean (Parker) Apr 84
Shera, Jesse H(auk) obit Jun 82
Shevardnadze, Eduard (Amvrosiyevich) Feb 86
Shevchenko, Arkady N(ikolayevich) Sep 85
Shields, Brooke Oct 82
Shinwell, Baron See Shinwell, E. obit
Shinwell, Emanuel obit Jun 86
Shivers, Allan obit Mar 85
Sholokhov, Mikhail A(leksandrovich) obit Apr 84

Shoup, David M(onroe) obit Mar 83
Sidney, Sylvia Oct 81
Signoret, Simone obit Nov 85
Silber, John R(obert) Feb 84
Siles Zuazo, Hernán Jun 85
Sills, Beverly Feb 82
Silvers, Phil obit Jan 86
Simmons, Richard May 82
Simpson, George Gaylord obit Jan 85
Simpson, Howard E(dward) obit Apr 85
Sinclair, Adelaide Helen Grant Macdonald See Sinclair, Mrs. D. B. obit
Sinclair, Mrs. D. B. obit Jan 83
Singh, Giani Zail Sep 87
Six, Robert F(orman) obit Nov 86
Slade, Roy Jun 85
Slatkin, Leonard Feb 86
Slezak, Walter obit Jun 83
Slick, Grace Apr 82
Sliwa, Curtis Feb 83
Sloane, Eric obit May 85
Smith, Carleton obit Jul 84
Smith, James H(opkins), Jr. obit Feb 83
Smith, Kate obit Aug 86
Smith, Liz May 87
Smith, Mary Elizabeth See Smith, Liz
Smith, Red obit Feb 82
Smith, Roger B(onham) May 86
Smith, William French Jan 82
Smuin, Michael Oct 84
Smyth, H(enry) D(eWolf) obit Nov 86
Sneider, Vern obit Jun 81
Snell, George D(avis) May 86
Snyder, John W(esley) obit Jan 86
Soames, (Arthur) Christopher (John), Baron of Fletching Aug 81 obit Oct 87
Sobhuza II, King of Swaziland Mar 82 obit Oct 82
Söderström, Elisabeth Nov 85
Solarz, Stephen J(oshua) Nov 86
Soong Ching-ling. See Sun Yat-sen, Mme. obit
Soss, Wilma (Porter) obit Jan 87
Souvanna Phouma, Prince of Laos obit Mar 84
Sovern, Michael I(ra) Feb 81
Sowell, Thomas Jul 81
Soyer, Isaac obit Sep 81
Sparkman, John J(ackson) obit Jan 86
Speakes, Larry Mar 85
Speer, Albert obit Oct 81
Speidel, Hans obit Feb 85
Spelling, Aaron May 86
Sperry, Roger W(olcott) Jan 86

Spiegelman, Sol(omon) obit Mar 83
Spillane, Mickey Sep 81
Springer, Axel (Caesar) obit Nov 85
Sprinkel, Beryl (Wayne) Jul 87
Stankiewicz, Richard (Peter) obit May 83
Starr, Mark obit Jul 85
Stavropoulos, George (Peter) Mar 85
Stein, Jules (Caesar) obit Jun 81
Steiner, (Francis) George Oct 83
Stenmark, Ingemar Apr 82
Stephanie, Princess of Monaco Aug 86
Sterling, J(ohn) E(wart) Wallace obit Aug 85
Stevens, Robert T(en Broeck) obit Mar 83
Stevenson, William E(dwards) obit May 85
Stever, H(orton) Guyford Jan 81
Stewart, Potter obit Feb 86
Stigler, George J(oseph) Jul 83
Stilwell, Richard Feb 86
Sting Jul 85
Stockman, David (Alan) Aug 81
Stoddard, George D(insmore) obit Feb 82
Stoessel, Walter J(ohn), Jr. obit Feb 87
Stokes, Anson Phelps, Jr. obit Jan 87
Stoltzman, Richard Mar 86
Stone, Oliver Jun 87
Stone, Robert (Anthony) Jan 87
Strasberg, Lee obit Apr 82
Straus, Jack I(sidor) obit Nov 85
Strauss, Franz Josef Feb 87
Strawberry, Darryl Jun 84
Streibert, Theodore C(uyler) obit Mar 87
Streit, Clarence K(irshman) obit Sep 86
Stroessner, Alfredo Mar 81
Struble, Arthur D(ewey) obit Jul 83
Stuart, Jesse obit Apr 84
Stutz, Geraldine (Veronica) May 83
Styne, Jule May 83
Styron, William (Clark, Jr.) Jun 86
Sullivan, John L(awrence) obit Oct 82
Sumner, Gordon See Sting
Sunay, Cevdet obit Aug 82
Sun Myung Moon See Moon, S. M.
Sun Yat-sen, Mme. obit Jul 81
Suslov, Mikhail A(ndreyevich) obit Mar 82
Susskind, David obit Apr 87

Sutherland, Donald Feb 81
Suzuki, Zenko Jan 81
Swaggart, Jimmy (Lee) Oct 87
Swanson, Gloria obit May 83
Sweeney, James Johnson obit Jul 86
Swigert, Ernest G(oodnough) obit Feb 87
Swing, Joseph M(ay) obit Feb 85
Syberberg, Hans Jürgen Apr 83
Szent-Györgyi, Albert (von Nagyrapolt) obit Jan 87

Tabb, Mary Decker See Decker, Mary
Taft, Charles P(helps, 2d) obit Aug 83
Talvela, Martti Oct 83
Tambo, Oliver Apr 87
Tandy, Jessica Aug 84
Tange, Kenzo Sep 87
Tartikoff, Brandon Apr 87
Tati, Jacques obit Jan 83
Taussig, Helen B(rooke) obit Jul 86
Taylor, A(lan) J(ohn) P(ercivale) Nov 83
Taylor, Cecil Mar 86
Taylor, Elizabeth Oct 85
Taylor, Glen H(earst) obit Jul 84
Taylor, Maxwell D(avenport) obit Jun 87
Taylor, Peter (Hillsman) Apr 87
Tcherkassky, Marianna Nov 85
Teague, Olin E(arl) obit Apr 81
Teale, Edwin Way obit Jan 81
Tebbit, Norman (Beresford) Nov 87
Teller, Edward Nov 83
Tennstedt, Klaus Sep 83
Tenzing Norkey obit Jul 86
Terra, Daniel J(ames) Nov 87
Terry, Luther L(eonidas) obit May 85
Theorell, (Axel) Hugo (Teodor) obit Oct 82
Thicke, Alan Jun 87
Thiebaud, Wayne Mar 87
Thomas, Charles Allen obit May 82
Thomas, Charles S(parks) obit Jan 84
Thomas, D(onald) M(ichael) Nov 83
Thomas, Franklin A(ugustine) Oct 81
Thomas, Lowell (Jackson) obit Oct 81
Thompson, Daley Nov 86
Thompson, Hunter S(tockton) Mar 81
Thompson, Paul See Rotha, Paul obit

Thornton, Charles B(ates) obit Jan 82
Thurman, Howard obit Jun 81
Tiegs, Cheryl Nov 82
Tiger, Lionel Jan 81
Tillstrom, Burr obit Feb 86
Timerman, Jacobo Nov 81
Tinker, Grant A. Mar 82
Tisch, Laurence A(lan) Feb 87
Tobin, James Oct 84
Todd, Richard May 82
Tomás, Américo (Deus Rodrigues) obit Nov 87
Tomasson, Helgi Apr 82
Tormé, Mel Mar 83
Torrijos Herrera, Omar obit Sep 81
Tors, Ivan (Lawrence) obit Aug 83
Touré, (Ahmed) Sekou obit May 84
Towle, Katherine A(melia) obit May 86
Townshend, Peter Aug 83
Trapp, Maria Augusta obit Jun 87
Trevor, William Sep 84
Trevor-Roper, H(ugh) R(edwald) Sep 83
Trippe, Juan T(erry) obit May 81
Trottier, Bryan Jun 85
Truffaut, François obit Jan 85
Truman, Bess (Wallace) See Truman, Mrs. Harry S obit
Truman, Mrs. Harry S obit Jan 83
Truman, (Mary) Margaret Jun 87
Trumka, Richard L(ouis) Apr 86
Trump, Donald J(ohn) Feb 84
Tsarapkin, Semyon K(onstantinovich) obit Nov 84
Tsongas, Paul E(fthemios) Jul 81
Tubb, Ernest Oct 83 obit Oct 84
Tuck, William M(unford) obit Aug 83
Tudor, Anthony obit Jun 87
Tully, Alice Jan 84
Tune, Tommy Jan 83
Turner, John (Napier) Nov 84
Turner, Kathleen Jun 86
Turner, Tina Nov 84
Tutu, Desmond (Mpilo) Jan 85
Twining, Nathan F(arragut) obit May 82
Tworkov, Jack obit Oct 82
Tyler, Anne Jun 81

Ueberroth, Peter V(ictor) Apr 85
Ullman, Al(bert Conrad) obit Jan 87

Umberto II, King of Italy obit
May 83
Underhill, Ruth M(urray) obit
Oct 84
Unruh, Jesse M(arvin) obit
Sep 87
Updike, John (Hoyer) Oct 84
Urey, Harold C(layton) obit
Mar 81
Urquhart, Brian E(dward) Jun
86
Urrutia Lleo, Manuel obit Aug
81

Vadim, Roger Jan 84
Vagnozzi, Egidio Cardinal obit
Feb 81
Valenzuela, Fernando Oct 82
Vallee, Rudy obit Aug 86
Van Arsdale, Harry obit Apr
86
Van den Haag, Ernest Oct 83
Vane, John R(obert) May 86
Vaness, Carol Sep 86
Van Wagoner, Murray D(elos)
obit Aug 86
Van Zandt, James E(dward)
obit Mar 86
Vaughan, Harry H(awkins)
obit Jul 81
Veeck, Bill obit Feb 86
Velde, Harold H(immel) obit
Jan 86
Vendler, Helen May 86
Vera-Ellen obit Oct 81
Vidal, Gore Jun 83
Vidor, King obit Jan 83
Viguerie, Richard A(rt) Jan 83
Vila, George R(aymond) obit
Aug 87
Vinson, Carl obit Jul 81
Visser 't Hooft, Willem A(dolf)
obit Aug 85
Vogel, Hans-Jochen Jan 84
Vollenweider, Andreas May
87
Von Zell, Harry obit Jan 82
Voorhis, (Horace) Jerry obit
Nov 84
Vorster, Balthazar Johannes
obit Nov 83

Wadsworth, James J(eremiah)
obit May 84
Wagner, Robert Jun 84
Waite, Terence (Hardy) Sep 86
Waitz, Grete Apr 81
Wajda, Andrzej Jul 82
Walcott, Derek (Alton) Apr 84
Waldheim, Kurt Jan 87
Walesa, Lech Apr 81
Walker, Alice Mar 84
Walker, Herschel Mar 85
Wallace, DeWitt obit May 81
Wallace, Lila (Bell) Acheson
obit Jul 84
Wallenstein, Alfred obit Mar
83

Wallop, (John) Douglass obit
Jun 85
Walton, Sir William Turner
obit May 83
Wang, An Jan 87
Wang Shih-chieh obit Jun 81
Ward, Barbara (Mary) obit Jul
81
Warhol, Andy Jul 86 obit Apr
87
Waring, Fred obit Sep 84
Warren, Harry obit Nov 81
Washington, Harold Feb 84
Wasserburg, Gerald J(oseph)
Mar 86
Waters, Muddy May 81 obit
Jun 83
Waterston, Sam Sep 85
Watt, James G(aius) Jan 82
Wattenberg, Ben J. Jun 85
Watts, Heather May 83
Weaver, Earl Feb 83
Webb, Jack obit Mar 83
Webb, James H(enry), Jr. Aug
87
Webber, Andrew Lloyd See
Lloyd Webber, A.
Wechsberg, Joseph obit Jun 83
Wedel, Cynthia Clark obit Oct
86
Weidenbaum, Murray L(ew)
Mar 82
Weidlein, Edward R(ay) obit
Nov 83
Wein, George (Theodore) Oct
85
Weinberg, Robert A(llan) Jun
83
Weir, Peter Aug 84
Weiss, Peter obit Jul 82
Weiss, Ted Oct 85
Weizsäcker, Carl Friedrich
von Jan 85
Weizsäcker, Richard von Mar
85
Welch, Robert (Henry Win-
borne, Jr.) obit Mar 85
Welles, (George) Orson obit
Nov 85
Wenders, Wim Jul 84
Werner, Oskar obit Jan 85
Wertham, Fredric obit Jan 82
Wesley, Charles H(arris) obit
Oct 87
West, Jessamyn obit Apr 84
West, Mae obit Jan 81
West, Dame Rebecca obit May
83
Westheimer, (Karola) Ruth Jan
87
Weston, (Theodore) Brett Feb
82
Wharton, Clifton R(eginald),
Jr. Feb 87
White, Betty Jun 87
White, E(lwyn) B(rooks) obit
Nov 85
White, Katharine Elkus obit
Jun 85

White, Mark (Wells) Aug 86
White, Robert E(dward) May
84
White, Theodore H(arold) obit
Jul 86
Whitehead, Don(ald Ford) obit
Mar 81
Whitney, John Hay obit Apr
82
Whittemore, Arthur obit Feb
85
Wick, Charles Z. Mar 85
Wiesel, Elie Feb 86
Wilcox, Francis O(rlando) obit
Apr 85
Wilde, Frazar B(ullard) obit
Aug 85
Wilder, Alec obit Feb 81
Wilder, Billy Oct 84
Wilkins, Roy obit Oct 81
Will, George F(rederick) Sep
81
Williams, Billy Dee Apr 84
Williams, Emlyn obit Nov 87
Williams, Eric (Eustace) obit
May 81
Williams, Gluyas obit Apr 82
Williams, Joe Apr 85
Williams, John Jul 83
Williams, John Bell obit May
83
Williams, Mary Lou obit Jul 81
Williams, Paul Jun 83
Williams, Tennessee obit Apr
83
Williams, Vanessa May 84
Willis, Bruce Feb 87
Willis, Paul S. obit Aug 87
Wills, Garry Jun 82
Willson, Meredith obit Aug 84
Wilson, August Aug 87
Wilson, Carroll Louis obit Mar
83
Wilson, Kenneth G(eddes) Sep
83
Wilson, Peter (Cecil) obit Aug
84
Winchell, Constance M(abel)
obit Sep 84
Windsor, Wallis (Warfield),
Duchess of obit Jun 86
Winfield, Dave Jan 84
Winfrey, Oprah Mar 87
Winger, Debra Jul 84
Winter, Paul Oct 87
Wise, James DeCamp obit Apr
84
Wolfenden, Lord See Wolfen-
den, Sir John obit
Wolfenden, Sir John (Freder-
ick) obit Mar 85
Wolper, David L(loyd) Oct 86
Wood, John Apr 83
Wood, Natalie obit Jan 82
Wood, Robert D(ennis) obit Jul
86
Woodhouse, Barbara (Black-
burn) Feb 85

Woodhouse, (Margaret) Chase
Going obit Apr 85

Woodruff, Judy Sep 86
Woods, Donald Feb 82
Woods, George D(avid) obit
Oct 82
Woodson, Carter G(odwin)
obit Yrbk 84 (died Apr 50)
Woodward, C(omer) Vann
May 86
Wright, Louis B(ooker) obit Jun
84
Wu, K(uo) C(heng) obit Aug 84
Wurf, Jerry obit Feb 82
Wu Yifang obit Jan 86
Wyeth, Andrew (Newell) Nov
81
Wyler, William obit Sep 81
Wyman, Thomas H(unt) Jun 83

Wyszynski, Stefan Cardinal
obit Jul 81

Yadin, Yigael obit Aug 84
Yamasaki, Minoru obit Apr 86
Yankelovich, Daniel Mar 82
Yarborough, Cale Jan 87
Yeager, Jeana May 87
Yeh, George K(ung-)C(hao)
obit Jan 82
Yost, Charles W(oodruff) obit
Jul 81
Young, John A(lan) Oct 86
Young, Milton R(uben) obit Jul
83
Young, Philip obit Mar 87
Young, Stephen M(arvin) obit
Feb 85
Youngerman, Jack Nov 86
Youngman, Henny Oct 86

Yourcenar, Marguerite Nov 82
Yukawa, Hideki obit Nov 81

Zablocki, Clement J(ohn) Jun
83 obit Jan 84
Zacharias, Jerrold (Reinach)
obit Sep 86
Zevin, B(enjamin) D(avid) obit
Feb 85
Zhao Ziyang Jun 84
Ziaur Rahman Jun 81 obit Jul
81
Zimbalist, Efrem obit Apr 85
Zorin, Valerian
A(lexandrovich) obit Mar 86
Zulli, Floyd, Jr. obit Jan 81
Zwilich, Ellen (Taaffe) Jan 86
Zworykin, Vladimir K(osma)
obit Sep 82